Managing
Global
Issues

A Public Role for the Private Sector: Industry Self-Regulation in a Global Economy
Virginia Haufler

Africa's New Leaders: Democracy or State Reconstruction?
Marina Ottaway

Aiding Democracy Abroad: The Learning Curve
Thomas Carothers

Caught in the Middle: Border Communities in an Era of Globalization
Demetrios G. Papademetrious and Deborah Wallter Meyers, Editors

Citizenship Today: Global Perspectives and Practices
T. Alexander Aleinikoff and Douglas Klusmeyer, Editors

From Migrants to Citizens: Membership in a Changing World
T. Alexander Aleinikoff and Douglas Klusmeyer, Editors

Funding Virtue: Civil Society Aid and Democracy Promotion
Marina Ottaway and Thomas Carothers, Editors

The Third Force: The Rise of Transnational Civil Society
Ann M. Florini, Editor

Managing Global Issues

Lessons Learned

P. J. Simmons
Chantal de Jonge Oudraat
Editors

CARNEGIE ENDOWMENT FOR INTERNATIONAL PEACE
Washington, D.C.

Carnegie Endowment for International Peace
1779 Massachusetts Avenue, N.W., Washington, D.C. 20036
202-483-7600   www.ceip.org

The Carnegie Endowment normally does not take institutional positions on public policy issues; the views and recommendations presented in this publication do not necessarily represent the views of the Carnegie Endowment, its officers, staff, or trustees.

To order, contact Carnegie's distributor:
The Brookings Institution Press
Department 029, Washington, D.C. 20042-0029, USA
1-800-275-1447 or 1-202-797-6258
Fax 202-797-2960, E-mail bibooks@brook.edu

Printed in the United States of America on acid-free, recycled paper with soy inks.
Typesetting by AlphaWebTech, Mechanicsville, Md.

Library of Congress Cataloging-in-Publication Data

Simmons, P. J., 1967- Managing global issues : lessons learned / P. J. Simmons, Chantal de Jonge Oudraat
    p.   cm.
    Includes bibliographical references and index.
    ISBN 0-87003-183-X (pbk. : alk. paper) 1. Globalization. 2 Globalization—Case studies. I. Jonge Oudraat, Chantal de. II. Title.
JZ1318.S56 2001   2001004156
303.48'2—dc21

---

07 06 05 04 03 02 01   5 4 3 2 1   1st Printing 2001

Contents

Foreword

THE OPEN, HYPERCONNECTED WORLD of the twenty-first century offers individuals and societies the promise of vast new benefits. It also holds comparable dangers. Terrorism and crime can cross borders and oceans almost as easily as can liberating knowledge and democratic ideas. Pollution and disease travel at high speeds and over great distances in much the same manner as capital and communications.

Despite its unnerving by-products, globalization is not a process that can be reversed. Yet, as this book documents, it can be steered. Indeed, managing global problems more effectively has become a necessity. That imperative means more cooperative governance: to curb terrorism, to block the international transit of crime, disease, and narcotics, to control the proliferation of weapons of mass destruction, to reduce non-tariff trade barriers, to ensure environmental protection, to protect intellectual property, and so on. A broad, if shallow, international consensus defines many of the desired ends. The debate over means, however, often reveals differences so intense as to stymie sound and timely responses.

Unlike the single-mindedness with which terrorists or advocacy groups can focus on their goals, the world's sovereign states face a rapidly expanding agenda of international challenges against which political will has mobilized unevenly at best over the last half century. In an already complicated setting, such globalizing forces as the information and communications revolutions not only propel more challenges to center stage but also rewrite the roles of various protagonists. This profoundly reshapes the ways and means of problem solving. The multifaceted diplomacy of the future will need to blend very old methods and attitudes with less-tried, more ambitious strategies for promoting interstate accord and action. In the experiences of recent decades, we should be able to discern the shape of things to come and the hope of stronger performance.

Managing Global Issues is a unique mapping of this new international territory. It examines the mechanics of recent global diplomacy, analyzing its failures and its successes. The book poses a common set of questions to experts on sixteen issues about the four key phases of international governance: agenda setting, negotiation, implementation, and reactions to noncompliance. The editors chose the case studies based on their potential to yield lessons (track records long enough to display both promise and defeat) that might be transferable to other longstanding challenges, such as terrorism and population growth, and newer issues, such as Internet privacy and biotechnology. The result—analyses that use the same compass to map diverse terrain—is valuable in part because it is so rare. Most scholars and practitioners investigate their own specialties in great depth but miss the broader, sometimes the more obvious, positive and negative lessons that might be drawn from one field and applied in another.

That time-honored approach is showing its age. Today's international governance (and certainly tomorrow's) demands a steeper learning curve and an approach that does not depend on reinventing the wheel for each new challenge. While not a manual for global problem solving, Managing Global Issues offers an extraordinarily useful inventory of what has been tried so far, how these tools and approaches have worked, and other possible options for alleviating global problems. The lessons chronicled by the volume's editors and contributors form a rich base of learning on which to build a rigorous field of knowledge and solid practical experience for addressing difficult new circumstances. At the Carnegie Endowment we see this volume as the centerpiece of our early work in the Global Policy Program. I am confident that legions of readers will find it equally pathbreaking and useful in their own endeavors.

Managing Global Issues is the product of a lengthy, disciplined inquiry by experts working on their own and together. This work was made possible by the farsighted support of the Rockefeller Brothers Fund and the Ford Foundation. The Carnegie Endowment for International Peace owes them the profound thanks I am glad to express here.

JESSICA T. MATHEWS
President
Carnegie Endowment for International Peace

Acknowledgments

OUR FIRST DEBT OF GRATITUDE is to the chapter authors from whom we asked and received so much. Not only did they meet the demand of writing ambitious chapters within a strict framework, but they also cheerfully attended long preparatory meetings. There, taking on more than the standard role of commentators, they even summarized each other's drafts to the group as a way to test for clarity and accessibility to non-experts. In addition, the authors penned several drafts in response to comments from us, each other, and outside reviewers. We thank them for the rich variety of their labors and for making the process so enjoyable.

Many individuals whose names do not appear in the table of contents helped to make this book possible. P. J. Simmons is indebted to the members of a 1998 study group who met almost a dozen times to identify key governance questions and themes that heavily informed the book project: Robert Boorstin, Nancy Zucker Boswell, Daniel Bradlow, Reba Caruth, Joseph Cirincione, James Connaughton, Lynne Davidson, Renee DeNevers, Lee Feinstein, Martha Finnemore, Ann Florini, Hilary French, Sumit Ganguly, Alene Gelbard, James Gibney, Virginia Haufler, Jeffrey Laurenti, Marc Levy, Jamie Metzl, Kathleen Newland, Annie Petsonk, Molly Reilly, Peter Richardson, Daniel Rosen, John Sammis, Frances Seymour, David Victor, and Paul Williams. Simmons also deeply appreciates the help and guidance of Geoffrey Dabelko, Ann Florini, Aaron Frank, John Gibson, John Harper, Vida Johnson, Shanthi Kalathil, Laurie Kohn, Thomas Lovejoy, Walter Lubelczyk, David Maxwell, Christopher Murphy, E. J. Simmons, Sarah M. Terry, Jon Wolfstahl, and, above all, Will Gartshore.

Our preparatory meetings with authors were greatly enhanced by the participation of Michael Brown, Thomas Carothers, Shepard Forman, Fen Hampson, Alexandre Kiss, Ed Luck, Gordon Smith and David Victor. In addition, we appreciate the help of several expert commentators on individual chapters: Nancy Birdsall,

Jeff Boutwell, Fran Carr, I. M. (Mac) Destler, Kimberly Ann Elliot, Richard Falk, Cathleen Fisher, Isaiah Frank, David Freestone, Julio Frenk, Sherm Garnett, Virginia Haufler, Lynne Holloway, John Jackson, William Korey, Dan Morrow, Auguste Noanga Malonga, Elinor Ostrom, Andrew Pierre, Wolfgang Reinicke, Asad Sayeed, Amy Smithson, Stephen Stedman, Staci Warden, and Oran Young.

Many further thanks are due to the individuals who helped transform a manuscript into a book. Even editors need editors, and we were fortunate to receive help from two outstanding ones—Diane McCree, who was instrumental over many months in working on the issue chapters, and Alfred Friendly, Jr., who challenged our thinking and added grace to our prose as we developed our introduction and conclusions. Among the superb group of researchers and assistants who helped in countless ways were Jonathan Blavin, Dianna Christenson, Jared Feinberg, Elaine French, Jennifer Haefeli, and Radha Kuppali. Carnegie's librarians—Jennifer Little, Kathleen Higgs, and Chris Henley—graciously filled countless requests for help. Trish Reynolds, Sherry Pettie, and Jacqueline Edlund-Braun handled the nuts and bolts of the production process with great skill, speed, and patience.

Finally, we are grateful to the Carnegie Endowment for the supportive base from which to launch this endeavor. In particular, we thank Jessica Mathews, Thomas Carothers, and Paul Balaran for their encouragement and guidance. And on behalf of all the contributors, we thank the Rockefeller Brothers Fund for making this project possible, as well as the Ford Foundation, the William and Flora Hewlett Foundation, and the John D. and Catherine T. MacArthur Foundation for their generous support of the Carnegie Endowment's Global Policy Program.

Part I

Introduction

Managing Global Issues:
An Introduction

P. J. Simmons and Chantal de Jonge Oudraat

CONTAGIOUS DISEASES AND FINANCIAL CONTAGION, civil conflicts and regional security, carbon sinks and ozone layers, patent infringement and human rights infringement, biodiversity and biological weaponry, refugee flights and capital flows. Diverse and, at first glance, unrelated, these topics share a common identity. They are all global concerns that cannot be successfully addressed unilaterally, bilaterally, or even regionally. They and a swelling roster of topics are the stuff of almost ceaseless international discourse that sometimes inaugurates cooperation and sometimes dissolves in discord. Over the last generation, the international community has scored a number of impressive victories in dealing with issues requiring extensive cooperation across borders. But overall, the track record is decidedly mixed, while the number of challenges is increasing.

In this book, sixteen respected experts investigate a number of global challenges in areas where changing settings are altering familiar assumptions about who sets policy, how, and with what results. Collectively, their essays amount to coloring outside the neat lines that define academic disciplines and diplomatic practice and too frequently insulate both scholars and practitioners from others with complementary knowledge and concerns.

The intent is not to examine particular issues so much as successful and failed attempts to manage them. The goal is to draw practical lessons from the recent past for their relevance to the near future. The forecast is for more such global challenges, more difficult to compartmentalize, more demanding of innovative responses. Early lessons like the ones our authors extract can help shape policies that have yet to be formulated for threats already with us and for many that are still indistinct.

SHRINKING PLANET, PROLIFERATING ISSUES

Depending on the size of your globe, there have always been global issues—from Attila the Hun's rampages to the Black Death to the European colonizers' grab for Africa. Until relatively recently, most such matters fell under the general rubric of security—military, political, and economic. If states could or had to deal with these challenges, they designated high-level representatives to do the dealing. At formal encounters, behind closed doors, the envoys attempted to make the world "safe for democracy" or "determined to save succeeding generations from the scourge of war."[1]

But the familiar ordering of international dealings is giving way to a very different modus operandi as the pressures of globalization reshape the nature of policy challenges, the efficacy of traditional responses, and the attributes of actors needed as problem solvers. Globalization—a magnified version of interdependence—is occurring on multiple fronts: *economic* (including the spread of consensus around a basic economic model and vast increases in international trade and capital flows); *political and social* (including increased democratization, expanding civil society, the spread of ideas, information, and people); *technological* (brought about by revolutions in information and telecommunications technologies); and *environmental and biological* (including transboundary flows of materials that affect human health and well-being, from climate-changing gases to viruses).[2] Although various forms of interdependence have been present for centuries, contemporary globalization is marked by an unprecedented degree of integration of markets, states, and technologies—all of which are "enabling individuals, corporations and nation-states to reach around the world farther, faster, deeper and cheaper than ever before."[3] The implications of such pervasive mutations for the work of managing global issues are profound.

Crowding In

One change is numerical. Clubby gatherings of ministers and central bankers from the affluent Atlantic states and Japan could once make the rules for world trade and finance and make them stick. But UN membership has grown 370 percent since 1945, and powerful nations increasingly find themselves challenged by assertive coalitions of lesser states. The claims of these newer arrivals can complicate even such seemingly simple matters as the allocation of orbital slots for communications satellites. When only a few countries launched satellites, it was easy to divide the pie. Now, with governments often fronting for the thousands of commercial enterprises in the field, the bargaining over lucrative berths in space is anything but routine.

Places at the bargaining tables, moreover, are no longer limited to sovereign states. They are also occupied by multinational enterprises, technical experts, and, with increasing frequency, independent organizations that may even have served as catalysts for the gathering. Thousands of highly motivated, skillful, and often antagonistic private groups—businesses, labor unions, and nongovernmental organizations (NGOs)—dedicated to causes as varied as Tibetan independence, fossil fuels, debt relief, children's rights, and the gospel of Ayn Rand not only throng the corridors of power but penetrate the conference rooms as well.

In environmental affairs, particularly, the power of NGOs to thrust issues into the spotlight and force the pace of negotiation has been not just novel but astonishing. They, not just the governments that signed it, were principal authors of the 1992 Rio Framework (Rio) Convention on Global Climate Change. Some see NGOs as hugely productive forces—the most effective grass-roots agents of many otherwise top-down multilateral assistance initiatives. Others find them obstructionist if not obscurantist. Tariff reductions on manufactured goods, for example, were far easier to negotiate when the parties were like-minded countries that had shared the traumas of the Great Depression and World War II. Iconoclastic NGOs that inserted labor and human rights issues and environmental concerns into the equation of global commerce have undone the older consensus. Similarly, government ministers lost their freedom to operate in cozy confidentiality in 1997 when protesters disrupted and helped to scuttle negotiations on what was to have been the Multilateral Agreement on Investment (MAI).

The near-monopoly on information once enjoyed by government officials has also blurred into the cacophony of the wired world. Journalists who used to get by on a communiqué and a background, not-for-attribution briefing may now have ringside seats or multiple ringside sources inside any international assembly. More significantly, inside information has moved outside and into the hands and analytical competence of corporations, citizens' groups, scholars, and others able and often eager to put their own spin on the data and disseminate it more widely. Technology—fax machines and the Internet—has strengthened governments, but it has empowered legions of free agents, jostling for position and the chance to influence policy.

Linking Up, Down, and Sideways

These added participants—known in the literature and throughout this book as nonstate actors—may enrich the process, but they do not simplify it. Simplicity, in any case, is bound to be elusive in dealing with issues that are not only complex in and of themselves—development assistance, refugee relief, and nuclear nonproliferation, for example—but that add layers of difficulty as they intertwine with other issues. Development, once quantified in gross domestic product (GDP) or miles of roadway or rates of infant mortality, has become inseparable from concerns for environmental sustainability. Intellectual property rights—drug patents—are sacrosanct, except when the lives of AIDS victims in poor countries are at stake.

Globalization is spinning new strands of complexity, stitching issues and actors together in a world where economic, humanitarian, health, and environmental concerns respect no national frontiers. Domestic conflicts drive refugees from their homes and across national borders, sometimes in desperate, disorderly flights that threaten to destabilize whole regions such as the upper Congo in the aftermath of the Rwandan genocide of 1994. "As with 'chaos' theories, and in weather systems," Keohane and Nye have commented, "small events in one place can have catalytic effects, so that consequences later and elsewhere are vast."[4] Ozone-depleting chemicals consumed in the United States raise anxiety levels in Chile, Argentina, and Australia where a thinning shield against ultraviolet rays threatens a higher incidence of skin cancer. Diseased food from one continent may reach consumers in another before contamination is detected.

New kinds of links are also making the formerly internal affairs of states into international issues. "Since 1990 the Security Council has declared a formal threat to international peace and security 61 times, after having done so only six times in the preceding 45 years," Jessica Mathews observed in 1997. She continued: "[I]t is not that security has been abruptly and terribly threatened: rather, the change reflects the broadened scope of what the international community now feels it should poke its nose into."[5] Now a Bosnian Serb accused of overseeing multiple rapes is taken before an international tribunal in another country to answer for alleged war crimes.

Globalization's synthesizing effect creates more connections across distances and disciplines and more occasions where people and issues mingle at greater and greater depth. Its attributes include mounting speed of exchanges (not just capital and information but also diseases and cures), swelling scale of all kinds of activity (financial, criminal, and technological, and all three together), and constantly expanding scope of both opportunities and risks. All of this makes the protection and advancement of human welfare more complicated.

Raising the Bar

Complexity is generally unsettling. The impulse to undo a Gordian knot with one swift swordstroke is understandable. In a nuclear world of 189 nations, six billion people, and trillion-dollar economies, however, quick, neat solutions are impractical and even potentially self-defeating. Banning arms flows to a war-torn country, for instance, would seem to offer a promising response to genuine threats. In practice, though, the action may paradoxically expand opportunities for criminals to circumvent restrictions and supply combatants with weapons.[6] The shortages created by arms embargoes increase the price of goods and thus, the profit margins—luring suppliers willing to ignore restrictions. The same is true, on a grander scale, of shortages created by international campaigns to dry up the flow of opium, cocaine, and their derivatives. Such efforts may cut supply but also raise profits and unintentionally encourage both smuggling and commerce in other drugs to satisfy hungry, illicit markets.

As intricate international dealings become labyrinthine, globalization drives not just the pace of transactions and their multiplicity but the twisting turns of the follow-through as well. In some respects, the easy part is over. Conventional negotiation—tying norms and goals into discrete issue packages—begins to looks like child's play compared to the exacting demands of setting standards and reaching accords where technical intricacies and disparate interests proliferate. Trade negotiations that once concentrated on reciprocal lowering of border tariffs have now become arenas for debates over workers' rights, environmental protection, and claims of equity—issues that penetrate deeply into domestic affairs. What were once issues of coordination mutate into clashes of values.

Even more daunting, though, is ensuring compliance with proliferating agreements ranging from the highly specialized (the UN Agreement on the Conservation and Management of Straddling and Highly Migratory Fish Stocks) to the highly general (the 1995 intergovernmental pledge to reduce poverty by half by 2015). Banning landmines, for instance, is an easier and cheaper goal to proclaim than detecting and removing them. Nations far more law-abiding than Iraq resist verification measures on the production or destruction of chemical, biological, and nuclear weapons because the intrusive activities undercut sovereignty and may expose corporate or state secrets. Controlling the output of pollutants, whether from cruise ships at sea or from furnaces on land, depends on enlisting, rewarding, and punishing private enterprises that have entrenched interests in business as usual. Controlling transnational criminal organizations is proving a task beyond the means and ingenuity even of the states most harmed by their activities. For customs and immigration inspectors in 1999 at the United States' 301 ports of entry and 3,700 terminals, globalization was a nightmare of "475 million people, 125 million vehicles, and 21.4 million import shipments. . . . Intercepting the ripples of danger in this tidal wave of commerce is about as likely as winning a lottery."[7] The chances are no better in Singapore where mechanization enables stevedores in eight hours, on average, to unload 3,000 of the over one million freight containers that pass through the port each month.[8]

The threats are real. Collective response, however, is uneven, uncertain, in some cases unformed. Financial volatility is no longer controlled by central banks or national boundaries, but international emergency rescue mechanisms still operate more ad hoc than as systems. Multilateral agreements among states take years to negotiate, often resulting in inadequate lowest-common-denominator solutions. For most issues covered in this book, effective implementation of such accords requires targeting the behavior of multiple actors, including individuals, businesses, and criminals. But successful monitoring and regulating of private actors can be a political or logistical ordeal. To complicate matters, sometimes the would-be enforcers disagree intensely about which actors to target. To curb transnational organized crime, for instance, should the emphasis be on changing the behavior of states, the crooks, or the consumers of illegal goods and services? Effective solutions in these circumstances require action on multiple fronts, which are easier to prescribe than to perform.

VARIETIES OF GOVERNANCE

New players, thorny problems, spillover effects, and the magnitude of cross-border flows together inflate the difficulty of coherent action at almost all levels of international affairs. These variables are, in a sense, products of the technologies and intergovernmental decisions that have brought countries and markets and people inexorably into both collision and cooperation. At the same time, these offshoots of escalating interdependence strongly influence the direction in which globalization will move—either toward tighter teamwork in meeting multiple challenges or toward division. This book does not seek to predict the direction of the future. Its authors, though, make clear that the stakes are rising, that the hazards for global statesmanship are profound and novel, and that collective responses to different issues in differing circumstances have been uneven.

Most of the tasks that our authors describe—whether keeping the peace after intrastate conflict, reversing climate change and widespread species extinction, tackling deeply entrenched corruption, or alleviating poverty and disease—necessarily demand long-term planning and sustained engagement as the foundation of successful implementation and compliance. Governments, however, tend to demand quick results. Keeping them involved for the long haul will require modifying mindsets to respond as diligently to enduring complexity on a global scale as to crises along the way. It also calls for changing institutional cultures within governments to create new connections across bureaucracies so that in-house dealings can mirror the multifarious linkages among global issues.

Those are problems for government, but governance is not government. Rather, the term signifies a diverse range of cooperative problem-solving arrangements, state and nonstate, to manage collective affairs. "It includes formal institutions and regimes empowered to enforce compliance, as well as informal arrangements that people and institutions either have agreed to or perceive to be in their interest."[9] Governance is the use of "mechanisms for steering social systems towards their goals."[10] It takes place through "laws, norms, markets, and architecture," not necessarily or exclusively the field of action of governments alone but rather in association with one another, with multinational bodies, with corporate and sometimes academic research entities and with NGOs. Such collective activity, structured or improvised, produces governance, sometimes without governmental authority.[11]

Over 2,000 multilateral agreements (among three or more states) already exist, establishing norms and rules that govern a broad range of global issues from maritime transport to fish stocks.[12] Of these arrangements, only some have near-universal participation—such as the International Treaty to Ban Landmines, the Universal Declaration on Human Rights, and the Non-Proliferation Treaty. The remainder are minilateral accords among a smaller set of partners, such as the Basel agreements on standards for banking adequacy; or regional, such as the North American Free Trade Agreement. In addition, a multitude of bilateral agreements, such as the 1972 U.S.-Soviet Anti-Ballistic Missile Treaty, have varying effect on global issues. Moreover, unilateral actions can also shape global practices. Y2K standards set by the United States quickly became internationally accepted.[13] For some issues such as weapons of mass destruction, elaborate institutional frameworks and binding rules exist. For others such as corruption, institutions and rules are far less developed.[14] In the description given by Robert Keohane and Joseph Nye, multiple "islands of governance" engage in problem solving—islands that, while more "densely concentrated among developed states, . . . often have global extension."[15]

Some of the products of past multilateral cooperation have proved so beneficial that the process is taken for granted in many areas. Global agreements on international trade that reduced tariffs significantly have helped trade flows grow at an average annual rate of six percent since 1947. International cooperation on telecommunications has built today's global information infrastructure, ordering the airwaves and the framework within which national networks connect. Multilateral assistance—initially premised on Cold War economic and political security concerns—has become a humanitarian given, a powerful instrument for cutting infant mortality, child malnutrition, and the incidence of such diseases as polio and smallpox. The negotiation and spread of international norms on basic human rights and labor rights contributed to an overall improvement in the treatment of individuals by governments and employers around the world. And the decision by state leaders to heed scientists' warnings and negotiate an agreement on the Earth's ozone layer checked a looming threat to human health and well-being. The benefits of cooperative action in many areas are as significant as the attendant progress in overcoming intense philosophical disagreements about how to shape international cooperation in a world of sovereign states.

Agreements among governments do not hold the monopoly on governance. Business leaders, citizen activists and NGOs, individual government elites, international organizations, and others have launched supplementary rule-making and problem-solving actions—alone and in partnerships that leapfrog national boundaries and sectoral lines. Coalitions of private actors monitor and enforce their own negotiated rules, as through the Worldwide Responsible Apparel Manufacturing Principles. Hybrid decision-making forums include the World Commission on Dams, whose commissioners include representatives from government, private industry, and NGOs. Some global private authorities, such as private bond-rating agencies, in effect force governments to accept their rules. Canadian leaders responded quickly after Moody's Investors Service threatened to downgrade the country's rating if it did not align its deficit-to-GDP ratio with global expectations.[16] Government elites compare techniques and then imitate each other—the result sometimes being common, even higher criteria on issues of global concern such as human rights. The Israeli Supreme Court has long researched U.S. Supreme Court precedents before ruling on freedom of speech, privacy rights, and other matters.[17] NGOs, private foundations, and businesses—beyond serving merely as contract agents for states and international organizations—increasingly provide services, money, normative values, and even leadership where governments and international organizations do not. One example is the Medicines for Malaria Venture that seeks to redress private sector underinvestment in vaccine research and production.

Transnational governance, however, is only as good as the effort that goes into matching laudable principles with actual practice. Nothing guarantees that all things multilateral will always prove benign. In reality, international regimes can bend to suit the priorities of the powerful: for example, the protectionist interests of the United States in textile trade or of the European Union (EU) in agriculture. Ideological or other coalitions can steer a global body away from its responsibilities as occurred when the International Labor Organization (ILO) in the mid-1970s routinely ignored Soviet and East European violations of international labor rights law. Governance strategies developed by private, self-selected groups can strain the limits of democratic accountability and give rise to complaints, for instance, about the unelected NGOs that worked with the World Bank to shape guidelines for the development of an oil pipeline in Chad. Understandably then, scholars and practitioners hold legitimate, fundamentally different views on how best (and who best) to approach the governance of global issues.

Innovation is the one common thread in this diverse assortment of management modes and approaches to governance. It has turned the "islands of governance" into an archipelago, connecting many of them along cooperative causeways. The concept of governance as something larger than government is itself relatively new. Its practical application has been more than a little uncertain. But there is no returning to the simplicities of an earlier age, and there are few roadmaps to show the way to a successful passage through the burgeoning complexity of global issues. Through a scholarly mining of the record of governance across a large range of fields for the nuggets of insight that can improve performance in the future, this book aims to provide one such map.

SURVEYING COMMON GROUND

This book tries to bridge disciplines in much the same way that its authors believe states must try to do. The exercise of producing it was a challenge from the start. Experts from different fields speak their own languages. What might be a fascinating insight from environmental management, for example, becomes a dull study of detail to a trade expert if issue-specific jargon obscures the point. In other cases, language can mislead: Certain already vague buzzwords like "civil society" have very different connotations in different fields.

An additional challenge was that the theoretical underpinnings for such a broad-based study—encompassing all phases of managing global problems—are scattered across a voluminous literature. The literature on global governance has ill-defined boundaries overlapping work on international relations theory, political science, multilateralism, international organizations, globalization, and other related topics.[18] Nearly all the relevant practical literature focuses on single-issue areas or specific regimes.[19] Very few studies in comparative governance address multiple issue areas; those that do are highly concentrated in a few fields (economics, environment, and arms control.)[20] Even those tend to focus on only single aspects of governance such as negotiations, sanctions, or the role of a particular set of actors.[21] As a result, lessons learned in one domain are seldom transposed to others. Furthermore, most studies have focused on interstate cooperation, with few works on the emergence of non-state-centric approaches to global problems.[22]

To draw comparative lessons, we invited sixteen experts to assess successes and failures of cooperation in the fields they know best based on a common set of questions. Following a common framework, these contributors distinguished among four related but analytically distinct components of governance: agenda setting, negotiation, implementation and compliance, and reactions to noncompliance. While these phases do not always occur sequentially and often blur together, this simple division greatly facilitates communication across fields.[23] We gave the authors a Herculean task: describe for nonexperts the nature of the principal governance issues in their respective fields; review the record of success and failure in problem solving; identify which actors, techniques, and types of regimes were most effective in each phase; and explain the factors that determined the overall outcomes. We asked authors to analyze intergovernmental efforts larger than bilateral ones, as well as any noteworthy alternative approaches involving nonstate actors or state/nonstate partnerships. In two concluding chapters, we sum up the authors' insights and offer our own analysis.

- *Actors.* Throughout this book we distinguish among five broad categories of actors. *States* include associations of them (such as G-8, G-10, EU). We define *international organizations* as including intergovernmental bodies (such as UN organizations, Bretton Woods institutions, development banks, treaty secretariats, and regional organizations) as well as hybrids.[24] The latter comprise some mix of government agencies, individual experts, NGOs, and private corporate actors (such as the International Organization for Standardization, the International Labor Organization, and the International Corporation for Assigned Names and Numbers.) We use *business* and *private sector* interchangeably to describe for-profit entities and nonprofit associations promoting business interests (such as the International Chamber of Commerce.) We use *NGOs* and *civil society* to include the diverse universe of interest groups, advocacy groups, and citizens' associations representing public, if sometimes specialized, interests.[25] Finally, we use *experts* to refer to government and nongovernment individuals with specialized technical, regulatory, or scientific knowledge who advise or make decisions in global rule making and regulation; and we use *epistemic communities* to refer to transnational groups of experts who meet sporadically and conduct common discourse based on shared knowledge.[26] These groupings are admittedly somewhat artificial given the diverse cast of characters and the networks they are forming— but they provide a useful categorization.

- *Agenda Setting.* Agenda setting involves raising an issue's profile on the international stage and in some cases framing specific goals for negotiation and action. Effective agenda setting is largely measured by the actions taken to deal with the problem. An issue may emerge following a carefully prepared strategy or unintentionally, as the result of some catalytic event or crisis, or as a side effect of some other issue. We were chiefly concerned with understanding which actors and techniques are successful in pushing issues into the international spotlight, and why.

- *Negotiation.* Negotiation is the stage in which participants exchange information on issues, stake out their positions, and may enter into coalitions to move debate toward agreed action. It is the point at which intentions are transformed into stated goals, norms, or commitments. The scope and complexity of intergovernmental negotiations have increased enormously in recent decades—because of the dramatic increase in the number of states active in the international system, the presence of more authoritative nonstate actors, and the greatly expanded substantive content of issues brought to the bargaining table. In addition, negotiations are taking place in hybrid decision-making forums and even exclusively among private actors. We asked authors to examine three questions: (1) What role do different types of actors play in negotiations? (2) How are negotiating instruments and strategies selected and employed? (3) What outcomes are achieved, and how effective are these outcomes in addressing the problems at hand?

- *Implementation and Compliance.* In this phase of governance, actors translate the intent behind agreements into action. *Implementation* takes in the broad range of activities that state and nonstate actors undertake to promote actions and behavioral changes in accordance with agreements. Within that range are the incorporation of governance norms into domestic laws, reforms within a corporation, NGO actions to push states or corporations to implement norms and comply with rules, programs of international organizations to improve states' capacity for implementation, and many other activities.

Compliance broadly describes the condition of state or nonstate parties' actual adherence to binding or nonbinding rules or to aspirational goals. Sometimes, achieving compliance may necessitate undertaking strenuous implementation measures; in other cases, compliance might come accidentally, or where governance merely codified existing practice, compliance might simply represent business as usual. Within this phase, actors use a range of techniques to monitor, review, and verify implementation and compliance. The term *monitoring* is used both to describe efforts to gather information and data about compliance and to describe efforts to collect data about developments within the issue or problem itself. *Verification* is a more limited concept to describe the process of certifying that a party or target is in compliance. Our chief concern in this phase was to evaluate the role and weight of various actors and to identify techniques and mechanisms that work best in influencing targeted actors to undertake desired actions or change behavior.

- *Reactions to Noncompliance.* Reactions to noncompliance—including incentives, technical assistance, diplomacy, public shaming, economic sanctions, and military force—are rarely formalized in intergovernmental or private agreements. It is unusual for such pacts to specify who is responsible for determining noncompliance and what should happen if parties do not abide by agreed-upon rules. When such provisions do exist, they tend to be vague. We asked authors to examine three questions: (1) What roles do the different types of international actors play in formulating and implementing responses to noncompliance? (2) What strategies are employed? (3) Which strategies are most effective?

IMPROVING THE ODDS

This book's underlying concern is *effectiveness*—the approaches that solve or help to solve problems. Effectiveness goes beyond formal compliance; parties may come into compliance with agreements effortlessly for a time and without undertaking any measures that change behavior or contribute to solving the problem. Agreements themselves may not be ambitious enough to provide more than temporary or cosmetic relief of global problems.

This book points to a grab bag of options. Sometimes effectiveness comes from a few powerful states acting first—rather than 189 trying to march in step. Other times it means a network of several governments working alongside business and civil society leaders to forge new means to address an issue. Or, it can mean a transnational advocacy group publicizing an issue and prompting changes in behavior absent a formal treaty.

Throughout their studies, the authors tried to answer the same, bottom-line question: What works? It would be rash to claim that they found formulas, magic or otherwise, but the inquiries reveal patterns, good and bad, that point toward approaches that may be required for the future. The authors concur that global issues management is the product of many hands trying to move many levers—not always in sync and not always with the desired results. The complexity of international issues, their overlapping nature, and the turmoil of the arena in which they surface defy tidy theorizing about effective management.

Instead, observers seeking to decipher the action and even the outcome need to know and weigh nuances of policy and politics and the roles played by a large and shifting cast of states and actors. The value to be derived from subjecting a range of global issues to a comparative scrutiny, as this book attempts, does not lie only in learning what has already been tried. The exercise can also serve as a stimulus to creative thinking and experimentation. Given the magnitude of the challenges this book describes, both are needed.

NOTES

1. Preamble to the Charter of the United Nations.
2. See Carnegie Endowment for International Peace, Global Public Policy Program, at <http://www.ceip.org>. See also Robert O. Keohane and Joseph S. Nye Jr., "Introduction," in Joseph S. Nye Jr. and John D. Donahue, eds., *Governance in a Globalizing World* (Washington, D.C.: Brookings Institution Press, 2000), pp. 4–7.
3. Thomas L. Friedman, *The Lexus and the Olive Tree* (New York: Farrar, Straus, and Giroux, 1999), pp. 7–8. For description of various forms of interdependence or globalism, see Keohane and Nye, "Introduction," esp. pp. 2–12.
4. Keohane and Nye, "Introduction," p. 11.
5. Jessica Tuchman Mathews, "Power Shift," *Foreign Affairs*, vol. 76, no. 1 (January/February 1997), pp. 59–60.
6. See Phil Williams, Chapter 3, in this volume.
7. Stephen E. Flynn, "Beyond Border Control," *Foreign Affairs*, vol. 79, no. 6 (November/December 2000), p. 57.
8. Stephen E. Flynn, "The Global Drug Trade Versus the Nation-State: Why the Thugs Are Winning," in Maryann K. Cusimano, ed., *Beyond Sovereignty: Issues for a Global Agenda* (New York: Bedford/St. Martin's Press, 2000), p. 52.
9. Commission on Global Governance, *Our Global Neighborhood* (Oxford, U.K.: Oxford University Press, 1995), p. 2. The UN Development Program (UNDP) defines governance as "the exercise of political, economic and administrative authority in the management of a country's affairs at all levels. Governance is a neutral concept comprising the

complex mechanisms, processes, relationships and institutions through which citizens and groups articulate their interests, exercise their rights and obligations and mediate their differences." See UNDP, *Governance for Sustainable Human Development* (New York: UNDP, January 1997). Oran Young defines governance in terms of "a social function centered on the making of collective choices regarding matters of common concern to the members of human groups." See Oran R. Young, *Global Governance: Drawing Insights from the Environmental Experience*, Occasional Paper (Hanover, N.H: Dickey Center, Dartmouth College, 1995), p. 1.

10. James Rosenau, "Toward an Ontology for Global Governance," in Martin Hewson and Timothy J. Sinclair, eds., *Approaches to Global Governance Theory* (Albany, N.Y.: State University of New York Press, 1999), p. 296.

11. Keohane and Nye, "Introduction," p. 12.

12. Union of International Associations, ed., *Yearbook of International Organizations: Guide to Global Civil Society Networks, 2000–2001* (Munich: K. G. Saur Verlag, 2000), p. 2406.

13. Keohane and Nye, "Introduction," p. 21.

14. When analyzing and measuring levels of institutional development, one might consider whether the following exist: (1) generally accepted principles and norms; (2) codes of conduct; (3) partnerships and networks; (4) consultation and negotiating mechanisms; (5) legally nonbinding agreements; (6) legally binding agreements; (7) international organizations; (8) monitoring mechanisms; (9) verification mechanisms; and (10) enforcement mechanisms.

15. Keohane and Nye, "Introduction," p. 20.

16. Friedman, *The Lexus and the Olive Tree*, pp. 91–2.

17. See, for example, Robert O. Keohane and Joseph S. Nye Jr., *Power and Interdependence* (Glenview, Ill.: Scott, Foresman, and Co., 1989); and Robert W. Cox and Harold Jacobson, *The Anatomy of Influence: Decision Making in International Organization* (New Haven, Conn.: Yale University Press, 1973). More recently, see Anne-Marie Slaughter, "The Real New World Order," *Foreign Affairs*, vol. 76, no. 5 (September/October 1997), pp. 183–97.

18. Suggested additional reading on governance appears at the end of this chapter. See the literature review on global governance in Craig Murphy, "Global Governance: Poorly Done and Poorly Understood," *International Affairs*, vol. 76, no. 4 (October 2000), pp. 789–803. See also John Gerard Ruggie, *Multilateralism Matters: The Theory and Praxis of an Institutional Form* (New York: Columbia University Press, 1993); and Nye and Donahue, eds., *Governance in a Globalizing World*. For a searchable database on global governance literature, visit the Managing Global Issues Information Network at <http://www.ceip.org>.

19. We use the term *regime* to describe a wide range of "sets of norms and rules spelling out the range of admissible behavior of different kinds of actors." See Peter Mayer, Volker Rittberger, and Michael Zuern, "Regime Theory: State of the Art and Perspectives," in Volker Rittberger, ed., *Regime Theory and International Relations* (Oxford, U.K.: Oxford University Press, 1995), p. 403. These sets of norms and rules may be formalized in treaties or they may be based on informal—legally nonbinding—agreements and understandings. Regimes may include international organizations—that is, material entities

possessing offices, personnel, budgets, equipment, and often legal personality—but are not limited to them. They may also comprise other institutions such as consultative mechanisms, negotiating bodies, partnerships, and networks. For a discussion on regime definitions and classifications, see also Marc A. Levy, Oran R. Young, and Michael Zuern, "The Study of International Regimes," *European Journal of International Relations*, vol. 1, no. 3 (September 1995), p. 274.

20. One notable exception is John Braithwaite and Peter Drahos, *Global Business Regulation* (Cambridge, U.K.: Cambridge University Press, 2000)—the product of a remarkable ten-year effort to analyze multiple actors in all phases of governance for thirteen issue areas.

21. Major comparative works across issue areas on one aspect of governance include Fen Osler Hampson, *Multilateral Negotiations: Lessons from Arms Control, Trade, and the Environment* (Baltimore, Md.: Johns Hopkins University Press, 1995); and Abram Chayes and Antonia Handler Chayes, *The New Sovereignty: Compliance with International Regulatory Agreements* (Cambridge, Mass.: Harvard University Press, 1995). Representative analyses of the role of particular actors in governance across issue areas include Margaret Keck and Kathryn Sikkink, *Activists Beyond Borders: Advocacy Networks in International Politics* (Ithaca, N.Y.: Cornell University Press, 1998); and Ann M. Florini, *The Third Force: The Rise of Transnational Civil Society* (Washington, D.C.: Carnegie Endowment for International Peace, 2000). On implementation in the environment field, see David G. Victor, Kal Raustiala, and Eugene B. Skolnikoff, eds., *The Implementation and Effectiveness of International Environmental Commitments: Theory and Practice* (Cambridge, Mass.: MIT Press, 1998); and Oran Young, ed., *The Effectiveness of International Environmental Regimes: Causal Connections and Behavioral Mechanisms* (Cambridge, Mass.: MIT Press, 1999). For a detailed listing of recommended readings on managing global issues, see the suggested additional reading at the end of this chapter.

22. See Wolfgang Reinicke, *Global Public Policy: Governing Without Government?* (Washington, D.C.: Brookings Institution Press, 1998); Cusimano, ed., *Beyond Sovereignty*; Wolfgang Reinicke and Francis Deng, *Critical Choices: The United Nations, Networks, and the Future of Global Governance* (Ottawa: International Development Research Centre, 2000); and Nye and Donahue, eds., *Governance in a Globalizing World*.

23. In many cases, such as the international movement to reverse depletion of the ozone layer, or the arms control field, analysts can consider these four components as "phases" that occur sequentially: a period of awareness building on the severity of a problem generates public pressure and political will to act; and an international treaty is negotiated and implemented, with subsequent efforts to enforce legally binding obligations by signatories. In other cases, the four components seem to blur together, and these distinctions are more difficult to make.

24. The United Nations comprises six "principal organs": the General Assembly, the Security Council, the Economic and Social Council (ECOSOC), the Trusteeship Council, the International Court of Justice, and the Secretariat. Each of these organs has a specific mandate under the 1945 UN Charter. Numerous subsidiary bodies and specialized agencies operate under UN auspices to compose the UN system. These specialized agencies, each with its own constitution, membership, and budget, include bodies like the World

Health Organization (WHO), the Food and Agricultural Organization (FAO), the UN Environment Program (UNEP), and the UN Educational, Scientific, and Cultural Organization (UNESCO).

The Bretton Woods institutions are the International Monetary Fund, the World Bank Group, the General Agreement on Tariffs and Trade (GATT), and the GATT's successor organization, the World Trade Organization (WTO). Similarly, development banks such as the Inter-American Development Bank, the Asian Development Bank, and the African Development Bank are lending institutions composed of member nations, operating under a charter and with a professional staff.

Under our definition, the Secretariat of the Convention on International Trade in Endangered Species (CITES), for example, would be considered an international organization. The ILO is a subsidiary organization of the United Nations. However, its tripartite structure of governments, employers, and workers makes it a hybrid international organization.

Like all international organizations, regional organizations also differ in their mandates and level of cooperation. Such is the case, for example, among the EU, the Organization of American States (OAS), the Organization of African Unity (OAU), and the North Atlantic Treaty Organization (NATO). While the EU has an exceptionally high degree of supranational political and economic integration, it is fundamentally an intergovernmental international organization.

25. P. J. Simmons, "Learning to Live with NGOs," *Foreign Policy*, no. 112 (Fall 1998), p. 83.
26. Braithwaite and Drahos, *Global Business Regulation*, pp. 24, 29. See also Peter Haas, "Epistemic Communities and International Policy Coordination," *International Organization*, vol. 46, no. 1 (Winter 1992), pp. 1–35.

SUGGESTED ADDITIONAL READING

Additional suggested readings on governance of specific global issues are listed at the end of each chapter.

Governance and International Cooperation

Axelrod, Robert. *The Evolution of Cooperation.* New York: Penguin Books, 1990.
Cox, Robert W., with Timothy J. Sinclair. *Approaches to World Order.* Cambridge, U.K.: Cambridge University Press, 1996.
Hasenclever, Andreas, Peter Mayer, and Volker Rittberger. *Theories of International Regimes.* Cambridge, U.K.: Cambridge University Press, 1997.
Hewson, Martin, and Timothy J. Sinclair, eds. *Approaches to Global Governance Theory.* Albany, N.Y.: State University of New York Press, 1999.
Katzenstein, Peter J., Robert O. Keohane, and Stephen D. Krasner, eds. *Exploration and Contestation in the Study of World Politics.* Cambridge, Mass.: MIT Press, 1999.

Keohane, Robert O. *International Institutions and State Power: Essays in International Relations Theory*. Boulder, Colo.: Westview Press, 1989.

Krasner, Stephen D. *International Regimes*. Ithaca, N.Y.: Cornell University Press, 1983.

Levy, Marc A., Oran R. Young, and Michael Zürn. "The Study of International Regimes." *European Journal of International Relations*, vol. 1, no. 3 (Fall 1995), pp. 267–330.

Murphy, Craig N. "Global Governance: Poorly Done and Poorly Understood." *International Affairs*, vol. 76, no. 4 (October 2000), pp. 789–803.

Rittberger, Volker, ed. *Regime Theory and International Relations*. Oxford, U.K.: Clarendon Press, 1993.

Rosenau, James N., and Ernst-Otto Czempiel, eds. *Governance Without Government: Order and Change in World Politics*. Cambridge, U.K.: Cambridge University Press, 1992.

Ruggie, John Gerard. *Multilateralism Matters: The Theory and Praxis of an Institutional Form*. New York: Columbia University Press, 1993.

Sandler, Todd. *Global Challenges: An Approach to Environmental, Political, and Economic Problems*. Cambridge, U.K.: Cambridge University Press, 1997.

Slaughter, Anne-Marie, Andrew S. Tulumello, and Stepan Wood. "International Law and International Relations Theory: A New Generation of Interdisciplinary Scholarship." *American Journal of International Law*, vol. 92, no. 3 (July 1998), pp. 367–97.

Young, Oran R. *Governance in World Affairs*. Ithaca, N.Y.: Cornell University Press, 1999.

Zacher, Mark W. *The United Nations and Global Commerce*. New York: United Nations, Department of Public Information, 1999.

How Globalization Affects Governance

Boli, John, and Frank J. Lechner, eds. *The Globalization Reader*. Malden, Mass.: Blackwell, 1999.

Cusimano, Maryann K. *Beyond Sovereignty: Issues for a Global Agenda*. Boston, Mass.: Bedford/St. Martins, 2000.

Edwards, Michael. *Future Positive: International Cooperation in the 21st Century*. London: Earthscan, 1999.

Florini, Ann M. *The New Rules for Running the World* (forthcoming).

Friedman, Thomas L. *The Lexus and the Olive Tree*. New York: Farrar, Straus, and Giroux, 1999.

Globalization, Governance, and Civil Society. Tokyo: Japan Center for International Exchange, 1998.

Held, David, et al. *Global Transformations: Politics, Economics, and Culture*. Cambridge, U.K.: Polity Press, 1999.

Homer-Dixon, Thomas. *The Ingenuity Gap*. New York: Alfred A. Knopf, 2000.

Kaul, Inge, Isabelle Grunberg, and Marc A. Stern, eds. *Global Public Goods: International Cooperation in the 21st Century*. Oxford, U.K.: Oxford University Press, 1999.

Kennedy, Paul. *Preparing for the Twenty-first Century*. New York: Random House, 1993.

Lechner, Frank J., and John Boli, eds. *The Globalization Reader*. Oxford, U.K.: Blackwell, 2000.

Mathews, Jessica. "Power Shift." *Foreign Affairs*, vol. 76, no. 1 (January/February 1997), pp. 50–66.

Nye, Joseph S., Jr., and John D. Donahue, eds. *Governance in a Globalizing World*. Washington, D.C.: Brookings Institution Press, 2000.

Our Global Neighborhood: The Report of the Commission on Global Governance. Oxford, U.K.: Oxford University Press, 1995.

Prakash, Aseem, and Jeffrey Hart. *Globalization and Governance*. New York: Routledge, 1999.

Reimagining the Future: Toward Democratic Governance. Victoria, Australia: Department of Politics, La Trobe University, 2000.

Reinicke, Wolfgang. *Global Public Policy: Governing Without Government?* Washington, D.C.: Brookings Institution Press, 1998.

Rosenau, James N. *Along the Domestic-Foreign Frontier: Exploring Governance in a Turbulent World*. Cambridge, U.K.: Cambridge University Press, 1997.

Simai, Mihaly. *The Future of Global Governance: Managing Risk and Change in the International System*. Washington, D.C.: U.S. Institute of Peace, 1994.

Smith, Gordon, and Moises Naím. *Altered States: Globalization, Sovereignty, and Governance*. Ottawa: International Development Research Centre, 2000.

Comparative Studies Across Global Issues

All Phases of Governance

Braithwaite, John, and Peter Drahos. *Global Business Regulation*. Cambridge, U.K.: Cambridge University Press, 2000.

Negotiations

Hampson, Fen Osler. *Multilateral Negotiations: Lessons from Arms Control, Trade, and the Environment*. Baltimore, Md.: Johns Hopkins University Press, 1995.

Implementation and Compliance

Chayes, Abram, and Antonia Handler Chayes. *The New Sovereignty: Compliance with International Regulatory Agreements*. Cambridge, Mass.: Harvard University Press, 1995.

Downs, George W., David M. Rocke, and Peter Barsoom. "Is the Good News About Compliance Good News About Cooperation?" *International Organization*, vol. 50, no. 3 (Summer 1996), pp. 379–406.

Shelton, Dinah, ed. *Commitment and Compliance: The Role of Non-binding Norms in the International Legal System*. Oxford, U.K.: Oxford University Press, 2000.

Verification. London: Verification Research, Training, and Information Centre (VERTIC), Annual Yearbook.

Sanctions

Cortright, David, and George Lopez. *The Sanctions Decade: Assessing UN Strategies in the 1990s*. Boulder, Colo.: Lynne Rienner, 2000.

Crawford, Neta C., and Audie Klotz, eds. *How Sanctions Work: Lessons from South Africa.* New York: St. Martin's Press, 1999.

de Jonge Oudraat, Chantal. "Making Economic Sanctions Work." *Survival,* vol. 42, no. 3 (Autumn 2000), pp. 105–27.

Haas, Richard N., and Meghan L. O'Sullivan, eds. *Honey and Vinegar: Incentives, Sanctions, and Foreign Policy.* Washington, D.C.: Brookings Institution Press, 2000.

Hufbauer, Gary Clyde, Jeffrey J. Schott, and Kimberly Ann Elliott. *Economic Sanctions Reconsidered.* Washington, D.C.: Institute for International Economics, 1990.

Weiss, Thomas G., David Cortright, George Lopez, and Larry Minear. *Political Gain and Civilian Pain: Humanitarian Impacts of Economic Sanctions.* Lanham, Md.: Rowman and Littlefield, 1997.

Actors in Governance

All Actors

Braithwaite, John, and Peter Drahos. *Global Business Regulation.* Cambridge, U.K.: Cambridge University Press, 2000.

Mathews, Jessica. "Power Shift." *Foreign Affairs,* vol. 76, no. 1 (January/February 1997), pp. 50–66.

Reinicke, Wolfgang, and Francis Deng. *Critical Choices: The United Nations, Networks, and the Future of Global Governance.* Ottawa: International Development Research Centre, 2000.

States

Strange, Susan. *The Retreat of the State: The Diffusion of Power in the World Economy.* Cambridge, U.K.: Cambridge University Press, 1996.

World Bank. *World Development Report 1997: The State in a Changing World.* New York: Oxford University Press, 1997.

International Organizations

Diehl, Paul F., ed. *The Politics of Global Governance: International Organizations in an Interdependent World.* Boulder, Colo.: Lynne Rienner, 2001.

Jacobson, Harold K. *Networks of Interdependence: International Organizations and the Global Political System.* New York: Knopf, 1984.

Keohane, Robert O. *International Institutions and State Power: Essays in International Relations Theory.* Boulder, Colo.: Westview Press, 1989.

Murphy, Craig. *International Organization and Industrial Change: Global Governance Since 1850.* Oxford, U.K.: Oxford University Press, 1994.

Paolini, Albert J., P. Jarvis, and Christian Reus-Smith. *Between Sovereignty and Global Governance: The United Nations, the State and Civil Society.* New York: St. Martin's Press, 1998.

Proceedings of the 92nd Annual Meeting: The Challenge of Non-state Actors. Washington, D.C.: American Society of International Law, 1998.

Reinalda, Bob, and Bertjan Verbeek, eds. *Autonomous Policy Making by International Organizations*. New York: Routledge, 1998.

Zacher, Mark W. *The United Nations and Global Commerce*. New York: UN Department of Public Information, 1999.

Nongovernmental Organizations

Boli, John, and George Thomas, eds. *Constructing World Culture: International Nongovernmental Organizations since 1875*. Stanford, Calif.: Stanford University Press, 1999.

Charnovitz, Steve. "Two Centuries of Participation: NGOs and International Governance." *Michigan Journal of International Law*, vol. 18, no. 2 (Winter 1997), pp. 183–286.

Edwards, Michael. *NGO Rights and Responsibilities: A New Deal for Global Governance*. London: Foreign Policy Centre, 2000.

Florini, Ann M., ed. *The Third Force: The Rise of Transnational Civil Society*. Washington, D.C.: Carnegie Endowment for International Peace, 2000.

Higgott, Richard A., Geoffrey R. D. Underhill, and Andreas Bieler, eds. *Non-state Actors and Authority in the Global System*. London: Routledge, 2000.

Keck, Margaret, and Kathryn Sikkink. *Activists Beyond Borders: Advocacy Networks in International Politics*. Ithaca, N.Y.: Cornell University Press, 1998.

Mathews, Jessica. "Power Shift." *Foreign Affairs*, vol. 76, no. 1 (January/February 1997), pp. 50–66.

O'Brien, Robert, Anne Marie Goetz, Jan Aart Scholte, and Marc Williams. *Contesting Global Governance: Multilateral Economic Institutions and Global Social Movements*. Cambridge, U.K.: Cambridge University Press, 2000.

Risse-Kappen, Thomas, ed. *Bringing Transnational Relations Back In: Non-state Actors, Domestic Structures and International Institutions*. Cambridge, U.K.: Cambridge University Press, 1995.

Wapner, Paul. *Environmental Activism and World Civic Politics*. Albany, N.Y.: State University of New York Press, 1997.

Weiss, Thomas G., and Leon Gordenker, eds. *NGOs, the U.N., and Global Governance*. Boulder, Colo.: Lynne Rienner, 1996.

Private Sector

Cutler, A. Claire, Virginia Haufler, and Tony Porter, eds. *Private Authority and International Affairs*. Albany, N.Y.: State University of New York Press, 1999.

Haufler, Virginia. *A Public Role for the Private Sector: Industry Self-Regulation in a Global Economy*. Washington, D.C.: Carnegie Endowment for International Peace, 2001.

Mitchell, John, ed. *Companies in a World of Conflict*. London: Earthscan, 1998.

Experts

Braithwaite, John, and Peter Drahos. *Global Business Regulation*. Cambridge, U.K.: Cambridge University Press, 2000.

Haas, Peter. "Epistemic Communities and International Policy Coordination." *International Organization*, vol. 46, no. 1 (Winter 1992), pp. 1–35.

The United States and Multilateralism

Karns, Margaret P., and Karen A. Mingst, eds. *The United States and Multilateral Institutions: Patterns of Changing Instrumentality and Influence*. Boston, Mass.: Unwin Hyman, 1990.

Maynes, Charles William, and Richard S. Williamson, eds. *U.S. Foreign Policy and the United Nations System*. New York: W.W. Norton, 1996.

Patrick, Stewart, and Shepard Forman, eds. *Multilateralism and U.S. Foreign Policy*. Boulder, Colo.: Lynne Rienner, 2001.

Washburn, John L. "United Nations Relations with the United States." *Global Governance*, vol. 2, no. 1 (January 1996), pp. 81–96.

For a searchable database on governance literature, visit the Carnegie Endowment's Managing Global Issues Information Network at <http://www.ceip.org>.

Part II

Global Issues

1

Communications

William J. Drake

HOW ARE GLOBAL COMMUNICATIONS GOVERNED? Twenty years ago, the answer to this question would have been straightforward. Governments collaborated in the International Telecommunication Union (ITU) to devise multilateral regimes for the organization of international networks and services and the distribution of radio frequency spectrum and satellite orbital slots. Similarly, they partnered in the International Telecommunications Satellite Organization (Intelsat) and ancillary organizations to provide and govern satellite communications. These three international regimes—for telecommunications, radio frequency spectrum, and satellite services—formed the overarching policy architecture of the global communications order. They extended to the international level a pattern of industry organization that in most countries was defined by extensive state control and regulation, rather than by private ownership and competitive market forces. Nested within the framework established by these regimes, governments cooperated in regional and plurilateral organizations to set locally specific rules and manage programs for the development of infrastructures and services. In addition, they cooperated in other forums to tackle, with rather less success, questions raised by international mass media and information flows.

Over the past twenty years, the globalization of pressures unleashed by the information revolution has undermined much of this orderly policy architecture. New technological opportunities created by the merging of telecommunications and computing provided transnational corporations (TNCs) with the incentives and means to pressure governments to liberalize domestic and international markets. In parallel, the spread of new ideas about the role of telecommunications and its optimal governance in an information-based economy encouraged governments, first in the industrialized world, and later in the developing world, to consider the case for liberalization in a more accommodating light. As a result of domestic factors, the speed of conversion from the old beliefs and institutional arrangements varied considerably across countries, and these asymmetries generated substantial conflict between the United States and other industrialized countries, in particular over the extent and terms of competition. Nevertheless, by the 1990s, the bulk of the global communications industry was transitioning to competition and private sector control, and even the more reluctant developing countries were following suit.

As governments liberalized and privatized their domestic industries, corresponding changes in the multilateral rules of the game for international networks and services became the order of the day. Under pressure from the global business community and pro-liberalization governments led by the United States, the international telecommunications and satellite regimes were transformed to facilitate the shift to a multiprovider, business-friendly global marketplace. In parallel, while the radio regime's organizing principles and mechanics did not change, its underlying politics are now largely driven by the competing demands of corporations. In addition, the efforts of some governments to establish multilateral regulations on international mass media and networked information flows collapsed, thereby strengthening the momentum toward corporate freedom and market organization. And capping off the transition, the 1986–1994 Uruguay Round negotiations produced the first multilateral regime liberalizing international trade in services, including telecommunications and information services.

As if these changes were not enough, the rise of the Internet sealed the fate of the old state-centric order. Since the mid-1990s, the globalization, commercialization, and mass popularization of the Internet have radically transformed the world of international communications. The technologies, transactions, and actors that are increasingly driving the worldwide restructuring of the sector emerged outside the old communications industries and are not easily governed by traditional forms of national and international public authority. In consequence, the Internet has raised significant challenges for the international telecommunications and trade in services regimes, as well as for a range of ancillary institutions at the regional and plurilateral levels. At the same time, the Internet also has given rise to new and unique patterns of international cooperation. The management of Internet infrastructure is dominated by companies working in a wide array of industry forums to devise private systems of rules. In parallel, both governments and firms are collaborating—with varying degrees of success—in a diverse range of forums to devise shared rules on communications behavior and global electronic commerce conducted over that infrastructure.

The net effect of all these developments, then, has been a transformation of the global communications order. Global governance has moved away from the long-stable model of states working in a limited number of organizations to devise heavily administrative rules, and toward a more fluid and heterogeneous policy architecture in which states and a hyper-empowered global business community cooperate and compete in a wide range of forums to devise market-enabling rules. The diversity of these management efforts reflects the explosive growth and differentiation of communications behavior and the issues it raises; in many cases the very notion of uniform, universal regulatory frameworks has become archaic and counterproductive. To be sure, many of the legacy system institutions of previous eras are still around and battling to preserve their positions. The resulting tensions between the old and new "networld" orders have rendered international cooperation a far more complicated, contested, and fluid arena than in the past. But the game and the balance of power within it have clearly changed, and the trajectory going forward will clearly be in the direction of ever increasing transnationalism and private control of the global communications environment.

It would be well beyond the scope of this chapter to provide a systematic overview of this transformation process, or to map out the myriad issues and organizational dynamics involved in each substantive domain of international cooperation at the bilateral, regional, plurilateral, and multilateral levels. Instead, my purpose is necessarily much more modest: to survey some of the major features of the principal foundations of multilateral communications policy to draw out a few general lessons about what has worked, what has not, and why. My focus is not on issues and dynamics of interest primarily to specialists who are deeply engaged in the intricacies of global communications policy. Rather, in keeping with the objectives of this book, I concentrate on broader lessons that may be of relevance to analysts and practitioners of international cooperation in general.

Even this nominally modest goal presents challenges that warrant two caveats. First, the scholarly literature on multilateral communications policy is very thin; although much has been written about some of the issues encompassed by the regimes, there has been far less on the regimes as a whole, and even less than that on the ways in which agenda setting, negotiation, implementation, and reactions to noncompliance (the four shared focuses of this volume) have worked in each or any of them. As such, what is presented here is a first-cut interpretation based more on primary research and news accounts in trade publications than on a well-developed scholarly consensus. Second, pulling back from the trees to depict the forest means that the potentially generalizable lessons one can draw from the diverse experiences of communications regimes are necessarily broadly framed and even somewhat generic. Nevertheless, in keeping with the objectives of this volume, they should provide a basis for drawing comparisons and contrasts with the dynamics of global governance in other international issue areas.

NATURE OF THE PROBLEM

Managing international communications requires that states confront a sharp trade-off between competing values. On the one hand, the control of communications networks and services has always been viewed as an essential component of national sovereignty. Telecommunications is both a key infrastructure that underlies and integrates a country's economy and society and a leading high-technology sector that drives innovation and wealth creation in other industries. Similarly, mass communications are central to the public sphere of ideas and sociocultural development. In light of these and related considerations, the desire to retain national political control over their communications industries has been keenly felt by all governments for 150 years. On the other hand, the ability to communicate internationally also is of critical importance to a country's prospects and prosperity, and fostering that ability requires cooperation with other countries to establish shared rules of the game. As a result, the history of global communications policy has been shaped by states' efforts to balance these political and functional imperatives.

In broad terms, multilateral communications policy involves managing five sets of issues. First, varying kinds of electronic networks located in different countries have to be physically interconnected and logically interoperable so that information can be transported across borders and effectively utilized. As technology has progressed over the years, ensuring that an increasingly heterogeneous array of networks, services, applications, and customer terminals can work together has become a progressively more demanding task. The means by which this goal has been pursued is international technical standardization. Technical standards ensure compatibility between different pieces of hardware or software by selecting common design parameters and, conversely, deselecting other possible configurations.

Second, the scarce international resources underlying certain elements of communications infrastructures must be distributed and managed. These resources may be physical or logical. Scarce physical resources include the radio frequency spectrum through which wireless communications flow and satellite orbital slots. In both cases, there are natural limits on the usable spaces available, so particular segments of those spaces must be devoted to services and users on an exclusive basis to avoid interference. Although technological progress sometimes allows services to share or utilize narrower slices of these resources, in the end their physical scarcity and consequent overcrowding remain intractable realities. And as the development of new spectrum-dependent services usually requires the displacement of incumbent services or users, the intergovernmental management of the reallocation process can become a highly politicized affair. Similarly, scarce logical resources include telephone numbers and, in the case of the Internet, both IP (Internet Protocol) numbers and domain names—including country codes such as .us, global top-level domains such as .org, and second-level domains such as www.ceip(.org).[1] Here too, the challenge is to allocate these resources to unique users so that messages are properly directed across complex networks of networks, recognizing that particular names may be prime real estate desired by multiple competing contestants.

Third, once networks and equipment are standardized and the resources underlying them are allocated, providers in different countries must agree on the terms and conditions according to which traffic will be passed from one interconnected system to the next. Such operating agreements need to cover not only the technical requirements of making systems work together, but also the economic aspects of providing services and managing exchanges across national borders. The dominant way of doing this in the telecommunications environment historically has been for operators in different countries to provide the facilities and services jointly on a noncompetitive basis and to exchange compensation for terminating each other's outbound traffic. Although the operating agreements between carriers are generally embodied in bilateral contracts, the desire for predictability of terms and a measure of transnational uniformity encourages countries to establish multilateral rules governing intercarrier relations. Alternatively, in the Internet environment, in the era of exclusively research and educational networking, operators used to simply agree to "peer" and exchange traffic without the corresponding exchange of compensation. With the Internet's transformation into a commercial medium, however, these peering agreements often have broken down and been replaced by compensation schemes that operate on a different basis from those employed in public telephone networks.

Fourth, governments may wish to facilitate the international commercial exchange of services. For example, rather than having carriers in different countries partner to provide telecommunications, they could allow a given carrier to build solely owned networks that span national borders to provide the end-to-end transmission of messages, or they could allow foreign carriers to build cross-border networks that then interconnect with local ones for a fee. Further, they may wish to allow trade in telecommunications services that use capacity leased from a network owner, or in information-based services embodying different types of content. In these and other cases, trade agreements are needed on the terms of market access, and in some cases on a wide range of ancillary questions related to the sale of commercial products (for example, intellectual property protection, consumer protection, competition policy objectives, and so on).

Fifth, apart from any trade agreements on the commercial exchange of services, some governments may want to have shared rules on the substantive types of information that can flow across national borders. Historically, this issue primarily pertained to mass media flows, such as the international dissemination of radio or television broadcast signals, although in the contemporary era of networked information the matter also has arisen with respect to private data communications over corporate networks and the Internet. In truth, the problem here is more political than functional, because such agreements are not technically required for communications to occur. And in fact, because the issue has been so politically divisive, governments to date have not established strong and coherent universal international regimes, although there are some regional arrangements among broadcasting agencies, particularly where geographic density and irregular borders raise questions of signal spillover.

In extremely truncated and stylized form, these then are the major issues that give rise to international policy cooperation on communications. In the next section, I consider some of the main responses to them that have been adopted over the years.

TRACK RECORD OF INTERNATIONAL RESPONSES

International communications regimes have taken a variety of forms over the past 150 years. Indeed, as noted above, the global communications order comprises a plethora of bilateral, regional, plurilateral, and universal multilateral arrangements of varying scope and strength. Here the focus is only on the most important, top-level arrangements employed in seven key issue areas: (1) the international telecommunications regime; (2) the international radio regime; (3) the international satellite regime; (4) international principles for information flow; (5) the international trade in services regime; (6) the international private management of Internet infrastructure; and (7) potential international regimes for Internet communication and commerce.

International Telecommunications Regime

Until recently, the international telecommunications regime provided the central foundation of the global communications order. The regime establishes a framework for the organization of global markets, interconnection of national networks and equipment, and international exchange of traffic. Its core principles were established in the 1850 Treaty of Dresden, which created the four-member Austro-German Telegraph Union, and they influenced the design of the Western European Telegraph Union formed in 1855. The principles then were elaborated on in the 1865 Treaty of Paris, in which twenty countries established the world's first international organization—the International Telegraph Union. As the membership expanded (to 189 nations in 2000) and telegraph, telephone, and radio issues became increasingly interrelated, in 1932 governments decided to replace it with a broader International Telecommunication Union (ITU). The ITU was restructured and expanded in scope by conferences held in 1947 and 1992, and along the way evolved into a semifederalist array of bodies. Those involved in deciding telecommunications regime matters included the diplomatic Plenipotentiary Conferences, the Administrative Conferences, and the technical committees on telegraph and telephone, which were merged in 1956 and became part of a unified International Standardization Section in 1993.[2] The section includes the World Telecommunications Standardization Assemblies, the study groups, and a business advisory group. In addition, the ITU's annual management council also makes decisions at times that can affect regime issues.

The telecommunications regime that has developed since 1865 is codified in three sets of instruments. First, the Plenipotentiary Conferences periodically meet to revise the ITU's Convention and, from 1993, a separate Constitution. While both of these treaties deal with the organizational management and decision-making procedures of the ITU, the convention also lays down some overarching principles specific to the regime. Second, the Administrative Conferences also meet on a periodic, as-needed basis to revise a treaty that, since 1988, has been called the International Telecommunication Regulations. This treaty elaborates principles and norms on how the union's objectives are to be met in the organization of networks and services. Third, each of the standards section's dozens of study groups and working parties meets several times per year to devise recommendations, which are nonbinding but generally followed rules—including technical standards and economic and operational prescriptions—that specify in minute detail exactly how the governing treaties' principles and norms are to be operationalized in particular circumstances. At present, more than 2,600 recommendations laid out in more than 60,000-plus pages are in force.

The *ancien* regime that lasted from 1850 to 1988 rested on three overarching principles. The national sovereignty principle meant that, internally, states could configure and govern their networks and industries however they pleased as long as they played by the rules where international correspondence was concerned. With a few exceptions—most prominently, the United States and Canada—a government Ministry of Posts, Telegraphs, and Telephones (PTT) controlled the telecommunications industry in most countries. The PTTs served as both the principal policy maker and the monopoly or near-monopoly providers of public switched telephone networks and services. In this dual role of umpire and sole or dominant player, their control over the game at the national level was complete. Externally, the sovereignty principle meant that international correspondence had to be conducted in accordance with the mutual consent of the countries involved. The principle was broadly interpreted to justify a wide range of rules that buttressed the power of national monopolies and restricted both competitive market entry by private suppliers and what the carriers deemed to be potentially undesirable uses of systems and services by corporate customers.

The joint service provision principle meant that services moving traffic from an outbound country to an inbound country were provided jointly by the carriers in each, with the revenues collected divided evenly between them and a fixed share going to the carriers of any transit countries in between. Over the years, ITU members utilized a number of methods for managing the division of revenues from joint services, the most important of which—the international accounting and settlements system—attained dominance in the 1960s. The joint service provision principle, and the complex norms and rules operationalizing it, established an international order in which monopolists could exchange traffic without competing against one another. This was the fundamental political glue that held the system together and ensured broad intergovernmental support for and compliance with the regime.

The third principle required interconnection between national networks via technical standardization. This was not a simple matter, because key ITU members in the industrialized world saw the promotion of domestic manufacturers as a sovereign right. Standardization therefore long concentrated to the extent possible on the connection points between national networks. But as technology progressed and became more complex, it reached further and further into the national domain, thereby making the task more politically demanding.

The international telecommunications regime has gone through four developmental phases over the past 150 years. From 1850 to the 1970s, it evolved in a largely stable manner with new technologies and services being slowly incorporated into the dual system of national monopoly control and international joint service provisioning. But from the mid-1970s to the mid-1980s, the information revolution, U.S. domestic deregulation, corporate demands for worldwide market liberalization, and the spread of new ideas about telecommunications governance progressively undermined the foundations of the old order. The asymmetric international spread of these pressures generated substantial conflict between pro-liberalization and pro-monopoly governments, especially within the industrialized world.

By 1988 the opposition in principle to liberalization began to collapse, and ITU members undertook the progressive renegotiation of the regime to allow a shift toward a market-based and more privately controlled global order. Regulations and recommendations on market organization and corporate networking that were previously justified by the sovereignty and joint services principles were relaxed, while technical standardization for interconnection was reformed to be more responsive to an increasingly heterogeneous industry and moved to a significant degree out of the ITU nexus. By the mid-1990s, the cumulative result of these dynamics was a fundamental transformation of the regime's social purpose and of some of its key instruments. The three overarching principles that shaped the regime during the long century of monopoly control remained in place, but they were now interpreted and implemented in a manner that puts far fewer restrictions on market forces and private control. Nevertheless, the institution remained too limiting for leading segments of the increasingly empowered private sector, and governments—led first and foremost by the United States—began to defect selectively from the rules of the game. At the same time, new technologies and players increasingly worked around the regime's restrictions, while new international trade agreements shifted the locus of economic cooperation on telecommunications rules out of the ITU. In consequence, since 1998 the world's oldest international regime has entered a state of drift and decline, with its instruments remaining in force but governing less and less of the global industry's actual behavior.

International Radio Regime

The international radio regime provides a universal policy framework for the management of the natural resources and services involved in wireless transmission. Its origins lie in the 1903 Treaty of Berlin, in which six states agreed that wireless telegraph stations should avoid interference with one another. Three years later, twenty-seven nations met again in Berlin to adopt the first International Radiotelegraph Convention and Regulations. Signatories agreed to provide technical and operational information about their uses of radio frequency spectrum to the Berne Bureau, the administrative organ of the ITU. In 1932 governments decided to establish the Telecommunication Union and brought radio policy fully into the new body. The organs focused on developing the radio regime included the Plenipotentiary Conferences; the World Administrative Radio Conferences, the Regional Administrative Radio Conferences, and specialized Administrative Conferences; and a technical committee that had been independently created in 1927. In 1947 a restructured ITU replaced the radio functions of the Berne Bureau with a new and stronger organ, the International Frequency Registration Board (IFRB). The 1992 Plenipotentiary Conference restructured the ITU again and grouped all radio-related organs into a new International Radiocommunication Section. The section includes the World Radiocommunication Conferences and Regional Radiocommunication Conferences, the study groups and their Plenary Assemblies, a business advisory group, a permanent Radiocommunication Bureau, and a more functionally limited Radio Regulations Board.

The radio regime that has developed in the ITU is codified in four sets of instruments. First, the ITU's plenipotentiaries periodically revise the convention that, inter alia, lays down some of the overarching principles of the radio regime. Second, the radiocommunication conferences meet on a more regular basis to revise the International Radio Regulations. This treaty comprises administrative and operational principles and procedures on how the union's objectives are to be met in the wireless sphere, and a Table of Frequency Allocations around the world. Third, the Radiocommunication Bureau, and before 1993 the IFRB, maintains an exhaustive and continually updated Master International Frequency Register of assignments. Fourth, the radio study groups and working parties meet several times per year to devise nonbinding recommendations on technical standards and related issues.

The radio regime is based on five overarching principles. First, the national sovereignty principle allows ITU members to organize their domestic spectrum use as they please as long as this is consistent with the principles below and international services are operated by mutual consent of sending and receiving countries. Second, the shared resource principle holds that international radio frequency spectrum and satellite orbital slots are global resources that cannot be owned by anyone, although they can be devoted to the exclusive or shared use by certain services and users. Third, the noninterference principle means that radio frequency spectrum and satellite orbital slots must be employed in a manner that facilitates communication and avoids harmful interference with legal uses. The adoption of technical standards serves this function, as do the other, subsidiary principles.

Fourth, the allocation and allotment principle spells out how resources are to be distributed. Allocations pertain to frequency bands that are designated for use by particular services. Allotments pertain to specific frequencies or channels that may be used by national administrations or services in particular countries or regions. Allotments can be done in one of two ways: *a posteriori,* or on a first-come, first-served basis; and *a priori,* or through collective planning. Both methods have been widely used over the years depending on the technical properties of and competing demands on the frequencies in question. In the early postwar era, the United States was an advocate of planning. More recently, the industrialized countries often have favored the *a posteriori* approach on the grounds that it is more efficient, whereas the developing countries have favored the *a priori* approach on the grounds that it is more equitable.

Fifth, the assignment notification principle requires that states inform the ITU of their authorized frequency assignments and satellite positions. The bureau (and before 1992, the IFRB) then assesses these to determine if they conform with the treaties and the table of allocations and avoid harmful interference with existing, legally registered users. If the judgment is favorable, the notifications are added to the master register and enjoy legal status. If it is unfavorable they do not attain that status, although the ITU has no power to force a member to give up an unapproved use and may even include a rejected assignment in the register if it does not cause interference.

The radio regime has developed in four stages. From 1903 to 1946, the international rules developed slowly and were subject to much contestation and widespread violations, which the ITU's early radio instruments were not equipped to handle. The organizational restructuring of 1947 changed the regime by giving ITU members clearer rights and obligations, and by providing the IFRB with an expanded ability to rule on the legality of spectrum usage (although it lacked any real enforcement power to act on adverse judgments). This year also saw the advent of concerted efforts to plan spectrum usage on an *a priori* basis. Although grandiose proposals to thoroughly plan the entire spectrum have failed, planning has been successful in certain frequencies.

Since 1963 the ITU has extended the regime's principles and procedures to cover the allocation of geostationary orbital slots and spectrum usage by satellites, which has required a corresponding increase in the level and complexity of the activities involved. Finally, since 1992 the politics of the radio regime have been transformed, even if the regime's fundamental principles and modalities have not. In earlier eras, the radio regime tended to revolve around interstate battles over allocations and allotments and the balance between the *a posteriori* and *a priori* approaches—first among the United States, Europe, and the Soviet bloc, and later between the industrialized and the developing countries. In today's context of global market liberalization and privatization, the real action is among competing TNCs seeking space for their new systems and services, with their home governments playing more of a supporting role.

International Satellite Regime

The international satellite regime is a somewhat unusual, hybrid arrangement. On the one hand, it comprises multilateral rules on the organization of the global satellite services market. On the other hand, it establishes the dominant actor in that market—the 144-member Intelsat. In other words, Intelsat has acted as both the umpire and main player in the game, although today that game is changing rapidly and its de facto rule-making role for the market as a whole is receding.

A U.S.-led initiative, Intelsat was created in 1964 as a consortium of government-designated institutions, which in most cases were the PTTs. In contrast, the United States was represented in most contexts by a private firm, the Communications Satellite Organization (Comsat), which was created by a U.S. law in 1962. During Intelsat's first decade, Comsat served not only as the largest shareholder in the organization, but also as its manager. In 1973 Intelsat's "interim arrangements" were superseded by the "definitive arrangements." These include the intergovernmental Intelsat Agreement, which establishes Intelsat as an international organization and defines its purpose and structure; and the Intelsat Operating Agreement among the government-designated shareholders, which deals with more detailed technical, operational, and financial issues. The Intelsat Agreement created a four-part governance structure comprising an Assembly of Parties, or sovereign states; a Meeting of Signatories, or operating entities; a Board of Governors elected to oversee policy; and a Director-General and staff responsible for day-to-day management.

Until recently, the satellite regime had three main components. First, members agreed to jointly fund and operate Intelsat as a near-monopoly provider of international satellite services. Second, they agreed that it should follow certain technical and operational standards in interconnecting with national public networks; employ tariffs that among other things facilitated developing countries' access to the global system; and provide links only to shareholder organizations, rather than directly to end users. And third, they agreed to coordinate any other satellites they might establish with Intelsat. This is a key principle, because it effectively meant that Intelsat members collectively would decide whether and on what terms other entities from their countries could enter the marketplace. Different technical and economic criteria were involved depending on the type and scope of services contemplated, but the key was that members would not launch competing systems that could pose "economic harm" to Intelsat, which generally was interpreted to mean taking away more than 3 percent of its market. Hence, when some members formed the International Maritime Satellite Organization (Inmarsat) or regional satellite systems in the 1970s, they had to ensure that no technical or economic harm would ensue. Of course, this clause did not apply to Intersputnik, the parallel and negligibly significant organization established by the Soviet bloc in 1972, because its members were not also in Intelsat.

The satellite regime has developed historically in four stages. During the interim arrangements of 1964–1972, the principal political battles were between the United States and Europe over Comsat's managerial role and the allocation of equipment procurement contracts. Following the definitive arrangements, Intelsat became a truly multilateral institution and greatly expanded the scope of its operations, providing crucial interconnectivity to developing countries in particular. The major political challenge from the mid-1970s to the mid-1980s was to ensure that the burgeoning development of domestic and regional satellite systems (and, less explicitly, fiber optic cables) run by member operators did not detract from Intelsat's position of preeminence.

By the mid-1980s, though, Intelsat's near-monopoly power came under direct attack from its former patron, the United States. The Reagan administration unilaterally decided to satisfy growing corporate demands and allow private companies to enter the global market, subject to successful coordination with Intelsat. Although these private entrants argued that their initial service offerings would not pose economic harm to Intelsat, Intelsat's defenders correctly saw their plans as a harbinger of increasing and unwanted competition in the years ahead. A highly politicized and divisive struggle ensued, but in the end the new U.S. policy prevailed, and in ensuing years other leading governments followed suit by authorizing their own companies to launch competing systems. American pressures yielded further changes in the 1990s. Intelsat not only rescinded the "no economic harm" test, but also split off a commercially oriented independent company. Going even further, members subsequently decided to undertake a complete privatization of the intergovernmental organization, scheduled for 2001. Hence the satellite regime has been thoroughly transformed from a system of rules protecting and operating a meta-monopoly to one that allows competition in international services, albeit with Intelsat as the still dominant player.

International Principles for Information Flow

The three regimes discussed above focus primarily on the systems and services that move information across borders, rather than on the substantive content of that information. Historically, the overarching political problem in this arena was the tension between the competing principles of national sovereignty and the free flow of information. The former has been interpreted to mean that states can decide what types of information will be allowed to cross their frontiers, while the latter means that people have a right to send and receive information of their choosing without impediment. The functional need to set universal rules was so weak and the political differences among states were so deep that strong and coherent international regimes were impossible. Instead, what emerged was a patchwork of ambiguous, conflicting, nonbinding, or unenforceable international principles embodied in different instruments.

In the pre-Internet era, multilateral debate focused on international point-to-multipoint mass communications, most notably broadcasting, and international point-to-point communications via telecommunications networks. With regard to the former, three kinds of universal instruments are especially relevant, the first of which are the ITU agreements. Under the ITU Convention, members reserved the right to intercept, monitor, and stop transmissions that are deemed threatening to national security and public order, both of which could be defined however a government liked. With the advent of radio broadcasting in the 1920s, many nations became alarmed that their publics could receive signals from abroad, including from hostile powers. Hence, when communist governments took to jamming incoming signals, the practice was challenged in the ITU primarily insofar as sloppy efforts generated harmful interference with the signals of third parties. Similarly, after the rise of direct television broadcasting by satellite, a 1971 radio conference established a doctrine of "prior consent," which held that broadcasters should reduce as far as possible any signal spillover into other countries unless otherwise authorized.

Second, in the 1960s, the Soviet bloc and the developing countries launched campaigns to reinforce and extend the sovereignty principle in nontechnical instruments. For example, in the 1966 Covenant on Civil and Political Rights and in a 1972 resolution, the UN General Assembly inserted language that buttressed the right of sovereign states to control cross-border information flows. Similarly, from the 1970s to the mid-1980s, developing countries pushed in the UN Educational, Scientific, and Cultural Organization (UNESCO) for a New World Information and Communications Order. In this context, the organization adopted a Mass Media Declaration that among other things called for increased state sovereignty and regulatory authority in global media relations. But third, and in contrast, the United Nations also has adopted similarly soft law instruments calling for freedom of communication, most notably the 1948 Universal Declaration of Human Rights. Hence, that both competing principles are embodied in broad-based multilateral instruments has produced a good deal of ambiguity and highly charged political debates as to which takes precedence.

With regard to point-to-point communications, in the telegraph era some states availed themselves of the right to intercept, monitor, and stop particular messages or links. Although the ITU treaties invoked the public's right to private communications, including coded messages, reasons of state clearly trumped that right. But in the 1960s, the right of states to project territorial control onto private communications grew progressively more difficult to enforce, as the number of communications channels and the diversity of information forms increased with the development of international direct dial telephony and data communications. This problem came to a head in the 1970s in the worldwide debate over transborder data flows (TDF).

Many governments from the industrialized and developing worlds alike feared that the use of TDF by TNCs, particularly those based in the United States, would have negative consequences for their economic and legal independence and sociocultural integrity. As such, a debate raged to the mid-1980s about the wisdom and feasibility of devising national and international rules for TDF that would restrict any problematic corporate uses of TDF and promote national sovereignty. At the multilateral level, this debate played out in two forums in particular: the Organization for Economic Cooperation and Development (OECD); and the Intergovernmental Bureau for Informatics (IBI), an organization in Rome comprising over forty developing countries. The debate ranged widely over an array of complex issues, and for awhile the voices calling for various forms of regulation—especially France, the developing countries, and on some points Canada and the Scandinavians—gained ground.

In the end, an intensive U.S. and corporate campaign for preserving free flows combined with the difficulties of actually monitoring, evaluating, and controlling TDF led the industrialized countries away from broad regulatory solutions. Only in the case of protecting the privacy of personal data did the Europeans insist: they established domestic laws and regulations; adopted a convention in the Council of Europe; backed the OECD's establishment of nonbinding guidelines, which was all the Americans would agree to; and in the 1990s adopted a European Union directive, all in the hope of ensuring protection of their citizens' privacy when personal data are transferred across borders. Enforcing and monitoring compliance with these arrangements is difficult, however, and the adamant refusal of the United States to abide by meaningful protections significantly undercuts their intent.

On the wider range of issues raised in the TDF debate, several years of negotiation in the OECD resulted in 1985 in a nonbinding Declaration on Transborder Data Flows that allowed both sides to claim victory by acknowledging the importance of both free flow and national sovereignty and focusing more on networked trade in and access to data. The industrialized world's backing off voided any hope the developing countries had of adopting and enforcing restrictions, and the IBI not only relented but was later disbanded. The net effect of all this, then, was to establish a variably enthusiastic and lightly institutionalized international understanding that the content-based regulation of networked information is technically difficult and too politically divisive, and thus will not be pursued. Nevertheless, many of the issues are now being revisited, albeit with important differences, with respect to the Internet.

International Trade in Services Regime

The establishment of the General Agreement on Trade in Services (GATS) was one of the key results of Uruguay Round negotiations launched in September 1986. The agreement signed in April 1994 by members of the General Agreement on Tariffs and Trade (GATT) covered a wide range of issues, and among other things replaced the GATT organization with a stronger World Trade Organization (WTO), which has 140 members. With respect to global communications, the GATS regime includes separate provisions dealing with the dual roles of telecommunications mentioned above. As a sector in its own right, governments undertook market-opening commitments on trade and investment in telecommunications. As a medium for the exchange of other services, telecommunications is treated as the dominant form of the cross-border "modes of supply" for services trade.[3]

The GATS regime comprises three major elements. The first is the Framework Agreement, which includes fifteen principles or General Obligations and Disciplines, such as most-favored-nation status, that usually apply to national commitments. In addition, the agreement includes Specific Commitments, which are negotiated undertakings by governments to liberalize the provision of service sectors or subsectors. In other words, a given type of service transaction is opened to competitive supply only insofar as a government agrees to do so; it can pick and choose what to liberalize or not (for example, by allowing the cross-border supply of a particular service but not its supply via other means). There are three such commitments: to provide market access by removing quantitative restrictions; to ensure national treatment; and to undertake any additional commitments that governments choose.

The second component of the GATS regime is the eight annexes. These clarify or modify how the general obligations apply to issues unique to certain services sectors and modes of supply and establish the legal basis for future negotiations on them. The Annex on Telecommunications deals with telecommunications as a mode of supply for other services and obliges governments to ensure access to and use of public telecommunications transport networks and services. Public systems must be accessible to foreign service providers for domestic and international service provisioning once governments have agreed to liberalize the service in question, be it financial services, professional services, or whatever. The annex requires that public systems be provided on a reasonable and nondiscriminatory basis and that foreign suppliers can access and use private leased circuits, interconnect such circuits with public networks, and so on. In addition, governments must ensure that foreign suppliers can transfer TDF and access databases abroad.

The third component of the GATS is the National Schedules in which governments list their commitments. Comprising several thousand pages, the schedules include a wide range of market-opening measures in different services sectors, including telecommunications. During the Uruguay Round, sixty governments made commitments on telecommunications as a trade sector in its own right. In general these focused on computer-enhanced or "value-added" services, with only a few countries making limited commitments on basic telecommunications services such as international telephony that comprise the lion's share of the global market.

Hence, in accordance with another GATS annex, in 1994 countries willing to contemplate more substantial basic telecommunications commitments launched a new negotiation. In February 1997, the Group on Basic Telecommunications (GBT) completed a deal among sixty-nine governments, which others have joined subsequently. Essentially, the participants—who account for more than 90 percent of the global market—deepened their national schedules, and most also endorsed in their additional commitments sections a Reference Paper comprising six key principles for the redesign of national regulatory rules and institutions to ensure compatibility with trade disciplines. These require market-opening actions with respect to competitive safeguards, network interconnection, the protection of universal service, the public availability of licensing criteria, the establishment of independent regulators, and the allocation and use of scarce resources such as radio frequency spectrum.

The GATS and its Reference Paper constitute the biggest institutional change in the global communications order since 1850. For the first time, governments have erected a multilateral system of rules designed to progressively open up trade and investment in services sectors, including communications and information. Where national commitments allow, companies can build or buy into networks abroad to provide telecommunications services on an end-to-end basis, rather than under the joint service provisioning arrangements of the telecommunications regime. At the same time, while the accounting and settlements system has yet to be formally subjected to GATS rules through dispute resolution, the intercarrier exchange of traffic under the joint service scheme is increasingly viewed as a matter of trade in traffic origination and termination services. And where governments have made commitments, the delivery of information and mass media services is also subject to trade disciplines. In short, the GATS represents a fundamentally different policy architecture for the organization of global communications systems and services, which will progressively deepen the transformation from statist to market-based global governance.

International Private Management of Internet Infrastructure

Both the overarching architecture of Internet governance and the approaches to tackling individual issues are of recent vintage, heavily contested, and rapidly changing. As such, and in contrast with the other cases above, it is somewhat difficult to provide a snapshot of Internet cooperation or to draw many firm lessons from its still emerging forms. That said, broadly speaking, Internet governance may be said to involve two arenas of collective action. One concerns the management of the under-lying infrastructure, or the array of networks, services, and core applications that define the medium; the other concerns the governance of communication and com-merce conducted over that infrastructure, which is covered in the next section. Gov-ernments sometimes have had indirect influence on specific dimensions of infra-structure management, but in general private companies have been the key players in this arena since the Internet's commercialization in the early 1990s. Most of the activity involves the coordination of projects and policies among firms, rather than the establishment of transparent and generalized systems of authoritative rules akin to formal international regimes. However, to the extent that the leading firms in the field have undertaken much of this effort, their private decisions and contrac-tual relationships de facto have the effect of setting rules for third parties. A listing of the diverse firms and industry organizations that have played prominent roles in infrastructure issues would read like a large alphabet soup of acronyms. It is thus easier to say simply that there are groupings working on four broadly framed sets of issues.

First, there is extensive private coordination among the providers of the underly-ing infrastructure. Internet service providers and backbone operators have to inter-connect their networks and hand off traffic, a process that increasingly involves the exchange of payments between large and small operators. Second, there is a wide range of industry groups indigenous to the Internet working on the development of the technical standards and protocols required for network interconnection and interoperability. Historically, the most important of these has been the Internet En-gineering Task Force (IETF), which in coordination with the Internet Architecture Board has elaborated many of the key specifications. Third, there are industry orga-nizations involved in managing and setting private rules among themselves on such issues as network security, digital signatures, electronic contracting, and so on. In a few cases, these organizations have established so-called self-regulatory or private regimes that affect third parties; the various private frameworks for the voluntary protection of World Wide Web users' privacy are the most obvious example of this.

Fourth, the domain of private cooperation that is popularly thought to be synony-mous with "Internet governance" is the management of Internet names and num-bers. In the Internet's early years as a research and education network, this function was performed by a one-man organization called the Internet Assigned Number Authority under contract with the U.S. government. With the Internet's globaliza-tion and commercialization, the government decided that the function should be performed on a cooperative basis by a range of private industry organizations and invited proposals. After an intensely politicized power struggle in which a variety of domestic and international bodies attempted to assert their authority, in 1998 the United States selected the Internet Corporation for Assigned Names and Numbers (ICANN) to serve as the lead authority.

A private, not-for-profit corporation registered in California, ICANN represents a new hybrid form of international organization. Its semicorporatist organizational structure includes a president and chief executive officer, a secretariat, and a board of directors, the latter of which has ultimate decision-making authority; a Domain Name Supporting Organization, an Address Supporting Organization, and a Protocol Supporting Organization, each comprising various industry factions; and an At-Large Membership of Internet users around the world that elects five of the board's nineteen directors. In addition, ICANN has a Government Advisory Committee comprising representatives (usually from communications ministries) of dozens of governments. Unfortunately, although ICANN's articles of incorporation and bylaws spell out fairly clear procedures for the operation of all this machinery, in fact rather fundamental decisions—such as the selection of board members and policies—often have been taken in a loose and nontransparent manner that many observers argue deviates wildly from the purported rules. Either way, through its contract with the U.S. government, which controls the root server that routes messages around the Internet, ICANN is charged with setting global policies for the management of Internet names and IP numbers, including the number and variety of global top-level domains. To effect these policies, it maintains contractual relationships with the private registrars and registries that commercially allocate these resources. It also has enunciated a uniform domain name dispute resolution policy (UDRP) that is supposed to provide a neutral mechanism for sorting out competing claims arising from the *a posteriori* allotment of names.

Incipient International Regimes for Internet Communications and Commerce

Governments have moved aggressively since the mid-1990s to fill the perceived policy void on Internet communications and commerce through a combination of uncoordinated national actions and multilateral dialogue. At the same time, concerned that governments will adopt retrograde policies that could damage the Internet's development, private sector actors are working to advance so-called self-regulatory solutions to certain problems, in some cases with the support of noncommercial actors, leading governments, and international institutions. The extent to which these and related dynamics have played out and resulted in the institutionalization of widely accepted governance arrangements varies from issue to issue, but in most cases we are still early in the process.

Among the issues in play are market access, customs and taxation, the terms of electronic contracting and authentication, consumer protection, intellectual property, encryption, personal privacy, and content questions such as the balance between freedom of speech and restrictions on objectionable material. The U.S. government has worked hard to take the lead in shaping the international debate on these points in the hopes of preemptively setting agendas compatible with its interests, although the European Commission in particular has moved quickly to establish itself as a countervailing force. In addition, the European Union has adopted a slew of measures to promote the harmonized development of Internet commerce laws and regulations among its members. Other industrialized countries also have weighed in in various forums, whereas the developing countries have had fewer opportunities to participate in devising solutions to any of these issues.

Efforts to establish governance mechanisms have proceeded on two tracks: informal agreements and consultations, and calls for legally binding agreements under formal international organizations. With regard to the former, the United States has reached a number of bilateral memorandums of understanding (MOUs) with other industrialized countries, and members of the OECD and the Asia-Pacific Economic Cooperation (APEC) have developed nonbinding declarations and guidelines on several issues. The ITU has adopted a number of recommendations related to Internet standardization and traffic exchange and has sought, unsuccessfully, to carve out a central role in domain name management. In addition, the UN Commission on International Trade Law (UNCITRAL) has adopted a draft model law on electronic signatures, the World Customs Organization has developed recommendations on related issues, and the UN Centre for Trade Facilitation and Electronic Business has devised recommendations to promote electronic transactions.

With regard to the latter, the World Intellectual Property Organization (WIPO) established a treaty in 1996 to protect the interests of major content owners in global markets and has been given a central role in the ICANN domain name dispute process. In 1998, the WTO adopted a work program to bring Internet commerce under its instruments in the pending round of trade negotiations. In addition, the industrialized countries have been working in several forums to devise firm rules to deal with network security and cybercrime. In sum, most of the activity to date has involved reaching informal agreements designed to facilitate global electronic commerce, particularly among the industrialized countries. However, in the years ahead it is likely that formal arrangements will play a greater role with respect to certain issues, most notably market access and intellectual property, and that the developing countries will demand a greater voice in shaping the rules of the game.

LESSONS LEARNED

The schematic overview above provides a context within which lessons from communications regimes can be considered. Below are eighteen lessons, grouped in keeping with this volume's framework into four categories: agenda setting, negotiation, implementation and compliance, and reactions to noncompliance. The first few lessons are somewhat specific to the communications environment but provide important background on the political dynamics at work in this field. In contrast, the rest are more broadly framed and may provide some leverage in thinking about international cooperation more generally.

Agenda Setting

In the monopoly era, incremental change and overall stability in the operational environments of communications regimes facilitated state control of the international agenda. From the 1840s to the 1980s, most countries for most of the time had government-owned communications systems, and those that had any private telecommunications networks or broadcasters regulated them heavily. This pattern of control at the national level tightly constrained both the progress of technological change and deployment and private sector challenges to the forms of global governance favored by states. But precisely which governments had the most power over the international agenda varied across regimes.

European PTTs dominated the international telecommunications regime. As the creators of the regime and the ITU, the Europeans had a substantial first-mover advantage, and countries that joined subsequently had to buy into the fundamental parameters they had defined. Working together in a club-like atmosphere, the Europeans organized the policy process and designed regime instruments in a manner that buttressed their national monopoly control. The framing of new issues had to map with their material interests, technocratic organizational culture, and normative conceptions of how national correspondents should work together. New ideas or demands that did not fit within these parameters were reworked to become acceptable or filtered out of the system. Moreover, they utilized their colonial and postcolonial connections with much of the developing world—which generally had little independent influence on the agenda—to broaden support for their preferred models of national and global governance. As the ITU's membership grew in the twentieth century, the PTTs of other industrializing countries like Japan and upper-tier developing countries such as Brazil and India began to play a greater role in agenda setting, but they too supported the European vision.

In contrast, the U.S. government had much less influence on the agenda. After all, the United States did not join the ITU until the 1930s and hence had no role in designing the global policy architecture. After it did join, the government generally deferred to its private sector—primarily, the American Telephone and Telegraph Co. (AT&T), which also favored the intermonopoly model of joint service provision, even if it opposed the intergovernmental regulation of rates and related issues. With some support from Canada, which also had private carriers and did not join the ITU until the 1930s, the United States frequently and unsuccessfully argued against key elements of the European-born PTT agenda.

The situation was different with respect to the radio and satellite regimes. Because the United States was the single largest user of frequency spectrum and the creator, biggest shareholder, and initial manager of Intelsat, its influence over the agendas of these regimes was correspondingly greater. At times the two sides of the Atlantic had significant disagreements, but over the broad sweep of history these differences were generally sorted out enough to facilitate the agenda-setting process. For their part, the developing countries at times were able to exercise much greater influence on the radio regime agenda than they could in the other two cases. ITU voting rules in the Administrative Conferences give every country one vote, and since the late 1970s, developing countries have used this procedural opening to band together and demand preferential treatment and greater planning of allocations. These efforts usually did not yield their desired results once power was brought to bear in the negotiating process, but they did affect the items included on the agenda.

Although in the nineteenth century the vast majority of intercontinental submarine cables were controlled by a cartel of private firms largely based in the United Kingdom, the PTTs were able to use their collective authority to bring these companies and subsequent private carriers into the telecommunications regime on their terms. After the United States joined the ITU, the decision-making procedures were amended somewhat to enhance the role of the private sector, but overall its independent influence on nontechnical aspects of the agenda remained heavily constrained by procedural rules and PTT power. What influence the private sector did have was exercised by participation in certain (most notably, U.S.) national delegations or consultations outside of ITU forums. Much the same was true of the radio regime, under which governments negotiated the allocation of spectrum to different services, which in turn would assign it to users at the domestic level. Similarly, the notable exception of Comsat, private sector influence was negligible in the satellite regime. And as a monopoly carrier with the sole right to provide access to the Intelsat system within the United States, Comsat's core interests with regard to the organization of the global market and its influence on the agenda were hardly representative of wider corporate interests.

The information revolution and global liberalization have greatly increased private sector influence on the international agenda. The rapid growth and differentiation of systems and services provided by firms outside the traditional PTT nexus has made it impossible for governments to dictate how the global communications order should be structured. At the same time, TNCs—especially those based in the United States—have been at the forefront of a worldwide private sector revolt against the traditional monopoly order. As a result, communications industries have been woven into the fabric of global capitalism, and the cooperative central planning favored by the PTTs is now a thing of the past. Indeed the PTTs themselves are becoming a thing of the past: in all of the industrialized countries and in a growing majority of developing countries, the PTTs have been broken up, with postal services split off from what are now called Public Telecommunications Operators (PTOs). These PTOs have been privatized throughout the industrialized and much of the developing world, although in many cases the government remains a leading shareholder, at least for now. More-over, they are acting as commercial entities that compete within each other's own markets even as they cooperate in the ITU and Intelsat.

With regard to the telecommunications regime, private sector influence on the agenda is exercised from within and outside the ITU. Internally, especially impor-tant today are a dozen or so international "super carriers," including some former PTTs, that are invading national markets and forming interfirm alliances to provide corporate users with integrated, end-to-end solutions on the most lucrative and high-volume routes. Their regime preferences are somewhat mixed: on the one hand, many remain dominant in their home markets and at times seek to use multilateral mechanisms to shore up those positions through anticompetitive regime rules. On the other hand, their involvement in multiple markets abroad sometimes gives them incentives to seek international rules of the game that are flexible and business friendly. More singular in their objectives are corporate users and many equipment manufac-turers, both of whom are increasingly influential on certain issues and tend to favor thorough liberalization.

In contrast, other PTOs and residual PTTs, particularly from the developing coun-tries, often want only to preserve their traditional national positions rather than com-pete internationally. They have become increasingly active in the agenda-setting pro-cess and seek to use multilateralism to slow the pace of change so as to better cope with the transitions under way. Hence much of the intra-ITU regime politics today revolves around competitive tensions among private network operators, with the support of their respective home governments. In addition to these insider dynamics, private companies also shape the agenda externally simply by pursuing strategies in global markets that stimulate responses within the ITU. Among them is a variety of new competitors that, as is discussed below, do not participate heavily or at all in ITU affairs.

Increasing private sector influence also has redefined agenda setting in the other two traditional arenas of cooperation. In the radio regime, technological change has provided opportunities to provide a range of new mobile voice and data services, and companies have pushed hard in the ITU to secure the necessary spectrum realloca-tions. In the 1990s, two major groupings have dominated the agenda. The first are companies, based mostly in the United States, that hope to provide personal digital communications services from new nongeostationary satellites. Several of these ven-tures have failed in their early stages because of high costs, soft demand, and compe-tition from terrestrial systems, but sorting out their technical requirements and op-erational arrangements has nevertheless been a major and time-consuming issue. The second are companies, based mostly in Europe and Asia, that hope to provide third-generation mobile services over terrestrial links. Similarly, in the satellite regime, separate systems operators' calls for market liberalization and the competitive responses of Intelsat's PTO membership have dominated the agenda.

What about the new regimes formed in the 1990s? Although other players such as the European Community and policy analysts also played crucial roles, it is clear that the private sector (particularly U.S.-based TNCs) and the U.S. government were the leading proponents of getting international trade in services on the agenda and pushing through the GATS and the GBT deal. Companies and multinational trade associations have also driven current efforts to establish market-friendly rules for global electronic commerce in the WTO and other forums, the development of the WIPO's regime for online intellectual property, and the creation of the ICANN-based regime Internet names and numbers. In cases in which sociopolitical rather than commercial objectives are dominant, however, it has been governments rather than firms that have driven the Internet policy agenda. Indeed some of the proposals to establish arrangements for cybercrime, encryption, and the restriction of access to certain types of content have been opposed by otherwise dominant business interests. As these examples underscore, governments have hardly disappeared from the game; nevertheless, the balance of influence between them and the global business community has definitely shifted.

In an increasingly competitive global environment, inadequate private sector participation can preclude effective agenda setting. Although the influence of the private sector as a whole has greatly increased in recent years, many relevant companies do not participate in multilateral policy discussions. One problem is that small- and medium-sized firms often lack the means to participate effectively. Another is that some governments are selective about which firms they will consult with or allow to participate in multilateral forums. And still another hurdle is the rules of the forums themselves. Some, like the WTO, do not allow private sector participation; others, like Intelsat, allow only selected firms, in this case shareholders; and still others, like the ITU, are open to all but discourage many companies, whether intentionally or not, from taking advantage of the opportunity. For example, historically in most ITU bodies, companies were denied the right to participate independently and vote; joining government-led delegations was thus the primary option. Recognizing that its legitimacy, technical work, and financial resources would all be enhanced, in the 1990s the ITU reformed its procedures to allow the independent representation of business interests in some of its bodies, subject to the payment of membership fees. Even so, most of the big decisions are still made in bodies in which only governments can vote, so dues-paying firms may find themselves sitting on the sidelines while decisions they oppose are being adopted.

More generally, even if corporate participation is allowed, the configuration of power within some of the organizations is such that doing so seems pointless to many firms. This is especially a problem with respect to the ITU. Many of the new competitors that are launching systems, services, and markets are engaged in what the ITU calls "new modes of operation." These are types of service provisioning—international simple resale, callback, refile, Internet telephony—that bypass the traditional cooperative model and are not standardized and regulated in accordance with ITU instruments. In general, these firms see the regime's regulatory dimensions as being overly restrictive and view the ITU as essentially a clubhouse for semireformed PTTs in which their demands for open competition cannot prevail. That attitude is particularly prominent in the Internet industry, which increasingly is the driving force of all global communications.[4] Hence, while the PTOs continue to coordinate within the ITU, a growing percentage of the industry is in the hands of firms that are not involved in the organization and are working whenever necessary and possible outside its policy framework. The result is an increasing decoupling of the global market and the regime that is supposed to govern it. Power dynamics are also a problem in ICANN, where the dominance of trademark interests and major registrars has constrained competition and thrust many smaller firms into positions of often vociferous opposition.

Whatever the reasons for it may be in a given case, a lack of participation by the full range of private sector stakeholders can be deleterious for both agenda setting and subsequent stages of cooperation. To the extent that many of the new competitors are playing key roles in driving the development of technologies and markets, not having them at the table robs the process of important expertise and perspectives and increases the possibility that the dominant actors will define issues in a self-serving and anticompetitive manner. In turn, a lack of buy-in by the new actors increases the likelihood that the agreements subsequently forged will not be recognized as legitimate and implemented by the industry as a whole.

Nongovernmental organizations sometimes can make valuable contributions to the agenda-setting process, but special measures may be needed to facilitate their participation. Civil-society-based nongovernmental organizations (NGOs) historically have had little impact on international communications regimes. In those countries that had consumer groups and labor unions with interests in communications policy, these organizations tended to focus their attention on domestic rather than international affairs. Moreover, the relevant international organizations made no allowance for independent NGO participation, and their inclusion in government-led delegations was very rare. Even today, when the question of the role of NGOs in global governance is all the rage, efforts to bring them into the traditional global communications organs have been decidedly half-hearted. For example, in 2000 the ITU established a new associate category of membership that could be used for this purpose, but associates are only entitled to participate in a single technical study group and must pay a fee to do so and to access documents. Given the number of meetings these groups hold in Geneva and the costs and other demands of participating, this small change in procedures is unlikely to result in a major increase in noncommercial participation.

In light of these constraints, only two examples of NGOs playing notable roles in the traditional regime debates come readily to mind. First, with support from the United States in particular, amateur or "ham" radio operators were able to secure some spectrum to carry on with their activities and even managed to obtain a small office in the ITU headquarters. Similarly, one NGO recently has managed to get a place on the agenda for its proposal to set aside some spectrum for noncommercial development programs in developing countries. Second, some NGOs have been involved in international mass media issues, most notably in support of the developing countries' calls for a New World Information and Communication Order. Their efforts were not independently consequential in terms of policy outcomes, however, and no international mass media regime was ever agreed.

In general, it is only with the mass popularization of the Internet in the 1990s that a significant number of NGOs have gotten involved in international communications policy. By providing diverse groups with powerful information resources, the current distributed stage of the information revolution gives them a heightened sense of having stakes in how such resources are governed. Concern that governments and TNCs will devise international rules that favor commercial objectives over other uses, restrict speech, expand state surveillance and police powers, and so on have spurred the development of Internet policy NGOs and the formation of coalitions across national frontiers.

With regard to infrastructural issues, academics and other noncommercial experts that share perspectives with or even have links to user-oriented NGOs have long participated in agenda setting in the IETF and other technical bodies. They have also been centrally involved in other arenas of technological development, such as the current worldwide movement to develop the Linux operating system as an open-source alternative to the Wintel environment. To the extent that widely adopted standards and computer code come to have lawlike properties that structure behavior, such efforts could be said to constitute participation in a form of global governance.[5]

In terms of more legally grounded arrangements, ICANN finally has established a mechanism for NGOs to participate in some of its work, and the New York–based Markle Foundation has provided NGO members with the funds to attend important meetings. In addition, in 2000, ICANN held an online election in which more than 34,000 people around the world participated—despite significant procedural and technical problems—in selecting regional representatives, including some from the noncommercial sector. Insofar as many people in the sector are intensely critical of ICANN's policies and procedures and have mobilized to express their concerns, it is possible that the civil society constituency could become an important voice affecting ICANN's agenda.

With regard to Internet communications and commerce issues, NGOs are increasingly organizing but generally have not been given the opportunity to participate in agenda setting. Instead they have been left to react post hoc to agendas set by governments and powerful corporations. In a few cases, NGOs have been allowed to express their views directly in intergovernmental meetings. For example, in 1998 the OECD invited trade unionists and members of the Global Internet Liberty Campaign—an international coalition of organizations concerned with free speech, privacy, and related matters—to address a conference at which nonbinding guidelines were adopted on privacy and consumer protection. Both the agenda and the guidelines had been agreed beforehand, however. Usually even such nominal offers of inclusion are not extended, and NGOs' main options are to express their views through online or offline activism, publications, conference punditry, meetings with any receptive national officials, and the like. Nevertheless, these forms of post hoc participation sometimes do matter; in 2000, the Council of Europe decided to rework a draft treaty on cybercrime after an outpouring of vociferous protest from NGOs and other stakeholders.

The experience with the cybercrime treaty reflects a new reality: because the management of global communications affects a growing array of technologically empowered stakeholders, for some types of issues it may become increasingly difficult to devise legitimate and effective forms of global governance without including NGOs from the outset. As with the private sector, important segments of the noncommercial sector may not passively abide by regimes that are directly contrary to their interests, especially where they have the technical ability to circumvent such rules. But involving relevant NGOs in communications agenda setting would require some significant changes. Governments and firms would need to be willing to bring them into the domestic consultation process as real partners and perhaps include them in delegations to international conferences. International organizations would have to increase significantly their transparency by using the World Wide Web to disseminate much more information; amend their rules on participation; not require that NGOs pay fees to attend meetings or obtain documents; and allow remote online participation in their deliberations, as is the IETF's practice. However, given the attitudes toward communications policy–oriented NGOs that have been displayed by many businesses and governments, most notably in the developing world, it is far from clear that measures such as these will be adopted anytime soon.

Prior forms of institutionalization can have a powerful impact on the paths that new issues follow to the international agenda.   Over the past 150 years, new international communications issues have arisen from a wide variety of sources—technological change, market behavior, new ideas, the demands of powerful companies and governments, the demonstration effect of domestic experiences, the internal debates of international organizations, and so on. But regardless of their origins, new issues have not moved seamlessly onto the international agenda. Instead they have been filtered through a maze of existing interest configurations and conflicts, organizational cultures and procedures, conceptual frameworks, and the like.

Particularly important has been whether or not there was an international organization and/or regime with clear jurisdiction, and if there was, whether addressing the issues would be supportive or disruptive of the status quo. When there have been institutions in place, new issues that comported with the existing order generally were brought onto the agenda without great difficulty. For example, the progressive elaboration of technical standards and operational rules for international telegraph service or spectrum management in the monopoly era was not the product of some apolitical functionalist logic at work; rather it reflected the shared interests and institutional orientations of ITU members who wanted centralized technical and policy architectures under their control.

In contrast, potentially disruptive issues often received a different reception. Sometimes such issues were addressed slowly and reluctantly; it took almost a half-century after the invention of the telephone for the ITU to begin serious work on developing international service, in large part because the PTTs wanted to recover the costs of their telegraph network investments before contemplating a competing service. In a different vein, even though the Uruguay Round provided a logical and facilitative environment in which to tackle trade in services, many developing countries insisted that the issue not be negotiated under the legal aegis of the GATT, and ultimately made rather limited commitments under the GATS. Or, sometimes disruptive issues were addressed more promptly, but in a distorted manner. The advent of private computer networking in the early 1960s was viewed not as a boon to global communications that should be strongly encouraged to develop unfettered, but instead as a potential threat to monopoly networks that should be carefully reigned in through collective regulation. And although these restrictive dynamics were especially prominent in the monopoly age, they are visible even in today's environment. For example, conservative members of the ITU still respond to pro-competitive technologies such as the Internet or callback systems by attempting to circle the wagons and impose PTO control.

More interesting have been cases involving potentially disruptive issues over which there were no intergovernmental institutions in place with clear jurisdiction. TDF in the 1970s–1980s and many Internet issues today are obvious examples. In these cases, governments struggled to determine whether existing concepts and international arrangements provided elements of possible solutions, or whether new ones would have to be created. Moreover, not only were the issues complex, but many governments were unclear as to what solutions would be most in their interest. Absent familiar guideposts to frame and channel them down a pre-established track, the issues remained fluid and bounced around in various institutional arenas.

This sort of distributed issue institutionalization can be constructive from the standpoint of raising international awareness, generating an unfettered and multiperspective debate, and highlighting different aspects of complex problems in a manner that slowly builds consensus on their optimal framing and resolution. Moreover, some issues that do not fit tidily into existing institutional boxes may not in fact require broad-based multilateral solutions, particularly of the intergovernmental treaty variety. For example, given the very asymmetric participation in Internet communications and commerce, formal and informal deals struck among groups of like-minded industrialized countries could provide enough international order on issues such as the balance between freedom of expression and pornography, hate speech, cybercrime, privacy protection, encryption, digital signatures and electronic contracting, and so on, at least in the near term (although developing countries may balk at being left to buy into arrangements that were not of their making). But on the minus side, as Internet usage deepens around the world, truly global responses to some of these issues might be needed, and distributed issue institutionalization may not provide a clear path from issue identification and debate to focused agenda setting for multilateral negotiations and rule making.

Negotiation

The quality of powerful states' leadership is important, particularly when negotiating changes to the status quo. When the solutions to global problems are clear and the costs and benefits of solving them are properly distributed, leadership might not matter that much. But as these happy circumstances often do not apply, it can be important to have some state or core group of states that can articulate a compelling vision on ends, elaborate viable proposals on the means to achieve them, and push the process along to a successful conclusion—including by making commitments and concessions that make it palatable for others to follow suit. Over the past fifty years, the United States has played this role in many international issue areas, including some of those covered in this book.

In the field of international communications, the picture has been more mixed. To be sure, the broad trajectory of recent regime development has been a shift from state control to market-oriented rules, and to the extent that the United States has been the chief advocate of this transformation, one might conclude that it has successfully exercised leadership. Two caveats are in order, however.

First, although the United States has usually won in the end, it often has won "ugly." In the early postwar period, a hegemonic United States willingly bore a disproportionate share of the cost of cooperation in arenas such as international trade and monetary policy to bring along other countries. In contrast, in international communications the United States has bargained more like an ordinary power that is concerned above all with satisfying the demands of its vocal private sector and increasingly has pressured governments to accept solutions that were perceived as yielding benefits slowly and pain immediately. Accordingly, many governments have accepted U.S. solutions rather grudgingly as faits accomplis, and conflicts have arisen over foot-dragging in the implementation phase.

Second, that other governments eventually went along with U.S. demands in such cases had more to do with the private sector and the new technology environment than with state power or deft diplomacy. Transnational firms based in the United States and other comparatively liberal countries such as the United Kingdom have pushed governments toward market-oriented policies through a variety of mechanisms including demands for market access and better treatment, investment (and disinvestment) decisions, and the like. Moreover, their enhanced competitiveness in both communications supply and user markets (everything from automobiles to banking and insurance and beyond) has encouraged domestic firms abroad to push their own governments toward liberalization so as to better equip them for global competition. Further, the demonstration effect of companies and economies thriving amid liberalization also has had a substantial if diffuse impact on how governments around the world evaluate their national interests.

Hence, insofar as the U.S. government has championed the private sector's agenda, it might appear to have been the prime mover, but it really has been more of a prime follower. It has a loud voice and can credibly threaten to exit agreements it does not like and act unilaterally because it has legal jurisdiction over many of the companies that are driving the global industry's evolution. Even so, although other governments may have come around to the general proposition that market-oriented approaches are the only viable way forward, many do not necessarily share America's values and vision, are seeking to promote their own companies' causes, and often resist U.S. positions on specific issues. In consequence, international communications policy has become a far more contested and conflictual terrain than ever before.

As intergovernmental, hybrid, and private negotiations all have strengths and weaknesses, the desirability of one model or the other depends on the issues and interests involved. Most of the major international communications regimes are grounded in intergovernmental treaties. But in fact, only the GATS process has involved negotiations solely among government representatives. Of course, WTO members may coordinate closely with their respective private sectors before and during the negotiation process, but trade ministries conduct the actual bargaining, at times with some support by colleagues from other relevant state agencies.

The principal benefit of this model has been that it allowed trade negotiators to wheel and deal within and across economic sectors without being overly encumbered by nonstate actors that might be unwilling to make concessions to move the process forward. Because cutting trade deals requires that domestic constituencies adjust to increased competition, directly involving such groups in the GATS bargaining process undoubtedly would have made it more difficult for governments to concede on one point to gain on another. Moreover, the "governments only" approach increased the probability that participants would have the requisite expertise in trade law and WTO mechanics. But purely intergovernmental negotiations also have limitations on the flip sides of these coins. In some countries, vocal constituencies in other government agencies, the private sector, and civil society have strongly opposed concessions made in their absence. In addition, trade ministry personnel were not always fully aware of the technical and operational difficulties of applying trade disciplines to services industries, in which a wide variety of regulatory and other rules may serve important objectives but be vulnerable to challenge as market access barriers. Accordingly, some countries' trade negotiators made commitments that key actors at home did not want or simply did not know how to implement. In short, although an intergovernmental approach is probably advisable for multisectoral trade negotiations and certainly made cutting the GATS and GBT deals easier to manage at the time, the lack of participation by a broader array of stakeholders may be causing problems in the implementation phase.

In light of these kinds of shortcomings, some analysts have argued for hybrid negotiations—including governments, the private sector, and NGOs—as a new and better approach to managing global issues.[6] In fact, two types of hybrid negotiations have a long pedigree in international communications policy. The first, which I will call Hybrid Type 1, involves the participation of nonstate actors in government-led delegations to regime negotiations. In contrast, Hybrid Type 2 involves nonstate actors directly representing themselves in negotiations.

The Hybrid Type 1 model has long been employed in the ITU. Although until recently the majority of countries were represented by their PTTs, those countries that had any private carriers, equipment manufacturers, or other important corporate stakeholders often included these actors in government-led delegations. The most notable and consistent country to adopt this practice has been the United States. The United States not only has had by far the largest delegations—including diverse corporate representatives and even the odd academic or industry analyst from time to time—but frequently appoints businesspersons as ambassadors to lead delegations to treaty-making conferences. With the spread of liberalization and market entry, hybrid delegations are becoming increasingly common, particularly among the industrialized and upper-income developing countries that account for most of the global industry's revenues.

Relative to a purely intergovernmental approach, Hybrid Type 1 negotiations can increase the level of stakeholder buy-in on the process and product. Further, they can help to ensure that diverse types of expertise are brought to bear in cases where this is useful. But multisectoral delegations also can be more difficult for their government leaders to manage, especially if the companies involved are in competition with one another and have different preferences on tactics and objectives. Moreover, some delegation members may not be fully aware of the relevant institutional history and the bargaining strategies in play. In addition, if they lack a certain deftness in multilateral negotiations, they may fail to sing from the same hymnal in explaining their delegation's positions and hence get played off against one another by crafty counterparts. These problems have arisen at times with U.S. delegations to ITU meetings, and it is likely that other governments will have similar experiences in the future.

The Hybrid Type 2 model was used in the International Telegraph Union. The Union's 1871 conference decided that henceforth private carriers could independently participate in the Administrative Conferences and accede to the regulations adopted, albeit without the right to vote. This option was not retained when the ITU was created, although some companies and industry associations were allowed to participate (without a vote or right of recognition) in meetings of the technical committees that produced nonbinding recommendations.

As noted previously, in the 1990s the ITU changed the rules to enhance corporate participation. Companies can now be full voting members in the technical committees, and they can participate fully in the occasional World Telecommunications Policy Forums set up to debate and reach nonbinding agreements on policy matters. Similarly, companies can directly represent themselves in ICANN's supporting organizations, although their recommendations to the board are only advisory. Still another variant on this model involves Intelsat. Although the U.S. government is a signatory to its intergovernmental agreement, in most contexts Comsat represents the United States. Comsat is legally accountable to the government, but in practice the company has had a good deal of latitude to pursue its own commercial objectives. This often has generated conflict with the U.S. government and ultimately strengthened its resolve to liberalize satellite markets and privatize the multilateral carrier.

Hybrid Type 2 negotiations naturally are favored by stakeholders who wish to have their own distinctive voice in multilateral proceedings. This is especially true of companies or NGOs that have a global profile and do not want to have their views folded into and potentially submerged in the positions of a national delegation. It is clear, however, that many governments, particularly in the developing world, are not comfortable conducting negotiations or even discussions in the presence of what they often perceive to be interlopers. In consequence, they have at times either resisted giving such actors a voice or a vote, or moved their maneuverings out of the official sessions and into the corridors. An important factor contributing to this reaction is that many of the corporations or NGOs seeking direct participation have been based in the United States. Rightly or wrongly, countries that have less robust business communities and third sectors may be prone to view the independent participation of such actors as a ploy to strengthen U.S. bargaining power even further.

Given these perceptions and related issues, Hybrid Type 2 negotiations have proven useful in developing some kinds of nonbinding agreements but have not been employed in treaty negotiations.

Finally, a fourth model employed in international communications has been private sector negotiations. Although one could argue that in today's liberalized world contractual arrangements between firms are a key source of international order, here the focus is only on multilateral rule making. Pure private rule making is represented by the work on Internet technical standards carried out in bodies such as the IETF and the World Wide Web Consortium and by the so-called self-regulatory frameworks that have been devised by several industry associations. In contrast, the example many people would cite as best representing private policy making actually presents a somewhat murky picture. Although ICANN is a not-for-profit corporation whose key members and sources of financial support are other private companies, its Government Advisory Committee and the U.S. Department of Commerce have notable behind-the-scenes influence. Whether one should characterize its decision-making process as fully private is hence somewhat debatable.

Purely private negotiations may be an effective way for companies to make decisions on matters of mutual interest such as technical standards, rules for business-to-business global electronic commerce, and so on. In a rapidly changing Internet environment that many states might not entirely understand, this may well be preferable at times to establishing intergovernmental frameworks. When private negotiations have a direct impact on third parties such as small businesses and consumers, however, they can suffer from problems of legitimacy and accountability that far exceed those of intergovernmental agreements. In such cases, governments may need to exercise some oversight and adopt complementary multilateral rules (for example, on privacy and consumer protection).

The excessive formalization of regime negotiations and instruments can diminish their effectiveness and impede change. The principal communications regimes have always been developed in accordance with very detailed procedural rules and embodied in binding treaties. A high degree of formalization can have its virtues, especially when it comes to managing an international organization or locking in essential commitments from which defection might be attractive. Moreover, it can be favorable to less powerful actors, who often equate calls for quick and flexible decision making with backroom deals from which they would be cut out, and who may be able to use formalized rules to guarantee due process, play for time, and offset their lack of resources.[7] But as an approach to governing rapidly changing arenas such as global communications, formalization does have some significant liabilities. This is most clearly evident in the case of the two ITU-based regimes, the fundamentals of which were erected in vastly different eras from today.

The ITU approach to decision making is famously mind-numbing, in both a figurative and—as many delegates have attested—literal sense. Over the past century, the Plenipotentiary and Administrative Conferences have turned into marathon affairs running three to six weeks and involving thousands of people and documents, elaborate and minutely detailed procedural rules, and massively overloaded and nearly unmanageable agendas. The preconference preparatory phase is almost equally demanding for both the ITU secretariat and the national delegations. Similarly, the ITU's technical standardization work over the years has been rigid and slow, as topics are filtered through a complex array of committees, study groups, and working parties employing rococo procedures, and important decisions often are delayed from one study cycle to the next.

Perhaps governments could get away with all this in the monopoly era, but today the technologies and markets are in the hands of an increasingly heterogeneous global private sector that cannot afford to wait for the system to inch forward. Recognizing this, the ITU revised its procedures in the 1990s to cut the lag time between treaty-revising conferences, to allow the accelerated adoption of certain standards, and so on. Nevertheless, these reforms fall short of what is needed, and although the spectrum allocation process leaves firms no choice but to wait until decisions are finally made, they increasingly are moving key technical standardization activities out of the ITU and into other, more nimble industry forums.

Related problems apply to the treaty instruments adopted. For more than a century, the telecommunications regime's regulations needlessly specified in extraordinary detail the operational procedures and rates carriers should employ. In 1973, the ITU decided to "deformalize" much of this text by moving it into the voluntary recommendations and reducing the regulations on telegraphy and telephony from 186 to 21 (still rather restrictive) pages. Although the revised regulations of 1988 provided greater latitude for market forces, they arguably still include too many details and limitations on what is after all an increasingly private industry. But rather than further shrinking and liberalizing the International Telecommunication Regulations, a majority of ITU members are now pushing—over U.S. objections—for a new mega-conference to expand them and spell out rules of the game on a wide variety of points. Unless they somehow turned out to be very liberal, in which case the need for them is unclear, such rules would probably be unevenly enforced upon some firms and circumvented by others. Similarly, the International Radio Regulations still comprise 1,000-plus pages of extraordinarily detailed prescriptions and proscriptions that encumber much of the industry, some of which doubtlessly could be deformalized. In short, the processes and products of international cooperation need to match the operational environments they are supposed to govern, which in the case of global communications suggests a more flexible approach.

A capacity for innovation is necessary to facilitate agreement. Multilateral cooperation on communications policy is densely institutionalized; with its federal structure of organizations, many of which have multiple subgroups, the ITU alone holds well over a hundred meetings per year involving thousands of people to work on technical standards, operational rules, and the like. Given the highly iterative and nested nature of these negotiations, historically many disagreements were simply rolled over to future meetings in the hope that consensus eventually would emerge. But often governments cannot get away with this sort of incrementalism, especially in today's competitive environment. In such cases, having the flexibility to innovate to break deadlocks and facilitate agreement becomes key.

Various tactics have been employed in different contexts. A first is to redefine the issues. When the TDF debate was framed as a binary trade-off between national sovereignty and the free flow of information, parties were encouraged to align with one side or the other, thereby hardening positions and making it difficult to consider the middle ground. But when the problem was redefined in terms of access to and trade in information, it became possible to forge a consensus in the OECD and elsewhere that better accommodated both sets of concerns.

A second approach is to redefine the procedural aspects of the negotiations. When developing countries balked at the idea of discussing trade in services within the GATT (for fear of establishing a presumption that a deal necessarily would result from the Uruguay Round), a parallel, nominally independent negotiation track was created. Meetings were held in the GATT building but not legally as GATT activities, and in this less threatening environment the process proceeded to a reasonably fruitful conclusion. Another procedural maneuver employed in the WTO and elsewhere is to focus first on the low-hanging fruit in order to build confidence and leave the more difficult calls to later stages. Although often this results in suboptimal eleventh-hour compromises among exhausted parties, even half measures can be better than an early deadlock if there is agreement to revisit the issues subsequently.

A third option is to bring in outside mediators, such as the heads of international organizations. The success of their interventions has depended to a significant degree on whether or not the third parties were perceived to be interested only in forging a workable compromise, rather than in pushing one side's agenda or the other's. For example, in 1988, the United States was threatening not to sign the new International Telecommunication Regulations that had been drafted by a group of conservative PTTs because the treaty appeared to be overly restrictive and was opposed by much of the business community. With both sides dug in and failure looming, the ITU Secretary-General produced an alternative draft that softened the controversial language and added new provisions, thereby clearing the way for willing countries to pursue a more market-friendly approach without requiring the unwilling to follow suit. This saved the conference and resulted in new regulations that initiated the transformation of the regime into an arrangement that could accommodate the expansion of competitive supply and user control. That the Secretary-General was perceived as interested in protecting the institution rather than forcing or blocking liberalization undoubtedly contributed to the success of this unprecedented intervention in an ITU negotiation.

In contrast, when the Reagan administration unilaterally declared its intention to license private competitors to Intelsat, the organization's director strongly and publicly took the majority's side in opposition. Indeed he undertook a highly controversial and ultimately damaging crusade that included lobbying the U.S. Congress to reverse the administration's course. To make matters worse, not long afterward he was removed from office on corruption charges involving the construction of Intelsat's new headquarters in Washington, D.C. Although it is not clear whether a more neutral leader would have been able to broker a compromise, it is abundantly clear that this activism deeply alienated U.S. policy makers of all political persuasions and added weight to calls for liberalization and privatization of the organization. Similarly, rather than remaining neutral in the highly charged battle over the New World Information and Communications Order, UNESCO's Secretary-General opted to align himself closely with the developing countries' agenda and their controversial Mass Media Declaration. In response, the Reagan administration and its supporters unleashed an unprecedented campaign of demonization against the head of an international organization, and having failed to get him removed, withdrew the United States' membership.

A fourth option is to redefine the payoffs to the parties. A standard technique is to offer side payments and concessions on other issues to bring along holdouts. This was done in the GATS negotiations, in which developing countries were led to believe that accepting a services deal would yield benefits in other sectors such as agriculture. Similarly, in radio regime negotiations, spectrum reallocations of interest to industrialized countries often have been matched with changes in other frequency bands favored by developing countries.

A fifth approach is to change the requirements on the parties, most notably by accepting differential commitments. The telecommunications regime has long employed this solution. In the monopoly era, the ITU divided the world into zones for the purposes of tariffs and accounting, and stronger regulatory regulations and recommendations were applied to Europe and the developing world than to North America. Similarly, even in the case of prescriptions that are supposed to be universal in nature, countries have the option to select their levels of conformity by issuing reservations to particular treaty provisions. This was especially important in keeping the United States more or less in the fold; the U.S. government was allowed to participate in the ITU without accepting the treaty regulations in full until 1973.

Differential commitments are also used in the GATS, under which governments can pick and choose the sectors and subsectors in which they will make commitments. Only general obligations such as most-favored-nation treatment are nominally required to be applied across the board, and even then it is possible to take exemptions. Furthermore, many of the telecommunications commitments undertaken by governments, especially those in the developing world, are to be phased in over time. Predictably, critics of the agreement argued upon their completion that all these limitations greatly diminish the significance of the GATS and the GBT deal. That may be true in a narrow, short-term sense for companies that would like to break into particular national markets, but from an institutional perspective it misses the point. By binding themselves to the GATS framework, governments set themselves up for pressures for progressive liberalization that will open their markets over time, and this strengthens the institutional development of the international trading system.

Finally, a sixth approach is to change the nature of the agreement being sought. As noted, because the United States repeatedly refused to sign on in full to the telecommunications regime's treaty regulations, other governments eventually decided to move major chunks of the text into the nonbinding recommendations. The decision to deformalize meant that the government would not be expected to apply strict rules on rates to U.S. carriers and cleared the way for the United States to accept the remaining, slimmed down obligations.

Nonbinding instruments can be very useful tools with which to build international consensus.   Critics scoff that such instruments are weak and not worth the paper they are written on, and undoubtedly many fit that description. Nevertheless, in multilateral communications policy, they have proven to be important and even preferable to treaties in some cases.

Technical standards offer a clear example. In the early years of telegraphy, ITU treaties mandated the use of specific technologies, such as Morse code. But as the rate of technological change increased over the years, it made less and less sense to lock regime members into treaty commitments to deploy one system or another. Voluntary standards could be more frequently revisited and updated by specialized experts in light of new conditions. Moreover, voluntary standardization would allow members some flexibility to pursue different national implementation options without fully defecting from the coordination process, although in some cases (such as television standards), there were enough incentives to do so. Accordingly, since 1924 the ITU has produced tens of thousands of pages of recommendations that have played a central role in the evolution of the global network of networks.

It is commonly believed that historically most of the ITU membership followed these recommendations most of the time. However, compliance undoubtedly has eroded in the current competitive environment, and a good deal of the standards activity has shifted out of the ITU and into more market-responsive industry forums. These trends are due to companies' substantive problems with the standards (and the ITU's decision-making processes), rather than with the standards' voluntary nature. Indeed, that they are voluntary has allowed the market to pursue alternatives as the ITU model began to lose favor.

Another type of nonbinding instrument that is growing in usage is the MOU. Memorandums of understanding, which could be said to occupy the middle ground between legal agreements and mere declarations, have proven particularly attractive for policy agreements on the rapidly changing economic aspects of communications. For example, in 1996 the ITU adopted a widely praised MOU on global mobile personal communications by satellite which, together with frequency allocations under the Radio Regulations, helped clear the way for the development of mobile voice and data communications via non-geostationary satellites. In addition, MOUs are increasingly used in bilateral and regional intergovernmental consultations on market access and related issues in telecommunications and global electronic commerce, as well as in private coordination on Internet infrastructure issues.

In addition, although they are softer than MOUs, declarations and guidelines can still create helpful normative presumptions about what constitutes appropriate behavior. The OECD's various nonbinding instruments on such issues as TDF, privacy protection, encryption, and online consumer protection reflect collective learning and an evolution toward common positions. Indeed, the OECD's work has proven critical in forging a level of international consensus on such topics as telecommunications, TDF, trade in services, the Internet, and global electronic commerce that significantly impacted dialogues in other forums. Of course, participants in this gentlemen's club have not attempted to bring strong pressure on counterparts that failed to implement the agreements. On the other hand, some UN members have employed the various declarations on mass media issues in this manner.

Finally, in cases involving highly charged political issues on which there is no consensus, nonbinding instruments allow groups of regime members to express their collective sentiment on the record while backing down from further conflict. The dozens of resolutions and opinions that ITU members routinely append to treaties often illustrate this safety-valve function. Because such proclamations can be claimed by their proponents to have a certain normative force, they may provide enough satisfaction to keep really divisive issues from infecting and threatening negotiations over binding agreements.

Implementation and Compliance

Technological change and market liberalization sometimes can make it difficult to determine whether private firms are behaving in accordance with the commitments undertaken by their home country governments. This is a significant problem. While the major communications regimes are intergovernmental arrangements, the private sector controls the lion's share of the global market. Hence the effectiveness of regime implementation suffers if companies do not act in accordance with the international rules and the commitments undertaken by their governments. But technological progress allows firms to undertake an increasingly wide range of activities that may or may not comport with those commitments. Some of these activities cannot be monitored unless governments undertake draconian measures that would generate business outrage and risk stifling economic activity or promoting exit to more hospitable investment locations. In addition, liberalization has greatly increased the number and variety of firms engaged in these activities, and some governments are increasingly reluctant even to attempt to monitor the behavior of their private sectors and to impose the rules on them.

Two examples illustrate the problem. First, as noted earlier, the telecommunications regime requires that international communications be conducted in accordance with the mutual consent of the countries involved. Nevertheless, companies—especially in the United States—are making extensive use of new modes of operations such as refile and callback to route traffic around the world in ways that violate that principle but are technically difficult to detect.[8] The overwhelming majority of ITU members denounce these practices, and developing countries have pushed through resolutions demanding that they be curtailed. But believing that such services increase international competition, the U.S. government has made rather limited efforts to do so.[9]

Second, the OECD's guidelines and the various "self-regulatory" private sector agreements on privacy protection set out fair use rules for handling of personal data. But trusting firms to police themselves means that there really is no way to know what they are doing with the data they accumulate unless an unusual circumstance brings this to light. Moreover, data about World Wide Web usage is just the tip of the iceberg; a staggering amount of personal information about citizens is culled from other sources, stored in databases, electronically shipped across national borders, and used by companies to make all kinds of decisions without much constraint. Nevertheless, the U.S. government has consistently opposed efforts to devise firm multilateral rules on privacy protection and has championed unenforceable guidelines and self-regulation as an alternative.

More generally, as global electronic commerce over the Internet continues to blossom, it will be increasingly difficult to be certain that all the transactions undertaken conform with applicable national and international laws. And while audits and other post hoc, offline mechanisms may not be entirely adequate to the task, the more proactive alternatives that some governments apparently wish for may be technically unworkable and unduly interventionist. As such, it will be difficult for governments to agree on and implement international rules that territorialize intangible transactions in cyberspace without overburdening a key component of the global economy.

Centralized monitoring systems are more demanding but more effective than are decentralized systems. Centralized or partially centralized systems have been employed in cases involving joint facilities tasked with managing scarce resources. The ITU's radio bureau examines the frequencies and satellite slots notified by governments to determine whether they conform to the rules and avoid harmful interference with legal allocations. However, as monitoring the day-to-day operation of the services would be beyond the bureau's means, this function is performed from the bottom up via other members. Similarly, because they operate the mechanism through which cooperation is effected, Intelsat staff can readily determine whether members have paid into the system, are using the prescribed technical standards linking satellites and terrestrial networks, have coordinated any separate private or regional satellite systems, and so on. In parallel, ICANN can assess the behavior of the companies with which it has contractual relationships, although any issues pertaining to the use of names and numbers (such as alleged trademark violations) are brought to its attention from the bottom up. In all these cases, resource scarcity and the need for central management of certain operations create functional bottlenecks that increase the visibility of behavior.

However, centralized systems would be very demanding to operate and politically controversial in other environments. Hence the other major communications regimes have employed decentralized monitoring systems. Although international organization staff may do some information gathering, member governments and companies perform most of the monitoring. With regard to the telecommunications regime, over the years the ITU secretariat has sent members questionnaires to gather operational statistics concerning traffic levels on different routes, the number and type of lines laid in national territories, and so forth so as to facilitate network planning. But it has not attempted to monitor compliance with regulatory rules, technical standards, or other prescriptions. Member governments are jealously expansive in guarding their sovereignty, and public and private service providers alike regard much of the information that would be needed to be proprietary. Accordingly, it is left up to governments and firms to detect any noncompliance in the course of their operational relationships. Monitoring of compliance with the GATS is similarly decentralized, with companies complaining of problems in foreign markets to their respective host governments.

Although this decentralized approach helps to preserve members' autonomy and is easy to implement, it does raise some problems. Most obviously, absent a neutral mechanism to gather and assess information, it is difficult to know just how widespread compliance or noncompliance may be at any given point in time. Lacking such information, it is also difficult to know whether regime members and international organization staff are spending their time wisely. For example, ITU members have spent an enormous amount of time over the years producing tens of thousands of pages of recommendations, but it does not have any independent and systematic means of knowing how widely and fully these are being implemented. Critics charge that much of this work serves narrow PTO interests and is either irrelevant or counterproductive in a competitive environment, but it is difficult to empirically assess their claims or the ITU's objections to them.

Private sector monitoring can help to fill in the gaps of decentralized systems. Given the private sector's increasing control of the global communications industry, it is no surprise that it often has better information about regime-related practices around the world than do governments. In consequence, governments and international organization secretariats are to some extent dependent on businesses to monitor and report on instances of noncompliance, as well as other industry trends.

Private sector monitoring takes two forms. First, as indicated above, the high level of operational interdependence between network and service providers in the day-to-day conduct of global communications puts these companies at the front line of the detection process. Accordingly, when any deviations from the rules arise that affect their interests, they can take up the matter with the relevant government agencies and companies in the hope of resolving the issue. If such efforts fail to bear fruit, the affected firms may then bring the matter to the attention of their home country governments in the hope of garnering support and triggering consultations. Alternatively, or in addition, in some cases they can raise the matter at the multilateral level in discussions with regime members or with an international organization's secretariat. Often the issues are resolved quietly with little public notice, but when they are not the information may percolate up and disseminate in a manner that increases transparency for all.

Second, the private sector also plays a wider role in gathering, analyzing, and disseminating information on industry and policy trends. The many multinational industry associations representing diverse market segments regularly generate reports and position papers detailing problems their members are encountering in international markets, including alleged violations of regime commitments. Similarly, scores of consulting firms produce single and multiclient reports that do the same, a function that is buttressed by the activities of journalists, industry pundits, and academics.

Although all these private efforts are integral to the decentralized monitoring systems used in communications regimes, relying on them can lead to some problems that presumably would be less prevalent under centralized intergovernmental systems. Most obviously, to the extent that competing service providers, industry associations, or the clients for consultant reports have material interests at stake, there may be questions about the objectivity of the analyses proffered. Accordingly, governments and firms accused of noncompliance may dispute their findings and question their motivations, with the results that regime surveillance becomes a contested, interest-driven struggle rather than a neutral process of fact finding. Moreover, companies based in the industrialized world (most notably in the English-speaking countries) overwhelmingly carry out this private monitoring, which opens an additional avenue for players at the receiving end to claim that the analyses are biased. Hence, although private sector monitoring is an essential part of the mix, it is not without potential shortcomings, nor is it a complete substitute for the sort of unbiased and professional assessment one would hope for from international organization staff.

The behavior of leading actors can have a significant effect on the compliance of other regime members. When the states or firms that have the greatest degree of influence on a regime are unambiguously in compliance with national commitments, this helps to establish a normative context in which any deviations by less powerful actors would appear to be contrary to the global consensus, and it increases the prospect that power could be deployed to pressure them to change course. Conversely, when the leading actors refuse to comply with such commitments, this makes deviations by others appear to be more normatively acceptable, and it may decrease the prospect of pressure being applied to keep them in line.

The experience of the telecommunications regime illustrates both dynamics. In the monopoly era, the European PTTs that dominated the regime firmly complied with its detailed stipulations. They had professional interests and reputational stakes in seeing the rules they created implemented, attached a great deal of normative value to comity within the club, saw compliance as essential to ensuring a stable and predictable operating environment, and understood that a strong group commitment to cartel-like practices precluded divisive competition among members. The European bloc's firm attachment to implementing the rules meant that the vast majority of countries that subsequently joined their club were socialized into conformity with long-standing practices, which generally served their own state-building interests. Further, the Europeans' strong compliance meant that private carriers, including American carriers, had to follow suit if they wanted to maintain landing rights and operational agreements with the PTTs.

By the 1990s, the information revolution and liberalization had increased the power of the private sector, a significant portion of which sees key elements of the regime as counterproductive or irrelevant. Moreover, that many of these dissident and powerful firms are based in the United States has greatly strengthened the U.S. government's hand in demanding thorough liberalization and refusing to comply with rules it does not like. In turn, the growing noncompliance of leading firms and the United States has eroded other players' commitment to the rules, a problem complicated by the difficulty of detecting some types of cheating. Hence other governments are now allowing their firms to engage in forms of bypass that are contrary to the traditional obligation for mutual consent between countries. Similarly, to justify their own foot-dragging, some governments have charged that the United States has failed to implement fully its GATS commitments. And when the United States left the fold and authorized private competitors to Intelsat, other countries—after a period of decrying American unilateralism—began to do the same thing. In short, when the leading actors defect and profit thereby, there may be strong incentives for others to follow suit.

Obtaining the compliance of developing countries often requires technical assistance, resource transfers, and flexibility. Many developing countries have difficulties implementing their communications regime commitments in a full and timely manner. Sometimes the problems begin in the negotiation phase because they do not have experts on the issues at hand or cannot afford to send them to all the meetings. Indeed, when the frameworks of pending agreements are being established, poorer countries are often represented by consular officers who pick up the documents and read out prepared statements but cannot engage in complex problem-solving dialogues. Particularly on demanding issues such as technical standardization work or the GATS, such deficiencies have resulted in some developing countries signing on to instruments the details and requirements of which they do not fully understand. And even if the negotiators are up to snuff, the people and institutions at home that would have to implement the commitments and make them credible may not be fully prepared to do so. In such cases, the industrialized countries and international organization secretariats need to provide much more technical support than they have to date.

A second and related problem is that compliance with commitments that alter the status quo sometimes entails high short-term adjustment costs and is slow to yield offsetting benefits. Implementing ITU recommendations calling for lower accounting and settlements rates; opening markets under the GATS; changing domestic frequency spectrum assignments to accommodate new services promoted by industrialized countries; adapting tariffs and revenues to competition with Intelsat—these and other steps can require painful changes on the parts of national PTOs and state budgets, government employees, formerly subsidized consumers, and so on. Not surprisingly then, many countries fail to implement their commitments fully and promptly and thus find themselves under attack from U.S. trade officials, TNCs, and other proponents of tough love reform. Development assistance, or even side payments in unrelated arenas, could do much to help such countries through such transitions, but these too are often in short supply. Under these circumstances, at a minimum, regimes need to provide some flexibility on the pace and thoroughness of compliance so that developing countries can manage the necessary transitions and experience softer landings.

Reactions to Noncompliance

The lack of strong enforcement mechanisms in the regulatory regimes has made it difficult to deal with noncompliance. The ITU lacks any mechanisms to penalize noncompliance and cannot compel members to engage in institutionally convened dispute resolution. In the case of the telecommunications regime, this was not a major defect during the monopoly era because most members found that the benefits of compliance outweighed any incentive to cheat, and the normative pressures on club members generally were adequate to the task. The main exception of sorts was the North American countries, which as noted earlier insisted on playing by somewhat different rules with regard to certain economic issues. But as key countries began to shift toward a more pro-competitive stance in the 1980s, the cartel-like coherence of the past began to break down, and the ITU majority had to rely on more vigorous arm-twisting and unprecedented bilateral threats to keep potential defectors in line.

For example, in 1981, the U.S. Federal Communications Commission (FCC) unilaterally announced its intention to extend resale and sharing to international circuits. Resale involves the competitive provision of services using capacity leased from facilities-based carriers such as AT&T, whereas sharing involves groups of corporate users such as banks or travel agencies linking their operations together over private leased circuits. PTTs abroad correctly viewed both services as threats to their monopoly control and had adopted ITU recommendations limiting them. They therefore complained to the FCC and threatened to revoke U.S. corporate users' access to leased lines in their markets, complaints that were backed up by the ITU's leadership. In consequence, worried U.S. businesses convinced the FCC to back off. Similarly, when British Telecom reduced its rates to Europe in the hope of strengthening its role as a "hub" for traffic between the United States and the continent, European PTTs argued that the rules on transit routings prohibited such competitive practices and forced their British counterpart to relent. This proved to be a short-lived victory, however, because as competition spread in subsequent years, Great Britain proceeded to strengthen its hub status.

As liberalization spread in the 1990s, the lack of collective enforcement mechanisms became a much bigger problem for the ITU majority. The most obvious and consequential example concerns U.S. defection from the norms of the accounting and settlements system. U.S. outbound telephone traffic was booming because of the comparatively low rates charged by its competing carriers, the propensity of U.S. firms to engage in traffic reorigination techniques such as refile and callback, and demographic factors. PTTs typically maintained both high collection charges, which discouraged their customers from calling abroad, and high accounting and settlement rates for the receipt and termination of inbound traffic. As a result, U.S. carriers were running up a significant trade deficit with their foreign counterparts, particularly in the developing world. The United States pushed through an ITU recommendation calling for lower rates, but many countries did not reduce them far enough fast enough under this voluntary agreement to solve the United States' problem. By 1998, U.S. carriers were paying out more than $5 billion dollars more per year than they received back.

In response, the FCC adopted its "Benchmark Order" that unilaterally set new and far lower rates at which U.S. carriers could compensate their counterparts. Greatly reduced settlements income has very serious consequences for developing countries and hence has caused an enormous battle within the ITU, where again questions of comity and legality have been raised at great length but have fallen on deaf American ears. In effect, the U.S. unilateral move gutted the ITU's authority over the issue and rendered irrelevant both the recommendations and those provisions of the treaty regulations that specify that accounting rates should be set by mutual consent between corresponding carriers. In light of their own liberalization efforts and traffic imbalances, other industrialized countries wanted lower rates as well—albeit not by these means—so they criticized the United States but backed away from real confrontation. Because the ITU's developing majority has no collective mechanism at its disposal to sanction this noncompliance and its bilateral threats against the United States ring hollow in the contemporary environment, the Benchmark Order stands, and the telecommunications regime has been rendered irrelevant to a major element of the industry's economic organization.

The lack of enforcement mechanisms has been a much more long-standing problem for the radio regime. The ITU has no way to force off the airwaves or out of the skies users of spectrum and satellite slots that are found to be in violation of its instruments. Such uses lack legal standing and protection, and the offending countries could find it a bit more difficult to subsequently assert their rights and complain about interference from others. If, however, they are willing to run those risks there are no stronger penalties—for example, suspension of membership—that can be applied. Not surprisingly, violations were widespread throughout the twentieth century, with governments claiming thousands of assignments that did not to conform with the rules and often refusing to budge when informed of that fact.

In addition to harmful interference, the ITU has been unable to deter or penalize squatting. Bogus claims to resources not actually in use have a long pedigree as well. To note an especially egregious example, in the 1930s "several administrations, particularly the USSR, took advantage of [the system] by submitting long, largely fictitious lists of frequencies in use. By 1938 the USSR was registered on virtually every available frequency."[10] Although most governments have usually been more circumspect, especially in modern times, the fact remains that excessive squatting in the scarce spectrum resource has caused problems for other users and the ITU staff that post hoc evaluations and findings of legality do not overcome.

A similar problem has arisen in recent years regarding the allocation of satellite orbital slots. With the liberalization of the global satellite market and the increasing value of real estate in the sky, about a dozen countries have been overfiling notices of new commercial satellite systems. The excess systems are "paper satellites" that have not been and probably never will be launched. Instead the filers hope to resell or lease the slots to the highest bidder. This speculative hoarding has resulted in a situation in which paper satellites outnumber real systems recorded with the ITU by two to one, and the administrative backlog caused by processing bogus claims has significantly slowed ITU processing of legitimate requests. Given the need to coordinate existing and new satellites and the high costs of building and launching systems, these delays can have a substantial negative impact in a competitive global market.

In an effort to discourage overbookings, in 1997 the ITU adopted an "administrative due diligence" procedure under which filing governments must disclose implementation data about the system and contracts involved (for example, the names of the spacecraft manufacturer, satellite operator, and launch vehicle provider). But while this procedure has yet to improve the situation whatsoever, ITU members have been unable to agree on the establishment of a "financial due diligence" requirement, under which governments would pay filing, registration, and other fees for the slots they claim. The developing countries currently abusing the process argue that such fees would be discriminatory, and more generally many ITU members oppose secretariat proposals to enhance the organization's efficiency by charging incrementally for services rendered to members. Nevertheless, absent any financial disincentive, the paper satellite problem surely will continue unabated.

In the case of the satellite regime, the situation is more mixed. On the one hand, the Intelsat agreements do provide for binding arbitration to settle certain kinds of disputes that might include claims of noncompliance. Further, they also allow the suspension or expulsion of members under extreme conditions; for example, a number of developing countries have been suspended for nonpayment of their capital contributions to the organization. On the other hand, Intelsat has been unable to deal with behaviors that strongly violate the spirit perhaps but not the letter of the law, most notably the United States.

Conversely, the presence of strong enforcement mechanisms in the more market-enabling communications regimes has promoted compliance. The WTO has a new dispute resolution system that is stronger than the one formerly used in the GATT organization. The details of the system's working are covered elsewhere in this volume and so are not repeated here.[11] To date, no cases involving telecommunications and information services have been brought under the system; nevertheless, its mere presence has already proven useful in strengthening compliance with the GATS and GBT commitments. For example, since the completion of the GBT deal, the United States has had significant disagreements with countries such as Germany, Japan, and Mexico over whether they are applying the Reference Paper's principles concerning network interconnection and related issues. Although the governments involved have denied that their domestic policies are out of synch with their WTO commitments, the prospect of facing a panel, losing a decision, and being subject to U.S. trade sanctions clearly has concentrated their minds on ways to accommodate U.S. demands and avoid that eventuality. As such, in these and similar cases, lengthy bilateral consultations have been undertaken that eventually yielded workable compromises. And while the United States has been the primary actor to employ such threats, what is important to the strength and legitimacy of the regime is that the mechanism is equally available to all WTO members. Moreover, from the standpoint of developing countries in particular, having a strong multilateral alternative to the unilateral application of U.S. or other national trade laws is extremely important.

ICANN has been more widely tested and has proven effective, if not necessarily even-handed, in sanctioning certain forms of noncompliance. The UDRP is incorporated into registrars' agreements with customers and sets forth the conditions under which a name registration may be challenged and ultimately transferred from one user to another, as well as the mechanisms that may be employed (for example, WIPO arbitration or alternative dispute resolution systems). In addition, ICANN has established guidelines that have deterred cybersquatting on lucrative domain names to some extent. These operations have proven exceedingly controversial, however, and ICANN's approach suffers from substantial legitimacy problems. In general, large corporations holding trademarks have routinely won out over individuals and small firms, and have used ICANN rules to suppress speech such as World Wide Web sites that criticize or mock big corporations and famous personalities. Given that an adverse ruling can result in the loss of a domain name, this is an effective stick to wield in enforcing policy. Whether it has been used fairly is an entirely separate question.

Some variability in compliance does not undermine the overall value of regime cooperation. It would be easy to survey the record of international communications regimes, focus on the frequent violations of their rules, and come to the conclusion that these are weak and not terribly useful institutions. In fact, nothing could be further from the truth. International cooperation on communications policy has proven enormously productive and important over the past 150 years. For all its faults, the telecommunications regime has provided a framework within which national networks have been interconnected and progressively upgraded to provide the foundation of today's global information infrastructure. Similarly, the radio and satellite regimes played absolutely critical roles in the development of worldwide wireless communications, and it is entirely probable that in their absence these vital resources would not be what they are today. Moreover, multilateral cooperation, particularly in the ITU, has been enormously important to information sharing and collective learning, especially on the part of the developing countries. Hence, that some actors have violated certain rules from time to time, or ignored them and acted unilaterally to change the rules of the game for everyone, does not detract from the general utility of regime cooperation. One suspects that the same will prove true for the newer and less-tested regimes as well.

CONCLUSION

Relative to many other international issue areas, for all its problems, international cooperation in communications has worked fairly well. There are no pending disasters or unmet challenges in this arena on the order of global warming, rampant arms proliferation, massive human rights violations, or the like. But if global communications has not broken down and left the world incommunicado, the lessons above suggest that there is still ample room for significant improvements in the institutional organization of its governance. In particular, as global communications becomes increasingly the province of a transnational private sector that does not need or want bureaucratic regulation, governments and international institutions will have to find new, more flexible, and market-enabling forms of governance that are appropriate to this environment. At the same time, they will also have to find new ways to help developing countries manage the transition to a competitive global information economy and to maintain public accountability and oversight in situations in which corporate decisions potentially can harm small businesses and individual consumers or citizens. In this regard, if there is one key lesson from this assessment for the field itself, it is that international communications policy is too important to leave to the communications ministries and dominant carriers.

NOTES

1. It should be noted that some of the scarcity here is human made. That is, while there can only be one domain name called www.ceip.org, a vast array of similar names would be possible if there were more global top-level domains. Alas, decisions made at the behest of trademark interests in particular have artificially limited the number of global top-level domains and have thus generated both distributional conflicts over and wildly inflated prices for choice names.
2. Since 1993, the Administrative Conferences are called World Conferences on International Telecommunications. None have been held under the new rubric.
3. Cross-border supply (via telecommunications, postal systems, and so forth) is one of four designated "modes of supply" for services under the GATS regime, the others being movement of the consumer to the producer's country, movement of a natural person producer to the consumer's country, and the "commercial presence" of producer firms in consumer countries, notably via foreign direct investment (FDI).

4. The Internet emerged outside the PTO nexus, is based on non-ITU standards, represents a completely different vision of networking and services, and is increasingly driving much of the global telecommunications agenda, often in directions many PTOs would not prefer. Indeed, when the Internet first began to take off as a global commercial medium, most ITU members reacted with a mixture of denial (it was just an academic plaything, and not invented here) and fear. For many PTOs, especially in the developing world, that fear has only grown with the burgeoning explosion of Internet telephony, which entirely bypasses their tariffs and the telecommunications regime's accounting and settlements system. For others, especially in the industrialized world, "if you can't beat it, join it" is the operative phrase, and they are working to adapt their network architectures and service portfolios to take advantage of the Internet's possibilities. Even so, the most significant technological sea change in global telecommunications since the advent of satellites has arisen from outside the ITU, and members are having to adjust their agendas to that reality.

5. See Lawrence Lessig, *Code, and Other Laws of Cyberspace* (New York: Basic Books, 1999).

6. See, for example, Wolfgang H. Reinicke, *Global Public Policy: Governing Without Government?* (Washington, D.C.: Brookings Institution, 1998).

7. This is clearly true of developing countries, which have championed and benefited from highly formalized procedures in the ITU and other intergovernmental forums. But it can also be true of other comparatively powerless actors. For example, ICANN has often made decisions in an ad hoc, informal manner that is inconsistent with its own charter, and the results have often been favorable to powerful insiders like the trademark lobby. Hence, NGOs and small businesses have demanded that ICANN follow more formal and transparent procedures.

8. Refile involves routing around countries' high accounting rates to offer cheaper services to corporate customers. If a company wants to send traffic from country A to country B, but country B's accounting rate on the direct route is higher than the combined accounting rates from country A to country C and from country C to country B, the traffic is sent to country C (typically, the United States) and then on to country B. To the carrier in country B, the traffic appears to originate in country C, and it receives a lower settlement payment (one half the accounting rate) than it would have if that traffic had come in from country A. Country B clearly loses out here and has not agreed to the service relationship, but it can neither detect nor stop the practice. Callback also involves traffic reorigination. In the most common form, a customer in a country with a high collection charge (the retail price) on international calls dials a computer in a country with low collection charges (usually the United States), gets a tone, and then hangs up before a call is actually completed and a charge is rendered. The computer then calls the customer back and provides a dial tone allowing the customer to place an international call as if it originated in the United States. If the call goes to a third country, the customer's home country loses entirely—the call is billed as a call from America to wherever. If the call destination is in the United States, the high-cost country still gets a settlements payment on the minutes exchanged, but this is less than what it would have gotten if the call had been originated and tariffed within its borders.

9. For example, the United States suggested that ITU members unable to enforce their domestic prohibitions on callback could obtain assistance from the Federal Communications Commission (FCC) by submitting a copy of legislation that specifically bans callback, the name and address of the specific U.S. provider that allegedly provides services illegally, specific evidence that there are violations of the domestic prohibition, and evidence that unsuccessful enforcement procedures have been undertaken. Given the technical difficulty of detecting callback, this is setting the bar rather high, especially for the developing countries. And while the FCC did nominally proscribe the "constant calling" and "answer supervision suppression" callback methods on the grounds that these impede efficient network operation and may cause technical harm, these practices persist.

10. James G. Savage, *The Politics of International Telecommunications Regulation* (Westview, Colo.: Westview Press, 1989), p. 70.

11. See the chapter in this book by Vinod Aggarwal.

SUGGESTED ADDITIONAL READING

Codding, George A. *The International Telecommunication Union: An Experiment in International Cooperation.* Leiden: E. J. Brill, 1952.

Codding, George A., and Anthony M. Rutkowski. *The International Telecommunication Union in a Changing World.* Dedham, Mass.: Artech House, 1982.

Cowhey, Peter F. "The International Telecommunications Regime: The Political Roots of Regimes for High Technology." *International Organization*, vol. 44 (Spring 1990), pp. 169–99.

Drake, William J. "Asymmetric Deregulation and the Transformation of the International Telecommunications Regime." In Eli M. Noam and Gerard Pogorel, eds. *Asymmetric Deregulation: The Dynamics of Telecommunications Policies in Europe and the United States.* Norwood, N.J.: Ablex, 1994, pp. 137–203.

Drake, William J. "The Rise and Decline of the International Telecommunications Regime." In Christopher T. Marsden, ed. *Regulating the Global Information Society.* London: Routledge, 2000, pp. 124–177.

Drake, William J. "Territoriality and Intangibility: Transborder Data Flows and National Sovereignty." In Kaarle Nordenstreng and Herbert I. Schiller, eds. *Beyond National Sovereignty: International Communications in the 1990s.* Norwood: Ablex, 1993, pp. 259–313.

Drake, William J., and Eli M. Noam. "Assessing the WTO Agreement on Basic Telecommunications." In Gary Clyde Hufbauer and Erika Wada, eds. *Unfinished Business: Telecommunications after the Uruguay Round.* Washington, D.C.: Institute for International Economics, 1998, pp. 27–61.

Drake, William J., and Kalypso Nicolaïdis. "Global Electronic Commerce and the General Agreement on Trade in Services: The 'Millennium Round' and Beyond." In Pierre Sauvé and Robert M. Stern, eds. *GATS 2000: New Directions in Services Trade Liberalization.* Washington D.C.: Brookings Institution Press, 2000, pp. 399–437.

Drake, William J., and Kalypso Nicolaïdis. "Ideas, Interests and Institutionalization: 'Trade in Services' and the Uruguay Round." In Peter Haas, ed. *Knowledge, Power and International Policy Coordination, A Special Issue of International Organization*, vol. 45 (Winter 1992), pp. 37–100.

Hamelink, Cees J. *The Politics of World Communication: A Human Rights Perspective*. Thousand Oaks, Calif.: Sage Publications, 1994.

Kahin, Brian, and James H. Keller, eds. *Coordinating the Internet*. Cambridge, Mass.: MIT Press, 1997.

Leive, David M. *International Telecommunications and International Law: The Regulation of the Radio Spectrum*. Dobbs Ferry, N.Y.: Oceana Publications, 1970.

Martinez, Larry. *Communications Satellites: Power Politics in Space*. Dedham, Mass.: Artech House, 1985.

Mueller, Milton. "ICANN and Internet Governance: Sorting Through the Debris of 'Self-Regulation.'" *Info*, vol. 6 (December 1999), pp. 497-520.

Nicolaïdis, Kalypso. "International Trade in Information-Based Services: The Uruguay Round and Beyond." In William J. Drake, ed. *The New Information Infrastructure: Strategies for U.S. Policy*. New York: Twentieth Century Fund Press, 1995, pp. 269–302.

Pelton, Joseph N. *Global Communications Satellite Policy: INTELSAT, Politics, and Functionalism*. Mt. Airy, Md.: Lomond Books, 1974.

Preston, William, Edward S. Herman, and Herbert I. Schiller. *Hope and Folly: The United States and UNESCO, 1945-1985*. Minneapolis, Minn.: University of Minnesota Press, 1989.

Sauvant, Karl P. *International Transactions in Services: The Politics of Transborder Data Flows*. Boulder, Colo.: Westview Press, 1986.

Savage, James G. *The Politics of International Telecommunications Regulation*. Boulder, Colo.: Westview Press, 1989.

Snow, Marcellus S. *The International Telecommunications Satellite Organization (INTELSAT): Economic and Institutional Challenges Facing an International Organization*. Baden-Baden: Nomos Verlagsgesellschaft, 1987.

Zacher, Mark W., and Brent A. Sutton. *Governing Global Networks: International Regimes for Transportation and Communications*. Cambridge, U.K.: Cambridge University Press, 1996.

Internet Sites

International Telecommunications Union (ITU) <http://www.itu.int>

INTELSAT <http://www.intelsat.int>

International Corporation for Assigned Names and Numbers (ICANN) <http://www.icann.org>

Electronic Commerce, Organization for Economic Cooperation and Development (OECD) <http://www.oecd.fr/dsti/sti/it/ec/index.htm>

United Nations Economic, Social, and Cultural Organization (UNESCO) <http://www.unesco.org>

World Trade Organization (WTO) <http://www.wto.org>

2

Corruption

Peter Richardson

MANY SOCIETIES ONCE REGARDED CORRUPTION as inevitable and, although wrong, not particularly harmful.[1] Historically, for a government or an international organization to try to convince another government to crack down on domestic corruption was not only rare but also thought to be naïve, not to mention insensitive to the prerogatives of national sovereignty. Although providers of international economic aid sought to prevent corruption directly related to the assistance they provided, they seldom addressed the overall problem.

This chapter examines the methods and the success of the campaign—internationally, in countries and in business organizations—to create pressures and bring about changes that will reduce corruption. The corruption may be "grand corruption," often found in relation to international contracts, or "petty corruption," involving small bribes often demanded from national citizens by relatively low-level officials. Although the players and amounts may differ, the systemic remedies for each have much in common and, in the long term, sustainable progress requires advances on both fronts.

Corruption remains widespread and is pervasive in some countries. Yet high levels of corruption are no longer regarded as inevitable. Consensus now exists that corrupt behavior reduces economic growth, invariably benefits the few at the expense of the many, is especially injurious to the poor, and can destabilize governments. Both nationally and internationally, the need to reduce corruption has taken on increasing urgency. It has become a subject in discussions not only among governments but also between international organizations and governments. Reflecting (although perhaps overstating) the change, U.S. Congressman James Leach, Chairman of the House Banking Committee, wrote recently that "the struggle of the last half century was to defeat Communism; the challenge in the years ahead will be to constrain corruption."[2]

Growing recognition of the detrimental effects of corruption has spurred countries to consider practical ways to reduce it. For example, the governments of many developed countries have begun to implement agreements to criminalize the bribing of foreign officials. Also, multinational corporations are increasingly formulating codes of conduct to guide their behavior when dealing with government officials. In addition, country-level anticorruption coalitions have been created and have become active.

How were these changes brought about? What strategies were used to bring corruption to the forefront of national and international attention and what general lessons can we draw from the anticorruption campaign thus far? Although it is too soon to talk about victory—defined as actual reductions in bribery—the campaign's rapid progress in generating attention and mobilizing political will to act is clearly a success and holds some valuable lessons for global governance.

At least four such lessons stand out. First, the availability and dissemination of information about the extent and detrimental effects of corruption—especially in the form of comparative indices—have been a powerful tool in drawing attention to corruption, the necessary prelude to action. Second, an approach that features cooperation is more effective than an approach that emphasizes confrontation. Countries with serious corruption problems require deep changes involving governments, the private sector, and civil society. Because such changes cannot be brought about overnight, engaging these various actors in a sustained and constructive dialogue is key. Third, without the development and dissemination of expert knowledge on how to design and implement systemic changes, the campaign would not have been as successful. Fourth, to offset concerns that bribers might enjoy a competitive advantage over nonbribers, building trust among all parties that no one will cheat is essential. Effective monitoring, implementation, and enforcement of anticorruption measures are therefore at least as important as the formal establishment of a legal framework for dealing with those engaged in corruption.

NATURE OF THE PROBLEM

While the clandestine nature of corruption makes estimation difficult, the annual cost of corruption to developing countries may well exceed the annual total of all economic assistance. The World Bank has estimated corruption to cost $80 billion worldwide—a figure that the Organization for Economic Cooperation and Development (OECD) believes may represent only "the tip of the iceberg."[3] According to research at the International Monetary Fund (IMF), corruption can reduce a country's economic growth rate by more than 0.5 percent of gross domestic product (GDP).[4] Minxin Pei has estimated that in China corruption amounts to about 5 percent of GDP.[5] Petty bribes are the most difficult to estimate, even though their amounts are obvious to the very large numbers of people who have to pay them. While petty bribes are individually small, their aggregate cost is not—and such bribes are especially injurious to the poor, who can least afford them.

At least six obstacles impeded serious progress against corruption. First, until the early 1990s, few efforts had been made to gauge the magnitude of corruption, and few recognized either its harmfulness or its international contagiousness. Indeed, in many countries there was a commonly held, but erroneous, belief that bribery was acceptable and that it was even a potentially useful tool in combating bureaucratic lethargy or intransigence.[6] Many deemed corruption inevitable in many countries, especially those with immature institutions and a tradition of bribery. Partly as a result, most countries not only permitted the bribing of foreign officials but also, in some cases, allowed tax deductions for such bribes. An exception was the United States, where the Foreign Corrupt Practices Act (FCPA) went into force in 1977.[7]

Second, corruption was a taboo subject in international relations. No government wanted to admit that its high officials could be bribed, and no country or corporation wanted to admit that it got its competitive edge through bribery. Moreover, Cold War objectives often led aid-providing countries to avoid raising corruption issues that could heighten aid fatigue and offend friendly aid-recipient governments. Also, most multilateral assistance agencies believed corruption was a political issue and therefore beyond their purview.

Third, many governments dismissed U.S. pressures to reduce corruption elsewhere as a mere business-induced effort to increase U.S. competitiveness by leveling the playing field.

Fourth, an effective anticorruption campaign required action on multiple fronts and required the cooperation of all actors concerned. The willingness of international businesses to offer bribes or to "export" corruption was as pernicious as the propensity of officials to demand them. Unless all actors in a particular sector agreed not to bribe (and could be expected to honor such an agreement), few would be likely to stop doing so. To complicate matters more, officials with the power to initiate reforms had little incentive to change since they were often beneficiaries of corruption.

Fifth, many developed countries were reluctant to devote resources to assist anticorruption efforts in developing countries because they considered the prospects for success poor.

Sixth, globalization and the accompanying rise in trade and capital flows (including foreign direct investment) helped to protect the corrupt by increasing opportunities for money laundering and hiding illicitly acquired funds in "safe haven" banks.

TRACK RECORD OF INTERNATIONAL RESPONSES

Several events in the 1990s gave impetus to the anticorruption campaign. First, revelations of major corruption scandals in Brazil, Colombia, France, India, Italy, Japan, Mexico, Pakistan, Russia, Tanzania, Turkey, and Venezuela showed that corruption was widespread even in democracies and developed countries. Second, contrary to hopes that it would reduce the scope for corruption, privatization became a major new source of corruption, particularly in formerly communist countries. Third, research showed that corruption significantly retards economic growth and penalizes the poor, as shown in box 2-1. Moreover, it easily spreads across national boundaries and weakens corporations that bribe by diluting their reliance on quality and cost to remain competitive. Fourth, the general recognition that good governance and sound policies are required for maximum acceleration of economic growth heightened the awareness (especially in finance ministries) that corruption in developing countries is a significant impediment to growth and poverty reduction. This awareness also contributed to the willingness of development assistance agencies to take on corruption. Finally, in the early 1990s, the U.S. government began aggressively to promote anti-corruption activism at every opportunity.[8]

International Actors

Two nongovernmental organizations (NGOs) were largely responsible for the growing awareness of the pernicious effects of corruption. The most influential of these was Transparency International (TI); the other was the International Chamber of Commerce (ICC). Key multilateral organizations—with which TI had extensive interaction—were the OECD, the World Bank, the IMF, and the regional development banks. The fact that two of the founders of TI and several of its activists were former World Bank officials helped TI persuade the financial institutions to move forward on this issue. Finally, TI was able to engage the international business community, with U.S. businesses particularly keen on seeing the campaign succeed. In this section, we will briefly examine the role of these different actors as well as the instruments they put in place.

Transparency International. TI was established in 1993 under the leadership of Peter Eigen, former World Bank director for East Africa, and with the support of several prominent individuals from developing countries, including Nobel Laureate Oscar Arias and the current president of Nigeria, Olesegun Obasanjo. TI's activists, most of them volunteers, included other World Bank alumni, a former director of GTZ (the German technical assistance program), former staff of the U.S. Agency for International Development, the Commonwealth Secretariat, the European Union, and a former associate general counsel of General Electric. In addition to these leaders and to energetic young enthusiasts, TI was able to draw on many highly experienced retirees who had valuable access to key international organizations, government ministries, and multinational corporations. All of these activists were complemented by

Box 2-1. *Corruption's Consequences Especially Harmful to Developing Countries*

- Deterrence of honest individuals from entering public service
- Provision of incentives for public officials (who may have bought their jobs) to focus their energy on self-enrichment rather than public benefit
- Generation of counterproductive regulatory requirements that provide opportunities for officials to demand bribes
- Introduction of a bias against social sectors and maintenance of infrastructure in favor of military procurement (which is often secret) and new capital-intensive projects
- Facilitation of over-invoicing and substandard work by contractors
- Reduction of tax revenues, resulting in higher tax rates
- Undercutting of environmental regulation and other necessary regulations such as building codes
- Discouragement of foreign direct investment and encouragement of capital flight
- Reduced respect for law
- Undermining of human and civil rights
- Erosion of political stability
- Facilitation of other crimes (such as drug trafficking)

Note: For the disproportionate impact of corruption on the poor, see World Bank, *World Development Report 2000/2001* (New York: Oxford University Press, 2000), ch. 6.

numerous luminaries in TI's national chapters and by an advisory committee containing, among others, six former heads of state and one sitting president.

The organization rapidly grew into a global organization with nearly eighty national chapters.[9] Creating and supporting national anticorruption coalitions was and is a top priority of TI. The TI national chapters serve as broad-based instruments for (1) analyzing country-specific shortcomings that abet corruption; (2) setting priorities and establishing action plans for achieving them; and (3) monitoring progress.[10] Because the change in public expectations and government policies, procedures, and practices inescapably has a political dimension, the national coalitions have to be genuinely nonpartisan and widely viewed as such if they are to be effective as sustainable instruments for building consensus.

Typically, the national anticorruption coalitions are composed of representatives from civil society, business, and government. Often, the coalition representatives are chosen by participants from an initial "national integrity workshop" that is attended by members of the press, academia, NGOs, government, and business. TI and the

World Bank's Economic Development Institute jointly organized many of the early workshops. Although there is no set formula for how to begin, the principal task of the first workshop usually involves getting corruption-related reform on the national agenda. Follow-up workshops, often sponsored by the national coalition, then elaborate and revise priorities, propose approaches, and track progress.

While TI's national chapters opened dialogues with their governments on how to curb corruption, TI's international secretariat in Berlin spearheaded intensive behind-the-scenes discussions with the OECD, the Organization of American States (OAS), the World Bank, and the IMF on how to integrate anticorruption measures into their programs. The Belgian chapter engaged in similar discussions with the European Union. Concurrently, TI produced numerous articles, speeches, briefings for journalists, press releases, radio and television interviews, and helped in organizing special regional workshops and global and regional conferences.

Perhaps the most influential activity in elevating the issue of corruption on the national and international agendas has been TI's annual publication of the Corruption Perceptions Index (CPI). Begun in 1995, this composite index based now on fourteen independently conducted surveys of business people, academics, and country analysts, represented the first attempt to rank countries by levels of corruption.[11] Each year, the CPI receives extensive international publicity and discussion and has created political embarrassment in countries ranked near the bottom. For countries waging a battle against corruption, the index can provide a useful tool in helping them assess their relative progress—or lack of it—from year to year. International investors have used the index to help estimate country-related risks. The CPI has also helped spawn a substantial increase in empirical research related to corruption.[12]

Many developing countries considered the index unfair because it did not reflect the supply side of the equation by ranking countries according to how many bribes are offered by their international businesses. In response, TI developed the Bribe Payers Index (BPI) to show from where and in which sectors bribes were most likely to originate. The BPI was intended to increase public pressure on developed countries to criminalize the bribery of foreign officials. It revealed that the most corruption-prone sectors were the public works, construction, oil and other energy-related sectors, as well as the arms and defense industry.[13]

In addition to these indices, TI has published a *National Integrity Systems Sourcebook*, which describes the anticorruption elements of good governance and provides examples and case studies of relevant laws, institutions, procedures, standards, and good practices.[14] The Sourcebook has not only fostered the view that corruption can be reduced; it has also helped establish TI as an NGO with a practical rather than quixotic approach to the problem. Altogether, the Sourcebook, the BPI, and the CPI helped to establish TI's credibility in the international anticorruption campaign and cemented its role as a major player.

TI has been pragmatic rather than moralistic in its approach. It has sought to engage all actors involved and to maintain government support. Placing its emphasis on economic development rather than scandals and past offenses, the TI campaign has tended to give low priority to exposing and prosecuting corrupt individuals, particularly in the early stages of a country's reform program.

TI's initial attention vis-à-vis the developed countries focused on the OECD member states. With relatively few members—most of whom had well-developed legal systems and institutions but did not criminalize bribery of foreign officials—the OECD was a prime target for the anticorruption campaign. Businesses from its member countries—accounting for 70 percent of world trade and 90 percent of foreign direct investment—were responsible for supplying some of the largest and most corrosive international bribes.[15] Reducing the willingness of international businesses to supply such bribes could, in the long run, be expected to help reduce the demand for them. Moreover, OECD members were also in a position to strongly influence the international financial institutions.

International Organizations. The World Bank, the IMF, and the regional development banks, as multilateral institutions, were better positioned than the bilateral aid providers to raise corruption issues in member countries, and they are vital players in helping developing countries introduce reforms that address the demand side of bribery. Initially, many of these institutions were reluctant to take on the problem of corruption beyond the scope of the activities they financed. Five factors worked against their active involvement.

First, the economic costs of corruption were not as widely recognized as they are today. Second, they wished to avoid the divisiveness they could expect from insulting borrowers who in return would be likely to criticize developed country members whose businesses were allowed to "export" bribes. Third, corruption seemed to have political implications that the institutions—with the exception of the European Bank for Reconstruction and Development (EBRD)—believed could not be considered under their mandates. Fourth, they were not clear what, if anything, could be done about the corruption problem. And, finally, their agendas already seemed overly ambitious without adding the corruption issue.

The World Bank's Economic Development Institute, a training facility for mid-level and senior officials from developing countries, did not, however, share these concerns. For several years the institute, which was not in the mainstream of Bank operations, had been running corruption-related courses on how to conduct investigative journalism, had arranged seminars for parliamentarians, and, in collaboration with TI, had conducted national integrity workshops.[16]

The World Bank's position on reducing corruption became less rigid a year after the arrival in 1995 of James Wolfensohn as president. Wolfensohn, a lawyer by training, did not find the Legal Department's argument for avoiding the corruption issue convincing. His opinion was shared by the Bank's new vice-president/controller, Jules Muis. Additional support came from Bank staff who were becoming increasingly restless with senior management's apparent tolerance of activities that undermined development assistance objectives. Also influencing this shift was the reluctance of the U.S. Congress to release funds for the replenishment of the Bank's concessional lending facility. This reluctance was supported by growing public awareness (echoed by the U.S. Treasury Department) that corrupt regimes waste country resources and often divert economic assistance from its intended uses.

In 1996, the World Bank—no longer convinced that the problem of corruption was peripheral to economic development, intractable, purely political, or unduly divisive among its membership—changed its stance. At their annual meeting in Hong Kong in October 1996, the heads of the World Bank and the IMF committed themselves and their institutions to address issues of corruption head on—not only when providing loans and credits, but also when designing country assistance strategies, determining lending levels, providing macroeconomic advice, addressing systemic governance issues in adjustment lending, and providing technical assistance for the design and introduction of corruption-reducing reforms. During the meeting, the two institutions adopted a Declaration on Partnerships for Sustainable Growth, which states that "ensuring the rule of law, improving the accountability of the public sector and tackling corruption" are essential elements of lasting prosperity. The two heads of the institutions also pledged to play an active role in urging countries to outlaw the bribing of foreign officials.

Action followed shortly thereafter. The Bank greatly expanded the budget for the Economic Development Institute's governance-related activities.[17] In 1997, the Bank approved and published an action-oriented strategy paper, *Helping Corrupt Countries Combat Corruption: The Role of the World Bank*. In his foreword, James Wolfensohn, stated: "The international community simply must deal with the cancer of corruption because it is a major barrier to sustainable and equitable development."[18] In 1999, the Bank's widely read and influential *World Development Report* devoted a chapter to corruption. In addition, the Bank tightened its procurement guidelines, which traditionally have set the standard for other multilateral development banks, bilateral assistance agencies, and even countries. The guidelines now require disclosure of payments to business agents and the public advertisement of major consultancy contracts, permit the use of "integrity pacts" (see below), and allow suspension of disbursements, cancellation of loans, and the barring of offending firms from future work if corruption is discovered.

Also in 1997, the IMF approved what it described as "a more proactive approach in advocating policies and the development of institutions and administrative systems that eliminate opportunities for bribery, corruption, and fraudulent activity in the management of public resources."[19] To meet this objective, the IMF increased its research on the corruption problem and issued a guidance note entitled *The Role of the IMF in Governance Issues*. Research was soon followed by concrete action. For example, after allegations that Russia had misused IMF funds, Russia agreed to keep any disbursement from an IMF credit of $4.5 billion in an account at the IMF. When the initial installment of $640 million was disbursed, it was transferred to Russia's IMF account and then used to pay down prior debt to the IMF. Similarly, in the face of allegations that Ukraine's central bank had misrepresented its foreign currency reserves, the proceeds of IMF loans to that country were also kept in an account at the IMF.

In December 1996, the UN General Assembly approved a nonbinding Declaration Against Corruption and Bribery in International Commercial Transactions that included among other things a code of conduct for public officials and a call on member states to criminalize the bribery of public officials, eliminate tax deductibility for bribes paid, and assist each other in investigations and extradition. The UN Development Program (UNDP) followed suit and began to incorporate anticorruption efforts in its work. Other UN agencies also became more willing to allow corrupt staff to be prosecuted, even when that entailed waiver of their diplomatic immunity.

Also in December 1996, the World Trade Organization (WTO) Ministerial Conference established a Working Group on "Transparency in Government Procurement" "to conduct a study on transparency in government procurement practices, taking into account national policies, and, based on this study, to develop elements for inclusion in an appropriate agreement."[20] The OECD, the OAS, and the Council of Europe all originated conventions, as will be discussed shortly.

Not surprisingly, the growing interest in the anticorruption campaign was complemented by a host of international conferences. Three were of particular significance. First, the Eighth International Anticorruption Conference, which was held in 1997 and attended by more than 1,000 people from ninety-three countries, produced the comprehensive Lima Declaration, a blueprint for action. The conference pledged to review the signatories' progress at its meeting two years later.[21] Second was the February 1999 Global Forum on Fighting Corruption and Safeguarding Integrity among Justice and Security Officials. Delegates from eighty-nine countries with then-U.S. Vice-President Al Gore as their host attended the forum. The delegates endorsed several agreements on corruption (including those of OECD, the European Union, OAS, the Council of Europe, and the Global Coalition for Africa), encouraged evaluation of one another's implementation measures, subscribed to a set of guiding principles, and agreed to hold a follow-up conference a year later, in addition to annual global ministerial forums on the fight against corruption.[22] Third was the ninth International Anticorruption Conference, held in 1999 in Durban, which attracted more than 1,400 delegates from 135 countries. Featured speakers included presidents Mbeki of South Africa, Mogae of Botswana, and Wolfensohn of the World

Bank, and chief executives of Interpol, UNDP, the UN Drug Control Program, and the Rio Tinto Group. Among the many topics addressed in forty-one workshops, the conference focused particular attention on the problem of money laundering and the need to promote the return of money stolen by corrupt leaders.

In addition to focusing the attention of the world on the problem of corruption, these conferences have strengthened the will of reformers and provided opportunities to compare experiences and identify common problems and solutions. They enabled the dissemination of research and helped to forge linkages among government officials, academics, and international civil servants.

Taken together, these actions placed corruption firmly on the agenda of key international organizations and bilateral assistance agencies, which have substantial leverage in influencing standards and promoting reform—especially when they reflect broad consensus.

Further reflecting the consensus, the communiqués of several G-7/G-8 summits, beginning in 1996, mentioned the need to reduce corruption. And in June 2000, more than a hundred democracies in the Community of Democracies Ministerial Meeting recognized corruption as a threat to "core democratic principles and practices." They agreed, in the Warsaw Declaration, that "government institutions [should] be transparent, participatory and fully accountable to the citizenry of the country and take steps to combat corruption, which corrodes democracy," and they resolved to "strengthen cooperation to face the transnational challenges to democracy, such as . . . corruption and money laundering."[23]

International Business. International businesses—particularly those based in the United States—have been natural allies in the international campaign against corruption for two reasons. First, those that do not bribe or yield to extortion are often put at a competitive disadvantage.[24] Second, those that do bribe often have to hire dishonest agents; keep two sets of books to preserve secrecy; bypass corporate controls; incur the unpredictable risks of discovery, unenforceable performance, and blackmail; and condone dishonest behavior or the tolerance of it by their own executives. When it became clear that the global campaign against corruption was making progress, many international businesses joined the campaign.

In 1994, the ICC created an ad hoc committee to review its 1977 rules of conduct for enterprises. In 1996, ICC's Executive Board approved new "Rules of Conduct to Combat Extortion and Bribery" and created a Standing Committee to "stimulate action by enterprises and business organizations in support of self-regulation, as an important factor in effectively combating extortion and bribery."[25] In addition, local affiliates of the ICC, including partners and subsidiaries of a number of multinational corporations, often used their influence to help convince others to take action and frequently made their staff available to TI at no charge.

For several years, the widely publicized annual meetings of the World Economic Forum (sometimes referred to as the "Davos Group"), an influential informal association of heads of government and senior international business executives, have provided a useful venue for addressing corporate responsibility in combating corruption.

In the summer of 1999, the OECD agreed to sponsor jointly with the World Bank a Global Forum on Corporate Governance to "respond to the growing need of individual countries that want to strengthen corporate governance. . . provide the basis for a global dialogue on corporate governance reform and . . . bring together relevant international institutions, developing and developed countries, as well as private sector participants and stakeholders."[26] The forum, whose secretariat is housed in the World Bank, is assisted by a Private Sector Advisory Group, an Investors Responsibility Task Force, and a Media Task Force. The forum is seeking to fund a three-year budget of about $15 million. The forum's activities include national and regional roundtables, information exchanges (including a web site and publications series), technical assistance, capacity building, and task forces to address areas of special concern such as audit and accounting. Under the forum's principles, one of the responsibilities of a corporate board of directors is "[to ensure] the integrity of the corporation's accounting and financial reporting systems, including the independent audit, and that appropriate systems of control are in place, in particular systems for monitoring risk, financial control, and compliance with the law."[27]

With respect to banks and their role in abetting money laundering, the Financial Action Task Force on Money Laundering—a multidisciplinary, intergovernmental, policy-making body composed of twenty-nine member countries and housed in OECD—publicly named fifteen "noncooperative" countries as potential havens for ill-gotten wealth. This effectively put banks (and also brokerage houses) on notice to scrutinize their customers' transactions when they involved accounts in those countries.[28]

International Instruments

In the second half of the 1990s, a number of additional international agreements were concluded and nongovernmental codes of conduct adopted.

OECD Convention. The OECD Convention on Combating Bribery of Foreign Public Officials in International Business Transactions was signed in December 1997 by all twenty-nine of the organization's members and five other countries.[29] It came into force on February 15, 1999, having by then been ratified by twelve of the signatories.[30]

The OECD Convention requires that bribery of foreign public officials "be punishable by effective proportionate and dissuasive criminal penalties" and that "the range of penalties shall be comparable to that applicable to [bribery of the country's] own public officials."[31] To oversee compliance, the convention requires a system of "self- and mutual-evaluation." Accordingly, the OECD created a Working Group on Bribery (WGB), which in mid-1998 approved "a rigorous process of multilateral surveillance" to ensure full and effective implementation.[32] The WGB consists of all the signatories to the convention. It holds regular consultations with the OECD's Business and Industry Advisory Council and its Trade Union Advisory Council, as well as with the ICC and TI. The WGB regularly provides information to the public on its own activities.[33]

The convention provides for a two-phase verification process. In the first phase, a signatory country completes a standard detailed questionnaire on existing legislation. Then the WGB Secretariat, assisted by two experts selected from a roster of officials nominated by participating countries, prepares a report on which the country is given an opportunity to comment. After a review meeting during which the lead experts and all members of the WGB may pose questions to the subject country's representative(s), the WGB formulates conclusions and recommendations. Although business and civil society groups do not participate in the formal WGB meetings, the schedule of country meetings is made public in time for such groups to formulate their opinions and make them known.[34]

In the second phase, which is scheduled to start in 2001, countries will again be asked to respond to a standard questionnaire. Following site visits by OECD experts, the WGB Secretariat will prepare a report on each country's enforcement performance. If the country reviews indicate a need, subsequent cross-cutting reviews on particular implementation issues may also be conducted.

This verification system should reassure each signatory that all other signatories are complying with the convention's obligations in a timely and reasonable manner. The convention has no formal sanctions, but the prospect of wide publicity and domestic and international opprobrium is expected to be enough of a disincentive to cheat. As a further safeguard, TI has created its own working group to monitor compliance with the OECD Convention. It has developed a checklist that its national chapters can use in reviewing countries' draft legislation and also intends to play an active role in helping the WGB monitor enforcement.[35]

Consistent with the convention but going beyond its specific requirements, OECD members agreed in December 2000 to include antibribery measures in their officially supported export credit and credit guarantee programs. They agreed to require an undertaking by applicants that "neither they, nor anyone acting in their behalf, have been engaged or will be engaged in bribery in the transaction."[36] Proven breach of the undertaking would, they also agreed, result in "appropriate action, such as denial of payment or indemnification, refund of sums provided and/or referral of evidence of such bribery to the appropriate national authorities."[37]

Council of Europe Conventions. In November 1998, the Council of Europe (composed of forty-three foreign ministers, many of whom represent non-OECD countries in Central and Eastern Europe) adopted a Criminal Law Convention on Corruption. It goes beyond the OECD Convention in addressing the demand side of bribery. Moreover, it covers private-to-private bribery. In addition, it recommends making "trafficking in influence" a crime, and it recommends lifting the immunity of members of parliament from prosecution in such cases. Its relatively strong stance on bribery reflects the law enforcement perspective of its drafters.

In addition to the Criminal Law Convention, the Council of Europe approved in September 1999 a Civil Law Convention on Corruption. This convention calls on signatory states to protect whistle blowers and to compensate parties injured as a result of corruption by their public officials. Neither the Criminal Law nor the Civil Law Convention has entered into force. Both need ratification by fourteen signatories. Also in 1999, the Council of Europe established the "Group of States Against Corruption" (GRECO) to oversee an OECD-style monitoring process with respect to three specified dimensions important to enforcing compliance.[38]

OAS Convention. In March 1996, the OAS adopted the Inter-American Convention Against Corruption. This was followed by a comprehensive Plan Against Corruption in June 1997 and the formation of a group to negotiate a regional agreement on government procurement in 1998 at the Summit of the Americas in Santiago.[39] The Inter-American Convention Against Corruption (also known as the OAS Convention) has been signed by twenty-six OAS member countries and ratified, as of November 2000, by twenty-one. Both the OAS Convention and the OECD Convention call upon signatories to cooperate with each other in information sharing and investigation, and both lack explicit sanctions for noncompliance, but the OAS does not yet have a counterpart to the OECD's effective peer evaluation process. Recognizing this need, the Council of Presidents and Prime Ministers of the Americas, in the May 1999 "Transparency for Growth" Conference at the Carter Center, called for creation of a peer review mechanism similar to OECD's—to "promote consistent and effective implementation of criminal laws . . . and share best practices and model laws."[40] The OAS Convention goes well beyond its OECD counterpart by, among other things, calling upon its parties to establish as a corruption offense "illicit enrichment," defined as "a significant increase in the assets of a government official which he cannot reasonably explain in relation to his lawful earnings during the performance of his functions." More generally, the OAS Convention—unlike the OECD one—is more concerned with domestic corruption than with the bribery of foreign officials.

Nongovernmental Codes of Conduct. In 1996, the U.S. national chapter of TI completed a "best practices" study of codes of conduct and related programs used by U.S. businesses.[41] In the same year, the ICC undertook to serve as an information clearing house, conduct seminars, and work with international organizations and national governments to promote more effective laws against extortion and bribery and to work with ICC national committees in sixty-two countries to have them adopt or adapt its Rules of Conduct.[42] In 1999, the ICC published what it described as "a practical handbook for corporate managers, lawyers, and accountants responsible for developing and administering corporate compliance programs."[43]

In October 2000, after meeting intermittently with TI for two years, eleven of the world's largest banks agreed to a set of global anti–money laundering principles and guidelines for international private banks. Each signatory bank would "endeavor to accept only those clients whose source of wealth and funds can be reasonably established to be legitimate." The "Wolfsberg Principles" stated that "numbered or alternate name accounts will only be accepted if the bank has established the identity of the client and the beneficial owner." The principles prescribed "heightened scrutiny to clients and beneficial owners resident in and funds sourced from countries identified by credible sources as having inadequate anti-money-laundering standards or representing high-risk for crime and corruption." The principles also committed the banks to "establish an adequately staffed and independent department responsible for the prevention of money laundering."[44] A collaborative effort will now be made to extend the Wolfsberg Principles to additional banks and to extend similar principles and guidelines to other segments of the financial sector, including investment firms, brokers, insurance companies, and asset management firms.

The combination of international conventions, implementing legislation, and model corporate codes has begun to change norms relevant to the conduct of transnational business. TI and the ICC have collaborated closely and effectively in helping bring about this basis for future progress in the effort to reduce corruption.

LESSONS LEARNED

Because the long-term challenge of reducing corruption has only recently been recognized as a global as well as national problem, it is still too early to assess the results of the anticorruption campaign. Nevertheless, some preliminary observations are possible.

Agenda Setting

To date, most of the work of the anticorruption campaign has focused on raising the visibility of the corruption issue and getting it placed on national and international agendas. The prerequisites for anticorruption reform include governmental checks and balances, a respect for the rule of law, independent judiciaries, competent prosecutorial capabilities, financial disclosure standards, free and independent media, and an expectation that bribery is not necessary in business relations. In developed countries, most of these prerequisites are already in place—even if they sometimes fail to function properly. As democracies with active civil societies, most developed countries tend to be responsive to public opinion. Organizations like TI can mobilize or threaten to mobilize against domestic corruption and also against governments that tolerate the bribing of foreign officials—or worse, subsidize it through tax deductibility.[45]

Targeting the developed countries was a high priority for the TI anticorruption campaign because its activists believed that these countries could achieve progress faster and more easily than most developing countries, which were thought to require more comprehensive programs of long-term reform. Moreover, developed countries were influential in the multilateral development banks, the IMF, and the OECD. Without the support of these countries and international organizations, the campaign would have been much less effective for two reasons. First, the multilateral development banks and the IMF finance a substantial share of the business between developed country corporations and developing country governments. Second, even when aid financing is not involved, corporations based in the OECD countries supply a substantial portion of the bribe money involved in international transactions with governments.

Taken together, the host of activities by international organizations and businesses constituted—or reflected—an agenda that could not be ignored by democratically elected governments, governments whose actions would ultimately contribute importantly to the success of the global campaign. Nor could it be ignored by the media, whose impact in many countries is formidable.[46]

Getting corruption issues onto the agendas of developing country governments—especially the nondemocratic ones—has been more difficult given the number and diversity of developing countries and the magnitude of the task involved. It required different approaches, and with some notable exceptions, has proceeded more slowly. From the outset, the campaign recognized that sustained impetus for broad-based reform in societies that lack many of the essential barriers to corruption has to come from within. Although external involvement (for example, from sources of capital and expertise) can certainly help, there is no practical alternative to reforms that are internally initiated and supported by broadly representative national anticorruption coalitions. For this reason, the campaign properly emphasized efforts to create country-level coalitions that could heighten national recognition of the corruption problem, press for demand-side systemic and institutional improvements, help identify priorities, and play a role in monitoring progress. In parallel, the campaign sought to have international businesses adopt and enforce codes of conduct banning bribery.

Four factors helped the campaign convince developed countries, developing countries, multilateral institutions, and the business sector that corruption deserved priority attention. First, the campaign was successful in showing how corruption threatens economic growth, undermines corporate governance and spreads across national borders. Second, it began to demonstrate that large-scale corruption is not inevitable and that pragmatic steps can be taken to combat it. Third, the campaign devised practical means to make existing relative levels of corruption—particularly the bribery of public officials—more visible. The widely publicized comparative country rankings have been a remarkably effective catalyst for change. Fourth, the strong support of a small number of governments (especially that of the United States) was an important factor in the success of the anticorruption campaign.

Negotiations

Several factors influenced the speed and ease of negotiating the 1997 OECD Convention on Combating Bribery of Foreign Public Officials in International Business Transactions. Careful preparation by the OECD's anticorruption unit was one. Another was the decision to adopt a flexible approach, which made it unnecessary to design and spell out in detail binding undertakings that would have to fit within the diverse legal systems of the signatories. Yet another was the carefully designed program of "self- and mutual-evaluation," which helped allay concerns that countries that effectively implemented the convention would be put at a disadvantage vis-à-vis those that did not.

In addition, earlier concerns about extraterritoriality had been overtaken by the realization that in the economic sphere globalization had greatly reduced the relevance of national borders. Finally, the active involvement of the international business community and national TI chapters in OECD's member countries (especially Germany, Great Britain, and the United States) demonstrated that key sectors of society were in favor of the convention.[47]

Implementation and Compliance

Reducing corruption is necessarily a long-term challenge, and it is too soon to claim success—defined here as actual reductions in corruption. It is not too soon, however, to outline how to maintain pressure for reform and what processes for tracking progress in achieving it need to be put into place. Nor is it too soon to describe the major elements of reform sought within countries where corruption is pervasive.

In countries with major systemic and institutional deficiencies, a holistic multi-faceted approach to implementing reform is essential for success. Short of that, corruption will inevitably find its way through gaps in the system, and the resulting contagion and cynicism will be likely to undermine the broader country-level effort. This is not to say, however, that all aspects have to be addressed simultaneously from the outset. When devising and implementing needed reforms, it will be important to set priorities and seize targets of opportunity.

Ultimately, widespread corruption will substantially decrease only when citizens and businesses come to believe that bribery is risky, costly, and wrong, and when public officials are made to fear that seeking or accepting bribes might well result in disclosure, prosecution, and severe penalties. To be effective, national reform packages must therefore: (1) reduce the incentives and opportunities to extort and bribe; (2) greatly increase the risks to future bribers and bribees of detection; and (3) increase the likelihood and severity of penalties when bribery is detected.

Although national needs and internal negotiations vary widely and there is no single ideal approach to such reforms, national reform programs usually have to include improvements in both the public sector and the private sector. While the optimal sequencing of reforms is sure to vary from country to country, and the determination of what to do next will often have to be opportunistic, in nearly all countries the first four areas of reform should probably be judicial reform, creation of prosecutorial capacity, codification of disclosure requirements, and media freedom. Box 2-2 contains a fuller description of the main requisites of a "national integrity system."

Helping to determine the priorities for reform, identifying targets of opportunity (such as a sympathetic minister, a receptive local government, or a major contract), building and maintaining pressure, negotiating, and monitoring progress all are important roles of the national coalitions already described. Even where the head of state supports broad-based reform, these kinds of activities are required to help reduce the influence of those with vested interests in the continuance of corruption. For example, before his election in 1995, President William Mkapa of Tanzania signed an "integrity pledge" that had come out of a national integrity workshop held by TI and the Economic Development Institute in August. Yet in 1999 Tanzania was ranked among the bottom five countries in the CPI.[48] Where the head of state does not support the effort, the coalitions' principal role is to build and maintain internal pressure and pursue targets of opportunity.

Three types of national survey instruments are proving useful to countries in spurring the development and execution of reform programs. The first, a powerful domestic variant of TI's international CPI, is a country or provincial "service delivery survey" of consumers of public services that seeks to create, and then publish with respect to each government unit, a "report card" indicating the incidence and magnitude of bribes typically demanded and paid.[49] A second instrument identifies, by government unit, outputs delivered in relation to the budgetary inputs provided, to identify unexplained discrepancies. The third instrument is the compilation of so-

Box 2-2. *Elements of an Effective National Integrity System*

Systemic Improvements

- *Civil Service Reform.* Civil service and ministerial pay must be set at levels that make corruption unnecessary, by enabling public officials to live on their government compensation in reasonable comfort. Criteria and procedures for appointments, promotions, and dismissals should be clear, published, and followed.
- *Regulatory Reforms.* Regulatory reforms (including such measures as tax simplification, reduction of nontariff barriers to trade, and elimination of unnecessarily elaborate requirements) must be introduced to reduce the requirements for public officials to be involved and to narrow the scope for discretion when they are.
- *Privatization.* The privatization of selected public sector activities can help reduce corruption if it can be accomplished with appropriate safeguards and accompanied, as necessary, with suitable competition-enhancing measures or regulatory regimes (including pricing standards and transparent performance benchmarks).[a]
- *Procedures and Criteria.* Procedures and criteria relevant to obtaining licenses, permissions, customs clearance, and government contracts, subsidies, and grants should be reformed as necessary, published, and adhered to. For licenses and the like, time norms should be established and prominently displayed. Where the opportunity for corruption is great, helpful procedural tools should be introduced—including joint decision-making, frequent job rotation, random selection among judges, spot checks, required reporting of gifts, financial disclosure to reveal illicit enrichment, and close management oversight, as well as competitive bidding for—and transparent decision-making with respect to—contract awards.
- *Financial Management and Transparency.* Appropriation, budgeting, accounting, audit, and financial disclosure requirements and practices must make money flows fully traceable.

Note: These elements are elaborated, with discussion and examples, in Transparency International's *National Integrity Sourcebook*.

a. See Ira W. Lieberman, Stilpon S. Nestor, and Raj Desai, eds., *Between State and Market: Mass Privatization in Transitional Economies* (Washington, D.C.: World Bank and OECD, 1997) and, for a briefer treatment, <http://www.imf.org/external/pubs/ft/fandd/1999/06/nellis.htm>.

- *Criminalization of Bribing Foreign Officials.* All countries should criminalize bribery of foreign as well as domestic officials and should not permit such bribes to be tax deductible.
- *Government Publication.* Legislative debates and government, administrative, and judicial decisions must be promptly published.
- *Political Finance.* Rules should be devised and enforced to prevent bribes provided in the form of political contributions.

Enforcement
- *Judicial Reform and Prosecutorial Capabilities.* Countries must have an honest and independent judiciary as well as competent, independent, and well-resourced prosecutorial capabilities. Countries should cooperate with one another in investigations and extraditions.
- *Whistle-Blowers and Watchdogs.* Whistle-blowers must be protected and watchdog organizations should be created (for example, anticorruption commissions, national public sector audit institutions, inspectors general, public accounts committees in parliaments, independent auditors, ombudsmen, TI national chapters). To permit public monitoring of progress, major construction projects should publicly display their costs, financial sources, and schedules. A framework of accountability is crucial.
- *Penalties and Private Enforcers.* Targets of corruption should have the right to sue and recover damages in civil proceedings. Government contracts that are proven to have been awarded through corruption should be invalidated.
- *Asset Declarations.* Public declarations of personal and family assets by parliamentarians and senior government employees upon assumption of office and periodically thereafter until departure should be required and monitored, to help deter "illicit enrichment" and protect honest individuals.
- *Free Media.* Media must be freed from government control or unreasonable restraint of content and allowed to keep their sources confidential. Libel laws that intimidate honest competent journalists should be changed, and the truth of what is written or said should be a recognized defense in a lawsuit. The widest possible access to government information should be the norm (subject to narrow restrictions on grounds of national security or personal privacy).
- *Surveys and Investigations.* Periodic and targeted surveys and investigations should be conducted to determine the extent to which anticorruption mea-

Continued on next page

Box 2-2. Continued

sures are working and in what countries, localities, activities, and agencies they are not.

Standards

- *Public Sector Codes of Conduct.* Public sector (civil service and political) codes of conduct that address conflict-of-interest issues should be adopted, published, and enforced.
- *Corporate Codes of Conduct.* Corporations should have and enforce codes of conduct and should make management responsible for taking all reasonable measures to ensure that their employees, subsidiaries, and agents do not engage in corrupt practices.
- *Professional Ethical Standards.* Professions such as accounting and the law should establish ethical standards and deny or suspend accreditation to those who breach them.[b]

---

b. Omitted from the above list is decentralization to local government, often supported on the grounds that it is likely to increase civil society involvement, social capital, and government responsiveness. The omission reflects my view that local governments tend to be more corrupt than central ones and that introducing the necessary systemic reforms to local as well as central governments would exponentially increase the magnitude of the effort and the number of skilled reformers required. In China, for example, according to Minxin Pei, "an investigation by the central government reported that almost 90% of the fees collected by local governments [fees that account for about half of total government revenues] were either unauthorized or illegal." See Minxin Pei, "Will China Become Another Indonesia?" *Foreign Policy* (Fall 1999), p. 101. When a central government has been "cleaned up" and self-fulfilling expectations of extortion and bribery have been reduced, it may become more appropriate to consider decentralizing authorities to the country's local governments. An exception, however, could be made when a particular local government has been selected as an "island of integrity."

---

called Big Mac Indexes—indexes that can reveal unexplainable cost discrepancies within a country for similar commodities (such as school lunches, aspirins in a hospital, and so on). TI/Argentina conducted a Big Mac survey, which revealed that a school lunch in Buenos Aires cost the equivalent of $5. A comparable lunch in Mendoza, which had been implementing anticorruption measures, cost the equivalent of $0.80. Within days of publication of the survey's result, the cost of a school lunch in Buenos Aires was more than halved.[50] The use of all three instruments is growing.[51]

Another approach is "integrity testing," whereby police are given, say, a $20 bill that was "found on the street" to see whether they turn it in. Or, they are "tipped off" about a cache of illicit money, drugs, or stolen goods, and a video is made of what is done with the contents.

One more approach to the problem of compliance is the development of international performance objectives. The World Customs Union, for example, has established a standard program for measuring the time required before goods are released from customs. A pattern of major deviations from the standard could be the result of either inefficiency or extortion (or both) and would provide cause for closer investigation. The World Bank has also, in some countries, compared the total value of imported goods, calculated from macroeconomic data, with the value shown for customs purposes, and found very large differences indicative of corruption. Customs operations have long been magnets for transborder corruption.

In addition, TI and the Global Coalition for Africa—an intergovernmental policy forum of which former World Bank president Robert McNamara is chairman emeritus—have pioneered the "islands of integrity" approach, which is intended to produce visible results more rapidly than the required comprehensive reform programs would. An "island of integrity" can be a large contract, an industry segment such as large power generators that have relatively few suppliers, or a location such as a city with a reformist mayor. The purpose is to deter bribery within the "island" by increasing the likelihood of discovery, successful prosecution, and the imposition of severe penalties. By signing an "integrity pact," all bidders for a contract agree to: (1) adopt and enforce a code to avoid bribery by their employees, subsidiaries, or agents; (2) provide information about all payments to third parties; and (3) submit to appropriate monitoring. Each chief executive officer or senior corporate official must accept in writing the terms of the pact, so that he or she cannot subsequently disclaim knowledge of the terms. The government commits itself to provide full public disclosure of the criteria and all relevant data regarding the evaluation of the competing bids. Breach by a bidder of the integrity pact will entail liability for damages, loss of the contract, removal from consideration for future contracts, forfeiture of bid security, and penalties on high-level officials (if they cannot demonstrate reasonable preventive efforts) as well as against the firm. The pact explicitly gives competing bidders and the government legal standing to bring suit—perhaps before an international arbitrator (such as the ICC's Arbitration Court), if the local court system is inefficient or not to be trusted. Businesses, in short, are empowered to police one another. The integrity pact approach has been applied, for example, with respect to a refinery rehabilitation project in Ecuador, a telecommunications privatization plan in Colombia, and a subway project in Buenos Aires, Argentina.[52]

One test case for the anticorruption campaign may be Nigeria. Ranked as one of the world's most corrupt countries, it elected Olesegun Obasanjo as president in 1999. Obasanjo was for many years (some of them spent in jail as a political prisoner) the chairman of TI's Advisory Council. If he is able to turn Nigeria around and bring it up to, say, the middle of the CPI's annual ranking, that improvement would provide good evidence that reform is possible even in the most egregiously corrupt countries.

Reactions to Noncompliance

If, pursuant to their obligations under the OECD Convention, the developed countries enforce laws criminalizing the bribing of foreign officials, these will be a substantial deterrent to bribery by their business sectors. For developed countries that, despite the OECD Convention, do not have adequate anticorruption laws or are lax in enforcing them, the sole but powerful sanction will be public (domestic and international) opprobrium. This sanction is strengthened by publication of the TI Bribe Payers Index, which in 1999, for example, ranked nineteen leading exporting countries in terms of the degree to which their corporations are perceived to be paying bribes abroad.

In developing countries, externally applied penalties for sustained corruption and failure to address corruption will be more severe. One powerful force, as mentioned earlier, is TI's annual CPI. Where a country's level of corruption is egregious and there is little governmental effort to reduce it, the international financial institutions and bilateral assistance agencies may reduce or eliminate their aid packages, as happened in Kenya in 1997. Many of these countries are also being penalized by the world's financial markets. For example, PricewaterhouseCoopers has recently developed an "opacity index" to measure the "lack of clear, accurate, formal, and widely accepted practices" and to provide a basis for measuring the deleterious impact of opacity. The index, a composite, encompasses corruption, laws governing contracts or property rights, economic policies, accounting standards, and business regulations. Using the index, PricewaterhouseCoopers has estimated the impact of low opacity rankings on a country's cost of raising capital through sovereign bond issues. The "opacity risk premium" of Russia, for example, is estimated to exceed 12 percent, a burden equivalent to a tax on investment in Russia of 43 percent.[53] Further, as the OECD Convention takes hold and increases the risks of bribing, potential sources of foreign direct investment and foreign contractors may decide to avoid doing business with particularly corrupt countries.[54] As a result of these penalties, the economic growth—and perhaps in some cases the political stability—of laggard countries will be impaired.

Lastly, consideration is being given to the creation of an electronic mail account or hot line that international businesses could use if they believed that they were the victims of extortion or that a competitor was providing bribes. The ambassadors from the countries involved would receive notification of the complaint. Then, assuming the complaint was plausible, an investigation would be launched—requiring the cooperation at least of those countries that had ratified one of the anticorruption conventions or subscribed to the Warsaw Convention.

CONCLUSIONS

Revelations of major corruption scandals in developed as well as developing countries placed the issue of corruption on the agendas of many politicians. The annual CPI, followed by the BPI, helped keep it there. The increased awareness of corruption's damage to economic growth and poverty reduction—combined with the related threat of growing aid fatigue—encouraged other actors to join the campaign, including development assistance institutions, the IMF, and citizen groups from developing countries. These actors were well positioned to increase the pressure for—and then assist with—reform in developing countries.

The actor chiefly responsible for ensuring sustained attention to the problem was TI. Its effectiveness was due largely to an experienced, internationally balanced, and well-connected leadership and to its close relations with the OECD Secretariat, the World Bank, and the ICC. In addition, the U.S. government and numerous businesses played important roles in pushing for international conventions and higher standards of conduct. Strategically, TI's decision to aim one part of the anticorruption campaign at OECD countries was sound as well as politically astute. Addressing the supply side of corruption was essential, and the even-handed approach enhanced the campaign's credibility in developing countries, where public officials commonly demand bribes.

Nevertheless, many obstacles remain in the effort to reduce corruption—an effort that has to be long-term, multipronged, and multinational. For developed countries, the most difficult obstacle will be lax enforcement. For developing countries, the principal obstacle will be the difficulty of organizing effective and sustainable national anticorruption coalitions that are strong enough to overcome opposition by corruption's beneficiaries.[55] Another obstacle everywhere will be the resourcefulness of corrupt individuals and organizations in devising new ways to circumvent whatever anticorruption measures are adopted. Related to this obstacle is the shortage—in developing countries, assistance agencies, and the relevant professions—of skills needed to design and implement anticorruption reforms. Finally, a fundamental obstacle nearly everywhere will be the view that the struggle against corruption is hopeless and therefore quixotic, that bribery is inevitable and therefore necessary.

NOTES

1. Corruption can take many forms including: nepotism, embezzlement, tax evasion, theft of state property, election fraud, and bribery. As used in this chapter, corruption is de-

fined as the abuse of public office for private gain. It excludes modest disclosed gift giving if no quid pro quo other than goodwill is expected. It also excludes so-called private-to-private corruption (that is, fraud, bribery, and embezzlement not involving public officials), which, although a serious problem, is more diffuse and less directly harmful to the public, especially the poor. Some private-to-private corruption, however—such as a widespread Ponzi scheme or a private monopoly that provides an indispensable service or commodity such as electricity or water—can be directly harmful to the poor.

2. James A. Leach, "The New Russian Menace," *New York Times*, September 10, 1999, p. A25.

3. See <http://www.oecd.org/daf/nocorruption/faq.htm>.

4. Paulo Mauro, "Corruption and Growth," *Quarterly Journal of Economics*, vol. 110, no. 3 (1995), p. 705.

5. Minxin Pei, "Will China Become Another Indonesia?" *Foreign Policy* (Fall 1999), p. 99.

6. Once fashionable arguments that "speed" and "grease" payments—payments to accelerate an action that is legal, as opposed to payments to break the law—can promote efficiency are refuted in Daniel Kaufman, "Revisiting Anticorruption Strategies: Tilt towards Incentive-Driven Approaches," in Sahr Kpundeh and Irene Hors, eds., *Corruption and Integrity Improvement Initiatives in Developing Countries* (New York: UNDP and OECD Development Centre, 1998). The incidence of corruption, including speed payments, correlates positively with the time people have to spend dealing with government officials. In addition, the expectation of bribes often leads to the imposition of additional requirements for government approval. See Daniel Kaufman and Shang-Jin Wei, *Does "Grease Money" Speed the Wheels of Commerce?* NBER Working Paper No. 7093 (Cambridge, Mass.: National Bureau of Economic Research, 1999).

7. The FCPA was introduced following the disclosure that Lockheed had paid $25 million to Japanese officials to secure the sale of its Tristar L1011 aircraft. The act: (1) criminalized certain payments to foreign officials (but excluded payments to expedite routine government actions and payments that were legal under host country law); (2) required accurate accounting of all transactions; and (3) made U.S. managers liable to prosecution, fines, and imprisonment if they were aware of or showed conscious disregard of the payments' illegality. Given the skepticism in some quarters about the extent to which the act has been enforced, it is not clear that the FCPA has been an effective deterrent to those U.S. firms that are inclined to bribe. U.S. enforcement, however, may become more vigorous as the signatories of the OECD Convention pass and begin implementing similar legislation.

8. Five factors influenced the U.S. government to launch its anticorruption campaign: (1) the end of the Cold War and with it the reduced need to avoid offending friendly governments or prop up corrupt regimes; (2) the arrival of a new administration which, under President Bill Clinton, hoped to build corporate support for and from the anticorruption campaign, given that the Foreign Corrupt Practices Act disadvantaged U.S. corporations; (3) the desire to clean up and reduce waste in both U.S. and international aid programs and reduce aid fatigue; (4) the increased visibility of corruption; and (5) the growing perception that the corruption problem was not intractable.

9. TI has received support from more than a dozen foundations, more than seventy corporations, and more than twenty-five public sector agencies. In 1993, the Global Coalition

for Africa (an intergovernmental forum cochaired by former World Bank president Robert McNamara) became the first multilateral organization to contribute funding to TI. The diversity of sources in funding has helped dampen occasional suspicions that TI is a stalking-horse for the U.S. government.

10. The coalitions also provide some protection against the vindictiveness of governments against putative reformers and make it less likely that sustained support for reform would be undermined by changes of government. For more information about TI, see Frederick Galtung, "A Global Network to Curb Corruption: The Experience of Transparency International" in Ann Florini, ed., *The Third Force: The Rise of Transnational Civil Society* (Washington, D.C.: Carnegie Endowment for International Peace and Japan Center for International Exchange, 2000), pp. 17–47. See also Frederik Galtung and Jeremy Pope, "The Global Coalition Against Corruption: Evaluating Transparency International," in Andreas Shedler, Larry Diamond, and Mark Plattner, eds., *The Self-Restraining State: Power and Accountability in New Democracies* (Boulder, Colo.: Lynne Rienner, 1999), pp. 257–82.

11. Ninety countries were ranked in 2000. The CPI's methodology is documented on the TI web site, <http://www.transparency.org>. An alternative methodology, building on numerous indicators of good governance and the grouping of countries' degree of corruption by quartile, is described in Daniel Kaufman, Aart Kraay, and Pablo Zoido-Lobatón, *Aggregating Governance Indicators*, Policy Research Working Paper No. 2195 (Washington, D.C.: World Bank, October 1999). The paper is available at <http://www.worldbank.org/wbi/governance/pubs/aggindicators.htm>. This "finer grained" methodology is more useful than TI's for country-specific research and the design of country-level remedial measures, but less valuable as a source of pressure to act.

12. Through empirical analyses, corruption has been correlated positively with time spent by business managers with government officials and with policy distortion, and negatively correlated with civil liberties, women's rights, investment in education, merit-based recruitment in the civil service, civil service wages, predictability of the judiciary, foreign direct investment, the ratio of gross investment to GDP, and national environmental performance. At the Annual Meeting of the World Economic Forum 2001 in Davos, Switzerland, Dan Esty, Project Director of Columbia University's Center for Earth Science Information and Director of the Yale Center for Environmental Law and Policy, commented: "This striking correlation [of corruption with poor environmental performance, as indicated by the new Environmental Sustainability Index] underlines the importance of Transparency International's CPI as a measure of much more than corruption. Corruption contributes to environmental degradation, but is also an indicator of the way societies develop in terms of open government. . . ." See TI press release, January 26, 2001. For a guide to the empirical studies, see Johann Graf Lamsdorff, *Corruption in Empirical Research—A Review*, available at <http://www.transparency.org/documents/work-papers/lambsdorff_eresearch.html>. See also "Empirical Studies of Governance and Development," *Helping Countries Combat Corruption: Progress at the World Bank Since 1997*, Annex IV (Washington, D.C.: World Bank, 2000).

13. See <http://www.transparency.org/documents/cpi/index.html> and <http://www.transparency.org/documents/cpi/bpi_framework.html>. Following the release of

the CPI and BPI in 1999, TI's web site received more than 50,000 hits per day for several days.

14. TI posted the Sourcebook on the Internet. See <http://www.transparency.org>. By 2001, the original English-language version of the Sourcebook had been translated into fifteen languages: Arabic, Azeri, Bahasa Indonesian, Bosnian, Chinese, French, Hungarian, Korean, Polish, Portuguese, Romanian, Russian, Serbian, Slovak, and Spanish. The Latin American chapters of TI adapted the Sourcebook to the Latin American context and developed teaching manuals based on it. In 2000 a French translation of the English-language common law version was being adapted to French civil law, and a Russian translation had been adapted to the Russian context. A greatly expanded revision of the Sourcebook—entitled *Confronting Corruption: The Elements of a National Integrity System*—was completed in 2000 for publication and distribution in 2001.

15. TI, *Combating International Corruption,* Transparency International Annual Report (Berlin: TI, 1998), p. 29.

16. The Economic Development Institute is now called the World Bank Institute. The former's early involvement, contrary to Bank skepticism, helped to establish that the Bank could do such work without negative fallout. The World Bank Institute has traditionally taught lessons drawn from the Bank's experience, but with respect to corruption—where Bank operational experience was negligible—it was and still is at the leading edge of Bank work. In its anticorruption core course, the World Bank Institute emphasizes that the reform process requires "*KI+L+CA*"—that is, knowledge/information and data + leadership (including political) + collective action for change. (See, for example, Maria Gonzalez de Asis, *Reducing Corruption: Lessons from Venezuela*, PREM Note No. 39 (Washington, D.C.: World Bank, 2000).

17. From a level of $400,000 in FY1996, the budget for such activities grew to $600,000 in 1997 and then to $1.25 million in 1998 and 1999.

18. World Bank, *Helping Corrupt Countries Combat Corruption: The Role of the World Bank* (Washington, D.C.: World Bank, 1997), p. 2. During this "gearing up" period, in which Bank anticorruption strategies were developed, the Bank sought and received substantial advice and support from TI, which had the expertise, perspectives, and access to civil society that the Bank lacked. In addition to these actions, the Bank greatly increased its number of procurement specialists, began a program of special procurement audits by independent international firms, established a special confidential hot line, and in 1998, created a top-level Oversight Committee on Fraud and Corruption. At the Bank's 1999 annual meeting, World Bank President Wolfensohn reported that the Bank was spending $5 billion a year on governance and was working on corruption programs in over two dozen countries. Corruption, mentioned thirteen times, received extensive attention throughout his opening speech to the Board of Governors. As of November 2000, the Bank, on the recommendation of its Sanctions Committee (created in November 1998), had debarred fifty-three firms and individuals from competing for Bank-financed contracts. See http://www.worldbank.org/html/opr/procure/debarr.html>.

19. IMF News Brief No. 97/15 (August 1997). Subsequently, IMF Managing Director Camdessus, paraphrasing an adviser to Louis XVI, said, "It's not progress . . . it's a revo-

lution!" See IMF, "The IMF and Good Governance," address by Michel Camdessus at TI, Paris (January 21, 1998). Available at <http://www.imf.org/external/np/speeches/1998/012198.htm>.

20. WTO Working Group on Transparency in Government Procurement, 1998 Report to the General Council, WT/WGTGP/2 (November 17, 1998), available at <http://www.wto.org/english/tratop_e/gproc_e/tran98_e.htm>.

21. TI functioned as secretariat/organizer for the international anticorruption conferences in 1997 and 1999. Many of the conference papers and the Lima Declaration are accessible on the TI web site.

22. See <http://www.state.gov/www/global/narcotics_law/global_forum/appendix2.html>.

23. See <http://www.state.gov/www/global/human_rights/democracy/000627_cdi_warsaw_decl.html>.

24. Assuming that increased business integrity and corporate unwillingness to bribe are a public good, those businesses that continue to offer bribes (and find takers) become free riders with an advantage over their competitors. To offset the advantage, the likelihood of discovery and punishment must be increased. (See, for example, the discussion in this chapter of "integrity pacts.") Interestingly, the BPI revealed a body of opinion that U.S. diplomatic aggressiveness in promoting U.S. business is itself coercive and may reduce the need for U.S. firms to bribe.

25. "ICC: Extortion and Bribery in International Business Transactions," 1999 Edition of ICC Rules of Conduct, available at <http://www.iccwbo.org/home/statements_rules/rules/1999/briberydoc99.asp>. See also Fritz Heimann, "Combating International Corruption: The Role of the Business Community," in Kimberly Ann Elliott, ed., *Corruption and the Global Economy* (Washington, D.C.: Institute for International Economics, 1997). The ICC Rules of Conduct were revised in 1999.

26. World Bank, news release no. 99/2217/S, Washington, D.C.

27. Section V.D.5 of the Principles.

28. Joseph Kahn, "Fifteen Countries Named as Potential Money-Laundering Havens," *New York Times*, June 23, 2000, p. A4.

29. The five non-OECD signatories were Argentina, Brazil, Bulgaria, Chile, and the Slovak Republic. Prior to the OECD Convention (in May 1996), OECD's Ministerial Council had agreed that member countries should stop granting tax deductions for bribes of foreign officials, and the Group of Seven (G-7) heads of government, at their June 1996 summit in Lyon, had endorsed the recommendation. It may be noted that in September 1996, the European Union, reacting to numerous well-publicized scandals involving some of its member states, had adopted a protocol requiring its members to criminalize the bribery of foreign public officials. Unfortunately, the protocol—which was overtaken by the OECD Convention—did not address the bribery of foreign officials of nonmember countries. Nor did it address the issue of tax deductibility.

30. By March 2001, thirty of the convention's signatories had ratified it. In 1998, after the convention was signed but before it went into effect, OECD's anticorruption unit launched a series of outreach efforts designed to encourage non-OECD members to sign on. In addition, it began to manage anticorruption networks for "transition economies" (formerly communist ones) and for Latin American countries, and it commissioned studies

of five subjects not encompassed in the convention: payments to political parties and their officials, payments to candidates for public office, coverage of foreign subsidiaries, private sector bribery, and money laundering.

31. See OECD, *Public Sector Corruption: An International Survey of Preventive Measures* (Paris: OECD, 1999), which surveys the measures that fifteen OECD countries are currently using to protect their domestic public institutions against corruption.

32. For the full-compliance monitoring process go to <http://www.oecd.org/daf/nocorruption/selfe.htm>. The WGB's monitoring process was modeled on that of the Financial Action Task Force.

33. The OECD web site, <http://www.oecd.org/daf/nocorruption>, also has links to the relevant implementing laws and draft new laws of signatory countries.

34. The WGB, in June 2000, prepared a wide-ranging overview report to the ministers of progress during phase one of the implementation process—in which they summarized country findings and progress, identified related initiatives and issues requiring further study or negotiation, and found the process to be "comprehensive and rigorous." See OECD, *Report by the CIME: Implementation of the Convention on Bribery in International Business Transactions and the 1997 Revised Recommendation* (Paris: OECD, p. 3), available at <http://www.olis.oecd.org/olis/2000doc.nsf/LinkTo/c-min(2000)8>.

35. Information on compliance, in addition to that coming from the WGB, is provided in a new quarterly journal, *The International Trade Corruption Monitor*. The journal, which is available from <http://www.cameronmay.com>, tracks relevant national legislation, regulations, and case law. It is edited by two TI directors. In addition, TI's comments on countries' drafts of implementing legislation are published on TI's web site.

36. OECD, "Action Statement on Bribery and Officially Supported Export Credits," December 2000, p. 1. Available at <http://www.oecd.org/ech/docs/bribery-en.pdf>.

37. Ibid., p. 2.

38. The dimensions are: (1) independence, autonomy and powers of persons or bodies in charge of preventing, investigating, prosecuting, and adjudicating corruption offenses; (2) immunities from investigation, prosecution, or adjudication of corruption offenses; and (3) training of persons or bodies in charge of fighting corruption.

39. See OAS web site at "Fighting Corruption: Programs and Plans of Action," at <http://www.oas.org>.

40. Final Statement from the Atlanta conference, p. 3.

41. The study, *Corporate Anticorruption Programs: A Survey of Best Practices,* is available at <http://www.transparency-usa.org/survey_96.htm>. Adoption of corporate codes of conduct and related compliance programs had, of course, been spurred by passage of the FCPA. The creation of such codes had been given further impetus when the U.S. Justice Department's sentencing guidelines provided for more lenient treatment of convicted senior executives whose companies had generally effective codes and compliance programs.

42. For the 1999 edition of ICC's Rules of Conduct, see <http://www.iccwbo.org/home/statements_rules/rules/1999/briberydoc99.asp>.

43. François Vincke, Fritz Heimann, and Ron Katz, eds. *Fighting Bribery* (Paris: ICC, 1999). Mr. Heimann is chairman of TI's U.S. chapter.

44. The Wolfsberg Principles are available at <http://www.wolfsberg-principles.com/wolfsberg_principles.html>.

45. In contrast, many developing countries have systems and institutions designed to prevent corruption that are weak and also lack publicly accountable governments, adequate standards of financial disclosure, and media experienced in and free to pursue investigative journalism. Equally important, many in these countries expect that bribes are simply unavoidable in dealing with government.

46. A Lexis-Nexis search of articles published in the *Economist* and the *Financial Times* shows than an average of 229 articles per year mentioned the word "corruption" from 1982 to 1987. The yearly average from 1996 to 1998 increased to 1,307 articles.

47. In the OECD countries, the involvement of TI and, to a lesser extent ICC, took the form of writing letters to and giving briefings for key ministers and parliamentarians; building personal contacts; participating in television and radio discussions and interviews; writing press releases; participating at conferences and seminars; testifying before legislative committees (at the ratification stage); and orchestrating an "open letter" from European business leaders to European economics ministers urging signature and ratification of the OECD Convention. A few OECD members who were reluctant to sign the convention had argued that the bribery of foreign officials by their nationals was actually beneficial because it created jobs at home, but in the face of all the favorable publicity about the convention, they found it politically impossible to withhold their support.

48. During Mkapa's campaign, he disclosed and accounted for his assets and those of his family, and after the election he frequently referred to the proceedings of the workshop and then commissioned and had published the "Warioba Report," which named corrupt officials and made numerous recommendations for systemic improvement. Nevertheless, in the 1999 CPI, Tanzania ranked ninety-fifth out of ninety-nine countries. Despite Mkapa's lead, follow-up to the Warioba Report had been weak, and it is possible also that the perceptions of corruption were heightened by the report's disclosures. In the CPI of 2000, Tanzania's ranking had improved to 76 out of 90, perhaps indicating that reform cannot happen quickly or that even if it does, perceptions take time to change.

49. The use of this type of survey in India is described in K. Gopakumar, *TI Working Paper: Citizen Feedback Surveys to Highlight Corruption in Public Services: The Experience of Public Affairs Centre, Bangalore*, prepared for Annual General Meeting of TI, Kuala Lampur, Malaysia, September 1998. The document is available at <http://www.transparency.org/documents/work-papers/kgopakumar.html>. See also Samuel Paul, *Making Voice Work*, Working Paper No. 1921 (Washington, D.C.: World Bank, 1998). A variant type of country survey—to use as a basis for an integrity workshop—has been used by the World Bank for diagnostic purposes in Albania, Georgia, and Latvia. See World Bank, *New Frontiers in Diagnosing and Combating Corruption*, PREM Note No. 7 (Washington, D.C.: World Bank, 1998). See also material on corruption surveys in Bangladesh at <http://www.ti-bangladesh.org/docs/index.htm>.

50. See Daniel Kaufman, "Beyond Rule of Law: On Alternative Anticorruption Strategies in Emerging Economies," in TI, *Combating International Corruption*, p. 81.

51. See *Using Surveys for Public Sector Reform*, PREM Note No. 23 (Washington, D.C.: World Bank, 1999).

52. Possibly, a specialized international tribunal could be created to adjudicate integrity pact disputes. See Susan Rose-Ackerman, "Corruption and the Global Economy," in *Corruption and Integrity Improvement Initiatives in Developing Countries* (New York: UNDP and OECD Development Centre, 1998). The World Bank Group has tended to resist integrity pacts on the grounds that they might reduce the number of bidders. For a fuller discussion of integrity pacts, see <http://www.transparency.org/activities/integrity-pact.html>. For a status report on their use and plans for future use, see <http://www.transparency.org/activities/ip_annexes.html>.

53. See <http://www.opacityindex.com>.

54. For the overall negative correlation between corruption and investment, see Shang-Jin Wei, *How Taxing Is Corruption on International Investors?* NBER Working Paper No. 6030 (Cambridge, Mass.: National Bureau of Economic Research, 1997). Wei's empirical analysis (p. 11) indicates that an "increase in corruption level from that of Singapore to that of Mexico is equivalent to raising the tax rate [and thereby lowering the incentive to invest] by over twenty percentage points." In countries such as China, which are considered large markets, foreign investment may remain substantial (albeit less than otherwise, as shown in Wei) even when corruption is common. In smaller economies, corruption is likely to be a more serious deterrent to capital flows. See, for example, the following excerpt from a *New York Times* story on corruption in Bosnia: "The rampant corruption has discouraged foreign investment. Most foreign companies, including MacDonalds, have refused to set up operations after demands by officials to pay bribes and do business exclusively with local party officials. Other companies—like the Italian construction company Aluveneto and Gluck Norm, Germany's largest maker of door and window frames—have pulled out with heavy losses, complaining of interference from the state, an inability to collect debts and demands by officials for kickbacks and bribes to stay in business. Volkswagen is also considering pulling out of Bosnia, according to European diplomats." See Chris Hedges, "Leaders in Bosnia Are Said to Steal up to $1 Billion," *New York Times*, August 17, 1999, p. A1.

55. In addition to bribees and those who defeat competitors by successfully bribing, potential beneficiaries include those who through bribes can accelerate legal government action or who violate existing laws, regulations, or standards. As used here, "sustainable" means sustainable politically (that is, with respect to governments' long-term willingness to introduce and implement necessary reforms), socially (that is, with respect to civil society's willingness over the long term to generate necessary pressures for reform), and technically (that is, with respect to the creation and maintenance of the required indigenous technical expertise).

SUGGESTED ADDITIONAL READING

Elliot, Kimberly Ann, ed. *Corruption and the Global Economy*. Washington, DC: Institute for International Economics, 1996.

Galtung, Fredrik, and Jeremy Pope. "The Global Coalition Against Corruption: Evaluating Transparency International." In Andreas Schedler, Larry Diamond, and Marc Plattner, eds. *The Self-restraining State: Power and Accountability in New Democracies*. Boulder, Colo.: Lynne Rienner Publishers, 1999, pp. 257–82.

Galtung, Fredrik. "A Global Network to Curb Corruption: The Experience of Transparency International." In Ann Florini, ed. *The Third Force: The Rise of Transnational Civil Society*. Washington, D.C.: Carnegie Endowment for International Peace, 1999, pp. 17–47.

Kpundeh, Sahr John, and Rick J. Stapenhurst, eds. *Fighting Corruption: A Model for Building National Integrity*. Washington, D.C.: World Bank, EDI Seminar Series, 1997.

Ofosu-Amaah, W., Raj Soopramanien, and Kishor Uprety. *Combating Corruption: A Comparative Review of Selected Legal Aspects of State Practices and Major International Initiatives*. Washington, D.C.: World Bank, 1999.

Pope, Jeremy, ed. *Confronting Corruption: The Elements of a National Integrity System* [also known as the TI Sourcebook (revised)]. Berlin: Transparency International, 2000.

Rose-Ackerman, Susan. *Corruption and Government: Cause, Consequences, and Reform*. New York: Cambridge University Press, 1999.

Transparency International and World Bank Economic Development Institute. *New Perspectives on Combating Corruption*. Washington, D.C.: World Bank, 1998.

Vincke, François, Fritz Heimann, and Ron Katz, eds. *Fighting Bribery*. Paris: International Chamber of Commerce, 1999.

Internet sites

Transparency International (TI) <http://www.transparency.org>

Transparency International Working Paper, "Corruption in Empirical Research – A Review" <http://www.transparency.org/documents/work-papers/lambsdorff_eresearch.html>

Organization for Economic Cooperation and Development (OECD), Anticorruption Unit <http://www.oecd.org/daf/nocorruption>

World Bank <http://www.worldbank.org/publicsector/anticorrupt/index.htm>

World Bank Institute, Governance and Anti-Corruption <http://www.worldbank.org/wbi/governance>

International Chamber of Commerce (ICC) <http://www.iccwbo.org/home/menu_extortion_bribery.asp>

United Nations Development Program (UNDP), "Corruption and Integrity Improvement Initiatives in Developing Countries" <http://www.undp.org/dpa/publications/corruption/index.html>

U.S. Department of State, Global Forum on Fighting Corruption <http://www.state.gov/www/global/narcotics_law/global_forum/appendix2.html>

3

Crime, Illicit Markets,
and Money Laundering

Phil Williams

ORGANIZED CRIME IS PERHAPS BEST UNDERSTOOD as the continuation of commerce by illegal means, with transnational criminal organizations as the illicit counterparts of multinational corporations. During the 1990s, transnational organized crime—and the related phenomena of illegal markets and money laundering—were transformed from an unrecognized problem to an issue taken seriously by governments, both individually and collectively. Indeed, there has been a growing sensitivity to the problem and increased willingness to address transnational organized crime, illegal markets, and money laundering as serious challenges to international security and governance rather than simply domestic issues.

Transnational criminal organizations pose a major challenge for governance at both the national and global levels. They are inherently hostile to domestic or international efforts to control their behavior, because their ability to continue their activities depends on their capacity to negate governance efforts. Complicating matters is the added paradox that governance in certain domains can provide criminal organizations with major opportunities to expand their activities and enhance their profits. The creation of regulatory regimes in certain areas can create perverse incentives for criminal organizations to engage in entrepreneurial activities that undermine regimes and embargoes.

It is now widely recognized that purely national or even bilateral responses are simply inadequate to deal with the problem. The dynamics of illegal markets, the activities of criminal enterprises, the reach of criminal networks, and the pervasiveness of money laundering all militate in favor of multilateral responses. So too does the lack of capacity of weak governments to respond adequately, the unwillingness of corrupt governments to take decisive action against indigenous criminal organizations, and the reluctance of many offshore financial centers and bank secrecy jurisdictions to initiate measures that would keep out the proceeds of crime. Also fueling the growing efforts at governance in this area is the recognition that in some cases, governments themselves are part of the problem. This is not simply a competition between sovereign states and what James Rosenau termed "sovereignty-free actors"; in some cases, state structures and institutions have been neutralized, compromised, or coopted by criminal organizations.[1] This makes collective governance simultaneously more important and more difficult.

This chapter focuses on the efforts by governments to respond to the growing challenges posed by transnational criminal organizations. It examines this issue very broadly and considers not only criminal organizations and the illicit markets within which they operate, but also the money that is generated by a wide range of illegal activities, much of which goes into licit businesses and the global financial system. Illegal markets involve at least four separate categories of commodities and services: (1) prohibited goods or services, such as drugs or commercial sex; (2) regulated commodities, such as antiquities or fauna and flora; (3) differentially taxed commodities, such as cigarettes; and (4) stolen goods, such as cars.

Accordingly, this chapter does several things. First, it elucidates the nature of transnational organized crime, illicit markets, and money laundering, and in so doing highlights why during the 1980s and 1990s these issues became a serious challenge for international governance. Second, it outlines the major international responses, identifying the multilateral institutions and agencies that have been involved and delineating the major initiatives they have taken to establish more effective governance in dealing with criminal organizations, the markets in which they operate, and the proceeds of their activities. These range from the creation of norms to efforts to enhance the effectiveness of national law enforcement agencies through improved sharing of information and intelligence. Third, it identifies the major lessons from this experience, identifying those approaches that have worked and that hold considerable promise for the future, as well as those that have proved less effective. Fourth, it delineates the major obstacles to the establishment of more effective governance in this area. Some of these obstacles stem from the fact that even where governments are fully in compliance with international norms and conventions, criminal organizations will still find ways to circumvent them. Finally, it concludes, somewhat pessimistically, that governance in the area of organized crime, drug trafficking, and money laundering is seriously inadequate because of systemic conditions that might prove impossible to change. Nevertheless, some recommendations can be made for enhancing governance.

NATURE OF THE PROBLEM

Criminal organizations have a long history. The Sicilian Mafia developed during the nineteenth century, providing protection, contract enforcement, and debt collection in a region where the Italian government was weak. The criminal activities of Chinese triads can be traced back to the early part of the twentieth century. Initially established as secret societies to oppose the Qing dynasty, the triads lost their political rationale with the collapse of the dynasty and the establishment of the Republic of China in 1912. Whereas some members entered politics, "those who were not absorbed by the political machine returned to the well-established Triad organizations for power and status. However, without a patriotic cause to pursue, the secretive and anti-establishment nature of the organizations helped transform them into criminal groups."[2]

For its part, organized crime in the United States has witnessed a pattern of ethnic succession with Irish, Jewish, and Italian criminal organizations enjoying periods of dominance before gradually giving way to the current kaleidoscope of organizations, many of which are ethnically based. The "new ethnic mobs," as they have been termed, include: Colombian, Dominican, and Mexican drug trafficking groups; Russian émigré networks involved in a wide variety of criminal activities, ranging from car theft to health-care and insurance fraud and stock manipulation; Nigerian criminal networks engaged in drug trafficking and imaginative fraud schemes; Chinese criminal entrepreneurs smuggling illegal aliens and operating protection rackets within their own community; roving Vietnamese gangs engaged in home invasions; and Albanian organizations adept at supermarket robberies.[3] In effect, the United States has become host to foreign criminal organizations, attracted by large illicit markets and lucrative opportunities.

Organized crime has long had a transnational dimension—a characteristic that becomes even more important in an interdependent world. During prohibition in the United States, for example, liquor was not only manufactured illegally in the United States but also brought from Europe and Canada. Similarly, the drug trafficking industry had a transnational dimension almost from the outset, simply because those countries that historically were the main growers, processors, or manufacturers of narcotic and psychotropic substances were not the major consumers. Even more striking, smuggling—an inherently cross-jurisdictional or transnational activity—is one of the world's oldest professions, based as it is on differential opportunities for profit. (It has long been argued, for example, that the Caribbean could better be described as the sea of contraband.)[4]

Trafficking, of course, has not been limited to goods: trafficking in women for commercial sex also has a long history. In the late nineteenth century, for example, Argentina and Brazil emerged as lucrative markets for traffickers in women. Those who controlled the business were predominantly French, Jewish (from Poland and Russia), and Italian.[5] Among those trafficked were significant numbers of Slavic women taken to work as prostitutes in a wide variety of places, including the Ottoman Empire and Argentina as well as New York and other major cities in the United States.[6] As one of the predecessors of today's nongovernmental organizations (NGOs) lamented in 1903: "The white-slave traffickers are in close contact in all parts of the world, in great cities as in small villages . . . in order to benefit fully from the techniques of the traffic and the advantages of combination."[7] Moreover, "the advantages of the traffickers were indeed substantial. They had the steamship and the railway to move women quickly and the telegraph to help dispatch them efficiently. With the exception of Britain and Germany, the police were corrupt or compliant to varying degrees everywhere."[8] The difference in today's world is not the trade as such, but the speed, ease, and variety of the flows of women—and even this is a difference in degree rather than kind.

New Dimensions of Old Problems

Acknowledging the antecedents for contemporary transnational organized crime and illegal markets is not to ignore the very real increases in the phenomenon in the 1980s and the 1990s. There are several reasons for this increase. First, the globalization of trade, technology, transportation, communications, information, and financial systems provides new opportunities for criminal enterprises to operate across national borders. The free trade system has made it easy to embed illicit products in the vast amounts of imports and exports that now characterize international trade. Indeed, illicit trade often develops a parasitic relationship with licit trade, as is evident in the growing number of seizures of drugs being transported in intermodal containers.

Second, one of the characteristics of globalization has been significant population movements driven by a mix of push and pull factors that range from ethnic conflict and environmental degradation to the desire for economic betterment. The increase in migration and the growth of ethnic networks that transcend national borders have proved valuable to the operations of criminal organizations. Although most immigrants are law-abiding citizens and are in fact more likely to be the victims than the perpetrators of crime, the dispersal of Colombians in the United States, Turks in Western Europe, and Nigerians throughout Southeast Asia, Western Europe, and the United States has greatly facilitated the creation of network structures for the supply of illicit goods. Diaspora-based ethnic communities are an important resource for transnational criminal enterprises. They provide recruitment opportunities, cover, and support. Recruitment based on ethnic loyalties is particularly easy when the immigrant groups have not been fully integrated into their adopted society. As one analyst observed: "Many immigrant groups have been totally marginalized in Europe, some live in cultural ghettos. They readily provide some of the personnel for international organized crime."[9] The low status and poor living conditions of many Turkish immigrants in Western Europe, for example, means that the rewards offered by Turkish criminal organizations for assistance in smuggling heroin from Southwest Asia into Western Europe are attractive. Even casual participation or involvement on the margins can yield greater rewards than can be obtained through the licit economy. At the same time, many immigrant communities such as the Chinese are not only very resourceful but also engage in a wide range of commercial and trading activities that can provide excellent cover for illicit activities. Such groups are also very difficult to penetrate. The barriers of language and culture provide built-in defense mechanisms that are strengthened by ties of kinship and inherent suspicion of authority. Just as transnational corporations have their local subsidiaries, transnational criminal organizations have their ethnically based criminal groups within immigrant communities.

The third reason for the rise in transnational organized crime is that the global financial system is increasingly based on digital or "megabyte" money. Such funds can be moved rapidly and anonymously and can be traded, exchanged, and cleaned or legitimized via an array of financial instruments such as derivatives and futures.[10] The global financial system has multiple points of access and, once in the system, money can be moved with speed and ease and with a minimum of interference from regulators. To some extent this was a result of deliberate government choices, with competitive deregulation of financial systems in the 1970s encouraging a more permissive approach to capital, whatever its source. The growth of offshore financial centers and their use for tax advantages by licit corporations established patterns that were soon followed by criminal enterprises, which increasingly use offshore financial centers and bank secrecy havens to hide their money. The proceeds of crime are often moved through several jurisdictions, making it difficult for law enforcement to follow the money trail. Indeed, following the money across multiple jurisdictions is a complex and costly task for law enforcement; and even if criminal money is identified, obtaining it from offshore financial centers and bank secrecy havens is a formidable task. Criminal organizations engage in a form of jurisdictional arbitrage using offshore financial centers that promise maximum protection for their funds and in effect are financial safe havens. In many respects, the contemporary global financial system has become a money launderer's dream. Conversely, it is a nightmare for law enforcement agencies that have to work through a jurisdictional and bureaucratic morass in their efforts to follow and seize the money.

The fourth factor is the growth in attractive markets or sources. During the 1980s and the 1990s, there was a massive growth in drug markets. Drug trafficking and drug abuse have been transformed: they are no longer simply a "U.S. problem" but have become problems affecting other large consumer countries such as those of Western Europe, Russia, and China. They have also become a problem for source and transshipment states. Criminal enterprises are particularly attracted to host countries where there is significant demand for illicit drugs and other products and services. Moreover, such host countries might be a significant source of products that can be stolen and trafficked to meet a burgeoning market elsewhere. In the United

States, for example, many criminal organizations are involved in supplying illicit drugs to a large body of consumers. At the same time, American cars and sport utility vehicles are stolen for markets elsewhere. According to the State Department estimate, several hundred thousand of the 1.5 million vehicles stolen annually in the United States are illegally exported to Central America and Eastern Europe.[11] In some instances, the same organizations that are involved in bringing drugs or illegal aliens into the country are also responsible for the theft and trafficking of cars to other destinations. In other words, although some countries are more obviously attractive markets than others, the flows of illicit products are not all in the same direction. Women from the newly independent states of the former Soviet Union, for example, are trafficked to Western Europe, where they are in high demand, while luxury cars stolen in West European countries are trafficked to the east.

A fifth contributing reason is found in differential profits. The most attractive markets of course are not only those in which there is large-scale consumer demand, but also those in which prices—and profit levels—are high. Differential profits in different national markets provide incentives for criminal organizations to penetrate these markets. Drugs are not unique in accumulating a markup as they move through the chain from producer country to the consumers; what is distinctive is simply the extent of the markup. In other cases of course the problem is not illicit products, but licit products that have large variations in prices from one market to another—often because of taxation policies. Where there are significant variations in prices of products (such as cigarettes) and a highly permeable border, then either new criminal enterprises will emerge to meet the demand for cross-border trafficking—as happened with American Indian involvement with cigarette smuggling on the U.S.-Canada border—or existing criminal groups will diversify into this area.

Sixth, differential regulations and laws spur transnational crime. Nikos Passas uses the term *criminogenic asymmetries* to describe differences among states that encourage transnational criminal activity.[12] One of these differences concerns national regulations. Where regulations are relatively lax or poorly implemented in critical sectors such as finance and banking, this is an invitation for criminal organizations to move into the state and exploit the lacuna. Once again, there is a form of jurisdictional arbitrage at work.

Finally, the differential abilities of states to impose risks encourage crime. It bears emphasis that the distinctiveness of illicit business lies not in the profit side—all enterprises seek to maximize profits—but in the risks transnational criminal organizations face, especially but not exclusively from law enforcement and government. All businesses have to deal with the risks posed by competition, by government intervention in the market, by changing consumer tastes, and so on. The risks facing criminal organizations, however, are distinctive: they stem from the illicit nature or their activities; neither they nor their rivals are bound by rules, norms, and regulations in the way that licit corporations are; and they operate within an industry where violence is an integral means to resolve interorganizational disputes. Perhaps most important, however, are risks resulting from the activities of governments that attempt to put criminal organizations out of business. Considerable efforts and resources therefore are devoted to neutralizing or circumventing law enforcement, thereby reducing risks to the business. Indeed, there is a constant dialectic between illicit business and law enforcement that does much to shape the character of transnational criminal organizations and to determine in which jurisdictions they operate.[13] This is not to imply that transnational criminal groups will avoid high-risk states. If such states provide attractive and lucrative markets, they will also become host states, as South Africa has done with criminals from China, Italy, Nigeria, and Russia. Where feasible, however, criminal organizations will engage in illicit activities primarily from a low-risk jurisdiction.

Nature of the Challenge

This combination of opportunities and incentives for organized criminal activity helps to explain why organized crime has increased in both scale and diversity. These developments have been accompanied by a marked expansion in both illicit markets and informal economies. Indeed, during the 1990s criminal organizations became more powerful, more varied, and more prevalent. Traditional organized crime groups such as the Italian Mafia, Chinese Triads, and Japanese Yakuza now share the stage with relative newcomers such as Turkish clans, Albanian drug trafficking organizations, Nigerian networks, Russian criminal organizations, Colombian and Mexican drug trafficking organizations, and the like. Organized crime has become a major problem in many parts of the world, and criminal organizations have displayed a capacity to amass enormous wealth; a willingness to confront, corrupt, and even coopt governments; a propensity to infiltrate legal sectors of national economies; a tendency to develop cooperative linkages; and a remarkable resistance to government efforts to put them out of business.

One factor that promises to enhance further the power of criminal organizations is information technology. Indeed, criminal organizations exploit information technologies in three ways. First, they adopt information technologies as force multipliers: using devices such as global positioning systems to carry out certain crimes more effectively, computer systems to enhance managerial efficiencies, and encryption technologies to protect their communications from governments and law enforcement agencies. Second, they use information technologies as the means to commit certain crimes. (The use of Internet banks based in offshore jurisdictions to commit fraud provides merely one of many possible examples.) Finally, criminal organizations target information technologies, especially information systems, to extort businesses and degrade and deter the response capabilities of governments and law enforcement agencies.[14] In other words, information technologies provide new opportunities and new targets for transnational organized crime.

Two dimensions of transnational criminal organizations pose problems for governance and, indeed, for national security: (1) the concentration of illegal power that can threaten democratic institutions and the rule of law; and (2) a set of criminal activities that not only provide the source of wealth and power for organized crime but also inflict considerable physical harm on both societies and individuals. Criminal enterprises undermine state sovereignty, challenge state authority (either directly through confrontation or indirectly through corruption), and subvert government monopoly of the use of violence.[15] The activities of criminal organizations involve gross violations of human rights (trafficking in women and children for the global sex trade); undermine regulatory regimes (chlorofluorocarbons, hazardous waste trafficking, trafficking in endangered species); threaten nonproliferation and arms embargoes (trafficking in nuclear materials and conventional weapons); and undermine licit trade and commerce (through the theft of intellectual property and counterfeiting).

In terms of the threat posed to states, however, the challenge from criminal organizations varies considerably, depending on the vulnerabilities of the state. For stable democracies with high levels of legitimacy, vibrant civil societies, and established mechanisms for rooting out corruption, the issue rarely becomes more than a law enforcement problem. For weak states or states in transition, however, the situation is rather different. States with a low level of capacity and legitimacy, with undeveloped traditions of democratic government or civil society, and with few safeguards against corruption are ideal targets for penetration by criminal organizations. Most of the Caribbean islands, for example, are relatively weak states and have been penetrated by Colombian drug traffickers, Sicilian organized crime groups, and, increasingly, Russian criminals. Many of these islands are used for transshipment of drugs or illegal immigrants, while their offshore financial sectors are used to launder and hide the proceeds of crime. In this vein, hopes for a smooth transition to a free market and liberal democracy in Cuba after Castro could well be dashed: a rapid influx of major criminal organizations will no doubt seek to control what is currently a disorganized market for commercial sex and to use Cuba for both drug transshipment and money laundering. The problem, however, is not confined to small states. Even large states are vulnerable to the power of criminal organizations. In Russia, for example, organized crime has not only penetrated most sectors of the economy but has also forged alliances with members of the political and administrative elites and with business. Indeed, it is arguable that in Russia an iron triangle of business, crime, and politics has derailed the transition to a functioning liberal democracy. In effect, organized crime has neutralized the criminal justice system, superseded some state functions, and captured parts of the state apparatus. The extent of the symbiosis between crime and politics warrants describing Russia as a captured state. Indeed,

Louise Shelley has argued persuasively that the authoritarianism of the Communist Party will be replaced not by liberal democracy but by the authoritarianism of organized crime.[16] Even if such an outcome is avoided, the capacity of organized crime to infiltrate and distort government is growing. In states as diverse as Mexico and Turkey, the pattern is similar, developing into what Roy Godson has termed a "political-criminal nexus."[17] China may be moving in the same direction, with a serious increase in organized crime–related corruption.

Neutralizing and capturing the state apparatus is clearly the preferred option for organized crime. In some cases, though, such an approach—generally as a result of disappointed expectations about the benefits of collusion—is abandoned in favor of confrontation. Most dramatically, during the 1980s and early 1990s in Italy and Colombia, major criminal organizations confronted the state authorities with large-scale campaigns of violence that were ultimately defeated but nevertheless proved very costly for the state. Direct confrontation, however, is relatively unusual. Most criminal organizations choose cooption rather than confrontation, collusion rather than coercion, and the development of symbiotic rather than adversarial relations with state authorities. Ultimately, however, their use of corruption as an instrument is probably even more pernicious than the use of violence: it undermines the integrity of institutions (especially in the area of criminal justice), has a distorting impact on the functioning of government, and generally inhibits the development of civil society and the rule of law. For states in transition, such consequences are particularly debilitating.

In some cases, of course, state authorities go from being passive beneficiaries to initiating and controlling much organized crime activity. This has happened in Nigeria during the Abacha era and is a pattern that could become even more prevalent in Africa. Indeed, the prospects for Africa in relation to organized crime are gloomy to say the least: in some countries, organized crime will attempt to neutralize or capture state authorities; in others, state authorities themselves will engage in activities normally associated with criminal organizations; while in yet others, subnational politico-military factions trying to obtain control over the state will use crime to fund their military activities.[18] Whether the state is captured, criminal, or contested, however, organized crime could have a major impact on the future of many African states. The moves to democracy will not necessarily end the spoils system so much as require its diffusion.

The other multifaceted dimension of the challenge to governance reflects the relationship between organized crime and ethnic conflicts and terrorism. First, factions within terrorist organizations, insurgencies, or separatist movements such as the Kurdistan Workers Party (PKK) in Turkey, the Kosovo Liberation Army (KLA) in Kosovo, and the Liberation Tigers of Tamil Elam (LTTE) often resort to criminal behavior such as drug trafficking to fund their political struggles. They also benefit from criminal activities by members of the diaspora, who funnel money back to the organization.

Tamil networks around the world, for example, have extended their activities beyond drug trafficking, becoming proficient at credit card fraud in Great Britain and Canada, extortion in Germany, social security fraud in France, and counterfeiting of currency in several European countries and Australia.[19] There is also a link between organized crime activities and LTTE military activities in Sri Lanka. In a 1999 report, the Royal Canadian Mounted Police claimed to have "clear evidence" that Tamil street gangs in Toronto were sending the proceeds from bank and casino fraud, immigration fraud, drug smuggling, and trafficking in weapons to the LTTE to support terrorist activities.[20] Similarly, during the late 1990s, Kosovar Albanians became more prominent in heroin trafficking in Western Europe, and there was considerable concern about the profits from this and other criminal activities going to fund the KLA struggle against the Serb government in Belgrade. The second aspect of this linkage reflects the opportunities for criminal entrepreneurship and the supply of illegal goods created by the collapse of authority and the emergence of conflict. These opportunities are particularly attractive where an international embargo is imposed on one or more of the combatants. In essence, criminal organizations can exploit the opportunities arising from the gap between demand for weapons and other goods and restrictions on supply. During the war in Bosnia in the first half of the 1990s, an estimated $2 billion worth of arms per year were supplied to the combatants, circumventing the UN arms embargo. A third kind of linkage arises when insurgents tax or extort criminal organizations (often along with licit businesses), especially drug traffickers. The PKK has a reputation for doing this both in Turkey and in the Netherlands, while the Revolutionary Armed Forces of Colombia (FARC) in Colombia derives a substantial income from its "protection" of drug traffickers.

Inextricably linked to the rise of criminal organizations is the emergence of what H. Richard Friman and Peter Andreas term "the illicit global economy," which consists of large transnational criminal markets in a wide range of goods that are either illegal in most jurisdictions (such as drugs) or legal but exported or imported illegally. As suggested above, in some cases the issue is not the product so much as its theft, its diversion from licit purposes to illicit, and its supply to end users such as terrorist organizations or rogue states. Furthermore, "smugglers do not limit their operations to stolen goods or illicit products such as drugs. Through clandestine trade in licitly produced commodities, smugglers also seek to circumvent trade duties or to take advantage of variations in domestic taxes on high-demand products."[21] Looking at the issue in economic rather than organizational terms encourages a focus on the dynamics of illicit markets, the factors of demand and supply, the scale of activities, and those factors that facilitate or inhibit transactions.[22] It also helps to highlight collusion between criminals and a wide variety of individuals and institutions in the "upper world." The market in stolen antiquities, for example, depends in part for its effectiveness on either complicity or active collusion by antique businesses and auction houses. Similarly, trafficking in children for commercial sex generally starts with villagers in countries such as Burma selling their daughters to agents who transfer them to brothels in Thailand or elsewhere, and depends on the connivance of immigration officials, local police, and the like. Fauna and flora trafficking is similar in that much of what is trafficked is incorporated into traditional Asian medicines or used by Asian craftsmen to create artifacts that are subsequently sold by legal businesses. Although none of these markets rival the illegal drug trade in scope, pervasiveness, or impact, they contribute to a global illicit economy that presents a major challenge to governance.

Whether the emphasis is on organizations or markets, one concern is the huge profits that are generated—and the power that such financial clout gives to criminal organizations. Measuring the proceeds of crime, however, is problematic. Although figures such as the $500 billion drug trade or $1 trillion organized crime industry provide sensational headlines, such estimates have more to do with sound bites than with sound financial calculations. If the precise figures are elusive, however, it is clear that the proceeds of crime are substantial and that in some economies they can have a significant impact. Moreover, criminal proceeds can add to the volatility of capital markets, distort economic development efforts, and undermine the integrity of financial institutions.

In short, organized crime has ceased to be simply a domestic problem, becoming instead a challenge to stability and security at a variety of levels. In a sense, transnational organized crime forced itself onto the international agenda. Governments became increasingly aware of the problem in the 1980s and with U.S. leadership took major initiatives in the late 1980s. (The Vienna Convention of 1988 on drugs and money laundering and the Financial Action Task Force are discussed below.) As long as the Cold War lasted, however, combating organized crime or drug trafficking was secondary to competing with the Soviet Union. As a result, U.S. and Western intelligence agencies conveniently overlooked criminal or drug trafficking activities that helped to fund anti-Soviet or anticommunist activities. Seen in this context, the end of the Cold War contributed to the increased salience of organized crime.

Equally if not more important were the collapse of the Soviet Union and the move toward liberal democracy and market economies in the states of the former Soviet bloc. What few observers initially realized, however, was that communist governments had repressed not only their populations but also organized crime—even while using criminal groups to feed the black markets and provide luxury goods to the political and economic elite. In effect, the authoritarian systems had incubated organized crime, but within limits and in ways determined by the state. With the collapse of state authority, the incubation period was transformed into one of rapid growth.

Moves toward a market economy without any rules and regulations, the capacity for debt collection and contract enforcement, and the evolution of legal protection provided ideal opportunities for criminal groups to develop regulatory functions that in most Western democracies were the prerogatives of the state. When combined with privatization efforts that offered enormous opportunities for corruption, these conditions meant that the early 1990s was a period of rapid growth for organized crime in the former Soviet Union. Moreover, the collapse of the coercive apparatus of the Soviet state meant that opportunities could be grasped with impunity. The criminal justice system was ill equipped to meet the new challenge, while a prohibitive taxation system provided perverse incentives for tax evasion that contributed in several ways to a culture of criminality. Moreover, it became clear that the problem was not confined to the states of the former Soviet Union. In the early 1990s, Berlin became a battleground for rival Russian organized crime groups, and such groups increasingly extended both their activities and their influence to Western Europe, the United States, and perhaps most notably of all, Israel. Although in some quarters the threat was exaggerated (with global organized crime and particularly Russian organized crime described as the "new empire of evil") and oversimplified (for example, claims regarding the emergence of a Pax Mafiosa), organized crime groups from the former Soviet Union have not only become transnational in scope but have also forged cooperative linkages with other criminal enterprises from Colombia and Italy.

TRACK RECORD OF INTERNATIONAL RESPONSES

Although organized crime was traditionally seen as a domestic law-and-order problem and not something that required major collective efforts, some cross-border criminal activities have been on the international agenda for some time, the subject of rudimentary attempts at establishing governance and control.[23] However, it was only during the late 1980s and the 1990s that transnational organized crime became a clear focus of efforts at international governance. There have been three distinct levels of governance in dealing with organized crime, drug trafficking, and money laundering. First is the creation of international norms: various conventions on drug trafficking and the slave trade. Second is information sharing to enhance law enforcement, especially through the creation of Interpol, which had its origins in the capacity of criminals to escape justice simply by crossing borders. Interpol instituted a system of notices about international fugitives that remains one of its major functions today. Third is the creation of education, eradication, and interdiction programs at the regional and global levels to respond to particular criminal activities, especially drug trafficking.

This analysis of existing responses starts with global efforts at agenda setting and norm creation in relation not only to transnational organized crime but also to specific criminal activities such as money laundering and trafficking in women and children. It will examine in particular the work of the United Nations, the Group of 8 (G-8), and the Financial Action Task Force (FATF). Following this, it will consider the more operational aspects of governance—law enforcement cooperation at both the regional and global levels.

United Nations: Agenda Setting and Norm Creation

Efforts by the United Nations to combat organized crime can be traced to 1975, when the Fifth UN Congress on the Prevention of Crime and the Treatment of Offenders examined changing dimensions of criminality, focusing on the notion of crime as business.[24] Although the focus on organized crime continued, it was overshadowed for much of the 1980s by more specific concerns over drug trafficking and money laundering. These concerns resulted in the UN Convention Against Illicit Traffic in Narcotic Drugs and Psychotropic Substances, adopted in December 1988. This superseded earlier conventions signed in 1961 and 1971 and, in effect, established the framework for subsequent efforts to combat drug trafficking and money laundering. It was designed to promote cooperation among the signatories so that they could more effectively combat drug cultivation and trafficking. Parties to the convention were also obliged to "take necessary measures, including legislative and administrative measures" to "establish as criminal offences" drug cultivation, manufacture, transportation, and sale and to develop laws allowing the confiscation of the proceeds of drug trafficking. The convention also included clauses on extradition and mutual legal assistance, and in 1990 the UN General Assembly adopted Model Treaties on Extradition and on Mutual Assistance in Criminal Matters. Initiatives during the 1990s reflected a broadening of UN efforts at agenda setting and norm creation, to include not only drug trafficking and money laundering but also transnational organized crime. In 1991 the UN General Assembly established a Commission on Crime Prevention and Criminal Justice within the UN Economic and Social Council (ECOSOC). This ensured the involvement of national governments in the efforts to combat transnational organized crime. At the inaugural meeting of the commission, Judge Giovanni Falcone, a renowned anti-Mafia figure in Italy who was subsequently assassinated by the Mafia, proposed a global conference to establish the basis for enhanced international cooperation against organized crime. The international community was receptive to this proposal, partly because the end of the Cold War allowed new issues to appear on the international agenda, and partly because the emergence of newly independent states particularly vulnerable to organized crime gave the issue unprecedented urgency.

Falcone's vision came to fruition with the World Ministerial Conference on Organized Transnational Crime, held in Naples in November 1994. The conference had more than 2,000 participants, with 142 national delegations, 86 of which were at the ministerial level.[25] This was a landmark event in crystallizing concerns about transnational organized crime and resulted in a declaration and action plan elucidating various ways to combat a phenomenon that was becoming increasingly pervasive. The declaration and action plan emphasized: the need for enhanced knowledge about the organized crime challenge and the capacity of criminal justice systems to respond effectively to it; the need for assistance to states in drafting legislation and regulations against organized crime; and the need for improved international cooperation and the provision of technical assistance to enable recipients to enhance their capacity to combat transnational organized crime. It appeared that there was broad agreement on objectives and how to attain them.

Initially, developing countries supported the idea of moving to a convention against transnational organized crime, while many Western countries were skeptical. The latter group was concerned not only about the conceptual and legal problems, but also that a convention would be based on the lowest common denominator and would therefore lack "teeth."[26] During 1995 and 1996, however, several developments would ultimately facilitate agreement on the desirability of a convention. A survey by the UN Secretariat revealed that a majority of states favored the idea. In addition, the G-8 states established a Group of Senior Experts (see below) that developed forty recommendations to help combat transnational organized crime and helped to transform the approach among governments that previously had been skeptical about a convention. Finally, in September 1996, Poland, one of the most vigorous supporters of the idea of a convention, introduced a draft framework. This gradually transformed the discussion from an abstract debate about desirability to a more specific focus on what the convention would look like. An intergovernmental group of experts, established by the General Assembly, met in Warsaw in February 1998 and began to explore "options for the convention"—a euphemism for a preliminary draft.[27] Specific concerns also began to emerge about: illicit manufacturing and trafficking in firearms (of particular concern to Japan and Canada), trafficking in women and children for commercial sex (an issue pushed by Argentina), and smuggling of illegal migrants (of grave concern to both Austria and Italy). It was then decided that these should be linked to the convention as additional instruments. A meeting in Buenos Aires in September 1998 gave further momentum to the process, partly because of the emergence of a core group of delegates committed to developing an effective and acceptable text. The commission then created an Ad Hoc group—officially established in December 1998—to elaborate the convention and the additional instruments in the three areas of concern identified by particular nations. Ironically, at this stage, some developing countries became concerned about the resource implications of implementing the convention. Nevertheless, the Ad Hoc group made sufficient progress to make the deadline of December 2000 a realistic one.

The draft convention focuses on organized crime actors and the concept of serious crimes. Its focus on criminal organizations rather than particular activities reflects the capacity of these organizations to move from one product line to another, as well as the fact that in some areas conventions already exist against specific criminal activities. The Vienna Convention is the most obvious case in point, but also relevant is the Convention on International Trade in Endangered Species (CITES) convention prohibiting trafficking in endangered fauna and flora. Similarly, the 1970 UN Educational, Scientific, and Cultural Organization (UNESCO) Convention on the Means of Prohibiting and Preventing the Illicit Import, Export, and Transfer of Ownership of Cultural Property was intended to prevent illicit trafficking in art and antiquities. In contrast to these earlier initiatives, the draft convention focuses not on particular items that are trafficked but on more generic issues. Accordingly, it establishes four offenses: participation in an organized criminal group, money laundering, corruption, and obstruction of justice. The convention also promotes international cooperation through its articles on extradition, mutual legal assistance (which goes well beyond existing norms to include the use of modern technology and the unrequested provision of information and assistance), transfer of criminal proceedings, and law enforcement cooperation, including the exchange of intelligence. Detailed provisions on countering money laundering and the sharing of confiscated assets are accompanied by provisions for witness protection, including relocation, and for the protection of victims. As a result of these provisions, signatories will need to adopt new legislation and enhance the capacity of their criminal justice and law enforcement systems. Provisions for technical assistance are intended to facilitate this process and enable developing states to meet their obligations under the convention. The draft convention also includes a Conference of the Parties that will oversee implementation and provide a system of peer review, designed in part to identify areas where technical assistance is necessary. In addition—and this is very innovative—the draft includes an article on prevention that is designed to encourage countries to take measures to develop procedures that will "safeguard the integrity of public and private entities" and make it more difficult for organized crime to infiltrate legal markets and institutions.[28]

In addition to the draft convention, there are three protocols. The first of these, the Protocol Against Trafficking in Persons, Especially Women and Children, combines measures against offenders with steps to protect the victims of trafficking. The Protocol Against Smuggling of Migrants promotes international cooperation to protect the human rights of the smuggled migrants, while also advocating preventive measures including enhanced document security. The Protocol Against Illicit Manufacturing of and Trafficking in Firearms promotes the marking of firearms to ensure that they can be uniquely identified and traced across borders.[29]

Disagreements on the precise language concerning a number of the provisions were worked out in July and August 2000, and the convention was opened for signature in December 2000. When it does come into force, it will establish a set of norms for combating transnational organized crime that go far beyond anything previously envisaged by the international community. Although there are many outstanding questions about the extent to which these norms will be implemented, the convention is nevertheless a major step forward in the area of global governance to deal with transnational organized crime, money laundering, and illegal markets. Norm creation is only a first step, but the explicit consideration given to implementation in the convention acknowledges that effectiveness depends in large part on the willingness and capacity of signatories to implement the norms that they have formally recognized.

G-8: Agenda Setting and Symbolizing Commitment

If the UN initiatives can be understood as reflecting the will of the global community of states, the effectiveness of these initiatives in almost all areas of governance depends on a basic congruence between the global community and the great powers. In this connection, the work of the United Nations in agenda setting and establishing norms to combat transnational organized crime has been complemented and strengthened by the activities of the G-7/G-8. In July 1994, for example, in its meeting at Naples the G-7 noted that it was alarmed by the growth of organized transnational crime, with countries in transition increasingly targeted by criminal organizations. It also made clear that it was determined to strengthen international cooperation to address this situation and welcomed the forthcoming UN World Ministerial Conference. In 1995 the G-7 heads of state created a group of experts to counter transnational organized crime and prepare recommendations for the annual G-7/G-8 summits. This group, the Senior Experts Group on Transnational Organized Crime (sometimes known as the Lyon Group) developed forty recommendations, most of which focused on practical matters rather than more conceptual issues such as definitions. The recommendations underlined the importance of mutual legal assistance and extradition even if there was no "dual criminality," the need for a central authority within states to expedite cooperation, and the importance of coordinating prosecutions. In addition, they covered techniques for mutual education (such as secondments and personnel exchanges); witness protection, including reciprocal arrangements and the use of video links; the need to criminalize technological abuses and the smuggling of persons; the importance of removing safe havens for criminals; better firearms regulations; and the development of international cooperation on electronic surveillance, undercover operations, and controlled deliveries—that is, allowing the delivery of illegal goods to go ahead under surveillance so that all involved can ultimately be arrested. The Senior Experts Group also advocated new laws for technology crimes and recommended that Interpol and the World Customs Organization (WCO) extend their support for operational activities by national law enforcement agencies. To enhance cooperation among national law enforcement agencies, it was recommended that nations prepare brief guides to their legal systems and identify liaisons to facilitate exchanges. In addition, it was recommended that alien smuggling be criminalized and that governments exchange information not only on trafficking patterns but also on the false documentation that facilitates the process. The group also urged that states consider adopting measures for asset seizure, as well as passing laws to combat corruption.[30]

The forty recommendations were endorsed by the G-7 at the Lyon Summit in June 1996, even though the summit was in fact preoccupied with terrorism rather than organized crime. At the Denver Summit in June 1997, the leaders noted that combating transnational crime would remain a priority, and they committed themselves to intensifying efforts to implement the Lyon recommendations. They also emphasized the prosecution and punishment of high-tech criminals. The concern over the capacity of criminal organizations to exploit information technologies was evident in the deliberations, and the summit stressed the need to provide technical and legal capabilities to respond to high-tech crimes wherever they were committed. In the Birmingham Summit in May 1998, participants agreed to implement an action plan on high-tech crime. Cooperation with industry on a legal framework for obtaining, presenting, and preserving electronic data as evidence was also emphasized, as was the need for agreements on sharing evidence of high-tech crimes with international partners. In the 1999 summit at Cologne, the issue of transnational organized crime was given less attention, and it was clear that the main forum for dealing with the challenge was once again the United Nations.

The first significant aspect of the G-7/G-8's work concerns the substance of the forty recommendations. Although little was new, they offered a systematic checklist of initiatives that would help in combating transnational organized crime. The second important aspect was the symbolism: the Senior Experts Group's recommendations, in effect, endorsed the direction in which the United Nations was moving and helped to convince the major powers that the convention was an important step.[31] In effect, the activities of one international forum fed into another in a very positive way. Third, and closely related to this, the work of the G-7/G-8 made clear that major states had placed the fight against transnational organized crime high on their agendas and recognized the need for a vigorous response using comprehensive strategies.

FATF: Norm Creation and Peer Pressure

Another area where the G-7 and the United Nations have complemented each other's activities concerns the efforts by criminal organizations to legitimize the proceeds of their activities, a complex process summarized in the term *money laundering*. The 1988 Vienna Convention highlighted the need to do something about the proceeds of drug trafficking. Subsequent efforts to create a global regime against money laundering encompassed a wide variety of initiatives including the Basel Committee on Banking Regulations and Supervisory Practices Statement of Principles of December 1988; the FATF; the Council of Europe Convention on Laundering, Search, Seizure, and Confiscation of Proceeds of Crime of September 1990; and the sixty-one recommendations of the Caribbean Drug Money Laundering Conference of June 1990.

Perhaps most significant was the creation in 1989 by the G-7 of the FATF, charged with combating money laundering.[32] In April 1990, the FATF issued forty recommendations, which were amended and strengthened in 1996. These recommendations covered the criminal justice system and law enforcement, the regulation of the financial system, international cooperation, and the criminalization of money laundering, with predicate offenses that went beyond trafficking in drugs. The FATF emphasized the need for legislative measures to enable authorities to identify, trace, evaluate, and confiscate laundered money or property of corresponding value. In addition, it opposed anonymous accounts and highlighted the need for measures to obtain information about the true identity of persons on whose behalf an account was opened or a transaction conducted. In effect, the recommendations can be understood as an attempt to establish an anti–money laundering regime with two broad components. The first is a domestic regulatory regime that encompasses monitoring and reporting of cash transactions above a certain amount ($10,000 in the United States), the reporting of suspicious transactions, and a mandate that banks should meet know-your-customer and due diligence requirements.[33] The second component is a regime for international cooperation against money laundering that encompasses mutual legal assistance treaties (MLATs) and extradition, cooperative investigations, and the sharing of information, including greater responsiveness to requests for information about suspicious transactions and to requests by foreign countries to identify, freeze, and confiscate proceeds.

Although not a formal convention, the forty recommendations have provided a benchmark for the member states (the twenty-six original members and those that joined subsequently) and provided the basis on which the FATF subsequently developed a threefold role. The first role is to monitor the progress of the member states in implementing measures to counter money laundering through annual self-assessments and more detailed mutual evaluations. This is done through review processes that provide opportunities to put considerable moral and political pressure on governments not in compliance with the recommendations. Under FATF pressure, for example, Austria grudgingly agreed to deal with anonymous savings accounts that ran counter to notions of transparency and accountability.

The second role is to review money laundering trends, techniques, and countermeasures and their implications for the recommendations and share this information with the members to enhance their capacity to respond to innovations in laundering.

This has resulted in an annual meeting and report on money laundering typologies. In recent reports, for example, FATF members have focused attention on specific money laundering mechanisms such as trade-related schemes, informal remittance systems, Internet banking, and the role of company-formation agents.

The third role is to extend the adoption and implementation of the FATF recommendations in an attempt to build a global anti–money laundering network. This process has two separate but complementary components: broadening membership to include new countries; and creating regional groupings with a mandate similar to the FATF's. The Eastern and Southern African Anti–Money Laundering Group (ESAAMLG), created in August 1999, is an example of the second variant, while states that have recently joined the FATF itself include Argentina, Brazil, and Mexico.

In effect, the FATF has constantly sought to extend the scope of anti–money laundering measures geographically, sectorally, and functionally. In 1996 it recommended that money laundering crimes be extended beyond the predicate offense of drug trafficking, and that consideration be given to imposing restrictions on the use of new technologies to conduct financial transactions that are remote, anonymous, and outside traditional institutions. Not surprisingly, these proposals were accompanied by the recommendation that the same laws and regulations that have been developed for the banking sector be extended to nonbank financial institutions. More recently, the FATF has attempted to give teeth to its efforts. In 1999 and the first half of 2000 it published criteria for identifying "noncooperative jurisdictions" and reviewed a number of jurisdictions with these criteria in mind. Fifteen jurisdictions with serious systemic problems were identified: Bahamas, Cayman Islands, Cook Islands, Dominica, Israel, Lebanon, Liechtenstein, Marshall Islands, Nauru, Niue, Panama, Philippines, Russia, St. Kitts and Nevis, and St. Vincent and the Grenadines. The FATF initiative was a mixture of carrot and stick, encouraging these jurisdictions to remedy the deficiencies identified and offering technical assistance where appropriate, while also making clear that should they "maintain their detrimental rules and practices," FATF members would consider countermeasures.[34]

Complementing these systematic efforts by the FATF to develop and extend an anti–money laundering regime has been the creation of informal networks among Financial Intelligence Units (FIUs), such as the U.S. Treasury's Financial Crimes Enforcement Network (FINCEN) and Australia's Austrac. This cooperation has been formalized through the establishment of what has been called the Egmont Group. Although there are regular meetings of the members, the essence of this approach remains the sharing of information through the network of financial intelligence units linked by secure Internet connections. The formal meetings merely provide a framework to enhance the cooperative effort. In some respects, the Egmont Group represents an innovative approach to combating money laundering. Operating within the formal framework of norms developed by the FATF, the group gives these standards real meaning at the practical level of law enforcement operations. At the same time, the emphasis on information sharing has a surprisingly long tradition in law enforcement, a tradition enshrined most obviously in Interpol. Indeed, this provides another level in the complex of governance efforts against transnational organized crime, money laundering, and criminal markets. Whereas the international efforts described above look at governance from the top down, through the creation of rules, norms, and regulatory regimes, a more practical approach is based on functional cooperation, which comes at the problem from the bottom up.

International Police Cooperation: Interpol

No discussion of international cooperation to combat transnational crime would be complete without some consideration of Interpol. Established in 1923 and based in Lyon, France, Interpol has National Central Bureaus (NCBs) in member states, operates in four official languages (Spanish, French, English, and Arabic), and seeks to facilitate mutual assistance between law enforcement agencies in different countries. Interpol is governed by a General Assembly of delegates appointed by member states and an Executive Committee that meets three times a year. The committee consists of thirteen delegates elected by the assembly on the basis of geographic equity. The General Secretariat is responsible for implementing recommendations of the General Assembly and the Executive Committee, and plays a critical coordinating role that includes centralizing information on crime and criminals, and dealing with national and international authorities.[35]

The General Secretariat operates in conjunction with the NCBs, which provide a focal point for requests for information or actions and act as critical network nodes in a global system of information dissemination. Indeed, the NCBs play a pivotal role in Interpol's formalized system of notices, which includes requests for arrest of suspects with a view to extradition; requests for information about suspects; circulation of information about those who have committed or are likely to commit a crime; circulation of information about corpses, missing persons, and stolen property; and notification of criminals' methods of operation and places of refuge. In recent years this system has been enhanced by a secure electronic mail network linking 177 NCBs. Interpol databases, containing 120,000 records with fingerprints, photographs, and biographical data on criminals that are available to member countries through the Automated Search Facility, have been extended to include stolen vehicles. Furthermore, the establishment of an Analytical Section within Interpol has enhanced the quality of intelligence provided to members. As well as sharing information, Interpol is encouraging the standardization of ways in which national law enforcement agencies collect and analyze information about crimes and criminals.

Interpol has also strengthened its relationship with the United Nations and has extended its concerns to cover environmental crimes, child pornography, and trafficking in women and children. In 1992 an expert group was created in Interpol to study responses to a questionnaire on crimes against children that was circulated to member countries. In 1993 Interpol established subgroups to look into law enforcement, legislation on child prostitution, international cooperation, liaison networks, sex tourism, victim assistance, police structures, missing children, free telephone helplines, prevention models, training, and research and statistics. The Working Party has met regularly since then and in 1998 published a *Handbook on Good Practice for Specialist Officers Dealing with Crimes Against Children,* providing advice on all aspects of investigating sexual crimes against children. Interpol has also worked closely with a leading NGO, End Child Prostitution in Asian Tourism (ECPAT), a working relationship that combines law enforcement expertise with considerable field experience in dealing with the trafficking of minors.

In addition, the Interpol General Secretariat assists in international investigations. One example of this was "Operation Black Powder," an investigation of a Colombian drug trafficking organization that was mixing cocaine hydrochloride with iron filings and other substances, thereby making it difficult to detect. Interpol's role was in demonstrating that seizures in a variety of countries were linked to Colombian traffickers.

For all its successes, however, Interpol has always been limited because its legal status has been somewhat hazy. Moreover, it is still often described as a "policemen's club" rather than a more formal international organization.[36] Yet if this is a weakness of Interpol, it is also one of its strengths. Interpol both benefits from and contributes to the professional trust police have in one another. Indeed, in the long term, Interpol is almost as important for the transnational trust networks it creates among police from different jurisdictions as for its formal operations. If its global membership is a unique asset, however, it is also a weakness, arousing concerns on the part of some member states that information supplied to other members of Interpol might be compromised. Furthermore, Interpol's system of notices depends for its effectiveness largely on obtaining rapid responses from particular states, something that is not always forthcoming, often because of limits in state capacity. Consequently, this has led to efforts to supplement Interpol with regional cooperation. This has been especially the case in Europe.

Europol

The creation of Europol can be understood in terms of the confluence of three distinct impulses: growing concern over transnational organized crime; continued, if muted, dissatisfaction with the services provided by Interpol; and a spillover effect of European integration into justice and home affairs. Largely an initiative of former German Chancellor Helmut Kohl, Europol is designed to counter transnational crime within the boundaries of an enlarged European Union. Starting as a European Drugs Unit, Europol is based on a convention signed by member states in July 1995. The convention was ratified in June 1998 and entered into force on October 1, 1998. Europol's task is to enhance cooperation and effectiveness in combating serious crimes. Its mandate covers drug trafficking; illicit trafficking in radioactive and nuclear material; illegal immigration and trafficking in people; the theft and trafficking of motor vehicles; and money laundering. Europol facilitates data exchange and provides operational analysis and technical support for member states. Specific projects have included maritime intelligence and analysis of Albanian criminal networks in Europe. Europol has developed encrypted electronic mail links with fourteen member states, and its computer system will be fully operational in 2001.

One of the problems facing Europol, however, has been the need to establish safeguards for protection of both data and personal privacy. Another issue concerns sensitivities over sharing of national data. Relations with non-European police agencies and other international bodies are also important since criminal networks extend beyond the bounds of national and regional law enforcement. Cooperative arrangements of this kind are currently being established but are not yet fully developed. Nevertheless, within these limits it is likely that Europol will enhance the capacity of the states of the European Union to counter transnational organized crime.

World Customs Organization

The other international body that is important in combating smuggling is the WCO. In 1952 the Customs Cooperation Council (CCC) was established as "an independent intergovernmental body with world-wide membership whose mission is to enhance the effectiveness and efficiency of Customs administrations."[37] In 1994 it adopted the informal working name "World Customs Organization," which gives a far better indication of its status and its 145-state membership. The WCO pays attention to issues such as the harmonization of customs procedures, and it also has a role in supporting "members' efforts to secure, through control and enforcement, compliance with their legislation, in particular by endeavoring to maximize the level and effectiveness of members' cooperation with each other and with international organizations (and) agencies in order to combat customs offenses." In recent years, this enforcement role has become increasingly important as national customs agencies have found themselves on the front line in efforts to combat trafficking of all kinds. In 1996, for example, customs authorities worldwide seized 16.8 tons of opiates and more than 76 tons of cocaine. The WCO has established a good working relationship with both the UN International Drug Control Program and Interpol, and memoranda of understanding (MOU) to promote cooperation have been signed with a variety of bodies. In July 1996, for example, the secretariats of the WCO and

CITES signed a MOU that led to greater emphasis on the role of customs in combating trafficking in fauna and flora. In August 1997, another MOU was signed between the WCO and the Motion Picture Association to combat intellectual property theft and smuggling.

LESSONS LEARNED

In considering the track record of international responses to transnational organized crime, illegal markets, and money laundering, two broad perspectives yield very different interpretations. The first perspective is what might be termed the "synoptic strategic approach." A synoptic strategic conception of governance places considerable emphasis on overall strategic design—a top-down methodology in which all components are carefully coordinated. From this perspective, governance efforts in the area of transnational organized crime have been grossly inadequate. They have been poorly coordinated and characterized by overlapping responsibilities, and thus the gap between the creation of norms and effective implementation remains enormous. Although some progress has been made in developing cooperative approaches to combating transnational organized crime, it has been hindered by inherent problems of cooperation among states, the elevation of form over substance, the lack of overall strategy, duplication of effort (combined with significant shortfalls in resources), and gaps in regulations and implementation and enforcement. There is an urgent need for a strategic approach to governance that includes forging agreement on the problem; sharing information about its major manifestations; initiating comprehensive law enforcement attacks on transnational criminal organizations, their leadership, structures, and profits; and developing a broader approach designed to create barriers to illicit markets and thereby reduce their profitability. Because the problem is multidimensional—it is partly about criminal organizations, but also about illegal markets and corrupt processes—effective action requires attacking organizations and markets as well as reducing corruption. This is an essential component of a strategic vision for making real progress. Unfortunately, not only is such a perspective lacking, but the realities of practical cooperation also leave a great deal to be desired.

The alternative approach to a synoptic strategic conception of governance is what might be termed an "incremental evolutionary approach." From this perspective, the record is much more positive than suggested by the preceding appraisal. The recent past has seen a remarkable diffusion of awareness in the international community of transnational organized crime. Such awareness has resulted in various international institutions and agencies taking on different but complementary roles. The mechanisms of governance in this area remain seriously underdeveloped, but this is hardly surprising given the rapid emergence of the transnational organized crime challenge. Furthermore, it is important to recognize the complexity of governance, and the different stages involved, before a fully mature, comprehensive approach can be developed and implemented. In the meantime, a multilevel approach in which different institutions fulfill different but complementary roles is essential. The downside to this, of course, is duplication of effort, lack of coordination, interagency rivalry, and uncertainty about the appropriate venue for certain kinds of initiatives. Nevertheless, it is clear that governance in the area of combating transnational organized crime, drug trafficking, and money laundering has to be multilayered. Activity at each layer can make a different contribution. For example, the United Nations and the FATF play critical roles in setting international norms that can then be used to hold states accountable and put pressure on them to live up to the standards to which they have agreed. The United Nations does this through conventions, while the FATF has established a mechanism for performance review of national governments and the imposition of peer pressure. This has proved effective in establishing a regulatory approach to money laundering (although the impact of the regulations in preventing money laundering, as opposed to displacing it, is far from clear). In reality, not all states are signatories to international conventions dealing with transnational crimes. Furthermore, formal adherence to a particular convention and implementation of its injunctions are often far from synonymous. The critical point, however, is that conventions highlight areas in which there is a convergence of views among states on certain criminal activities. In this connection, the UN Convention Against Transnational Organized Crime, which was completed in August 2000 and was opened for signature in December 2000 in Palermo, Sicily, will help to bring a greater semblance of order to the issue. At the same time, there are broad areas of transnational criminal activity where conventions—or even national laws—are not yet in place. The digital realm, for example, is an area in which international governance as well as many national jurisdictions are striving to catch up with the explosion of both licit and illicit activities associated with the Internet and the World Wide Web. An incremental evolutionary model of governance, however, recognizes that although such lacunae are inevitable, eventually measures will be taken to deal with the problem. Governance is a long-term endeavor, and short-term difficulties are unavoidable. Responding creatively to these difficulties is one of the key components of the incremental evolutionary approach. Indeed, the virtues of this approach are flexibility, pragmatism, and the capacity to adapt as the challenge itself adapts.

Agenda Setting

This section identifies the key variables and actors associated with agenda setting, including: the importance of symbolism; the influential role of NGOs; the importance of leadership, as well as bureaucratic innovation and commitment; the role of public-private partnerships; and the need for careful management of the transition from agenda setting to negotiations.

Symbolism. It is difficult to exaggerate the importance of symbolism in agenda set-ting and in developing momentum toward the creation of more effective governance mechanisms. Major high-level initiatives, such as the World Ministerial Conference on Organized Transnational Crime, held in Naples in 1994, are well-orchestrated events that receive considerable attention and highlight transnational organized crime as a global challenge. The symbolism of holding the conference in a stronghold of the Mafia was also evident. The Convention Against Transnational Organized Crime that was unveiled in December 2000 in Palermo will have equal if not greater sa-lience. It promises to do to transnational crimes and transnational criminal organiza-tions what the Vienna Convention of 1988 did to drug trafficking and money laun-dering—formally identify these activities and the organizations that carry them out as international evils that states should outlaw and attack. Another highly symbolic meeting that helped to push an issue much higher on both international and national agendas was the World Congress Against the Commercial Sexual Exploitation of Children held in Stockholm in 1996.

Role of NGOs. NGOs have been particularly important in agenda setting in several areas where transnational organized crime is active and where the issue has important connections with human rights. The most pertinent example is trafficking in women and children for the commercial sex trade. Two organizations have been particularly important here. One is ECPAT, which has worked closely with Interpol in assessing the problem and identifying some components of the response. ECPAT has chapters in many countries and carries out a continued campaign for more effective actions against child prostitution and trafficking in children. It uses publicity to focus atten-tion on an issue that both populations and governments prefer to ignore and puts pressure on law enforcement agencies to become more vigorous in attacking the problem and to close the gap between laws and their implementation. ECPAT works with both law enforcement and social welfare agencies to increase sensitivities to the problems of dealing with children who have been trafficked or otherwise sexually abused. One result of its efforts has been a willingness of a growing number of states to adopt legislation that has extraterritorial impact—for example, in punishing its citizens who travel overseas and engage in sexual activities with minors. Australia, Germany, Holland, Norway, and Sweden have all successfully prosecuted pedophiles who have traveled to Thailand or other countries for sex with children. Furthermore, other countries including the United States have passed legislation prohibiting citi-zens from traveling overseas to engage in sex with minors.

While such legislation is far from universal—in fact, only a small number of coun-tries have such legislation in place—without ECPAT there would be even less will-ingness to contemplate laws with extraterritorial reach. ECPAT also played a major role in organizing the World Congress Against the Commercial Sexual Exploitation of Children and has done more than any other single organization to place this issue on the agenda of both governments and international organizations.[38] Significantly, the philosophy behind ECPAT's approach is evident in the United Nations' protocol on trafficking in persons, and especially women and children.

If ECPAT has been important internationally, in the United States the organization with perhaps the greatest impact in putting trafficking in women on the national policy agenda has been the Washington-based NGO Global Survival Network (GSN). GSN's research, publications, and outreach have drawn national attention to the phenomenon of trafficking in women from Eastern Europe and the former Soviet Union to the United States and Israel. Indeed, largely as a result of GSN's activities, the United States has gradually moved toward a more comprehensive response. In March 1998 President Bill Clinton issued a memorandum directing both the attorney general and the secretary of state to give the issue greater attention. The attorney general was required to take steps to ensure the safety of victims and witnesses and to guarantee their safe return to their country of origin. Temporary or permanent legal status for victims of trafficking was also to be considered, as were legal changes to ensure that trafficking is criminalized and prosecution efforts are more effective. The secretary of state was required to cooperate with source, transit, and destination countries to develop strategies for protecting and assisting victims of trafficking. Preventive efforts based on public awareness campaigns were to be accompanied by assistance in drafting legislation to combat trafficking and provide assistance to its victims. In fact the United States, working in cooperation with the European Union, has initiated educational programs in Ukraine and Poland and is also working closely with Italy and Israel. Such initiatives are useful. Nevertheless, much more needs to be done at the international level before human commodity trafficking—a phenomenon sometimes described as the most modern form of slavery—is seriously inhibited. The phenomenon is widespread; the results often tragic; and the countermeasures, for all the recent flurry of initiatives, still far short of what is required. With one of the protocols to the UN Convention on Transnational Crime dealing with trafficking in women and children, more attention will be devoted to the issue. The real measure of success, however, will only be evident when many more states criminalize trafficking in women and impose more severe penalties. The protocol is an important development, but the obligations imposed by existing conventions must be incorporated into laws that are vigorously enforced at the national level. In effect, this is the point at which NGOs face limits. They can create awareness and help to put issues on the political agenda at either the national or the international level, but they cannot determine what happens once these issues are on the agenda.

Importance of Leadership.   Even if one accepts the notion that global governance is usually advanced through an incremental evolutionary approach rather than through the top-down imposition of norms and regulations, this does not mean that it can develop spontaneously. Although governance in a particular area does not necessarily require a hegemon, it does require that states with authority regard the topic as important. In this connection, the United States has played a vital role in highlighting transnational organized crime. In the Fiftieth Anniversary Speech before the United Nations, President Clinton stressed the need to respond to the challenge posed by transnational organized crime, thereby providing a major signal to the international community that the United States regarded the issue as important. This was followed by tangible evidence of the salience of the issue when, in 1998, the United States unveiled a detailed strategy against international organized crime. Although the strategy includes many measures that are national and unilateral, the strategy also emphasizes the need for international cooperation.

The role of the G-7/G-8 has also been crucial in placing transnational organized crime on the agenda of issues requiring a vigorous international response. The annual great power summits have allowed heads of state to share concerns about high-tech crimes, for example, and to provide broad endorsement for efforts to combat transnational organized crime. When one looks closely at the G-7/G-8 through the 1990s, it appears that with the creation of the Group of Experts, it was poised for more direct involvement. Having put forth the forty recommendations, however, the G-7/G-8 adopted a supporting role, allowing the United Nations to provide the major forum. Nevertheless, at a critical point in deliberations about whether a convention was feasible or desirable, the G-7/G-8's support for the idea—generated largely by the Group of Experts—was pivotal. Leadership can be expressed in terms of broad support as well as detailed planning, and it is in the former mode that the G-7/G-8 has proved most significant.

Importance of Bureaucratic Innovation and Commitment.   Although it is tempting to see leadership in agenda setting as simply a matter of high-level endorsement, an important organizational dimension should not be overlooked. Indeed, the United States has adopted a strategic response to transnational organized crime at the international level in part because of the efforts of the International Narcotics and Law Enforcement Bureau (INL) in the State Department. INL has provided an organizational basis for efforts to coordinate national policies against transnational organized crime and illegal markets. It represents an organizational innovation that other countries could usefully adopt. Although its efforts through most of the Clinton years were particularly impressive because of the energy, commitment, and vision of Deputy Assistant Secretary of State Jonathan Winer, the organizational commitment was also important. Although some law enforcement agencies, such as the U.S. Drug Enforcement Administration or indeed many national customs authorities, are closely attuned to the needs of international cooperation, these tend to be the exceptions rather than the rule, and they operate at the practical rather than the diplomatic level. Efforts at international governance will be successful only if they have genuine supporters at the diplomatic level who can contribute to effective cooperation. In this respect, operation of INL provides an important example for other states to follow. Establishing units dedicated to combating transnational organized crime and illegal markets in ministries of foreign affairs could be a key innovation in enhancing governance in response to the challenge posed by transnational organized crime. Such units would not be a replacement for direct contacts among law enforcement agencies but would provide a basis for enhanced international cooperation at both the formal and informal levels. Indeed, they are essential as efforts are made to expand the number and reach of formal frameworks for legal cooperation. Most important at this formal level are extradition treaties and mutual legal assistance treaties that allow information sharing for use in trials. Progress has been made in this area, but the existing web of international agreements needs to be expanded. Units dedicated to the fight against transnational organized crime that combine diplomatic and negotiating skills with both legal and subject-area knowledge will greatly facilitate this process, especially once the UN Convention Against Transnational Organized Crime comes into force.

Success of Public-Private Partnerships and Reciprocity.   Coopting the private sector and forging public-private partnerships to combat organized crime, drug trafficking, and money laundering are essential. The private sector provides many targets for transnational organized crime and money laundering, and governments cannot combat the challenge without considerable cooperation from business. Indeed, banks—albeit rather reluctantly—have countered money laundering through reporting requirements and the pursuit of due diligence and know-your-customer rules. They do not always live up to their commitments in these areas, however. The assistance given by Citibank to Mexican President Raoul Salinas in placing money in Swiss banks revealed that in the world of private banking, due diligence requirements are not always met. Similarly, the Bank of New York developed correspondent relationships with Russian banks without serious due diligence. When combined with lax internal supervision, this provided opportunities for money laundering and capital flight. Both Citibank and the Bank of New York have been severely criticized for these failures. Other banks, however, in the United States and elsewhere have institutionalized reporting activities for suspicious transactions, and on occasion these reports have led to significant investigations and arrests for money laundering. Although the partnership is not an easy one, with many banks feeling that some of the requirements are rather onerous, it remains essential.

Similar relationships are being forged between governments and transportation industries concerned about their conveyances being used for various forms of smuggling, as well as about cargo theft. Governments are sometimes willing to establish MOUs with freight-forwarding companies, whereby they will expedite inspection processes connected with both imports and exports in return for information from the industry about any suspicious activities. Such policies could be extended to include any industry (for example, hazardous waste disposal) that is vulnerable to infiltration by organized crime groups. Programs devised to make companies less vulnerable to infiltration and hostile takeover could also be devised by government and industry, working together. In effect, the agenda has to be both broadened and extended into the private sector, emphasizing the interest of the private sector in working more closely with the government. The key to success here is reciprocity: both government and private industry must feel that they are gaining from the relationship. Indeed, this is one of the keys to effective agenda setting.

Management of the Transition from Agenda Setting to Negotiations. The transition from agenda setting to practical negotiations is often neglected. In the case of the UN Convention Against Transnational Organized Crime, this was a particularly critical juncture. The idea of a convention was on the agenda, but the debate focused more on principle than practicality. An initiative of the Polish government helped to tip the momentum toward specific negotiations; their draft framework shifted the terms of the debate to substance rather than principle and gave important impetus to substantive negotiations. This situation suggests that a government's willingness to take ownership of a problem can have a decisive impact in moving from agenda setting to actual negotiations.

Negotiations

This section discusses some of the key aspects of successful negotiations, including: avoiding dilution, establishing ownership of the problem, and creating substantive measures of effectiveness.

Avoiding Dilution. The problem with the multilateral approaches required by any serious effort at international governance is that even if agreement is obtained, it is often based on the lowest common denominator, and some states expect that they will subsequently have opportunities to dilute the governance effort even further at the implementation stage or act as free riders. In effect, breadth of participation is achieved, but only at the expense of depth of cooperation. Consequently, multilateral cooperation can all too easily become an excuse for doing nothing or moving very slowly. Similarly, it can become a substitute for more decisive unilateral action or can be used as an alternative to making more specific commitments in a narrower bilateral relationship. This is clearly the danger with global efforts at responding to transnational organized crime—the more players there are, the less coherent the play. If the sensitivities and predilections of all governments are taken into account, negotiations can be protracted. The more serious danger, however, is that the resulting agreement will be significantly diluted for the sake of consensus. There is some danger of this in the UN Convention Against Transnational Organized Crime. Having the provisions dealing with illegal manufacturing and trafficking in firearms, trafficking in women and children, and smuggling of illegal aliens as protocols to the convention rather than part of it is a case in point, given that the protocols carry less weight than the convention. At the same time, this sort of compromise has allowed the process to go forward more rapidly than might have been expected. Furthermore, there also seems to have been an awareness among the participants of the danger of dilution, and efforts have been made to avoid it. The UN Secretariat has provided expertise both on the nature of the transnational crime challenge and on what some governments have done in response.

Establishing Ownership of the Problem.   One critical component of large, protracted multilateral negotiations is that certain participants care very much about a successful outcome and assume considerable responsibility for bringing the negotiations to fruition. In the case of the UN Convention Against Transnational Organized Crime, individuals within the UN Secretariat have nursed the process along, providing institutional support and informal expertise, and acting as effective liaisons among delegations. The UN Secretariat arranged follow-up meetings in several regions, building participation and support. Moreover, key governments also committed themselves to a favorable outcome of the negotiations. Poland, for example, through the latter half of the 1990s championed the convention; it was not coincidental that in February 1998 Warsaw was the venue for the meeting of an intergovernmental group of experts established by the General Assembly. Argentina's consistent support for action against trafficking in children was also an important factor, and its offer to host an informal preparatory meeting of the intergovernmental ad hoc committee in Buenos Aires helped to maintain momentum through 1998. Two other developments extended the sense of ownership. One was the formation of a group known as "friends of the chair," which met in July 1998 in Rome. Second, at the Buenos Aires meeting there emerged "a core group of delegates who were experts in their field and shared considerable experience from previous negotiations. One important feature of the core group was that it was highly participatory, in the sense that it included representatives from virtually all regions and all legal systems of the world. The formation of this core group brought with it a gradually increasing sense of ownership regarding the text, which is a key element of the success of the endeavor."[39] That there were some participants with a sense of ownership provided a degree of consistency and stability that survived the vagaries of the negotiation, especially the loss of enthusiasm by the developing countries.

Creating Substantive Measures of Effectiveness.   Another lesson concerns aims and objectives. In combating transnational organized crime and its attendant activities such as money laundering, sometimes a certain vacuousness in negotiations succeeds in establishing procedural norms rather than creating substantive norms with real impact. In other words, the issue becomes one of conformity with FATF procedures rather than an assessment of the effectiveness of these procedures in inhibiting or detecting money laundering. Cooperation is sometimes seen as a goal in its own right, rather than simply a means to an end, and the cooperative venture becomes fundamentally flawed by elevating form over substance. Although the FATF has obtained major plaudits for imposing an anti–money laundering regime, the congratulatory rhetoric hides a reality that is more complex and somewhat disappointing. Indeed, there are two problems with the FATF. First, in spite of its efforts to expand its geographic reach, it remains circumscribed geographically; thereby instead of halting money laundering, in some cases it merely displaces it to locations where the risks are lower. Second, the FATF has established a set of standards that require considerable effort to implement but do not yield commensurate results. For example, the FATF requires that states adopt certain forms of regulation—such as filing reports for cash transactions over a certain amount—designed to inhibit or help detect and prosecute money laundering. Although this procedure has probably had some impact in obstructing and displacing money laundering, the achievements measured in substantive terms have been disappointing. This is not surprising: cash transaction reports and suspicious transaction reports are enormously time consuming and yield vast amounts of information, but they have led to very few successful prosecutions. Turkey provides a particularly instructive case. Under pressure from the FATF, Turkey responded in two ways: it pushed money laundering activities into Turkish Cyprus, and then it met the FATF requirements. This suggests that the FATF's approach to combating money laundering results in the wrong questions being asked. The focus is on whether participating states meet FATF standards rather than the far more important question of whether participating states are effective in combating money laundering. The result is self-delusion and an impression that far more is being achieved than is actually the case. To many observers and adherents of the FATF approach, such judgments will seem unduly harsh, especially given the developments in 1999 and 2000 whereby the FATF publicly identified noncooperative jurisdictions found to have systemic problems in dealing with money laundering. The point is, however, that in combating transnational organized crime, money laundering, and illicit markets it is essential to know what works and what does not, and to develop measures of effectiveness that reflect real rather than ostensible results.

Implementation and Compliance

This section covers the following themes regarding implementation and compliance: the need for systematic implementation; the dangers of asymmetrical implementation; the need to complement global negotiations with bilateral, regional, and multi-lateral efforts; and the importance of functional cooperation.

Need for Systematic Implementation. One lesson that emerges clearly from even a rudimentary history of efforts to control illicit markets is the need to focus more on implementation. Governance measures that are long on conventions, laws, and regulations but short on implementation are grossly inadequate, if not spurious.

Efforts to suppress trafficking in women and children, for example, include conventions from 1922 and 1930 that deal with child prostitution as part of the broader issue of the abolition of forced labor. Another important international instrument targeting sexual exploitation was the 1949 Convention on the Suppression of Traffic in Persons and of the Exploitation of the Prostitution of Others. This document targeted those who procured and exploited prostitutes rather than the prostitutes themselves. The 1979 Convention on the Elimination of All Forms of Discrimination Against Women provides that signatories "shall take all appropriate measures, including legislation, to suppress all forms of traffic in women and exploitation of prostitution of women."[40] The 1959 UN Declaration on the Rights of the Child and the 1989 Convention on the Rights of the Child focused specifically on how children should be treated, requiring adherents to "undertake to protect the child from all forms of sexual exploitation and sexual abuse." Taken together, these measures constituted an international legal and normative framework against the exploitation of children, explicitly including sexual exploitation.

As with most international conventions, however, there has been a major gap between aspiration and achievement. The international norms enshrined in these declarations and conventions have been far less effective than desired. Even when states have acceded to them there has been insufficient or ineffective monitoring of compliance, while national implementation has been only sporadic. During the 1990s there was growing acknowledgment of the gap between formal norms and effective implementation of policies designed to disrupt the markets for illicit products. One report, focusing on the problem of trafficking in children, emphasized the need for effective actions designed both to "stop the supply and eliminate the demand."[41] This, it was noted, required substantive laws at the national level making child prostitution and child pornography criminal offenses, as well as the introduction of procedural provisions to protect children during criminal proceedings.[42] The media, education, and criminal justice systems were identified as the three main actors positioned to respond to commercial sexual exploitation of children.[43] In terms of law enforcement, considerable emphasis was placed on the need for enhancing national capabilities. Priority was also to be given to international cooperation, ranging from information sharing and synchronization of national laws to "arrangements by which abusers in a foreign country may be subject to prosecution either where the offence took place or in the country of the offender. This could be done through either extradition or expansion of jurisdiction through extraterritoriality."[44] In other words, a prohibition regime is in place; the requirement therefore is not to add further regulation but to ensure that states bring their criminal laws fully into line with their international obligations. Efforts still have to be made to move from the declaratory level and both introduce and enforce tougher laws and sentences for those who traffic in women and children for commercial sex. The Protocol on Trafficking of Persons, Particularly Women and Children, to the Convention Against Transnational Organized Crime will be useful if it focuses attention on the need for implementation rather than merely serves as another declaration.

Dangers of Asymmetrical Implementation.   Implementation is significantly weakened by states that are formally part of governance regimes or declarations, but in practice defect from that effort. A serious obstacle to the establishment of effective global governance mechanisms to deal with transnational organized crime is overt defections by states. One of the difficulties in combating transnational organized crime is that criminal organizations often operate very effectively from safe havens. These are generally jurisdictions in which criminal justice systems are particularly weak or so corrupt that criminal organizations can operate with a minimum level of risk. As long as this is the case, efforts to increase the risk of criminal behavior are seriously hampered. As Ernesto Savona has argued, it is important not only to raise the risks that organized crime confronts from law enforcement but also to equalize those risks across all states.[45]

Three categories of states are likely to defect: corrupt states where organized crime has made some inroads into the state apparatus and created a climate of acquiescence to criminal activities; captured states where organized crime has neutralized much of the state apparatus; and criminal states where the state, in effect, has taken over organized crime. In criminal states, government personnel are deeply involved in the commission and orchestration of crimes at either the domestic or the transnational level. This phenomenon of criminal states is relatively rare, but examples include North Korea, Nigeria under Abacha, and Serbia under Milosevic. In these cases criminal activities are or were endorsed or even organized by government leaders or members of their families. Under Slobodan Milosevic, for example, members of the government dominated an underground economy created in large part by the imposition of sanctions. Cabinet members and leading politicians controlled the distribution and sale of products such as oil, gas, consumer goods, stolen cars, computers, telecommunications, foreign currencies, illicit drugs, agricultural products and other foods, and spare parts. Exploitation of official positions was enormous, especially as Milosevic and his family rewarded political supporters with government monopolies. Among the major activities were: trading in foreign currency; bribery and corruption to obtain permission to run small businesses; the use of monopolies to trade agricultural products; distribution of stolen cars; smuggling of cigarettes into Serbia and from Serbia into the European Union; control over gasoline imports; and complicity with Turkish trafficking organizations and Serbian officials allowing free passage of heroin to Western Europe. The problem arose in large part from the existence of a seamless web between the state and private entrepreneurship, both legal and illegal. In North Korea, the issue has been one of using transnational crime to assist the financing of a state that was until recently internationally isolated and all but bankrupt. In Nigeria under Sonny Abacha, the military regime was not only a participant in such criminal schemes as advance fee frauds—which were all the more effective when there appeared to be official endorsement—but also looted the state, with some estimates claiming that Abacha amassed over $4 billion.[46]

More typical than explicitly criminal states are those that establish collusive relationships with criminal organizations and that can appropriately be regarded as captured states. Examples include Turkey (where there is a close relationship between major organized crime clans and government officials), Mexico (where *mordida* or bribery has become a way of life at the highest levels of government), and Russia (where relationships involving government officials, business oligarchies, and criminal organizations have become a dominant feature of political and economic life). Captured states are characterized by the tendency of at least some criminal organizations to cloak their power in the mantle of state authority. This is not to suggest that the criminal symbiosis will determine all aspects of state behavior. Where the state is captured by organized crime, the state will still carry out many of its traditional functions in international relations. At the same time, state authorities will take measures to ensure that organized crime functions unhindered in its pursuit of wealth. The implication is that there will continue to be states that provide sanctuaries for criminal organizations. Indeed, their number could well increase as transnational criminal organizations continue to entrench themselves in weak states in the former Soviet Union, Africa, Latin America, and parts of Asia. Captured states are likely to become particularly prevalent in Africa where, ironically, democratization and the simultaneous cutbacks in Western aid and assistance provide new opportunities for transnational criminal organizations to exert influence through the electoral process.

Until now, however, efforts at international governance in this area have shied away from dealing seriously with criminal or captured states partly because of sensitivities over national sovereignty and partly because other concerns have inhibited the adoption of stringent measures. Even Nigeria under Abacha had no serious costs imposed on it, because the criminality was seen as a nuisance rather than a security threat meriting the imposition of sanctions, and because of trade-related (oil) considerations. Russia poses even more of a problem; Western interests in the success of the Russian transition militate against full recognition of the extent to which the state has been compromised by organized crime.

Nor is defection the only problem when it comes to implementation of governance efforts against transnational organized crime. Perhaps or even more serious is the problem of capacity, which led some developing states to temper their enthusiasm for the Convention Against Transnational Organized Crime. Indeed, implementation of norms, regulations, laws, and policies in accordance with the dictates of governance suffers critically from gaps in national capacity. Even if some states want to participate fully in international regimes and other efforts at governance, they do not have the capability to implement appropriate laws. Many states that have gone along with the anti–money laundering regime, for example, have little or no capacity to oversee their banking sectors to ensure that they are not recipients of the proceeds of crime. Moreover, the situation is not static. States that lack the capacity to implement governance mechanisms targeted against transnational organized crime are themselves likely targets for these same criminal organizations. Indeed, organized crime flourishes where state capacity is limited, where states do not have complete control over their territory, and where state institutions are open to external influence. Organized crime will also seek to perpetuate the weakness of the state and to ensure that it remains a congenial environment. As a result, weak states can all too easily become captured states, thereby joining the ranks of the overt defectors from efforts at international governance.

In short, weak and captured states seriously hinder multilateral efforts to combat transnational organized crime, ensuring that global regimes will remain seriously incomplete and that criminal organizations will continue to enjoy geographic and jurisdictional loopholes. Sanctuary states will continue to put transnational criminal organizations out of the reach of those states whose laws they have violated and whose population provides customers for their illicit products and services. The result will be not the containment of criminal activity but its adaptation. Indeed, partial regimes and uneven regulatory measures displace—both geographically and methodologically—rather than inhibit the activities of criminal organizations and the operation of criminal markets. Criminal activities do not necessarily diminish in response to regulation or law enforcement efforts; they simply adapt—often by becoming increasingly sophisticated—or move to where they can be conducted with greater ease and less risk.

The implication of this analysis is that regional rather than global cooperative efforts, or partial rather than comprehensive regimes, may be of limited value. Although their establishment can give the impression of progress, this impression is created by a relocation of criminal activities and organizations rather than any diminution of the market or the capacity of the organizations. This is not to say that they are useless; rather, it suggests that their potential is connected to the effectiveness of the overall global framework.

Need to Complement Global Negotiations with Bilateral, Regional, and Multilateral Efforts. Global negotiations are particularly suited to the promulgation of norms that are applicable to the international community as a whole. In many other cases, however, a select group of states will establish cooperative efforts when they share a similar perception of a problem and believe that common action can be advantageous. This is particularly useful at the operational end of governance efforts against transnational organized crime and has resulted in multinational task forces that have had striking successes against drug trafficking organizations and other forms of organized crime. Operation Green Ice in the early 1990s, for example, resulted in around 200 arrests in countries as diverse as Canada, Colombia, and Spain.[47] Indeed, where the target is a transnational criminal network operating in multiple jurisdictions, it can effectively be dismantled only by cooperation.

Importance of Functional Cooperation. Closely related to the development of these multinational task forces, but a step up from it in terms of sustained cooperation, is the growing importance of functional agencies in negotiating with their counterparts in other countries. Financial Intelligence Units, for example, largely under the leadership of the U.S. Treasury's FINCEN, have developed an international network that employs both meetings and information sharing using technology. As suggested above, the Egmont Group is an important mechanism for information sharing and adds enormously to the capacity of governments to track the proceeds of crime as they move through multiple jurisdictions. In some respects the Egmont Group is an important model, reflecting the point made by John Arquilla and David Ronfeldt that it takes a network to defeat a network.[48] The creation of law enforcement networks that transcend national borders in the same way as do criminal organizations can be enhanced through negotiation among functional units. For the most part, however, law enforcement networks that establish trust among agencies in different nations and facilitate the pursuit of crimes involving more than one jurisdiction emerge not from formal negotiations but from experience, training efforts, and international conferences. At the same time, incentives can be created for cooperation among law enforcement agencies from different nations, such as sharing assets forfeited by criminals. Concerns about "bounty hunting" and lack of provision for asset forfeiture in many legal systems, however, set limits to this. Nevertheless, if used with care, such schemes could enhance international cooperation at the operational level.

Reactions to Noncompliance

Significant potential dangers and inadvertent consequences are associated with effective enforcement, which requires long-term capacity building.

Difficulties of Enforcement and the Need for Long-Term Capacity Building. Until recently there have been few penalties for noncompliance with governance efforts by states, reflecting uncertainty about culpability. In dealing with organized crime, there is perhaps an inherent confusion about whether the target of enforcement is primarily states, criminal organizations, or criminal markets. In some cases, governance is essentially about the regulation of state behavior; in others it is about encouraging states to regulate the behavior of its citizens, as either consumers of illegal goods and services or participants in criminal enterprises. States often lack the capacity or the inclination for serious enforcement, so the predominant effort of governance has been to encourage compliance through capacity building rather than the imposition of penalties. This makes sense. If a state is weak, external sanctions are likely simply to exacerbate the weakness, making the state an even easier target for criminal organizations (as has been demonstrated in Serbia, where sanctions actually facilitated the criminalization of the state). The problem, however, is that capacity building is a slow process and one in which the results are not easy to measure. The lesson here is the need for patience and the development of an approach that can be sustained over the long term.

Dangers of Enforcement. Another trend, however, might be gaining momentum: a more punitive approach to noncompliance. The United States took the lead in this during the mid-1990s with its use of the International Emergency Economic Powers Act (IEEPA) against Colombian companies involved in drug trafficking and money laundering. The recent actions by the FATF in pressuring Austria to deal with anonymous bank accounts and in publicly identifying noncooperative jurisdictions was a step in the same direction, although naming and shaming is still a long way from formal sanctions. The trend toward serious enforcement, however, could become much stronger following the adoption of the Convention Against Transnational Organized Crime.

Indeed, the distinction between states that uphold global governance against transnational organized crime and those that decline to be included in this effort may become much sharper. It is not inconceivable that during the first half of this century one of the major global divides will be caused not by competing ideologies, the struggle for power, or Samuel Huntington's "clash of civilizations," but by conflict between states that uphold law and order and those dominated by criminal interests. This vision of the future as one in which private power masquerades as state authority is chilling. To be effective, enforcement will have to go well beyond the measures envisaged thus far, but in so doing could actually precipitate conflicts between the two kinds of states. Even if these stark consequences are avoided, however, another problem can arise—that of inadvertent consequences.

Problem of Inadvertent Consequences. There are two dimensions of the problem of inadvertent consequences of efforts to establish more effective global governance. The first is the inadvertent spin-offs that can arise from governance efforts intended to deal with problems other than transnational organized crime but nevertheless create new opportunities for criminal organizations. Negotiating an overly restrictive approach to environment issues, or trying to bring warring parties to a settlement through the imposition of an international embargo, feed directly into what might be termed the restriction-opportunity dilemma. Although governance is anathema to criminal organizations, restricted activities (for example, prohibitions on drugs or chlorofluorocarbons) paradoxically provide inroads for the creation of new criminal markets or the enlargement of existing markets. International arms embargoes on countries where there is civil strife or ethnic conflicts, for example, create enormous opportunities for criminal organizations and unscrupulous entrepreneurs to circumvent restrictions and supply combatants with weapons. Indeed, embargoes represent an excellent example of governance efforts that contain the seeds of their own failure: embargoes create shortages; shortages increase the price of goods; increased price means increased profits; and the potential for increased profits brings in new suppliers willing to ignore the restrictions.

The second dimension of the enforcement problem concerns the inadvertent consequences that sometimes arise when enforcement efforts succeed. For example, success against the Medellin and Cali cartels in Colombia benefited Mexican drug trafficking organizations, which have become dominant in a large part of the U.S. market for cocaine. In the same vein is what might be termed the "sophistication race": as governments introduce more effective measures to combat organized crime, so criminal enterprises become more sophisticated in response. Furthermore, government and international measures to combat organized crime, drug trafficking, and money laundering are most effective against the least well organized groups, thereby diminishing the competition facing the more established and efficient criminal enterprises and encouraging the survival of the fittest.

CONCLUSIONS AND IMPLICATIONS

If the efforts at establishing more effective mechanisms of international governance are fundamentally flawed, simply improving them will not help. There are limits to what can be achieved given the problems of weak states, the capacity of criminals to circumvent law enforcement efforts, the advantages transnational criminal organizations possess in dealing with governments, and the fact that criminal activities often reflect market dynamics that are not easily weakened—and can sometimes even be strengthened—by government interventions. Obstacles to more effective governance include the existence of legal systems based on different principles and criminalizing different activities, which sometimes makes it difficult for states to cooperate. The difference between civil law and common law jurisdictions can obstruct the development of concerted approaches. A good example of this is that many civil law countries have a rule of compulsory prosecution that limits prosecutorial discretion and makes it more difficult to use criminal informants to obtain information. This obstacle is reinforced by continued adherence to the notion of sovereignty. The prevailing attitude that national law is one of the last bastions of sovereignty makes states reluctant to move toward harmonization of laws or to countenance extraterritoriality, even though sacrificing some of the formalities of sovereignty might be the only way to retain real sovereignty in the face of transnational organized crime.

The other difficulty, even for governments committed to combating transnational organized crime and illegal markets, is that they are pursuing other, conflictual goals. As Peter Andreas has so effectively pointed out, trade liberalization facilitates increased trade flows that provide additional cover for drugs; and both privatization and financial liberalization offer increased opportunities for money laundering.[49] The United States emphasizes market liberalization, especially in developing countries, but some of these countries' most marketable products are illegal commodities. Similarly, it is difficult to interdict illegal products effectively while facilitating the more rapid flow of international trade. Governments want to continue enjoying the benefits of globalization and are somewhat reluctant to deal with its dark side by taking any measures that might interfere with these benefits.

Finally, there are important links between organized crime and drug trafficking, and underlying problems such as poverty, wealth disparities, failure of national governments, social and political instability, and ethnic conflicts. Yet governance efforts treat organized crime as an unmitigated evil, ignoring the benefits that organized crime and illegal markets provide—benefits that extend well beyond the immediate members of the organizations. At least some of the money earned by criminal organizations has significant and beneficial multiplier effects in local, regional, and even national economies. Similarly, illicit trafficking can be a major source of export earnings for states that have few licit products. Moreover, organized crime often provides a form of employment when few other opportunities are available. In societies where large segments of the population do not have ready access to the legitimate avenues of advancement, or where these avenues are simply not well developed, becoming a member of a criminal organization can appear attractive. It is no coincidence that criminal organizations often develop amid poverty or as an accompaniment to social upheaval, economic dislocation, or political disruption. In such circumstances, the ability of criminal organizations to provide patronage to the local community sometimes elevates their leaders to the status of folk heroes. None of this is intended to condone transnational criminal organizations or their activities. It is simply that understanding their positive aspects is a prerequisite for implementing more effective strategies against them. To the extent that transnational criminal organizations emerge from specific conditions, changing the conditions should be a major element of preventive strategies.

One implication is that it is impossible to establish effective governance against transnational organized crime in a vacuum. Transnational organized crime has become so pervasive and so linked with globalization that it needs to be considered much more carefully in relation to a range of governance initiatives. One recent development in the fight against corruption, for example, was the Organization for Economic Cooperation and Development (OECD) Convention Against Bribery. Although widely regarded as a major step forward in dealing with corruption of governments by international business, it focused on only one part of the problem. In effect, it attempted to stifle the supply of bribes to government officials from transnational corporations. Although this is a start, it deals only with the supply of corrupt payments, while doing nothing about the demand. Indeed, the demand for bribery in many developing countries is likely to continue. This is especially the case as democratic reforms lead to greater emphasis on elections. In many countries campaign finance will be very difficult to obtain. This is likely to offer transnational organized crime an enormous opportunity to obtain influential political partners through support for their campaigns—the pattern was set by Cali drug trafficking organizations that contributed to the Samper campaign for the Colombian presidency in the mid-1990s. This pattern will increasingly be emulated elsewhere. As a result even more countries will become vulnerable to criminal infiltration and end up as captured states. Use of political corruption by organized crime, therefore, is likely to be an increasingly important challenge.

Unfortunately governance efforts against transnational organized crime and against corruption are inadequately coordinated. Although it is important not to conflate crime and corruption—they are separate and distinct in many respects—there are important relationships between them. Corruption is not simply a condition that exists in many social, political, and economic systems; it is also an instrument of organized crime and is in fact the most important single weapon used by criminal organizations to protect themselves from governments and law enforcement agencies. Consequently, transparency—one of the major anticorruption weapons—should also be used against transnational organized crime. Indeed, support and encouragement for a vigorous and independent media is critical and should assist in the identification of the political-criminal nexus that facilitates criminal activities and protects criminal organizations. Furthermore, organized crime considerations need to be taken into account when other policies are implemented, such as aid to states in transition. In some cases, the lack of safeguards has enabled corrupt officials and their criminal partners to grow rich at the expense of donors.

In addition to viewing governance efforts against transnational organized crime, money laundering and illegal markets from a broader perspective, it is perhaps most important to develop an overall strategy that relates ends and means, targets resources more effectively, and attacks criminal enterprises and their various support structures. In the same vein, it is essential to develop measures of effectiveness and to determine what is meant by successful governance.

It is also important to accept that developing effective governance will be a long, difficult process that requires sustained effort and that will always be fraught with problems and characterized by setbacks. Moreover, although it is tempting to suggest that most governance efforts seem to have grown piecemeal and that the emphasis should therefore be placed on rationalization and consolidation, it is perhaps even more important to acknowledge that this is a multipronged exercise involving several layers of activity. Formal and informal approaches will continue to be essential. At the level of implementation, for example, it is vital to build on the benefits of informal cooperation especially in the creation of transnational networks. Yet the process must go well beyond formal state-to-state cooperation. Governance through informal functional cooperation might be the answer—and in this connection the Egmont Group might prove to be a pioneering example.

At the same time, the overall strategy should not be lost. In the final analysis, the two approaches to governance discussed above—the synoptic strategic model and the incremental evolutionary mode—are not mutually exclusive. Rather than being seen as alternatives, they should be regarded as complementary, for both are necessary ingredients of good governance. Yet even if they are combined far more effectively than has been possible so far, this is still no guarantee of success. As the preceding analysis has shown, combating transnational organized crime, illegal markets, and money laundering remains one of the most problematic governance issues, both domestically and internationally. Unfortunately, it is also one of the most urgent.

NOTES

1. James Rosenau, *Turbulence in World Politics: A Theory of Change and Continuity* (Princeton, N.J.: Princeton University Press, 1990).
2. Ko-lin Chin, *Chinese Subculture and Criminality: Non-traditional Crime Groups in America* (New York: Greenwood Press, 1990), p. 9.
3. W. Kleinknecht, *The New Ethnic Mobs: The Changing Face of Organized Crime in America* (New York: The Free Press, 1996).
4. Lance Grahn, *The Political Economy of Smuggling: Regional Informal Economies in Early Bourbon New Grenada* (Boulder, Colo.: Westview Press, 1997), pp. 3–4. In eighteenth-century New Grenada, the Spanish colony that subsequently became Colombia, contraband smuggling was pervasive. Furthermore—in a development that foreshadowed similar problems today—connivance by the authorities, "prejudiced the quality of law enforcement . . . and made official dishonesty a fixture of public life" (Grahn, *The Political Economy of Smuggling*, p. 5). Nor was the problem limited to the overseas colonies of European great powers. Throughout the eighteenth and nineteenth centuries, there was a flourishing and well-organized contraband trade in luxury goods such as liquor and fine silks smuggled into England from France by well-organized groups. Men of status within the local community in the counties of Kent and Cornwall often organized the groups and developed sophisticated methods of concealment for their products. See David

Phillipson, *Smuggling: A History, 1700–1970* (Newton Abbot, United Kingdom: David and Charles, 1973).

5. Edward J. Bristow, *Prostitution and Prejudice: The Jewish Fight Against White Slavery, 1870–1939* (New York: Schocken Books, 1983), p. 118.

6. See the analysis in Bristow, *Prostitution and Prejudice*, for a fuller discussion of these destinations.

7. The Hamburg-Jewish Committee Against White Slavery, quoted in Bristow, *Prostitution and Prejudice*, p. 124.

8. Ibid., p. 124.

9. Frank Bovenkerk, "Crime and the Multi-ethnic Society: A View from Europe," in *Crime, Law, and Social Change*, vol. 19 (1993), pp. 271–80 at p. 279.

10. This is a major theme in Joel Kurtzman, *The Death of Money* (New York: Simon and Schuster, 1993).

11. Office of International Criminal Justice, U.S. Department of State, Bureau for International Narcotics and Law Enforcement Affairs, <http://www.ncjrs.org/ineloicj.htm>.

12. For example, in his presentation at the IASOC Panel at the American Society of Criminology 49th Annual Meeting, San Diego, November 19–22, 1997.

13. The author is grateful to Ernesto Savona for his insights on the importance of risk for criminal organizations.

14. John Picarelli and Phil Williams, "Organized Crime and Information Technologies," in Dan Papp and David S. Alberts, eds., *The Information Age Anthology, Part II: National Security Implications of the Information Age* (Washington, D.C.: NDU Press, 2000).

15. For example, in Russia there are more than 500 contract killings per year, in which the victims include politicians, government officials, business people, journalists, and criminal leaders.

16. Louise Shelley, "Transnational Organized Crime: The New Authoritarianism," in H. Richard Friman and Peter Andreas, eds., *The Illicit Global Economy and State Power* (Lanham, Md.: Rowman and Littlefield, 1999), pp. 25–52.

17. See *Trends in Organized Crime*, vol. 3, no. 1 (Fall 1997), pp. 4–7.

18. This theme is developed in Jean-Francois Bayart et al., *The Criminalization of the State in Africa* (Bloomington, Ind.: Indiana University Press, 1999).

19. Mackenzie Institute, *Funding Terror: The Liberation Tigers of Tamil Eelam and Their Criminal Activities in Canada and the Western World* (Toronto: Mackenzie Institute, 1996).

20. Amran Abocar, "Canada: Canada Police Say Tamil Gangs Funding Rebels," *Reuters,* March 28, 2000.

21. "Introduction: International Relations and the Illicit Global Economy," in Friman and Andreas, *The Illicit Global Economy*, pp. 1–24 at p. 6.

22. I am grateful to Tom Naylor for this point.

23. Some attempts were made in the early and mid-twentieth century to deal with transnational markets (such as those for trafficked women and illegal drugs) through a series of international conventions. Few of these measures, however, had any teeth. Moreover, the issues were seen as separate from one another rather than as part of a larger whole in which criminal organizations operated in interlocking and reinforcing criminal markets. Re-

sponses were also inhibited because organized crime was viewed as a domestic problem with few if any implications for international governance or multilateral cooperation.

24. This section draws heavily on Dimitri Vlassis, "The United Nations Convention Against Transnational Organized Crime and Its Three Protocols," paper presented at Conference on International Organized Crime in the Global Century, All Souls College, Oxford, U.K., July 5–6, 2000. This paper provides an excellent overview of the negotiations in which Dimitri Vlassis was intimately involved.

25. Ibid.

26. Ibid.

27. Ibid.

28. The analysis in this paragraph draws heavily on Vlassis. Ibid.

29. The Protocol Against Illicit Manufacturing of and Trafficking in Firearms was not completely negotiated by December 2000 when the Convention was unveiled.

30. G-7/G-8 Senior Experts Group on Transnational Organized Crime, "G-7/G-8 Senior Experts Group Recommendations," Annex 4, Paris, 12 April 1996. Excerpts can be found in *Trends in Organized Crime* (Summer 1997), pp. 72–6.

31. This is a point emphasized by Vlassis, "The United Nations Convention."

32. Based in Paris (with the OECD), the FATF maintains an excellent, up-to-date web site that features its annual reports, news releases, and other publications. See <http://www.oecd.org/fatf/>. The following analysis draws heavily on the FATF documents provided on this site.

33. Know-your-customer regulations require banks to take steps to determine the identity of their customers and the sources of the customers' funds—and to report any activities that appear suspicious. The notion of due diligence is that banks should exhibit a reasonable degree of prudence in judgments about financial transactions.

34. The naming of names marked a new stage in the effort to establish an effective global anti–money laundering regime, although the FATF acknowledged in 1999 that ten years after its creation, "continued mobilization at the international level to deepen and widen the fight against money laundering" remained essential. *FATF-X*, Financial Action Task Force on Money Laundering, Annual Report 1998–1999 (Tokyo, July 2 1999), p. 40, available at <http://www.oecd.org/fatf/FATDocs_en.htm#Annual>.

35. The information in this section is drawn from the Interpol web site, <http://www.interpol.int>.

36. For a good, if rather critical, discussion of Interpol's role and legal status, see Paul Swallow, "Of Limited Operational Relevance: A European View of Interpol's Crime-Fighting Role in the Twenty-first Century," *Transnational Organized Crime* (Winter 1996), pp. 106–30.

37. This and the subsequent information on the organization can be found on its informative web site, <http://www.wcoomd.org>.

38. The Stockholm Congress was attended by more than 1,300 participants from 125 countries and included representatives from governments, intergovernmental organizations, and NGOs. The delegates formulated a declaration and agenda for action that provided guidelines for specific initiatives at the local, national, regional, and international levels. The agenda included the development and implementation not only of "comprehensive,

cross-sectoral and integrated strategies and measures" but also of monitoring mechanisms. Vitat Muntarbhorn, *World Congress Against Commercial Sexual Exploitation of Children: The Report of the Rapporteur-General,* Stockholm, Sweden, August 27–31, 1996, p. 4. Among the principles to guide the development of these strategies, the congress emphasized: the participation of the children themselves; the need for prevention through education and the creation of early warning systems; the protection of children through more effective laws against child trafficking, and child pornography, as well as the provision of hotlines, mobile services, and shelters; the recovery and reintegration of children; the collection and diffusion of information regarding all aspects of the problem and appropriate responses; and international cooperation at all levels. See *World Congress,* pp. 14–21.

39. Vlassis, "The United Nations Convention," p. 16. The analysis here draws heavily on Vlassis.

40. Article 6 of the 1979 Convention on the Elimination of All Forms of Discrimination Against Women.

41. *Sale of Children, Child Prostitution, and Child Pornography: Note by the Secretary-General,* General Assembly Document, Fifty-first Session, Agenda item 106, A/51/456/, 7 October 1996, p. 11.

42. Ibid., p. 13.

43. Ibid., p. 16.

44. Ibid., p. 24.

45. This theme was developed by Ernesto Savona in one of the background papers for the Naples World Ministerial Conference. See Phil Williams and Ernesto Savona, eds., *The United Nations and Transnational Organized Crime* (London: Cass, 1995).

46. For an analysis of advance fee frauds, also known as 4-1-9 fraud, see "Prepared Statement of Mr. Dana Brown, Deputy Special Agent-in-charge, Financial Crimes Division, United States Secret Service, at Hearing on Financial Instruments Fraud," *Senate Banking, Housing, and Urban Affairs Committee,* September 16, 1997, available at <http://iafci.org/nf/news/articles/970916hearing.htm>.

47. Operation Green Ice was an undercover or sting operation involving law enforcement agencies from Canada, the Cayman Islands, Colombia, Costa Rica, Great Britain, Italy, Spain, and the United States. The Drug Enforcement Administration used undercover agents to launder money for Cali drug trafficking organizations and used the information they obtained to attack the financial infrastructure of these organizations and to seize over $50 million of their assets.

48. This is one of the main themes developed in John Arquilla and David Ronfeldt, eds., *In Athena's Camp* (Santa Monica, Calif.: RAND, 1997).

49. The insights offered by Andreas can be found in Friman and Andreas, *The Illicit Global Economy.* They are developed most fully in Peter Andreas, *Border Games: Policing the U.S.-Mexico Divide* (Ithaca, N.Y.: Cornell University Press, 2000).

SUGGESTED ADDITIONAL READING

Andreas, Peter. *Border Games: Policing the US-Mexico Divide.* Ithaca, N.Y.: Cornell University Press, 2000.

Bayart, Jean-François, Stephen Ellis, and Béatrice Hibou. *The Criminalization of the State in Africa*. Bloomington, Ind.: Indiana University Press, 1999.

Blum, Jack, Michael Levi, R. Thomas Naylor, and Phil Williams. *Financial Havens, Bank Secrecy and Money Laundering*. New York: United Nations, 1999.

Bovenkerk, Frank. "Crime and the Multi-ethnic Society: A View from Europe." *Crime, Law and Social Change*, vol. 19 (1993), pp. 271–80.

Chin, Ko-lin. *Chinese Subculture and Criminality: Non-traditional Crime Groups in America*. New York: Greenwood Press, 1990.

Finckenauer, James, and Elin Waring. *Russian Mafia in America: Immigration, Culture, and Crime*. Boston, Mass.: Northeastern University Press, 1998.

Friman, H. Richard, and Peter Andreas. "Introduction: International Relations and the Illicit Global Economy." In H. Richard Friman and Peter Andreas, eds., *The Illicit Global Economy and State Power*. Lanham, Md.: Rowman and Littlefield, 1999.

Kleinknecht, William. *The New Ethnic Mobs: The Changing Face of Organized Crime in America*. New York: The Free Press, 1996.

Kurtzman, Joel. *The Death of Money*. New York: Simon and Schuster, 1993.

Less, Rensselaer W. *Smuggling Armageddon: The Nuclear Black Market in the Former Soviet Union and Europe*. New York: St. Martin's Press, 1998.

Robinson, Jeffrey. *The Merger*. New York: Outlook Press, 2000.

Williams, Phil. "Emerging Issues: Transnational Crime and Its Control." In Graeme Newman, ed., *Global Report on Crime and Justice*. Published for the United Nations Office for Drug Control and Crime Prevention, Center for International Crime Prevention. New York: Oxford University Press, 1999, pp. 221–42.

Williams, Phil, ed. *Illegal Immigration and Commercial Sex: The New Slave Trade*. London: Frank Cass, 1999.

Winer, Jonathan M. "International Crime in the New Geopolitics: A Core Threat to Democracy." In William F. McDonald, ed., *Crime and Law Enforcement in the Global Village*. Cincinnati, Ohio: Anderson Publishing Company, 1997.

Internet Sites

Organization for Economic Cooperation and Development (OECD), Financial Action Task Force on Money Laundering (FATF) <http://www.oecd.org/fatf>

World Customs Organization (WCO) <http://www.wcoomd.org>

Interpol <http://www.interpol.int>

4

Development Assistance

Catherine Gwin

INTERNATIONAL DEVELOPMENT ASSISTANCE is a post–World War II phenomenon. In the aftermath of the Great Depression and the massive destruction of a second world war in less than a half-century, governments agreed to reform the international economic system and, through processes of international cooperation, lay the foundation for a new era of international peace supported by economic stability and growth. The innovation of financial and technical assistance, provided by nations in support of reconstruction and renewed growth, was one of the central pillars of the postwar international architecture.

The International Monetary Fund (IMF), the International Bank for Reconstruction and Development (IBRD, subsequently referred to as the World Bank), and the General Agreement on Tariffs and Trade (GATT) were established to advance the new economic order. The founders had two dominant concerns: to encourage rapid postwar recovery and to prevent a return to the "beggar thy neighbor" policies of the 1920s and 1930s involving closed trading blocs and competitive exchange rates that were seen in retrospect as major contributors to depression and war.

The creation of the United Nations further established international development assistance as a responsibility of the international community. As stated in the preamble of the UN Charter, one of the four aims of the institution was "to promote social progress and better standards of life in larger freedom." To this end, member governments committed themselves "to employ international machinery for the promotion of the economic and social advancement of all peoples."

At the outset, international development assistance was viewed as a transitional need. That is, aid for reconstruction and development was designed to cover the limited period of time expected for wartorn countries to get back on their feet and for international capital markets to return to a pre-1930s pattern of widespread lending. Circumstances quickly altered this expectation, however. First, postwar reconstruction needs exceeded the resources of the newly created IBRD. Perceiving a rising communist threat in key European countries, the United States initiated the massive Marshall Plan as a separate bilateral aid program for Europe. Second, the onset of the Cold War stimulated a globalization of the U.S. aid effort—motivated by the notion that "underdevelopment" provided conditions conducive to the spread of communism and that Western support of countries' economic growth and development could serve as an important countermeasure. Third, the rapid decolonization of large numbers of countries in the 1960s increased the number of independent member governments in the new international institutions and, with that, demands for a broader development assistance effort. Moreover, these circumstances made clear that the challenges of development were not only larger and longer term but also far more complex than initially perceived. As a result, both the rationale for development assistance and its size and scope changed markedly in the first two decades after World War II. Ideas about development and how best to provide development aid have continuously evolved since then.

Some fifty years after the advent of international development aid, enormous improvements have been made in the standard of living around the world. All of the postwar European recipients of aid have become major donors, and a number of developing countries have joined their ranks. Yet needs for international assistance remain. More than 1 billion of the world's 6 billion people live in conditions of absolute poverty. Even as the phenomenon referred to as "globalization" offers increasing opportunities for worldwide access to capital, technology, and ideas, many of these absolute poor are at risk of being left behind.

Moreover, since 1980 more than fifty countries (most of them low-income developing countries) have experienced significant periods of conflict, with some resulting in complete breakdown of the state and massive needs for assistance in postconflict reconstruction. Fifteen of the twenty poorest countries have experienced major conflict in the past fifteen years.[1] At the same time, former Soviet bloc nations have sought aid to meet their needs. Intermittent financial crises in one or another developing country have required international action to contain the spread of economic turmoil, and in recent years a host of global health, environmental, and other problems has created needs for new international assistance efforts.

Clearly, the eradication of mass poverty and achievement of sustainable development are primarily the responsibility of individual countries. Evidence shows, moreover, that countries' own efforts are by far the most important determinants of the overall success or failure of development programs. The promotion of development is nonetheless a core global problem for at least three reasons. First, extreme deprivation and economic disparity are an ethical issue that knows no boundaries. This is a principle embedded in the UN Charter, which stems from the recognition that concerns with the human condition are not divisible in the modern world. Second, development (or the lack thereof) has important positive (or negative) spillover effects on other countries—manifest in such things as the control of the spread of disease, the potential economic opportunity gains of more efficient production, and reduced pressures of both population growth and refugee flows. Third, development is an essential underpinning for the solution of many other global problems, which depend on the interest and capacity of poor countries to engage effectively in shared problem solving.

The provision of official development assistance (ODA) is not the only way that external actors affect the development of poor countries. International markets now account for more than $250 billion of private capital flows to developing countries annually, as compared to $50 billion in ODA (see figure 4-1). Access to markets in goods and services is one of the more powerful inducements to economic growth, the reduction of poverty, and structural change in developing societies. This makes it difficult to isolate the effects of aid on development. Moreover, the political and commercial interests of donor countries have always weighed heavily in their decisions regarding the allocation of aid—development impact not always being the primary concern.

The use of multilateral institutions for the mobilization and provision of aid has somewhat mitigated the distorting effects of donor countries' nondevelopmental objectives. But multilateral programs have not eliminated these effects, for two reasons. First, bilateral aid—that is, assistance provided by a donor country directly to recipient countries—still accounts for more than half of all development aid, despite the buildup of numerous multilateral aid programs over the years. Second, member governments provide the resource base and set the policies of the multilateral institutions. Still, the stated objective of the multilateral assistance system has been development, and this chapter addresses the record of the management of that objective.[2]

Unlike most other areas of global management, development assistance is a resource-based domain of cooperation. It is fundamentally about the mobilization and allocation of resources (financial, technical, and informational) from "haves" to "have-nots." In that sense, it differs from other areas of global management that are more rule based (such as trade) or norm based (such as human rights).

This is not to say that rules and norms are absent from development assistance. Donor governments have agreed on certain principles of international aid procurement, for example. The multilateral development institutions operate under specific articles of agreement and resource allocation policies. Moreover, the coordination of governments' actions is a factor of aid effectiveness. Yet development aid has rarely taken the form of negotiated support for a specific, international objective, and lack of adequate coordination has been a perennial weakness. International assistance may move toward a more coordinated, rules- and norms-based system if it is sustained beyond the next ten to fifteen years. The traditional approach to aid, focused on an individual country's development challenges, would then shift to an approach focused instead on the provision of specific international public goods (such as devel-

Figure 4-1. *Net capital flows to developing countries, 1985–2000*
Billions of Dollars

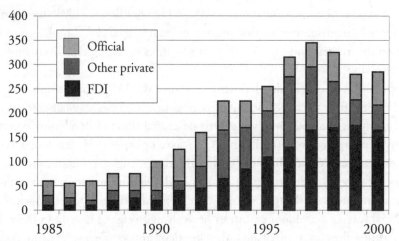

Note: Amounts for 2000 are estimated.

Source: Global Economic Prospects and the Developing Countries 2001 (Washington, D.C. World Bank, 2000). Available at <http://www.worldbank.org/prospects/gep2001/chapt1.pdf>.

opment of an AIDS vaccine, international efforts to stem drug trafficking or the spread of financial crises, or prevention of environmental degradation).

Development aid is therefore defined here as a weak form of global management. Yet it is at the forefront of the management of global problems in many regards. First, promotion of development has been for the last fifty years the area that has garnered the largest continuous mobilization of public resources from one group of countries for use by another group. Second, development aid has given rise to a host of institutional arrangements, policies, and instruments and to public-private partnerships that have been trendsetters with relevance for cooperation on other global problems. Third, the international promotion of development has pioneered the move in international relations to engage in activities previously thought to be within the sovereign domain of national governments.

This chapter seeks to elaborate on this view of development assistance as a relatively weak but nonetheless innovative and significant tool of global management. It begins with a brief discussion of the development challenge and the evolving international responses to it over the last half-century. This discussion highlights four key features of the international development assistance system that have shaped both the delivery of aid and aid's effectiveness.

Against this background, the chapter reviews the record of multilateral development assistance. The story is complex, affected by many factors including shifting trends in global economics and politics, and highly varied performance of donors and recipient countries. It will be possible, therefore, to make only broad summary observations.

The main lesson is that aid can—but does not automatically—contribute to development. What determines effectiveness is that aid be: (1) provided by donors and used by recipients for development purposes; (2) allocated to countries in accordance not only with their level of need but also their demonstrated commitment to sound development policies and transparent accountable governance procedures; (3) provided in support of country-led national development strategies rather than donor-driven country assistance programs; (4) implemented in ways supportive of the long-term and comprehensive nature of development and the consensus building and institutional development in recipient countries required to sustain structural reforms and societal changes; (5) tailored to individual countries' political as well as economic conditions and to realistic objectives; (6) coordinated among donors to avoid not only wasteful duplication but also excessive administrative burdens on countries' limited public sector capacities; and (7) focused on achieving specified results. It has also become increasingly clear that there are reasons to extend the focus of development assistance beyond traditional country-based efforts to the provision of international public goods—for example, international agricultural research, development of an AIDS vaccine, and the development of regional economic integration agreements. Although these lessons may seem obvious, the management of development aid to date has not fully exemplified them, which accounts in large part for aid's mixed record of success.

DEVELOPMENT CHALLENGE AND RESPONSES TO IT

There is no one right way for countries to develop; their natural resources, underlying economic conditions, and particular constellation of social forces and political tendencies determine the strategies followed and the trade-offs made. As a result, there has been considerable diversity in development experiences, with some countries managing the process more successfully than others. This record has led to a range of "best practices" in development policies. But beyond certain fundamentals—macroeconomic stability, social sector investment, and "good governance"—one country's experience is at best an imperfect guide for any other.

In support of countries' national efforts, international development assistance has involved the financing of specific projects; the provision of general balance of payments and budget support, technical assistance, and policy advice; and the dissemination of wide-ranging information on development issues. The general rationale for this assistance is that the development it promotes contributes to world economic growth and political stability and is thereby of mutual benefit to donors and recipients.

Although this cooperation may sound straightforward in principle, it has been anything but that in practice. Development has been more challenging and development assistance more difficult and controversial than could possibly have been anticipated from the outset. How individual countries have responded to their own development challenges has been the primary determinant of progress made. Nevertheless, four key features of the international development assistance system have significantly influenced aid's record of effectiveness: (1) the mix of motives on the part of both donor and recipient governments that has affected their uses of development aid; (2) the continuous change in concepts of development and ideas about aid; (3) the asymmetrical and decentralized structure of the aid system; and (4) the intergovernmental nature of development assistance.

Mixed Motives

The development impact of aid would have undoubtedly been stronger had both donor and recipient governments not used aid resources to support a variety of purposes: domestic and international political aims, public and private economic interests, social divisions and conflicts, and public officials' pursuit of private gain. This mix has affected the size, allocation, and uses of aid in ways often less than optimal from a development perspective.

Although humanitarian concerns have always played a role in sustaining public support for aid and shaping the content of donors' aid programs, diplomatic and commercial interests have dominated decisions on the allocation of aid resources. As a result, the bulk of aid flows have not gone to the best-performing developing country governments or to the most needy.[3] Instead, donors have provided large amounts of aid to countries with governments only weakly committed to development. For example, despite its poor development record, Zaire was a major aid recipient through most of the Cold War because of its perceived strategic importance to the West; Latin American dictators of the 1960s were prominent aid recipients despite their human rights abuses; and mineral-rich countries tended to attract more outside aid than those that were resource poor. This mix of motives has also sustained a preference in most donor countries for bilateral aid over aid channeled through the multilateral agencies.

Moreover, because development has been for donors the proximate but not the ultimate goal in the provision of aid, the actual size of aid flows has always been small relative to the scope and complexity of the development challenge. At its height, aid from the U.S. Marshall Plan amounted to some 5 percent of U.S. gross national product (GNP). Although aid levels from the United States and other donor countries grew in absolute amounts from that time through the early 1990s, they have never again amounted to such a large percentage of donor countries' GNP.

As a part of the "United Nations Second Development Decade" of the 1970s, donor countries formally accepted an aid target of 0.7 percent of gross domestic product (GDP), but only a few, small donors have ever come close that to level, and in 1997 the figure for all donor countries combined was only 0.22 percent As a result, aid has never contributed more than a small fraction to the total resources of any country (the notable exception being the very high level of aid dependence in Sub-Saharan Africa today). Moreover, from 1992 to 1997, aid flows declined in absolute amounts, even as rising numbers of poor people in the world, countries in transition, countries emerging from internal wars or other crises, and the intensification of concern over specific global problems have placed heavy new demands on international assistance funds. Since 1998, concessional aid flows have turned moderately upward. However, development aid in 2000 was still less than in the early 1990s and the recent increase has reflected some temporary factors (notably a rise in Japanese aid in response to the financial crisis in East Asia). (See table 4-1.)

A combination of strong social forces and political tendencies have driven recipient governments in their uses of aid. How well they have integrated aid into their national development strategies has therefore reflected varied (and often competing) objectives. There has been wide variation in the management of economic policies and significant differences in attention given to the development of public institutions—both key determinants of the effectiveness of aid. There have been differences in the pace and scope of opening the economy to trade and private investment; in patterns of public expenditures for such things as basic health and education; and in the emphasis given to agriculture and rural development relative to urban-based industrial development. Government officials have varied widely in their commitment to national development objectives as distinct from private or group gains. To the extent that these mixed motives have led to weak commitments to development on the part of donor and/or recipient governments, aid's development impact has been limited, if not counterproductive.

Evolving Concepts of Development and Aid

International development assistance has also reflected continuously evolving and sometimes sharply competing notions about development and aid. Indeed, development assistance, perhaps more than any other field of global management, has been based on constantly shifting intellectual sands.

Dominant theories of development have evolved through several phases since the economic development of poorer countries became an international concern.[4] Two main themes have predominated: ideas about what makes economies grow, and prevailing views regarding how best to reduce poverty. Changing ideas on both topics and their interrelationships have in turn shaped approaches to aid. In addition, in the last decade and a half, new concerns about environmental sustainability, gender equity, and governance have arisen not only as factors affecting growth and poverty reduction but also as causes in their own right.

Table 4-1. *Official Flows to Developing Countries by Type and Source, 1990-2000*
(US$ billion)

	1990	1991	1992	1993	1994	1995	1996	1997	1998	1999	2000[a]
Official development finance	55.2	60.9	56.5	53.6	48.0	55.1	31.9	42.8	54.6	45.3	47.1
Official development assistance	43.2	49.5	46.4	41.7	48.1	46.2	39.7	35.6	38.4	40.3	41.6
Grants (excluding technical cooperation grants)	28.2	35.1	30.5	28.3	32.7	32.7	28.1	26.1	27.3	28.9	29.6
Bilateral	24.6	29.5	23.9	22.5	24.6	26.1	21.8	19.8	20.5	22.0	22.6
Multilateral	3.6	5.6	6.6	5.8	7.9	6.6	6.3	6.3	6.8	6.9	7.0
Concessional loans	15.0	14.4	15.9	13.4	15.4	13.5	11.6	9.5	11.1	11.4	11.7
Bilateral	8.3	6.3	8.5	6.7	6.5	4.9	3.0	1.5	3.1	4.3	5.1
Multilateral	6.7	8.1	7.4	6.7	8.9	8.6	8.6	8.0	8.2	7.1	6.6
Nonconcessional loans	12.0	11.4	10.1	11.9	-0.1	8.9	-7.8	7.2	16.2	5.0	5.5
Bilateral	2.9	3.9	4.5	3.5	-2.6	5.2	-12.4	-6.5	-4.4	-7.1	-5.5
Multilateral	9.1	7.5	5.6	8.4	2.5	3.7	4.6	13.7	20.6	12.1	11.0
Memo items											
International Monetary Fund	0.1	3.2	1.1	2.6	1.6	16.8	1.2	14.7	19.3	-12.6	…
Technical cooperation grants	14.1	15.6	17.7	18.2	16.9	20.0	18.7	15.7	16.2	16.6	17.1

a. Estimate.
Note: Inflows of debt are net of amortization payments. For this reason, these flows are sometimes referred to as "net" resource flows.
Source: World Bank, *Global Development Finance* (Washington, D.C.: World Bank, 2001), ch. 4.

In the 1950s and 1960s, economic thinking emphasized the accumulation of capital as the engine of growth. Growth in turn was viewed as the key to poverty reduction. A large public sector was seen as the essential counter to weak markets and inadequate private sector forces. Except for possible inefficiencies in resource allocations (which it was assumed could be resolved through dynamic government planning), developing countries and the problems confronting them were portrayed early on as identical to more developed countries and their challenges. Thus much early development assistance mainly took the form of "nonconcessional" (or near–market rate) loans, and the focus of most of this lending was on large-scale infrastructure.

By the early 1960s experience had led to the beginnings of change in this thinking. Two events in particular played major roles. A foreign exchange crisis in India in 1958 made it clear that poor countries could not manage the burden of debt that resulted from nonconcessional borrowing on the scales required. The subsequent Indian food crisis in 1960 underscored the need for a broader development agenda, including explicit attention to agriculture and rural development.

By the end of the 1960s, confidence in the trickle-down approach to poverty reduction had waned because progress was so slow. Studies undertaken at the time showed that despite improved rates of economic growth, hundreds of millions of people in developing countries were still living in poverty, lacking safe drinking water, adequate nutrition, and access to basic health care and education. These conditions, it was argued, stifled productivity and kept earning capacity low, causing a self-perpetuating cycle of poverty. Poverty, which was concentrated in rural areas, persisted not only because of insufficient investment in agriculture and rural development, but also because of the absence of broad-based (that is, labor-intensive) growth and social sector development that extended education and health to the poor. The findings concluded that although growth was necessary, it was not sufficient to reduce poverty in any reasonable period of time.

In the early 1970s, the United States and other bilateral donors turned to more proactive approaches to combating poverty, through the direct address of "basic human needs." By mid-decade, the World Bank began to devote much more analysis and lending to direct efforts to reduce poverty and promote "pro-poor growth." Accordingly, the development assistance agenda broadened to include greater attention not only to agricultural and rural development but also to family planning, education, health, water, and sanitation. Still, aid continued to take the form largely of project financing, together with associated technical assistance.

At the same time, however, a deep rift began to appear in ideas about promoting and sustaining growth. Through the 1960s and into the 1970s, state-led development strategies and inward-looking (import-substitution) policies held sway in many countries throughout the developing world. For a time, these policies achieved high rates of growth; but the global recession of the late 1970s halted the state-led investment boom; and numerous countries, especially in Latin America and Africa, began a descent into economic stagnation, prolonged by the debt crisis of the 1980s. While developing country governments tended to blame international economic events for their troubles, development researchers and practitioners in Europe and the United States were becoming increasingly critical of the policies and practices of these governments.

Thus, by the early 1980s, even before the international debt crisis broke, the World Bank (and subsequently other multilateral donors) began to offer a new form of nonproject aid, conditioned on recipient governments' adoption of macroeconomic policy reforms. Mexico's default on its external debt in 1982 and the debt crisis that followed focused attention still more sharply on macroeconomic stabilization measures and the need for liberalization, especially of financial markets and trade. The design of macroeconomic reforms emphasized market-based policy fundamentals, including fiscal discipline; market-determined prices, interest rates, and exchange rates; and trade liberalization. This approach reflected many influences, including the steady growth of the East Asian countries in contrast to the chronic inflationary pressures and populist cycles in Latin America and stagnation in Sub-Saharan Africa.

This paradigm initially provoked bitter controversy and resistance. In most developing countries, it challenged long-established ideological leanings and threatened deeply entrenched political and economic interests. Yet in the course of the 1980s and early 1990s, its core elements gradually prevailed, including acceptance of a limited public sector role in direct economic activities (though differences remained on the particulars of such issues as financial and regulatory reform, industrial policy, and privatization). This so-called Washington consensus was strengthened by failed alternative attempts to stabilize and resume growth (for example, in Brazil and Peru), by the increasingly impressive economic performance of Chile, and most dramatically by the collapse of communism in the Soviet Union and Eastern Europe.

Economic growth did not, however, ensue as quickly or as strongly as envisioned in countries that undertook reforms; and many other countries got bogged down in incomplete reform efforts. Both circumstances led to still further new thinking on development and aid. Whereas rhetoric in the mid-1980s supported the idea that "government is best that governs least," by the mid-1990s the World Bank and other aid agencies were beginning to emphasize good governance as an element in promoting growth and reform.

In the first few years of the debt crisis, overriding preoccupation with restoring international financial stability had sidelined poverty concerns in many developing countries and in their interactions with the international financial institutions (IFIs). As it became clear that stabilization and structural adjustment would take years, and as the social costs of protracted economic crisis became painfully evident, pressures grew—especially from nongovernmental organizations (NGOs) within and outside reforming countries and from the UN Children's Fund (UNICEF)—for adjustment programs to build in safety-net programs to protect the most vulnerable groups. Although this initial return to poverty concerns was limited primarily to measures to deal with the short-term costs of adjustment, by the early 1990s it had become apparent that despite modest (and in some cases robust) revival of economic growth, poverty remained pervasive. This recognition returned poverty reduction to the center of development efforts—built around a new approach focused on both increasing poor people's access to basic social services (education, health, water, and sanitation) and encouraging more labor-intensive growth. Over the course of the 1990s, more attention was also focused on the impact of existing or increasing inequalities as an impediment to poverty reduction and sustained growth. Moreover, development advocates began to stress gender equity as an essential component of development, in recognition that women make up the majority of the poor in the developing world.

Beginning in the mid-1980s, environmental sustainability had moved onto the development agenda. Although this new concern led to a fairly rapid buildup of aid programs aimed at environmental protection, the much broader concept of sustainability has yet to be fully reconciled with the objectives of either growth or poverty reduction, and there is much debate within the intellectual and policy community over how this reconciliation should be achieved.

Comparative successes and failures among developing countries are one set of factors that have provoked changes in development thinking over the years. The successful development experience of the so-called East Asian tigers in the late 1970s to mid-1990s, for example, encouraged increasing emphasis on both social sector investment and more export-oriented economic policies.

In addition, the international political and economic context for development cooperation has been fundamentally altered by the end of the Cold War (and the collapse of the socialist model) and by accelerated global economic integration. On the positive side, both developments have reinforced trends toward economic liberalization and democratization already under way within an increasing number of developing countries. On the negative side, however, the changes in context have also heightened political instability and increased economic risk and inequality. The benefits and the harmful effects of globalization are provoking still further debate about strategies of development and uses of aid.[5]

Along the way, the aid relationship between donors and recipients has changed dramatically. Aid programs have become involved in activities previously viewed as the domestic affairs of recipient countries, and aid agencies have become engaged with a wider array of domestic actors. With these changes, weaknesses in the nature of the aid relationship have become the focus of explicit attention in the search for more effective practices. This constant churning has brought much positive innovation. It has also fueled tensions between donors and recipients as the rules of the game have shifted; led to "mission creep" on the part of virtually all aid agencies as each sought to remain relevant to a constantly changing agenda; and impeded coordination among donor institutions that have emphasized different notions about development and the best ways of supporting it.

Asymmetry and Decentralization in the International Aid System

The highly asymmetrical and decentralized structure of the international aid system reflects the fact that aid comes from voluntary contributions of multiple donor countries. There are no automatic sources of finance—for example, funds provided by international taxes or fees—nor any formally agreed requirements for periodic appropriations. As a result, donor governments dominate the management of international development assistance through the power of the purse. Moreover, each donor country decides individually on the level of its annual aid flows, sets its own aid policies, and determines its allocation of resources among countries and between its own bilateral aid agency(ies) and the various multilateral development institutions.

The resulting asymmetry between donor and recipient countries in the governance of international development aid is moderated to some extent by the channeling of some resources through multilateral institutions, which have governing boards composed of representatives of all member countries. International goals on aid levels and objectives have often been set through the deliberations of these institutions, and their broad membership has enabled them to serve as forums for debating ideas, seeking consensus, and setting international norms.

Still, decisions taken by the multilateral institutions must be broadly consistent with donor country perspectives and interests. In general, it is true that the larger the donor, the larger the voice, regardless of formal decision-making procedures.[6] Moreover, different multilateral development agencies operate on the basis of different voting structures, and donor countries have historically vested more resources and more responsibility in those institutions (such as the World Bank) in which their votes are more heavily weighted. In addition, donor governments expressly use multilateral aid "pledging" negotiations as occasions for advancing their agendas.

Donor preferences have also led to a plethora of international development agencies and programs. Both within and among donor countries, competing interests have exerted strong influence over the allocation of international aid resources. To maintain a broad base of public support, funding has been directed to multiple areas of emphasis.

At the outset, the United States was by far the dominant donor. As demands for development aid expanded, it supported the creation of new international agencies as a way to involve other developed countries in the provision of aid. The global politics of the 1950s and 1960s contributed further to a decentralized system, producing a rift between the United Nations (with its universal membership and governance rule of one country/one vote) and the Bretton Woods institutions (dominated by the West as a result of the early withdrawal of the Soviet Union and a system of voting weighted by member countries' positions in the world economy). The rift reflected the two international fault lines of the times: between the noncommunist developed countries of the so-called West and the Soviet empire of the East, and between the developed countries of the North and the developing countries of the South. Nothing better exemplifies the impact of these two divides on the system of international development assistance than the near simultaneous creation of the International Development Association (IDA) as an affiliate of the World Bank and what became over time the UN Development Program (UNDP).

This fragmentation has allowed recipients to play one donor agency against another. In the absence of a single path to development, many observers endorse the pluralism in the system ensured by the many separate aid agencies. The asymmetry and decentralization in the international aid system, however, have limited aid's development effectiveness.

Intergovernmental Character of Aid

Most aid channeled through bilateral and multilateral agencies has been intergovernmental. It has involved official resource transfers from governments or from intergovernmental institutions to government entities in recipient countries. This intergovernmental process prevails even though aid deals with issues that are by definition domestic and that require the participation of not only government officials but nonstate actors as well.

This official character of aid reflects that aid monies are public funds, appropriated through regular budgetary processes in donor countries. Aid agencies are obligated to account for the uses to which these public resources are put. Private voluntary contributions, raised by a wide variety of NGOs, complement ODA. However, the total private contribution has amounted to only a small fraction of total ODA.

Especially in the 1990s, as the development agenda has focused more sharply on poverty reduction and broadened to include issues of social sector and private sector development and environmental sustainability, aid agencies have come to rely more on NGOs to implement aid programs. Still, most aid is transferred through public agencies (bilateral and multilateral) to or through government agencies in recipient countries. And in the case of the World Bank and the regional development banks, a recipient government must guarantee the loans even if the investment activity is carried out by a nongovernmental entity.

This intergovernmental character of aid has been consistent with the dominant rationale for aid as an instrument of donor country foreign policy and the initial thinking about development as a process driven by government. Aid has therefore been managed through the public sector and largely focused on public sector activities in developing countries. In the 1990s, this feature began to change for two principal reasons: the shift in development strategy to a more market-based approach, which gives increased recognition to the private sector as an engine of development; and the spread of democratic processes in an increasing number of recipient countries, which has brought with it an increasing role for civil society organizations. Still, current analyses show that aid effectiveness remains limited by the failure of both official aid agencies and recipient country governments to deal adequately with nonstate actors in the design and implementation of development policies, programs, and projects.

TRACK RECORD

Not surprisingly, the overall record of aid in support of development has been mixed. There has been impressive progress throughout the developing world over the past half century, and especially in the last twenty-five to thirty years. In the 1990s alone, rich countries voluntarily contributed more than $500 billion of ODA to poorer countries, and a number of onetime major recipients have joined the ranks of donors. These facts alone are indications of success. Moreover, the majority of aid projects evaluated over the years have achieved their objectives. Accompanying this broad record of success, however, have been major problems, and alongside effective programs have been discouraging failures.

Progress and Remaining Challenges

Over the past generation, more has been done to reduce poverty and raise the quality of life than during any equivalent period of time in history. Since 1960, infant mortality rates have been cut in half, and life expectancy has increased from fifty-five to sixty-four years. Per capita food production and consumption have risen by 20 percent. The percentage of the population with access to clean water has doubled to 70 percent. Child malnutrition rates have declined by almost one-third. Primary school enrollment has reached almost 80 percent, and gender disparities have narrowed. Adult literacy has also risen from less than half to more than two-thirds.[7] Developing countries as a group are also more integrated into the world economy than they were only two decades ago. Flows of private investment capital to the developing countries as a whole increased fivefold since 1990 alone. And developing countries' access to markets for goods, services, and knowledge has expanded greatly.

But progress has been uneven, and major challenges remain. The 1980s, which came to be called the "lost decade of development," were a period of marked economic decline. Countries that carried through on reforms saw a return of reasonable rates of economic growth and investment by the mid-1990s, but others that followed a more erratic approach have yet to recover fully. Moreover, the financial crisis of the late 1990s temporarily set back even the most successful developing countries of East and Southeast Asia.

Even more troubling, in today's high-tech world of increasing wealth, an estimated 3 billion people live on less than $2 a day, and 1.3 billion live on less than $1. Moreover, progress toward reducing poverty during the past decade has been very disappointing. Although the proportion of the world's population living in poverty has declined, the number of poor people has increased. In South Asia, where about half of the world's poor live, India and Bangladesh have made only modest gains in reducing the number of poor (although the proportion of absolute poor in the population has declined), and Pakistan probably has made no gains at all. Across Sub-Saharan Africa, growth in per capita GDP turned positive for some countries in the second half of the decade, but other countries were embroiled in violent conflicts; and there has been no significant decline in poverty rates. Among the poor transitional economies, economic recovery has not yet begun, and poverty rates have increased sharply. The 1997–1998 financial crisis in East Asia returned numbers of people there to the ranks of the poorest. Among large countries, only China has succeeded during this decade in achieving a significant decrease in the number of its poor.

The record is less bleak in terms of social indicators than in terms of income. But by either measure, developing countries, especially those in Africa, have fallen far short both of the achievements in East Asia prior to the 1997 crisis and of hopes at the beginning of the decade. In 1990 the World Bank projected that if a strategy of pro-poor growth combined with public investment to increase access to social services for the poor were followed in developing countries, the number of poor in 2000 would decline to some 825 million, but it is now expected that the number will be closer to 1.4 billion.[8]

Aid's Impact on Development

Assessing the impact of aid on developing countries' progress is a complicated (and controversial) matter. The lack of a strong commitment to development on the part of both donors and some recipient governments, the small size of aid relative to the problems it aims to affect, and the long-term nature of the development process make it difficult to assess aid's development impact.

Nonetheless, it is possible to cite some notable examples of where aid has had a transforming effect, such as the green revolution that greatly increased agricultural yields in South Asia and the spread of family planning practices worldwide. Aid programs have also helped to reduce the prevalence of diseases such as river blindness and polio, and vastly expanded immunization against childhood diseases. In some instances, aid has made important contributions to policy reform and helped to improve public sector management. For example, adjustment assistance supported trade policy liberalization in Latin America and accelerated transition in some of the former Soviet republics in the 1980s and 1990s. Botswana and the Republic of Korea in the 1960s, Indonesia in the 1970s, and Uganda, Mozambique, and Vietnam in the 1990s are examples of countries that have gone from crisis to accelerated development. Aid played a significant role in each case, contributing ideas, training for public officials, and finance in support of reforms, improvements in public services, and a rebuilding of infrastructure.

At the same time, many aid programs either failed to achieve their goals or had a negative impact. It is therefore useful to look beyond the anecdotal evidence to more comprehensive assessments of what has worked, what has not, and why.

For most of the first forty years, reviews of aid focused on two things: (1) the content of the development strategy being pursued, especially the adequacy of the "growth model" at the heart of the early development and aid policy designs; and (2) the effectiveness of aid delivery mechanisms and how best to design and implement aid projects to ensure a satisfactory economic rate of return on investments. The last decade and a half, however, has witnessed a more profound questioning of aid effectiveness that has focused directly on the aid relationship itself—that is, the interactions of donors and recipients and their impact on the effectiveness of aid in promoting development.

The 1986 study *Does Aid Work?* was the first comprehensive assessment of aid. Looking at both bilateral and multilateral aid, the study concluded that most aid does indeed work: it succeeds in achieving its development objectives, contributing positively to recipient countries' economic performance and not substituting for activities that would have occurred anyway. But the study went on to say that aid had not worked in every instance and that its performance depended on both the aid provided and the policies of the recipient countries—a collaboration in which aid is definitely the junior partner.[9]

The reasons for failures, where they occurred, had to do with actions of both donors and recipients. On the donor side, problems arose from the intrusion of commercial or political motives; technically poor project designs resulting from both lack of attention to local conditions and an emphasis within aid agencies to the quantity rather than the quality of aid flows; and, less reprehensibly, the efforts by donors and recipients to do ambitious things in difficult circumstances. In the case of the recipients, both poor policies and weak administrative capacities were identified as major impediments to effective use of aid. These problems were exacerbated in countries where governments did not take keen interest in implementing aid projects or where there was excessive interest in prestige projects driven by nondevelopmental political or commercial considerations.

In the last ten years, a spate of additional aid effectiveness studies have reinforced and extended these findings—though their assessment of aid's impact on development is rather more sobering.[10] They show that although aid can promote development, it has not always done so. Indeed, a recent study relating aid flows to recipient country economic growth shows no systematic correlation, positive or negative.[11] Large flows of aid have not necessarily "bought more development," as supporters of aid would have one believe; nor have they automatically retarded development, as critics of aid on both the left and the right have argued for years. Rather, factors other than the size of aid flows have mattered to how constructive an impact aid has had—factors related to the performance of both donors and recipients.

One of those factors, emphasized even more strongly in the recent studies than in 1986, is the policy and institutional setting of the countries receiving aid. Aid works in good policy and institutional environments where governments are committed to reforms. Indeed, it has been estimated that under these conditions the effect of aid can be quite large: with the equivalent of 1 percent of GDP in assistance translating into a 1 percent decline in poverty.[12] But in a weak policy and institutional environment, external resources have had much less of a constructive impact (and some would argue have even done harm).

Yet aid has not succeeded for the most part in leveraging good policies. Efforts to "buy" policy improvements in recipient countries where there has been no active commitment to reform and institutional strengthening have typically failed. One reason is that aid allocations by donors have not adequately rewarded good policy performance. That is, neither the rewards for good performance nor the punishments for poor performance have been strong enough to make a difference in cases of reluctant reformers. How aid has succeeded in encouraging sustained policy change, most analyses suggest, is through the power of ideas (such as policy dialogue) backed by resources and the time it takes for learning by doing.

Any number of reasons explain why aid allocations have not been reflected in recipient country performance. As noted above, donors have sometimes chosen, for diplomatic reasons, to provide large amounts of aid to governments with little demonstrated commitment to development. Donor agencies have also been driven by internal factors, including pressures to disburse funds so as not to lose subsequent budget allocations and, especially in the case of the IFIs, to lend "defensively" to prevent countries from falling into arrears or defaulting on their accumulated debt. These pressures have tended to create a pretense of good performance where it has not existed. In contrast, where reforms have been implemented and sustained, recipient country "ownership" of the reform process, not conditional aid, has been key.

Yet numerous practices of aid agencies undermine rather than enhance the capacity to manage aid in recipient countries that is required if aid programs are to be implemented successfully. These practices persist not because donors and recipients lack awareness of the problems, but because they have not yet resolved several basic dilemmas, including: (1) the difficulties poor countries face in absorbing needed economic aid in the absence of adequate institutions; (2) the fact that program aid (that is, aid not tied to a single project), introduced to support policy reforms and ease absorptive problems, has tended to require even more local capacity than project aid; (3) the incompatibility between giving control to donor aid agendas, which seek quantifiable results, and building local ownership; and (4) the tendency of large amounts of aid, intended to promote sustainable progress, to induce a sense of passivity on the part of recipient officials.[13]

Although studies differ on whether high levels of aid, in and of themselves, are inherently a problem, they generally agree that donors have played too large and recipients too small a role in the design and management of aid; donor agencies have been too driven by pressures to "move money" and have often acted in too much haste; aid programs have often been excessively complex, overly ambitious, and insufficiently focused on institutional strengthening and other forms of capacity building. Moreover, programs have been weakly coordinated at best; they have not held recipient governments sufficiently accountable for the efficient use of funds; and neither donors nor recipients have, until recently, adequately acknowledged the importance of good governance as an underpinning of development success.

Roles of the Different Multilateral Aid Institutions

Within this overall record, a plethora of international aid institutions have demonstrated a wide variety of strengths and weaknesses. The main multilateral aid institutions include: the UN funds and programs; the IFIs (that is, the IMF, World Bank, and regional development banks for Africa, Asia, and Latin America); the aid program of the European Union; and certain special-purpose organizations, including a number of coordinating mechanisms. In addition, there are more than twenty major bilateral aid programs, which are referred to in this assessment only where comparisons with the multilateral agencies are particularly significant.

In reviewing the track record of these institutions, three points warrant highlighting. First, multilateral and bilateral aid agencies exhibit distinct comparative advantages. The bilaterals, which provide the greater share of total aid, tend to have particular knowledge based on historical ties with particular recipients. Most also have expertise in specific areas of development to which they have devoted particular attention, which is often superior to that of the multilaterals—or at least in advance of them. This was true for many years of the U.S. Agency for International Development's population programs and of Swedish aid's support for gender equity. Moreover, bilaterals tend to take the lead in new areas of development assistance, ahead of the establishment of broad international consensus. Often their early support paves the way for the multilateral agencies to expand consensus and financing for a new issue.

Further, that they are seen to be serving national purposes promotes public support for aid as a whole.

Nonetheless, multilateral aid agencies have been expanded over the years in large part to redress deficiencies in bilateral aid. As aid statistics show, multilateral aid makes the allocation of aid among countries more development-oriented and more supportive of poor countries. The international membership of multilateral agencies makes them better able to carry out policy dialogues on sensitive issues such as macroeconomic policy and social sector reforms. The channeling of aid resources through multilateral agencies has led to norms of procurement and other best-practice procedures of aid delivery. Last but not least, the multilateral agencies offer a unique economy of scale in the provision of aid to poor countries. The multilateral development banks (MDBs) in particular have created a combined financial, analytic, and technical capacity that greatly exceeds what could be offered effectively by the sum of individual bilateral donor agencies. Not only are they able to provide a mix of financial assistance (in the form of loans, guarantees, and on a more limited scale, grants), but also their finance is combined with economic and sector analysis of borrowing countries, advisory services, research, and information on best practices. Moreover, although the international organizations are not likely to take the lead on new issues, the substantive and geographic scope of MDB operations makes their accumulation of knowledge an unrivaled source on many issues.

A second point in reviewing the track record of multilateral aid institutions is that there are marked differences in the relative strengths and weaknesses of the different groups of multilateral aid institutions that reflect their differing mandates, governance structures, and institutional competencies. The key contrasts are between the UN development programs and the MDBs; the World Bank and the regional development banks (RDBs); and the World Bank and IMF in the area of structural adjustment lending. Space does not permit more than a summary discussion of these three pairings.

The United Nations and the MDBs. Differences between these development institutions were greater in the past, when MDB assistance was more narrowly focused on promoting economic growth primarily through infrastructure investment and membership was less than universal (because the centrally planned economies chose not to join). Still, four main differences persist today. First, the UN programs provide aid in the form of grants, and the MDBs primarily (though not exclusively) provide loans. This has enabled the United Nations to support capacity-building and institution-building activities for which recipients have been reluctant to borrow money on any significant scale. But the overall scale of MDB financial assistance far exceeds that of the United Nations, and the MDBs are more able to leverage their lending through cofinancing with national entities (such as export-import banks and, to a limited extent, the private sector). Second, the United Nations traditionally has focused on technical assistance and the MDBs on project investments and program loans—although this distinction has become blurred over time as the MDBs have increased the amount of technical assistance they provide. Third, the United Nations has historically had a broader mandate, including political and social as well as economic concerns, which in theory should put the UN programs in the lead on matters of human development and conflict prevention and response. Sectoral specialization has sometimes helped to make this so, as with the role of the UN Fund for Population Activities (UNFPA). But as thinking about development has changed, the agenda of the MDBs has broadened and the distinctions have come to reside more in the policies and instruments than in the areas of assistance. Fourth, whereas UN programs are governed on the basis of one country/one vote, the MDBs give more voice to member countries with larger financial subscriptions. This has tended to give developing countries a greater sense of ownership over the UN programs, while vesting the MDBs with greater donor resources with which to assist the developing world.

World Bank and the RDBs. Although similar in mandate and in the provision of concessional and nonconcessional loans, the World Bank and the African, Asian, and Latin American RDBs have distinct institutional characters, competencies, and resource levels. Given its global membership and reach, the World Bank has developed a broad substantive scope that enables it to provide client countries with a worldwide knowledge of issues and policy responses. Its global character and lending capacity also help the World Bank to advance economy- and sectorwide reforms. At the same time, the World Bank is sometimes criticized for applying a global standardized approach to problems and not being sufficiently attuned to local realities. In contrast, the regional banks, with their geographic focus and greater regional member-country voice, are said to have a better understanding of the sociopolitical context in which they operate, a better feel for local conditions affecting their delivery of assistance, and greater empathy for their clients. Yet they have not tended to play as proactive a policy reform role as the World Bank; nor have they emphasized structural and sectoral adjustment lending. Although their comparative strengths and weaknesses might have usefully led to a marked division of labor between the World Bank and the regional banks, the institutions have been reluctant to move toward specialization, and their member governments have not until recently encouraged them to do so. Rather, recipients have chosen to play one against the other, and donors have pushed their preferred agendas in all institutions simultaneously.

World Bank and the IMF. The distinctions between these two original Bretton Woods institutions derive from differences in their core mandates: the IMF is a monetary institution designed primarily to help countries manage short-term macroeconomic problems, and the World Bank is a financial institution created to help foster long-term development, largely through project lending to countries' productive and social sectors. With the advent of structural adjustment assistance in support of countries' medium-term macroeconomic policy reforms, areas of overlap developed. When a country is faced with a major crisis in its balance of payments or external financial debt, the IMF—with its procedures for quick-disbursing, short-to-medium–term assistance—is in theory the institution better able to assist with economic stabilization; the World Bank—with its long-term lending and broader sectoral expertise—is better suited to help with the processes of structural adjustment (for example, in trade and investment policies, labor markets, and other economic and social policy reforms). But both institutions have been active in the large gray area between short-term stabilization and long-term sectoral reform. Also, as crises in the 1980s and 1990s made clear, social dimensions of stabilization and adjustment efforts deserve attention, which neither institution was well equipped to provide. The two institutions have increasingly interacted in support of adjustment programs, with Bank support often dependent on a country's agreement with the IMF on an program of stabilization and adjustment measures. Also, joint preparation of policy framework papers (PFPs) has underpinned adjustment assistance. Continuous tension between the two institutions' approaches to problems and lack of close coordination in specific circumstances, however, have led some observers to maintain that the institutions should be merged, while others argue that the IMF should limit its role in poor countries to short-term stabilization efforts. Because neither view has garnered much support, however, there is a continuing push to get the IMF and World Bank to better coordinate their efforts in partnership with client countries and to deal more effectively with the social as well as economic dimensions of adjustment. In September 1999, the World Bank and the IMF agreed to an enhanced multilateral debt relief effort to be underpinned by countries' preparation of Poverty Reduction Strategy Papers (PRSPs). In support of the new PRSP, it was also agreed that there would be a rationalization of Bank and Fund support and more structured coordination. This new country-designed PRSP process has the potential to serve as the basis for greater country-level coordination among all major donors.

A third point in examining the record of multilateral aid institutions is that differences among these sets of multilateral institutions notwithstanding, they all face a number of shared problems in defining and implementing their contractual arrangements (that is, projects and programs) with recipient countries. These problems include: (1) proclivity toward ever-expanding agendas; (2) pressures to disburse funds at the expense of effective implementation; (3) a tendency both to overestimate their own and their recipients' capacities to carry out stated objectives and to neglect incentives needed to garner support for change; (4) difficulty in coming to grips with the underlying political/governance imperatives of effective development; and (5) a reluctance to coordinate and to seek out strategic alliances, despite clear evidence of the high costs of not doing so.

Effectiveness of the Different Aid Instruments

Aid instruments as well as institutions have different strengths and weaknesses. As the development agenda has broadened, the uses of all three main instruments—project aid, program aid, and technical assistance—have evolved.

Project Aid. Project investments have been by far the primary mode of assistance over the past fifty years. The study *Does Aid Work?*, which reviewed evaluations of projects of all the major bilateral and multilateral donor agencies, concluded that projects produce satisfactory results in a large proportion of cases—roads get built, water reaches farmers' land, and there are measurable production benefits. At the same time, the study pointed to a set of concerns that cut across projects of different agencies and in different countries and sectors, including: the sustainability of projects after aid transfers had ended; the impact on the quality of project design and implementation of pressures within agencies to commit funds; the tendency of donors to overdesign projects in an effort to advance multiple objectives simultaneously; the weakness of the capacity-building features of projects, especially those that entailed separate administrative units rather than the incorporation of project management into recipients' normal administrative structures; the fact that both donor and recipient understandings of institutional, political, and social constraints tended to lag behind economic and technical competencies in virtually all agencies; and the general insufficiency of project feedback, including the lack of development of evaluation capacity in recipient countries.

Subsequent experience has highlighted three related shortcomings. First, as concerns about the need for economic policy reform mounted in the 1970s, the limitations of project aid as a vehicle for encouraging broad policy adjustments and related institutional development became clear. This limitation spurred the introduction of structural adjustment lending (provided in the form of balance of payments or budget support, rather than discrete project investments). Second, in the 1980s and early 1990s, the experience with adjustment lending showed the central importance of recipient performance. Hence "ownership" of policies, programs, and projects and the need to make projects stronger vehicles of knowledge transfer, best practices, and institutional development gained greater attention (along with the recommendation to tailor all forms of aid more closely to recipient performance and capacity). Third, some recent studies contend that because all aid is fungible—that is, aid resources intended to finance a particular project could end up indirectly funding any other activity—aid could have a bigger impact if provided not in the form of project financing but as general budget support and technical assistance in support of national programs and projects.[14]

Program Aid. The second mode of development assistance, program aid, has provided financing not for investment in individual projects but rather to supplement recipients' balance of payments or budgetary resources. Used only sporadically before 1980, usually in response to balance-of-payments crises, program aid took new shape and became a more prominent form of assistance thereafter, as a way both to provide quick-disbursing balance-of-payments support and to serve as a vehicle for leveraging improvements in recipient countries' economic policy.

This new form of policy-based program aid, which has involved the heavy use of what came to be called "aid conditionality," brought about a major change in the field of development aid. In particular, it shifted the focus of attention from resources to policy and, in particular, to the quality of the broad economic (and later sector) policy framework within which aid was being provided. This broadening of attention from project financing to policy environment has had a strongly positive effect on the whole enterprise of development assistance.

However, the way that aid conditionality has been applied has been of limited effectiveness at best. Indeed, most studies of aid conditionality have concluded that "the overall record is bleak."[15] Research has shown that adjustment programs (most of which have been funded by the IMF and World Bank) have achieved their economic objectives only to a partial extent: they have prompted improvements in the balance of payments and exports but have had little impact on inflation. Typically, they have not affected the pace of economic growth in either direction. They are consistently associated with reductions in investment levels, however, which threaten economic progress over the long term. Moreover, neither the IMF nor the World Bank has been able to show systematic connections between their programs and improvements in economic policies.[16]

Contrary to early criticisms, however, the social effects of the adjustment programs have not been uniformly negative, but rather, complex and varied. Social effects have proved to be strongly influenced by initial conditions, with burdens likely to fall disproportionately on urban populations; and large social consequences have been the exception, not the rule—with no systematic tendency for the poor to lose disproportionately.[17]

Early critiques of aid conditionality tended to focus on perceived deficiencies in the policy of conditional aid programs. But experience has shown that the conditionality approach to policy resulted in improved economic performance *where the conditions were implemented.* The main problems, in other words, have been in the implementation of conditional aid, not in its broad policy orientations. Evidence of this problem is the frequency of IMF programs breaking down and of World Bank lending being delayed.

There are several different dimensions to the implementation problems that have been encountered. One dimension, discussed above, has been the tendency of donors to continue financing despite a recipient's failure to comply with the myriad conditions attached to structural adjustment assistance.

Another part of the explanation has been that aid's leverage over most specific policy instruments in recipient countries is weak. That is, conditionality can make a decisive difference to policy instruments suited to serving as preconditions of aid. These include actions that are directly controlled by those parts of governments in the negotiations, capable of being undertaken quickly, and unambiguous and easily monitored. But conditionality does not work well with more complicated policy-making processes such as those that are politically sensitive, involve the actions of large numbers of bureaucrats and agencies, cannot be accomplished in a single step, require extensive institutional change, and lack strong technical consensus on their utility.

Furthermore, conditionality negotiations have tended to be closed affairs between donor agencies and recipient governments. And officials in recipient countries spent more time interacting with donors than working to build internal consensus for reform. One result is that the reforms have lacked legitimacy domestically. Another is that reforms appear to be undertaken at the behest of donors, which has undermined their catalytic effect on private investors. Investor decisions are heavily based on judgments about the quality of government decision-making, but the existence of an IFI program is not taken as an adequate proxy. And because the revival of private investment is crucial to achieving renewed growth in adjusting countries, this failure to instill confidence is damaging. Where recipient governments pass the buck to the IFIs in difficult adjustment situations—with the implication of government disavowal of policy change—this too has a negative consequence. Conditionality, studies emphasize, thus makes the crucial task of the political management of policy change difficult. Indeed, a common theme that runs through recipient government perceptions of their experience with structural adjustment assistance is the feeling of loss of control over both the policy content and the pace of implementation of the reform program.

Yet another problem is that adjustment programs have frequently been underfunded, and recipient governments have perceived the risks as too great relative to the funding available. This is a major difficulty, especially when the proposed reforms pose complex issues of managing winners and losers within resource-constrained societies.[18]

In a study of aid and macroeconomic policy reform in ten African countries, these general findings have been refined.[19] The ten case studies show that the results of aid aimed at stimulating policy reform have been varied. What policy reform has occurred has been driven primarily by the domestic political economy of individual countries, and most major reform efforts have come only after economic and political crises. Large amounts of aid to countries not prepared to undertake reforms have sustained rather than altered poor policies. In general, donors have not discriminated effectively among different countries or different phases of a reform process. Instead donors have tended to provide the same package of assistance everywhere and at all times, including large amounts of initial financing that gets phased out once reforms are under way. The cases show that a different composition of aid in different phases has proved to be more effective: in a pre-reform phase, technical assistance is most appropriate; during periods of rapid initial reform, conditionality backed with quick-disbursing finance is both useful and welcomed; but in the later stage of a reform process, as governments deal with the more politically and institutionally complex policy and structural changes, conditionality is no longer useful (although financing remains important).[20] Most recently, the World Bank has introduced a revised form of programmatic lending designed to meet new needs and to overcome many of the past weaknesses of structural adjustment lending. In particular, the new style programmatic lending offers multiyear budget support in the form of a series of single tranche disbursements made in support of actions actually taken, not promises made.

Aid in support of sectorwide reforms followed the evolution in recipient countries from macroeconomic stabilization and adjustment needs to "second-stage" sector-specific reform tasks. Since the mid-1990s, this has entailed the increasing use of integrated sectorwide reform programs (often referred to as "sectorwide approaches," SWAps) involving agreed sector reform strategies, government medium-term expenditure plans, coordinated funding commitments of donors, and a common monitoring process. In some SWAps, donors have agreed to pool their funding; in most others they have committed to direct their separate project investments or program financing to activities outlined in the agreed sectorwide framework. Although this approach embodies what has come to be understood as good aid practice, there are two main impediments to moving rapidly toward full-scale "common pool" arrangements. Many recipient countries lack the institutional capacity needed for donors to agree to common implementation arrangements over which they do not exercise traditional forms of program or fiduciary control. Of particular concern is the existing weakness in many countries of public expenditure management and accountability systems. Even where there is solid agreement on sector reform priorities and strategies, donor acceptance of implementation arrangements (in which donors essentially agree to pool their aid in support of a program that is recipient managed) will likely require long processes of capacity and confidence building.[21] Second, most bilateral donors confront legislative requirements and specific constituency interests that impede the pooling of their aid resources.

Technical Assistance. Technical assistance, the third main instrument of aid, has had the weakest record of all.[22] The institution- and capacity-building technical assistance components of loans fail about twice as often as the physical components. From the outset, technical cooperation was viewed as an essential aspect of development aid. Students of economic development saw it as a straightforward and powerful device that could make a major contribution to the economic transformation of developing countries. President Truman's "Point Four Program" in 1949 reflected this early vision. And for the next several decades it was seen as an indispensable adjunct to capital investment—needed not only to help build roads and universities, but also to develop the local capacity to maintain and run them. Technical assistance through the early decades was therefore built into project financing.

In the 1970s, as the development agenda broadened and concerns grew about the sustainability of project investments, the technical assistance components of aid projects expanded to cover a wider array of capacity-building and institutional development tasks. But the technical support was still directly tied to project activities, and as those activities became more complex—that is, involved assistance to the social sectors—aid agencies tended to set up separate project implementation units.

With the introduction of structural adjustment lending in the 1980s, the focus of technical assistance changed dramatically to emphasize problems of institutional development and capacity building in developing countries generally, not just in terms of specific project tasks. Moreover, this heightened awareness of the importance of institutional change to policy reform was reinforced by advocates of more participatory approaches to development. Thus technical assistance came to be viewed not only as a way to transfer skills and fill knowledge gaps, but also as an essential element of a broader process designed to create and disseminate knowledge for development purposes at all levels of society.

Reviews of this form of aid have shown that it can make important contributions, especially in effective project implementation and where focused explicitly on skills training. Still, it is subject to wide-ranging criticism, with dissatisfaction greatest in the most heavily aided countries.[23] The main points of criticism include: (1) the ineffectiveness of technical assistance within the overall objective of achieving greater self-reliance in recipient countries by building institutions and strengthening local capacities in national economic and sector policy management; (2) the high costs of technical assistance, which has for a long time relied mainly on the use of resident expatriate advisors and failed as an instrument of capacity building; and (3) the supply-driven nature of technical cooperation, which has been said to result in its excessive use, inefficient allocation, and weak local "ownership" and commitment to institution and capacity building.

The reasons for the poor record of technical assistance are many—including that it is inherently difficult—in part because of long-standing weakness in the intellectual underpinnings of institutional development and human capacity building as compared to other areas of development cooperation. In addition, the historical division of labor between UN technical assistance and MDB project financing has posed major coordination problems. Moreover, technical assistance has often been provided as a part of a project or program package to make up for a recipient's lack of institutional capacity. Where the preexisting incapacity is relatively minor compared to the needs of the project or program, this added component can lead to both capacity building and a successful outcome. But too often technical assistance has been provided because the funded activity is too complex for the entity being assisted. In these cases a better solution is to finance more appropriately sized and designed projects.

Finally, as the central importance of institution and capacity building has gained recognition, more efforts have been made to grapple with the sources of weakness in the provision of technical assistance. Donors have sponsored more "free-standing" institutional development projects and more research into best practices. Still, most institution-building efforts have assumed that capacity is solely a matter of organizational capability that can be developed through training and technical assistance. These aspects are necessary, but they are not sufficient to attain institutional development goals. Other elements are required, including transparent institutional rules and incentive structures and broader mechanisms that promote citizen "voice" and political and market competition.

Aid Coordination

No record of the aid experience would be complete without reference to the issue of aid coordination, a much discussed but ongoing problem. Attention to the importance of development coordination has intensified over the years as donors, development institutions, projects, and programs have proliferated. Many heavily aid-dependent countries now receive assistance from more than a hundred bilateral, multilateral, and NGOs—each with its own priorities, procedures, planning cycles, and reporting requirements. Along with this proliferation of actors has been a blurring of the functional lines of responsibility among donor agencies, as each extends its role in the ever-widening aid agenda.

Poor coordination has not only resulted in duplication and waste in the development business, it has also put a heavy burden on the limited management capacities of recipient governments, which must deal with donors' multiple procedures, policy directives, and stand-alone projects. Multiple projects of multiple donors place demands on recipient countries' budgets for local and recurrent costs, and on their often weak administrative capacities for the handling of each donor's separate monitoring and reporting requirements. Tanzania is said to have had some 2,000 projects supported by 40 donors in the 1990s—albeit several of them operated through small NGOs.[24] As a result, the diverse aid activities of the donors engaged in any particular country does not add up to a coherent contribution to development.

Donors have acknowledged this problem for a long time. Recent donor documents emphasize the need to find solutions, especially in an environment in which low-income countries remain heavily dependent on stagnating aid flows, development performance has been disappointing, and there are increasing demands in donor countries for better accountability. Yet as a recent set of case studies concluded, "The need for greater coordination of aid is noted by both donors and recipients alike. However, coordination of aid remains recognized in principle, but rarely in practice."[25]

Numerous mechanisms have been devised over the years to deal with coordination problem among donors and between them and individual recipient countries. The main formal aid coordination mechanism is the World Bank–chaired aid Consultation Groups (CGs). These CGs now exist for some sixty countries and are supplemented by a number of UNDP-chaired roundtables for another twenty countries. Initially, in the late 1950s and early 1960s, these mechanisms concentrated on aid mobilization to meet the resource gaps implied by crude investment-driven growth models. Subsequent decades introduced new objectives, including harmonization of donor policies and practices, support of macroeconomic reforms, and broadening of attention to governance issues. Experience indicates, however, that these country-focused and regional coordination mechanisms have been generally less than satisfactory.

Another significant coordination mechanism is the Development Assistance Committee (DAC), a "donors' club" of members of the Organization for Economic Cooperation and Development (OECD). The DAC has compiled annual data on bilateral aid flows and served as a forum in which bilateral donors can discuss aid practices and, at times, agree on reforms in such areas as aid tying and procurement regulations. DAC also frequently issues sets of principles on aid practices, but the bilateral agencies are left to follow up—or not. Overall, DAC has made no significant contribution to overcoming the obstacles to improved aid coordination.

A notable exception to the lack of success in donor aid coordination is the Special Program of Assistance for Africa (SPA). Established to deal with the deepening economic crisis in Africa in the 1980s, the SPA was conceived as an informal association of donors, both bilateral and multilateral. Its specific aim is to support countries' structural adjustment programs with IDA and the IMF. A recent major review of this mechanism concluded that the SPA proved effective in responding to the immediate challenge it was designed to meet.[26] Free of formality, donors were able to test ideas, develop mutual understandings, and engage in frank and open exchanges on African economic and social policy issues. High-level donor representation was maintained throughout and provided important opportunities for meaningful interaction between bilateral donors and the IFIs; and peer pressure exerted in the context of SPA meetings helped mobilize quick-disbursing aid and improve donor procedures.

As the immediate macroeconomic stabilization crisis in African countries eased and the SPA agenda became more complex, increased attention was given to promoting and improving sectorwide programs and to building closer interaction with African partners. An evaluation of the SPA's initial phase concluded that, while open to African participation in its working groups and planning sessions, the SPA has not done enough to foster real partnership with African recipients. Moreover, communication between donor agencies and project administrators proved inadequate; links with country-focused mechanisms for donor coordination remained weak; and monitoring and evaluation of reforms and developments were not systematic. Overall, this experience supports the general point that effective coordination of ongoing aid needs to occur at the country level, led by the recipient government; and it needs to be reinforced by agency-level harmonization of policies and procedures.

LESSONS LEARNED

This mixed record of aid provides one overarching lesson about aid effectiveness and numerous subordinate lessons related to each stage of aid management, from agenda setting through negotiations, implementation, and reactions to noncompliance.

The main lesson, stated repeatedly in evaluations, is that aid can provide important support to development efforts—in the form of both money and ideas—but it can also impede development "unless it carefully avoids reinforcing flawed policies and poor governance, weakening local institutions, and creating dependence."[27] What makes the difference is both donor and recipient commitment to the uses of aid for core development purposes, recipient ownership of its own development policies and programs, donor allocations on the basis of country need and performance, and approaches to the delivery of aid that are tailored, participatory, and transparent.

Agenda Setting

Three general observations can be made about agenda setting in the field of international development aid. First, agenda setting takes place in numerous venues and on several different levels, including global forums such as UN conferences; multilateral organizations at both the global and regional level, such as the MDBs, the European Union, and the more tightly focused entities such as the Paris Club and the SPA; and within donor and recipient countries. This obviously creates many points of entry for interested parties to advance agenda items. But the fragmentation also makes it difficult to ensure that the whole is greater than the sum of its parts, that linkages and trade-offs among issues are adequately taken into account, and that agendas are adequately funded, monitored, and evaluated.

Second, international political and economic events have largely determined the broad rationale for which development aid has been given and, to a large extent, set policy parameters for aid agendas. Within the broad framework established by geopolitical and economic trends, new ideas and the accumulation of experience have contributed to changing concepts of how best to aid the development process. In turn, the pressure of special interest groups has been able to affect the definition of specific aid objectives and processes.

There has been a marked incoherence in the ways that these sets of forces have acted on the development agenda. The problem stems from the top-down way that agendas have been formed and the lack of attention paid in the agenda-setting stage to devising incentives for those actors essential to the attainment of objectives. The effect has often been discontinuity between the agenda set at the global level and the actions taken in individual countries, both by aid agencies and by recipient governments.

Third, the aid agenda has always been largely donor driven. Even where there has been a galvanizing event, when and how an issue gets on the aid agenda is largely determined by donor country interests. And the aid agenda has tended to reflect most markedly the mixed motives and multiple interests of the largest aid-giving country, the United States.

Seven main lessons can be drawn from this experience.

First, aid agenda setting is of necessity a very open process. This is so because aid lacks a single powerful constituency in any donor country, and maintaining public support for aid therefore requires broad participation of multiple actors each with their individual constituencies, mandates, and procedures. There is no single "right way" to achieve sustainable development.

Second, as long as development aid is based on voluntary contributions from donor countries, they will dominate the international agenda-setting process. But serious weaknesses stem from the inevitable limitations of donors' knowledge of conditions within recipient countries; the fact that implementation determines results; and that recipient ownership of its development strategy and management of its aid resources largely determines effective implementation. In other words, donors control the purse but cannot force their will. Rather, setting the international aid agenda in a way that is most likely to achieve effective implementation requires identifying issues that donors can support and recipients can "own."

Third, global-level aid agenda setting can foster consensus building among donors and recipients around broad objectives, but it takes time. And it requires sharing information on problems, amassing credible evidence on the mutual benefit of addressing them, and developing convincing solutions. It took years, for example, to put population on the development agenda and to build a body of knowledge on the benefits to development and on best practices for successful action.[28]

Fourth, for consensus building on broad goals, intergovernmental institutions in general and the United Nations in particular have played important roles. Of particular significance have been the various UN conferences convened over the past decade, although not all have been equally influential (often depending on the "ripeness" of the issue). Of greatest impact have been the UN Conference on Environment and Development (UNCED) in Rio de Janeiro in 1992; the Third International Population Conference in Cairo in 1994; and the World Conference on Women in Beijing in 1995. All served to alter the policy debate and intensify collective action.

The conferences have provided measuring sticks for development assistance efforts. The United Nations has conducted a process, led by the Economic and Social Council (ECOSOC), to track an integrated and coordinated implementation and follow-up of major UN conferences and summits. The World Bank now keeps data on how goals are being met. In 1996, the DAC made a number of goals agreed to by UN conferences the core of a new aid policy statement, *Shaping the Twenty-first Century: The Role of Development Cooperation*. NGOs have begun to use the international goals—and the failure of both donors and recipients to live up to them—as the focus of aid campaign efforts. For example, Oxfam International has recently launched a global campaign to advance the goal of universal primary education.

International organizations—which convene these agenda-setting conferences, provide follow-up resources, and act as forums for additional dialogue—represent the global good by: providing a forum in which multiple voices can be heard; offering what is perceived as legitimate sources of information on what is at stake, thereby countering specific political or commercial interests; making available information on best practices and on possible approaches to solving problems; and being a voice for the "dispossessed," that is, poorer and weaker countries and groups within countries.

Fifth, nonstate actors—private NGOs such as international commissions or issue-specific NGOs—have also been important in drawing attention to problems and pressuring both governments and international organizations to act. Past examples include the 1968 Pearson Commission, which sought to counteract mounting aid fatigue in the major donor countries by defining the mutual benefits of accelerating poor country development and the priority issues amenable to effective development cooperation; and the 1987 Brundtland Commission, which put the issue of sustainable development on the agenda.

A more diffuse nongovernmental effort has been the Roman Catholic Church's Jubilee 2000 campaign, which has pressured donor governments to do more to relieve the debt of the poorest countries. This massive campaign, extending over many years, combined moral suasion, global mobilization of campaign activists, and persistent use of evidence on the shortcomings of existing policies to pressure developed country governments to come up with a more generous policy. The campaign was aided by the active support of three major players: the Pope, the U.S. secretary of the treasury, and the president of the World Bank.

Sixth, beyond creating awareness of the importance of specific problems, achieving consensus on broad goals, and occasionally getting agreement on a wholly new initiative (such as the establishment of a new fund for a specific action), however, global agenda-setting efforts are not likely to be effective. The many hours spent arriving at "plans of actions" at the global level have been largely wasted. Such plans are not linked to formal resource commitments, and the resources provided are often inadequate. This lack of support has been notably true, for example, for the goals set at the Cairo conference on population and development, after which U.S. funding for population programs was sharply cut due to domestic debates about abortion. Global agenda setting creates problems of unfunded mandates and contributes to an erosion of confidence in multilateral cooperation. In the past decade, the tendency has been to negotiate such plans globally and then to include, as a part of that global plan, the commitment to develop national action plans for implementation. Rarely if ever has the order been reversed—starting with national plans that are then compared and enhanced through global conferences—although that may well be the more effective process.

Seventh, where agenda setting is sharply focused on a single problem, it tends to be easier to translate concern into meaningful action. In these situations, there is a greater role for both technical expertise and skilled practitioners from both donor and recipient countries. International efforts to eliminate river blindness (a public-private effort involving governments, international organizations, NGOs, and a major pharmaceutical company) and to immunize children are two prominent examples.

Negotiations

Aid negotiations deal mainly with amounts and terms of allocations. In the absence of norms, rules, and procedures, development assistance is a constant process of negotiation. This can be seen as a strength inasmuch as it provides for flexibility in the granting of aid and for midcourse corrections; but on balance it is an enormous weakness that has distorted the development effort and drained energies from the implementation and monitoring of development programs.

Negotiations occur periodically among donors, around issues of funding the multilateral agencies, including the conditions attached to those funding replenishments; of improving aid donor practices, such as the untying of aid; and of enhancing donor coordination at the international and country level.[29] At times, resource levels have also been "negotiated" among donors and recipients within international forums, but this has done little more than set normative targets that have usually not been met.[30]

Donor-recipient negotiations most often focus on the conditions to be attached to aid allocations and on the design of specific programs and projects. As during agenda setting, donors have tended to dominate negotiations. What has provided some balance is that the donors' drive to disburse aid funds has been as strong as the recipients' need to obtain them. But this "disbursement dance" has seriously undermined development effectiveness.

Over the years, aid negotiations have become both more complex and more problematic affairs. This trend reflects several developments discussed above, including: the proliferation of donor agencies and programs; the broadening of the aid agenda and, as part of that, the move of development assistance into new areas involving complex internal political and social factors; and the introduction in the late 1970s and early 1980s of aid conditionality as an explicit means of linking aid allocations to recipient countries' promises of specific policy reforms.

Occasionally, special arrangements (such as the SPA) have been made—often in response to crises—to coordinate and speed allocation decisions. Although these arrangements have usually succeeded in meeting initial objectives, problems linked to aid negotiations have remained. In the last several years, aid reviews have pointed to one overarching lesson and several subordinate lessons for improving the situation. The core lesson, in the words of an independent review of the IMF Enhanced Structural Adjustment Facility (ESAF) program, is that "the challenge is to foster strong country ownership and at the same time to provide adequate assurances to donors that resources will not be wasted."[31] From this lesson several others follow.

First, aid needs to be allocated selectively, on the basis of actual—not promised—sound policy frameworks and government adherence to accountable expenditure procedures. Given what has been demonstrated about the central importance of recipient performance, it makes little sense for donors to negotiate the same kinds of aid packages and programs with strong and weak performers.

Second, within a framework of internationally agreed performance standards, negotiations need to be driven more by recipient countries. Recipients, not donors, need to identify the priorities for which support is sought. And donors need to negotiate the amounts, terms, and conditions of their funding within the context of that policy framework, in accordance with their own agency mandates and policies, international standards of accountability, and country performance.

As far as individual country circumstances permit—and certainly in the case of strong performers—the starting point for the provision of aid should be the recipient country's national budget (or public expenditure program). Donors should agree with the recipient on assistance needed in support of that program, and then refrain from committing resources to activities falling outside the framework of national priorities. Rather, within those priorities donors should identify areas of activity on which they choose to focus in accordance with their own mandates and constituent interests; and provide funding in those areas on the basis of a multiyear rolling program, subject to continuing public expenditure reviews and accepted monitoring procedures. This does not preclude donor support for specific programs and projects. But it does mean that donors should fund only what fits within national strategies and implementation capacities. For this to work, it is important not only for a recipient country's top leadership and finance or planning ministry to be involved, but also for other relevant ministries to be part of the negotiation and program design process.

A recent example of an effort that moves in this direction is the Mozambique Health Sector Recovery Program. The background of this program was the near complete collapse of government health services outside the urban centers during the long civil war, and the involvement of a large number of aid agencies in providing emergency assistance. The challenge for the health sector recovery effort was to reestablish national coverage while bringing donor operations within a common program framework. Two main achievements of the program have been the development of a plan for rehabilitating health facilities and service provision within a sector policy worked out by the government in close cooperation with key donors; and the establishment of a framework for donor cooperation and for shared implementation procedures.

Third, for recipients to "own" development programs, there must be broad public participation and buy-in of the policies and programs proposed by the government, especially among those likely to be most affected. This requires a transparent and participatory process within the recipient country involving relevant stakeholders in the design of the national strategy, programs, and projects. In sectorwide programs, for example, stakeholder consultations should be led by government to inform public expenditure decisions, and all levels of government that will have a responsibility for implementation should be involved at an early stage of program design. That process of consultation requires that time be spent in advance of negotiations with donors, which tends not to occur today.

Fourth, donors and recipients need equal access to information on the situation within the country and on the resource gaps and other constraints confronting successful program implementation. The credibility of the source of the information matters, however; therefore more use of independent experts and joint donor-recipient analyses is likely to improve the pace and the outcome of negotiations. The involvement of experts could also be a useful antidote to the tendency of both donors and recipients to overreach.

Fifth, the recipient country's national strategy as a whole, rather than individual projects, is the most important focus for development aid negotiations. Both the long-term comprehensive nature of the development process and the fungibility of aid make a country-level focus essential. This means that in countries where a donor plays a major role as is increasingly the case, the donor ought to develop, in consultation with the recipient, a comprehensive country assistance strategy that considers recipient absorptive capacity and the role of other donors before beginning negotiations on specific aid programs.

Sixth, aid negotiations need to focus on results, not just inputs. Therefore negotiations should include clear statements of objectives, benchmarks for measuring progress, and procedures for monitoring and evaluation—and they should leave the details of implementation to the recipient.

Seventh, where multiple donors are involved in support of an individual country, negotiations ought to be far more coordinated than they have been in the past. Where able, the recipient should take the lead in fostering that coordination. Also, in the interest of better-coordinated, more effective aid, individual donors ought to become more selective in the services they agree to provide and the areas in which they operate. This would mean reversing the trend over the past couple of decades of donors seeking to do all things as a way of maintaining their relevance. Instead, contributions by different donors should reflect a deliberate division of labor based on institutional comparative advantage. The proposal by World Bank President James D. Wolfensohn for a Comprehensive Development Framework (CDF) takes a long-term, holistic view of development and proposes a "partnership approach" between donors and recipients, including recipient leadership in the design of development strategies, and advocates a division of labor among donors in support of those strategies.[32] One specific action would be to reform the CGs and roundtables as the main forums for negotiations between a recipient and its various donors. As noted above, this should include the move to country-based CG meetings (which have occurred in the last couple of years, but not with regularity) to foster broader participation in the aid negotiation process and donor support for a shift to country-led (rather than donor-led) CGs.

Implementation and Compliance

Once aid "bargains" have been struck, donors have limited ability to enforce their implementation, which depends on the policy and institutional environment of the recipient. How aid is designed and managed, however, can do much to support or undermine recipients' efforts. In 1992, the World Bank released a report on the performance of its loan portfolio whose main message was that "effective implementation is the key to development impact."[33] Although the point may seem obvious, the report's message represented a major shift within the development community from a focus on aid disbursements to an emphasis on effective aid use.

As emphasized in this and other studies, a pressure to lend on the part of aid agencies has undercut effective implementation. The procedure for reversing this situation—basing allocations on ownership and performance—has been noted. In addition, numerous changes are required in what recipients and donors need to do, separately and together, to make the implementation of assistance more supportive of effective country-driven development efforts. Four main implementation lessons derive from the accumulation of experience and analysis.

First, for recipients, the challenge is to develop, build consensus behind, and carry out programs capable of achieving sustainable development. Effective implementation, however, requires good governance. Although a recognition of the importance of good governance has figured into aid program design from the earliest days as a matter affecting the implementation of individual projects, in the past decade a framework of good governance has come to be seen more broadly as a precondition for good country performance overall. Key components include: good public sector management, with accountable public institutions that give priority to sound policies; transparent policy making and implementation; and clarity, stability, and fairness in the rule of law essential to a well-functioning private sector and equitable development outcomes.

To cite one example of change in this direction: a newly elected government in Tanzania in the mid-1990s took several major steps to improve and make more accountable government processes, including taking greater control over the management of aid and improving relations with donors. Although Tanzania still has a way to go in improving public sector processes (including combating corruption), the government has led the preparation of the recent policy framework paper that underpins its IMF and World Bank support and effectively involved line ministries and the entire cabinet in the process; chaired a public expenditure working group (composed of professionals from government, the donor community, academic institutions, and local consulting firms) that has planned, evaluated, and effectively used the budget and related material to assess experience, draw lessons, and make projections for the future in a highly transparent way; and begun to build a significantly improved financial data storage and retrieval system and strengthen the treasury's budget management.

Second, donors, for their part, need to provide aid in ways that reinforce rather than undermine recipient ownership and effective policy and aid management. In addition to allocating aid more selectively, donors must improve the design quality and fit of aid programs, the modes and instruments for the delivery of aid, the incentives and skills mix within donor agencies, and the rationalization and coordination of aid programs.

In particular, aid programs need to be made less intrusive and more flexible. This requires that donors simplify their procedures; diversify the modalities of aid to encourage both experimentation and learning; move more from project to program or budget support, where circumstances permit design projects as vehicles of knowledge and best practice (supportive of policy reform, skill transfers, and institutional development); build project management into recipients' existing administrative structures, and strengthen them rather than create separate project management units; and build in adequate contingency mechanisms.[34]

Incentives in donor agencies need to be structured to ensure a focus on the quality, not the quantity, of aid. Stemming the pressure to disburse requires establishing internal incentives to reward implementation, experimentation, and a willingness to say no where conditions are not conducive to effective use of aid monies. In addition, it is generally held that a decentralization of agency staff to the field helps to ensure greater knowledge and understanding of the local conditions within which to design aid—although there are attendant costs and risks of even greater donor intrusiveness and dominance in aid management.

Third, if progress is to be made in improving implementation, both donors and recipients need to give more attention to capacity building, especially in the form of institution building, as a central element of aid. Too often donors have overestimated their own and recipients' capacities. This stems in part from the pressure to lend and from impatience with slow results. But the record clearly shows that effective development assistance depends on the institutional capability of recipient countries to design and implement national development strategies, including ways to integrate aid in a manner consistent with national priorities. Countless aid programs have faltered because of overly ambitious efforts not well suited to existing capacity and lack of attention to capacity mobilization and institutional development in the program design.

Capacity building is time-consuming and expensive, however, and is not likely to be emphasized by either donors or recipients unless the effectiveness of technical assistance can be improved. Given the weak intellectual underpinnings of capacity-building efforts to date, considerable investment must be made in research and experimentation. And there is need for the development of appropriate standards, instruments, staff training (in both donor and recipient agencies), institutional analyses, and, overall, more realism in institution-building efforts.

Closely related is the need to invest in monitoring and evaluation. Experience shows that effective monitoring and evaluation design, including the selection of limited numbers of appropriate indicators and attention to responsibility and capacity for data collection and analysis, enhances a focus on results and increases the likelihood of achieving the desired development impact.

Fourth, the development community must think beyond individual donor-financed projects to the broader challenge of effective implementation of national development strategies. And for this, aid coordination is essential in the implementation as well as the negotiation phase. Recent analyses have brought together the various lessons about aid effectiveness into proposals for a "partnership approach" to aid that emphasizes both country ownership and aid coordination. In this new approach, the issue of coordination is addressed at the country and interagency level.[35]

Coordination between a recipient and its many donors must be fostered through mechanisms such as regular country-level meetings, joint studies and assessments, and increased cofinancing. Coordination is crucial at the sector level, where it seems likely that donors and recipients could go furthest in agreeing on an overarching policy framework within which different donors would agree on their respective assistance roles. And, country capacities permitting, donors would agree to sector support in the form of a multiyear package of budget support and, as appropriate, project financing.

Among the multiple aid agencies, the new partnership approach calls for enhanced coordination based on three things: the rationalization of the aid program of each agency, reflecting an institutional division of labor; the harmonization of disbursement, implementation, accounting, and reporting procedures to ease the burden on recipients; and the "transformation of the aid agency's institutional culture" to strengthen its capacity for collaboration with others—through joint analyses, joint aid missions, staff exchanges, and the commitment of money and time to build collaborative processes.

Reactions to Noncompliance

Noncompliance in the field of aid can occur on at least three levels: projects, policies, and program objectives. The first and more formal aspect of noncompliance entails nonperformance in regard to specific project contracts between donor and recipient. Fairly rigorous international standards and procedures have been developed over the years, ranging from international bidding on aid procurements to the monitoring and apportioning of aid disbursements. One of the main functions of the DAC has been to encourage adherence to those standards by all bilateral donor countries, while the World Bank has often the led the way for the multilateral agencies.

Second, with the shift to policy-based adjustment assistance in the 1980s, the issue of noncompliance became more complicated, as the above discussion on the failures of conditionality reveals. In this case, it was not the specific terms of a project contract that were at issue, but the carrying out of multiple policy and institutional reforms. And, as indicated, many structural adjustment programs broke down because of the inability or unwillingness of recipient governments to meet the many policy conditions.

A third and more difficult aspect of noncompliance in the aid field has to do more with nonperformance on broad goals and objectives—the issue of aid effectiveness. The above discussion has sought to make clear that both donors and recipients must share responsibility here. On both sides, mixed motives have tended to undermine aid's development impact. In the post–Cold War world of increasing globalization and democratization, however, both groups of countries (if not always their government officials) have increasing interests in strengthening aid's development effectiveness.

The ultimate "weapon" is of course the ability of either donor or recipient to say no. But this is a rather blunt instrument, not likely to be frequently used. For the recipient, the problem is clear: the need for external resources often leads to a willingness to accept aid on donors' terms even when it is clear to the recipient that the terms do not align with its own priorities or conditions.

The problems for donors, in contrast, are more numerous: First, getting agreement among donors on cutting off aid to a particular recipient has often proved difficult, and without agreement the sanction is ineffective. Second, the comprehensive nature and multiple dimensions of development make it hard to determine when performance warrants an aid cutoff. Thus, for example, a country may be performing well on economic and poverty reduction policy grounds but poorly on governance. Third, a complete cutoff of aid is likely to hurt the poor the most. Donors have therefore tried to limit their aid in badly performing countries to targeted efforts designed specifically to help the poor. But a weak policy environment or corrupt, mismanaged regime often hurts the poor the most, by denying them efficient delivery of public services. Fourth, and perhaps most important, donors worry that they will lose the ability to encourage improved performance if they make deep cuts to aid allocation.

There is the additional matter of the compliance of multilateral aid institutions with the policies set for them by their member governments. In principle, the governing boards of these institutions perform the main oversight function. But member governments, especially donors, have sometimes taken the view that policies are not being followed, despite the functioning of the boards. This has led in the last decade to several initiatives, including the creation of an independent inspection panel at the World Bank to review complaints of institutional noncompliance with established policies; independent reviews, such as the recent study of ESAF by an outside group of experts commissioned by the IMF board; and the insistence, by donor member governments at the urging of NGOs, for much greater openness and transparency in the workings of the international agencies.

In sum, various forces are pushing for far greater aid effectiveness today. Pressures include the change in the rationale for the provision of aid, the evolution of democratic governments in many developing countries, and the emergence of NGOs as increasingly active players in the development sphere.

Greater selectivity in the provision of aid is an important improvement, although not yet as widespread in practice as it ought to be. The World Bank is far ahead of other donors in implementing a system of performance-based allocations for its concessional resources, but other donors have begun to devise systems of their own. Making this work effectively is not easy and depends on a credible system of assessing performance. A key to this is the transparency of any performance assessment system, and reasonable coordination among donors on performance criteria.[36] Neither feature is fully in place, but both would be fully consistent with the proposed CDF put forward by the World Bank.

Peer pressure has also served as an effective instrument for fostering compliance. This is more a feature among donors than among recipients today, but it is worth asking whether it has a place (perhaps on a regional or subregional basis) in encouraging adherence, particularly in regard to new and sensitive issues such as governance.

Finally, there is the powerful impact of transparency, and especially its value in empowering nongovernmental groups to hold both governments and intergovernmental institutions accountable for their actions. NGOs have exerted effective pressure over the past decade to open the World Bank to greater information disclosure. But that institution still has far to go and others, including the IMF and the regional development banks, lag behind.

CONCLUSIONS: THE WAY AHEAD FOR AID EFFECTIVENESS

The lessons on aid effectiveness have led to the embrace, at least rhetorically, of two new overarching approaches to aid: "performance-based" assistance that allocates resources not on the basis of promised performance, but on demonstrated actions; and "development partnerships" that give recipients more control over the process, thereby overcoming many of the long-standing aid implementation and compliance problems.

These new approaches are not yet firmly in place, although there has been considerable movement on both fronts in the last couple of years. Some people question whether they go far enough and propose as an alternative what they call "a common pool approach to aid"; while others question the prospects for even the innovations under current discussion.

A different approach would entail a shift from today's country-based aid to a problem-focused, international public goods approach. This would require changes in rules and procedures for a number of agencies and a new kind of agility in forming coalitions for action. The opportunities are many, and there is the potential for large development benefits.[37] Current examples would include more concerted international efforts to combat communicable diseases in particular the HIV-AIDS pandemic; improved international machinery to reduce the "contagion effect" of financial crises; and global support to countries for the protection of forests as the bases of biodiversity preservation and carbon sequestration. As long as poverty persists and public and private sector institutions remain weak in low-income countries, there is no case for abandoning traditional country-based aid, but there is a strong case for beginning to do more in the name of international development assistance to increase the provision of scarce international public goods.

Relevance of Aid Lessons for Other Areas of Global Management

Where the provision of external resources is used as a tool to advance objectives in other domains of global management (such as preservation of the environment or control of infectious diseases), the lessons laid out here would seem to be broadly relevant. Moreover, some lessons from the development assistance field should have relevance in other domains, even where resource transfers are not a principal tool. These include:

- the importance of developing country "ownership" and capacity for their participation in international problem solving;
- the role of knowledge in building the momentum for change;
- the need to pay attention to constituency building and the management of winners and losers in fostering sustainable reforms;
- the high costs of lack of coordination among donors;
- the value of international institutions in all phases of global management, but also the need for international norms, rules, and procedures to provide room for national diversity; and
- the importance of transparency in holding both governments and international institutions accountable.

NOTES

1. World Bank, *Post-conflict Reconstruction: The Role of the World Bank* (Washington, D.C.: World Bank, 1998).
2. Consistent with the other studies in this volume, this review deals only with multilateral aid (that is, aid provided through formal international institutions) and not with bilateral

aid. Also, because of the nature of the overall project, this chapter is necessarily more about the process of development assistance than about the content (although the issue of aid's changing role is a subtheme throughout).

3. World Bank, *Assessing Aid: What Works, What Doesn't, and Why* (New York: Oxford University Press, 1998).

4. This section draws heavily on Catherine Gwin and Joan Nelson, "Development and Aid: New Evidence and New Issues," in Catherine Gwin and Joan Nelson, eds., *Perspectives on Aid and Development* (Washington, D.C.: Overseas Development Council, 1997), pp. 1–17.

5. Dani Rodrik, *The New Global Economy and Developing Countries: Making Openness Work* (Washington, D.C.: Overseas Development Council, 1999).

6. See, for example, Catherine Gwin, *U.S. Relations with the World Bank* (Washington, D.C.: Brookings Institution, 1994).

7. "Eliminating World Poverty: A Challenge for the 21st Century," White Paper on International Development, Secretary of State for International Development, United Kingdom (London: Her Majesty's Stationery Office, November 1997).

8. World Bank, *World Development Report 1990: Poverty* (New York: Oxford University Press, 1990).

9. Robert Cassen, *Does Aid Work?* (Oxford, U.K.: Clarendon Press, 1986).

10. See such recent examples as World Bank, *Assessing Aid*; Carol Lancaster, *Aid to Africa* (Chicago: University of Chicago Press for the Century Fund, 1999); Nicolas van de Walle and Timothy A. Johnston, *Improving Aid to Africa* (Washington, D.C.: Overseas Development Council, 1996); Finn Tarp, ed., *Foreign Aid and Development: Lessons Learnt and Directions for the Future* (London: Routledge, 2000).

11. Craig Burnside and David Dollar, "Aid Policies and Growth," World Bank Policy Research Working Paper No.1777 (Washington, D.C.: World Bank Development Research Group, 1997).

12. Paul Collier and David Dollar, "Aid Allocation and Poverty Reduction," Development Research Group paper (Washington, D.C.: World Bank, 2000).

13. Elliot Berg, "Dilemmas in Donor Aid Strategies," in Gwin and Nelson, *Perspectives on Aid and Development*, pp. 79–94; see also Lancaster, *Aid to Africa*; and van de Walle and Johnston, *Improving Aid to Africa*.

14. Shantayanan Devarajan and Vinaya Swaroop, "The Implications of Foreign Aid Fundability for Development Assistance," Policy Research Working Paper No. 2022 (Washington, D.C.: World Bank, 1998).

15. See, for example, Tony Killick, *Aid and the Political Economy of Policy Change* (London: Routledge, 1998); Paul Mosley et al., *Aid and Power: The World Bank and Policy-Based Lending*, 2 volumes (London: Routledge, 1991); and Paul Collier, "The Failure of Conditionality," in Gwin and Nelson, *Perspectives on Aid and Development*.

16. This, it should be noted, is a different point than the assertion that adjusting countries have performed better than nonadjusting countries, as concluded in the study of "Higher Impact Adjustment Lending (HIAL): Initial Evaluation," Operations Evaluation Department (Washington, D.C.: World Bank, 1999).

17. "External Evaluation of ESAF," Report by a Group of Independent Experts (Washington, D.C.: International Monetary Fund, 1998).

18. World Bank, *Assessing Aid*.

19. Shantayanan Devarajan, David Dollar, and Torgny Holmgren, eds., "Aid and Reform in Africa," World Bank Development Research Group (Washington, D.C.: World Bank, 2000).

20. Devarajan et al., "Aid and Reform in Africa."

21. Stephen Jones, "Sector Investment Programs in Africa: Issues and Experience," World Bank Technical Paper No. 374 (Washington, D.C.: World Bank, September 1997); and Stephen Jones, "Scaling Up: Issues in Moving from Projects to Programmatic Aid" (Oxford, U.K.: Oxford Policy Management, August 1999).

22. See, for example, the assessment of the institutional impact in World Bank projects in *1998 Annual Review of Development Effectiveness,* Operations Evaluation Department (Washington, D.C.: World Bank, 1998). The problem is by no means one limited to World Bank operations.

23. Elliot Berg, *Rethinking Technical Cooperation* (New York: UN Development Program, 1993).

24. van de Walle and Johnston, *Improving Aid to Africa*.

25. Jerker Carlsson, Gloria Somolekae, and Nicolas van de Walle, *Foreign Aid in Africa* (Uppsala, Sweden: Nordiska Afrikainstitutet, 1997), pp. 214–15.

26. "The Special Program of Assistance for Africa (SPA): An Independent Review," Operations Evaluation Department (Washington, D.C.: World Bank, 1998).

27. Lancaster, *Aid to Africa,* p. 221.

28. Robert Cassen, *Population Policy: A New Consensus* (Washington, D.C.: Overseas Development Council, 1994).

29. Two examples to note are the role of the DAC and the periodic IDA replenishment negotiations.

30. The prime example was the setting of 0.7 percent of donor GNP as a target for annual aid contributions. Although this figure was used as a rallying cry, only a few Nordic countries ever reached it, and today total aid from all donors amounts to the smallest share of their GNP since aid statistics began to be kept in the 1950s—less than one-quarter of one percent.

31. "External Evaluation of ESAF," p. 21.

32. "A Proposal for a Comprehensive Development Framework," discussion draft (Washington, D.C.: World Bank, January 21, 1999).

33. World Bank, "Effective Implementation: Key to Development Impact," Report of the World Bank's Portfolio Management Task Force (Washington, D.C.: World Bank, 1992).

34. Relations between Uganda and its aid donors stand out as a good example of movement in this direction. As described in a recent speech by Uganda's Permanent Secretary/Secretary of the Treasury, E. Tumusiime-Mutebile:

    Government has moved from a project driven approach to the development of comprehensive, co-ordinated, sector-wide programmes and investment plans, involving the participation of all stakeholders, including donors. This has entailed the development of a three year Medium Term Expenditure Framework (MTEF). The MTEF incorporates both recurrent and development components of the Government budget, and aims to ensure that all expenditures accord with strategic budgetary priorities and the medium term resource availability which is consistent with macroeconomic stability.... The Medium Term Expenditure Framework has given the donors greater confidence in Uganda's capacity for budget management and encouraged them to channel a larger share of their aid to the Government in the form of budget support, as opposed to directly funding projects outside the domestic budget.... The increase in the share of aid disbursed as budget support is a welcome development. It enhances national ownership and control over the budget, because it enables a larger share of development expenditures to be brought under the control of the Finance Ministry and subjected to the normal processes of budgetary planning.... It is also important because, by channeling aid through the Government budget, these funds become subject to the normal Parliamentary appropriation process and scrutiny by the Public Accounts Committee of Parliament.

As the secretary noted, more needs to be done on both sides. The government needs to strengthen further its adherence to rules and procedures of budget and program management. And the donors need to do more to consolidate and coordinate their aid in support of the government-led program. Still 60 percent of the aid to Uganda takes the form of separate donor projects, and the value of the MTEF would be considerably enhanced if donors would give the government indications of levels of aid (or even aid scenarios) over the medium term. But the trend is clearly in accordance with recent evidence on how to improve aid effectiveness and efficiency. "From Aid Co-ordination to Development Partnership: Uganda's Experience with Aid Co-ordination," Development Partnership Forum, Paris, December 7–8, 1999.

35. See, for example, World Bank, "Partnership for Development: From Vision to Action," (Washington, D.C.: World Bank, September 23, 1998); and the CDF proposal.

36. Catherine Gwin and Stephen Eccles, *Supporting Effective Aid: A Framework for Future Concessional Funding of Multilateral Development Banks* (Washington, D.C.: Overseas Development Council, 1999).

37. Three recent studies advance arguments in favor of this new approach and give concrete examples of development-related international public goods. See Ravi Kanbur, Todd Sandler, and Kevin Morrison, *The Future of Development Assistance: Common Pools and International Public Goods* (Washington, D.C.: Overseas Development Council, 1999); Wolfgang H. Reinicke, *Global Public Policy: Governing Without Government?* (Washington, D.C.: Brookings Institution, 1998); and Inge Kaul, Isabelle Grunberg, and Marc Stern, eds., *Global Public Goods: International Cooperation in the Twenty-First Century* (New York: Oxford University Press, 1999).

SUGGESTED ADDITIONAL READING

Cassen, Robert. *Does Aid Work?* Oxford, U.K.: Clarendon Press, 1986.

Gwin, Catherine and Joan Nelson, eds. *Perspectives on Aid and Development.* Washington, D.C.: Overseas Development Council, 1997.

Helleiner, Gerald K. "Changing Aid Relationships in Tanzania." Paper prepared for the Tanzania Consultative Group Meeting, May 3–4, 1999.

Kanbur, Ravi, Todd Sandler, and Kevin Morrison. *The Future of Development Assistance: Common Pools and International Public Goods.* Washington, D.C.: Overseas Development Council, 1999.

Kapur, Devesh, John P. Lewis, and Richard Webb. *The World Bank: Its First Half Century,* 2 vols. Washington, D.C.: The Brookings Institution, 1996.

Killick, Tony. *Aid and the Political Economy of Policy Change.* London: Routledge, 1998.

Lancaster, Carol. *Aid to Africa.* Chicago: Chicago University Press for the Century Fund, 1999.

OECD/DAC. *Shaping the 21st Century: The Contribution of Development Cooperation.* Paris: OECD, 1996.

World Bank. *Assessing Aid: What Works, What Doesn't, and Why.* New York: Oxford University Press, 1998.

5

Economics: Global Finance

Robert E. Litan

TO MANY, THE BUSINESS OF FINANCE conjures up images of needless middlemen, taking a cut off the top, as it were, as money changes hands. In fact, finance performs three vital economic functions: supplanting barter with far more convenient means of payment; spreading risk across time and space; and perhaps most important, channeling funds from savers to investors—a process known as "intermediation."

The importance of these functions is self-evident (if not fully appreciated) to those living in developed countries, who are accustomed to using banks and credit cards for paying their bills, buying insurance to spread risk, and using a variety of financial intermediaries (banks, mutual funds, and the markets themselves) to invest in and borrow from. But there is also compelling evidence that the development of a strong financial infrastructure—sound financial institutions and well-functioning markets, the physical and intellectual capital on which both depend to operate, and an effective system of government oversight—facilitates rapid economic growth in developing countries as well.

History has demonstrated, however, that things often go wrong in financial markets and institutions. Banks and other financial institutions fail, threatening to trigger contagious runs of depositors and other creditors. Stock and bond markets have crashed, displaying a similar type of contagious behavior by panicky investors. If sufficiently serious, these financial malfunctions can significantly disrupt the wider economy—much as the breakdown of a car's transmission would bring the car itself to a halt.

Continuous improvements in financial technologies, aided by the extraordinary expansion of computing power at ever lower costs, has driven finance to become increasingly international in scope, helping to integrate developing economies with the rest of the world. But the same process of globalization has also facilitated the transmission of financial crises across national borders. This has become evident in

196

each of the last three decades: when the Bankhaus Herstatt of Germany failed in 1974, triggering a panic on international currency markets; the sovereign debt crisis of the 1980s, which threatened the solvency of a number of the largest banks in the world, especially the money center banks headquartered in the United States; and the series of currency crises in the 1990s, beginning with Mexico in 1994–1995 and continuing with Southeast Asia and Russia in 1997–1998, which sent a shudder through even developed country capital markets.

Policy makers have responded to these events by escalating their efforts to coordinate the supervision of financial institutions and markets, while implementing or seeking to implement minimum prudential standards. Further, they have increasingly relied on an international financial safety net: emergency loans provided by the International Monetary Fund (IMF) designed in large part to stop contagious behavior in currency markets. In turn, the IMF has acted as a global economic governor by imposing a variety of conditions on borrowing countries. Each of these developments has been accompanied with controversy.

This chapter distills several key lessons about the way in which financial issues get on the international agenda, how they are negotiated, and how negotiated agreements are monitored and enforced.[1] Eight broad themes emerge from this discussion.

First, by definition, successful international agreements result when there is consensus among the negotiating parties. In each of the successful episodes reviewed below, however, it is noteworthy that the United States—and, in some cases, Great Britain—played leading roles in inducing the other participating countries to join that consensus. The leaders set the agenda and were instrumental figures in the subsequent negotiations.

Second, the successful international efforts in the financial arena generally have emerged in response to *crises*. At the same time, not all of the agreements emerged immediately. In one case—the development of the Bretton Woods agreement—the parties faced an imminent deadline: the coming end of World War II. The pace of negotiations for the other agreements depended on both the need for immediate action and the degree of consensus among the parties going into the negotiation.

Third, none of the international financial arrangements surveyed in this chapter have lasted intact in their original form. One—the system of fixed but adjustable exchange rates—no longer exists, largely because market forces made the original system impossible to enforce. Meanwhile, each of the other arrangements has been modified in response to subsequent events. This pattern suggests that for agreements to endure they must be flexible enough—and more specifically, the parties to them need to be sufficiently flexible—to accommodate change.

Fourth, for most of the post–World War period, international efforts to make global finance run more smoothly have involved technical issues familiar only to financial policy makers (finance ministries and central banks, and their staffs) and to officials in firms providing financial services. The technocrats set the agenda and conduct the negotiations. The relatively narrow range of participants has facilitated agreements on these technical issues.

In recent years, however, global finance has become increasingly intertwined with broader, nonfinancial issues. In the process, the range of players is also expanding, from the public officials and financial specialists who have traditionally been occupied with financial matters, to now include nonfinancial, nongovernmental organizations (NGOs) and their members and constituents. NGOs with interest and expertise in these other issues have made their presence felt and want to be part of any future international efforts aimed at facilitating cross-border financial operations. This has been most powerfully demonstrated in the opposition to further liberalization of restrictions on cross-border foreign direct investment (FDI). If policy makers and financial services firms want further liberalization of country rules that now inhibit financial flows, they will have to find some way to take these broader interests into account.

Fifth, only one of the international financial regimes—the Bretton Woods regime of fixed exchange rates and associated international financial institutions (IFIs)—is truly global. The multinational bank capital standards developed in the 1980s involved only like-minded industrialized countries. Similarly, the attempt to negotiate a liberalized investment framework was conducted only within the Organization for Economic Cooperation and Development (OECD), also a group of like-minded advanced countries. These experiences demonstrate that not all multinational agreements need be global arrangements.

Sixth, international financial agreements have tended so far to rely heavily on command-and-control regulatory techniques to minimize any negative consequences associated with increased financial integration. Yet market forces undermined the effectiveness of fixed exchange rates, while the command-and-control approach to international bank safety and soundness—represented by "capital standards"—also has come under increasingly stiff market pressures. A key challenge for policy makers is finding ways of harnessing market forces to assist them in their efforts to provide stability in global finance.

Seventh, a related point is that states have had uneven success in enforcing their international financial agreements. To some extent, the Bretton Woods system of fixed exchange rates was self-enforcing because countries running deficits in their balance of payments had to make changes in their domestic economic policies or else devalue—otherwise they would run out of foreign exchange. But there was no self-enforcing mechanism within Bretton Woods for countries running consistent balance-of-payments surpluses (although the agreement envisioned that these countries, too, were obligated to make changes in their domestic economies to reduce those surpluses).

The IFIs also have had the means to enforce the policy agreements they have negotiated with borrowing countries: if countries want the money, they have to comply. In this sense, the IFIs have accumulated power akin to a domestic sovereign government. At the other extreme, however, the states that have negotiated minimum bank capital standards have found it impossible to enforce those standards through international fiat; instead, the market has done some of the job, although imperfectly.

In the end, the challenge for policy makers in the twenty-first century is to learn from both the successes and mistakes of the past, while constructing institutions that better enable economies to reap the benefits of modern finance without suffering the pitfalls that plagued so many countries in the century. The challenge is akin to that discussed in the chapter in this volume on international efforts to address health problems: like diseases, financial crises cannot be eliminated, but their likelihood can be reduced and their adverse impacts can and should be minimized and contained.

NATURE OF THE PROBLEM

Not all banking problems have global implications. But in an increasingly global financial marketplace, the links between banking systems and capital markets continue to grow stronger, ensuring that problems in one arena can easily spill over into problems in others. These so-called financial externalities can, at times, lead to crises—a circumstance that has often justified interventions by national or supranational governments. These dangers—and the responses to them—are the main subjects of this section.

Finance is important not just for its own sake but because it is central to the process of economic growth. Financial intermediaries (banks, securities firms, mutual funds, and insurers) and markets enhance both saving and investment, thereby enlarging the capital stock and thus increasing the productivity of workers. In addition, because they are able to take advantage of economies of scale in collecting and evaluating information about investment projects and their sponsors, financial intermediaries in particular can help efficiently allocate capital to its most productive uses. These are not merely theoretical propositions. Empirical evidence confirms that the level of financial development is highly correlated with economic growth, controlling for other factors.[2]

Financial intermediation need not be, and indeed increasingly is not, confined within national borders. Much of the economic history of the world since the end of World War II centers on the rising mobility of capital across national borders and resuming a trend toward increasing integration. This was also true for several decades prior to World War I but was interrupted between the two world wars. Indeed, cross-border capital flows have been rising for some time now at an annual rate that is as much as 10 percentage points higher than world output.[3] In the process, the integration of capital markets across borders has lowered the cost of borrowing, while offering savers opportunities to earn higher risk-adjusted rates of return. It is sometimes noted that, even so, capital markets are no more integrated today—as measured by capital flows as a ratio of gross domestic product (GDP)—than they were before World War II. This is a misreading of the available evidence, however. A century ago, cross-border, long-term investments in the United States in particular were far more narrowly concentrated in a few sectors (such as railroads) than is true today, while trading in foreign exchange was virtually nonexistent compared with the vast sums that slosh around in world capital markets now.[4]

Economists debate the relative importance of various causes of the postwar expansion of cross-border financial activity, but all of the following clearly have played a role: the continuous decline in the costs of communicating, storing, and evaluating information (which facilitates investment in faraway places); the gradual lifting of controls on movements of capital; and the increasing importance of trade in goods and services that capital flows are required to finance.

It is customary to distinguish between two types of cross-border financial flows. So-called portfolio capital consists of investments that are potentially short term in nature, including loans between banks and investments in traded bonds and equities. Cross-border interbank lending now exceeds $6 trillion, up from $1.2 trillion as recently as 1983.[5] The globalization of stock markets also has facilitated the movement of portfolio capital between countries. The shares of portfolios invested in foreign stocks and bonds has been rising steadily in the United States, Western Europe, and even Japan, although investors in all countries continue to favor disproportionately firms headquartered at home.[6] Bond markets, too, have become increasingly international in scope, with sovereign and private firms in both the developed and developing countries issuing debt to investors around the world.

In contrast, FDI consists of equity holdings aimed at controlling or exercising significant influence over the management of local firms.[7] FDI has become increasingly linked to trade. It no longer suffices to simply ship many products across borders to customers waiting in foreign lands to purchase them. Consumer and business products often require local servicing operations, as well as research and development and marketing enterprises, if they are to be sold effectively in other countries. Moreover, financial and professional services, among others, typically can only be supplied by an on-the-ground presence in other countries (although this need not be true for services supplied via the Internet).

It is also important to distinguish the sources and destinations of capital movements. Given that most trade takes place among developed countries, it is not surprising that most capital flows have followed the same pattern. Significantly, however, Asia and Latin America have also recently become major destinations of FDI (the same is not true for FDI outflows, which remain relatively small in both regions).

The financial and currency crises of 1997–1998 in Southeast Asia and Russia have called special attention to capital flows into developing countries and emerging markets. Table 5-1 shows that inflows of all types in developing countries rose dramatically during the 1990s, hitting a peak in 1997. Perhaps most remarkably, all of the increase was in private capital. Official capital flows actually declined from 1990 to 1997, picking up only in 1998 to help ease the pain of the financial crises.

Finally, not only is capital increasingly crossing borders, but so are financial institutions. Although Japanese financial institutions were in the vanguard in the globalization movement during the 1980s, in the 1990s U.S. and European institutions undertook major cross-border expansion.[8] Indeed, by the end of the 1990s, U.S. banks collectively derived as much as 15 percent of their profits from foreign operations, and for the five largest banks, the foreign profit share was much higher, close to 45 percent.[9] Meanwhile, many foreign financial institutions are active in the U.S. market, and almost 350 companies are listed on the New York Stock Exchange. During this decade, much cross-border consolidation among European banks and other financial institutions is expected in the wake of the new euro, which has exposed pricing differentials between countries and thus encouraged the exit of inefficient firms, often by acquisition.

When functioning well, finance is critical to facilitating economic growth. But when finance malfunctions, economic growth can be stalled or thrown into reverse. In fact, between 1975 and 1997, there were 158 exchange rate crises and fifty-four banking crises in a representative sample of roughly fifty countries around the world.[10] Given that financial activity increasingly crosses borders, it is inevitable that financial problems in one part of the world can and will cause damage in other parts as well. Three broad concerns have been raised about global finance: two relate to capital flows, the third relates to financial institutions (specifically to commercial banks).

The first concern about capital flows—specifically about portfolio capital movements—is about their volatility or instability. As the recent Asian and Russian financial crises have demonstrated, when investors lose confidence in a country's currency and its economic policy, they can and do act in a hurry. More often than not, the first investors to run are those best acquainted with local circumstances, namely domestic residents.[11]

In fact, the dangers of capital flight have been recognized for many decades. The Bretton Woods arrangement of fixed but adjustable exchange rates, for example, explicitly permitted countries as part of that arrangement to maintain capital controls to assure that their exchange rates could be defended (without having to raise interest rates to punishingly high levels in a crisis).

A different concern has been voiced about the cross-border movement of long-term capital, or FDI: that it is helping to drive a race to the bottom in the setting of

Table 5-1. *Net Long-term Resource Flows to Developing Countries*
(US$ billion)

Type of flows:	1990	1991	1992	1993	1994	1995	1996	1997	1998[a]
Net long-term resource flows	100.8	123.1	152.3	220.2	223.6	254.9	308.1	338.1	275.0
Official flows	56.9	62.6	54.0	53.3	45.5	53.4	32.2	39.1	47.9
Private flows	43.9	60.5	98.3	167.0	178.1	201.5	275.9	299.0	227.1
From international capital markets	19.4	26.2	52.2	100.0	89.6	96.1	149.5	135.5	72.1
Private debt flows	15.7	18.6	38.1	49.0	54.4	60.0	100.3	105.3	58.0
Commercial bank loans	3.2	4.8	16.3	3.3	13.9	32.4	43.7	60.1	25.1
Bonds	1.2	10.8	11.1	37.0	36.7	26.6	53.5	42.6	30.2
Others	11.4	3.0	10.7	8.6	3.7	1.0	3.0	2.6	2.7
Portfolio equity flows	3.7	7.6	14.1	51.0	35.2	36.1	49.2	30.2	14.1
Foreign direct investment	24.5	34.4	46.1	67.0	88.5	105.4	124.4	163.4	155.0

a. Based on preliminary data.
Source: World Bank, Debtor Reporting System.

domestic policies and regulatory standards. Unlike the volatility of capital flows that primarily has occupied the attention of policy makers, the concerns about a race to the bottom were voiced initially by NGOs—environmental organizations, labor unions, and some "consumer" activists—who fear that companies and investors in developed economies increasingly are being driven to build facilities in developing countries where wages are far lower and the social safety net is much less well established than it is in rich countries. This process, it is claimed, inhibits rich countries from maintaining their costlier social welfare policies and regulatory standards. Although the evidence for these claims is sparse—and the lion's share of FDI goes to other rich countries—the fears about companies fleeing to lower-cost locations are very real in developed countries.[12]

The third set of concerns relates to the cross-border financial "spillovers" entailed in the activities of large financial institutions, primarily banks. The focus on banks is readily understood. As shown in table 5-2, except for the United States and South Korea, banks dominate finance throughout the world.

Bank failures can have international or cross-border consequences in several ways, and to the degree these occur or threaten to occur, they generate support for multinational policy solutions. A large bank that has many counterparties, directly or through a bank clearinghouse such as CHIPS (the largest private sector clearing and settlement system in the United States, which also handles dollar clearings for large foreign banks), can send shivers through the financial system if it fails and causes large losses to cascade to other banks.[13] In addition, weak banking systems can slow economic growth, or even threaten to trigger a recession. In a world where economies are increasingly interlinked, therefore, severe banking problems in one country or region of the world can adversely affect the economies of other countries or regions. Indeed, this possible chain of events was very much on the minds of policy makers during the sovereign debt crisis of the 1980s, which posed real risks to the solvency of major banks in the United States and elsewhere.

Policy makers have been driven to join hands not only to prevent financial problems, but also to protect the business interests of home country financial institutions. Because of their importance to the economy, and more recently, because governments insure their deposits, banks have been subject to government regulation to ensure their safety and soundness. The prime regulatory instrument used in most countries has been a minimum capital requirement, or a rule that some fraction of bank assets be supported by shareholders' equity and possibly subordinated debt (uninsured bonds), rather than deposits, which often are insured by the government by law or by practice.

In a global economic environment, capital requirements in different countries can have powerful effects on the abilities of banks to expand, because the level of capital requirement determines the amount of leverage an institution can adopt. The higher

Table 5-2. *Bank Share of Assets of Financial Intermediaries, Selected Countries, 1994*

Country	Percentage
Argentina	98
Brazil	97
Chile	62
Colombia	86
Germany	77
India	80
Indonesia	91
Japan	79
Malaysia	64
Mexico	87
Singapore	71
South Korea	38
Taiwan	80
Thailand	75
United States	23

Source: Morris Goldstein and Philip Turner "Banking Crises in Emerging Economies: Origins and Policy Options," Economic Paper No. 46 (Basel, Switzerland: Bank for International Settlements, 1996).

the capital requirement, the lower the degree of permissible leverage. Developed countries have adopted minimum capital standards to minimize cross-border risks arising out of bank failure. These international rules, however, were motivated as much by concerns of competitive equity across countries—to ensure that banks from no single country had an artificial advantage because of more relaxed capital rules—as they were to shore up the safety and soundness of the global banking system.

Finally, it bears mention that the first and third concerns—those relating to excessive capital volatility and to the global consequences of weak financial systems—can be and have been intertwined. By sending tremors across global currency markets, the failure of Bankhaus Herstatt provided an early demonstration of the links between banks and cross-border flows. The recent Southeast Asian financial crisis provided even more powerful proof: it began with the failure of a little-known financial institution in Thailand. This crisis, and subsequently the one in Russia, illustrates that cross-border effects also can run in the other direction. Capital flight can lead to the depreciation of local currencies, which in turn significantly enlarges the domestic currency burden of debt denominated in foreign currencies, thereby threatening the solvency of financial institutions that are not properly hedged (or that do not have assets and liabilities in matching currencies and maturities).

TRACK RECORD OF INTERNATIONAL RESPONSES

Since the end of World War II, there have been several international responses to the challenges posed by excessive volatility in capital flows and potential cross-border spillovers from failures of financial institutions (primarily banks). The main effort relating to capital flows actually was the more far reaching of the two, representing a true attempt to establish a "global financial architecture" for the postwar era. That effort of course was embodied in the Bretton Woods agreement of 1944, initiated primarily by the two principal victors—the United States and Great Britain—and joined by forty-two other allied countries. As part of the agreement, the parties established the IMF and the World Bank. The linchpin of the new architecture was a system of fixed but adjustable exchange rates. That system was designed to correct what was then perceived as one of the great international economic problems of the prewar era: successive rounds of competitive exchange rate depreciations that, along with heightened trade barriers, deepened the Great Depression of the 1930s.

Under the Bretton Woods system, countries would fix the exchange rate of their currencies in terms of gold, which in turn meant that the exchange rates between different currencies were also fixed. However, unlike the era of the gold standard, which existed before the Depression, the Bretton Woods system permitted countries to change their exchange rates if their currencies became significantly undervalued or overvalued. This exchange rate "escape clause" was rarely used through the first two decades of the Bretton Woods system but began to be invoked more frequently in the late 1960s until the breakdown of the entire fixed rate system in the early 1970s.

The Bretton Woods arrangement addressed capital flows—specifically short-term flows not related to trade—only indirectly, as part of the larger effort to maintain fixed exchange rates. The U.S. and British negotiators at Bretton Woods—Harry Dexter White and John Maynard Keynes, respectively—did not view flows of capital between countries in the same benign light as flows of goods and services. To the contrary, they believed that the interwar period had demonstrated cross-border movements of short-term capital to be volatile and disruptive, and although the Bretton Woods agreement did not actually encourage countries to enact capital controls, it also did not discourage them from doing so. At the same time, both men—and the countries they represented—wanted a postwar system much freer of trade restrictions than the protection-laden system of the 1930s. Accordingly, in creating the IMF, the negotiators made sure that although countries were permitted to restrict currency conversions related to capital movements, they were required to convert their currencies into others for so-called current account transactions, or those relating to trade.[14] As a result of the IMF's position on capital account controls, many developing countries that emerged from the war with strong balance-of-payments positions nonetheless adopted restrictions in later years when they ran into payments difficulties.[15]

The IMF was created to administer the exchange rate system and to act like a bank for countries needing temporary assistance in financing their balance-of-payments deficits. If those deficits were truly temporary, or could be made temporary through appropriate adjustments in macroeconomic policy, then the IMF "bridge financing" would enable the country to avoid having to change its exchange rate. In this way, the IMF buttressed the system of fixed rates. In launching the World Bank, the negotiators at Bretton Woods sought to provide long-term project financing to countries that could not access global capital markets at reasonable rates of interest. Later, regional development banks were formed for Africa, Asia, Latin America, and eventually Eastern Europe. These regional institutions, however, have tended to take their lead on policy matters from the World Bank, although it is not clear this will continue in the future if the Bank and its sister institution, the IMF, are limited in their financing by member governments.

Financial institutions have long engaged in cross-border activity, but it was not until the mid-1970s that nations began to take collective action to deal with the potential "spillovers" that failed institutions in one country could generate in others. As in the case of Bretton Woods, it took a crisis for nations to come to this realization: the failure in 1974 of the Bankhaus Herstatt, a medium-sized West German bank that had large foreign currency exposures. The bank's failure briefly threatened the interruption of foreign currency and interbank lending markets.

This brush with disaster led central banks in the major industrialized countries in Europe, Japan, and the United States—where 90 percent of the world's international banking activity was located—to form the Standing Committee on Banking Regulation and Supervisory Practices, since named the "Basel Committee," and to agree on principles of bank supervision embodied in a concordat. In its initial version, the agreement established the principle that the country of a parent bank has primary responsibility for ensuring its solvency and that of its subsidiaries and branches in foreign countries.[16] The concordat was subsequently revised to permit the exchange of sensitive information about banks among national supervisors and to recognize the importance of supervising international banks on a "consolidated basis," taking into account both banking and nonbanking activities.

Yet another crisis, this time with sovereign debt in the 1980s, led the Basel Committee to move beyond facilitating coordination of national supervisory policies and into the setting of regulatory standards themselves. The committee was spurred into action by the United States and Great Britain, whose financial authorities grew alarmed at the threat that large losses on loans to developing countries posed to the solvency of many of the largest international banks. To address that problem, central banks from the two countries agreed in 1986 on a set of minimum requirements relating to the amounts of capital, or shareholders' equity, banks had to maintain to support their assets. The Basel Committee followed two years later with its own "risk-based" system of capital rules.

The risk-based standards had the effect of requiring different amounts of capital to back various categories of assets and off–balance sheet exposures. For example, at one extreme, no capital was required to support bank investments in securities issued by governments of OECD countries. In contrast, most loans had to be backed by an 8 percent capital requirement (at least half to consist of equity). In the middle, residential mortgage loans required 4 percent capital backing, while interbank loans required capital of 1.6 percent.

Interestingly, although the Basel countries were moved to act because of bank lending problems in developing countries, the minimum standards set by the Basel Committee applied only to banks in developed countries. By the mid-1990s, the Group of Seven Industrialized Countries (G-7) (a smaller group of the largest members of the Basel Committee) recognized this anomaly and called on the committee to stimulate improvements in banking supervision in emerging market and developing countries. Ironically, the committee released the results of its efforts—*Core Principles for Effective Banking Supervision*—in September 1997, or just two months after the failure of a bank in Thailand triggered the Southeast Asian financial crisis.[17] The IMF has since made improvements in local banking supervision a key condition in its lending to countries affected by that crisis.

The fact that international financial standard setting came first to banking is not surprising given the dominance of banking in virtually all financial systems outside the United States (see table 5-2). Nonetheless, international efforts also have been under way for some time to enhance cooperation among national regulators and to develop prudential standards for other types of financial institutions.

The International Organization of Securities Commissions has focused primarily on encouraging the development of common accounting standards (through the International Accounting Standards Committee based in the United Kingdom) that issuers of securities can use to offer stock in multiple countries without having to comply with the separate disclosure requirements of each. At this writing, most of these standards have been developed and in fact are used in many countries—with the notable exception of the United States, whose Securities and Exchange Commission has been concerned that the international standards might have the effect of watering down the U.S. rules. Ultimately, however, it is likely that one day even the United States will adopt some form of the standards, and when this occurs, it will be much easier for multinational companies to list their shares in multiple exchanges throughout the world, and it will be much easier for investors in different countries to compare the performance of companies headquartered in various countries (because their accounts will have been prepared on a common basis).

In the insurance sector, regulators from many countries have developed prudential standards for insurance companies through the International Association of Insurance Supervisors. This effort is only several years old and too much in its infancy to judge its success.

Assessment of International Efforts

The success of the first two multinational efforts addressing financial issues—those aimed at cross-border capital flows and potential spillovers from financial failures—has been mixed. All three pillars of the Bretton Woods system—fixed exchange rates, the IFIs, and toleration of limits on cross-border capital flows—remained intact for several decades after the agreement was signed. In particular, the Bretton Woods system of fixed exchange rates, supported by the international financial institutions, "worked" for twenty-five years, in the sense that the exchange rate system did not break down.

However, because most global trade and finance was conducted in dollars, the system was also dependent throughout this period on the ability and willingness of the United States to supply liquidity—in the form of additional dollars year in and year out to finance trade and development around the world. The United States did this by consistently running current account deficits (and thus investing more than it was saving), by shipping abroad more dollars to pay for imported goods than it took in when selling exports abroad. This process might have continued indefinitely had the United States not begun to suffer an accelerating rate of inflation beginning in the late 1960s and continuing in the early 1970s, as a by-product of the country's unwillingness to pay for its Vietnam War defense spending. The continued erosion of the purchasing value of the dollar eventually caused investors at home and abroad to doubt the commitment of the United States to maintain its Bretton Woods commitment: to exchange its steadily larger supply of dollars for a fixed amount of gold (at the rate of $35/ounce). So after one devaluation in 1971, the United States shortly thereafter let its exchange rate float. By 1973 the Bretton Woods system of fixed rates, which hinged on the U.S. commitment to maintain a fixed gold parity, was officially dead.

The demise of fixed exchange rates, however, did not end either of the two major IFIs created under Bretton Woods. To the contrary, each continued to grow; however, as shown in table 5-1, official financing became relatively less important to many developing countries as private financing—bank loans, bonds, and equity—grew at a more rapid pace. Nonetheless, both IFIs have become more controversial, especially the IMF, in the wake of the series of major international financial crises of the 1990s triggered by banking problems and/or exchange rate devaluations associated with each of the following countries or regions: Mexico (1994–1995), Southeast Asia (1997–1998), Russia (1998), and Brazil (1999).

Simply put, with its obligation to support the system of fixed exchange rates no longer relevant, the IMF has transformed itself into a quasi lender of last resort for countries that have suffered bouts of financial crisis—and specifically, runs on their scarce holdings of foreign exchange. The IMF has justified this role as an effort to prevent financial contagion, while providing bridge financing to countries that agree to reform their economies as a condition for the loans. Such "conditionality," which was controversial at the outset of the Fund, traditionally has taken the form of macroeconomic "belt-tightening" or reductions of government deficits and increases in domestic interest rates designed to encourage investors (domestic and foreign) to maintain holdings of domestic currency. In the Southeast Asian financial crisis, the IMF broadened its conditions to include reforms in various domestic functions as well: financial regulation, bankruptcy regimes, and systems of corporate governance, among others.

With the anchor of fixed exchange rates gone, policy makers and academic scholars continue to debate vigorously the IMF's role, as well as the appropriate exchange rate regime. Perhaps the most controversy surrounds the future of the IMF. Critics argue that with fixed exchange rates gone, the Fund should disappear. That it has continued to exist and thus provided a financial safety net in repeated crises, these critics argue, has only encouraged unsound lending and borrowing, leading to more and deeper financial crises. This is the so-called problem of moral hazard, a term originally used in the insurance context to refer to the tendency of insureds to take greater risks knowing they have insurance coverage if the risks turn sour. At the other extreme are those who grant the need for the IMF to provide bridge financing to countries experiencing temporary runs on their foreign exchange reserves, but who believe that the Fund's conditions on its loans are inappropriate in some fashion: either its macroeconomic belt-tightening is uncalled for when countries are experiencing a collapse in domestic demand or its new microeconomic conditions aimed at reforming borrowers' domestic policies represent an unwarranted intrusion on borrowers' sovereignty and entail the risk of a severe political backlash.[18]

At this writing, the IMF has so far survived all of these criticisms but also has adopted a series of reforms or policy changes. Among other things, for example, the Fund now provides more information about its lending arrangements and assessments of the macroeconomic conditions of its members. At the behest of the United States, it has created a new Contingency Credit Line aimed at supplying credit in advance to countries following sound economic policies to insulate them from sudden, contagious runs on their foreign exchange reserves. Confounding its critics, the Fund has in rare cases—Russia in 1998 being a notable example—refused to lend to countries that do not follow its prescriptions. And the Fund's leaders have put private lenders on notice that they will have to share in some of the pain of working out the debts of countries that run into financial trouble (for example, Ecuador's inability to meet its foreign bond obligations in the fall of 1999).

Meanwhile, there appears to be a growing consensus among policy makers in the developed world that restrictions on the inflow of short-term foreign capital—such as the foreign reserve requirements that Chile once imposed on foreign investments of less-than-year maturity—can be an appropriate means of discouraging excessive short-term indebtedness.[19] But there continues to be strong skepticism in policy circles of restrictions on capital outflows, as well as restrictions on FDI, or long-term equity, that can and does bring foreign money and ideas to developing countries.

Indeed, it was precisely because of this consensus about the strengths of FDI that the developed country members of the OECD attempted to negotiate liberalization of remaining restrictions against FDI following the completion of the 1994 Uruguay Round of trade negotiations. In fact, multilateral trade negotiators began to address investment issues in the Uruguay Round itself through the agreement on trade-related investment measures, which prohibits trade-distorting restrictions on investment (such as local content and export performance requirements) and the General Agreement on Trade in Services (GATS), which is aimed at relaxing restrictions on cross-border investments in services industries in particular.

The OECD investment initiative, the Multilateral Agreement on Investment (MAI), would have clearly established that governments must abide by the rule of "national treatment" (whereby foreign and domestic firms are treated alike), refrain from imposing performance requirements (such as adhering to local content rules or export requirements) as a condition of investing, and not expropriate property without full compensation. If governments had violated these principles, an international tribunal could force them to pay damages. In short, the MAI would have established much the same open regime for cross-border investment as now exists for trade in goods under the rules of the General Agreement on Tariffs and Trade (GATT) and now the World Trade Organization (WTO).

Although such an objective may have seemed reasonable to many policy makers at the time, they unexpectedly encountered stiff opposition from various NGOs—environmental organizations, labor unions, and "consumer" groups—in different countries. These organizations expressed fears that if barriers to further cross-border investment were relaxed, developed country governments would be induced to weaken their regulatory standards and social welfare policies to deter their firms from locating facilities (and jobs) abroad where wages are lower and environmental controls are weaker. Putting aside whether such fears are justified—my view is that they largely are not—they had a powerful effect in halting any further discussions of the MAI within the OECD.[20] Moreover, these fears cast a cloud over the WTO ministerial meeting in Seattle in December 1999, where the agenda of the next round of trade negotiations ground to a halt. The Seattle debacle (and subsequent demonstrations at the World Bank/IMF meetings in Washington, D.C., in April 2000 and Prague in September 2000) clearly highlighted that amid vociferous demonstrations from various opponents to globalization and deep splits among Europe, the United States, and the developing countries on what that agenda should look like, concerns about mobility of capital and jobs will continue to be part of a larger campaign by the same

NGOs to include labor and environmental provisions in any future multilateral trade agreement (assuming one comes about).[21]

Finally, the jury is still out on the effort to establish international prudential standards for financial institutions—banks in particular. In the political realm, the Basel capital accord has been a striking success, illustrating that states with a common interest can indeed come together to form a potentially far-reaching international agreement. On strictly economic grounds, however, the Basel capital accord has been less successful: the standards established in the late 1980s quickly became outdated and, at this writing, are being considered for fundamental revision. In addition, the original agreement had no real mechanism—other than the market—to ensure its enforcement. That teaches a lesson: in the realm of international finance, markets often trump, and certainly tend to outpace, efforts of national regulators and policy makers.

LESSONS LEARNED

What lessons can policy makers take away from the various efforts at international cooperation and, to some extent, governance in global finance? To address this key question, it is useful to turn to each of the major topics just surveyed: how each became an international agenda item, how the negotiations subsequently proceeded, how the agreements were implemented, and what steps were taken to address noncompliance.

Agenda Setting

It is often said that necessity—or crisis—is the mother of invention. That aphorism has been amply confirmed in the case of two of the major efforts to address cross-border volatility: (1) the creation of the Bretton Woods system of fixed exchange rates and associated IFIs; and (2) more recently the development of common international prudential financial standards for financial institutions—especially banks. In contrast, the effort to put FDI liberalization on the international negotiating agenda did not follow from crisis, but instead flowed logically from the prior sequence of trade liberalization. Following their success in reducing virtually all tariff barriers to trade, as well as some nontariff barriers, the next step for negotiators seemed to be the removal of barriers to rights of establishment and thus long-term foreign investment.

Crisis alone does not necessarily set an agenda, for at least three reasons. First, recognition of a crisis may trigger calls for action, but the agenda-setting process is a separate issue. The experience in the financial arena teaches that the dominant actors—or the nations most wanting agreement and having the clout eventually to persuade and/or motivate others to reach agreement—set the agendas. For example, the two main impending victors of World War II, the United States and Great Britain, set the Bretton Woods agenda. Similarly, the same two countries were the first to set common bank capital standards in the 1980s, motivating the other members of the Basel Committee to adopt similar standards later in the decade.

Second, the contents of the agendas themselves in the financial arena have been shaped heavily by relevant preceding history. The system of fixed exchange rates at the heart of the Bretton Woods agreement was aimed at preventing a reoccurrence of the competitive exchange rate depreciations that, coupled with heightened tariff barriers, deepened the Great Depression of the 1930s. The initial impetus for the Basel agreement on bank capital standards came from the United States, and specifically the Congress, which in the International Lending and Supervisory Act of 1983 instructed U.S. bank regulators to work with their counterparts in other "major banking countries" to strengthen the capital bases of banks. The Congress in turn was responding to the weakened financial condition of the U.S. money center banks resulting from the sovereign debt crisis that was then unfolding.[22]

The Basel Concordat, and later the Basel capital standards, responded to very real concerns at the time that weaknesses in the banking systems of the major industrialized countries not only could act as a drag on economic growth, but in a worst case, could trigger or fuel a broad financial and economic collapse. More recently, the sudden occurrence and aftermath of the Asian financial crisis helped set the agenda for reform of the global financial architecture, and more specifically, of the way the IMF does business.

A third reason is that, apart from the experience with the MAI, financial agendas have been set by finance ministers and other technocrats, not necessarily by heads of state. Thus Keynes of Great Britain and White of the United States heavily guided Bretton Woods. The Basel Committee consisted of central bankers and has operated outside of the formal political sphere since it was created. In both cases, the dominance of financial technocrats should not be surprising given that the subject matter of finance is so heavily technical.[23]

At the same time, the agendas for international financial agreements have not been set in a vacuum. The Basel capital accord was driven not only by regulators' concerns about the adequacy of bank capital, but also by bankers' concerns that regulators not raise capital standards unless they coordinated any increase with other countries. The reason was so that U.S. and other banks would not be placed at a competitive disadvantage relative to other banks—notably those in Japan—where capital standards were perceived to be weaker.[24] More recently, banks have actively lobbied their governments and officials at the IMF in the wake of the Asian financial crisis to promote reforms, while broadly resisting efforts to have private lenders contribute to the costs of cleaning up after crises have occurred. Until the Russian crisis of 1998 and the IMF's implicit blessing of the default by Ecuador on its "Brady bonds" (bonds issued in the late 1980s and early 1990s to repay previous bank debts in part) in the fall of 1999, banks were not disappointed.

Meanwhile, as financial and trade policy makers attempted to broaden their agenda to cover FDI, they found themselves—quite unexpectedly—running head-on against the competing agenda of NGOs, who feared greater mobility of capital. The NGOs prevailed, making heavy use of a new technology—the Internet—to communicate the depth of their concerns to policy makers around the world. The NGOs succeeded also because the most important intended beneficiaries of the MAI—multinational companies—did not display much enthusiasm for the agreement, perhaps in large part because they believed they already had as much freedom as they needed to locate facilities in different countries without the agreement. In any event, the failure of the MAI, coupled with recent attempts by labor unions urging the IMF to pay attention to core labor standards when disbursing its loans to borrowing clients, demonstrates powerfully that international financial agreements and institutions are no longer the province of financial technocrats. In a world where everything seemingly becomes linked to everything else, other interests and their "experts" have become relevant players as well.

Negotiation

Although each of the major financial initiatives on which this chapter has focused—the Bretton Woods agreement, the various initiatives pursued by the Basel Committee, and the recent efforts aimed at reforming the financial architecture in the wake of the Asian financial situation—responded to a crisis, the pattern and pace of negotiation proceeded very differently. Accordingly, one of the main lessons from the negotiation phase of these agreements is that agreement is reached more rapidly the more severe and dangerous the crisis.

This was clearly evident in the case of Bretton Woods, as negotiators were facing the impending end of the war and the need to construct an economic framework that would be ready when that event arrived. Similarly, the Basel Committee was created, and the first concordat was reached, within one year after the failure of Bankhaus Herstatt, which awakened policy makers to the dangers of cross-border spillovers from failed financial institutions. Agreement on the Basel capital standards took longer to reach, in contrast, because the weaknesses in large banks exposed by the substandard condition of their loans to developing countries did not appear to pose an imminent threat to the stability of the world's financial system. In contrast, that threat appeared very real in the case of the Asian financial crisis, especially in August–September 1998 following the default of the Russian government on its bonds and the devaluation of the ruble. Finance ministers met quickly and repeatedly following these events and agreed on the reforms of the IMF and the financial architecture already discussed, although these initiatives were not as far-reaching as other observers wanted at the time—precisely because there was no consensus among policy makers about the merits of more ambitious or radical reform proposals.[25]

A second lesson is that the countries that drive the agenda of international financial arrangements not surprisingly also dominate the negotiation of the outcomes. This was clearly the case with the United States and Great Britain in Bretton Woods and more recently with the Basel capital accord. In the case of the IMF, the United States is the major financial supporter and thus has appeared to be the driving force behind recent IMF reforms. At the same time, the United States shares its power at the Fund with other industrialized countries and must gain the consent of the others before the Fund adopts or changes policy. In the case of the Basel capital accord, the United States was not successful in forging a consensus in Basel until it was able first to reach agreement with regulators from Great Britain. Only then did regulators from Japan consent to a similar arrangement, which paved the way for the full Basel Committee to put its seal of approval on a final arrangement in 1988. It is widely believed that Japan was pressured to join the accord only after the United States threatened to withhold further access to the U.S. market if the Japanese did not go along.[26]

There have been disagreements among the principal negotiating countries from time to time, however, on specific issues. For example, the British and the U.S. negotiators disagreed over one central element of the Bretton Woods architecture. Led by Keynes, the British favored the creation of a new international money (bancor) to facilitate lending to countries experiencing liquidity problems, so that the IMF would not be limited to lending only the foreign exchange that was contributed to it by each of its members. In contrast, the United States feared the creation of an institution that would have had such far-reaching lending authority—the equivalent of a world central bank—fears that have continued to this day.

In another instance Keynes strongly opposed having the IMF interject itself or get actively involved in overseeing the economic policies of borrowing countries. The U.S. negotiators, led by White, took the opposite view, wanting the Fund to have the authority to override a borrowing country's economic policies and, if necessary, to force it to change its exchange rate. A strong subtext to the U.S. position was that the U.S. negotiators expected that for some period after the war the United States would be the main creditor (through the IMF) to other countries, and if U.S. money was going to be used, the United States wanted assurances that it would be used wisely.

The British negotiators, however, had good company in advancing their more restricted view of the Fund's supervision of borrowing country policies: the U.S. Congress, which simultaneously was nervous about the IMF having too much money in reserve and getting too heavily involved in the internal affairs of borrowing countries.[27] The compromise that was reached cut back on the Fund's authority to dictate policy, but also rejected the British proposal for a new international money.

With the passage of time, however, the U.S. view about what has since been called "conditionality" gradually began to prevail. The more countries sought to borrow (in relation to their initial contribution to the IMF's reserves, or their "quota"), the more active the IMF became in attaching conditions to the funds, generally requirements that governments reduce their budget deficits or adopt other measures to restrain consumption, and therefore imports, to help rectify payments imbalances.[28] As already noted, in the 1990s the IMF embarked on a more ambitious course, adding to the standard macroeconomic policy adjustments a series of microeconomic conditions to its loans to transition economies and more recently to Asian countries. Among the newer conditions are reforms in local legal and financial systems, reductions in tariffs and other at-the-border restrictions, and changes in domestic corporate and bankruptcy laws.

A third lesson is that negotiations are far more likely to succeed where the parties have agreed on the agenda in advance, the negotiations are conducted by technical experts, and outside interests are relatively narrowly focused. Each of these conditions was present in the case of Bretton Woods and the Basel capital accord. In the case of Bretton Woods, there was an overriding objective shared by the parties, who were led by the United States, to prevent the financial nightmare of the 1930s that helped lead to World War II.

The Basel capital accord, meanwhile, emerged as the product of a highly technical exercise requiring the specialized input of policy makers and, to a lesser extent, representatives of the financial community.[29] The technical nature of the subject matter limited the degree to which groups outside the financial and policy-making communities wanted to or could get involved. And without outside involvement, agreement was easier to reach, especially once U.S. regulators had agreed on a set of standards with their counterparts in Great Britain. Further, the decision by U.S. regulators to take seriously the concerns of the U.S. banking industry that any increase in capital standards be implemented only in the context of leveling the international playing field helped remove any serious opposition to the capital accords, which in turn meant that Congress had no reason to become involved either.

The failure of the MAI stands in stark contrast to the Basel experience. Although the negotiators were trade technocrats from the various OECD countries, they failed to attract the enthusiastic support of the business communities they ostensibly thought they were representing. Meanwhile, interest groups previously uninvolved in financial issues—and in this particular case openly hostile to the liberalizing agenda formulated by the negotiating parties—in effect "crashed the party" and eventually helped ruin the entire effort.

Implementation and Compliance

Agreements to which parties have paid considerable attention during the negotiation phase are highly likely to be implemented, if only because of the time and effort that each has invested in them. At the same time, international agreements—like contracts between private parties—are essentially voluntary: parties join them when they perceive that they have more to gain from participating than any costs that may be entailed in compliance.

Agreements are rarely one-shot deals, however. Instead, like constitutions, they require continued interpretation and good faith by the parties to adhere to any refinements or new interpretations that may come along.

Both the Bretton Woods and Basel agreements fit this pattern. Each has required flexibility and continued evolution beyond the original agreement. In particular, the international financial agreements were forced to adapt to market developments— and in the case of the Bretton Woods agreement on fixed exchange rates, eventually to give way entirely to the market. In the case of the IMF lending designed to cushion the impacts of financial crises, the conditionality program has evolved from one centered on macroeconomic factors to programs entailing much more detailed microeconomic measures. The reason is straightforward although not without controversy: whereas financial and exchange rate crises prior to 1997 stemmed largely from macroeconomic imbalances—which can be cured by fiscal austerity and/or tighter monetary policy—the Asian financial crisis taught policy makers the lesson that even countries with apparently sound macroeconomic policies can still be victimized by runs on their currencies. This in turn is more likely to happen when firms or governments borrow excessively in foreign currency with short maturities.

Similarly, national bank regulators that are members of the Basel Committee have had to play catch-up to the markets almost from the very first day the capital accord was finalized in 1988. Indeed, at the outset there was widespread recognition that the "risk-bucket" approach embodied in the standards—whereby required capital is based on the measurement of the risks of individual assets but not on the risk of a bank's entire portfolio—had significant shortcomings. In addition, the initial standards centered only on credit risk and ignored other types of risks common to banks: liquidity, managerial, and trading. Accordingly, the committee has introduced several revisions of the original standards, most notably grafting onto those standards in the mid-1990s a purportedly market-based approach to requiring separate capital backing for trading risks. After initially attempting to impose a single method on banks of measuring the risks of their trading portfolio, the committee eventually deferred to the banking industry and let banks use their own "internal models" to assess these risks.

Given their origins in committees, each of the international agreements has maintained a committee-like structure to develop these refinements. For Bretton Woods, however, the committee turned into permanent institutions—the IMF and the World Bank—each run by a permanent full-time staff, but reporting to an executive committee consisting of the states that helped create them. At the same time, reflecting the dominant role of the United States and United Kingdom in creating the two IFIs, the major decisions of each organization are made by a system of weighted voting under which the countries supplying the largest funding also receive the greatest weights. These weights have changed over time to reflect the changing distribution of the contributions.

By contrast, the Basel Committee operates by true consensus. Although the members seem to accord implicit deference to the United States, this is not always the case. The Bundesbank representatives on the committee have been especially influential in gaining special discounts in the risk weighting system for bank capital for mortgage lending, for example.

Earlier, an assessment was offered regarding the "success" of each of the major international financial agreements. In that context, success was narrowly defined to encompass primarily the degree to which the agreements have lasted. There is another, arguably more important, metric of success: by how much, if at all, the agreements have improved economic performance. There is no clear consensus, however, on this issue. It is hard to know how economic events would have unfolded under different regimes. Moreover, the agreements discussed in this chapter themselves have evolved with changes in events. Nonetheless, it is useful to review some of the prevailing views about the ways in which each of the major agreements—Bretton Woods and Basel—has actually worked, and what their effects have been.

Scholars have continued to debate whether the Bretton Woods system of fixed exchange rates—and the subsequent demise of the regime—was good or bad for the world economy. Supporters of the original system, such as former U.S. Federal Reserve chairman Paul Volcker, point to the strong record of economic growth from the end of World War II to 1973, when the system came apart.[30] The following decades were marked by bouts of inflation and slower productivity growth, evidence that supporters of the original system of fixed rates cite to support their view that the demise of the fixed rate system helped usher in a period of inferior economic performance. Accordingly, certain policy makers in Europe and some economists have favored a return to fixed rates or to one step removed—a system allowing countries to float their currencies only within relatively narrow bands, which themselves might change, or "crawl," over time.[31]

So far, this seems to be the minority view. Most economists continue to believe that the demise of the fixed rate system was inevitable. By the 1970s, too many dollars were outstanding on world markets to sustain the belief that the United States would be able to honor the commitment to exchange its dollars for its scarce gold reserves at the fixed rate of $35 per ounce, a price upon which all other exchange rates were pegged. In this view, the world economy faced unsettling events after 1973 not because of the end of fixed exchange rates, but because of a series of exogenous shocks, notably large increases in oil prices in 1973–1974 and 1979–1980, which inevitably led both to reduced output and higher inflation in the oil-consuming nations. More to the point, one of the lessons that has emerged from the Asian financial crisis is that countries fix their exchange rates at great peril, and attempts to prop them up when foreign exchange reserves are limited run a high risk of failure. To be sure, the introduction of the euro in place of the previous system of fixed exchange rates (the European Monetary System) throughout Western Europe is a stark exception, but its development arose more out of political than economic factors. In addition, the European Union has created institutions—such as the European Central Bank—to help support the new currency. Eventually there may be more currency blocks, centered perhaps around the dollar and the yen, but at this date, most of the countries outside Europe now let the values of their exchange rates be determined by the market rather than by fiat.

Sentiment also has shifted on capital controls, which were a linchpin of the original Bretton Woods system. Since the establishment of that agreement, capital controls and restrictions on the convertibility of domestic currencies into foreign exchange (for trade purposes) have been substantially relaxed. With the United States and other developed economies paving the way in the 1970s and 1980s, many emerging market countries have repealed at least some of their capital controls in the 1990s to attract financing from abroad to facilitate more rapid growth. The United States and the IMF have cheered this process on.[32]

Here again, the Asian crisis seems to have induced a change in thinking. One of the most important lessons from that experience is that countries with weak systems for monitoring and ensuring the health of their financial institutions and corporations run great risks if they also peg their exchange rates and open up to short-term capital inflows from abroad. Under these circumstances, there is a great temptation for local residents to engage in "currency arbitrage": that is, borrowing from abroad at low interest rates, often at short maturities, in the hope of investing the proceeds locally to generate much higher returns. This game may go on for a time, but if not appropriately supervised and constrained, it will lead to bubbles—that will burst. And when they do, both domestic and foreign holders of the currency will dump it before the government is forced to devalue the currency. That is exactly what happened in Asia.

Accordingly, there is an emerging consensus among policy makers in developed and developing states that it is permissible, if not recommended, for countries with weak financial infrastructure—imperfect financial supervision and inadequate means of corporate governance—to inhibit inflows of short-term capital, especially short-term foreign currency debt.[33] This can be done by *temporarily* imposing reserve requirements on short-term capital inflows, as Chile has done (but since abandoned because governmental leaders had come to believe that the controls had outlived their usefulness), or through explicit regulatory limits on banks in particular (for example, by requiring their foreign currency borrowings to match the foreign currency composition of assets and their maturity).

The jury is also still out on the impact of the Basel capital accord. It is uncontestable that since the original accord, implemented in 1989, capital ratios at major banks throughout most of the world—Japan being a significant exception about which more is said below—have improved substantially. Indeed, in the United States the banking system at the end of the century looked healthier, measured by both capitalization and profitability, than it has been in several decades.

Nonetheless, it would be inappropriate to attribute all, or perhaps even much, of this improvement to the Basel agreement. For example, because of its severe banking problems of the 1980s, the United States went ahead anyhow and changed its domestic laws in both 1989 and 1991 to force banks and thrift institutions to have higher capital cushions. Scandinavian countries that experienced severe banking problems in the late 1980s and 1990s, which as a percentage of GDP were worse than those in the United States, also almost surely would have done so had Basel not been in place.

More fundamentally, the Basel standards from the outset have had at least three well-recognized weaknesses—apart from the lack of an effective enforcement mechanism. First, the initial risk-based system, which assigned different capital requirements to different asset "buckets," was admittedly crude. It took no account of other types of risk to which a bank was exposed, such as interest rate risk arising from the mismatching of maturities of assets and liabilities, managerial risks, and market risks. In addition, the system took no account of the risks of a bank's overall portfolio, which according to modern finance theory should be the central focus of regulatory attention. The Basel Committee was sensitive to these omissions and over time gradually attempted to refine—some would say further complicate—the initial standards to take some of these additional considerations into account.

A second shortcoming of the current standards, exposed by the Asian crisis, is in the risk weights. Interbank loans in particular have required only 20 percent of the capital backing (1.6 percent versus 8 percent) as is required of most ordinary bank loans. It is now generally recognized that this risk differential encouraged excessive lending by large foreign banks to banks in Asia and Russia.

A third weakness is that the Basel Committee lags developments in the market and thus is always in the role of constantly trying to catch up to unanticipated events. In part, this is inherent in any multinational decision-making process that operates by consensus. But it can be especially problematic in a field such as finance where technological advances are threatening to outrun the abilities of national regulators to monitor them adequately, let alone those of an international body such as the Basel Committee.

The committee is in the process of responding to at least the last two of these concerns. In early June 1999, it proposed a major revamping of the risk weights, one that would rely on the ratings that borrowers receive from major credit rating agencies. Among other things, this new system would have the effect of raising the capital required on interbank lending, while allowing the risk weights for certain types of borrowers to reflect market developments, to the extent they are reflected in the ratings. The committee proposed further refinements to the standards in early 2001 but postponed a final decision during the summer of 2001, probably until some time in 2002.

Ultimately, despite their substantive weaknesses, the Basel standards are a testament to the political agility of the central bankers of the developed world to establish and adhere to agreement on a complicated, technical matter. In addition, the developed country members of Basel have helped to create a precedent by developing prudential safeguards for financial systems—a lesson that at least some emerging market countries seem to be taking to heart since the Asian financial crisis revealed the dangers that economies face from weak banks and even weaker systems of financial regulation.

Reactions to Noncompliance

Some agreements are self-enforcing; others require some supervening authority—such as a judiciary or a panel of the parties—to enforce their terms. Perhaps the most striking lesson to emerge from the international financial agreements reached during the postwar period is that the more agreements rely on self-enforcing techniques, the more effective—in terms of their original goals—they are likely to be.

The best example of this principle, of course, is the system of fixed exchange rates under Bretton Woods, which, while they lasted, were largely (although not entirely) self-enforcing. Countries that ran large and consistent balance-of-payments deficits faced the exhaustion of their foreign exchange reserves, without which they could not conduct further trade and commerce. This system provided strong discipline to government policy makers who were thus compelled to pursue macroeconomic policies that kept exchange rates fixed. If they allowed too much inflation, for example, exportable products would be priced out of world markets, and the country would lose foreign exchange reserves.

In extreme cases—that is, where the domestic adjustments were too great—governments had a choice: they could claim they faced a "structural" current account deficit and ask the IMF for permission to devalue, which would make their exports cheaper in terms of foreign currency, while raising the domestic currency price of foreign imports. In combination, exchange rate depreciations, at least in principle, would help correct current account deficits and thus bring in more foreign exchange. Alternatively, governments could seek temporary financing from the IMF in an effort maintain their current exchange rates.

This system worked reasonably well for the twenty-five years or so fixed rates were in effect, but it is notable that its enforcement mechanism was asymmetric. Only countries experiencing payments deficits actually were forced to do anything under the Bretton Woods system. If they did not, they would run out of foreign exchange and thus be unable to participate in international commerce. In theory, the IMF's

Articles of Agreement had an enforcement mechanism for countries running consistent payments surpluses: if they failed to adopt policies to end those surpluses—for example, by stimulating their economies to increase imports—they were exposed to discriminatory trade sanctions from other countries under the "scarce currency clause" of Article VII. But punishment for surpluses was not automatic, or action forcing, in the same way as was true for countries running payments deficits. Not surprisingly, therefore, surplus countries were not disciplined.

The asymmetry in enforcement eventually contributed to the demise of the fixed rate system. For a combination of reasons, one country—the United States—consistently ran payments deficits, while many other countries ran surpluses. Faster productivity growth abroad enabled other countries to expand exports more rapidly than the United States. Meanwhile, the U.S. government sent dollars abroad in the form of foreign aid, while private U.S. firms invested abroad in foreign markets. In the process, the Bretton Woods system of exchange rates tied to gold gradually became transformed into a "dollar standard," because the U.S. dollar became the key currency in which most international trade and finance was carried out. Most significant, bank deposits and other short-term securities held around the world were denominated in dollars.

The proliferation of dollars was useful, if not essential, in providing liquidity for firms and investors to conduct commerce. At the same time, however, the more dollars the United States pumped out, the less credible became its commitment to redeem gold for dollars at the official exchange rate of $35 per ounce. As discussed earlier, largely because of rising inflation brought on by heavy spending for the Vietnam War and domestic programs, the United States lost credibility in the early 1970s over its gold-for-dollars commitment. As a result, the United States was forced to devalue and ultimately to float its currency. At no point during this period did other countries consistently running payments surpluses volunteer to raise the values of their currencies.

A second lesson regarding enforcement is that agreements that entail the commitment of financial resources seem to gravitate toward the use of conditions as an instrument of enforcement. The key example here is the gradual emergence of conditionality as a critical element in IMF lending. In effect, for those countries that need IMF assistance, the IMF has become the economic "grandmother" that Keynes so vigorously opposed when the design of the Fund was originally debated.

The World Bank has moved in a similar direction. Whereas the Bank once was confined to providing only project-based financing, during the past two decades it has increased its structural adjustment lending (that is, loans to facilitate broad economic reform programs in borrowing countries). The structural adjustment loans also carry conditions: they are disbursed only as countries continue to follow the reforms that were originally negotiated with the Bank. The Bank's structural adjustment lending has blurred the distinction between its activities and those of the IMF.

The steady expansion of the types of conditions imposed by the Fund (and to a lesser extent the Bank) has not been without controversy. In the late 1990s, the IMF defended the use of broader, microeconomic conditions by arguing that macroeconomic adjustments alone are not likely to be sufficient to restore investor confidence in a country's currency, especially where as in the case of the Asian countries, fiscal and monetary policies were not unsound at the time the crises broke out. Instead, as the Fund and others have pointed out, the seeds of the crises were planted by inadequate financial supervision, corporate governance, and weak accounting practices, among other things, that permitted too much borrowing in the wrong currencies and maturities and too much investment in the wrong places.

Critics of the Fund respond that it has been guilty of mission creep. The IMF is said to lack the expertise to impose and monitor these more intrusive conditions. More disturbing, by attempting to micromanage the economic affairs of borrowing countries, the Fund arguably is usurping national sovereignty and planting the seeds of a major political backlash against not only the institution but its main country-directors—namely, the United States.[34] Other critics argue that the Fund has been too harsh in applying its traditional macroeconomic medicine: tight budgets and tight money.[35]

IMF analysts have conducted a thorough analysis of the Fund's conditionality programs up through the mid-1990s, or just before the Asian crisis. The evaluation suggests a mixed record.[36] Based on a review of forty-five conditionality arrangements (covering thirty-six countries) approved between mid-1988 and the early 1990s, this study found that the external positions of the borrowing countries generally had improved, but that developments on the domestic front were less impressive. Very few countries achieved dramatic reductions in their inflation rates; many continued to experience moderate inflation, with some actually seeing an upward movement in inflation. For countries outside Central Europe, growth generally improved and savings rates increased, but few saw an increase in overall investment rates (although the mix of investment shifted toward the private sector and away from the public sector). On balance, the pre–Asian financial crisis experience suggests that conditional lending by the IMF remains very much a work in progress. Many observers would say that the Asian crisis has not changed this assessment.

A final lesson is that financial agreements without a mechanism for correcting noncompliance, at best, can work by persuasion and by influencing market actors, rather than through explicit enforcement actions. A central shortcoming of the Basel capital standards, for example, was the lack of a system for forcing countries to implement the standards, a shortcoming that persists. Of course, this is understandable: the standards were negotiated by a committee of central banks, not one of which was willing to surrender its sovereignty to a multinational body. The absence of an enforcement system was illustrated most dramatically during the 1990s by the severe and growing problems with Japanese banks in the 1990s—whose nonperforming loans may total $1 trillion. Indeed, it is ironic that Japanese banks have been so weak since the accord came into being given that one of the major motivations of the United States and other members in forming the agreement was to strengthen the capital bases of banks in all countries, including those in Japan.

Still, it is only fair to note that although the Basel standards lack a formal means of international enforcement, the market provides some discipline. Japanese banks, for example, have been forced by the market to pay a premium for the funds they seek in the interbank market, largely because investors perceive the banks not to fully comply with the Basel rules (although Japanese regulators may formally say that they do). The Basel Committee has also encouraged more disclosure by banks of their derivatives positions. Nonetheless, market forces are blunted by inadequate reporting of problem loans by banks and regulators in Japan and conceivably other Basel member countries, as well as by the implicit protection that the Japanese government (like governments in other industrialized countries) extends to large depositors to prevent runs on the banking system.[37]

CONCLUSIONS AND IMPLICATIONS

What else lies ahead? The Asian crisis has stimulated a vigorous debate around the world about overhauling the global financial architecture. At this point, at least four things are clear about the outcome of this debate.

First, for the time being, there will be no radical changes in direction. The advice of free market critics that the IMF should be dismantled or severely restricted in its activities—to provide stronger incentives for countries to adopt suitable economic policy measures on their own without having a safety net to catch them—will be rejected. The memories of contagious currency runs, especially during the fall of 1998 after the Russian default and devaluation, are too fresh and unsettling for any of the major industrialized countries to risk removing the only international source of liquidity in the event of a multicountry financial crisis. At the other extreme, the calls for new supranational institutions to regulate finance—to serve as an international bankruptcy court or as supranational regulator of financial institutions—also will be ignored. The industrialized nations are not ready to sacrifice their sovereignty to such institutions, although they do not object to the fact that when developing and emerging market countries seek aid from the IMF they must give up some of their sovereignty or autonomy as a price for obtaining the assistance.

Instead, a policy of cautious incrementalism has emerged, one that seeks to reduce the likelihood and severity of future crises. This policy, to which a growing number of countries are subscribing, contains several elements: more intensive financial regulation by governments in emerging markets; a bias against supporting pegged exchange rates; the establishment of a Contingent Credit Line to insulate countries with well-designed economic policies from contagious currency runs (by providing an up-front line of credit to countries following sound policies but threatened with global financial instability); in the wake of the IMF's refusal to provide loans to Russia in the fall of 1998, a policy of "constructive ambiguity" on crisis lending by the Fund, which should encourage more prudent economic policies from countries that can no longer count on IMF loans (beyond a country's quota) as a matter of right; and a continuation of some kind of policy loan conditionality, although the details of the conditions are likely to change as the Fund and member states gain more experience with them.[38]

Second, the Basel standards for bank capital appear to be the leading edge of a movement to harmonize regulations and practices across the financial services industry. As already noted, parallel efforts are under way to set minimum standards in the regulation of securities and insurance firms and in the development of an internationally accepted system of accounting rules. Although these various processes will take time to bear fruit, it is clear that the countries party to these efforts—principally the industrialized countries—are slowly building an international legal and regulatory infrastructure to support finance that is akin to the more fully developed infrastructure that now exists within each country.

Several questions remain, however. To what degree and at what pace will these standards be applied to emerging market countries? A representative list of such standards for the banking industry in particular, which are mirrored in the Basel Committee's *Core Principles* released in September 1997, is shown in box 5-1.

It would be wildly optimistic to project that emerging market countries will be able to replicate any time soon the legal and regulatory infrastructure now found in industrialized countries. Indeed, many so-called advanced countries have room for significant improvement themselves. It was only a little more than a decade ago that the United States, for example, suffered through its savings and loan debacle and the worst banking crisis since the Depression. At this writing, Japan is struggling with an even greater banking crisis, while many European countries have only recently emerged from similar crises.

At the same time, two powerful forces will drive emerging market countries to move toward Western-style financial architecture, or in the words of Thomas Friedman, to put on the "golden straitjacket."[39] One is the market. Countries that want foreign capital to encourage faster growth will put on whatever parts of the straitjacket that investors demand. The other force is the IMF. Rather than impose its own conditions, the Fund will be looking to internationally negotiated standards and requiring adherence to them as conditions for lending (or, instead of adding compliance as a condition, imposing an interest penalty for noncompliance), where it is judged that the absence of an effective infrastructure has contributed significantly toward a country's existing payments or currency crisis.

Box 5-1. *Banking Reform Measures for Developing and Emerging Market Countries*

- Implement and enforce capital standards for banks that are above those for developed countries.
- Publish timely, accurate, and audited information on the financial condition of individual banks.
- Adopt internationally recognized loan classification and provisioning practices.
- Enforce requirements that banks maintain internal procedures and safeguards.
- Make government involvement in the banking sector more transparent (through disclosure of banking system costs to government, data on non-performing loans of state-owned banks, and disclosure of the nature and extent of government instructions to banks on the allocation of credit).
- Limit bank lending to "connected" parties (major shareholders or affiliates of banks).
- Limit deposit insurance and offset its "moral hazard" through a system of "prompt corrective action" (now embodied in U.S. banking law).

Source: Morris Goldstein, *The Case for an International Banking Standard* (Washington, D.C.: Institute for International Economics, 1997).

The use of international standards as a component of conditionality partially answers the second question about the new international standards: How will they be enforced? The answer is partially, because conditions can be placed only on countries that borrow from the IMF, and even then, not all international financial standards will be part of every conditional lending package. What will motivate other countries, especially developed economies that have no need to go to the Fund, to adhere to new standards in accounting, insurance, securities, and so forth? For the time being, the only answer is: the market. If investors value adherence to the standards, then they will penalize countries—by demanding higher rates of return—that do not comply. This may not be the perfect means of enforcement, but it is likely to be the best that can be achieved for the foreseeable future.

A third question is whether and to what extent countries will introduce market-like rules and compliance incentives to replace the commands and controls that are familiar to the financial marketplace. The question is made relevant by the increased use of incentives in the United States and elsewhere in controlling pollution (through taxes rather than hard limits and tradable pollution permits) and in moderating traffic congestion (by imposing congestion taxes rather than explicit driving limits). Can similar market-like incentives be used in finance? The answer surely is "yes."

Already, the safety and soundness of nonbanking institutions generally are policed by the market rather than by government regulators, although government lends a helping hand by mandating certain types of disclosures. Historically, the financial soundness of banks has been accomplished differently—through mandated capital requirements, lending limits, and activity restraints—in large part because government guarantees of their deposits have limited or destroyed market discipline. Yet the Asian crisis, as well as the banking crises in various developed economies over the past two decades, has taught that government-mandated banking supervision has significant weaknesses. Supervisors can be and often are subject to political interference. In addition, financial innovations can and do outrun the ability of supervisors to keep up. Hence, one challenge that should be uppermost on the minds of financial policy makers is to find ways of harnessing the forces of the market to help ensure the stability of the financial system.

Although on the surface, the recent proposal by the Basel Committee to incorporate credit ratings in setting risk weights appears to be market-based, closer inspection reveals a more complicated picture. The views of the rating agencies are not those of the market, but rather the views of a limited set of analysts from organizations that have a poor record of predicting crises.[40] In addition, the risk weights remain highly arbitrary. Once an asset is classified in a different risk "bucket" based on the credit ratings, the bucket itself is still assigned an arbitrary risk weight ranging from 20 to 150 percent.

I believe that a superior approach to incorporating the views of the market into capital standards would rely explicitly on the judgments of the market itself. One way to do that is to require the large multinational banks that are subject to the Basel standards to back a certain portion of their assets with uninsured, long-term debt (or "subordinated debt"). Unlike deposits, such debt could not be redeemed except at par and thus could not "run." Moreover, because the holders of such debt do not share in the upside of a bank's fortunes but do bear the risks of downside losses, they have strong incentives to discourage banks from excessive risk taking and to induce banks to provide more disclosure. Although many large banks now voluntarily issue subordinated debt, a requirement would subject all large banks to the same level playing field. Regulators and market participants could then use the interest rates on these debt issues as signals for appropriate action (in the case of regulators, as signals for adopting progressively stiffer limits on bank risk taking).[41]

A final set of issues—concerns that more freedom for FDI to move across borders will encourage a race to the bottom in regulatory standards and social welfare policies—are so new that comparatively little can be said about them. After all, at this writing, it is only a few years ago (since 1998) that a loosely organized revolt of NGOs from around the world helped to stop the MAI negotiations dead in their tracks.

The merits of the NGOs' fears are outside the scope of this chapter (although I have already indicated my skepticism). The plain political fact is that unlike the issues raised by exchange rates and bank capital rules, which however important are also highly technical and often abstract, the issues raised by the movement of plants and facilities across national borders collide head-on with "Main Street" concerns about job stability. Furthermore, the MAI must be viewed against the backdrop of several WTO decisions that have implicated U.S. environmental rules (such as those banning the use of fishnets to catch tuna or those requiring the use of devices to avoid catching sea turtles when fishing for shrimp) as trade barriers, and in the process aroused the ire of the environmental community. Many of the same NGOs see the MAI's proscription of "performance standards" relating to cross-border investment as potential threats to other environmental regulations. More broadly, these NGOs fear that if capital becomes even more footloose than it is already, it will increasingly find its way into locales with less stringent environmental rules than those applicable to U.S.-based activities, and thus pressure U.S. regulators to relax those rules in the interest of keeping capital at home.

In short, the movement of FDI across national borders strikes very different political nerves than does the cross-border movement of portfolio capital, or stocks, bonds, and bank loans. The latter is intangible and classic "Wall Street." The former is very real on Main Street in the form of plants and facilities that citizens see in their local communities.

Hence, if policy makers and financial companies want further relaxation of at-the-border restrictions on the movement of FDI, they will have to engage the NGOs on some level. At a minimum, they will have to explain why the cross-border movement of FDI is not the threat that some may fear. For starters, they can explain that incoming FDI has brought great benefits to the economy, not only lowering interest rates but bringing with it new ideas and technologies that have made firms more competitive in world markets. Although the same is also true for outgoing FDI, defenders of agreements like the MAI can and should point out that most such outgoing investment is associated with the delivery of services or facilitates the exports of goods made at home, and so is a clear net plus for the economy.

But good arguments alone are not likely to be sufficient to qualm the fears of the NGO critics, who either want no further liberalization of investment rules, or if they do, want it conditioned on countries agreeing to a set of minimum environmental and labor rules. One challenge for policy makers interested in removing remaining restrictions on cross-border FDI thus may be to find a formula that will satisfy the critics of such a move without at the same time frustrating the very objective the negotiations would be designed to achieve: more integration of investment across national borders.[42]

Yet another challenge for the negotiators will be to find ways of energizing the business community to support further relaxations in investment restrictions. One additional reason for the failure of the MAI—apart from the opposition generated by the NGOs—was that large multinational corporations found little in the proposed agreement to motivate them to actively support it. As it is, under the current system, these corporations tend to find a way around investment restrictions; indeed, their capital and expertise often are openly courted by recipient countries. The lack of transparency and discrimination embedded in many countries' investment rules instead acts as an impediment to cross-border investment by small- and medium-sized enterprises. These smaller businesses, however, seem more interested in expanding their domestic business than in looking for overseas investment opportunities. Inducing them to broaden their interest in foreign opportunities will not be easy. For this reason alone, therefore, the subject of investment restrictions may not be on the multilateral negotiating agenda anytime soon.

As the foregoing discussion demonstrates, it is not difficult to understand why the increasing globalization of finance and capital flows has been accompanied by significant efforts by countries to cooperate with another to ensure that the benefits of increased integration are not offset by its downsides. The process is an ongoing one.

A critical issue is whether international forums will prove too cumbersome to keep up with the rapid pace of change in the financial world. Complex new instruments and trading strategies continue to come on the scene, with seemingly greater rapidity. It is hard for national regulators to keep up. Can or should we expect international bodies to do the same?

It is tempting in the face of unsettling change to try to halt it, regulate it, or slow it down. Regardless of whether any of those objectives is possible, the more realistic approach is to search for effective ways to manage new risks or at least contain their impacts. That challenge is one that will keep all concerned busy for a long time to come.

NOTES

1. The author wishes to thank his Brookings Institution colleague, Ralph Bryant, who has provided extremely helpful advice and guidance on the issues addressed in this chapter, and to other members of the Shadow Financial Regulatory Committee, which the author co-chairs (with George Kaufman), for stimulating some of the ideas contained here.
2. See Robert King and Ross Levine, "Finance and Growth: Schumpeter Might Be Right," *Quarterly Journal of Economics*, vol. 108, no. 3 (1993), pp. 717–37; Ross Levine and Sara Zervos, "Stock Markets, Banks, and Economic Growth," *American Economic Review*, vol. 88, no. 3 (1998), pp. 537–58; and Raghuram G. Rajan and Luigi Zingales, "Financial Dependence and Growth," *American Economic Review*, vol. 88, no. 3 (1998), pp. 559–86.
3. See Lawrence Summers, "Reflections on Managing Global Integration," *Journal of Economic Perspectives*, vol. 13, no. 2 (Spring 1999), pp. 3–18.
4. Michael D. Bordo, Barry Eichengreen, and Douglas A. Irwin, "Is Globalization Today Really Different Than Globalization a Hundred Years Ago?" in Susan M. Collins and

Robert Z. Lawrence, eds., *Brookings Trade Forum*, vol. 2 (Washington, D.C.: Brookings Institution Press, 1999), pp. 1–50.

5. Ibid.

6. Linda L. Tesar and Ingrid M. Werner, "The Internationalization of Securities Markets Since the 1987 Crash," in Robert E. Litan and Anthony M. Santomero, eds., *Brookings-Wharton Papers on Financial Services*, vol. 3 (Washington, D.C.: Brookings Institution Press, 2000).

7. A widely used convention is to classify equity as FDI if the investor acquires 10 percent or more of the outstanding shares of a firm.

8. Both have been bottom-feeding in Southeast Asia, picking up financial institutions rendered insolvent by that region's financial crisis. Some U.S. giants also have been doing the same thing in Japan, acquiring firms or remnants of firms that have been brought down by that country's prolonged economic downturn. Well-known examples include Citigroup-Travelers' investment in Nikko Securities, Merrill Lynch's pickup of the remnants of Yamichi Securities, and GE Capital's significant investments in Japan.

9. Council on Foreign Relations, *Safeguarding Prosperity in a Global Financial System: The Future International Financial Architecture.* Report of an independent task force (New York: Institute for International Economics, 1999).

10. Stephen S. Roach, "Learning to Live with Globalization," Testimony before the United States House Banking Committee, May 20, 1999.

11. For example, there is strong evidence that domestic residents in Asian countries were the first to sell their currencies and only later did some foreigners follow. See Barry Eichengreen et al., "Hedge Funds and Financial Market Dynamics," *Occasional Paper*, no. 166 (1998). Similarly, the Mexican peso crisis of 1994–1995 was triggered by capital flight of Mexican residents who lost confidence that the government was going to maintain the peso-dollar exchange rate peg.

12. See Gary Burtless, Robert Z. Lawrence, Robert E. Litan, and Robert J. Shapiro, *Globaphobia: Confronting Fears of Open Trade* (Washington, D.C.: Brookings Institution, Twentieth Century Fund, and Progressive Policy Institute, 1998). Many countries also have resisted incoming FDI, fearing takeover by foreigners of companies deemed important to national interests.

13. To its credit, however, CHIPS has taken a series of measures—many of them in the wake of the October 1987 stock market crash—to reduce the risk of the system's collapse. Currently, the system is capable of withstanding the simultaneous collapse of its two largest members. See Robert E. Litan and Jonathan Rauch, *American Finance for the 21st Century* (Washington, D.C.: Brookings Institution Press, 1998), p. 123.

14. Indeed, the articles made contracts that violate the exchange controls of any member country unenforceable in all member countries. See Joseph Gold, *International Capital Movements Under the Law of the International Monetary Fund* (Washington, D.C.: International Monetary Fund, 1977).

15. See Richard Cooper, "Should Capital Controls Be Banished?" in William C. Brainard and George L. Perry, eds., Brookings Papers on Economic Activity, no. 1 (Washington, D.C.: Brookings Institution Press, 1999), pp. 89–125.

16. Richard J. Herring and Robert E. Litan, *Financial Regulation in the Global Economy* (Washington, D.C.: Brookings Institution Press, 1995).

17. Goldstein has made a powerful case that because of additional risks in the macroeconomic environment, developing and emerging market countries should set their bank capital standards at higher levels than those applicable in developed economies; see Morris Goldstein, *The Asian Financial Crisis: Causes, Cures, and Systemic Implications* (Washington, D.C.: Institute for International Economics, 1997).

18. For a flavor of the critiques, see Martin Feldstein, "Refocusing the IMF," *Foreign Affairs* (March/April 1998), pp. 20–33; and Jeffrey Sachs, "Brazil's Fever: First, Do No Harm," *The Milken Institute Review*, Second Quarter (1999), pp. 16–25.

19. Nonetheless, there is not universal support for Chilean-type restrictions on short-term capital inflows.

20. As one piece of evidence that the race-to-the-bottom effects are much overrated, consider that upwards of $100 billion of FDI now flows into and out of the United States each year. This has not stopped the United States from having one of the more stringent regulatory regimes for health and safety in the world. To be sure, the social safety net is not as well developed in the United States as it is in Europe, but this is not because the United States is somehow constrained by global economic forces. Rather, it reflects more deep-seated voter skepticism of new, broad, and potentially costly federal programs (the failure of the Clinton universal health care initiative provides a good example). For a fuller elaboration of this thesis, see Jonathan Rauch, *Government's End: Why Washington Stopped Working* (Washington, D.C.: Public Affairs Books, 2000).

21. Momentum for the MAI was also blunted by the relative lack of interest shown in the negotiations by the business communities in the developed countries.

22. For an excellent historical account of the events surrounding the development of the Basel capital accord, see Wolfgang Reinicke, *Global Public Policy: Governing Without Government?* (Washington, D.C.: Brookings Institution Press, 1998), pp. 102–34.

23. Similarly, the agenda behind the recent Kyoto agreement on climate change, which entails complex issues of science and economics, has been driven by environmental experts rather than heads of state (the late-hour intervention of Vice President Gore at Kyoto was an aberration, but Al Gore was known to all as an environmental "expert" himself).

24. Reinicke, *Global Public Policy*.

25. The more extreme suggestions ranged from abolition of the IMF to suggestions that national financial institutions be subject to a new and far-reaching system of global financial regulation. There was also a wide range of views about desirable exchange rate regimes, with some suggesting that developing countries adopt currency boards or even abandon their currencies in favor of the dollar, while others claimed that exchange rates should always be flexible. Relatively few commentators have advocated a middle course, or some kind of "managed" floating exchange rate arrangement. For an excellent summary of the various proposals for reforming the global financial architecture, see Barry Eichengreen, "Kicking the Habit: Moving from Pegged Rates to Greater Exchange Rate Flexibility," *The Economic Journal*, vol. 109, no. 454 (March 1999), pp. C1–C14; and

Barry Eichengreen, *Toward a New International Financial Architecture: A Practical Post-Asia Agenda* (Washington, D.C.: Institute for International Economics, 1999).

26. Reinicke, *Global Public Policy*, p. 111.

27. See Richard Cooper, *The Economics of Interdependence: Economic Policy in the Atlantic Community* (New York: Council on Foreign Relations, 1968); and Sidney Dell, "On Being Grandmotherly: The Evolution of IMF Conditionality," *Princeton Essays in International Finance*, no. 144 (October 1981).

28. At the urging of the Americans, the IMF construed its initial Articles of Agreement to permit it to impose conditions. In 1969 the articles were formally amended to explicitly sanction their use.

29. See Reinicke, *Global Public Policy*.

30. See Paul Volcker and Toyoo Gyohten, *Changing Fortunes: The World's Money and the Threat to American Leadership* (New York: Times Books, 1992).

31. See C. Fred Bergsten and John Williamson, "Is the Time Ripe for Target Zones or the Blueprint?" in Bretton Woods Commission, ed., *Bretton Woods: Looking to the Future* (Washington, D.C.: Bretton Woods Commission, 1994).

32. In September 1997, the Interim Committee of the IMF agreed that the Fund's articles should be amended to add the promotion of capital account liberalization as a specific purpose of the IMF.

33. The IMF itself has acknowledged since the Asian financial crisis that capital flows can be destabilizing, especially movements of short-term money across borders.

34. See Feldstein, "Refocusing the IMF."

35. Sachs, "Brazil Fever."

36. Susan Schadler et al., *IMF Conditionality: Experience Under Stand-by and Extended Arrangements* (Washington, D.C.: International Monetary Fund, 1995).

37. To their credit, Japanese regulators have revamped their loan classification procedures, which have improved the accuracy of problem loan disclosure. In addition, the new Japanese regulatory body, the Financial Supervisory Agency, has toughened policies toward nonperforming loans.

38. Controversy remains on the extent to which the IMF should publicize the adherence of its borrower states to its conditions and/or to improving the effectiveness of their financial supervision. Proponents of information release argue that the IMF is in the best position to judge countries' progress in these areas because of the unique access of its officials to counterparts within country governments. Opponents counter that once the IMF begins to publicize or rank country performance, its officials will be denied access to key information. Furthermore, the downgrading of a country in any one area may itself trigger a run on its currency, thus bringing about a crisis that the IMF very much wants to avoid. It is the judgment of this author that over time market forces will induce the IMF to become more, rather than less, involved in publicizing its judgments about borrower states. Indeed, the IMF already has moved toward public disclosure of its judgments on borrower nations' macroeconomic policies through its Article IV consultations. It is not much of a step to have the fund release its judgments on the microeconomic policies of borrower states as well.

39. Thomas L. Friedman, *The Lexus and the Olive Tree* (New York: Farrar, Straus & Giroux, 1999).
40. Frank Partnoy, "The Siskel and Ebert of Financial Markets? Two Thumbs Down for the Credit Rating Agencies," draft manuscript (March 1999).
41. For a fuller critique of the June 1999 Basel capital proposal and the proposal for mandatory subordinated debt, see *Reforming Bank Capital Regulation: A Proposal by the U.S. Shadow Financial Regulatory Committee* (Washington, D.C.: AEI Press, 2000); and Charles Calomiris and Robert E. Litan, "Financial Regulation in a Global Marketplace," in Robert E. Litan and Anthony M. Santomero, eds., *Brookings-Wharton Papers on Financial Services*, vol. 3 (Washington, D.C.: Brookings Institution Press, 2000).
42. One possible approach is for developed countries, especially the United States, to strengthen their income support programs for displaced workers. Working with other colleagues, I have been advocating for some time a system of wage insurance that would compensate displaced workers for some portion of their lost earnings for some limited period (say, two years) following a job layoff. Such a system would encourage workers to find new jobs quickly (because they would not receive the compensation until they found new jobs) and at the same time make up for some of the loss in firm-specific capital that workers had acquired on their old jobs. See Burtless et al., *Globaphobia: Confronting Fears of Open Trade*.

SUGGESTED ADDITIONAL READING

Bordo, Michael D., Barry Eichengreen, and Douglas A. Irwin. "Is Globalization Today Really Different Than Globalization a Hundred Years Ago?" In Susan M. Collins and Robert Z. Lawrence, eds., *Brookings Trade Forum*, vol. 2. Washington, D.C.: Brookings Institution Press, 1999, pp. 1–50.

Burtless, Gary, Robert Z. Lawrence, Robert E. Litan, and Robert J. Shapiro. *Globaphobia: Confronting Fears of Open Trade*. Washington, D.C.: Brookings Institution Press, Twentieth Century Fund, and Progressive Policy Institute, 1998.

Calomiris, Charles, and Robert E. Litan. "Financial Regulation in a Global Marketplace." In Robert E. Litan and Anthony M. Santomero, eds., *Brookings-Wharton Papers on Financial Services*, vol. 3. Washington, D.C.: Brookings Institution Press, 2000.

Cooper, Richard. "Should Capital Controls Be Banished?" In William C. Brainard and George L. Perry, eds., *Brookings Papers on Economic Activity*, no. 1. Washington, D.C.: Brookings Institution Press, 1999, pp. 89–125.

Council on Foreign Relations. *Safeguarding Prosperity in a Global Financial System: The Future International Financial Architecture*. Report of an independent task force. New York: Institute for International Economics, 1999.

Eichengreen, Barry. *Toward a New International Financial Infrastructure: A Practical Post-Asia Agenda*. Washington, D.C.: Institute for International Economics, 1999.

Feldstein, Martin. "Refocusing the IMF." *Foreign Affairs*, vol. 77, no. 2 (March/April 1998), pp. 20–33.

Friedman, Thomas L. *The Lexus and the Olive Tree.* New York: Farrar, Straus, & Giroux, 1999.

Goldstein, Morris. *The Case for an International Banking Standard.* Washington, D.C.: Institute for International Economics, 1997.

Summers, Lawrence. "Reflections on Managing Global Integration." *Journal of Economic Perspectives*, vol. 13, no. 2 (Spring 1999), pp. 3–18.

6

Economics: International Trade

Vinod K. Aggarwal

OVER THE LAST FIFTY YEARS, states have utilized a host of measures to regulate international trade flows, including unilateral restraints, bilateral agreements, regional accords, and multilateral arrangements. Depending on the number of products and the geographical participation of countries, we can consider three important specific governance approaches: sectoralism, regionalism, and globalism. Sectoralism refers to industry-specific arrangements that can be unilateral, bilateral, minilateral, or multilateral, and may be driven by market opening or protectionist objectives. Regionalism refers to arrangements by a limited set of geographically concentrated countries that involve either free trade arrangements or customs unions with common external tariffs, either on a single or multiproduct basis. Finally, globalism refers to multilateral, multiproduct arrangements such as the General Agreement on Tariffs and Trade (GATT) and its successor organization, the World Trade Organization (WTO).

Several important lessons emerge from the analysis of previous and more recent efforts to manage trade at different levels, the details of which are discussed later in this chapter. In addition to those lessons, two key themes can be drawn from analyzing the dynamic interaction among governance arrangements at different levels.

First, a new challenge in global trade management has arisen from the increasing tension and potential conflicts among sectoral, regional, and global approaches to liberalization. Although there is still debate about whether regional blocs serve as building blocks for global liberalization, the conventional wisdom is that liberalization on a sectoral basis is good for the trading system. I argue, however, that the evidence suggests that the recent effort to develop liberal multilateral sectoral arrangements such as the Information Technology Agreement (ITA) or the WTO's Basic Telecommunications Agreement (BTA) may make it more difficult to conduct global trade negotiations. As potential supporters of multilateral trade liberalization achieve liberalization in their respective sectors, they become less willing to lobby for the more general public good of trade liberalization. A similar but lesser danger exists for the negotiation of regional arrangements; such accords may also decrease the commitment of various groups to global solutions, thus leaving strongly protectionist forces in the multilateral global negotiation arena. For example, the post–Asian financial crisis collapse of the U.S. voluntary sectoral approach in the Asia-Pacific Economic Cooperation (APEC) forum has left unresolved divisions among the United States, Japan, and other Asian countries over liberalization of agricultural and industrial sectors.

This concern about the development of sectoral and regional arrangements is not simply a wholehearted endorsement of global negotiations as the only route to reconciling trade conflicts. Ferreting out protectionist groups for special treatment through sectoral agreements may indeed allow for the advancement of broader global liberal trading arrangements. And, with respect to regional arrangements, some elements of the North American Free Trade Agreement (NAFTA) and APEC regional agreements have, in their own ways, contributed to the reinforcement of WTO norms and principles.

The second theme concerns the costs and benefits of the formalization of compliance and dispute settlement mechanisms. It may well be that the recent further legalization of this process in the WTO will generate greater conflict among major powers, as evidenced in the recent European Union (EU)–United States hormone-beef dispute—rather than forcing them to abide by the rule of law. In some cases, more informal consultations rather than formalized procedures may diminish trade conflict and achieve balanced and progressive liberalization.

This chapter focuses on providing an analytical account, rather than a detailed history of trade negotiations, of governance approaches that states have used. I begin with a discussion of the motivation for developing governance arrangements in trade and the evolving nature of trade issues. Next I focus on different types of possible trade arrangements and then offer an empirical overview of sectoral, regional, and global accords with an eye to examining their impact on enhancing cooperation. Then I review the lessons to be learned in the four components of the governance process of agenda setting, negotiations, implementation, and reactions to noncompliance on a sectoral, regional, and global basis. In conclusion, I evaluate the lessons learned and consider how different forms of governance might be reconciled.

NATURE OF THE PROBLEM

The underlying premise behind the benefits of international trade goes back to Adam Smith, who argued that it would be foolhardy to purchase higher-priced domestically produced goods if such goods were available elsewhere at a lower price. The case for mutual gains from trade has now become an article of faith among liberal economists.[1] At the same time, the benefits of free trade have continued to be questioned from other perspectives. For example, dependency theorists have argued that declining terms of trade—particularly declining prices of primary commodities without corresponding drops in prices of manufactured goods—could permanently impair the ability of developing countries to compete in the global economy. To cope with this perceived problem, the more radical theorists argued for a break with the capitalist world, suggesting that trade with rich, advanced capitalist countries will always be detrimental to the less developed. Less radical analysts called for policies of temporarily restricting imports so that countries could develop a comparative advantage in higher value-added products. From a different perspective, neomercantilists have suggested that the strategic nature of some industries, economies of scale, or the possibility of manipulating trading arrangements to improve one's terms of trade signify that open trade may not always be an optimal policy.[2]

Despite these criticisms, there continues to be a strong consensus, particularly among liberal economists, on the benefits of open markets. Even the mainstream view, however, recognizes that labor and firms often face significant adjustment costs. Although some believe that no compensation is necessary to ensure smooth transitions to changing comparative advantage in the global economy, others have called for various forms of adjustment assistance, and many countries have implemented schemes to help displaced workers and firms.

In the absence of smooth adjustment or sufficient compensation, groups negatively affected by shifts in comparative advantage are likely to press governments to intervene in international trade on their behalf. If these groups are politically powerful enough to secure the support of their governments, they may be able to secure unilateral measures such as tariffs, quotas, antidumping responses, or threats of trade restrictions to open foreign markets. These measures have commonly led to a series of countermeasures by other states, and this process of reaction and counter-reaction may lead to a downward spiral of trade protection and economic contraction as in the 1930s. Following World War II, the United States and others responded to the widely held belief that trade protection had exacerbated the Depression by making efforts to control the use of unilateral measures through the negotiation of the GATT. And although multilateral multiproduct negotiations have been the dominant form of negotiations over the last fifty years, a variety of other trade measures on a bilateral and minilateral basis have also been common, and unilateral trade restraints have also continued. Moreover, trade arrangements have also been concluded on a narrower basis, covering only a limited set of products. Thus, whereas broad agreement holds on the benefits of open trade, there is much less consensus on the impact of different types of arrangements and their contribution to greater trade liberalization or protectionism.

Although specific types of trade measures have been a key subject of debate, a more recent questioning of which issues should properly be included in trade negotiations has come from environmentalists and human rights activists. Environmentalists worry that increased trade promotes greater consumption that will undermine the environment; they also argue that mandated reductions in trade barriers prevent states from using domestic regulations to achieve their environmental objectives. Human rights groups, particularly those concerned about the conditions of labor in the developing world, claim that trade encourages firms to seek low-cost production sites, reducing wages and undermining efforts to improve working conditions.[3] Through lobbying and the use of new forms of communication such as the Internet, both environmentalists and human rights activists have increasingly challenged the current arrangements for governance in international trade.

In summary, because both state and nonstate groups have different preferences for open trade and propensities to intervene in international trade, national intervention decisions create externalities that in turn spread to other states and nonstate actors. This stimulates pressure to collaborate on a bilateral or regional basis to avoid conflict generated by unilateral actions. Such bilateral and regional agreements can themselves in turn generate externalities that spill over to other states and interest groups, further stimulating pressure for global negotiations. At the same time, because consensus at the global level is far from assured, weaker states may simply end up bearing the costs of negative externalities generated by the actions of stronger states that prefer to pursue unilateral or nonglobal governance mechanisms.

TRACK RECORD OF INTERNATIONAL RESPONSES

Before examining the empirical record of globalism, sectoralism, and regionalism, it is useful first to analyze these mechanisms within a broader context of trade measures. As noted, we can focus on three dimensions to characterize different forms of governance mechanisms: (1) the actor scope (number of actors); (2) the product scope (few or many); and (3) the geographical focus of accords (dispersed or concentrated). The dimensions are illustrated in table 6-1 along with some empirical examples of arrangements in each resulting category.

As this table shows, one can consider twelve different cells based on the three dimensions.[4] In general, analysts do not adequately specify what regionalism or globalism means, with the two terms often being used interchangeably. From my perspective, the most useful analytical definition of globalism refers to negotiations on a multiproduct, multilateral basis. By contrast, sectoralism can come in many forms, essentially referring to cells 1–6. Of course, whether sectoralism takes place with only a few actors or with many is an important political economy question, and

Table 6-1. *Categorizing Modes of Governance in Trade*

Actor Scope

Product Scope	Unilateral	Bilateral		Minilateral		Multilateral
		Geographically dispersed	*Geographically concentrated*	*Geographically dispersed*	*Geographically concentrated*	
Few products (sectoralism)	Specific quotas or tariffs or U.S. Super 301 1	U.S.- Japan Voluntary export restraints 2	U.S.-Canada auto agreement 3	Single sector commodity agreements 4	European Coal and Steel Community 5	Information Technology Agreement 6
Many products	Tariffs such as Smoot-Hawley, or unilateral liberalization 7	Mexico-Chile free trade agreement 8	U.S.-Canada free trade agreement 9	Agreement on government procurement or LOME 10	Multiactor free trade agreements or customs unions such as EU 11	GATT or WTO *(globalism)* 12

one worth investigating. Finally, regionalism is often used to describe geographically proximate countries, but as the table makes clear, cells 3, 5, 9, and 11 are all forms of regionalism. Here again, the political economic implications of arrangements in these different cells have been a subject of analytical scrutiny.

Globalism

Even before the end of World War II, governments in North America, Western Europe, and elsewhere understood the importance of international institutions, developing the International Monetary Fund (IMF) and International Bank for Reconstruction and Development (or World Bank)—known collectively as the Bretton Woods regime—to cope with fluctuating exchange rates and provide for postwar reconstruction.[5] In trade, the counterpart organization to the Bretton Woods financial arrangements was to be the International Trade Organization (ITO).

This system of international management depended on U.S. leadership. With a dominant military force, a large market, enormous productive capacity, and a strong currency and financial system, the United States was well positioned to assume this global responsibility. In addition, with Western Europe and Japan ravaged by the war, the Cold War context further reinforced the U.S. desire for rebuilding these economies. Nevertheless, a coalition of protectionists and free traders in the United States, who thought that it was an excessive compromise, prevented the ITO from securing congressional approval and thus led to its demise.[6]

With the ITO moribund, the United States promoted a temporary implementing treaty, the GATT, as the key institution to manage trade on a multilateral basis. GATT negotiations were successfully concluded and signed in Geneva in October 1947. As a trade institution, the GATT got off to a difficult start, representing a stopgap agreement among contracting parties—rather than a true international institution. The twenty-three GATT members negotiated a series of tariff concessions and free trade principles designed to prevent the introduction of trade barriers. Under the agreement, more than 45,000 binding tariff concessions were covered, constituting close to $10 billion in trade among the participating countries.

As the sole interim framework for regulating and liberalizing world trade, the GATT was highly successful at overseeing international trade in goods and progressively reducing trade barriers. Whereas the Annecy Round of 1949 resulted in 5,000 more tariff concessions and the entry of ten new GATT members, the Torquay Round of 1951 led to an overall tariff reduction of close to 25 percent and the inclusion of four new contracting parties. The 1956 Geneva Round that followed fostered further agreement of tariff reductions worth approximately $2.5 billion. Under the terms of the Dillon Round of 1960–1961, for the first time, a single schedule of concessions was agreed for the recently established European Economic Community (EEC), based on the Common External Tariff. Tariff concessions worth more than $4.9 billion in trade were also negotiated. In total, tariff reductions for the first five rounds amounted to 73 percent.[7]

The Kennedy Round of 1962–1967 proved to be the most dramatic facilitator of trade liberalization. GATT membership increased to sixty-two countries responsible for more than 75 percent of world trade at the time. New tariff concessions surpassed 50 percent on many products as negotiations expanded from a product-by-product approach to an industry/sectorwide method, while overall tariff reductions were 35 percent.[8] In addition, an agreement establishing a Code on Anti-Dumping was also brokered. This period from 1945 until the end of the 1960s is often dubbed the golden age of trade liberalization, witnessing a dramatic reduction of border barriers. With the United States acting as the world's central banker, providing the major impetus for international trade liberalization and dominating manufacturing production, these two decades were marked by unprecedented economic growth and development.

By the 1970s, however, the Bretton Woods financial system faced severe challenges. A weakening dollar and balance-of-trade deficit throughout the decade prompted President Richard Nixon to take the United States off the gold standard and devalue the dollar. By the mid-1970s, the Organization of Petroleum Exporting Countries (OPEC) "oil shocks" produced stagflation and a rise of new domestic "inside the border" protectionism in the form of voluntary export restraints (VERs) and support for declining industries. Although the developed countries remained the dominant agenda setters, developing countries increasingly sought to become more influential in obtaining the benefits of international management.[9] Finally, the liberal consensus had begun to erode, both among the advanced industrialized countries and the developing world. The United States continued to run large deficits but was unable to get Europeans or the Japanese to revalue their currencies. The most vocal critics of the trade and financial order came from developing countries, which argued that the open monetary, trade, and financial system perpetuated their underdevelopment and dependence on the richer Northern countries.

It is in this context of increasing complex interdependence that the next GATT round was negotiated. In the Tokyo Round of 1973–1979, a record ninety-nine countries agreed to further tariff reductions worth more than $300 billion of trade and an average reduction in manufacturing tariffs from 7 to 4.7 percent. In addition, agreements were reached on technical barriers to trade, subsidies and countervailing measures, import licensing procedures, government procurement, customs valuation, and a revised antidumping code. Yet for most participants, the Tokyo Round was a disappointment. With inadequate implementation and enforcement mechanisms in place, disputes involving nontariff barriers and agricultural and industrial subsidies remained relatively unsolved. Still, the Tokyo Round marked the first time that GATT dealt with significant nontariff barriers arising from domestic policies.

Following significant difficulties in setting the agenda for a new round, the Uruguay Round got under way in 1986, with the United States again taking the major initiative. The high level of contentiousness that threatened the conclusion of the round was unprecedented. In part, this reflects the changing balance of power among more actors in the system, the dissolution of the liberal consensus and inclusion of diverse interests, and the unwillingness of the United States to continue to be the lender and market of last resort. The era of détente and the subsequent end of the Cold War also served to weaken the security argument for continuing economic cooperation. Finally, the United States was no longer the undisputed hegemon of the system. In addition to a rise of a "fortress Europe" and a "Japanese miracle" replicated by the East Asian newly industrialized countries, the debt crisis of the 1980s led to power- and burden-sharing arrangements with Europe and Japan.

After several delays from the original target conclusion date of 1990, the Uruguay Round was finalized in 1993. Despite serious conflicts during the round, it succeeded in establishing the WTO. This new institution is equipped with both a Trade Policy Review Mechanism (TPRM) to increase the transparency of trade laws and practices across borders, and a strengthened Dispute Settlement Mechanism (DSM). In addition, many issues that had previously been absent or not subject to GATT discipline such as services, trade-related investment, and intellectual property are now incorporated into the WTO. Market access for agricultural products has also been dramatically improved as countries have committed to transforming their quotas to tariffs and then implementing reductions.

Most recently, an effort to start a new round of global negotiations under the appellation of the "Millennium Round" was marred by unprecedented conflict surrounding the WTO ministers meeting in November 1999 in Seattle. Although dispute among the major powers on how best to move forward with a new round was hardly unprecedented, the active protests by environmentalists, labor activists, human rights activists, and many other self-styled antiglobalists were unanticipated.

In summary, despite recent problems, under the global trade regimes of GATT and the WTO, tariffs have been significantly reduced, and global trade has grown at an annual average of 6 percent from 1947 to the present.[10] Still, although tariff rates have been drastically reduced, the decline of tariffs has been accompanied by a rise of various nontariff barriers. Thus, despite the dominance of GATT in the trade arena, we have seen the parallel development of sectoralism and regionalism.

Sectoralism

Sectoralism first emerged in the 1950s and accelerated in the 1980s. The first such market-sharing arrangements were in textiles, steel, electronics, autos, footwear, and semiconductors. These include such accords as VERs (also known euphemistically as orderly marketing agreements, OMAs) and sector-specific international regimes such as those in the textile trade known as the Multi-Fiber Arrangement (MFA).[11] VERs seek to allocate market shares between exporters and importers, stipulating that low-cost exporting countries "voluntarily" restrict their exports to countries where they threaten industry. VERs were temporary sectoral responses to evade the strictures of Article 19 of the GATT, which prevents exporters from being singled out for import protection. These arrangements have typically started out as bilateral sector-specific measures in mature low-cost and labor-intensive industries.[12]

The most prominent international export-restraining regime is the MFA that grew out of the Short-Term Agreement and Long-Term Agreement on Cotton Textiles (LTA) in the 1960s. It provided for the application of selective quantitative restrictions when surges in imports of particular products caused, or threatened to cause, serious damage to the industry of the importing country.[13] The MFA was a major departure from basic GATT rules and particularly the principle of nondiscrimination.

The persistence of VERs has varied depending on sectors.[14] For example, the United States negotiated an OMA with Japan for color televisions in 1977, which expired in three years, and with Korea and Taiwan, in 1980, which lapsed after two years. In footwear, OMAs negotiated with Taiwan and Korea in 1977 expired in 1981. In steel, the extent of protectionist arrangements among the European Community, Japan, and the United States has varied over time. In textiles and apparel, protectionism became multilateral and institutionalized during the 1960s and 1970s.

The success of a VER can be measured based on whether it maintains orderly international efforts to prevent states from engaging in detrimental protectionism. The success and failure of VERs have depended on whether the industry covered by VERs was securely protected and had an opportunity for competitive adjustment.[15] In textiles and apparel, the difficulty of providing secure protection and adjustment alternatives led to a bilateral VER in the 1950s with Japan, which was later expanded to include more countries and multilateralized in the MFA to include most fabrics. The most restrictive protectionist regime in the postwar era, the MFA progressively became more protectionist and thus increased conflict between the South—the main exporters—and the North—the main importers. The Agreement on Textiles and Clothing reached during the Uruguay Round gradually eliminates the MFA over ten years, but it remains to be seen whether this will actually take place.[16]

By contrast, VERs in the television industry succeeded in providing temporary protection and facilitating competitive adjustment of the industry, because the barriers to entry and exit as well as the size of the industry were small.[17] During the 1970s, Japan's rising television exports to the United States led Zenith to file countervailing duty suits against Japanese firms. In 1977, Zenith won an OMA with Japan. The subsequent increase of imports from Korea and Taiwan led to further OMAs with each of them, but by the mid-1980s, twelve of the seventeen producers assembling televisions in the United States were foreign owned, and most firms, including Zenith, had adjusted to find another competitive niche. The OMAs were soon eliminated, leading once again to free trade in this sector.

In addition to these classic protectionist sectoral arrangements, a new trend in promoting sector-by-sector liberalization has begun, most notably the ITA model developed in 1996 and championed as a model for other sectors by the U.S. Trade Representative (USTR). Building on the momentum generated by the successful conclusion of the Uruguay Round, the United States was able to expeditiously push an APEC-brokered ITA agreement through the WTO. Covering more than 90 percent of the total trade in information technology products among sixty-nine participant countries, the ITA forms the foundation upon which further liberalization of the information technology sector is currently being negotiated in WTO committees. In addition, the BTA seeks to extend the same sectoral liberalization principle to trade in telecommunications products.

Regionalism

The second key deviation from the multilateral process has been the development of regional accords. Beginning in the 1950s, we have seen among others the formation of the EEC, the European Free Trade Area (EFTA), the Latin American Free Trade Area (LAFTA), and the Association of Southeast Asian Nations (ASEAN). In the 1990s, subregionalism grew with Mercosur, NAFTA, and the ASEAN commitment to form the ASEAN Free Trade Agreement (AFTA). Each of these institutions has developed distinct sets of regime objectives, rules, and procedures.

Regional arrangements have liberalized trade among members, but many analysts have warned of the problem of trade diversion resulting from such accords. Moreover, there continues to be considerable debate over whether these arrangements will strengthen or undermine the WTO. In the case of the EU, one could make the argument that internal trade liberalization has led its member states to be more open to liberalizing trade with the rest of the world, rather than a turn toward "fortress Europe" that many feared in the 1980s. It is worth noting the often important role played by major powers in the formation of some of these regional arrangements and the close connection to security issues.

In addition to these geographically circumscribed regional arrangements, new transregional arrangements have emerged. These include links between North America and Asia (APEC), the EU and United States, and the EU and East Asia (Asia Europe Meeting, or ASEM). We have seen growing links among the United States, Latin America, and the EU as well. The current negotiation to create a Free Trade Area of the Americas (FTAA) is an ambitious effort to nest all subregional groupings in the Western Hemisphere. Here, as with regional agreements, the question of whether such transregional accords might prevent a possible inward focus by countries has become a key element of research and policy debate.

Owing to space constraints, my discussion of regional trade accords focuses primarily on NAFTA and APEC.[18] Moreover, NAFTA represents a notable achievement in terms of widening the scope of the market and facilitating the exchange of available labor skills, and it is an example of a legalized formal free trade agreement (FTA).[19] By contrast, in the Asia-Pacific region, APEC has a much softer and diffuse form. It has been in existence since 1989 but in 1993, heads of state met in Seattle and enhanced its role, in the process giving the Uruguay Round of negotiations a strong boost. Since then, with the Bogor Declaration, issued in November 1994 in Indonesia, APEC members set a target for achieving open trade in the region for developed nations by 2010 and developing nations by 2020. The Bogor accord also supports the acceleration and the implementation of commitments under the WTO, promotes the notion of "open regionalism," and calls for an expansion of trade and investment. Distinct from the "closed regionalism" developing in the EU, the APEC "open" concept is based on the belief that APEC should be part of the broader GATT/WTO efforts to promote further liberalization.[20]

* * *

An important issue that remains to be resolved is the relationship among globalism, sectoralism, and regionalism. As noted, debate over the compatibility of these arrangements has been active. One way to think about the issue of appropriate institutional design is to consider three types of possible relationships. As I have argued elsewhere, arrangements can be linked in nested or parallel fashion, or not linked at all.[21]

Nested institutions are nicely illustrated by the relationship between the international regime for textile and apparel trade (the LTA and its successor arrangement, the MFA) and the GATT. To cope with these competing pressures, the United States promoted the formation of a sector-specific international regime under GATT auspices. This "nesting" effort ensured a high degree of conformity both with the GATT's principles and norms and with its rules and procedures. For an example of the nesting of regional institutions, we can consider APEC's relationship to the GATT and WTO. APEC's founding members were extremely worried about undermining the GATT, and thus the notion of "open regionalism" provided an alternative to the use of Article 24 of the GATT, which permits the formation of free trade areas and customs unions, to justify this accord.

An alternative mode of reconciling institutions would be to simply create parallel institutions that deal with separate but related activities, as exemplified by the GATT and the Bretton Woods monetary system. By promoting fixed exchange rates through the IMF and liberalization of trade through the GATT, policy makers hoped that this parallel institutional division of labor would lead to freer trade. On a regional basis, one can see the development of the European Economic Coal and Steel Community and the Western European Union (WEU) as parallel organizations. The first was oriented toward strengthening European cooperation in economic matters (with important security implications), while the WEU sought to develop a coordinated European defense effort.

Of course institutions could simply be not linked. Thus in the past, environmental institutions and trade organizations were seen to be independent. As a result of politicization and new perceptions about the impact of issues on one another, however, attempts are being made to connect what were previously separate institutions. The question of how institutions at the sectoral, regional, and global level might be appropriately linked is thus crucial for policy makers.

LESSONS LEARNED

The history of international trade negotiations offers a number of lessons for the future. With respect to the four elements of agenda setting, negotiations, implementation and compliance, and enforcement, I first review the lessons to be learned about each phase. By focusing on specific themes that cut across global, sectoral, and regional trade regimes, I provide detailed but general lessons. Naturally, not all of the lessons learned will apply to all types of arrangements.

Agenda Setting

The process of setting agendas has varied considerably among different forms of governance. Generally speaking, five sets of actors have been involved in agenda setting: hegemonic powers, middle powers, domestic interest groups, transnational interest groups, and epistemic communities. In the regional context, the hegemonic power does not automatically refer only to the United States. For example, Germany has acted a regional hegemon in bearing the startup cost and assigning obligations to other countries in the formation of the European Monetary Union.[22] Why certain issues become salient on an agenda and the mechanisms through which they arise are two key points I address below.

Eight major lessons emerge with respect to agenda setting.

First, the agenda of trade negotiations has been heavily influenced by the general security environment. If an issue can be framed as a domestic security concern, it will be dealt with more expeditiously. The core idea behind the creation of a post–World

War II trading system emerged from the conviction of U.S. policy makers that they must take world leadership in coordinating collective action. Acutely mindful of the tariff wars following the Great Depression and the looming Cold War with the Soviet Union, the United States set out to create a liberal international trading system that would simultaneously bolster its own economy and those of allied countries.

As the postwar hegemon, the United States acted as the military leader of the Western alliance, served as the world's central banker, and provided the major impetus for international trade liberalization. In particular, the subordination of the international trading system within the overall security system gave the U.S. president leverage over domestically oriented protectionist groups by allowing him to argue for the primacy of Cold War concerns over narrow parochial interests.[23] Thus the United States maintained a coherent approach to the trading system—founded on its interest in promoting multilateralism—and ensured that its trading partners grew to buttress the Western alliance against Soviet encroachment.

For much of GATT's history, the U.S. government, pressed in part by domestic interests, has been able to pursue its national objectives by leveraging its hegemonic position and thus remained the prime mover in setting the international trade agenda. U.S. negotiators were the initiators of all eight rounds of GATT. The GATT rounds in the 1950s and 1960s were successful due to the concentration of market and military power, and the accepted leadership of the United States during the postwar recovery phase and within an overarching Cold War security context. For the most part, Europeans feared U.S. isolationism—not U.S. hegemony. With the Cold War in full force, the United States was often willing to allow the rest of the developing world to free ride on its open markets in exchange for political influence.

At the same time, despite the U.S. commitment to multilateralism, security concerns also influenced decisions about regional arrangements. For example, when the European Coal and Steel Community came under challenge as a violation of the GATT (which prohibited sector-specific regional arrangements under Article 24), the United States strongly supported this arrangement for security reasons and pressed for an exception in the GATT in support of the Germans and French. At the sectoral level, the U.S. textile and apparel industry as well as the steel industries have often argued that they need protection for reasons of national security. Indeed, in the Pastore hearings on the textile industry in the 1950s, the industry went so far as to argue the case for protection successfully by claiming that woolen blankets would be necessary for protection against radiation in the event of an atomic war![24]

By the 1960s, it had become increasingly clear that U.S. trading partners were disproportionately benefiting from progressive tariff reductions. With persistent European and Japanese exchange controls and industrial policies, trade concessions provided only limited returns for U.S. exporters and tangible damage to import-competing sectors. Yet as long as economic growth continued and the Cold War raged on, the U.S.-led liberal system worked well for all participants.

By the late 1970s, however, the conditions conducive to further liberalization had deteriorated. Protectionism was on the rise. Increased economic interdependence and surging merchandise trade growth resulted in higher political sensitivity over issues such as jobs and the persistent trade imbalance. As U.S. manufacturing productivity declined relative to that of other developed economies, U.S. competitiveness in many sectors deteriorated. In addition, rising foreign direct investment led to a shift of manufacturing to the newly industrializing economies. Finally, Japan and Western Europe began to challenge the U.S. lead in high-technology industries. Whereas international trade management up to the end of the Kennedy Round occurred under high economic growth, low unemployment, and increasing world trade, the 1970s was marked by stagflation and oil shocks. In this context, the institutional flaws and "gray areas" embedded in the GATT became painfully clear and politically volatile. Consequently, the eagerness of the United States to bear a disproportionate amount of the costs associated with providing the public goods of global trade liberalization waned.

Two historical moments marked the turning points in U.S. trade policy. The collapse of the Bretton Woods system in 1971 signaled the end of the postwar monetary order, challenging the conventional view that international economic institutions were necessarily enduring. The difficulties in starting the Uruguay Round, followed by the end of the Cold War and growing global interdependence, redefined the commercial interests of the United States. These changes have influenced U.S. bargaining leverage in trade issues vis-à-vis historical U.S. trade partners and emerging markets such as China, and the political alignment and policy influence of trade-affected domestic groups. As a consequence, U.S. trade policy has failed to sustain an overarching vision and an effort to move toward a strategy of multiple institutional commitments in the face of difficulties in various trade forums.[25]

Second, U.S. interest groups have been very effective in setting the international trade agenda, and their influence has grown since the end of the Cold War. Influenced by particular national institutional configurations and state/society relationships, interest groups have pursued various political strategies with varying degrees of success in advancing their trade agendas. With the diminution of security priorities in the post–Cold War era, however, interest groups have increased their ability to set the trade agenda.

Interest groups often have multipronged strategies. They may attempt to influence the agenda by putting direct pressure on the various branches of government. In addition to lobbying legislators and negotiators, they may lobby administrative agencies with the hope that new interpretations of existing trade arrangements may change the state's agenda. When faced with growing imports from Japan in the 1950s, the U.S. textile industry pressed for protection. Although labor and business were at odds on many matters, they came together on the protection issue. Using access to

Congress and pointing to job losses, the coalition was able to halt progress on trade acts that authorized the president to negotiate tariff reductions. In addition, they used the Tariff Commission mechanism to investigate imports to produce new information in support of their protectionist cause.

Given that the United States was committed to free trade in the postwar golden years for economic and security reasons, the administration faced the dilemma of how to help the industry without directly violating the GATT. The result was the 1957 U.S.-Japan bilateral protectionist agreement on cotton textiles, which set off a wave of protectionism.[26] First, as textile input prices increased, apparel manufacturers began to lobby for protection. Second, the export-restricting agreement on cotton between Japan and the United States led to increasing exports of cotton from other countries into the United States, prompting the coalition to demand protection against more countries. Finally, the rapid rise in imports of noncotton fibers, such as wool and man-made fibers, led other parts of the textile and apparel industry to focus on these fibers. Accordingly, beginning in 1974, the MFA covered a variety of fibers.

Agriculture is another case of U.S. producer interests leading to a significant departure from GATT's liberal principles. For example, provisions made in the original treaty and amended in the Torquay and Geneva Rounds provided for a separate agricultural trading regime. In fact, in 1955 the United States even obtained a waiver under a GATT rule that provided it with authority to impose quotas on agricultural products.[27] Over time U.S. agricultural interests have changed their trade objectives. The Clinton administration has attempted to pressure European and other protected agricultural markets to eliminate export subsidies, lower tariffs, and reduce barriers against biotechnology, which is one of the U.S. agrochemical business's strong suits. Because Europe, Japan, South Korea, and others have very little interest in agriculture liberalization, the American farming groups could expect little from these ambitious goals.[28]

In addition to putting political pressure on governments, interest groups often attempt to create a fertile ideational environment for their cause. In the early 1970s, U.S.-based service firms faced increased regulations and restrictions abroad. As a result, they instigated the initial lobbying for action on trade in services.[29] The Coalition of Service Industries was formed in 1982 to advance the interests of a larger group of firms in this sector. This group was influential in getting the U.S. government to persuade the other contracting parties of GATT to initiate a new round and to place services on the agenda.

In the post–Cold War, post–Uruguay Round environment, the coalition for free trade has increasingly frayed. Thus in the service sector, liberalization is supported aggressively by some groups, but not by all. Because of the sector-specific liberalization agreements that have been concluded in their favor, some of the most politically powerful groups, such as the telecommunications and information technology sectors, are not as interested as before in a new round of the WTO. Consequently, business interests do not include the full panoply of committed supporters to the extent that they did before the start of the Uruguay Round.

At the same time, protectionist-oriented interest groups have a freer hand than they did in the 1950s and 1960s, when the U.S. government often resorted to security arguments to deny protection to affected interests. Among the anti–Millennium Round coalition, the strongest protectionist interests have been the sunset industries such as steel, textiles, and apparel. These industries may exert a powerful public influence, depending on the parties in office. Their pressure does not of course guarantee protection for these industries, as the recent defeat of a protectionist steel bill in the U.S. Congress indicated, but as their alliances with other groups expand, their power increases.

For example, environmental and human rights groups have increasingly allied themselves with older protectionist industries in their advocacy of "fair trade." Although the strength of these groups varies, the highly educated and well-organized environmental and human rights groups together with their labor allies can mount strong opposition to further trade liberalization. Because these groups often pale financially in comparison to many of the proliberalization business interests, they have attempted to influence state behavior through mobilizational and educational strategies. Enhanced organizational tactics such as voter mobilization or call-in drives can be quite effective. In addition, they may also attempt to frame trade issues through education and media campaigns.

In short, with the end of the Cold War, the fraying of the pro–free trade coalition, and the rise of a new multifaceted coalition that includes industries in decline, environmentalists, and human rights activists, trade liberalization faces an uphill battle.

Third, agenda setting offers an opportunity for the control of international and domestic actors. Different governance structures and negotiating arenas offer different options and payoffs for actors. Thus a country's size, relative power, and objectives will influence the choice of arena in which it pursues its agendas. Moreover, trade agreements may serve as an instrument for controlling the behavior of other states as well as moderating pressures arising from domestic actors.

Even the undisputed role of the United States as a global hegemon has not always directly resulted in trade agreements. Instead, U.S. power must be conscientiously translated into trade strategies during the agenda setting and negotiation stages. At the same time, middle and small countries have taken advantage of the leveling effect of multilateral institutions to counter the influence of the United States. Examples of opportunities for control in regional negotiations can be seen in the agenda-setting history of NAFTA and APEC.

The most important motivation for all countries and nonstate actors in setting the agenda for negotiations in NAFTA has been the opportunity to control other actors through a rule-based system. When the United States and Mexico began negotiations for a bilateral FTA in the early 1990s, Canada decided to engage in trilateral negotiations rather than stand aside and have its own FTA with the United States possibly undermined. If the United States and Mexico formed an exclusive agreement, other such agreements would soon follow (for example, with Chile), and hemispheric trade would be on its way to a "hub-and-spoke" model. The United States would control a bilateral trade agreement with each country, making it the only one with unrestricted access to all the markets of the "spoke" countries. In this way, U.S.-Mexican negotiations set the agenda for Canada.

In NAFTA negotiations, Mexico set the initial agenda by pressing for a free trade agreement for a host of motivations. The government of Carlos Salinas, faced with slow movement in the Uruguay Round, worried about retaining market access to its primary export market. By binding the United States into an agreement, Mexico hoped to ensure that protectionist measures would not threaten its newly outward-oriented focus. In particular, the objective was to firmly lock in economic reforms, particularly those related to investment to attract capital. At the same time, Salinas saw NAFTA as an arrangement that would strengthen his hand vis-à-vis domestic interest groups.

Turning to APEC, its coming of age was to a large extent a response by Australia and Japan to the negative spillovers of U.S. unilateralism in the Asia-Pacific region and regionalism in North America. Many smaller Asian states wished to draw their largest partners—the United States and Japan—into an organization that would diminish U.S. pressure for market openness and prevent isolation if the trend turned toward discriminatory trading blocs. This consideration appears to have been the driving force behind Australia's promotion of APEC: it was concerned about both potentially exclusionary Asian (ASEAN) and North American (NAFTA) blocs.

The United States was motivated to promote APEC for a number of reasons, but a key motivation was the view that the creation of APEC norms, principles, and rules might prevent a turn toward an exclusive East Asian free trade area.[30] Pressuring the Europeans on the Uruguay Round also was a critical motive.

Precisely because of the individual APEC members' motivation for controlling others' actions, agenda setting in APEC has been particularly controversial. Most Asian countries have attempted to secure an agenda that focuses only on voluntary trade and investment liberalization. But Australia, Canada, the United States, and other countries, pressed by a variety of domestic and transnational lobbies, have pushed a number of other issues onto the agenda. As a result, APEC's scope now includes trade and investment liberalization, the environment, social issues, infrastructure, women's issues, and, recently, efforts at financial coordination in the aftermath of the Asian crisis.

With respect to sectoralism, efforts to control domestic and international actors have been common. In the 1960s, the United States sought to develop an international textile regime for multiple purposes: it would open up European and other closed markets, control imports from developing countries, and diminish pressure from domestic interest groups by tying the U.S. administration's hands to an international accord. More recently, a liberal sectoral approach to manage market opening has been pursued with mixed success. Following on the success in information technology with the ITA, the United States saw an opportunity to champion the model of sectoral liberalization in the context of APEC. In Vancouver in 1997, ministers agreed to consider nine additional sectors for fast-track trade barrier reduction and to create detailed market-opening plans in the nine areas by the first half of 1998, aimed at beginning implementation in 1999 (Early Voluntary Sectoral Liberalization, or EVSL). The United States led a movement to make the nine-sector liberalization a package to discourage countries from picking and choosing sectors based on domestic concerns. But at Kuala Lumpur at the Sixth Leaders' Summit in November 1998, Japan, supported by other Asian countries concerned about moving forward with liberalization in their weakened economic state, refused to liberalize fishing and forestry products. This development threw into disarray the U.S. strategy of using APEC as the vanguard for sectoral liberalization and forced the participants to send the whole package to the WTO for negotiation.

The EU and Japan, instead of the United States, have provided the main impetus for a comprehensive new round of global talks. This so-called Millennium Round would have emphasized unique opportunities of control for the EU, Japan, and the United States. The EU's tactic was to put everything that anyone wanted on the agenda—to conduct the negotiations as a single undertaking to ensure that all agreements would be accepted by everyone and concluded within a two- to three-year span. Such an undertaking would have covered the built-in issue of further liberalization of agriculture, where the United States and the Cairns Group have demanded substantial concessions from the EU, Japan, and others in terms of import liberalization and reducing domestic support and export subsidies.[31] In addition, both the United States and the EU pushed for some type of sectoral negotiations on industrial tariffs. Some of the major developing countries, with relatively high average bound tariffs and the potential to industrialize and compete, were to be the focus of further WTO-driven trade liberalization.

The EU has argued that without a comprehensive round in which there could be some trade-offs, it would be politically unable to undertake the major concessions expected of it in agriculture. The EU also tried to tie agricultural concessions to trade and investment, impose multilateral rules and disciplines on governments, and expand the rights of foreigners to invest in countries with all kinds of capital. In contrast, developing countries were wary that putting all the new issues in an omnibus round would lead to further marginalization of the developing countries within the multilateral trading system. Instead, they have emphasized the need to evaluate implementation of Uruguay Round agreements and keep off the table any issue on which there is no consensus, including the labor and environmental concerns of advanced industrialized countries. The insistence on special treatment of developing countries in the various WTO agreements has become vehement, as developing countries feel that they have paid an enormous price in disproportionate concessions under the Uruguay Round.

Fourth, mobilizing political action on a specific issue or limited set of issues along sectoral or regional lines is generally easier than mobilizing political action on a wide array of issues. Due to high start-up costs, problems of free riding, and the anxiety over disproportional contributions, agenda setting has often been marred by significant disagreements arising from fear of losses from trade liberalization. Generally, the smaller the group in question, the easier it is to overcome collective action problems. Despite these challenges, there have been several instances of successful collective action in the international arena. Below I explore how some actual problems were confronted and resolved.

As the history of GATT illustrates, global trade talks have been plagued by problems of collective action arising from their multiproduct nature and inherently large membership. Compounding factors have been the erosion of the postwar U.S.-centered world order and the rising relative autonomy of middle powers. Sectoralism and regionalism partially address this problem by limiting the scope of issues and participants, although they have their own downsides.

Sectoral initiatives, in both liberal and protectionist incarnations, often aim to resolve issues that have been raised, but not resolved, by global or regional governance structures. In fact, the Uruguay Round's "build-in agenda" amounted to a series of ongoing sectoral talks. The key difference between liberal and protectionist sectoralism is the presence or absence of transnational collective action among the affected industries and their governments. The domestic coalition behind protectionist agreements is inward looking, and in the case of the hegemon pursuing protectionism, other countries are compelled to enter into a managed-trade concession or to face unilateral actions such as the U.S. Super 301 clause.[32] Protectionism in middle or small countries historically has not produced sectoral agreements but has created distortions in the global liberalization framework. One such example is the persistence of the European Common Agricultural Policy as a barrier to agricultural liberalization. Protection in small and middle countries has also caused the breakdown of sectoral liberalization negotiations, such as the stalemate over ITA-II and APEC's EVSL negotiations in the aftermath of the Asian financial crisis.

The opposite is true for liberal sectoralism. The ITA, BTA, and the Financial Services Agreement (FSA) show that intense lobbying by transnational and domestic industrial groups in advanced countries similarly positioned in the global economy can overcome collective action problems in crafting a sectoral agreement. For example, numerous high-technology business lobbies supported by the USTR and the

Department of Commerce initially promoted the ITA as an effective way to liberalize trade in technology equipment associated with the information superhighway by 2000. With Internet-related demand booming on a global scale, U.S. firms and their business associations have become increasingly influential transnational actors.[33] In short, sectoral liberalization strongly depends on the ability of certain industries to convince a hegemon or a critical mass of middle powers to use their influence to overcome resistance from countries that may be wary of accepting a liberal agenda in their uncompetitive sectors.

Theoretically, overcoming collective action problems at the regional level should be easier than at the global level. After all, there are fewer actors and clearer payoff schemes. The success of regional cooperation, however, depends on how the regional market is defined and how ambitious the goals of integration are. The core treaties of what was to become the EU were established by a group of six original members that were relatively culturally homogeneous and generally in agreement on the means and ends of their regime. And in agenda setting for NAFTA, the presence of the United States as a hegemon clearly facilitated the process of starting negotiations. By contrast, APEC is now a twenty-one-member organization with a vast array of cultures, histories, and ideas about the proper approach to regionalism. In the EU many of the rules and institutions were in place before the organization expanded to the current size of fifteen members; but as the EU expanded, it became clear that qualified majority voting would have to be extended if any substantial progress was to be made. By contrast, given its larger size and more diverse makeup, APEC has been saddled with significant collective action problems from the beginning, despite strong leadership initiatives from Australia, Japan, Malaysia, and the United States, and thus the agenda-setting process has become extremely complex.

Fifth, liberal sectoralism can become a stumbling block for global multiproduct trade negotiations. Despite the relatively easier process of agenda setting for sectoralism and regionalism, these types of arrangements have an important downside. Because sectoral (and regional) agenda setting involves a limited and easily polarized set of domestic interests, the margin for coalition building and political give-and-take is much slimmer. Thus, ironically, industries that have succeeded in securing sectoral liberalization may pose a threat to a global liberalization agenda. These groups may see little reason to take the risk and expend energy in relocating the basis of their existing benefits onto the global multilateral level.

After the end of the Tokyo Round (1973–1979), faced with an increasingly protectionist Congress and pressed by certain outward-looking sectoral interests to place new issues on the GATT agenda, the U.S. government began pushing for a new round of talks. However, the 1982 GATT ministerial meeting was marked by conflict over possible new items on the agenda, as the United States pressed to include areas in which its producers enjoyed competitive advantages—services, investments, and intellectual property. The major problem facing early attempts to promote action in services was that no one considered services important enough for international trade negotiations.[34] Eventually, of course, information technology and telecommunications firms got the sectoral agreements they wanted with the ITA, BTA, and FSA.

By the mid-1980s, with the problems in starting the Uruguay Round, the United States was no longer solely committed to the multilateral route. The regional and sectoral alternatives were in full bloom, and both the Bush and Clinton administrations pursued a mixed trade strategy of "opportunistic liberalization" while exercising their bilateral leverage to defend job and trade balance concerns. In the end, the mixed strategy has led to a lack of focus and sustainable commitment to these alternatives, as well as a deterioration of the U.S. hegemonic leadership in the WTO process.[35]

The concrete realization of the risk of sectoral liberalization undermining global liberalization has become evident in the surprisingly weak lobbying effort and conservative agenda-setting priorities of U.S. information technology and telecommunications industries in the recent Seattle WTO summit. It appears that these sectors have come to rely on extant sectoral agreements and bilateral pressures to open key emerging markets, most notably China, and have lost interest in global institutions.

Sixth, mobilizing support for protective policies is easier than mobilizing support for the removal of protection for other actors to lower input prices. Historically, industries have rarely lobbied for the removal of protection or major domestic adjustment programs if securing their own protection was an option. Thus from a theoretical economic standpoint, one might have expected the auto industry to argue for the removal of protection for the upstream steel industry that raised their input prices; similarly apparel producers might be expected to press for the removal of protection on textiles. In practice, however, because of the political dynamics of coalition building and issue framing, this has not been the case in the United States. For example, in the 1950s, after a bilateral agreement with Japan that raised prices for textile products, the apparel industry asked for its own protection, rather than attempting to remove protection for textiles. And the textile industry itself had sought and received protection in 1955, arguing that the agricultural price support system in the United States had raised their input prices for cotton.[36]

Seventh, deregulation and internationalization have pushed industries to lobby for open markets. A country's domestic deregulation or its industries' success in becoming internationally competitive often has an impact on how firms and states perceive their optimal trade strategy. For example, deregulation of the U.S. financial services industry under the Reagan administration intensified competition at home, leading to increased demand for market access and national treatment of U.S. services abroad.

The subsequent creation of the FSA fits the pattern of the U.S. government heeding the demands of globally competitive domestic businesses to bring liberalization to the trade agenda.

As U.S. firms developed a clear competitive advantage in the booming global financial service industry in the early 1980s, they began to organize and put pressure on the government to pay more attention to services in the formulation of trade policy.[37] However, the service lobby did not primarily seek unilateral action. In fact, representatives of key financial firms seemed opposed to bilateral accords, arguing that the introduction of services into the GATT's framework of multilateral trade would provide the critical mass of countries necessary to achieve a comprehensive liberalization of the sector.[38] As a part of a broader Coalition of Service Industries, the U.S. financial service industry staged a campaign to influence U.S. policy makers to push for a reorientation of U.S. trade policy to put greater emphasis on liberalization of trade in services. Attempting to link the inclusion of services in GATT's negotiating agenda with the general health of the U.S economy, the financial lobby focused on trade and investment barriers that restricted U.S. firms' penetration of foreign markets. These barriers, they argued, would hurt the U.S. economy, resulting in lost jobs and weakened national competitiveness.[39]

The United States officially raised the issue at a GATT ministerial meeting in November 1982. But already in July of that year, William Brock, the key U.S. trade representative in the GATT negotiations, had called for the inclusion of services in the upcoming Uruguay Round as a U.S priority.[40] The U.S. initiative unleashed fierce debate and opposition. Still, the United States initially refused to make any concessions, threatening not to participate in the Uruguay Round if services were not on the agenda. In the end, only ten of the thirty developing countries that had first voiced reservations against the U.S proposition remained. Eventually in 1986, a compromise was reached: negotiations on services would take place simultaneously with negotiations on goods, but in a separate forum.[41] This track of negotiations became the General Agreement on Trade in Services (GATS).[42]

Deregulation of certain domestic industries within the United States and the EU has left the winning firms with an outward orientation and a desire to push for international agreements that would open up emerging markets. Thus it is clear that the effects of national policy on domestic firms' global competitiveness will influence the demand for modifying national trade agendas. The question remains if deregulation will have this effect on all industries, or whether strategic regulation may enhance competitiveness in qualitatively different industries.

Eighth, academic research has often helped in generating a shared understanding of the trade problem and its solutions. In highly complex and technical issues, policy makers often must rely on experts, or "epistemic communities," to help them construct and justify what they believe to be their best interest.[43]

The American academic community has long advocated a multilateral approach to U.S. relations with the Asia-Pacific region, for example. Winston Lord, Clinton's Assistant Secretary of State for East Asian and Pacific Affairs from 1993 through 1996 and former president of the Council on Foreign Relations, authored the Clinton administration's policy of multilateral cooperation in its approach to the region.[44] Clinton subsequently promulgated Lord's embrace of multilateralism in his own speeches during his July 1993 trip to Asia. Moreover, by the late 1980s, many officials in foreign affairs and national security condemned the Bush administration's continuing resistance to Asia-Pacific cooperation as short sighted.[45] Their new support of multilateral cooperation helped provide acceptance of a shift in policy that occurred under the Clinton administration.

Formal think tanks associated with APEC also enjoy considerable access and influence over agenda setting and the subsequent momentum of negotiation. The Eminent Persons Group led by C. Fred Bergsten was critical in defining the principle of "open regionalism."[46] The Pacific Economic Cooperation Council—a forum of government officials, business representatives, and academics—played a large role in creating the consensus for establishing APEC.[47]

Negotiations

Trade negotiations at different levels have involved different actors and a variety of strategies. For the most part, sectoral trading arrangements tend to arise from strong industry pressure on dominant states in the system such as the United States, or in the case of the EU, a supranational entity. But many opportunities for smaller states to broker arrangements or to promote their interests in view of the broad agenda of negotiations arise on the multilateral level. Regional arrangements fall somewhere in between, with clear domination by one or two states, but with some opportunities for compromise and strategic maneuvering by smaller countries. Nonstate actors play a role at all three levels, often in attempting to affect individual states' behavior, but also in serving as experts or affecting the ideational environment of negotiations via media and educational campaigns. Three key lessons can be drawn from the effects of international power structures and the choice of direction and pace of global liberalization on the outcome of trade negotiations.

First, although major powers generally determine negotiating outcomes, middle and small powers can gain considerable maneuverability in negotiation by alternating between the roles of "supporter" and "spoiler" of hegemonic initiatives. In the postwar period, given its military and economic superiority, the United States has dominated negotiations at the sectoral, regional, and global levels. Although power asymmetry has often resulted in the United States having the primary say in determining outcomes, actual negotiations are often mediated by the institutional setting and the specific issues. Both factors may give middle and small powers disproportionately high leverage over the dominant state. In addition, the dynamics of negotiations often depend on how closely interests are aligned between the hegemonic and middle powers, with the lesser powers often having little influence.

An example of sectoral negotiations reflecting the power asymmetry between the North and South is the FSA. The profound divergence of national interests between the industrialized and developing countries was revealed before the Uruguay Round. The issues motivating the developing countries to resist the inclusion of services into global trade talks under WTO auspices (that is, the lagging competitiveness of their service industries, and the politically sensitive nature of deregulating their services sectors) applied also to the financial services industry. For the developing countries, the gains for market-opening reforms were far from obvious. Their financial firms were small, underdeveloped, and incapable of competing with their U.S. or European counterparts and wished to keep control over the pace of deregulation and the terms on which foreign firms penetrated their financial markets.[48]

The industrialized countries, however, faced significant incentives. For leading exporters of financial services, the perceived benefits of expanded markets were substantial. In addition, as most OECD countries' financial systems were already relatively open, the cost of liberalizing their financial sectors would be marginal.[49] Not surprisingly, then, while the United States and European countries argued for extensive liberalization, most developing countries were reluctant to endorse extensive market-opening reforms. Over a protracted negotiation period of ten years, the United States withdrew its offer several times and pressured countries individually to wear down the anti–financial services coalition. Still, the end of the Uruguay Round did not bring an agreement on financial services because of continued opposition from developing countries. Indeed, financial services were not subject to an accord, the 1997 FSA, until 1999.

As with sectoral negotiations, regional negotiations are often dominated by one or two regional great powers that strongly influence, if not dictate, whether progress is made. Small or middle powers are sometimes able to wield significant influence, however, through their strategic positioning as spoilers or supporters of the dominant agenda.

The U.S. regional approach to liberalization in the Western Hemisphere is characterized by a strategic leveraging of hegemonic power. Recognizing its market appeal and political persuasion, the United States has sought to bring its trade partners into a "hub-and-spoke" negotiation relationship, with the United States at the center. Despite the advantages of its hegemonic bargaining position, the United States often encounters resistance during negotiations. Middle powers have consistently asserted their rights as members of an economic club in haggling over terms of concession and preferential treatments, or played a catalytic role in leading other regional players to consensus. This is most clearly illustrated in the formation cases of the FTAA.

The hemispheric initiative, the first meeting of leaders of thirty-four countries in the Western Hemisphere in more than a generation, was launched at the Miami summit in 1994 and calls for completion of negotiations by 2005. On paper, FTAA is currently the most ambitious trade initiative in the world, building on the trend of regional trading blocs of the past five years. For the United States, FTAA represents a strategic opportunity to shore up its leadership of Western Hemispheric trade arrangements, even as its capacity to lead continues to be hampered by the absence of congressional approval of fast-track authority.

The need for the United States to exercise persuasion rather than power can be seen during the pre–FTAA summit meetings. Latin American delegations harbored considerable resentment toward what they perceived as a U.S. strategy of using the hub-and-spoke approach to enhance the U.S. bargaining position. In the months leading to Miami, the USTR met separately with various subregional groups (Caricom, Central American Common Market, Andean, Mercosur) and with Mexico and Canada individually in Washington, D.C., to gain support for the U.S. position. The U.S regional strategy of basing FTAA on the NAFTA model posed serious redistributive concerns to members of Latin and Central American subregional organizations. The Latin Americans expressed numerous reservations about the U.S. advocacy of NAFTA disciplines. Points of contention included the linking of trade and labor and environmental protection, flexibility in the timing of implementation, and differential treatment in the process of liberalization.

Similarly, the structure of negotiation in APEC is designed to downplay the role of regional hegemonic power and reduce the anxieties of forced redistribution. The process of negotiation in APEC reflects its "consensus-building, non-binding, 'soft law' approach" to multinational cooperation.[50] The executive decision-making structure in APEC is the annual summit, where the host country asserts considerable leverage over the selection of issues to be discussed. Leaders at the summit tend to put a premium on politically visible accomplishments, making pledges of action that are largely symbolic and uncoordinated rather than on the outcome of substantial negotiations.

The notion of give-and-take negotiations is problematic in the APEC setting, as most Asian countries have placed a great deal of emphasis on reaching consensus. After the summits, operational measures and plans for public-private cooperation are drafted by working groups of technical experts. Although one might expect more concrete negotiations in these arenas, little real progress has emerged from this process.

The norms of consensus do not imply absence of controversies and stalemates. The lack of practical results exhibited in APEC is not simply a product of organizational softness, but also reflects political tensions within the APEC regime. Several geographic, economic, and political dividing lines among member nations have vitiated against consensus on norms and procedures. The central debates in APEC continue to concern alternative mechanisms for liberalization and for rendering APEC compatible with GATT/WTO. More recently the central debates have expanded to include sectoral liberalization and the potential roles of APEC in regional financial supervision and monetary coordination. Thus although U.S. hegemony may have been contained in APEC, the institution's lack of progress illustrates the difficulty of concluding agreements when there is no clear consensus. In such cases, other states might regret the lack of exercise of hegemonic power to ensure the provision of public goods.

The United States has long dominated negotiations at the global level. As the regional and sectoral examples illustrated, however, the particular trajectory of negotiations often depends on the constellation of interests of hegemonic and middle powers. In an increasingly interdependent global economy, states or economic blocs with large markets have a decisive reservoir of clout that they can wield in negotiations. This situation of asymmetric interdependence often allows the larger economies to dominate the agenda as well as the negotiations because they can threaten to limit access to their markets. The Uruguay Round negotiations were primarily dominated by the United States and the EU for this reason. When consensus existed between the United States and the EU, the developing countries had few options. On nearly every issue of trade liberalization, the major industrial countries successfully shaped the talks according to their interests and often at the expense of the developing countries, producing an increasingly polarized situation.

Developing countries are not completely subject to the whims of the developed countries, but their room to maneuver is circumscribed. Even in areas where developing countries made gains in asserting their interests, they often found themselves ultimately forced to grant concessions to the developed countries. The Uruguay Round Agreement on Trade-Related Aspects of Intellectual Property Rights (TRIPs) was initially negotiated along a North-South divide but soon refocused on North-North issues. In the end, developing countries proved willing to trade their support for the TRIPs accord for improved access to industrial markets in agriculture and light manufacturing products.

The general pattern appears to be that global and sectoral negotiations succeeded when U.S. and EU norms were in agreement and failed when talks required the United States to change significantly its existing laws or practices.[51] The North-South bargaining pact is consistent with an economic club interpretation of the multilateral institution and is similar to the ongoing efforts in Europe to incorporate Eastern European countries into the economic sphere of their wealthier Western neighbors. In short, the less developed countries want access to capital and markets, and due to the asymmetric dependence on the more developed regions, they have much less influence in negotiations.

Second, domestic politics may affect ongoing international negotiations. Whether states are negotiating at a sectoral, regional, or global level strongly influences the ability of negotiators to trade among competing domestic interests. In addition, states' bargaining room depends on the strength and flexibility of domestic interests. In short, a more circumscribed sectoral negotiation, or an influential lobby with a rigid agenda, leaves negotiators with less bargaining room in comparison to a more multilateral arena where interests can be played against each other or compensated via creative package deals.

Although the United States had been a catalyst in putting trade liberalization in financial services on the international agenda, the uncompromising position of its domestic business interests prevented swift agreement. The United States was unwilling to sign any agreement that did not fulfill its very stringent demands presented at the onset of negotiations. On two occasions, under pressure from domestic interests, the United States withdrew its offers, almost precipitating a breakdown of the negotiations.

The problems that U.S. negotiators faced can be understood by consideration of the financial services lobby. As noted above, the financial service industries were instrumental in pressuring the United States to bring the issue of financial services liberalization to GATT's agenda in the early 1980s. The U.S. financial lobby made it clear at an early stage of the negotiation process that it would play an assertive role.[52] It was suspicious of any limited agreement that would grant developing countries' firms a free ride to the U.S. market while their own operations in foreign markets continued to be hampered by restrictions. During critical phases of the negotiation process, the financial lobby pressured the U.S. delegation not to accept offers it did not consider forthcoming enough.

A window of opportunity opened in 1997, as actors who previously had obstructed a comprehensive agreement seemed more reluctant to jeopardize the accord. Some propitious factors can be discerned. One was the outburst of the financial crises, which began with the Thai currency crisis on July 2, 1997. As the Asian financial crises spread, Southeast Asian countries came to see an agreement as a quick remedy that would boost their reform efforts and restore some of the credibility that had been lost to foreign investors.[53]

Also the financial lobby had become increasingly weary of the consequences of another breakdown in negotiations. In the spring of 1997, U.S. and European financial services firms joined together in a transatlantic initiative aimed at coordinating their lobbying efforts. They rallied around the Financial Leaders Group, a new lobbying group consisting of thirty leading financial firms with a stake in securing an agreement.[54] In addition, the tension between the EU and the United States that had marked the negotiations that led to the interim agreement of 1995 evaporated as negotiations progressed. At the end of 1997, a new joint leadership had emerged between the EU and the United States for bringing the negotiations to a successful conclusion.[55]

Third, the commonly espoused "bicycle theory"—the notion that unless liberalization moves forward constantly, protection will become rampant—appears to have little merit. In fact, poorly planned, piecemeal liberalization often derails the global liberalization momentum. Conversely, although the granting of sectoral protectionism to the textile and apparel industries through the LTA has distorted trade patterns in these industries, it allowed the Kennedy Round of trade negotiations to go forward and the United States to ratify the resulting agreement.

For example, the aim of completing an ITA-II pact that would remove duties on 200 high-technology products by 2002 (2007 for some poorer countries) has been aggressively pushed forward by the United States and the EU and has met considerable resistance from some Asian developing countries—especially Malaysia and India.[56] Due to the impact of the Asian crisis, both Malaysia and Thailand wanted more consumer electronic products included despite the fact that many of their industrial lobbies were opposed to further liberalization during a recession. Another sticking point in the negotiations occurred when India strongly objected to the inclusion of dual-use technologies and other non–information technology (IT) items such as radar/navigation equipment and satellite parts. As Indian producers have made no secret of their desire to be an IT superpower, few were sympathetic to their concerns. These examples illustrate two main points: (1) the dissension among countries as well as among their domestic producers; and (2) how the inclusion of additional products tends to snowball in response to individual domestic lobbies. Consequently, rushing toward global liberalization without addressing key potential interest groups has led to the weakening of pro–free trade coalitions and created little interest in future WTO negotiations.

The collapse of sectoral initiatives in the APEC context also created difficulties of negotiation at the WTO level. The U.S.-led momentum of regionalism through EVSL initially appeared to be viable but quickly ran into difficulties. Mexico opposed the sectoral approach, preferring multilateral liberalization through the WTO. Chile opted out because of its flat tariff rate structure. Then in Kuala Lumpur at the sixth Leaders' Summit in November 1998, Japan (supported by China, Indonesia, Malaysia, and Thailand) refused to liberalize trade in fishing and forestry products. With an economy that was still moribund, the Japanese government was unwilling to take the political heat from interest groups that strongly opposed liberalization in this area. Further regional cleavages in APEC have manifested themselves primarily because Japan and the United States failed to narrow the gap between their approaches during the APEC meetings. Japan wanted a single undertaking approach (supported by South Korea), whereas the United States wanted to allow participating economies to implement accords as soon as they are reached.[57] Following the Auckland APEC meeting, the United States won out, and APEC members decided that tariff reductions would be delivered sector by sector according to each economy.

Disagreement in APEC led to the failure of any APEC member country to implement unilateral EVSL tariffs cuts, essentially ending EVSL as an effective means for reducing tariff barriers. The resulting tension carried over to the Seattle WTO summit in November 1999. Japan preferred to take up a variety of issues, but the United States wanted a limited agenda, and they continued their disputes over liberalization of fish, timber products, and agriculture. Paradoxically, at the same time, many developing nations, particularly Malaysia, were cautious of moves to widen the scope of WTO negotiations to include nontrade issues. In fact, Malaysian ministers were glad that APEC did not set a decisive time for new trade negotiations in the Millennium Round, despite U.S. pressures to do so.[58]

Although the welfare merits of sector-specific arrangements are debatable, it is arguable that in the early 1960s textiles and apparel protection was simply the necessary price to be paid for the broader objective of what became known as the Kennedy Round of GATT negotiations. And most crucially, the LTA and the MFA were carefully nested in the GATT, and indeed, the implementation and enforcement structures were housed in Geneva. In short, states may have to appease certain interest groups demanding some protection as the price of global liberalization.

Implementation and Compliance

After states agree to trade agreements, the question of how such accords become translated into domestic laws and regulations in line with the multilateral commitment is critical. Some measures require little effort, while others are more ambiguous, expensive, and technically complicated. In assessing this stage of trade governance, we can focus on two key aspects: (1) what helps or obstructs the implementation of measures; and (2) what mechanisms are in place to determine if states are complying. For example, is it mainly a lack of financial or technical resources that prevents a state from full implementation, or does flawed institutional design give actors incentives to delay implementation? Similarly, are problems with compliance caused by inadequate monitoring mechanisms or ambiguity over what "compliance" in fact is? Five main lessons with respect to implementation and compliance can be drawn.

First, formal institutionalization has a better track record of advancing the reduction of tariffs than the alternatives. Because situations of "voluntarism" closely resemble the uncontrolled situation that existed before any trade agreements, it can be presumed that voluntarism will not often be strong enough to overcome national protectionist tendencies and the temptation to free ride on other states that might have complied. In addition, legalistic institutions with a stronger independent means of gathering information are better at highlighting noncompliance.

Voluntary implementation makes it difficult to distinguish between states that comply and those that do not. Without developed criteria and interventionist mechanisms to verify noncompliance or effective enforcement mechanisms, voluntary governance structures mainly rely on the persuasive power of norms and the ability of more powerful actors to enforce compliance through arm-twisting diplomacy. At the same time, the conventional threat of unilateral retaliation or collective action against laggard states is often restrained by the trade regime itself.

These points are well illustrated by APEC's voluntary tariff reduction program. The evidence shows that this approach has not worked consistently and independently of global or regional momentum. The 1994 Bogor Declaration called for free and open trade by 2020 for all countries and by 2010 for developed countries, but this objective has been implemented mainly through Individual Action Programs (IAPs) undertaken by member governments following the guidelines set by the Osaka Action Agenda.[59] The IAP commitments to tariff reduction are nonbinding and voluntary. Few developed members of APEC, however, have proposed anything beyond their existing Uruguay Round obligations; at the same time the ASEAN countries have sometimes circumvented APEC in pursuing initiatives started in the subregional context. Ongoing political negotiations and institutional efforts have focused on resolving the ambiguities left by the Osaka Agenda, including the issues of endpoints, benchmarks, time path, and extension of reduced tariffs to nonmembers. The slow progress of IAPs and the success of the ITA in 1996 have revived the enthusiasm for a more coercive sectoral approach, but as noted earlier, the nascent EVSL multisectoral framework has met significant resistance.

The positive effect of transparency in inducing compliance via institutional processes such as information sharing is best captured by more formal, legalistic governance structures. An agreement to simply provide information—even without the threat of enforcement—may be a useful beginning point for putting pressure on other states or for states to persuade domestic interests to go along with multilateral accords.

A formal system of monitoring based on information gathering and verification enhances transparency. Consequently, it is more probable that states will implement and comply if their actions are observable to others, for two reasons: (1) generally, states will find it embarrassing to confront information that contradicts their public claims; and (2) if there are enforcement mechanisms in place, they will ex ante know that noncompliant behavior is likely to be noticed and other states will respond.

A possibly powerful counterpoint to the APEC problematic model of voluntarism is the EU's attempt to intensify monitoring and information gathering in employment (and quite recently social protection) areas. Essentially, what has been called the Luxembourg process institutionalizes a process of centralized coordination on employment issues begun in 1997 before it even had a legal basis in the EC Treaty.[60] In exchange for states being required to provide certain information (quantifiable whenever possible), they are allowed to comply voluntarily.

Each year, the European intergovernmental Council of Ministers and the European Commission are to publish a joint report communicating specific employment guidelines. The fifteen member states must take these guidelines into account in formulating their National Action Plans for that year. Then, at the end of the year, the council can make recommendations to the member states concerning their employment policies. They analyze each state's action taken in that year in relation to the common objectives and the specific National Action Plans. The most severe sanctioning mechanism member states face, however, is a nonbinding recommendation from the council.

In contrast to other issue areas, such as the promotion of a single market via binding supranational legislation, the institutional framework put in place for employment policy is facilitative rather than prescriptive. Member states maintain control over their own employment policies, and the principle of subsidiarity has been further enshrined. The perceived success of this process has led to an interesting case of institutional mimicry. In December 1999, the European Council of Ministers and the European Commission created a High Level Working Party on Social Protection. The council underlined the need for cooperation in modernizing social protection, based on a structured and permanent dialogue, follow-up and exchange of information, experience, and good practice between member states.

An implicit assumption is that the production and dissemination of quantifiable information that can be compared to a state's behavior will put enough pressure on states to comply. Although it is still too early to make any categorical judgments about the effects of increased transparency on implementation and compliance, the perceived success does not mean that such an institutional mechanism can readily be transferred to other regions. The EU is relatively culturally homogeneous, currently dominated by social democratic governments, and economically and legally integrated. In addition, this process depends on states being concerned with whether they appear—to their own public, the transnational public, and the regulatory regime—to be acting consistently with their stated plans. In short, increased transparency can exacerbate the fact that states within the EU are probably more susceptible to shaming than states in other regimes. The ostracization of Austria since the government's inclusion of the far-right Freedom Party, a right-wing party led by Joerg Haider, is a compelling example.

By comparison, the WTO is a good example of a fully codified Trade Policy Review Mechanism (TPRM) designed to provide greater transparency of national laws and practices and to examine the impact of member policies on other countries. TPRM reviews are simple consultations that are not intended to judge the consistency or conformity of national practices with trading regime rules. Rather, under the permanent Trade Policy Review Board, the TPRM has become the repository of all notifications for WTO member country obligations and is required to conduct reviews of major countries (Canada, the EU, Japan, and the United States) every other year. Through seminars, reviews, publication of reports, and meetings, the TPRM has made a significant contribution to the transparency objective. It is worth noting, however, that the implementation of these agreements has strained limited WTO resources, especially in the legal and economic analyses divisions.[61] Ironically, the United States has resisted budgetary increases despite indications that it stands to benefit disproportionately.[62]

Second, formal institutions frequently encounter problems of politicization. Although formal institutional mechanisms appear superior to voluntary implementation and compliance, formal institutions are not a universal panacea and have their own practical shortcomings. The crucial questions concern what kind of formal institutions are in place, and how impervious to political manipulation they are. An example that illustrates some of the potential pitfalls of formal institutions is the development of VERs.

Even though VERs are generally negotiated on a bilateral or multilateral basis, they must be implemented by the national governments of exporting countries and monitored by importing countries. Exporting countries have incentives to circumvent their self-imposed restraints because their exports are artificially restricted, while the importing countries have incentives to monitor compliance to protect their industries. The typical process has been for the governments of exporting countries to instruct industries to restrict their exports to the bilaterally or multilaterally agreed level. The industries and the national agencies of the importing countries usually carry out monitoring and verification of compliance. For example, if an import-competing industry suspects that imports are larger than permitted under a VER, it can appeal to its home government for retaliation.

An example of the politicization of formal monitoring mechanisms is in textiles and apparel trade. Here the sectoral-specific MFA regime governing the rules of bilateral VERs established an international monitoring mechanism called the Textiles Surveillance Board (TSB) under the auspices of the GATT. The organization was set up to monitor compliance with the agreement. The TSB's mandate emphasized conciliation of disputes through a multilateral mechanism, which reviewed all actions taken under the provisions of the arrangement and made recommendations to the participating countries to facilitate implementation.[63] The TSB examined bilateral and unilateral actions of its member countries and reported the findings to the Textiles Committee of the GATT forum.

The TSB consisted of members of various importing and exporting countries. The delegates to the TSB were to serve as technical experts in monitoring agreements, although in reality, political criteria have often determined their actions. For example, the flexibility clauses that allowed departures from the agreed rates of growth in import quotas create a problem for maintaining compliance with the MFA guidelines of VERs. Under these clauses, developed importing countries negotiated increasingly restrictive trade agreements, claiming disruptions to their markets, but the TSB was not able to criticize their actions, and it also did not force compliance. And the periodic renewal requirement of certain agreements makes them vulnerable to domestic pressures at times of renewal. The MFA is an example in which the requirement of periodic renewals hurts compliance. As domestic industry increased pressure for protectionist measures, the developed countries weakened the agreement in successive renewals. Thus, overall compliance has decreased over time.[64]

Third, formal institutions may encourage and exacerbate the use of available exceptions. Three types of measures within the GATT/WTO regime provide exceptions or a temporary pause in the implementation of a state's multilateral commitments: antidumping measures (ADM), subsidies and countervailing duties, and safeguard measures (SGM). The Uruguay Round tried to prohibit the use of VERs in favor of formal SGMs, but at the same time it limited the potential restrictiveness of SGMs and thus diminished their appeal. Moreover, the United States and the EU had managed to blunt efforts to restrain ADMs, thus creating a dynamic favoring ADMs as trade remedies.[65]

ADMs are special tariffs on imported goods that are priced below home market prices. Because of the difficulty for states to prove that they are not dumping, such measures have become the most frequently used trade remedy in Western countries. They have been employed by protectionist-minded groups with a higher success rate than SGMs, reflecting the selective rules- and power-based enforcement of these measures.[66] ADMs also impose relatively low costs for their uses—they do not require the provision of trade compensation, and they shift a high procedural burden onto responding firms, which must provide information to the dumping authorities.[67] The GATT permits the use of ADMs in Article IV but provides little guidance as to the proper procedure and bases for determining injury. The Tokyo Round Code and the Dunkel Draft of 1991 tightened up the procedures somewhat, but in the necessary process of translating the code into domestic law, the United States and European countries have been able to preserve considerable leeway for domestic import-competing industries to claim injury from dumping.[68]

SGMs, commonly known as the "escape clause" of GATT Article XIX, are formal procedures by which governments may suspend or withdraw GATT commitments affecting an injured industry. Prior to the Uruguay Round, there was no multilateral legal code governing the use of SGMs. The Uruguay Round SGM Code specified general rules, especially for the phasing out of VERs and constraining the use of SGMs. It also gave developing countries benefits through a longer phase-in period, exempting their exports from SGMs in some cases and lengthening the effective period of SGMs to ten years. By contrast with ADMs, SGMs have been used far less as a means of modifying states' GATT/WTO commitments. The problem is mainly one of complex legalism. To qualify for import relief, an industry has to show that it was experiencing serious injuries caused in major part by increased imports, and furthermore it has to demonstrate that the increased imports were caused in major part by past tariff concessions. The key difficulty is in showing the second link; and even if it is demonstrated, the complainant must compensate the trading partner for the granting of import restrictions as relief. As Jeffrey Schott argues, the remaining attraction of SGM is as an option for its main users—the EU and the United States— to act against import surges from emerging trading powers such as China.[69]

Fourth, material incentives and flexibility may assist compliance. Financial assistance used to support poorer countries in implementation and to create monitoring systems for developing countries increases the likelihood of efficacious implementation and compliance. For example, sectoral liberalization programs have been better implemented when there were financial incentives for the poorer countries. Flexibility in implementation may also encourage the broader objective of overall compliance.

The ITA provides an example of the benefits of material incentives to encourage compliance. Implementation and compliance with the ITA have focused on making the IT trading processes transparent, setting up uniform data-gathering methods, creating monitoring systems, and establishing verification procedures. Because the ITA was negotiated by and for WTO members, it utilized the TPRM as the chief implementation and compliance mechanism. The concern for transparency and monitoring is most evident in setting up a uniform schedule for phasing out tariffs and other customs and duties. The financial resources and technological know-how needed for monitoring and verification, however, are not always in ample supply in developing countries.

For their part, the exporting countries have been reluctant to complain very vocally to the GATT for fear of jeopardizing exports. Moreover, because limiting exports can lead to increased prices, in some cases, exporting countries have been able to secure quota rents and have not been unduly harmed by the restraints. Because restraints are quantitative, another negotiating effort has been to avoid any restrictions on the prices of goods, thus allowing them to export higher-priced goods and still maintain an overall quantitative limitation to meet the demands of the importing country. Thus, although compliance with the overall goal of reducing export growth has been met, the willingness of U.S. negotiators to be flexible on specifics has allowed them to meet competing political imperatives.

Fifth, open regionalism sometimes reinforces globalism through supportive norms and rules. Although the lack of compliance mechanisms has retarded the progress of tariff reduction in the context of Asia-Pacific integration, APEC's principles of "open regionalism" have tended to reinforce the existing global regime.[70] "Open regionalism" is a code phrase that reflects a certain Asian skepticism for Western-style institution building and serves as a defense against bureaucratic, regionwide rule making. Nevertheless, a central substantive tenet of open regionalism is an institutional commitment to consistency and convergence with the global liberal momentum.

At the level of elite consensus formation and socialization, the APEC forum can be said to have had some influence on member states' general economic orientation and state-society relations; however, these effects are difficult to quantify. Member bureaucracies have on occasion looked to APEC for reinforcement of a liberal economic policy line against domestic interests who do not share the free market ideology. For example, it would have been unlikely for China to make the across-the-board tariff cuts it offered at the 1995 Osaka APEC meeting without the justification of needing an impressive down payment for APEC.[71] Participation in the APEC process may have helped to moderate U.S. trade unilateralism and to provide impetus for Japan to carry out long-delayed deregulation.[72] Thus there is some evidence that states are using APEC to reduce pressure from domestic interests by using APEC as a focal point that justifies some modicum of voluntarism. But the bottom line remains that without more effective mechanisms, implementation and compliance will remain in short supply.

Open regionalism has encouraged APEC countries to abide by the GATT/WTO regime in trade and similar global conventions. Through its information exchange and training, APEC may apply pressure for improved enforcement or help overcome technical deficiencies or simply ignorance. For example, "soft" mechanisms in such areas as intellectual property protection, customs classification, value-added network services, and transportation may help overcome the considerable deficiencies in some APEC members' compliance with global regimes. Moreover, the normative APEC vocabulary is full of other more operationally meaningful principles such as transparency, nondiscrimination, comprehensiveness, WTO consistency, and mutual benefit. These guiding principles influence national, bilateral, and subregional rule making and serve as a basis for other governments to challenge actions inconsistent with them.

Thus, institutional developments in one arena may support or stifle agreements made in other arenas. In the operational rule-making, implementation, enforcement, and adjudication arenas, APEC facilitates the effectiveness of other regimes. It does so, however, by acting to strengthen the operation of global regimes at the regional level rather than creating new regional regimes or pushing for major extensions of global regimes. Although not all members of APEC are members of the WTO, there is a significant amount of membership overlap. Indeed, with such overlapping membership in different governance structures that, in principle, have complementary goals, it is intuitive that rules in one would strengthen those in the other. That is not to suggest, however, that regional structures cannot cause tensions with global structures, as the legacy of political tension and institutional fatigue upon the collapse of the U.S-led sectoral initiative in the APEC context demonstrates.

Noncompliance

Although the enforcement of trade agreements is tightly linked with implementation and compliance, they are distinct phases of a trade regime. Enforcement refers to the problem of dealing with states that have clearly failed to comply. A trade deal can be implemented but not effectively enforced. The causes of states' failure to comply largely determine the types of enforcement mechanisms needed. If one believes that noncompliance is unintentional and rare, then a managerial approach may be preferred.[73] If noncompliance is believed to be the outcome of willful deceit, then more coercive measures that significantly raise the costs of noncompliance would prove useful. Once noncompliance has been detected, the two most important factors in enforcement are the party in charge of reacting to noncompliance and the enforcement mechanisms. Five key lessons were learned from our survey of the history of enforcement with respect to different trading arrangements.

First, without strong legal-rational mechanisms of dispute settlement, collective international responses to noncompliant behaviors are hard to organize. Formal institutions at all three levels have had more success in enforcing implementation and compliance than voluntary and nonbinding mechanisms. The differences between NAFTA and APEC illuminate the strengths and weaknesses of legalism and soft-law approaches. NAFTA has demonstrated that regional dispute settlement mechanisms can provide an effective alternative to unilateral actions, while APEC shows that a deliberate avoidance of enforcement mechanisms has seriously impeded progress in the reduction of trade barriers.[74]

Second, dispute resolution mechanisms may vary in design depending on the nature of the parties involved. NAFTA's dispute settlement mechanisms have generated many valuable ideas for future designs of dispute settlement mechanisms; one involves the differential treatment of states and individual or corporate entities as parties in disputes. A strong case has been made that although transparency is essential to the monitoring and verification of state behaviors, and thus helps organize collective responses to noncompliant state behaviors, in cases involving individual or corporate entities, the benefits of transparency must be balanced against the need for confidentiality in facilitating mediation and arbitration.

Third, countermeasures from major powers are effective in correcting violations of bilateral and multilateral agreements. Historically, early flaws in the GATT dispute settlement process made enforcement of trade agreements difficult. Long delays in panel proceedings, the ability of disputants to block the necessary consensus to approve panel findings and authorize retaliation, and the difficulty of securing compliance with rulings threatened to derail the entire global trading regime. Partly in response to the GATT's weak dispute resolution mechanism, the EU and the United States began to resort to unilateral laws such as Super 301. When or why would states believe that certain unilateral threats are better than the current arrangement, and whose threats are likely to be credible? Power asymmetry and national strength in the affected industries are two of the most salient factors. A powerful state with a large market can often use unilateral threats as an effective weapon to enforce compliance.

In the background of successive rounds of GATT negotiations was the fear of U.S. unilateralism. Under pressure from highly competitive European and Asian firms, the United States adopted trade remedy laws for unilateral retaliation in the form of Section 301 of the Trade Act of 1974. Section 301 has been tailored to promote the enforcement of U.S. rights under international trade agreements and to deter foreign countries from unfair trade practices. Although it is nominally consistent with GATT, it exploits the gray area through which the United States could continue to exercise unilateralism.

The strengthening of the GATT/WTO dispute settlement mechanisms (DSMs) in the Uruguay Round has predictably challenged the use of Section 301 and increased the additional costs of U.S. unilateralism, but perhaps not to the degree hoped for and expected by developing countries. As a formal "equalizer" between the enforcement powers of great and lesser powers, the DSM is expected to impair substantially the use of unilateralism by great powers to pry open emerging markets and dismantle restrictive business practices. Although the Japanese believed that "the era of bilateralism is over" and the Japanese system of import and investment protection would henceforth be immune to U.S. sanctions, this has not been the case in practice.[75] The strengthened DSM is broadly compatible with the continuing creative use of Section 301. U.S. firms and policy makers have attempted to recast their claims as trade remedies in response to unfair trade practices, in conjunction with GATT/WTO-sanctioned measures of antidumping, subsidies and countervailing duties, and safeguards.[76] In the most drastic scenario, the United States can simply choose to ignore the rulings of the DSM.

Thus, an economic powerhouse like the United States can credibly threaten with unilateral action, because many other countries are asymmetrically dependent on the U.S. market. It generally follows that states with smaller economies can use this option less often and most likely only with other economies of similar size. Of course, one must look not only at the size of the economy, but also at the affected industry.

Fourth, recent strengthening of the GATT/WTO dispute settlement mechanism represents an effort to shift enforcement from a power-based system of the Cold War era to a rules-based system. The Uruguay Round addressed three basic flaws in the GATT's DSM: long delays in the panel proceedings, difficulties in achieving consensus needed for approval of panel findings and authorization of retaliation, and difficulties in securing compliance with panel rulings.[77] Closely resembling a judicial regime of appellate review operating on a strict time schedule, the Dispute Settlement Understanding (DSU) established a unified system to settle disputes arising under all multilateral trade agreements covered by the WTO. Under the new WTO agreement, a new standing appellate body—consisting of third-country nationals to review appeals of panel rulings and procedures to monitor compliance, as well as allow for automatic retaliation in the event of noncompliance—was established. Finally, a new Dispute Settlement Body was created to administer dispute settlement rules and procedures with the ability to disapprove noncompliance retaliation by consensus.[78] From start to finish, the dispute process is supposed to take no longer than twenty months.

The DSU represents a dramatic move from a power-based system to a rule-based system. Although its scope is limited, its jurisdiction is compulsory. The preferred solution is the removal of the offending measure, not award of damages for trade lost during the process. It has some potential advantages and many more practical disadvantages for smaller and developing countries. The DSU is the primary way by which the Uruguay Round commitments of the larger countries can be enforced through a rule-based system, and it restricts the use of unilateral measures like the U.S. Section 301 that have targeted exporters from developing countries. However, the function of enforcement is potentially most effective when the WTO dispute settlement institution is willing to take on the enforcer role, rather than its current position as a passive third party that encourages settlement.[79] The final resort to retaliation by the complainant state clearly disadvantages smaller countries that value the markets of their major trade partners and have few resources to risk an escalation of the trade dispute. Paradoxically, the dispute settlement procedures actually restrain the complainant state from retaliation until a neutral panel has reviewed its case and the panel's ruling is affirmed by the Appellate Body and adopted by the Dispute Settlement Body. Meanwhile, the defendant state simply agrees to participate in the process.[80] Furthermore, when the weak state takes on politically entrenched programs of powerful states, the latter might choose to ignore a dispute settlement decision, thus precipitating a legal crisis that could undercut confidence in the dispute settlement regime itself. One may argue that "the real sanction of the system is the value that the parties—especially the large parties—place on it."[81]

Fifth, global mechanisms of enforcement can support regionalism or sectoralism. Procedures and monitoring mechanisms in one arena may support dispute resolution in another arena if institutions have been designed to be compatible and if states have overlapping memberships in various agreements. For example, the WTO has been used as an effective and efficient tool to implement and enforce a sectoral agreement.

The role of the WTO as the arbiter of trading rules remains under intense scrutiny domestically. Both liberals and conservatives from the U.S. Congress, for example, have openly questioned the decisions of the dispute resolution panels established under the WTO's dispute settlement understanding, arguing that such WTO decisions interfere with national sovereignty. It remains unclear whether the DSU will be an effective mechanism for resolving noncompliance disputes.

CONCLUSIONS AND IMPLICATIONS

This chapter has examined the process of agenda setting, negotiations, implementation, and reactions to noncompliance in the trading arena. The focus has been on understanding the interplay of various state and nonstate actors in three different categories of governance in this issue area: sectoralism, regionalism, and globalism.

With respect to agenda setting, the most significant factor has been the general security environment. In an effort to secure protection, interest groups have often framed their concerns as those of national security. At the same time, the U.S. government, for one, was able to use the threat of communism as a means to resist protection from vested interests. Moreover, it was often able to use various types of trade arrangements, particularly multilateral ones, as a means of controlling both domestic interest groups (by arguing that its hands were tied once an international agreement was negotiated) and other states once it was able to get them to commit to an agreement. But with the end of the Cold War, interest groups have now been able to lobby more effectively for their specific interests. The most interesting recent manifestation of this is the advent of liberal sectoral arrangements in new industries such as telecommunications and information technology. A similar phenomenon can be seen in the financial services industry. Faced by deregulation domestically in the United States and similar changes in other countries, industry groups in these sectors have been able to obtain sector-specific multilateral agreements. At the same time, protectionist groups such as textiles, apparel, and steel producers have become more active in opposing liberalization and have even opposed developments such as China's accession to the WTO.

Sectoral arrangements must be analyzed more carefully in the future. Protectionist agreements need not impede global liberalization, if they are marked by clearly delimited commitments and designed to provide a temporary respite for affected industries to permit them to adjust to competition or exit the industry. The most egregious example that does not meet these criteria has been the textiles and apparel industries, with the MFA evolving into a multifaceted protectionist mechanism that has eroded the ability of the developed countries to make moral entreaties to developing countries in the name of liberalism. In the second best of all possible worlds, sectoralism may allow policy makers to move forward with broader trade objectives, but this path can also lead to protectionism.

Sectoral openness, as manifested in the ITA, might seem to be an ideal means of promoting liberalism when global trade efforts stall. Yet this approach is potentially fraught with danger. When successful, by giving highly motivated liberal-minded interests what they want in their specific sector, sectoralism undermines the ability to make trade-offs among a variety of different sectors that has been the hallmark of the GATT process. When unsuccessful, such as in the cases of the aborted U.S.-led EVSL in APEC and the OECD-originated MAI campaign, sectoral initiatives threaten to disrupt regional or multilateral cooperation and create entrenched domestic opposition on the same issue. Thus, liberalism for its own sake can be destructive—without concern for the creation of a broader political-economic coalition that will propel global negotiations forward.

In international trade negotiations, major powers have generally been able to determine outcomes. Yet middle and smaller powers that are adroit in forming coalitions (as well as in working to set the agenda for trade negotiations) may often have a much larger role than one might predict from their economic position alone. Domestic actors, particularly with the end of the Cold War, have also been able to exert a great deal of power during international state-to-state negotiations, often placing negotiators in untenable positions or undermining national stances. The so-called bicycle theory of trade, which argues that unless liberalization moves forward constantly, protection will become rampant, appears to have little merit.

The success of implementation and compliance of multilateral agreements depends largely on the incentives and institutional mechanisms targeting the national level. Although the track record of international trade regimes demonstrates that formal institutionalization is more effective in advancing tariff reductions than the alternatives (including the soft-law, voluntary approach of APEC), states may respond to formal constraints by political manipulation of the monitoring mechanism, or by increasing resort to trade relief measures that put the multilateral commitments on hold. Moreover, developing countries or "laggards" in the multilateral trade liberalization efforts predictably require additional institutional incentives for cooperation. In this regard, material incentives and flexibility in implementation have proven useful in eliciting compliance from countries concerned with their capability to bear the costs and develop domestic institutional capacities for liberalization. Furthermore, where compulsory, legalistic mechanisms of compliance face insurmountable cultural or political resistance, such as in the Asia-Pacific regional context, a principled commitment to consistency and convergence with the global regime, promoted by continual renewal of consensus and socialization of member-state bureaucrats, can be useful in raising the probability of voluntary compliance. Nevertheless, the slow progress in sectoral liberalization of APEC in recent years casts doubt on this soft-law approach. This development stands in sharp contrast to regional integration in Europe and North America, which has continued to deepen through the developing of formal monitoring systems and rule-based DSMs that aim to close loopholes for domestic noncompliance.

The two most important factors in dealing with states that have failed to comply with their multilateral commitments are (1) the party in charge of reacting to non-compliance whether it is the injured country(ies) or the international community at large; and (2) the enforcement mechanisms in place, whether power-based or rules-based. Supranational, legalistic DSMs, as exemplified by NAFTA's Chapter 11, have had greater success in redressing deviations from implementation and compliance than voluntary and nonbinding mechanisms. These mechanisms, however, must make sufficient distinctions among parties involved in disputes, such as by granting confidentiality to private investors while insisting on transparency in monitoring and verifying state behaviors. The reasons for the differential treatment are the reduction of transaction costs inherent in a legalistic process and the provision of incentives for mediation and arbitration.

The institutionalization of rule-based enforcement mechanisms also tends to create an equalizing effect among member states, as weaker countries gain leverage to bind the commitments of powerful countries and restrain them from unilateralism. This objective of empowering weaker states through supranational legal mechanisms has also been incorporated into post–Uruguay Round modifications in the GATT/WTO DSMs. This effort to shift enforcement from a power-based system of the Cold War era to a rule-based system, however, does not entirely rule out the advantages of and domination by strong states, in particular the United States, because the WTO has been unwilling to take on the enforcer role, thus leaving weaker states to face the real risks of retaliation in confronting their major trade partners.

Finally, well-functioning global mechanisms of enforcement provide support for sectoral and regional liberalization initiatives—if proper institutional linkages are established to provide the alternatives of dispute settlement and enforcement through global institutions. The question of the factors that permit such "nesting," or some type of parallel arrangements that enable a division of labor among trade institutions, is of great relevance for policy makers who wish to design new multilateral institutional solutions to problems arising from global interdependence.

Still, further WTO legalization brings about problems of its own. Although many lawyers and some economists are enthusiastic about the direction that the WTO has taken, an excessive preoccupation with formalization may undermine the objective of minimizing hostilities among countries. Simply developing rules and procedures—without due attention to creating a consensus on the appropriateness of certain kinds of intervention and retaliation—does not provide a solution to conflicts arising from ideational differences and power asymmetries. The continuing controversy and escalating protectionism between the EU and the United States over hormone-fed beef, despite a ruling from the WTO in favor of the latter, demonstrate the limits of DSMs in the absence of shared norms on proper justification of national regulation for health and safety reasons.

Calling for efforts to develop a consensus on a host of issues may seem naïve and not the stuff of international politics. In the absence of such discussion, however, institution building is meaningless. I hope that this chapter provides a small step in our efforts to better understand the dynamics of goverance in international trade and to improve our ability to formulate policy in this arena.

NOTES

1. Many economists have contributed to the basic theory of comparative advantage, including Eli Hecksher, Abba Lerner, John Stuart Mill, Bertil Ohlin, David Ricardo, Paul Samuelson, and Robert Torrens.
2. See, for example, the work on strategic trade theory. For a survey, see Paul R. Krugman, ed., *Strategic Trade Policy and the New International Economics* (Cambridge, Mass.: MIT Press, 1986).
3. It is worth noting that what should properly be included in the area of "trade" goes beyond recent environmental and labor concerns. In the early period of post–World War II negotiations, the focus at all levels was on the manufacturing sector. Especially at the global level, agriculture was left out of negotiations and only began to be seriously addressed in the Uruguay Round of GATT negotiations from 1986 to 1993. Moreover, issues such as intellectual property, trade-related investment measures, and government procurement came to be seen as legitimate questions for discussion in the GATT/WTO only over a long period of time. Thus, at least in principle, the scope of the trade issue is subject to fluctuation based on an evolving consensus and political pressures.
4. The dimension of geographical dispersion applies only to the bilateral and minilateral categories, although one could imagine a focus on unilateral measures that were oriented toward geographical neighbors or to more distant actors.
5. See Joan E. Spero and Jeffrey Hart, *The Politics of International Economic Relations* (New York: St. Martin's Press, 1997), for a detailed historical narrative.
6. See William Diebold, Jr., "The End of the I.T.O.," *Princeton Essays in International Finance*, no. 16 (October 1952).
7. *Economic Report of the President* (Washington, D.C.: U.S. Government Printing Office, 1995), p. 205.
8. Ibid., p. 205.
9. See Stephen D. Krasner, *Structural Conflict: The Third World Against Global Liberalism* (Berkeley, Calif.: University of California Press, 1985).
10. See WTO web site at <http://www.wto.org/wto>.
11. For an analysis of the MFA, see Vinod K. Aggarwal, *Liberal Protectionism: The International Politics of Organized Textile Trade* (Berkeley, Calif.: University of California Press, 1985).

12. Vinod K. Aggarwal, Robert O. Keohane, and David B. Yoffie, "The Dynamics of Negotiated Protectionism," *American Political Science Review*, vol. 81, no. 2 (1987), pp. 345–48.

13. See WTO web site at <http://www.wto.org/english/tratop_e/texti_e/texintro.htm>.

14. See Aggarwal, Keohane, and Yoffie, "The Dynamics of Negotiated Protectionism," for extensive discussion on these sectors.

15. Ibid., pp. 347–52.

16. See WTO web site at <http://www.wto.org/english/tratop_e/texti_e/texintro.htm>.

17. Aggarwal, Keohane, and Yoffie, "The Dynamics of Negotiated Protectionism," pp. 356–37.

18. The literature on the complex institutional history of the European Community (EC)/EU is beyond the scope of this chapter and is relatively well known. For an excellent review of the EC/EU's history, see Loukas Tsoukalis, *The New European Community Revisited* (Oxford, U.K.: Oxford University Press, 1997).

19. See John C. Condon, *Good Neighbors: Communicating with the Mexicans* (Yarmouth, Maine: Intercultural Press, 1997) for an empirical overview.

20. See Vinod K. Aggarwal and Charles Morrison, eds., *Asia-Pacific Crossroads: Regime Creation and the Future of APEC* (New York: St. Martin's Press, 1998).

21. See Aggarwal, *Liberal Protectionism*, for a discussion of nested systems and institutions in the context of sectoral arrangements. See also Vinod K. Aggarwal, "Comparing Regional Cooperation Efforts in Asia-Pacific and North America," in Andrew Mack and John Ravenhill, eds., *Pacific Cooperation: Building Economic and Security Regimes in the Asia-Pacific Region* (Sydney: Allen and Unwin, 1994), for analysis of institutional nesting in a regional context in North America and the Asia-Pacific region and APEC's options. These ideas are elaborated in Vinod K. Aggarwal, ed., *Institutional Designs for a Complex World: Bargaining, Linkages, and Nesting* (Ithaca, N.Y.: Cornell University Press, 1998).

22. See Beverly Crawford, "Explaining Germany's Decision to Participate in European Monetary Union," University of California at Berkeley (1998), unpublished manuscript.

23. See Aggarwal, *Liberal Protectionism*, for a discussion of the nesting of economic issues with a security context.

24. U.S. Senate, *Problems of the Domestic Textile Industry*, Committee on Interstate and Foreign Commerce, 1959–1963.

25. See Vinod K. Aggarwal and Kun-Chin Lin, "Strategy Without Vision: U.S. and Asia-Pacific Economic Cooperation," in Jürgen Rüland, Eva Menske, and Werner Draguhn, eds., *APEC: The First Decade* (London: Curzon Press, 2001).

26. Vinod Aggarwal, with Stephan Haggard, "The Domestic and International Politics of Protection in the U.S. Textile and Apparel Industries," in John Zysman and Laura Tyson, eds., *American Industry in International Competition* (Ithaca, N.Y.: Cornell University Press, 1983), p. 26.

27. See Dale E. Hathaway, *Agriculture and the GATT: Rewriting the Rules* (Washington, D.C.: Institute for International Economics, 1987).

28. "Press Briefing by National Economic Advisor Gene Sperling, United States Trade Representative Charlene Barshefsky, and Secretary of Agriculture Dan Glickman," released by the White House Office of the Press Secretary, October 13, 1999.

29. Jonathan Aronson, "Negotiating to Launch Negotiations: Getting Trade in Services onto the GATT Agenda," Teaching Material Case 125 (Pittsburgh, Penn.: University of Pittsburgh New Program, 1988), p. 7. This paragraph draws on this work.

30. For American motives to promote APEC, see Richard J. Baker, "The United States and APEC Regime Building," in Aggarwal and Morrison, *Asia-Pacific Crossroads*, pp. 170–71. For the United States' key motive to promote APEC, see Joseph M. Grieco, "Political-Military Dynamics and the Nesting of Regimes: An Analysis of APEC, the WTO, and Prospects for Cooperation in the Asia-Pacific," in Aggarwal and Morrison, *Asia Pacific Crossroads*, pp. 245–46.

31. Formed in the mid-1980s, the Cairns Group is a fifteen-member body that seeks to reform high levels of protection on agricultural goods through the WTO.

32. Super 301 refers to U.S. trade law that allows for unilateral trade sanctions against countries whom the USTR's office identifies as unfairly restricting U.S. exports. The unilateral nature of this approach has often been criticized as undermining the principle of multilateralism in global trade negotiations.

33. Some estimates predict that 70 percent of the demand for computers will come from outside the United States by the year 2000. See Frost and Sullivan, *1996–98 IT Market Reports*.

34. See Vinod K. Aggarwal, "The Political Economy of Service Sector Negotiations in the Uruguay Round," *The Fletcher Forum on World Affairs*, vol. 16, no. 1 (Winter 1992), pp. 35–54.

35. See Aggarwal and Lin, "Strategy Without Vision."

36. See Aggarwal, *Liberal Protectionism*, for a discussion of this.

37. Jeffrey J. Schott, *The Uruguay Round: An Assessment* (Washington, D.C.: Institute for International Economics, 1994), p. 99.

38. Clyde H. Farnsworth, "New Trade Struggle: Services," *New York Times*, November 23, 1982, p. 1.

39. Wendy Dobson and Pierre Jacquet, *Financial Service Liberalization in the WTO* (Washington, D.C.: Institute for International Economics, 1998), p. 71.

40. Clyde H. Farnsworth, "Trade Topics Are Determined," *New York Times*, January 18, 1982, p. 1.

41. For more information on the content of the compromise, see William Dullforce, Ivo Dawnay, and Punta Del Este, "Farm Trade to Come Within GATT," *Financial Times*, September 22, 1986, p. 6; and Felix Dearden, "Trade Round to Ignore Big Imbalances," *Journal of Commerce*, September 23, 1986, p. 3.

42. For an extensive account of the position of developing and industrialized countries, see Aggarwal, "The Political Economy of Service Sector Negotiations in the Uruguay Round," pp. 48–53.

43. See Peter Haas, "Do Regimes Matter? Epistemic Communities and Mediterranean Pollution Control," *International Organization*, vol. 43, no. 3 (Summer 1989), pp. 377–403.

44. Baker, "The United States and APEC Regime Building," p. 174.

45. Ibid., p. 176.

46. Fred C. Bergsten, ed., *Whither APEC? The Progress to Date and Agenda for the Future* (Washington, D.C.: Institute for International Economics, 1997), p. 99.

47. Aggarwal and Morrison, *Asia-Pacific Crossroads*, pp. 11–12. It had provided the intellectual rationale for open regionalism by characterizing trade liberalization as a "prisoner's delight," with unilateral liberalization being a high-payoff strategy. See Aggarwal, "Comparing Regional Cooperation Efforts in Asia-Pacific and North America," p. 48.

48. For a discussion, see Dobson and Jacquet, *Financial Service Liberalization in the WTO*. On the link between comparative advantages and developing country stances, see Murray Gibbs and Michiko Hayashi, "Sectoral Issues and the Multilateral Framework of Trade in Services: An Overview," in *Trade in Services: Sectoral Issues* (New York: United Nations, 1989), pp. 3–8; and Francois J. Outreville, "Trade in Insurance Services," in *Trade in Services*, pp. 177–78.

49. Dobson and Jacquet, *Financial Service Liberalization,* pp. 78–9.

50. Lyuba Zarsky, "APEC, Globalization, and the Environment," *BASC News*, vol. 1, no. 2 (Summer/Fall 1998), p. 3.

51. See Jeffrey J. Schott, "The World Trade Organization: Progress to Date and the Road Ahead," in Jeffrey J. Schott, ed., *Launching New Global Trade Talks* (Washington, D.C.: Institute for International Economics, 1998).

52. William Armbruster, "US Business Urged to Prod Trade Talks," *Journal of Commerce*, June 8, 1990, p. 1.

53. Dobson and Jacquet, *Financial Service Liberalization*, p. 83.

54. For a list of participating companies, see "Business Leaders See WTO Accord on Financial Services as Vital," *Financial Times,* September 22, 1997, p. 20.

55. Dobson and Jacquet, *Financial Service Liberalization*, p. 81.

56. "WTO Talks Delayed Again," *Financial Times*, December 15, 1998, p. 9.

57. "APEC Ministers End Morning Session in N.Z.," *Japan Economic Newswire*, September 8, 1999.

58. "MSIA Happy No Date Set to Launch New WTO Negotiations," *Bernama–The Malaysian National News Agency*, September 19, 1999.

59. Fred C. Bergsten, *Whither APEC?* p. 62.

60. The process began in 1997, but the Treaty of Amsterdam did not come into force until May 1999.

61. Schott, "The World Trade Organization," pp. 10–11.

62. Ibid., ch. 1. Schott argues that if we use U.S. success in panel rulings and the amount of trade at stake as indicators, the United States has the most to gain.

63. This and the following paragraph draw heavily on Aggarwal, *Liberal Protectionism*.

64. The MFA has begun to be phased out since January 1, 1995, by the new Agreement on Textiles and Clothing reached during the Uruguay Round. Under the Agreement, WTO Members have committed themselves to remove the quotas in the industries by January 1, 2005, by integrating the sector fully into GATT rules. A Textiles Monitoring Body (TMB) will oversee the implementation of commitments under this new agreement and prepare reports for major periodic reviews. Available at WTO web site, <http://www.wto.org/english/docs_e/legal_e/ursum_e.htm#cAgreement>.

65. Kenneth W. Abbott, "Trade Remedies and Legal Remedies: Antidumping, Safeguards, and Dispute Settlement After the Uruguay Round," in A. Panagariya, M. G. Quibria, and N. Rao, eds., *The Global Trading System and Developing Asia* (Oxford, U.K.: Oxford University Press, 1997), pp. 366 and 376.

66. Ibid., p. 367.

67. Ibid., p. 386.

68. Ibid., p. 376; and Schott, *The Uruguay Round*, pp. 84–5.

69. Schott, *The Uruguay Round*, p. 98.

70. The following two paragraphs are excerpted from Aggarwal and Morrison, *Asia-Pacific Crossroads*, pp. 403–04.

71. See Yunling Zhang, "China and the APEC," in Aggarwal and Morrison, *Asia-Pacific Crossroads*.

72. See Baker, "The United States and APEC Regime Building," and Yoshinobu Yamamoto and Tsutomo Kikuchi, "Japan's Approach to APEC and Regime Creation in the Asia-Pacific," in Aggarwal and Morrison, *Asia-Pacific Crossroads*.

73. Abram Chayes and Antonia Handler Chayes, *The New Sovereignty: Compliance with International Regulatory Agreements* (Cambridge, Mass.: Harvard University Press, 1995).

74. The strength of the NAFTA structure as an alternative to other forms of implementation and compliance is demonstrated in that its dispute mechanisms have practically eclipsed the WTO mechanisms as a forum for Canada, Mexico, and the United States to settle their formal trade disputes. Indeed, from 1995 to 1997, only two disputes among the parties have been taken to the WTO.

75. Thomas R. Howell, "The Trade Remedies: A U.S. Perspective," in Geza Feketekuty with Bruce Stokes, eds., *Trade Strategies for a New Era: Ensuring U.S. Leadership in a Global Economy* (New York: Council on Foreign Relations, 1998), p. 311.

76. Ibid., p. 313.

77. Schott, *The Uruguay Round*, p. 125.

78. Consistent with GATT Article XXIII, the DSU also can adjudicate disputes involving measures that affect benefits accruing to a WTO member but do not violate any provision of the WTO agreements. However, such "nonviolation" cases are subject only to nonbinding recommendations by the panel and cannot require the withdrawal of the disputed measure. As Sylvia Ostry has noted, the WTO obligations to include a broader range of trade and investment in goods and services than under GATT without the requisite capability to bind national sovereignty toward a single liberalization standard are likely to result in a sharp increase in trade disputes over time. See Sylvia Ostry, *Reinforcing the WTO*, A Group of Thirty Occasional Paper No. 56 (Washington, D.C.: Group of Thirty, 1998).

79. Abbott, "Trade Remedies and Legal Remedies," p. 394.

80. David Palmeter, "Comments by David Palmeter on Kenneth Abbott," in Panagariya, Quibria, and Rao, eds., *The Global Trading System and Developing Asia*, p. 430.

81. Ibid., p. 429.

SUGGESTED ADDITIONAL READING

Aggarwal, Vinod K., ed. *Institutional Designs for a Complex World: Bargaining, Linkages, and Nesting*. Ithaca, N.Y.: Cornell University Press, 1998.

Aggarwal, Vinod K., and Charles Morrison, eds. *Asia Pacific Crossroads: Regime Creation and the Future of APEC*. New York: St. Martin's Press, 1998.

Bergsten, Fred C., ed. *Whither APEC? The Progress to Date and Agenda for the Future*. Washington, D.C.: Institute for International Economics, 1997.

Chayes, Abram, and Antonia Handler Chayes. *The New Sovereignty: Compliance with International Regulatory Agreements*. Cambridge, Mass.: Harvard University Press, 1995.

Dobson, Wendy, and Pierre Jacquet. *Financial Service Liberalization in the WTO*. Washington D.C.: Institute for International Economics, 1998.

Feketekuty, Geza, and Bruce Stokes, eds. *Trade Strategies for a New Era: Ensuring U.S. Leadership in a Global Economy*. New York: Council on Foreign Relations, 1998.

Krugman, Paul. "Regional Trade Blocs: The Good, the Bad and the Ugly." *The International Economy* (November/December 1991), pp. 54–56.

Lawrence, Robert Z. "Emerging Regional Arrangements: Building Blocks or Stumbling Blocks?" In R. O'Brien, ed., *Finance and the International Economy*, vol. 5. Oxford, U.K.: Oxford University Press, 1991.

Ostry, Sylvia. *Reinforcing the WTO*. A Group of Thirty Occasional Paper No. 56. Washington, D.C.: Group of Thirty, 1998.

Schott, Jeffrey J., ed. *Launching New Global Trade Talks*. Washington D.C.: Institute for International Economics, 1998.

For major help in writing this chapter, I would like to thank Kun-Chin Lin. Significant research assistance was also provided by Chris Tucker, Tuong Vu, Rishi Chandra, Grace Wang, and Brandon Yu. For comments, I would like to thank Chantal de Jonge Oudraat, P. J. Simmons, and the participants in the project.

7

Environment: Nature Conservation

Peter H. Sand

IT IS SOMEWHAT HAZARDOUS to label specific environmental regimes successes or failures, given the abysmal overall record of global environmental quality—virtually all indicators point downward. In few areas is the speed of decline as well documented as in the case of wildlife (animals and plants), mainly because the international machinery for worldwide scientific assessment and cooperation in this field is well established and matched by considerable public attention and media interest.[1] We are thus witnessing the most staggering loss of our planet's living resources, at a rate of extinction that is one hundred to one thousand times as great as it was before the coming of humanity: this roughly translates into the disappearance of about three species per hour, or approximately 30,000 species per year.[2]

So what is wrong with our global management systems? Or are some of the remedial and precautionary instruments recently put in place beginning to have an effect? This chapter reviews international institutions for nature conservation that emerged in the twentieth century, with a view to identifying some of the mechanisms likely to assist in averting—or at least containing and reducing—the risks of further environmental degradation. The chapter deals exclusively with lessons from regimes to manage and protect wild living resources, that is, terrestrial and aquatic animals and plants. It does *not* deal with global pollution regimes, covered elsewhere; nor is it concerned with international regimes for cultivated food and fiber resources and commodities.

The chapter argues first that wildlife resources and their natural habitats are grossly undervalued as economic assets, which contributes substantially to their worldwide decline. Second, a range of innovative institutions and techniques for international governance in this field—especially in the form of market incentives for positive measures and external trade sanctions for noncompliance—suffer from a lack of "WTO-proof" intergovernmental endorsement. Finally, the traditional legal concept of permanent sovereignty over natural resources has yet to be reconciled with the emerging environmental concept of public trusteeship over resources of common concern.

NATURE OF THE PROBLEM

Wild plants and animals are renewable or "flow" resources; that is, they replenish themselves by natural reproduction or propagation. Together with other renewable resources (such as water or the atmosphere), they are part of the complex ecosystem supporting life on Earth. They provide essential and irreplaceable services: cleaning the air and water we pollute; recycling organic matter into usable form; sustaining our food chains; replenishing our supplies of fiber, medicine, and all the natural products and genetic building blocks of our civilization. Characteristically, however, they have a critical zone below which their depletion—from natural causes or human interference—may become irreversible and lead to extinction. Among the potentially fatal risks are not only those of overexploitation and habitat destruction, but also careless human mismanagement; for example, accidental displacement of native plants and animals by invasive exotic species or genetically modified organisms.

These natural assets are typically common property goods: their use is subject to regimes of open access. Because most of them are not fully captured in commercial markets or quantified in terms comparable with economic services and manufactured capital, however, they are often given too little weight in policy decisions. When a first estimate of the value of the world's ecosystem services and natural capital put their total price tag at $33 trillion a year—more than the gross national product of all countries in the world combined in 1995—the reaction of conservative economists ranged from skepticism to incredulity.[3] There is a common tendency of decision makers to favor short-term uses and economic gains over long-term resource conservation (and in particular, to discount potential future benefits to generations yet unborn). This tendency, together with the lack of agreed economic valuation criteria for the use (or precautionary non-use) of natural assets, continues to skew international management decisions—be it the investment priorities of bilateral and multilateral aid agencies, or the ranking of environmental concerns in regional and global trade regimes.[4]

TRACK RECORD OF INTERNATIONAL RESPONSES

Management of living natural resources has long been a subject of international treaty making, with the earliest bilateral (transboundary) agreements on hunting and fishing regimes going back to the eighteenth century, regional fishery treaties emerging in the nineteenth century, and the first multilateral convention on endangered African species being signed in 1900. There has been a steady increase in both "hard" and "soft" international law making for wildlife and nature conservation ever since. A baseline survey carried out on the eve of the 1992 Rio de Janeiro Conference on Environment and Development (UNCED) counted some thirty multilateral conservation instruments, representing about 25 percent of the total volume of existing environmental agreements surveyed and ranking second in numbers after the top category of antipollution treaties (approximately 44 percent) at the time. That percentage has remained more or less constant, with another twenty instruments added to the conservation category since Rio.

In terms of geographical participation (as of July 2001), the most widely accepted multilateral conservation agreements are the 1992 Convention on Biological Diversity (CBD, 180 member states, still not including the United States); the 1994 Convention to Combat Desertification (CCD, 174); the 1972 Convention for the Protection of the World Cultural and Natural Heritage (WHC, 164); the 1973 Convention on International Trade in Endangered Species of Wild Fauna and Flora (CITES, 154); and the 1971 Convention on Wetlands of International Importance (Ramsar, 124). Another potential global regime, the 1979 Convention on the Conservation of Migratory Species of Wild Animals (CMS, 74), never achieved universality mainly because it failed to overcome the continuing resistance of some important maritime powers to its claim for regulatory jurisdiction over endangered marine species. In addition to these comprehensive regimes, a wide range of international agreements for particular natural areas and species exist at the global, regional, or bilateral level.[5]

The international community has tended to develop conservation regimes around two issue categories: area-based (habitat) conservation and species-based conservation. These issues are highly interdependent, however, with the continuous reduction of natural habitats inexorably leading to further depletion of wildlife species. In the case of species-based conservation, the most significant development in recent years has been a shift from the management of geographically defined wildlife populations to the global allocation of access to genetic wildlife resources. As a result, conservation regimes experience regulatory competition and friction not only with international trade regimes but also with regard to intellectual property rights and sometimes with traditional rights of indigenous users.

The plethora of treaty regimes is matched by a multitude of international institutions. Initial organizational attempts again go back to nineteenth- and early twentieth-century fishery commissions and a remarkable (if abortive) initiative by U.S. President Theodore Roosevelt to convene a Hague Peace Conference on global nature conservation in 1909. What actually emerged after the 1972 UN Stockholm Conference and the 1992 Rio de Janeiro Conference is a less-than-coherent aggregate of global and regional intergovernmental institutions with partial or sectoral mandates for the management of living natural resources, the centerpiece of which remains the UN Environment Program (UNEP). One of the key global players in the management of economically significant marine resources continues to be the UN Food and Agriculture Organization (FAO), which serves as administrative focal point for several regional fishery conventions and commissions.

One area where regime building for preserving the global natural heritage has been notoriously unsuccessful is forest management, even though rainforest decline and forest die-back caused by acid rain are widely publicized environmental issues, epitomize worldwide "green" concerns, and have direct links to climate change, desertification, and transboundary air pollution. Yet global responsibilities for forest resources continue to be hotly contested among several bodies within the UN system, including the FAO Committee on Forestry (COFO) in Rome; the International Tropical Timber Organization (ITTO) in Yokohama, established under the auspices of the UN Conference on Trade and Development (UNCTAD); and the UN Forum on Forests (UNFF) set up in New York by the UN Economic and Social Council (ECOSOC). Efforts to negotiate an International Convention on Conservation and Development of Forests (proposed in FAO/COFO since 1990) met with deadlock at the 1992 Rio Conference. All the conference produced on this topic was a "non-legally binding authoritative statement of principles for a global consensus on the management, conservation and sustainable development of all types of forests [sic]," which has been said to fall "100% short of providing even the most elementary basis for an international regime for the protection of the world's forests."[6]

That failure has of course much to do with North-South politics: a misplaced focus on tropical forests, reflecting the reluctance of Northern countries to subject their own exploitation of boreal forests to comparable sustainability criteria; misguided issue linkage, reflected in attempts by the European Union at Rio to trade off Northern agreement to a desertification treaty for Southern agreement to a forest treaty; and the general underestimation of Southern sensitivities on matters of sovereignty, reflected in insinuations of "ecological intervention" by "UN green helmets" in Amazonia or the Himalayas. Almost a decade after the Rio negotiations, there are only two fragmentary legal instruments in this field: the 1993 Central American Convention on the Management and Conservation of Natural Forest Ecosystems and Forest Plantation Development; and the 1994 International Tropical Timber Agreement, which is essentially a commodity market arrangement between producer and consumer countries, supplemented by nonbinding ecological guidelines. No diplomatic consensus exists on the need for a forest convention—or even a forest protocol to the conventions on climate change or biodiversity—on the global agenda.

In terms of overall effectiveness, it would be premature to assess the Rio and post-Rio regimes, which are still shaping their follow-up institutions and procedures through continuing negotiations. By contrast, there is ample material regarding the major pre-Rio regimes; in fact, there have probably been more comparative ad hoc assessments of international wildlife agreements than of any other category of environmental regimes, with at least nine external evaluations undertaken from 1992 to 1999.[7] The following discussion draws on these findings.

Building on an institutional tradition of continuous scientific monitoring and assessment drawn mainly from the experience of international marine fishery agreements, conservation regimes have developed their own systems for implementation review (SIRs) to assess both the performance of the regime in meeting its objectives and the performance of member states in implementing their treaty commitments.[8] For instance, CITES—which establishes worldwide trade controls based on mandatory permits and certificates covering the export, import, and reexport of plant and animal species or products listed in the appendices to the convention—has an extensive implementation and review process. The Conference of the Parties to CITES periodically undertakes species-by-species assessments of the trade and conservation status of fauna and flora regulated (or to be regulated) under the convention, as well as country-by-country assessments of national legislative implementation. In 1996 the signatories conducted an overall external evaluation of the treaty's effectiveness.[9] SIRs thus function in part as a device for monitoring compliance (with 125 CITES member countries surveyed since 1993, legislation in only 24 countries was found fully up to the treaty's standards, in 47 countries inadequate, and in another 54 countries at least partly deficient). SIRs are more than just routine inspection and maintenance services, however. If the mandate of a review is policy reorientation in light of new knowledge, it must include the option of consequential institutional change. The reviews not only help to determine which species are listed in the appendices, but also offer decisions on future recommendations to improve international regime performance and national implementation.

LESSONS LEARNED

The systematic implementation reviews may be seen as a built-in feedback loop, reflecting a new fluid model of environmental agreements, envisioned as a "rolling process of intermediate or self-adjusting agreements that respond to growing scientific understanding."[10] Yet the ongoing process of "social learning" in the field of global environmental management also has an essential ethical dimension. It has been pointed out that "the values of dominant decision-makers and epistemic communities must agree, otherwise governments will not tolerate the policy innovations recommended."[11] The point is illustrated by (1) the rise of the sustainable development paradigm at Rio, which took twenty years to emerge from the wide ideological gap between Northern pro-environment and Southern pro-development positions affirmed at the 1972 UN Conference on the Human Environment in Stockholm;[12] and (2) the checkered diplomatic history of the precautionary principle (championed before and during the 1992 Rio Conference by industrialized countries but subsequently espoused by developing countries, against U.S. opposition, during negotiation of the Biosafety Protocol in 1999).[13]

The overview that follows will focus on some of the institutional innovations pioneered by nature conservation regimes in response to global change, in terms of agenda setting, regime formation, implementation and compliance, and reactions to noncompliance.

Agenda Setting

Priorities on the global environmental agenda are never exclusively set by objective factors such as external events, crises, or new scientific insights. They are largely determined by regime politics, which are in turn shaped by powerful governmental and nongovernmental interests, and their interaction. That process may be illustrated by two case histories: the ivory trade ban and the whaling moratorium.

Ivory Trade Ban. The 1973 Endangered Species Convention (CITES) is one of several conservation treaties sponsored or cosponsored by the World Conservation Union (IUCN), which was founded in 1948. Partly because of its hybrid membership—currently including 78 governments, 112 governmental agencies, and more than 700 nongovernmental organizations (NGOs)—IUCN has served a unique bridging role in the "green epistemic community" of administrators, scientists, and activists involved in international environmental decision making. IUCN's own internal agenda underwent a radical change in 1956, when the organization changed its name from International Union for the Protection of Nature to the International Union for Conservation of Nature and Natural Resources. The change reflected a transition from so-called preservationist approaches—rooted in a predominantly European tradition of romantic naturalism with a distinct colonial touch of green paternalism for the rest of the world—toward the more utilitarian concept of conservation as rational long-term resource management. The 1980 IUCN World Conservation Strategy then codified this latter concept as sustainable development, a term that eventually made its way into the 1987 Brundtland Report of the World Commission on Environment and Development and the 1992 Rio Conference (Agenda 21). Yet the debate on global conservation priorities is not closed, and the preservationist/ protectionist faction—albeit outvoted—remains a powerful legitimate minority within IUCN, particularly within its more donor-driven offshoot, the Worldwide Fund for Nature (founded in 1961 as World Wildlife Fund, WWF).

An opportunity for articulating that debate came in 1989, when the Conference of the Parties to CITES had to decide the fate of the international ivory trade. Until then, exports of African elephant ivory had been permitted, on the assumption (backed by IUCN) that some 1.3 million elephants survived in their African range states, and that the income from controlled hunting and from sales of legally taken ivory would ensure sustainability of the species as a source of tourism revenue. By the late 1980s, however, the poaching and smuggling of illegal ivory had spiraled out of control, partly as a result of civil wars in some range states (with both sides using poached ivory to buy weapons abroad) and unabashed free-rider behavior by nonmember states like Burundi, the United Arab Emirates, and Singapore (serving as entrepôts for huge stockpiles of smuggled ivory destined for the Far East). The 1989 CITES Conference in Lausanne—after heavy lobbying by NGOs (including the WWF) and the imposition of unilateral import bans in North America and Western Europe— placed the African elephant on Appendix I of the convention, which lists species and products banned from international trade. This move was decided by the required two-thirds majority but against the votes of nine range states and China.

Opinions were divided on the effectiveness of the ensuing worldwide trade ban, and after intensive further negotiations the 1997 CITES Conference in Harare decided to move certain "sustainably managed" elephant populations (in Botswana, Namibia, South Africa, and Zimbabwe) back to Appendix II—the list of species and products eligible for export. While some experimental controlled sales of raw ivory and other elephant products from those countries were authorized since 1998, the Nairobi CITES Conference in April 2000 maintained a general ban on ivory trading, subject to further review at the next conference to be held in Santiago, Chile, in 2002. The pendulum of management policies under the convention thus tends to swing back and forth between the extremes of a total trade ban (reflecting the preservationist agenda) and permissive trade regulation (reflecting the sustainable-use agenda).

Whaling Moratorium. During the same period, the agenda of the international whaling regime faced an equally radical split—affecting a popular wildlife resource that quickly took on a wider symbolic meaning for global environmental governance. The International Whaling Commission (IWC) had initially been set up as an intergovernmental management board to administer the 1946 International Whaling Convention, with the stated goal of conserving whale resources for future generations, though clearly also aimed at supporting current economic uses; among the unarticulated political objectives at the time were food and employment security for postwar Japan and Korea. The commission set out to implement these goals by allocating annual catch quotas, based on a management policy of maximum sustainable yield (MSY). After it became clear in the 1960s that the MSY policy had led to overexploitation and a dramatic decline in whale stocks, and after several original signatories stopped whaling altogether, the annual IWC meetings turned into increasingly acrimonious confrontations between whaling and antiwhaling interests. On the one hand, the whaling industry engaged in "pirate whaling," circumventing

IWC rules by using non-IWC fleets (for example, Onassis ships operating under Panamanian registry). They also applied economic pressure or selective incentives to influence voting in the commission. On the other hand, nonwhaling member countries such as the United States used, or threatened to use, unilateral trade sanctions against noncompliance with IWC restrictions.

Starting with the 1972 UN Stockholm Conference (Recommendation 33), a majority of nonwhaling countries outside the regime repeatedly called for at least a temporary ban on whaling. The involvement of environmental NGOs (such as Greenpeace) in IWC matters expanded from observer status to massive lobbying, worldwide monitoring and public exposure of noncompliance, direct harassment of whaling activities, scientific and financial support for developing-country participation in the commission, and recruitment of new antiwhaling state members. As a result, the composition of the IWC changed from fourteen member countries in 1972 to thirty-nine in 1982, when it finally reached the two-thirds antiwhaling majority required to pass a moratorium on all commercial whaling, effective from 1986 onward. The moratorium survived several subsequent votes, notwithstanding a cautiously optimistic reassessment of recovered whale stocks by the IWC Scientific Committee and some legitimate whaling continuing through the convention's loopholes (Japanese scientific permits, Norwegian coastal whaling, and Native American subsistence hunting).

Thus, within less than four decades, the IWC had to change its agenda from consumptive "whale mining" to nonconsumptive "whale saving." That change—based primarily on ethical rather than scientific grounds—was brought about in large measure by pressure from nongovernmental groups (effectively using a combination of diplomacy, media campaigns, and direct civic action to raise public awareness and support) and to some extent by increased participation from developing countries. Paradoxically, though, successful accomplishment of the whaling regime's conservation objective was accompanied by manifest failure in regard to its other declared objective (orderly development of the whaling industry)—perhaps because the two goals were incompatible from the start.[14]

Regime Formation

The traditional institution for multilateral regime building is the ad hoc diplomatic conference to negotiate and adopt a treaty, which then has to undergo national ratification to become legally binding. There are two notorious drawbacks to this conventional approach. First, treaty-based regimes are entirely voluntary, and no sovereign state is obliged to join any treaty. Second, the formal requirement of parliamentary ratification by a specified minimum number of states delays the entry into force of international agreements (and their amendments) by an average of five years—and by as much as twelve years, as in the case of the 1982 Convention on the Law of the Sea.

These drawbacks are especially serious for global environmental regimes, which require both universal participation and flexible adaptation in the face of changing natural circumstances and continuous scientific-technological progress. A number of regimes in this field therefore had to find innovative ways of coping with these shortcomings—in particular, selective incentives to encourage wide participation, and recourse to "soft-law" arrangements to bypass the need for formal ratification.

Selective Incentives. To induce states to participate (and to discourage free riding), several conservation regimes have developed schemes that offer an array of incentives to join a treaty—most notably, access to resources, markets, and funding.

The prospect of access to valuable natural resources is an economic incentive for states to participate in international regimes, even at the price of having to accept restrictions in the interest of rational resource use and other onerous commitments. Most regimes for international management of wildlife resources in the global commons have used quota systems to regulate access. For example, annual catch quotas on fish or whales are allocated to member states as an incentive to comply with other regime rules, such as management and reporting standards.

Similarly, the promise of access to lucrative consumer markets for wildlife and wildlife products has proven one of the most effective incentives for participation in regulatory regimes such as CITES. After most wildlife-importing countries had joined the regime, exporting countries found themselves shut out from the luxury leather, fur, and pet trade markets abroad unless their export products were certified to be in conformity with the convention. Acceptance of the treaty's regulatory requirements thus became the price of entry into what otherwise had turned into a closed market. The question has indeed been raised whether the CITES system, with its manifest discrimination against nonmember states, is compatible with global free trade principles as interpreted by the World Trade Organization (WTO); so far, however, none of the multilateral CITES restrictions has been challenged.

Finally, access to funding has also been a powerful incentive for countries to adhere to international conservation regimes. The 1972 WHC first developed a system to attract global participation by offering the prospect of financial aid for nature conservation. The World Heritage Fund (WHF) does not provide assistance for charitable reasons, but rather as financial compensation to the host countries of heritage sites for the special conservation efforts they make on behalf of the international community ("for the present and future benefit of the entire world citizenry"), and in exchange for their compliance with specific custodial obligations.[15] That concept—subsequently expressed in terms of agreed incremental costs incurred for global environmental benefits—became a model for the establishment of a number of other "eco-funds" during the 1990s. The most significant of these is the Global

Environment Facility (GEF), which was set up in 1991.[16] According to the 1994 Instrument for the Establishment of the Restructured Global Environment Facility, GEF grants for activities within focal areas addressed by a convention—such as the Biodiversity Convention—"shall only be made available to eligible recipient countries that are party to the convention concerned" (Article 9). Participation in a treaty regime thus becomes a condition for funding, adding yet another variety to the ubiquitous growth of "green conditionality."

Soft Law.   As in other areas of international environmental law, legally nonbinding soft instruments, which do not require a formal process of treaty ratification and entry into force, have achieved prominence in living resource management. It is important, however, to distinguish between two categories of soft law in this area. The first category consists of purely declaratory instruments, which were never intended to become regulatory regimes (such as the 1982 World Charter for Nature adopted by the UN General Assembly), or which are merely remnants of unsuccessful treaty negotiations (such as the 1992 UNCED Forest Principles). By contrast, the second category includes quasi-binding instruments that provide operational structures for global resource management (such as the 1983 FAO International Undertaking on Plant Genetic Resources and the 1995 statutory framework of UNESCO's World Network of Biosphere Reserves). Sometimes these instruments establish a fast track for action, pending the ratification of formal treaty arrangements (as in the case of the 1995 FAO Code of Conduct for Responsible Fisheries, paving the way for entry into force of the 1993 Agreement to Promote Compliance with International Conservation and Management Measures by Fishing Vessels on the High Seas). Sometimes these instruments encourage the subsequent development of hard national/ regional laws or bilateral agreements. That was the effect of the Moratorium on Fishing with Large-Scale Driftnets adopted as UN General Assembly Resolution 46/ 215 in 1991, which in turn triggered implementing regulations by the European Union in 1992 and bilateral arrangements backed up by the threat of trade sanctions (such as the 1996 U.S.-Italian Agreement to Stop Illegal Driftnet Fishing in the Mediterranean).

Implementation and Compliance

The institutions established by multilateral conservation regimes—mainly conferences of contracting parties and their subsidiary bodies—essentially deal with international standard setting and are not empowered to apply those standards (that is, to exercise regulatory authority) directly vis-à-vis either member states or persons under the jurisdiction of member states. Instead, authority for implementation is delegated (by a process known as "dédoublement fonctionnel," in the term coined by Georges

Scelle) to a different operational level. Governmental (and in some cases, nongovernmental) institutions are designated for specific regulatory functions such as certification of compliance, compliance monitoring, and enforcement and compliance assistance.[17]

Role of Nonstate Actors.   Participation by civil society in international environmental affairs has traditionally been more prominent and more active than in most other regimes. Alongside the two leading global umbrella NGOs (IUCN and WWF), a broad spectrum of other transnational nonstate groups are involved. This spectrum encompasses one of the most lively (and some would say, most chaotic) sectors of the NGO universe, ranging from scientific associations (such as ornithologists) to business interests (such as fur traders). NGO participation in multilateral conservation agreements has become a standard feature of treaty negotiations, following the model clause taken from CITES Article 11, according to which "technically qualified" NGOs are routinely accredited as nonvoting observers unless one-third of the governmental representatives at the meeting object. NGO participation has also become common at various stages of treaty administration and implementation. For example, IUCN provides official secretariat services to the 1971 Ramsar Convention on Wetlands and official scientific advisory services to the 1972 WHC.

Environmental NGOs have also played a pivotal role in "green development aid," with the aim of assisting developing countries to meet their obligations under multilateral conservation treaties. The budgetary capacity and professional expertise of NGOs such as WWF for overseas field projects in this area far exceed that of intergovernmental bodies such as UNEP. Among pioneering NGO financial initiatives were "debt-for-nature swaps"—bilateral agreements rewarding developing countries for local conservation efforts (such as the establishment and management of nature reserves or protected forests) by writing off a portion of their foreign debt, purchased for this purpose from creditor banks. Following the first pilot agreement (between Bolivia and Conservation International in 1987), more than thirty swaps were completed over the next decade in fifteen developing countries. Governments of several creditor countries then emulated the example by writing off public bilateral debt in exchange for environmental commitments from debtor countries (for example, Kenya and Germany, 1989; Bulgaria and Switzerland, 1995; and the brief Enterprise of the Americas Initiative between the United States and seven Latin American and Caribbean countries, 1990–1993). Even though the overall significance of debt-for-nature swaps in the context of global debt relief negotiations remains marginal—and may eventually be overtaken by calls for unconditional debt forgiveness—it demonstrated the capacity of the NGO community to induce intergovernmental action.[18]

Certification of Compliance.   In the absence of a supranational regulatory authority, multilateral conservation regimes had to develop mechanisms to ensure compliance on a basis of reciprocity, that is, mutual recognition of foreign certificates attesting compliance with the regime, based on agreed uniform standards and subject to periodic reporting and verification. Notably, the worldwide control of wildlife trade by the CITES regime is not operated by some new international bureaucracy but relies entirely on reciprocal acceptance of national certificates (permits for export/import/reexport) attesting conformity with the requirements of the treaty.

This mutual recognition process is similar to the reciprocal acceptance of foreign passports or of motor vehicle licensing, which are also subject to the observance of agreed minimum standards. In practice, international governance functions in this field have to a large extent been delegated to national wildlife and customs authorities. The incentive for governments to participate in any such regime (and the primary sanction of the regime) is its reciprocity and the economic advantages this offers to the participating state, for example, where compliance facilitates the export of certain products.

There have been innovative attempts at introducing similar certification schemes for other natural commodities not currently regulated by global treaties. In June 1992, Austria enacted legislation requiring all imported tropical timber to be certified and labeled as derived from environmentally sustainable harvesting and subjecting such imports to an "eco-tax" to finance international projects for sustainable forest management. Malaysia, in response, complained to the Council of the General Agreement on Tariffs and Trade (GATT), hinting at retaliatory action, and the Austrian parliament had to rescind the law in December 1992.[19] On the other hand, the GATT panel in the first tuna-dolphin case (*Mexico v. USA*, 1991) had expressly stated that a voluntary certification scheme, such as the "dolphin-safe" label created under the 1990 U.S. Dolphin Protection Consumer Information Act, was compatible with GATT rules. The panel reasoned that unlike the 1972/1988 Marine Mammals Protection Act, the 1990 act did not impose mandatory restrictions on tuna imports.[20] Accordingly, several NGO initiatives now promote voluntary international certification and eco-labeling of sustainably harvested timber by the Forest Stewardship Council (FSC) and several other bodies, and marine fishery products by the Marine Stewardship Council (MSC) in cooperation with Unilever.[21]

Compliance Monitoring. One of the difficulties with governmental self-reporting and mutual verification under a multilateral agreement is the risk of cheating at the expense of the community's collective interest. Such a risk was illustrated by the IWC's reciprocal observer scheme, which lent itself to mutual cover-up deals between Japanese and Russian whalers. To cope with that problem, conservation regimes had to develop new methods of compliance monitoring to track down treaty infractions by individual and corporate offenders or eventually by governments.

In international marine resource management, compliance controls—in the form of mutual observer, boarding, and inspection procedures—have a long-standing tradition, expanded more recently by Part VI of the 1995 UN Agreement on the Conservation and Management of Straddling Fish Stocks and Highly Migratory Fish Stocks. An example comes from among existing regional regimes. On the basis of the 1992 Niue Treaty on Cooperation in Fisheries Surveillance and Law Enforcement in the South Pacific Region, the Forum Fisheries Agency (FFA) coordinates a satellite-based surveillance and communications network, as well as patrol boat and aerial surveillance facilities (provided by the Australian and New Zealand armed forces) to monitor vessel movements and fishing operations in the region. There are also examples of active NGO involvement in compliance monitoring. For instance, in the context of CITES, the nongovernmental Trade Records Analysis of Flora and Fauna in Commerce (TRAFFIC) network has successfully supported and supplemented the intergovernmental secretariat's infraction reporting practice. The TRAFFIC network's monitoring started on a voluntary basis, but later operated under contract with the secretariat and with formal authority from the Conference of the Parties.

Enforcement and Compliance Assistance. As part of the efforts of governments to cope with infringements (including criminal infractions) of nature conservation treaties, a number of arrangements for concerted transnational law enforcement have been concluded, similar to the regional port state memoranda of understanding for the enforcement of global marine environment regimes.[22] For example, a task force established under the 1994 Lusaka Agreement on Cooperative Enforcement Operations Directed at Illegal Trade in Wild Fauna and Flora coordinates subregional implementation of CITES in parts of Eastern and Southern Africa. In addition to memoranda of understanding among the CITES secretariat, the World Customs Organization (WCO), and the Interpol Subgroup on Wildlife Crime, joint action against illegal wildlife trade is also on the agenda of the International Network for Environmental Compliance and Enforcement (INECE) of the U.S. Environmental Protection Agency established in 1990; the European Union's Network on the Implementation and Enforcement of Environmental Law (IMPEL), established in 1992; and more recent projects to combat environmental crime by UNEP and the Group of Eight Industrialized Countries (G-8), as part of the Lyon Group of Experts on Transnational Crime set up in 1998. Along the same lines, the Council of Europe's 1998 Strasbourg Convention on the Protection of the Environment through Criminal Law lists among the offenses that will incur criminal sanctions in all member states "the unlawful causing of changes detrimental to natural components" of protected areas and "the unlawful possession, taking, damaging, killing or trading of or in protected wild flora and fauna species."

At the same time, there is growing recognition that the causes of noncompliance with environmental treaties in many countries (as documented in the series of effectiveness surveys carried out since 1992) are less related to weaknesses in criminal enforcement than to a general lack of administrative capacity for implementation.

Capacity building at the local level—including professional training and managerial infrastructure—has thus become a high priority for technical assistance under several conservation agreements (expressly referred to as "compliance assistance," for example, in Article 23 of the 1992 Convention for the Protection of the Marine Environment of the North-East Atlantic), as part of active treaty management and as part of the legitimate incremental costs of treaty participation for developing countries in particular.[23] Critics have argued that subsidized compliance—financial side payments to countries for meeting their treaty obligations—may undermine the credibility of international environmental law and the principle of *pacta sunt servanda*.[24] Conversely, withholding such support, or the mere threat of withholding it, turns into a sanction to penalize noncompliance: what may have seemed like a carrot when granted tends to become a stick when denied.[25] That trend is confirmed by the recent practice of the WHF, in which reporting duties and compliance controls—in return for financial assistance—are gradually being tightened, or "deepened," in the jargon of enforcement theory.[26]

Reactions to Noncompliance

Part of the strategy of living resource regimes to maintain both flexibility and a high level of participation has been to allow for a margin of tolerable noncompliance. This is achieved by giving dissenting members the right to opt out of specified majority decisions without abandoning the regime altogether. Examples are the "objections" procedure of the IWC (Article 5/3, modeled after the opt-out clauses found in many regional fisheries agreements) and the "reservations" procedure of CITES (Article 15/3, which is a misnomer and actually serves as an opt-out clause for outvoted dissenters). In the case of the controversial 1982 whaling moratorium vote in the IWC (25 in favor, 7 against, and 5 abstaining), only one of the outvoted whaling countries left in protest but did not resume whaling; the four others entered objections (two of which were later withdrawn), which one of them has since used as a legal basis for unilaterally continuing limited whaling "within the regime." In the case of the equally controversial 1989 ivory trade ban vote in CITES (76 in favor, 11 against, and 4 abstaining), seven of the outvoted states initially entered reservations, six of which were later withdrawn, mainly in light of subsequent arrangements to exempt specified elephant populations from the ban; two have since participated in bilateral controlled ivory trade "within the regime."

In both cases, the system of tolerated noncompliance was arguably successful, enabling the regime to cope with minority dissent or even defections without losing its majority support. Once a formal breach of the rules is established, however, a regime that does not wish to lose its credibility must respond—either by formal legal proceedings (hardly ever used) or by other, mostly economic, means (hardly ever publicized).

Legal Remedies. There are two reasons why noncompliance by states with multilateral conservation commitments rarely ends up in court. First, the dispute settlement clauses of most environmental treaties make recourse to third-party adjudication or arbitration optional (by common consent only), and virtually none of those clauses has ever been invoked in practice. Adjudication of disputes between sovereign states generally hinges on consensual submission by the parties, and even states accepting the jurisdiction of the International Court of Justice (ICJ) as compulsory are free to make reservations for sensitive issues. Canada did so in 1994 regarding conservation and management measures for fisheries in the Northwest Atlantic, which is why the ICJ had to decline jurisdiction in a case involving seizure of a Spanish fishing trawler (*Spain v. Canada*, 1998).

Second, obligations laid down in multilateral conservation treaties normally do not lend themselves to adversarial proceedings. Environmental obligations of states are typically collective duties, owed to a community of contracting parties or to the international community at large, rather than to any particular party injured by another state's noncompliance with the treaty.[27] The difficulty of identifying an injured party also explains why noncompliance with environmental treaty obligations is rarely raised in national courts. There is, however, one notable exception: in legal systems where civic NGOs are granted custodial standing to sue on behalf of collective community interests, international environmental agreements have indeed been invoked against governments. Governmental noncompliance with conservation treaties was thus successfully challenged by NGOs with regard to application of CITES in the United States (for example, in *Defenders of Wildlife v. Endangered Species Scientific Authority*, D.C. Circuit Court of Appeals, 1981), application of the Ramsar Convention in India (*People United for Better Living in Calcutta v. State of West Bengal*, Calcutta High Court, 1993), and—albeit unsuccessfully—application of the WHC in Australia (*Friends of Hinchinbrook Society v. Minister for Environment*, Federal Court of Australia, 1997).[28]

NGOs do not have standing to sue before the ICJ or the International Tribunal for the Law of the Sea (ITLOS); and attempts by nonstate actors to obtain standing on behalf of collective environmental interests before the Court of Justice of the European Union (ECJ) were unsuccessful (*Stichting Greenpeace Council and Others v. the Commission*, ECJ, 1998). Still, European NGOs and individuals at least have a right of complaint against governmental infringements of EU environmental directives, which in turn may trigger legal action by the European Commission in its capacity as guardian of treaty implementation. In one of the infringement actions so initiated (the 1990 Bolivian Furskins case), the European Court found the French

Republic in noncompliance with its CITES treaty obligations as implemented by EU regulations.[29]

Whether the resulting judicial law making has always strengthened conservation policies is open to debate. For instance, in the often-quoted Leybucht case (*Commission v. Germany*, ECJ, 1991), the European Court did indeed uphold the duty of member states not to encroach for solely economic and recreational reasons on natural areas protected under both the 1971 Ramsar Wetlands Convention and the EU's 1979 Directive on the Conservation of Wild Birds. But then the same member states in their next revision of the directive in 1992 changed its wording to legalize that very type of encroachment "for imperative reasons of public interest, including those of a social and economic nature."[30] What had seemed like an advance in EU environmental law making thus turned out to be a Pyrrhic courtroom victory.

Economic Sanctions. None of the existing living resource conventions contains formal provisions for the imposition of penalties against noncomplying states. Yet both the CITES and the IWC regime managed to retrofit themselves with economic sanction mechanisms for effective enforcement of multilateral decision making.

The CITES Conference of the Parties has repeatedly recommended the temporary suspension of transnational wildlife trade with individual countries found in persistent noncompliance—including failure to enact implementing national laws or (starting in 2001) continued failure to submit the required annual reports. Over the past fifteen years, that procedure was invoked at least twelve times, most recently against Greece, Guyana, and Senegal. In the case of the United Arab Emirates, the country withdrew from the convention after being targeted by an embargo in 1987, and then readhered when the embargo was lifted in 1990. CITES sanctions have even been used against nonmember countries to penalize persistent refusal to provide "comparable documents" pursuant to Article 10 of the treaty; in the cases of El Salvador (1986–1987) and Equatorial Guinea (1988–1992), the embargoes were lifted after the countries targeted became parties, thus turning them from free riders into "forced riders."[31] In other cases, bilateral retaliation was used to enforce the convention, including national embargoes under the U.S. Lacey Act, or certifications of noncompliance under the 1971 Pelly Amendment (against Singapore in 1986 and Taiwan in 1994), as well as collective embargoes by the EU's CITES Committee (restricting EU wildlife trade with Indonesia, 1991–1995).[32]

The same type of economic disincentives—known as *gaiatsu,* or "foreign pressure" in Japanese—has been credited for effective enforcement of the IWC.[33] Although the most prominent penalties here again were U.S. governmental trade sanctions, NGO-led consumer boycotts (or the mere risk of boycotts) against products from targeted countries also played a key role, especially in the case of Iceland's vital seafood exports to Europe. As a result of 1988–1989 antiwhaling boycotts in German supermarkets, Iceland is reported to have suffered a total annual loss of export revenues of approximately $29 million.[34] After leaving the IWC in disgust over the moratorium issue, Iceland cosponsored a new regional organization with potential free-riding objectives (the 1992 North Atlantic Marine Mammal Commission, or NAMMCO). It has, however, so far preferred not to defy the moratorium by resuming commercial whaling.[35]

CONCLUSIONS

There are no single-track institutional solutions in sight for global environmental management problems. Although the proliferation of multilateral agreements on living resources and nature conservation has led to a certain amount of "treaty congestion," there is ample scope for synergies too.[36] An advantage of the present structure is its openness and adaptability to change, which any new institutional arrangements in this field should actively promote. In many ways, diversity is an asset, providing a precious flow of alternative remedies for common problems, present or future; and as with other environmental assets, we should endeavor to preserve it.

A number of opportunities exist for strategic progress. First, the current undervaluation of our planet's natural assets (wild living resources and habitat areas) is in urgent need of correction by realistic new standards of economic valuation, national accounting, and long-term discounting. Ongoing programs for scientific resource monitoring (in particular by the UNEP/IUCN/WWF World Conservation Monitoring Centre, or WCMC) need to be supplemented with new capacity to quantify those resources and habitats in terms of ecological economics.[37] Ongoing programs for the development of environmental quality indicators (in particular by the World Bank and the UN Commission on Sustainable Development) need to be translated into new databases for decision makers, both at the macro level and at the level of individual development projects.[38] Paradoxically, it is only in light of catastrophic losses of natural assets—in the course of compensation for pollution disasters such as the *Amoco Cadiz* and *Exxon Valdez* tanker accidents, or the Gulf War oil spills and oil fires—that the question of their monetary value is recognized as a global concern, through the work of institutions such as the International Oil Pollution Compensation Funds (IOPC) and the UN Compensation Commission (UNCC).[39]

Second, market-oriented incentives and disincentives are available to promote the rational use of living natural resources, but they are still inadequately integrated in international management regimes. Both the FSC and the MSC now promote worldwide acceptance of eco-labels that certify sustainably harvested timber and marine fishery products.[40] Yet mere voluntary certification and labeling inevitably operates at a competitive disadvantage with regard to free riders who refuse to internalize the social (environmental) costs generated by their products. The CITES experience demonstrated that only mandatory certification schemes had a chance to curtail environmentally unsustainable trade practices; however, mandatory eco-labeling is precisely what the WTO tends to consider as potentially incompatible with GATT.[41] At the same time, targeted "green" trade embargoes (for example, against countries found in noncompliance with CITES) continue to lead a twilight existence in latent conflict with the WTO regime.[42] Sooner or later, the international community will have to resolve that issue—preferably by recognizing the regulatory authority of multilateral conservation regimes to certify trade in certain natural goods as environmentally harmful, and by depriving such goods of market access as unequivocally as in the case of, say, international trade in slaves or narcotics.[43]

Third, among the farthest reaching, and least explored, developments of new international law has been the gradual nationalization of access to living natural resources once considered part of the common heritage domain. First, the 1982 Convention on the Law of the Sea formally extended the territorial sovereignty of coastal states up to 200 miles, to the vast new area of exclusive economic zones (EEZ); then the 1992 Biodiversity Convention extended the functional sovereignty of *in-situ* states to another vast new domain, the genetic resources occurring within their territories. In both cases, the economic consequences were momentous—with the combined EEZ areas accounting for 90 percent of the world's fish catch and 43 percent of the world's ecosystem services, and with genetic resources emerging as the natural basis of biotechnology, one of the fastest-growing new industrial sectors worldwide.[44]

Will the governance challenges of these issue areas be met by mere extensions of the traditional legal cliché of "permanent sovereignty over natural resources"?[45] Alternatives are on the horizon, and among them is the concept of public trusteeship or stewardship: the idea that the earth's natural heritage might not be the property of nation-states after all, but a kind of public trust for the benefit of all people (present and future generations), with governments as trustees accountable for their diligent exercise of mere fiduciary rights and obligations.[46] As early as 1893, in the *Bering Sea Fur Seal Arbitration*, the United States had argued that governments must act as trustees "for the benefit of mankind and should be permitted to discharge their trust without hindrance."[47] The public trust concept has made its appearance not only with regard to resources in the global commons but also for natural assets partly or fully under national jurisdiction, such as living marine resources in the EEZ, natural heritage sites, endangered forests, and genetic resources of global concern.[48] The rights of coastal states over their EEZ, as well as the rights of *in-situ* states over their genetic resources, are expressly limited by specified duties to other states and to the international community (UN Convention on the Law of the Sea Articles 61–70, Biodiversity Convention Articles 8 and 15/2). Those obligations may indeed be viewed as fiduciary and hence would imply accountability of the trustees, to beneficiaries, for diligent discharge of such duties.

The revival of the public trust is perhaps the single most significant trend in the contemporary law of nature conservation and living resource management. The concept of trusteeship—with historical parallels in a number of the world's legal systems, from Roman to Islamic law traditions—thus reemerges in modern environmental legislation of countries like Sweden and Italy; and in the landmark environmental decision of *Mehta v. Kamal Nath,* the Supreme Court of India in 1996 declared the public trust doctrine "a part of the law of the land."[49] The idea of extending that approach to international environmental governance was indeed foreshadowed by Roscoe Pound.[50] He suggested to limit the role of states in common natural resource management to "a sort of guardianship for social purposes"—which turns out to have yet another unexpected forerunner over a century ago[51]:

> Even society as a whole, a nation, or all contemporary societies together, are not owners of the Earth. They are merely its occupants, its users; and as diligent guardians, must hand it down improved to subsequent generations.[52]

NOTES

1. For background and detailed bibliographical references, see Peter H. Sand, "A Century of Green Lessons: The Contribution of Nature Conservation Regimes to Global Governance," *International Environmental Agreements: Politics, Law, and Economics,* vol. 1 (2001), pp. 33–72.
2. Edward O. Wilson, quoted in "A Field Guide to the Sixth Extinction," *New York Times Magazine,* December 5, 1999; see also Edward O. Wilson, "Biodiversity: Vanishing Before Our Eyes," *Time,* vol. 155, no. 16A (Special Earthday Edition, April-May 2000), pp. 28–34.
3. See Robert Costanza et al., "The Value of the World's Ecosystem Services and Natural Capital," *Nature,* vol. 387 (May 15, 1997), pp. 253–60; and Gretchen Daily, ed., *Nature's Services: Societal Dependence on Natural Ecosystems* (Washington, D.C.: Island Press, 1997). For comparison with combined 1995 GDP figures, see Table 12 in World Bank, *World Development Report 1997* (Oxford, U.K.: Oxford University Press, 1997); and David W. Pearce, "Auditing the Earth," *Environment,* vol. 40, no. 2 (1998), pp. 23–8.
4. See David W. Pearce, "Natural Environments and the Social Rate of Discount," in John Weiss, ed., *The Economics of Project Appraisal and the Environment* (Cheltenham, U.K.: Edward Elgar, 1994), pp. 31–51; David W. Pearce, "Valuing the Environment: Past Practice, Future Prospects," in Ismail Serageldin and Andrew Steer, eds., *Valuing the Environment* (Washington, D.C.: World Bank, 1994), pp. 47–57; and Timothy M. Swanson, ed., *The Economics and Ecology of Biodiversity Decline: The Forces Driving Global Change* (Cambridge, U.K.: Cambridge University Press, 1995). On trade versus environment decisions in the GATT/WTO context, see notes 19 and 20 below.
5. For an overview, see Peter H. Sand, "Wildlife Protection," in Rudolf Bernhardt, ed., *Encyclopedia of Public International Law,* vol. 4 (Amsterdam: Elsevier, 2000), pp. 1471–78.
6. Alberto Szekely, "The Legal Protection of the World's Forests After Rio 1992," in Luigi Campiglio, ed., *The Environment After Rio: International Law and Economics* (London: Graham and Trotman/Nijhoff, 1994), pp. 65–69, at p. 67.

7. In addition to the seven independent "effectiveness surveys" published since 1992 covering one or more wildlife regimes (CITES, the International Whaling Convention, the International Tropical Timber Convention, and the World Heritage Convention), as listed in Sand, ("A Century of Green Lessons," pp. 38, 56–57), see the reports of two further surveys commissioned by the French Environment Ministry, Claude Impériali, ed., *L'effectivité du droit international de l'environnement: contrôle de la mise en oeuvre des conventions internationales* (Paris: Economica, 1998); and Jean-Marc Laveille, ed., *Conventions de protection de l'environnement: secrétariats, conférences des parties, comités d'experts* (Limoges: PULIM, 1999).

8. See Lee A. Kimball, *Treaty Implementation: Scientific and Technical Advice Enters a New Stage*, Studies in Transnational Legal Policy No. 28 (Washington, D.C.: American Society of International Law, 1996); John Lanchbery, "Reviewing the Implementation of Biodiversity Agreements," in John B. Poore and Richard Guthrie, eds., *Verification' 95* (Oxford, U.K.: Westview, 1995), pp. 327–50; and John Lanchbery, "Long-Term Trends in Systems for Implementation Review in International Agreements on Fauna and Flora," in David G. Victor, Kal Raustiala, and Eugene B. Skolnikoff, eds., *The Implementation and Effectiveness of International Environmental Commitments: Theory and Practice* (Cambridge, Mass.: MIT Press, 1998), pp. 57–87.

9. John Horberry and Daniel Navid, *Study on How to Improve the Effectiveness of the Convention on International Trade in Endangered Species of Wild Fauna and Flora (CITES)* (London: Environmental Resources Management, Ltd., 1996); see also Robert Hepworth, "The Independent Review of CITES," *Journal of International Wildlife Law and Policy*, vol. 1 (1998), pp. 412–32.

10. Jessica T. Mathews, "Redefining Security," *Foreign Affairs*, vol. 68 (Spring 1989), pp. 162–77, at p. 176.

11. Peter M. Haas and Ernst B. Haas, "Learning to Learn: Improving International Governance," *Global Governance*, vol. 1 (1995), pp. 255–85, at p. 273; see also the comments by Joshua D. Sarnoff on a paper by Lynton K. Caldwell, *Colorado Journal of International Environmental Law and Policy*, vol. 10 (1999), pp. 251–58, at p. 252: "We will need to generate international consensus on environmental values if we are to generate environmental 'world law.'"

12. Compare Peter B. Stone, *Did We Save the Earth at Stockholm? The People and Politics in the Conference on the Human Environment* (London: Earth Island, 1973), especially pp. 100–21; and Stanley B. Johnson, "Did We Really Save the Earth at Rio?" *European Environmental Law Review*, vol. 1 (1992), pp. 81–2.

13. See *International Legal Materials*, vol. 39 (2000), p. 1027; see also Aaron Cosbey and Stas Burgiel, *The Cartagena Protocol on Biosafety: An Analysis of Results* (Winnipeg, Canada: International Institute of Sustainable Development, 2000); and Peter H. Sand, "The Precautionary Principle: Coping With Risk," *Indian Journal of International Law*, vol. 40 (2000), pp. 1–13, at p. 4.

14. Sebastian Oberthür, "The International Convention for the Regulation of Whaling: From Over-Exploitation to Total Prohibition," *Yearbook of International Co-operation on Environment and Development*, 7th ed. (1998–1999), pp. 29–37; and Daniel Bodansky, "The Legitimacy of International Governance: A Coming Challenge for International Envi-

ronmental Law," *American Journal of International Law*, vol. 93 (1999), pp. 596–624, at pp. 605–06; see also notes 34–35 below.

15. As formulated at the 1965 White House Conference on International Cooperation, by a Committee on Natural Resources Conservation and Development, which launched the first draft of the treaty; see Richard N. Gardner, ed., *Blueprint for Peace* (New York: McGraw-Hill, 1966), pp. 154–55.

16. Peter H. Sand, "Carrots without Sticks? New Financial Mechanisms for Global Environmental Agreements," *Max Planck Yearbook of United Nations Law*, vol. 3 (1999), pp. 363–88.

17. Georges Scelle, *Précis de droit des gens*, Part I (Paris: Sirey, 1932), p. 43; see Antonio Cassese, "Remarks on Scelle's Theory of 'Role-Splitting' (*dédoublement fonctionnel*) in International Law," *European Journal of International Law*, vol. 1 (1990), p. 210.

18. Cord Jakobeit, "Nonstate Actors Leading the Way: Debt-for-Nature Swaps," in Robert O. Keohane and Marc A. Levy, eds., *Institutions for Environmental Aid: Pitfalls and Promise* (Cambridge, Mass.: MIT Press, 1996), pp. 127–66.

19. Lilly Sucharipa-Behrmann, "Austrian Legislative Efforts to Regulate Trade in Tropical Timber and Timber Products," *Austrian Journal of Public and International Law*, vol. 46 (1994), pp. 283–92; and Brian F. Chase, "Tropical Forests and Trade Policy: The Legality of Unilateral Attempts to Promote Sustainable Development Under the GATT," *Hastings International and Comparative Law Review*, vol. 17 (1994), pp. 349–88.

20. Report of the GATT Dispute Settlement Panel (*United States Restrictions on Imports of Tuna*) of August 16, 1991, paras. 5.42–5.44; *International Legal Materials*, vol. 30 (1991), p. 1594, at p. 1622.

21. On eco-labeling of forest products, see Eleonore Schmidt, "The Forest Stewardship Council: Using the Market to Promote Responsible Forestry," *Yearbook of International Co-operation on Environment and Development*, 7th ed. (1998–1999), pp. 23–7. Other voluntary certification schemes include forest sector guidelines (ISO/TR 14061) developed by the International Standardization Organization (ISO); the Pan European Forest Certification (PEFC), launched in 1998; and the WWF/World Bank Alliance for Forest Conservation and Sustainable Development (aiming at independent certification of 200 million hectares of managed production forests by the year 2005). See Steven Ruddell, James A. Stevens, and I. J. Bourke, "International Market Access for Wood Products: Post-Uruguay Round Issues," *Forest Products Journal*, vol. 48, nos. 11–12 (1998), pp. 21–6; Deborah Goldemberg, Kristina Leggett, and Farhana Yamin, "Forests," *Yearbook of International Environmental Law*, vol. 9 (1998), pp. 316–19; and World Bank, *Environment Matters: Annual Review 1999* (Washington, D.C.: World Bank, 1999), p. 57. On eco-labeling of marine products, see MSC, position paper submitted to the 7th Session of the UN Commission on Sustainable Development 1999 (CSD-7, New York, April 1999); for background, see David Freestone and Zen Makuch, "The New International Environmental Law of Fisheries: The 1995 UN Straddling Stocks Convention," *Yearbook of International Environmental Law*, vol. 7 (1996), pp. 3–51, at pp. 48–9.

22. On recent extensions of port state enforcement to fishery agreements, see David Anderson, "Port States and Environmental Protection," in Alan Boyle and David Freestone,

eds., *International Law and Sustainable Development: Past Achievements and Future Challenges* (Oxford, U.K.: Oxford University Press, 1999), pp. 325–44, at pp. 337–42.

23. See Peter H. Sand, "Institution-Building to Assist Compliance with International Environmental Law: Perspectives," *Heidelberg Journal of International Law*, vol. 56 (1996), pp. 774–95, at pp. 780–76; Markus Ehrmann, *Erfüllungskontrolle im Umweltvölkerrecht* (Baden-Baden: Nomos, 2000), pp. 256–66; and Antonia H. Chayes, Abram Chayes, and Ronald B. Mitchell, "Active Compliance Management in Environmental Treaties," in Winfried Lang, ed., *Sustainable Development and International Law* (London: Graham and Trotman/Nijhoff, 1995), pp. 75–89, at p. 83.

24. Thilo Marauhn and Markus Ehrmann, "Workshop on 'Institution-Building in International Environmental Law': Summary of the Discussion," *Heidelberg Journal of International Law*, vol. 56 (1996), pp. 820–27, at p. 827; see also Ulrich Beyerlin and Thilo Marauhn, *Law-Making and Law Enforcement in International Environmental Law after the 1992 Rio Conference*, Federal Environmental Agency Report No. 3/97 (Berlin: Erich Schmidt Verlag, 1997), p. 160.

25. Sand, "Carrots Without Sticks?," p. 388; and Mary E. O'Connell, "Enforcing the New International Law of the Environment," *German Yearbook of International Law*, vol. 35 (1992), pp. 293–32, at p. 319 (withholding of financial assistance as legitimate "retorsion").

26. See Resolution on Periodic Reporting adopted at the 29th General Conference of UNESCO, transmitted to the World Heritage Commission at its 21st session (Naples, 1997), WHC-97/CONF.208/17, Annex V; and George W. Downs, "Enforcement and the Evolution of Cooperation," *Michigan Journal of International Law*, vol. 19 (1998), pp. 319–44, at p. 342.

27. Peter H. Sand, "New Approaches to Transnational Environmental Disputes," *International Environmental Affairs*, vol. 3 (1991), pp. 193–206; and Ellen Hey, *Reflections on an International Environmental Court* (The Hague: Kluwer Law International, 2000), pp. 21–5.

28. Daniel Bodansky and Jutta Brunnée, "The Role of National Courts in the Field of International Environmental Law," *Review of European Community and International Environmental Law*, vol. 7 (1998), pp. 11–20.

29. Case No. C-182/89 of November 29, 1990, *European Court Reports* (1990), vol. I, p. 4337.

30. Council Directive 92/43/EEC of May 21, 1992, on the Conservation of Natural Habitats and of Wild Fauna and Flora, *Official Journal of the European Communities* (1992), L 206/7, article 6(4); see André Nollkaemper, "Habitat Protection in European Community Law: Evolving Conceptions of a Balance of Interests," *Journal of Environmental Law*, vol. 9 (1997), pp. 271–86, at p. 276. On the Leybucht case (No. C-57/89) of February 28, 1991, *European Court Reports* (1991), vol. I, p. 383, see Ludwig Krämer, *European Environmental Law Casebook* (London: Sweet and Maxwell, 1993), pp. 217–21, 397–407.

31. Term coined by Charles Pearson; see Steve Charnovitz, "Encouraging Environmental Cooperation Through the Pelly Amendment," *Journal of Environment and Development*, vol. 3 (1994), pp. 3–28, at p. 4.

32. For background, see Peter H. Sand, "Whither CITES? The Evolution of a Treaty Regime in the Borderland of Trade and Environment," *European Journal of International Law*, vol. 8 (1997), pp. 29–58, at pp. 38-40; Sand, "A Century of Green Lessons," pp. 47–8.

33. Phyllis Mofson, "Protecting Wildlife from Trade: Japan's Involvement in the Convention on International Trade in Endangered Species," *Journal of Environment and Development*, vol. 3, (1994), pp. 91–107, at p. 100.

34. On U.S. governmental trade sanctions, see James W. Brennon, "Enforcing the International Convention for the Regulation of Whaling: The Pelly and Packwood-Magnuson Amendments," *Denver Journal of International Law and Policy*, vol. 17 (1989), pp. 293–324; and Gregory Rose and George Paleokrassis, "Compliance with International Environmental Obligations: A Case Study of the International Whaling Commission," in James Cameron, Jacob Werksman, and Peter Roderick, eds., *Improving Compliance with International Environmental Law* (London: Earthscan, 1996), pp. 147–75. On Iceland's economic losses, see Steinar Andresen, "The Making and Implementation of Whaling Policies: Does Participation Make a Difference?" in Victor, Raustiala, and Skolnikoff, eds., *Implementation and Effectiveness of International Environmental Commitments*, pp. 431–74, at p. 458.

35. Including Iceland, Norway, the Faroe Islands, and Greenland; see David D. Caron, "The International Whaling Commission and the North Atlantic Marine Mammal Commission: The Institutional Risks of Coercion in Consensual Structures," *American Journal of International Law*, vol. 89 (1995), pp. 154–67.

36. On treaty congestion, see Edith Brown Weiss, "International Environmental Law: Contemporary Issues and the Emergence of a New World Order," *Georgetown Law Journal*, vol. 81 (1993), pp. 675–710, at pp. 697–702; and Bethany L. Hicks, "Treaty Congestion in International Environmental Law: The Need for Greater International Coordination," *University of Richmond Law Review*, vol. 32 (1999), pp. 1643–74. On treaty synergies, see United Nations Development Program, *Synergies in National Implementation: The Rio Agreements* (New York: UNDP, 1997); United Nations University, *Synergies and Coordination Between Multilateral Environmental Agreements* (Tokyo: UNU, 1999); United Nations Environment Program, *Synergies: Promoting Collaboration on Environmental Treaties*, Newsletter No. 2 (Geneva: UNEP, 2000); and Lyle Glowka, *A Guide to the Complementarities Between the CMS and the CBD*, UNEP/CBD/COP/5/Inf.28 (Nairobi: UNEP, 2000).

37. The WCMC was originally established in Cambridge under the auspices of the IUCN Species Survival Commission in 1979, cosponsored since 1987 by WWF, and formally reconstituted as a UNEP unit in 2000.

38. See *Expanding the Measure of Wealth: Indicators of Environmentally Sustainable Development* (Washington, D.C.: World Bank, 1997); Thomas Fues, *Das Indikatoren-Programm der UN-Kommission für nachhaltige Entwicklung: Stellenwert für den internationalen Rio-Prozess und Folgerungen für das Konzept von Global Governance* (Frankfurt: Lang, 1998); Stuart L. Pimm, "The Value of Everything," *Nature*, vol. 387 (May 15, 1997), pp. 231–32. Alexander N. James, Kevin J. Gaston, and Andrew Balmford, "Balancing the Earth's Accounts," *Nature*, vol. 401 (September 23, 1999), pp. 323–24, estimate the global costs of a preventive/precautionary program to conserve the Earth's biological resources at

$300 billion per year; in other words, about half of the cost of Agenda 21 (the action plan developed by the 1992 Rio Conference) as quantified in paragraph 33.18, UNCED Report A/CONF.151/26/Rev.1, vol. I, p. 417 (1993). By way of comparison, the current total volume of official development assistance (bilateral and multilateral) is less than $50 billion per year, according to the Organization for Economic Cooperation and Development, *Development Co-operation: 1999 Report* (Paris: OECD, 2000); detailed tables available at <http://www.oecd.org/dac/htm/online.htm>.

39. The two International Oil Pollution Compensation Funds were established under the auspices of the International Maritime Organization (IMO) in 1978 and 1996, respectively. The UN Compensation Commission was established under the auspices of the UN Security Council in 1991. The claims for environmental and natural resource damage now before the commission's "F4" Panel (established in 1998) amount to more than $47 billion.

40. See note 21 above; and United Nations Environment Program, *Global Environment Outlook 2000* (London: Earthscan, 1999), pp. 18–19.

41. Pre-CITES arrangements between IUCN/WWF and the International Fur Trade Federation (IFTF) to prevent trade in endangered species by voluntary commitments failed, mainly because compliance by traders was spotty and self-enforcement by IFTF ineffective; see Tim Inskipp and Sue Wells, *International Trade in Wildlife* (London: Earthscan, 1979), p. 41. On the WTO and eco-labels, see the cases of Austria's tropical timber label and the U.S. "dolphin-safe" label, notes 19–20 above.

42. See note 33 above.

43. The international community rigidly enforced free trade in opium (as in the Opium Wars of 1839–1842 and 1856–1860 against China) until the adoption of the first International Opium Convention in 1912; see Peter H. Sand, "International Economic Instruments for Sustainable Development: Sticks, Carrots and Games," *Indian Journal of International Law*, vol. 36, no. 2 (1996), pp. 1–16, at pp. 6–7.

44. See Independent World Commission on the Oceans, *The Ocean: Our Future* (Cambridge, U.K.: Cambridge University Press, 1998), p. 59; the research outline by Alf Hakon Hoel, *Performance of Exclusive Economic Zones*, Institutional Dimensions of Global Environmental Change: Scoping Report No. 2 (Hanover, N.H.: IDGEC, 2000); and generally Dominic Moran and David W. Pearce, "The Economics of Biodiversity," in Thomas H. Tietenberg and Henk Folmer, eds., *International Yearbook of Environmental and Resource Economics: A Survey of Current Issues* (Cheltenham, U.K.: Edward Elgar, 1997), pp. 82–113.

45. Nico Schrijver, *Sovereignty over Natural Resources: Balancing Rights and Duties* (Cambridge, U.K.: Cambridge University Press, 1997); B. S. Chimni, "The Principle of Permanent Sovereignty over Natural Resources: Toward a Radical Interpretation," *Indian Journal of International Law*, vol. 38 (1998), pp. 208–17; Karen T. Litfin, ed., *The Greening of Sovereignty in World Politics* (Cambridge, Mass.: MIT Press, 1998); and Stephen D. Krasner, *Sovereignty: Organized Hypocrisy* (Princeton, N.J.: Princeton University Press, 1999).

46. On the development of a public trust doctrine by the U.S. Supreme Court since 1892, see especially the seminal study by Joseph L. Sax, "The Public Trust Doctrine in Natural

Resources Law: Effective Judicial Intervention," *Michigan Law Review*, vol. 68 (1970), pp. 471–556; for recent re-assessments, see the symposium issue, "Taking, Public Trust, Unhappy Truths, and Helpless Giants: A Review of Professor Sax's Defense of the Environment Through Academic Scholarship," *Ecology Law Quarterly*, vol. 25 (1998), pp. 325–438. See also William D. Brighton and David F. Askman, "The Role of Government Trustees in Recovering Compensation for Injury to Natural Resources," in Peter Wetterstein, ed., *Harm to the Environment* (Oxford, U.K.: Clarendon, 1997), pp. 177–206.

47. *Great Britain v. United States* (August 15, 1893), *Moore's International Arbitration Awards*, vol. 1 (1893), p. 755, at pp. 813 and 853; see Philippe J. Sands, *Principles of International Environmental Law*, vol. 1 (Manchester, U.K.: Manchester University Press, 1995), pp. 417–18.

48. On the global commons, see, in particular, the report of the Commission on Global Governance, *Our Global Neighborhood* (Oxford, U.K.: Oxford University Press, 1995), pp. 251–52 ("trusteeship for the global commons"); the report of the UN Secretary-General to the General Assembly, *Renewing the United Nations: A Programme for Reform*, A/51/950 (New York: United Nations, July 14, 1997), para. 85 (UN Trusteeship Council to be reconstituted "as the forum through which member states exercise their collective trusteeship for the integrity of the global environment and common areas such as the oceans, atmosphere, and outer space"); and the report of the Independent World Commission on the Oceans, *The Ocean*, pp. 45–46 ("treating the 'high seas' as a public trust"). See also Alexandre C. Kiss, "La notion de patrimoine commun de l'humanite," *Hague Academy Recueil des Cours*, vol. 175 (1984), pp. 99–256, at pp. 128–33 ("common heritage of mankind" as international public trust); Keith Suter, *Antarctica: Private Property or Public Heritage?* (London: ZED, 1991), pp. 169–81 (analogy from the public trust concept to "public heritage of humankind" as applied to the Antarctic); Jon M. Van Dyke, "International Governance and Stewardship of the High Seas and Its Resources," in Jon M. Van Dyke, Durwood Zaelke, and Grant Hewison, eds., *Freedom for the Seas in the 21st Century: Ocean Governance and Environmental Harmony* (Washington, D.C.: Island Press, 1993), pp. 13–22, at p. 19 (drawing analogies from the public trust concept as applied to U.S. territorial waters); Alan E. Boyle, "Remedying Harm to International Common Spaces and Resources: Compensation and Other Approaches," in Wetterstein, ed., *Harm to the Environment*, pp. 83–100, at p. 84 (common heritage as "a form of international trusteeship"); Jessica L. Brown, "Stewardship: An International Perspective," *Environments: A Journal of Interdisciplinary Studies*, vol. 26 (1998), pp. 8–17; W. M. von Zahren, "Ocean Ecosystem Stewardship," *William and Mary Environmental Law and Policy Review*, vol. 23 (1998), pp. 1–108; and Francesco Morandi, *La tutela del mare come bene pubblico* (Milan: Giuffré, 1998). On EEZs, see Jack H. Archer and Casey Jarman, "Sovereign Rights and Responsibilities: Applying Public Trust Principles to the Management of EEZ Space and Resources," *Journal of Ocean and Shoreline Management*, vol. 17 (1992), p. 251; and Richard G. Hildreth, "The Public Trust Doctrine and Coastal and Ocean Resources Management," *Journal of Environmental Law and Litigation*, vol. 8 (1993), pp. 221–36. On the similar custodianship rationale put forward by Canada for its 1970 Arctic Waters Pollution Prevention Act, see John Allan Beesley, "The Canadian

Approach to International Environmental Law," *Canadian Yearbook of International Law*, vol. 11 (1973), pp. 3–12, at p. 6. On natural heritage sites, see Gardner, *Blueprint for Peace*, and Russell E. Train, "A World Heritage Trust," in E. R. Gillette, ed., *Action for Wilderness* (Washington, D.C.: Sierra Club, 1972), at p. 172. See also Percy H. C. Lucas, Michael Beresford, and John Aitchison, "Protected Landscapes: Global and Local Stewardship," *Environments: A Journal of Interdisciplinary Studies*, vol. 26 (1998), pp. 18–26. On endangered forests, see the comments on Russian proposals for a "global biosphere trust" under the auspices of the UN Trusteeship Council, by Thomas M. Franck, "Soviet Initiatives: U.S. Responses—New Opportunities for Reviving the United Nations System," *American Journal of International Law*, vol. 83 (1989), p. 531, at p. 541 (suggesting international debt relief to compensate countries such as Brazil, as "administering power," for the opportunity costs of holding its tropical rain forests in trust on behalf of the global community). On genetic resources, see Titus Gebel, *Der Treuhandgedanke und die Bewahrung der biologischen Vielfalt: Einschränkung der territorialen Souveränität durch treuhänderische Verwaltung von lebenden Umwelt-Ressourcen* (Sinzheim: Pro Universitate 1998); and Pierre-François Mercure, "La proposition d'un modèle de gestion integrée des ressources naturelles communes de l'humanité," *Canadian Yearbook of International Law*, vol. 36 (1998), pp. 41–92, at p. 64 (states exercising "a sort of guardianship" over genetic resources on behalf of humanity). In October 1994, twelve research centers of the Consultative Group on International Agricultural Research (CGIAR) entered into identical agreements with FAO to place their genebanks under the auspices of FAO as part of an International Network of *Ex-Situ* Germplasm Collections. The centers undertook not to claim ownership over designated germplasm but to hold it in trust for the international community.

49. On historic parallels, see William F. Fratcher, "Trust," *International Encyclopedia of Comparative Law*, vol. 6, ch. 11 (Tübingen: Mohr, 1973), pp. 84–141; Donovan W. M. Waters, "The Institution of the Trust in Civil and Common Law," *Hague Academy Recueil des Cours*, vol. 252 (1995), pp. 113–454; Richard H. Helmholtz and Reinhard Zimmermann, eds., *Itinera Fiduciae: Trust and Treuhand in Historical Perspective* (Berlin: Duncker and Humblot, 1998); and Stefan Grundmann, "Trust and *Treuhand* at the End of the Twentieth Century: Key Problems and Shift of Interests," *American Journal of Comparative Law*, vol. 47 (1999), pp. 401–28. In Italy, the Court of Accounts (and since 1986, the Environment Ministry) acts as trustee for claims of damage to national heritage (*danno erariale*) in the field of natural resources; see Andrea Bianchi, "Harm to the Environment in Italian Practice: The Interaction of International Law and Domestic Law," in Wetterstein, ed., *Harm to the Environment*, pp. 103–29, at p. 104. For the Supreme Court of India judgment, see Judgment of 13 December 1996 (by Judges Kuldip Singh and S. Saghir Ahmad, with extensive references to U.S. jurisprudence and to the alleged Roman origins of the concept), *Supreme Court Cases* (1997), vol. I, p. 388; reprinted in UNEP/UNDP, *Compendium of Judicial Decisions on Matters Related to Environment: National Decisions*, vol. 1 (Nairobi: United Nations Environment Program, 1998), pp. 259–74. See also Rajkumar Deepak Singh, "Response of Indian Judiciary to Environmental Protection: Some Reflections," *Indian Journal of International Law*, vol. 39 (1999), pp. 447–63, at p. 458.

50. On extending the public trust doctrine to environmental governance, see Ved P. Nanda and William K. Ris Jr., "The Public Trust Doctrine: A Viable Approach to International Environmental Protection,"" *Ecology Law Quarterly*, vol. 5 (1976), pp. 291–319; Edith Brown Weiss, *In Fairness to Future Generations: International Law, Common Patrimony, and Intergenerational Equity* (Tokyo: United Nations University, 1988); Catherine Redgwell, *Intergenerational Trusts and Environmental Protection* (Manchester, U.K.: Manchester University Press, 1999); and the reference to the "principle of trusteeship of earth resources" in Judge Christopher G. Weeramantry's separate opinion in the 1997 decision of the International Court of Justice, "Case Concerning the Gabcíkovo-Nagymaros Project," *International Legal Materials*, vol. 37 (1998), p. 213; reprinted in David Hunter, James Salzman, and Durwood Zaelke, eds., *International Environmental Law and Policy* (New York: Foundation Press, 1998), p. 246. See also Christopher G. Weeramantry, *Nauru: Environmental Damage Under International Trusteeship* (Melbourne: Oxford University Press, 1992), pp. 151–13, 340.

51. Roscoe Pound, *An Introduction to the Philosophy of Law*, revised edition (New Haven, Conn.: Yale University Press, 1954), p. 111.

52. Karl Marx, *Das Kapital*, vol. 3, ch. 46 (Friedrich Engels, ed., 1894): "*Selbst eine ganze Gesellschaft, eine Nation, ja alle gleichzeitigen Gesellschaften zusammengenommen sind nicht Eigentümer der Erde. Sie sind nur ihre Besitzer, ihre Nutzniesser, und haben sie als boni patres familias den nachfolgenden Generationen verbessert zu hinterlassen.*" [Note: The reference to the concept of *boni patres familias* (literally "good family fathers," that is, caretakers, stewards, or guardians) of Roman law—in which Marx had been trained—defines a fiduciary standard of care comparable to the due diligence of a common law trustee.]

SUGGESTED ADDITIONAL READING

See also Peter M. Haas's recommended readings on pollution.

Carlowitz, Hans Carl von. *Sylvicultura Oeconomica*. Leipzig: Brauns, 2nd ed., 1732.

Chayes, Abram, and Antonia Handler Chayes. *The New Sovereignty: Compliance with International Regulatory Agreements*. Cambridge, Mass.: Harvard University Press, 1995.

Ciriacy-Wantrup, Siegfried von. *Resource Conservation: Economics and Policies*. Berkeley, Calif.: University of California Division of Agricultural Sciences, 3rd ed., 1968.

Holdgate, Martin. *The Green Web: A Union for World Conservation*. London: Earthscan, 1999.

Hunter, David, James Salzman, and Durwood Zaelke. *International Environmental Law and Policy*. New York: Foundation Press, 1998.

Klemm, Cyrille de, and Clare Shine. *International Environmental Law: Biological Diversity*. Geneva: United Nations Institute for Training and Research, 1998.

Lyster, Simon. *International Wildlife Law: An Analysis of International Treaties Concerned With the Conservation of Wildlife*. Cambridge, U.K.: Grotius Publications, 1985.

Mathews, Jessica Tuchman, ed. 1991. *Preserving the Global Environment*. New York: W.W. Norton & Company, 1991.

Orrego Vicuña, Francisco. *The Changing International Law of High Seas Fisheries.* Cambridge, U.K.: Cambridge University Press, 1999.

Sand, Peter H. *Lessons Learned in Global Environmental Governance.* Washington, D.C.: World Resources Institute, 1990.

Wijnstekers, Willem. *The Evolution of CITES: A Reference to the Convention on International Trade in Endangered Species of Wild Fauna and Flora.* Geneva: CITES Secretariat, 6th abridged electronic ed., 2001.

Yearbook of International Environmental Law. Vols. 1–10. London: Graham & Trotman, 1990–1999.

Selected Internet Sites

Databases

ECOLEX: A Gateway to Environmental Law (jointly operated by IUCN and UNEP) <http://www.ecolex.org>

Environmental Treaties and Resource Indicators (ENTRI) at the Center for International Earth Sciences Information Network (CIESIN), Columbia University, New York <http://sedac.ciesin.org/pidb/pidb-home.html>

International Regimes Database (IRD) at the Technical University of Darmstadt, Germany <http://www.ifs.tu-darmstadt.de/pg/ird_home.htm>

TRAFFIC: Trade Records Analysis of Flora and Fauna in Commerce (IUCN and WWF) <http://www.traffic.org>

World Conservation Monitoring Centre (WCMC), operated by UNEP at Cambridge, U.K. <http://www.unep-wcmc.org>

Yearbook of International Co-operation on Environment and Development, on-line at the Fridtjof Nansen Institute, Oslo, Norway <http://www.ngo.grida.no/ggynet>

Intergovernmental Sites

Biodiversity-Related Conventions (CBD, CITES, CMS, Ramsar, WHC): Joint Website <http://216.95.224.234/rioconv/websites.html>

Food and Agriculture Organization of the United Nations (FAO) <http://www.fao.org>

Global Environment Facility (GEF) <http://www.gefweb.org>

International Network for Environmental Compliance and Enforcement (INECE) <http://www.inece.org>

International Tropical Timber Organization (ITTO) <http://www.itto.or.jp>

International Whaling Commission (IWC) <http://ourworld.compuserve.com/homepages/iwcoffice>

South Pacific Forum Fisheries Agency (FFA) <http://www.ffa.int>

UN Commission on Sustainable Development (UNCSD) <http://www.un.org/esa/sustdev/csd.htm>

UN Environment Program (UNEP) <http://www.unep.org>

Nongovernmental Sites
Forest Stewardship Council (FSC) <http://www.fscoax.org>
Greenpeace International <http://www.greenpeace.org>
International Institute for Sustainable Development (IISD) <http://www.iisd.ca/linkages>
IWMC World Conservation Trust <http://www.iwmc.org>
Marine Stewardship Council (MSC) <http://www.msc.org>
World Conservation Union (IUCN) <http://www.iucn.org>
Worldwide Fund for Nature (WWF) <http://www.wwf.org>

8

Environment: Pollution

Peter M. Haas

THE TWENTY-FIRST CENTURY, suggests renowned biologist E. O. Wilson, will be the age of the environment.[1] Despite the convenience of millennial accounting, this age started earlier—with the 1972 UN Conference on the Human Environment (UNCHE), when the international community first became aware of the widespread impact of human behavior on the natural environment. Before then, national leaders were by and large unfamiliar with environmental issues, scientific understanding was rudimentary; and there were few national or international institutions available for promoting environmental protection. Over the last thirty years, however, the environment has become firmly established on the international diplomatic agenda, and, through regime formation, binding rules have been developed for most human activities affecting environmental quality. Almost all areas of human economic activity are now subject to at least one international environmental accord, and most countries are bound by a number of international environmental commitments. One feature of international environmental governance is particularly striking: national governments have become increasingly aware of the complexity of the threats to the world's ecosystems and of the need for more comprehensive and collective responses. Accordingly, the substance of regional and international legal arrangements on the environment has begun to reflect this awareness. Environmental governance—the ever-expanding network of legal obligations and formal institutions influencing states' environmental policies—has evolved principally through the development of better scientific understanding about the behavior of the physical environment combined with a growing appreciation of the role that international institutions can play. These regulations and institutions have contributed to a structural change in the world economy and to the development of markets for clean technology.

UNCHE provides the benchmark against which progress in international environmental governance has occurred. UNCHE, which took place in Stockholm in

1972, was the first global governmental conference on the environment. It popularized the environment, putting the environment firmly on the international agenda, as well as triggering administrative reforms in most governments of the world that had to designate environmental bodies to be responsible for producing reports on national environmental problems. UNCHE provoked states to take initial positions on the environment that revealed deep cleavages that have persisted throughout subsequent negotiations. Industrialized countries expressed principal concern about matters of industrial pollution, whereas developing countries were primarily concerned with natural resource usage and that they would have to forgo economic development to protect the environment. In addition, UNCHE was the first UN conference to have a parallel nongovernmental organization (NGO) forum, marking the beginning of the formal involvement of NGOs and civil society in international conference diplomacy. UNCHE adopted both the Stockholm Declaration establishing twenty-six principles of behavior and responsibility to serve as the basis for future legally binding multilateral accords and the Action Plan for the Human Environment that specified 109 recommendations in the areas of environmental assessment, environmental management, and supportive institutional measures.

The conference also created the UN Environment Program (UNEP). Based in Nairobi, Kenya—the first UN agency to have headquarters in a developing country—UNEP served as the environmental conscience of the UN system for over twenty years. UNEP urged other UN agencies to internalize environmental concerns into their programmatic activities, engaged in public environmental education, helped draft dozens of international environmental treaties, trained developing country officials in environmentally sensitive natural resource management techniques, helped monitor the environment, and tried to empower environmental NGOs in many countries.

The UN Conference on Environment and Development (UNCED), held in Rio de Janeiro in 1992, marked the twentieth anniversary of UNCHE. UNCED adopted the Rio Declaration with 27 principles for guiding environmental policy and a sweeping action plan to promote sustainability. The action plan was called Agenda 21 and provided 2,509 specific recommendations with elements applying to states, international institutions, and members of civil society.[2] UNCED created the UN Commission on Sustainable Development (UNCSD) and cemented the tacit North-South compromise that environment and development were complementary in the long term, so long as the North contributed financial assistance to developing countries to pay for much of their pollution control that would affect conditions elsewhere in the world. In 2002 there will be a Rio Plus 10 Conference held in Johannesburg, South Africa, to continue the efforts by the international community to protect the global environment and to encourage sustainable development.

This chapter looks at the creation and evolution of multilateral regimes that address transboundary and global pollution threats—what the UNEP calls multilateral environmental agreements (MEAs). It seeks to describe the major trends in international environmental policy since the 1970s and explain the principal policy factors that account for the dramatic increase in concern about and commitment to improving the quality of the Earth's environment. Multilateral regimes help to coordinate and influence state actions, and although they do not directly stop human activities that degrade the environment, they do offer a set of institutional expectations and pressures on states to develop and enforce policies toward that end.

Ecological ideas introduced by environmental scientists, NGOs, and international institutions over the last thirty years have evolved against a backdrop of new trends in international politics.[3] Transnational networks of environmental scientists grew influential in the 1970s in the aftermath of the UNCHE. Until the end of the Cold War, dominant attitudes toward international institutions remained burdened with dominant calculations about national security and geopolitics, to which environmental concerns were subordinated. However, with the end of the Cold War, interest in developing more powerful international institutions has increased worldwide, as people have become more comfortable with the notion of globalization, and geopolitical calculations no longer dominate the mind-sets of elite policy makers in the West. Popular interest in environmental quality issues has also grown in this period as the emergence of green parties in most advanced industrial societies would attest. To some extent, the decline of profound North-South cleavages in the 1980s facilitated consensus on sustainable development as a policy goal. Lastly, the spread of civil society and democratization since the early 1990s has increased the influence of environmental voices both at home and abroad through complex networks of transnational influence that are beginning to make governments accountable not only to their own citizens but also to citizens from other countries and to international institutions. Still, the majority of these background changes, which surely contributed to an acceleration of environmental governance, only occurred in the early 1990s, following twenty years of real progress in the development of environmental regimes. Many of the ideas and actors were already present, but UNCED focused attention on them.

NATURE OF GLOBAL ENVIRONMENTAL THREATS

Global environmental problems should be of great concern not only because of nature's intrinsic value or because of ethical concerns for future generations. They also matter because environmental problems can harm human health and well-being, impose disruptive costs on national economies, and even fuel political instability and violent conflict by exacerbating inequalities and tensions in resource-poor areas.[4]

Environmental degradation is the collateral damage of modern economic growth based on fossil fuel consumption and industrial production. Most industrial and other human activities generate contaminants that accumulate in the physical environment, leading to unanticipated environmental risks and often irreversible consequences. Ironically, environmental threats can be the unanticipated result of well-intentioned efforts at improving prosperity.

Ecosystems transfer pollutants geographically. Thus contaminants from emissions in one area may eventually appear elsewhere. Contaminants that accumulate in ecosystems may have nonlinear effects on environmental quality, so that even in small quantities they could have unanticipated and sometimes disastrous results. For instance, in 1972 many were shocked to learn that DDT, a chemical pesticide widely used for the elimination of malaria-transmitting mosquitoes, had been detected in Antarctica. Scientists determined that the pesticide caused penguin eggshells to become more fragile, which ultimately meant that fewer penguins were born alive. Chlorofluorocarbons (CFCs), industrial coolants that have been widely used since the 1930s for refrigeration and insulation, were found to accumulate in the stratospheric ozone layer. Not only do CFCs contribute to seasonal thinning of the ozone layer, but also to the increase of ultraviolet rays reaching the surface of the earth. According to some, these rays are responsible for the increase in the skin cancer rate in humans and declines in fisheries and agricultural productivity.

Climate change is humankind's most recent global environmental problem and its most politically challenging. Recent scientific consensus suggests that the use of fossil fuels will lead to the warming of the Earth's climate by 2050 to an extent that may lead to widespread interference with vital ecosystems. The Intergovernmental Panel on Climate Change (IPCC) is a body of government-nominated scientists, created in 1988, responsible for ascertaining the state of scientific consensus on climate change. In 1996, it concluded that "the balance of evidence suggests a discernible human influence on the global climate." The IPCC now predicts that if current emissions rates continue, the average temperature on the planet will rise by 2.5-10.4 degrees Fahrenheit over the next 100 years—the most rapid change in ten millennia and 60 percent higher than the IPCC predicted six years ago—leading to widespread coastal flooding and submersion of small islands and deltas, changes in growing seasons and agricultural productivity, more acute weather patterns, widespread loss of biodiversity, and the spread of tropical diseases, although estimates of the full magnitude or timing of the impacts of human-induced climate change remain unclear.

Political Problems Impeding Effective Environmental Governance

Transboundary and global environmental risks have been politically difficult to manage at the international level for several reasons. Technically, efforts to cope with environmental threats must be comprehensive if they are to address the complex array of causal factors associated with them. Yet comprehensiveness is difficult to achieve, because few governments or international institutions are organized to cope with the multiple dimensions of environmental problems, and many states lack the technical resources to develop and apply such efforts.[5]

Many tools of international environmental governance can help to address these political problems. For instance, through providing new information to all actors and by empowering NGOs, imaginative efforts at environmental governance by international organizations may improve national abilities to anticipate environmental threats. They also create domestic constituencies for dealing with them and for verifying or overseeing compliance with environmental regulations. Building national scientific competence and educating the public and elites about the behavior of complex ecosystems can also transform states' notions of their national interests when negotiating international environmental regimes. This, in turn, can make them more likely to accept voluntary constraints on economic growth and on state authority to preserve international environmental resources.

Many neorealist and institutionalist analysts characterize international environmental politics principally in terms of problems of collective choices.[6] Although collective action may be desirable to address shared problems, neorealists and realists believe that the international system is institutionally and administratively too weak to leverage sufficient political pressure on states to act. As such, the ability of states to manage shared problems is inadequate to the task of protecting the environment.

Most environmental problems require joint action because they are typically created by large numbers of countries, and because many of their consequences extend beyond the jurisdiction of any one country (including the atmosphere and open oceans). Individual countries accurately assume that their environmental policies will not yield significant benefits unless most states agree to cooperate. Some observers assign principal blame for this to the persistence of state sovereignty. This view may be overstated, however, given that much effective environmental governance has been successful despite continuing claims of national sovereignty.[7]

Governments frequently have different experiences with environmental problems and thus do not share common preferences about which problems should be addressed or the importance accorded to various environmental protection efforts. For instance, developed countries typically express concern with transboundary and global pollution threats, whereas developing countries voice greater concern about national problems associated with resource use and environmental degradation. Moreover, most developing countries stress the urgency of economic development and are leery of the short-term opportunity costs associated with environmental protection.

Political factors often influence states' environmental policies. National governments, for example, find that most international environmental issues are politically difficult to address because they are Olsonian public goods problems: that is, the costs of solving them are concentrated, whereas the benefits are diffuse. This means generally that those responsible for paying for the short-term costs of pollution control are usually more politically organized than those who benefit from environmental protection.

Domestic and international political systems are typically ill-equipped to create and implement environmental policy. Problems of both information availability and of political power and practice inhibit their rapid and effective application. Governments vary broadly in their administrative ability to develop and enforce environmental policies. Most governmental agencies and international organizations are designed to address disjointed problems and thus lack the knowledge base or administrative influence needed to address the full range of complex interactions that characterize environmental issues. For instance, agricultural ministries are responsible for increasing food production, typically through intensive agriculture, but they do not heed the social or environmental consequences of increasing reliance on chemical inputs. National regulatory bodies are usually organized to consider and apply management styles designed for discrete problems rather than cross-cutting ones; timely environmental quality data are often absent; and the relevant holistic or ecological models, when they exist, tend to remain restricted to the scientific community. In addition, environmental experts must contend with a government administration that at times can appear either ignorant or indifferent.[8] The institutional barriers are the consequences of long-held public administration orthodoxy, developed at the turn of the century for military and civilian organizations. They established iron triangles and patronage relationships between the government and society and weakened transmission channels connecting universities and environmental research institutions with relevant government agencies.

Lack of knowledge about the environment compromises effective management. Ecologists stress the need for comprehensive models of ecosystems, ecosystem health, and the human activities that influence ecosystems and are affected by them. Yet governments and modern institutions—as well as specialized modern scientific disciplines—are organized functionally to address only parts of such a broad problematique. Fragmented and incomplete scientific understanding of environmental threats and the behavior of ecosystems also inhibits the formulation of sweeping environmental measures. Moreover, the scientific myopia is reinforced by research funding imperatives from government sources that often stress narrow mission-based research rather than broader ecological studies. Consequently, most national and international efforts have sought to address specific environmental threats rather than work toward the protection of broad transboundary or global ecosystems.

Government officials' unfamiliarity with environmental problems has often hindered their ability to appreciate how their states' national interests can be harmed by environmental degradation. Further, it has retarded the development of effective environmental quality. For instance, in the early 1970s, Mediterranean governments responded to alarms about the decline of the sea's health and created the robust Mediterranean Action Plan, which has reversed much of the decline of the Mediterranean Sea. Officials in the Mediterranean were genuinely unaware of the pollutants their countries were emitting, the concentrations of these pollutants in the sea, the human health and long-term consequences of these activities, and what to do about them. Such uncertainty in fact opened up political opportunities. Because the political leaders were uncertain about how their state interests would be affected by pollution, they turned to scientists for advice. Politicians, uncertain of the domestic coalitions likely to support or oppose environmental protection—although the tourism industry was vigorously opposed to any public admissions of environmental risk—could afford to take political gambles that they would not have likely taken if they had better anticipated the degree of domestic opposition by industry.

Most states now have national agencies for environmental protection, as well as sustainable development agencies. Governments have experimented with various institutional designs to make their agencies more effective. Some have focused on making their environmental agencies highly centralized, which proved useful for devising and enforcing environmental policies. Others have tried interagency coordination as a way to ensure that environmental concerns are reflected in the policies of other agencies responsible for managing activities that have an environmental impact. The most effective environmental agencies are found in states party to the Organization for Economic Cooperation and Development (OECD). In Eastern Europe and in most developing countries, however, such bodies still suffer from a lack of budgetary resources, political authority, popular support, and competent technical staff.

TRACK RECORD

International efforts to protect the environment have taken off since the creation of UNCHE. The number of multilateral treaties has more than doubled, a variety of new regimes have been established, and many innovative institutional support arrangements have been introduced. More than half of the 140-plus multilateral environmental treaties signed since 1920 have been adopted since 1973.[9] Since UNCHE, the catalyzing event of 1972, the international focus has shifted to a new set of environmental threats—from oil pollution of the seas and endangerment of whole species to atmospheric and marine pollution caused by, among other things, politically and economically costly industrial manufacturing (see table 8-1).

In the last thirty years, the adoption of treaties dealing with the environmental effects of economic activities, and framework treaties laying out agendas of interrelated issues for subsequent collective action, has greatly increased. This change signals a move away from trying to conserve individual species to controlling the negative consequences of economic activities that have traditionally been dealt with in isolation.

Table 8-1. *Changing Substantive Focus of Environmental Treaties*

Substantive area of coverage	Percent of treaties signed pre-1973	Percent of treaties signed post-1973
Species conservation	37	25
Plant disease and pest control	14	0
Framework treaties	3	19
Air pollution	0	9
Land-based sources of marine pollution	5	7
Marine oil pollution	11	16
Marine dumping	6	4
Worker protection from environmental hazards	5	7
Nuclear regulation and safety	6	6
Other	19	6

Note: Totals may not add to 100 because of rounding.

The substance of global environmental governance has expanded to capture the broad scale and functional scope of environmental threats. Global action has been taken to confront threats to the atmosphere. Marine treaties for global commons problems (such as pollution from shipping) have also acquired a global scope. Meanwhile efforts to confront problems with regional characteristics (such as coastal marine management) remain regional, although efforts are under way to develop global guidelines for managing land-based sources of marine pollution and for creating integrated coastal management. Before the 1970s, marine environmental law focused almost exclusively on preventing oil spills from tanker-related emergencies and operational activities. Recently, however, marine pollution control moved from controlling tanker-based sources of pollution to controlling marine dumping and the politically more difficult and economically costly land-based sources of pollution and air pollution, and to protecting ecosystems in which valued species dwell.

Attention has also shifted more generally from local and regional risks to global ones. For example, the conservation of localized bird species (as characterized by environmental law through the 1950s) has given way to efforts, starting in the 1970s, to protect migratory birds' habitats. Negotiations have also moved away from global regional approaches to issues (such as acid rain) in the 1970s and 1980s to global atmospheric issues such as stratospheric ozone protection and climate change in the 1980s and 1990s.

Substantively, environmental governance arrangements have become increasingly ecological in form, heeding the ecological laws espoused by environmental scientists and focusing on the sustainable management of ecosystems rather than containing threats to environmental quality. The laws of man are increasingly based on understandings of the laws of nature. Species management is cast in terms of a habitat's ability to support multiple species rather than in terms of protecting individual populations living in the area. Environmental impact assessments are now widely required by governments and international organizations so that they may weigh the environmental consequences of economic or development decisions. International debates now regularly consider new concepts such as "ecological sensitivity values" to bound the rates of economic growth. Richard Gardner notes that the preamble to the UN Framework Convention on Climate Change (FCCC) commits signatory states "to the goal of stabilizing greenhouse gas concentrations in the atmosphere at a level that would prevent dangerous interference with the earth's climate, and to do so in a time frame that will permit ecosystems to adapt."[10] The 1987 Montreal Protocol on Substances that Deplete the Ozone Layer (the Montreal Ozone Protocol), with 168 parties, has a design that reflects a growing willingness to accept scientific uncertainty when applying science to environmental management. Mandated reductions in CFC use are scheduled to take effect unless scientific consensus determines that such reductions are unnecessary, thereby indicating a readiness to stop using scientific uncertainty to avoid action. Such provisions shift the burden of proof from those pressing for environmental action to those urging delay.[11]

A number of national and international organizational innovations have been introduced since 1972. In addition, most governments have created national environmental authorities, and, since 1992, sustainable development bodies as well. Countries have experimented with various forms of institutional design, with some opting for centralized bodies capable of creating and enforcing environmental policy. Often, however, these bodies have little or no influence over other important governmental agencies responsible for making policy affecting the generation of environmental stresses. Others have chosen more coordinated arrangements that encourage other agencies to internalize environmental considerations. Some of these, however, lack the resources to monitor compliance. Many national pollution control and environmental protection programs have become more comprehensive during this period as well. For example, by the mid-1990s, 150 integrated coastal zone management efforts were in place in sixty-five countries.[12]

International institutional innovations occurred as well. UNEP was established in 1973, with a mandate to spur environmental action within the UN system. Other UN agencies developed new institutional resources to monitor environmental quality, foster policy research, create international laws, and verify state compliance. They have sought to do this by building national concern, transferring technology, training, and institutional lessons to governments to improve state capacity, and reaching out to NGOs and civil society. Since 1986 the World Bank has taken increased account of the consequences of its development projects, seeking, in particular, to minimize environmental damage. In addition, it has spent more money on environmental remediation and in helping governments develop national environmental plans.

Gaps remain, however, in the institutional structure for environmental governance. Better early warning systems are needed; compliance mechanisms are weak and increasingly vulnerable to challenge when they infringe on free trade; more research is necessary for what is now widely called sustainability; and verification of state compliance is often weak. Substantively, few institutional efforts exist in the areas of soils protection, toxic waste management in developing countries, and freshwater pollution control.

Major international conferences have only had limited impacts on international environmental diplomacy. The UNCHE, the UNCED and its follow-up conferences, and the European Conferences on the European Environment have generated momentary public attention to the environment, but they have not been able to mobilize longer-term resources or induce governments to change their policies. Such conferences are better at stimulating public concern and galvanizing administrative reforms (member states must designate responsible national agencies) than they are at sustaining momentum in international environmental protection.

Some regimes have been highly effective in protecting the quality of the environment. The ozone regime is credited with virtually eliminating CFCs that once threatened the stratospheric ozone layer. The rate of environmental decline caused by organic and inorganic contaminants has been slowed in the Mediterranean, North Sea, and Baltic. The quality of the marine environment may have stabilized in the South Pacific and Southeast Pacific regions, although the data are much scantier for those areas. Airborne emissions of sulfur in Europe declined by 35 percent from 1980 to 1991, and a slight reduction in nitrogen emission from 1987 to 1991 has been recorded.[13] These achievements are all consequences of regime influences over state actions because the political pressures and information generated by relevant regimes influenced states to enforce their environmental commitments.[14]

More general assessments about environmental conditions are limited by data availability. Seldom are high-quality time series environmental data available to determine real changes in the quality of the environment (or even to measure changes in the activities giving rise to environmental stresses). Analysts are often forced to make proxy judgments by looking at states' activities (such as political or administrative reforms) that are likely to result in better environmental policy making and thus improve environmental quality.

Other improvements in environmental conditions have been documented, but they are not causally attributable to the multilateral governance efforts discussed in this chapter. Ronald Mitchell calls these "spurious accomplishments." The intensity of materials usage in modern industrial economies has declined, as has the energy intensity of modern advanced industrial societies. Energy and materials usage is growing disconnected from economic growth. The spread of wastewater treatment plants, and thus the reductions in contamination of many freshwater resources, is attributable to broader growth of economic prosperity in many developing countries.

LESSONS LEARNED ABOUT ENVIRONMENTAL GOVERNANCE

International relations studies of international environmental politics have proliferated since the early 1970s.[15] The literature began by documenting global environmental harm and trying to explain the various reasons for such widespread unanticipated consequences from actions that were not ill intentioned. More recently, international relations scholarship has begun to look at explanations of collective responses to shared environmental threats. Most explanations of international environmental governance study the five groups of actors involved in environmental governance and their interactions: national leadership, international institutions, NGOs and civil society, consensual knowledge, domestic politics, and multinational corporations (MNCs). Most work has focused on the interplay of institutions and knowledge. Domestic pressure, NGOs and civil society, and MNCs have only recently come to play significant roles. This section first explores the roles of each of these actors in environmental governance. It then examines environmental governance within the framework of this book—agenda setting, negotiations, compliance, and reactions to noncompliance—while noting the imaginative and novel practices that may result from different stages of international governance.

Role of the Main Actors in Environmental Governance

National Leadership. States are the legal authorities responsible for adopting treaties, and they are increasingly subject to influence from a variety of other actors. However, state leadership has not played an especially important role in international environmental politics. In fact, much successful cooperation actually has occurred in the absence of strong state leadership, and the United States—the presumptive international hegemon—has not demonstrated any systematic pattern of behavior across environmental regimes in which it has been involved.[16] The United States has vigorously promoted strong environmental regimes for stratospheric ozone protection, vigorously opposed strong environmental regimes for biodiversity, and straddled the fence on climate change and many regional seas arrangements. Congress has held only a few hearings on issues other than climate change and these only after 1989. At times the United States has been a unilateral leader, for example, in trying to stem operational oil pollution and pushing for the passage of requirements for double-hull tankers—even in the absence of harmonized policies by other states. The United States has been highly selective, however, in its attention to UNEP activities, of which it is the largest funder.

Robert Paarlberg attributes this inconsistency in U.S. foreign environmental policy to the separation of powers and the pluralist nature of the American state.[17] Congress is responsive to domestic groups, and domestic interests are highly issue-specific.

Thus, in the case of ozone depletion, where domestic environmental coalitions have been dominant, the United States has taken a leadership role. In other cases, such as biodiversity and climate change, where environmental groups have been weaker than their industry counterparts, the United States has opposed international environmental efforts.

International Institutions. Formal international institutions, when permitted by their member states, can play an important role in promoting environmental governance and sustainable development. They can help to build more comprehensive regimes and encourage compliance by providing a venue for international cooperation, building national capacity, and strengthening political will. In particular, this means providing politically tractable instruments to groups within countries that are interested in, for example, supporting sustainable development and marine protection, and building stable political coalitions that can press their governments and others to support such issues.

Major research by international relations scholars conducted in the 1980s and 1990s identified a variety of properties that helped international organizations to effectively steer environmental governance.[18] Influential institutions were able to provide a forum for international negotiations. Their members met often to maintain the political saliency of certain issues. It also helped to convene periodic high-level meetings, so that parliamentary environmental ministers could garner the domestic political benefits of being seen as environmental leaders by their constituencies. For instance, the North Sea ministerial conferences are convened roughly every three years, although annual lower-level meetings are held within the Paris and Oslo Commissions. UNCED negotiations were held for nearly two weeks, capped by a three-day ministerial session. Linkages among institutions—such as the partially overlapping memberships of the European Union, the Oslo and Paris Commissions for the North Sea, and the Baltic Commission—amplify the influence of any one institution and regional decision by providing a political mechanism for having the policies endorsed in other institutions as well, and thus spread the number of countries and environmental media subject to environmental controls. Links between the UN Economic Commission for Europe (UNECE) and the European Union (EU) have a similar salutary effect on air pollution regulations for Europe.

Oran Young and Robert Keohane have suggested that institutions with small numbers of members, at least under seven, are likely to be more effective than those with larger memberships, because diplomacy is easier and not as many countries' activities will have to be monitored for compliance. This would suggest that in negotiations regional bodies are preferable to global, universal bodies, or that some form of weighted or bloc voting should be developed to streamline negotiations. In practice, though, the most influential institutions have been of intermediate size: UNEP has a governing council of fifty-four members, the UNECE has fifty-five members, and strong regimes have emerged from regions with as many as sixteen participants in the Mediterranean Action Plan.

Institutions that can build national environmental concern are also more likely to exercise influence in international environmental governance. The key activities in this effort include: popularizing issues, setting agendas, generating new information, encouraging public participation, public education, and engaging in training programs, involving new actors (including NGOs), requiring national reporting, environmental monitoring, and conducting policy verification of states' compliance activities.

Influential international institutions also have the ability to build member states' administrative and political national capacity for environmental protection. National capacity can be improved by the provision of environmental information, as well as through environmental monitoring activities, training programs for government officials, the transfer of technology, and the supply of financial assistance. Through public education and the dissemination of information, the capacity of the public to engage effectively in national environmental discussions can also be improved.

Not all international organizations have these properties. The UNCSD, for example, lacks resources to advance the sustainable development agenda. In the environmental realm, the most influential international organizations have been the World Bank, the UNEP, and the UNECE. These are organizations whose members have endowed them with sufficient resources to play an important role in international environmental politics, and they operate as autonomous actors and "provide independent inputs into the policy process, or somehow amplify the outputs of the process."[19] In UNEP's case, this autonomy was the result of widespread popular concern with the environment at the time of its creation, and the absence of profound geopolitical schisms associated with its mission. Established in 1972 during a period of détente, the UNEP was spared the geopolitical calculations that informed the creation of most UN bodies after World War II. Similarly, the UNECE is a détente body, and the World Bank became environmentally constructive after 1986, when concern in the United States led to profound institutional reforms in the organization.

These institutions have been able to play a role independent from the interests of their member states because their missions command widespread support, their governing bodies are devoid of deep political schisms, they have been led by deft executive heads, they command sufficient financial resources, they have maintained relationships with outside policy networks, and their staffs have been recruited based on merit. In addition, institutionalized science leads to regimes that are more comprehensive, more judicious, and slower to negotiate than regimes that are negotiated through institutions in which science is not allowed to play a significant role, or where scientific consensus does not exist.

UNEP has played a powerful role in environmental protection the last thirty years. It has successfully maintained political support for its activities from the Group of Seventy-Seven (G-77). With a staff of less than 200 professionals and a budget now on the order of $100 million a year, UNEP has led global environmental monitoring efforts, catalyzed environmental protection activities in other UN bodies, served as the environmental conscience of the UN system, and sponsored the conclusion of dozens of international environmental treaties.

Despite these successes in the 1990s, the United States grew disillusioned with UNEP's influence and its ability to drive negotiations beyond what the United States was willing to tolerate in both climate change and biodiversity. Indeed, the United States has supported the World Bank in its endeavors and tried to create organizational structures from scratch for climate change negotiations that did not involve UNEP. More recently, the United States has become more willing again to rely on UNEP for regime creation, as seen by the recent development of a Persistent Organic Pollutants Protocol and global guidelines on land-based sources of pollution. Given the proliferation of international institutions with environmental competencies, the United States no longer has to rely on UNEP for developing all international environmental regimes and thus only defers to UNEP when the United States already supports strong environmental controls on a particular issue.

NGOs and Civil Society.   Analysts have often stressed the importance of NGOs and civil society in international environmental politics.[20] They highlight, in particular, that NGOs can shape public perceptions and values about the environment and press governments to adopt and comply with more vigorous environmental positions. UNCED was a transformational international conference at which NGOs exercised a strong presence.

Although potentially contributing to effective regional governance, domestic pressure and NGOs have not played a strong role in environmental governance to date.[21] In Europe, concern about the environment was very modest until the late 1980s and only took off in the rest of the world in the early 1990s. A Gallup poll prepared for UNCED in 1992 noted increased worldwide concern for the environment, but it also suggested very little interest on transboundary and global issues. Public opinion seemed highly issue specific, such as the sites for individual factories rather than developing regional plans.[22]

In general, NGOs, when involved in environmental regimes, have expressed preference for pursuing principled norms and pressing for strong commitments of principles to which governments may subsequently be held accountable. Most NGOs avoid recourse to precise formulations of regime rules, because they often lack the resources to carefully observe compliance. NGOs' own abilities to garner financial resources from public contributions often rest on their ability to put forward principled positions and to embarrass governments and firms found in violation of their commitments. NGOs prefer regimes based on the prohibition of certain activities, rather than efforts to shape tolerable ranges of action (there is a parallel here between disarmament and arms control) or other doctrinal approaches such as the precautionary principle, which urges firms and governments to exercise environmental caution even in the absence of scientific consensus that specific activities may cause environmental damage.[23]

For instance, Greenpeace has been seeking to establish a moratorium on whaling—in the face of more nuanced schedules of tolerable whaling harvests suggested by cetologists, estimates of the population dynamics, and degree of threat to individual whale species—and the creation of a marine sanctuary in the Southern Ocean. In the North Sea, Greenpeace's Brent Spar campaign successfully induced Shell Oil to dispose of obsolete oil drilling platforms on shore, rather than at sea, with higher economic costs but with clearly higher environmental benefits. With regard to the Convention on Trade in Endangered Species (CITES), Greenpeace has pushed to ban poaching of endangered species, rather than set tolerable limits on takings.

Knowledge and Epistemic Communities.   Transnational networks of policy professionals who share common values and causal understandings, called epistemic communities, are the principle developers and disseminators of new scientific understandings for public policy. When they become involved in national policy making, epistemic community members inform national preferences and policy agendas with their own preferred visions. Epistemic community members have typically served as consultants to national governments engaged in environmental negotiations and as officials at international institutions engaged in environmental politics (most notably UNEP, UNECE, and the World Bank). Epistemic communities often work in conjunction with broader policy networks, functional bureaucrats, transnational scientists, NGOs, and international civil servants.[24]

Members of epistemic communities seek to introduce national measures consistent with their beliefs and utilize the enforcement mechanisms of the bureaucratic units in which they operate. Patterns of regime support and compliance are thus based on the extent to which these members are able to acquire influential positions in national administrations and international institutions.

The epistemic community pattern may have differential impacts on advanced industrialized and developing countries. Advanced industrial countries, given their greater resources and ability to evaluate new information, are more likely to defer to transnational scientific advice. Epistemic communities are most likely to gain prompt entrée in democratic states that have a high degree of technical competency in the substantive area in question. Conversely, many developing countries are highly suspicious of foreign technical advice and will only heed scientific advice provided through domestic channels. The development of indigenous scientific capability reinforces the authority of those scientists giving advice to decision makers.

In the environmental realm, epistemic communities have been active in negotiating and implementing a number of regimes on specific topics. Epistemic community members have a shared understanding of complex systems requiring management subject to consensus about the tolerable concentrations of contaminants that individual ecosystems can sustain. For instance, when involved in negotiating the Montreal Ozone Protocol, atmospheric chemists identified substances to control that had the highest ozone-depleting potential and set reduction targets to achieve environmentally sustainable goals. In the Mediterranean, oceanographers, marine biologists, engineers, and environmental planners helped to establish emission and ambient standards for individual substances that reflected the scientists' understanding of the Mediterranean's ability to recycle wastes. They also helped to design national policy programs to reduce coastal zone stresses. Scientists involved in making multilateral environmental policy agree that the environment must be preserved, but that emissions need not be reduced to zero. Rather, they argue, emissions should be controlled subject to the scientific consensus about the behavior of the particular ecosystems with which policy makers are concerned. The "critical loads" concept that underlies efforts to reduce European acid rain uses a similar approach.

Finally, epistemic communities seek to develop common national policies that will ultimately reduce environmental stresses, rather than merely stipulate uniform environmental standards for governments. In the Mediterranean, for example, treaty negotiations on pollution control standards have been conducted in parallel with policy research on demographic patterns, land-use planning, and broader coastal zone management, so that governments would be able to make more macroeconomic policy changes that would be environmentally beneficial as well as focusing narrowly on drafting pollution control standards.

Multinational Corporations. MNCs were largely absent from international environmental politics until the creation of UNCED. Initially, most firms seemed to misjudge the depth of environmental concern and the potential influence of scientists and international institutions. Analysts suggest that MNCs are important forces for environmental improvement if they choose to use green and efficient technology and to develop new cleaner products and production techniques. Institutionally, MNCs they have helped to provide information exchange about timely and valuable technologies.

Many MNCs have guidelines and codes of conduct for environmental practices, ecological accounting procedures, and public environmental accounting, either through the International Standards Organization's ISO 14000 procedures for conducting environmental audits or through voluntary sectoral guidelines developed by industry groups.[25] Some of the world's largest MNCs associated with the Business Council for Sustainable Development, an industry forum created before UNCED to facilitate input from MNCs, have called for global uniform environmental standards based on some of the most stringent national measures currently in force. For obvious reasons, the private sector prefers voluntary standards over regulation. Further, MNCs argue that they are more dynamic over the long run when they can avoid locking in premature or obsolete technologies into command-and-control–based policies.

International Relations of the Environment. Analysts of international environmental politics fall into one of two schools of thought: the transformative school and the neoliberal institutionalist school.[26] Members of both schools aspire to make treaties that can be negotiated promptly, quickly enter into force, enjoy widespread compliance, are designed to address the key environmental threats confronting the parties, and are likely to yield significant improvements in the quality of the environmental medium in question. All agree that most regime dynamics are principally the consequence of the interplay of knowledge and institutional forces, with some reinforcing action from NGOs and possibly amplification by domestic politics in democratic societies.

On the one hand, a transformative view sees regimes as dynamic, open-ended social forces that evolve over time and may help to transform national calculations of self-interest as well as redistribute material capabilities among countries.[27] Peter Sand in 1990 listed a number of potentially transformative institutional activities.[28] This school sees uniform patterns across the stages of regime development, depending on the configuration of actors and influences at early stages of regime development. In this perspective, strong institutions capable of mobilizing and deploying ecological epistemic communities may be able to introduce new ecological perspectives on environmental policy making. Not all regimes are evolving, open processes. Transformative regimes are only likely to occur with particular configurations of institutional properties (strong institutions) combined with the presence of an epistemic community.

On the other hand, a more static view, associated with most neoliberal institutionalists, sees institutions as serving a more mechanical role—one that allows states to achieve preexisting goals. Institutions thus serve principally as formal arrangements to reduce transactions costs and increase the availability of useful information to state actors.

Of the two views, the dynamic school has been superior at accounting for changes over time in environmental governance because it has been better able to account for the mechanisms by which states' notions of the national environmental interest have changed as a consequence of their involvement in international environmental regimes and their exposure to international institutions.

Agenda Setting

Agendas are typically set by a highly publicized galvanizing event. For instance, the establishment of UNCHE followed in the wake of widespread concern about limits to growth, alarms about oil spills, and the unknown long residency times of inorganic chemicals in the environment. Mediterranean pollution control was spurred by Jacques Cousteau's widely publicized proclamations that the ocean was dying. The 1989 Basel Convention on the Control of Transboundary Movements of Hazardous Wastes and Their Disposal was catalyzed by the publicity accorded to the voyage of the toxic-waste-carrying barge Khia Khan that was denied dumping permission around the world. North Sea pollution control was similarly catalyzed by a similar waste-dumping episode, and the ozone regime has sparked alarms of seasonal Antarctic stratospheric ozone thinning.

Scientists, credible NGOs, and international institutions typically sound these alarms in high-level conferences. In the absence of such events, actors have used lower-profile meetings or even the media to launch a call for action. Once the alarm has been sounded, transnational policy networks try to keep the issue politically salient by convening workshops, publishing, and speaking out. Few national environmental agencies have sufficient international standing or conduct monitoring of truly global or transboundary ecosystems to sound the alarm. Some international organizations and regime secretariats have been created to perform selective environmental monitoring of the ecosystems within their regulatory purview, although they are seldom prompt or particularly accurate.

Agenda setting has two dimensions. The first is to get the issue onto the international agenda and into negotiations. More subtle and important in the long term is the framing of the issue that can greatly influence the final outcome or predispose the subsequent field of possible outcomes. If an authoritative actor sets the agenda, then the particular presentation and institutional venue in which the agenda is set will have lasting influence over subsequent negotiations. The rhetoric associated with an issue will establish a baseline against which national positions must be couched (for example, environmental threats versus economic costs). The international institution in which the issue has been submitted will influence the array of actors likely to participate, the form of discourse, and the voting rules by which decisions will be reached (consider the consequence if GATT rather than UNEP had been made the principal international organization after UNCHE).

A consequence of agenda setting is to privilege subsequent types of collective responses. For instance, North Sea environmental threats were initially viewed as marine pollution problems that required the banning or control of certain contaminants. Thus, at later stages of the regime states banned offshore incineration, even though scientists did not widely regard this as a major source of marine pollution and it was considered a superior mode of waste disposal compared to storage on land. But if the frame had been one of waste reduction, then offshore incineration would have been encouraged as a more efficient means of disposal leading to less waste accumulation in Europe.

UNEP helped to set the international agenda for a variety of environmental issues and has helped to frame the way in which the issues were addressed. In 1981, for example, UNEP identified land-based sources of marine pollution, damage to the ozone layer, and the transport, handling, and disposal of toxic and hazardous waste as serious environmental concerns. Less urgent but still serious were lack of international cooperation in coastal zone management, soil erosion, transboundary air pollution, pollution of inland waterways, the absence of legal and administrative mechanisms for prevention or redress of pollution damage, as well as the methods of environmental impact assessment.[29]

At best, agenda setting has been haphazard. It has relied on prompt publicity recast about environmental disruptions. Not all alarms are heard by the media, however, and not all disasters generate policy responses. Conducting widespread environmental monitoring and publication of the results in, for example, the UNEP annual *State of the World Environment* reports and triennial *Global Environment Outlook* assessments, could improve ongoing monitoring of global ecosystems by among other things signaling early warnings for disruptions. If necessary, new regimes could be created or modifications made in existing regimes that are performing poorly. Appraisals of the environment are offered at annual meetings of regimes by secretariats, secretariats' networks, and the conferences of parties.

Standing monitoring bodies could also generate the information for triggering prompt responses to newly identified problems. The UN system is currently underinstitutionalized to perform this function, however, and there is also a need for a regularized early warning system. Creating standing bodies of environmental scientists—akin to the Group of Experts on Scientific Aspects of Marine Environment Protection (GESAMP) for marine issues or the IPCC for climate change—would make possible prompt environmental assessments and announcements of warnings, thus accelerating the agenda-setting process in environmental governance.

Negotiations and Regime Formation

International law can take one of two forms: "hard law" or "soft law." The overwhelming majority of international environmental obligations are granted in hard law as are environmental regimes, which are established by treaties. Soft-law commitments are expressed in, for example, conference declarations, UN resolutions, and the UNEP nonbinding guidelines drawn up between 1978 and 1987 covering ten areas of environmental management: managing shared natural resources (1978), weather modification (1980), offshore mining and drilling (1982), a World Charter for Nature (1982), banned and severely restricted chemicals (1984), marine pollution from land-based sources (1985), environmentally sound management of hazardous wastes (1987), environmental impact assessment (1987), and the exchange of information about chemicals in international trade (1987).

Soft law can also be used as a precursor to hard-law instruments. Soft-law instruments can establish norms and habits. UNCHE adopted the Stockholm Declaration, establishing twenty-six principles of behavior and responsibility to serve as the basis for future legally binding multilateral accords. The Action Plan for the Human Environment specified 109 recommendations in the areas of environmental assessment, environmental management, and supporting institutional measures. UNCED adopted the 1992 Rio Declaration with 27 principles guiding environmental action and a sweeping environmental policy to promote sustainability (Agenda 21), with 2,509 specific recommendations applying to states, international institutions, and members of civil society.[30]

In the environmental area, diplomats generally fall back on soft law when there is insufficient political support for anything stronger or as an initial step to achieve more significant commitments in the future. For instance, UNEP's voluntary guidelines on hazardous waste and toxic chemical management, which were initially developed by expert groups and endorsed by the governing council, served as the foundation for later treaties on the transport of hazardous wastes and persistent organic pollutants. In adopting a soft-law principle, diplomats also do not have to worry about a contentious ratification process or an unfriendly reception by Congress or parliament.

There are three types of environmental treaties and regimes: social learning, institutional bargaining, and least-common-denominator results.[31] Each is characterized by a distinctive set of discrete political patterns of participation, agenda setting, interest formulation, compromise, and resilience, and each is associated with discrete configurations of actors and influence.

Most environmental regimes have a strong command-and-control orientation, rather than market-based instruments or the precautionary principle. Despite current policy debates in climate change discussions about the efficiency gains from the use of market instruments in environmental regimes, for example, or the NGO arguments about the desirability of the precautionary principle, regimes retain a presumptive approach based on uniform cuts or scientifically derived differential obligations. The absence of economic frames is largely due to control of negotiations by international institutions staffed principally by environmental scientists rather than by economists. The Bretton Woods institutions, which are dominated by economic styles of policy making, were not active in international environmental negotiations until the 1990s, so that the vast majority of treaties concluded before the 1990s reflected an environmentalist approach to command-and-control-type environmental policy making.

When regimes are negotiated with the involvement of epistemic communities and strong international institutions, they develop through a process of "social learning." Negotiations occur within a scientific discourse, in which political debate and compromise reflect expert consensus on the behavior of ecosystems and their ability to sustain stress. The substance of regimes reflects scientific consensus about the most important environmental threats, and negotiated standards reflect consensus about the degree of environmental stress the target environment can sustain. Social learning generates treaties with differentiated national obligations and substantive commitments, based on expert consensus on causes and environmental effects. For instance, the 1980 Land-Based Sources Protocol for the Mediterranean requires more stringent emission controls on the industrialized countries than on the developing countries, because the magnitude of degradation of the northern coast of the Mediterranean was much more severe than it was on the southern coast.

The most effective regimes are those in which strong norms, institutions, and science have all been brought to bear. Enduring organizations are built around clear normative references supported by a body of knowledge. Institutionalized science leads to regimes that are more comprehensive and judicious than regimes negotiated through institutions in which science is not allowed to play a significant role or for issues for which scientific consensus does not exist. Regimes developed through social learning include the stratospheric ozone protection regime, the 1979 Geneva Convention on Long-Range Transboundary Air Pollution (LRTAP), subsequent treaties addressing European acid rain, and pollution control efforts for the Mediterranean, Persian Gulf, South Pacific, and South East Pacific.

Maurice Strong, Secretary-General of UNCHE and UNCED and UNEP's first executive director, helped design the outlines of this process of social learning. Strong believed that "the policy is the process": that is, by generating an open political process in which states are exposed to consensual science, government officials may be persuaded to adopt more sustainable policies, and individual scientists may gain heightened political profiles at home that may ultimately increase their effectiveness as well. Most social learning treaties have standing environmental monitoring and research committees, to provide timely warnings of new problems, monitor achievements of regime goals, and educate politicians and policy makers on environmental issues.

However, social learning takes time. Comprehensive treaties are slower to negotiate than are others, because they require persuasion and consensus rather than mere compromise. From a policy perspective, though, comprehensive regimes are likely to be superior in their ability to protect the environment in a cost-effective and politically acceptable manner.[32] Moreover, treaties developed with help from the scientific community typically enter into force more rapidly than without it, presumably because of the weight that involvement of scientists carries in the ratification process.[33]

Strong institutions alone yield regimes concluded through institutional bargaining. Goals are reached through political compromise and thus are less likely to generate technical results at an optimal economic cost than are arrangements worked out in conjunction with experts. Environmental regimes developed through institutional bargaining contain legal efforts that are uniform and commitments that tend to entail across-the-board emission cuts. A typical example of institutional bargaining is the 1990 North Sea Ministerial Declaration calling for 50 percent reductions for thirty-seven pollutants and 70 percent reductions for emissions of dioxins, mercury, cadmium, and lead. The coastal states adopted 30 and 50 percent cuts on emissions of more than thirty chemicals into the sea. The percentages were chosen based on their political appeal, not on scientific conclusion. Interestingly, it is not clear if the thirty chemicals identified in the agreement are in fact the most important contaminants. It is also unclear what the environmental effects will be of achieving the mandated cuts.

Limiting negotiations to small groups or bargaining blocs accelerates negotiations because logistically these are more efficient, and there are usually fewer naysayers.[34] This method was useful in attaining agreement in European acid rain negotiations and is consistent with bargaining theorists' focus on "k-groups."[35] If not carefully designed, however, limited negotiations may alienate developing countries if they are not members of the bargaining bloc. Because developing countries control so many votes in UN-sponsored negotiations, their opposition may scuttle any talks.

Horizontal linkage between institutions, both functionally and geographically, has allowed environmentally progressive states to "forum shop" (that is, to find institutions likely to be receptive to their ideas). For instance, a decision by a group of states to control the emission of certain contaminants into the North Sea could spur another group of perhaps some of the same states to push for similar control in the Black Sea. Similarly, the EU and UNECE agreed on setting standards on sulfur emissions in Europe. Attention to equity concerns did not permeate regime rules, although they were widely expressed by developing countries.

Finally, with only thin institutional contexts and no epistemic communities, states create regimes based on a least-common-denominator pattern. Regimes in this category are grounded in weak treaties with only limited national obligations. They are unlikely to have a strong impact on environmental quality. In the absence of any compelling external political pressure to induce states to adopt strong environmental treaties, the most vocal and reluctant party will exercise the most influence in seeking compromise. Consequently, in the absence of strong institutions or persuasive scientific consensus, negotiations will be driven by a race to the bottom because collective agreement must be acceptable to the least willing (and dirtiest) participant. Most multilateral fisheries agreements have been of this type, as have efforts to protect the Caribbean, West African seas, and East African seas. Similar difficulties also marred talk on the North Sea until 1987, when the negotiations were transferred from low-profile bureaucratic forums to higher profile ministerial meetings at which environmental ministers had an incentive to reach an understanding—and in the process distinguish themselves to be environmentally progressive to their increasingly green domestic constituencies.

Social learning is becoming increasingly common, as a result of the growing institutionalization of ecological understanding, and a greater willingness among states to defer to key institutions that are to some extent beyond the immediate control of major states. As the scientific understanding of different ecosystems has improved, ecological epistemic communities have grown more vocal. Regime dynamics are thus increasingly driven by the spread of consensual knowledge about the environment and in turn have helped to increase the number of epistemic communities across issue areas.

UNEP has developed a growing confidence in exercising leadership in a wide variety of environmental negotiations, including those focused on pollution, ozone protection, and the preservation of natural habitats. The UNECE has been a leader in European acid rain, using many of the same techniques to institutionalize the role of science. Some of the key secretariat members in UNECE once worked in UNEP and with UNEP "administered regimes." The principal resources that helped these institutions to institutionalize knowledge included their access to and control over technology transfer, training, and public education. In addition, high-tech, high-profile diplomatic meetings exposed political leaders to new ideas and to networks of experts. With the growth of domestic environmental consciousness and the end of the Cold War, governments have been increasingly willing to grant a greater autonomy to international institutions that they believe would help improve the environment.

Mostafa Tolba has identified several techniques that he argues helped UNEP move along negotiations of environmental agreements: the use of selective incentives in treaties, differential obligations, regionalization, and the promotion of overachievement of environmental goals by lead countries.[36] Tolba does not specify when such techniques are likely to be attractive or on which types of countries they may exercise an influence. Differential obligations will appeal to developing countries that are worried about equity considerations in treaties. The application of differential obligations is a signal that the treaties reflect their norms of equity. In general, these are techniques that can be applied only if the negotiators are willing to accept them (that is, that little substantive disagreement exists).

Environmental lawyers have developed a variety of legal innovations to accelerate the regime formation process and to make treaties more comprehensive. These include signing framework treaties that are tied to specific protocols, drafting black lists that ban highly toxic substances and gray lists that regulate less toxic substances, allowing modification of these lists by expert agreement without having to reconvene the political parties, pursuing an iterated negotiating process for each regime so that individual problems get addressed separately while the corpus of the regime grows over time, establishing trust funds so that regimes may be self-supporting, and creating committees for monitoring treaty compliance.[37] The Montreal Ozone Protocol, for example, has eliminated a number of ozone-depleting substances by allowing the Conference of Parties to approve environmental regulations without having to go through governmental ratification.

Any of these techniques are widely used and help to provide the institutional framework in which new perspectives and actors can participate in regime development and promote social learning. The social learning regimes have been concluded using these diplomatic techniques.

Other reviews of social learning efforts provide a complementary set of lessons about how to generate scientific consensus within environmental regimes. First, an epistemic community's most important political resource is its reputation for impartiality (coupled with its own socialized consensus process for truth). Members of the epistemic community are thus likely to give advice that will be relatively untainted politically, and decision makers, in turn, are likely to treat such advice with confidence. Consequently, epistemic communities are most influential when scientific consensus precedes the policy negotiations. In instances when consensus is being built concurrently with policy talks, the network must be protected from overt political influence.

Based on comparative studies of most of the social learning regimes, including UNEP's Regional Seas Program and UNECE's efforts for European acid rain control, the following lessons about how to build policy networks of scientific expertise for environmental governance can be drawn.[38]

Scientific policy networks are not self-organizing. International institutions had to provide the initiative to identify and organize people with shared beliefs and understandings. Once organized within the institutional framework provided by UNEP, these individuals were able to exchange information and operate as a policy network.

UNEP carefully surveyed the population of marine scientists in the Mediterranean to assure a commonality of views. In the Mediterranean, a UNEP consultant spent nine months visiting national laboratories around the region to inventory national capabilities and to build a scientific network before any meetings were convened. UNEP then carefully recruited individuals, paying particular attention to the scientific reputations of the national and regional institutions from which they recruited to help assure that those chosen would be able to contribute to collective monitoring, research, and policy. They based recruiting decisions on individuals' professional credentials and networking ability. UNEP avoided relying on any one national institution to provide research and training, out of a concern that this could compromise the political authority of the work and make longer-term financial support contingent on capricious national science budgets. UNEP provided professional outlets for members by organizing conferences and publications in refereed professional journals, which enhanced the domestic profile of individual scientists who could then be recruited to fill positions in national administrations.

UNEP now recognizes that it is necessary to maintain momentum within the scientific community by continuing to sponsor projects and make research opportunities available so those members do not drift away. In the Mediterranean, collective efforts have slowed tremendously because the first generation of epistemic community members have retired or moved on to other projects and have not been replaced within the UNEP network. Maintaining a vital scientific enterprise prevents the need of having to reconstitute the community every time a new problem emerges. In the Regional Seas Program, UNEP provided opportunities for exchanges of experts among institutions, countries, and even regimes to encourage the dissemination of knowledge and experiences and to strengthen environmental networks. At the same time, however, UNEP had to strive, however, to avoid spreading the network too thin and overloading key individuals with networking and administrative responsibilities.

UNEP and other institutions have taken care to create international interdisciplinary panels for environmental risk assessment. This is vital to ensure a network of experts free of state influence. They selected individuals for both their areas of expertise and their ability to work with experts from other field. Institutions sought to ensure the participation of individuals from multiple scientific disciplines to avoid capture of the network by any one scientific discipline or school of analysis, because this would limit the ability of the policy advice to capture externalities. It would also undermine the political authority of the experts if they were not seen as impartial. UNEP avoided government-nominated scientists, choosing instead to designate experts itself. That governments have sometimes appointed scientists has compromised the authority of the policy panels they sit on—including those of the IPCC. International institutions arranged for focused interactions among scientists, diplomats, and policy makers to discuss the technical substance of the issues. In European discussions on acid rain, this proved an effective technique for educating diplomats about the technical aspects of sulfur emissions, and for familiarizing them with the critical loads approach to policy making. By encouraging environmental ministry officials to attend international meetings, UNECE and the International Institute for Applied Systems Analysis (IIASA) were able to expand and reinforce membership in transnational policy networks. IIASA was responsible for modeling transport patterns and the environmental efforts of acidic depositions in different ecosystems, and IIASA modelers were able to explain their findings to diplomats.

A comparison of cases and the lessons above yield some guidelines for building social learning dynamics into international environmental negotiations. Relying on thick international institutions provides the basis for independent political planning and deploying sufficient institutional resources to be able to influence the environmental positions of many governments. The lessons about the care and feeding of scientific networks provide some ideas for how to design and organize a scientific network for use in multilateral environmental regime making. It must be remembered that scientific consensus and the existence of a transnational epistemic community are not always present. In their absence, institutional bargaining is the best prospect for regime development.

Compliance

Discussions about the determinants of compliance with environmental regimes have been extensive.[39] This is a particularly important theme, because not all MEAs are in effect. Most still require the participation and ratification of one major polluting party, and the entry into force after ratification is often disappointingly slow. For example, the United States is not a party to the Kyoto Protocol, and the EU Commission often finds that as many as half of its members are not carrying out their obligations under some EU environmental directives.

In fact, information on compliance and effectiveness is available for only a small number of the seventy major international environmental treaties that were concluded after UNCHE and are currently in force. The results are highly mixed across the nineteen treaties for which there is evidence. It seems that if there were widespread state compliance with international environmental treaties, then international relations scholars would have more data about the subject, and analysts would know more about patterns and determinants of compliance. The relative ignorance about the topic, seen politically, is caused by an absence of information or reluctance on the parts of states to reveal information on noncompliance because it may be embarrassing before domestic or foreign audiences.

Consequently, most studies of compliance proceed from more general insights about compliance with international law in other functional areas. Recent studies by Harold Jacobson and Edith Brown Weiss, and by David Victor, Kal Raustiala, and Eugene Skolnikoff develop a number of complementary hypotheses about factors that may influence state compliance with environmental commitments.[40] Both works proceed from more general insights about compliance with international law in other functional areas.

Most analysts agree that implementation requires states to enjoy the political will and bureaucratic or administrative capacity to enforce regimes.[41] Implementation with environmental commitments is usually a matter of calculation because compliance entails economic costs. Many industrialized societies have the capacity to comply, but the political will is less predictable. In developing countries and economies in transition, states lack the institutional capacity—and often the political will—to carry out their obligations. In many newly industrialized countries, political will is also absent, due to the national priority accorded to economic development, even if capacity exists.

Not all countries attach the same degree of importance to compliance. In the United States, diplomats like to talk of a culture of compliance: the United States does not like to sign treaties with which it will not comply, or with which others will not comply. Diplomats are worried that Congress will not ratify a treaty that will commit U.S. financial resources when others may not reciprocate. But in practice, the United States will often tolerate escape clauses or overlook noncompliance out of a recognition that other countries are less concerned about compliance or that other parties may be able to comply later on even if they cannot comply immediately. Most other countries are much less insistent on firm compliance provisions, and some countries may actually prefer not to have stringent compliance requirements as they wish to show environmental concern but are unable to enforce the law. For instance, Eastern European governments have signed treaties knowing they could not satisfy their requirements—such as European acid rain commitments—hoping that by signaling a desire to comply, they might receive financial support to help facilitate future compliance. They further hope that it will indicate their subscription to broader norms supported by other institutions they hope to join one day (such as the EU). In short, compliance decisions are often taken independently of decisions about joining a regime, and the United States should display greater tolerance of marginal noncompliance by nondemocratic countries in the hope of being able to improve the compliance process over the longer term.

Harold Jacobson and Edith Brown Weiss develop three factors that may influence the decision to comply with environmental regulations: characteristics of the activity involved, characteristics of the treaty or regime, and the international environment.[42] The major characteristics of the activity include a relatively small number of actors, so that supervision of compliance is easy; the availability of economic incentives for compliance; and the involvement of a small number of MNCs in the activity, so that few activities have to be controlled. In addition, because of concern for their global reputations, MNCs may be willing to eliminate environmentally unfriendly activities. Still, not all MNCs are equally concerned about their reputations. Those that are likely to help states comply with strong environmental obligations have exposure in markets where they are prone to consumer boycotts. Thus, Jacobson and Weiss add a fourth dimension to the characteristic of the activity: the environmentally degrading activity must be concentrated in major countries, where states are capable of exercising regulatory control, and citizens or NGOs have recourse to the legal system.

Jacobson and Weiss identify eight factors characteristic of the treaty or regime that may also influence compliance: perceived equity of the obligations, so that developing countries will be willing to commit scarce resources to compliance; clearly defined obligations, so that noncompliance may be readily identifiable and states would worry about their reputations if they did not comply; the availability of scientific and technical advice; reporting requirements on compliance; the provision of other forms of monitoring of state behavior; an independent and technically able secretariat; informational, financial, and technological incentives; and sanctions for noncompliance.

They also specify six background factors that may encourage state compliance: major international conferences; worldwide media and public opinion; NGOs; a critical mass of countries already adhering to the treaty; the involvement of international organizations; and international financial institutions that provide monetary incentives. Further discussion of each factor and the cluster of factors is not necessary because all the analysis by Jacobson and Weiss and by Victor, Raustiala, and Skolnikoff is explicit that each factor is indeterminate. Jacobson and Weiss argue that "each factor interacts with the others to produce a combined effect on implementation, compliance, and effectiveness."[43] Victor, Raustiala, and Skolnikoff conclude that the influence of each factor varies by case and by target country.[44] They argue that "different national circumstances have led countries to take different approaches," but that compliance more generally is positively affected by a system of interacting influences. In short, more is better, and it is difficult to differentiate the tangible impacts of each factor.

Rather, lessons about compliance focus on the aggregation of factors, subject to the application of some background innovations involved with international society, such as the influence of soft law, a culture of compliance, and the interaction of institutions and policy networks to induce states to comply with commitments out of broader notions of national interest rather than any particular concern about environmental protection. The current array of compliance-related factors remains weak and requires strengthening if it is to truly affect state compliance decisions.

Weiss offers some propositions about general lessons for facilitating or permissive factors that may contribute to compliance.[45] She stresses the influence of dense linkages between treaties, so that commitments in one area are substantively connected with those in others. When international relations are based on a tight network of interactions with other actors, concerns about reputation and concessions in linked negotiations may encourage states to live up to their obligations. Related to this is the notion of an ongoing relationship among the participants, which is likely to have similar effects. In addition, norms of compliance may shape states' decisions. Institutional structures that encourage transparency and accountability may reinforce a culture of compliance. Threats of sanctions for noncompliance may also induce states to fulfill their obligations. Finally, if states believe that their public welfare and ecological survival will be satisfied by compliance, then they are also more likely to comply.

In the following section, some of the more powerful propositions about compliance are discussed. These propositions come from the works previously discussed as well as from the broader international relations literature on international institutions.

Soft law may be more politically effective than hard law, although less environmentally beneficial. Weiss also suggests, along with Victor, that compliance with soft law may be easier than compliance with hard law and thus may be more effective. The appeal of this idea is that soft-law commitments may be established without a formal, difficult ratification process, yet states will choose to comply with those commitments through an array of domestic and institutional incentives. Yet this does not appear to be borne out in practice. Few soft-law obligations have the precision of hard law, so it is difficult to ascertain if states are in compliance. Moreover, many soft-law commitments, such as Agenda 21, call for expanded political participation, rather than for substantive policy decisions by governments. To the extent that such commitments are complied with, then, they would be merely instrumental to institutional and political capacity for compliance. However, even this does not always appear to be true. For example, the 1992 Climate Change Convention commitments are in essence voluntary but have not led to significant reductions in greenhouse gas emissions in most of the world, nor have they significantly added to the political constituency behind such efforts.

A culture of international compliance can improve national compliance. Most neoliberal institutionalist analysts believe that if a set of aspirations and shared expectations about compliance exists, reinforced by a dense set of interlocking institutions, then states (and firms) may have incentives to comply with their international commitments. The problem for compliance in the environmental realm, compared to other areas of international relations, is that no real culture of compliance with international environmental law exists, and the density of relationships in the environmental realm remains fairly thin. Broader norms of environmental protection are not widely accepted by governments, in part because of the relatively recent entry of environmental issues onto the international agenda. The Stockholm Declaration, for instance, is singularly ambivalent in its assertion that states with an obligation to maintain resource quality can still enjoy full national sovereignty. The development of an Earth Charter and other normative instruments of soft law could help build the foundations for such a compliance culture.

Linkages between issues, between institutions, and between governments are not as dense in the environmental arena as they are in others, particularly those focused on economic issues. Although density of linkages between institutions and policy networks has contributed to regime formation, the hurdles to compliance are also higher. The effects of national environmental practices do link countries closely, but these links are not always well understood or recognized by decision makers or publics. Environmental regimes are not tightly linked together because their policy networks seldom overlap. Problems in different environmental media are addressed by different government agencies with only a weak environmental body coordinating them. There are no mechanisms either within or between governments to tie together the policy networks of various environmental regimes. In addition, no single environmental regime has a strong social or cultural identity. Consequently, the actors responsible for compliance in one environmental regime have no reason to consider seriously the nature of their broader involvement with international society.

The inclusion of target groups in environmental regimes may help to encourage compliance and effectiveness. The strongest finding of Victor, Raustiala, and Skolnikoff is that the participation of target groups in multilateral negotiations and institutions can improve compliance. An example of this is the design standards of the International Convention for the Prevention of Pollution from Ships (MARPOL), which seek to reduce operational oil pollution from tankers. Enforcement falls, in practice, to the insurance industry, because insurance providers do not want to be liable for oil spill cleanups or for paying for faulty tankers. Consequently shipyards and tanker owners have no choice but to comply with the state's written regime.[46] In climate change, Greenpeace has been trying to involve the insurance industry by publicizing the unusual frequency and expense of cleanups after major weather-related disasters (such as hurricanes) that Greenpeace argues are the consequence of global warming. Careful thought needs to be given to the potential role of the insurance industry in helping to improve compliance with other environmental regimes. Establishing key liability standards for pollution and ecosystem disruption in all environmental regimes would provide a strong motivating force for involving the insurance industry.

The involvement of key groups also helps to generate better information about policy options, technical feasibility, and environmental benefits, thus leading to more effective treaties and compliance. This is an interesting finding, because in the 1970s and 1980s most target groups opposed all international regimes and, when involved in the negotiations, would try to either dismiss the need for the regime or urge voluntary measures instead. For instance, in the Montreal Ozone Protocol, the initial response of the CFC manufacturers was to oppose any controls and to challenge the scientific authority behind calls for them. In MARPOL, tanker owners and shipyards opposed any tanker designs that would introduce additional production costs. Moreover, not all target groups contribute to compliance. So a tension is involved at the moment appropriate for including target groups in environmental governance: if they help design the regime they may develop weak measures that do not significantly contribute to improvements in environmental quality, yet it is difficult to involve them just at the compliance stage without having them involved in the drafting. Jacobson and Weiss note that timber companies actively oppose efforts for sustainable forestry within the International Tropical Timber Organization. There has to be an affinity between the potential for market gains for the target groups and compliance: the net benefits of pollution control must offset the additional costs of such control, which means that there have to be penalties for continuing to pollute and market opportunities for new product development. These conditions are likely only for highly profitable firms in countries where they justly anticipate regulatory costs or loss of reputation for noncompliance.

However, with the increase in domestic environmental consciousness, the heightened willingness in the industrialized societies to pay for green products, and the growth of demand for environmental cleanup technology, more firms may be interested in contributing to environmental negotiations and adhering to their commitments than in the past.

Compliance is most successful when it is within a system for implementation review. Compliance is the consequence of multiple interacting forces. For key groups to engage in compliance, they must be subject to accountability, review, and surveillance pressures. Victor, Raustiala, and Skolnikoff term the institutionalized arrangements through which parties share information, review performance, handle noncompliance, and adjust commitments a system for implementation review (SIR). Thus, they accurately conclude, actor groups and states must be bound together in a synergetic set of institutional forces that combine policy verification with participation.

No single SIR for environmental regulation exists. In practice, however, the enforcement of multilateral environmental regimes has occurred against a backdrop of decentralized systems for implementation review. Most international governance schemes have had to rely on a small number of institutional- and knowledge-based incentives to spur state compliance. The most important activities for inducing compliance have been environmental monitoring, policy verification, and technological and financial assistance. In addition, international institutions and NGOs have engaged in bureaucratic training programs and public and elite education to instill norms of environmental protection, a culture of compliance, and notions of environmental self-interest, as well as to increase the density of relationships among environmental actors.

Environmental monitoring contributes to compliance by providing information about the quality of the environment, and thus indirectly about whether a state's efforts are worthwhile and whether other states are living up to their obligations. It may also mobilize public concern and stimulate pressure for compliance.

Monitoring efforts worldwide remain largely the domain of governments, although most treaties require the provision of periodic reports to international authorities. National reporting to secretariats on state environmental protection activities (which may include monitoring environmental quality or providing information on compliance efforts) is often poor, and many secretariats lack the resources or authority to check data submitted by governments. A 1991 U.S. General Accounting Office survey found that only about 60 percent of the parties to the 1972 London Dumping Convention were complying with reporting obligations; only 30 percent of the members of the MARPOL convention on oil pollution submitted reports; and many reports under the Montreal Ozone Protocol and the Helsinki Sulfur Dioxide Protocol are incomplete and impossible to verify.[47] Reporting under the 1982 Memorandum of Understanding on Port State Control in Implementing Agreements on Maritime Safety and Protection of the Marine Environment is much better, suggesting that well-designed questionnaires may evoke higher response rates than poorly designed ones, and further research is necessary on optimal designs for reporting and verification questionnaires.

Many NGOs are now capable of monitoring environmental quality as well as national compliance and are becoming involved as a source of shadow verification of government obligations in the EU and elsewhere. Their activities help compensate for the dearth of reliable environmental quality data and also provide an independent quality check on data collected through other sources. Greenpeace International seeks to keep track of national compliance with many treaties, and the Natural Resources Defense Council collects data on national compliance with the FCCC. The World Conservation Union (IUCN) and Greenpeace also try to track national compliance with many of the species conservation treaties.

The World Meteorological Organization (WMO) and UNEP routinely monitor of atmospheric quality. UNEP, the Food and Agricultural Organization (FAO), and the World Health Organization (WHO) conduct studies of freshwater quality in lakes and river basins. UNEP and the Intergovernmental Oceanographic Commission (IOC) monitor the oceans. These efforts provide background information on environmental quality.

Much of the environment can be monitored remotely from satellites and does not require the active collection and submission of data by governments, although not all environmental conditions are equally accessible to remote monitoring. Remote sensing and satellite monitoring can enhance verification of trends in natural resource use and pollution from organic sources and from oil. It is also useful in monitoring levels and production of greenhouse gases, although double checking from ground-based instruments and by human personnel is still necessary to confirm remote sensing data. Satellite- and airplane-based monitoring is less effective at monitoring inorganic marine contamination and urban air quality, for instance, which requires localized sampling and monitoring. Institutional problems still exist with the use and dissemination of such remote sensing data once they have been collected.[48] With the proliferation of private satellites, NGOs will find it increasingly easy to acquire tailor-made monitoring data.

Direct verification of state compliance may affect state choices to comply. Prompt access to information about other's actions not only enhances early detection of violations but also reduces concerns of free riding. Also, by making information available of one's own activities, verification may indirectly deter noncompliance by increasing the likelihood of detection. To seriously influence compliance, verification data must be timely and reliable. Verification may not be equally feasible in all cases and is easier when the actions to be verified are large: that is, a few activities conducted by easy-to-identify actors.

Many actors are responsible for performing verification functions. Fifty-eight international environmental treaties stipulate some provisions for verification. Governments are required to produce verification reports in 72 percent of the treaties, although it is not specified to whom the reports are to be made available. Governments have to submit reports to international institutions in only 7 percent of the cases, and international institutions are held responsible for conducting verification studies in 3 percent. The remaining 18 percent are unspecified.

Policy verification may be most credible when not performed by states. Some international organizations conduct periodic verification assessments of national compliance with environmental standards. The OECD has been regarded as having successfully provided such assessments for a number of its members, publicizing infractions and identifying areas for improvement.

NGOs are also increasingly active in verifying state compliance with environmental accords, and the EU has sought to expand participation in its development of sectoral policies to include such alternate NGO submissions of information about compliance and noncompliance. In international regimes, Greenpeace now regularly monitors trade in hazardous wastes and in flora and fauna, and it publicizes shipments in violation of international treaties. TRAFFIC, the wildlife trade monitoring program of IUCN and the World Wildlife Fund, for instance, verifies compliance with the CITES regime on trade in endangered species. The publicity generated by these activities is often sufficient to pressure recipient governments to enforce their international commitments as well as to refuse entry of such products. Many NGOs have become virtual watchdogs over private activities in the field as well, replacing or supplementing the monitoring activities of national enforcement agencies. Because governments are often unwilling to cede the semblance of authority to NGOs, private monitoring of governments' actions and of the environment may best be accomplished through independent scientific panels that have access to a variety of sources of information. Surprise visits by independent inspectors are used in some regimes as a means of verification and have long been a part of the nuclear nonproliferation regime and the Antarctic Treaty System. The 1980 Convention on the Conservation of Antarctic Marine Living Resources (CCAMLR) provides for such visits, and the Helsinki Commission, in managing the Baltic Sea area, has also considered them. Eastern European and OECD countries accept the concept, but developing countries are suspicious that acceptance will lead to further forms of World Bank and International Monetary Fund conditionality.

Technology and financial transfers may also help states comply with their environmental obligations by providing new equipment with which to reduce emissions. Technology panels that parallel international regimes exist with government, MNC, and mixed participation. Technologically advanced states and firms can serve a constructive role on technology panels by being invited to serve as lead countries, allowing them the opportunity to foster demand in export markets for environmentally clean technologies. Technology panels organized on this principle exist for the following regimes: European acid rain, Mediterranean, ozone, North Sea, and Baltic.

None of these factors are uniformly implicated in compliance decisions because not all governments face the same difficulties in fulfilling their obligations. Thus, they require different technical or political incentives to comply. For instance, democratic societies with strong national environmental administrations, such as the OECD countries, are likely to have their compliance decisions shaped by the provision of verification and monitoring provisions. Verification helps the state guard against free riding, and monitoring reinforces public demands for compliance. In nondemocratic strong states, including many newly industrialized countries, compliance decisions are driven largely by verification and monitoring activities, as these would influence states' expectations of the behavior of others but would not be tied in to domestic-level pressures on the government. Weak states are much more prone to the inducements provided by technology and financial transfers. States with significant science and technology resources are less likely to find the limited offerings of international institutions significant in their calculations of national policy.

Reactions to Noncompliance

Compliance mechanisms are fairly modest. Most analysts are unsure about the extent of state compliance with international commitments. Reliable data are lacking, and the institutions for verifying compliance remain haphazard. If there were more compliance, then international lawyers would likely have more data about the subject, and analysts would likely know more.

Few formal mechanisms exist for addressing noncompliance in the environmental realm. Most efforts rely on sanctions and dispute resolution panels. NGOs have successfully penalized noncompliant actors through public campaigns and may contribute to effectiveness well in excess of formal legal obligations. Similarly, consumer boycotts against endangered tropical hardwoods have led producers to engage in environmentally more sustainable forestry practices, and World Bank threats of green conditionality on financial flows if environmental guidelines were not met led Brazil to reform some of its unsustainable development policies in the Amazon. In each of these cases, NGOs did not launch their campaigns in the country they were trying to influence. Keck and Sikkink call these innovative NGO campaigns a "boomerang effect," as NGOs exercise their political influence on nonstate actors over whom they enjoy some influence.[49] For instance, NGOs successfully launched a campaign against the dumping of the Shell Oil Brent Spar drilling platform in the North Sea by focusing a consumer boycott in Germany, where Shell had a large market presence, rather than in England, where Shell Oil headquarters were located. Consumer boycotts in Europe against imports of tropical timber grown with nonsustainable forestry practices led exporters in Southeast Asia to modify their practices. In the Brazilian case, U.S. NGOs lobbied Congress to exercise its influence over the World Bank to induce the World Bank to threaten to withhold loans to the Brazilian government until the Brazilian government reformed its policy in the Amazon.

Sanctioning noncompliance is seldom possible. A number of agreements contain provisions for trade sanction against violators (including the Montreal Protocol, CITES, the Basel Convention on Control of Transborder Movements of Hazardous Wastes and their Disposal, and ten species conservation treaties), but these have seldom been invoked and are increasingly losing legitimacy in the anticipated WTO legal battles against trade-restricting environmental regulations.[50] To the extent that they may actually be invoked, it would be more likely part of a conscious challenge of the WTO's authority by groups that were challenging the principles of unrestricted free trade.

Even though most treaties contain language providing for adjudication and the creation of dispute resolution panels, no countries have ever convened an arbitration panel to enforce a regime. This is probably because most regimes cover a number of different activities, and every government anticipates that it is not in compliance with some set of them. Consequently, no state wishes to launch proceedings against another party, when they may have to face a reciprocal challenge.

Two limited examples exist of arbitration proceedings that are not limited to state choices. The World Bank Inspection Panel solicits submissions from NGOs and has found favorably for NGO complaints against projects that were likely to be environmentally destructive. However, the Bank panel has no formal authority over the Bank, so its reports are merely advisory. The North American Free Trade Agreement (NAFTA) has a unique arrangement in which an NGO can submit protests about its own government's noncompliance with NAFTA environmental rules. Despite recent efforts by Mexican NGOs to use this mechanism to protest their government's environmental lapses, the panel operates by a majority vote of two of the three governments, which makes it difficult for NGO submissions to be upheld.

The Montreal Ozone Protocol has experimented with encouraging voluntary reporting of noncompliance. Yet in an extensive study of verification systems and compliance with the Montreal Ozone Protocol, David Victor found few examples of voluntary reporting and compliance. Those he did find related to self-reporting countries with hopes of attracting financial assistance to achieve compliance. Effective self-reporting requires additional institutional mechanisms for financial and technology transfers to reward the self-reporters.[51]

CONCLUSION AND IMPLICATIONS

Rio Plus 10 provides the next major opportunity for reforming and streamlining multilateral environmental governance. A delicate web of regimes and actors has developed over the last thirty years, creating a new global policy network of environmental actors. To date, agenda setting and regime development have been far more successful than compliance. NGOs are most active in agenda setting. States continue to be responsible for regime development and compliance. International institutions are involved in all three steps, as are scientists and epistemic communities. MNCs have remained largely involved with just compliance.

This chapter has focused principally on the activities of international institutions. Although these institutions perform a variety of functions, substantive gaps remain in the environmental realms subject to governance. Further inventory of governance activities performed by NGOs and the private sector is necessary.

The international environmental governance system has not been significantly overhauled in three decades. After UNCHE, UNEP was the only international institution responsible for environmental protection. Since then, however, most international institutions have assumed some environmental responsibilities. To some extent, UNEP's success has led to its own obsolescence because it is no longer equipped to conduct its activities or to serve as the UN system's conscience on environmental issues now that the system has become so robust and decentralized. Recent evaluations suggest that there are administrative overlaps in the system, as institutions have assumed new responsibilities for the environment, as well as inefficiencies in the system. There is also growing disenchantment with UNEP's remote location in Kenya and its lack of resources. Suggestions for improvements focus on reforming UNEP and on the creation of a Global Environmental Organization (GEO). These improvements seemed a more likely political agenda for a U.S. Democratic administration before the 2000 U.S. presidential election.[52]

At present, UNEP lacks the resources to perform all functions effectively and to pressure states to pursue environmentally sustainable policies. UNEP nonetheless has a comparative advantage in the UN system for its scientific expertise and should be preserved as a monitoring and environmental assessment body. UNEP should also help develop rosters of experts for use by governments, international organizations, NGOs, and the private sector for assessing new environmental risks as they are identified. UNEP also has long-standing experience with coordinating loose, decentralized networks around the world. Thus it may still be capable of serving a coordinating function to ensure that the multiple elements of SIRs are coordinated, to anticipate any gaps, and to keep members of international policy networks in touch with one another. It would serve as an air-traffic controller for issues on the international environmental agenda, as well as for the multitude of associated ongoing studies and negotiations.

A GEO should be established to fulfill the policy and technology-based functions that provide institutional support for multilateral environmental governance. A GEO would consolidate environmental policy research, technology databases, and clearinghouses; conduct training; and centralize the secretariats that administer current environmental regimes. Centralizing these secretariats would facilitate the creation of a broader global policy network across specific environmental issues and justify the creation of national environmental embassies to represent states and participate in future negotiations. A GEO could also serve as a legal advocate for environmental protection and regulations to counterbalance the WTO by collecting a roster of international environmental lawyers to participate in WTO panels. The GEO should have high-profile annual ministerial meetings to address all environmental issues to assure widespread involvement in environmental policy networks and galvanize rapid responses to new alerts. Ongoing efforts would continue to be addressed through the existing secretariats and conferences of parties. The GEO could even have a panel of environmental inspectors available to verify compliance by states and firms with MEAs.

Much progress has been made in international environmental policy since Stockholm. The system remains fragile, however, and requires continual support and new recruitment to bolster its many policy networks and to maintain the pressure on governments for continued environmental protection.

NOTES

1. Edward O. Wilson, "On the Age of the Environment," *Foreign Policy*, no. 119 (Summer 2000), p. 34.
2. Michael Grubb et al., *The "Earth Summit" Agreements: A Guide and Assessment, An Analysis of the Rio '92 Conference on Environment and Development* (London: Earthscan and Royal Institute of International Affairs, 1993).
3. James Rosenau, *Turbulence in World Politics: A Theory of Change and Continuity* (Princeton, N.J.: Princeton University Press, 1990).
4. P. J. Simmons, "Environmental Security," in *Routledge Encyclopedia of Political Economy* (London: Routledge, 2001).
5. See Sheldon Kamieniecki, ed., *Environmental Politics in the International Arena: Movements, Parties, Organizations, and Policy* (Albany, N.Y.: SUNY Press, 1993); Miranda Schreurs and Elizabeth C. Economy, eds., *The Internationalization of Environmental Protection* (Cambridge, U.K.: Cambridge University Press, 1997); Martin Jänicke and Helmut Weidner, eds., *Successful Environmental Policy: A Critical Evaluation of 24 Cases* (Berlin: Edition Sigma, 1995); The Social Learning Group, *Social Learning and the Management of Global Environmental Risks* (Cambridge, Mass.: MIT Press, 2001); William Ascher, "Understanding Why Governments in Developing Countries Waste Natural Resources," *Environment*, vol. 42, no 2 (March 2000), pp. 8–18; Ruth Greenspan Bell, "Building Trust," *Environment*, vol. 42, no. 2 (March 2000), pp. 20–32; and Arild Underdal and

Kenneth Hanf, eds., *International Environmental Agreements and Domestic Politics: The Case of Acid Rain* (Aldershot: Ashgate, 2000).

6. See Elinor Ostrom and Robert O. Keohane, eds., *Local Commons and Global Interdependence: Heterogeneity and Cooperation in Two Domains* (Thousand Oaks, Calif.: Sage Publications, 1995); and Oran R. Young, *Governance in World Affairs* (Ithaca, N.Y.: Cornell University Press, 1999).

7. See Ken Conca, "Rethinking the Ecology-Sovereignty Debate," *Millennium*, vol. 23, no 3 (1994), pp. 701–11; Ronnie Lipschutz and Ken Conca, eds., *The State and Social Power in Global Environmental Politics* (New York: Columbia University Press, 1993); and Karen Litfin, ed., *The Greening of Sovereignty in World Politics* (Cambridge, Mass.: MIT Press, 1998).

8. Viktor Sebek, "Bridging the Gap Between Environmental Science and Policy-Making," *Ambio*, vol. 12, no. 2 (1983), pp. 118–20; Martin W. Holdgate, "The Environmental Information Needs of the Decision-Maker," *Nature and Resources*, vol. 18, no. 1 (January–March 1982), pp. 5–10.

9. The number is over 900 if one includes soft law, bilateral agreements, and EU directives. See Edith Brown Weiss, Daniel Barstow Magraw, and Paul C. Szasz, *International Environmental Law: Basic Instruments and References, 1992–1999* (Ardsley, N.Y.: Transnational Publishers, 1999).

10. Richard N. Gardner, *Negotiating Survival: Four Priorities After Rio* (New York: Council on Foreign Relations, 1992), p. 37.

11. Arild Underdal and the Oslo School refer to this class of problems as "malign problems" that are unlikely to yield effective collective responses.

12. Biliana Cicin-Sain and Robert W. Knecht, *Integrated Coastal and Ocean Management: Concepts and Practices* (Washington, D.C.: Island Press, 1998), pp. 32–6.

13. OECD Compendia, UNCSD, "Global Change and Sustainable Development," E/CN.17/1997/3; UNCSD, "Overall Progress Achieved Since the United Nations Conference on Environment and Development," E/CN.17/1997/2/Add.7.

14. Indur M. Goklany, "Factors Affecting Environmental Impacts: The Effects of Technology on Long-term Trends in Cropland, Air Pollution, and Water-related Diseases," *Ambio*, vol. 25, no. 8 (December 1996), pp. 497–509.

15. Early work includes Richard A. Falk, *This Endangered Planet: Prospects and Proposals for Human Survival* (New York: Vintage Books, 1971); and Harold Sprout and Margaret Sprout, *Toward a Politics of Planet Earth* (New York: Van Nostrand Reinhold Company, 1971). Since then the major works of primary research include David Kay and Harold Jacobson, eds., *Environmental Protection: The International Dimension* (Totowa, N.J.: Allanheld Osmun, 1983); Peter M. Haas, Robert O. Keohane, and Marc A. Levy, eds., *Institutions for the Earth: Sources of Effective International Environmental Protection* (Cambridge, Mass.: MIT Press, 1993); Nazli Choucri, ed., *Global Accord: Environmental Challenges and International Responses* (Cambridge, Mass.: MIT Press, 1993); Oran R. Young, ed., *Global Governance* (Cambridge, Mass.: MIT Press, 1997); Marvin S. Soroos, *The Endangered Atmosphere: Preserving Global Commons* (Columbia, S.C.: University of South Carolina Press, 1997); Oran R. Young and Gail Osherenko, eds., *Polar Politics: Creating International Environmental Regimes* (Ithaca, N.Y.: Cornell University Press, 1993); Oran

R. Young, ed., *The Effectiveness of International Environmental Regimes: Causal Connections and Behavioral Mechanisms* (Cambridge, Mass.: MIT Press, 1999); Edith Brown Weiss and Harold K. Jacobson, eds., *Engaging Countries: Compliance with International Environmental Accords* (Cambridge, Mass.: MIT Press, 1998); David Victor, Kal Raustiala, and Eugene Skolnikoff, eds., *The Implementation and Effectiveness of International Environmental Commitments: Theory and Practice* (Cambridge, Mass.: MIT Press, 1999); Mostafa K. Tolba and Iwona Rummel-Bulska, *Global Environmental Diplomacy: Negotiating Environmental Agreements for the World, 1973–1992* (Cambridge, Mass.: MIT Press, 1998); Steinar Andresen et al., *Science and Politics in International Environmental Regimes: Between Integrity and Involvement* (Manchester, U.K.: Manchester University Press, 2000); and Peter Sand, *Lessons Learned in Global Environmental Governance* (Washington, D.C.: World Resources Institute, 1990).

16. See Stephen Hopgood, *American Foreign Environmental Policy and the Power of the State* (Oxford, U.K.: Oxford University Press, 1998); and Robert Paarlberg, "Lagged Leadership," in Norman Vig and Regina Axelrod, eds., *The Global Environment: Institutions, Law, and Policy* (Washington, D.C.: CQ Press, 1999), pp. 236–55. Strong environmental leadership need not lead to positive environmental outcomes. For instance, the United States exercised its leadership in opposing the biodiversity treaty and in seeking to water down a climate change treaty. From the perspective of climate change skeptics conducting policy analysis, the United States is exercising hegemonic leadership to promote social welfare by opposing a set of unwarranted commitments and thus preventing policy based on a diagnosis of a false positive.

17. Paarlberg, "Lagged Leadership."

18. For similar inventories of properties of institutions capable of inducing behavior change by member units, see Haas, Keohane, and Levy, eds., *Institutions for the Earth*; Elinor Ostrom, *Governing the Commons: The Evolution of Institutions for Collective Action* (Cambridge, U.K.: Cambridge University Press, 1990); Young, *Governance in World Affairs*; Weiss and Jacobson, eds., *Engaging Countries*; Ernest Haas, *When Knowledge Is Power: Three Models of Change in International Organizations* (Berkeley, Calif.: University of California Press, 1990); Victor, Raustiala, and Skolnikoff, eds., *The Implementation and Effectiveness of International Environmental Commitments*; see also earlier international institutions literature: John Gerard Ruggie, "International Responses to Technology," *International Organization*, vol. 29, no. 3 (Summer 1975), pp. 557–84; Eugene Skolnikoff, *The International Imperatives of Technology, Technological Development and the International Political System* (Berkeley, Calif.: Institute of International Studies, University of California Press, 1972); and Kay and Jacobson, eds., *Environmental Protection*.

19. Arild Underdal, "The Roles of IGOs in International Environmental Management," in Michael H. Glantz, ed., *The Role of Regional Organizations in the Context of Climate Change* (Berlin: Springer-Verlag, 1994), p. 153. See also Peter M. Haas and Ernst B. Haas "Learning to Learn," *Global Governance*, vol. 1, no. 3 (September 1995), pp. 255–85.

20. See Paul Wapner, *Environmental Activism and World Civic Politics* (Albany, N.Y.: SUNY Press, 1996); Ronnie Lipschutz with Judith Mayer, *Global Civil Society and Global Envi-*

ronmental Governance (Albany, N.Y.: SUNY Press, 1996); Sheila Jasanoff, "NGOs and the Environment," in Thomas Weiss, ed., *Beyond UN Subcontracting: Task-sharing with Regional Security Arrangements and Service-providing NGOs* (New York: St. Martin's Press, 1998), pp. 203–23; Kal Raustiala, "States, NGOs, and International Environmental Institutions," *International Studies Quarterly*, vol. 41 (1997), pp. 719–40; and P. J. Simmons, "Learning to Live with NGOs," *Foreign Policy*, no. 112 (Fall 1998), pp. 82–109.

21. Russell J. Dalton, *The Green Rainbow* (New Haven, Conn.: Yale University Press, 1994).

22. See Riley E. Dunlap, George H. Gallup Jr., and Alec M. Gallup, *Health of the Planet Survey* (Princeton, N.J.: Gallup International Institute, 1992). The countries are Brazil, Canada, Chile, Denmark, Finland, Germany, Great Britain, Hungary, India, Ireland, Japan, Mexico, Nigeria, Netherlands, Norway, Philippines, Poland, Portugal, Russia, South Korea, Switzerland, Turkey, United States, and Uruguay.

23. The Delaney Clause in U.S. pharmaceutical regulations is an early example of such an approach. The Delaney Amendment of 1985 states that no additive shall be deemed safe if it is found to induce cancer when ingested by man or animal. Thus, it sets an absolute regulatory standard, subject to evolving determination of dose-response relationships that cause cancer.

24. Wolfgang H. Reinicke and Francis Deng, *Critical Choices: The United Nations, Networks, and the Future of Global Governance* (Ottawa: International Development Research Centre, 2000).

25. See Naomi Roht-Arriaza, "'Soft Law' in a 'Hybrid Organization': The International Organization for Standardization" in Dinah Shelton, ed., *Commitment and Compliance: The Role of Non-binding Norms in the International System* (Oxford, U.K.: Oxford University Press, 2000); Riva Krut and Harris Gleckman, *ISO 14001: A Missed Opportunity for Sustainable Global Industrial Development* (London: Earthscan 1998); Aseem Prakash, *Greening the Firm: The Politics of Corporate Environmentalism* (Cambridge, U.K.: Cambridge University Press, 2000); Ronie Garcia-Johnson, *Exporting Environmentalism: U.S. Multinational Chemical Corporations in Brazil and Mexico* (Cambridge, Mass.: MIT Press, 2000); and Stephen Schmidheiny with the Business Council for Sustainable Development, *Changing Course: A Global Business Perspective on Development and the Environment* (Cambridge, Mass.: MIT Press, 1992).

26. See Michael Zurn, "The Rise of International Environmental Politics," *World Politics*, vol. 50, no. 4 (July 1998), pp. 617–49. Compare with George W. Downs, Kyle W. Danish, and Peter N. Barsoom, "The Transformational Model of International Regime Design," *Columbia Journal of Transnational Law*, vol. 38, no. 3 (2000), pp. 465–514; and Ronald B. Mitchell, "Structures, Agents, and Processes in International Environmental Politics," in Thomas Risse, Beth Simmons, and Walter Carlsnaes, eds., *Handbook of International Relations* (Thousand Oaks, Calif.: Sage Publications, 2001).

27. Peter M. Haas, "Do Regimes Matter? Epistemic Communities and Mediterranean Pollution Control," *International Organization*, vol. 43, no. 3 (Summer 1989); Abram Chayes and Antonia Handler Chayes, *The New Sovereignty: Compliance with International Regulatory Agreements* (Cambridge, Mass.: Harvard University Press, 1995).

28. Sand, *Lessons Learned in Global Environmental Governance*.

29. Tolba and Rummel-Bulska, *Global Environmental Diplomacy*, p. 6.

30. Grubb et al., *The "Earth Summit" Agreements*.

31. Other analysts have similar taxonomies of regime patterns. See Ethan Nadelmann, "Global Prohibition Regimes: The Evolution of Norms in International Society," *International Organization*, vol. 44, no. 4 (Autumn 1990), pp. 479–526; Oran R. Young, *Governance in World Affairs*; and Stacey VanDeveer, "Protecting Europe's Seas," *Environment*, vol. 42, no. 6 (July/August 2000), pp. 10–26.

32. Peter M. Haas, "Scientific Communities and Multiple Paths to Environmental Cooperation," in Anathea Brooks and Stacy VanDeveer, eds., *Saving the Seas: Values, Scientists, and International Governance* (College Park, Md.: Maryland Sea Grant College, 1997), pp. 206–07.

33. From data presented in Bertram I. Spector and Anna R. Korula, "Problems of Ratifying International Environmental Agreements," *Global Environmental Change* (December 1993), pp. 369–81; Peter M. Haas and Jan Sungren, "Evolving International Environmental Law," in Choucri, ed., *Global Accord*, pp. 401–30.

34. Sand, *Lessons Learned in Global Environmental Governance*.

35. The concept of a k-group, introduced by Thomas Schelling, is a small core group of countries that are responsible for enough of a problem that if they reach an agreement, then the problem is likely to be resolved, making it easier for other countries to join the regime out of an anticipation that their costs will not be futile.

36. Tolba and Rummel-Bulska, *Global Environmental Diplomacy*, pp. 17–21.

37. See Patrick Szell, "The Development of Multilateral Mechanisms for Monitoring Compliance," in W. Lang, H. Neuhold, and K. Zemanek, eds., *Environmental Protection and International Law* (London: Graham & Trotman, 1991); Peter H. Sand, *Trusts for the Earth* (Hull, U.K.: University of Hull Press, 1994). UNEP administers twelve trust funds for the Regional Seas Program and CITES. The World Bank administers the Montreal Trust Fund for the ozone regime, while the Global Environment Facility (GEF) exists to finance the international component of projects intended to preserve biodiversity, protect the ozone layer, curtail climate change, control marine pollution, and limit desertification.

38. For UNEP's regional seas experiences, see Peter M. Haas, "Save the Seas," in Elisabeth Mann Borgese et al., *Ocean Yearbook 9* (Chicago: University of Chicago Press, 1991), pp. 188–212; and Peter M. Haas, "Prospects for Effective Marine Governance in the NW Pacific Region," *Marine Policy*, vol. 24, no. 4 (July 2000), pp. 341–48. For acid rain in Europe, see Leen Hordijk, "Task Force on Integrated Assessment Modelling," *Monitair*, vol. 4, no. 6 (October 1991), pp. 8–11.

39. See Ronald B. Mitchell, "Compliance Theory: A Synthesis," *Review of European Community and International Environmental Law*, vol. 2, no. 4 (1993), pp. 327–34; and Ronald B. Mitchell, "Compliance Theory: An Overview," in James Cameron, Jacob Werksman, and Peter Roderick, eds., *Improving Compliance with International Environmental Law* (London: Earthscan, 1996), pp. 3–28; and Ruth Greenspan Bell, "Developing a Culture of Compliance in the International Environmental Regime," *The Environmental Law Reporter*, vol. 27, no. 8 (August 1997), pp. 10402–12.

40. Harold K. Jacobson and Edith Brown Weiss, "Assessing the Record and Designing Strategies to Engage Countries," in Jacobson and Weiss, eds., *Engaging Countries*, pp. 511–54; and Kal Raustiala and David G. Victor, "Conclusions," in Victor, Raustiala, and Skolnikoff, eds., *The Implementation and Effectiveness of International Environmental Commitments*, pp. 659–707. Young, ed., *The Effectiveness of International Environmental Regimes*, provides a similar analysis.

41. See Peter M. Haas, "Choosing to Comply: Theorizing from International Relations and Comparative Politics," in Dinah Shelton, ed. *Commitment and Compliance*, pp. 43–64; and Peter M. Haas, "Compliance with EU Directives," *Journal of European Public Policy*, vol. 5, no. 1 (March 1998), pp. 17–37.

42. Harold K. Jacobson and Edith Brown Weiss, "Assessing the Record and Designing Strategies to Engage Countries," in Jacobson and Weiss, eds., *Engaging Countries*, pp. 511–54.

43. Ibid., pp. 520–21.

44. See Kal Raustiala and David G. Victor, "Conclusions," in Victor, Raustiala, and Skolnikoff, eds., *The Implementation and Effectiveness of International Environmental Commitments*.

45. Edith Brown Weiss, "Concluding Remarks," in Dinah Shelton, ed., *Commitment and Compliance*.

46. Ronald B. Mitchell, "Regime Design Matters," *International Organization*, vol. 48, no. 3 (Summer 1994), pp. 425–58; and Ronald B. Mitchell, *International Oil Pollution at Sea* (Cambridge, Mass.: MIT Press, 1994).

47. Peter H. Sand, "Introduction," in Peter H. Sand, ed., *The Effectiveness of International Environmental Agreements* (Cambridge, U.K.: Grotius Publications, 1992), pp. 13–14; U.S. General Accounting Office, *International Environmental Agreements Are Not Well Monitored* (Washington, D.C.: U.S. General Accounting Office, January 1992).

48. "Remote Sensing and Environmental Treaties," available at <http://sedac.ciesin.columbia.edu/rs-treaties/>.

49. Margaret Keck and Katherine Sikkink, *Activists Beyond Borders: Advocacy Networks in International Politics* (Ithaca, N.Y.: Cornell University Press, 1998).

50. Steve Charnovitz, "Trade Measures and the Design of International Regimes," *Journal of Environment and Development*," vol. 5, no. 2 (June 1996), pp. 168–96.

51. David Victor, "The Operation and Effectiveness of the Montreal Protocol's Non-Compliance Procedure," in Victor, Raustiala, and Skolnikoff, eds., *The Implementation and Effectiveness of International Environmental Commitments*, pp. 137–76.

52. See Frank Biermann, "The Case for a World Environment Organization," *Environment*, vol. 42, no. 9 (November 2000), pp. 22–31; Calestous Juma, "The UN's Role in the New Diplomacy," *Issues in Science and Technology*, vol. 17, no. 1 (Fall 2000), pp. 37–8; Dan Esty, "The Case for a Global Environmental Organization," in Peter B. Kenen, ed., *Managing the World Economy: Fifty Years After Bretton Woods* (Washington, D.C.: Institute for International Economics, 1994), pp. 287–309; and Dan Esty, "An Earthly Effort," *Worldlink* (September/October 2000), available at <http://www.worldlink.co.uk/stories/storyReader$334>.

SUGGESTED ADDITIONAL READING

See also Peter H. Sand's recommended readings on nature conservation.

Andresen, Steinar, T. Skodvin, Arild Underdal, and J. Wettestad. *Science and Politics in International Environmental Regimes: Between Integrity and Involvement*. Manchester, U.K.: Manchester University Press, 2000.

Benedick, Richard Elliot. *Ozone Diplomacy: New Directions in Safeguarding the Planet*. Cambridge, Mass.: Harvard University Press, 1998.

Benedick, Richard Elliot et al. *Greenhouse Warming: Negotiating a Global Regime*. Washington, D.C.: World Resources Institute, 1991.

Haas, Peter M. *Saving the Mediterranean: The Politics of International Environmental Cooperation*. New York: Columbia University Press, 1990.

Haas, Peter M., and Ernst B. Haas. "Learning to Learn." *Global Governance*, vol. 1, no. 3 (September 1995), pp. 255–85.

Mathews, Jessica Tuchman, ed. 1991. *Preserving the Global Environment*. New York: W.W. Norton & Company, 1991.

Mitchell, Ronald B. "Structures, Agents, and Processes in International Environmental Politics," in Thomas Risse, Beth Simmons, and Walter Carlsnaes, eds., *Handbook of International Relations* (Thousand Oaks, Calif.: Sage Publications, 2001).

Skodvin, Tora. *Stucture and Agent in the Scientific Diplomacy of Climate Change: An Empirical Case Study of Science-Policy Interaction in the Intergovernmental Panel on Climate Change*. Dordrecht: Kluwer Academic Publishers, 2000.

Victor, David G., Kal Raustiala, and Eugene B. Skolnikoff, eds. *The Implementation and Effectiveness of International Environmental Commitments: Theory and Practice*. Cambridge, Mass.: MIT Press 1999.

Weiss, Edith Brown, and Harold K. Jacobson, eds. *Engaging Countries: Compliance with International Environmental Accords*. Cambridge, Mass.: MIT Press, 1998.

Young, Oran R., ed. *The Effectiveness of International Environmental Regimes: Causal Connections and Behavioral Mechanisms*. Cambridge, Mass.: MIT Press, 1999.

Young, Oran R. *Governance in World Affairs*. Ithaca, N.Y.: Cornell University Press, 1999.

Young, Oran R., and Gail Osherenko, eds. *Polar Politics: Creating International Environmental Regimes*. Ithaca, N.Y.: Cornell University Press, 1993.

Zurn, Michael. "The Rise of International Environmental Politics." *World Politics*, vol. 50, no. 4 (July 1998), pp. 617–49.

Internet sites

International Treaties and Institutions

The Interlinkages Initiative: Synergies and Coordination Between Multilateral Environmental Agreements <http://www.geic.or.jp/interlinkages/>

Yearbook of International Cooperation on Environment and Development <http://www.ngo.grida.no/ggynet/>

Environmental Treaties and Resource Indicators (ENTRI) at the Center for International Earth Sciences Information Network (CIESIN), of Columbia University, New York <http://sedac.ciesin.org/entri/texts-home.html>

International Institutions
UN Environment Program (UNEP) <http://www.unep.org>
Rio Plus 10: The World Summit on Sustainable Development <http://www.un.org/rio+10>
UN Commission on Sustainable Development (UNCSD) <http://www.un.org/esa/sustdev>
World Bank <http://www.worldbank.org>
Intergovernmental Panel on Climate Change (IPCC) <http://www.ipcc.ch>
Global Environment Facility (GEF) <http://www.gefweb.org>
U.S. Department of State, Bureau of Oceans and International Environmental and Scientific Affairs <http://www.state.gov/www/global/oes/index.html>

Global Environmental Assessments
Global Environment Outlook, UNEP <http://www.unep.org/Geo2000>
World Conservation Monitoring Centre <http://www.wcmc.org.uk>

9

Global Commons: The Oceans, Antarctica, the Atmosphere, and Outer Space

Christopher C. Joyner

THE ABILITY OF STATES TO REGULATE usage of the global common spaces in the twenty-first century has far-reaching consequences for the environment and for humankind. Global common spaces are domains lying beyond the exclusive jurisdiction of any state that states or their nationals may use for resource extraction, waste disposal, scientific research, and so on. Throughout history conflicts have arisen over who can use these areas, how they can be used, and whether one actor can exclude use by another. This chapter assesses why and how states have cooperatively sought to manage and regulate their activities in common space areas. It examines the conditions under which mechanisms for international governance of activities in these areas can be most effective.[1]

Among the areas traditionally considered as global common spaces are the world's oceans, Antarctica, the atmosphere, and outer space. Each has important geophysical distinctions and different potential uses. The oceans cover nearly three-quarters of the Earth's surface and touch more than 150 states. They are used for fishing and mining and contain a variety of energy resources. The Antarctic commons region includes the massive ice-covered continent surrounded by the open Southern Ocean. Its seas are abundant with marine living resources while the continent is rich with unharvested minerals and hydrocarbons. The atmosphere includes the troposphere above the Earth (where weather patterns begin), the stratosphere (where the ozone layer is located), the mesosphere, and beyond.[2] The atmosphere—the blanket of gases that surrounds the planet—contains carbon dioxide, which plants need for photosynthesis, a process that generates oxygen that all living creatures need to survive. Beyond the atmosphere is the limitless void of space, which includes countless celestial bodies with unknown resource potential. Although outer space extends far beyond the Earth, it is regarded as a global commons not only because of its "global" effects on the earthbound, but because all humans can use it. Admittedly, the "commons" character of all these spaces is subject to debate and, as such, has given rise to conflicting economic and political interpretations for both user and conservationist.

Failure to manage properly the global commons could have profound consequences. The unregulated exploitation of world fisheries will lead to growing scarcity. The unregulated emission of man-made chemicals into the atmosphere will further diminish the capacity of the ozone layer to filter ultraviolet radiation from the sun. Left unchecked, this trend will result in increased cancer rates. Persistent emissions of carbon dioxide and other gases will continue to contribute to the gradual warming of the planet's atmosphere and surface, a phenomenon that may have dramatic and unwelcome consequences for the quality of life on Earth.

In response to growing concern for the global commons, states have established near-universal regimes to guide governments in working together to manage activities in commons spaces. These efforts have on the whole been quite successful and contain many valuable governance lessons in the areas of agenda setting, negotiation, implementation and compliance, and reactions to noncompliance.

With regard to setting the agenda, this chapter argues that, first, ideological cleavages between developed and developing states often dominate the framing of issues and determine which issues are put on the international agenda. Second, technology and scientific breakthroughs are important drivers of the agenda, creating new opportunities for human activities that subsequently need regulation. Third, nongovernmental organizations (NGOs) also play a key role in pushing new items on the agenda.

Regarding negotiation, this chapter identifies six major lessons. First, widespread participation and near-universal membership in global commons negotiations can help to legitimize these negotiations, but they do not necessarily translate into more effective negotiations. Second, negotiations are more effective if membership is restricted to governments with direct interests in, and control over, issues relevant to the regime. Third, political coalitions of all kinds can occur, with coalition structure changing dramatically depending on the problem under consideration and the national interests of the states involved. That said, global commons negotiations often pit states from the North against states from the South. Fourth, negotiations must adopt a progressive approach to problem solving. The convention-cum-protocol approach was particularly useful in negotiating regimes for the commons. Fifth, instead of negotiating specific obligations, states have in some instances successfully negotiated nonlegally binding agreements that outline the preferred conduct by states. Sixth, rules must appear fair and equitable—both in the way they are developed and in their substance.

With respect to implementation and compliance, national governments implement and comply with international rules and norms because such behavior is perceived to enhance their national interests. Regime success results largely from the self-interested considerations of the regime's members. Regimes and rules are strong only if they are implemented by each and every member state. Six additional lessons emerge from the commons regimes in terms of implementation and compliance. First, regimes with institutions that can manage and regulate activities of states are generally more effective than regimes without such central institutions. Second, if rules for managing the global commons are too rigid, they are more likely to be ignored or broken, and are therefore less likely to be agreed to by governments. Third, decisions made with consensus support are more likely to be supported than those taken by majority voting procedures. Fourth, a successful and effective global commons regime must have leadership from the technologically developed world, most notably from the United States. Fifth, NGOs can become salient and influential players in the effective implementation of a commons regime, particularly when pervasive global environment stakes are perceived to be at risk. Sixth, and most important, if a global commons regime functions successfully, that success can be attributed in large part to self-interested considerations among member governments.

Finally, with respect to enforcement and reactions to noncompliance five lessons spring to the fore. First, if common space regimes are to be enforced, verifiable monitoring of the activities of states in the area is essential. Second, if rules for managing common space regimes are actually to be enforced, governments of member states must be willing to make them enforceable on their own nationals, as well as other member states. Third, international institutions, even if they have no formal enforcement authority, can become powerful shapers of state behavior with respect to the global commons. Fourth, inadvertent cases of noncompliance can be overcome with the help of international organizations. Fifth, if the environment and the natural resources in global common spaces are to be protected, reliable means must be available for settling international disputes.

NATURE OF THE COMMONS PROBLEM

Fundamental to the global commons concept is the problem often referred to as the "tragedy of the commons." In his famous essay by the same name, Garrett Hardin explains the principal dynamic of commons abuse using a typical English village common green.[3] Hardin depicts a traditional commons pasture open to all, where herders can freely graze their cattle. The arrangement works to everyone's benefit so long as the number of cattle does not exceed the carrying capacity of the pasture. The logic of individual greed, however, is likely to transform the freedom of open access into a collective tragedy. According to this logic, each herder will want to graze as many cattle as possible to reap greater profits from their sale. The addition of more cattle by one herder, however, will cause others to follow suit. Inevitably, the herders become trapped in a competition, as each seeks to increase his herd on a finite piece of pastureland, and herein lies the tragedy. Eventually, the carrying capacity of the pasture will be exceeded, and the negative effects of overgrazing will become evident. In the end, the freedom to exploit a commons area for individual profit brings ruin to all. Thus the perceived rational choice to maximize individual benefit produces the irrational outcome of universal loss.

Determining who has access to common areas, and to what extent, is at the heart of the commons dilemma.[4] Common areas are not private property. They are open to all, and barring international agreement to the contrary their resources are free for the taking. In the above scenario, a rational herder can make greater personal gains by overusing the pasture's resources, whereas a herder who does not add to his herd— perhaps in an effort to conserve the pasture—will make fewer such gains. This "free-rider" notion has many applications. For example, the fisherman who takes fewer fish to conserve overall stocks or the industrialist who complies with air pollution laws both depend on others to do the same. Otherwise their individual efforts at conservation will be wasted. To avoid this outcome, Hardin's public goods model prescribes the establishment of a central authority to compel all users to refrain from overexploiting and otherwise abusing limited public resources.[5] In the absence of such an authority, the exploitation and abuse of the common area would continue. In general, then, if the global commons are to remain economically productive for all, they must remain environmentally solvent. To that end, regimes must be devised and effectively implemented for the sustainable management of those areas.[6]

International law has long recognized the right of all peoples to use common spaces. This right of access, however, is not unqualified. Norms and laws have evolved that require governments to use reasonable regard to the interests of other states when dealing with common spaces. To wit, although the contemporary law on the oceans ensures the right of nationals from all states to fish or otherwise use the high seas, this right is subject to a variety of restrictions, including treaty obligations and the rights of coastal and other seafaring states. As another example, government activities in the Antarctic, both on the continent and in its circumpolar waters, are restricted so that this unique environment may be preserved. Toward this end, states have adopted legal measures to ensure that the area remains demilitarized. Likewise, although outer space is free and open for exploration and use to all states, such activities must be carried out exclusively for peaceful purposes for the benefit of, and in the interests of, all states.

Thus the fundamental question concerning common space areas is: How can states use them in a way that accommodates the needs of the largest number of people in a safe, efficient, and environmentally responsible manner? Since the late 1950s, this has been accomplished through the creation and expansion of multilateral legal regimes for each major commons area.[7]

TRACK RECORD OF GLOBAL COMMONS REGIMES

International responses to the need for managing the global commons have been significant, but ad hoc. Over the past four decades, states have established sophisticated regimes to regulate national activities on the high seas and in the Antarctic, the atmosphere, and outer space. For the first two areas, these efforts have evolved into highly institutionalized regimes that incorporate strongly rooted norms and many treaties. In the latter two cases, the regimes are also based on treaties but are less developed. In all four areas, regime development has been driven by technological change and the perception of governments that grave threats to a commons area exist. The involvement of powerful states has been key to regime growth in each of these areas. The absence of their leadership has frustrated regime development.

High Seas

The oldest recognized commons are the oceans or, more accurately, the high seas, which cover 71 percent of the Earth's surface and serve as a main conduit for international commerce. In addition, they contain a storehouse of food, mineral, and energy resources, the potential of which has yet to be fully realized. At the same time, however, the oceans have become a sink for waste materials, whether by way of intentional discharge into rivers that empty into the sea, the release of land-based effluents, or accidental oil spills from giant tankers.

States' economic interests in exploiting high seas resources have slowly produced a patchwork of rules, principles, and treaty law.[8] Since the late 1950s, negotiations have taken place in UN Conferences on the Law of the Sea (UNCLOS), as well as in ad hoc multilateral arrangements.[9]

Negotiations culminated in 1982 with the signature of the UN Convention on the Law of the Sea. Its 320 provisions contain generally accepted principles—variously identified as rules, standards, regulations, procedures, and practices—relating to the use of oceans. The convention establishes a 12-mile territorial sea, a 200-mile exclusive economic zone for coastal states, as well as an area called "the high seas." In addition, it sets out rights and duties for the following: passage through international straits and archipelagoes, flag state control over ships, behavior of vessels on the high seas, and conservation of ocean resources. It also created the International Seabed Authority, an international organization charged with regulating and supervising deep ocean mining for seabed minerals.[10]

Linked to the UN Convention on the Law of the Sea are subsidiary regimes designed to address distinct maritime needs and problems. For example, the International Maritime Organization (IMO) administers the regime for international shipping and navigation. The IMO has taken a leading role in drafting binding legal measures, and its members have negotiated some forty conventions and protocols dealing with the efficiency of maritime services, safety standards, and marine environmental protection—the most prominent of which involve issues such as dumping of vessel-source pollution, safety in commercial traffic, and the hijacking of ships at sea.[11] In addition, during the 1980s eleven regional seas conventions were negotiated under UN auspices.[12] These deal principally with promoting antipollution norms and conservation measures among littoral states.

In the 1990s the United Nations has given particular consideration to creating regimes for managing fisheries and other living resources in the high seas. Chief among these are the 1993 UN Food and Agriculture Organization Compliance Agreement to regulate the reflagging of fishing vessels and the 1995 Fish Stocks Agreement to deal with the problem of straddling stocks. A number of regional fishery institutions have also been established, among them the Northwest Atlantic Fisheries Organization, the Commission for the Conservation of Atlantic Tunas, and the Indian Ocean Tuna Commission.

Separate but integral to ocean resource management are two regimes that oversee the conservation of whales and seals. In 1946, motivated by the long history of overexploitation of whales, the International Convention for the Regulation of Whaling created the International Whaling Commission (IWC). The IWC sets quotas on the number of whales its members can take and has adopted voluntary moratoriums for member states that aim to prevent the taking of certain whale species. In 1994 the IWC established a long-term ban on whale-taking, creating, in effect, a global whale sanctuary south of 40 degrees south latitude.[13] In 1972, stemming largely from concerns about the overexploitation of seals in southern polar waters, a group of states negotiated the Convention on the Conservation of Antarctic Seals. The convention prohibits its members from engaging in the commercial harvesting of six species of seals south of 60 degrees south latitude. The signatories include those states most engaged in seal hunts throughout the nineteenth and twentieth centuries—Canada, Japan, Norway, Russia, the United Kingdom, and the United States.

Antarctica

Surrounded by the Southern Ocean, Antarctica is the size of the United States and Mexico combined—5.4 million square miles. It is the world's largest desert—in terms of precipitation—yet contains 70 percent of the world's freshwater frozen in its massive ice cap. Although the ice sheet depresses Antarctica's land surface to a very low elevation, the thickness of the ice makes Antarctica the highest continent above sea level. Antarctica is the most isolated and inhospitable of continents. There are no trees, grasses, reptiles, land mammals, or amphibians, and it is the only continent without an indigenous population.

Seven countries—Argentina, Australia, Chile, France, New Zealand, Norway, and the United Kingdom—have claimed territory in the Antarctic. In the case of Argentina, Chile, and the United Kingdom, these claims overlap. Following a successful collaborative science project, known as the International Geophysical Year (IGY) in 1957/1958, the seven claimants plus Belgium, Japan, South Africa, the Soviet Union, and the United States agreed to set aside territorial disputes in favor of international cooperation in the region. In 1959 they negotiated the Antarctic Treaty, which entered into force in 1961.

The treaty is an unprecedented example of conservation and research values codifying national interests, and in the process it has forged sophisticated cooperation among erstwhile international rivals. The Antarctic Treaty totally demilitarizes the continent and pledges that the treaty area, which includes the circumpolar ocean space south of 60 degrees south latitude, will only be used for peaceful purposes. Nuclear explosions and radioactive waste disposal are prohibited. Scientific investigation, exchange, and cooperation are guaranteed, and parties to the treaty can conduct unannounced inspections of other countries' stations and facilities on and around the continent.

Growing conservation and environmental protection concerns in the early 1960s made necessary new rules to regulate activities in the region. These concerns, combined with the successful experience of cooperation lent by the 1959 Antarctic Treaty, led to the adoption of additional treaty measures in 1964 and to the negotiation of other international agreements to deal with new strategies and technologies affecting resource exploitation in the southern commons. The 1972 Antarctic Seals Convention noted above was followed in 1980 by the negotiation of an international instrument aimed at conserving living marine resources, especially krill, within the Antarctic Convergence Zone.[14] This agreement has global significance because of the critical place krill occupies in the Southern Ocean's food chain. Throughout the 1980s, negotiations proceeded on an Antarctic minerals agreement. Although completed, France and Australia blocked the treaty's entry into force in 1989 because of serious concerns over the environmental implications of any mineral exploration and mining activities—in particular, marine pollution, displacement of Antarctic wildlife, and damage to the pristine continent. Subsequently, in 1991 an environmental protection protocol providing a more comprehensive approach for regulating activities potentially harmful to the circumpolar environment was negotiated for the Antarctic Treaty.

The constellation of Antarctic Treaty agreements has been negotiated and implemented by the Antarctic Treaty Consultative Parties (ATCPs), that is, those states party to the Antarctic Treaty that have asserted special national interests in the Antarctic and have undertaken scientific activities to support those interests. Although there is no formal organization or secretariat per se, representatives of ATCP states meet annually to decide policy for their nationals in the Antarctic.

The Antarctic Treaty System (ATS) is highly developed and has operated smoothly in addressing a range of environmental, scientific, commercial, and military issues concerning the polar south. That this regime functions as well as it does—even in the face of standing sovereignty claims by key states to overlapping portions of the continent and absent any formal standing secretariat—is largely the result of the leadership of Australia, New Zealand, the Soviet Union (now Russia), the United Kingdom, and the United States, as well as the relatively small numbers of states with tangible stakes in Antarctic management.

The number of states participating in the ATS has increased dramatically, from twelve in 1961 when the Antarctic Treaty entered into force to forty-four in 2000. This growth not only complicates decision making but also poses new challenges. These include supervising and regulating increased shipborne tourism to the area; stemming the depletion of fisheries in circumpolar seas; and agreeing on a formal liability regime that covers accidents from vessel-source pollution or operator mismanagement in the region.[15]

Atmosphere

The Earth's atmosphere provides virtually limitless sources of oxygen, carbon dioxide, and nitrogen—all essential for the survival of plants and animals. It also provides the water needed to sustain life and dissipates many of the waste products of biological life and human industry through its circumglobal reach. The atmosphere transmits radiation from the sun that is essential for photosynthesis. It shields the Earth from ultraviolet radiation as well as from cosmic rays and meteors that shower down upon the planet from space. The atmosphere acts as a blanket to maintain a higher temperature on Earth than would otherwise exist and moderates the planet's climate, warming the polar regions and cooling the tropical areas. The atmosphere is essential for communications. Air readily transmits sound and electromagnetic (light and radio) waves, and an electroconductive layer in the upper atmosphere reflects radio waves, thus permitting communication beyond the horizon.[16]

Three man-made threats that affect the atmospheric commons have led to the development of three international regimes. The legal principle underpinning each regime is the responsibility of the state to do no harm—that is, to ensure that activities within its national jurisdiction or control do not cause damage to the environment of other states or to areas beyond the limits of national jurisdiction.[17]

The first threat concerns the stratosphere and the human-induced chemical changes that affect solar radiation penetrating the upper atmosphere, commonly known as the ozone hole. The release of chlorofluorocarbons (CFCs) into the atmosphere has resulted in substantial ozone layer reduction, exposing the Earth's surface to more intense ultraviolet radiation. In reaction to growing scientific information and popular concern about this threat, a group of states in 1985 negotiated the Vienna Convention for the Protection of the Ozone Layer. The convention did not specify how to combat ozone depletion. Instead, it was a framework instrument that provided the basis for more substantive future action by confirming the existence of a serious worldwide problem. It called for information exchange, monitoring, and research. The Vienna Convention thus offered quick, widespread acknowledgment of a global problem, even while the policy implications of this problem were still being debated.[18] In September 1987, the Montreal Protocol on Substances That Deplete the Ozone Layer was concluded, and it set out a schedule for the progressive phaseout of CFCs. The protocol, though not wholly satisfactory, furnished a useful precedent for rapid, remedial action to address a pressing problem of commons preservation.

The key to the Montreal Protocol's flexible development, implementation, and enforcement lies in its decision making and institutional provisions. The powers enjoyed by the Conference of the Parties are unique. For example, if the Conference of the Parties cannot reach a consensus, a two-thirds majority can still make certain decisions that will bind all members, even those that voted against a proposed action. Such decisions must be supported by a complement of developed and developing states.[19] Further, the protocol provides for a formal noncompliance procedure, whereby an implementation committee can hear complaints and report to the Conference of Parties, which can then decide on an appropriate course of action. One measure of the success of the Vienna Convention and the Montreal Protocol is the size of its membership. In 2000 the convention and the protocol had 175 members, including Germany, Russia, the United Kingdom, the United States, and other members of the European Union. Evidence of substantial progress among members in adhering to the protocol's requirements suggests that it will likely be effective at solving the problem.

The second threat to the atmosphere is global climate change that, although no one is certain about its severity or future effects, is nonetheless recognized as potentially serious. In 1995 the UN Intergovernmental Panel on Climate Change issued a report asserting that notable increases in carbon dioxide emissions had occurred since 1750, and that greater concentrations in the twenty-first century were expected.[20] We now know that human activities—most important, deforestation and the burning of fossil fuels such as coal, oil, and natural gas—are altering the atmosphere's composition and contributing to climate change. Global warming could cause glaciers and polar ice caps to melt, thus raising sea levels and threatening islands and low-lying coastal areas. Other likely effects include shifts in regional rain patterns and agricultural zones, which could lead to famine and population displacement.[21]

To respond to the global warming threat, state representatives at the 1992 Rio Summit of the UN Conference on Environment and Development (UNCED) negotiated the Framework Convention on Climate Change (FCCC). The FCCC is a framework for international action and a process for agreement on policy action. It commits governments to voluntary reductions of greenhouse gases and other steps, including the enhancement of greenhouse gas sinks—that is, enlarging areas of the Earth's surface such as tropical forests that absorb these gases. These actions were aimed mainly at developed countries by requiring them to stabilize their emissions of greenhouse gases at 1990 levels by the year 2000. Even so, developing countries will have to accept more responsibility for their emissions as their industrialization programs progress and their share of greenhouse gas production increases. Industrialized countries are expected to render fiscal and technological assistance to economically developing countries to facilitate the latter's control of indigenous greenhouse gases. All parties are encouraged to share information about sources and sinks of greenhouse gases and the measures being taken to control any local emissions of those gases.

The FCCC's action plan, though notable, has suffered from being more of a pledge to principle than a hard, legally binding commitment. Moreover, it became apparent that major greenhouse gas producers such as the United States and Japan would not meet their voluntary stabilization targets by 2000. Recognizing the need for firmer commitments, the FCCC signatories negotiated a special protocol in Kyoto, Japan, in December 1997. It commits the industrialized states to legally binding reductions in greenhouse gas emissions of an average of 6 to 8 percent below 1990 levels between the years 2008 and 2012.

The third threat concerns the atmosphere as a carrier of harmful substances. The air serves as a medium for many forms of pollutants, although much attention since the 1970s has focused on the transnational acid precipitation generated by the burning of fossil fuels. Emissions from northern Germany and the United Kingdom, for example, are carried across the North Sea and fall out over Scandinavia. Similarly, transnational acid rain from industrial centers in the midwestern United States has caused serious degradation of forests and lakes in southeastern Canada.[22]

An early attempt to redress this form of air pollution was the negotiation of the 1979 International Treaty on Long-Range Transboundary Air Pollution (LRTAP), which entered into force in 1983 and now has forty-seven parties, among them Canada and the United States. The LRTAP is the only major international agreement devoted to the regulation and control of transboundary air pollution. Under the agreement, the European air mass is treated as a shared resource, and parties are required to coordinate pollution control measures and common emission standards. The instrument, however, does not contain provisions for assessing liability for air pollution damage, nor does it provide tangible commitments to require specific reductions in air pollution. Parties are pledged instead to broad, vague principles and objectives for pollution control policy.[23]

Outer Space

Outer space is regarded as a global commons area because it lies beyond the limits of national jurisdiction and is subject to common use. In the early years of space exploration, all launch vehicles and satellites were the property of national governments. Beginning in the 1970s, however, private corporations and other entities began developing their own satellites (and financing their own launches from government facilities). This was most notable in the field of communication satellites, but considerable attention has also focused on remote sensing and manufacturing possibilities. The increasing number of activities by state and private actors in the commercial exploration of outer space, especially in launching vehicles and in stationing orbital satellites, made necessary the creation of a special regime for outer space.[24]

Since its establishment in 1959, the UN Committee on Peaceful Uses of Outer Space (COPUOS) has been the central forum for discussing legal and technical outer space issues. Dominated from the 1960s to the 1980s by the Soviet Union and the United States, COPUOS drafted all five space treaties that together comprise the legal regime for managing the outer space commons: the Outer Space Treaty of 1967, which sets out the core freedoms and duties of states in using outer space; the Rescue and Return Agreement of 1968, which supplies international legal means for assisting astronauts and returning space objects that fall back to Earth; the Liability Convention of 1972, which furnishes the general obligations for liability for damage caused by space objects; the Registration Convention of 1976, which mandates that its parties furnish the UN Secretary-General with information on the general purpose of the objects they launch into outer space; and the Moon Treaty of 1979, which established a common heritage of mankind (CHM) regime for the exploration and exploitation of the moon and other celestial bodies.

This body of international space law is characterized by the following principles. Outer space is the province of all humankind, where all communal interests should be accommodated. Outer space, including the moon and other celestial bodies, is not subject to national appropriation by sovereign claim, occupation, or any other means. States are obligated to use outer space for exclusively peaceful purposes. Objects carrying nuclear weapons or other weapons of mass destruction may not be placed in orbit, nor may weapons tests or military maneuvers be conducted in outer space. The resources and benefits of space exploration and exploitation must be shared with the international community. In addition, states are free to explore and use outer space without interference from other states or international organizations. They can do so as long as their activities are peaceful, they do not establish claim to title, and they do not seek to evade state responsibility.

Thus state responsibility has evolved as a principle of outer space law; and as with transboundary air pollution, governments are liable for their activities in outer space. The Outer Space Treaty of 1967 and the Liability Convention of 1972, as they have evolved through state practice, make states liable for their activities in space that result in damage on Earth, in the atmosphere, or in outer space. The launching state is also liable for the actions of its nationals, even if they act in a private capacity. In 1978, for example, the Soviet satellite Cosmos 954 fell from orbit and crashed, scattering radioactive debris in a remote part of Canada. To be allowed to recover the remnants of its satellite, the Soviet Union had to pay Canada $3 million in compensation for the damage done.

Increasingly, states and other entities are sending up Earth-orbiting satellites for communications, broadcasting, and remote sensing. The operation of these satellites relies on the use of radio frequencies; hence consideration of outer space as a global commons is linked to use of the radio spectrum. One outer space orbit—the geostationary orbit (GSO), which is located 22,300 miles (36,000 kilometers) above the Earth's equator—has emerged as paramount. A satellite placed in this orbit and traveling in the same direction as the Earth's rotation will be stationary relative to points on the Earth's surface. The GSO has become critically important for satellite television and for making cost-effective telephone and data communication links.

For telecommunications technologies to operate effectively, a high level of technical international cooperation is required. Governments must establish transnational networks for standardizing technology for broadcast and reception. Throughout the twentieth century, governments used the International Telecommunications Union (ITU), originally the International Telegraphic Union, as the principal forum for standardizing and regulating international telecommunications technologies.[25]

The role of the ITU has notably expanded with the advent of communication satellites. Because radio signals are fundamental to satellite activities, states have enabled the ITU to require advance notification of satellite system plans. Moreover, in addition to producing laws, regulations, agreements, procedures, and practices for assuring the operation of international telecommunications, the ITU is also responsible for regulating use of the GSO and sets technical standards for GSO use, many of which are found in its radio regulations, which guide worldwide frequency use.

LESSONS LEARNED FROM MANAGING THE GLOBAL COMMONS

The effective management of the global commons is brought about by state compliance with internationally agreed-upon norms. These norms are typically codified in binding legal agreements and are often enshrined in an institutional framework to ensure proper monitoring and promote compliance. The negotiation of instruments for managing global commons areas has been notable and significant. Still, promulgation and even entry into force of such agreements is not sufficient. Implementation, government compliance, and reactions to noncompliance are critical if the global commons are to be successfully managed and conserved.

Agenda Setting

Two major developments drove states to conclude multilateral agreements to coordinate and regulate their activities in the global commons: (1) pressure from developing states during the 1970s for a global redistribution of wealth and for right of access to commons resources; and (2) the availability of new technologies as well as the growing awareness of the dramatic pace and extent of resource depletion in commons areas, if these technologies were left unchecked. In addition, NGOs played a key role in pushing items on the agenda, particularly those items related to preserving the environment.

Pressures from Developing Countries. Ideological cleavages between developed and developing states often dominated the framing of issues and what issues were placed on the international agenda. The significance of ideological differences was demonstrated by the rift that resulted following the collapse of the Bretton Woods system in the early 1970s and the oil price shocks later that decade. These events spurred calls from developing countries for a New International Economic Order (NIEO), including calls for a reformulation of the legal status of the global common spaces. Developing countries argued that the exploitation of natural resources in the commons and the revenues derived from those efforts should be used to subsidize development programs. The notion of a CHM was central in this regard. The CHM principle holds that the commons areas are not subject to state appropriation, rather they are owned by all humankind. As such, the economic benefits from a CHM area must be shared with all peoples, as opposed to only certain persons, corporations, or governments.[26] The economic demands of developing countries suggested a certain redistributive justice implicit in the CHM, in which greater benefits might be allocated to poorer countries. The CHM concept also considers commons areas to be held in trust for future use, not just as regions to be exploited for present needs.[27] It follows that a common heritage management regime cannot rely on the goodwill of governments. Instead, CHM requires permanent international administration over a commons area, theoretically done by all peoples, but practically performed through a supranational management and monitoring agency. Typical of such an institution is the International Seabed Authority created under the 1982 UN Convention on the Law of the Sea.

During the 1970s and 1980s developing countries also tried to apply the CHM principle to issues involving the management and use of outer space and the moon as well as Antarctica.[28] Developing states wanted access to potentially valuable resources in these areas. Their arguments, however, emphasized immediate political and economic returns rather than legal propriety or ethical considerations for future generations and therefore produced no appreciable legal changes to the regimes in these areas. NIEO aspirations and the CHM concept remain alive, but the prospects for realizing either have dimmed markedly over the past two decades. Indeed, despite the emergence of CHM as a legitimate treaty-based principle of international law, as in the UN Convention on the Law of the Sea, the principle still lacks acceptance as a customary legal norm.[29]

The NIEO movement and the CHM principle did, nonetheless, contribute to the developed states' desire to establish stronger regimes for managing global common spaces. The movement had revealed developing countries' intense dissatisfaction with their economic situation, and developed states saw structured commons management as a low-cost way to accommodate them. Moreover, they believed that legally based regime structures could supply stronger internationally approved rules and norms for the long-term conservation and protection of the global commons. By the time UNCED convened in Rio de Janeiro in 1992, many governments had begun to realize that economic development and environmental protection should be seen as inseparable goals that could be reconciled philosophically and politically through international law. Thus, to the extent that CHM survives as a guiding principle for commons management, it is related more closely to conservation than to exploitation.

New Technologies. The availability of new technologies has moved issues onto the agenda or kept them off. In each commons area discussed here, governance regimes emerged in the wake of technological developments or new information gained from scientific research.[30] New exploitation technologies and concern that particular resources in the commons might be severely depleted, in effect, drove regime development. For example, new harvesting technologies for high seas fisheries and deep seabed minerals resources created concern that states with these technologies would exploit those resources before the have-not states could enjoy their share.[31] In November 1967, Arvid Pardo, the Maltese Ambassador to the United Nations, articulated these concerns in a dramatic, three-hour speech before the UN General Assembly. His plea to stop the race against chaos in the oceans led the United Nations to establish in 1968 the Committee on the Peaceful Uses of the Seabed. It became the bureaucratic vehicle for preparing the Third UN Conference on the Law of the Sea (UNCLOS III) that convened at various times from 1973 to 1982. Similarly, in the polar south, new concerns over possible uses of the area's resources created new needs for law and policy regulation.

Technological developments have also helped frame issues regarding the atmosphere and outer space. For the atmosphere commons, the agenda to create legal regimes was set in motion with the realization that human activities are damaging the atmosphere by depleting the stratospheric ozone layer and exacerbating the greenhouse effect, thus producing global warming, possible climate change, and widespread environmental degradation from acid precipitation. States came to view each of these processes as severely threatening to the integrity of the atmospheric commons and the vitality of life on the planet.

Outer space remained an esoteric legal consideration until the Soviet launch of *Sputnik* in 1957. That event heralded the arrival of space exploration. Accordingly, if several governments developed the technological capability to send satellites into orbit, then rules to govern those activities had to be established. Similarly, the development of satellite broadcast technologies made new regulations desirable to manage orbits and frequencies, primarily to minimize possible interference from other satellites.

Nongovernmental Organizations. NGOs have played a key role in agenda setting. They have been greatly responsible for increasing pressure at both the domestic and international levels to engage in environmental diplomacy. NGOs stimulate public awareness and help shape public opinion, by educating the public about threats to common spaces at the national level. They assist in formulating policy by mobilizing constituencies and employ special tactics toward these ends. NGOs lobby policy makers and other public officials to encourage them to pursue a particular objective or policy. They provide factual information and expert advice on critical issues to government representatives and international civil servants to substantiate and secure support for their objectives.

NGOs also can be catalytic agents by facilitating international agreement on particular issues. They can sponsor informal meetings with officials in whom they can candidly exchange views and work to find common ground. For example, Greenpeace International and the Antarctic and Southern Ocean Coalition (ASOC) played significant roles in shaping the legal development of environmental protection instruments eventually adopted by governments for managing the polar south. Similarly, European branches of the Friends of the Earth, the National Wildlife Federations, and the National Clean Air Coalition were salient influences in shaping the LRTAP conventions and subsequent protocols.

Negotiation

The establishment of a management regime acceptable to all parties requires negotiation of rules, including agreement on mechanisms for decision making, monitoring, and enforcement of norms. Six lessons from past negotiations of common space regimes are notable.

First, widespread participation and near-universal membership in global commons negotiations helped to legitimize these negotiations, but they did not necessarily translate into more effective negotiations. Indeed, the greater the number of parties, the more opportunities for conflicting interests and priorities, and thus defection. For example, consensus decision-making procedures used by 160 governments in the negotiations on the Convention on the Law of the Sea protracted the process for nearly a decade and eventually contributed to the United States' refusal to accept the entire convention as a package deal.

Second, negotiations are more effective if membership is restricted to governments with direct interests in, and control over, the issues under negotiation. Having fewer parties generally facilitates consensus building. The difficulty, however, comes in dealing with states that have specific interests in issues over which the regime has control but who are not involved in the negotiation. For instance, in the case of deep seabed mining, the absence of the United States, the largest holder of ocean mining technology, from the series of Preparatory Commission meetings convened for institutionalizing the Seabed Authority severely undercut the practical value of those negotiations. Similarly, the failure of the two greatest space-faring states—the United States and the former Soviet Union—to support the 1979 Moon Treaty have rendered many of the treaty's provisions meaningless.

Third, governments negotiate agreements for global common spaces to create obligations that further their national policy objectives and to eschew legal obligations that might impair their national interest. In the politics affecting the negotiation of the regimes, developed states were often pitted against developing states.

For example, at UNCLOS III the Group of 77 (G-77) argued that the principle of freedom of the seas was deficient, because it enhanced the position of the strongest maritime powers. The developing states favored extending national jurisdiction seaward to gain more offshore ocean space and greater access to living marine resources. To this end, the G-77 advocated 200-mile offshore jurisdiction in the form of an exclusive economic zone. This, the group believed, would not only protect developing states' economic sovereignty over those areas but would also promote greater fairness in North-South relations and foster the establishment of a CHM regime for the oceans.

The most severe North-South fault line appeared over the issue of deep seabed minerals. Who should benefit from the riches on the deep ocean floor? The industrialized states with the money and technology to exploit those resources or the poorer, have-not states that needed greater revenues to finance their development objectives? The Convention on the Law of the Sea adopted in 1982 responded by creating the International Seabed Authority, which would be responsible for both overseeing development of the minerals resources on the deep ocean floor and distributing revenues derived from that exploitation. The United States and other Western governments, however, viewed this institution as a developing-country, socialistic cartel that would operate to benefit developing countries at the technological and financial expense of the developed states, and the United States refused to sign the treaty.[32] Over the next decade, the political and economic impracticability of an institution that lacked the participation of the United States became clear. By 1994 modifications to the convention were negotiated to remedy U.S. concerns, although domestic politics in the Congress have precluded the United States from formally becoming a party to the regime.

The negotiation of the outer space regime in COPUOS also played out largely along North-South lines. During the 1979 Moon Treaty negotiations, the developed states refused to agree with the developing states' position that the moon and its natural resources are considered CHM. Interestingly, the treaty, which entered into force in 1984, includes no space-faring states among its nine parties. As for the issue of remote sensing from outer space, developing countries argued that not only must launching states obtain prior consent from the government whose territory is being sensed, but if photographs or readings are taken, the sensed state should have proprietary rights to those images on national security grounds. Developed states countered, however, that they are under no obligation to perform either service, because the use of and access to space are free and unrestricted for all peoples—so long as the activity being performed is exclusively for peaceful purposes. This continues to be the prevailing view.

During ITU deliberations in the 1970s, developing states argued for guaranteed equal access and national rights to orbital positions in the general spectrum regime. Given that the orbital spectrum is limited in its accommodation of satellites and frequencies, these states wanted to reserve slots for future satellite and broadcast use, arguing that to deny them access to orbital slots in the GSO or to broadcast frequencies would be unfair and inequitable. Nonetheless, the 1980s and 1990s underscored most governments' realization that the management of spectrum and orbit use is a technical enterprise that is dependent on technological and engineering solutions, rather than on the politics of attaining equity in orbit. Equity in managing outer space cannot be arrived at by a majority of states imposing international legal rules on the minority of governments that control these communication technologies, or without considerable cooperation from the multinational corporations that develop, operate, and sell those technologies.

For climate change, politics became fundamental to the economic problem. Clearly, the industrialized states—the United States and Europe—bore the brunt of the responsibility for producing the greenhouse problem. But also at stake were those states' industrial priorities and economic well-being. At the same time, questions arose over what compensation, if any, would be appropriate as an inducement for developing countries to adhere to any agreement, as well as the implications for national economic sovereignty posed by the need to monitor and enforce the agreement. The Kyoto Protocol on Climate Change underlined the critical rift between the United States and developing countries over the latter's meaningful participation in the protocol. The G-77 and the Association of Small Island States proposed that if industrialized countries reduced carbon dioxide emissions to 35 percent below 1990 levels, then developing countries would be exempt from any emissions reductions. The United States insists that before it ratifies the instrument, developing countries make meaningful commitments to the protocol by becoming subject to binding emissions targets. This split between developed and developing states has hobbled the Kyoto regime's effectiveness.

The ozone regime—Vienna Convention and Montreal Protocol—was negotiated mainly by developed states that had been major producers of the chemicals that deplete the ozone layer, in particular, Japan, the United States, and Western European countries. Even so, the regime had to take into account the eventual integration of developing states, especially China and India, as they embarked on intensive modernization programs. The political solution was agreement on a program for North-South compensation, in which developing countries were given special consideration, including the right to delay compliance with the Montreal Protocol for ten years after the target dates set for the reduction and phaseout of specific controlled substances.

Finally, the negotiations affecting the Antarctic regime throughout 1959–1982 were confined mainly to the ATCPs. During the 1980s, the UN General Assembly became interested in the management of Antarctica. Led by Malaysia, some developing countries contended that Antarctica should be declared part of the CHM, as had the deep seabed and the moon. They also argued that the ATCPs constituted an exclusive, secretive club and that one of the parties—the white minority government of South Africa—should not be considered a legitimate ATCP. Furthermore, they believed that the minerals regime being contemplated for the continent would benefit only those states that were members of the Antarctic Treaty System at the expense of the majority of humankind. Interestingly, between 1983 and 1988, the ATCPs—which counted developing countries among their members, including Argentina, Brazil, Chile, China, and India—stood fast as a group on every issue except the status of South Africa and refused to participate in the General Assembly votes on the Antarctic question. The demise of the Antarctic Treaty minerals regime in 1990 prompted Malaysia to abandon its perennial call for Antarctica to be made part of the common heritage, leaving the Antarctic Treaty System as the implicitly lawful regime for administering activities of states interested in the polar south.

Fourth, to be successful and enduring, negotiations must adopt a progressive approach to problem solving. Common space negotiations must develop and adjust to deal with new problems, political realities, and scientific discoveries. The convention-cum-protocol approach, whereby parties negotiate a broad convention first and then follow up with negotiations on protocols containing specific obligations, has been very successful in managing the global commons. This approach has been applied to Antarctica, the Law of the Sea, global climate change, and ozone depletion. In all these cases, the parties would agree first on how to articulate key principles in defining a problem and then on how to address it. For example, global warming exists; it is caused by carbon dioxide emissions; these emissions should be restricted. Often these initial agreements would be nonbinding but would represent a clear commitment to resolve a particular issue. National scientific research programs would then determine a response to correct the problem. For example, scientific research during the negotiation of the 1979 LRTAP treaty laid the diplomatic groundwork for the 1985 Vienna Convention on the Protection of the Ozone Layer for reducing CFC emissions. In turn, the Vienna Convention gave rise to the even more effective 1987 Montreal Protocol. The Climate Change Convention that emerged from the 1992 Rio Summit also followed this model: by omitting specific targets and timetables in favor of more general commitments to reduce greenhouse gas emissions, it was able to garner widespread support.[33] The convention was followed by the Kyoto Protocol, which strives to set targets for reducing the emission of greenhouse gases.

The convention-cum-protocol approach has a major drawback, however: it risks politicizing issues and can give disproportionate influence to developed states. Most states involved in international negotiations on the global commons are reluctant to proceed without a scientific consensus on the nature of a core problem and without agreement on the most appropriate means to resolve it. Developed states have greater technological and scientific knowledge and capabilities—an advantage that gives them a weighted, sometimes preponderant, capacity to shape the debate and negotiate the outcomes.[34] Governments of developed states can argue—consonant with their interests—that insufficient scientific information is available be able to proceed with restrictions on, for instance, acid rain or greenhouse gas emissions. For example, the United States' paralysis over the Kyoto Protocol after a well-funded media assault by industry undermined public confidence in the facts of global warming and solidified domestic opposition to binding emissions cuts. Absent U.S. participation, the prospects for obtaining significant emissions reductions are slight at best.

Fifth, and related to the above, is that states, instead of negotiating specific obligations, may decide to negotiate nonlegally binding agreements that indicate preferred permissible state conduct. This so-called soft-law approach has been used successfully in the management of the global commons. Soft law is often criticized for being vague and nonbinding, yet this approach has helped to develop and expand the jurisdiction of global commons regimes by means of negotiating general precepts, promulgating principles, and reinforcing customary international law.[35] It is precisely because international resolutions and declarations containing broad normative statements lack binding enforcement authority that governments can be persuaded to accept them. Soft-law agreements have been particularly valuable as pragmatic first steps when scientific consensus on critical issues is lacking. They are also helpful when agreement on binding resolutions is elusive because large groups of states are involved; soft law can provide interim hortatory measures that move rulemaking in a constructive direction.

Soft law can also provide enough of a noncommittal cushion for states to test a regulatory policy for its utility and later to create legally binding measures. For example, concerns since the 1970s about poor management in the shipping industry led states to adopt voluntary standards on safety and environmental issues, as well as procedures for reporting accidents, responding to emergencies, and undertaking internal audits. The voluntary code gradually evolved into a legally binding agreement. After securing sufficient commitments based on shipping tonnage by carrier states, states became sufficiently confident that many would comply, and on July 1, 1998, the International Safety Management Code became mandatory for all oil tankers, chemical tankers, bulk carriers, gas carriers, and passenger ships on international voyages. By 2000 the code covered 78 percent of merchant ships.[36]

Finally, soft law can help to overcome interstate disputes that would otherwise obstruct regime formation. For example, in the 1970s when developed countries began launching satellites capable of collecting high-resolution images, many equatorial developing countries objected on the grounds that this constituted an invasion of their national privacy, encroached on their national security, and intruded on their economic sovereignty.[37] Not surprisingly, tensions arose in international negotiations during the 1980s over whether remote sensing should be considered a freedom of the use of outer space, or whether the legal principle of sovereignty gives a "sensed" state the right of prior consent. In late 1986, following discussions in COPUOS, the UN General Assembly adopted fifteen principles relating to the remote sensing of Earth from outer space. Among them is the principle that remote sensing is to be carried out for the "benefit and in the interests of all countries, irrespective of their degree of economic, social, or scientific development," with particular consideration given to the needs of developing states.[38] In addition, it was stated that remote sensing must be conducted in accordance with international law, and that sensing states should promote international cooperation and environmental protection of the Earth.[39] Although these principles do not require prior consent for remote sensing, many governments regard them as a body of soft law for managing remote sensing activities.[40]

In some cases, however, soft law has been little more than a feel-good measure. On the issue of Direct Broadcast Satellites (DBS), for example, a loose body of soft law exists, but it is largely ignored by those states that own and operate the satellite technology. Efforts to establish a regime began in the 1970s with debates in COPUOS. In 1982, the UN General Assembly adopted a nonbinding resolution, *Principles Governing the Use of Artificial Earth Satellites for International Direct Television Broadcasting*, which stipulated that before using DBS, governments must obtain consent from other states. Most Western states objected vehemently to the resolution and instead sought to develop a DBS regime within the ITU. Discussions in the ITU during the 1980s and 1990s, however, failed to produce a regime for the space commons that would either regulate broadcast information or permit complete freedom to broadcast across national borders.

Sixth, for a commons regime to be successful, its rules must appear fair and equitable—both in the way they are developed and in their substance.[41]   In some cases, this means developing rules that create equal obligations on the part of all states. In other cases, fairness is achieved by negotiating differential obligations. For example, in some environmental agreements, states that pollute the most are often expected to assume more commitments than states that pollute the least. Two examples highlight the appeal to fairness. As stipulated in the 1982 Convention on the Law of the Sea, for ocean floor mining, contributions to the International Seabed Authority were to be based on parties' relative gross national product, which would make the United States the largest contributor to the authority's budget. As such, the United States, being the state with corporations that controlled the greatest amount of mining technology, would be mandated to transfer the most technology to start up the enterprise, the mining arm of the authority. In this instance, equity and fairness were integrated into the core convention, but with the perverse effect of dissuading the very state most critical to the regime's effectiveness from participating.

Implementation and Compliance

Governments may adhere to and comply with a global commons agreement simply because doing so requires little or no change in their behavior.[42] This is undoubtedly the case for the majority of states party to the 1967 Outer Space Treaty and its family of three other agreements. Indeed, most of these states have no space-faring capabilities. This is also true for most of the nonconsultative parties to the Antarctic Treaty that are not engaged in any activities in the polar south. Similarly, governments may adhere to and comply with global commons agreements when such agreements proscribe undesirable actions that they do not presently, or in the near future, wish to undertake. For example, the Antarctic Environmental Protection Protocol prohibits drilling or mining in the Antarctic, even though neither is currently viewed as desirable or commercially profitable. Another example is deep seabed mining, which is not expected to be commercially attractive until the mid-twenty-first century, if then. In addition, governments are generally inclined to adhere to agreements that involve potential threats or where the real prospects for developing natural resources are unknown and where barring such activities seems to leave all parties better off. For example, the multifaceted regimes for ocean space and the atmosphere have largely been reactions to the recognition that certain activities are seriously threatening those commons areas. By contrast, the 1959 Antarctic Treaty and the 1967 Outer Space

Treaty are examples of successful preclusive agreements that were negotiated in anticipation of potential problems.[43]

That said, most commons agreements require that states actually modify their behavior and deliver on their commitments. At the national level they must usually develop, adopt, or modify existing national legislation to enact the treaty's provisions. Once such laws are enacted, governments must ensure that they are obeyed; that is, persons under that state's jurisdiction and control must comply with these obligations. Some international agreements may require that parties secure such compliance by imposing criminal penalties. National implementation efforts are key to the effectiveness of commons regimes. At the international level, governments usually are expected to report to international bodies on measures adopted for the implementation of their international legal obligations. Typically governments are required to submit to such bodies copies of national laws relating to, for example, resource exploitation and waste disposal, annual reports detailing breaches of those laws, and the sanctions that were imposed in response to those breaches. In addition, governments are often required to provide statistical information on, for example, catch limits or harvests taken, licenses and permits issued, scientific information on pollutant production and distribution, or evidence of breaches or violations by nationals of a state party. Taken together this information permits regime institutions to assess the extent to which parties are complying with their obligations under the relevant agreement.[44]

Six lessons emerge from the commons regimes in terms of implementation and compliance.

First, regimes with institutions that can manage and regulate activities of states are generally more effective than regimes without such institutions.[45] Some commons regimes have international organizations with extensive regulatory authority. For example the IMO, a functional agency of the United Nations, makes much of the specific law that manages and regulates vessel passage and navigational standards.[46] Similarly, the ITU has extensive management and regulatory capacity. Given its legally binding, standard-setting authority, the ITU, rather than COPUOS, became the natural vehicle for bringing legal order to space telecommunications, including the regimes for managing remote sensing and direct satellite broadcasts.[47]

Other commons regimes have institutions with mostly monitoring and oversight functions, and little management or regulatory authority. The FCCC creates three institutions to assist efforts to monitor and minimize climate change. Its supreme body, the Conference of the Parties, meets regularly to promote and review implementation of the treaty and, if appropriate, proposes ways to strengthen it.[48] The 1979 Long-Range Transboundary Pollution Treaty and its series of protocols operate under the aegis of the UN Economic Commission for Europe (UNECE), with a view to coordinating national efforts aimed at curbing air pollution. Its principal institution is the Executive, composed of environmental advisers of UNECE governments who meet annually and a secretariat. These institutions mainly review how well the convention is being implemented (that is, the effectiveness of national policies), collect information on emissions and their distribution, and enable parties to better determine where remedial measures might be needed. Although these special institutions are important indicators of regional collaboration and facilitate international cooperation in decision making, they are generally considered weak in terms of their regulatory authority and management capability.[49]

Finally, there are commons regimes that function without any formal organization or secretariat. In the case of Antarctica, the regime is nonetheless effective—in large part because of the leadership of Australia, New Zealand, the Soviet Union (now Russia), the United Kingdom, and the United States, and the fact that this small group of states has tangible stakes in the Antarctic. The increasing number of participants, however, will undoubtedly complicate decision making in the future.[50]

Second, compliance with global commons regimes—and their effectiveness—will be low if the rules of the regime are too rigid. The key question for effectiveness is how to provide binding rules that are flexible enough to adapt to rapid technological change, especially in the area of environmental protection. A reasonable test of flexibility for global commons regimes rests in the ability to generate and incorporate scientific knowledge into the regime's evolving policies. Most international commons regimes are based on treaty law, which embodies the most binding and least flexible type of regime rule.[51] Importantly, legal provisions of modern regimes for managing common space activities formally preclude reservations, which allows the regime to be negotiated within a more legally balanced context, yet does not give much flexibility. At times, governments may facilitate compliance with commons regimes by negotiating vague and ambiguous provisions. Ambiguity may reflect the desire to agree, despite sincere differences over the specific content of the rules. Excessive resort to such tactics, however, can render compliance meaningless in practical terms.[52] The less clear the provision, the greater the wiggle room for governments to violate the spirit of the agreement.

Third, the effectiveness of global commons regimes often also depends on the decision-making processes of a regime. Most commons regimes have regular conferences and meetings of the parties at which decisions are made, typically by consensus; formal voting is generally regarded as a last resort. Decisions reached by consensus are more likely to be implemented than those taken by majority voting procedures. For example, COPUOS usually drafted, negotiated, and adopted the treaties and principles for outer space by consensus. The consensus procedure aims to promote compromise on issues while fostering willingness to ratify and respect treaties. Yet, while attaining consensus is desirable, problems can arise from the process: the quest for consensus can exacerbate negotiations, dilute the legal strength and scope of an agreement, and render the product more prosaic but less clear as a set of legally binding obligations.

Fourth, for a global commons regime to function successfully and persist, it must have leadership from the technologically developed world, most notably, the United States. The active involvement of the great powers is a key ingredient in making the regime succeed. The United States not only has technological wherewithal, but also political presence and diplomatic clout. Multilateral regimes for global common spaces evolve because the great powers recognize that a problem affects their mutual interests or constituencies, and they take action to deal with that concern. Given the close association among international economics, communications, maritime, and environmental matters, the dominant players in commons regimes are likely to be developed states. But salient exceptions occur. As a major space power, the Soviet Union/Russia figured importantly in DBF and remote sensing negotiations. In Antarctic Treaty meetings, Chile and Argentina, by virtue of being claimant states and closest to the continent, play exceptional roles. In the ozone negotiations, not only the European Community, Japan, Russia, and United States have a great deal of influence, but so too do China and India.

Fifth, NGOs, although they lack full-fledged international legal status, have become prominently involved in the implementation of rules designed to conserve resources in commons areas, in particular high-seas fisheries and Antarctica.[53] NGOs influence states directly by pressuring governments to comply with international agreements. They often have their own international legal staffs and challenge government arguments that tend to minimize the scope of substantive obligations. Further, NGOs lobby government officials and delegates to international conferences.[54] For example, the role of the ASOC and Greenpeace was enormous in scotching the Antarctic minerals treaty and in establishing and promoting priorities for the negotiation of the Environmental Protection Protocol under the Antarctic Treaty. Indirectly, NGOs affect ways of thinking about the commons environment by fostering greater sensitivity to ecological issues and the consequences of unregulated use. High-profile public campaigns generate a sense of civic responsibility, which in turn can put pressure on governments to alter their policies toward the oceans, the atmosphere, or Antarctica. Moreover, NGOs can act like watchdog agencies, independently checking official information and compelling governments through the courts to uphold environmental obligations in treaty commitments. For example, the World Wildlife Federation monitors global fishing activities in the world's oceans independently, the Antarctica Project reports on "pirate" fishing activities in the Southern Ocean, and Greenpeace monitors national whaling activities by Norway and Japan.

Sixth, and more generally, if a global commons regime functions successfully, that success can be attributed in large part to self-interested considerations among member governments. The underlying motive for global commons regimes is that cooperation is self-interested. Regimes are created and sustained because they deal with problems of market failure at the interstate level. Regimes improve the quality of information and provide a stable set of expectations that enhance the prospects for cooperation. In essence, institutions minimize transaction costs, while allowing for monitoring to check compliance and provide indirect suasion for enforcement for effective management of the high-seas stocks in question.

Reactions to Noncompliance

There are three main reasons for noncompliance with global commons regimes. First, a government might not comply with certain rules because it perceives the benefits of compliance to be less than the costs of noncompliance. Even though there might be strong domestic and international pressures to adhere to an agreement for managing some facet of the global commons regardless of the costs, narrower national interests might prevail. For example, pressures from domestic fishing industries might overwhelm the government's willingness to comply with a straddling stocks fisheries agreement, as happened when domestic considerations in the Soviet Union and Japan frustrated efforts by the Convention on the Conservation of Antarctic Marine Living Resources (CCAMLR) to have those governments report their fishermen's Antarctic catch levels. Second, governments might lack sufficient resources to comply with existing regulations. Violation of agreements affecting the Antarctic region can come from administrative or technological incapacities. A government might not be technologically capable of monitoring or preventing prohibited actions by domestic actors that pollute the water or atmosphere. Third, noncompliance may be inadvertent. For example, a private commercial consortium might launch a vehicle into space that fails, falls back to Earth, and causes damage to some other state's territory.

These three examples of noncompliance call for different types of responses. In the first case, the response requires proof that a state has willfully violated its obligations. Once the evidence clearly indicates that a government has failed to fulfill a legal treaty obligation, the question is: What legal means should be exercised by which legal entities to enforce that obligation internationally? In the second case, assistance by other states or international organizations may redress the problem. The third case is not really a case of noncompliance and requires at best compensation mechanisms to help third parties recover their losses.

Enforcement of common space regimes depends on many things: clarity of the rights, duties, and obligations of states party to an international instrument, or subregional or regional organizations or arrangements; state party investigations and assistance from other states or organizations; identification and reporting of parties suspected of undermining conservation measures; accumulation and sharing of evidence; and actions taken to deter nationals of parties from activities that would violate or undermine conservation and management measures.

As connections are tightened between economic development and environmental integrity, compliance with international environmental agreements can be linked with increasing effectiveness to incentives for governments, rather than coercion against them. Incentives build trust between states, whereas coercion breeds anxiety. For example, efforts by more affluent governments to use aid, grants, technology, and other assistance as inducements to developing countries should enhance their compliance with international environmental agreements. If the Kyoto Protocol is to be applied effectively to developing countries, these kinds of incentives will be essential.

More specifically, five lessons concerning noncompliance and reactions to noncompliance to common space regimes have emerged from state practice.

First, monitoring and verification mechanisms are essential to deter and detect treaty violations. Key for assessing information gathered by monitoring mechanisms is the availability of adequate scientific information on the state of a commons and its resources. Without such information one cannot adequately assess resource exploitation, perform surveillance, and trigger enforcement against offenders.[55]

To facilitate availability of the information necessary to enforce common space regimes, parties are generally obliged to exchange information, including evidence relating to activities that might undermine conservation and management measures. In this respect, port states may investigate fishing vessels to determine whether violations have occurred, and parties are obliged to enter into global, regional, or bilateral agreements to promote objectives of the agreement. In the polar south, parties to the Antarctic Treaty may inspect vessels and facilities of other parties, as well as those of their own nationals, to ensure compliance with the ATS regulations. For monitoring vessels engaged in high-seas fishing activities, the flag state retains primary responsibility. The 1982 Convention on the Law of the Sea clearly places this duty on each state.[56] It is essential in this regard for governments to monitor the fishing activities of their fishermen and the vessels under their flag of national jurisdiction.

In the case of the south polar commons, the Scientific Committee on Antarctic Research (SCAR) provides essential, long-term impartial assessment and monitoring functions for the Antarctic Treaty regime. For the Southern Ocean, a special scientific committee conducts studies and furnishes data critical for decisions taken on fishing and conservation policies considered annually by the Commission of the 1980 CCAMLR. The 1959 Antarctic Treaty permits unannounced, on-site inspection of any scientific station. Requiring that specified data be collected and submitted to a central authority may influence government behavior and deter possible treaty violations. Similarly, satellite surveillance of commons areas has a deterrent value by enhancing global monitoring of potential harmful activities, such as ocean dumping, pollution output, ozone depletion, and drift-netting activities.

Regional or subregional organizations also play roles in enforcing compliance through agreed-upon observer schemes and joint inspection schemes. In addition, states that are engaged in national activities in a global commons are generally obliged to cooperate in monitoring activities. Although most reactions to noncompliance—in particular prosecutions of individuals—will remain in the hands of the flag state or state of national origin, more serious attention should be given to the possibility of having regional and subregional organizations make arrests, prosecute, and impose penalties on persons who engage in unlawful activities. It would strengthen enforcement efforts and help deter would-be violators. In the final analysis, however, enforcement by a state or multilateral organization rests on state willpower and resolution.

Second, the governments of member states must be willing to enforce the regime's rules on their own nationals. Indeed, none of the international institutions established to manage the global commons have the authority to determine whether a state or its nationals are violating a convention or to enforce sanctions against a state or its nationals for detected violations. National governments remain the ultimate arbiters of compliance and enforcement. For example, responsibility for enforcement of the Convention on the Law of the Sea rests with national governments. Maritime conventions such as the International Convention for the Prevention of Pollution from Ships (MARPOL), the International Convention for the Safety of Life at Sea (SOLAS), or the Convention on the International Regulations for Preventing Collisions at Sea (COLREGS) do not provide the IMO with any enforcement powers.

Formal enforcement authority under those conventions lies with the appropriate flag states, port states, and nonport coastal states. State enforcement, however, is often weak: individuals responsible for treaty violations are not always prosecuted. Similarly, responsibility for enforcement of the formal legal agreements, recommended measures, and special norms adopted under the ATS falls to governments party to the Antarctic Treaty.[57] None of the ATS instruments includes provisions for formal multilateral sanctions to enforce the agreements. Enforcement of outer space law is also the responsibility of national governments. Neither COPUOS nor the ITU has any real powers to sanction or punish governments or nonstate actors that violate legal principles or legal agreements. Ultimately, enforcement of rules and regulations in the international telecommunications domain rests on member states recognizing that the effects of failure to conduct their policies in a responsible manner can harm everyone, including themselves. Put bluntly, to ignore decisions of ITU World Administrative Radio Conferences, other broadcast coordinating agencies would increase mutual radio signal interference, thus creating negative effects for all states.

Third, international institutions, even if they have no formal enforcement authority, can become powerful shapers of state behavior with respect to global commons. For example, states are required to report to the IMO on matters relating to the application of conventions, including violations or alleged violations. IMO committees try to ensure that reports are submitted and to follow up on possible violations. To this effect the IMO publishes lists of the names of vessels that are reported as noncompliant with agreed-upon standards. By publicizing these lists, the IMO is attempting to mobilize international opinion to shame governments that are delinquent not only in submitting reports, but in correcting alleged deficiencies in their ships and facilities. The lists can also help to spotlight willful violations of marine safety standards for NGOs to target, lead to new opportunities for IMO assistance or member governments to help deficient or delinquent governments enforce and monitor violations, as well as improve safety conditions in their shipping industries.

Fourth, administrative and technical cases of noncompliance can be overcome with the help of international organizations. For example, states often fail to submit reports, and when they do, the reports are sometimes inaccurate or incomplete. Most of these violations are not committed in willful disregard of norms or regulations, but stem more from the inability of governments to exercise proper supervision because of a lack of expertise or funds. The IMO, for example, maintains technical assistance programs to help states comply with their treaty obligations. It assists in running competent maritime administrations, formulating maritime legislation, upgrading merchant shipping and facilities, and training qualified maritime personnel.

Fifth, reliable means must be available for settling international disputes between states. Competing national interests and the lack of scientific consensus on most commons issues make disputes between regime participants inevitable. Accordingly, dispute settlement mechanisms are critical to maintaining cooperative governance of the global commons. Most core instruments establishing a commons regime make special provision for dispute settlement among parties. Next to bilateral negotiations, they include inquiry, mediation, conciliation, arbitration, judicial settlement, and resort to regional agencies or arrangements.[58] For example, the 1982 Convention on the Law of the Sea mandates compulsory, binding procedures for dispute settlement in most cases. Settlement is compulsory because either party in a dispute may submit its case for arbitration or adjudication, and the other party is bound by the convention to comply with that option. Both parties are expected to comply with the decision rendered by a court or arbitrative tribunal. Similarly, each ATS instrument includes provisions that call for resolving disputes over treaty provisions through negotiation, inquiry, mediation, conciliation, arbitration, judicial settlement, or "other peaceful means." Importantly, however, as of 2001, there has never been a reported dispute concerning any ATS agreement sufficiently severe to require resort to any of these dispute settlement techniques.

The 1987 Montreal Protocol on ozone depletion provides for an unusual formal noncompliance procedure. In 1990 members devised an "implementation committee" to hear complaints and receive submissions from the parties concerned. The committee reports to the Meeting of the Parties, which decides on the measures that should be taken to bring about full compliance. The Multilateral Fund for the Implementation of the Montreal Protocol was created to assist developing countries to comply with controlling ozone depleting substances as provided for in the protocol. Paid for by industrial states, the fund has thus far granted more than $1 billion to finance 3,300 projects in 121 developing countries. In addition, the 1985 Vienna Convention does provide in Article 11 for optional acceptance of compulsory arbitration or judicial settlement in the event of a dispute. Alternatively, parties are required to negotiate a solution, ostensibly through good offices or mediation. Even so, these are not strong dispute settlement stipulations because the multilateral noncompliance procedure emphasizes greater collective control and multilateral negotiation, rather than reliance on bilateral resolution or formal adjudication. The Climate Change Convention in Article 14 mandates dispute settlement between parties through negotiation or any other "peaceful technique of their own choice," including resort to the International Court of Justice, arbitration, and a conciliation commission. The key sticking point, however, remains the political will of the parties to compromise on an agreed-upon solution.

Indeed, disputes under contemporary global commons law may be subject to compulsory dispute settlement procedures, as in the case of the high seas, or to a somewhat lesser extent under the Antarctic Treaty and the Montreal Protocol. In the case of the Climate Change Convention, dispute settlement is supposed to be mandatory, but no special juridical body is created to manage settlement of the dispute. Consequently, the ways, means, and timing for dispute resolution rest mainly with the disputants.

* * *

In sum, compliance with rule-based governance for a global common space is a process that is based on positive political will rather than negative intimidation through sanctions. In global commons agreements, no formal sanctions have been negotiated into management regimes. It is generally believed that the willingness of governments to obey rules governing the global commons can be influenced by suasion, inducement, or intimidation. Moreover, a government's decision to comply with a norm is in great part determined by that state's perceptions of how its national interests will be affected, irrespective of whether the incentive comes from opportunities of inducement, enforcement, sanctions, or dispute settlement.

CONCLUSION

The industrial revolution forever changed the relationship between nature and humanity. There is genuine concern that within this century human activities will alter the fundamental conditions that have permitted life to survive on Earth. Protecting global common spaces is key for preventing catastrophic changes in the weather and the oceans, and in our ability to use natural resources to meet human needs. To overcome this multifaceted threat, states have devised regimes to manage activities in the global commons. These regimes work principally by facilitating collective choices, setting standards, making rules, monitoring activities, and enforcing compliance among participant governments. The regimes have been established to coordinate national activities out of common concern, mutual expectation, and agreement on common rules and goals. In some cases, the regimes have prompted creation of intergovernmental organizations for dealing with an issue or area of mutual international concern. Mostly, global commons governance is carried out by individual states acting in accordance with agreed-upon rules.

Global commons regimes are institutions in a sociological sense. They involve actors with recognized roles conforming to agreed-upon rules through set decision-making procedures. But, as noted above, compliance and enforcement occur at the level of the individual state. Global commons regimes are thus a means of governance without formal government. International regimes governing the use of global commons areas are dynamic. World conditions (including scientific advancements and technological change), the interests of individual states and other actors, and ideas about proper conduct and organization all change. These changes constantly put pressure on regimes. Thus regimes for managing use of the global commons tend to evolve in phases. First, states must realize that a multilateral solution for a certain problem is needed. Then, following scientific appraisals, informal consultations, and perhaps an international drafting conference, a regime is created, usually through the negotiation of a formal multilateral agreement. Mandatory rules are set out, norms are asserted, and legal obligations are affirmed. To ensure its continued success, the regime then enters a second, or maintenance, phase. Governments apply the agreed-upon rules and procedures to situations as needed. Rules become standard operating procedures for national and international bureaucracies supporting the regime. So long as international conditions and governments' perceptions of their own national interests remain stable, the regime can operate through the intergovernmental organization with relative ease and effectiveness. If difficulties arise, member governments may have to adjust the regime through revision of its rules or shifts in priorities.

The management of the commons is driven by a utilitarian rationale, namely to establish means for self-interested cooperation. The use of global common spaces is earmarked by interdependence among users. Interdependence, however, can increase the possibilities for conflict, which can spark instability and disorder in international relations. Regimes for managing common spaces coordinate the avoidance of mutually harmful conduct among parties. Securing mutual gains through institutional mechanisms in a commons regime is less the motivation than managing shared vulnerabilities arising from unregulated activities. Put another way, global commons regimes are not designed to increase the efficiency of harvesting fish, or mining ocean minerals, or disposing of wastes, or establishing enlarged communications facilities. Rather, the motivation is to secure the protection of mutual welfare through jointly agreed-upon rules and norms. Mutual vulnerability necessitates mutual management for mutual protection. That highly pragmatic motive explains in large measure why states have created regimes to manage problems affecting the global commons.

That legal regimes have been fashioned for internationally managing activities in the oceans, Antarctica, the atmosphere, and outer space highlights a critical realization by governments: No state or group of states can deal satisfactorily with these global problems alone. If man-made threats to global common areas are to be seriously redressed, or at least curbed, a concerted international effort is required. There is greater international safety in numbers when the behavior of all parties is guided by the same set of rules and guidelines.

The key lesson for success, however, is galvanizing the requisite political will of governments to adhere to those rules and laws already created for various global commons regimes. A regime's ability to influence the political will of states will be determined largely by the extent to which the regime is seen as enhancing each member state's national interests, at costs perceived to be fair and not disadvantageous when compared to that state being outside the regime. Governments must be willing to comply with and enforce these regulatory regimes to ensure that the oceans, polar regions, and atmosphere survive humankind's abuse. This is clearly an ambitious challenge, but one that must be met if an acceptable quality of life on our planet is to be preserved and protected for future generations.

NOTES

1. This chapter does not focus specifically on environmental protection, preservation, or conservation needs in these global commons areas; these issues are substantially treated in other chapters of this volume.
2. Although no universally agreed-upon legal ceiling has been placed on how high up national air space extends, an upper limit of between 50 and 100 miles is often suggested in legal treatises.
3. See Garrett Hardin, "The Tragedy of the Commons," *Science,* vol. 162 (1968), pp.1243–48. See also Garrett Hardin and John Baden, eds., *Managing the Commons* (San Francisco, Calif.: W. H. Freeman and Co., 1977).

4. See Elinor Ostrom, *Governing the Commons: The Evolution of Institutions for Collective Action* (Cambridge, U.K.: Cambridge University Press, 1990); D. W. Bromley, ed., *Making the Commons Work: Theory, Practice, and Policy* (San Francisco, Calif.: Institute for Contemporary Studies, 1992); and D. W. Bromley, *Environment and Economy: Property Rights and Public Policy* (Oxford, U.K.: Basil Blackwell, 1991).

5. See William Ophuls, *Ecology and the Politics of Scarcity: A Prologue to a Political Theory of the Steady State* (San Francisco, Calif.: W. H. Freeman and Co., 1977), pp. 148–49; Ostrom, *Governing the Commons*; and J. Samuel Barkin and George E. Shambaugh, eds., *Anarchy and the Environment: The International Relations of Common Pool Resources* (Albany, N.Y.: State University of New York Press, 1999).

6. See Oran R. Young, *International Cooperation: Building Regimes for Natural Resources and the Environment* (Ithaca, N.Y.: Cornell University Press, 1989); and Oran R. Young, *International Governance: Protecting the Environment in a Stateless Society* (Ithaca, N.Y.: Cornell University Press, 1994).

7. See M. J. Peterson, "International Organizations and the Implementation of Environmental Regimes," in Oran R. Young, *Global Governance: Drawing Insights from the Environmental Experience* (Cambridge, Mass.: MIT Press, 1997), pp. 115–52.

8. See *The Ocean Our Future: The Report of the Independent World Commission on the Oceans* (Cambridge, U.K.: Cambridge University Press, 1998); Anne Platt McGinn, *Safeguarding the Health of Oceans*, Worldwatch Paper no. 145 (Washington, D.C.: Worldwatch Institute, March 1999); and Elisabeth Mann Borgese, *The Oceanic Circle: Governing the Seas as a Global Resource* (Tokyo: United Nations University Press, 1998).

9. UNCLOS I took place in 1958; UNCLOS II in 1960; and UNCLOS III was a marathon negotiation that lasted from 1973 to 1982.

10. See Bernard H. Oxman, "Law of the Sea," in Christopher C. Joyner, ed., *The United Nations and International Law* (Cambridge, U.K.: Cambridge University Press, 1997), pp. 309–35.

11. See, for example, the 1965 Convention on the Facilitation of International Maritime Traffic; the 1972 Convention on the Prevention of Marine Pollution by Dumping of Wastes and Other Matter; the International Convention for the Prevention of Pollution by ships (MARPOL 73/78); the 1974 International Convention for the Safety of Life at Sea (SOLAS); the 1972 Convention on the International Regulation for Preventing Collisions at Sea (COLREGS); and the 1988 Convention on the Suppression of Unlawful Acts Threatening the Safety of Maritime Navigation.

12. These regional conventions cover the following areas of the ocean commons: the Mediterranean Sea, the Persian/Arabian Gulf, the West African coast, the southeast Pacific, the Red Sea and the Gulf of Aden, the Caribbean Sea, the East African region, and the southwest Pacific. See Christopher C. Joyner, "Biodiversity in the Marine Environment: Resource Implications for the Law of the Sea," *Vanderbilt Journal of Transnational Law*, vol. 28 (1995), pp. 672–79; and Peter H. Sand, *Marine Environmental Law in the United Nations Environmental Programme: An Emergent Eco-Regime* (New York: Tycooly, 1988). Outside the UN system, regional sea agreements have been negotiated for the Baltic Sea and the circumpolar Antarctic waters.

13. Despite the IWC ban, Iceland, Japan, and Norway persist in taking minke whales for "scientific" purposes.

14. The Antarctic Convergence Zone, sometimes called the Antarctic Polar Frontal Zone, marks the circumpolar boundary where the cold Antarctic surface water flowing northward meets the warmer subantarctic water flowing southward. This biological zone provides a readily identifiable ocean zone some 50 kilometers wide circumscribing the Antarctic area.

15. See Christopher C. Joyner, "Managing Common-Pool Marine Living Resources: Lessons from the Southern Ocean Experience," in Barkin and Shambaugh, *Anarchy and the Environment*, pp. 70–96; and Christopher C. Joyner, *Governing the Frozen Commons: The Antarctic Regime and Environmental Protection* (Columbia, S.C.: University of South Carolina Press, 1998), pp. 220–58.

16. See Marvin S. Soroos, *The Changing Atmosphere: The Quest for Global Environmental Security* (Columbia, S.C.: University of South Carolina Press, 1997).

17. Importantly, this reflects the cardinal notion of international environmental law found in Principle 21 of the 1972 Declaration of the UN Conference on the Human Environment at Stockholm. See UN Doc. A/CONF/48/14/REV.1, June 16, 1972.

18. The 1985 Vienna Convention for the Protection of the Ozone Layer established two bodies: a Conference of Parties and a secretariat. The conference reviews implementation of the convention, receives reports from parties, adopts policies, and establishes necessary programs.

19. The decisions are to be made by consensus whenever possible. When impossible, decisions are made with a two-thirds majority of states present and voting, representing a majority of developing states (defined in Article 5 of the protocol) as well as a majority of "other" (that is, developed) states. The types of decisions involve matters relating to Meetings of the Parties and decisions taken there, the program budget of the Multilateral Fund, and the allocation of assistance to developing countries from that fund.

20. See Intergovernmental Panel on Climate Change, *Climate Change 1995: Second Assessment* (Cambridge, U.K.: Cambridge University Press, 1996).

21. See Wayne A. Morrissey and John R. Justus, "89005: Global Climate Change," *CRS Issue Brief for Congress*, January 11, 1999, <http://www.cnie.org/nle/clim-2.html>; O. P. Obasi, "The Atmosphere: Global Commons to Protect," *Our Planet*, vol. 7.5 (February 1996), <http://www.ourplanet.com/imgversn/75/obasi.html>. See also the web site prepared by the Intergovernmental Panel on Climate Change, *Common Questions about Climate Change*, <http://www.gcrio.org/ipcc/qa/cover.html>.

22. See Gareth Porter and Janet Welsh Brown, *Global Environmental Politics,* 2nd ed. (Boulder, Colo.: Westview Press, 1996), pp. 69–72; John McCormack, *Acid Earth: The Global Threat of Acid Pollution* (Washington, D.C.: Earthscan, 1985); and Lynton Keith Caldwell, *International Environmental Policy: From the Twentieth to the Twenty-First Century,* 3d ed. (Durham, N.C.: Duke University Press, 1996), pp. 209–10.

23. At least eight protocols have been negotiated to augment the LRTAP, including a Protocol on the Reduction of Sulphur Emissions or their Transboundary Fluxes that entered into force in 1987 and required parties to reduce sulphur emissions by 30 percent by 1993. Other protocols dealing with the reduction of nitrous oxide emissions, ozone-

depleting substances, and fiscal matters to facilitate prevention of transboundary air pollution have yet to enter into force.

24. See Ralph G. Steinhardt, "Outer Space," in Joyner, ed., *The UN and International Law*, pp. 336–61; and N. Andasiri Jasentuliyana, ed., *Space Law: Development and Scope* (Westport, Conn.: Praeger, 1992).

25. Other organizations dealing with telecommunications internationally include: The International Telecommunications Satellite Organization (Intelsat) established in 1964; the International Maritime Satellite Organization established in 1979; and Intersputnik, the (Soviet) Russian effort established in 1971 to rival Intelsat. Arabsat for the Middle East and Eutelsat for Europe provide more limited regional coverage.

26. For an authoritative and provocative study, see Kemal Baslar, *The Concept of the Common Heritage of Mankind in International Law* (The Hague: Martinus Nijhoff Publishers, 1998). See also Christopher C. Joyner, "Legal Implications of Common Heritage of Mankind," *International and Comparative Law Quarterly*, vol. 35 (1986), pp. 190–99.

27. See Edith Brown Weiss, *In Fairness to Future Generations: International Law, Common Patrimony, and Intergenerational Equity* (Dobbs Ferry, N.Y.: Transnational Press, 1989).

28. See Article XI in the Moon Treaty. See also Joyner, *Governing the Frozen Commons*.

29. Article 136 of the 1982 Convention on the Law of the Sea asserts that: "The Area [that is, deep seabed] and its resources are the common heritage of mankind." By August 2001, at least 158 states had signed and 135 had ratified the convention, thereby becoming legally obligated to treat the deep seabed as the CHM.

30. See Olav Schram Stokke, "Regimes as Governance Systems," in Young, *Global Governance*, pp. 27–64.

31. On the governance of fisheries on the high seas, see, for example, David A. Balton, "The Bering Sea Donut Hole Convention: Regional Solution, Global Implications," and Alex G. Oude Elferink, "The Sea of Okhotsk Peanut Hole: De Facto Extension of Coastal State Control," in Olav Schram Stokke, ed., *Governing High Seas Fisheries: The Interplay of Global and Regional Regimes* (Oxford, U.K.: Oxford University Press, 2001), pp. 143–77 and 179–205.

32. For the powers and functions of the International Seabed Authority, see the 1982 UN Convention on the Law of the Sea, Articles 156–183. Controversy over the nature of the authority led to the eventual modification of its structure, powers, and functions in order to make the convention acceptable to developed states as a whole. See Christopher C. Joyner, "The United States and the New Law of the Sea," *Ocean Development and International Law*, vol. 27 (1996), pp. 41–58.

33. See William K. Stevens, "Lessons of Rio: A New Prominence and an Effective Blandness," *New York Times*, June 14, 1992, p. A10. General agreement among the European Community, for example, was to stabilize emissions at 1990 levels by the year 2000. See also William K. Stevens, "With Climate Treaty Signed, All Say They'll Do Even More," *New York Times*, June 13, 1992, p. A1.

34. See Frederick R. Anderson, "Of Herdsmen and Nation States: The Global Environmental Commons," *American University Journal of International Law and Policy*, vol. 5 (1990), pp. 217, 218.

35. See Edith Brown Weiss, ed., *International Compliance with Nonbinding Accords* (Washington, D.C.: American Society of International Law, 1997); and Dinah Shelton, ed., *Compliance with Non-Binding Legal Instruments* (Washington, D.C.: American Society of International Law, 2000).

36. Other examples of "soft law" on commons issues abound. There are special IMO codes containing detailed standards for maritime navigation and commerce. Such formally nonbinding instruments include the Construction and Equipment of Ships Carrying Dangerous Chemicals in Bulk (1971) and International Bulk Chemicals (1983); the Code for the Safety of Nuclear Merchant Ships (1981) aims to minimize chances of nuclear accidents at sea; the IMO International Maritime Dangerous Goods (IMDG) Code (1965) aims at prohibiting the carriage at sea of harmful substances in packaged form; and the International Gas Carrier Code (1983) sets out minimum standards for the construction and equipment of liquefied natural gas carriers. These codes and recommendations provide guidance for governments in framing national regulations and requirements for maritime safety and control of marine pollution. IMO soft laws have been integrated into more than forty nonmandatory instruments. Similarly, for managing the polar south, the ATCPs have produced a network of "soft" rules and norms for their activities in Antarctica. The Antarctic Treaty process is all consensual, yet more than 200 recommended measures have been adopted, many of which ATCP national governments have approved as legally binding for their own nationals. These recommended measures pertain to a vast range of activities, from international telecommunications, postage regulations, and meteorology to logistics, tourism, and the designation of specially protected areas and scientific sites. See Christopher C. Joyner, "Recommended Measures Under the Antarctic Treaty: Hardening Compliance with Soft International Law," *Michigan Journal of International Law*, vol. 19, no. 2 (Winter 1998), pp. 401–43.

37. See the so-called Bogota Declaration of 1976. See also Carl Cristol, *The Modern International Law of Outer Space* (1982), pp. 891–96.

38. UN General Assembly Resolution 41/65 of December 3, 1986, principle II.

39. Ibid., principles III-X.

40. With the advent of commercial remote sensing satellites this consensus is crumbling. Since the 1980s, governments have neither closely monitored nor regulated commercial enterprises engaged in remote sensing of other states, largely because those activities are viewed as being the peaceful, and therefore lawful, exercise of private, free enterprise in outer space.

41. This lesson is of equal importance for implementation and compliance.

42. See Michael Faure and Jurgen Lefevere, "Compliance with International Environmental Agreements," in Norman Vig and Regina Axelrod, eds., *The Global Environment: Institutions, Law, and Policy* (Washington, D.C.: Congressional Quarterly Press, 1999), pp. 138–56; and Abram Chayes and Antonia Handler Chayes, *The New Sovereignty: Compliance with International Regulatory Agreements* (Cambridge, Mass.: Harvard University Press, 1995).

43. Similarly, many states believed that it was better to get a minerals agreement in place for Antarctica before any exploitable minerals were actually discovered. See Christopher C.

Joyner, "Fragile Ecosystems: Preclusive Restoration in the Antarctic," *Natural Resources Journal*, vol. 34 (Fall 1994), pp. 879–904.

44. That said, the full extent to which multilateral regime norms and rules force states to modify their behavior is often difficult to ascertain, much less to assess. Quantifiable criteria and objective targets are available in only a few instruments—for example, the ozone regime and the Climate Change Convention—and even then, developed and developing countries often disagree over the means of evaluation. Most notably, global common space regimes generally do not have strong provisions for monitoring and verification. Thus, determining a regime's effectiveness may well hinge on the extent to which state compliance can be verified or national conduct can be independently assessed.

45. See Marvin S. Soroos, "Global Institutions and the Environment: An Evolutionary Perspective," in Vig and Axelrod, *The Global Environment*, pp. 27–51.

46. The IMO has two main organs: an Assembly and a Council. The Assembly is composed of the IMO's 158 member states. It meets every two years to approve the IMO's work program and budget, and to make recommendations to member governments for the adoption of regulations and guidelines on maritime safety and pollution control. The thirty-two-member Council is responsible for coordinating the activities of IMO bodies and supervising the work of the organization at the executive level. Elected by the Assembly, the Council includes the eight states with the largest interest in international shipping. Two main committees—the Maritime Safety Committee and the Marine Environment Protection Committee—play critical roles in drafting new rules and standards, while the Legal Committee considers issues regarding the legal responsibility of states and shipowners in shipping. The IMO also has special committees dealing with marine environmental protection, technical cooperation, and facilitation of maritime traffic. For information on the structure and functions of IMO, see IMO web site, at <http://www.imo.org>.

47. The ITU is the mechanism in which radio frequencies used by satellites are determined and agreed. The ITU strives to fix the actual location of transmitters and receivers to minimize mutual interference between systems, and it allocates frequencies through special administrative conferences. The ITU's Plenipotentiary Conference, which consists of all members, is the institution's supreme organ. The conference convenes every four years to determine general ITU policies and the budget. Mention should also be made of the World Administrative Radio Conferences (WARCs), to which all ITU members are invited. They are critical means of devising and setting uniform international standards. Regulations adopted by WARCs are legally binding on members and have the same juridical status as the ITU Conventions. These conferences discuss and set standards for operating telecommunications equipment, in particular, international telephone systems, radio spectrum use, and satellite orbit allocation.

48. The FCCC also establishes a subsidiary body to provide scientific and technological advice on policy alternatives for governments, as well as a special body to facilitate implementation of the convention.

49. Regional or subregional organizations can also play roles in the monitoring of agreements through agreed-upon observer and joint inspection schemes. For example, regional fish-

ery organizations usually have as part of their arrangement a secretariat with headquarters to serve as a clearinghouse for managing national reports and scientific information concerning the fishery area. For example, the Asia-Pacific Fishery Commission has its headquarters in Bangkok, the Indian Ocean Fishery Commission in Rome, the Indian Tuna Commission in the Seychelles, the Western Central Atlantic Fishery Commission in Barbados, and the Commission for Antarctic Marine Living Resources in Hobart, Tasmania, Australia. See FAO Fisheries Department, "Regional and Sub-regional Offices," at web site <http://www.fao.org/fi/regsubof/regsubof.asp>.

50. While there is no formal organization or secretariat per se, representatives of ATCP states meet in annual meetings to discuss and decide policy for their nationals in the Antarctic. The ATCP group includes the twelve original members of the treaty and fifteen other states whose status has been approved over the years by consensus among the member ATCPs. A second group of seventeen parties to the 1959 Antarctic Treaty, the so-called nonconsultative group, has opted not to apply for Consultative Party status and its members are content to attend ATCP meetings as observers, while still being legally bound to regime policies generated by ATCP decisions under the Antarctic Treaty.

51. See, for example, the Antarctic Treaty, Vienna Convention on Ozone Depletion, Climate Change Convention, Outer Space Treaty, and the Convention on the Law of the Sea.

52. See Abram Chayes and Antonia Chayes, "On Compliance," *International Organization*, vol. 47 (1993), pp. 188–92.

53. Prominent among NGOs concerned about world fisheries are the Cousteau Society, the Environmental Defense Fund, Greenpeace International, the International Wildlife Management Consortium, the World Conservation Union, the World Wide Fund for Nature, and the World Wildlife Federation.

54. See John McCormack, "The Role of Environmental NGOs in International Regimes," in Vig and Axelrod, *The Global Environment*, pp. 52–71.

55. It also indicates what type of regulatory approach would be most effective. For example, two general techniques have been used to foster national compliance with international fishery management in the high seas and in the circumpolar Southern Ocean. One involves putting controls on fishing effort, including restrictions on the type of gear and size of mesh, limits on vessels, including vessel type, length and horsepower, and restrictions on fishing seasons and areas. The other is to impose controls on fishing catches. It remains for governments, however, to decide whether to manage fishery resources by effort controls or through catch quotas. For instance, in cases where scientific data on the condition of stocks are adequate, and proper monitoring and enforcement are possible, determination of total allowable catch and specific allocation of quotas to take that catch might be considered appropriate for effective management of the high-seas stocks in question. See *The Law of the Sea: The Regime for High Seas Fisheries: Status and Prospects* (New York: Division for Ocean Affairs and the Law of the Sea, Office of Legal Affairs, United Nations, 1992), p. 33.

56. As Article 117 in the 1982 UN Convention on the Law of the Sea affirms, "All States have the duty to take, or to cooperate with other States in taking, such measures for their respective nationals as may be necessary for the conservation of the living resources of the high seas."

57. The obligation to abide by these regulations accrues only to parties of the ATS instruments. Third-party states are not legally obligated to comply with ATS norms. However, the harsh Antarctic conditions have made this concern irrelevant, since nonparty states have little incentive, revenues, or interests to pursue Antarctic activities. If they do, it is usually by "piggybacking" their programs with an agreeable ATCP.

58. For contemporary ocean law, see the 1982 Convention on the Law of the Sea, Articles 279–299 (Settlement of Disputes); the 1993 FAO Compliance Agreement, Article IX, para. 2; and the 1995 Straddling Stocks Agreement, Articles 27–32 (Peaceful Settlement of Disputes).

SUGGESTED ADDITIONAL READING

Baslar, Kemal. *The Concept of the Common Heritage of Mankind in International Law.* The Hague: Martinus Nijhoff Publishers, 1998.

Caldwell, Lynton Keith. *International Environmental Policy: From the Twentieth to the Twenty-first Century*, 3rd ed. Durham, N.C.: Duke University Press, 1996.

Hardin, Garrett. "The Tragedy of the Commons." *Science*, vol. 162 (1968), pp. 1243–48.

Independent World Commission on the Oceans. *The Ocean Our Future: Report of the Independent World Commission on the Oceans.* Cambridge, U.K.: Cambridge University Press, 1998.

Joyner, Christopher C. *Governing the Frozen Commons: The Antarctic Regime and Environmental Protection.* Columbia, S.C.: University of South Carolina Press, 1998.

Ostrom, Elinor. *Governing the Commons: The Evolution of Institutions for Collective Action.* Cambridge, U.K.: Cambridge University Press, 1990.

Sebenius, James K. *Negotiating the Law of the Sea.* Cambridge, Mass.: Harvard University Press, 1984.

Soroos, Marvin S. *The Changing Atmosphere: The Quest for Global Environmental Security.* Columbia, S.C.: University of South Carolina Press, 1997.

Stokke, Olav Schram, ed. *Governing High Seas Fisheries: The Interplay of Global and Regional Regimes.* Oxford, U.K.: Oxford University Press, 2001.

Vig, Norman, and Regina Axelrod, eds. *The Global Environment: Institutions, Law, and Policy.* Washington, D.C.: Congressional Quarterly Press, 1999.

Weiss, Edith Brown. *In Fairness to Future Generations: International Law, Common Patrimony, and Intergenerational Equity.* Dobbs Ferry, N.Y.: Transnational Press, 1989.

Internet sites

International Maritime Organization (IMO) <http://www.imo.org>

UN Framework Convention on Climate Change (FCCC) <http://www.unfccc.de/resource/protintr.html>

UN Environment Program (UNEP), The Ozone Secretariat <http://www.unep.ch/ozone/>

10

Health

Octavio Gómez-Dantés

GLOBALIZATION—THE RAPID GROWTH of international commerce, the increasing ease of travel, and the communications revolution—has eroded national borders, encouraging the movement of goods, services, people, ideas, and lifestyles from one country to another. One of the side effects of this new world dynamic is that disease is no longer a local phenomenon. National health systems, particularly in the developing world, already burdened by internal challenges—such as maintaining hygiene and providing adequate health care for the sick—must now worry about disease threats from outside their borders. Migrant workers may spread illnesses prevalent in their own countries (such as Egyptians who bring the hepatitis C virus to the Persian Gulf States), and imported foodstuffs may bear new and devastating contagions (such as the bovine spongiform encephalopathy found in some British beef). States and their health care institutions and organizations cannot handle these new threats alone. Indeed, as the scholar Lincoln C. Chen has pointed out, we are entering "an era of global 'health interdependence,' the health parallel to economic interdependence."[1]

This new era of global health interdependence is accompanied by a new understanding of the part that health plays in economic and social development. No longer is improving health conditions simply a humanitarian issue. In recent years, there has been increasing appreciation of the vicious cycle of illness and poverty—poor national health leads to poverty, and poverty in turn leads to ever worsening health. In addition, globalization has intensified fears that the spread of certain diseases may actually threaten international peace and security.

Because of the shift in the focus on health from the humanitarian level to the economic and political plane, the actors who traditionally dominated the global health arena—national governments, the World Health Organization (WHO), and various NGOs—have been joined by development banks, aid agencies, and other private sector groups who wish to shape the response to the threat of disease. However, this increasing and welcome attention on eradicating illness, with the profusion of actors and ideas and agendas, has rendered the coordination and implementation of health policy an extremely complicated proposition.

Initiatives to tackle international health problems have evolved in the twentieth century from simple sets of measures and actors devoted to controlling the regional spread of some diseases to a complex global regime with an increasing number of functions, institutional arrangements, objectives, and players. This international health regime has evolved along two main lines. First is the development of norms and standards and the spread of knowledge and technical information related to diseases, their prevention, and their cure. Second is the development of programs geared toward specific health needs and problems in the developing world. International initiatives to treat health problems in developing countries have often been motivated by humanitarian and developmental concerns, but security, economic, political, and military interests have also weighed heavily at times.

More generally since the late 1920s, two schools of thought have competed for attention on how to address global health challenges. On the one side are those who support the development of general health services to control all major health threats. On the other side are those who favor the control of specific diseases. Those who favor more comprehensive approaches—heirs to the European social reformers of the nineteenth century—have argued that ill health is not due to specific ailments but to a coming together of circumstances that result from poverty, dirt, and ignorance. Those who favor focused interventions argue that without the control of specific diseases, no development is possible.

There is no doubt that without improvements in overall living conditions (access to clean water, sanitation, good nutrition, and education) and effective health systems, no long-term solution to the vast majority of health problems can be envisaged. This should be the emphasis of strategic approaches to health threats in developing countries. Some specific disease initiatives, however, have acted as opening wedges for more comprehensive health care, and some others have produced spillover benefits to health systems development in general.

In this chapter, I will discuss the nature of global health threats—primarily those involving communicable diseases and developing countries—and examine the international responses to them in the period since World War II.[2] I pay particular attention to the work of the WHO and to the competing views of development banks and multilateral health agencies regarding health policy issues. I then look at six case studies that best illustrate the changing concerns and approaches of the international regime: the malaria control program, the smallpox eradication campaign, the expanded program on immunization, the infant formula debate, the action program on essential drugs, and the fight against AIDS. I also describe the current state of affairs in the field of international health: the increasing role of new actors, most notably development banks; the institutional and leadership crisis of WHO; and the debate about the core functions of international health agencies.

The case studies provide the groundwork for the main focus of this chapter—the lessons learned about what makes for successful approaches to managing global health. I explore the challenges of balancing donor and recipient priorities during the agenda-setting process; the challenges of negotiation among the increasing number of actors (bilateral and multilateral agencies, private foundations, academic institutions, development banks, NGOs) involved in shaping international initiatives; the difficulties of implementing the initiatives and ensuring compliance; and the ways of responding to noncompliance.

NATURE OF THE PROBLEM

The twentieth century was a period of tremendous progress in health and health care worldwide. Infant mortality rates declined, life expectancy increased, and the gap in life expectancy between rich and poor nations narrowed (from twenty-five years in 1955 to thirteen years in 1995).[3] This was mainly due to improvements in income and living conditions and advances in disease control. However, more than one billion people remain untouched by the progress of the last century. They suffer from malnutrition and succumb to common infections and reproductive problems for which relatively cheap and effective remedies are available. Pneumonia, diarrhea, malaria, and measles—easily overcome in the developed world—remain major causes of death in many poor countries, which also have to cope with new, virulent infections such as the Ebola virus and HIV.[4] Add to this grim picture the appearance of new variants of old diseases such as cholera, diphtheria, malaria, and tuberculosis (TB), as well as the declining investment in research for new antimicrobial products, and it is easy to predict a reversal of the recent decline in mortality rates due to communicable diseases.

Among the communicable diseases that pose a global threat, AIDS is probably the most prominent. More than thirty-four million people are living with HIV/AIDS, 70 percent of whom reside in Sub-Saharan Africa. Infection rates in the former Soviet Union are skyrocketing, and infection rates in the Middle East, Eastern Europe, and Central Asia are also on the rise. Since the early 1980s, close to twenty million people have been killed and more than thirteen million children have been orphaned by AIDS.[5] By 2010, it is expected that in Africa alone some forty million children will have lost one or both parents to the disease. The implications of this epidemic for social and economic development are staggering, yet policy makers around the world have only just begun to face the problem.

AIDS is by no means the only peril. Tuberculosis, once thought to be under control, is making a spectacular comeback. Each year, TB kills almost two million people. It is estimated that between 2000 and 2020, nearly one billion people will become infected with the bacteria that causes TB, 200 million will develop the disease, and thirty-five million will die.[6] Southeast Asia is hit particularly hard, with nearly three million new cases each year. Drug-resistant TB, caused by inconsistent or partial medical treatment, is climbing at alarming rates in Russia and other former Soviet republics.[7] According to Hans Kluge, the regional coordinator for TB Programs for Médecins Sans Frontières (Doctors Without Borders), TB is set to become the principal epidemic of the twenty-first century.[8]

There is no doubt that the threat of infectious disease is growing—the last ten years have seen the emergence of no fewer than thirty new pathogens, and there is no telling which one could prove to be the next AIDS—but noncommunicable diseases such as cancer and heart disease are beginning to make up an increasing proportion of the global disease burden. This is in large part due to the effects of globalization and economic development. People in poorer countries are living longer and consuming more, and much of what they are consuming—imported fast foods, tobacco products—are not good for them. Chronic diseases prevalent in the developed world— like certain cancers, Type 2 diabetes, heart disease, stroke, and pulmonary diseases— are now on the rise in the developing world. Worldwide, noncommunicable diseases—mainly heart disease, stroke, cancer, and lung disease—account for nearly 60 percent of deaths and are the main drivers of demand for health resources.[9] The WHO has estimated that by 2020 noncommunicable afflictions will account for 73 percent of the disease burden worldwide, as opposed to 43 percent in 1998.[10]

The health challenges described above impose enormous burdens on health care systems. Wealthy countries face an explosion in demand for health care services from an aging population and skyrocketing costs resulting from physician dependence on advanced medical technology. In fact, in 1994, 90 percent of all health care spending was done in the industrialized countries.[11] For developing countries, the challenge is more daunting. Most poor nations lack adequate health care infrastructures, and government investment in basic medical services is almost nonexistent. Multinational programs to help stem the tide of disease may founder because poor domestic conditions make it difficult to implement them.

Developing countries bear 92 percent of the world's disease burden but possess only 10 percent of the world's health care resources. The major pharmaceutical companies would save countless lives by developing drugs to combat tropical diseases, but they prefer to focus their resources on developing drugs in high demand for ailments in the developed world. Any drugs that are of use in the developing world are often too expensive, and international trade regimes—designed to protect patents and copyrights—mean that poorer nations do not have the option of producing their own generic versions of the needed medicines.

The search for rational responses to these challenges has resulted in the formation of a kind of global health care reform movement.[12] Although the main challenges and reasons for reform vary across countries, some of the proposals are remarkably similar. Among the most prominent of these common proposals are the following:

- Separate the basic functions of the healthcare system—regulation, financing, and delivery—in order to establish incentive structures that promote competition and accountability;
- Establish mechanisms to evaluate the cost and effectiveness of health interventions and to define priorities;
- Create mechanisms that ensure the proper use of health technologies;
- Develop programs that assure the continuous improvement in health care quality and responsiveness to patients' needs; and
- Promote the participation of the public in the development and implementation of health care policy.

Despite the recognition of the need for health care reform, no consensus exists regarding the role of markets and government intervention in health care. Many countries, influenced by development banks, are considering "turning to the market to put things right," and some policy makers would like to limit the participation of governments in health care to the design and implementation of regulations.[13] Others believe that governments should finance health care themselves. The latter view is shared by Gro Harlem Brundtland, the new Director-General of the WHO. She wrote:

> Our values cannot support market-oriented approaches that ration health services to those with the ability to pay. Not only do market-oriented approaches lead to intolerable inequity with respect to a fundamental human right, but growing bodies of theory and evidence indicate markets in health to be inefficient as well. Market mechanisms have enormous utility in many sectors and have underpinned rapid economic growth for over a century in Europe and elsewhere. But the very countries that have relied on market mechanisms to achieve the high incomes they enjoy today are the same countries that rely most heavily on governments to finance health services.[14]

It is clear that the increasing complexity of regional and global health threats demands more innovation and cooperation between the national governments and multinational organizations that make up the international health regime. The regime should modify its traditional role of responding to vulnerable populations in need and confront current health challenges by concentrating on regional and global epidemiological surveillance; developing norms and standards for health care; helping design and implement policy; identifying regional or global health problems for which multinational action is required (the eradication of poliomyelitis or the control of resistance to antibiotics, for example); and promoting research. The definition of the basic role of the health regime, however, should also take into account the record of previous international efforts in this field.

TRACK RECORD OF INTERNATIONAL EFFORTS TO CONTROL HEALTH THREATS

International efforts to control health risks date back to the second century, when traveling healers from China, Japan, and Korea spread their knowledge all over the Far East. In the fourteenth century, in an attempt to control the spread of the Black Death, the city-states of northern Italy set up Public Health Councils, and similar bodies were established within the Ottoman Empire. In the early nineteenth century, inspection and quarantine policies were common, designed to protect international trade in the Mediterranean and the Black seas from the spread of cholera, yellow fever, and plague. By the end of the nineteenth century, the control of infectious diseases had become a staple of international diplomacy.[15] At this time international health activities also began to have a more multilateral and institutional character.

The International Sanitary Conferences convened between 1851 and 1907 stimulated the development of international health surveillance systems based on notification and control. That said, it was not until the twentieth century that permanent international health organizations were established.

The Pan American Sanitary Bureau was the product of the Second International Conference of American States, held in Mexico City in 1901. The purpose of this organization was to act as an information clearinghouse through which the countries of the region could keep one another informed regarding epidemics of international importance. The bureau was also involved, upon the request of national governments, in developing studies and assistance programs to combat outbreaks of infection or to improve sanitation.

The Office International d'Hygiène Publique (OIHP), the first worldwide international health organization, was set up in Paris in 1907 as a technical commission for the study of epidemic diseases, a permanent body for the administration of international conventions, and a center for the exchange of epidemiological data. Information was required on cholera, plague, yellow fever, typhus, and relapsing fever—diseases "that Western European countries, which dominated the creation of the health regime, feared would spread from Asia, Latin America and Eastern Europe."[16]

In 1920, the League of Nations called for the reexamination of international cooperation in all fields and created its own health organization. The rationale was that there was a need for broader surveillance and more active disease control based on well-organized national health services.

To many, the coexistence of several permanent international health organizations made no sense. In fact, efforts were developed to place the OIHP under the authority of the League of Nations. But these efforts were opposed by France—which did not want to lose control of what it considered its organization—and the United States, which was not a member of the League of Nations. Not surprisingly, there was considerable overlap in the programs of the OIHP and the League's health organization.

Much of the information distributed by these international organizations was superfluous. Indeed, the European powers knew a great deal about health conditions in their colonies and had first-hand access to local epidemiological information. The same was true for the United States in Latin America. Moreover, the increasing availability of sanitation facilities and clean water in Europe and North America; the development of new drugs, vaccines, and insecticides; and the improved understanding of the mechanisms of disease transmission reduced the fear of the spread of tropical diseases.

Probably as a consequence of this decreasing fear, after World War II and during the creation of the United Nations, health was overlooked at first as a matter of global concern. It was eventually recognized, however, as a field in which the United Nations should be involved. In 1946 the International Health Conference convened in New York and adopted the constitution of the future WHO, which was officially established in September 1948.[17]

The new organization absorbed and unified all the existing health organizations into a single worldwide intergovernmental body with broad responsibilities and the power to adopt conventions, agreements, and international regulations. At least formally, WHO was not going to limit itself to controlling the international spread of infectious diseases but was now responsible for "the attainment by all peoples of the highest possible level of health" through the development of at least twenty-two functions specified in Chapter II of its constitution.[18]

Much of the initial work of the WHO would be influenced by the progress made during and after World War II in the field of communicable diseases, including the development of insecticides, improvements in the production and application of vaccines, and the development of antibiotics. The Interim Commission of WHO, in fact, placed malaria first on its list of priorities, a decision that was ratified by the first World Health Assembly, which agreed on the immediate implementation of action plans for malaria, TB, and venereal diseases.

This emphasis on communicable disease was strengthened during the 1950s and 1960s. In the early 1950s, after the introduction of sulphone therapy, leprosy was included in the list of priorities of international health. In 1955 WHO accepted a resolution to eradicate malaria. Mass penicillin campaigns against yaws, pint, and bejel were also implemented in the 1950s. Finally, the late 1960s was dominated by the campaign against smallpox and the Expanded Program on Immunization (EPI).

In the early 1970s, decolonization and the worldwide focus on development lead to a broadening of the international health agenda. Under the leadership of Halfdan

Mahler, Director-General of the WHO from 1973 to 1988, the WHO began to adopt a comprehensive, primary-care approach designed to improve a population's overall health profile rather than just eradicate a certain disease. Early successful experiments in comprehensive health care include the development of a network of health care units in Kenya and Indonesia in the 1950s and the idea of integrated health care systems in the Philippines in the early 1960s. Yet, the efforts to advance this kind of approach failed due to the lack of a clear strategy, limited resources, and strong opposition from major donor agencies on the grounds that scarce resources should be spent on those interventions that yielded the highest return per unit of investment.

The 1980s and early 1990s were dominated by top-down, narrowly focused programs including the EPI, the UN Children's Fund (UNICEF) GOBI (growth surveillance, oral rehydration, breastfeeding, and immunization) initiative, and the World Bank's Safe Motherhood program. However, these strategies were overshadowed by the development of the health system reform movement, the WHO's recent concern for "effective health systems," and, most notably, the World Bank's "sectorwide approach."

The sectorwide approach is an effort to facilitate aid coordination in global health governance. To date, most aid for health activities in developing countries has come in the form of projects, such as national immunization programs, essential health services, or reproductive health education programs. Project-based aid has come under increasing scrutiny by international agencies and governments, as it tends to lead to fragmentation and duplication of efforts, especially when many donors are involved, and often causes local staff to focus on competing donor interests rather than the project's. By contrast, in the sectorwide approach, donors contribute funds to the health sector of a certain country and help shape the process of developing national health policies. In this way, focus shifts to the improvement of the health sector as a whole.

Indeed, the World Bank's intellectual and policy leadership has been a new and significant development in international health governance. The Bank has emerged as the largest external financier of health activities in low- and middle-income countries and is now a major player in health policy debates and research. With its enormous financial contributions to health activities, the World Bank has elevated the profile of health policy and highlighted the importance of good health to successful economic development. According to Kent Buse and Catherine Gwin, "By the end of 1996, the cumulative HNP [health, nutrition, and population] portfolio [of the World Bank] had reached US$13.5 billion (in 1996 dollars), encompassing 155 active projects in 82 countries and an additional 70 completed projects."[19]

The rise of the World Bank in international health governance highlights the changing role of the WHO. Whereas the Bank has been able to marshal extensive resources, from money to economic research to access to national finance ministries, toward supporting health sector reform, the WHO has maintained a largely technical role and dealt with national ministries of health. Although WHO's technical and medical expertise and legitimacy give it a unique position in health governance, its overall funding has stagnated and donors have tended to fund special programs—some of which operate outside the WHO—instead of contributing to the organization's core budget. As Buse and Gwin have written, some observers saw World Bank's publication of its 1993 report, *Investing in Health*, as the turning point "when leadership in international health passed from the WHO to the World Bank."[20]

Although the power and influence of different international agencies have varied over the last century, NGOs—including church groups and large-scale organizations like Doctors Without Borders—continue to play a significant role in health governance. NGOs usually try to provide much needed primary care to the poorest segments of a population. In many African countries, religious organizations have sometimes provided such services in partnership with the local government. But sometimes, NGOs end up replacing the state as the major provider of health services, especially when government is deficient or has broken down. For example, the Somalia Red Crescent Society manages the Integrated Health Program, with the support of the International Federation of the Red Cross, the Red Crescent Society, and the Northern National Societies. The Afghan Red Crescent Society runs the Integrated Health and Development Program in Afghanistan.[21]

Finally, a new aspect of the global governance of health has been the use of telecommunications technology for disease verification and monitoring. For example, the WHO has established WHONET, a global surveillance network that links microbiology labs around the world to a central database in an effort to detect and prevent the spread of drug-resistant microbes. The Program to Monitor Emerging Diseases (ProMED), founded in 1993 by a group of American scientists, is a global electronic mail network that disseminates reports on disease outbreaks around the world. It now boasts more than 10,000 subscribers in over 120 countries.

However, surveillance networks like ProMED and WHONET face significant limitations. Communications and medical capabilities are often lacking in developing countries, where diseases are most likely to emerge. "Moreover," according to Dennis Pirages and Paul Runci, "it is of little use to report on disease outbreaks if adequate national or transnational response capabilities do not exist. In the absence of such capabilities, local doctors, scientists, and public health officials have little reason to participate in reporting networks."[22] Local governments also have an incentive not to facilitate the reporting of disease outbreaks because of the potential loss of revenue from lowered tourism and investment.

The evolution of the international health regime in the second half of the twentieth century and the lessons learned in the process are best illustrated through the six case studies that follow.

Malaria Eradication Program

In 1955, WHO resolved to eradicate malaria.[23] This idea was strongly prompted by Fred Soper, director-to-be of the Pan American Health Organization (PAHO), who had done extensive work for the International Health Division of the Rockefeller Foundation and prided himself as almost single-handedly having resurrected the idea of eradication as an attainable goal.[24] Almost one-third of the world population was then living in malarious areas, and the yearly number of cases of this disease was reaching 300 million.

The idea was based on the efficacy of the insecticide DDT—proven through the eradication of malaria from British Guyana, Ceylon, Greece, Italy, Puerto Rico, Sardinia, and Venezuela—and the new synthetic antimalarial drugs developed by the British and the Americans during World War II. The U.S. government donated $1 billion to the effort between 1958 and 1963. The WHO itself earmarked one-third of its regular budget during these years to the malaria campaign.

In addition to the obvious humanitarian reasons behind the effort to eradicate malaria were the ideological concerns of the Cold War period. In a 1955 report, the International Development Advisory Board of the United States argued:

> American support for malaria control could be received throughout the world only as a humanitarian action on the part of the people of the United States and their government toward their fellow human beings. This would do much to counteract the anti–United States sentiments, which have been aroused by subversive methods in these countries. If properly carried out, programs like these will challenge the Russian approach.[25]

By the mid-1960s malaria had been eliminated from the United States, Western and Eastern Europe, most of the Soviet Union, and some developing countries, and global incidence had been reduced to around 120 million cases per year.

However, by the late 1960s, the program began to lose momentum—and eventually, support from donor countries—when the effectiveness of DDT and antimalarials started to diminish. In 1969, India reported 349,000 cases, up from only 62,000 in 1962. In Pakistan, the number of cases reached 108,000 in 1971, up from only 9,500 in 1968. Increases were also registered in Afghanistan, Bangladesh, Burma, Costa Rica, El Salvador, Haiti, Honduras, Indonesia, Nepal, Sri Lanka, and Thailand.

The global campaign came to an end in 1969, when it was decided that eradication could not be achieved. This declaration signaled the exclusion of malaria from the scientific, media, and political agenda for nearly thirty years.

As malaria deaths continued to rise through the 1990s, efforts to combat malaria made a comeback. The Roll Back Malaria initiative—a partnership among WHO,

UNICEF, the UN Development Program (UNDP), and the World Bank—attempts to build on the lessons learned from the failures of past initiatives. A WHO press release announcing the initiative stated:

> Roll Back Malaria (RBM) is different from previous efforts to fight malaria. RBM will work not only through new tools for controlling malaria but also by strengthening the health services to affected populations. RBM will implement its activities through partnerships with international organizations, governments in endemic and non-endemic countries, academic institutions, the private sector and nongovernmental organizations. Above all it will be a united effort by the four international agencies concerned with malaria and its effects on health and economic development.[26]

The focus on partnerships at the global, regional, and national levels is aimed at fostering sustained international interest in combating malaria. The RBM initiative also devises a new tool for combating malaria, the Medicines for Malaria Venture (MMV). MMV brings together the knowledge and expertise in drug discovery and development of the pharmaceutical industry and the policy and field studies expertise of the public sector. The mission of MMV is to raise capital for the discovery, development, and distribution of antimalarial drugs that are affordable to populations most afflicted with the disease.[27]

Eradication of Smallpox

While the attention of the world health regime was focused on eradicating malaria, a parallel debate was taking place about the possible eradication of smallpox, a deadly disease that afflicted between 10 and 15 million people worldwide in the 1960s.[28] Proponents of smallpox eradication were encouraged by the elimination of the disease from North America and Europe in the 1940s, and by the initial success of the campaign to eliminate it from the Americas in the 1960s. In 1966, the World Health Assembly voted a special budget of $2.5 million annually for an intensive program to eradicate smallpox by 1976.

The technical rationales for the eradicability were that an effective and simple vaccine was readily available, the disease was easy to diagnose, had a short period of infectiousness, no animal reservoir, and provided complete natural immunity. However, memories of the failed antimalaria campaign still rankled, and there was much resistance to the idea that any disease could be eradicated. As a result, cash support from industrialized countries was extremely scarce. Fortunately, donors began to extend in-kind support. In the initial phases of the program, more than 140 million doses of vaccine were provided by the Soviet Union and 40 million more by the

United States. Eventually, donations were received from more than twenty countries and vaccine production in developing countries increased considerably. By 1970, seven of the twelve most endemic countries of the world were rendered free of small-pox; Brazil and the Americas followed in 1971; Indonesia eliminated the infection in 1972; and India saw its last case in 1975.[29] On May 8, 1980, the 33rd World Health Assembly declared: "The world and all its peoples have won freedom from smallpox . . .[and] calls this unprecedented achievement in the history of public health to the attention of all nations, which by their collective action have freed mankind of this ancient scourge."[30]

Expanded Program on Immunization

The success of the smallpox eradication program strengthened the leadership of WHO and prompted extensive international work in immunizations. In 1974, after a historic conference held at the Rockefeller Foundation Center in Bellagio, Italy, WHO and UNICEF launched the Expanded Program on Immunization (EPI), aimed at eradicating poliomyelitis—a goal supported by a $400 million grant from Rotary International—and immunizing 80 percent of the world's children against measles, tetanus, pertussis, diphtheria, and TB.

By the early 1990s, vaccinations prevented more than three million deaths from measles, neonatal tetanus, and pertussis each year. Globally, the reported incidence of poliomyelitis declined by over 80 percent since 1988 and was eliminated in the Americas by 1991. In addition, better surveillance systems were put in place, new paradigms for community participation in public health emerged, and national immunization days, identified as efficient means for vaccine delivery, were established on a regular basis worldwide.

These results gave UNICEF the necessary leverage to negotiate ambitious goals with national health authorities—not only for immunizations but also for reductions in infant and maternal mortality rates—and allowed it to expand its presence in the health field. This move was welcomed by those who were concerned that WHO could not adequately exercise the world's mandate for health by itself.[31] However, this also fueled a rivalry between WHO and UNICEF that would last for several years.[32]

However, despite the strong leadership UNICEF provided to pull various global actors together to improve immunization rates in developing countries in the 1970s and 1980s, immunization rates faltered by the 1990s. Inadequate local health care infrastructure, donor fatigue, insufficient information about the disease burden and vaccine effectiveness, and the high costs of vaccines plagued efforts at immunization. Also, operational problems related to the use of vaccines in the field (heat sensitivity, sterilization problems, and waste disposal) persisted in several places. By 1995, six of the world's most populous developing countries reported coverage levels below 70 percent and twelve African nations reported figures below 50 percent.[33] Today at least two million children die from diseases preventable through relatively inexpensive immunizations, and UNICEF, plagued by decreased budgets, has difficulties affording vaccines for hepatitis B and Haemophilus influenzae type b (Hib).[34]

In the late 1990s a new immunization effort was introduced—the Global Alliance for Vaccines and Immunization (GAVI). GAVI promotes a method of vaccine pricing known as "planned pricing tiering." This 1999 initiative, which replaced the Children's Vaccine Initiative (CVI), is an international coalition of national governments; international organizations such as UNICEF, WHO, and the World Bank; philanthropic institutions such as the Bill and Melinda Gates Foundation; the private sector; and private research institutions.[35] Central to the initiative is the Global Fund for Children's Vaccines, created with a $750 million grant from the Gates Foundation. The initial grant was intended to encourage other donors to contribute to the fund. The Gates Foundation is working with the international public health community, including pharmaceutical companies, to develop new strategies to get the new vaccines to children in the poorest countries. As in the past, poor domestic health infrastructure remains a significant obstacle. Despite the very low price of the older vaccines, the lack of transportation networks and trained medical personnel keeps immunization rates low in many areas.

Infant Formula Controversy

The controversy over the use of infant formula underscores the importance of NGOs in the international health arena and remains one of the best examples of international mobilization against practices detrimental to public health.[36] By the 1970s NGOs and some health and development experts became increasingly concerned that infant morbidity and mortality in developing countries could be aggravated by the infant formula industry's aggressive promotion of breast milk substitutes and the decline of breastfeeding. Several studies had suggested a direct relationship between diarrhea and malnutrition and bottle-feeding when carried out amid the poverty hazards of developing countries, including the use of contaminated water for preparation of the formula. The industry, however, claimed that no sound evidence supported the hypothesis that marketing practices for infant formulas had actually contributed to the decline of breastfeeding in poor nations or elsewhere.

By the end of the decade, several coalitions of consumer groups—most prominently, the Infant Formula Action Coalition (INFACT) and the National Council of Churches' Interfaith Center on Corporate Responsibility—were lobbying for a highly restrictive international regulatory code. The controversy became extremely political because it involved substantial economic interests ($1.5 billion in sales annually in developing nations).[37]

The matter was eventually taken to the WHO with the expectation that an international code, satisfactory to all parties, could be developed. In May 1981, the International Code of Marketing of Breast Milk Substitutes, drafted by the WHO, UNICEF, several NGOs, and representatives from the food industry, was adopted.[38] The code had originally been proposed as a regulation, which would have become binding on all member states once adopted by the World Health Assembly, but in final form it took on the quality of a recommendation and left to each country the choice of how to implement it. The WHO Executive Board, before presenting the code to the assembly, "agreed that the moral force of a unanimous recommendation could be such that it would be more persuasive than a regulation that had gained less than unanimous support."[39]

One hundred and eighteen nations voted to approve the code. The United States alone voted against it, with abstentions from Argentina, Japan, and Korea. Supporters of the code argued that the United States had capitulated to the lobbying pressures from the industry, and that its vote against the code should serve as a signal to the rest of the world that the United States would favor the protection of corporate profits above the health and welfare of children.[40] Opponents of the code argued that its endorsement infringed upon trade and constituted an attempt at international regulation by the WHO.[41]

In 1996, support for the code was reaffirmed by 191 member states of the World Health Assembly. Its translation into national laws, however, has been relatively slow. In fact, a recent report by the Interagency Group on Breastfeeding Monitoring—a coalition of NGOs, churches, academic institutions, the British Medical Association, and leading international agencies such as UNICEF—demonstrated that fifteen years after the adoption of the code, the marketing practices of the leading infant food industries had changed very little.[42]

Action Program on Essential Drugs and Vaccines

The pharmaceutical industry eyed the infant formula debate warily, fearing it might be a prelude to increasing scrutiny of the health care field in general. The WHO's growing efforts in the realm of prescription drugs in the late 1970s and the early 1980s confirmed these fears.

The WHO's concept of essential drugs was developed in the 1970s in response to the scarcity of medicines in poor rural and urban areas, the proliferation of ineffective drugs, and the increasing expense of drugs. In the beginning, WHO's activity in this area consisted of compiling a list of such drugs, but in 1981 the organization established its Action Program on Essential Drugs and Vaccines, which was designed to make recommendations on the exclusive use of generic names and the purchase and distribution of drugs, suggest the establishment of quality programs, and help set guidelines for the design of national regulations.

The program was strengthened considerably by the financial contributions of several European states and by the participation of the growing international consumer movement. In 1981, several organizations, including the International Organization of Consumers' Unions, Social Audit, OXFAM, and BUKO collaborated to form Health Action International (HAI), whose goal was: "To further the safe, rational and economic use of pharmaceuticals worldwide, to promote the full implementation of the WHO Action Program on Essential Drugs, and to look for non-drug solutions to the problems created by impure water and poor sanitation and nutrition."[43]

The coalition of multilateral agencies, European governments, and international consumer groups favored the implementation of national health programs on essential drugs in countries as diverse as Bangladesh, Democratic Yemen, Mexico, Mozambique, the Philippines, Sri Lanka, Vietnam, and Zimbabwe. The depth, emphasis, and results of these drug policies, however, were uneven at best and depended mostly on the different strengths and negotiating abilities of the local officials and nonprofit groups favoring reform, on the one hand, and the pharmaceutical industry on the other. Overall, centrally planned economies were more able to introduce comprehensive policies, while mixed economies implemented just a few aspects of the essential drug policies, often limited to the public sector.[44]

Fight Against AIDS

The decline of the idea of the comprehensive approach to health threats coincided with the appearance of a disease that became the model of emerging infections—AIDS. Just when many health specialists were stating that infectious diseases were no longer a threat in the developed world, AIDS made its appearance in the United States in 1981.

Twenty years after the beginning of this devastating epidemic, the figures are daunting: nineteen million people have died of AIDS, and before the end of 2000 the number of people living with HIV/AIDS reached thirty-five million. In Botswana, 35 percent of adults are infected with HIV, and in South Africa this figure has reached 20 percent, up from 13 percent just two years ago.[45] In Latin America and the Caribbean there are twenty countries in which adult prevalence of the infection is above one percent, and in Eastern Europe there were more infections registered in 1999 than in all previous years together.[46]

The initial response to the epidemic came too late. Thousands of people had to die, including a Hollywood star, and the group initially most affected by the epidemic, the gay community, had to build an enormous political infrastructure before the medical and research establishments, the funding agencies, and the media reacted, as Randy Shilts put it, "the way they should in a time of threat."[47]

Once prejudice was overcome and the magnitude of the threat was established, major international initiatives were put in place. In 1986 the First Global AIDS Strategy was formed. In 1987 the WHO created its Special Program on AIDS, which became the Global Program on AIDS (GPA) a year later. In six years GPA was able to gather $700 million in support, making it the largest international health program ever established.

The major achievements of the GPA were that it raised awareness about the epidemic and its eventual spread, defended the rights of those afflicted with the disease, advanced the notion that AIDS policies should be driven by evidence and not morality or politics, and promoted the idea that AIDS policies in general should be implemented on the basis of persuasion and not enforcement.[48]

The GPA entered into a number of partnerships with several NGOs, providing funding for some, seeking the participation of others on its advisory and technical committees, and working with them helping to organize international AIDS conferences.

In the late 1980s and early 1990s, HIV figures began to rise in Africa, and the epidemic spread to Asia and Eastern and Central Europe. It was then that the health officials started to acknowledge that AIDS was a major development and security issue that demanded a comprehensive response. However, a body was needed that could coordinate the work of the different—and sometimes competing—UN agencies involved in the fight against AIDS. An Inter-Agency Advisory Group had been created since the inception of GPA in anticipation of such coordination problems. This group did not have sufficient authority, however, and never developed the ability to resolve conflicts or coordinate activity.

In May 1993, the World Health Assembly requested the Director-General of WHO to evaluate the establishment of a joint United Nations AIDS program (UNAIDS) to provide interagency coordination. This idea was eventually endorsed by the governing councils of a number of other UN agencies and led to the creation of UNAIDS on January 1, 1996. UNAIDS—which replaced GPA—was an attempt to draw on the experience of all UN agencies in combating AIDS. UNAIDS, composed of a Secretariat and six cosponsor agencies, has coordination, guidance, and advocacy functions and is charged with developing and implementing strategic anti-AIDS plans at the country level.

The story of AIDS is far from over. The disease continues to spread, despite the fact that we now have a better understanding of the dynamics of the epidemic, that there is acceptable international and national coordination, and that successful prevention campaigns have been implemented in most developed countries.

Potent new drug combinations called "AIDS cocktails" have enabled doctors to delay the onset of full-blown AIDS in individuals who have contracted HIV, and they have alleviated the symptoms of thousands more. But the hope offered by these therapies is limited mainly to patients in the developed world, where the pharmaceutical companies that developed the drugs can charge exorbitant sums for them. The average annual cost for an AIDS cocktail in the West is about $15,000 per patient. This amount is unthinkable in the poorer countries of the world.

Developing nations like Brazil and Thailand have pioneered a new approach to dealing with the high cost of AIDS drugs—they produce generic versions of the drugs locally.[49] Although the legality of such efforts is in doubt—Brazil, for example, is a signatory to international agreements requiring it to respect Western patents—the benefit to AIDS patients in poor countries is enormous. In February 2001, an Indian drug company, Cipla, offered to supply generic versions of the cocktails to the African anti-AIDS campaign of Doctors Without Borders for $350 per patient per year.[50]

The WHO has also been working to secure cheaper drugs for AIDS victims in poor countries. Last year, several major multinational drug makers, after talks with WHO, agreed to sell AIDS drugs to developing countries at heavily discounted rates—approximately $1,000 per patient per year. But getting the agreements has been a slow and tedious process, as they must be negotiated on a country-by-country basis. Today, only Rwanda, Senegal, and Uganda have agreements. Moves like Cipla's may be just the impetus multinational corporations need to work faster to conclude more agreements with the WHO, lest they be beaten out of the market altogether.

The U.S. government has had a mixed record in this field. In August 2000, it offered South Africa and Namibia $1 billion in loans to purchase AIDS drugs, but the offer was rejected by governments not eager to plunge themselves into more debt. But in May 2000, President Clinton issued an executive order pledging that the U.S. government would not interfere with patent violations by African countries seeking to manufacture cheap AIDS drugs. Although many African countries lack the technology to take advantage of the executive order, Brazil has expressed its willingness to share its know-how with other developing nations, which means, as Tina Rosenberg wrote recently in the *New York Times*, "The debate over whether poor countries can treat AIDS is over. The question is how."[51]

Challenges Ahead

Despite considerable achievements, the international health regime has been under increasing fire since the 1990s. Critics declare that international health activities are disparate and often uncoordinated, that priorities follow donor preferences rather than rational evaluations of problems, and that there is a leadership vacuum in the field. (The origin of this last charge lies in the extremely political election of Hiroshi Nakajima to the post of Director-General of WHO in 1988—his two unpopular administrations were even accused of fraud.)[52]

Part of these problems arises from the number of actors involved. In addition to WHO and its regional offices, the health care arena is crowded with a number of other specialized UN agencies and programs—including UNAIDS, UNICEF, the UN Food and Agriculture Organization (FAO), and the UN Educational, Scientific, and Cultural Organization (UNESCO)—as well as multilateral development banks, such as the World Bank. A variety of NGOs devoted—either through research, awareness building, interest representation, or direct action—to specific causes are also an influential group of actors in the health field. Finally, there are the multinational corporations—such as pharmaceuticals companies—responsible for the worldwide production of a large percentage of health-related goods and services.[53]

These new international health actors have often proven unable to work together to achieve common goals and now must reinvent themselves to meet the challenges of the future. The agenda for reform includes issues like redefining mandates for multilateral agencies, setting priorities and tasks, redesigning governance structures, developing efficient coordination mechanisms, and adopting reliable means of accountability. Among these issues, one of the most controversial is the identification of priorities, which must be done before any of the other challenges can be tackled. At the moment, however, there is little consensus about what the essential functions of international health organizations should be. In fact, there seems to be a broad spectrum of views with respect to the scope of responsibility that international health agencies should assume in the coming years.[54]

At one end of the spectrum we find what might be called the "essentialist" point of view, which identifies functions in which international organizations have a comparative advantage over national entities, because it is more cost-effective for these organizations to carry them out and because these functions fall outside the sovereignty of any one nation. There are two major functions that the essentialists want to make the permanent responsibility of international agencies: (1) the production of international public goods, including conducting research and development, compiling information and databases, setting norms and standards, and building consensus on health policy issues that can help mobilize political will within each country, and (2) the management of international health threats, such as the spread of pathogens and microbial resistance to antibiotics and of environmentally related health problems.

At the other end of the spectrum are those who desire a broader, more activist role for international health organizations. Based primarily on arguments of social justice, proponents of this view want to redistribute resources from rich to poor countries, actively advocate certain national health policies, regulate transnational corporations, and intervene in planning or implementing national health projects.

In the middle are those who identify two general types of functions for international agencies: core and supportive.[55] Core functions are basically those proposed by the essentialists, and supportive functions, seen as temporary obligations of the international community, include the protection of the dispossessed—especially in countries where state structures are weak—and the mobilization of resources such as knowledge and money to support countries with special developmental needs.

The health regime has changed dramatically in size and complexity in the twentieth century and is again poised on the brink of reform. Whatever the shape of the next incarnation of the international health system, if it is to be successful, it will have to take into account the hard lessons learned through five decades of experience.

LESSONS LEARNED

The uneven record of international attempts to meet health challenges provides several key lessons about each stage of health care governance: agenda setting, negotiation, implementation, and reactions to noncompliance.

Agenda Setting

Donors have driven the international health agenda since the inception of the regime in the late 1800s. Issues important to developing countries have always been prominent, but their growing importance in the agenda has reflected the fears and concerns of the major interest groups of Western nations. For example, the international disease surveillance activities of the early twentieth century were focused mainly on those tropical diseases that could represent a real threat to the security of European nations.

Humanitarian and developmental concerns are key components of the international health agenda, but economic, commercial, security, political, and ideological interests have also been important. Economic interests, for example, guided the international health activities of several countries and firms in the early twentieth century. Frederick T. Gates, who would help found the Rockefeller medical philanthropies, stated in 1905: "Our export trade is growing by leaps and bounds. Such growth would have been utterly impossible but for the commercial conquest of foreign lands under the lead of missionary endeavor."[56] The conquest of these lands for Western commerce, in turn, would not have been possible were its exotic diseases not kept in check. Indeed, at a joint WHO/FAO meeting on tropical diseases in 1948, Alberto Missiroli made clear the relationship between the eradication of tropical diseases and the filling of Western coffers when he pointed out that, "Africa cannot be fully exploited because of the danger of flies and mosquitoes. If we can control them, the prosperity of Europe will be enhanced."[57]

During the Cold War, eradicating disease was no longer just a financial matter to Western governments—battling pathogens was akin to battling Communism. At a 1950 Conference on Health Problems of Industries Operating in Tropical Countries, attended by representatives of twenty-three multinational corporations, the dean of Harvard University's School of Public Health, James Simmons, declared:

> Powerful Communist forces are at work in this country and throughout the world, taking advantage of sick and impoverished people, exploiting their discontent and hopelessness to undermine their political beliefs. Health is one of the safeguards against this propaganda. Health is not charity, it is not missionary work, it is not merely good business—it is sheer self-preservation for us and for the way of life which we regard as decent. Through health we can prove to ourselves and to the world, the wholesomeness and rightness of Democracy. Through health we can defeat the evil threat of Communism.[58]

In recent years, development banks have become involved in reforming national health systems, and there are now loans earmarked for health system reform in almost a hundred countries. Such programs are useful when health care problems have been clearly identified, but often they are implemented in nations where their need is unclear. This is the case in Central Europe, where programs of health reform are undertaken with little preparation and even less thought about what they are eventually supposed to achieve.[59]

Multilateral agencies, however, have helped lessen the influence of donor governments and agencies by building up awareness of health issues in the developing world. This was the role of WHO in the promotion of primary health care, immunizations, and essential drugs, for example. It is an especially important role considering the low priority that health aid tends to have in the domestic political agenda of donor governments.

But the international health agencies can only do so much. For an issue to gain traction, it must attract the interest of a major donor—if an issue does not gain such support, or if it fails to maintain it, it falls by the wayside. The antimalaria campaign is a good example of how waning donor support can help sink an important initiative. However, when donor agencies, foundations, and private corporations are interested in an issue, such as children's vaccination, efforts in that arena receive a major boost. Witness the March 1999 WHO-UNICEF meeting in Bellagio, Italy, to explore the creation of a new, major vaccination program, attended by leaders of the vaccine industry and representatives of bilateral aid agencies and major foundations, and strongly influenced by the recent creation of the Bill and Melinda Gates Children's Vaccine Program.[60]

NGOs have also become important actors in this field. With increasing access to the media and electronic methods of communication, NGOs are able to introduce major issues in the international health agenda. In fact, the infant formula debate and the essential drug policy program are good examples of this, with open participation not only of consumer groups but also of industry associations. NGOs have been particularly vigorous in adding their voices and concerns to the debate over the shape of international health initiatives to deal with AIDS.

NGOs are not only participating in the debate over the international health agenda, they are actually providing the forums in which much of the most important discussion of health policy issues takes place. Two recent examples are the Conference on Health Reform in Latin America, convened by the Forum of the Civil Society of the Americas, and last year's People's Health Assembly, coordinated by the Asian Community Health Action Network, Consumers International, Health Action International, the Dag Hammarskjöld Foundation, the International People's Council, and others. Some of these organizations have been active in the international scene since the early 1980s and have successfully participated in the design and implementation of several health initiatives.

Any body that wishes to participate in the agenda-setting process can have no more powerful weapon at its disposal than science. States, international organizations, and NGOs have consistently used scientific knowledge as a key instrument to advance health initiatives. Progress in medical knowledge and technology in this century has been so impressive that since the early 1940s, the merest suggestion by technical experts and the scientific community of an issue's importance is enough to place it on the agenda. In fact, practically each step in the progress of international health can be linked to a scientific and technological breakthrough. The yaws and malaria campaigns, for example, were triggered by the introduction of two new technologies: an injectable, single-dose, long-acting penicillin for the treatment of yaws; and DDT, an inexpensive insecticide for use against the malaria mosquito. New oral rehydration therapy quickly became the cornerstone of antidiarrheal programs, and immunization-related initiatives such as EPI and the Task Force for Child Survival were given successive boosts by the biotechnology breakthroughs of the 1980s, which eventually gave birth to the CVI.

In fact, until development banks and economists arrived on the scene, the international health field was dominated by people who were trained in public health and medicine, which produced "an ethos that looked at global health problems as medical-technical issues to be resolved by the application of the healing arts."[61] Organizations like the Rockefeller Foundation, for example, have traditionally used scientific and academic leadership to rally the international health community around new initiatives. In 1997, 100 scientists and public health experts from all over the world, summoned by the heads of the U.S. National Institutes of Health and France's Institut Pasteur, gathered in Dakar to kick off a new program to combat malaria in Africa.[62]

For many, health problems can be seen essentially as technological challenges and not as problems that have strong behavioral, political, and economic components. Sometimes only those health challenges that seem to lend themselves to technical solutions are included on the agenda, and, in extreme cases, problems that demand strong political mobilization or broad societal interventions are actively excluded.[63]

Disease-specific and technically oriented initiatives can sometimes act as opening wedges for other essential health activities. In the Americas, for example, the effort to combat polio necessitated the development of a surveillance system that is now used to report cases of other infectious diseases. However, all too often, resources earmarked for specific disease programs are not available for other purposes. A striking example is the recent SmithKline Beecham donation of drug supplies worth more than $2 billion solely for the eradication of lymphatic filariasis.

In addition, the traditional emphasis of international health activities on specific disease investments has changed considerably in the last decade with the adoption by the World Bank of its comprehensive, sectorwide approach, the implementation of which has been associated with an almost tenfold increase (to $2.5 billion in 1996) in the Bank's loans for health, nutrition, and family planning.

Negotiation

Donor countries and agencies have dominated the negotiation process in the health field, frequently disregarding local concerns, imposing their views and priorities on the recipients, and dictating how health initiatives are to be implemented. This is a clear reflection of the conviction in the 1950s and the 1960s that Western science, technology, and managerial abilities were sufficient to transform the developing world.[64] This attitude is particularly ascendant in the broader policy initiatives in which clear donor interests are at stake and in programs designed to help the least developed countries where their dependence on external aid is so high that they are forced to accept any suggestion or condition.

However, the increasing number of actors in the health arena and the lessons of the past have helped even out somewhat the balance of power between donors and recipients, allowing more local control of international initiatives, thus increasing their legitimacy. The smallpox eradication campaign, for example, was considerably more attentive to local interests and views than was the malaria program, which was rigidly imposed from abroad and neglected the opinions and concerns of local officials, technicians, and communities. A recent example is the health system reform proposal in El Salvador to be financed by an Inter-American Development Bank (IADB) loan. The proposal was submitted to a consensus exercise as a result of the pressures generated by Congress and several professional and civil society groups, such as the National College of Physicians and the Salvadoran Foundation of Economic and Social Development.[65]

Finally, conflicting interests between donor and recipient and the diverse values of local interest groups have often demanded a certain degree of ambiguity in the negotiation process to reach formal acceptance by different national parties or interest groups.[66] These ambiguities are carried through in conventions and agreements, which leave to local authorities the responsibilities of the form of implementation. The result is that important issues are never really resolved, locking participants in a constant process of negotiation and redefinition. WHO's international code on the marketing of breast milk substitutes, for example, is widely violated (or creatively interpreted) and must be constantly monitored, supported, negotiated, and redefined at international and local levels.

Implementation and Compliance

The successful implementation of disease control or eradication programs has depended on a few factors: the local health infrastructure, local capacity to implement health initiatives, and the technology involved in the initiatives, especially the efficacy of the drug chosen for disease control. The international experiences with malaria and smallpox provide a valuable comparison. The malaria program failed for several reasons: drugs and pesticides were used inconsistently, thus encouraging the emergence of resistant mosquitoes and parasites; no new research was being done; national eradication programs did not have enough money or technical know-how; basic health care services were lacking; the program was run in a hierarchical manner; and socioeconomic conditions were too poor to sustain such a program. Since that initial failure, malaria has begun to be addressed as a social and economic issue, not just a health concern.[67] The Roll Back Malaria initiative, for example, assumes that malaria "flourishes in situations of social and environmental crisis, weak health systems and disadvantaged communities" and makes its control dependent on the integration of disease-specific interventions with "existing primary health care activities, and the strengthening of health care services in general."[68]

Although malaria eradication efforts hobble along, a thorough assessment of the lessons learned from their costly failure helped lead to the successful eradication of smallpox. The malaria program illustrated the need for flexibility and for the ability to implement a program using existing health services. It also demonstrated the importance of continued research and involving local communities in eradication programs. And it demonstrated that a careful analysis of the eradication potential of the disease and the efficacy of the treatment was required. For smallpox, such analysis demonstrated that it was easier to eradicate than malaria and that the available vaccine was effective and easy to apply in adverse field conditions. Finally, the malaria failure demonstrated that strong international commitment to cooperate toward a common goal was required—an attitude that has been absent in more recent health initiatives.

Often, broad disease control initiatives require that smaller local or regional experiences demonstrate their effectiveness and feasibility. The supporters of the eradication of smallpox in the 1960s pointed to regional elimination experiences in Europe, North America, the Philippines, and some countries of Central America in the 1940s and 1950s. The elimination of malaria from Cyprus, Sardinia, and Venezuela served as a strong argument for the approval of the worldwide malaria eradication campaign. The strategy for global poliomyelitis eradication was built on the initial successes of pilot programs in the Americas in the early 1990s.

Even when a program to combat infectious disease fulfills all of these requirements, it still may falter. Compliance with certain international regulations is problematic. For example, providing information on outbreaks, which is required by international law, can harm commerce and tourism. The cholera outbreak in Peru in the early 1990s, for example, cost the country $800 million in lost trade and tourism. Therefore, states have an incentive not to participate or support disease control programs. Some of the blame lies with the excessive, inappropriate measures implemented by the international community in response to disease outbreaks.

Governments and localities cannot fight vicious diseases on their own, however. Just as it is necessary to get an item on the global health agenda, sustained interest and support by donor countries and agencies are needed for successful implementation of global health initiatives, especially those that affect significant business and economic interests. We have already seen how the lack of U.S. support for the breast milk code has meant that manufacturers of baby formula have not changed their marketing practices in developing countries, even though a large number of countries have signed onto the code.

An important and creative example of how business and national interests have met in the health field is PAHO's Revolving Fund. Participating Latin American and Caribbean countries contribute toward the fund, a common fund used to finance the bulk purchase of vaccines and immunization-related supplies. The increased purchasing power allows the participating countries to negotiate with pharmaceutical companies to obtain lower prices. Countries are also allowed to pay for the vaccines in local currency after they are delivered, thereby eliminating two major obstacles developing countries face in the international marketplace: the lack of hard currency and the need to pay in advance.

One of the main challenges to successful implementation of health initiatives is the proliferation of and lack of coordination among the myriad independent actors in the global health arena. In the early 1990s the number of organizations involved in international health assistance in the United States alone amounted to more than 400, and the number of NGOs in developing countries working to promote people's health was estimated at around 20,000.[69] In most African countries, ten to fifteen major external sources of health assistance deal regularly with local health authorities. These organizations often have competing or overlapping agendas, and the recipient country must spend considerable resources to satisfy all of them. "It's a common experience," says Richard Feachem, former director of health, nutrition, and population at the World Bank, "to go to ministries of health in smaller countries and see most of the talented people devoting their time to servicing the needs of the donors rather than developing the policies and health services for their country."[70]

One of the most promising recent experiments in increasing coordination is the UNAIDS program, which provides the highest visibility for the challenge of AIDS and coordinates the activities of a plethora of actors. The other is the sectorwide approach. In Bangladesh, for example, a consortium of ten donors funds around one-third of the health ministry's budget and coordinates the activities of more than thirty multilateral and bilateral organizations.[71]

Reactions to Noncompliance

International organizations have limited capacity to enforce or guarantee compliance with international agreements. Several mechanisms have been tried, including reporting, external monitoring, conditioned disbursements, and periodical evaluations, with variable results. International events, such as the World Summit for Children or AIDS World Day, are also used to encourage national health authorities to commit themselves to the attainment of precise health goals in a particular period of time (for example, they are challenged to attain a certain percentage of vaccination coverage, or a specific reduction in infant mortality rates or in the number of cases of a specific disease).

The situation is different when it comes to development banks and broad policy issues. A senior World Bank economist recently made the following comment:

> Policy based lending is where the Bank really has power—I mean brute force. When countries really have their backs against the wall, they can be pushed into reforming things at a broad policy level that normally in the context of projects, they can't. The health sector can be caught up in this issue of conditionality.[72]

In contrast to the power of the purse of development banks, the WHO and the World Health Assembly are relatively powerless. Most of the World Health Assembly's decisions are recommendations that are legally nonbinding. This position is consistent with the public health ethos that traditionally supports the idea that disease-prevention and health-promotion activities should depend mostly on education and persuasion. Legal experts argue that international law in the field of health is nothing more than a loose moral code because it cannot be enforced.[73]

However, the Framework Convention on Tobacco Control, on which negotiations began in October 2000, may mark the WHO's entry into regulation of a product. Tobacco policies enacted by the World Health Assembly will become binding under Article 19 of the WHO Constitution, which states that a measure accepted by two-thirds of the votes of the World Health Assembly "shall come into force for each Member" state.[74] In other words, the World Health Assembly will finally use its long-dormant power to make law.

But this increased enforcement power—and the controversy it will no doubt engender—might not be a good thing. Compliance with international recommendations has been best when supporting resources are available and when issues are recognized as clear national priorities. As of September 1997, for example, only seventeen countries had approved laws fully compliant with the International Code of Marketing of Breast Milk Substitutes.[75]

CONCLUSION

The twenty-first century promises to bring tremendous advances in world health, but it also promises to be an era fraught with challenges. Although new technologies and breakthroughs may allow us to cure once devastating diseases, new contagions and long-dormant ones will pose new threats. And as increasingly dynamic economies lead to increased life spans and greater consumption, rich people's diseases will become all people's diseases: obesity, diabetes, certain cancers, and heart disease will become equal-opportunity killers.

The international health care regime must be reformed if it is to cope adequately with the challenges and promise of the new century. The reform process will require input from all relevant actors: health care professionals, multinational institutions, donors, and recipients. It will require better means of ensuring compliance without trampling on the fragile sovereignty and national pride of developing nations, and it will require a recognition on the part of wealthy nations that poor health anywhere in the world affects us all.

Any successful reform effort should be grounded in a thorough examination of what came before. During the first half of the twentieth century, regional and global health challenges were few and international health activities were limited and controlled by Western countries. In the second half of the century, however, the number of global challenges increased dramatically, as did the number of actors in the health field. The creation of the WHO and the emergence of NGOs gave recipients a voice, helped their concerns become part of the international health agenda, and changed the way international initiatives were negotiated and implemented at local levels. In the next century, the challenges of setting an inclusive, well-defined agenda, of conducting effective negotiations that produce results, of ensuring international compliance with agreed-upon rules, and of developing means of enforcing those rules will remain paramount. They can be met, however, if we do not forget the lessons of the past, including the importance of:

- Fostering local control of health initiatives;
- Taking local capabilities and concerns into account during the agenda setting process;
- Coupling responses to specific diseases with efforts to improve local health infrastructure and the socioeconomic conditions that foster disease;
- Using regional programs to build momentum for broader initiatives;
- Coordinating the work of NGOs and multinational health organizations;
- Finding ways for recipients to pool their resources and work as equals with donors; and
- Continuing research into new methods.

NOTES

1. Lincoln Chen, D. Bell, and L. Bates, "World Health and Institutional Change," in *Pocantico Retreat: Enhancing the Performance of International Health Institutions* (Cambridge, Mass.: Rockefeller Foundation, Social Science Research Council, Harvard School of Public Health, 1996), pp. 9–21.
2. Except for the work of the International Health Division of the Rockefeller Foundation, no mention will be made of either the work of bilateral private and public institutions or the activities of the missionary societies in the first half of the century because their work tended to have a limited regional scope. The same is true for the International Committee of the Red Cross, which was basically involved in the relief of acute suffering or aid of persecuted populations.
3. This section is based on Jaime Sepúlveda et al., "The New World Order and International Health," *British Medical Journal,* vol. 314 (May 1997), pp. 1404–07.
4. Malaria, the world's most important tropical parasitic disease, is second only to tuberculosis in terms of number of deaths. Of the estimated 300–500 million cases of malaria per year, one million die, the vast majority of whom are young children in Sub-Saharan Africa.
5. UNAIDS, *Report on the Global HIV/AIDS Epidemic* (Geneva: UNAIDS, 2000).
6. Nearly two billion people—one-third of the world's population—have latent TB infection. Poorly managed TB programs and patients who go through partial treatments have given rise to drug-resistant TB, which threatens to make TB incurable. See WHO web site <http://www.who.int/health-topics/tb.htm>.
7. David Remnick, "More Bad News from the Gulag," *New Yorker,* February 15, 1999, pp. 27–8.
8. G. York, "A Deadly Strain of TB Races Toward the West," *Globe and Mail,* March 24, 1999, pp. A1, A12.

9. See WHO Noncommunicable Diseases web site at <http://www.who.int/ned/>.

10. WHO, *The World Health Report, 1999—Making a Difference* (Geneva: WHO, 1999), p. 16.

11. G. Schieber and A. Maeda, "Health Care Financing and Delivery in Developing Countries," *Health Affairs*, vol. 18, no. 3 (May–June 1999), pp. 193–205.

12. To give an idea of the magnitude of the health system reform movement, we can mention that the Inter-American Development Bank has loans earmarked for health system reform in every country in Latin American and the Caribbean, and that the World Bank has more than ninety active projects in the area of health worldwide, many of them devoted to the local implementation of the Bank's sectorwide approach.

13. "The Americas Shift Toward Private Health Care," *The Economist*, May 18, 1999, pp. 69–70.

14. Gro Harlem Brundtland, "Message from the Director General," in WHO, *The World Health Report, 1999—Making a Difference*, pp. vii–xix.

15. Inge Kaul, Isabelle Grunberg, and Marc Stern, "Health," in Inge Kaul, Isabelle Grunberg, and Marc Stern, eds., *Global Public Goods: International Cooperation in the Twenty-First Century* (New York: Oxford University Press, 1999), p. 264.

16. Mark Zacher, "Global Epidemiological Surveillance: International Cooperation to Monitor Infectious Diseases," in Kaul, Grunberg, and Stern, eds., *Global Public Goods*, pp. 266–307.

17. Neville Marriot Goodman, *International Health Organizations and Their Work* (Edinburgh: Churchill Livingstone, 1971).

18. WHO, *Basic Documents*, 39th edition (Geneva: WHO, 1992).

19. See Kent Buse and Catherine Gwin, "The World Bank and Global Cooperation in Health: The Case of Bangladesh," *The Lancet*, vol. 351 (February 28, 1998), pp. 665–69.

20. Ibid., p. 666.

21. Pal Jareg and Dan C. O. Kaseje, "Growth of Civil Society in Developing Countries: Implications for Health," *The Lancet*, vol. 351 (March 14, 1998), p. 820.

22. Dennis Pirages and Paul Runci, "Ecological Interdependence and the Spread of Infectious Disease," in Maryann K. Cusimano, ed., *Beyond Sovereignty* (New York: St. Martin's Press, 2000), p. 189.

23. The term *eradication* has a very precise definition and should be distinguished from the terms *elimination* and *control*. WHO defines eradication as the achievement of a status whereby no further cases of a disease occur anywhere and continued control measures are unnecessary. Elimination is defined as the reduction of case transmission to a predetermined low level. Finally, the control of a disease implies the implementation of operations or programs aimed at reducing its incidence.

24. Socrates Litsios, "René J. Dubos and Fred L. Soper: Their Contrasting Views on Vector and Disease Eradication," *Perspectives in Biological Medicine*, vol. 41, no.1 (Fall 1997), pp. 138–49.

25. H. Cleaver, "Malaria and the Political Economy of Public Health," *International Journal of Health Services*, vol. 7, no. 4 (1977), pp. 557–79.

26. WHO, "Four International Organizations United to Roll Back Malaria," Press Release WHO/77, October 30, 1998. Available at <http://www.who.int/inf-pr-1998/en/pr98-77.html>.

27. See <http://www.malariamedicines.org/>.

28. Smallpox is a disease caused by a virus that spreads from person to person in droplets discharged from the mouth or nose. After ten to twelve days of inhaling the virus, the infected person develops a high fever and aching sensations. After two to four days a rash appears on the face and then spreads over the entire body. The papules quickly become enlarged vesicles filled first with a clear serum and then with pus. In severe cases the pustules may be so close together, particularly on the face, that there is no normal skin; the face is swollen and the patient may be unrecognizable. A few days later scabs begin to form and by the third week they fall off, leaving depigmented areas that become disfiguring scars. Some patients are left blind and those afflicted by the virulent Asian form of the virus may die. Once smallpox has been contracted, there is no effective treatment for it.

29. Donald R. Hopkins, "Smallpox: Ten Years Gone," *American Journal of Public Health*, vol. 78, no. 12 (December 1988), pp. 1589–95.

30. F. Fenner et al., *Smallpox and Its Eradication* (Geneva: WHO, 1988).

31. William Muraskin, "Origins of the Children's Vaccine Initiative: The Intellectual Foundations," *Social Science and Medicine*, vol. 42, no. 12 (June 1996), pp. 1703–19.

32. Strong competition between UNICEF and WHO dates back to the early 1980s, when UNICEF launched the "Children's Revolution" and started promoting children's health in a direct way, a responsibility traditionally attached to WHO. The idea of developing health initiatives outside WHO arose from an extended impression that WHO was turning extremely bureaucratic, a feeling exacerbated during the highly politicized election campaign of 1988 that made Hiroshi Nakajima Director-General. Disagreements between these two agencies were also common around style and approach.

33. F. T. Cutts, "Advances and Challenges for the Expanded Programme on Immunization," *British Medical Bulletin*, vol. 54, no. 2 (1998), pp. 445–61.

34. See U.S. General Accounting Office, "Global Health: Factors Contributing to Low Vaccination Rates in Developing Countries," GAO/NSIAD-00-4, October 1999.

35. The CVI was founded following the World Summit for Children in New York in 1990. Its cosponsors were the UNICEF, UNDP, the World Bank, the WHO, and the Rockefeller Foundation. The CVI Secretariat is located in Geneva, Switzerland. The annual CVI Meeting of Interested Parties in June brings together country representatives, cosponsors, and other collaborators, including industry, to examine CVI activities during the year past and its plans for the year to come. See <http://www.who.int/inf-fs/en/fact169.html>.

36. Andrew Chetley, *Lessons from Baby Food Campaign* (Geneva: International Fund for Development Alternatives, 1986).

37. S. C. Joseph, "The Infant Formula Controversy: An International Health Policy Paradigm, *Annals of Internal Medicine*, vol. 95, no. 3 (1981), pp. 383–84.

38. WHO, *Code of Marketing Breastmilk Substitutes* (Geneva: WHO, 1981).

39. Introductory statement by the representative of the Executive Board to the Thirty–Fourth World Health Assembly on the subject of the Draft International Code of Marketing of Breast Milk Substitutes quoted in K. Tomasevski, "Health," in Oscar Schachter and Christopher Joyner, eds., *United Nations Legal Order* (Cambridge, U.K.: Cambridge University Press, 1985), pp. 859–906.

40. S. C. Joseph, and E. N. Babb, "Of Babies, Profit and the Question of Conscience," *Los Angeles Times*, May 21, 1981.

41. E. Abrams, "Infant Formula Code: Why the United States May Stand Alone," *Washington Post*, May 21, 1981.

42. Anna Taylor, "Violations of the International Code of Marketing of Breastmilk Substitute: Prevalence in Four Countries," *British Medical Journal*, vol. 316 (April 1998), pp. 1117–22.

43. M. Reich, "Essential Drugs: Economics and Politics in International Health," *Health Policy* (1987), pp. 39–57.

44. London School of Hygiene and Tropical Medicine, Koninklijk Institut voor de Tropen, *An Evaluation of WHO's Program on Essential Drugs* (London: London School of Hygiene and Tropical Medicine, and Koninklijk Institut voor de Tropen, 1989).

45. UNAIDS, *Report on the Global HIV/AIDS Epidemic* (Geneva: UNAIDS, 2000).

46. UNAIDS, *Global Strategy for HIV/AIDS* (Geneva: UNAIDS, 2000).

47. Randy Shilts, *And the Band Played On: Politics, People, and the AIDS Epidemic* (New York: St. Martin's Press, 1987), p. xxii.

48. M. Merson, "Experiences in the Global Program on AIDS," paper presented at the Thirteenth International AIDS Conference, Durban, South Africa, July 13, 2000.

49. Tina Rosenberg, "Look at Brazil," *New York Times Magazine*, January 28, 2001.

50. Doug McNeil Jr., "Indian Company Offers to Supply AIDS Drugs at Low Cost in Africa," *Boston Globe*, February 6, 2001, p. A1.

51. Rosenberg, "Look at Brazil," p. 28.

52. Fiona Godlee, "WHO in Crisis," *British Medical Journal*, vol. 309 (November 1994), pp. 1424–28. See also Fiona Godlee, "WHO in Retreat: Is It Losing Its Influence?" *British Medical Journal*, vol. 309 (December 1994), pp. 1491–95.

53. With the liberalization of trade, the international market for health products and services has greatly expanded. Medicinal and pharmaceutical exports from OECD countries, for example, increased 1,000 percent since the late 1970s. Trade in health services has also expanded in all its forms, and already several health care firms—Aetna, Healthcare, Cigna, Health Partners, Humana, Kaiser, United HealthCare—operate globally.

54. Kelley Lee, "Shaping the Future of Global Health Cooperation: Where Can We Go From Here?" *The Lancet*, vol. 351 (March 1998), pp. 899–902. Also, see Frenk et al. "The Future of World Health."

55. Dean Jamison, Julio Frenk, and Felicia Knaul, "International Collective Action in Health: Objectives, Functions, and Rationale," *The Lancet*, vol. 351 (February 1998), pp. 514–17.

56. Quoted in R. Brown, "Public Health in Imperialism: Early Rockefeller Programs at Home and Abroad," *American Journal of Public Health*, vol. 66, no. 9 (1976), pp. 897–903.

57. Randall Packard, "Malaria Dreams: Postwar Visions of Health and Development in the Third World," *Medical Anthropology*, vol. 17, no. 3 (1997), pp. 279–96.

58. Quoted in Litsios, "René J. Dubos and Fred L. Soper."

59. A. Nichols, "Health and Wealth," *Business Central Europe*, vol. 6, no. 62 (1999), pp. 12–15.

60. Gustav J. V. Nossal, "Global Immunization for the 21st Century," *Science*, vol. 284 (April 1999), p. 587.

61. David Fidler, "The Future of the World Health Organization: What Role for International Law?" *Vanderbilt Journal of Transnational Law*, vol. 31, no. 5 (1998), pp. 1079–1126.

62. Elliot Marshall, "African Malaria Studies Draw Attention," *Science*, vol. 275 (January 1997), pp. 299.

63. An important sector of the public health community supports the idea that international health initiatives should focus on problems about which we can actually do something. Health threats related to economic, social, or political determinants are traditionally viewed as beyond the reach of reform efforts.

64. Judith Tendler, *Inside Foreign Aid* (Baltimore, Md.: Johns Hopkins University Press, 1975).

65. G. Leal, "Voces, salidas, lealtades, oportunidades, denominación de origen," interés y tempo de una política pública: la reforma mexicana de la salud y la seguridad social, *Gestión y Política Pública* (1998), pp. 115–41.

66. Reich, "Essential Drugs."

67. Octavio Gómez-Dantés and A. E. Bim, "Malaria and Social Movements in Mexico: The Last Sixty Years," *Parassitologia* (2000), p. 42.

68. WHO, "Rolling Back Malaria," in *World Health Report 1999—Making a Difference*, pp. 49–63.

69. Jareg and Kaseje, "Growth of Civil Society in Developing Countries," pp. 819–22.

70. Kamran Abbasi, "The World Bank and World Health: Interview with Richard Feachem," *British Medical Journal*, vol. 318 (April 1999), pp. 1206–08.

71. Kamran Abbasi, "The World Bank and World Health: Focus on South Asia—I: Bangladesh," *British Medical Journal*, vol. 318 (April 1999), pp. 1066–69.

72. Kamran Abbasi, "The World Bank and World Health: Healthcare Strategy," *British Medical Journal*, vol. 318 (April 1999), pp. 933–36.

73. Fidler, "The Future of the World Health Organization."

74. WHO, *Basic Documents*.

75. Anthony Costello and Harshpal S. Sachdev, "Protecting Breast Feeding from Breast Milk Substitutes," *British Medical Journal*, vol. 316 (April 1998), pp. 1103–04.

SUGGESTED ADDITIONAL READING

Abbasi, Kamran. "The World Bank and World Health," (series of six articles). *British Medical Journal*, vol. 318 (April 1999).

Fenner, F., D. A. Henderson, Y. Arita, Z. Jezek, and I. D. Ladnyi. *Smallpox and Its Eradication*. Geneva: World Health Organization, 1988.

Godlee, Fiona. "WHO in Retreat: Is It Losing Its Influence?" *British Medical Journal*, vol. 309 (December 1994).

Godlee, Fiona. "The World Health Organisation" (series of three articles). *British Medical Journal*, vol. 309 (December 1994), pp. 1424–28, 1566–70, 1636–39.

Godlee, Fiona. "The World Health Organisation" (series of two articles). *British Medical Journal*, vol. 310 (1995), pp. 110–12, 178–82.

Goodman, Neville Marriott. *International Health Organizations and Their Work*. Edinburgh: Churchill Livingstone, 1971.

Jamison, Dean T., Julio Frenk, and Felicia Knaul. "International Collective Action in Health: Objectives, Functions, and Rationale." *The Lancet*, vol. 351 (February 14, 1998), pp. 514–17.

Jareg, Pal, and Dan C. O. Kaseje. "Growth of Civil Society in Developing Countries: Implications for Health." *The Lancet*, vol. 351 (March 14, 1998), pp. 819–22.

Lee, Kelley. "Shaping the Future of Global Health Cooperation: Where Can We Go from Here?" *The Lancet*, vol. 351 (March 21, 1998), pp. 899–902.

Tendler, Judith. *Inside Foreign Aid*. Baltimore, Md.: Johns Hopkins University Press, 1975.

UNAIDS. *Global Strategy for HIV/AIDS*. Geneva: UNAIDS, 2000.

Zacher, Mark W. "Global Epidemiological Surveillance: International Cooperation to Monitor Infectious Diseases." In Inge Kaul, Isabelle Grunberg, and Marc A. Stern, eds., *Global Public Goods: International Cooperation in the 21st Century*. New York: Oxford University Press, 1999, pp. 266–83.

11

Human Rights

Dinah L. Shelton

GOVERNANCE OVER HUMAN RIGHTS is multifaceted, including different levels of action (subregional, regional, global), multiple actors (states, intergovernmental organizations, nongovernmental organizations, experts, and, increasingly, business entities), and a variety of techniques, from legal standard setting and litigation to grassroots mobilization. Its scope of action can be seen in the development of new techniques as wide ranging as technical assistance/capacity building and criminal prosecution before national and international criminal tribunals. The proliferation of norms, institutions, and techniques reflects both the importance of the issue on the international agenda and the variety of problems needing attention.

This chapter assesses the accomplishments and limitations of the human rights regime as it has developed since the end of World War II.[1] It concludes that human rights governance has led to an overall improvement in the treatment of individuals by governments around the world. Despite continuing controversy about its aims, normative content, and powers of the institutions it created, human rights governance can be said to have restrained many dictatorial powers and established the criteria for transition to democracy and the rule of law. It also has succeeded in challenging many totalitarian and authoritarian governments, although it cannot claim sole credit for the democratization of South Africa, Central and South America, and Central and Eastern Europe over the past two decades.[2]

Success in human rights governance can be attributed to several linked factors. First, unlike many global issues, human rights is aided by its moral and ethical dimensions and the innate desire of every human being for protection from abuse. The very idea of human rights as a legitimate claim of every individual, founded in theology, morality, and philosophy, is thus a powerful governance tool.[3]

Second, civil society has insisted on the right to participate in the development of international human rights governance structures. Nonstate actors, particularly human rights nongovernmental organizations (NGOs) have played an essential role at every stage—from negotiating norms and standards to enforcing them—creating a global human rights movement. NGOs represent actual or potential victims of human rights violations who are concerned with preventing governmental actions that are contrary to human rights guarantees. NGOs are often the first to focus attention on new issues. They may take the lead developing the content of specific human rights and pressing states to make them law; in some instances they bypass the states altogether, writing human rights standards to govern key nonstate actors.[4] They provide legal assistance to victims of human rights violations, gather evidence, and bring cases before international tribunals. Their roles as watchdogs and whistle-blowers are crucial to the effectiveness of human rights guarantees. Any state that is concerned with domestic or international political support cannot afford to ignore broad-based NGOs.

Third, the human rights movement of civil society and like-minded states produced relatively early consensus about the general normative content of human rights, reinforced by repetition in subsequent global and regional treaties and declarations.[5] This recasting of human rights policy as international law encouraged greater compliance. Governments are composed of individuals who have a general habit of obedience to law—to norms that are adopted through procedures recognized as legitimate. The sense of obligation makes it more difficult for states to ignore human rights claims that are formulated in treaties and custom. For example, states that have undergone transformation or conflicts often seek to legitimize themselves in the eyes of the international community by adopting international human rights norms in domestic law and portraying themselves as respectful of international standards.

Fourth, states are held accountable through an evolving set of interlocking institutions with a mandate to address human rights issues through a variety of techniques. Global and regional intergovernmental institutions provide the means through which NGOs place issues on the human rights agenda. In turn, states and intergovernmental institutions rely on the information brought to them by human rights groups to expose violations and pressure states to conform to their obligations. The UN system initiated the human rights revolution through its early standard setting, but regional systems have been most innovative in building institutions to effect internationally recognized rights. Regional courts are proving particularly effective in securing redress for individual victims and consequent changes in the laws and practices of member states, in part because of the prestige attached to courts, and in part because of the quality of the judges and their carefully crafted judicial opinions. This has led to a virtually unblemished record of compliance with judgments of human rights courts.

Fifth, some of the major human rights successes stem from linking the topic to other issue areas, such as peace and security, economic development, and environmental protection. Such linkage can provide incentives for states less motivated to respect human rights, increasing compliance and the effectiveness of human rights guarantees. Developments in Central and Eastern Europe initiated by the Helsinki Conference on Security and Cooperation in Europe and its transformation into one of the largest regional organizations concerned with human rights are instructive in the value of linking human rights to other topics of international concern. The United Nations represents the largest example of issue linkage. A state wishing to join the United Nations and participate in its economic, cultural, or scientific programs must in turn accept human rights obligations.

Although there have been successes, human rights governance has failed in some highly visible instances to prevent or halt massive abuses, including genocide. The reasons for these failures are many. First, there are legal restraints. Human rights has been hampered by traditional concepts of state sovereignty and domestic jurisdiction, as well as by the consent-based nature of many international obligations that prevents enforcement of norms against nonconsenting states. This legal barrier is reinforced by the conflict of interest inherent in a system where those violating human rights participate in standard setting, compliance monitoring, and enforcement. At an extreme, this leads to challenges to the normative basis of human rights governance from ruling elites who seek to retain power by invoking cultural relativism. They challenge the universality of human rights despite their participation in drafting normative instruments guaranteeing such rights and subsequent voluntary consent to them through ratification.

Second, and more generally, most states exhibit a reluctance to criticize others for human rights violations, unless there are independent political reasons to do so, such as ideological conflicts or unfriendly relations. In many cases, the reluctance stems from concern about reciprocal complaints, but it also derives from the multifaceted nature of international relations. States usually must balance, and often subordinate, consideration of human rights issues to other international concerns, including trade, military and strategic policy, and foreign investment. When human rights does become a cornerstone of bilateral and multilateral relations, particularly on the part of a powerful state or a group of states, it can have a significant positive impact on compliance with human rights norms.

Third, human rights governance is limited by its own design, which had in mind restraining powerful government agents. It has not succeeded in addressing the massive violations that occur in weak or failed states where anarchy and civil conflict prevail, because violations by nonstate actors that cannot be controlled by a state generally fall outside the scope of most human rights law. Humanitarian law and international criminal standards concerning crimes against humanity and war crimes cover nonstate actors, but these topics are usually, if mistakenly, treated separately from human rights in international law. International human rights institutions and systems thus lack the power to step into failed states and have been so far unable to develop new institutions and procedures to prevent or remedy violations in anarchical states or those in which armed conflict is occurring. Even where there are functioning states, increasing deregulation and globalization are creating powerful nonstate actors outside the governance structure. These will call for new governance mechanisms in the future as states voluntarily renounce some of their power in favor of the private sector.

NATURE OF THE PROBLEM AND INTERNATIONAL RESPONSES

Human rights became a matter for international governance because human rights abuses by a government necessitate international action. Victims and those who see themselves as potential victims demand such action, and states see it as in their interest to respond. Human rights advocates understand that when the government of a state turns on those within its power, torturing or summarily executing them, discriminating against minorities, or simply looting the resources of the state and its people, those subject to abuse have few ways to halt what is in almost all cases a disregard of the state's own constitutional and statutory protections. In the absence of respect for the rule of law, they can attempt to rebel against the government, they can flee, or they can call on help from outside the state.[6] Millions who were unable to rebel or flee, and who received no outside help, suffered and died during World War II. An evident source of postwar concern with international protection of human rights is the absence of prewar legal norms and mechanisms that would have permitted action on behalf of the victims of Nazi denials of human worth and dignity. The call "never again" expresses the demand by individuals and groups for action to create an "international safety net" to protect those within a state from abuse by the government.

States also perceived an interest in protecting human rights because human rights violations create problems outside the violating state. Streams of refugees cross borders; rebellion and armed conflict spill into neighboring countries; nonnationals are often arbitrarily arrested, tortured, and executed; and foreign trade and investment are affected. The influx of refugees into other countries can create wider destabilizing effects. Dictatorial governments often target foreign investment for seizure or control or foster a culture of corruption that is both costly and unpredictable for business.

Humanitarian impulses and self-interest thus led the international community to create a theoretical and legal construct that views human rights as a matter of general international concern.[7] The international community had long taken up human rights issues when they had an obvious interstate dimension, whether because of trade, jurisdictional conflicts, or transnational religious affiliations.[8] States also acted to protect the rights of their nationals in other countries, while generally ignoring the foreign state's treatment of its own nationals. The right of diplomatic protection centered on a doctrinal debate over whether aliens were entitled to "national treatment" or whether there existed an "international minimum standard," a debate now resolved by guaranteeing human rights for all.

After World War I, concern focused on guaranteeing rights by treaty for certain racial, religious, and linguistic minorities in the defeated states. The Fourteen Points of President Woodrow Wilson stressed the ideals of minority rights and of self-determination. Wilson proposed that the Covenant of the League of Nations include norms protecting minorities, but this approach was rejected in favor of a series of "minorities treaties" imposed on new and reconfigured states in Central and Eastern Europe and the Balkans.

The victorious states accepted no similar obligations for themselves or their colonies, however. The League of Nations system of minority protection, established in the peace treaties after World War I, functioned well for about fifteen years, but the treaties ultimately failed because the norms and institutions were inadequate and key states did not participate, nor was there an active lobby of human rights NGOs.[9] Furthermore, there was no consensus on human rights as a global issue; those bound by the treaties often complained that other states were not similarly obligated. Finally, the treaties themselves aimed more at collective protection of groups than at guarantees of individual rights and freedoms, although the instruments did contribute to eroding claims of state sovereignty over the treatment of those within national borders. The incorporation of the Minorities Treaties into the League of Nations structure in 1919 provided the first general multilateral forum for discussion of human rights issues. Other international organizations were also beginning to address human rights issues. For example, the ILO, which was created at approximately the same time, began considering many workers' rights issues. On the regional level, the creation of a Central American Court of Justice allowed individuals from the states party to the treaty to bring actions against a government other than their own for "denial of justice" or violation of a treaty or convention. The court existed only between 1907 and 1923 and had few disputes submitted to it.[10]

World War II finally convinced states that human rights is a global issue. Franklin Roosevelt's speech to Congress on January 6, 1941, discussed the relationship between domestic liberties and international peace, proclaiming the need to secure "four essential human freedoms" for all: freedom of speech and expression, freedom of worship, freedom from want, and freedom from fear "everywhere in the world." Roosevelt declared, "Freedom means the supremacy of human rights everywhere. Our support goes to those who struggle to gain those rights or keep them."

The experience of the war heightened awareness of human rights and demonstrated the extreme consequences of the doctrine of national sovereignty. It forced the Allied governments to look inward and admit that human rights problems existed in most countries (although no government was keen to subject itself to international scrutiny), and it galvanized a crusade for international guarantees of human rights.[11]

The Atlantic Charter, promulgated on August 14, 1941, by Franklin Roosevelt and Winston Churchill, reaffirmed faith in the dignity of each human being and supported "the right of all peoples to choose the form of government under which they will live" and the right of "improved labor standards, economic advancement, and social security." The incorporation of human rights in the UN Charter, which was adopted on June 26, 1945, subsequently made it impossible for member states to claim credibly that the matter is exclusively within their domestic jurisdiction. The great powers thus accepted, albeit reluctantly, that human rights is a matter of international concern, but they also insisted on the principle of nonintervention in domestic affairs. Much of the early period of the United Nations was dominated by tension between proponents of human rights and states that invoked the doctrine of nonintervention in matters of domestic jurisdiction. Defining the extent of permissible international action remains a significant problem, but the UN Charter created a legal framework for the norms and institutions of human rights governance.

Within this framework, one important characteristic dominates the field of human rights: its unilateral nature. Unlike "contractual" treaties that contain reciprocal benefits and burdens, such as agreements on arms control and tariff reductions, human rights guarantees are viewed as imposing burdens without benefits, being almost exclusively concerned with how states treat those within their territory and jurisdiction. This characteristic makes traditional approaches to international law and relations inapplicable because they are based on the possibility of retaliatory action in case of a breach injuring another state (for example, breach of a tariff-lowering agreement may result in the reciprocal raising of tariffs by the affected state or states). It also makes apparent the reason why issue linkage is an important part of human rights governance.

The difficulties in applying traditional international legal approaches stemming from the unilateral nature of human rights obligations are counterbalanced by the existence of shared moral, ethical, and religious foundations for human rights. Although different priorities are attached to certain rights, shared values with common underpinnings facilitate universal commitment to the identification and protection of human rights.

The international community responded to problems of human rights violations by first agreeing on the list of rights to be internationally protected, a process that dominated global efforts until the late 1960s. It then turned to the establishment of institutions to monitor state compliance with the agreed rights and duties. Recently efforts have shifted to prevention and to capacity building through the development of early warning systems and advisory services. In addition, the international community is attempting through the development of international criminal law and procedures, such as the establishment of an International Criminal Court, to deter and punish individuals who perpetrate the most serious violations.

This section examines global and regional institutions concerned with human rights and each system's successes and failures. Actions to promote and protect human rights at the global and regional levels have had similar results in standard setting but have utilized different institutions. Only regional organizations have courts that issue binding decisions in cases brought by individuals against governments, while global institutions utilize state reporting, fact finding, and public discussion. Global institutions also tend to focus more on gross and systematic violations or overall state behavior than on individual complaints. The global system has been most successful when it has taken an issue-based rather than a country-based approach, targeting a particular type of violation for stigmatization and action. Regional institutions have shown strength in addressing individual cases and have a more mixed record in combating systematic violations.

UN Human Rights System

Concern for the promotion and protection of human rights is woven throughout the UN Charter.[12] Indeed, one of the basic purposes of the United Nations is to achieve international cooperation in promoting and encouraging respect for human rights and fundamental freedoms.[13] The UN Charter does not define the term *human rights*, although it contains a clear prohibition of discrimination based on race, sex, language, or religion. The absence of a human rights catalog in the UN Charter led to a continuing effort to define and codify human rights, beginning with the adoption, on December 10, 1948, of the Universal Declaration of Human Rights (UDHR) and continuing with several other important documents.[14] The codification effort in the United Nations and its specialized agencies has resulted in a vast body of international human rights law.[15]

International organs and procedures have been created by many human rights instruments to monitor state compliance with prescribed norms. The International Covenant on Civil and Political Rights (CCPR), for example, establishes a Human Rights Committee that supervises compliance by reviewing and commenting on periodic reports that parties to the treaty must submit and by administering the CCPR's optional interstate complaint mechanism. The First Optional Protocol to the CCPR enables victims of a violation of the covenant to file a complaint against a state party to the covenant and the protocol. The Convention Against Torture and Other Cruel, Inhuman, and Degrading Treatment also provides for optional interstate and individual complaints, patterned after the CCPR. The Convention on the Elimination of All Forms of Racial Discrimination (CERD) provides for an optional individual complaint procedure and a mandatory interstate complaint process. The Convention on the Elimination of All Forms of Discrimination Against Women (CEDAW) has recently adopted a protocol that will also create complaint machinery.

The International Covenant on Economic, Social, and Cultural Rights (CESCR), in contrast, contains obligations that are monitored only via examination of periodic state reports. There are no individual or interstate complaint procedures, although efforts are under way to adopt an optional protocol containing a petition procedure. (The CEDAW and the Convention on the Rights of the Child contain comparable reportable mechanisms.) The 1948 Convention on the Prevention and Punishment of the Crime of Genocide creates no permanent institution to monitor compliance and leaves punishment of offenders to national courts and to the law of state responsibility.[16] It was the lacuna in enforcement of international criminal law that led first to ad hoc tribunals for Rwanda and the former Yugoslavia, and second to a treaty to establish a permanent international court.

In addition to the treaty-based mechanisms, virtually all UN Charter bodies deal with human rights matters. Although the General Assembly and the Economic and Social Council (ECOSOC) are important in standard setting, it is the Human Rights Commission and its Sub-Commission on the Promotion and Protection of Human Rights that take up most human rights issues. The UN Commission, composed of state representatives, meets annually, but since 1992 it has been authorized to hold emergency sessions and has done so with regard to Rwanda and the former Yugoslavia. The UN Sub-Commission, which consists of twenty-six independent experts elected by the UN Commission, also meets annually and has proved more progressive on human rights issues than the UN Commission, whose work is often politicized.

The UN Commission and the UN Sub-Commission initiate studies on human rights problems, draft instruments for adoption by ECOSOC or the General Assembly, and take action in response to violations. The last function has evolved the furthest since the UN Commission was created. For the first twenty years of the United Nations, the UN Commission officially and repeatedly stated that it had no power to take any action in regard to complaints concerning human rights. But between 1967 and 1978, the UN Commission gradually assumed a greater role in responding to violations, initially because newly independent states were seeking additional ways to combat apartheid in South Africa.

Any assessment of UN efforts since 1945 must conclude that immense progress has been made in the human rights of millions of people throughout the world. It is a system strong on promotion, based on accepted standard-setting procedures, and international assistance for the national implementation of agreed-upon norms. It is weak, at least over the short term, in achieving human rights in the face of deliberate and massive violations by states at the two ends of the power spectrum: in wealthy and powerful states and in failed states. In both circumstances, positive changes are possible in the long term and may be accelerated through international pressure, as was the case in South Africa and countries of Latin America and Eastern Europe. Intransigent states, however, can be moved only through the mobilization of considerable resources by international institutions, states, and nonstate actors. It is far easier to remedy the lapses or violations by states that are generally committed to the rule of law, accepting of outside scrutiny, or in a position to be pressured into compliance.

Regional Human Rights Systems

Regional systems drew inspiration from the human rights provisions of the UN Charter and the UDHR and were further stimulated by a variety of historical and political factors. One such factor was the nearly two decades it took from the creation of the United Nations to the final approval of the two UN covenants, during which time it became clear that the compliance mechanisms at the global level would not be strong.[17] As a result, beginning with Europe, regional systems focused on the creation of procedures of redress, establishing machinery to supervise the implementation and enforcement of the guaranteed rights.[18] The functioning European and inter-American courts are one of the great contributions to human rights by regional systems.

European Human Rights System. Europe, the theater of the greatest atrocities of World War II, felt compelled to press for international human rights guarantees as part of European reconstruction and created the first regional human rights system to be fully operational.[19] It began with the creation of the Council of Europe by ten Western European states in 1949 and has since expanded to include Central and Eastern European countries, bringing the total membership to forty-three.[20] Every member state must accept the principles of the rule of law and of the enjoyment by all persons within its jurisdiction of human rights and fundamental freedoms.[21]

The European Convention on Human Rights (ECHR) to which additional guarantees have been added over time was adopted to "to take the first steps for the collective enforcement of certain of the rights stated in the Universal Declaration" (ECHR Preamble). The European system was the first to create both an international court to protect human rights and a procedure for individual complaints. (An earlier, more limited effort was made in 1907 with the creation of the Central American Court of Justice.) The European system is characterized by the adoption of treaties and protocols, and, through its Parliamentary Assembly, the Council of Europe has drafted a series of human rights instruments that form a network of mutually reinforcing human rights protections. It is also worth noting that the assembly adopts recommendations on human rights, some of which are influential in shaping the laws and policies of member states. In some cases the Committee of Ministers requests governments to inform it of measures they have taken to implement specific recommendations.

Initially, the victims' role was limited, admissibility requirements were stringent, and the jurisprudence of the European Court of Human Rights was relatively conservative, reflecting concern to maintain state support and the then-optional jurisdiction of the court. As the system has matured, the institutional structures and normative guarantees have been considerably strengthened. Although most of the changes result from efforts to improve the effectiveness of the system and add to its guarantees, some of the evolution has been in response to the activities of other regional organizations, and still others reflect the impact of expanding membership.

Other European Institutions. The Helsinki Final Act (1975), which created the Conference—now Organization—on Security and Cooperation in Europe (OSCE), developed human rights in the context of peace and security, linking the issues. Follow-up meetings strengthened human rights protections, sometimes adding provisions not found in other regional or global instruments.[22] The OSCE has used diplomatic intervention and mediation for conflict prevention. The OSCE also has linked the development of regional democracy with human rights. The Office for Democratic Institutions and Human Rights in Warsaw assists the democratization process in OSCE states and monitors the implementation of human rights programs. Parallel to OSCE efforts, the Council of Europe created a program in 1990 to strengthen democracy and to facilitate the integration of new member states into the Council of Europe.[23]

Although originally concerned with economic integration, the European Union has also been involved with human rights. Since the 1970s, the European Court of Justice has held that respect for basic rights is an integral part of European Community law.[24] Both the basic legal instruments and the jurisprudence of the court have expanded the rights of individuals, not just in the economic field but in regard to political rights as well.[25] The court has been particularly active in enforcing equal rights in employment.[26] The court refers to the European Convention in its jurisprudence and has expressly recognized the right to respect for private life and the right to pursue a trade.[27] The European Parliament has adopted a Declaration of Fundamental Rights granting broader guarantees than the European Convention.[28] In addition, the European Parliament's Human Rights Sub-Committee produces an annual report on human rights in countries throughout the world.

Inter-American System. The Americas have a tradition of regional approaches to international issues, including human rights, growing out of solidarity developed during the movement for independence. Pan-American conferences took action on several human rights matters well before the creation of the United Nations.[29] The modern inter-American system began with the transformation of the Pan-American Union into the Organization of American States (OAS). The OAS Charter proclaimed the "fundamental rights of the individual" as a founding principle.[30] The 1948 American Declaration on the Rights and Duties of Man, adopted some months before the United Nations completed the UDHR, gives definition to the charter's general commitment to human rights.[31]

In 1959, the OAS created a seven-member Inter-American Commission on Human Rights, which had a mandate to further respect for human rights.[32] In 1965, the OAS expanded the role of the Inter-American Commission, giving it the power to receive complaints from victims, request information from governments, and make recommendations to bring about more effective observance of human rights.[33] The American Convention of Human Rights, signed in 1969, conferred an additional mandate on the Inter-American Commission to oversee compliance with the convention.[34] The convention, which entered into force in 1978, also created the Inter-American Court of Human Rights, which has jurisdiction over contentious cases submitted against states that accept its jurisdiction and may issue advisory opinions. Like the European system, the inter-American system has expanded its protections over time through the adoption of additional human rights instruments.[35]

The Inter-American Commission's jurisdiction extends to all thirty-five OAS member states (virtually the entire Western Hemisphere is included). The twenty-five states that have ratified the convention are bound by its provisions, while other member states are held to the standards of the 1948 American Declaration. Communications or complaints may be filed against any state; the optional clause applies only to interstate cases. Standing for nonstate actors to file communications is broad. Article 44 of the American Convention states that "[a]ny person or group of persons, or any non-governmental entity legally recognized in one or more member states of the Organization, may lodge petitions with the Commission containing denunciations or complaints of violation of this Convention by a State Party." The Inter-American Commission's regulations provide the same extensive standing for complaints to be filed against OAS member states that are not party to the convention.

The Inter-American Commission may also prepare country reports and conduct on-site visits to individual countries, examining the human rights situation in the particular country and making recommendations to the government. Country reports have been prepared on the commission's own initiative and at the request of the country concerned. The Inter-American Commission may also appoint special rapporteurs to prepare studies on hemisphere-wide problems.

African System. As independent African states emerged from colonization, human rights became a recognized part of the regional agenda within the framework of the Organization for African Unity (OAU). The African Charter on Human and Peoples' Rights (African Charter), adopted in 1981, differs from other regional treaties in its inclusion of "peoples' rights"—that is, rights whose violation inevitably extend beyond the individual to affect whole groups.[36] The African Charter includes the right to self-determination, the right to a healthy environment, the right to development, and the right to peace. It also includes economic, social, and cultural rights to a greater extent than either the European Convention or the American Convention.

The African Charter establishes the African Commission on Human and Peoples Rights, which has four functions: promotion of human and peoples' rights; protection of those rights; interpretation of the charter; and the performance of other tasks that may be entrusted to it by the Assembly of Heads of State and Government. The African Commission may undertake studies, conduct training and teaching, convene conferences, initiate publication programs, disseminate information, and collaborate with national and local institutions. The African system envisages not only interstate and individual communications procedures but a special procedure for gross and systematic violations.

Nascent Middle East System. The League of Arab States approved an Arab Charter on Human Rights on September 15, 1994, building on earlier texts adopted by regional nongovernmental and intergovernmental organizations. The founding Charter of the League of Arab States, adopted on March 22, 1945, does not mention human rights. On September 12, 1966, the Council of the League of Arab States adopted its first resolution on human rights, calling for the establishment of a steering committee to elaborate a program for the celebration of Human Rights Year in 1968. The steering committee recommended the establishment of a permanent Arab Committee on Human Rights and the convening of an Arab Conference on Human Rights. The latter was held in December 1968 in Beirut.[37]

Article 41 of the Arab Charter requires periodic reporting by states and implies that the Arab League Human Rights Committee may request a report. The committee studies the reports and distributes its own report to the Human Rights Committee. The charter specifies no other promotion or protection functions for the committee. Until the charter enters into force, there are no regional institutions or procedures for monitoring human rights. The emerging Middle East system is probably marked more than other regional systems by controversy concerning human rights issues, such as gender equality and religious liberty, which has slowed progress in achieving a functioning human rights system.

Asia. Despite efforts by NGOs and the United Nations, no human rights system exists in Asia.[38] In 1993, more than a hundred Asia-Pacific NGOs adopted an Asia-Pacific Declaration of Human Rights supporting the creation of a regional system.[39] At a 1996 UN-sponsored workshop, however, the thirty participating governments concluded that "it was premature, at the current stage, to discuss specific arrangements relating to the setting up of a formal human rights mechanism in the Asian and Pacific region," although they agreed to explore "the options available and the process necessary for establishing a regional mechanism."[40]

There are several hurdles to creating an Asia-Pacific regional system despite widespread NGO support. First, there is far greater diversity of language, culture, legal systems, religious traditions, and history in the Asia-Pacific region than in other regions of the world. Second, the geographical limits of the region are unclear but vast.[41] These two factors suggest that the region may be better served by subregional mechanisms that could be more quickly and easily developed because of the closer ties of states in smaller areas.[42] A third factor hindering the development of a regional system is that governments in the region have been unwilling in general to ratify human rights instruments, making it unlikely that an effective regional system would garner widespread support in the near future. Among the thirty Asian countries that participated in the 1996 workshop, only Australia, Nepal, New Zealand, the Philippines, and the Republic of Korea have ratified both UN covenants and the optional protocol on individual communications. As of March 2000, twenty-seven states in the region, including virtually all the Pacific island states, had not signed or ratified either of the UN covenants.

The 1990s economic crisis in Asia put pressure on governments trying to survive in the wake of growing unrest and created a risk of repression in the short term. During such periods, "Asian values" may become even more "a tool of some authoritarian regimes to suppress individual rights, especially freedom of expression and association which are at the heart of democratic aspirations."[43] In fact, the regional economic and political crisis led many to question the concept of "Asian values" as a means to progress. As a result, political movements and NGOs have renewed efforts to ensure greater respect for human rights in the region. The chances of creating a regional system thus appear better than at any point in the past.

Normative Development: Defining the Scope of Human Rights

Human rights governance began with agreement that human rights is a matter of international concern; the international community then sought to agree on a list of human rights to be internationally promoted and protected as legal obligations of states. On the whole, international attempts to define the content of human rights have succeeded. Most efforts today are devoted to giving greater detail to the agreed-upon rights, although the list of human rights is not and probably cannot be a closed one.

Governance is made easier when there is consensus on the particular right (such as freedom from torture) and more difficult when there is disagreement over its content or its inclusion among the rights states are legally obliged to promote and protect (such as right to development). Reservations to human rights treaties are perhaps the best indication of nonacceptance of particular norms. Reservations suggest that rights of women, aliens, and prisoners are the least favored.[44] When rights are widely accepted and reiterated in numerous instruments, it becomes more difficult for a state to deviate from the norm. The basic legal instruments are widely ratified, and many states have made good faith efforts to implement the provisions in national law. For example, the CCPR has been accepted by 144 states and the CESCR by 142 state parties. The Convention on the Rights of the Child has been ratified by every state in the world (191) except the United States and Somalia.

The norms are also reiterated in global and regional instruments. Virtually all human rights treaties and declarations refer to the UDHR and the UN Charter, providing a measure of uniformity and reinforcing the universality of the declaration.[45]

Regional treaties also incorporate the norms set forth in other global instruments, in particular the CCPR and CESCR. For example, the economic, social, and cultural rights contained in the UDHR and the CESCR are also found in the American Declaration, the European Social Charter, and the African and Arab Charters. The Arab Charter includes the right to work, to equal employment opportunities, to equal pay, to trade union freedoms, to an adequate standard of living, to social security, to education, and to the right to participate in cultural life and to be "given the chance to advance his artistic thought and creative talent." Article 26 of the American Convention calls for progressive realization of the economic, social, and cultural standards set forth in the OAS Charter. In Europe, only the right to education and the right to property are guaranteed by the European Convention, Protocol 1. Other economic and social rights are specified in the European Social Charter while cultural rights are guaranteed within the new Framework Convention on National Minorities.

Provisions in the treaties and principles of interpretation that require states to enforce the most favorable rule to the individual lead to further convergence in the norms, despite some differences in formulation of the rights.

Although based on universal norms, regional instruments also contain additional guarantees and emphases; indeed, the preambles of all the regional instruments refer to their regional heritages.[46] For example, the European Convention focuses on civil rights, especially due process, while the American system is strongly concerned with democracy and the rule of law. The Arab Charter takes religion as its starting point. The African Charter focuses on economic development, paying particular attention to the right to development. Although the regional instruments sometimes omit rights found in global texts, they more often add new rights not found in the Universal Declaration.[47] Often inspired by the work of other systems, these new guarantees have included the abolition of the death penalty, action to combat violence against women, right to a satisfactory environment, and strengthened guarantees in regard to economic, social, and cultural rights. It is notable that a right has never been limited or withdrawn by a later instrument.

Procedures and Mechanisms

Human rights obligations are reinforced through institutional mechanisms and procedures that seek to hold states accountable for compliance with the legal norms. The most widely used treaty mechanisms are state reporting, interstate complaints, and individual complaints. In addition, fact-finding studies and investigations, technical assistance and capacity building, and procedures to hold individuals accountable for human rights violations have emerged as techniques to enhance compliance. The effectiveness of each of these procedures varies, as discussed below, not only in comparing one type of procedure to another, but also among different versions of the same procedure, such as state reporting.

Human rights monitoring organs have given a dynamic reading to human rights guarantees as circumstances change and new problems arise. They have recognized that the standards for assessing state compliance with most civil and political rights are necessarily different from those applicable to most economic, social, and cultural rights. While the former largely require a state's abstention from action, implementation of the latter group often directly depends on socioeconomic factors. Compliance with social and economic rights in Haiti could not be equated with compliance in the United States. Capacity to comply, then, is a consideration.

Judicial power in the regional systems is significant. Regional conventions are written in general terms, leaving ample scope for judges and commissioners to apply and creatively interpret their provisions. The jurisprudence of the regional human rights bodies in Europe, where the European Court of Human Rights has delivered close to 1,000 judgments, has thus become a major source of human rights law. In general, judges and commissioners have been willing to substantiate or give greater authority to their opinions by referencing the decisions of other global and regional bodies, although differences in treaty terms or approach sometimes have led to a rejection of precedent from other systems.[48] Liberal standing rules, as found in the inter-American and African systems, greatly aid this process. Victims and their lawyers often draw attention to the relevant case law of other systems, thus expanding human rights protections by obtaining a progressive ruling in one system and invoking it in another. Many complaints are filed by NGOs that operate in more than one system and bring expertise and professional reputation as "repeat players" before the regional courts.

LESSONS LEARNED

Human rights governance started with a revolutionary concept—that a government's treatment of those within its power is a matter of international concern—but it began with a modest objective, declaring and defining a set of fundamental rights, leaving to states the choice of means and policies to implement the norms. Over time, as the norms became more detailed, it became clear that international supervision of compliance with human rights obligations was required as part of the normative framework. International human rights law now usually progresses through similar stages: issue identification, debate, adoption of nonbinding declarations, negotiation of binding agreements (treaties), establishment of supervisory institutions and procedures, and further elaboration of the rights through decisions and judgments of the supervisory institutions. At all of these stages, a multiplicity of actors is involved because the issues touch individuals, governments, businesses, religious institutions, indeed, all parts of society. Success on any human rights issue usually involves coalition building. Coalitions are possible because personal relationships develop among people who work in the field, leading to agreement on issues, especially in intergovernmental and nongovernmental organizations, within networks and through informal links. In addition, as the system has evolved, it has become clear that the synergy between regional and global systems furthers human rights.

Regional systems are increasingly dominated by judicial mechanisms to redress individual wrongs, while the global system maintains a focus on gross and systematic violations. The results may appear to make the regional systems more effective, but individual cases are less threatening to states than attacks on the entire governance system when there are widespread violations. The difficulties the European system has faced in obtaining Italian reform of its judiciary to eliminate unwarranted procedural delays in hearing cases indicate the limits of the individual case approach; the remedies awarded individual victims are an inadequate deterrent to further violations because the government finds it economically and politically less costly to pay the damages than to undertake reform. In such cases, the risk is that patience will give out before results are seen and the system will be deemed a failure, leading to instability or even violence. By taking an approach that focuses on litigation or quasi-judicial mechanisms to enforce rights, the governance system often fails to address root causes of social discord, such as disparities in wealth, religious and racial prejudice, and historic conflicts.

Agenda Setting

As with other legal regimes, the agenda is set in reaction to perceived problems. The media plays an important role in identifying human rights issues that need resolution by documenting abuses and often creating an emotional response. For example, the famine in the early 1980s in Ethiopia had been in existence for two years before the international media drew attention to it and produced a movement for humanitarian aid. The outrage factor is very important in mobilizing public opinion and creating coalitions of NGOs and others; compelling media imagery thus can be a significant factor in bringing an issue forward. For this reason, NGOs, victims, and their families use the media to expose human rights abuses and raise consciousness about particular issues, helping to shape the global agenda. The paucity of grassroots organizations capable of attracting international media coverage is one reason African human rights problems receive less attention than others. In contrast, the high profile of sweatshops and child labor abuses reflects the ability of a well-organized and well-financed coalition of human rights groups and labor unions to push an issue into international consciousness.

States do raise human rights issues on their own, usually motivated by strategic and political considerations or historic rivalries. The United States, for example, raises the issue of human rights in Cuba at every session of the Human Rights Commission; Turkey and Greece regularly trade charges of human rights abuses in Cyprus and accuse each other of mistreatment of national minorities. This can be useful because political motivation does not minimize real human rights problems. Indeed, during the Cold War, U.S. emphasis on the right to leave and the misuse of psychiatric institutions in the Soviet Union, and Soviet accusations of U.S. racism, usefully pointed to abuses that required response. At the same time, the political motivation may undermine any effort to change state behavior by creating suspicion about the veracity of the complaints. It also may make the target state more intransigent when hostile states or traditional enemies raise issues.

NGOs and international civil servants working exclusively on human rights issues are clearly a major factor in agenda setting. One commentator called human rights NGOs "the engine for virtually every advance made by the United Nations in the field of human rights since its founding."[49] States often lag in pressing for human rights, which is only one of many matters of international concern for them. In addition, governments resent being criticized and do not want to promote consideration of human rights issues where they know they have problems. The topic of indigenous rights, for example, was placed on the agenda by indigenous groups working primarily with countries that had no indigenous peoples. Some of the most criticized states repeatedly seek to limit the role of NGOs and challenge their findings, accusing them of bias or political motivation.

State power has waned to some extent because of the proliferation of independent expert bodies, the growth in human rights secretariats, and the participation of NGOs. Although UN member states were able to block petitions in 1947, claiming that any discussion of human rights violations constituted an unlawful intervention into domestic affairs, the "domestic jurisdiction" defense has been largely abandoned. Instead, violators seek to be elected to the UN Commission and ECOSOC in order to manipulate the agenda and water down resolutions. Many remember that Uganda was elected to the Human Rights Commission during the reign of Idi Amin, who succeeded in both delaying and limiting UN action regarding human rights abuses in Uganda. More recently, particularly egregious violators have sometimes failed to achieve the votes necessary for election, with NGOs and pro–human rights states playing a role in the elections. The moral claim of human rights also probably plays a role as it has become clear that the composition of the human rights bodies is extremely important to agenda setting, in terms of both putting matters on the agenda and keeping matters off it.

Some states do take a crucial leadership role; in particular, Costa Rica, the Netherlands, Norway, and Senegal are known as leaders on human rights issues. Other states may step forward when national reforms have been instituted to address particular problems. The impartiality, credibility, and moral leadership of states on human rights impart more than traditional measures of state power; in many cases the United States has alone voted against measures (for example, the Declaration Against Torture and the Convention on the Rights of the Child) that it has later come to approve (the United States is now a party to the Torture Convention). As David P. Forsythe has noted, U.S. policies are not congruent with those of much of the rest of the world, which has hampered its effectiveness as an advocate of human rights issues.[50] The U.S. criminal justice system, for example, lags far behind those of other states in prison reform, abolition of the death penalty, and treatment of juvenile offenders. The United States is one of only seven countries in the world that as of August 2000 permit the execution of those convicted of crimes they committed before they were eighteen years old. In the last ten years, the United States has executed more juvenile offenders than the other six countries (Congo, Iran, Nigeria, Pakistan, Saudi Arabia, and Yemen) combined.[51]

NGOs have been effective at getting issues on the international agenda. For example, Amnesty International's campaign on the death penalty led to three treaties being drafted: the Second Protocol to the CCPR, the Sixth Protocol to the European Convention on Human Rights, and the Inter-American Protocol on the Abolition of the Death Penalty. Amnesty works through a grassroots, membership-based system that is global and well funded, which enables it to have considerable impact. Indigenous and women's groups at the United Nations and its specialized agencies also have been effective in maintaining a high profile for their issues at meetings because they are vocal, well organized, and knowledgeable.

Foundations and other funding sources also shape the human rights agenda, sometimes as a result of internal changes in policy reflecting the personal interests of their management or boards. NGOs face a constant problem of limited resources, which can undermine coalitions and lead to competition for both funding and credit for results, making them dependent to varying degrees on foundation grants and similar funding sources. When the priorities of the donors shift, NGO priorities tend to shift with them. Concern at the Rockefeller Foundation with weapons of mass destruction shaped the Arms Watch Program of Human Rights Watch, eventually leading it to create a separate division on arms control for what had begun as a program to look at the export of weaponry to human rights abusers. Similarly, Amnesty International has begun a program on human rights and the environment, as this is now a priority issue with several donor groups.

Negotiations

Successful negotiations on human rights issues involve coalition building among states and nonstate actors because of the multiplicity of actors with divergent interests who participate in any negotiations for new human rights norms. For example, indigenous groups and supporting NGOs recently proposed the creation of intellectual property rights for traditional indigenous knowledge. States, indigenous groups, pharmaceutical companies, the World Intellectual Property Organization, environmental associations, the International Labor Organization (ILO), the World Health Organization, interested scholars, and the UN High Commissioner for Human Rights have participated in meetings on the topic. Trade-offs are made between the ideal and the possible; often the form as well as the content of the negotiated instrument reflect compromise and efforts to achieve consensus. It has proved easier to negotiate consensus on a new normative instrument if it is made legally nonbinding; nearly all human rights treaties today are preceded by a nonbinding declaration.

Nonstate actors have been observers/participants in intergovernmental bodies since the beginning of the modern human rights movement and have often had an impact on the outcome. During the drafting of the UN Charter, a coalition of states, particularly those from Latin America and Europe that saw the link between peace and human rights, joined nongovernmental groups reacting to the Holocaust to press for the creation of an international bill of rights. They were able to succeed because they articulated strong moral claims for action, identified key leaders among governmental delegations, including Eleanor Roosevelt, represented sometimes powerful domestic political lobbies, and came from around the globe rather than simply constituting a Western European movement. Subsequent negotiations for human rights treaties reflect the continued importance of these elements. In particular, rights issues pressed by only one geographic region are unlikely to be adopted; even those supported by a majority will be ineffective in the face of significant minority opposition. Although this makes progress slow, it does ensure that there is political support behind any concluded text: most states will support it and will attempt to bring in those that do not, through issue linkage, public discussion, or media campaigns.

The negotiations surrounding the creation of the United Nations and its charter illustrate the successful techniques involved in the negotiation process. The Dumbarton Oaks proposal for a United Nations, prepared by the great powers, did not contain references to human rights, despite the earlier rhetoric of Roosevelt and the Atlantic Charter. A diverse group of states, but mostly younger and middle-sized ones, objected to the omission. Latin American governments ultimately called for their own meeting to develop a collective policy toward creation of a new international system. Meeting in Chapultepec, Mexico, representatives of twenty nations declared that fundamental principles for the postwar era must include "the rights of Man," and they expressed support for a "system of international protection of these rights." Their role was important because they championed human rights and also held twenty of the fifty votes at the San Francisco Conference that drafted the UN Charter.[52] States from other regions also proposed including human rights language in the charter.[53]

The proposals benefited from the geographic and political diversity of support as well as from the enormous participation of NGOs. Domestic political pressure was exerted on key states.[54] NGOs participating in the conference with the U.S. delegation drafted a detailed memorandum arguing that human rights are essential not only to domestic life but to international peace. The organizations met with U.S. Secretary of State Edward Stettinius and argued that if human rights provisions were not in the charter, the support of the American people would be lost and the charter would never be ratified. The secretary of state reversed U.S. policy and declared the government in favor of human rights in the charter.[55]

On many issues, this global coalition of NGOs and medium and small powers achieved considerable success. For example, several groups representing torture survivors and other victims of abuse succeeded in obtaining provisions on victim compensation in the Statute of the International Criminal Court through alliance with key states, such as France, that saw the provisions as furthering continental legal approaches over common-law legal systems. In addition, these global coalitions championed an increased role for the General Assembly, giving it explicit power to initiate studies and make recommendations concerning human rights. They made ECOSOC a principal organ with clear responsibilities in the human rights area. As a result of the pressure, the great powers submitted a collective package of amendments incorporating some of the suggestions on human rights, although insisting on a reaffirmation of the principle of domestic jurisdiction.

In subsequent human rights negotiations, the strategy of coalition building has been enhanced by the leadership exercised by "repeat players," those known to have expertise and an impartial commitment to human rights. In addition, an effective negotiating strategy to bring forward the human rights agenda has been to link it to other subjects, including economic assistance (U.S. Foreign Assistance Act, World Bank funding) and security arrangements (OSCE), to import elements of reciprocity and strengthen the leverage of those concerned with human rights. Some of these regimes (such as the OSCE) have been particularly effective.

Implementation and Compliance

Once the human rights catalog was largely completed in the late 1960s, attention turned to the problem of strengthening implementation and compliance mechanisms. One of the major developments in human rights governance has been to take much of the compliance review away from direct governmental control and to give it to independent experts. The result has been positive because the experts generally have created regular and transparent procedures for fact finding and determination of levels of compliance, which have in turn enhanced the credibility and legitimacy of the findings. In cases where political bodies monitor human rights compliance, the politicization of the debate usually results in a loss of effectiveness (for example, the UN Human Rights Commission). In addition to the creation of independent bodies, new approaches have emerged to addressing human rights issues. First, as described further below, thematic mechanisms and procedures have been established to supplement treaty bodies and institutions (such as thematic rapporteurs at the United Nations and OAS, the High Commissioner for Human Rights, the OSCE High Commissioner on National Minorities). These new mechanisms have some-times proved more effective because they are thematic rather than directed at a single state. The thematic approach helps to avoid the claims of "double standard" when one or a few states are singled out for scrutiny. Another trend is the use of proactive, preventive mechanisms such as technical assistance, training, and technology, which offer incentives to states instead of condemnation. This is particularly effective where the state has the will but lacks the capacity to effectively implement human rights.[56]

Several obstacles hamper the effectiveness of human rights governance. Expert bodies at both global and regional levels are chronically underfunded, understaffed, and given inadequate time to meet—all of which hamper their ability to oversee implementation of treaty obligations. (The European Court of Human Rights is the only full-time international body in existence, and it was only made so on November 1, 1998.) Another problem is normative: international human rights standards do not provide methods or measurements for determining whether a given country is in compliance or if its situation is improving or deteriorating, leading states to reject findings that they consider subjective or biased, including the conflicting assessments prepared by NGOs such as Amnesty International and Freedom House. There is no generally accepted methodology for comparing different countries' human rights practices. Assessing compliance through reference to domestic legal norms has the benefit of some ease of application, but this method does not reveal whether human rights are in fact respected. Successful assessment of compliance with international human rights norms requires a more complex analysis of the extent to which a gov-ernment permits diversity and dissent, refrains from interference with personal lib-erty, and maintains a socioeconomic framework in which basic needs are satisfied. Increasing the variables chosen to evaluate compliance increases both the arbitrary nature of the study and disagreements among monitoring bodies, but such analysis is often attempted by supervisory organs, states, NGOs, and scholars.

Monitors may count reported violations of those rights where quantification is deemed possible; that is, the number of persons reported to be tortured, summarily executed, raped, enslaved, or subjected to forced labor. Others work from a basis of "standards" rather than "events" by setting levels of performance that are deemed to indicate compliance. These may vary considerably from one organization to another, as they are often arbitrary or subjective, for example, basing assessments of due process on the number of defense attorneys per population unit. The link between the concept (due process) and the variable or indicator (number of defense attorneys) is rarely explained, nor why a particular number is deemed adequate. There are considerable problems with the use of such statistical measurements to analyze compliance, even though the country reports mentioned above are often treated as conclusions derived from methodologically sound quantitative data.

States as a whole are much less involved with monitoring implementation and compliance than are the treaty-monitoring bodies, members of the secretariats of international organizations, and NGOs. States no doubt find it easier to proclaim rights than to review implementation and compliance when criticism of other states may create political problems. The other groups have considerable interaction. A June 1994 meeting of special rapporteurs and experts on working groups appealed "to non-governmental organizations whose work and information is crucial to human rights protection and to the effective discharge of our own mandates to continue providing us with relevant information and ideas."[57] The UN Secretariat established a special human rights hotline after appointment of the first UN High Commission for Human Rights, which makes it easier for NGOs to provide early warning of emerging conflicts.[58] NGOs also work informally with members of treaty bodies that do not formally accept NGO participation.

State Reporting Procedures. State reporting mechanisms are the most common procedure found in human rights treaties. States submit periodic reports on the measures they have taken to implement the guaranteed rights, the obstacles they face, and the changes they have made. Generally, independent review bodies inquire about the incorporation of international norms into domestic constitutions and laws and review these provisions for conformity with international standards. Other domestic law may also be reviewed, including judicial decisions, executive orders (local, state/ province, national), administrative agency regulations, and codes of conduct or regulations of quasi-public entities (such as bar associations and medical boards).

Reporting procedures would be ineffectual if each state could determine the subjects to be reported on, or if they stopped with formalistic inquiries about constitutions and laws without questioning the implementation of the laws, including remedies for their violation. Effective reporting procedures have been elaborated, however, that include guidelines for states on reporting, detailing the information to be submitted. Most reporting procedures also now include public questioning of state representatives and involve demands for additional information. They have proved effective in highlighting problem areas and encouraging positive change in state behavior.

The leadership of the experts on the initial committees, in particular those on the Racial Committee and the first and long-time chairman of the Human Rights Committee, was very important in advancing the reporting procedure toward effective compliance review. The Racial Committee initiated the practice of inviting state representatives to appear in public sessions to answer questions about the reports. After the first few showed up, either for reasons of prestige or out of ignorance, it became very difficult for subsequent states not to follow the same procedure. The precedents turned into habit. Moreover, media coverage and public participation force states to be relatively truthful and open. The Human Rights Committee also began, first as individuals, then openly as a committee, to accept information from NGOs, on the basis of which committee members could question or verify claims made by states. For example, in October 1998, the review of Israel's state report on compliance with the CESCR involved almost two dozen Israeli and West Bank NGOs supplying information and questions to the committee on demographics, basic needs, and other issues within the scope of the committee's mandate. The government took very seriously their presence and the resulting reporting "back home"; there can be domestic political implications for governments preparing and submitting reports.

This process of open questioning on the basis of outside information has made the reporting procedure far more effective in highlighting good and bad state practices, and inducing positive changes, than anyone expected. The transparency of the process, the quality of the membership of the early committee, and the quasi-judicial but nonconfrontational nature of the committee's reporting procedure may explain why the views are given weight by both the NGOs and the states involved, more so than those of other bodies. The frequent reference by committee members and state representatives to the procedure as one of "constructive dialogue" conveys the nonadversarial approach that engages states in the process.

Outside intergovernmental organizations, the reports of nonstate actors are an extremely important part of human rights governance. Amnesty International and the Watch Committee reports are widely disseminated and viewed as credible. The UN Working Group on Arbitrary Detentions reported in 1995 that 74 percent of its cases in 1994 had been brought by international NGOs, another 23 percent came from national NGOs, and only 3 percent came directly from families.[59] Such reports can have an impact on national policies toward particular states and on attitudes within international organizations.

The African Commission has developed a periodic reporting system based on the procedure followed by the UN Human Rights Committee. The African Commission determines the required content of the reports, invites states to appear for discussion, and addresses observations to reporting states when it finds that the state has not discharged any of its obligations. If the commission determines that a report does not contain adequate information, it may request additional information by a specific date. Although the procedures are progressive, the reporting system has not been a success. Many reports are more than ten years overdue, and thirty-three of the fifty-one states party to the African Charter have not submitted any reports. The reasons are probably found in the lack of political support from the OAU and the lack of African NGOs. Ironically, given the commission's limited resources and meeting time, the lack of reports has probably enhanced the effectiveness of the African Commission by leaving it more time to focus on individual communications and situations of gross and systematic violations.

Thematic Rapporteurs. The establishment of the Working Group on Enforced or Involuntary Disappearances, the first UN thematic study of human rights abuses, was motivated by NGO reports about disappearances in Chile and Argentina. Amnesty International undertook a 1977 mission to Argentina, exposing the problem and mobilizing public opinion.[60] The *junta* in Argentina attacked the credibility and legality of action by NGOs, the UN Secretariat, and individual experts.[61] The decision to adopt a thematic approach allowed the investigation to go forward by implying that the problem was not limited to Argentina but occurred in other countries as well. The use of thematic rapporteurs has become widespread in the United Nations and regional organizations and has represented a major advance in global governance.

The Working Group on Enforced or Involuntary Disappearances set a precedent for the 1982 creation of the Special Rapporteur on Summary or Arbitrary Executions.[62] In 1985, the UN Human Rights Commission appointed a Special Rapporteur on Torture, and in 1991 it created a Working Group on Arbitrary Detention.[63] Each rapporteur or working group has its own mandate conferred by the commission for a renewable three-year term. The approaches and working methods of the various individuals and groups have expanded and converged over time. Generally the working groups seek information from governments, propose "urgent action," make country visits, and report to the commission.[64] In some instances, the thematic groups can accept petitions and raise the issue of redress for victims of violations.

The African and the Inter-American Commissions have adopted the use of thematic rapporteurs, giving them broad mandates to address problems specific to their regions. In 1998, the Inter-American Commission had rapporteurs studying women's rights, indigenous populations, migrant workers, prison conditions, and freedom of expression. The African Commission has appointed rapporteurs on extrajudicial executions, prisons, and women. The African rapporteur decided to pay specific attention to wars and ethnic conflicts in Africa and announced a program of cooperation with the Rwanda Tribunal in gathering information for prosecutions for the genocide and other crimes committed in Rwanda in 1994 and has served to supplement and enhance the effectiveness of UN human rights efforts.[65]

The effectiveness of the thematic procedures varies considerably because the resources allocated to the special rapporteurs are extremely limited, and the rapporteurs vary considerably in personal expertise and commitment. The best of them have proved to have excellent legal and diplomatic skills, writing convincing and detailed reports and negotiating closely with governments to bring about improvements. At the opposite extreme, some rapporteurs have been viewed as apologists for particular governments or as simply ineffectual, leaving the investigation and reports to overworked UN staff members.

On-Site Visits. Both UN human rights programs and those of regional systems include on-site visits. The Inter-American Commission has long claimed this power and has exercised it frequently.[66] More recently, the European Committee for the Prevention of Torture and Inhuman or Degrading Treatment was given the power to visit prisons and other places of detention, making both periodic visits with notice and unannounced visits. The Torture Committee decides where to visit on the basis of information supplied by NGOs. It is not a judicial body; it studies the places visited, reports on its findings, and makes recommendations. Reports are normally confidential but can be published at the request of a party or if a two-thirds majority of committee members decides that a state has failed to cooperate with the committee or refused to act on its recommendations [Torture Convention, Article 10(2)]. The publication sanction was used against Turkey in 1992, when the committee found that its recommendations regarding serious police abuse had been persistently ignored.

On-site visits enable regional bodies to both gather and verify information, increasing public knowledge and the number of private persons who can be heard. On-site visits also allow national officials to explain the context and complexity of situations when rights have been violated. Finally, the mere presence of an outside group may deter violations. Unlike communications procedures, which begin only after a violation has occurred and local remedies have been exhausted, the visits of the Torture Committee and the Inter-American and African Commissions can occur whenever indications are received that violations may be taking place, or when a state seeks assistance in evaluating and improving its human rights performance. Visits can be cooperative, rather than confrontational, offering the same advantages as the constructive dialogue entered into through UN reporting mechanisms, but with better information. On-site visits are particularly important in avoiding regression during periods of political transition and in dealing with massive violations of rights where it may be impracticable to open individual cases. Given the importance of on-site visits, it is not surprising that the Inter-American Commission has visited the large majority of OAS member states and that the practice of on-site visits is becoming the rule, not the exception, in Africa.

Although on-site investigation and interviewing can be extremely important in acquiring data, it is also the most difficult method to undertake, because it requires state consent. It also enhances the likelihood of subjective assessment unless a well-developed and reliable methodology is utilized. At the same time, obtaining direct testimony of victims or eyewitnesses is extremely important to documenting violations.

Many of the successes of on-site visits are unknown to the public because the price for improvement is secrecy. In response to the moral claim of human rights and the potential power of shaming and other sanctions, governments engaged in human rights violations have been known to release political prisoners, "find" disappeared persons, and allow dissidents to leave the country in exchange for an on-site investigator not publicizing that the persons were detained or disappeared in the first place.[67] The practice is controversial because it distorts the record of violations and improvements, but there is no doubt that hundreds of individuals have benefited. The threat of publicity as a sanction has thus proved to be a major governance tool for the improvement of human rights.

Interstate and Individual Complaints Procedures. One of the greatest contributions of the human rights systems is the establishment of complaint mechanisms for judicial or quasi-judicial redress of human rights violations. Europe was the first to create a commission and court that could hear complaints, followed by the Americas and now Africa. For example, the Inter-American Commission on Human Rights, from its creation in 1960, interpreted its powers broadly to include the ability "to make general recommendations to each individual state as well as to all of them." This was deemed to include the power to take cognizance of individual petitions and use them to assess the human rights situation in a particular country, based on the normative standards of the American Declaration. The inter-American system was thus the first to make the complaints procedure mandatory against all member states.[68]

The UN system also has complaint procedures for the Racial Convention, the CCPR, and the CEDAW, as well as mechanisms at the ILO and the UN Educational, Scientific, and Cultural Organization (UNESCO). Several of the UN special rapporteurs also may accept complaints. In general, one state party to a treaty may file interstate complaints against another state party (the inter-American system being the exception). In contrast, individual complaint mechanisms are optional in all UN treaties and require explicit acceptance by states; individuals automatically have the right of individual petition in the regional systems. Despite this, interstate proceedings are almost nonexistent. None have ever been filed at the Inter-American Commission or before UN treaty bodies. A handful have been brought in the European system and at the ILO. By any measure, the use of interstate complaints to induce compliance has little utility. In contrast, individuals have filed tens of thousands of cases at regional and global bodies. The consequences have been dramatic. To date, every judgment of the European Court has been complied with, resulting in constitutional, legislative, and administrative changes throughout Europe. Inter-American Court judgments also have been followed, albeit slowly. Nonbinding recommendations of bodies such as the Human Rights Committee and the regional commissions are less successful. The lesson seems to be that states will accept legally binding judgments, out of a habit of obedience, but feel themselves free to stall or disregard "mere" recommendations, even when delivered by the institution created to give authoritative determinations about matters of compliance.

As states have become more accepting of individual petitions procedures, the regional commissions and courts have gradually strengthened their procedures for handling complaints. In the European system, a slow evolution toward individual standing first allowed individuals to appear before the court in the guise of assistants to the European Commission. A protocol later permitted them to appear by right. With the entry into force of Protocol 11, complainants will now have sole standing. The European Social Charter has been strengthened through amendment and practice.[69] Additional rights have been added by the 1988 Protocol, and a second protocol radically revises the system of supervision. Although the latter protocol is not yet in force, most of its provisions have been implemented by the supervisory organs.[70] An even greater change was envisaged by the 1995 Additional Protocol that provides for collective complaints from trade unions and employers' organizations and from NGOs.[71]

The African system has evolved quickly through the African Commission's interpretation of its powers and revision of its rules of procedure. The African Commission, like the Inter-American Commission, may "give its views or make recommendations to Governments" and since 1990 has published annual reports containing them. Like the other commissions, the African Commission negotiates friendly settlements.[72] The African Commission has developed its procedures on communications to include country reports and on-site visits to countries suspected of systematic violations of human rights. In regard to the latter, it has sent missions to Burundi, Mauritania, Nigeria, Rwanda, and Sudan.[73] The African Commission also sent a mission to Senegal to offer its good offices in the aftermath of an armed clash with separatists.[74] The situations in Chad and Zaire also have been characterized as constituting grave and massive violations of human rights.[75] The African system may undergo dramatic change with the approval of an African Court on Human Rights. The protocol creating the court was adopted on June 8, 1998, by the OAU Assembly of Heads of State and Government and signed by thirty of the fifty-three member states.

The African Court on Human Rights will have jurisdiction over all cases and disputes submitted to it concerning the charter, the protocol, and "any other applicable African human rights instrument." Cases can be submitted by the African Commission or a state party involved in a case as complainant or defendant. Article 6 highlights the "leapfrogging" effect of regional systems as it provides broader standing than other regional courts allow. It opens the African court to public-interest litigation by individuals and by NGOs with observer status. They may submit to the court urgent cases and those involving serious, systematic, or massive violations of human rights against states that file a declaration accepting Article 6.

In general, all the systems have enhanced their complaints procedures through providing means for greater participation by victims and their representatives. In most cases, these changes have occurred through action by the supervisory bodies rather than by amending the basic texts. The result of these changes has been a large increase in the number of cases filed. All the systems are now facing backlogs and overload. The regional governance bodies and the conferences of parties of the UN treaties have shown little inclination for making the human rights machinery more effective by increasing resources or staff. This may prove to be one of the largest problems in the future.

Reactions to Noncompliance

Global and regional institutions are weakest in follow-up mechanisms to respond to noncompliance with treaty obligations and judicial decisions. Most of the commissions and courts demand that states inform them of the measures they have taken to comply with decisions. Some institutions have gone further. After the African Commission recommended the release of Nigerians it deemed were wrongfully detained, it decided "to bring the file to Nigeria for the planned mission in order to verify that . . . [the victims] had been released."[76]

Individual and NGO complaints work well at the regional level but are less effective and useful globally where situations of widespread violations are encountered more frequently. The special rapporteur on summary or arbitrary executions annually receives information concerning between 65,000 and 70,000 cases. It would be extremely difficult to establish a workable individual complaint mechanism for all human rights violations around the world. The United Nations thus has created specialized treaty bodies and thematic rapporteurs and at the same time has focused its attention on those states in which gross and systematic violations occur, deeming these a violation of the UN Charter obligations to promote and respect human rights.[77]

The UN Charter–based procedures initially failed to produce any reaction to violations by Pol Pot in Kampuchea, Idi Amin in Uganda, Bokassa in the Central African Empire, or the military regimes in Argentina and Uruguay. The problems stemmed from the initial limitations and conservatism of the procedure. States were not interested in a public investigation and condemnation of human rights violations and wrapped the UN Charter procedures in secrecy and delay, apparently providing more protection to the governments than to the victims. NGOs had virtually no ability to participate apart from filing the complaints and holding press conferences. From 1979, the procedures became more public, and fact-finding and quasi-judicial proceedings substantially increased, reflecting the development of the thematic procedures.

The obvious evolution in norms and procedures does not address the fundamental question of whether human rights noncompliance procedures have brought about compliance, but there can be little doubt in this regard. There is considerable evidence that many states have responded to recommendations of the UN Human Rights Committee, CERD, and the thematic rapporteurs. Judgments of the regional tribunals have led to even more changes in laws and practices. In Europe it is relatively easy to demonstrate the effect of the convention and court judgments: Austria, for example, has modified its Code of Criminal Procedure; Belgium has amended its Penal Code, its laws on vagrancy, and its Civil Code; France has strengthened the protection for privacy of telephone communications; Germany has modified its Code of Criminal Procedure regarding pretrial detention, given legal recognition to transsexuals, and taken action to expedite criminal and civil proceedings; the Netherlands has modified its Code of Military Justice and the law on detention of mental patients; Ireland has created a system of legal aid; Sweden has introduced rules on expropriation and legislation on building permits; and Switzerland has amended its Military Penal Code and completely reviewed its judicial organization and criminal procedure applicable to the army.[78] According to Thomas Buergenthal,

> The decisions of the European Court are routinely complied with by European governments. As a matter of fact, the system has been so effective in the last decade that the Court has for all practical purposes become Western Europe's constitutional court. Its case law and practice resembles that of the United States Supreme Court.[79]

The impact of the system in Europe is relatively easy to demonstrate because of the follow-up procedure that requires states to report to the Committee of Ministers on their compliance with decisions of the European Court. In a similar fashion, the Inter-American Court maintains open files on cases until the defendant state carries out the judgment. It has closed a number of cases following compliance. The impact of Inter-American Commission decisions is harder to measure, but in the field of criminal justice there have been significant changes in laws and practices throughout the hemisphere, for example in regard to amnesty for human rights violators. According to a former member of the Inter-American Commission,

> In many ways the Inter-American system has not been as efficient as the European regional system, though its mandate is notably broader. The challenges the Inter-American system has faced are, however, severe and make its accomplishments all the more impressive. The fact that government leaders, diplomats, commission and court members, and many non-governmental organizations in the Americas

have been able, often in an ongoing adversarial collaboration, to fashion and implement a useful human rights instrument may be of particular importance to those interested in establishing regional human rights systems.[80]

Even without undertaking a detailed empirical analysis of the impact of the regional human rights systems, it is clear that they contribute to the functioning and improvement of human rights governance.

CONCLUSIONS AND IMPLICATIONS

In the human rights field, states set standards and monitor violations, but states are also the primary violators and the target of enforcement efforts. This inherent conflict of interest can present serious obstacles to greater progress, as reflected in the underfunding of monitoring bodies and efforts to undermine the independence of international commissions and committees. Over time, however, respect for human rights has increasingly become a test of legitimacy for governments, and incentives are greater for governments not to ignore other states' violations.

The ability of governments to conceal evidence and control information makes it difficult to monitor violations, as does the lack of criteria for measuring or evaluating performance in regard to many rights. Traditional legal principles, such as placing the burden of proof on the accuser, pose problems when the evidence is in the hands of the state. Furthermore, human rights measures were designed to deal with totalitarian, authoritarian governments but have yet to develop adequate responses to violations resulting from ineffective governments or the absence of government. Finally, there is sometimes the perception that human rights is not a mainstream problem but a fringe concern raised by "troublemakers" that gets in the way of serious subjects.

Human rights governance provides some lessons for other areas of global governance, particularly areas where much of the standard setting is complete and attention has been turned to implementation and monitoring compliance. The essential role of NGOs will be felt in any effort to govern states' internal behavior. Additionally, state reporting is an effective tool for monitoring compliance and easily translates to any field of international law. The importance of linking subject areas so that states may gain in one area only by giving in another is likely to transfer to other areas if it remains successful, as in the OSCE.

All the regional systems have seen dramatic changes in their environments, and with a breakdown of authoritarian, repressive regimes, a large decrease in the worst governmental abuses. New member states have joined regional systems, bringing new possibilities and problems. Countries in transition face enormous challenges in building democratic institutions, including the creation of independent judicial systems, professional police and military, a free press, and accountability for violations. Regional systems also face unprecedented problems from the resurgence of minority nationalism and ethnic tensions. There is a "mainstreaming" of human rights, as regional bodies are increasingly occupied with issues of democracy, armed conflict, transnational crime, environmental protection, economic development, science and technology, and indeed, the full range of human activities. Unfortunately, limited time and resources require that hard choices be made to accomplish the enormous tasks of preventing as well as remedying violations. The promise of regional systems is conditioned on the willingness of member states to increase resources for regional institutions in the future.

All the human rights systems are expanding their efforts to consider a broad range of issues related to human rights. The UN Center for Human Rights has developed an extensive program of technical assistance and training and has opened an increasing number of regional offices and operations. The Inter-American and African systems have increasingly become involved in internal armed conflicts and democratic institution building. The Council of Europe moved on the issue of human rights and biotechnology with its adoption of a Convention on Human Rights and Bioethics and a 1997 protocol on the prohibition of cloning human beings. It is the first legally binding international text on cloning. The protocol prohibits without reservation or derogation any intervention intended to create a human being genetically identical to another, whether living or dead. States are to legislate criminal or other sanctions, revoke licenses for laboratories or clinics, and issue bans on research or medical practice in case of offense.

Human rights governance is suffering from expanding work and diminishing resources. The success of the systems is in part responsible for the difficulties they face. Beginning in the early 1980s, the caseload of the European system, for example, began to double approximately every five years.[81] During its first eighteen years, the European Court decided twenty-six judgments, while the next eighteen years brought 472 decisions. At the end of 1993, the system had a backlog of 3,100 cases. The Inter-American Commission's caseload is also expanding; as of January 1, 2000, it had 945 cases under consideration and a staff of twelve lawyers to handle them. The question is whether even a full-time commission or court can cope.

At the United Nations, human rights activities account for less than 2 percent of the budget of the organization. The African Commission has repeatedly complained of shortages of staff and equipment. An OAU budgetary crisis has meant that several projects of the African Commission had to be suspended and one session was cut from two weeks to eight days. As of June 2, 1998, OAU member states owed more than $48 million in contributions, an amount that represented 1.5 times the annual budget of the organization.[82] Only twenty of the fifty-three members are up-to-date in their assessments. Two states have not paid for twelve years and two others for ten years.[83]

Finally, there is always the risk of backsliding. Barbados, Guyana, Jamaica, and Trinidad announced their intention to establish a Caribbean Court of Justice in 1999 in large part out of disagreement with inter-American standards on due process in death penalty cases.[84] On May 26, 1998, Trinidad and Tobago denounced the Inter-American Convention on Human Rights, the only state ever to do so. It also denounced the Optional Protocol to the CCPR. In January 1998, Jamaica withdrew from the CCPR Optional Protocol on the death penalty, and the Government of Barbados announced that it was considering denouncing the Inter-American Convention. Although these events challenge both regional and global standards, so long as the states remain members of the OAS, they are bound by regional norms and subject to the jurisdiction of the Inter-American Commission.

All systems are strengthened by the variety of subsystems that interact and even compete as parts of them.[85] As each subsystem attempts to optimize its functioning, the interaction of the subsystems at various meeting points changes the nature of the problems to be solved by them. The adaptive moves by each further modify the problems, stimulating additional evolution. The variety of responses leads to overall sustainability and resistance to threats, because each component can respond as it is differently adapted. Each subsystem benefits from the response of the others, learning and evolving in an ongoing interdependent process.

In just over half a century, the international protection of human rights has emerged as a fundamental value of modern society. Its foundation in religion and moral philosophy energizes civil society to maintain pressure on governments to respect and ensure human rights. Global and regional action to enact human rights into legally binding obligations imposed on all states has enhanced the pull toward compliance that is already provoked by the moral claim human rights exert. Although powerful elites often seek to maintain power through repression, and a resurgence of ethnic and religious conflict poses intractable problems, victims, human rights NGOs, and sympathetic states maintain the pressure on recalcitrant governments through fact finding and dissemination of information to the media and intergovernmental organizations capable of taking responsive action. Incentives and disincentives to compliance are provided by the establishment of international institutions that review state performance and can mobilize shame or issue binding judgments against noncomplying states.

It is a significant reflection of the power of human rights demands that repeated failures by governments to respect human rights lead advocates and activists not to abandon their efforts, but to strive toward strengthened international legal and political guarantees. Thus, the past decade has witnessed the first ad hoc international criminal tribunals since the Nuremberg and Tokyo war crimes trials after World War II. The new courts, like the older ones, have been established to ensure individual accountability for the most serious violations of international human rights. In addition to the ad hoc tribunals, the movement toward a permanent International

Criminal Court is yet another manifestation of the acceptance of international human rights as a matter of international concern. Such developments also reflect recognition of the need to continue developing the mechanisms of global governance to make respect for human rights a reality.

NOTES

1. The chapter is limited to multilateral action and thus does not address bilateral responses such as linking human rights compliance to most-favored-nation trade status, or unilateral sanctions like the termination of economic assistance to countries engaged in a pattern of gross and systematic violations of human rights. These measures, taken by states individually in an attempt to enforce international human rights norms, are often effective but are not expressly authorized by global institutions. Indeed, such measures may be resisted because they are outside the treaty regimes and multilateral framework created for the promotion and protection of human rights.

2. Demonstrating causality in the field of human rights is a perennial problem. Governments generally deny that human rights abuses are taking place and are not inclined to admit that any positive changes are the result of international pressure. Much of the evidence for the impact of human rights norms and institutions is therefore anecdotal or circumstantial, apart from those instances where evidence of compliance must be transmitted by a state, as is the case with judgments of the European and Inter-American Courts of Human Rights.

3. See P. G. Lauren, *The Evolution of International Human Rights: Visions Seen* (Philadelphia, Penn.: University of Pennsylvania Press, 1998).

4. The Sullivan and MacBride Principles are examples of nongovernmental standard setting. The Sullivan Principles were developed for use by multinational enterprises doing business in South Africa during the apartheid regime. The Reverend Leon Sullivan proposed the Sullivan Principles while serving as a member of the Board of Directors of General Motors Corporation in 1977. The code was intended to promote social justice and contribute to the elimination of apartheid. The principles called for integrated workplaces, fair employment practices, and affirmative action. Companies had to express written commitment to the principles and prepare and submit an annual report or self-evaluation of progress. A system was developed for measuring compliance. By 1984, there were 125 signatories to the code, representing about 80 percent of U.S.-employed South Africans. The MacBride Principles applied this approach to Northern Ireland. See Christopher McCrudden, "Human Rights Codes for Transnational Corporations: What Can the Sullivan and MacBride Principles Tell Us?" *Oxford Journal of Legal Studies*, vol. 19 (1999), p. 167.

5. Subsequent debates about the details of the rights have emerged, of course, as well as questions about priorities and resolution of problems when rights conflict. These developments, as well as recent efforts to add to the catalog of human rights, show the importance of normative consensus. Claims that development, environmental protection, safe

drinking water, and similar goals constitute human rights have provoked political debate and division rather than consensus at the United Nations and other international bodies, slowing consideration of them as human rights matters.

6. The Preamble to the Universal Declaration of Human Rights states that "it is essential, if man is not to be compelled to have recourse, as a last resort, to rebellion against tyranny and oppression, that human rights should be protected by the rule of law."

7. See, generally, Louis B. Sohn and Thomas Buergenthal, *International Protection of Human Rights* (Indianapolis, Ind.: Bobbs-Merrill, 1973).

8. Throughout the nineteenth century, antislavery societies worked to persuade governments to abolish the slave trade and slavery itself. Most of the antislavery movement was motivated by religion and morality, but those engaged in international trade also saw the economic value in the abolition of unpaid labor. Fear of competitive disadvantage in the growth of transnational trade, coupled with humanitarian concern for child labor and other abuse of workers, also led to the creation of the International Labor Organization (ILO) and concern for workers' rights at the beginning of the twentieth century.

9. The 1919 Treaty between the Principal Allied and Associated Powers and Poland served as a model for the interwar system. It provided for protection of life and liberty and religious freedom for all inhabitants of Poland. Polish citizens were guaranteed equality before the law and the right to use their own language in private life and judicial proceedings. Members of racial, religious, and linguistic minorities were guaranteed "the same treatment and security in law and in fact" as other Polish nationals, and the right to establish and control at their expense their own religious, social, and educational institutions. An equitable share of public funds was to be set aside for minorities in areas where they were concentrated, for educational or religious purposes. Specific guarantees were provided for Polish Jews. The League of Nations supervised compliance and developed procedures to implement its duties, including a right of petition for minorities claiming violation of any of the treaty guarantees.

10. See Manley Ottmer Hudson, *The Permanent Court of International Justice* (New York: The MacMillan Company, 1934) at p. 49.

11. Human rights activists included H. G. Wells, the Movement for Federal Union, the Institut de Droit International, the Catholic Association for International Peace, Jacques Maritain, and Hersch Lauterpacht.

12. The preamble "reaffirm[s] faith in fundamental human rights, in the dignity and worth of the human person, in the equal rights of men and women and of nations large and small." Article 55 calls on the United Nations to promote "universal respect for, and observance of, human rights and fundamental freedoms for all without distinction as to race, sex, language, or religion." In Article 56, "All members pledge themselves to take joint and separate action in cooperation with the Organization for the achievement of the purposes set forth in Article 55." UN Charter, June 26, 1945, 59 Stat. 1031, T.S. 993, 3 Bevans 1153.

13. Ibid., Art. 1(3).

14. UDHR, G.A. Res. 217A (III), UN Doc. A/810 (1948). See also Convention on the Elimination of All Forms of Racial Discrimination, Dec. 21, 1965, entered into force January 4, 1969, 660 U.N.T.S. 195; International Covenant on Civil and Political Rights,

Dec. 16, 1966, entered into force March 23, 1976, G.A. Res. 2200A (XXI), UN Doc. A/ 6316 (1966), 999 U.N.T.S. 171; International Covenant on Economic, Social, and Cultural Rights, Dec. 16, 1966, entered into force Jan. 3, 1976, G.A. Res. 2200A (XXI) 993 U.N.T.S. 3.

15. Other major UN human rights treaties include the Convention on the Prevention and Punishment of the Crime of Genocide, December 9, 1948, in force January 12, 1951, 78 U.N.T.S. 277; the Convention on the Elimination of All Forms of Discrimination against Women, Dec. 18, 1979, in force September 3, 1981, G.A. Res. 34, 180, 34 UN GAOR, Supp. No. 46, UN Doc. A/34/46, 193, 19 I.L.M. 33 (1980); the Convention Against Torture and Other Cruel, Inhuman, or Degrading Treatment, December 10, 1984, in force June 26, 1987, G.A. Res. 39/46, 39 UN GAOR, Supp. No. 51, UN Doc. A/39/51, at 197 (1984), 23 I.L.M. 1027 (1984); and the Convention on the Rights of the Child, November 20, 1989, in force September 2, 1990, G.A. Res. 44/25, Annex, 44 UN GAOR Supp. No. 49, p. 167, UN Doc. A/44/49 (1989), 28 I.L.M. 1448 (1989).

16. The issue of state responsibility for the crime of genocide has come before the International Court of Justice in the *Case Concerning Application of the Convention on the Prevention and Punishment of the Crime of Genocide [Bosnia and Herzegovina v. Yugoslavia (Serbia and Montenegro)]*, ICJ Reports 1993, pp. 3 and 325; 32 I.L.M. 888 (1993). Bosnia alleged that Yugoslavia is responsible for breaches of the genocide convention. On July 11, 1996, the International Court of Justice rejected the Preliminary Objections raised by Yugoslavia, emphasizing that the rights and obligations contained in the genocide convention are *erga omnes* duties (owed to the international community as a whole) and that each state is obligated to prevent and punish the crime of genocide regardless of the type of conflict or territorial limits. Art. IX of the convention does not exclude any form of state responsibility. ICJ Rep. 1996, paras. 31–32.

17. The UN legal advisor held in 1949 that the United Nations could not consider human rights complaints.

18. "We desire a Charter of Human Rights guaranteeing liberty of thought, assembly and expression as well as the right to form a political opposition; we desire a Court of Justice with adequate sanctions for the implementation of this Charter." *Message to Europeans*, adopted by the Congress of Europe, 8–10 May 1948, quoted in Council of Europe, *Report of the Control System of the European Convention on Human Rights*, (H(92)14) (Dec. 1992), p. 4. A resolution adopted by the Congress stated that it "is convinced that in the interest of human values and human liberty, the (proposed) Assembly should make proposals for the establishment of a Court of Justice with adequate sanctions for the implementation of this Charter, and to this end any citizen of the associated countries shall have redress before the Court, at any time and with the least possible delay, of any violation of his rights as formulated in the Charter." The previous quote is also taken from Congress of Europe, *Message to Europeans*.

19. In the preamble to the European Convention on Human Rights, the contracting parties declared that they were "reaffirming their devotion to the spiritual and moral values which are the common heritage of their peoples and the true source of individual freedom, political liberty and the rule of law, the principles which form the basis of all genuine

democracy." European Convention on Human Rights, Pmbl., 213 U.N.T.S. 221, ETS No. 5. See J. G. Merrills, "The Council of Europe (I): The European Convention on Human Rights," in Raija Hanski and Markku Suksi, eds., *An Introduction to the International Protection of Human Rights* (Turku: Institute for Human Rights, Åbo Akademi University, 1997). Merrills states, "Many statesmen of the immediate post-war epoch had been in resistance movements or in prison during the Second World War and were acutely conscious of the need to prevent any recrudescence of dictatorship in Western Europe" (p. 221). Merrills also views the emergence of the East-West conflict as a stimulus to closer ties in Western Europe.

20. The Statute of the Council of Europe was signed in London on May 5, 1949, on behalf of Belgium, Denmark, France, Ireland, Italy, Luxembourg, Netherlands, Norway, Sweden, and the United Kingdom. Statute of the Council of Europe, May 5, 1949. ETS No. 1, Gr. Brit. T.S. No. 51 (Cmnd. 8969). Russia joined in 1996, Georgia in 1999, Azerbaijan and Armenia in 2001.

21. Membership in the Council is de facto conditioned on adherence to the ECHR and its protocols. See Committee of Ministers, Declaration on Compliance with Commitments Accepted by Member States of the Council of Europe, adopted on 10 November 1994, reprinted in Council of Europe, Information Sheet No. 35 (July–December 1994) (1995), Appendix I, 146. All forty-one member states have ratified the convention, as restructured by Protocol 11, and the European Torture Convention, ETS No. 126. Armenia and Azerbaijan were the last states to become members of the Council of Europe, on January 25, 2001.

22. Follow-up conferences have been held in Madrid (1983), Vienna (1989), Copenhagen (1990), and Budapest (1994). The Madrid meeting focused on the issue of trade union freedoms in light of the advent of the Solidarity movement in Poland. Specific and detailed guarantees regarding freedom of religion, nondiscrimination, minority rights, freedom of movement, conditions of detention, and capital punishment were added at the Vienna meeting. See Concluding Document of the Vienna Conference on Security and Cooperation in Europe, adopted January 15, 1989, reprinted in *Human Rights Law Journal*, vol. 10 (1989), p. 270. Copenhagen also resulted in considerable standard setting in several areas of human rights protections, especially concerning national minorities. It was also one of the first documents to refer to the right of conscientious objection to military service, a right not contained in the ECHR.

23. See Andrew Drzemczewski, "The Council of Europe's Cooperation and Assistance Programmes with Central and Eastern European Countries in the Human Rights Field," *Human Rights Law Journal*, vol. 14 (1993), p. 229.

24. Case 11/70, *International Handelsgesellschaft mbH v. Einfuhr- und Vorratsstelle für Getreide und Futtermittel*, [1970] European Case Reports 1125.

25. Article 8b creates citizens' rights to vote and stand as a candidate in European elections throughout the European Union. There is also a right to petition the European Parliament. Treaty on European Union, O.J. No. C 224, August 31, 1992. EC documents on environmental protection stress rights of information, public participation, and redress. See, for example, EEC Directive on the Assessment of the Effects of Certain Projects on

the Environment, 85/337/EEC, O.J.E.C. L. 175 of July 5, 1985; EEC Directive on Freedom of Access to Information on the Environment, 90/313/EEC, O.J.E.C. L. 158 of June 23, 1990.

26. See, for example, Case 152/84, *M. H. Marshall v. Southampton and South-West Hampshire Area Health Authority (Teaching)*, [1986] ECR 723. The case is based on the EC Equal Treatment Directive.

27. For the right to respect for private life, see Case 165/82, *Commission of the European Communities v. United Kingdom of Great Britain and Northern Ireland*, [1983] ECR 3431. For the right to pursue a trade, see Case 249/83, *Vera Hoeckx v. Openbaar Centrum voor Maatschappelijk Welzijn Kalmthout*, [1985] ECR 973.

28. O.J. No. C 120/51 of 16 May 1989.

29. For a history of the inter-American system, see Thomas Buergenthal and Dinah Shelton, *Protecting Human Rights in the Americas*, 4th ed. (Arlington, Va.: N. P. Engel, 1995), pp. 37–44. At the International American Conference of War and Peace, held at Chapultepec, Mexico, in March 1943, twenty-one American states asked for a bill of human rights to be included in the UN Charter. Three of these countries (Cuba, Chile, and Panama) were the first to submit a draft for such a bill. At the San Francisco Conference they lobbied for inclusion of a bill of rights in the charter. Other Latin American countries prepared other drafts that became part of the background to the drafting of the UDHR. The text submitted by the Inter-American Juridical Committee was particularly influential, as were the Chilean draft and the work of the Chilean delegate, Hernan Santa Cruz.

30. Art. 3, OAS Charter.

31. American Declaration of the Rights and Duties of Man (1948), in OAS, *Basic Documents Pertaining to Human Rights in the Inter-American System* (hereinafter *Basic Documents*), OEA/Ser.L/VII.92, doc. 31, rev. 3 (1996) p. 17. See Interpretation of the American Declaration of the Rights and Duties of Man within the Framework of Article 64 of the American Convention, 10 Inter-Am.Ct.H.R. (Ser.A) (1989).

32. Interpretation of the American Declaration of the Rights and Duties of Man, pp. 7–9. The statute of the commission described it as an autonomous entity of the OAS having the function to promote respect for human rights (1960 Statute, Art. 1). In 1967, the Protocol of Buenos Aires amended the charter to make the commission a principal organ of the OAS.

33. Interpretation of the American Declaration of the Rights and Duties of Man, p. 10. Reflecting state ambivalence about the new procedure, this and other human rights texts avoid the word "complaints," referring instead to "communications" or "petitions."

34. American Convention on Human Rights, November 22, 1969, reprinted in 9 I.L.M. 673 [hereinafter American Convention].

35. The major instruments are: the Inter-American Convention to Prevent and Punish Torture, OAS T.S. No. 67, reprinted in *Basic Documents*, p. 87, entry into force on February 28, 1987; Additional Protocol to the American Convention on Human Rights in the Area of Economic, Social, and Cultural Rights, OAS T.S. No. 69, OAS doc. OEA/Ser.A/ 42 (SEPF), reprinted in *Basic Documents*, p. 69, entry into force November 1, 1999; Protocol to the American Convention on Human Rights to Abolish the Death Penalty, OAS T.S. No. 73, reprinted in *Basic Documents*, p. 83, entry into force on August 28,

1991; Inter-American Convention on the Prevention, Punishment, and Eradication of Violence Against Women, General Assembly Resolution 1257, reprinted in *Basic Documents*, p. 109, entry into force 5 March 1995; Inter-American Convention on Forced Disappearance of Persons, OAS T.S. No. 80, reprinted in *Basic Documents*, p. 99, entry into force on March 28, 1996; IACHR, Press Communique of 3/97, reprinted in OAS, Annual Report of the Inter-American Commission on Human Rights 1997, OAS doc. OEA/Ser.L/V/II.98, Doc.7 rev. (1998), p. 1081 (The Declaration of the Rights of Indigenous Peoples).

36. African Charter on Human and Peoples' Rights, OAU Doc. CAB/LEG./67/3/Rev. 5, reprinted in 21 I.L.M. 59 (1982), entry into force on October 21, 1986.

37. See Mohamed Noman Galal, "The Arab Draft Charter for Human Rights," in *Human Rights: Egypt and the Arab World*, vol. 37, no. 17 (Cairo Papers in Social Science, 1994). See Arab Charter on Human Rights, September 15, 1994, Council of the League of Arab States, 102nd sess., Resolution 5437. An unofficial translation of the charter appears in *The Review of the International Commission of Jurists*, vol. 56 (1996), and at *International Human Rights Reports*, vol. 4 (1997), p. 850. Resolution 5437 was approved after a motion by Kuwait to adjourn discussion of the charter was defeated. The defeat was interpreted by the Jordanian chairman as an endorsement of the charter. A Standing Committee on Human Rights in 1968 began drafting the charter in 1970 and completed its work in 1985. See *Report and Recommendations of the Arab Standing Committee on Human Rights at Its Eleventh Session Held at Cairo from 10 to 14 January 1993*, E/CN.4/1993/90. For a history of the drafting of the Arab Charter, see Galal. For early background on the League and its human rights activities, see S. Marks, "La commission permanente arabe des droits de l'homme," *Revue Droit de l'Homme*, vol. 3 (1970), p. 101. Regarding NGOs, in 1981 a Universal Islamic Declaration of Human Rights was prepared by representatives from countries in the Middle East under the auspices of the Islamic Council, an NGO. Furthermore, a larger organization of all Islamic states, the Islamic Conference, endorsed human rights in its 1972 charter, reaffirming the commitment of Islamic states to the UN Charter and fundamental human rights. On August 5, 1990, a meeting of foreign ministers of the conference member states adopted the Cairo Declaration on Human Rights in Islam. For an English translation of the declaration, see UN GAOR, World Conference on Human Rights, 4th Sess., Agenda item 5, UN Doc. A/CONF.157/ PC/62/Add.18 (1993). For a critique of the declaration, see Ann Elizabeth Mayer, "Universal Versus Islamic Human Rights: A Clash of Cultures or a Clash with a Construct?" *Michigan Journal of International Law*, vol. 15 (1994), p. 307. For background on the Islamic Conference, see Hasan Moinuddin, *The Charter of the Islamic Conference and Legal Framework of Economic Cooperation Among Its Member States* (New York: Oxford University Press, 1987).

38. One of the early regional efforts in Asia resulted in a 1983 document entitled "The Declaration of Basic Duties of ASEAN People's and Governments." A regional NGO, the Law Association for Asia and the Pacific (LAWASIA), and the Association of Southeast Asian Nations (ASEAN) Law Association have supported the creation of a regional human rights mechanism. The UN Center for Human Rights has sponsored a series of government workshops in Manila, Jakarta, Seoul, Kathmandu, Amman, and Teheran

for officials from countries in the Asia-Pacific region. See, for example, United Nations, *Fourth Workshop on Regional Human Rights Arrangements in the Asian and Pacific Region*, HR/PUB/96/3 (1996).

39. Bangkok NGO Declaration on Human Rights (Asian Cultural Forum on Development, 1993).

40. See UN Workshop, especially note 38, p. 3. The rejection of a regional system continued at the 1997 and 1998 regional meetings. At the 1997 meeting in Amman, participants agreed on incremental steps—some of which are positive, others seemingly intended to slow implementation of human rights in the region. The steps include ratification of human rights instruments, promotion of national institutions, recognition of NGOs and the role of civil society, promotion of the right to development, advocacy against human rights conditionality, attention to vulnerable groups, support for universality, "objectivity and nonselectivity" of human rights, more technical cooperation, information sharing, capacity building, and programs for regional cooperation. C. Dias, "From Building Blocks to Next Steps: The Task Ahead at Teheran," background paper for the Sixth Workshop on Regional Arrangements for the Promotion and Protection of Human Rights in the Asian and Pacific Region (1998), p. 15. The 1998 workshop in Teheran reaffirmed the universality, indivisibility, and interdependence of human rights "in a region proud of its rich cultures, religions and diversities" and pledged commitment to the Vienna Declaration and Program of Action.

41. The "Asian" members of the UN Human Rights Commission have included not only China, Indonesia, Japan, and the Philippines, but also Cyprus, Pakistan, and India. The United Nations lists forty countries in the region. See E/CN.4/1998/50, p. 10 (1998).

42. ASEAN member states created working groups for a human rights mechanism. In 1997, members met in Kuala Lumpur and adopted conclusions supporting the development of a regional human rights mechanism, including the possibility of drafting an ASEAN Convention on Human Rights. According to UN classifications, the Arab Charter represents an Asian regional instrument.

43. According to Vitat Muntabhorn, "Asian values" are now seen as comprising "profligate expenditure, over-borrowing, excessive investment in the real estate sector, inadequate regulation, and an admixture of vested interests and cronyism." He argues that this could be a blessing in disguise because it enables the region to question the legitimacy of the region's economic and political bases. See Vitat Muntabhorn, "Protection of Human Rights in Asia and the Pacific: Think Universal, Act Regional?" in *Collection of Lectures, Twenty-Ninth Study Session, International Institute of Human Rights I* (Strasbourg: International Institute of Human Rights, 1998), p. 3.

44. See Dinah Shelton, *State Practice on Reservations to Human Rights Treaties*, 1983 Canadian Human Rights Yearbook 205; William Schabas, "Reservations to the Convention on the Elimination of All Forms of Discrimination Against Women and the Convention on the Rights of the Child," *William and Mary Journal of Women and Law*, vol. 3 (1997), p. 79.

45. Only the American Declaration of the Rights and Duties of Man does not mention the UDHR, because it was adopted prior to the completion of the UDHR. The American Declaration indicates its origin in the "repeated occasions" that the American states had

"recognized that the essential rights of man are not derived from the fact that he is a national of a certain state, but are based upon attributes of his personality" (Preamble). It also asserts that "the international protection of the rights of man should be the principal guide of an evolving American law" (Preamble).

46. The European Convention refers to the "common heritage of political traditions, ideals, freedom and the rule of law." The American Declaration refers not only to prior meetings and actions of the American states but to "evolving American law," while the American Convention reaffirms the intention of the states party to the agreement to consolidate a system of rights "within the framework of democratic institutions." The African Charter states that it takes into consideration the virtues of African historical tradition and "the values of African civilization." The Arab Charter states that it stems "from the Arab Nation's faith in the dignity of man; from when God favored it by making the Arab nation the cradle of monotheistic religions and the birthplace of civilization; which has reaffirmed man's right to a life of dignity based on freedom, justice and peace" (Preamble).

47. The Arab Charter is unique in omitting explicit mention of slavery, although its prohibition on forced labor could be intended to include slavery. The charter also omits the right to free and fair elections, specifying only the right of citizens to occupy public office. Article 19 of the charter adds that "[t]he people are the source of authority. Political capacity is a right for every citizen of a legal age to be exercised in accordance with the law." The rights of aliens are limited in many texts. The Arab Charter limits to citizens the rights to leave and not to be expelled, to political asylum, to private property, to freedom of assembly and association, to work and to social security, to equal opportunity in employment and equal pay for equal work, to political rights, and to education. The CESCR allows states to limit economic rights for aliens. All human rights treaties limit political rights to citizens, while other civil rights guarantees for aliens have provoked a relatively high number of reservations to the CCPR. In terms of additional rights, the Arab Charter's regulation of the death penalty uniquely prohibits the execution of a nursing mother, until two years have passed from the date of her child's birth (Art. 12). The prohibition on torture specifies that it extends to both physical and psychological torture, and mandates criminal penalties for performing or participating in an act of torture. The Arab Charter also expands on the right of political asylum, adding that "political refugees shall not be extradited" (Art. 23). The Council of Europe's Parliamentary Assembly, even before the signing of the European Convention, proposed the inclusion of additional rights, which were added by Protocol 1.

48. For example, the European and Inter-American Courts take very different approaches to their remedial powers based on the different language of their respective treaties. In case law, the Inter-American Court has also rejected the European doctrine of "margin of appreciation."

49. See Felice D. Gaer, "Reality Check: Human Rights NGOs Confront Governments at the UN," in Thomas G. Weiss and Leon Gordenker, eds., *NGOs, the UN, and Global Governance* (Boulder, Colo.: Lynne Rienner, 1996).

50. David Forsythe, "The United States, the United Nations and Human Rights," in Margaret P. Karns and Karen A. Mingst, eds., *The United States and Multilateral Institutions* (Boston: Unwin Hyman, 1990).

51. Sara Rimer and Raymond Bonner, "Whether to Kill Those Who Killed as Youths," *New York Times*, August 22, 2000, p. 1.

52. Brazil, the Dominican Republic, and Mexico submitted an amendment calling for the organization to ensure respect for human rights and fundamental freedoms without discrimination on the basis of race, sex, condition, or creed. Amendments to the Dumbarton Oaks Proposals, Doc. 2, G/25, 5 May 1945, 3 UNCIO Documents 602. Uruguay proposed that the organization endorse "the essential rights of mankind, internationally established and guaranteed," New Uruguayan Proposals, Doc. 2 G/7(a)(1), 5 May 1945, 3 UNCIO Documents 35. Panama suggested inserting a declaration of "essential human rights" and a clause guaranteeing equal protection against discrimination because of race, religion, sex, or "any other reason." Additional Amendments Proposed by the Delegation of the Republic of Panama, Doc. 2, G/7 (g)(2), 5 May 1945, 3 UNCIO Documents 269.

53. Proposals to include human rights provisions came from Egypt, Iraq, the Philippines, China, India, New Zealand, Mexico, France, Norway, Guatemala, Paraguay, South Africa, Lebanon, and Cuba.

54. The United Kingdom was petitioned, inter alia, by the London-based Council of Christians and Jews, which included the archbishops of Canterbury and Westminster, the Chief Rabbi, and the moderator of the Church of Scotland to view human rights as an essential matter to be given prominence by the British delegation.

55. See Gaer, *Reality Check*.

56. Not all of these cases are in the field of economic, social, and cultural rights. Mauritania sought UN assistance in the eradication of slavery.

57. UN Doc. E/CN.4/1994/para. 25(h).

58. See Weiss and Gordenker, *NGOs, the UN, and Global Governance*.

59. UN Doc. E/CN.4/1995/47, p. 12, para. 48.

60. Reports of the Working Group are contained in: E/CN.4/1435 and Add. 1 (1981); E/CN.4/1492 and Add.1 (1982); E/CN.4/1984/21 and Add.1-2; E/CN.4/1985/15 and Add.1; E/CN.4/1986/18 and Add.1; E/CN.4/1987/15 and Add.1; E/CN.4/1988/19 and Add.1; E/CN.4/1989/18 and Add.1; E/CN.4/1990/13; E/CN.4/1991/20 and Add.1; E/CN.4/1992/18; E/CN.4/1993/25; E/CN.4/1994/26; E/CN.4/1995/36; E/CN.4/1996/38; E/CN.4/1998/43. On disappearances, see Iain Guest, *Behind the Disappearances: Argentina's Dirty War Against Human Rights and the United Nations* (Philadelphia, Penn.: University of Pennsylvania Press, 1990), pp. 79–86.

61. Despite the attacks, the report led to an innovation in UN practice when the chairman of the Human Rights Commission allowed Amnesty to mention Argentina by name, holding that NGOs could provide information about but not "attack" governments. Prior to this, mentioning a country by name could get an NGO ruled out of order. The change made the threat of public denunciation more credible and thus a more powerful tool for NGOs.

62. Now entitled the Special Rapporteur on Extrajudicial, Summary, or Arbitrary Executions, reports of the Special Rapporteur are found in: E/CN.4/1983/16; E/CN.4/1984/29; E/CN.4/1985/17; E/CN.4/1986/21; E/CN.4/1987/20; E/CN.4/1988/22 and Add.1-2; E/CN.4/1989/25; E/CN.4/1990/22; E/CN.4/1991/36; E/CN.4/1993/46; E/CN.4/1994/7; E/CN.4/1996/60; E/CN.4/1997/60 and Add.1; E/CN.4/1998/68 and Add.1.

63. Reports of the Special Rapporteur are found in: E/CN.4/1986/15; E/CN.4/1987/13; E/CN.4/1988/17 and Add.1; E/CN.4/1989/10; E/CN.4/1990/17 and Add.1; E/CN.4/1991/17; E/CN.4/1993/26; E/CN.4/1994/31; E/CN.4/1995/34; E/CN.4/1996/35 and Add.1; E/CN.4/1998/38 and Add.1. Reports of the Working Group are found in: E/CN.4/1995/31 and Add.1-2; E/CN.4/1996/40 and Add.1; E/CN.4/1997/4; E/CN.4/1998/44 and Add.1.

64. The urgent action procedure "is basically humanitarian" and intended to prevent or halt violations rather than provide redress for prior victims; "hence the emphasis is laid on the element of 'effectiveness' and on the adoption of preventive measures." See *Torture and Other Cruel, Inhuman, or Degrading Treatment or Punishment,* Report of the Special Rapporteur, Mr. P. Kooijmans, pursuant to Commission on Human Rights Resolution 1992/32, E/CN.4/1993/26, para 15.

65. See also the report of the special rapporteur on prisons in Africa, whose mandate is to examine prison conditions and recommend improvement, pushing relevant international human rights norms and standards. The mandate also extends to creating a special communications procedure for persons deprived of their liberty and taking preventive measures. The rapporteur initiated his work with an on-site visit to Zimbabwe, where he met with NGOs and prison officials.

66. The Inter-American Commission has issued country reports, usually on the basis of on-site visits, on Argentina, Bolivia, Brazil, Chile, Colombia, Cuba, Dominican Republic, Ecuador, El Salvador, Guatemala, Haiti, Nicaragua, Panama, Paraguay, Peru, Suriname, and Uruguay.

67. Author interviews with UN special rapporteurs and staff members of the Inter-American Commission on Human Rights.

68. Inter-American Commission on Human Rights, First Report 1960, OAS Doc. OEA/Ser.L/V/II.1, Doc. 32 (1961).

69. For a general review of the evolution of the European Social Charter, see David Harris, *The Council of Europe (II): The European Social Charter*, in Hanski and Suksi, p. 243.

70. Although interim application of treaty commitments is common in the environmental field, it is extremely rare in international human rights law. This may in fact be a unique example. Among the changes implemented prior to the entry into force of the protocol, the Committee of Ministers agreed to expand the Committee of Independent Experts (CIE) that reviews state reports from seven to nine members. The Amending Protocol also codifies the practice of the CIE in assessing from a legal standpoint the compliance of national law and practice with the obligations imposed on states by the charter [Art. 24(2) Amending Protocol]. Finally, there has already been implementation of the provisions of the Amending Protocol that provide for meetings between the CIE and representatives of a state party at the request of either. This brings the CIE process of reviewing state reports into conformity with the practice of UN treaty-monitoring bodies such as the Human Rights Committee. One difference, however, is that the CIE reviews of state reports during meetings with state representatives are generally closed meetings.

71. ETS No. 158. The protocol requires five ratifications to enter into force.

72. Communication 44/90, *Peoples' Democratic Organization for Independence and Socialism v. the Gambia*, concerned voter registration irregularities. A new government acknowl-

edged the problem and expressed its intent to correct it by establishing an independent electoral commission and team of experts to review the electoral law.

73. The resolution on Burundi expressed concern with the "serious violations" and "abuses" in Burundi, "considering that impunity is one of the main causes of the worsening situation." It referred to "hate media" in the country and urged the government to conduct transparent and impartial investigations into the violations and abuses, guarantee the independence of the judiciary, and allow on-site investigations by several international organizations including the African Commission. The resolution also asked the United Nations to send a commission of inquiry. On Rwanda, see Ninth Annual Activity Report of the African Commission on Human and Peoples' Rights, 1995–1996, OAU Doc. AHG/207 (XXXII), p. 7, para. 20.

74. The African Commission's mission included fact finding to establish the basis of future negotiations between the separatists and the government. After its one-week trip, it found that "in sum the arguments developed to support the separatist positions lack pertinence. They cannot justify the grave attacks against human rights in the course of the conflict." The African Commission also rejected some of the government's arguments and made recommendations to both sides to assist in resolving the dispute.

75. On Chad, see Communication 74/92, Commission Nationale des Droits de l'Homme et des Libertés/Chad, AHG/207(XXXII) Annex VIII, p. 12. The commission held hearings on the case, after which it decided that the communication provided evidence of serious and massive violations of human and peoples' rights. The OAU Assembly was notified. The finding regarding Zaire followed the consolidation of four communications asserting torture, killings, arbitrary detention, unfair trials, restrictions on the right to association and peaceful assembly, suppression of freedom of the press, and denial of the rights to education and to health. In regard to the latter, the commission said "Article 16 of the African Charter states that every individual shall have the right to enjoy the best attainable state of physical and mental health, and that States Parties should take the necessary measures to protect the health of their people. The failure of the Government to provide basic services such as safe drinking water and electricity and the shortage of medicine as alleged in communication 100/93 constitutes a violation of Article 16." AHG/207(XXXII), Annex VIII, p. 8.

76. Case 60/91 8th p. 4. Also Case 87/93, *The Constitutional Rights Project in re Zamani Lakwot and Others v. Nigeria*, pp. 7–9.

77. First in 1967 and then in 1970, ECOSOC invited the UN Commission on Human Rights to consider the question of violations of human rights, making particular reference to policies of racial discrimination, segregation, and apartheid. UN Economic and Social Council Resolutions 1235 (XLII) of June 6, 1967, and 1503 (XLVIII) of May 27, 1970, permit consideration by the UN Commission of information relevant to gross violations of human rights. According to Resolution 1235, the UN Commission may undertake a thorough study and report its finding to ECOSOC where there is found to be a consistent pattern of such violations. Pursuant to this authority, the UN Commission has appointed working groups and special rapporteurs to report on large-scale violations in

specific countries throughout the world. Resolution 1503 establishes a limited petition system for the UN Sub-Commission on Promotion and Protection of Human Rights to consider nonstate communications that "appear to reveal a consistent pattern of gross and reliably attested violations of human rights and fundamental freedoms." The UN Sub-Commission may forward the information to the UN Commission, which may either undertake a thorough study according to the provisions of Resolution 1235, undertake an investigation by an ad hoc committee with the consent of the state concerned, or take no action.

78. On Austria, see *Neumeister v. Austria*, 8 Eur.Ct.H.R. (Ser.A)(1968); *Stogmuller v. Austria*, 9 Eur.Ct.H.R. (Ser.A)(1969); *Matznetter v. Austria*, 10 Eur.Ct.H.R. (Ser.A)(1969); *Ringeisen v. Austria*, 13 Eur.Ct.H.R. (Ser.A)(1971); and *Bonisch v. Austria*, 92 Eur.Ct.H.R. (Ser.A)(1985). On Belgium, see *De Wilde, Ooms, and Versyp v. Belgium* (Vagrancy Cases), 12 Eur.Ct.H.R. (Ser. A) (1970) and *Marckx v. Belgium*, 31 Eur.Ct.H.R. (Ser. A)(1979)(discrimination between legitimate and illegitimate children). On France, see *Kruslin and Huvig v. France*, 176B Eur.Ct.H.R. (Ser.A)(1990)(wiretapping). On Germany, see, for example, *Luedicke, Belkacem, and Koc v. Germany*, 29 Eur.Ct.H.R. (Ser. A)(1978)(interpreters fees). On the Netherlands, see *Engel v. Netherlands*, 22 Eur.Ct. H.R. (1976)(military penal code) and *Winterwerp v. Netherlands*, 33 Eur.Ct.H.R. (Ser.A)(1979)(mentally ill). On Ireland, see *Airey v. Ireland*, 32 Eur.Ct.H.R. (Ser. A)(1979). On Sweden, see *Sporrong and Lonnroth v. Sweden*, 88 Eur.Ct.H.R. (Ser. A)(1985). *Eggs v. Switzerland*, Application 7341/76, Decisions and Reports, vol. 6, p. 170.

79. Thomas Buergenthal and Dinah Shelton, *Protecting Human Rights in the Americas* (Alexandria, Va.: Engel Verlag, 1996), p. 34.

80. W. Michael Reisman, "Practical Matters for Consideration in the Establishment of a Regional Human Rights Mechanism: Lessons from the Inter-American Experience," *St. Louis-Warsaw Transnational Law Journal* (1995), p. 89.

81. In 1982, the commission registered more than 500 applications for the first time; in 1988 more than 1,000 applications were registered. By 1992, the number of registered applications reached 2,037. ECHR, Survey of Activities and Statistics (1993). The number of court judgments has similarly risen. During its first fifteen years, it issued seventeen judgments in regard to eleven cases. During the next ten years, fifty-nine judgments were adopted. From 1984 to 1993, the number jumped to 372.

82. Sidy Gaye, "OAU Owed 48 Million by Member States," *Pan African News Agency*, June 2, 1998.

83. Ibid.

84. "Four Nations Shedding Curbs on Executions," *Chicago Sun-Times*, July 5, 1998. Trinidad and Tobago is to be the seat of the new court, which will replace the Privy Council as the last court of appeal for death row cases in the four countries. "Trinidad and Tobago to Be Centre for Caribbean Court," *The Lawyer*, vol. 36 (August 4, 1998), p. 36.

85. Stuart Kauffman, *At Home in the Universe: The Search for Laws of Self-Organization and Complexity* (New York: Oxford University Press, 1995), p. 247.

SUGGESTED ADDITIONAL READING

Buergenthal, Thomas. *International Human Rights in a Nutshell.* St. Paul, Minn.: West Publishing Co., 1988.

Buergenthal, Thomas, and Dinah Shelton. *Protecting Human Rights in the Americas,* 4th ed. Arlington, Va.: N. P. Engel, 1995.

Guest, Iain. *Behind the Disappearances: Argentina's Dirty War Against Human Rights and the United Nations.* Philadelphia, Penn.: University of Pennsylvania Press, 1990.

Humphrey, John P. *Human Rights and the United Nations: A Great Adventure.* Dobbs Ferry, N.Y.: Transnational Press, 1984.

Hurst, Hannum, ed. *Guide to International Human Rights Practice.* Ardsley, N.Y.: Transnational Press, 1999.

Lauren, Paul Gordon. *The Evolution of International Human Rights: Visions Seen.* Philadelphia, Penn.: University of Pennsylvania Press, 1998.

Sohn, Louis B., and Thomas Buergenthal. *International Protection of Human Rights.* Indianapolis, Ind.: Bobbs-Merrill, 1973.

Steiner, Henry J., and Philip Alston. *International Human Rights in Context: Law, Politics, Morals, Text, and Materials,* 2nd ed. New York: Oxford University Press, 2000.

Internet sites

Human Rights Watch <http://www.hrw.org>
Amnesty International <http://www.amnesty.org>
OAS Human Rights, Inter-American Commission on Human Rights <http://www.cidh.oas.org>
UN High Commissioner for Refugees (UNHCR) <http://www.unhchr.ch>

12

Labor Rights

Brian Langille

KARL POLANYI PROVOCATIVELY OBSERVED that "labor is the technical term for human beings."[1] In our time, discussions of international labor rights put a human face on discussions of international economic integration or, more simply, "globalization." Not everyone is a refugee, the victim of terrorism, or involved in the weapons trade. But almost everyone is involved in productive activity, or seeks to be. The way in which productive economic activity is structured is the concern of labor law, the ambition of which is to secure justice in this aspect of the lives of people around the world. This chapter analyzes labor regulation not as a domestic legal phenomenon, but rather as an issue of global management. It adheres to the view that a discussion of management of this issue (whether in terms of agenda setting, negotiation, monitoring compliance, or enforcement) that proceeds without a grasp of its unique structure will necessarily be shallow.

This essay begins with a description of the peculiar structure of the labor rights agenda domestically and how that agenda becomes even more complex at the international level. A central insight is that the labor rights agenda rests on one of the core political controversies of our time: the virtues and limits of markets.

Given the centrality of labor market regulations to the lives of individual workers and to the social and economic progress of states, it is not surprising that labor law has almost always been a central regulatory preoccupation of domestic politics. International governance, too, has a lengthy history, with most historians tracing the origins of modern global labor regulation to the early nineteenth century.[2] Since then numerous states, intergovernmental organizations, labor unions, firms, industry organizations, nongovernmental organizations (NGOs), and consumer and social movement groups have advocated perhaps every known strategy of international governance. In so doing, these actors have interacted within a broad spectrum of international spaces ranging from large international institutions such as the International Labor Organization (ILO) with elaborate bureaucratic and political processes to the unstructured space of the consumer marketplace. They have also pursued an equally broad range of remedial strategies—ranging from hard trade sanctions to weak sanctions (such as the sanction of shame) and incentives and capacity-building assistance. Multilateral, intergovernmental institutions such as the ILO, the Organization for Economic Cooperation and Development (OECD), and the World Trade Organization (WTO) have played important roles. Within these institutions nonstate actors (especially unions and employers) have participated actively. Regional economic arrangements—most notably the European Union and the North American Free Trade Agreement (NAFTA), but also including Mercosur in South America and South African Development Community in southern Africa—are also sites of contest for the labor rights agenda. Subnational activities, including international collective bargaining and coalition building by trade unions; firm-based or industrywide initiatives (such as codes of conduct); and consumer-driven campaigns involving boycotts and product labeling also abound. But these are not watertight compartments. There is evidence of what David Trubek and others, following Margaret Keck and Kathryn Sikkink, have described as "transnational advocacy networking," resulting in a complex mixture of complicated overlapping interactions among various actors at different levels seeking to deploy a wide variety of strategies.[3] The current state of play involves a rich cross-cutting variety of roles for all actors at all levels at all phases of governance. To give but one example, the ILO is an institution in which governments and nongovernmental actors (workers and employers) play official roles; it is simultaneously an important player in international debates about labor rights, a site of contestation over labor rights, a leader in private sector developments such as corporate codes of conduct, and a participant in regional and national development projects regarding labor rights such as the International Program for the Elimination of Child Labor.

BASIC CONFLICTS IN THE DEBATE OVER INTERNATIONAL LABOR RIGHTS

What is the structure of the labor rights issue? It is important to see that perhaps unlike other global issues studied in this volume, there is genuine disagreement about whether labor rights are a global good or a global evil. There is no doubt that more clean air is a global good and more corruption an evil. Whether more respect for labor rights is good or bad is contested, both normatively and empirically. The reasons are not hard to identify. Even in a nonglobalized world of imagined "island" jurisdictions with no trade, no foreign investment, and no interchange among them, labor rights are at the core of productive human activity. As Paul Krugman points out, "A country's ability to improve its standard of living over time depends almost entirely on its ability to raise output per worker"; or, more pointedly, "Productivity isn't everything, but in the long run, it is almost everything."[4]

Thus a society's approach to its development and use of human capital is of profound long-term importance. Growth can be achieved only by putting more people to work and making each worker more productive. Labor law structures productive relations between employers (firms and shareholders) and employees. Getting it right is important but difficult, because productive activity is a human activity and the labor market is a social institution, as Polanyi and others remind us.[5] Work is a vital human institution and an end in itself, not just a means to aggregate societal wealth. Human values are centrally implicated in the market in labor, or to put it more familiarly, "Labor is not a commodity."[6] Thus there is ample room for a contest of visions of employment regulation as "economic" or as "human."

In most states—certainly in OECD nations—labor law is conceived of as a debate about the virtues and limits of markets ordering labor. The history of domestic labor law in these countries is the history of a dialogue among capital, labor, and consumers, through democratic processes, that has resulted in a complex legal regime structuring, legitimizing, and limiting the operation of a free market in labor.[7] These labor laws are embedded in and help constitute complex systems of industrial relations, which in turn are embedded in and help constitute different models, as it is commonly put, of capitalism. Thus we talk of the Japanese model, the American model, and the European model (although for the last we should more appropriately say the German model, the Dutch model, and so on). Even among the successful liberal democratic OECD capitalist nations, there is rich differentiation in labor market regulation.

In the domestic debate about labor policy, those concerned disagree along a number of dimensions. Some, including conservative economists and libertarians, see labor law as a set of unwanted rigidities blocking required labor market flexibility, generating allocative inefficiency (unemployment), fostering distributive perversity (unionized employees earn more at the expense of the unemployed), and interfering with individual liberty. Others see interventions in the labor market as required to secure the optimum mix of economic efficiency and fairness by adjusting for market defects (such as information asymmetries between workers and employers) and by seeking to secure justice along dimensions (income equality, democratic participation, respect for freedom of association) that markets are not designed to address. Domestic political disputes revolve around questions both normative—are labor markets coercive?—and empirical—are unionized employees more productive? Does a minimum wage cause unemployment?

These legitimate debates are complicated by the basic distributional struggle between labor and capital. Even if labor laws help create a larger pie, both sides in the bargaining process would like to have a larger slice. Even if unionized firms are more productive, there are still questions about whether they will turn out to be more profitable for shareholders. In the political struggle over domestic labor law, arguments of principle are often tainted by self-interested, rent-seeking behavior by those with a stake in the distributive outcome.

But we do not live in a world of isolated island jurisdictions concerned only with domestic labor law. Our world is characterized not only by free trade, but also by what is referred to as "deep economic integration," in which not only goods but ideas, knowledge, data, semiprocessed goods, services, and most critically capital are mobile, and in which revolutions in transportation and communication technology have made possible systems of global production and consumption.[8] In this world where most factors of production are increasingly mobile, labor for the most part is not, for reasons both de facto and de jure. This is the central if somewhat oversimplified dilemma of the labor rights agenda as a global issue: capital is mobile; labor is not. Economic theory predicts the mobile factors will always play immobile factors against one another.

The normative and empirical debates do not disappear at national boundaries. These disagreements remain lively at the global level, and the distributional struggle between capital and labor remains unsurprisingly in place as well. But new dimensions to these disagreements and the distributional conflict are introduced in the shift from a world of "island" jurisdictions to an integrated world economy. Those who see labor regulation as a set of rigidities imposed by rent-seeking pro-labor interests will celebrate the escape of capital from the fetters of domestic government and its ability to tax and regulate. They welcome the introduction of a competitive world market in labor regulation, among other things.[9] But those less sanguine about the market will see the new world economy as a threat to the idea of labor law itself, which is to establish the legitimate limits of market ordering in labor through democratic dialogue. The questions of where and to what extent to deploy the market mechanism cannot be answered conceptually by saying "Leave it to the market." These are not questions internal to markets but about markets. Rather than see a useful international market in labor market regulation, they will see a collective action problem in which states, through their efforts to attract investment and jobs, will undermine the politically and democratically achieved social consensus, in the end without reward because every other state will follow suit. At the international level is a parallel set of empirical questions, such as: Is investment attracted by "lower" labor standards? These developments simply represent the transfer of the empirical and normative national debate about the limits of markets to the international level.

Globalization will also bring into the lives of many citizens increased awareness of the undemocratic and repressive regimes that systematically deny basic human rights, including labor rights, to their citizens. Images of foreign child laborers, sweat-shop workers, and state brutalization of citizens become more common in developed nations as communication technology reveals the conditions under which globally produced goods were made. But individual liberal democratic states wishing to address human rights violations abroad will be confronted with collective action problems, as they will have an incentive to maintain the gains from trade and investment rather than attempt to discipline repressive regimes unilaterally.

Distributional issues also acquire new dimensions at the global level. In addition to the struggles between labor and capital, the legitimate demands of the developing world take center stage. The result is not simply two problems instead of one, but rather the creation of a complex interplay between the two distributional concerns. Simply put, the integration of the world economy—particularly via trade and investment liberalization—has provided developing countries with access to markets and capital that are the required preconditions to economic and social progress. From the point of view of global equity, it is essential that investment be directed to these nations. At the same time, it is in the self-interest of workers in the developed world to resist the exit of capital (and jobs). A principled response to this reality would be to attend to the demands of global equity and the theory of comparative advantage. This would involve taking the gains from trade, avoiding the losses of protectionism, and compensating those in losing sectors in developed nations. It would also involve rejecting ill-conceived arguments for "level playing fields" in labor costs. If labor costs are lower because of differing levels of development, productivity, and so on, then loss of jobs to the developing world is both the economic and moral point of global integration. But self-interest on the part of labor in the developed world will take the form of resisting trade and investment liberalization, and failing that, of conditioning liberalization on respect for a strong set of labor standards designed to remove even legitimate cost advantages in poorer nations. Thus, in the developed world, labor rights will increasingly become a smokescreen for protectionist interests.

Meanwhile, capital and developing countries will ally to resist efforts at global labor regulation, even those that would otherwise be viewed as congenial to labor in the developing world, because any degree of regulation may be perceived as a barrier to trade and investment flows. Thus global labor regulation is confronted by a cross-cutting interplay of distributional concerns, with developing world labor resisting labor regulation that it would otherwise find in its interest. In addition, undemocratic regimes will use the rhetoric of globalization and "comparative advantage" as a smokescreen for denial of fundamental labor rights.

Thus the five core issues that inform the whole debate about the global labor rights agenda can be described as follows:

- The domestic debate about principles and empirics will continue to be transferred to the international arena.
- An increased perception of labor rights as human rights will be driven in part by the insight that substantive differences in labor law force us to focus on processes rather than outcomes, and in part by an increased and accurate perception of

these labor rights as human rights. But even regarding issues about which there is little disagreement (such as violations of basic human rights as in exploitive child labor), liberal democratic regimes will still face collective action problems in addressing abuses unilaterally.

- Developed nations may be induced by capital to engage in either competitive or "beggar thy neighbor" (depending on one's view) regulatory arbitrage of otherwise optimal labor policies.
- Self-interested behavior by labor in the North will lead to attempts to limit integration or heavily condition trade and investment liberalization on inappropriate standards. At the same time, governments and workers in developing nations will have an incentive to oppose international labor regulation of any sort.
- These developments engender a sense of loss of democratic control that threatens the project of economic integration.

Finally, all of this is taking place in a world not only of economic globalization but of what Harry Arthurs has called "globalization of the mind."[10] This is the world view of the "market ascendant," of the Washington consensus, of the beneficial disciplining of domestic and social economic policies by international markets (for the lucky) and by international financial institutions (for the not so lucky). It is a worldview that is at worst hostile to, but always suspicious of, nonmarket values.

These five specific elements and the general ideological context of our time structure the global labor rights issue and must be kept in mind to understand the history and current state of efforts at global labor rights governance. Only an understanding that takes into account these elements can assess the record of establishing the global labor rights agenda, its negotiation, efforts at securing compliance, and techniques of dealing with noncompliance. As this account of the structure of the labor rights issue makes apparent, the record is bound to be partial, tentative, and contested—but always interesting.

TRACK RECORD OF INTERNATIONAL RESPONSES

The strategy pursued here is to focus on three levels of governance—global, regional, and subnational—and three specific sites of contest—the ILO, NAFTA, and codes of conduct (using as a prime example the U.S. Apparel Industry Partnership, or AIP)—to observe successes and failures in securing compliance with labor rights and norms.

Global Responses: The ILO

The ILO is a UN agency headquartered in Geneva, with regional offices around the world. Almost every nation is an ILO member. Formed in 1919, the ILO was the first specialized UN agency, and it had a dramatic birth. At the end of World War I, the negotiators of the Treaty of Versailles turned their attention to the inclusion of labor clauses in the peace treaty; from their deliberations emerged the idea of the ILO, which would be an autonomous body within the League of Nations structure. Its bold mandate took the long view that the attainment of lasting world peace required the pursuit of social justice.

The most striking feature of the ILO is its tripartite structure. In all its activities, it operates through institutions and processes constituted by representatives of three groups: governments, employers, and workers (with a ratio of 2:1:1). The International Labor Conference (the legislative branch) and the fifty-six-member Governing Body (the executive branch) are of tripartite composition, while in the International Labor Office (the administrative branch), professional administrators and experts, widely representative of the membership, oversee processes and undertake projects through tripartite mechanisms. The Director-General, currently Ambassador Juan Somavia of Chile, heads the International Labor Office and is the Secretary-General of the International Labor Conference. One of the ILO's best-known accomplishments has been the establishment of an international labor code in the form of conventions and recommendations adopted by the conference, which meets annually in Geneva and in which every member country is represented by two government delegates along with one employer and one worker delegate. Even after the conference adopts a convention, it is binding in only those countries that ratify it. Recommendations are simply that and are not binding. Yet membership in the ILO carries with it a commitment to certain core or human rights labor values, such as freedom of association; the ILO has a long-established special procedure for reviewing violations of freedom of association in all member countries, whether or not they have ratified the relevant conventions. In 1998 the conference adopted the Declaration on Fundamental Principles and Rights at Work, which expanded this idea of commitment through membership rather than through ratification of conventions beyond freedom of association to include child labor, forced labor, and nondiscrimination.[11]

One hundred eighty-two ILO conventions cover many aspects of labor relations and labor standards, including collective representation, the employment of children, health and safety issues in a broad variety of contexts, nondiscrimination, and equal pay. Some conventions are narrowly defined and occupationally specific (for example, a series of conventions about conditions of work at sea), whereas others are broad ranging and articulated at a level of general principles, such as the conventions dealing with freedom of association. The record for ratification of conventions is high for those related to the core values, but some nations, such as the United States and Canada, do not have a good record of ratifying of even the core conventions. The constitution of the ILO establishes procedures for both monitoring compliance with conventions and investigating complaints of noncompliance. It also has a long-established procedure for reviewing the performance of countries that have not ratified conventions.[12] It is important to note, however, that even regarding ratified conventions:

> The ILO is empowered, under Article 33, of its constitution, to take such action as may be considered wise and expedient to secure compliance by a state against which another member country has filed a complaint, with the terms of the Convention which both member countries have ratified. However, in practice, the ILO relies on technical assistance, peer pressure, and persuasion to encourage greater compliance. It does not impose sanctions, financial, commercial or other.[13]

Or, as former ILO Director-General Michel Hansenne recently put it, "It is essentially voluntary."[14]

The ILO is not merely a Geneva-based "law-making machine." The ILO, both from Geneva and through its regional offices, in partnership with individual member states or through programs such as the International Program for the Elimination of Child Labor, expends much of its institutional and budgetary resources on technical assistance and field program work.

Regional Responses: NAFTA/NAALC

In 1988, Canada and the United States negotiated a free trade agreement that came into force on January 1, 1989. The agreement contained no explicit labor rights provisions, even though debate on its potential labor rights, environmental, social, and cultural effects had dominated the 1988 Canadian federal election. When in 1991 trade ministers from Mexico, the United States, and Canada began negotiation for a wider NAFTA, the issue of the labor rights impact of such an agreement became relevant to U.S. interests as well. As a result, NAFTA was supplemented by two "side agreements" on labor and environmental issues. The labor side agreement is officially known as the North American Agreement on Labor Cooperation (NAALC).[15] The NAALC is significant because it created a formal link between the labor rights agenda and an economic treaty governing not just trade but also investment and other elements of regional economic integration. Yet the NAALC responds to the labor rights agenda in a limited though complex manner. Unlike the ILO, the NAALC does not seek to establish international labor rights norms through negotiation or other means. Rather, the basic strategy of the NAALC is to respect the sovereignty of each of the three member states and to commit those states to the enforcement of their own labor laws. The NAALC is also unlike the ILO in that it is an extremely lightweight administrative apparatus in terms of personnel and budgetary resources. A Commission for Labor Cooperation was established and headquartered in Dallas. Each member country maintains a National Administrative Office (NAO) in its own jurisdiction. In 1997, the annual budget for the Commission on Labor Cooperation was $1.9 million. By comparison, the budget of the ILO for 2000–2001 is $481 million.[16] But again unlike the ILO, the NAALC has the capability to impose some form of hard trade or other economic sanctions for violations of some labor rights: the use of child labor, not adhering to minimum wage laws, and failure to enforce occupational health and safety laws. Of more subtle significance is that allegations of violation of NAALC norms may be brought by private parties and laid before an NAO outside of the jurisdiction in which the violation is alleged to have occurred. Thus violations of NAALC labor principles by the Mexican government must be filed in Washington or Ottawa. This has led to an interesting and unintended secondary impact of the NAALC, discussed at length below.

National Responses: The Apparel Industry Partnership and SA 8000

The strategy of global or regional intergovernmental regulation stands in stark contrast to the complex variety of strategies pursued by nongovernmental actors—firms, unions, NGOs, social movement groups, industry bodies, or sectoral groups—in the unstructured space of the marketplace, both local and global. A good overview of the multiple strategies deployed by private sector actors, sometimes with the assistance of governmental and intergovernmental organizations, is contained in the recent ILO document entitled *Overview of Global Developments and Office Activities Concerning Codes of Conduct, Social Labeling, and Other Private Sector Initiatives Addressing Labor Issues.*[17] In this document, the ILO uses the term *private sector initiatives* and then subdivides them into three categories: codes of conduct, social labeling programs (labeling of products based on social criteria), and investor initiatives (such as "responsible investing"). The ILO notes that the wide variety of initiatives currently being pursued are further divisible into initiatives led by: enterprises or enterprise associations; workers' organizations; NGOs and coalitions; and professional consultants, auditors, and educational enterprises. The ILO also notes that many initiatives actually involve private-public partnerships. The strengths and weaknesses of these activities flow from the fact that they occur within "the unstructured space of the marketplace" and by appeal to market values and mechanisms. The disciplining forces here are not formal legal regulation and enforcement, but rather the law of supply and demand, most especially consumer demand. Of the many examples that could be selected, the AIP within the United States and the SA 8000 Initiative of the Council on Economic Priorities serve as the focus of concern here. These initiatives are what the ILO terms "hybrid" systems involving enterprises, workers' organizations, NGOs, and, in the case of the AIP, government support. The White House's AIP was initially composed of ten major apparel and footwear companies, two unions, and four civic groups or NGOs (most crucially the International Labor Rights Fund, based in Washington, D.C.). With the support of President Bill Clinton and the White House, in April 1997 the partnership produced a historic agreement establishing a workplace code of conduct addressing nine labor rights issues (child labor, forced labor, discrimination, harassment, freedom of association, wages, health and safety, hours of work, and overtime compensation). Each company participating in the partnership agreed to adhere to the code and to "as soon as reasonably practicable implement a monitoring program consistent with established principles of monitoring" that would involve independent external monitoring processes. In November 1998 an AIP working group reached agreement on a charter document for the creation of a new organization to be known as the Fair Labor Association (FLA), a nonprofit entity that oversees monitoring of compliance with the code. The association is structured to have equal representation from companies and labor/NGO members and to be chaired by someone accepted by both groups. The FLA accredits independent monitors to inspect factories of participating companies for code compliance. At the end of the negotiation process, the major U.S. labor union involved— the Union of Needle Trades, Industrial, and Textile Employees (UNITE)—withdrew its support from the FLA and did not endorse the charter document. The FLA has now appointed fifteen directors and officers and has begun the process of accreditation of monitors. To date, three monitoring agencies (all nonprofit) have been accredited with twenty-four more applications pending. Nine firms with approximately 3,500 factories in twenty countries have been approved for participation. As many as 300 other firms are in various stages of applying for approval. UNITE meanwhile continues its opposition to the FLA through a variety of strategies including supporting student groups urging universities not to participate in the FLA.

LESSONS LEARNED

In assessing the lessons learned, this section reviews three levels of governance— global, regional, and subnational—in the context of agenda setting, negotiation, implementation and monitoring compliance, and reactions to noncompliance.

Agenda Setting

At the global intergovernmental level of the ILO, one has to distinguish between two separate aspects of the agenda-setting process: first, agenda setting concerning the ILO itself (that is, its creation and its ongoing story of institutional and constitutional evolution); and second, agenda setting within established ILO procedures and practices relating to ILO law making and field program design and implementation.

If we turn to agenda setting concerning the institution itself, we can identify three defining moments in its history, beginning with the creation of the ILO in 1919, when many of the now central elements of the problem of global labor law were countervailed by the following important considerations. Although the world was highly globalized and integrated in the era before World War I, several crucial differences are noteworthy.[18] The organization's founding moment followed a period of economic and human catastrophe in Europe, making peace and its stable preconditions the preeminent political concern. The creation of the ILO was primarily a developed nation affair. The modern distributional tensions between developed and developing nations were largely obscured by the existing colonial framework. Moreover, the 1917 Russian Revolution provided the incentive required for Western governments and capital to adopt the ideas of nineteenth-century liberal reformers and support the formation of an international organization designed to protect labor interests.[19] Events in Russia cast a long shadow over the institutional history of the ILO, both within and without the organization, and have led many to voice concerns about the continued viability and relevance of the ILO in a post-communist world.

ILO's second great constitutional moment occurred at the end of the social and economic cataclysm of World War II. The basic preconditions for consensus remained in place, reinforced by the extraordinary chain of events since 1914 in which the global economy was destroyed and the world's nations engaged in the "beggar-thy-neighbor" trade, currency, and economic policies of the Great Depression.[20] Eric Hobsbawm labels the period the "age of catastrophe."[21] After World War II, there followed what economists of all stripes agree was a time of substantial rates of economic growth through a "golden era" (to use Hobsbawm's term) lasting until the mid-1970s, when growth rates in the developed world collapsed to about one-half of what they had been.

The third constitutional moment for the ILO came with the 1998 Declaration on Fundamental Principles and Rights at Work. The troubled story of the declaration's appearance on the ILO agenda captures almost perfectly the complex interplay of the previously cited five factors that structure the labor rights agenda. The large lesson is that when fundamental disagreements persist, only credible threats or serious incentives can prompt meaningful reform. In the interim, however, reformers can make progress by publicly exposing their opponents' failure to act in accordance with their rhetoric.

From the point of view of the ascendant pro-market forces (for whom globalization offered the ability of capital to escape regulation by states and the introduction of an international market in labor policy), the ILO in the 1990s was a problem, not a solution. So too the developing world saw ILO regulation as acceptable as long as compliance was entirely voluntary. The ILO's containing role as a bulwark against communism was now a thing of the past. Yet some interests—notably labor unions and some governments in the developed world—had protectionist reasons to seek to use the ILO to condition trade and investment flows by linking them to respect for ILO labor standards. Therefore there was simultaneously an urge to dispense with the ILO and an impulse to upgrade radically its enforcement policy from purely voluntary to that based on sanctions. The leadership of the United States in pursuit of the declaration was perceived by many—especially those in the developing world—as both perverse distributionally and hypocritical insofar as there exists a double standard between respect for labor standards at home and abroad. Meanwhile the increased perception in the developed nations of labor issues as human rights issues—child labor, for example—provided impetus to a renewed interest in the ILO and its processes, especially on the part of human rights NGOs.

In this vortex of players and interests, the agenda adopted by the ILO is quite understandable. First, the threat of labor standards being considered as appropriate subject matter at the Singapore WTO Ministerial Meeting of December 1996—and the subsequent derailing of the OECD negotiation toward a Multilateral Agreement on Investment (MAI) by NGOs raising labor and environmental issues—caused proponents of liberalization to reconsider the ILO as a still viable and safe repository for these issues.[22] Simultaneously, an evolving consensus that the labor rights agenda should be pared down to a core of fundamental labor/human rights gave new momentum to ILO reform. The consensus holds that the core consists of: (1) freedom of association and collective bargaining; (2) elimination of child labor; (3) elimination of forced labor; and (4) nondiscrimination in employment. Within the ILO, labor was concerned about marginalizing the rest of the ILO conventions, but anxious to harness whatever momentum in favor of ILO reform existed in the post-Singapore context. The lesson here is that the conceptual shift from a purely political and distributive framing to a human rights conception of the problem offered increased space for agenda setting and consensus.

Thus the idea of a declaration, floated in Director-General Hansenne's 1997 report, was pushed onto the agenda through 1997 and 1998.[23] Strongly supported by the United States and various developed country governments, Northern labor, and the human rights community, it nonetheless faced opposition from developing world governments, which fought the declaration to a bitter but losing end. But the developed world wisely assured that the declaration was "strictly promotional" and that no hint of conditionality or link to trade or the international financial institutions was permitted.

I turn now to agenda setting within the ILO and its tripartite structures. The International Labor Code of the ILO is constituted by nearly 200 ILO conventions and numerous recommendations associated with them. As indicated above, the ILO manifests itself in the world not just through the production of legal documents, but through its field activities such as the International Program for the Elimination of Child Labor, "active partnership programs" with individual states, and "technical assistance" through a variety of techniques and partnerships. The Governing Body—tripartite, with twenty-eight government members (ten of which are constitutionally guaranteed to be from the world's most significant economies), fourteen labor, and fourteen employer members—formally sets the agenda for the Annual International Labor Conference and controls the work of the office and the budgetary process. The agenda-setting lesson is, however, the profound significance of the personal influence of the Director-General, the professional influence of the International Labor Office, the lobbying efforts of the independent caucuses of worker and employer representatives, the power of informal groupings of governments such as Industrialized Market Economy Countries (or IMEC, the developed OECD nations essentially) and the Asian and Pacific Group, and most obviously the power of the large dues-paying and off-budget program financing countries, which come mostly from the IMEC group. Field programs are often driven by external funding commitments from member states and other institutions such as the World Bank. Agenda setting here is thus often in the hands of those willing to provide funding.

The history of the proliferation of ILO conventions, and the rising calls for less rigid and more general conventions focused on fundamental rights, has been well documented.[24] This process reached its culmination in the first annual report (1999) of Director-General Somavia, entitled *Decent Work*, which does not concentrate on standard setting at all.[25] Rather, it takes the existing standards, most critically the 1998 declaration, as a given and concentrates on internal institutional restructuring, budgetary reform in accordance with "management by objectives," and insistence on internal efficiency and reform organized around the four core objectives. It clearly reaffirms the declaration's commitment to voluntarism and to absolute nonlinkage of labor rights to trade or investment. The agenda established in *Decent Work* is the logical result of the post-Singapore, post-declaration ILO world. The lesson is that, as discussed below, forum switching can be used to advantage by those resisting reform or change.

When we move to the regional NAFTA/NAALC regime, we must again distinguish between agenda setting regarding the institution itself and agenda setting within the institutional framework so established.

It is common to begin discussions of the NAFTA side agreement on labor with an account of the Bush/Clinton campaign in 1992. For Canada, however, NAFTA and the debate over economic integration with the United States and its impact on labor and other social policies has a lengthy history, going back to the beginning of the Canadian Confederation in 1867. So too, Mexico's nationalist and sovereign instincts regarding domination by the United States are well known and have a long history. In Canada the most recent installment of this national debate was the hotly contested 1988 federal election in which the dominant issue was whether Canada ought to enter into a new free trade agreement with the United States. Prime Minister Brian Mulroney promoted the agreement and won the election, and a free trade agreement between Canada and the United States was entered into on January 1, 1989. That debate had been precisely about the *direct* impact of economic integration on the Canadian job market and the *indirect* impact on Canadian labor policy if capital were freer to move to the "low labor standards" jurisdictions of the United States.[26] Two of the major political parties in Canada were profoundly influenced by these arguments, as were a majority of the Canadian population (the Conservatives won because the larger opposing vote was split between two parties). Labor unions and NGO activists such as Maude Barlow of the Council of Canadians then joined the debate; for many Canadians it became almost instinctively the dominant issue of the day because economic integration was perceived as a direct threat to Canadian sovereignty. But in the United States the issue of the free trade agreement with Canada—the country's major trading partner by far—was not an issue in the 1988 election. Canadians were more than slightly bemused therefore when Americans, confronted by the possibility of a NAFTA involving Mexico, suddenly perceived the nature of the threat posed by the allegedly low labor standard jurisdiction to its south. Undoubtedly Ross Perot and his famous "giant sucking sound" helped invigorate the American national debate. And as Trubek and others put it,

> NAFTA became a divisive issue during the 1992 U.S. presidential election. President Bush enthusiastically supported the agreement. Ross Perot was firmly opposed. Fearful of losing the support of the American Federation of Labor–Congress of Industrial Organizations (AFL–CIO), a vocal opponent of NAFTA, then democratic presidential nominee Bill Clinton sought a compromise. He supported NAFTA because he thought it would expand markets for U.S. goods and grow the economy, and create high wage, high skill jobs. However, he agreed with opponents, that the pact's failure to address labor and environmental standards was a serious flaw. His solution was to support NAFTA but require the addition of side agreements on labor and the environment. This position was sufficient to maintain labor support, and with Clinton's election standards became a recognized trade issue in North America.[27]

The successful negotiation of the two side agreements allowed Clinton to win congressional approval of NAFTA in 1994.[28]

We have seen that the core obligation under the NAALC is for each of the three signatories to enforce effectively its own domestic labor law. Unlike the European Union, or the ILO, the NAALC specially repudiates the establishment of uniform labor standards for Canada, the United States, and Mexico, and instead dedicates itself to "recognizing the right of each party to establish its own domestic labor laws," and maintaining "due regard for the economic, social, cultural and legislative differences between them."[29] Nonetheless, the NAALC does commit the three nations to observance of their own labor laws and provides a minimalist institutional structure within which private parties can complain that a state is not living up to the obligations in its own domestic labor law. Thus, as Lance Compa puts it,

> While the countries have not yielded sovereignty with respect to the content of their laws or the authorities and procedures for enforcing them, they have transcended traditional notions of sovereignty by opening themselves to critical international and independent reviews, evaluations, and even arbitrations over their performance in enforcing their labor laws. In three key areas—minimum wage, child labor, and occupational safety and health—the countries created a prospect of fines or loss of NAFTA trade benefits for a persistent pattern of failure to effectively enforce domestic law.[30]

The key to the idea of NAALC review is that an allegation of a failure by Mexico, for example, to apply its own labor laws fairly must be made in Washington or Ottawa. The actual legal process is widely viewed as weak, but it is designed to be so. Although private parties may file a complaint with a NAO in a jurisdiction other than the one complained of, only the NAO may recommend ministerial consultations and only a government party to the NAALC can recommend further stages in the process. Thus even the legal process is highly political and as Compa states, "Lobbying skills and political pressure are needed for the private parties to push their complaints forward through the process."[31]

Faced with this situation, many labor unions and NGOs in North America have realized that the NAALC is not really about the negotiation of or compliance with international norms, nor about remedies for noncompliance with such norms. Nor is it directly about negotiations of domestic norms or sanctions for noncompliance. Rather, the procedures the NAALC sets out are most creatively used as a domestic agenda-setting device. The lesson here—the significance of unintended side effects of international agreements—is profoundly important. Labor rights activists and trade unions can use the NAALC as a vehicle for publicizing labor rights abuses, inadequate labor laws, and so forth. Given that complaints have to be lodged outside the jurisdiction complained of, the ability to seize the institution and use it for agenda setting and indirect domestic political purposes has provided a strong incentive for cross-border coordination between those interested in bringing labor issues to public attention. As Trubek and others put it:

> Since NAALC provides no sanctions for failure to honour [freedom of association] rights, all that process can do is cast a spotlight on questionable practices. . . . whatever its shortcomings NAALC can increase the visibility of various failures to enforce existing national labor laws and has been used as part of broader transnational campaigns as one tool in the armoury of transnational labor advocates in North America.[32]

As the International Labor Rights Fund notes: "NAALC is a good model for access to the process and transparency. There is ample opportunity for the involvement of trade unions and NGOs to use the NAALC both in filing complaints and in participating in public hearings and other events."[33] In short, in spite of and because of its inadequacies, the NAALC has become a means for labor rights activists to place labor rights issues on a high-profile agenda designed to secure the attention of governments at a ministerial level. But equally important is the less overt effect and lesson of NAALC. As the International Labor Rights Fund states,

> Other benefits stemming from NAALC relate to the unprecedented increase in exchange, communication and collaboration among trade unionists, labor rights advocates, and labor researchers at the tri-national level. Under the agreements procedures, complaints about violations in one country must be initiated in another country. Thus, unions and labor rights activists are compelled to collaborate across North American borders to use the NAALC. Labor solidarity is growing. . . . Workers in the three NAALC countries are co-operating . . . trade unionists and allied groups in the three NAALC countries now regularly send delegates to each other's conventions, conferences and other activities. . . . In some instances union organizers have crossed borders to assist in organizing campaigns in another country. While it is not only the labor side agreement driving these actions, the NAALC creates a framework for concrete work nourishing long-term gains in labor solidarity.[34]

Agenda setting at the global intergovernmental level of the ILO is difficult and highly structured. Agenda setting in the regional context is also difficult, although as we have seen concerning the NAALC, there may be unintended side effects that enable agenda setting by those interested in domestic labor rights. Undoubtedly, it is possible to overestimate the impact of this agenda-setting function. But it is at the subnational, marketplace level—dominated by nonstate actors including business interests—that the agenda is most available and unconstrained by requirements of consensus on a global or regional basis. The difficulty here with agenda setting in some sense is not the difficulty of setting an agenda, but the ease of doing so. Even a brief study of codes of conduct, social labeling, and other direct initiatives centered on private marketplace activity makes clear that in an age of communication revolutions ("CNNization") it is quite easy to bring an issue to the public agenda, but extremely difficult to negotiate norms and secure compliance with them. The issue here is whether any particular labor rights issue will simply have its fifteen minutes on the world stage and then be quickly forgotten.

The AIP offers particularly instructive lessons in this regard. In common with many private or hybrid arrangements involving codes or consumer product labels, public exposés of the questionable labor practices of firms have played an extraordinarily important role in pushing these issues onto the agenda and getting consumers involved. As the International Labor Rights Fund relates,

> In 1991 it was revealed that jeans maker, Levi-Strauss, was using a contractor in Northern Marianas where young women from China and Thailand were being shipped in to work in factories under near-bonded conditions and denied any access to labor law protection. Dismayed by the negative publicity, Levi-Strauss adopted a code of conduct both for this own operations and for those of its suppliers and contractors. This was the first known example of a voluntary company code of conduct.
>
> Shoemakers, Nike International and Reebok International were the subjects of series of reports starting in the early 1990s and continuing to the present day about labor rights abuses in their production facilities in China and South East Asia. Reebok responded by adopting the first code of conduct to contain language protecting workers' rights to associate freely and to bargain collectively. Wal-Mart was the subject of a television exposé that revealed that garments it retailed containing a "Made in U.S.A." label were actually produced by child labor in Bangladesh. The National Labor Committee found and publicized the fact that the "Kathy Lee" label owned by TV personality Kathy Lee Gifford, was being produced in factories in Honduras employing 13 year old girls.[35]

In this context U.S. Labor Secretary Robert Reich urged the apparel industry, the relevant unions, and interested NGOs to develop a strategy to address these public concerns. Out of this effort came the "No Sweat" campaign, which in turn led to the creation (with White House support) of the AIP. It is no accident that the partnership included Kathy Lee Gifford, Nike, Reebok, and Liz Claiborne among its important corporate members. Agenda creation in this context, however, has limitations. First, it seems that the issues generally require a high-profile and sensational aspect such as child labor or sweatshop conditions. Second, it is significant that the No Sweat campaign and the AIP got under way with the support of the domestic labor union UNITE, which represented workers in a generally low-skilled and thus threatened sector of the economy whose interests were clearly at stake. Third, the firms involved have high-profile labels or brand names that are their key asset. When these factors converge with dramatic media presentations of abuses, an agenda is created.

The most interesting question posed by initiatives such as the AIP is whether and in what circumstances will firms find it in their self-interest to respect labor rights not merely to avoid negative publicity, but rather to gain a competitive edge in a consumer market. The Council on Economic Priorities is pursuing this latter agenda through its SA 8000 program. SA stands for "social accountability" and represents an effort to provide standards that can be monitored by professional firms to declare individual factories or work sites socially accountable. Other multinational firms can then contract with them with the assurance that they have been declared acceptable. The model here is the International Standards Organization (ISO) series of codes for quality standards. The logic is compelling, if the reality is somewhat distant. With the ISO standards, firms in a globally integrated world find it in their self-interest to advertise recognized approval of their quality control and territorial management systems so that other firms can safely contract with them. The difficulty for SA 8000 is the creation of circumstances in which respect for labor rights is viewed as an unqualified good in the way in which quality control processes are. Nonetheless, it is necessary that projects such as SA 8000 are operational when and if sufficient demand manifests itself, and that they work to stimulate that demand.

One of the most compelling lessons we have for agenda setting at the subnational level is the starkness of the contrast between the ease with which these sorts of labeling programs move onto the public agenda in the marketplace as compared to the difficulty of moving them onto the agenda of the ILO. In the ILO, developing country governments immediately rejected proposals for social labeling contained in the 1997 report of Director-General Hansenne.[36] Any effort to attach the labor rights agenda to any mechanism, no matter how market friendly (such as the market itself), was rejected. The distributional concerns of the developing world overwhelmed any other basis for action, no matter how principled in moral or economic terms.

Negotiation

Concerning negotiation of standards, the familiar distinction is between negotiation internal to the organization and negotiation about the organization itself. Within the ILO, the formal constitution dedicates the organization to the process of what is called "standard setting," meaning law creation via conventions primarily and recommendations secondarily. As a law-making institution, the ILO is an extremely formidable machine with highly developed rules, practices, and traditions. Some general lessons seem clear, however.

First, negotiation is easy when standards are sanctionless. There is no doubt that the scope of the International Labor Code, in terms of both the number of conventions and their level of detail, would not have been possible if the standards were hard. Second, the negotiation of standards within the ILO is a lengthy process involving many formal steps, but also taking place in the context of intense negotiation and lobbying outside the formal structures. The Governing Body sets the agenda for the conference. Once subject matters are decided, negotiation of standards takes place in the context of very broad technical and research support provided by the office, and negotiations carried on by the workers, the employers, and various government groupings. Formally, the conference discusses a proposed convention in a preliminary form one year and in a final form the next. This provides an opportunity for protracted consultations by the office with the tripartite interests. At the conference separate committees are established, with membership generally open to all to draft proposed conventions and recommendations. The work of these committees is often lengthy and sometimes difficult. The Legal Adviser (the ILO's chief lawyer) and his or her representatives are often asked to give interpretations of certain drafting questions or options. Because of the wide range of both formal and informal negotiations, it is extremely rare for negotiations on a convention to fail. The process of negotiation is a highly managed one in which consensus is generally secured.

Negotiations on the basic constitutional structure and fate of the organization itself reveal very important lessons, and not only about the ILO, but about other institutions as well. This was certainly true of the debates and negotiations concerning the 1998 declaration. The results of the WTO Ministerial Meeting in Singapore in December 1996 left the ILO with a large challenge. On the one hand, the WTO Singapore Declaration included reaffirmation of the importance of core labor rights and of the centrality of the ILO in advancing the core labor rights agenda.[37] On the other hand, the subtext of the declaration was obvious: the rejection of labor standards, core or otherwise, as a fit subject matter of WTO debate, and the dismissal of the ILO as marginal to the efforts of the WTO to set the ground rules for production and trade in the global economy. The WTO mandate ranges across a number of issues that go well beyond the traditional trade agenda (in other words, trade in goods) and is legitimately considered to include competition policy, intellectual property, the environment, and investment—but not labor. But the lesson of Singapore seems clear: the labor rights issue is dominating and controversial, a fact to which the Seattle WTO Ministerial Meeting in December 1999 seemed to have resigned itself.

The referral of these issues back to the ILO could be as both a reaffirmation of the ILO mandate and an attempt to undermine it. Our contradictory sets of values and interests conspire to produce precisely such a contradictory answer when the issue of labor rights is addressed as a separate agenda item.

The options facing the ILO after Singapore were not altogether attractive. One obvious option was to accept the official WTO text at face value and carry on as before, but with awareness of the risk of compromise this involved—the continued marginalization of labor issues. Another option was to use the results of Singapore as an impetus for change.

The strategy actually adopted was to take the official WTO text at face value, put the best possible spin on it, publicly ignore the subtext, and use the official position to as much advantage as possible to promote internal institutional renewal. In effect, this option amounted to calling the bluff of those speaking so favorably of the ILO in Singapore.

The concrete manifestation of this strategy—to make the most out of a difficult situation—was revealed by the Director-General's 1997 report to the June Conference entitled *The ILO, Standard Setting, and Globalization*.[38] Two of the proposals for institutional renewal are of interest here: (1) the idea of a declaration on funda-mental rights; and (2) the idea of social labeling. Although these ideas share much in common, as already noted, only the declaration proposal garnered support. The so-cial labeling idea was rejected immediately.[39]

The idea of a declaration is both evocative and amorphous in the ILO context. The ILO Constitution does not mention declarations—nor for that matter does the constitution of any other international organization.[40] Yet declarations are a familiar part of the institutional vocabulary of many international organizations, the Univer-sal Declaration of Human Rights being the most obvious example. And within the ILO context the idea of a declaration has particular historical resonance. The ILO's second great constitutional moment, described above, occurred when the ILO adopted the Declaration of Philadelphia in 1944 (subsequently enshrined in the constitution through constitutional amendment in 1946). That declaration involved a sweeping rearticulation of institutional purposes and constitutional values and is now viewed as one of the important milestones in ILO history.

Yet the ILO is clearly empowered to act, and it has acted in a more direct manner through the creation of conventions that, once ratified, are binding international trea-ties with attached monitoring and complaint processes (although no hard sanctions). The ILO is also expressly empowered to adopt nonbinding recommendations aimed at guiding policies within member states. What then is the point of a declaration of gen-eral principle concerning core labor rights? Is there not a risk of detracting from the seven concrete conventions dealing with the four core rights? This was an obvious concern to worker representatives at the ILO—that a declaration of principle would be a vehicle for weakening concrete and detailed obligations contained in the relevant conventions. From the perspective of governments and employers, however, conven-tions concerning the core rights often remained unratified because of states' difficulty in reconciling domestic legislation with the specific demands of the conventions.[41]

Yet another historical precedent within the ILO cast a long shadow over the pro-posal for a declaration: the precedent of the "freedom of association machinery." In 1951 the ILO established the Committee on Freedom of Association (CFA), techni-cally a tripartite committee of the Governing Body of the ILO.[42] The constitutional idea sustaining the CFA is of profound importance: that all member states of the ILO, simply by virtue of membership, are constitutionally committed to the promo-tion, recognition, and respect of the principle of freedom of association. The consti-tutional language supporting this assertion is contained in Article 1 of the ILO Con-stitution:

A permanent organization is hereby established for the promotion of the objects set forth in the Preamble to this Constitution and in the Declaration concerning the aims and purposes of the International Labor Organization adopted at Phila-delphia on 10 May 1944 the text of which is annexed to this Constitution.

The key word here is "promotion." The often cited constitutional basis for the CFA's mandate is that it is simply a mechanism established by the Governing Body for the promotion of one of the values articulated in the preamble to the constitution—"recognition of the principle of freedom of association."[43]

The CFA and its processes were originally conceived as a promotional mechanism. Nonetheless, it is commonly observed that the 1951 Special Procedure on Freedom of Association has increasingly moved away from a promotional mandate to a more legalistic, complaint-driven, heavily used mechanism.[44] This has resulted in a complex and detailed jurisprudence, although not technically based on the details of the relevant conventions, which is large and now distributed in an ILO monograph of approximately 200 pages.

Thus the CFA precedent offers the appealing prospect for workers of a "hard process" applying to all states regardless of whether the relevant conventions have been ratified. But it demonstrates to others the difficulty of preventing mechanisms designed for the promotion of fundamental values from becoming another layer of detailed institutional complication aimed at enforcement.

In this complex and sometimes contradictory interplay of interests—principle versus detailed commitment, constitutional versus normal legislative grounding of obligations, and promotion versus enforcement—lies the possibility of political compromise, coalition building, and the finding of common ground through negotiation, especially when the credibility of the ILO is an important value, albeit for different reasons for all concerned.

Within the ILO the familiar tripartite groups are employers, workers, and governments. On the issue of the declaration, however, distinctions within groups, and coalitions across groups, are defined by other dimensions—most often developed versus developing nations. In general, workers' representatives at the ILO were in favor of the idea of a declaration if appropriately worded and equipped with a powerful follow-up mechanism. Employers generally supported the idea of a declaration conceived of as a promotional statement of principle—rather than insistence upon conventional detail—and as long as it was sanctionless. Governments in Europe and North America backed the declaration as a vehicle for institutional renewal and focus. Those absolutely opposed to the declaration turned out to be a group of nations led vocally by the Government of Egypt and including representatives from the Persian Gulf, Asia, and Latin America. Among the dissenters were splits among the positions of government, employer, and worker members, although on occasion these nations did present a united front of the three interests. The negotiation of the declaration was long, acrimonious, and fraught with procedural trickery. But the central lesson is revealed by focusing on items in dispute.

The ILO Declaration on Fundamental Principles and Rights at Work contains the following language in its paragraph 5:

Stresses of labor standards should not be used for protectionist trade purposes and that nothing in this Declaration and its follow-up shall be invoked or otherwise used for such purposes; in addition, the comparative advantage of any country should in no way be called in question by this Declaration and its follow-up.

These words tell a great deal about the political realities in which the ILO operates and about its ability to articulate an uncontested role for itself in the new world economy. This sentence was included, in the operative part of the declaration, after a long, bitter debate. The workers opposed any such language. The employers, not wishing to establish a link between trade and labor standards, thought that at most this idea deserved some mention in the preamble. Developed countries were cool if not hostile to the idea. But many developing world governments vigorously supported the inclusion of such language.

The language in paragraph 5 of the ILO Declaration is drawn from, and meant to be parallel with, language contained in the WTO Singapore Ministerial Declaration. In that declaration, paragraph 4 states: "We reject the use of labor standards for protectionist purposes, and agree that the comparative advantage of countries, particularly low-wage developing countries, must in no way be put into question."[45]

Remarkably, the WTO in its Singapore Declaration actually articulated an institutional competence regarding labor issues—in the face of a simultaneous denial of such competence—and thereby staked a claim on one side of the debate over the very link it was anxious to deny. One may perhaps partially excuse the WTO for its declaration, using the following line of reasoning. The mandate of the WTO is to foster and expand the rules-based, liberal trading regime. Some vested interests in developed states may well use the international labor standards issue to protect themselves from international trade competition through veiled protectionism. It is therefore within the WTO's mandate and certainly in its interest to issue a declaration warning against, and making an institutional commitment to avoiding, such protectionist practices. We might say that the WTO, perhaps in a way it is nonetheless anxious to deny, is merely trying to protect it own turf, its own values, and its own mandate.

The WTO Singapore Ministerial Declaration addresses one half of a dilemma with which the new economy and its attending politics confront us: arguments about labor standards are sometimes used for illegitimate protectionist purposes. But the ILO Declaration on Fundamental Principles and Rights at Work fails to address the other half of the problem: allegations of protectionism and differences of comparative advantage are sometimes used as a justification for the violation of core labor rights and as a bar to sensible collective action concerning these violations. This is what the ILO had to set right. Instead, it was politically, diplomatically, substantively, and procedurally unable to deliver this fundamental rejoinder. Why? What is the lesson? At the conceptual level, the lesson is that the ILO, at the insistence of the developing world, succumbed to the logic of what might be called simple impact analysis. We live in a world in which it is rational for some developing countries to take the view that anything that has a negative impact on their ability to trade or attract investment is protectionism, which illegitimately undermines their comparative advantage. But impact alone is never enough. In a competitive economy, whether domestic or global, participants are meant to be disciplined by the action of others in the marketplace. That indeed is the whole point. Thus the real question is always whether the impact is legitimate or illegitimate. This involves deciding on substantive questions of right and wrong. The ILO Declaration *seems* to make just such a dramatic normative decision regarding the four core rights. But ultimately, the ILO failed to be as robust as the WTO and provide the other half of the required equation. When negotiations are structured by the complex interplay of interests that inform the global labor rights agenda, the unreconstructed distributional concerns of the developed world remained an obstacle because of the ILO's inability to offer compensating initiatives.

As we have seen, there are no processes in NAFTA, such as in the ILO, for ongoing negotiation or elaboration of labor standards. Rather the NAFTA processes have created incentives for cross-border organizing and agenda setting about domestic labor concerns. Hearings held in response to complaints provide a platform for publicly airing inadequacies in domestic labor law. In the cases that have successfully moved forward to the stage of ministerial consultations, the result has been research studies and consultations. But very little in the way of overt negotiation or renegotiation of domestic standards has occurred, although the treaty may be having a more subtle impact. For example, it is commonly believed in Canada that NAFTA influenced the Alberta provincial government when it threatened to pass legislation privatizing certain aspects of employment law enforcement. It is thought that the threat of a NAFTA complaint caused the government to retreat from this change in labor legislation. Thus the impact of NAFTA may be not to initiate negotiations but rather to forestall derogation from existing legislation.

Finally, it must be noted that the processes under the NAALC can be used by anti-union as well as pro-union or labor rights activists. For example, the *Wall Street Journal* recently printed a story entitled "Anti-Union Group Files NAFTA Suit: Complaint Against U.S. Filed with Canada Pushes for Employers' Rights."[46] Thus the NAALC processes are being used for agenda-setting/publicity purposes—confirmed by the fact that the group filing the complaint gave the newspaper interview before the complaint had been received by the Canadian NAO. The anti-union group sought to raise the profile of an issue (non-union forms of employee representation) for the domestic labor law agenda in the United States, not to use the NAALC as a negotiating forum.

The fate of the negotiations carried on by the AIP confirms the complex nature of the labor rights governance issue. In April 1997 the partnership announced its workplace code of conduct covering the issues of forced labor, child labor, harassment or abuse, nondiscrimination, health and safety, freedom of association and collective bargaining, wages and benefits, hours of work, and overtime compensation. The negotiations also enabled the partnership to announce certain "principles of monitoring," most critically the use of independent external monitors. The April 1997 announcement also committed the partnership to the formation of an association "over the next six months" to recruit new members to the partnership and develop a monitoring strategy. In fact it took until November 1998 for the partnership to develop a "charter document" for the formation of the FLA, the purposes of which are: (1) to accredit independent external monitors to conduct monitoring and inspection; (2) to certify whether the applicable brands of each participating company are produced in compliance with FLA standards; (3) to continue to address questions critical to the elimination of sweatshop practices; and (4) to serve as a source of information to consumers about the workplace code, the monitoring principles, and participating companies.

The charter for the FLA outlines an institutional structure, participation criteria for companies, accreditation criteria for external monitors, a monitoring process, and an outline of a complaint procedure that would allow third parties to file complaints about noncompliance with the code or the monitoring with respect to any participating company. But the core purpose of the FLA's processes will be to certify publicly compliance with the code by participating companies—that is, to act as a "seal of approval" for the brands.

The most remarkable part of the negotiations for the new FLA and its code and monitoring processes is that at the last moment the major American textile union, UNITE, refused to sign on. While offering many reasons, "the union's biggest criticism is the accord's failure to require that companies pay a living wage."[47] This was so even though other members of the partnership agreed upon a U.S. Department of Labor study on the minimum and prevailing wages in relevant countries and how those wages compare with the amount needed to meet workers' basic needs. The withdrawal of the union from the agreement on the FLA has not dissuaded the other firms and various NGOs involved from proceeding, but its withdrawal from negotiations draws attention to the centrality of the distributional problem between the developed and developing world in any effort to secure global governance of labor rights. From the union's point of view, negotiating an agreement would in effect put a "seal of approval" on the export of its members' jobs. From the point of view of global equity and the theory of comparative advantage, this is the point of economic integration, but any negotiation that requires the consent of the losing party is bound to fail unless it is accompanied by some compensation. Thus private sector, single-issue initiatives must find it almost impossible to deliver. Even though the accord is viewed by the human rights and labor rights activists in the partnership as a way of advancing global rights, it legitimizes the further weakening of an already declining unionized sector in the United States. At the ILO the demands of the developing world almost derailed negotiations, whereas here the distributional concerns of labor in the developed world were the problem.

Implementation and Monitoring Compliance

The ILO has been remarkably successful in generating a large corpus of substantive labor law, often referred to informally as the "international labor code," consisting of 182 conventions and numerous associated recommendations. The absence of sanctions has made negotiation easy—perhaps too easy. The ILO is voluntary in two senses: First, even when conventions are adopted by the annual conference, ratification of each convention is left to individual member states. The only obligation to members is to put the convention before appropriate domestic authorities for consideration. Second, even for those members that have ratified conventions, there is no hard sanction for violation. But monitoring and supervision is the ILO's strength, and it has often been celebrated for this accomplishment.[48] The supervisory system is mandated by Article 22 of the ILO Convention. A useful summary was recently provided by the OECD:

> The first stage of the procedure is the provision of a report by governments which have ratified a particular Convention. Countries submit these reports every two or five years, depending on the Convention; they can sometimes be requested to submit reports more frequently. Copies of these reports are sent to the most representative employers and workers' organizations in the country under examination. The organizations are invited to comment on the report, and, if necessary, to contradict it or provide additional information concerning the application of the Convention in question.
>
> The report, together with any comments from employers and workers' organizations is then submitted by the Secretariat of the ILO to the independent Committee of Experts on the Application of Conventions and Recommendations, which meets annually. This committee comprises 20 independent legal experts, appointed by the governing body of the ILO, acting upon proposals with the Director-General. The Committee examines compliance. It can ask for additional information and, if necessary, call for changes in law and practice in order to secure compliance with the Convention.
>
> The Committee of experts, in turn, submits a report to the Tripartite Conference Committee on the Application of Conventions and Recommendations. This report, produced annually, contains a general overview of the main trends and problems, a review of the implementation of obligations by particular countries and the summary of national law and practices based upon reports submitted by

member states. In light of the report, the Tripartite Conference Committee may invite governments to appear for the discussion period in particular. It may ask governments to explain intended measures to fulfil their obligations. A final report is then discussed at the plenary session of the International Labor Conference.[49]

Much less well understood outside the ILO is the ILO's constitutional capacity to monitor and supervise the behavior of member states regarding unratified conventions. In 1946 the constitution of the ILO was amended in a number of ways, including the addition of words to Article 19 of the ILO Convention, which now reads:

> If the member does not obtain the consent of the authority or authorities with whose competence matter lies [regarding ratification] no further obligation shall rest upon the member except that it shall report to the Director-General of the International Labor Office, at appropriate intervals as requested by the governing body, the position of its law practice in regards to the matters dealt with in Convention, showing the extent to which affect has been given or is proposed to be given, to any of the provisions of the Convention by legislation, administrative action, collective agreement or otherwise and stating the difficulties which prevent or delay the ratification of such Convention.[50]

The important point is that although Article 19 states that all members are bound to place conventions adopted by the conference before the appropriate national authority for ratification, there is no obligation to ratify or even to urge or recommend ratification, which is purely voluntary. The addition of the wording to Article 19(5)(e) in 1946 created a flexible mechanism whereby pressure can be maintained upon, and assistance offered to, those states who continue not to ratify any particular convention.

As a result, two explicit reporting/monitoring mechanisms are contained in the ILO Constitution—one for ratified conventions (Article 22) and one for unratified conventions (Article 19). It seems clear that the reports on unratified conventions have been subordinate to the reports on ratified conventions in terms of institutional resources allocated to this exercise. This is because the constitution does not establish a procedure—such as the Committee of Experts under Article 22—to use in connection with Article 19 reporting on unratified conventions. The constitution does specify that Article 19 reports are to be distributed to relevant employer and worker groups in the member state concerned, but nothing else is provided. In fact, Article 19 reports have gone to the Committee of Experts by default, and this committee has not made extensive use of them. The Governing Body tends to request Article 19 reports on one or more conventions, generally dealing with one topic. These are used by the Committee of Experts in a limited way, though a practice has evolved of issuing general surveys on a particular subject. In 1997, for example, the general survey was on one of the conventions dealing with labor administration. In compiling the general surveys each year, the Committee of Experts uses both Article 22 and 19 reports. But the Committee of Experts makes no further use of Article 19 reports. Its Annual Report to the Conference contains detailed country-by-country analysis of the Article 22 reports, but not of the Article 19 reports. In 1995, the Director-General took an initiative to reinvigorate Article 19 and its reporting mechanism. As a result, the Governing Body adopted a schedule for Article 19 reports (every four years) concerning the seven labor conventions dealing with the four core labor rights: forced labor, child labor, nondiscrimination, and freedom of association and collective bargaining. Under this 1995 initiative, it was apparently contemplated that the Committee of Experts would continue in more or less its existing fashion to issue a general survey or special report on these core conventions once every four years.

This idea of members' obligations regarding nonratified conventions, through Article 19, has been recently seized upon as a prime follow-up mechanism to be used under the 1998 declaration. One of the questions concerning the construction of any mechanism within the confines of Article 19 is certainly that of the effectiveness of that reporting process. A review of the reports of the Committee of Experts over the years shows that there are obvious problems with member states meeting their reporting obligations under Article 19. Nicolas Valticos and Geraldo Von Potobsky's survey of reporting levels under Article 19 over a ten-year period reveal: 1987 (65.4 percent of the requested reports received); 1988 (72.7 percent); 1989 (67.4 percent); 1990 (57.9 percent); 1991 (59.6 percent); 1992 (66.6 percent); 1993 (58.2 percent); 1994 (52.8 percent); 1995 (65.7 percent); and 1996 (54.7 percent).[51]

Also not well understood by those outside the ILO are general constitutional obligations flowing from membership in the organization itself and not from the ratification or nonratification of any particular convention. By far the most significant of these is the constitutional value of freedom of association and the ILO Special Procedure on Freedom of Association established in 1951. That special procedure is more fully described below under enforcement, because it has in effect evolved into a complaint procedure, but the idea inherent in this special procedure—that obligations can flow from membership in the organization itself—is the central idea of the 1998 Declaration on Fundamental Principles and Rights at Work. In that declaration the ILO extends the idea of inherent constitutional obligation contained in the Special Procedure on Freedom of Association to the three other core labor rights (child labor, forced labor, and nondiscrimination), but it does so by explicitly avoiding a complaint-style process associated with that special procedure. The logic of the declaration is to take the idea of inherent constitutional obligation but then wed it to the existing monitoring and supervisory system contained in Articles 22 and 19. The idea is to use their existing systems to create a "promotional" supervisory process for the inherent constitutional norms, rather than some other complaint-driven, sanction-based (even if soft) technique. As we have seen, this was the maximum response possible within the ILO following the WTO 1996 Ministerial Meeting, and even then it was hotly contested. The mechanism contemplated by the 1998 declaration and subsequently clarified, by actions of the Governing Body and its relevant committees, consists of two parts. First is an annual follow-up concerning nonratified conventions relevant to the four fundamental rights. In effect, this simply adopts the 1995 initiative to use Article 19 to promote attention to the conventions relevant to the four core rights. The mechanism under the declaration also contemplates the appointment of a new group of experts by the Governing Body: "With a view to presenting an introduction to the reports thus compiled, drawing attention to any aspects which might call for more in depth discussion, the Office may call upon a group of experts appointed for this purpose by the governing body."[52] In addition, and perhaps more dramatically, the ILO Declaration's reporting and monitoring mechanism calls for a Global Report each year, dealing with one of the four core rights in turn. This report will be drawn up by the Director-General on the basis of the annual reports under Article 19 and reporting under Article 22 regarding ratified conventions. The use of the report is described as follows:

> This report will be submitted to the Conference for tripartite discussion as a report of the Director-General. The Conference may deal with this report separately . . . and may discuss it during a sitting devoted entirely to this report, or in any other appropriate way. It will then be for the governing body, at an early session to draw conclusions from the discussion concerning the priorities and plans of action for technical cooperation to be implemented for the following 4-year period.[53]

As has been emphasized, this provision makes clear that the declaration and its monitoring mechanism are to be promotional and tied to the program of work of the organization in terms of technical assistance to member states, with a view to improving respect for the core rights. The form of the declaration thus fits neatly with the strategy described in the 1999 Director-General's report, *Decent Work*, which is to focus the organization on streamlining its program delivery according to certain priorities, the first of which is the declaration and its follow-up.

In sum, the ILO did not use any "conditionality" or sanction-based initiatives during the 1990s because it failed to overcome any of the collective action problems and distributional divides that obstructed agreement. Rather, it focused on promotional activities supplemented by financed program delivery in member states.

In North America the NAALC contains no elaborate provisions for ongoing monitoring of obligations. The NAALC did create a secretariat charged to "periodically prepare background reports setting out publicly available information supplied by each party" on matters such as labor law, trends in administrative strategies, labor market conditions, and human resources issues as well as on any other topic the council ministers may request.[54] The first such report, entitled *North American Labor Markets: A Comparative Profile*, was published by the secretariat in 1997. Other studies, such as a study on plant closing law in the three jurisdictions, have flowed from ministerial consultations resulting from complaints filed by private parties under the NAALC. The core point remains, however, that under the NAALC respect for the sovereignty of the three signatories remains paramount, no international norms are established, no ongoing monitoring of compliance with domestic norms is provided, and the complaint mechanism is lengthy, complex, and beyond the initial stage controlled by the governments involved.

At the subnational level, monitoring compliance with negotiated norms among nonstate actors is profoundly difficult. The beauty of subnational strategies is that they avoid the complex of principled, distributional, and collective action problems afflicting multilateral efforts at international governance of the labor rights regime. But with these advantages come significant challenges. Although agreement on sanctions is difficult at the ILO, no one doubts the ILO's credibility, democratic legitimacy, expertise, competence, and budgetary ability to monitor compliance. At the subnational level, the opposite is true. Real sanctions and rewards—in the form of reduced or increased consumer demand for various brands—are at hand. The difficulty lies in obtaining a legitimate and competent system of monitoring compliance with negotiated norms. These impediments accompanying other well-known difficulties with private sector initiatives: they often tend to be limited in scope (to the export sector and to certain high-profile, media-sensitive issues such a child labor) and pertain to goods purchased directly by consumers in developed countries.

The fundamental problems of monitoring in the private sector are twofold: (1) the difficulty in knowing whether certain norms are being adhered to given global production chains involving many contractors and producers throughout the world; and (2) the incentive to cheat. Both of these problems raise further issues of competence and expertise as well as independence of the monitoring agency. The International Labor Rights Fund highlighted these problems as follows:

> An example of such an exercise in "bad faith" was the advertising campaign launched by GUESS? Inc. in December 1997. In previous years, GUESS? had been the target of consumer campaigns to publicize the company's labor abuses. In December, the company took out a full-page ad in the *New York Times,* and other regional newspapers advertising its jeans as "sweat free" and stating that the company had been given a clean bill of health by the Department of Labor. In fact, the Department of Labor had cited GUESS?'s suppliers in the United States for labor violations earlier in the year, and insisted that the company remove the claim from

its advertisements. The GUESS? strategy illustrates the problems consumers might face if their only source of information were companies themselves. . . .

When Nike hired Ernst & Young, it argued that the accounting firm was capable of handling the task because of their familiarity with wage slips and other financial documents. Such an argument ignores the fact that many, if not most, labor rights violations occur off paper. In Nike's suppliers in China and Indonesia, for example, the practice of mandating overtime until set quotas are fulfilled has been uncovered. Workers are expected to fulfill their quotas within an eight-hour period. If by the end of that workday that quota is not yet met workers are expected to stay until they have completed their work. This overtime never appears on the timesheets, nor is it compensated on wage slips. Mere examination of documents would be insufficient to uncover such a practice let alone such abuses as corporal punishment for workers who make mistakes, another abuse documented by NGOs among workers in export facilities. Such practices can only be reliably uncovered through extensive, confidential worker interviews. Confidential interviews are also the only way to discover examples of anti-union practices.[55]

Most discussions of private sector code monitoring involved discussions of both internal and external monitoring.[56] The AIP's charter document for the FLA has extensive provisions relating to both external and internal monitoring programs; participating companies are under an obligation to submit a monitoring plan. All external monitors must be independent and approved by the FLA. The charter document establishes six sets of requirements of those seeking to qualify as external monitors to ensure independence, expertise, and ability. The charter document also provides for reimbursement to participating companies for the cost of external monitoring during an initial implementation period (thereafter companies are responsible for full cost of the external monitoring). The point of this elaborate procedure is to produce a report to consumers assuring that the brand-name products of the participating companies have been certified by the association to be produced in compliance with FLA standards. The charter document forbids individual companies from making any public claims about their brands unless the association has issued a certification. After the initial compliance period, the association will advise on an annual basis whether the brands of a participating company should continue to be certified. The association also recommends the level of ongoing monitoring required by each participating company.

Reactions to Noncompliance

Although the ILO is generally and accurately characterized as a voluntary organization, this description must be used carefully. It is true that the ILO does not use hard sanctions. Its ultimate sanction is publicity, applied by the International Labor Conference Committee Proceedings, and its ability to name publicly repeat offenders. The ultimate sanction is therefore one of shame.[57] It is also true that ratification of conventions is strictly voluntary. As we have seen, however, member states do have obligations regarding unratified conventions under Article 19 as well as constitutional obligations under the Special Procedure on Freedom of Association and under the 1998 declaration regarding the four core labor rights. However, procedures under the ILO Declaration are strictly promotional. Nonetheless, in addition to the monitoring processes, two sorts of complaint procedures are contemplated by the constitution of the ILO. First, *representations* are complaints from employers or workers alleging noncompliance with a ratified convention. A special tripartite committee established by the Governing Body hears these cases. The representation, and government reply, may be published. If a serious problem is perceived, it will be drawn to the attention of the Committee of Experts. This process is little used, and only eighty-nine representations have made over the entire history of the ILO.[58] Second, *complaints* by a government against another government, where both have ratified the convention allegedly violated, can be examined by an Independent Commission of Inquiry set up by the Governing Body. The complaining government may accept its recommendations or may decide to take the complaint to the International Court of Justice. Since 1919, the complaint procedure has been initiated only twenty-three times.

Of far greater significance is the ILO's Special Procedure on Freedom of Association, mentioned above. Although established only in 1951, this procedure has been invoked in almost 2,000 cases involving almost 150 countries. This special procedure operates in the following manner. The Committee on Freedom of Association is a tripartite body comprising nine members of the Governing Body and chaired by an independent legal expert. It is unlike the Committee of Experts, which deals with the monitoring processes under Articles 19 and 22. The Committee of Experts is a committee composed of independent legal experts. The CFA, unlike the Committee of Experts, is a much less legalistic body. Its original purpose was not to render legal judgments about compliance with the letter of the law, but rather to offer advice about attaining the spirit of the constitutional value of freedom of association. The CFA and the special procedure were originally viewed as a promotional mechanism to enhance respect for the core constitutional value of freedom of association. However, as the numbers of complaints have grown and the jurisprudence of the committee arising out of its comments upon the cases brought before it has grown, it has become very much a complaint-driven and soft sanction process. A government found in violation of the principle is advised of that fact and of any recommendations made by the CFA. The CFA has, over the years, and in light of the hundreds of cases brought before it, developed a considerable and elaborate (if elusive) jurisprudence. This body of law is frequently summarized in the form of a digest, the most recent of which was published in 1996 and runs to over 200 pages.[59]

As we have seen, the central issue in the history of the ILO over the last decade has been whether to move from this system of promotion, voluntariness, and soft sanctions. The resounding answer has been "no," because the global multilateral ILO has been unable to overcome the distributional divide between developed and developing nations. This outcome is helped, if not guaranteed, by the accurate perception of strictly protectionist motives behind some of those advocating a change in fundamental ILO strategy.

The NAALC contains an extremely elaborate set of procedures on enforcement, which, when combined with the ability of any private party to file a complaint with any one of the three NAO, looks extremely inviting. This may have misled many labor lawyers into thinking that it provided an avenue for concrete remedies for victims of labor law abuses. This was a mistake, as Compa points out:

> Critics assailed the NAALC for failing to achieve reinstatement of dismissed workers for recognition of independent unions. However, such criticism misapprehends the power of the NAALC for it cannot substitute for domestic labor law. None of the three countries was prepared to have a new supranational body dictate remedies to its domestic authorities. Instead, the NAALC creates a new setting for international scrutiny of labor law matters and hopes that over time, the "sunlight" effect of such scrutiny will change the climate of respect for workers' rights.[60]

The complaint process under the NAALC has a number of stages. First, a private party can file a complaint with a NAO. Interestingly, the U.S. NAO has established procedures for holding public hearings on complaints. But in Canada this is not the case, as Roy Adams notes:

> The procedures to be used by the Canadian NAO are largely similar to those in the United States and Mexico, but the organization does not plan to hold public hearings . . . it is the judgment of the Canadian NAO that hearings at which accusations and responses are aired publicly are adversarial in nature and thus are contrary to the spirit of co-operativism that the agreement is intended to foster.[61]

If any NAO finds violations of the NAALC following whatever procedures it has adopted, it may recommend what the agreement calls "ministerial consultations." Ministerial consultations usually result in the ministers recommending a series of trinational workshops, public conferences, special studies by independent experts, and calls for ongoing monitoring of the enforcement of domestic labor law.[62]

The NAALC then goes on to provide for two further stages of proceedings. It is crucial to note that each of these stages is driven not by the private party initiating the complaint, but rather by one of the three member governments. Thus if one of the member governments is not satisfied that the matter has been resolved after ministerial consultations, it can request an evaluation by what is called an "evaluation committee of experts." At this stage the most fundamental values of freedom of association and collective bargaining, as well as the right to strike, are excluded from potential review. The function of the committee is to investigate the matter and to prepare a report containing what the NAALC calls "practical recommendations that may assist the parties in respect of the matter."[63]

If one of the parties to the NAALC remains unsatisfied following the committee's report and recommendations, it can move on to an additional stage in the process. But this stage is available only if the issue relates to health and safety, child labor, or minimum wages; the further one proceeds through the process, the fewer substantive standards are available to be considered. This stage involves an arbitration panel on which membership is controlled by the council. In theory, a panel finding may result in penalties and fines in the case of Canada, and suspension of NAFTA's trade benefits in the case of Mexico and the United States. It is highly unlikely, however, that this final stage of proceedings would ever be invoked. The complaint procedure is better viewed as a structured opportunity for intergovernmental negotiation rather than enforcement.

One of the major innovations of the AIP is that the charter document of the FLA not only establishes a code of conduct and elaborates a comprehensive system of internal and external monitoring and certification, but it goes on to provide what is referred to as a "third-party complaint procedure." The charter document states:

> The Association shall establish and implement a process to allow third parties to report any significant and/or persistent pattern of non-compliance or individual incident of serious non-compliance with the workplace code or monitoring principles with respect to any facility of a participating company.

The procedure outlined begins with a complaint to the executive director of the FLA. The executive director can call for a response by the participating company complained against and, eventually, prompt further investigation by one of the accredited independent external monitors. As always, the ultimate sanction is the decertification of the brands of participating companies for noncompliance with the code and monitoring procedures.

The lesson of experience here is that, perhaps paradoxically, the private sector or subnational strategy leads to potentially the strongest set of sanctions. Unhindered by the need for intergovernmental agreement, either global or regional, direct appeal can be made to the self-interest of the firms involved, which in turn rests upon an appeal to consumer preferences.

CONCLUSIONS AND IMPLICATIONS

Many lessons may be drawn from the rich history of the complicated interaction of the actors and institutions involved in these three levels and sites of contestation of the labor rights agenda. The most important is that the labor rights agenda is inherently complex and value laden. We can expect as a matter of theory—and do find as a matter of practice—that the project of global labor rights governance is motivated by, and simultaneously frustrated by, inherent ideological conflicts. In many places governance is hindered by a direct challenge to the very idea of the pursuit of a labor rights agenda. Nevertheless, fundamental to the project of labor regulation is that it be precisely about the virtues and limits of markets.

Some general lessons can, however, be distilled by stepping back from the details of our three levels and sites of contest for labor rights governance.

First, at the global ILO level, it is difficult to imagine reducing the level of distrust and distributional conflict between the developed and the developing world. This is particularly so within a "single-issue" institution, such as the ILO. The ILO is unable to offer any compensation—such as access to markets or capital—in return for respect for core rights. As we have seen, this has been the informing idea for many of those pursuing the project of fundamental ILO restructuring—that is, introducing some form of conditionality. Yet this is precisely what is resisted. By comparison, it seems that within the WTO the developed and developing world manage to reach consensus on other items on the international regulatory agenda (such as intellectual property) because developed nations are in a position to offer a quid pro quo to the developing world. This problem of the single issue also is evident in the difficulties of the AIP in sustaining its coalition. The concerns of UNITE could not be addressed via compensation, which can take place only within broader, almost certainly nonprivate, negotiations.

Second, one should not underestimate the concerns in many parts of the world about maintaining sovereignty and avoiding domination by the rich and powerful countries. This is true even within regional arrangements such as NAFTA—perhaps even more so. Both Canada and Mexico brought profound suspicions to the NAFTA bargaining table. The result was an agreement that cedes no authority over the labor rights agenda to any international organization, but—and this is an important lesson—adopts the strategy of committing the various nations to enforcement of their existing labor laws. This approach overcomes the problem of fashioning global labor law, while respecting sovereignty. It is similar to the strategy pursued in the ILO of paring down the international labor code to a set of four core concerns, a plan that makes the labor rights agenda more manageable. Obviously it has its costs as well. But the idea of using existing structures, institutions, and law is clearly one of the interesting lessons to be learned from experience of both the ILO and the NAALC.

Third, it seems that the struggle at the subnational, private, marketplace level has great appeal, but also many difficulties. Here the issues of principle are completely finessed, as the appeal is to the basic virtues of market ordering itself. There is a market for respect for human rights, but human rights activists will object to establishing fundamental rights on such instrumental grounds. The long-term challenge is to see this approach not as giving up ground, but as reclaiming common ground. The difficulty ultimately is one of reconciling ends and means, and establishing in a principled and empirically grounded way a productive and fair way of ordering labor markets.

Fourth, the particular structure of the labor rights problem conspires to produce a world in which the mechanisms of effective governance are split between the different levels and sites of contest. Agreement is possible at the ILO on substance, but not on remedies or conditionality. Remedies are available at the level of private initiative, but lack credible and effective mechanisms. It is tempting to think that one could simply combine the successful elements of each regime: ILO resources, NAFTA's local standards, and private sector remedies. But history tells us that such a melding is elusive—perhaps the largest lesson.

NOTES

1. Karl Polanyi, *The Great Transformation* (Boston: Beacon Press, 1957), p. 75.
2. Jean-Michel Servais, *International Labor Organization (ILO)* (The Hague: Kluwer Law International 1996), p. 9; and Virginia Leary, "Workers' Rights and International Trade: The Social Clause," in Jagdish Bhagwati and Robert Hudec, eds., *Fair Trade and Harmonization*, vol. 2 (Cambridge, Mass.: MIT Press, 1996), p. 177.
3. See David M. Trubek, Jim Mosher, and Jeff Rothstein, "Transnationalism in the Regulation of Labor Relations, International Regimes, and Transnational Advocacy Networks," manuscript (January 1999), available from the Labor and the Global Economy Research Circle of the International Institute of the University of Wisconsin (Madison). The reference to Keck and Sikkink is from *Activists Beyond Borders: Advocacy Networks in International Politics* (Ithaca, N.Y.: Cornell University Press, 1998).
4. Paul Krugman, *The Age of Diminished Expectations* (Cambridge, Mass.: MIT Press, 1994), pp. 14–5.
5. See Robert Solow, *The Labor Market as a Social Institution* (Oxford, U.K.: Blackwell, 1990).
6. International Labor Organization, *Declaration of Philadelphia* (1944), Annex to the ILO Constitution. All ILO texts can be found at <http://www.ilo.org>.
7. It is common to state that the contest is between visions of a "regulated" and an "unregulated" market in labor. But as every first-year law student knows, this is a serious misunderstanding. There is never no regulation—the only issue is what form of regulation. "Nonregulation" means re-regulation by a set of (usually) common or civil law rules of

contract, property, tort, and so on. Our goal cannot be less regulation, only smarter and better regulation.

8. UNCTAD, *World Investment Report* (Paris: United Nations, 1994), p. 117.

9. A good example of this can be found in John O. McGiniss, "The Decline of the Western Nation State and the Rise of the Regime of International Federalism," *Cardozo Law Review*, vol. 18, no. 3 (December 1996), p. 903.

10. Harry Arthurs, "Globalization of the Mind: Canadian Elites and the Restructuring of Legal Fields," *Canadian Journal of Law and Society*, vol. 12 (1977), p. 219.

11. Available at <http://www.ilo.org>.

12. *ILO Constitution*, Article 19. Available at <http://www.ilo.org>.

13. *OECD Trade, Employment, and Labor Standards* (Paris: OECD, 1996), p. 28.

14. Hansenne, speech at the Wilton Park Conference on Liberalizing Rules to Trade and Prospects for the Singapore Ministerial Meeting, March 6, 1996, p. 2.

15. The best source of information for both official texts and other documentation is the web site of the Commission for Labour Cooperation, available at <http://.www.naalc.org>.

16. Commission for Labour Cooperation, *1997 Annual Report,* available at <http://www.naalc.org>. For the ILO budgetary situation, see <http://www.ilo.org>.

17. International Labor Office, Geneva, November 1998. This is a document of the governing body, document GB.273/WP/SDL/1, available at <http://www.ilo.org> under the heading of Governing Body November 1998.

18. For a useful summary, see UNCTAD, *World Investment Report*, pp. 117–56.

19. Servais, *The International Labor Organization,* p. 12.

20. Arthur A. Stein, *Why Nations Cooperate* (Ithaca, N.Y.: Cornell University Press, 1991).

21. Eric J. Hobsbawm, *The Age of Extremes: The History of the World, 1914–1991* (New York: Pantheon Books, 1994).

22. For two accounts, see David Henderson, *The MAI Affair: A Story and Its Lessons* (London: Royal Institute of International Affairs, 1999); and William Dymond, "The I: A Sad and Melancholy Tale," in Fen Osler Hampson et al., eds., *Canada Among Nations, 1999: A Big League Player?* (Toronto: Oxford University Press, 1999).

23. International Labor Conference, 85th session, *Standard-setting and Globalization* (Geneva: ILO, 1997).

24. Ignacio A. Donso Rubio, "Economic Limits on International Regulation: A Case Study: ILO Standard Setting," *Queen's Law Journal,* vol. 24 (1988), p. 189.

25. Available at <http://www.ilo.org>.

26. See Brian Langille, "Canadian Labour Law Reform and Free Trade," *Ottawa Law Review*, vol. 23 (1992), pp. 581–623.

27. Trubek, Mosher, and Rothstein, "Transnationalism in the Regulation of Labour Relations," p. 20.

28. For further accounts of this process, see Charles Tiefer, "'Alongside' the Fast Track: Environmental and Labor Issues in FTAA," *Minnesota Journal of Global Trade*, vol. 7 (1998), p. 329; Lance Compa, "NAFTA's Labor Side Accord: A Three-Year Accounting," *NAFTA: Law & Business Review of the Americas*, vol. 3, no. 3 (Summer 1997); Roy J. Adams and Parbudyal Singh, "Early Experience with NAFTA's Labor Side Accord," *Comparative Labor Law Journal*, vol. 18, no. 2 (Winter 1997), p. 161; and

Armand De Mestral, "The Significance of the NAFTA Side Agreements on Environ-mental and Labor Co-operation," *Arizona Journal of International and Comparative Law*, vol. 15 (1998), p. 169.

29. See NAALC, Article 2; and NAALC, Article 011(3).

30. Compa, "NAFTA's Labour Side Accord," p. 7.

31. Ibid., p. 11.

32. Trubek, Mosher, and Rothstein, "Transnationalism in the Regulation of Labour Rela-tions," p. 22.

33. International Labour Rights Fund, "Developing Effective Mechanisms for Implement-ing Labor Rights in the Global Economy," August 28, 1998. Discussion draft available at International Labor Rights Fund, <http://www.laborrights.org>.

34. Ibid., p. 8. See also Compa, "NAFTA's Labor Side Accord," p. 21. The idea that NAALC should be best viewed in this nonlegalistic, unintended way is a central theme in Compa's work.

35. International Labour Rights Fund, "Developing Codes of Conduct with Independent Monitoring Systems to Improve Labour Rights Enforcement." Discussion draft available at <http://www.laborrights.org>, at p. 2.

36. Chakravarti Raghavern, "ILO Director-General Backs Away from 'Social Label' Propos-als," Third World Network at <http://www.twnside.org.sg/title/soc-cn.htm>.

37. See the WTO Singapore Ministerial Declaration, adopted December 13, 1996, at <http://www.wto.org/english/thewto_e/minist_e/min96_e/wtodec.htm >. Core labor rights are addressed in the fourth article.

38. Geneva, ILO, 1997.

39. For a more complete discussion of the ILO's declaration negotiations, see Brian Langille, "The ILO and the New Economy: Recent Developments," *International Journal of Comparative Law and Industrial Relations*, vol. 15 (1999), p. 225.

40. See Henry G. Schermers and Niels M. Blokker, *International Institutional Law*, 3rd ed. (Manchester: Kluwer International Law, 1995), para. 1247. See also N. D. White, *The Law of International Organizations* (Manchester, U.K.: Manchester University Press, 1996).

41. Failure to ratify occurs in OECD countries as well as others. Difficulty in reconciling domestic legislation with convention demands has occurred, for example, in Canada with regard to child labor.

42. The Governing Body is the twenty-eight-state executive body of the ILO that meets in November, March, and June and sets the agenda for the annual labor conference held in June.

43. This constitutional defense is set out in Clarence Wilfred Jenks, *The International Protec-tion of Trade Union Freedom* (London: Stevens, 1957), pp. 191–200. See also the Gov-erning Body document GB267/LILS/5 (November 1996), where this argument is reiter-ated and accepted.

44. Since 1951, 1,100 complaints have been filed as opposed to fewer than 100 complaints under the two complaint mechanisms established for the ratified conventions.

45. The complete paragraph reads: "We reject the use of labour standards for protectionist purposes, and agree that the comparative advantage of countries, particularly low-wage developing countries, must in no way be put into question. We renew our commitment

to the observance of the internationally recognized core labour standards. The International Labour Organization (ILO) is the competent body to set and deal with these standards and reaffirm our support for its work in promoting them. We believe that economic growth and development fostered by increased trade and further trade liberalization contribute to the promotion of these standards. In this regard we note that the WTO and ILO Secretariats will continue their existing collaboration."

46. "Anti-Union Group Files NAFTA Suit: Complaint Against U.S. Filed with Canada Pushes for Employers' Rights," *Wall Street Journal*, April 14, 1999.

47. Steven Greenhouse, "Groups Reach Agreement for Curtailing Sweatshops," *New York Times*, November 5, 1998, p. 8.

48. See, for example, Abram Chayes and Antonia Chayes, *The New Sovereignty: Compliance with International Regulatory Agreements* (Cambridge, Mass.: Harvard University Press, 1995).

49. OECD, *Trade, Employment and Labour Standards*, pp. 154–55. See also Servais, *International Labor Organization*, pp. 44–5.

50. ILO Constitution, Article 19(5)(e).

51. Nicolas Valticos and Geraldo von Potobsky, *International Labour Law* (The Hague: Kluwer Law International, 1995), para. 620.

52. ILO, *1998 Declaration*, Annex II(3).

53. Ibid., Annex III(b)(2).

54. NAALC, Article 14.

55. International Labour Rights Fund, "Developing Codes of Conduct with Independent Monitoring Systems," available at <http://www.laborrights.org>.

56. See ILO, "Overview of Global Developments and Office Activities Concerning Codes of Conduct, Social Labelling and Other Private Sector Initiatives Addressing Labour Issues," GB.273/WP/SDL/1 (November 1998), p. 27–31. Available at <http://www.ilo.org>.

57. This is often said (see above, for example, at note 14 and text), but it is not what the ILO Constitution says. Article 33 of the ILO Constitution actually states that the final step in the enforcement of ratified conventions is that "the Governing Body may recommend to the Conference *such action* as it may deem will be expedient to secure compliance therewith." The content of this power has not been explored by the ILO, although it has been discussed in connection with Burma's persistent refusals to abide by or deal with the recommendations of a Commission of Inquiry into its violations of the forced labor conventions. See Report 6B.27616, 276th Session (of the Governing Body), November 1999 (available at <http://www.ilo.org>). The legislative history of Article 33 reveals that it was added in 1946 to alter and expand the preexisting version of the article, which limited the ILO to *economic* sanctions. The institutional silence concerning Article 33 is deafening.

58. OECD, *Trade, Employment, and Labour Standards*, p. 57. The OECD does note that the number of representations seems to be on the increase. In 1994 alone there were thirteen representations', and in 1995, six.

59. *Freedom of Association Digest of Decisions and Principles of the Freedom of Association Committee of the Governing Body of the ILO*, rev. ed. (Geneva: ILO, 1996).

60. Compa, "NAFTA's Labour Side Accord," p. 19. See also the comments of John McKenniney, executive director of the Commission for Labor Co-operation, in *American University Journal of International Law and Policy*, vol. 12 (1997), pp. 825–26.

61. Adams and Singh, "Early Experience with NAFTA's Labor Side Accord," p. 166.

62. These cases are summarized in Compa, "NAFTA's Labour Side Accord," and Adams and Singh, "Early Experience with NAFTA's Labour Side Accord."

63. NAALC, Article 25.

SUGGESTED ADDITIONAL READING

Leary, Virginia. "Worker's Rights and International Trade: The Social Clause." In Jagdish Bhagwati and Robert Hudec, eds. *Fair Trade and Harmonization*, vol. 2. Boston, Mass.: MIT Press, 1996, pp. 177–230.

OECD Trade, Employment, and Labor Standards. Paris: OECD, 1996.

Servais, Jean-Michel. *International Labor Organization (ILO)*. The Hague: Kluwer Law International, 1996.

Trubek, David M., Jim Mosher, and Jeff Rothstein. "Transnationalism in the Regulation of Labor Relations, International Regimes, and Transnational Advocacy Networks." Manuscript (January 1999). Available from the Labor and the Global Economy Research Circle of the International Institute of the University of Wisconsin (Madison).

Internet sites

Commission for Labor Cooperation <http://www.naalc.org>
International Labor Organization (ILO) <http://www.ilo.org>
International Labor Rights Fund <http://www.laborrights.org>

13

Refugee Protection and Assistance

Kathleen Newland

INTERNATIONAL REGIMES CAN FALL APART as well as come together. The emphasis in this volume is on regime formation, but it may be instructive to examine at least one example of regime dissolution, or at least transformation. The set of international agreements, norms, and common practices to assist and protect refugees provides one such example.

The picture that follows is one of a once well-established regime now in disarray, whose main state supporters are no longer willing to conform consistently to its basic principles and expectations despite pressure from international institutions and nongovernmental organizations (NGOs). This shift is in part because the context in which the regime was formed has changed fundamentally, in part because the numbers and kind of actors involved have expanded dramatically.

The result of the current deterioration of the refugee regime is that escape from violence and persecution has become more difficult, and refugees who manage to reach a place of relative safety are less likely to be allowed to enter and remain there. Countries of asylum attempting to control illegal immigration have instituted measures that fail to discriminate between refugees and other unauthorized migrants. Those that experience uncontrollable flows of refugees across their borders are increasingly subjecting them to harsh and restrictive conditions, effectively foreclosing their chances to rebuild their lives in a new country. The core of the refugee protection regime—that people would not be forcibly returned to a place where their lives or liberty would be endangered—is increasingly disregarded. As wars and campaigns of repression continue to target civilian populations, the victims have fewer options for refuge from suffering and death.

What is distinctive about this picture is not the disarray but the deterioration that it represents from an earlier period, loosely defined as the Cold War era. From roughly

1950 to 1990, the international consensus on appropriate responses to refugee out-flows went largely unchallenged—even if observance was far from perfect.

If many governments appear ready to abandon, or at least alter profoundly, the "classic" refugee regime established and codified after World War II, other signifi-cant actors are determined to defend its central principles. The defenders include the intergovernmental institutions mandated to implement the refugee regime, although there are differences of opinion within and among them about how to mount the best defense of refugees' interests, and indeed about what those interests are. The intergovernmental institutions—most centrally, the Office of the United Nations High Commissioner for Refugees (UNHCR)—operate in coalition with a rich array of partners: nongovernmental institutions, private foundations, news media, aca-demic institutions, and individual advocates, analysts, and relief professionals. On many questions, governmental actors will be found on different sides of the debate.

As with so many issues of international governance, issues of sovereignty lie at the heart of many disagreements about the essence of states' obligations to refugees. Is the acceptance of these obligations an exercise of national sovereignty, or an example of sovereignty overridden by international governance? Is the fundamental purpose of the regime to protect refugees from states, or to protect states—and the state sys-tem—from refugees?

This chapter will analyze how and why the refugee regime has changed so pro-foundly from its post–World War II origins and in doing so attempt to illuminate some of the dynamics of global issues management. It will briefly review the forma-tion and content of the classic regime, but the major part of the discussion will look at the process of change that began in the 1980s and became manifest in the 1990s.

The elements that emerge as major influences on the evolution of the refugee regime include classic variables such as the converging interests of powerful states and new phenomena such as the impact on public opinion of real-time television coverage from remote locations. The changing structure and size of refugee flows have had a profound impact on the willingness and capability of states to offer asy-lum on their own territory and has led to questions about the appropriateness of doing so. At the same time, many politicians and some members of the public in many receiving countries have come to believe that the original purposes of the re-gime are being abused by people seeking asylum who are not bona fide refugees but voluntary migrants.

The end of the Cold War and the subsequent proliferation of violent internal conflicts overturned assumptions about the purpose and the limits of international action to assist and protect the victims of violence and persecution. The classic re-gime was focused on protection in exile. The international response to refugee flows in the 1990s focused much more heavily on preventing and on occasion even ob-structing such flows by providing in-country assistance to people who had fled or might flee from their homes. The older set of international responses was conceived as purely palliative and relatively static, offering a substitute to people for the irrevocably lost protection of their own national governments. By contrast, the current international response to refugee flows is developing preventive and remedial ambitions that render it unstable and much less sure of success.

This chapter will examine how refugee protection and assistance have been defined and redefined as matters of international public interest, and who responds with what means to that interest. It will track the evolving, and sometimes contradictory, practices and norms of both protection and assistance, and describe what has been learned from the experience of the latter half of the twentieth century. It will explore whether the deterioration of the classic regime represents a clearing out of obstacles to the formation of a new regime, or simply a growing deficit of international governance in an arena whose importance for human well-being can scarcely be exaggerated.

BACKGROUND: THE FORMATION OF A REGIME

While refugees are as old a phenomenon as man's inhumanity to man, they were not seen as a responsibility of the international community until the twentieth century. The League of Nations created a series of ad hoc, temporary offices to manage particular groups of refugees (Russians, Armenians, Germans) created by World War I and the Bolshevik Revolution, but these led to neither permanent institutions nor broad international agreements. Nongovernmental efforts were similarly sporadic. The International Committee of the Red Cross (ICRC), founded half a century earlier to protect and care for captured and wounded members of the armed forces, provided assistance to civilian victims of war, although this was not yet formally a part of its mandate.

World War II left more than 50 million people displaced in Europe alone, including some 11 million forced laborers and displaced persons working in the former Third Reich. In the months to come, they would be joined by another 13 million ethnic Germans who would be expelled from countries to the east. The victorious allies recognized that the consolidation of the peace and the reconstruction of Europe could not proceed without addressing this massive displacement. In addition, the consolidation of communist rule in Eastern and Central Europe was creating new refugees in whom the West had a keen political interest.

In the first five years after the war, the allies persisted in the ad hoc approach of earlier years, creating separate bodies to deal with refugees in Europe, Palestine, and Korea. By 1950, however, multiple crises associated with the mounting confrontation between East and West—the Berlin blockade, the division of Germany, Mao's victory in China, the subjugation of Eastern Europe, and the start of the Korean War—as well as the chaotic partition of India, made it clear that the refugee issue would persist past the postwar reconstruction phase.

In December 1950 the UN General Assembly voted to establish the UNHCR as a subsidiary organ of the General Assembly, reporting to the General Assembly through its Third Committee and to the Economic and Social Council (ECOSOC). In 1951, an international diplomatic conference adopted the UN Convention Relating to the Status of Refugees. Signatories to the convention were called upon, in Article 35, to cooperate with UNHCR in the exercise of its functions. UNHCR is unique among the subsidiary organs of the General Assembly in having this direct institutional link to an international convention.

Even these arrangements were intended to be temporary, however. UNHCR was established for three years, and the convention was to apply only to people who became refugees before January 1951. States that signed the convention could limit their obligations to refugees in Europe. The life of UNHCR has been extended for more than fifty years. Although its mandate still must be renewed every five years by the General Assembly, there is every reason to expect that the organization will continue. The geographical and temporal limits in the convention were removed by a protocol adopted in 1967.[1] With these acts, the foundation was laid for the management of human displacement as a global issue.

The convention establishes an accepted definition of a refugee as a person who is outside his or her country of origin and cannot count on the protection of that country owing to a well-founded fear of persecution on specified grounds.[2] It also codifies the obligations of states toward refugees. The most important obligation is not to expel or return a refugee to a territory where his or her life or freedom would be threatened on account of race, religion, nationality, membership of a particular social group, or political opinion. Signatories also pledge to promote and safeguard refugees' rights while in asylum in such matters as education, employment, freedom of movement, access to the judicial system, and so forth.

Significantly, the convention does not establish a general right to asylum. States were, and remain, unwilling to compromise their sovereign right to decide who may be admitted to their territories.[3] But once a person who qualifies as a refugee somehow gains access to the territory of a state that is party to the convention, that person cannot be deported to a place where his or her life or freedom would be threatened.

The principle of no forcible return, or *non-refoulement* in legal parlance, opened a rift between the Soviet Union and the other World War II allies. The Soviets demanded that assistance to refugees from the Soviet Union and the countries coming under its domination should be for repatriation only, whereas the Western allies insisted that the refugees should not be forced to return home against their will. UNHCR's mandate to find durable solutions for refugees, in the view of the Western governments that supported it, chiefly would involve resettling the residual caseload from World War II and the small number of people who managed to escape from behind the Iron Curtain.

The statute that established UNHCR mandated it to provide international protection to refugees and to seek permanent solutions to the problem of refugees by working with national governments and, subject to the approval of governments, with private organizations. Thus, from the moment of its institutionalization, the international refugee regime explicitly foresaw a partnership among state, nonstate, and intergovernmental actors. In fact, the first substantial sum of money that UNHCR received was not from a state but from the Ford Foundation, which made a grant of $3.1 million in 1951.[4]

The statute of UNHCR also established one of the most useful and durable fictions of the postwar era in stating that "the work of the High Commissioner shall be of an entirely non-political character; it shall be humanitarian and social. . . ." The convention also makes clear that when one state accepts refugees from another, it is not to be seen as a belligerent act toward the country of origin. The convention and statute sought to neutralize refugees as a political factor. In the tense and polarized climate of the early Cold War years, this was seen as a necessary device to allow the United Nations to act on refugee issues. Even so, the Soviet Union and its allies did not sign the convention or cooperate with UNHCR. As they feared, the Western powers, and particularly the United States, commonly used refugees as a political weapon in the Cold War confrontation. In fact, the United States did not contribute to UNHCR initially, preferring to fund its bilateral "U.S. Escapee Program" and an international organization created outside of the UN system in 1952, the Intergovernmental Committee on Migration. UNHCR was perhaps seen as "too European" to be entirely trusted with U.S. strategic interests in refugee movements. The political impact of refugee response, whether intended or unintended, has continued. In the civil conflicts that have come to characterize the post–Cold War period, in which displacement is as often an aim as a by-product of war, protecting refugees is often seen by parties to the conflict as a direct frustration of their political and military intentions.

Curiously, one of the features most associated with refugee crises in the public mind is not mentioned at all in the 1951 Convention or the UNHCR Statute: humanitarian assistance to refugees. It was assumed initially that host countries would manage relief needs independently. In the early postwar years, material aid to refugees was subsumed under postwar reconstruction and aid to the general populations of devastated Europe. In the 1950s, the international community did little to assist refugees who fled from China to Hong Kong after the Communist victory on the mainland, or for Tibetan refugees fleeing to India. It was not until the 1960s, as UNHCR and other humanitarian organizations became more active in the developing world, that the need to provide material assistance to refugees became inescapable. In the last quarter of the twentieth century and into the twenty-first, humanitarian assistance is one of the dominant forms of response to refugee crises.

The refugee crises of the 1950s through the 1990s provided a series of turning points for UNHCR, each of which changed the orientation and mode of operation of the organization.[5] UNHCR broke from its backward-looking, World War II perspective with the Hungarian crisis of 1956. The refugee flows associated with the wars of decolonization in Africa in the 1960s ended its Eurocentric focus. The negotiation of the 1967 protocol put the stamp of permanence on both of these departures from the founding framework. Throughout this period, however, its role was primarily legal and diplomatic.

UNHCR first played a larger role, within the UN system and beyond, during the South Asian crisis of the early 1970s that created independent Bangladesh. It coordinated the provision of assistance, working with the host government (India), donor governments, other UN organizations, and NGOs.

UNHCR first became operational in Indochina in the mid-1970s, as it built and managed camps that sheltered Cambodians and Laotians. As an operational organization, it developed a unique mode of working with NGOs as contractual "implementing partners" in the field. The size and budget of UNHCR grew enormously in the 1980s as a result of simultaneous Cold War–related crises in Indochina, the Horn of Africa, Central America, and Afghanistan. When these crises ended, UNHCR took on not only the physical repatriation of refugees, but also the much more complex task of trying to ensure that return would lead to reintegration rather than stand as a prelude to renewed displacement.

More people from the conflict zones of Africa, Asia, and Latin America sought asylum in Europe and North America during the 1980s. In many countries, the categories of unauthorized migrants and asylum seekers in need of protection blurred. These movements generated a backlash against asylum seekers that found expression in increasingly restrictive measures aimed at deterring entry. As a result, UNHCR found itself criticizing and at times quietly confronting the states that were its major donors and political supporters, as it sought to preserve refugees' access to asylum.

The early 1990s saw a breakthrough in UNHCR's relations with the successor states of the former Soviet Union, which through most of its history had been hostile to UNHCR. With the convening of a 1996 international conference on displacement in the former Soviet Union, UNHCR definitively put the Cold War behind it. It opened offices throughout the immense region to assist governments and people confronting the enormous complexity of migration flows and protection needs in the fifteen successor states.

In the early 1990s, UNHCR also confronted a series of megacrises in former Yugoslavia, northern Iraq, and Rwanda. They forced UNHCR to operate on an unprecedented scale and in the midst of armed conflict. The growing reluctance of states to offer open-ended, traditional modes of asylum to large inflows of refugees also compelled UNHCR to cooperate in seeking alternative forms of protection, such as temporary protection, safe havens, and in-country provision of humanitarian relief. The provision of humanitarian assistance soared in this period, leading to criticism that UNHCR was neglecting its protection mandate in favor of assistance because its major donors found it much easier to provide relief supplies than to offer territorial asylum.

The proportion of official development assistance spent on emergency aid by the industrialized countries rose fourfold between the early 1980s and 1999. Between 1990 and 1996, more than $30 billion was spent on humanitarian assistance. The annual amount peaked at about $7 billion in 1994, then leveled off at about $3 billion until the Kosovo crisis made 1999 another record year.[6] This in part reflects the enormous increase in the numbers of people forcibly displaced by the major crises of the early to mid-1990s in former Yugoslavia, Rwanda, and Liberia, among others. But it also illustrates the strength of the humanitarian impulse that demands a response to the visible suffering of innocent people.

It is a central paradox of refugee protection and assistance that as the international consensus on the purpose of the enterprise has eroded, the enterprise itself has grown enormously. By the year 2001, 140 states had ratified or acceded to the 1951 Convention and/or the 1967 Protocol. Many states that are not parties to the treaties do in fact respect the principles set forth in them and cooperate extensively with UNHCR. India, Saudi Arabia, and Thailand, for example, are not signatories but all have hosted major UNHCR operations. India even sits on the Executive Committee of UNHCR despite not having signed the convention or protocol. Thus the refugee regime has become one of the more universal manifestations of international convergence around a set of norms, rules, and procedures in a given area. In establishing a system for managing refugee issues, states established a cornerstone in international law, a strong central institution, and a well-defined set of principles and obligations—the major building blocks of an international regime.

The contemporary regime is still firmly rooted in the context of the Cold War, the geopolitical concerns of the Western allies, and the traditions of state sovereignty. The European concept of neutral and impartial humanitarianism, as embodied in the Red Cross movement (see box 13-1) was grafted rather uneasily onto what was a highly state-centric refugee regime. At the end of World War II, the Western allies recognized the potential for political disorder that unresolved refugee problems can bring, and they were willing to sacrifice a small part of their prerogatives as sovereign states to manage this element of the dangerous situation in Europe at the war's end. As the aftermath of hot war quickly merged into the beginning of the Cold War, the value of a set of humanitarian instruments that were formally designated as nonpolitical yet were adaptable to making political points was appreciated.

The uneasy relationship between humanitarian needs and political objectives has been a constant in the management of refugee crises for the subsequent half-century.

Box 13-1. *The Red Cross Movement and the International Humanitarian Regime*

The International Committee of the Red Cross (ICRC) came into existence in 1863 largely as a result of one man's actions. A Swiss businessman named Henri Dunant witnessed a battle between French and Austrian forces at Solferino, in northern Italy, in 1859 and was appalled to see that after the battle was over and the armies retreated, the wounded were abandoned where they lay amid hideous suffering. Dunant's published account, in "A Memory of Solferino," brought fame to him and impetus to a project to devise a treaty to permit medical attention to soldiers wounded in battle.[a] Four years after the battle, a committee—the precursor of the ICRC—was formed in Geneva to advance Dunant's ideas. In 1864, sixteen countries agreed to the first Geneva Convention. The convention established that medical staff and equipment were to be regarded as neutral and that the wounded would be treated impartially. Subsequent revisions and new conventions codified the laws of war and set standards for the treatment of prisoners.

Dunant was awarded the Nobel Peace Prize in 1901; by the time he died in 1910, many countries had established Red Cross or, in Muslim countries, Red Crescent, Societies to provide humanitarian assistance and promote the Red Cross principles. These principles and practices took hold with surprising speed in Europe and North America, even as the mechanization of warfare increased casualties in battle. The ICRC and national societies were extremely active and widely respected in World War I. The savagery of World War II tested the movement beyond its limits, however. The targeting of civilians, as in the siege of Stalingrad, and the extermination of the Jews in the Third Reich found no answer in the Red Cross movement's project to "civilize" warfare. In 1949 a new diplomatic conference was called; it produced four separate conventions, which dealt with members of the armed forces (I and II), prisoners of war (III), and civilians, particularly those in enemy or occupied territories (IV).

In 1977, two additional protocols were negotiated. They increased protection for civilians, including some protection for those affected by internal warfare, and limited the methods and means of warfare. The most relevant portions for refugees are found in Article 3, which is common to all four conventions and the two protocols. States party to the conventions and/or protocols have a collective responsibility for ensuring compliance by other states and armed

a. Henry Dunant, *Souvenir de Solférino* (Paris: Slatkine, 1900). Facsimile of the original edition.

Continued on next page

Box 13-1. Continued

opposition movements, and an obligation to bring violators to trial in their own courts. They may also turn them over to other states for trial.

The ICRC, which remains a committee of private Swiss citizens, was mandated by the conventions to oversee the application of international humanitarian law, as the conventions and protocols are collectively known.

International humanitarian law provides important protections to refugees, but it also has major limitations. It applies only in situations of recognized armed conflict, and to nationals of the states involved in such conflicts. Not all refugees fall into this category—for example, those who are persecuted by agents of a state that is not at war, such as refugees from Kosovo before the NATO bombing campaign began, from Cambodia after the Khmer Rouge victory, or from Burma today. Refugees who flee into a state that is not party to the conflict also fall outside the scope of international humanitarian law. In addition, ICRC will operate only under conditions of consent, and not all states agree to give it access to victims: Turkey refuses to allow access to Kurdish areas, for example. States have resisted further extension of the ICRC mandate in internal conflicts short of war, as was proposed in two instruments put forward in 1988, because of concerns about sovereignty and interference in their internal affairs.

But a great many other elements have entered the picture in that period, leaving states much less in control of the issue than they felt themselves to be in the early 1950s. These factors prefigure some of the lessons to be drawn from the past decade of refugee protection.

First, the appalling scale of suffering and death of civilians in World War II gave rise to a determination to prevent a repetition. The "never again" pledge may not have been taken literally by the world's political leaders, but indifference to persecution and the ravages of war was seen to be dangerous and destabilizing as well as immoral. The era of decolonization, and later the proxy wars of the 1970s and 1980s, globalized the refugee regime.

Second, with the advent of the television age, the suffering associated with refugee flows in even the most remote corners of the world became steadily more visible and immediate. Protagonists in refugee-producing conflicts also became more adept at manipulating the images of suffering and displacement. Members of the public in affluent Western countries demanded responses from their elected officials or took action themselves through voluntary associations or in some cases directly. The organization Médecins sans Frontières, for example, grew out of a French doctor's fury with the business-as-usual approach of governments, the United Nations, and the

ICRC to the Biafran conflict of 1969–1971. Churches and charitable organizations have long been in the business of providing relief to people in need, but the exponential rise in the number and kinds of actors engaged in refugee relief work is a third major change in the humanitarian response to refugee crises in the latter half of the century.

Fourth, the revolution in communications and transportation that gained momentum in the 1980s meant that people seeking escape from violence and persecution had better information about the refugee policies of the Western countries and a greater possibility of reaching them to present an asylum claim directly. Increasing numbers of spontaneous arrivals in the industrialized countries created a sense that the system was out of control and was being used to increase unauthorized immigration rather than to assist desperate people genuinely in need of protection. The increasing prevalence of mixed flows of refugees and migrants, and the responses of industrialized countries to this fact, has posed the most severe challenge to the classic refugee regime since its formation.

For a regime whose character was so closely tied to the Cold War context in which it was born, the end of the Cold War was bound to change its architecture. With the other changes described above, it has compelled all actors involved in responding to refuge flows to question whether the existing regime is serviceable in a new context. Closely examining the lessons of the past is a first step toward an answer.

TRACK RECORD OF REFUGEE RESPONSE

The refugee regime was formulated around three objectives: (1) establishing legal protection of refugees, (2) finding solutions to their plight, and (3) providing assistance to enable them to survive the separation from their homes and communities. The first two were codified in the 1951 Convention Relating to the Status of Refugees, while the third was pursued in the more diffused domain of host governments, NGOs, the Red Cross movement, and UN organizations acting simultaneously. The track record of international response may be measured against these goals.

In the 1990s, however, the objectives of the refugee regime became intertwined with international responses to the new generation of post–Cold War, mostly internal, conflicts. Goals such as early warning and prevention of refugee flows, intervention to reverse the causes of exodus, peace building and development to consolidate repatriation, and control of unauthorized migration were invoked in some situations along with the classic three objectives, with decidedly mixed results. New actors such as national military forces, regional organizations, and the political organs of the United Nations became involved in these efforts. The assessment that follows, however, will focus on the three objectives that form the base of the refugee regime and have been consistently pursued by UNHCR.

Protection

The protection that the international community extends to refugees is a response to the specific needs of people who have good reason to fear that their own governments cannot or will not safeguard their rights. It provides a temporary substitute for national protection, until refugees can either return to their country of origin or form a new and durable relationship with a government that will protect them as permanent legal residents or citizens. Above all, international protection is meant to prevent refugees from being returned against their will to a place where they reasonably fear being persecuted.

The normal means of international protection is the institution of asylum, by which refugees gain access to the territory of a state that will accord them the same civil and economic rights as other legal residents, without discrimination. This includes such key elements of national protection as physical security (guaranteed as best the state can through military and police protection), access to the courts in case asylees are attacked or their rights are violated, and protection against economic exploitation. Obviously, the capacity of countries of asylum to deliver these protections varies, but the international system seeks to ensure that a refugee is no worse off than the citizen or legal migrant in the country of asylum. UNHCR and other protection advocates also work to ensure that refugees are allowed to escape from danger and gain access to asylum.

This internationally agreed system of protection has provided safety to many millions of refugees in the last half-century. The number recognized as refugees meeting the terms of the 1951 Convention or otherwise falling within the mandate of UNHCR peaked at about 18 million in 1993, which did not include the nearly 4 million Palestinian refugees who have been assisted by the UN Relief and Works Agency rather than UNHCR since 1948.[7] At the beginning of the year 2000, the U.S. Committee for Refugees reckoned that there were some 14.1 million people in need of international protection, counting the Palestinians and many asylum seekers not included in UNHCR figures; if displaced people who remain within the borders of their own countries are added, the figure rises to almost 35 million.[8]

A strong record on international protection arises from three factors: access to protection, quality of protection, and respect for the principle of non-refoulement. Hosting refugees in large numbers places a considerable burden on the country of asylum. States have been most willing to shoulder this refugee burden when they have had a motive for doing so beyond devotion to refugee protection: support for the political cause in which the refugees are embroiled, sympathy for displaced co-ethnics or co-religionists, a desire to score political points at an adversary's expense, or a need for human resources. Resettlement of European refugees after World War II was relatively easy to arrange, in part because the United States, Canada, Australia, and other countries perceived a need to increase their populations. Throughout the

Cold War era, the overwhelming majority of refugees accepted into the United States originated from its Cold War adversaries in Eastern Europe, Cuba, and Indochina. Many countries welcomed South African exiles in the apartheid era as a demonstration of their solidarity with the anti-apartheid struggle. Albania welcomed ethnic Albanian refugees from Kosovo at considerable cost and peril to its own security.

In situations in which such factors are weak or absent, however, potential countries of asylum have gone to considerable lengths to deflect refugees and asylum seekers. Southeast Asian countries in the late 1970s and 1980s drove refugee boats from Vietnam away from their shores and into grave peril on the high seas until Western countries agreed to remove the refugees for resettlement elsewhere. The United States intercepted Haitian asylum seekers in the Caribbean in the 1980s and early 1990s and returned them directly to Haiti, charging that they were economic migrants rather than people fleeing persecution. Turkey refused to grant entry to hundreds of thousands of Kurds who massed on its borders in 1991, under attack from Iraqi government forces. In 1996, four West African countries refused landing rights to a decrepit oil tanker aptly named the *Bulk Challenge*, which was dangerously overcrowded with refugees from Liberia. The countries of Western Europe have erected what one analyst described as a "paper Berlin Wall" of visa requirements, carrier sanctions, and regulations designed to keep unauthorized entrants from Eastern Europe and the developing world from claiming asylum in the European Union.[9]

Collectively, the Western industrialized states have experimented with a series of alternatives to asylum. These include "safe havens" established in northern Iraq and in former Yugoslavia (whose record of safety varies from poor to disastrous), and temporary admissions, from Bosnia to Germany, for example, that offer less security and stability than traditional asylum status. At the same time, they have raised obstacles to admission and narrowed the interpretation of who qualifies for refugee status. The result of these and other measures is that uncounted numbers of people who have a well-founded fear of persecution are unable to get to a place of safety where they may enjoy international protection.

Refugees who have managed to reach asylum have often discovered that adequate protection is sadly lacking, as they continue to face danger in refugee camps or in local communities. In settings from the Afghan refugee camps of Pakistan, to the Thai-Cambodian border, to Eastern Zaire, refugee camps are highly militarized. Many refugees find themselves under the control of fighting factions who use the refugees (civilians by definition) as virtual human shields, and persecute dissidents as ardently as the authorities in the country of origin. Areas of refugee settlement often draw fire from the forces of the government they fled, as for example the Karen camps in Thailand facing the Burmese border. (Eventually, UNHCR helped the Thai government relocate the camps away from the border to discourage such attacks.)

Beyond the political and military dangers, many refugee camps are dangerous simply because of high levels of criminality; in Somali camps in northern Kenya, it is reckoned that a woman's chance of being raped is as high as one in three, and police protection against rape, robbery, and extortion are virtually nonexistent. International donors have not been willing to provide the military or police resources necessary to raise the quality of protection for refugees to meet acceptable standards, either by separating military forces from civilian populations or by combating crime.

Finally, the cornerstone of international refugee protection, non-refoulement, has been violated repeatedly. In the 1990s, refugees were forced back to Cambodia from Thailand, to Afghanistan from Iran, to Burma from Bangladesh, to Rwanda from Tanzania and the Democratic Republic of Congo, and to Haiti from the United States. In the year 2000, this sad record continued—for example, with Burmese refugees being forcibly returned from Thailand.

Solutions

The international community has pursued three kinds of durable solutions for refugees: repatriation, permanent integration into the country of first asylum, and resettlement to a third country. Each of the three has at times been viewed as the preferred solution. In the immediate postwar period, resettlement was favored as the solution for European refugees. In Africa in the 1960s and into the 1970s, many states showed tremendous hospitality to refugees from neighboring countries and made it possible for them to integrate into border regions where, often, the local population was ethnically related. Resettlement again had a vogue in Indochina in the twenty years after the Vietnam War, when more than 2 million refugees from Vietnam were resettled, mostly in the West. Fueled by optimism at the end of the Cold War, UNHCR declared that the 1990s would be the "Decade of Repatriation." Indeed millions of refugees did go home during the 1990s because peace agreements took hold in their countries, for example, in Cambodia, Mozambique, and the countries of Central America.

The preference for repatriation as the optimal solution for refugees has become strongly entrenched in the collective will of major donor states and countries hosting refugees. Yet attempts to compel repatriation have marred the track record of humanitarian response. Some of the repatriations of the 1990s took place in an atmosphere so coercive that the line between repatriation and refoulement was all but obliterated. This was the case in the return of Rwandan refugees from Tanzania to Rwanda in 1996, for example. Other repatriations helped people return to situations still dangerous and unstable enough to compromise basic protection principles—and pose a real threat of renewed flows, as happened with Angolan refugees who repatriated between 1994 and 1998. When a fragile peace agreement broke down definitively, renewed warfare displaced thousands of people for the second time.

The record of repatriation therefore is one of stunning success in some cases, such as: the return from India to the newly created nation of Bangladesh in 1972 of 10 million refugees in a safe and orderly fashion within a matter of weeks, the return to Cambodia of 350,000 people who had been in exile for ten years or more, and the remarkably swift voluntary repatriation to Kosovo in 1999. Yet even the relatively successful repatriations pose challenges as refugees return to lands devastated by war, having lost everything and sometimes facing resentment or hostility from people who stayed behind. Stabilizing the political and economic situation into which refugees repatriate has taken humanitarian agencies into new areas of activity designed to ensure that repatriation is truly a durable solution.

Assistance

Provision of life-saving humanitarian assistance to refugees is on the surface perhaps the least ambiguous of the elements of international response to refugee crises. It has unquestionably saved millions of lives. The intergovernmental organizations such as UNHCR, the World Food Program, and UN Children's Fund (UNICEF) as well as the ICRC and many of the large private humanitarian NGOs have learned a great deal from the experience of the past fifty years. They have acquired extraordinary technical skills in bringing relief to huge numbers of desperate people often in remote and inhospitable territory. They have learned to operate in harmony with military forces engaged in humanitarian work despite great differences in procedures, ethics, and approaches. They have developed and refined emergency response procedures, standby arrangements, and rapid response teams to be able to move quickly to minimize the loss of life.

Despite this formidable technical expertise, the record of assistance is mixed. Succor depends on visibility, access, political interest, and the still significant constraints on capability. The last of these are not just technical but also political. The international community has not devised effective ways (and has not been willing to expend the resources necessary to attempt to develop them) to provide assistance in the midst of armed conflict, as in Sierra Leone, or in the face of violent resistance from an armed faction, as at Srebrenica.

Despite the record of success in saving lives, humanitarian assistance also has a record of unintended negative consequences. It has been accused, with some justice, of undermining local coping mechanisms by flooding the field with externally supplied relief goods and foreign personnel.[10] The social structures, markets, labor relations, and lines of authority of many refugee communities have been disrupted, fostering dependency and retarding community development.

Even more serious is the contribution of assistance to prolonging and intensifying conflict. Humanitarian relief supplies are valuable commodities in territories devastated by war and are subject to siphoning off by armed elements associated with refugee populations as well as raiding by bandits or hostile forces. In Bosnia, UNHCR convoys were forced to accept the imposition of "taxes" on relief convoys by local militia roadblocks all along their routes. In Somalia, some critics have written about the emergence of a sophisticated war economy in which relief supplies and livestock are traded for arms. Vehicles stolen from humanitarian agencies have reappeared in military service. UNHCR was witheringly criticized for its provisioning of camps known to be run by Rwandan army and militia forces in Eastern Zaire who were intent on rebuilding their fighting forces. And military forces drawn to refugee camps by the availability of food, medicine, and so forth may draw fire on the civilians among whom they blend.

Humanitarian relief assistance may also prolong fighting by reducing the incentives for surrender that might prevail if the fighters' families were not being protected from terrible deprivation by international relief supplies. This was felt to be an element of the dynamic in the siege of Sarajevo, where UNHCR's success in keeping the city from starving while utterly failing to protect its residents from attack gave rise to bitter jokes about the "well-fed dead."

LESSONS LEARNED

The most general lesson learned from the experience of international response to refugee flows in the post–Cold War period is that a management regime cannot stand without the commitment, however reluctant, of those actors who have the means to turn its abstract rules and norms into reality. In the case of the refugee protection regime, the principal actors are national governments, particularly those of the industrialized states who provide the bulk of funding for international protection and humanitarian relief while also setting the parameters for legal and political responses. The governments of these states are influenced by other actors—international organizations, opposition forces, NGOs, churches, the media, advocates, and experts, among others—that may significantly alter their deliberations, but these actors will usually be effective through their influence on states rather than through direct action.

The effectiveness of international response to refugee issues has largely depended on the mix of interests, values, capabilities, and engagement that these powerful states have brought to bear on each refugee-producing situation. Since the end of the Cold War, the consensus among the Western industrialized states on the purpose and value of the traditional methods of refugee protection has eroded, robbing the regime of its coherence. Attempts to establish a new consensus around a "New International Humanitarian Order" or an "Agenda for Peace," or to reinvigorate the old consensus have not proved successful. Management of refugee issues in the post–Cold War period has therefore been mostly ad hoc and crisis driven, aimed at least as much at protecting the wealthy industrialized countries from refugees as at protecting refugees from their persecutors.

In the abstract, a new approach to international protection—built around prevention and sparing people the pain of exile—is highly desirable. But the states with material and political resources sufficient to implement a new approach of "bringing safety to people rather than people to safety" have not been willing to allocate them for this purpose. In the absence of a wholehearted collective commitment to this goal, the dispiriting lesson may be that a relatively narrow, palliative regime is the most ambitious that can be supported by international consensus at this time. To abandon the older, asylum-based model of the post–World War II period in favor of an elusive model in which people do not have to flee is to exchange some hard-won protection for a chimera.

Agenda Setting

Hitler and Stalin set the agenda for international response to refugee crises in two different and often contradictory ways. The reaction to Hitler's "final solution" can be summed up in the "never again" pledge that has been invoked to mobilize international revulsion against attempts to eliminate (through genocide, ethnic cleansing, or mass expulsion) whole groups of people defined by their ethnicity, religion, race, or social group. Similarly, the reaction to Stalin's violent suppression of all political dissent established the refugee regime as both an avenue of escape for the courageous dissident and an effective tool of geopolitical contest. Those who have tried to set the agenda for international response to particular crises ever since have had to work within the framework of these two poles. A number of lessons for agenda setting follow from this observation; others emerge from other technological and political trends.

The agenda for international response to refugee issues is heavily shaped by the crisis of the day and the political interests that powerful states have in it. Long-running refugee situations tend to fall lower on the agenda of policy concern. Several other factors help shape the agenda:

- *Historical analogy is a powerful attention-getter.* A refugee outflow is more likely to get the attention of Western politicians and publics if the perpetrator can be portrayed as a latter-day Hitler (Pol Pot) or Stalin (Saddam Hussein) and the threat to the targeted population is cast as genocidal. In the case of the Rwandan Tutsis in 1994, the genocide analogy was entirely accurate, although the deserved attention came too late to save 800,000 victims. In the case of the Biafran civil war, genocide was never the intention of Nigerian federal forces, but highly effective propaganda on the part of the Biafran separatists mobilized international support for their cause nonetheless. The coincidence of the forcible expulsion of the Albanian population from Kosovo in 1999 (some in railroad boxcars) with the release of a popular film about the persecution of Italian Jews (*Life Is Beautiful*) probably helped to mobilize European public opinion for military action in Kosovo.

- *Geography matters.* Refugees in the Middle East are high on the agenda of the Arab states and their people; Balkan refugees are of particular interest to Europeans; Australia's people and politicians took the lead in East Timor; and Nigeria's leaders in Liberia. The United States tends to give refugee flows in Europe and Central America and the Caribbean higher priority than those in other neighborhoods.

- *The mass media are a fulcrum for leveraging action.* International organizations such as UNHCR and operational NGOs such as Oxfam and Médecins sans Frontières have become immensely sophisticated in waging media campaigns directly, or feeding information to the media, to generate support for humanitarian response (which includes funding for their own operations). In addition, as BBC journalist Nik Gowing has written, the opposing sides in many refugee-producing conflicts have also learned the power of television images and attempt to provide the images of human suffering that will serve their political ends.[11] At the extreme, some have been accused of staging atrocities, such as the 1994 Sarajevo marketplace bombing, for the television cameras. The advent of new media, in particular the Internet, and the twenty-four-hour news cycle have opened access to a much larger group of players but have also increased the difficulty of getting serious attention from overloaded policy makers and gatekeepers in the major news organizations.

Invisibility is an enemy of people in need of protection. Both refugee advocates and persecutors have learned well this central fact of the age of mass media and attempt to influence (or manipulate) news coverage of displacement, its causes, and the suffering it generates. NGOs that have reporting and monitoring as a central part of their mission, such as the U.S. Committee for Refugees, the International Crisis Group, and Human Rights Watch, have played important roles in galvanizing governmental response to displaced people by reporting from the field directly to governmental decision makers and to the public through their own publications and the news media. These campaigns not only inform people about a particular issue but make it more difficult for governmental decision makers to justify inaction with protestations of ignorance.

"Compassion fatigue" is a myth, at least among the general public. Since the mid-1980s at least, pundits have predicted that the public would become inured to reports of suffering and that the sight of one more starving refugee child on a magazine cover would fail to move them to demand action from their leaders. But humanitarian issues still command a response from Western publics, manifest in private donations to relief organizations and communications to political representatives demanding that these issues are put on the policy agenda. The psychological burnout implied by compassion fatigue seems to affect reporters and policy makers more severely than front-line humanitarian workers or members of the public.

Policy makers may effectively satisfy media-generated public demands for action with ineffective action. A leaky sanctions regime as in Burma, protracted political negotiation as in the Middle East, or a humanitarian aid program in place of protection or political action, as in Bosnia prior to the Dayton negotiations, provide what is sometimes referred to as a "humanitarian fig leaf" to governments that are under pressure to "do something"—but are not willing to take decisive action.

Coalitions of human rights groups, refugee advocates, analysts, sympathetic bureaucrats, and politicians can shift the agenda on specific topics. For example, refugee resettlement agencies in the United States worked over the course of several years in the late 1990s to reverse the declining number of refugees brought to the United States for permanent resettlement—a number agreed upon by the U.S. Department of State and Congress each year. An analytical base was established in roundtable discussions at Washington think-tanks; politicians responded to old-fashioned constituency politics from local branches of the resettlement agencies and questioned State Department officials; sympathetic officials reported to their bosses on the (rare) domestic concern about a foreign policy issue. The decline in resettlement quotas was reversed, with budget appropriations to support the change.

The agenda for management of refugee issues lacks coherence in large part because it is set by a variety of actors with different goals. Amid the incoherence, however, the agenda has shifted discernibly since the end of the Cold War. The rigid, geopolitically driven framework of the earlier period has relaxed considerably. With strategic concerns no longer driving refugee policy in every case, there is more room for human rights concerns, ethnic constituencies, and other forces to influence the protection agenda.

Negotiation

Negotiations on refugee issues focus on access, admissions, recognition, levels of assistance, and conditions of return. Almost all negotiations involve some level of international funding, which itself requires negotiation. As the bearer of the mandate for refugee protection, UNHCR is normally involved in negotiations on refugee-related subjects, but occasionally they take place exclusively among states. Both UNHCR and some governments routinely enter into discussions with NGO representatives, advocates, and experts to test reaction to a proposed course of action and seek support for it. These exchanges are not negotiations in a formal sense, but they share some of the character of negotiations in that positions or plans are altered to accommodate other parties. Some brief examples illustrate the great range of negotiations on refugees issues.

Access to refugees and internally displaced people is often the necessary first step in providing assistance and protection, and the forces that control access to refugee-populated areas are often willing to use it as a bargaining chip. UNHCR has had difficult negotiations with local military authorities and militia groups in West Timor to gain entry to camps housing people who fled from East Timor and in some cases were forcibly prevented from returning home. UNHCR gained formal access to the Thai side of the Thai-Burma border only in 1999 (it still has no access to the Burmese side) and now is permitted to monitor the deliberations of Thai admissions boards. Access for international monitors and assistance providers is usually a part of negotiations on repatriation of refugee groups.

Admissions are perhaps the most contentious subject of negotiations between UNHCR and refugee advocates on the one hand and governments on the other. Governments use a variety of justifications for refusing entry to refugees and asylum seekers. They may label them as illegal immigrants motivated by the desire for economic advancement rather than fear of persecution, as the U.S. government did with most Haitian refugees in the 1980s and early 1990s, and as Thailand continues to do with respect to many Burmese refugees. They may acknowledge refugees' claims for international protection but insist that they should have sought it in another country, as is the practice of many European states toward asylum seekers who have transited through a third country where they could have filed their claim. Or states may simply close their borders to the extent they can, invoking national security concerns that override their protection obligations. Turkey used this rationale to refuse to admit Kurdish refugees in 1991, as did Macedonia vis-à-vis the Kosovar Albanians for a few critical weeks in 1999. In each case, UNHCR encourages the government concerned to fulfill the spirit as well as the letter of the Refugee Convention, while NGO advocates often campaign publicly to reinforce the message.

Recognition of refugee status turns on some of the same questions as admissions, such as whether a person's flight is motivated by a well-founded fear of persecution or another reason that would not entitle him or her to international protection. Most of the wealthy industrialized states have highly evolved refugee determination procedures that are meant to bring objective criteria to bear on status determination, but in less well endowed countries recognition is often a matter of negotiation with UNHCR and/or concerned states that take an interest in a particular group of refugees. Domestic constituency groups often play an important role in advocating for recognition of a particular group as refugees. In some cases, diplomatic, economic, or military support for the host state may be the de facto price of recognizing refugees as such. States also negotiate nonrecognition of refugee status with each other. Members of the Commonwealth of Independent States have agreed not to recognize each other's nationals as being in need of international protection. The European Union has entertained a similar proposal for its member states.

Outside assistance is often critical in shoring up a reluctant government's willingness to receive refugees, who in many cases do indeed place a large burden on host communities in economic, environmental, and social terms. NGOs and refugee advocates urge donor countries to provide generously for refugee assistance. The humanitarian interests and institutional self-interest of many of the large, private-sector refugee relief agencies coincide, as the agencies depend on government and UNHCR contracts for a large proportion of their operating budgets.

The conditions of return of refugees to their countries of origin must be negotiated among the refugees themselves, UNHCR, the host government, and the government of the country of origin (although many refugees repatriate themselves outside of any negotiated framework by just going home). In many cases, other interested parties join the process of either formally or informally negotiating return. Nongovernmental human rights groups and assistance agencies have played important roles in monitoring the treatment of returnees, sounding the alarm when they encounter danger, and putting pressure on UNHCR and concerned governments to take appropriate action—including the suspension of repatriation. Negotiations dealing with return are at their most complex when repatriation is one element of a comprehensive plan involving peace negotiations, reconstruction, democratization, and other elements of stabilization.

In addition to the above negotiations on specific issues, UNHCR, with the support of the governments that are members of its Executive Committee, initiated in 2000 a process of "global consultations" designed to shore up the base of international consensus on refugee protection as laid out in the 1951 Convention Relating to the Status of Refugees. UNHCR has stated firmly that the provisions of the convention itself are not negotiable, and that the consultations are meant to address problems of interpretation connected to the convention and gaps in the coverage of existing refugee law. Refugee advocates, however, have expressed concern that instances of retreat from core principles of international protection are often presented as legitimate issues of interpretation.[12] For example, French and German courts have recently begun to read the 1951 Convention as extending protection only to people who are persecuted by agents of a recognized state authority—leaving out those persecuted by an insurgent group such as the Islamic Salvation Front (FIS) in Algeria, an unrecognized de facto government such as the Taliban in Afghanistan, or any force in a "failed state" such as Somalia that has no functioning government. NGOs have insisted on being part of the global consultations, and UNHCR has agreed to include them in the process.

From the complex record of negotiations on refugee issues, a few general lessons stand out:

- *A commitment to burden sharing can shore up protection by relieving the financial burden on countries of first asylum, or by offering to resettle willing refugees to a third country.* Both techniques were used to persuade Macedonia to reopen its borders to Kosovar refugees in the spring of 1999. Germany, which received more refugees from former Yugoslavia than all the other Western European countries combined, has called for a preemptive plan for burden sharing associated with spontaneous arrivals in the European Union.

- *Incentives work, but not always.* The right to control admissions to one's territory is an acknowledged privilege of the sovereign state. Countries of first asylum have driven some hard bargains beyond the direct arrangements for burden sharing, securing promises of foreign investment, debt relief, and other concessions. So have countries of origin in negotiations over the return of their nationals. However, a government that perceives its fundamental security to be threatened by a refugee influx, such as Turkey in 1991, will not necessarily respond to incentives to open its borders.

- *Nonbinding agreements are easier to negotiate than binding agreements.* States will often actually do more than they will formally commit themselves to doing.

- *NGOs, intergovernmental organizations, and sympathetic governments can form effective coalitions to press for higher standards of protection in negotiations on admission, recognition, and repatriation.*

- *Norms of protection can work their way from mere aspirational guidelines to "soft law" to harder law.* The process begins with the systematic articulation of norms, proceeds through their adoption by intergovernmental organizations (regional or universal) or coalitions of states to the point where they are acknowledged as customary law and are written into domestic legislation or enter into domestic jurisprudence of some of the states that observe them. A binding international instrument may eventually result; many observers see this as the logical end of the process by which the protection of internally displaced people is currently being brought into the realm of soft law.

Implementation

In implementing controls over who may enter the territory of a state, migration-related concerns trump refugee protection. The early 1990s saw a sharp rise in the number of asylum seekers who came to Europe and North America and applied for recognition as refugees. In the same period, refugees from former Yugoslavia, Cuba, and Haiti overwhelmed the processing capacity and the political will of their wealthy neighbors, who cracked down on unauthorized entry in ways that made it difficult for refugees to access the asylum systems of the West. Refugee and human rights advocates insist on the primacy of refugee protection as a treaty obligation and a fundamental value, but the domestic political imperative to combat illegal immigration takes priority.

The wealthy industrialized states set the tone for other states. Increasingly restrictionist policies in European and North American states have been imitated and cited as justification for similar policies in places as distant as Thailand and Tanzania. If wealthy and stable countries cannot bear the burden of proportionally much smaller flows of refugees and asylum seekers, how should poor and struggling countries be expected to cope?

One of the lessons bearing on implementation is that an overloaded agenda is less likely to be realized successfully, but a narrower one risks becoming irrelevant. Refugee matters are intimately connected to issues of development, conflict resolution, democratization, gender equality, nation building, and much else. The tendency in the 1990s was to approach refugee issues holistically to address their causes, in hopes of preempting displacement, and to recognize their lingering consequences, to secure a stable resolution. The logic of this broadened agenda was impeccable, and there were some modest successes in applying a more comprehensive approach. The peace process in Central America, for example, embedded refugee repatriation in a comprehensive package of political reform, human rights protection, and development assistance. It was far from a panacea, but the returns did prove to be durable.

At the same time that the refugee agenda was expanding temporally from root causes to the postconflict period, it was also expanding to take in other groups of people—not just those seeking protection from persecution outside their own countries but also internally displaced people and populations affected by war who had not moved at all. The expansion—some would say explosion—of the refugee protection agenda into a much broader humanitarian agenda has diffused the focus and leadership of the actors involved, particularly UNHCR. The core legal obligation of non-refoulement risks being lost in an endlessly unmanageable menu in which the principles of protection may be traded off for more transitory practical gains. This debate has revealed deep fault lines within the refugee policy community, with one side caricatured as "protection purists" and the other as "unprincipled pragmatists."

Reactions to Noncompliance

The central instruments of international refugee law—the 1951 Convention and its 1967 Protocol—are not self-implementing. In other words, to be enforced through formal judicial proceedings, they must be incorporated into the domestic law of signatory states. Thus, for example, although the United States signed the 1967 Protocol in 1969, it did not reform its domestic law until the passage of the 1980 Refugee Act. Implementation of refugee protection imposes certain requirements on states party to the convention or protocol, or states that are not parties to the treaties but wish to comply with their provisions nonetheless. They must have some administrative procedure in place to distinguish refugees from other immigrants, and they must have officials trained to implement the regulations that govern the treatment of refugees on the territory of the state.

There are no mechanisms in international refugee law to compel a state to comply with its obligations as a signatory to the convention and/or protocol. Therefore, UNHCR, other states, and refugee advocates must rely on diplomatic pressure, persuasion, and incentives to encourage reluctant states to implement provisions for international protection. UNHCR assists states to comply by offering training to their officials and mobilizing resources to develop their protection infrastructure. Along with the ICRC and other intergovernmental organizations such as the Organization for Security and Cooperation in Europe (OSCE), UNHCR monitors compliance and gives feedback to governments on their performance. Private organizations also monitor and report on the implementation of refugee protection.

If the international mechanisms for encouraging compliance are relatively thin, domestic resources are much more ample in states that have incorporated refugee protection instruments into national law. Court cases brought by refugees themselves or by refugee advocates on their behalf have clarified and made more specific the requirements of compliance. There is, however, considerable inconsistency among countries and even among courts within the same country. UNHCR frequently files "friend of the court" briefs to support an interpretation of national laws consistent with its interpretation of the convention. NGOs also provide briefs, expert witnesses, and pro bono representation of refugees in court and often are the claimant on behalf of a class of refugees.

Increasingly, regional courts are emerging as venues for testing compliance with refugee law. This is especially true of the European Court of Human Rights, where individual claimants can submit cases.

Just as there is no formal international mechanism for compelling compliance with refugee law, there is no formal mechanism for sanctioning noncompliance. The informal mechanisms include shaming, the use of sanctions from outside the realm of refugee law, and further negotiation. The use of incentives as a reaction to noncompliance has created a serious problem of moral hazard by rewarding bad behavior. In the face of Turkish refusal to admit Kurdish refugees stranded in hostile mountain territory, Malaysian return of Vietnamese boat people to serious peril on the high seas, or Macedonian border closings that left unsheltered refugees exposed to harsh weather, the international community responded with exceptional measures to accommodate the fears of the receiving countries—through a "safe haven" created in Northern Iraq for the Kurds, a massive resettlement program for Vietnamese refugees in first asylum countries in Southeast Asia, and a humanitarian evacuation program for Kosovars in Macedonia. Surely a lesson for the future is that rewarding noncompliance will only encourage recalcitrance in the future.

CONCLUSION

Providing protection to the people who reside within the territory it controls is a central function of the sovereign state. The regime of international refugee protection was designed to shore up the system of sovereign states at those points of weakness where a state proved incapable or unwilling to observe that fundamental obligation. The remedy of international involvement would protect refugees who had been forced to flee to another country, but it would also protect the state system from the perils of dysfunctionality. In the twenty-first century, the state system is faced with many challenges to its functionality, ranging from transnational forces to atomizing local loyalties. It is perhaps not surprising that refugee protection based on Westphalian notions of sovereignty is under challenge. But it is at least somewhat surprising that the defenders of the sovereignty-based system of protection include many institutions and individuals who embody the challenges to that system: human rights activists, humanitarian NGOs, refugee advocates, and transnational networks that link them all. They have, however, shifted the debate on refugee protection away from the state-centered framework toward a human rights framework that is more firmly centered on the needs of refugees.

The deterioration of the classic, asylum-centered refugee regime can be seen as a reaction on the part of states to the increasing difficulty they have in managing their borders and ports of entry. Countries of asylum in the North—and increasingly in the South—are gripped by fear that providing asylum to people genuinely in need of protection will open the floodgates to a rising tide of economic migrants posing as refugees. Many of the new ways of reacting to actual or potential refugee flows are aimed at deflecting rather than protecting people.

Refugees today face increasingly limited choices of where to seek protection or when to return home. There is considerable convergence around a new set of rules and practices that emphasize state control of admissions, restrictions on access to and duration of asylum, an emphasis on humanitarian assistance over protection, and the erosion of refugee rights.

Much of the new mode of response is not readily acknowledged. While practices are converging, there is not much consensus on norms, principles, or laws. Few of the innovations are codified in international law. The public face of international protection of refugees is still the 1951 Convention Relating to the Status of Refugees, but by default. Verbal commitment to the principles embodied in the convention is common but increasingly empty as states continue to derive ways of breaking the spirit without necessarily violating the letter of the convention.

The Office of the High Commissioner for Refugees has been much criticized for going along too easily with some of the innovations in refugee protection, such as temporary protection and in-country protection, which have proven in specific instances to be unsatisfactory in filling the commitments of the Refugee Convention.

The office is urged by refugee advocates to stand firm on the convention. But many within UNHCR have recognized that to stand still is to go backward in the debate on refugee protection in the twenty-first century. Improvement in security for millions of refugees will be found in innovations—as will some of the deterioration. Innovation will be a high-risk endeavor, as some states and other actors see the possibility to erode further or to evade their responsibility for protection. The danger and the opportunity in opening a debate on new models of protection cannot be separated. New tools are undoubtedly needed to meet changed circumstances. Yet nothing can guarantee that they will be more protective of refugees' rights than the ones they replace except the strenuous engagement of stakeholders at every level in the continuing effort to shape the evolving protection regime.

NOTES

1. States signing the protocol were permitted to retain the geographic limitation to Europe if they so chose.
2. According to the 1951 Convention as amended by the 1967 Protocol, a refugee is a person who "owing to a well-founded fear of being persecuted for reasons of race, religion, nationality, membership in a particular social group or political opinion, is outside the country of his nationality and is unable to or, owing to such fear, unwilling to avail himself of the protection of that country; or, who not having a nationality and being outside the country of his former habitual residence . . . is unable or, owing to such fear, unwilling to return to it."
3. A diplomatic conference, convened by the UN Secretary-General, met in 1977 to consider and adopt a Convention on Territorial Asylum but was unable to fulfill its mandate. It had not been reconvened as of the beginning of 2001. See Volker Turk, "The Role of UNHCR in the Development of International Refugee Law," in Frances Nicholson and Patrick Twomey, eds., *Refugee Rights and Realities: Evolving International Concepts and Regimes* (Cambridge, U.K.: Cambridge University Press, 1999).
4. Shepard Forman, "Underwriting Humanitarian Assistance: Mobilizing Resources for Effective Action," paper prepared for the Center on International Cooperation, New York, January 1999.
5. For a detailed account of this history, see UNHCR, *The State of the World's Refugees, 2000: Fifty Years of Humanitarian Action* (Oxford, U.K.: Oxford University Press, 2000).
6. Forman, "Underwriting Humanitarian Assistance."
7. UNHCR, *The State of the World's Refugees, 1995: In Search of Solutions* (New York: Oxford University Press, 1995).
8. U.S. Committee for Refugees, *World Refugee Survey, 2000* (Washington, D.C.: U.S. Committee for Refugees, 2000).
9. Bill Frelick, "The Year in Review," *World Refugee Survey, 1997* (Washington, D.C.: U.S. Committee for Refugees, 1997), p. 14.

10. See Barbara E. Harrell-Bond, *Imposing Aid: Emergency Assistance to Refugees* (Oxford, U.K.: Oxford University Press, 1986).

11. Nik Gowing, "Real-time Television Coverage of Armed Conflicts and Diplomatic Crises: Does It Pressure or Distort Foreign Policy Decisions?" Working Paper 94-1 (Cambridge, Mass.: The Joan Shorenstein Barone Center on the Press, Politics, and Public Policy, John F. Kennedy School of Government, Harvard University, 1994).

12. Letter from Bill Frelick, U.S. Committee for Refugees, to Erika Feller, Director of International Protection, UNHCR, dated September 12, 2000.

SUGGESTED ADDITIONAL READING

Forsythe, David P. *Humanitarian Politics: The International Committee of the Red Cross*. Baltimore, Md.: Johns Hopkins University Press, 1977.

Goodwin-Gill, Guy S. "The International Protection of Refugees: What Future?" *International Journal of Refugee Law*, vol.12, no. 1 (2000), pp. 1–6.

Goodwin-Gill, Guy S. *The Refugee in International Law*. Oxford, U.K.: Oxford University Press, 1996.

Harding, Jeremy. *The Uninvited: Refugees at the Rich Man's Gate*. London: Profile Books and the London Review of Books, 2000.

Newland, Kathleen, and Demetrios Papademetriou. "Managing International Migration: Tracking the Emergence of a New International Regime." *UCLA Journal of International Law and Foreign Affairs*, vol. 3, no. 2 (Fall/Winter 1998–1999), pp. 637–57.

Nicholson, Frances, and Patrick Twomey, eds. *Refugee Rights and Realities: Evolving International Concepts and Regimes*. Cambridge, U.K.: Cambridge University Press, 1999.

Roberts, Adam. "More Refugees, Less Asylum: A Regime in Transformation." *Journal of Refugee Studies*, vol. 11, no. 4 (1998), pp. 375–95.

Steiner, Niklaus. *Arguing About Asylum: The Complexity of Refugee Debates in Europe*. New York: St. Martin's Press, 2000.

UN High Commissioner for Refugees. *The State of the World's Refugees*. New York: Oxford University Press, 1993, 1995, 1997, and 2000.

U.S. Committee for Refugees. *World Refugee Survey*. Annual publication of the U.S. Committee for Refugees. Washington, D.C.: U.S. Committee for Refugees.

Internet Sites

UN High Commissioner for Refugees (UNHCR) <http://www.unhcr.ch>
U.S. Committee for Refugees <http://www.refugees.org>
International Committee of the Red Cross (ICRC) <http://www.icrc.org>

14

Violence: Intrastate Conflict

Timothy D. Sisk

THE DAWN OF THE TWENTIETH-FIRST CENTURY witnessed twenty-seven major armed conflicts around the globe.[1] Twenty of these were in Africa and Asia, with the remainder occurring in the Middle East, Europe, and South America. With the exception of two international wars, today's conflicts are internal conflicts, or civil wars, taking place primarily within the borders of sovereign states.[2]

Civil wars rose to the top of the international peace and security agenda in the early 1990s.[3] Bosnia's civil war from 1991 to 1995, and the 1994 Rwanda genocide, which left nearly 800,000 dead in a hundred days and produced some 1.7 million refugees, poignantly demonstrated the severe consequences of internal conflicts and the tangible and moral dilemmas they present for both neighboring countries and broader international society.

Today's civil wars pose pressing global problems. They generate refugee flows that require expensive humanitarian assistance, regional instabilities that impede trade, and threats to civilian populations. Indeed, in many of these wars, international norms prohibiting attacks against civilian populations are ignored. In the worst cases, crimes against humanity are perpetrated.

International responses by regional and global powers have varied and ranged from doing very little to stem the killing, to diplomatic efforts to try to stop wars, to the launching of multidimensional peacekeeping operations, to the imposition of coercive measures such as economic sanctions, to the use of force. International intervention has been very strong in instances such as Kosovo in 1999, where military force by Western powers was used to respond to allegations of gross violations of human rights. In other cases, however, external powers have been reluctant to intervene in internal disputes, such as in Sudan. This inconsistency between action and inaction characterizes today's global responses to civil wars.[4]

Significant international interventions involving major commitment of personnel and resources (such as the deployment of military forces) are usually triggered under two conditions: (1) the interests of powerful states are directly affected (interest-based intervention) or (2) gross violations of human rights occur (norm-based intervention). Legitimacy for such interventions is usually sought in the UN Security Council.[5]

This chapter examines the rapidly evolving international responses to civil wars and other intrastate violence in the 1990s and draws lessons with regard to agenda setting, negotiation, implementation and compliance, and reactions to noncompliance.[6] I argue that the agenda for intervention is set by powerful countries that either seek to intervene or by those that seek to oppose intervention. Although the news media or nongovernmental organizations (NGOs) may shine the spotlight on a conflict and highlight the humanitarian and other externalities, policy makers at the national or international level ultimately decide on whether the United Nations, regional organizations, or states acting alone or in an ad hoc coalition will intervene with an assertive diplomatic and/or military initiative.

When the United Nations or others intervene, negotiations occur at two levels: (1) among intervening states and (2) among intervenors and disputants. The former set of negotiations involves coordination and agreements on burden sharing. A lesson learned from these negotiations is that one country or institution has to take the lead. Such a country or institution should serve as a focal point for the plethora of actors involved in a complex international intervention. Negotiations with the parties in the conflict involve efforts to move them toward peace agreements and to have them abide by agreements reached. The lesson here is that outside actors need to better coordinate the civilian and military elements of intervention.

Implementation requires action on two fronts. First, those intervening have to make sure that they provide sufficient resources to do the job. The 1990s was rife with examples in which this was not the case. Second, implementation and compliance with peace agreements requires establishing security in the short term, building new political institutions in the medium term, and promoting democracy and reconciliation in the long term. Noncompliance with peace agreements has taught lessons on managing those who would undermine a nascent peace: tools include isolation, punishment by force or with sanctions, or the provision of positive incentives to gain compliance. A critical lesson learned is that effective demobilization of combatants is key in avoiding the resumption of violence. When demobilization and disarmament do not occur voluntarily, intervening actors must be prepared to authorize and use military force to make parties comply with previously agreed-upon agreements.

Today's system for the promotion and maintenance of international peace and security through the UN Security Council was created to resolve a certain type of threat to peace: wars *between* states. The system is not yet well suited, however, to responding to war *within* states. With the new challenges to peace, major structural reform of the UN system is required to create a more effective system to maintain and promote peace and security. However, such reform is unlikely. In the meantime, modest evolutionary changes in the design and conduct of peacekeeping operations may improve the situation somewhat. The most promising feasible reform in the near term is the creation of a standing UN rapid reaction force, of 5,000 to 15,000 troops, with a militarily robust capability and global reach. Such a force should be created along with a set of clear criteria for deployment and operational guidelines that would allow intervention in those situations where gross violations of human rights are expected to occur or have already occurred. Together with the evolution of new norms and institutions, such as the International Criminal Tribunal for the prosecution of war crimes perpetrators, a standing UN force would significantly improve the international regime designed to end the scourge of war.

CIVIL WARS: CAUSES, CHARACTERISTICS, AND CONSEQUENCES

Although popular views of the 1990s describe all civil wars as ethnic group rivalries, in fact the causes of war have varied greatly. Some wars were caused by state failure, which occurred when a troubled regime finally imploded, as in Somalia or Afghanistan. In some—such as the wars in the successor states of the Soviet Union, including Russia, and in the former Yugoslavia—civil wars broke out as previously multinational federations disintegrated. Some civil wars featured classic characteristics of revolutions, such as the uprising in the Mexican province of Chiapas. Revolutions of this type are considered primarily class-based (although the rebels are fighting for indigenous group rights), but revolutionary violence in other instances (such as Algeria) is grounded in tensions between secular and religious views of society. Finally, some wars are caused by a scramble for riches, such as the so-called diamond wars in Sierra Leone and Angola, which feature struggles over mineral wealth. Exclusive nationalist ideologies, leaders who exploit group tensions for personal gain, economic disparities among groups, and dramatic transitions in economic and political structures (such as the collapse of the Yugoslav federation in 1990–1991) all played a role. Sometimes events such as failed elections or rapid changes in political leadership could be pointed to as the immediate causes of violent conflict.

Contemporary civil wars have markedly different characteristics from international—interstate—conflicts. Foremost are the high stakes particularly in internal conflicts that center on ethnicity and religion. An opponent's military may be defeated on the battlefield, but conquering an entire ethnic group requires genocide, forced assimilation, or "ethnic cleansing." It follows that attitudes and preferences are much more intense than in conventional international wars.

Second, today's civil wars are often multipolar, with splintering and factionalism among the parties. Governments and rebel groups, paramilitary militias, warlords, and organized criminal enterprises are usually involved. Often the parties are disparate, faction ridden, and incoherent, without a clear organizational structure, a single, well-integrated leadership, or a public mandate for action.

Third, although these conflicts are called "internal," there are almost always cross-border linkages among groups and organizations that obfuscate the arenas of conflict. Often insurgent groups and states have patron-client relationships (or special linkages) with neighboring states and groups, as well as networks with like-minded combatants in other conflict situations; these linkages provide important sources of material support and a feeling of legitimacy for their actions. Restive minorities in one state will often provoke grievances in neighboring states. Indeed, ethnic conflict spreads by diffusion (when violence in one state leads to heightened tensions among similar groups in other states) and escalation (where violence in one state helps instigate a conflict spiral and the outbreak of violence in a neighboring state).[7]

The consequences of civil wars must be measured not only in terms of regional stability but also in humanitarian costs, violations of human rights, forgone opportunities for trade and investment, and environmental degradation. In human terms, refugees and internally displaced persons reflect the impact of war on societies. Today there are 11.5 million refugees on the globe who have sought shelter in countries other than their own, and an additional 6.7 million people are displaced within their own countries.[8] The costs of caring for these refugees and providing emergency assistance in conflict situations are staggering. At present, governments spend about $4 billion per year in emergency aid. According to Shepard Forman and Rita Parhad, humanitarian assistance rose sharply in the 1990s. They report that

> the proportion of official development assistance (ODA) which the industrialized countries spend on emergency aid has quintupled since the early 1980s. Since 1990, over $30 billion has been spent on humanitarian assistance, with more than 80% coming from OECD governments. Annual aggregate funding levels peaked at around $7 billion in 1994, and have since leveled off at $3–4 billion per year.[9]

In addition to the high social and economic costs, the moral basis of international society is undermined by flagrant violations of international standards on human rights. In many recent civil wars, both human rights and the rules governing the conduct of war have been violated, and crimes against humanity—such as genocide and forced migration or "ethnic cleansing"—have been perpetrated.[10] In some interventions, such as Kosovo, action has been explicitly justified in reference to global norms on the prevention and halting of such crimes against humanity.

There are also very tangible economic and social consequences of war. The costs are tallied by losses in economic development and growth, limits on exports and food production, and higher infant mortality rates. Moreover, war-torn societies exhibit lower rates of savings and investment, and greater expenditures on military equipment and personnel in lieu of investments in social services. Researchers have shown a direct relationship between war and impoverishment, leading to a decline in social conditions that may in fact sow the seeds for further conflict.[11]

War also leads to serious environmental degradation. From the burning of Kuwait's oil fields by retreating Iraqi forces in 1991, to massive deforestation in eastern Democratic Republic of Congo, to the use of depleted uranium munitions in the Kosovo conflict, recent wars with modern technologies have left a legacy of environmental harm in their wake. Among the environmental impacts of war are devastated agricultural lands, hazardous waste, contaminated water, deforestation, threats to endangered species, and atmospheric pollution, among others.[12] Environmental problems during war also lead to conditions ripe for the incubation of infectious disease.

INTERNATIONAL INTERVENTION IN CIVIL WARS

The global consequences of civil wars are such that no single state, acting alone, can possibly muster the external legitimacy, resources, and staying power to intervene for peace. Single-state intervention has not been very successful. When India agreed to perform unilateral peacekeeping in Sri Lanka between 1987 and 1990, for example, it found its forces becoming embroiled in the war as a party to the fighting instead of acting as an impartial monitor. Even the United States, which has a long record of unilateral intervention in Central American states, felt compelled to seek UN Security Council mandates for its multilateral mission to promote peace in Haiti in 1994. Multilateral efforts spread the risks of intervention, and UN Security Council mandates, when they are possible, provide legal authority and external legitimacy.

Actors

One of the most rapidly changing aspects of global responses to civil wars is the proliferation of different types of intervenors in today's conflicts. Four different actors can be distinguished.

United Nations. The UN Security Council has primary political responsibility for the restoration and maintenance of international peace and security, and it retains a preeminent role in authorizing measures to promote peace and security—especially coercive measures.[13] Within the Security Council, the five permanent members (China, France, Russia, the United Kingdom, and the United States) are the critical actors. Russia and China have more consistently opposed multilateral intervention in civil wars, in part because they too have experienced internal conflicts in Chechnya and

Tibet, respectively. France, the United Kingdom, and the United States have been more interventionist.

Operational responsibilities lie with the UN Secretariat. Within the Secretariat the principal actors are the Secretary-General, the Department of Political Affairs, the Department of Peacekeeping Operations, and the special envoys appointed by the Secretary-General. In addition, specialized programs of the United Nations such as the UN High Commissioner for Refugees (UNHCR), the UN Development Program (UNDP), the World Health Organization (WHO), and other agencies have also had major operational responsibilities. Finally, international financial institutions—the World Bank in particular—have supported peacemaking and peace-building efforts in their economic assistance activities.[14]

Early in 2000, approximately 27,000 UN peacekeepers were deployed around the world, along with 8,600 civilian police officers. An additional 8,000 were authorized to deploy once conditions on the ground had been met. The UN Secretary-General has named dozens of high-level mediators in various conflict settings.[15] The goals of intervention are multiple and include preventive action, peacekeeping, peace enforcement, and postsettlement peace building.

Increasingly in intrastate conflict situations, expanded peace operations are organized and launched on an ad hoc basis, usually but not always authorized by the United Nations. Such operations by coalitions of the willing are unique responses to specific circumstances threatening to international peace. They differ from traditional peacekeeping operations in that they frequently do not involve local consent; moreover, they tend to reflect the post–Cold War realignment in regional and global coalitions.[16]

Although such ad hoc interventionist initiatives are now routinely legitimated by the UN Security Council, they are often directed by powerful states (within or outside the region) or regional organizations: for example, the U.S.-led intervention in Somalia in 1992 and in Haiti in 1994; the French intervention in Rwanda in 1994, Operation Turquoise; NATO intervention in Bosnia in 1995; the Italian-led intervention in Albania in 1997; and the Australian-led intervention in East Timor in 2000. Intervention by the Economic Community of West African States (ECOWAS) in Liberia and Sierra Leone in 1994 as well as interventions led by the Commonwealth of Independent States in Tajikistan in 1992 and in Georgia in 1994 were authorized after the fact. Finally, the NATO bombing of Yugoslavia in 1999 had no UN authorization. See table 14-1.

Regional Organizations. Regional organizations have been active in the affairs of their members and neighbors.[17] For example, the North Atlantic Treaty Organization (NATO) intervened militarily in Bosnia and Kosovo; the ECOWAS intervened in Liberia and Sierra Leone; the Intergovernmental Authority on Development, an

Table 14-1. *Types of Multilateral Peace Operations*

	Intervening Agent	
	Multilateral Organization	*State-led Coalition*
Regional	*Regional Collective Security Organization* NATO's involvement in Bosnia and Kosovo; ECOMOG intervention in Liberia	*Regionally Powerful State* Italy-led intervention in Albania
Global	*Global Collective Security Organization* UN Peace Operations	*Globally Capable State* U.S.-led in Haiti; Canada-led in Zaire/Great Lakes (1994); France in Rwanda

Reach of Operation

Note: SFOR is the North Atlantic Treaty Organization's (NATO's) stabilization force in Bosnia. ECOMOG is the Economic Community Cease-Fire Monitoring Group of the Economic Community of West African States (ECOWAS).

East African regional organization, has sponsored mediation efforts to promote peace in Sudan; and the Organization of American States tried to mediate in Haiti.[18]

There are both advantages and disadvantages to this trend of having regional organizations intervene. They offer international intervenors an opportunity to wield real leverage in their efforts to negotiate and implement peace agreements. With greater flexibility over mandates, burden sharing, command and control, rules of engagement, planning, coordination with diplomatic initiatives, and ability to assume risks, outside intervenors have a real capacity to influence rival interests caught up in intrastate conflicts—a capacity that the United Nations currently lacks.

The disadvantages of operations launched outside direct UN operational control are that a regionally dominant state will intervene merely to extend its power. It is often claimed that Nigerian-led intervention in other West African states has more to do with the extension of that country's power in the region than it does in a good-faith response to the problems of war-torn neighbors. Especially when such military forays lack the specific authorization of the Security Council, the operation's legitimacy is rightly questioned. Finally, ad hoc efforts may suffer from operational problems such as a lack of experience in complex peacekeeping, an incoherent doctrine, or problems of coordination among participating states.

Individual States. Individual states acting alone remain important actors. Despite the more extensive role played by multilateral organizations, individual states continue to be involved in peacemaking efforts. For example, the ongoing effort of the United States to promote peace among Arabs and Israelis is a largely unilateral state-based intervention. Norway's mediation of the Sri Lanka dispute, beginning in 2000, is another example of a single state engaged in a unilateral intervention. At the other end of the spectrum, in mid-1994, during the height of the Rwandan genocide, the French government launched Operation Turquoise. The French intervention was motivated by a combination of factors such as embarrassment over past military support for the predominantly Hutu regime of President Juvenal Habyarimana (allegedly allowing arms shipments to the Hutu-led Rwandan government even after the genocide had begun), the desire to rescue their allies by blunting the advance of insurgent forces (thereby enabling the Rwandan army to escape to Zaire), and an ambition to remain an important player in the region. Many members of the United Nations therefore regarded French intervention with considerable skepticism.[19]

Nongovernmental Organizations. NGOs have increasingly become involved in civil wars.[20] NGOs have been particularly effective in aspects of agenda setting, such as pressuring governments to stop waging wars and in documenting gross violations of human rights during wartime. For example, during the Kosovo crisis of 1999, the Washington-based NGO, Refugees International, repeatedly published statements and bulletins urging forceful deployment of ground forces to halt alleged ethnic cleansing by the Government of Yugoslavia. In one bulletin in April 1999, an official of the organization argued that "to save [the Kosovars] will require a ground intervention. This will cost more American lives than planned, but this situation is partly of America's making and the United States cannot turn away from it."[21] In addition, NGOs have been involved on the ground as mediators between warring parties or as providers of humanitarian assistance. The South African-based Center for Conflict Resolution has been deeply involved in the peace negotiations in Burundi, for example, and it also has peacemaking programs in Angola and the Democratic Republic of Congo. Thomas Weiss and Sir Brian Urquhart have documented the extensive roles of NGOs working in the context of multidimensional peacekeeping operations in providing humanitarian relief in civil war settings.[22] Because NGOs are usually perceived to be neutral actors with only the best intentions, they are sometimes better able to engage different parties in deeply conflicted societies. They are also generally accepted as ideal providers of humanitarian assistance; however, Mary Anderson argues that humanitarian aid is often abused by contending parties in war because they hijack charity for their efforts to win on the battlefield.[23]

Instruments

Outside actors have different instruments at their disposal. An important distinction is that between noncoercive instruments—mediation, fact finding, peacekeeping, humanitarian assistance, and the use of financial incentives to bring about and maintain peace—and coercive instruments—the threat or use of economic sanctions or military force. The apprehension of individuals indicted by international criminal tribunals may also be counted as a coercive measure.[24]

Despite the continuing strength of the countervailing principles of sovereignty and noninterference, the international community is becoming less timid in intervening in the internal affairs of states. This change occurred rapidly in the 1990s, and at times the line between coercive and noncoercive actions became blurred. In a few cases, such as Kosovo or East Timor, outside powers resorted to "coercive diplomacy," that is, the careful combination of the threat of force with diplomatic efforts such as mediation.[25]

Donald Rothchild, in *Managing Ethnic Conflict in Africa: Pressures and Incentives for Cooperation*, has identified coercive measures and noncoercive incentives that mediators have used in negotiating with parties in a civil war.[26] His typology includes relatively benign incentives that provide disputants with rewards for altering their behavior and acting in a cooperative manner, such as offers of money or other resources (purchase), security guarantees such as deployment of peacekeepers or monitoring of compliance with peace agreements (insurance), and recognition of a party's standing or legitimacy in talks (legitimization). These noncoercive measures are designed to reassure disputants, construct a level playing field for negotiation, and offer knowledge and information that might help in problem solving during peace talks. Coercive measures used by mediators include punishment through diplomatic pressure such as blaming parties for bad faith negotiation or for bad behavior or atrocities (shaming), economic sanctions such as blockades and the freezing of assets of key leaders, and ultimately threatening the use of military force if talks fail to progress.

The instruments used in intervention in civil war work best when the diplomatic mediation tools used to induce bargaining among contenders are well coordinated with measures to reassure combatants through the deployment of peacekeeping force. In general, it is fair to conclude that when possible noncoercive measures to end civil wars are better than coercive measures, because then the termination of war is based more on a desire of the parties to end the fighting than on threats to their welfare if they do not. Moreover, noncoercive measures are less costly to the intervenor. Under many circumstances, however, the international community must resort to using arm-twisting or assertive military force when global interests are so damaged by a costly civil war or when norms such as the 1948 UN Convention on the Prevention and Punishment of the Crime of Genocide are breached.

TRACK RECORD

The track record of international intervention in civil wars in the 1990s is decidedly mixed. In assessing the record, it is important to distinguish among the three goals of intervention: prevention of deadly conflict, management of the violence when it breaks out, and settlement of the conflict through the negotiation and implementation of peace agreements. In all three objectives, assessment of success is inherently difficult. Success is a moving target because peace agreements can break down and war can resume, as in Angola in 1992 and Rwanda in 1994. Failure, too, is hard to measure. Is the inability to stop the killing in today's most intractable conflicts a failure of the system of global governance, or do the barriers to peace lie primarily with the warring parties themselves?

Despite the inherent difficulty with defining success or failure, there are some clear-cut cases of successful prevention, management, and settlement of civil wars and internal conflicts by international actors.[27] Examples of successful conflict *prevention* include the reduction of tensions between Estonian- and Russian-language speakers in newly independent Estonia. In this case, international officials of the Organization for Security and Cooperation in Europe (OSCE) worked together with local and international NGOs to convene a series of dialogues among Estonian and Russian speakers to help design new language and education laws that helped stem the escalation of conflict between these groups. The prevention of a wider war in South Africa at the perilous time of transition from apartheid to democracy, despite the loss of 14,000 lives in political violence between 1989 and 1994, can also be counted as a success. Indeed, there were moments in 1993, for example, when the violence could have significantly escalated had the United Nations not deployed an international observer mission (UN Observer Mission in South Africa) and linked that mission to domestic dispute resolution structures.

Some efforts at conflict *management* to limit escalation or to clinch peace agreements have clearly failed, despite concentrated efforts by many external mediators to broker a peace. The clearest example of failed peacemaking efforts may be Rwanda, and Sudan provides yet another example of dismal failure. Many official and unofficial efforts to bridge the gap between the Islamist government in Khartoum and the rebel factions of the South, such as the Sudanese People's Liberation Army, have failed to secure an agreement. Among those who have attempted to mediate the brutal war in the Sudan are Nigeria, the United Nations, the Intergovernmental Authority on Development, and eminent individuals such as former U.S. president

Jimmy Carter. Negotiations have become stalled on fundamental principles of the postwar order, particularly the question of the relationship between religion and government.

As described more fully below, there have also been successes and failures in the implementation of peace *settlements*. Although the peace processes within El Salvador and Namibia have managed to move these countries from a period of intense violence to a path of reconciliation and reconstruction, the underlying social tensions that helped fuel these conflicts may never be resolved. Class differences remain acute in El Salvador, and racial tension persists in Namibia, yet peaceful politics has replaced armed struggle as the principal way in which these conflicts are addressed.

LESSONS LEARNED

The myriad lessons learned in prevention, management, and resolution of civil wars will be highlighted along the four governance dimensions that are central to this book: agenda setting, negotiation, implementation and compliance, and reactions to noncompliance.

Agenda Setting

Given the multiplicity of civil wars and other internal conflicts in the 1990s, what determines whether such conflicts get the attention of the international community? One conclusion is clear: the numbers of corpses a civil war generates is not the principal criterion. Human suffering in a brutal war such as Sri Lanka's or Algeria's has far outpaced the level of violence and loss of life in Kosovo. Clearly the international agenda is not a coherent mechanism, in which the most costly conflicts in terms of human lives or other losses get the most attention from policy makers. What then motivates major powers to organize coalitions, take on financial burdens, and risk their own troops to intervene in civil wars?

Agenda setting in response to civil wars is directly related to two factors: interests and norms. It is clear that the agenda is set by states with the power to have conflicts that affect their interests placed on the international agenda. A critical question is whether these governments intervene proactively or simply react to domestic pressures to "do something" when the international news media brings scenes of horrible suffering into the living rooms of their populations. Often it is difficult to determine whether the motivation of a state championing intervention is interest based or norm based, as intervention often occurs in support of direct interests, while the action is justified with reference to norms. The matter is frequently one of issue framing. For example, British Prime Minister Tony Blair is widely regarded as having successfully framed the issue of intervening in Kosovo in 1999 on the basis of moral justice for the oppressed Albanian Kosovars as well as Great Britain's national interest in the broader stability of Europe.

News media attention and NGO pressure in public fora can stimulate policy makers to build multilateral coalitions, commit resources, and undertake the risk of intervention. The impact of the media in prompting intervention is sometimes called the "CNN effect."[28] That said, the CNN effect from the news media and the responsiveness of policy makers to clarion calls from the NGO community are often overstated. NGOs have seen some successes on certain issues, such as the successful campaign of 1,200 organizations in sixty countries working together with states such as Norway and Canada to seal a new global treaty on to eliminate the use of antipersonnel mines.[29]

Politicians are responsive to public opinion in democracies, but the decision to commit governmental resources and reputation in an intervention, especially one that involves deployment of military forces, is made more autonomously by policy makers who weigh the likely risks and likelihood of success.[30] Indeed, agenda setting lies most squarely with policy makers in influential capitals pursuing national security interests in managing the externalities of civil war. When powerful states in a global or regional context see their interests negatively affected by the threat or reality of civil war, they muster the political will to respond. A poignant example is "Operation Alba," the Multinational Protection Force led by Italy and deployed to stem mounting anarchy in Albania in mid-April 1997. Italy initiated the operation in response to two national security threats emanating from its neighborhood. First was the need for Italy (and Greece) to end a growing stream of Albanian refugees to their shores. Second was the need to prevent the Albanian conflict from spilling over and affecting ethnic Albanian relations with other nationalities in neighboring Yugoslavia (especially Kosovo) and Macedonia.

Powerful states can also keep certain conflicts off the international agenda. Indeed, why do Western powers overlook massive human rights abuses by Turkey against its restive Kurdish population? And why has there been no significant intervention in India, where an estimated 15,000–20,000 lives were lost in the troubles in Indian-controlled Kashmir? It is clear that overriding interests of cooperation and engagement with India keep the Kashmir question off the list of possible external interventions considered by the Security Council despite UN involvement in the dispute since 1947. Neither the United States nor China seeks to irritate India by raising the highly sensitive conflict before the world body. Owing to Pakistan's persistent interest, however, the issue is routinely raised at the annual meetings of the UN Human Rights Commission in Geneva, embarrassing India. Yet the thought of an external military intervention in Kashmir, given Indian sensitivities and military power and its role as a regional power, seems farcical. Similarly, the international effort to intervene in Turkey's civil war has been inhibited by NATO allies; Turkey is too strategic a partner for Western interests in the Middle East and Caucasus to consider the possibility of assertive outside intervention, which might alienate the country from NATO. These states, such as the United States, have instead used quiet diplomacy and other noncoercive incentives to move Turkey toward ending the civil war.

Much of the work of those who advocate a more preventive and less reactive stance by states and other actors in the international system involves agenda setting. How can systemic responses to incipient civil wars be launched before the violence escalates? Even with very credible early warnings of incipient armed conflict, it is often difficult to generate the political will—that is, the intensity of effort needed and the resources demanded—to effectively prevent war.

One way in which the political will problem can be circumvented is to create new institutions within international—particularly regional—organizations that can more autonomously set the agenda and respond to imminent cases of conflict. One of the more promising developments is the creation within the OSCE of a High Commissioner for National Minorities. The High Commissioner's mandate and budget enable his office to monitor situations of ethnic strife before they erupt into violence and to launch preventive missions to negotiate an effective system of balancing majority and minority interests. Another answer to inconsistent agenda setting is the creation of institutions that have the mandate to intervene regularly and systematically to address the problems that can lead to civil wars in the first place.

Negotiation

Once civil wars are on the international agenda, negotiation occurs at two different levels. First, negotiation occurs among the actors engaged in intervention on the objectives and form of the response. At this level intervening states negotiate among themselves on lead actors, mandates, commitment of troops, operational guidelines, burden sharing, and the linkages between military and civilian aspects of promoting peace.

Multiparty intervention in internal conflicts (both as a coalition at a single moment and with multiple actors over time in a single conflict setting) entails many coordination problems, burden sharing, and the assumption of risk—all of which must be negotiated.[31] In peace operations, coordination also involves the pairing of diplomatic and military activities, which sometimes feature different organizations involved with different tasks. For example, in Bosnia the OSCE administers the political aspects of the mission, NATO is responsible for military action, and the United Nations runs the civilian police force; UNHCR is tasked with refugee return and resettlement. The reliance on the special representative of the UN Secretary-General to serve as the coordinator of international intervention, who often performs the same task for regional organizations, has proven in this regard very successful.

Mozambique also offers a good example of effective coordination among multiple outside actors as diverse as the Communità di Sant'Egidio (a Catholic lay society), the United Nations, the Organization of African Unity, and powerful states such as the United States.[32] They all worked together, and each intervened at different times to bring peace to Mozambique. There is indeed the recognition that at different phases of a conflict the effectiveness of different outside actors varies. In all instances, the challenge is to assure coordination and continuity of purpose among outside intervenors with different interests, roles, and capacities.

The second level of negotiation involves talks among warring parties and usually but not always outside actors as third-party mediators. The goal of negotiation in civil wars—to induce the parties to settle their dispute at the bargaining table—is controversial because peace agreements are arguably inherently unstable. Some research shows that peace agreements in civil wars are more prone to breakdown than are settlements of civil wars through military victory.[33] External actors affect both the process of negotiating settlements—in particular, the sequencing dynamics of peace talks—and the outcome parameters—or the terms of settlement—through pressures and incentives. The reliance on the use of coercive diplomacy (negotiation with the threat of sanctions or force) to induce parties to negotiate is particularly controversial.

A critical initial challenge to convincing adversaries to peacefully settle their conflict is gaining access to all parties involved. In many instances disputants put up high barriers to the entry of international mediators, fearing that mediation will result in unwanted concessions. States, particularly, often espouse the international norms of sovereignty, noninterference, and consent to prevent external facilitation of peace processes. Power too limits the international community's ability to intervene. At the UN Millennium Summit in September 2000, President Jiang Zemin of China said, "Respect for each other's independence and sovereignty is vital to the maintenance of world peace."[34] Few observers expect that the United Nations could intervene to address the tensions in Tibet, for example.

Many developing states, including China, are concerned that the United Nations will be used to legitimate the global extension of Western power. Although sovereignty and consent are not the ironclad normative constraints on intervention that they once were, they continue to limit outside actor engagement, particularly by international organizations that must continue to operate within the confines of these principles. The unwillingness of states to resist demands for international involvement, driven in part by fears and debates within countries about the ethics, feasibility, and costs of intervening abroad, limits intervention most.

Critical to the effectiveness of outside actors is the use of leverage, especially the means by which influential states, regional organizations such as NATO, and occasionally international organizations wield sanctions and incentives to move parties toward agreement.[35] Leverage generally refers to the use of power and resources by third parties to encourage progress in negotiation or compliance with agreements or norms. Early coordination among outside actors is necessary to maximize leverage.

In general, mediation efforts succeed when there is a congruence of domestic and international requisites for peace. Balances and imbalances of power are also important; perceptions of a relatively balanced power equation promote the securing of negotiated settlements. The ability to secure negotiated settlements also depends on the ability of third parties to structure a system of incentives that allows key elites to reach and sustain a settlement while ensuring their political survival.

The issue of sovereignty is key to agreements in most of today's civil wars, and it continues to confound the principles and practices of intervention. Although it is primarily the interests and power of the disputants that frame the terms of a settlement in an internal conflict, international mediators clearly influence (on the basis of either principle or interests) the outcomes of peace processes. By insisting on the territorial integrity of a state, such as in Yugoslavia during the Kosovo crisis, outside powers usually prefer power sharing or autonomy arrangements to partition; by insisting on the territorial integrity for Yugoslavia and denying a prima facie case for Kosovo's independence, the United States and other Western powers limited the range of possible political solutions to the crisis to autonomy or a power-sharing scheme (as in Bosnia). As outside powers tend to encourage parties to share, they may even seek to affect the terms under which groups live together. The September 1995 Agreed Basic Principles for Bosnia (which formed the basis of the Dayton Agreement) is a case in point. The terms of the accord were formulated by the mediator, and not by the parties to the dispute.

In general, international intervention limits the options on the table to power sharing.[36] The outcomes of civil wars—along a continuum from partition to power sharing—are related to the depth of the enmity and the conduct of the war. In 1993, it might have been possible to get the parties in Bosnia to agree to a more integrative power-sharing plan, as embodied in the Vance-Owen plan proffered at the International conference in London. But by 1995, after two more years of carnage and war crimes, attitudes had hardened and only a tripartite condominium was possible at Dayton. At the same time, the territorial integrity and multiethnic character of Bosnia was preserved.

Implementation and Compliance

Negotiating a peace agreement does not necessarily imply success in securing the peace. Peace agreements in Angola, Cambodia, Rwanda, Liberia, and Sierra Leone have at times broken down, precipitating new violence. Indeed, peace agreements are often merely pledges to stop the immediate bloodshed by ending military operations and establishing new rules for a longer-term, self-sustaining relationship without recourse to violence. Conflict among the parties does not dissipate but is instead managed through ongoing negotiation and problem solving in the implementation phase. It is hoped that during the course of negotiating the agreement—and the broader peace involving a wide range of local and international participants—attitudes and behaviors become more accommodating, thereby creating a foundation for democracy, reconciliation, and postwar reconstruction. A negotiated settlement, through the principles it espouses and the rules and institutions it creates, offers a specific promise for a more peaceful future.

Lessons learned on peace agreement implementation vary widely because the terms of agreements are so diverse, and so too are the social and political conditions in various postwar environments. Summary conclusions on tasks of peace building suggest that success, while difficult to achieve, has proven possible when certain guidelines are followed:

- Once outside powers have decided to intervene, they should make available the necessary resources both in terms of military manpower and hardware and in terms of financial assets.
- All UN peacekeeping operations should be authorized under Chapter VII, and peacekeepers should have the military capability to defend their units, uphold their mandates, and protect vulnerable populations.[37]
- Mediators must maintain momentum and deal forcefully with potential spoilers who seek to scuttle the peace agreement.
- The UN Special Envoy or other clearly preeminent official should serve to coordinate the activities of the range of actors involved in intervention.
- Outside forces should maintain coherent leadership of the implementation process by emboldening moderates among the parties in dispute.
- All parties should be wary of timetables and benchmarks that cannot be kept.
- Those supporting the peace process should not focus on early elections, especially before the disarmament and demobilization of combatants has occurred.

In addition, to be successful, the short- and long-term goals of the international community need to be more carefully and thoughtfully integrated. For example, when crafting peace agreements in civil wars, concern should be directed at how the human rights components of these agreements can be effectively promoted in the postsettlement peace-building phase. Short-term considerations for ending the war—which may lead to amnesty for some combatants—need to be weighed against the longer-term need for prosecution of serious war criminals and the demand for social justice by victims of war crimes. In sum, those designing international intervention should identify an overall strategy that addresses the short-term problem of resolving security concerns, the medium-term problem of establishing viable political institutions, and the longer-term task of promoting a democratic postwar political system.

As the war winds down, the most immediate imperative for outside actors is providing short-term security to address the problem of credible commitments. In this regard, the following recommendations apply.

- Peacekeeping and verification forces should be deployed rapidly and effectively, with significant military capacity to deter threats to their units, mandates, and vulnerable populations.
- Schedules for demobilization of forces, and disarmament and cantonment of weapons, should be flexible, as the demilitarization of society is an ongoing process; at the same time, every effort should be made to eliminate military threats to key events such as elections.
- Introducing mechanisms for conflict management is equally critical to providing short-term security. When crises arise, such as an incident of political violence, measures should be taken to ensure that the crisis does not derail the peace process. (This issue is discussed more fully below in the section on noncompliance and enforcement.)
- Intervenors should work especially hard to ensure that parties on the ground respect initial commitments made in the settlement. If a party to the negotiation defects on commitments made in the settlement, the reciprocity and exchange relationships among the parties are likely to deteriorate and the process can begin to unravel.
- Reconstituting military and police credibility in public security is a critical immediate-term task to lay the basis for peace building. Although external peacekeeping forces can assist in the military components of providing security, these forces are often not specifically trained for policing.[38] Considerable progress has been made in recent years in improving policing capacities in postwar environments, but more work needs to done.
- Securing the external environment is necessary to prevent regional instabilities. Instability in neighboring countries can spill over and dislodge a very delicate balance.

In the medium term, the challenge is to reconstruct society and nonviolent politics. If the peace is to be self-sustaining over the long term, then the initial legitimacy of postwar political institutions is paramount. The linkages among governmental capacity, civil society strength, and the postwar provision of the benefits of peace are increasingly clear. A strong civil society sector working with an open, participatory set of political institutions is best placed to deliver on the promises of human security and socioeconomic development that lie behind the pursuit of peace.

Some lessons learned about medium-term tasks are the following:

- Reestablishing legitimate political structures, reintroducing the rule of law, and providing minority rights require a flexible and dynamic process of constitution making. Initially, constitutional arrangements are the result of negotiation among elites (negotiators ending the civil war); later, however, active involvement of citizens and civil society is necessary to craft a legitimate pact. A critically important question for all postwar situations is the degree of inclusiveness of new political institutions. The more the political institutions are inclusive of all major factions in society, the less the likelihood that a given party may defect from the agreement.

- Elections are a necessary and desirable step in legitimating the postwar system of governance. Despite criticism that elections exacerbate conflict (as politicians mobilize their communities for support, often along nationalistic lines), preparing and holding elections remains a critical postsettlement task. The principal reason is that there is no substitute for elections to create a legitimate postwar government. Considerable thought has gone into improving postwar elections in recent years, spurred by the dismal failure of some attempts (for example, Angola's 1992 election) and the relative success of other efforts despite very unfavorable circumstances (for example, Cambodia in 1993; Bosnia in 1996, 1998, and 2000).[39]

- Aid to support the rebuilding of civil society is critical. Because wars often sharpen social divisions and lead to the creation of parallel civil societies (reflecting the various sides of the conflict), external aid is often directed at forging ties among civil society organizations and supporting those that build bridges among the factions.

- Human rights procedures—including prosecution of war criminals—must be established quickly. Some human rights advocacy organizations have become increasingly concerned that, in ending the internal conflicts of the 1990s, justice usually took a back seat to conciliation. An effective human rights strategy should contain specific operational plans, and it must ingeniously draw the parties in conflict into commitments that make human rights protections the immediate and long-term aims of a negotiated settlement.[40]

- To expect victimized groups to reconcile, there must be some attempt to pursue justice and end the cycle of impunity. It is now widely recognized that various mechanisms can help reconcile the need for prosecution in some instances—particularly when crimes against humanity have occurred (as in the case of the international criminal tribunals for the former Yugoslavia, Rwanda, and Sierra Leone)—and the need to promote reconciliation. Truth Commissions, ad hoc judicial processes that combine investigation of alleged crimes with opportunities for victims (and sometime perpetrators) to tell their side of events, have been used in El Salvador and South Africa, and more recently in Guatemala. They seem to be a particularly useful mechanism, although the conditions under which this process can stimulate progress toward reconciliation remain hotly debated.[41]

- Repatriation of refugees and resettling of internally displaced persons are difficult but necessary; more support should be provided for these efforts. Failure to devote sufficient will, attention, and energy to this task sets up longer-term problems of reconciliation and can generate new disputes over housing, land, and employment.
- In accomplishing these tasks, coordination by an effective leader is critical. Because of their unique legitimacy as institutions to which all states belong, international organizations—especially the United Nations —are best placed to coordinate management of implementation and compliance in post–civil war environments.

Long-term compliance with peace agreements implies two overarching imperatives for managers in the international arena. The first is to promote social reconciliation in an approach that addresses the core causes of conflict and focuses on the need to meet fundamental human needs and foster broad-based social development.[42] The second imperative specifically associates sustainable peace with democracy.[43]

Democracy, reconciliation, and reconstruction are the internal components of sustainable implementation and ongoing compliance after a deadly war. But there is an external dimension as well. Both long-term goals require continued commitment and stewardship by third-party mediators. The external dimension relates to the further development of international norms on democracy in multiethnic societies (minority and minority rights and obligations), response mechanisms to ensure compliance with these norms, and new mechanisms for quick and effective responses when the norms are breached. This will require lengthening the time horizon for the involvement of the international community to build peace beyond notions of "exit strategies."[44]

Reactions to Noncompliance

Given the typical characteristics of postwar societies, negotiated settlements are extremely fragile. Many people on all sides harbor intense and recent memories of violence, suffering, loss, and injustice. The war leaves a proliferation of arms in its wake and a reservoir of disaffected soldiers and militiamen. Social structures are devastated as families and communities have been torn asunder; many civilians have fled their homes, villages, towns, and livelihoods; farmland and water resources have been thrashed. Economic capacities have either been converted to war use or ruined in the course of the war; infrastructures are often wrecked; and "silent killers" such as landmines often prevent a rapid recovery, especially in rural areas. Throughout all levels of society, trust has been destroyed and belief in public institutions shattered.

In this context, it should be expected that threats to the peace often prevail; the obstacles to reconciliation and reconstruction are enormous.

Why do peace settlements often fail, with one party or another defecting from an agreement? How do outside actors respond to noncompliance? Settlements in internal conflicts contain inherent problems of enforceability. Even under the best circumstances, when outside actors agree to step in with a peacekeeping force to secure the pact, when the transitional election is over and the peacekeepers leave, there is no external party to further guarantee the accord.[45]

Perhaps the most important peril of settlement is that the agreements among erstwhile enemies are essentially self-enforcing. In her study of fifty-three settlements of civil wars from 1940 to 1990, Barbara Walter suggests that this problem explains why most negotiated settlements fail in the long run. She describes a theory of credible commitment as the most important factor in whether settlements will yield sustainable peace.[46] In sum, Walter sees the period after a settlement has been reached as a highly volatile time in which parties are subject to the uncertainty and unpredictability of the security dilemma; incentives encourage striking first for fear of being attacked by one's foes.

Managing the commitment problem often amounts to the deployment of peacekeeping operations, quickly and with significant force capabilities. In Bosnia, for example, SFOR—the NATO stabilization force—has dealt with noncompliance with security aspects of the agreement quickly and effectively, and its success is a direct function of its ability and readiness to exercise clearly superior force against would-be cheaters. In Cambodia, the UN Transitional Authority in Cambodia was insufficiently prepared (or willing) to confront the Khmer Rouge forces that violated the Paris Peace Accords and subsequent UN mandates. Assuring an appropriate response to noncompliance on security matters is a matter of deploying sufficient force.

The worst disasters occur when the international community fails to respond to noncompliance with a peace agreement. Violence perpetrated by spoilers—Angola in 1992, Rwanda in 1994—produced some of the most deadly encounters in the 1990s. In these and other cases, spoilers are those who have the drive, capacity, and zeal to negate a peace agreement through the use of violence; spoilers can be erstwhile parties to an agreement who renege on its terms, or those who have opposed the peace talks all along. In Rwanda, the parties reached what many observers felt was a reasonably good settlement (the Arusha Accords) in early 1994, but elements of the government of then-President Juvenal Habryimana acted at the earliest possible moment—in April, as the president was returning from peace talks—to undermine the implementation of these agreements. It is now clear, in retrospect, that early use of superior and convincing military force by the international community could have contained and possibly prevented the tragedy.[47] The most important factor is for the international community to signal to combatants that it is serious about sufficient military force to provide security in the immediate aftermath of peace agreement.

That said, reacting to spoilers involves making difficult judgments about the spoiler: Is this a party with a legitimate constituency that should be brought into a peace process, or an irredeemable perpetrator of war crimes that should be defeated with military force?

Another common cause of failed peace pacts is the inability or unwillingness of the parties, or even one major party, to demobilize forces and give up arms. Spoilers are generally thought of as those who reject the peace agreement, but inept disarmament and demobilization gives all parties an easy out when the initial goodwill of the peace settlement wears off and the hard tasks of peace building begin. Failure to prevent noncompliance on demobilization and disarmament has often scuttled peace agreements.

No case better demonstrates the contributions of inadequate demobilization and disarmament to the failure of peace implementation than the halting efforts to sustainably end the civil war in Angola. In 1991, elections under the auspices of the Bicesse Peace Accords failed when the opposition faction's leader, Jonas Savimbi, showed poorly in the country's election and was set to lose a runoff with his archrival, Angolan President José dos Santos. Later in Angola's tragic history, the peace process that emanated from the 1994 Lusaka Protocols also broke down in late 1998; many observers point to continued unwillingness of the parties to lay down their arms.[48]

Problems of noncompliance can sometimes also be traced to incomplete or insufficient planning by the international community during the peacemaking phase. It is now widely accepted that in many situations, international agencies that seek to help implement agreements have not arrived at coordinated plans or strategic approaches to address the root causes of the conflict. Highly sensitive issues such as repatriation of refugees, fundamental restructuring of the economy, prosecution of war criminals, and the terms of postsettlement elections are not always systematically considered while the peace accord is being negotiated; they are kept off the table precisely because they are so difficult to resolve.

When noncompliance with global norms and negotiated settlements occurs, the system of global management of civil wars is tested to the limit. At times, UN Security Council endorsement of enforcement actions is not possible because there is a lack of consensus among the veto-wielding five permanent members. This happened, for example, in the case of Kosovo. At such times, the legitimacy of a multilateral response is denied. Powerful states and regional organizations such as NATO will be tempted to act without UN support particularly when they perceive that their national interests require it, as in the case of Kosovo.

Finally, it must be mentioned that international actors have increasingly stressed individual accountability. Perhaps one of the most significant events in the 1990s was the creation of international criminal tribunals to prosecute perpetrators of genocide and ethnic cleansing in Rwanda and the former Yugoslavia; the jurisdiction of the tribunals was recently extended to Sierra Leone. The tribunals have subsequently convicted war criminals for crimes against humanity. The creation of ad hoc tribunals and the modest success in arresting, trying, and convicting perpetrators of war crimes is a very promising aspect of the development of global governance mechanisms to manage civil wars. In mid-1998, negotiators in Rome concluded a treaty to establish a permanent international war crimes tribunal. Significantly, the United States did not sign the treaty establishing the court, citing concerns that U.S. forces overseas might be unfairly prosecuted for war crimes, circumventing the U.S. military criminal justice system. The establishment of a permanent tribunal is a small, incomplete, yet critical step in the further evolution of international law.[49] Ideally, the permanent body may deter future noncompliance with international norms like those prohibiting genocide and other war crimes and thus help prevent this worst consequence of civil wars.

CONCLUSIONS AND RECOMMENDATIONS

In the longer term, effective international management of internal conflicts will require further evolution of international norms, institutions, and capacities. A more consistent method of decision making and coalition building and a more effective UN response mechanism—such as a rapid deployment force—offer the best hope in the long term for rule-based, timely intervention to promote peace. Efficient, capable, and well-supported UN peacekeeping operations are the most desirable form of intervention to end civil war and build postsettlement peace. Operations endorsed by the United Nations offer the highest degree of international legal legitimacy, and the United Nations is best placed to orchestrate the activities of a broad coalition of actors involved in these complex emergencies.

Intervention in civil wars should occur when these conflicts produce significant negative externalities in the international system or when genocide or other serious war crimes are carried out. A more fair and effective system of global governance requires mechanisms for legitimating action on a consistent and regularized basis. A move toward a more norm-centered basis of intervention, as opposed to an interest-driven system of responses, is needed to improve governance in this sphere. In practice, this means that the international community should seek to develop a more consistent set of principles and criteria as to when it will intervene to stem civil wars, and the track record to signal to combatants that response will be capable, robust, and long term.

At present, the UN Security Council, created in a different era for a different purpose, is fundamentally ill equipped to authorize and manage international intervention in times of crisis when consensus among the permanent five members of the

UN Security Council is absent. Although assigning special status to the five permanent members may have made sense in 1945, the Security Council is an anachronistic institution in today's world. Especially when crimes against humanity are about to occur, or have begun, the Council has proven itself to be too slow in responding, unable to reach consensus, inconsistent in its actions, and ineffective in many situations. This is especially true when the direct interests of a member state are affected by an internal conflict, such as in Chechnya.

The short-term term response of the powerful states when confronted with the inadequacy of the Security Council's set of decision rules has been to marginalize the United Nations. In the long run, however, coalitions of the willing—acting without UN Security Council authorization—risk undermining the principal actor and instruments for promoting peace in civil wars and the gains in global governance made in the 1990s. Short-term necessity should give way to longer-term thinking about improving the structures, decision-making procedures, and operational effectiveness of the United Nations. International norms must be developed further—for example, clarifying the criteria for legitimate international intervention when "ethnic cleansing" (a crime against humanity arguably not covered under the Genocide Convention) occurs. Reform of the Security Council and the amendment of its decision-making rules may prevent the world body from being kept in check in times of grave emergency.

A cataclysmic event would probably be necessary to revisit the current configurations of power in the United Nations, however, as fundamental change of this nature has occurred previously only in the aftermath of the world wars. In the meantime, work needs to continue on ways to coordinate better the efforts of various actors promoting conflict management in civil wars—for example, integrating global and local NGOs into peace operation decision making.[50] The following recommendations are feasible at this juncture:

- Regional organizations should further develop norms for relations among majority and minority populations. The efforts of the Organization of American States, for example, to develop a declaration on the rights of indigenous peoples could be replicated in other regions such as South Asia, Africa, and East and Southeast Asia. New institutions should be developed along the lines of the OSCE High Commissioner for National Minorities, especially in Asia and the southern Pacific or at the United Nations.
- Efforts to develop a more regularized system of agenda setting through the monitoring and early warning functions of the UN Secretariat and regional organizations should be reinvigorated. UN member states should expand UN fact-finding capabilities and be willing to address more forcefully problems of ethnic discrimination and economic inequality *before* violence erupts. Considerable attention was given to preventive action in the mid-1990s, but this emphasis has not been sustained.

- International actors should continue to improve the timing and design of interventions. The most effective time for a peace initiative is not necessarily when the fighting and humanitarian tragedy is at its peak; by then outside intervention is usually too late. The best times are early in the process of escalation, before violence starts, or after a costly stalemate, and just prior to the prospect of a dramatic turning point in the conflict. Consistency in intervention is also critical for success; when the world neglects some major crises such as Sudan and yet pours enormous resources into less costly encounters, the legitimacy of all intervention efforts suffers.

- The military and coercive aspects of global responses need to be more closely integrated with noncoercive aspects of global responses such as mediation. Complex peace operations involving the use of force work best when explicitly linked to a well-conceived plan for settling the conflict. Peacemakers need a strategic idea linking the process of negotiation to a desired outcome such as power sharing and the sequencing and holding of elections. Recommendations to create integrated civilian-military mission task forces should be implemented as soon as possible.[51]

- The continued emphasis on third-party mediation should be sustained. The role of third parties is vital in constructing and implementing an accord. Mediators bring leverage, ideas, mechanisms, legitimacy, packaging of issue areas, enforcement, sanctions, verification, incentives, membership in or access to multilateral organizations, and knowledge and experience.

- A longer-term time horizon for implementation of peace agreements should become more routine in policy planning. Peace accords cannot settle everything in a single stroke. Settlements are frameworks and outlines—targets with benchmarks. They must be viewed as part of a dynamic process that contains logic and balance. Similarly, the provision of external assistance needs to be more consistent and long term. Accords require painstaking implementation; they cannot succeed without long-term commitment and resources.

These measures can help improve the system of global responses to deadly civil wars. Yet the inherent tensions within the prevailing structure of the international system will continue to seriously limit consistent and effective responses to today's violent social conflicts. The continuation of the veto in the Security Council, the persistence of sovereignty as an overriding international norm, and the absence of a well-trained and well-armed rapid deployment force with global capability continue to hamstring efforts to prevent, manage, and resolve today's civil wars.

The trends in warfare seen in the post–Cold War period suggest that the international community will continue to be called upon to intervene within borders of sovereign states to promote international peace and security. We can expect more violations of international norms of human rights to include, regrettably, genocide and other heinous war crimes; until there are changes in the system of global governance, the international response will be inadequate.

The best hope for the moment is a continuation of the incremental changes in the global regime to foster peace and security that began in the early 1990s and continues today. The most important next step that could be made in this arena is the creation of a standing force of 5,000 to15,000 troops, expertly trained in the nature and dynamics of civil wars, that could intervene when civil wars threaten international peace or when norms against genocide and war crimes are breached. Not only would such a force be beneficial in responding to today's most grave crises, but also its presence and clear willingness to be deployed may serve to deter antagonists in internal conflicts from allowing the spiral into war in the first place.

NOTES

1. Research for this chapter was conducted with the generous support of a Research and Writing Grant from the Program on Global Security and Sustainability of the John D. and Catherine T. MacArthur Foundation. The author thanks Michael E. Brown, Donald Rothchild, Stephen John Stedman, and other members of the Managing Global Issues project of Carnegie Endowment for International Peace for their thoughtful comments on earlier drafts of this chapter.
2. For regularly updated data on contemporary wars, see the University of Uppsala Department of Peace and Conflict Research, Conflict Data Project at <http://www.pcr.uu.se/data.htm>. The two "international" or state-to-state conflicts in 1999 involved Eritrea and Ethiopia and India and Pakistan.
3. The peak year for civil violence is 1992, when twenty-two intense civil wars raged around the globe (producing 1,000 dead in a year) and an additional sixty internal conflicts occurred that were of lesser intensity. Although there was a brief decline in the frequency of war between 1992 and 1997, the trend since then is rising.
4. In this chapter "intervention" means initiatives by official (international organizations, states) or "unofficial" international actors (NGOs) to induce disputants in civil war to prevent, manage, or resolve deadly conflict. This encompasses intervention with or without the consent of local parties. It also refers to both coercive and noncoercive measures of inducement.
5. In some cases, such as the Western military campaign in 1999 to halt the fighting in Kosovo, a lack of consensus among permanent members of the Security Council has inhibited the ability of lead states to gain a mandate from the United Nations. Similarly, the deployment of Russian-led Commonwealth of Independent States peacekeeping forces in Tajikistan in 1992 and Georgia in 1994 were not authorized by the Security Council due to a lack of consensus among the permanent members.
6. For reasons of space, the chapter does not extensively address intervention by neighbors on behalf of a disputing party, that is, intervention aimed at helping one side in the conflict achieve a military victory. Nor does the chapter address certain aspects of civil

wars covered in other chapters in this volume (such as humanitarian relief, human rights, small arms proliferation, or landmines).

7. See David Lake and Donald Rothchild, eds., *The International Spread of Ethnic Conflict: Fear, Diffusion and Escalation* (Princeton, N.J.: Princeton University Press, 1998).

8. For up-to-date data on refugees, as well as extensive background information on individual countries, see <http://www.unhcr.ch/refworld>.

9. Shepard Forman and Rita Parhad, "Paying for Essentials: Resources for Humanitarian Assistance," paper prepared for meeting at Pocantico Conference Center at the Rockefeller Brothers Fund, *Journal of Humanitarian Assistance* (September 11–12, 1997), available at <http://www.jha.ac/articles/a021.htm>.

10. For a recent assessment of the Genocide Convention, see William Schabas, *The Genocide Convention at Fifty*, U.S. Institute of Peace Special Report (Washington, D.C.: U.S. Institute of Peace Press, January 7, 1999).

11. See Frances Stewart, Frank P. Humphreys, and Nick Lee, "Civil Conflict in Developing Countries over the Last Quarter of a Century: An Empirical Overview of Economic and Social Consequences," *Oxford Journal of Development Studies*, vol. 25, no. 1 (February 1997), pp. 11–43.

12. Jay Austin and Carl Bruch, eds., *The Environmental Consequences of War: Legal, Economic, and Scientific Perspectives* (Cambridge, U.K.: Cambridge University Press, 2000).

13. Under Chapter VII of the charter, the United Nations is tasked with preventing and ending violent international conflicts through noncoercive means such as fact finding, negotiation, and mediation. Under Chapter VII, the UN Security Council can authorize coercive measures including the use of force; today, such coercive measures generally fall under the rubric of the use of force to protect UN mission mandates (goals) and personnel. The UN Security Council has also at times authorized the use of force for "peace enforcement," or military action designed to impose peace (for example, in Somalia in 1991). Traditional peacekeeping, which is not specifically referred to in the charter but instead developed from UN practice, is sometimes referred to as a "Chapter VI ½" intervention. See Donald Daniel, Bradd C. Hayes, and Chantal de Jonge Oudraat, *Coercive Inducement and the Containment of International Crises* (Washington, D.C.: U.S. Institute of Peace Press, 1998).

14. On financial incentives, see John Stremlau and F. R. Sagasti, *Preventing Deadly Conflict: Does the World Bank Have a Role?* (Washington, D.C.: Carnegie Commission on Preventing Deadly Conflict, 1997).

15. For a current list, see <http://www.un.org/peace>.

16. See William Durch, ed., *UN Peacekeeping, American Politics, and the Uncivil Wars of the 1990s* (New York: St. Martin's Press, 1996), p. 7; and Carnegie Commission on Preventing Deadly Conflict, *Preventing Deadly Conflict* (Washington, D.C.: Carnegie Commission on Preventing Deadly Conflict, 1997), p. 3.

17. See Connie Peck, *Sustainable Peace: The Role of the UN and Regional Organizations in Preventing Conflict* (Lanham, Md: Rowman and Littlefield and Carnegie Commission on Preventing Deadly Conflict, 1998); and Etel Solingen, *Regional Orders at the Century's Dawn: Global and Domestic Influences on Grand Strategy* (Los Angeles: University of California Press, 1998).

18. In 1991 the Organization of American States had adopted the Santiago Declaration (Resolution 1080) that pledged multilateral responses in instances when democratic governments are threatened or overthrown in a coup d'état.

19. Bruce D. Jones, "Keeping the Peace, Losing the War: Military Intervention in Rwanda's Two Wars," in Jack Snyder and Barbara F. Walter, eds., *Civil War, Insecurity, and Intervention* (New York: Columbia University Press, 1999).

20. See David Smock, *Private Peacemaking* (Washington, D.C.: U.S. Institute of Peace Press, 1998), for a fuller description of the NGO role in various settings.

21. "The Ground Troops Must Be Deployed Immediately," by Shep Lowman, *The International Herald Tribune*, April 20, 1999, p.18.

22. Thomas Weiss and Brian Urquhart, eds., *Military-Civilian Interactions: Intervening in Humanitarian Crises* (Lanham, Md.: Rowman and Littlefield, 1999).

23. See Mary Anderson, *Do No Harm: How Aid Can Support Peace or War* (Boulder, Colo.: Lynne Rienner Publishers, 1999).

24. When noncoercive measures are authorized in the United Nations, it is usually justified under Chapter VI of the charter; coercive intervention requires reference to Chapter VII.

25. On coercive diplomacy, see Alexander L. George, *Forceful Persuasion: Coercive Diplomacy as an Alternative to War* (Washington, D.C.: U.S. Institute of Peace Press, 1991). A related concept is the notion of "coercive inducement," a form of coercive diplomacy that relies on the deployment and demonstration of military force rather than the actual use of force. See Daniel, Hayes, and de Jonge Oudraat, *Coercive Inducement: The Containment of International Crises*.

26. Donald Rothchild, *Managing Ethnic Conflict in Africa: Pressures and Incentives for Cooperation* (Washington, D.C.: Brookings Institution Press, 1997).

27. Prevention has been successful in several instances in which armed conflict among contending groups was considered likely if the international community had not intervened. See Carnegie Commission, *Preventing Deadly Conflict*.

28. This refers to the role that the Cable News Network (CNN) played in stimulating the United States to forge a coalition to intervene in Somalia in December 1992. Absent a clear national interest in Somalia, the United States intervened in the civil war to provide humanitarian relief after public pressure grew to alleviate the horrible suffering brought to American households through television.

29. See the International Campaign to Ban Landmines at <http://www.icbl.org>.

30. Reporter Warren Strobel writes that "the news media have less influence over American foreign policy and military policy than many observers believe to be the case. . . . The media can exert influence on policy regarding peace operations, but whether they do depends on many factors, most of which are within government officials' power to control. The CNN effect is highly conditional." See Warren Strobel, *Late-Breaking Foreign Policy: The Media's Influence on Peace Operations* (Washington, D.C.: U.S. Institute of Peace Press, 1997), p. 211.

31. See also P. Terrence Hopmann, *The Negotiation Process and the Resolution of International Conflicts* (Columbia, S.C.: University of South Carolina Press, 1996).

32. See Cameron Hume, *Ending Mozambique's War: The Role of Mediation and Good Offices* (Washington, D.C.: U.S. Institute of Peace Press, 1994).

33. Military victories arguably are more desirable than negotiated settlements, because they settle the conflict with a degree of certainty. Robert Harrison Wagner argues that military victories in civil wars lead to more stable outcomes than negotiated settlements. Negotiated settlements inevitably leave many issues ambiguous or insufficiently addressed, or circumstances change and then lead one or more parties to change their terms. See Robert Harrison Wagner, "The Causes of Peace," in Roy Licklider, ed., *Stopping the Killing: How Civil Wars End* (New York: New York University Press, 1993), pp. 235–68.

34. Quoted in David E. Sanger, "Clinton Warns U.N. of a New Age of Civil Wars," *New York Times*, September 7, 2000, p. A1.

35. On the use of financial and other positive incentives, see David Cortright, ed., *The Price of Peace: Incentives and International Conflict Prevention* (Lanham, Md.: Rowman and Littlefield, 1997).

36. For an overview of power-sharing options, see Timothy Sisk, *Power Sharing and International Mediation in Ethnic Conflicts* (Washington, D.C.: U.S. Institute of Peace, 1996); and Peter Harris and Ben Reilly, eds., *Democracy and Deep-Rooted Conflict: Options for Negotiators* (Stockholm: International Institute for Democracy and Electoral Assistance, 1998).

37. Chapter VII of the UN Charter authorizes the UN Security Council to use force for purposes other than pure self-defense.

38. A recent study outlines the importance of the policing task; see Robert B. Oakley, Michael Dziedzic, and Eliot M. Goldberg, eds., *Policing the New World Order: Peace Operations and Public Security* (Washington, D.C.: National Defense University Press, 1998) pp. 8–9.

39. See Timothy D. Sisk and Andrew Reynolds, eds., *Elections and Conflict Management in Africa* (Washington, D.C.: U.S. Institute of Peace Press, 1998), for an overview of arguments concerning elections in postconflict societies. Bosnian elections in 1996 and 1998 have been a test case of the feasibility of early elections to restore legitimacy in difficult circumstances. For a careful analysis of these elections, see John Menzies, Lauren Van Metre, Burch Akan, and Kristine Hermann, *Bosnia Report Card: Pass, Fail, or Incomplete?*, U.S. Institute for Peace Special Report, December 1998.

40. See "How Can Human Rights Be Better Integrated in Peace Processes?" Conference Report of the Fund for Peace, Washington, D.C., 1998.

41. See Neil Kritz, ed., *Transitional Justice: How Emerging Democracies Reckon with Former Regimes* (Washington, D.C.: U.S. Institute of Peace Press, 1995).

42. John Paul Lederach, *Sustainable Reconciliation in Divided Societies* (Washington, D.C.: U.S. Institute of Peace Press, 1997).

43. See Harris and Reilly, *Democracy and Deep-Rooted Conflict: Options for Negotiators.*

44. Michael Brown asserts that "the goal should be creation of a lasting peace that would allow international actors to walk away at some point: peace would be self-sustaining. This is not an impossible dream, but it most certainly is not a short-term proposition. Politicians in Western capitals who need immediate gratification and crave regular diplomatic triumphs need not apply. This is a job for serious international actors capable of making long-term commitments to deep-seated problems." See Michael E. Brown, "International Conflict and International Action," in Michael E. Brown, ed., *The International Dimensions of Internal Conflict* (Cambridge, Mass.: MIT Press, 1996), p. 624.

45. For this reason, Wagner writes, "One of the disadvantages of a negotiated settlement is that, because no combatant is able to disarm its adversaries, a settlement requires that all the adversaries retain some semblance of their organizational identities after the war, even if they are disarmed. While such an agreement may facilitate the ending of one civil war, it may also facilitate the outbreak of the next." See Wagner, "Causes of Peace," p. 261.

46. Barbara Walter, "The Critical Barrier to Civil War Settlement," *International Organization*, vol. 51, no. 3 (Summer 1997), pp. 335–37.

47. Scott Feil summarizes deliberations on how the early insertion of a strong peacekeeping force could have prevented the genocide in Rwanda; see Scott Feil, *Preventing Genocide: How the Early Use of Force Might Have Succeeded in Rwanda* (Washington, D.C.: Carnegie Commission on Preventing Deadly Conflict, 1998).

48. Suzanne Daley, "Angola's Exhausted People Confront War's Agony Again," in *New York Times*, December 23, 1998, pp. A1 and A9. See also David Smock and John Prendergast, *NGOs and the Peace Process in Angola*, U.S. Institute of Peace Occasional Paper (Peaceworks) (Washington, D.C.: U.S. Institute of Peace Press, April 1996), on obstacles to popular reconciliation in Angola. In addition to the underlying failure of demobilization efforts, other factors led to the demise of the Lusaka Protocol, including: the death of the UN envoy, Alioune Blondin Beye, in a plane crash in early 1999; instability in neighboring Congo (Kinshasa); internal squabbles in dos Santos's government that instigated him to launch preemptive military strikes against UNITA; and failure to take advantage of the brief window of peace from 1994 to 1998 to deliver much needed economic benefits from Angola's impressive oil revenues.

49. For further information on the proposed court, see the Coalition for an International Criminal Court, <http://www.igc.apc.org/icc/>.

50. See George A. Joulwan and Christopher C. Shoemaker, *Civilian-Military Cooperation in the Prevention of Deadly Conflict: Implementing Agreements in Bosnia and Beyond* (Washington, D.C.: Carnegie Commission on Preventing Deadly Conflict, 1998).

51. See the report of the UN panel of experts on peacekeeping, which made recommendations on August 23, 2000, at <http://www.un.org/peace>.

SUGGESTED ADDITIONAL READING

Brown, Michael E., ed. *The International Dimensions of Internal Conflict.* Cambridge, Mass.: MIT Press, 1996.

Carnegie Commission on Preventing Deadly Conflict. *Preventing Deadly Conflict: Final Report.* New York: Carnegie Corporation of New York, 1998.

Crocker, Chester A., Fen Osler Hampson, and Pamela Aall, eds. *Herding Cats: The Management of Complex International Mediation.* Washington, D.C.: U.S. Institute of Peace, 2000.

Durch, William J., ed. *UN Peacekeeping, American Policy, and the Uncivil Wars of the 1990s.* New York: St. Martin's Press, 1996.

Hampson, Fen Osler. *Nurturing Peace: Why Peace Agreements Succeed or Fail.* Washington, D.C.: U.S. Institute of Peace Press, 1996.

Harris, Peter, and Ben Reilly, eds. *Democracy and Deep-Rooted Conflict: Options for Negotiators*. Stockholm: International Institute for Democracy and Electoral Assistance, 1998.

Lake, David, and Donald Rothchild, eds. *The International Spread of Ethnic Conflict: Fear, Diffusion, and Escalation*. Princeton, N.J.: Princeton University Press, 1998.

Lederach, John Paul. *Building Peace: Sustainable Reconciliation in Divided Societies*. Washington, D.C.: U.S. Institute of Peace Press, 1997.

Peck, Connie. *Sustainable Peace: The Role of the UN and Regional Organizations in Preventing Conflict*. London: Rowman & Littlefield, 1998.

Weiss, Thomas, and Leon Gordenker, eds. *NGOs, the UN, and Global Governance*. Boulder, Colo.: Lynne Rienner, 1996.

Internet Sites

African Center for the Constructive Resolution of Disputes <http://www.accord.org.za>

European Platform on Conflict Prevention and Transformation <http://www.euconflict.org>

Department of Peace and Conflict Research, University of Uppsala, Sweden <http://www.peace.uu.se>

United Nations <http://www.un.org/peace>

U.S. Institute of Peace <http://www.usip.org>

University of Minnesota Human Rights Library <http://www1.umn.edu/humanrts/index.html>

15

Warfare: Conventional Weapons

Joanna Spear

THE RECORD OF GLOBAL GOVERNANCE EFFORTS designed to tackle problems caused by conventional weapons is patchy at best.[1] Indeed many of these arrangements have been short lived. However, changes in the global security environment and the use of tools such as transparency arrangements to build confidence and security are creating an atmosphere more conducive to lasting governance arrangements.

Global governance of conventional arms is necessary and desirable for three main reasons. First, indiscriminate procurement of weapons can destabilize regions and states and initiate arms races (with negative security and fiscal consequences). In addition, the "buyer's market" for conventional weapons is leading to the proliferation of increasingly sophisticated weaponry into regional theaters. Second, weapons are causing millions of deaths (and particularly in the case of light weapons, large numbers of civilian deaths).[2] Specific types of conventional weapons—for example, land mines—cause high levels of suffering to both civilian and military personnel. Third, the resources being spent on conventional weapons draw money away from social and economic priorities. Of these three reasons for governance, most attention tends to be paid to the first, relating to security. Since the Vietnam conflict, however, humanitarian arguments have enjoyed increasing support, and in the post–Cold War period many states have implicitly accepted the arguments about redirecting resources (given the decreased security threats) and have significantly cut their conventional weapons arsenals.

Each of the governance approaches examined in this chapter has been proposed as a response to a distinct problem: disarmament as a way to ban war or eliminate a certain category of problematic weapons; arms control as a way to deal with the problem of instability and the risk of war; export controls as a way to prevent technology loss to enemies and, in the form of sanctions, as a way to mitigate interstate and intrastate conflicts; and confidence- and security-building measures (CSBMs), including transparency measures, as a way to increase understanding between enemies. In addition, states have sought to regulate the conduct of war.

As the record of governance in the area of conventional weapons shows, some of the most dramatic advances have occurred in the aftermath of major (interstate or intrastate) wars when efforts have been made to implement effective disarmament and arms control agreements with the specific aim of avoiding a repeat of recent events. These treaties, however, often subsequently fall victim to changes in the political environment.

Some disarmament initiatives have targeted specific classes of weapons on the basis of the humanitarian consequences of their use. These measures have been most successful when the targeted weaponry has not been effectively integrated into military planning, and thus there are no relative gains concerns, but absolute gains for all.[3]

Export controls have been used by states to manage proliferation as well as to prevent or terminate conflict. It is in the former role that export controls have scored more successes, particularly during the Cold War. The fear of losing technologies to enemies imposed great discipline on states. In more benign international environments, export controls have fared poorly. Export controls to prevent or terminate conflict have a poor record, in large part because of problems of implementation and enforcement. Implementation is undermined by the growing number of nonstate actors (black-market companies, smugglers, and others) who make their money through evading export controls and sanctions.

CSBMs and transparency initiatives have scored some success in the European theater but have yet to be applied elsewhere. It seems that the environment that allows CSBMs to flourish—including an acceptance of the regional balance of power—cannot be easily created elsewhere.

Three factors complicated governance in the conventional weapons field. First, the possession of conventional weapons has long been regarded as the key to state survival. Every state in the international system has an interest in the conventional weapons issue, as either a supplier or a recipient, or both. That interest involves perpetuating the availability of conventional weapons. The intimate connection between conventional weapons and security means that governance attempts have often met with resistance.

Second, the possession of weapons, including conventional weapons, is often considered by states to enhance their political prestige. In the past this was particularly true of major systems such as battleships. Today prestige rests in major platforms such as aircraft carriers and advanced fighter aircraft. Consequently, "negotiations designed to curb arms—especially those which are status symbols—not only run up against the intractable difficulties of ensuring military security, but also raise the inevitable issues of national pride."[4]

Third, governance of lower technology areas of the conventional weapons market—such as small arms, light weapons, and even major systems such as tanks and helicopters—is difficult because of the existence of parallel legal and illegal weapons trades.[5] Thus implementing and ensuring compliance with agreements is a complex task, requiring coordination, trained personnel, and significant resources. Unfortunately, few conventional weapons governance initiatives have been seen by states as important enough to merit the investment of such resources. The only agreements that have had that level of commitment are those implemented in the aftermath of major (interstate or intrastate) wars and arms control and disarmament treaties such as the Conventional Armed Forces in Europe (CFE) Agreement. For these reasons the issue of conventional weapons has proved a particular challenge for global governance efforts.

NATURE OF THE PROBLEM

The international community does not generally consider conventional weapons a problem. Most states possess conventional weapons, and the international trade in these weapons has existed throughout recorded history. Moreover, the UN Charter recognizes a state's right of self-defense. States have often fought attempts to bring conventional weapons issues onto the international agenda. At times, however, states have considered that conventional weapons can cause, exacerbate, or prolong conflict.

During the Cold War, the concern was the quantitative level of weaponry being produced and traded in the international system. Subsequently between 1989 and 1998, global military expenditures declined significantly from about $1.05 trillion to about $696 billion.[6] However, this decrease has not solved the problem of the proliferation of conventional weapons. Indeed, the overall decline in defense spending has resulted in much fiercer competition to make sales, leading to technology bidding wars and weapons purchases by unstable and undesirable recipients. Moreover, relatively speaking, the weapons being procured are much higher technologies than were available for transfer a decade ago. This raises two major problems. First, it raises concerns about the proliferation consequences of these transfers. In their desperation to sell, supplier states are increasingly willing to transfer advanced power projection capabilities (for example, submarines, aircraft, and refueling equipment). These transfers can have destabilizing consequences. In addition, the introduction of more advanced weaponry or a new type of weapon into a region can precipitate conflict. Second, on the substate level there are concerns arising from the transfer of mobile weapons, which naturally favor the offense.[7]

As the possession of weapons is so tightly related to the security of states, governance initiatives in the realm of conventional weapons raise four particular problems for participants. First, trust that others will abide by an agreement is fundamental for an agreement to thrive. Yet trust is hard to come by in a situation where agreements are negotiated among adversaries. Where players have conflicting ideologies—as occurred during the Cold War—problems of trust are exacerbated. For example, "The Western conviction—that if the Soviet Union could cheat in an arms control agreement, then it *would* cheat—was particularly strong during the 1950s."[8] This assumption suffused all governance attempts of the period. In addition, a state may be concerned that governance efforts are an excuse for other states to obtain information about its military deployments, forces, and strategies.

Second, the fear that results of a governance effort may favor some parties more than others and the desire to prevent other players from making relative gains can harm the chances of reaching agreements, determine strategies of negotiation, influence the form of agreements, and affect the way agreements are implemented. Because military forces are inherently dissimilar (making it hard to calculate definitively the military power of a state), there is great potential for states to perceive others making relative gains through governance attempts.[9] Perceptions of relative gains may in this regard be as difficult to overcome as actual relative gains and derail governance initiatives. Trust and relative gains concerns are not static but are constantly recalculated by states. Charges of iniquity may thus come many years after a governance initiative comes into existence. Finally, perceptions of inequality can lead to defections. They can also be used to justify cheating and more generally will exacerbate trust problems.

Third, there is the problem of participation. Governance efforts in the conventional weapons field can succeed only if all the key players participate.[10] Failure to include all the relevant actors may prevent agreement from being reached or may ensure that an agreement is flawed and will fail at the implementation stage. Participation issues have historically bedeviled conventional weapons governance efforts. The growth in the number of states in the international system, as well as in the number of nonstate actors engaged in arms production and trade, further complicates this problem.

Fourth, governance efforts can have unintended consequences, also known as the "balloon effect."[11] In the realm of conventional weapons, the balloon effect is exhibited when competition in a particular weapons system is ended through a governance effort but then emerges in another weapons system or arena of competition.

TRACK RECORD

Governance efforts in the conventional weapons field have been highly dependent on context. Four alternative approaches have been developed by politicians to deal with the problem of conventional weapons: disarmament, arms control, export controls, and CSBMs.

Disarmament

Disarmament has been sought by states and NGOs as a solution to two distinct types of problems. First, it has been seen as a way to prevent wars. Second, it has been used as a means of limiting the use of weapons that cause unacceptable levels of human suffering.

Preventing War. Disarmament efforts were particularly prominent after World Wars I and II. Immediately after World War I, there was widespread revulsion against the large-scale loss of life that had occurred.[12] Many in the British and American policy elite believed that the arms race among the major European protagonists and the vast amounts of weaponry accumulated had caused the outbreak of the war.[13] At the time, many were convinced that "if only the nations would disarm, as had been provided for in the Covenant of the League of Nations, peace would be assured."[14] Both U.S. President Woodrow Wilson and British Prime Minister Lloyd George held the view that once the enemies had been disarmed, public opinion would pressure the Allies to follow suit.[15]

The Treaty of Versailles, which sealed the end of the war with Germany contained many disarmament measures and outlined far-reaching restrictions over the forces and weaponry that Germany would be allowed to possess. Implementation of the treaty proved very difficult, however, "with the German military and naval authorities doing everything in their power to frustrate and 'counter-control' the Control Commission," which was set up to oversee the disarmament effort.[16] Cheating was a significant problem—one that would be transformed into complete defiance by the Nazi regime, illustrated by the revolution in the Luftwaffe.[17] The motive for German cheating was a security dilemma.[18] According to Tanner, "The Versailles disarmament scheme represented to the German leaders the institutionalization of assured vulnerability towards armed coercion from Allied powers. The only way to respond to this threat was to engage in illegal rearmament."[19]

The Treaty of Versailles led to several "balloon effects"; for example, the program for disarmament did not include controls on military expenditure, "a fact that Germany exploited by investing heavily in the military R&D sector."[20] This loophole allowed technological innovations such as the "pocket battleship," a ship small enough to avoid contravening the peace treaty's prohibitions on large armored ships. Moreover, strict limits on the size of the German army contributed to the growth of paramilitary organizations.[21]

Following the armistice negotiations and the establishment of the League of Nations in 1919, new negotiations were launched that culminated in the 1932 First World Disarmament Conference. At this conference, representatives of more than sixty states sought to negotiate universal reductions and limitations of armed forces and all types of armaments (conventional, incendiary, chemical, and bacteriological). A far-reaching draft document produced by Great Britain was accepted as a provisional text. The negotiations were fraught with problems, however; many delegations used them to achieve relative gains. For example, Germany and France sought incompatible outcomes from the conference; Germany wanted to achieve quantitative equality in armaments, whereas France wanted to institutionalize inequality by upholding the Treaty of Versailles.[22] Ultimately delegates were unable to agree on a final text, and the negotiations ended in acrimony.[23] This outcome reflected the deteriorating international situation, with Japan leaving the League of Nations because of the League's opposition to Tokyo's aggressive policies in Asia, Hitler becoming chancellor of Germany, and many states beginning to rearm. Participation problems also hampered the negotiations. For example, the United States only had observer status because it had chosen not to join the League system.

Outside the League system, attempts to institute naval disarmament through the establishment of a formula of ratios for capital ships and aircraft carriers resulted in three treaties between the naval powers of the day: the 1922 Washington Naval Treaty, the 1930 London Treaty, and the 1936 London Treaty. Some heralded the Washington Treaty as the first step toward a disarmed world.[24] The two other treaties, however, were negotiated against a background of intense rivalry between the major naval powers—principally, the United States and Great Britain.[25]

The naval arms control negotiations of the 1920s and 1930s were implicitly about establishing a new balance of forces, which in turn raised many relative gains concerns.[26] At the 1922 conference France, anxious about British and U.S. attempts to ban submarines (which would have diminished France's naval power), managed to block that plan. During the 1930 London Naval Conference, the Japanese had reluctantly accepted a force ratio to the British and Americans of 5:5:3. This inequality became increasingly problematic as Japan's perceptions of its naval requirements were revised in light of the threat posed by the unification of China.[27] Moreover, the French and Italians refused to accept the ratios on offer, and consequently the most important part of the treaty was signed only by Great Britain, the United States, and Japan.[28] Japan's subsequent proposal for a common upper limit and claim for parity was not acceptable to Great Britain and the United States, and Japan gave notice of its intention to terminate the Washington and London treaties, and withdrew from the negotiations in 1936.[29] Moreover, Germany was not a direct participant in the Second London Conference of 1935–1936, even though it was rising German power that made the negotiations so desirable.[30] This left only Great Britain, France, and the United States.[31] They signed the 1936 London Naval Treaty but, recognizing the problems of regime participation, included in it a number of "escape clauses" that allowed suspension of obligations as long as the other parties were informed.

Thus, even though several naval disarmament treaties were signed in the 1920s and 1930s, issues of relative gains, trust, and participation remained. Moreover, in the aftermath of the treaties, there was evidence of balloon effects. For example, the

1922 Washington Treaty, which restricted battleships, cruisers, and aircraft carriers, did not cover destroyers and submarines. As a consequence, extensive construction in these weapons systems started soon thereafter. Moreover, together the naval arms limitation agreements in the 1920 and 1930s led to intense interstate competition in land and air systems.

Despite the failure of the League of Nations to prevent World War II from breaking out, efforts after 1945 focused again on disarmament. The 1947 peace treaty with Italy contained many disarmament measures, and in the case of Germany and Japan, the Allies took complete control and started implementing far-reaching demilitarization and denazification measures.[32]

The attention of the United States and the Soviet Union then briefly turned to discussions of disarmament in the conventional and atomic fields. General and universal disarmament talks started within the framework of the United Nations—in the UN Commission for Conventional Armaments.[33] The United States and the Soviet Union, however, sought to structure the UN agenda in such a way that each could make relative gains vis-à-vis the other.[34] The United States tried to preserve its atomic arsenal (in part because of Western weakness in conventional weapons), whereas the Soviet Union wanted atomic weapons dealt with prior to any conventional disarmament. As a consequence of these fundamental disagreements, the talks ended in acrimony.[35]

With the onset of the Cold War and the United States' loss of its atomic monopoly, the establishment of a stable deterrent relationship between the United States and the Soviet Union became the absolute priority. As a result, conventional weapons slipped off the agenda. The two countries focused instead on bilateral nuclear arms control negotiations.[36] There was no further serious talk of conventional weapons disarmament until the end of the Cold War.

Today disarmament is discussed in the context of preventing the recurrence of intrastate conflict rather than interstate conflict. There have been many civil war peace settlements involving disarmament, for example, in Angola, Cambodia, Haiti, and Mozambique.[37] These agreements often requested international actors, including the United Nations, to monitor and verify the disarmament of state and nonstate actors such as ethnic groups, paramilitaries, and other irregular forces.[38] The record of post–civil war disarmament is mixed. Successes include El Salvador and Mozambique.[39] Among the failed efforts are Angola (three times) and Cambodia.[40] The success of disarmament efforts rests on many issues, but the most crucial is the acceptability of the postconflict balance of power between the parties. That said, the international institutions can play a positive role in verifying disarmament and thus assisting in the building of confidence and security in the state.[41]

Limiting the Effects of Weapons. Dealing with weapons that cause unnecessary suffering is the second purpose of disarmament. The St. Petersburg Declaration of 1868 is the first known weapons limitation treaty.[42] It prohibited the use of explosive and/or incendiary bullets and is the foundation for the international humanitarian law tradition of "forbidden weapons." The St. Petersburg Declaration was followed by two international peace conferences held at The Hague in 1899 and 1907.[43] Interestingly, the 1899 Declaration (IV) banning dum-dum bullets (that is, soft-nosed bullets that spread out in the flesh causing extensive internal injuries and are therefore particularly harmful and difficult for doctors to deal with) has achieved success far beyond what was anticipated. The declaration prohibits the use of such bullets in conflict only between signatory countries and permits their use against nonsignatories.[44] Even though this type of bullet remains a potent weapon, the norm of nonuse has spread to become a global norm. The universalization of this norm is unusual. Crossbows, gunpowder, red-hot shot, and dum-dum bullets were all initially thought to be unnecessarily nasty, but only the latter "stayed under the ban placed by popular military culture on weapons too horrible (in imagination at least) to bear thinking of."[45]

The use of modern conventional weapons such as incendiary weapons, land mines, and small-caliber, high-velocity bullets in the Indochina war led to the negotiation of the 1981 Convention on Prohibitions or Restrictions on the Use of Certain Conventional Weapons Which May Be Deemed to be Excessively Injurious or to Have Indiscriminate Effects, also known as the Convention on Conventional Weapons (CCW). Efforts leading up to the negotiation of the CCW involved ". . . parallel, and not always coordinated, work by the United Nations General Assembly and Secretariat, the International Committee of the Red Cross (ICRC), and a few countries, notably Sweden and Mexico."[46]

In earlier discussions participants had considered a large list of weapons, including napalm; small-caliber, high-velocity projectiles; and delayed-action weapons. Their differences were so great, however, that restrictions could be successfully negotiated on only three categories of weapons (some fragmentation devices; land mines and booby traps; and incendiary weapons).[47] Even then, there were disputes between countries wanting outright prohibitions (Sweden and Mexico) and those that styled themselves "realists" (the United States and the Soviet Union), and which sought more limited measures over issues such as incendiary weapons.[48]

The CCW outlaws conventional weapons considered excessively injurious. It bans weapons that leave "fragments which in the human body escape detection by X-rays" and restricts the use of mines, booby traps, and other devices, as well as incendiary weapons.[49] Intriguingly, despite the title of the treaty, "The Conference ended with no finding that the restrictions and prohibitions contained in the weapons convention were imposed because of any agreed belief or finding that those weapons were in fact excessively injurious or had indiscriminate effects."[50]

This failure suggests that despite the successful negotiation, the humanitarian intention behind the CCW was less well accepted than the view that it was in essence an arms control agreement. The negotiations over the CCW reflected a form of relative gains problem, with the United States participating in them only because it desired to block any attempt to build retroactivity into the treaty (probably fearing retribution over its activities in Indochina).

Activists have used subsequent CCW review conferences as one route to try to impose a complete ban on land mines, with only partial success.[51] A clear achievement was the use of the CCW to prohibit blinding laser weapons.[52] The ban was possible because few states had developed them, and they were not yet integrated into military planning.

The CCW has experienced some implementation and compliance problems, reflecting continued trust issues. The convention has no institutionalized monitoring of compliance. Instead monitoring is done in an ad hoc fashion by national governments and somewhat more systematically by humanitarian organizations such as the ICRC. This lack of monitoring means that states can make relative gains by evading the CCW agreements.

The post–Cold War period has seen the signing of the landmark Convention on the Prohibition of the Use, Stockpiling, Production, and Transfer of Anti-Personnel Mines and on Their Destruction. As of January 2001, 139 countries had signed the 1997 treaty, and 109 had ratified it.[53] Participation issues remain, however; key international players (China, India, and the United States, all major manufacturers of land mines) have yet to sign the treaty, raising questions about effective implementation. In addition, land mines have continued to be used in recent intrastate conflicts, even by some of the treaty's signatories.[54] Compliance has been very uneven, with regions of tension continuing to see the deployment of land mines as a normal part of conflict, whereas more peaceful regions have seen much greater adherence to the treaty.

* * *

The interstate disarmament efforts of the twentieth century were not successful. Even when treaties were signed, they failed to prevent trust problems, relative gains concerns, and security dilemmas, ultimately allowing wars to reoccur. Looking at post–Cold War disarmament after intrastate conflicts, the record seems more promising. The acceptance by all parties concerned of the resulting balance of power seems crucial to success. Agreements can be supported by CSBMs such as international verification means, which may make it possible to avoid future trust and relative gains problems. These postconflict peace settlements, however, have not yet shown if they can endure new challenges.

Disarmament efforts to ban certain types of weapons (on the grounds of humanitarian concerns) have achieved an initially modest but growing level of success. The approach is increasingly favored by NGOs, as the relevant governance forums are more open to nonstate actor agenda setting and involvement in negotiation and implementation.

Arms Control

There is some confusion over where to draw the line between arms control and disarmament.[55] However, the era of arms control can be said to have effectively begun during the Cold War. By the early 1960s the major powers realized that disarmament was not possible, and the more limited goal of arms control was pursued. The classic formulation of arms control gives it three purposes: to reduce the risk of war; to limit the destructiveness of war; and to facilitate the redirection of resources away from producing weapons to more productive and peaceful ends.[56] Arms control was also regarded as a "tool for managing the military aspects of a relationship among potential adversaries."[57] More specifically, it was seen as a means to solve the security dilemma between the United States and the Soviet Union.

During the Cold War, instability in Europe was a problem common to both the North Atlantic Treaty Organization (NATO) and the Warsaw Treaty Organization (WTO). Each feared nuclear escalation, which might result from an imbalance of conventional forces. Consequently, in the 1970s the two sides started negotiations on Mutual and Balanced Force Reductions (MBFR). The MBFR talks ran between 1973 and 1988 and were intended to negotiate force reductions in Central Europe; however, they never achieved any tangible results.[58]

Trust problems were a major dimension of the difficulties experienced in the MBFR negotiations, particularly given the attempts to achieve relative gains, which were present from the outset. The United States had another pressing reason for action; Congress was planning to make unilateral cuts to U.S. forces in Europe. The talks were therefore an attempt by the executive branch to restore relative gains to be lost through legislative activity. Relative gains concerns meant that NATO wished to use the talks to curb the WTO's growing superiority in conventional arms. NATO also wanted to maintain and improve its own conventional forces. The WTO, by contrast, wanted to minimize Soviet force reductions in Central Europe. Hence even the title of the negotiations was a source of dispute. Whereas the West emphasized the concept of "balanced" force reductions from the outset, the WTO rightly interpreted this to mean bigger reductions of their forces than on the NATO side and refused to include the word "balanced" in the official title.[59] Moreover, as the negotiations continued, "Both sides consciously tailored their proposals so as to allow weapon modernization and to ensure that the weapons that might be bargained away were of minimum military value."[60]

Trust concerns also emerged in disputes over verification. The NATO allies demanded intrusive verification of all agreements, something that the WTO was not prepared to accept, fearing spying and attempts to undermine its alliance. Ironically, the MBFR process may have increased trust problems: "The negotiations did result in a closer scrutiny by NATO of WTO force levels and strategies, and may well have served to increase the West's distrust of the Soviet Union."[61] The result was greater NATO investments in weapons standardization.

The long-running negotiations over MBFR were also hindered by France's refusal to participate, following its 1966 withdrawal from NATO's integrated military command structure. Indeed France's absence made a realistic trade-off of conventional forces much more difficult to achieve.[62]

The same year the MBFR talks began, the Conference on Security and Cooperation in Europe (CSCE) was launched. The conference, whose aim was to improve relations among states, was primarily concerned with political and economic issues.

The Conventional Forces Europe (CFE) Treaty negotiation started in 1989 as a follow-on negotiation to MBFR. Its original aim was to eliminate the capability to launch surprise attacks. Early CFE discussions took place under the aegis of the CSCE, as requested by France. The CFE process benefited from the good working relationships built among the participants through the CSCE process and resulted in the signature of the CFE Treaty in 1990.[63] Parties to the CFE agree to unprecedented reductions in conventional weapons in a geographical region from the Atlantic Ocean to the Ural Mountains. Five categories of weapons are covered; battle tanks, artillery pieces, armored combat vehicles, attack helicopters, and combat aircraft. In addition to limits on total holdings, there are restrictions on the numbers of specific systems that can be kept in four specified geographical zones.[64] CFE involves cooperative (but nevertheless intrusive) verification of the agreement and includes CSBMs.[65] It "thus sought to further reduce fears and tensions in post–cold war Europe."[66] According to Richard Falkenrath, the verification regime also serves "a more generally useful function . . . to improve and institutionalize transparency in the military affairs of Europe."[67]

Implementation of the treaty has been impressive; by January 1998 more than 51,200 pieces of equipment had been either scrapped or converted to civilian use. Nevertheless, implementation has been slower in the case of the new states that emerged out of the Soviet Union.[68] Implementation is monitored through the Joint Consultative Group, which also operates as a forum for solving problems and considers measures to enhance the treaty.

The CFE Treaty was completed at the end of the Cold War and therefore needed to be adapted to the new geostrategic situation. The parties to the CFE began to discuss treaty adaptation in 1997, but negotiations were difficult, grinding to a halt at several stages. Some of the obstacles concerned relative gains and trust issues. For example, NATO slowed the negotiations in 1998 until it could determine whether Russia was going to meet its commitments to remove equipment from its flanks by a deadline of May 1999. Meanwhile Russia slowed down the negotiations because it was uneasy over the issue of NATO expansion. Despite these problems, in November 1999 thirty states signed the agreement to adapt the CFE Treaty to the post–Cold War realities of Europe.[69]

Implementation of the CFE Treaty caused several balloon effects. First, after the negotiation of quantitative limits on the systems it could have on its western borders, Russia transferred many of the surplus aircraft, tanks, and other weapons to its border with China, significantly raising tensions there. Second, the CFE Treaty has built-in provisions for the transfer of weapons from states that need to decrease their holdings to bring them into line with their treaty obligations. This process, known as the "cascade" of weapons, led to the supply of higher-technology weapons to Greece, Norway, Portugal, Spain, and Turkey (all of which destroyed older weapons and replaced them with these newer ones).[70] Third, there has been an informal balloon effect, with many European states actually transferring more weapons than they were mandated to under the treaty. These weapons (particularly from East European states) have been subsequently used in civil wars in several African countries.

Another significant multilateral arms control agreement is the 1996 Florence Agreement on Sub-Regional Arms Control, signed by Bosnia and Herzegovina and its two entities (Bosnia-Herzegovina and Republika Srpska) and Croatia and Yugoslavia (composed of Serbia and Montenegro). As Zdzislaw Lachowski has noted, the implementation of the Florence Agreement is proving more successful than other elements of the 1995 Dayton Accords, the peace agreement that ended the war in Bosnia-Herzegovina.[71] The parties have met all their obligations regarding equipment limited by the agreement. More than 6,600 items of heavy equipment have been scrapped or converted, and numerous verification inspections have been completed. The notification and inspection regimes have been consolidated, with the help of the Organization for Security Cooperation in Europe (OSCE).[72] Much remains to be achieved, however, including integrating the three armed forces existing in Bosnia and Herzegovina, establishing a common security policy, and increasing transparency.

One of the more promising non-European arms control initiatives is the Economic Community of West African States (ECOWAS) three-year moratorium on production and trade in conventional weapons. It is the only agreement so far to go beyond rhetoric to action, having entered into force in November 1998. However, problems remain as it has no verification mechanism.[73]

* * *

Until the signing of the CFE Treaty, conventional arms control achievements were quixotic. Although there was no clear conventional weapons governance outcome from the fifteen years of negotiations, the MBFR talks were nevertheless valuable as a line of communication between the Cold War enemies.

The CFE Treaty is the first substantial multilateral conventional arms control treaty to have been negotiated successfully. It was negotiated at a time of rapid geostrategic change in Europe and played a positive role in managing geostrategic changes that could have been its deathknell. This indicates that the treaty has already achieved a level of robustness lacking in previous arms control and disarmament efforts. Moreover, it seems that CFE has proved a useful model for application in the Balkans and is meeting some success there (facilitated by the interest of the international community in stabilizing the region).

Export Controls

In part because of the general failure of disarmament and arms control efforts to ameliorate tensions, states have sought to restrict illicit access to weapons through export controls. Some export controls are designed to prevent the spread of weapons and technology; others are designed to prevent or control violent conflicts—be they intrastate or interstate.

CoCom and the Wassenaar Arrangement.   The loss of important technologies to the enemy, and the security problems this could cause, was a particular issue for the NATO alliance during the Cold War. In response NATO members (minus Iceland, but joined by Australia and Japan) developed export control arrangements to protect strategically important technologies. The Coordinating Committee for Multilateral Export Controls (CoCom), established in 1949, was an informal agreement between Western states and involved ongoing negotiations over which weapons and technologies were to be restricted. Negotiations were relatively successful during the Cold War. By the 1980s, however, tensions between the United States and its European allies had increased over how restrictive the regime needed to be.[74] In 1989 the recalculation of relative gains, vis-à-vis both other regime participants and nonparticipants, led Great Britain to challenge the United States over the restrictions on trade. Great Britain won concessions that allowed freer trade.[75] As the Cold War waned, CoCom's members increasingly pitted economic issues against security concerns in CoCom, resulting in the triumph of the former.

In 1994 the decision was made to disband CoCom, even though negotiations over a follow-up regime were incomplete. The new regime—which eventually became the Wassenaar Arrangement on Export Controls for Conventional Arms and Dual-Use Goods and Technologies—took several years to bring into existence because of arguments between the United States and other prospective members over how restrictive the regime should be, what systems it should cover, who should be allowed to join, and who the targets of the regime were.[76] Negotiations saw relative gains concerns aggravated by the contraction of the international arms transfer market, which made every potential sale more desirable and states reluctant to accept restrictions on trade. For example, negotiations were held up by French and Russian objections to giving advanced notification of transfers.[77] Only after significant pressure from other members, particularly the United States, did Russia (supported by France) drop its objections and accept the reporting requirements.[78] The Wassenaar Arrangement was agreed in 1995 and began to work in September 1996. In January 2001 Wassenaar's membership stood at thirty-three including many states that were formerly part of the Eastern bloc. One of the agreed aims of the arrangement is to exchange information and views on transfers on a range of items contained on agreed lists of munitions and dual-use items. The goal is to promote transparency and greater responsibility, and thus prevent destabilizing accumulations of conventional arms and sensitive dual-use technologies.[79] A group of states led by the United States, however, also seeks to use the arrangement to prevent technologies from reaching so-called rogue states.[80] Not all the Wassenaar members agree with the U.S. agenda. As a consequence of these differences, together with relative gains concerns, new market conditions, and the low-threat environment, the restrictions of the Wassenaar Arrangement are much weaker than were those of CoCom. For example, members do not have the right to veto one another's sales decisions.

Export controls are an effective tool to protect technologies when there is a clear enemy. Conversely, where the degree of danger posed by the enemy is contested, or where there is no clear enemy, export control regimes are more difficult to operate and are beset by relative gains issues among the suppliers. This accounts for the contrast between the successful operation of the CoCom regime at the height of the Cold War and its successor, the near-moribund Wassenaar Arrangement, which operates more like a transparency regime than an export control mechanism.[81]

CAT Talks.   During the Cold War several attempts were made to avoid destabilizing sensitive regions through conventional weapons transfers. In terms of export controls designed to prevent or control conflicts between states, the most comprehensive global effort was the 1977–1978 Conventional Arms Transfer Talks (CAT Talks) held between the United States and the Soviet Union. The talks failed after four surprisingly constructive rounds of negotiations. "The immediate fate of the talks and the timing of their collapse can only be understood in the context of the bureaucratic battles within the Carter administration over the issue of arms transfer control and the wider question of relations with the Soviet Union and China."[82]

Trust and relative gains concerns were present from the outset of the negotiations. Some officials in the U.S. Joint Chiefs of Staff did not trust the Soviet Union's apparent enthusiasm for the negotiations, fearing that the Soviets would make relative gains by forcing the United States to commit to a unilateral restraint policy (pending a successful outcome to the CAT Talks) while dragging out the negotiations.[83] U.S. defense manufacturers also had relative gains concerns. They feared that the Europeans would seize their traditional markets while they remained tied down by the unilateral restraint policy of the administration.[84]

Another problem of the CAT Talks concerned participation. The talks were conceived originally as a multilateral negotiation. However, the United States' Western European allies resisted the CAT initiative, and even when they were offered the incentive of a greater share of the NATO arms market, they refused to participate.[85] Moreover, the West European suppliers noted with concern the U.S. interest in limiting arms transfers to Latin America—a region where they were dominant.[86] They therefore saw relative gains issues arising from the U.S. agenda, adding to their skepticism. Nonetheless, the talks continued but as a bilateral negotiation between the United States and the Soviet Union with the intention to include Europeans at a later date. Because significant Western arms suppliers remained outside of the negotiation, however, the Soviet Union feared that the United States planned to tie them down in negotiations while the Europeans made inroads into traditional Soviet arms markets. Thus, in addition to participation problems, there were trust issues and relative gains concerns on both sides, making progress difficult. Nevertheless, the talks did make notable progress before eventually falling victim to the internal contradictions of the Carter administration over China and stand out as a serious attempt to establish international controls over conventional weapons.[87]

Regional Initiatives. A significant attempt to limit the supply of conventional weapons to the Middle East was the 1950 Tripartite Agreement. Negotiated among Great Britain, France, and the United States, the accord was an attempt to avoid an arms race between Israel and its Arab neighbors and a recurrence of the 1948–1949 fighting. Recipient states subject to the agreement were severely restricted in the weapons they could obtain and had to commit not to attack any state in the region. In practice, the agreement was "more of a division of the market than a limitation on the sale of arms to countries in the region."[88] The agreement was implemented through a Near East Arms Coordinating Committee, which tracked and balanced (by refusing or granting transfers) the arms trading, in light of the security needs of states in the region. The committee became a forum for disputes between the allies over implementation, as relative gains and different security issues came to divide them.[89] The allies' interest was not in conventional arms transfer control per se, but in ensuring close ties with developing states in the "forward defense areas" as part of the strategy of containment. This raised a participation problem, however, as Soviet-bloc suppliers were obviously not party to the agreement. Thus, according to one observer, "All control efforts were eradicated and effectively reversed when the Western arms monopoly in the Middle East was broken."[90] In 1951 Cairo contacted Moscow to try to circumvent the restrictions placed on arms transfers and secured a deal for Czechoslovakia to supply Egypt with weapons, which were delivered in 1955.[91]

In 1991, immediately after the Persian Gulf War, the permanent members of the UN Security Council (China, France, Great Britain, Russia, and the United States) launched the so-called P-5 Initiative as a response to the perceived problem of excessive and destabilizing arms transfers to the Middle East that might precipitate inter-state conflict. Designed to ensure that the top five arms sellers controlled transfers to the region, the protoregime collapsed in acrimony within a short time. The Chinese had been somewhat reluctant to participate in the P-5 Initiative and were therefore looking for a reason for exiting from a negotiation that raised relative gains and trust issues for them. President George Bush gave them this exit; Bush, engaged in a fierce reelection campaign, sought to win votes in the key state of Texas by ensuring defense jobs through allowing sales of F-16s to Taiwan. To the Chinese, the F-16 sale broke U.S. agreements with China, and they therefore gratefully exited the P-5 Initiative. Other relative gains issues also emerged from the P-5 Initiative. Specifically, the West Europeans were angered that the United States made large transfer deals with Israel and Saudi Arabia while urging control on them.[92]

Another notable governance attempt to limit arms sales was undertaken in Latin America. In 1974 Argentina, Bolivia, Chile, Colombia, Ecuador, Panama, Peru, and Venezuela agreed to negotiate measures to limit military expenditures and weapons purchases and thus free up resources for development. The Declaration of Ayacucho set in motion five rounds of meetings before the initiative collapsed.[93] The Ayacucho process was riddled with relative gains problems, played out in disputes over whether to institute arms import limitations. The Chilean government wanted to establish a favorable regional military balance prior to instituting limitations on the import of conventional weapons (it was then completing a procurement cycle). By contrast, Argentina, Brazil, and Peru rejected the proposal. According to one observer, "Argentina and Brazil felt that a balanced reduction could endanger their arms industry and Peru saw it necessary to maintain its current military capability owing to the possibility of confrontation at both its northern and southern borders."[94] Brazil, a major regional power that both produced arms and imported them, was not directly involved in the Ayacucho process, resulting in imperfect participation. This led to the specter of Brazil making relative gains against the declaration's adherents and thus created a security dilemma. Relative gains concerns were also obvious in the negotiations over the permitted range of missiles.[95] The Ayacucho process paralleled attempts at Andean integration. Both suffered from the rising tensions in the region, however. The major cleavage was between the ideologically opposed military regimes in Peru and Chile. This rift inevitably polarized discussions, and in 1974–1975 the Chileans defected from both the Ayacucho process and Andean integration. Relative gains and trust issues were not solved in the negotiations, leading ultimately to their failure.

New Approaches to Export Controls.   The difficulty of achieving export controls in a low-threat (post–Cold War) environment in which the economic incentives to trade in weapons are high has led to an emphasis on establishing nonbinding agreements that recognize certain minimum standards when contemplating transfers. Moves to establish "codes of conduct" over arms transfers have occurred at both the regional and global levels.

Former Costa Rican president Oscar Arias and a group of fellow Nobel Peace laureates are leading global efforts to establish a code of conduct for arms transfers. A draft code, prepared by the Arias Foundation and five NGOs, was launched in May 1997.[96] These codes are designed to limit arms supplies to states engaged in external aggression or internal repression. The code efforts have not yet moved beyond setting the agenda on this issue, and no state has specifically adopted this code, although it is complementary and supportive of other codes.[97]

By contrast, the European Union (EU) has agreed to a Code of Conduct on the Arms Trade, despite various relative gains concerns. The result is a voluntary, nonbinding agreement related to arms exports. Although agreement by the entire EU was reached on a text, it is much weaker than the draft text and weaker than the policies unilaterally adopted by the United Kingdom and Spain.[98] The French were particularly active in ensuring the watering down of the original text and refused to accept the proposed strict consultation or prior notification arrangements.[99] The EU code does not seem to be having a noticeable effect on overall arms transfer levels, although it has limited transfers to individual states—for example, to Indonesia during the troubles in East Timor in 2000.

Since the end of the Cold War, many other attempts to control the international conventional arms trade have been launched. Given the newness of some of these governance efforts, judgments on their success are necessarily provisional. In addition, since 1992, when the issue first came to international attention, many multilateral initiatives focusing on small arms and light weapons have been launched.[100] This development reflects the growing consensus that focus should be placed on the weapons that do the majority of the killing and whose proliferation (in the aftermath of the Cold War) is having marked negative effects on both interstate and intrastate security. The issue was highlighted, for example, in the UN Secretary-General's 1995 Supplement to an Agenda for Peace. Activity to date has involved raising the profile of the issue and, to this end, a conference on the illicit trade in small arms and light weapons was held in 2001.[101]

There has also been an increase in the number of regional governance initiatives on small arms and light weapons. For example, the 1997 Inter-American Convention Against the Illicit Manufacture of and Trafficking in Firearms, Ammunition, Explosives, and Other Related Materials.[102] The negotiation of the convention was motivated by concerns about the destabilization of governments in the region due to the availability of illegal small arms and light weapons. The convention has resulted in greater cooperation among states to eradicate smuggling, and the numbers of weapons interdicted has increased. Law-enforcement concerns led the UN Economic and Social Council (ECOSOC) to elaborate a universal protocol against the illicit manufacturing of and trafficking in firearms, ammunition, and other related materials.[103]

The Organization of African Unity has taken some tentative steps and held a ministerial meeting on the issue in Mali in November 2000.[104] Two other initiatives have emerged recently from Southern Africa. First, in 1999 the Southern African Regional Police Chiefs Co-operation Organization adopted a declaration on small arms, focusing particularly on the problems caused by illicit weapons. Second, in 2000 the Southern African Development Community (SADC) developed a protocol on the control of firearms, ammunition, and other related materials, which should be ready for signing at SADC's August 2001 summit.[105] In East Africa the most significant initiative is the March 2000 Nairobi Declaration on the problem of the proliferation of illicit small arms and light weapons in the Great Lakes region and the Horn of Africa.[106]

Bennie Lombard has noted that two approaches to the problem of small arms and light weapons are emerging. One approach considers that the issue of small arms is essentially a police and crime prevention matter and therefore any international effort should focus only on illicit arms. The other approach, advocated by those who favor a more holistic approach, concludes that the problems are linked and that licit and illicit arms should be dealt with in a broader context of peace building, good governance, and disarmament.[107]

The more narrow focus on illicit small arms and light weapons raises the problem of relative gains issues for nonstate actors. The participants in these international, regional, and subregional negotiations tend to be states. They are generally satisfied because curbing the illicit trade tends to increase their power, particularly vis-à-vis insurgent groups and other substate challengers. These latter groups may face significant security dilemmas, however, as a result of the removal of their means to protect themselves and their communities.

Finally, the post–Cold War period has seen increasing use of the arms embargo as a tool for managing inter- and intrastate conflicts. Prior to the end of the Cold War, only one arms embargo had been imposed by the United Nations since its founding (on South Africa in 1977). By contrast, between 1991 and May 2000, eleven embargoes were imposed that were intended to manage conflict.[108] Export controls in the form of arms embargoes have increasingly been employed as a response to the problem of war within states. One important innovation was the September 1993 imposition of an arms embargo on the UNITA faction in Angola. This was the first time that a group other than a state had been the target of an embargo. The move was designed to prevent UNITA from making relative gains at the expense of the Angolan government.

The record of arms embargoes as a response to interstate conflicts is mixed. Governance efforts here have been most effective when action has moved beyond mere rhetorical support for sanctions to active implementation through interdiction of supplies. Since the end of the Cold War, the growing number of different state and nonstate weapons suppliers has greatly increased the difficulty of implementing embargoes. The investment required to make them work is often more than outside powers are prepared to make, particularly given that for many states the imposition of an embargo is an alternative to direct action. Indeed active policing of an embargo might blur the boundary between nonintervention and intervention.[109]

The renewed use of the UN arms embargo as a tool of conflict management has led to the reemergence of a black market in weapons. The black market, largely stagnant since the 1930s, has revived and expanded in response to the demand caused by the imposition of embargoes by the United Nations, the EU, and other regional actors. This is a manifestation of the balloon effect.

* * *

Export controls have had maximum effect when they have been supported by a clear consensus and where efforts have been made to guarantee their success—for example, through effective monitoring of exports. The only time when this systematically occurred was during CoCom's existence, when the Cold War bred a responsible attitude toward export controls. Once the discipline of the Cold War was lost, export controls became hard to maintain and subject to challenge from within (by states parties) and without (by nonstate actors such as black marketers). Even weaker forms of multilateral export controls such as codes of conduct have been difficult to negotiate and their achievements to date minimal.

CSBMs and Other Transparency Measures

The realization in the 1970s that disarmament and arms control governance efforts were fraught with problems of trust and relative gains led to a search for tools to overcome them. Confidence- and security-building measures, including transparency initiatives, and verification procedures were thought to be a solution. Using CSBMs, states can show benign intent.[110] These measures should not be regarded as an end in themselves but are intended to create the right conditions for arms control and disarmament. Transparency initiatives can (1) have a deterrent effect, (2) provide reassurance, and (3) reveal to a government the consequences of its practices.[111] They may involve information collection and exchange, prenotification of military activities, provision of details of domestic procurement, and arms imports and exports.

CSBMs were first discussed in the CSCE. Inaugurated in 1973, the CSCE was concerned primarily with political and economic issues, but in the Helsinki Final Act of 1975 a variety of confidence-building measures were included. The Stockholm Conference on Disarmament in Europe was set up under the aegis of the CSCE in 1984 and reached agreement on a range of CSBMs in 1986.[112] These were improved on in the 1990 and 1992 Vienna Documents.[113] Among the measures in the 1990 document was a requirement for advanced notification of any intent to introduce new weapons into the CSCE area.[114]

With the end of the Cold War, the aims of the CSCE have been expanded. Within the CSCE—now called the OSCE, reflecting the institutionalization of the process—the Forum for Security Cooperation (FSC) was established as a follow-on negotiation to CFE. It started work in 1992 and has a three-part mandate: (1) to negotiate on arms control, disarmament, and confidence and security building; (2) to enhance regular consultation and to intensify cooperation on matters related to security; and (3) to further the process of reducing the risk of conflict.[115] The OSCE approach reflects a sophisticated and expansive attitude to CSBMs. According to a Polish security official, "The aim is not to negotiate new limits that make preparations for war more difficult, but to establish a network of mutual dependencies and relationships that will make a conflict of interests impossible: to prevent new arms races not by deeper cuts and stricter verification regimes, but by enhancing democratic control of military forces."[116] The FSC provides space for what Jenonne Walker terms "socialization" to take place.[117] She also asserts that "sustained dialogue among civilians and military security officials from across Europe can do more to promote stability and prevent conflict, and possibly even to reduce and restructure military forces, than specific arms control measures of the traditional kind."[118]

At the global level CSBMs are promoted through the UN Register of Conventional Weapons. A key aim of the UN Register is to help the international community to identify and prevent "excessive and destabilising accumulations and transfers of conventional arms."[119] By publishing information provided by states on their imports and exports of seven categories of conventional weapons (adapted from the CFE categories), the Register is designed to improve transparency and openness and therefore end trust problems. The original intention was to expand quickly the reporting categories to include a wider range of weapons, more detailed information on weapons types, and information on domestic holdings.[120] The UN Register has experienced problems, however, in trying to negotiate expansion both in terms of the weaponry within its remit and in terms of being a reporting and transparency mechanism.[121] States have resisted this expansion for a mix of relative gains concerns and trust issues. Because the UN Register works through consensus, states opposed to such expansion have been able to halt progress.

When the UN Register came into operation information was to be available only to governments. However, given that one of its intentions was to provide information so that citizens could pressure governments to change their behavior, the lack of transparency was a big problem. Under pressure from academics at Bradford University in Great Britain, who did publish this kind of information, governments began to release the details themselves. The subsequent move to post the reports on the Internet has further enhanced transparency.[122]

The UN Register, whose efficacy relies on universality, has many participation problems, however. There is little involvement from states in the Middle East, North Africa, or Sub-Saharan Africa. Moreover, Albania, Bosnia, and Yugoslavia have not participated since 1997.[123] Many conflict-prone states are not involved because of relative gains concerns, which undercuts its usefulness. In 1998 China declined to participate in the UN Register, reversing five years of participation.[124] If sustained, this defection would be a serious problem. Because China is both a permanent member of the UN Security Council and a major arms exporter, its presence has been one of the transparency regime's key strengths.[125]

The UN Register does not have an institutional capacity to verify submissions. The assessment of the meaning of entries is left to the participants. Where both importers and exporters participate in the UN Register, their returns can be checked against each other. This provides a measure of verification.[126] Significant discrepancies remain, however, between import and export data, with a "matching rate" of only 40 percent. Ironically, these discrepancies could lead to the kind of trust problems that the UN Register is designed to help mitigate, particularly if transfers are overestimated (by either importer or exporter).

The UN Register was created as a global CSBM. The Canadian government has argued that it has proved an important stimulus for security dialogues, both governmental and "second track," at the regional and subregional levels.[127] For example, the Association of South East Asian Nations (ASEAN) Regional Forum, known as the ARF, has seen high regional participation in the UN Register, and ARF members have begun to circulate their returns to one another as a CSBM.[128] The Organization of American States (OAS) governments agreed in 1998 to improve and broaden the information submitted by the member states to the UN Register as one of a number of CSBMs.[129]

The UN Register is operating more effectively in some regions than in others. Unfortunately, the regions where it is most effective tend to be more peaceful anyway and where relative gains and trust issues have less importance. The failure of the UN Register to expand and have countries from conflict-prone regions participate is a concern and limits its utility as CSBM. A way to deal with some of these problems may be to move to regional arms registers, which may enable some regions to capitalize on their growing confidence and move toward deeper governance initiatives.

CSBMs may be able to help states resolve lingering trust problems. They can fulfill this role, however, only when there is agreement over the basic balance of power. Absent this, CSBMs will be unable to play this catalytic role.

LESSONS LEARNED

One of the enduring debates surrounding the issue of conventional weapons control focuses on a question: Which comes first, governance or an improved security environment? The answer has differed over time. For example, in the League of Nations, discussions focused on whether such agreements must await the establishment of more friendly relations among nations, or alternatively, whether disarmament agreements in and of themselves would succeed in reducing tension.[130] This question divided the League of Nations, and the unwillingness of key players to put their faith in disarmament meant that the governance initiative failed. Trust problems triumphed.

The UN system considered the same problem after World War II. Thanks to the machinations of the two ideological blocs, two different UN forums came up with different answers. Members of the UN Atomic Energy Commission assumed that disarmament should precede an improvement in atmosphere, but members of the UN Commission for Conventional Armaments assumed the opposite.[131] Once again trust problems prevented the international community from going ahead with arms control or disarmament in either forum.

A key lesson of the twentieth century is that better relations between states must precede an arms control or disarmament agreement if it is to achieve its aims and last. One of the major criteria for establishing better relations among states or groups is a willingness to accept the balance of power. If this acceptance is present, then lingering trust, relative gains, and participation issues can be addressed through CSBMs. For example, in the case of the CFE Treaty, it benefited from participants engaging through the CSCE process, which built confidence and demonstrated to the parties that they all accepted the regional balance of power.

Furthermore, some forms of governance (CSBMs) can be used to create better relations among states, which is necessary for deeper governance (arms control and disarmament) to be instituted. This suggests that CSBMs can play a vital catalytic role in moving the international community through the various phases of governance: agenda setting, negotiation, implementation, and compliance. Thus the international community is not left waiting for better relations to naturally evolve.

The experience of the Florence Agreement adds a note of caution to this assessment, however. In the Florence Agreement, CSBMs and arms control and disarmament were to be implemented in parallel. To date, although the agreement has achieved its arms control and disarmament objectives, an improved regional environment has yet to emerge—indeed, its successful implementation outstrips other elements of the Dayton Accords. The interests of external powers, including their physical military presence in the region, have kept the Florence Agreement on track. But the parties to the agreement are not fully reconciled to the balance of power reflected in Dayton and have thus been prevented by trust issues from placing faith in the CSBMs of the agreement, and therefore relations among the parties have not improved.

Agenda Setting

Nine lessons on agenda setting can be distilled from conventional weapon governance efforts.

First, wars are important motors for agenda setting. Several of the major attempts to institute controls over conventional weapons came in the wake of World War I, World War II, and the Persian Gulf War. The wars crystallized attention on the destructive power of conventional weapons, stirred considerable public revulsion against the instruments of war, and pushed governments to take action. Similarly, it was the humanitarian consequences of the use of antipersonnel landmines that led to the conclusion of a treaty banning such weapons. As Richard Price noted, "The case of AP [antipersonnel] land mines confirms the oft-argued thesis . . . that the perception of a crisis or shock is a crucial factor in precipitating ideational or normative change."[132]

Second, agenda setting is most successful when parties can trust one another, accept the balance of power, and have no relative gains concerns. That said, there must also be a reason to act and a fairly conducive international environment in which to do so. Unfortunately, such situations are relatively rare. Trust issues are present from the start and in an anarchic international environment can be difficult to overcome.[133] For this reason, many more governance attempts are initiated than ever move into serious negotiations.

Any decision to initiate discussions over a conventional weapons issue raises questions about the motives of the agenda setter and of other parties prepared to accept that agenda. For example, when the Carter administration proposed negotiations with the Soviet Union over conventional arms transfer control, Moscow responded warily. The Soviets could not understand U.S. motives for wanting to initiate talks. More serious problems of trust arose when the idea of controls on arms transfers was discussed with European states. In particular the French, fearing a trick, were adamant that they would not enter negotiations until the superpowers had shown that they were serious about limitations. Thus the issue of trust was relevant to all parties to the negotiations.[134]

Confidence-building measures can help overcome trust problems to some extent. Indeed several of the European CSBMs have acted as unexpected supports for arms control agenda setting and negotiations, having begun as entities in their own right.[135] This is particularly true of the CSCE process and the development of the Stockholm Conference on Disarmament in Europe, which facilitated the success of the CFE negotiations by having given states the opportunity to work together cooperatively and thus dampened concerns about trust and relative gains. The CSCE experience points to the role of CSBMs as an important precursor to successful agenda setting.

Third, cooperative agenda setting is more likely to succeed than hegemonic agenda setting. The CFE process provides evidence on how to avoid the trust and relative gains problems that can undermine attempts at agenda setting. In the CFE system, there is a process for cooperatively establishing the terms of reference for future work on the treaty and for informing nontreaty OSCE members of that work so that their views on security issues may be included and unnecessary security dilemmas prevented.[136]

Fourth, getting key states involved early in the process can help make agenda setting successful and ensure that the issue moves to negotiation. Convincing key states to adopt unilateral measures can also help in building support for a governance effort. For example, in the land mine campaign NGOs could not move beyond raising awareness of the issue. They realized early on that they needed to get key states involved. An important extra move was having these states adopt unilateral land mine bans. Also important was persuading French President François Mitterand to request the UN Secretary-General to convene a review conference of the CCW. Similarly, getting national arms transfer codes adopted in Great Britain and Spain proved essential in securing the adoption of a European Code of Conduct for Arms Transfers.[137] In some circumstances unilateral initiatives will not help though—for example, where imbalances of power and security dilemmas exist, causing trust problems. In such a situation, the trust problems of other states will ensure that the unilateralism cannot be capitalized on and will make the initiative vulnerable to internal sabotage by politicians and bureaucrats worried about the implications of unilateral concessions by the initiator. A prime example of this is the fate of President Jimmy Carter's unilateral conventional arms transfer control policy that preceded the CAT Talks, leaving the United States vulnerable to relative gains made by competitor arms suppliers.[138]

Fifth, the record of agenda-setting attempts in the realm of conventional arms reveals that on many issues states initiated efforts in response to strong pressures from NGOs and public opinion. For example, in the aftermath of World War I there was a strong push for disarmament by the general public, which was revolted by the waste of lives of that war. NGOs channeled the latent revulsion against the war into support for the development of the League of Nations, which was expected to abolish war.[139]

Sixth, NGOs are most successful in putting issues on the agenda if they can frame them in nonsecurity terms. For example, the ICRC played a crucial role in having certain weapons banned and in developing international law for the conduct of war.[140] The ICRC was largely responsible for putting excessively injurious conventional weapons on the agenda, and it played a considerable role in doing the same for land mines. Indeed work on land mines initially grew out of efforts to develop humanitarian law. A key basis of the claim for the ICRC to act on the issue was its framing as a humanitarian concern. The Arms Transfer Project of Human Rights Watch and other NGOs subsequently picked up the land mine campaign. NGOs staked their claims for involvement through recontextualizing the issue. As noted by Price, "It reflects an effort on the part of civil society to alter the conduct of violence by redefining it as a humanitarian concern, which is a realm where civil society and the NGO community often have special claims to expertise and authority."[141]

A similar level of NGO involvement was displayed in the establishment of a European Code of Conduct for Arms Transfers. Here too the issue was framed in a manner that deflected attention from security issues. For example, emphasis was placed on the human rights consequences of weapons transfers to undemocratic regimes. The NGO attempt to get a global UN code of conduct for arms transfers also focuses on the nonsecurity aspects of such a code.[142] Once issues are framed in security terms NGOs take a backseat.

Seventh, international organizations can legitimate NGO involvement in an issue and give NGOs the credibility they need to try to influence the policies of national governments on both agenda setting and responses to agenda setting. International organizations and NGOs can thus act synergistically to move an issue on the agenda. For example, the United Nations helped to facilitate NGO access when they tried to push forward the land mine campaign. According to Price, "Relationships with the UN provided NGOs with a stage for voicing their concerns and a primary point of access to the international political process in the form of international negotiations orchestrated by intergovernmental organizations."[143]

Eighth, the support of academics and other experts as well as of nonpolitical "experts groups" can help propel an issue onto the agenda. For example, in the realm of confidence-building measures in Europe, there is evidence to suggest a symbiotic relationship at work:

> It now appears that many confidence building analysts (mostly but not exclusively Western) actually may themselves have been participants in a substantial precursor confidence building process as they developed, wrote about, discussed, and promoted the confidence building approaches as part of a developing community of experts.[144]

Similarly, the support of medical groups (such as Physicians for Social Responsibility) for the ban against land mines was important in legitimating that issue. The burgeoning campaign to tackle the problem of small arms and light weapons proliferation has received a fillip from gaining the support of groups of doctors in the United States, who routinely deal with the consequences of gun violence.

Ninth, NGOs can maximize their role in agenda setting by forming international coalitions. For example, the development of an integrated network of NGOs working on the land mines issue, known as the International Campaign to Ban Landmines (ICBL), was one of the keys to the success of the campaign in getting the issue onto the agenda. An attempt is under way to capitalize on this networking technique to advance agenda setting on the issue of small arms and light weapons. In 1998 the International Action Network on Small Arms (IANSA) was established to facilitate NGO action to "enhance human security," by preventing the misuse and proliferation of small arms.[145] However, whereas in the ICBL there was unanimity in the aim of the campaign, this is not so in the case of IANSA, where at least two agendas have emerged, and where there cannot be the simplicity of a blanket ban given that small arms have legitimate functions (such as use by police forces).

Negotiation

Seven lessons emerge from conventional weapons negotiations.

First, as in agenda setting, negotiations are most successful if parties can trust each other and if they have no relative gains concerns. Willingness to negotiate can be undermined by the fear of the consequences of another player cheating. So if these fears can be shown to be groundless, or controllable through intrusive verification to prevent cheating, effective negotiation can be facilitated. CSBMs, including transparency initiatives, can help overcome trust problems. This is most likely to be the case if there is general acceptance of the balance of power, but there are lingering security dilemmas resulting from traditions of hostility. For example, the situation at the time the CSCE was initiated in 1973 can be characterized in this way.

How CSBMs actually improve security is an issue not much discussed in the literature, which focuses instead on the technical measures themselves. However, James Macintosh, in advocating a "transformation view" of CSBMs, suggests that "confidence building is a more comprehensive process. When it is successful, it must by its nature entail a process of positive change in the security relations of states, probably as a result of changes in basic security thinking and perhaps also as a result of the institutionalization of restructured security relations."[146] Many of the types of CSBMs that are instituted require systematic contact between states. The building of personal relations between state representatives can facilitate negotiations by establishing trust between officials, which then influences their attitudes toward moving forward with negotiations.

Second, negotiations are easier and agreement is less elusive if negotiations preempt threats before they become manifest. Similarly, negotiations on weapon systems that have not yet been deployed are easier and more successful than negotiations on existing systems. In such situations, relative gains concerns are absent because no state or party is yet benefiting from the new system, and there are absolute gains for all in preempting the deployment of a problematic system. Thus it has proved easiest to negotiate bans when the weapon in question—for example, dum-dum bullets and blinding laser weapons—is not yet integrated into the military arsenal. Once weapons systems are part of the political economy of a state and integrated in military planning, negotiations become very difficult because relative gains issues are manifest. For example, U.S. unwillingness to sign the land mine treaty stems in part from the fact that land mines are regarded by the military as a key part of its planning for defending the South Korean border against land invasion from North Korea.

Third, for negotiations to be successful—that is, leading to a meaningful agreement that can and will be implemented—all key parties need to be involved. Failure to solve the participation issue means that parties engaged in the negotiation have a reason to defect because of trust concerns about the parties who remain outside the negotiation. For example, during the inter-war period the League of Nations was a significant forum for initiatives to tackle the problem of conventional weapons. League membership, however, never really reflected the power politics of the period. Germany was a member only from 1926 to 1933, the Soviet Union was excluded until 1934 and expelled five years later, and Japan and Italy resigned in 1933 and 1937, respectively.[147] Hence, all of the disarmament negotiations initiated through the League of Nations were subject to concerns about participation. Similar problems emerged in the naval disarmament negotiations in the 1930s, because Germany was not a participant in the Second London Conference of 1935–1936.[148] Participation problems also plagued the CAT Talks. The absence of major Western European arms producers caused the talks to collapse. In a similar vein, the Ayacucho process was bound to fail once it was unable to ensure the participation of Brazil, a major regional power that both produced arms and imported them. Without full participation there are no incentives (and active disincentives) to moving from negotiation to a full governance agreement.

Whether the problem of participation can be remedied will depend on the reasons that lie behind it. If nonparticipation is motivated by disenchantment with the balance of power, then negotiation will not succeed even if the players were included. However, if balance-of-power issues are not present but less problematic trust problems and relative gains concerns lie behind nonparticipation, these can be mitigated by judicious use of various types of CSBMs. The granting of "observer status" to skeptical parties may also go some way to ease these problems.

Fourth, the success of negotiations can on occasion be improved by widening participation to states beyond the immediate antagonists. For example, the CSCE process benefited from the inclusion of neutral and nonaligned European states, which came to play constructive roles in pushing negotiations forward, mediating between erstwhile enemies and ensuring that the remaining trust problems and relative gains concerns of the major players were not allowed to obliterate progress.

Fifth, for negotiations to be useful they do not necessarily need to be successful. Sometimes the very process of negotiation has value. The institutionalization of negotiations such as MBFR served an important function during the Cold War; it ensured that the lines of communication between the superpowers always remained open. In the mid-1970s, talks such as MBFR were seen as a symbol of détente.[149] The CSCE process was also in part initiated as a means to establish lines of communication between important state players, even if the initial stated intention was not to address security issues, but rather to address common interests in the economic and political spheres.

Sixth, NGOs are often unable to play a key role once negotiations get under way. For example, in the lead-up to the 1995 review conference of the CCW, NGOs had been active participants. However,

> NGOs were excluded from full participation at the CCW review conference because members considered the discussions to be matters of disarmament and therefore national security. However, sympathetic governments such as Canada and Australia allowed NGO personnel to serve in their delegations and use this as a platform for prosetelisation.[150]
>
> Although this seems to imply a real inclusion of NGOs, as the negotiations became more intense, fewer governments were willing to include NGO members in their delegations and "the degree of inclusion of NGO members in the actual policy making process has varied from significant in the case of Canada to negligible in the case of Germany."[151]

Seventh, the chances of negotiations succeeding are increased if verification measures are built into the agreement being negotiated. As Trevor Findlay, Director of the Verification Research, Training, and Information Centre (VERTIC) has noted, verification of disarmament and arms control plays three important roles. First, it is a determination of compliance or noncompliance. Second, it is a deterrent to potential cheating. Third, it is confidence building, enabling the parties to the agreement to demonstrate to one another their compliance with the agreement.[152] Verification can help to remove any lingering concerns about relative gains and cheating. Building the confidence of potential signatories that the agreement will be fairly monitored can enhance the chance of successful negotiation. For example, "The CFE Treaty inspection and verification regimes require unprecedented openness at military installations throughout the area of application."[153] Those arrangements could only be agreed, however, in the transformed environment of the waning of the Cold War. Thus data exchanges and verification of them had been proposed in the MBFR negotiations but had never been accepted by the Soviet Union. It was only with the accession of President Mikhail Gorbachev that this impasse was cleared.[154] These measures are hard to negotiate unless a certain level of trust exists in the first place, and the parties are prepared to move forward.

Implementation and Compliance

Implementation of and compliance with conventional weapons agreements have generally been poor. Moreover, in the face of war or the threat of war implementation of many governance initiatives collapsed. This is true of the lead-up to World Wars I and II. The 1930 London Treaty and London Protocol of 1936 controlling naval forces did not survive the first few days of World War II.[155] When security issues become paramount, even minimal governance initiatives are threatened, for example, the international law restrictions on weapons use. That land mines are still being laid by states engaged in conflict—even signatories of the land mine treaty—is evidence of this problem.

Defections, be they explicit or implicit, are a classic response to trust problems encountered at the implementation phase. An explicit example is the case of Japan's defection from naval arms control agreements when faced with a security threat from China. Japan gave formal notice and withdrew from the 1930 naval treaty.[156] Implicit defections occur when states start to cheat, for example, German rearmament in defiance of the Treaty of Versailles. On occasion, defections are widespread, and governance initiatives fall into disuse despite apparently remaining in force.

In some cases implementation of a governance initiative can have an unanticipated, or a balloon, effect. A good example is the effect of the arms embargo imposed on South Africa during the years of apartheid.[157] The embargo was a relatively successful governance initiative because many major arms supplier states refused to trade with the regime (although a number of suppliers defied this, particularly Israel). In response to the market opportunity opened up by the embargo, however, many nonstate actors stepped in to supply weapons to South Africa (at a premium). In addition, the response of the South African state was to invest heavily in its military industrial complex and create an indigenous arms industry—prepared to sell to almost any interested party.[158]

Based on the limited experience we have with the implementation and compliance of conventional weapon governance efforts, five lessons stand out.

First, because conventional weapon agreements are fraught with trust problems, agreements should allow for a mix of national and international verification procedures to ensure that parties are prepared to implement them. It is at the implementation stage that the problem of cheating becomes most acute. As the Stockholm Institute for Peace Research (SIPRI) noted:

It is not only prior to the agreement that security considerations are decisive. Even at later stages, during implementation of a treaty, a state will continue to appraise it in the light of its security interests in order to ensure that the balance of power envisaged at the time of the treaty's inception is being maintained even after weapons have been reduced in quantity.[159]

Trust problems can be overcome if governance initiatives are accompanied by effective verification measures. For example, the 1955 Brussels Treaty, which established the Western European Union, a collective defense alliance composed of European states, contained several provisions for "verification among friends" designed to assuage any lingering fears about neighbors. The relevant provisions for this agreement were Protocol II about not exceeding agreed upper limits for weapons and troops, and Protocol IV, which established the Agency for the Control of Armaments (ACA) to monitor implementation. Data were received, checked, and confirmed by on-site inspections that could be very intrusive if necessary.[160] These arrangements confirmed that all parties were implementing their agreements, and thus the trust among them increased.

With conventional weapons issues of disarmament, arms control, export controls, and CSBMs, it should not be assumed that parties to governance initiatives sit back and wait for institutional verification. Because all are security issues, National Technical Means (or NTM, referring to the gathering of intelligence from electronic and human sources) will be deployed to ensure verification. Allowing both institutional verification and use of NTM will show faith in the agreement and speed implementation. When the results endorse the findings of institutional verification, this can act as a confidence-building measure.

Second, embedding agreements in an institutional framework can help alleviate trust problems. Institutions can provide a forum for regular contact between parties and a means by which difficulties within a governance initiative are solved before they become a crisis. For example, even though CoCom was the scene of increasing friction between the United States and the European states, disputes were settled through negotiation.[161] Several of the governance initiatives in the European theater discussed in this chapter include some form of institutionalization. The institutionalization of agreements and the use of verification techniques by the institutions created have eased problems of governance in the realm of conventional weapons.[162] Governance initiatives lacking this institutionalization are often weak, for example, the UN Register of Conventional Weapons. The existence of an institution does not in itself strengthen a governance initiative, however, as the Wassenaar Arrangement shows.

Third, having all relevant actors, including nonstate actors, is key to successful implementation and compliance. Indeed, the problem of imperfect participation can inhibit successful governance in the realm of conventional arms transfers. Trends in the international arms market, which have brought many new actors onto the scene, have worsened this problem. Developments in the political economy of conventional weapons—in particular the widespread privatization of defense industries since the end of the Cold War (in both Western Europe and the former Eastern bloc)— have lessened state control over conventional weapons.[163] A range of new actors are now involved in the international trade in conventional weapons. At the very least, this means bringing into the governance process a whole range of nonstate actors such as defense firms and arms brokers.[164] Implementation will be undermined unless these various actors are brought into all stages of the governance process. Their participation is necessary both because they have enough of a role in the realm of conventional weapons to thwart governance if excluded (in the case of defense firms, weapons brokers, and others) and because they have the potential to advance the governance process (in the case of NGOs). These nonstate actors need to be involved as partners in implementation, not merely the subjects of implementation. Indeed, firms and other nonstate players can potentially play a positive role in verification, because they would have a stake in ensuring that other nonstate actors were not cheating. Thus their relative gains concerns (about competitor firms) could be harnessed to the advantage of the governance initiative.[165]

NGOs and other nonstate groups have begun to carve out for themselves useful roles in the implementation phase. They have stepped in to monitor implementation of several disarmament treaties. For example, Human Rights Watch has increasingly become involved in "monitoring violations of the laws of war in internal military conflicts."[166] Similarly, NGOs have created the Landmine Monitor Initiative to help oversee the implementation of the 1997 treaty. A network of 115 researchers based in eighty-five countries contributes to reports on compliance.[167] One of the positive effects of the NGO role is to keep the issue on the international agenda by regularly reporting on the performance of states (both treaty parties and nonparties). This can be seen as a form of "citizen verification."[168] In addition, NGOs have pushed states and international organizations toward greater transparency. For example, the posting of UN Conventional Weapon Reports submitted to the UN Register on the Internet is a direct result of NGO pressure and enables a form of citizen verification.

Fourth, implementation of disarmament agreements—particularly disarmament agreements as part of a peace deal in civil war situations—is greatly facilitated if the people who negotiated the agreement are also involved and responsible for its implementation. Ensuring that the officials involved in negotiating the disarmament agreements have a continuing role in the process serves two functions. First, it allows them to communicate to their groups the confidence they have in the agreement and thus helps to mitigate trust problems. Second, it gives them a stake in the success of implementation. This lesson may be applicable to other governance agreements as well.

Fifth, implementation and compliance are greatly facilitated if a treaty or an agreement contains clear guidelines about what is permissible under the terms of the agreement. This is particularly important for peace agreements of civil wars. Unfortunately, many peace agreements contain "silences" on contested issues by not specifying what disarmament or arms control is required, and what constitutes breaching the settlement.[169] It therefore becomes a matter of perception what constitutes "cheating," leaving scope for genuine confusion, game playing, and plain cheating. In terms of postconflict disarmament, Findlay has pointed to the importance of having in place procedures for dealing with problems prior to any occurring because this can forestall major problems in the implementation phase.[170] If such a procedure has previously been endorsed by the parties, then its impartiality has been acknowledged and its conclusions are more difficult to dispute.

Reactions to Noncompliance

The enforcement of governance initiatives in the realm of conventional weapons is not a common occurrence. Few of the agreements reached have any enforcement measures built into them, because the participants are sovereign states that cannot be forced to undertake actions. Only in situations where states have lost wars can they be made to comply with the international community's wishes. Even then, forcing states to comply with the will of the international community can be difficult. Violations of agreements and responses to noncompliance are highly context dependent. They will be dictated in large measure by the international environment. For example, Italian noncompliance with the 1947 Peace Treaty became irrelevant, if not contrary to Western interest, with the advent of the Cold War.[171] Consequently, no meaningful international response was organized.

Three factors complicate the organization of international reactions to noncompliance. First, even at this stage, states frequently have relative gains concerns, which exist even among allies and prevent concerted action. For example, in the aftermath of World War I, "the enforcement of the armistice terms with Germany was not running smoothly between the British and the Americans, or between the British and the French."[172] The French were unhappy about the wide powers given to the British, and the Americans felt that Great Britain was trying to monopolize enforcement in German waters. Great Britain and the United States also engaged in fierce disputes over which powers were to receive the majority of the captured German warships.[173] As a result, Germany was able to play one ally against another to successfully neutralize actions by them.

Second, in many cases the cost of enforcing agreements may be considered too high. The ultimate response in case of noncompliance is the resort to the use of force and war, something never undertaken lightly.[174] Such a course of action is likely only where the concern about cheating and defection is backed by pressing balance-of-power concerns. The costs of punishing a noncompliant party may even be too high in civil war cases. Indeed outside powers are often hesitant to enforce disarmament and demobilization measures of peace settlements. They fear being dragged into a conflict peripheral to their national interests.

Third, determining whether a violation of an agreement has occurred may be difficult. This is the point at which the inclusion of verification in the governance agreement can really pay dividends. If, as Findlay advocates, procedures are in place to deal with this problem, identifying and tackling issues of noncompliance are at least possible.

In the conventional weapons field, four types of reactions to noncompliance have been employed: use of force, criminal prosecution, sanctions and aid conditionality, and shaming. These responses have had mixed results.

Use of Force. The use of force is successful only when international actors are united. Enforcement of the Treaty of Versailles suffered in this respect from French and British discord, particularly with regard to the use of force. The occupation of the Ruhr in January 1923 did not improve German compliance with the disarmament provisions of the Versailles Treaty.[175] Ultimately, enforcement of the settlement was subject to the will of the Allies to carry it through. Although there was some activity, by the time of the signing of the Locarno Pact in 1925, a treaty designed to promote the security of Western Europe, there was no longer any will to sanction Germany, because it was no longer the Allies' biggest problem. Concerns had shifted to the strategic alliance formed between Germany and the Soviet Union, which they viewed as a far greater threat to security than German cheating.[176]

Criminal Prosecution. Individual criminal prosecution for violations of the rules of war was used after World War II in the Nuremberg and Tokyo tribunals. For example, Grand Admiral Karl Doenitz was called to account for the German navy's use of unrestricted submarine warfare during the war in contravention of the Hague conventions and London naval treaties. Although it was accepted that the Allies had also contravened some of the stipulations, the tribunal nevertheless found the admiral guilty of attacking neutral vessels and of the failure of German submarines to pick up survivors.[177]

Sanctions and Aid Conditionality. Sanctions and aid conditionality have been used as a way to ensure implementation of disarmament provisions after civil wars. International organizations such as the World Bank—in particular—have begun to use this instrument. For example, aid to Sierra Leone is conditioned on disarmament, to be implemented by the National Committee for Disarmament, Demobilization, and

Reintegration (NCDDR).[178] More generally, they have proposed linking disarmament to development.[179]

Shaming. International shaming has also been used as a response to noncompliance. This might be instigated by states or NGO groups and might result in exclusion from favorable trade arrangements, denial of aid, and so on. Such techniques are successful in applying pressure to governments concerned about their international standing. The value of "name and shame" techniques is limited if recalcitrant states are preoccupied with what are regarded as overriding security problems (for example, South Africa during the apartheid era), or if the government either does not care how it is viewed or is able to prevent its citizens from discovering how it is viewed internationally.

CONCLUSION

Conventional weapons issues are primarily security issues and as such wax and wane in tune with the international and regional security environment. Certain types of governance initiatives can assist in the formation of a more positive international security environment, however. The CSBMs used as examples of this (CSCE, CFE, and others) have not been subject to the test of a steeply deteriorating security situation. They have, however, survived a fast-changing security environment (the end of the Cold War) and played an important role in ensuring a positive outcome from those changes.

When the governance effort can be defined as something other than a straight security issue, progress has been made. The redefinition of issues as "humanitarian" has also legitimated the involvement of players besides sovereign states. This seems to have borne fruit in terms of the Land Mines Treaty and may be a productive route for the light weapons campaign.

Only some conventional weapons issues can be "spun" in this way, however, and in the realm of traditional security concerns, states hold sway. That said, the increasing number of nonstate actors involved in arms transfers and whose compliance would be required to successfully implement a governance initiative has significantly reduced the traditional ability of states to manipulate the arms market to achieve their desired outcome.

As in other areas there is value to be gained from joining forces with other governmental and civil society networks working on allied issues. Given the connections between conventional weapons issues and other problem areas, successful action on the conventional weapons problem may have positive spillovers for these other issue areas, and vice versa. For example, instituting more effective customs monitoring of arms transfers may aid in the crackdown on drug smuggling (which often involves the same routes and even the same personnel).

A final cautionary note should be struck. Changes in defense technologies are making the institution of governance initiatives in the area of conventional weapons increasingly difficult. The international weapons trade is now less about the supply of whole weapons and more about the supply of modular systems, weapons kits (to be assembled in country), production facilities, software programs, and dual-use goods. All of these are harder to monitor for the purposes of governance than whole weapons systems, leading to problems of implementation and new trust and relative gains concerns. Moreover, the close connections between the dual-use goods at the leading edge of commerce (communications technologies, miniaturized products, advanced computers, software, and others) and those useful for enhancing the performance of weapons and realizing the revolution in military affairs suggest that problems lie ahead for existing export control and transparency agreements. Relative gains concerns mitigating against any new governance initiatives designed to address this balloon effect are also likely to emerge.

NOTES

1. The category of conventional weapons includes large-platform technologies such as aircraft carriers, fighter aircraft, ships, submarines, and ballistic missiles; medium-sized weapons systems such as tanks, heavy artillery, unmanned aerial vehicles, and armored personnel carriers; light weapons such as truck-portable artillery pieces, rocket-propelled grenades, howitzers, and heavy mortars; small arms such as assault rifles, sniper rifles, pistols, grenades, land mines, knives, and machetes. Although this weaponry is united under the generic label "conventional weapons," there is tremendous variance in the size, scale of destruction caused, and degree of seriousness with which they are treated by the international community.
2. For example, it is estimated that conflicts around the world between 1990 and 1995 resulted in 109,754,500 deaths. See Ruth L. Sivard, *World Military and Social Expenditures* (Leesburg, Va.: WMSE Publications, 1996).
3. The term *relative gains* refers to a situation in which some players gain more from a situation than others do, and players are concerned that others are advantaged by this. By contrast, *absolute gains* represents a situation where all gain equally.
4. April Carter, *Success and Failure in Arms Control Negotiations* (Oxford, U.K.: Oxford University Press and Stockholm International Peace and Research Institute [SIPRI], 1989), p. 14.
5. "... unlike in the past when the black market dealt mainly in 'light' material, today it can deliver virtually everything, from assault rifles to nuclear precursors." R. T. Naylor, "Gunsmoke and Mirrors: Financing the Illegal Trade," in Lora Lumpe, ed., *Running Guns: The Global Black Market in Small Arms* (London, Zed Books, 2000), p. 159.

6. In constant 1995 U.S. dollars. See SIPRI, *SIPRI Yearbook, 1999: Armaments, Disarmament, and International Security* (Oxford, U.K.: Oxford University Press and SIPRI, 1999), (hereafter SIPRI Yearbook), Appendix 7A, pp. 300–01. SIPRI identified a 2 percent increase in world military expenditure in real terms in 1999, however, reversing the trend of the rest of the decade. See SIPRI web site <http://projects.sipri.se>.

7. Mobile forces can be used for offense or defense but naturally favor the offense. If these weapons are introduced into an area, it may increase the incentives of a group feeling itself under threat to attack first to try to nullify the advantage of the opponent. For an argument that builds governance proposals on the basis of this, see Ian Bellany, "The Offensive-Defensive Distinction and the International Arms Trade," Bailrigg Paper No. 16 (Lancaster, U.K.: Centre for Defence and International Security Studies, Lancaster University, 1993).

8. Carter, *Success and Failure in Arms Control Negotiations*, p. 22. See also Joseph Douglass, Jr., *Why the Soviets Violate Arms Control Treaties* (Washington, D.C.: Pergamon-Brassey's International Defense Publishers, 1988).

9. As Barry Posen has noted, military forces are inherently dissimilar. The differences are exaggerated by different military strategies, doctrine, technologies, recruitment, training, armament, and organization. See Barry R. Posen, "Military Lessons of the Gulf War—Implications for Middle East Arms Control," in Shai Feldmen and Ariel Levite, eds., *Arms Control and the New Middle East Security Environment* (Boulder, Colo.: Westview Press, 1994), pp. 62–71.

10. See SIPRI, *Strategic Disarmament, Verification, and National Security* (London: Taylor and Francis and SIPRI, 1977), p. 4.

11. George Rathjens has called this the "displacement effect" of arms control. George W. Rathjens, Abram Chayes, and J. P. Ruina, *Nuclear Arms Control Agreements: Process and Impact* (Washington, D.C.: Carnegie Endowment for International Peace, 1974), pp. 21–24.

12. Winston S. Churchill, *The World Crisis: The Aftermath* (London: Thornton Butterworth, 1929), p. 146.

13. See Brian Bond, *War and Society in Europe, 1870–1970* (Leicester, U.K.: Leicester University Press and Fontana Paperbacks, 1983), pp. 40–99. There is some evidence that lends credence to the idea that the war was caused by the huge amount of arms stockpiles. The existence of stockpiles of weapons exacerbated trust problems and led to an assumption that the existence of these capabilities meant that there was an intention to attack. This itself created incentives to preempt an attack that was seen as inevitable. See Barbara Tuchman, *August 1914* (London: Papermac, 1980).

14. Stephen Roskill, *Naval Policy Between the Wars, I: The Period of Anglo-American Antagonism 1919–1929* (London: Collins, 1968), p. 19.

15. See E. H. Carr, *The Twenty Years' Crisis 1919–1939*, 2nd ed. (London: Papermac, reprinted 1989), p. 33.

16. Under the treaty, the Military, Naval, and Aeronautical Inter-Allied Commission of Control (known as the Control Commission) was set up to implement the disarmament and deal with difficult international questions. See Roskill, *Naval Policy Between the Wars, I*, p. 97.

17. Under the Versailles settlement, Germany was not allowed any air power. However, it defied this prohibition to create a world-class air force, the Luftwaffe. See Edward L. Homze, *Arming the Luftwaffe: The Reich Air Ministry and the German Aircraft Industry, 1919–1939* (Lincoln, Neb.: University of Nebraska Press, 1976).

18. The term *security dilemma* was first used by Robert Jervis. It refers to a situation in which insecurity results in arms racing between states. A state procures conventional weapons for purely defensive purposes, but a neighboring state may perceive the acquisition as aggressive and feel obliged to respond in kind, triggering other acquisitions and thus an arms race. This arms racing may result in war because a state may have an incentive to preemptively attack an opponent who acquires more arms. At the heart of this dynamic lies a dilemma; in trying to achieve security, the states have actually undermined their security and created a situation of constant fear between states. Robert Jervis, "Cooperation under the Security Dilemma," *World Politics*, vol. 30, no. 2 (January 1978), p. 169.

19. Fred Tanner, "Versailles: German Disarmament After World War One," in Fred Tanner, ed., *From Versailles to Baghdad: Post-War Armament Control of Defeated States* (New York: UN Institute for Disarmament Research, 1992), p. 25.

20. Ibid., p. 9.

21. This increase in extremist organizations was attributed directly to the Treaty of Versailles by the German General Wilhelm Groener. Cited in ibid., p. 21.

22. Stephen Roskill, *Naval Policy Between the Wars, II: The Period of Reluctant Rearmament, 1930–1939* (London: Collins, 1976), pp. 143, 135, and 137.

23. See Philip Noel-Baker, *The First World Disarmament Conference and Why It Failed* (Oxford, U.K.: Pergamon Press, 1979); and Roskill, *Naval Policy Between the Wars, II*, pp. 134–63.

24. See James R. Leutze, *Bargaining for Supremacy: Anglo-American Naval Collaboration, 1937–41* (Chapel Hill, N.C.: University of North Carolina Press, 1977), pp. 4–5.

25. Rivalry was also fierce between Great Britain and France, France and Italy, the United States and Japan, and Great Britain and Japan. See Roskill, *Naval Policy Between the Wars, I*, p. 20.

26. See Carter, *Success and Failure in Arms Control Negotiations*, pp. 14 and 38.

27. Emily O. Goldman, "Arms Control in the Information Age," in Nancy W. Gallagher, ed., *Arms Control: New Approaches to Theory and Policy* (London: Frank Cass, 1998), p. 43.

28. Roskill, *Naval Policy Between the Wars, I*, p. 62.

29. See Jozef Goldblat, *Arms Control Agreements* (New York: Praeger, 1983), p. 3.

30. Rear Adm. J. R. Hill, *Arms Control at Sea* (Annapolis, Md.: Naval Institute Press, 1989), p. 31.

31. By this time Italy was concerned more about rearming than disarming and played no part in the discussions.

32. See W. Friedmann, *The Allied Military Government of Germany* (London: Stevens and Sons and London Institute of World Affairs, 1947), pp. 110–25; Edwin M. Martin, *The Allied Occupation of Japan* (Westport, Conn.: Greenwood Press and Institute of Pacific

Relations, 1948), pp. 14–21 and 38–44; and Robert A. Fearey, *The Allied Occupation of Japan Second Phase: 1948–50* (Westport, Conn.: Greenwood Press and Institute of Pacific Relations, 1948), pp. 13–17.

33. See United Nations, *Documents on Disarmament, 1945–1959*, vol. 1: 1945–56 (New York: United Nations, 1960), p. 175.

34. Bernhard G. Bechhoefer, *Postwar Negotiations for Arms Control* (Washington, D.C.: Brookings Institution, 1961), p. 93.

35. Goldblat, *Arms Control Agreements*, pp. 15–16.

36. For details on nuclear arms control, see the chapter by Thomas Bernauer.

37. See UN Institute for Disarmament Research, *Managing Arms in Peace Processes: The Issues* (Geneva: United Nations, 1996); Marcos Mendiburu, Sarah Meek, and P. Martin, *Managing Arms in Peace Processes: Haiti* (Geneva: United Nations, 1996); Clement Adibe and J. W. Potgieter, *Managing Arms in Peace Processes: Somalia* (Geneva: United Nations, 1995); and Mats R. Berdal, "Disarmament and Demobilisation after Civil Wars," Adelphi Paper 303 (London: International Institute for Strategic Studies [IISS], 1996).

38. See Joanna Spear, "The Disarmament and Demobilisation of Warring Factions in the Aftermath of Civil Wars: Key Implementation Issues," *Civil Wars*, vol. 2, no. 2 (Summer 1999), pp. 1–22.

39. See David Holiday and William Stanley, "Building the Peace: Preliminary Lessons from El Salvador," *Journal of International Affairs*, vol. 46, no. 2 (Winter 1993), pp. 415–37; Christopher C. Coleman, *The Salvadoran Peace Process: A Preliminary Inquiry*, Norwegian Institute of International Affairs, Report No. 173 (December 1993), pp. 29–30; Jim Wurst, "Mozambique Disarms," *The Bulletin of the Atomic Scientists*, vol. 50, no. 5 (September/October 1994), pp. 36–39; and Eric Berman, *Managing Arms in Peace Processes: Mozambique, UNIDIR Disarmament, and Conflict Resolution Project* (Geneva: United Nations, 1996).

40. SIPRI, "Major Armed Conflicts," *SIPRI Yearbook, 1994*, p. 115; and Lt. Gen. John M. Sanderson, "Peacekeeping Operations in Cambodia," *RUSI Journal*, vol. 139, no. 6 (December 1994), pp. 20–26.

41. Spear, "The Disarmament and Demobilisation of Warring Factions," pp. 1–22.

42. SIPRI, *Arms Control: A Survey and Appraisal of Multilateral Agreements* (London: Taylor and Francis and SIPRI, 1978), p. 53.

43. The Hague conferences and the resulting conventions were an attempt to codify the laws of war and, through this, regulate European interstate war. The conventions were not perceived as an end in themselves but were a by-product of attempts to control the effects of modern warfare at a time when the pace of military change was perceived as speeding up dramatically.

44. Ingrid Detter De Lupis, *The Law of War* (Cambridge, Mass.: Cambridge University Press, 1987), p. 341.

45. Geoffrey Best, *Law and War Since 1945* (London: Clarendon Press, 1997), p. 23.

46. Cap. J. Ashley Roach, "Certain Conventional Weapons Convention: Arms Control or Humanitarian Law?" *Military Law Review*, vol. 105 (Summer 1984), p. 6.

47. See ibid., pp. 43–44.

48. Ibid., p. 14.
49. See Goldblat, *Arms Control Agreements*, pp. 242–48.
50. Roach, "Certain Conventional Weapons Convention," p. 35.
51. After the failure of the 1995–1996 review conference to ban the use of antipersonnel mines, campaign groups turned to other means to advance their cause. This was one of the precursors to the process that culminated in the 1997 Ottawa Convention Banning Landmines.
52. Jozef Goldblat, "Land-mines and Blinding Laser Weapons: The Inhumane Weapons Convention Review Conference," SIPRI, *SIPRI Yearbook, 1996* (Oxford, U.K.: Oxford University Press, 1996), pp. 761–64.
53. International Campaign to Ban Landmines, *Landmine Monitor Report 2000: Toward a Mine Free World* at <http://www.icbl.org>.
54. "Human Rights Groups Slam Angola on Landmines," *Reuters*, September 13, 2000.
55. Indeed, some authors conflate the two under the heading "arms control." See, for example, Stuart Croft, *Strategies of Arms Control: A History and Typology* (Manchester, U.K.: University of Manchester, 1996).
56. Thomas C. Schelling and Morton Halperin, *Strategy and Arms Control* (New York: Twentieth Century Fund, 1961), p. 2.
57. Richard A. Falkenrath, *Shaping Europe's Military Order: The Origins and Consequences of the CFE Treaty* (Cambridge, Mass.: MIT Press, 1995), p. XIII.
58. Carter, *Success and Failure in Arms Control Negotiations*, pp. 230–47.
59. Ibid., p. 234.
60. Ibid., p. 244.
61. Ibid., p. 247.
62. France had substantial conventional forces. See ibid., p. 246.
63. Ibid., p. 255.
64. Dorn Crawford, "The CFE Treaty: Key Elements and Maps," in Catherine McArdle Kelleher, Jane M. O. Sharp, and Lawrence Freedman, eds., *The Treaty on Conventional Armed Forces in Europe: The Politics of Post-Wall Arms Control* (Baden-Baden: Nomos Verlagsgesellschaft, 1996), pp. 297–346.
65. Sergey Koulik and Richard Kokoski, "The Verification Provisions of the CFE Treaty," in *Conventional Arms Control: Perspectives on Verification* (Oxford, U.K.: SIPRI and Oxford University Press, 1994), pp. 41–76.
66. Croft, *Strategies of Arms Control*, p. 129.
67. Falkenrath, *Shaping Europe's Military Order*, p. XVI.
68. Zdzislaw Lachowski, "Conventional Arms Control," in SIPRI, *SIPRI Yearbook, 1999* (Oxford, U.K.: Oxford University Press, 1999), p. 614.
69. Wade Boese, "Executive Summary of the Adapted Conventional Armed Forces in Europe Treaty," *Arms Control Today*, vol. 29, no. 7 (November 1999), pp. 24–5.
70. Koulik and Kokoski, *Conventional Arms Control*, pp. 35–6.
71. Lachowski, "Conventional Arms Control," p. 633.
72. Ibid., p. 635.
73. Ibid., p. 637.

74. Kevin Cahill, *Trade Wars: The High Technology Scandal of the 1980s* (London: W. H. Allen and Co., 1986).

75. Joanna Spear, "Britain and Conventional Arms Transfer Restraint," in Mark Hoffman, ed., *UK Arms Control in the 1990s* (Manchester, U.K.: Manchester University Press, 1990), p. 181–82.

76. See Jon B. Wolfsthal, "COCOM Dissolved: New Regime Under Negotiation," *Arms Control Today*, vol. 24, no. 4 (May 1994), p. 19.

77. Sarah Walkling, "Post-COCOM 'Wassenaar Arrangement' Set to Begin New Export Control Role," *Arms Control Today*, vol. 25, no. 10 (Dec/Jan. 1995–1996), p. 24; and "Wassenaar Talks Fizzle," *Arms Trade News* (April 1996), pp. 1 and 3.

78. Sarah Walkling, "Russia Ready to Join New Post-COCOM Organization," *Arms Control Today*, vol. 25, no. 7 (September 1995), pp. 31 and 33.

79. *SIPRI Yearbook, 1999*, p. 699.

80. The United States has dropped this term in favor of *states of concern*.

81. *SIPRI Yearbook, 1999*, pp. 699–700.

82. Joanna Spear, *Carter and Arms Sales: Implementing the Carter Administration's Arms Transfer Restraint Policy* (Basingstoke, U.K.: Macmillan, 1995), p. 116.

83. Ibid., p. 119.

84. Ibid., pp. 78–79.

85. Ian Anthony, ed., *Arms Export Regulations* (Oxford, U.K.: Oxford University Press and SIPRI, 1991), p. 198.

86. Jo L. Husbands and Anne H. Cahn, "The Conventional Arms Transfer Talks: An Experiment in Mutual Arms Trade Restraint," in Thomas Ohlson, ed., *Arms Transfer Limitations and Third World Security* (Oxford, U.K.: Oxford University Press and SIPRI, 1988), p. 114.

87. There were divisions within the administration over how far to progress in relations with China, with the State Department continuing to prioritize relations with the Soviet Union and unaware of the National Security Council's (NSC) moves to normalize relations with China. The NSC was the victor in this battle. Joanna Spear, "Governmental Politics and the Conventional Arms Transfer Talks," *Review of International Studies*, vol. 19, no. 4 (October 1993), pp. 369–84.

88. J. Klein, "France and the Arms Trade," in Cindy Cannizzio, ed., *The Gun Merchants: Politics and Policies of the Major Arms Suppliers* (New York: Pergamon, 1980), p. 158.

89. Frederick S. Pearson, "Problems and Prospects of Arms Transfer Limitations Among Second-Tier Suppliers: The Cases of France, United Kingdom, and the Federal Republic of Germany," in Ohlson, *Arms Transfer Limitations*, p. 143.

90. Thomas Ohlson, "Introduction," in ibid., p. 3.

91. Nicole Ball, "Third World Arms Control: A Third World Responsibility," in ibid., p. 46.

92. Joanna Spear, "On the Desirability and Feasibility of Arms Transfer Regime Formation," *Contemporary Security Policy*, vol. 15, no. 3 (December 1994), p. 99.

93. See Augusto Varas, "Regional Arms Control in the South American Context," in Ohlson, *Arms Transfer Limitations*, p. 180.

94. See ibid., p. 179.

95. For strategic reasons Colombia, Chile, and Ecuador wanted to prohibit long-range missiles, whereas Bolivia, Peru, and Venezuela wanted to keep long-range missiles but prohibit short-range ones. This impasse was not overcome. Ibid., p. 179.

96. See Nobel Peace Laureates' International Code of Conduct, 1997, available at <http://www.arias.or.cr/fundarias/cpr/code-span.htm>; and British-American Security Information Council, "Codes of Conduct: Co-ordination in the US, the EU, and the UN," *Campaign Update*, no. 13 (November 1997).

97. The Oscar Arias Foundation at <www.arias.or.cf>.

98. Amnesty International Spain, Greenpeace Spain, and Médicins Sans Frontières Spain, "The Killing Secrets Campaign Succeeds: All Political Parties Vote in Favour of Transparency and Parliamentary Control of the Arms Trade," *Press Release*, March 19, 1997; and Saferworld, "The EU Code of Conduct on the Arms Trade: Final Analysis," available at <http://www.saferworld.co.uk/armstrade/code.html>.

99. "European Ministers Meet on Code of Conduct," *Arms Transfer News* (November 1997), p. 3.

100. Mitsuro Donowaki suggests that an important factor in drawing international attention to the problem was the report of the ICRC on the conflict in Somalia. There, one million people—out of a population of seven million—died in a conflict mainly fought with small arms and light weapons. Mitsuro Donowaki, "The UN and the Small Arms Crisis: Preparing to Meet the Challenge," *Disarmament Diplomacy*, no. 49 (August 2000), p. 22.

101. Ibid., pp. 22–3.

102. See British-American Security Information Council, "Draft Inter-American Convention Against Illicit Trafficking," *BASIC Reports*, no. 61, November 12, 1997, pp. 2–5.

103. This is as a supplementary protocol to a universal Convention against Transnational Organized Crime. Donowaki, "The UN and the Small Arms Crisis," p. 25.

104. Bennie Lombard, "Small Arms and Light Weapons: A Neglected Issue, a Renewed Focus," *Disarmament Diplomacy*, no. 49 (August 2000), p. 29. Mali has played the role of catalyst both regionally and internationally on the small arms issue. In 1993 the president of Mali asked the UN Secretary-General to help with the collection of small arms and light weapons still in circulation in the state one year after the civil war there had been terminated. The resulting report highlighted, among other things, the regional dynamics of the problem and recommended a regional approach to the problem.

105. Ibid., p. 29.

106. Nairobi Declaration on the Problem of the Proliferation of Illicit Small Arms and Light Weapons in the Great Lakes Region and the Horn of Africa, March 15, 2000. Cited in ibid., p. 30.

107. Ibid., p. 30.

108. The embargoes were placed on the Republics of Former Yugoslavia (1991), Somalia (1992), Liberia (1992), Haiti (June and October 1993), UNITA and Angola (1993), Rwanda (1994), Sierra Leone (1997), Federal Republic of Yugoslavia (1998), and Ethiopia and Eritrea (2000). See Chantal de Jonge Oudraat, "Intervention in Internal Conflicts: Legal and Political Conundrums," Global Policy Program Working Paper No. 15 (Washington, D.C.: Carnegie Endowment for International Peace, 2000), p. 22.

109. Joanna Spear, "Arms Limitations, Confidence-Building Measures, and Internal Conflict," in Michael Brown, ed., *The International Dimensions of Internal Conflict* (Cambridge, Mass.: MIT Press, 1996), pp. 391–392.

110. Nancy W. Gallagher, "Bridging the Gaps on Arms Control," in Nancy W. Gallagher, ed., *Arms Control: New Approaches to Theory and Policy* (London: Frank Cass, 1998), p. 9.

111. See Ann M. Florini, "A New Role for Transparency," in ibid., p. 59.

112. Carter, *Success and Failure in Arms Control Negotiations*, pp. 247–51.

113. Zdzislaw Lachowski and Pia Kronestedt, "Confidence- and Security-Building Measures in Europe," in *SIPRI Yearbook, 1999*, pp. 644–54.

114. Don O. Stovall and Mitchell R. Audritsh, "The Future Direction of On-Site Inspections in Arms Control Through the Provisions of Confidence- and Security-Building Measures," *Arms Control*, vol. 13, no. 3 (December 1992), pp. 421–38.

115. Helsinki Document, 1992: The Challenges of Change, Helsinki Decisions, July 10, 1992, article 5, section 8. Document reproduced in Jenonne Walker, *Security and Arms Control in Post-Confrontation Europe* (Oxford, U.K.: Oxford University Press and SIPRI, 1994), p. 159.

116. Cited in ibid., p. 26.

117. Ibid., p. 48.

118. Ibid., p. 38.

119. Malcolm Chalmers and Owen Greene, "The UN Register of Conventional Arms: A Progress Report," *Disarmament Diplomacy*, no. 35 (March 1999), p. 16.

120. Malcolm Chalmers and Owen Greene, "Expanding the Register," in Malcolm Chalmers, Owen Greene, Edward J. Laurance, and Herbert Wulf, eds., *Developing the UN Register of Conventional Arms*, Bradford Arms Register Studies No. 4 (West Yorkshire, U.K.: Department of Peace Studies, University of Bradford, 1994), pp. 153–75.

121. *Report on the Continuing Operation of the United Nations Register of Conventional Arms and Its Further Development: Report to the Secretary-General*, UN General Assembly Document A/49/316, October 1994; and Malcolm Chalmers, Mitsuro Donowaki, and Owen Greene, eds., *Developing Arms Transparency: The Future of the United Nations Register*, Bradford Arms Register Studies No. 7 (Bradford, U.K.: University of Bradford and Centre for the Promotion of Disarmament and Non-Proliferation, 1997).

122. Chalmers and Greene, "The UN Register," p. 12.

123. Ibid., p. 13.

124. This was for reasons unconnected to the register itself. It was a protest against the inclusion in the U.S. report of sales to Taiwan, even though these exports were reported in a footnote, rather than in the text of the report.

125. Chalmers and Greene, "The UN Register," p. 14.

126. Ibid., p.16.

127. For a discussion of "second track" dialogues in the Asia-Pacific region, see *The ASEAN Regional Forum: Confidence Building* (Ottawa: Department of Foreign Affairs and International Trade, February 1997), pp. 7–9.

128. Lachowski, *Conventional Arms Control*, p. 639.

129. Ibid., p. 641.

130. Bechhoefer, *Postwar Negotiations for Arms Control*, p. 12.

131. Ibid., p. 89.

132. Richard Price, "Reversing the Gun Sights: Transnational Civil Society Targets Land Mines," *International Organization*, vol. 52, no. 3 (Summer 1998), p. 622.

133. F. A. Long, "Arms Control in the Nineteen-Seventies," *Daedalus*, vol. 104, no. 3 (Summer 1975), p. 5.

134. Spear, *Carter and Arms Sales*, p. 117.

135. Marie-France Desjardins, "Rethinking Confidence-Building Measures," Adelphi Paper No. 307 (London: IISS, 1996), pp. 8–11.

136. Lachowski, "Conventional Arms Control, "in SIPRI, *SIPRI Yearbook, 1997: Armaments, Disarmament, and International Security* (Oxford, U.K.: Oxford University Press, 1997), p. 484.

137. "European Ministers Meet on Code of Conduct," *Arms Transfer News* (November 1997), p. 3.

138. Spear, *Carter and Arms Sales*.

139. Churchill, *The World Crisis*, p. 146. Among the prominent NGOs of the time were the Quakers, trade unions, national League of Nations groups, the Peace and Disarmament Committee of the Women's International Organizations, and the Union of Democratic Control.

140. Maurice Aubert, "The International Committee of the Red Cross and the Problem of Excessively Injurious or Indiscriminate Weapons," *International Review of the Red Cross*, No. 279 (November 1990), pp. 477–97.

141. Price, "Reversing the Gun Sights," p. 638.

142. Wendy Cukier, "International Fire/Small Arms Control," *Canadian Foreign Policy*, vol. 6, no. 1 (Fall 1998), pp. 73–89.

143. Price, "Reversing the Gun Sights," pp. 623–24.

144. See James Macintosh, *Confidence Building in the Arms Control Process: A Transformational View*, Arms Control and Disarmament Studies, no. 2 (Ottawa: Non-Proliferation, Arms Control, and Disarmament Division, Department of Foreign Affairs and International Trade, 1996), p. 14.

145. The International Action Network on Small Arms (IANSA) at <http://www.iansa.org>.

146. Macintosh, *Confidence Building in the Arms Control Process*, p. 23.

147. See Roskill, *Naval Policy Between the Wars, I*, p. 19.

148. Hill, *Arms Control at Sea*, p. 31.

149. Carter, *Success and Failure in Arms Control Negotiations*, p. 242.

150. Price, "Reversing the Gun Sights," p. 639.

151. Ibid.

152. Trevor Findlay, VERTIC, "Post-Conflict Demilitarisation: The Role of Verification," paper presented to the MacArthur seminar on Regional Security in a Global Context, Department of War Studies, King's College London, February 2, 1999.

153. Zdzislaw Lachowski, "Conventional Arms Control and Security Cooperation in Europe," in *SIPRI Yearbook, 1996*, p. 714.

154. Jonathan Dean, "Verifying Conventional Force Reductions and Limitations," in Robert D. Blackwill and F. Stephen Larrabee, eds., *Conventional Arms Control and East-West Security* (Durham, N.C.: Duke University Press, 1989), p. 293.

155. Hill, *Arms Control at Sea*, p. 33.

156. Goldman, "Arms Control in the Information Age," p. 43.

157. See Croft, *Strategies of Arms Control*, p. 56.

158. Peter Batchelor and Susan Willett, *Disarmament and Defence: Industrial Adjustment in South Africa* (Oxford, U.K.: Oxford University Press and SIPRI, 1994), pp. 24–48.

159. SIPRI, *Strategic Disarmament*, p. 8.

160. See Harald Müller, "The Evolution of Verification: Lessons from the Past for the Present," *Arms Control*, vol. 14, no. 3 (December 1993), p. 334.

161. Richard T. Cupitt and Suzanne R. Grillot, "COCOM Is Dead, Long Live COCOM: Persistence and Change in Multilateral Security Institutions," *British Journal of Political Science*, vol. 27 (July 1997), pp. 361–89.

162. *Verification in All Its Aspects, Including the Role of the United Nations in the Field of Verification, A United Nations Report Prepared by a Group of Qualified Governmental Experts*, UN Document A/50/377 and Corr. 1, December 1995.

163. David Mussington, *Understanding Contemporary International Arms Transfers and Feasibility of Arms Transfer Regime Formation* (London: Brasseys and International IISS, 1994); Spear, "On the Desirability," pp. 87–189; and Ian Anthony, *Russia and the Arms Trade* (Oxford, U.K.: Oxford University Press, 1998).

164. Joanna Spear, "Beyond the Cold War: Changes in the International Arms Trade," *Harvard International Review*, vol. 16, no. 5 (Winter 1994), pp. 8–11 and 70–2.

165. This argument has also been used about the role of firms in implementing environmental legislation.

166. See Best, *Law and War Since 1945*, pp. 383–84.

167. Stephen Goose, "The 1997 Mine Ban Treaty: Making a Difference," *Disarmament Diplomacy*, no. 47 (June 2000), p. 7.

168. For an early version of this "inspection by the people," see Seymour Melman, "General Report," in Melman, *Inspection for Disarmament*, pp. 38–41.

169. Spear, "The Disarmament and Demobilisation of Warring Factions," p. 9.

170. Findlay, "Post-Conflict Demilitarisation."

171. Interestingly, in the aftermath of World War II, relative gains concerns meant that the Allies were prepared to sanction Italian noncompliance with the terms of the 1947 Italian peace treaty. See Ilaria Poggiolini and Leopoldo Nuti, "The Italian Peace Treaty of 1947: The Enemy/Ally Dilemma and Military Limitations," in Tanner, *From Versailles to Baghdad*, p. 36.

172. Roskill, *Naval Policy Between the Wars, I*, p. 77.

173. Ibid., p. 78.

174. For example, Germany's decision in 1917 to cease to obey the submarine-warfare rules of The Hague conventions ultimately led the United States to enter the war. In 1917 Germany began attacking merchant shipping. This contravened the laws of naval combat established

at the 1907 Hague peace conference and 1908–1909 London naval conference. Germany's decision was made not to stave off defeat, which might have been considered acceptable, but to secure victory. Germany justified its decision on the basis that Great Britain was arming merchant ships in contravention of Convention VII. Nevertheless, the result of this was international opprobrium and an encouragement to the United States to enter the war. Best, *Law and War Since 1945*, pp. 76–7, 305; and Hill, *Arms Control at Sea*, p. 29.

175. The Germans, however, perceived this as a cloak for French territorial aspirations, rather than a serious attempt to ensure arms restraint. See Tanner, "Versailles," p. 24.

176. Ibid., p. 24.

177. Hill, *Arms Control at Sea*, p. 34.

178. <www.worldbank.org/afr/afth2/crrp/bulletin3-30html>.

179. Jacques Fontanel and Jean-François Guilhaudis, "Arms Transfer Control and Proposals to Link Disarmament to Development," in Ohlson, *Arms Transfer Limitations*, pp. 213–26.

SUGGESTED ADDITIONAL READING

Carter, April. *Success and Failure in Arms Control Negotiations*. Oxford, U.K.: Oxford University Press, 1989.

Croft, Stuart. *Strategies of Arms Control*. Manchester, U.K.: Manchester University Press, 1996.

Gallagher, Nancy W., ed. *Arms Control: New Approaches to Theory and Policy*. London: Frank Cass, 1998.

Goldblat, Jozef. *Arms Control Agreements: A Handbook*. New York: Praeger, 1983.

Macintosh, James. *Confidence Building in the Arms Control Process: A Transformational View, Arms Control and Disarmament Studies, No. 2*. Ottawa: The Non-Proliferation, Arms Control and Disarmament Division, Department of Foreign Affairs and International Trade, 1996.

Ohlson, Thomas, ed. *Arms Transfer Limitations and Third World Security*. Oxford, U.K.: Oxford University Press, 1988.

Price, Richard. "Reversing the Gun Sights: Transnational Civil Society Targets Land Mines." *International Organization*, vol. 52, no. 3 (Summer 1998), pp. 613–44.

SIPRI. *SIPRI Yearbook 1999*. Oxford, U.K.: Oxford University Press, 1999.

Tanner, Fred. *From Versailles to Baghdad: Post-war Armament Control of Defeated States*. New York: UNIDIR, 1992.

Internet sites

United States Bureau of Arms Control <http://www.state.gov/www/global/arms/bureau_ac/reports_ac.html>

Federation of American Scientists (FAS), Arms Sales Monitoring Project <http://sun00781.dn.net/asmp>

Center for Defense Information (CDI) <http://www.cdi.org>

British American Security Information Council (BASIC) <http://www.basicint.org>

International Action Network on Small Arms (IANSA) <http://www.iansa.org>

Military Parade, the Magazine of the Russian Military Industrial Complex <http://www.milparade.com>

Stockholm International Peace Research Institute (SIPRI) <http://www.sipri.se>

The Wassenaar Arrangement <http://www.wassenaar.org>

UN Department for Disarmament Affairs <http://www.un.org/Depts/dda/DDAHome.htm>

UN Register of Conventional Arms <http://domino.un.org/REGISTER.NSF>

16

Warfare: Nuclear, Biological, and Chemical Weapons

Thomas Bernauer

DESPITE THE REDUCED INTENSITY of great power rivalry since the late 1980s, risks posed by nuclear, biological, and chemical (NBC) weapons, often referred to as weapons of mass destruction (WMD), persistently score at the top of global public security concerns. The technical feasibility of releasing from one single nuclear weapon more energy than was released by all conventional weapons in all wars in history remains the most powerful example of risks that human activity poses to life on Earth.

For decades the international community has invested great efforts into controlling and eliminating the risks posed by NBC weapons. These efforts have only been partially successful. Three global regimes organized around the 1968 Nuclear Nonproliferation Treaty (NPT), the 1972 Biological Weapons Convention (BWC), and the 1992 Chemical Weapons Convention (CWC) have been established. In addition, a variety of international export control arrangements as well as regional and bilateral arms control regimes have emerged. These arms control efforts are incomplete—several states have not given up possession of WMD while others seek to acquire such weapons—and compliance problems continue to plague most governance efforts in this area.

This chapter describes the successes and failures of global policies for WMD, seeks to explain differences in the performance of existing international regimes, points out the lessons learned, and puts forward policy recommendations. The analysis is structured around the four aspects of governance identified in this book: agenda setting, negotiation, implementation, and reactions to noncompliance.

Agenda setting in the area studied here has been largely reactive, has often been driven by instances of WMD use or threats thereof, and has been dominated by governments. In contrast with their involvement with other arms control issues, such as land mines or small arms, nongovernmental organizations (NGOs) have had only a very indirect influence on negotiating WMD-related agendas. Particularly in the areas of nuclear weapons and export controls, large military and industrial powers have dominated the agenda-setting process. They have succeeded in framing issues in ways that promote asymmetric policies, implying unequal rights and obligations for possessors and nonpossessors of WMD or related technology. In the medium to long term, the increasing integration of the world economy threatens to undermine these policies. Stable, long-term solutions to risks posed by WMD will have to become more symmetrical and self-enforcing, combining the benefits of open markets (including those in dual-use goods) with safeguards against the abuse of technologies for WMD purposes. To that end, international export control arrangements operating outside global regimes should be integrated into the latter.

The golden age of global negotiations in the Geneva-based Conference on Disarmament (CD) is probably over, because the CD has become too inflexible for managing complex trade-offs among large numbers of countries. Future negotiations on global arrangements are likely to be conducted in ad hoc forums. The negotiation of monitoring systems, a prerequisite for successful arms control, has been greatly facilitated by experimental inspections, particularly in the case of the CWC. This means they should be used more systematically in efforts to establish a monitoring system for the BWC and efforts to improve safeguards and special inspections under the NPT.

Failure of China, France, Russia, the United Kingdom, and the United States to implement fully their NPT commitments (notably the elimination of nuclear weapons) remains a major obstacle in implementing the NPT. A formal and unconditional ban on the use of nuclear weapons, deactivation of all nuclear weapons, the elimination of tactical nuclear weapons, as well as full implementation of the Comprehensive Test Ban Treaty (CTBT) and Strategic Arms Reduction Treaties (START II and III) would go a long way toward bolstering the normative underpinnings of the NPT and increasing the political pressure on the remaining holdouts. Delays in monitoring the U.S. chemical industry and in eliminating Russia's chemical weapons threaten to undermine confidence in the CWC. Providing technical and financial assistance to Russia for elimination of chemical weapons should become a top priority of all Western countries. Positive incentives (assistance) have often been more successful in the nuclear area than have sanctions, particularly in redressing involuntary implementation problems and attracting holdout countries. The safeguards system under the NPT would be greatly strengthened if all Western countries signed the new protocol (INFCIRC 540) providing for more intrusive safeguards, and if they tied acceptance of that protocol by other countries to all nuclear trade. Implementation of the BWC will remain deficient as long as the convention lacks an intrusive monitoring system. The appropriate balance between effective (intrusive) monitoring and the protection of business or military secrets unrelated to WMD could be found by increased use of experimental inspections. Terrorism with WMD remains a possibility, though the probability and possible damage are very difficult to assess. Effective implementation of global WMD regimes would ultimately lower this risk by creating ever stronger social norms against WMD use and making the acquisition of such weapons physically and economically more difficult. In the meantime, combating WMD terrorism requires intensified international collaboration between national intelligence agencies and police forces.

Compliance with WMD regimes is greater than frequently assumed. Noncompliance remains the exception and has been addressed largely outside the respective regimes. Cases such as Iraq, North Korea, and Russia suggest that sanctions alone cannot produce stable, long-term solutions and that positive incentives may be more conducive to cooperative behavior.

The greatest challenge in the years ahead is to redesign or implement international commitments in a way that creates more symmetry of rights and obligations as well as economic burdens. More symmetry would greatly strengthen the normative force and self-enforcing nature of global regimes. Full implementation by the United States and Russia—the possessors of the largest WMD arsenals—of their NPT, CWC, and BWC commitments, as well as the integration of all international export control arrangements into the three global WMD regimes, are the most effective measures toward this end. Together with intensified international efforts to settle regional conflicts, these measures would also increase the attractiveness of global WMD regimes to the few remaining holdouts.

NATURE OF THE PROBLEM

NBC weapons pose a variety of humanitarian, security, and environmental risks that governments must seek to address. When disagreements arise over these risks, they often influence the forms and effectiveness of international collaboration and institutions.

Effects of Nuclear, Biological, and Chemical Weapons

When used in armed conflict, NBC weapons have indiscriminate effects: damage to civilian targets is almost impossible to avoid. This is why the three types of weapons are often called weapons of mass destruction.

Nuclear Weapons. Around thirty states have the capacity to develop and produce nuclear weapons within variable time frames. Nine of these are known to have done so: China, France, India, Israel, Pakistan, the Soviet Union/Russia, South Africa, the United Kingdom, and the United States. The United States and Russia possess the largest nuclear arsenals.[1] The only country to have eliminated nuclear weapons under its possession and control is South Africa. Belarus, Kazakhstan, and Ukraine, on whose territories a large number of nuclear weapons were left after the collapse of the Soviet Union, did not acquire operational control of these weapons and ultimately transferred them to Russia for destruction. Thus they cannot be regarded as (former) nuclear weapons states.

If used in armed conflict, nuclear weapons can cause huge destruction of life, infrastructure, and the environment. No other weapon has the destructive power of nuclear arms. Humans, animals, and plants are affected through pressure, heat, and radiation. Infrastructure is damaged or destroyed by pressure and heat. The environment in a broader sense (that is, the atmosphere, soil, and water) is contaminated for periods ranging from days to many years by the radioactive fallout of nuclear explosions. In the case of large-scale nuclear war, scientists have predicted a worldwide cooling effect as dust particles blown into the atmosphere by nuclear explosions block incoming sunlight.[2]

Only two nuclear weapons have been exploded in armed conflict, those over the Japanese cities of Hiroshima and Nagasaki in 1945. Assessments of the effects of nuclear weapons are based on these two cases, more than 2,000 nuclear test explosions by seven countries since then (China, France, India, Pakistan, Soviet Union/ Russia, the United Kingdom, and the United States), computer simulations, and laboratory experiments. Nuclear test explosions have served to develop new weapon designs; calibrate the explosive power of weapons; assess the reliability, security, and safety of stockpiles; and demonstrate the nuclear capability of testing states to potential adversaries.

Chemical, Biological, and Toxin Weapons. Chemical warfare agents are substances that enter the human body through the respiratory system or the skin. They harm life by means of their toxic effects, for example, by damaging the respiratory or nervous system. Biological warfare agents are living organisms, such as viruses and bacteria, which cause illness. Toxins are toxic substances produced by living organisms, such as bacteria. In essence, toxins are chemical warfare agents. Chemical and biological weapons (CBW) can also contaminate infrastructure and the environment for periods ranging from hours to many years.

CBW in the arsenals of states today, even though labeled as WMD, may cause human suffering only on a much smaller scale than nuclear weapons. Chemical weapons have repeatedly been used in war on a tactical level. Their destructive capacity has never exceeded rather limited theaters of war and has never played a decisive role in the outcome of conflicts. Several states are known to have possessed chemical weapons at some time in their history, notably China, Egypt, France, Germany, India, Iran, Iraq, Italy, South Korea, Soviet Union/Russia, the United Kingdom, and the United States. Pending the elimination of their chemical weapons under the

CWC, Russia and the United States own the largest chemical weapon stockpiles.[3] Other states that have declared their possession of chemical weapons are India and South Korea. Other countries (such as Iran and Pakistan) are suspected of having such weapons. Iraq's large chemical weapons stockpile was destroyed under the supervision of the UN Special Commission for Iraq (UNSCOM) in the 1990s.

Some biological warfare agents and toxins could be produced in quantities sufficient to destroy all human life. This potential notwithstanding, most military experts question the strategic utility of such weapons, as they exist today, and no one has yet used biological or toxin weapons in war. Only a few countries (such as, Iraq, Japan, the Soviet Union/Russia, the United Kingdom, and the United States) have possessed biological weapons. Some other countries have engaged in biological warfare research but have probably not produced and stockpiled biological weapons. Biological weapons have been less attractive to the military than have nuclear or chemical weapons for several reasons. First, the delivery of such warfare agents is technically more difficult than the delivery of nuclear weapons. Even dissemination across smaller geographical areas, such as one medium-sized country, is, with today's technology, very hard to achieve. Second, the effect of biological weapons materializes only some time after the attack and tends to be quite unpredictable. Finally, protection of human life against biological, chemical, and toxin weapons is to a large degree feasible. By comparison, the destruction of entire countries with a few dozen nuclear weapons is possible and protection of large numbers of people against such weapons is prohibitively expensive or physically impossible. Presently, existing biological weapons may thus have significant military value in some asymmetrical conflicts. In relation to industrialized countries, they remain largely weapons of terror.

Some observers expect that technological innovation, particularly in molecular biology and biotechnology, will increase the threat posed by biological and toxin weapons by resulting in agents that are more potent, easier to disseminate, and harder to protect against. At present, such developments are largely a hypothesis.[4]

Military-Security Risks Posed by NBC Weapons

Nuclear weapons in particular can destabilize relations between countries and increase the risk of war. International strategic stability problems are much less pronounced in the case of CBW. The known possessors of nuclear weapons—China, France, India, Israel, Pakistan, Russia, the United Kingdom, and the United States— have maintained these weapons primarily to deter other countries from attacking them. However, stable deterrence—deterrence that reduces the risk of war—is contingent on a variety of circumstances, including: relatively symmetric military capabilities of the actors in a deterrence relationship; a reliable second-strike capability of all sides; sufficient information of the actors about one another's intentions and behavior (including reliable early-warning systems); rationality of decision makers; and safeguards against problems in the chain of command (that is, the problem of rogue subordinate officers).

Governments of states possessing nuclear weapons usually argue that most of these conditions for stable deterrence are met, but such assertions have remained a matter of dispute among military analysts. For example, several known instances of false alarms created by U.S. and Russian early-warning systems, supposedly the best in the world, highlight that such systems are not foolproof and that accidental launches of nuclear weapons remain possible. The risk of accidental nuclear war exists particularly when relations between countries are conflictual, warning times are short, and launch-on-warning rules are adopted. By contrast, the risk of unauthorized use of nuclear arms is, not least due to stringent safety systems installed by nuclear weapons possessors, somewhat smaller.[5]

Yet another problem—that of preemptive strikes (nuclear strikes to "decapitate" the arsenal of the adversary)—remains a source of instability in deterrence relationships. No such strikes have occurred, but available evidence suggests that military planners and political decision makers on both sides of the Cold War never ruled out this option. Similar problems exist with regard to nuclear rivalries between regional powers, such as India and Pakistan.

In contrast to the problem of preemptive war, a preventive strike has occurred in one instance. In 1981 Israel destroyed a nuclear reactor in Iraq in an effort to stop that country's military nuclear program. The war against Iraq in 1990–1991 was not explicitly designed to prevent Iraq from acquiring nuclear weapons but did serve that purpose among others.[6]

If NBC or related materials were to fall into the hands of terrorist groups, security problems of a predominantly domestic nature could also arise. As discussed below, very few instances are known where terrorist or other radical nonstate actors have acquired and/or used WMD. So far, this problem has been restricted largely to CBW. With growing availability of critical technology and know-how in global markets, however, this problem could become more pressing, particularly in the field of CBW.

Regulatory Problems

All of these risks posed by WMD are the subject of global regulatory efforts. Regulations in this realm perform three functions: they lessen the risk of armed conflict, reduce costs of arming in preparation for (possible) war, and limit damage should war break out.[7] In other words, states have adopted policies for controlling, reducing, and eliminating WMD because these weapons can destabilize relations among countries and increase the risk of war; they are a burden on the economies of states; they inflict unacceptable human suffering, destruction of infrastructure, and environmental damage if used in armed conflict; and predominantly domestic security problems could arise if terrorist or other radical nonstate actors were to acquire such weapons. Regulatory efforts have concentrated on reductions or the elimination of WMD by states possessing such weapons and on preventing nonpossessors from acquiring WMD.

Disputes about the fundamental goals to be achieved relate to military-security problems associated with WMD, much less to humanitarian, economic, or environmental effects. In essence, the question is whether the total elimination of WMD is, at the margin, preferable over stable and well-controlled deterrence systems. In addition, it is debated whether the deterrence system between Russia and the United States can be effectively replicated in regional contexts. In the field of CBW, this dispute, which had divided policy makers and the military throughout the twentieth century, was by the early 1990s resolved to a large degree in favor of total elimination of these weapons. The large majority of states have ceased to regard CBW as a means of deterring threats or attacks by WMD or other weapons. Only a few Arab countries still argue in favor of retaining the chemical weapons option as a deterrent against nuclear weapons (notably those of Israel). Most military strategists think that this argument does not make sense and will wane. Biological weapons could, due to technological breakthroughs, become more attractive to some states. So far, however, the existing taboo against such weapons remains strong.

In contrast to CBW, the dispute between supporters of stable deterrence and supporters of total elimination of nuclear weapons has not been resolved. Even though most governments of states possessing nuclear weapons tend to pay lip service to the goal of a world free of such weapons, few analysts think that this outcome will materialize soon. At best, Russia and the United States will reduce their arsenals from tens of thousands to a few thousand nuclear warheads on each side, still enough to destroy large parts of the globe.[8] Even though both nuclear superpowers have moved from doctrines of massive retaliation to minimum deterrence postures, it is unlikely that they will forswear the use of nuclear weapons completely. A few strategic analysts have taken to the extreme position of welcoming the spread of nuclear weapons to more countries. The basis of the "more may be better" view is that war among states will become less likely—as it did between the two military alliances during the Cold War—if stable nuclear deterrence can be established among a wider set of states.[9] Disagreement about the stability of existing nuclear deterrence systems and about evident problems of how to get to stable nuclear deterrence among a larger number of countries has led most policy makers to dismiss this proposition. However, arguments by nuclear weapons states and some of their allies that nuclear deterrence among a few possessor states is desirable, whereas the spread of nuclear weapons to more countries is undesirable, have also been rejected by the majority of states. This dispute about the legitimacy and logic of nuclear deterrence has constituted a serious liability on all global efforts to eliminate the risks posed by WMD.

A range of theoretically predictable cooperation problems also affect global regulatory efforts for WMD. The harshest critics of arms control have argued that when arms control is most necessary, it will not work; and when it is not necessary, it will be easy to achieve but meaningless.[10] This assertion derives from a radical interpretation of the so-called security dilemma, which scholars have traditionally regarded as the principle obstacle to arms control and disarmament cooperation. This dilemma means that international cooperation would be optimal from the collective standpoint but is difficult or impossible to achieve because it runs against the rational self-interest of individual countries. As long as information about actual and future intentions and behavior of states is incomplete, states cannot, in the eyes of potential partners, credibly commit to joint governance structures that reduce or eliminate WMD, even if collaboration would be the collectively optimal strategy. Under conditions of incomplete information and in the absence of a supraordinate authority able to enforce compliance, states operate with worst-case assumptions about other states and are reluctant to engage in substantive arms control or disarmament measures.[11] Research in political science has shown that the basic remedies to these problems are ongoing cooperation and greater transparency.[12] Most arms control efforts are therefore geared to establishing cooperative structures that are based on reciprocal step-by-step cooperation and monitoring and compliance systems.[13] The analysis of the three global regimes for WMD below underlines the importance of such mechanisms.

Another obstacle to effective governance that has been studied in more detail only recently is asymmetries in the preferences of the actors involved in a collaborative venture and asymmetries in their capacities to engage in and implement international commitments. These problems affect the possibilities of cooperation separately from problems of monitoring and enforcement. For example, countries that perceive little benefit in engaging in international regulatory efforts and/or lack the capacity to implement international commitments can seriously reduce the overall effectiveness of global governance efforts.

Changes Since the End of the Cold War

The regulatory problems involved in trying to reduce or eliminate risks posed by WMD did not disappear with the end of the Cold War. The end of East-West confrontation, however, has created some new problems as well as some new opportunities.

As the Berlin Wall fell, some analysts predicted that controlling or eliminating WMD would become much more difficult.[14] They argued that the number of states possessing WMD would increase as existing military alliances disintegrated, international nonproliferation and disarmament regimes forged under the leadership of the two superpowers weakened, and the bipolar system transformed into a multipolar balance-of-power arrangement similar to the one in Europe during the nineteenth century. Others also pointed to the risks emanating from a hitherto unknown or neglected problem: the declining regulatory capacity of states due to the forces of economic globalization.[15] All of the known regulatory approaches to removing the risks posed by WMD had presupposed that the problem was to get governments to master the collective will to conclude and implement international agreements. New about the post–Cold War situation is that, in two respects, the capacity of states to implement effectively international regulatory regimes has suffered a severe blow.

The first, and most dramatic, capacity problem emerged from the disintegration of the Soviet Union. The most acute risks have been theft of nuclear weapons, weapon-grade fissile material, and related technology, and their transfer to proliferator countries or nonstate actors, such as terrorist groups, as well as transfers of know-how by underpaid or unemployed personnel of the former Soviet Union's nuclear weapons complex to proliferator countries or nonstate actors. Similar problems have existed for missile technology, as well as materials and know-how that could be abused for the production of CBW.[16]

The second risk emerged even before the end of the Cold War but has been amplified by the transition of many formerly planned economies to market economies. Since the 1970s most countries have become much more open to international trade and foreign direct investment. This globalization of trade, investment, and industrial production has constrained the capacity of governments to control transfers of military and dual-use goods. Many analysts believe that socioeconomic disarray in former communist countries and processes of globalization have combined to increase significantly the risk of WMD or related materials technology and know-how falling into the hands of proliferator countries or terrorist groups.[17]

Other analysts have been more optimistic, arguing that governments have collaborated intensively and with considerable success over the past decade in an effort to reverse the potential loss of control capacities at the national and international levels.[18] They also highlight the new opportunities for cooperation created by the end of East-West conflict. Relations between countries in the North Atlantic Treaty Organization and former communist countries have improved enormously. These changes as well as evolving notions of sovereignty in general have led most states to accept much more intrusive international monitoring. These developments have improved the possibilities for successful collaboration.

INTERNATIONAL RESPONSES

The track record of governance efforts contains successes and failures. On the one hand, twenty years of negotiations on a chemical weapons treaty succeeded in 1992.

Several important holdouts have joined the NPT, making its membership almost universal. Nonproliferation measures for all WMD have been tightened considerably. On the other hand, several important countries have remained outside the regimes for NBC weapons. In 1998 the group of nuclear weapons possessors increased by two countries when India and Pakistan exploded several nuclear devices. Problems with Iraq and North Korea have not been fully resolved. The risk of "loose nukes" and illicit transfers of military or dual-use materials, technology, and know-how from states of the former Soviet Union to other countries has not been eliminated.[19] Since the use of poison gas by a Japanese sect in Tokyo, which in March 1995 killed twelve people and wounded hundreds of others, the specter of WMD acquisition and use by terrorist groups has been subject to much debate. Some observers also fear that, because of U.S. failure to ratify the CTBT, problems with the NPT and bilateral nuclear arms control, and other difficulties, the normative structure underpinning global regimes for WMD might gradually erode.[20] By which measures has the international community sought to address these risks, and with what degree of success?

Nuclear Weapons

The risks posed by nuclear weapons have only partially been eliminated. At the core of a large patchwork of governance arrangements restricting or banning various military activities in the nuclear field is the NPT, which was concluded in 1968 and entered into force in 1970. The NPT bars nuclear weapons states from transferring to any recipient nuclear weapons or nuclear explosive devices or control over such weapons or devices. The nuclear powers must not in any way assist, encourage, or induce nonnuclear weapon states to produce or acquire such arms or devices. The nonnuclear weapon states, for their part, have committed themselves not to receive nuclear weapons or other nuclear explosive devices or control over them. They are also barred from producing such weapons and from receiving assistance from anyone to that end. In other words, nuclear weapons states—defined as states having exploded a nuclear device before January 1, 1967—are allowed to retain their weapons for an undefined period of time, whereas nonnuclear weapon states are barred from possessing such weapons. Compliance by nonnuclear weapon states with their treaty obligations is monitored through so-called safeguards (that is, procedures designed to monitor the nuclear fuel cycle of nonnuclear weapon states in order to prevent illegal diversion of fissile material for weapon purposes). They are administered by the International Atomic Energy Agency (IAEA), an international organization that already existed when the NPT was concluded.[21]

Nonnuclear weapon states would probably not have accepted such unequal rights and obligations if no compensatory measures had been built into and around the

NPT. First, the nuclear weapons states promised to pursue negotiations on the cessation of the nuclear arms race "at an early date" and on nuclear disarmament. Second, they promised support to nonpossessors in their peaceful nuclear activities. Third, they provided, albeit qualified, assurances to nonnuclear weapon states to assist them if they were threatened or attacked with nuclear weapons, and not to attack them with nuclear arms.[22]

In assessments of the successes and failures of global efforts, the NPT serves as a useful starting point. Adherence and compliance with its provisions by nonnuclear weapon states indicate the degree to which the "horizontal" spread of nuclear weapons—increases in the number of states possessing such arms—has been stemmed. Disarmament efforts by the five nuclear powers under the NPT (China, France, Russia, the United Kingdom, and the United States), an obligation contracted by these states under Article 6 of the treaty, as well as by other nuclear weapons states outside the NPT indicate the extent to which "vertical" proliferation—the growth of existing nuclear arsenals—has been reduced or reversed.

In terms of adherence, the NPT is a success story. Around 190 countries have become parties to the treaty. Except for the cases of Iraq and North Korea, there is no evidence of noncompliance. In 1995 the NPT was extended for an unlimited period of time, and the monitoring (safeguards) system of the regime is being strengthened through the IAEA's so-called 93+2 program. The obligations of nonpossessors are reinforced by nuclear weapon free–zones covering parts of the Pacific (Treaty of Rarotonga, 1986), Latin America and the Caribbean (Treaty of Tlatelolco, 1967), Africa (Treaty of Pelindaba, 1996), Antarctica (1959), and Southeast Asia (1995). Most states, including most known nuclear weapon possessors, are committed not to deploy these weapons in the global commons, notably Antarctica, the seabed, and outer space. This success in stemming the further spread of nuclear weapons is all the more astonishing because some important promises to nonnuclear weapon states, designed to offset the unequal rights and obligations under the NPT, have not been fulfilled.

The five nuclear weapons powers under the NPT have far to go before their nuclear weapons are eliminated. In 1996 a global treaty, the CTBT, was signed, banning all nuclear test explosions. To enter into force, however, the CTBT must be ratified by all forty-four states possessing nuclear reactors. The CTBT expands on existing constraints on nuclear testing that prohibit tests in the atmosphere and space as well as the ocean floor, Antarctica, and other demilitarized areas or that limit the yield of nuclear test explosions. These older treaties on nuclear testing were more successful in preventing environmental contamination in some areas than in actually slowing the nuclear arms race.

Similarly, older nuclear arms control measures, such as the Strategic Arms Limitation Treaties (SALT I, SALT II) and the 1972 Antiballistic Missile Treaty, were designed only to facilitate a stable nuclear deterrence relationship between the two superpowers. They did not significantly constrain the qualitative and quantitative growth of nuclear arsenals. Only in the late 1980s did the United States and Russia begin reductions of their nuclear weapons stockpiles, both unilaterally and in the framework of bilateral nuclear disarmament treaties, particular the Intermediate Range Nuclear Forces (INF) and START agreements. Despite these reductions, the arsenals of the two countries at the end of the 1990s are still the size they were when the NPT was negotiated in the 1960s.[23] The United Kingdom and France have reduced and modernized their nuclear arsenals unilaterally but have not engaged in any cooperative measures. China has not engaged in any reductions. In the late 1990s, discussions on stopping the production of fissile material for weapons purposes started in the Conference on Disarmament, so far with no progress. This measure, even if it were to be successfully implemented, would have little effect on the five nuclear powers under the NPT because they already possess large stocks of weapon-grade fissile material. Rather it might contribute to preventing the emergence of yet more nuclear weapon states or the further growth of nuclear arsenals in India, Israel, and Pakistan, should these states accept such a commitment. At the year 2000 review conference of the NPT, the five nuclear powers reaffirmed their commitment to pursue nuclear disarmament, but without indicating any time frame.[24]

The NPT does not explicitly provide for security assurances to nonnuclear weapon states. But under pressure from the have-nots three of the original nuclear powers party to the NPT (Russia, the United Kingdom, and the United States) gave some assurances in a UN Security Council resolution. They promised assistance, in accordance with the UN Charter, to nonnuclear weapon states attacked or threatened with nuclear weapons. These assurances did not exceed the normal duties of all UN members to help victims of international aggression. Requests for further-reaching promises have been rejected by the nuclear powers. Nonnuclear weapon states have also asked for promises not to attack them with nuclear arms. All five nuclear powers under the NPT have accepted such commitments. But all these assurances have been conditional, declaratory, and worded in different terms. Proposals for an international treaty that would unconditionally bind all nuclear powers in the same way have fallen on deaf ears. A few days before the 1995 NPT review and extension conference, the UN Security Council adopted a resolution that took note of declarations made by four nuclear powers (not China). These declarations combine positive and negative assurances. Only China has declared that it will not, under any circumstances, use nuclear arms against nonnuclear weapon states party to the NPT or similar arrangements.[25]

To increase the attractiveness of the NPT to nonnuclear weapon states, these states were promised facilitated access to materials and know-how for peaceful uses of nuclear energy. Most of the expectations have not been met. Neither have nonnuclear weapon countries enjoyed significantly facilitated or even concessionary access to nuclear materials and technology on world markets, nor have proposals to use nuclear explosions for peaceful purposes (for example, building of reservoirs) proven environmentally and economically acceptable.

Two factors have constrained collaboration in the peaceful uses of nuclear power. First, there is a fundamental dilemma in assisting nonnuclear weapon states in their civilian nuclear programs. As long as the relevant materials are under IAEA safeguards, nonnuclear weapon parties to the NPT are, in principle, allowed to produce and use plutonium, highly enriched uranium, and other nuclear materials and technology. States in a position to do so are even encouraged by the NPT to provide assistance to other states parties in this regard. Because obtaining weapon-grade fissile material is the most important hurdle in any nuclear weapons program, and because even purely civilian nuclear programs can create a knowledge base that can be abused for military purposes, any far-reaching exports and assistance to NPT countries suspected of harboring military nuclear ambitions poses a problem. Most nuclear exporter countries have been cautious and have adopted rather restrictive interpretations of their NPT commitments, which has repeatedly led to conflict among NPT parties. One of the most prominent examples is the U.S. effort to prevent Russian exports of nuclear materials and technology to Iran, even though such exports are perfectly compatible with the NPT (to which Iran is a party) and the IAEA has not detected any signs of noncompliance in Iran. Second, environmental concerns, particularly since the Three Mile Island (1979) and Chernobyl (1986) nuclear accidents, as well as growing doubts about the economic efficiency of nuclear power, have led to a virtual standstill of civilian nuclear power projects in most countries. Consequently, the demand for nuclear assistance, as provided for in the NPT and the IAEA statute, has been declining. Proposals for peaceful uses of nuclear explosive devices have fared even worse. Experiments of the two biggest nuclear powers (Russia and the United States) with such explosions have shown that their utility is minimal to negative.

To sum up, a record number of countries have joined the NPT and have complied with its rules. This success is astonishing because the treaty appears to favor nuclear weapons states by granting them a military nuclear oligopoly, and because promises to offset this inequality with disarmament efforts, security assurances, and nuclear assistance have lagged far behind initial expectations. Since the end of the Cold War, some of the nuclear weapons–capable holdouts from the NPT have joined the regime, in particular Argentina, Brazil, and South Africa. The enormous problems associated with the collapse of the former Soviet Union have at least in part been resolved: Belarus, Kazakhstan, and Ukraine transferred to Russia the nuclear weapons that were on their territories at the time of the collapse and became nonnuclear weapon parties to the NPT; controls of Russia's nuclear weapon stockpile and exports of dual-use nuclear materials have been strengthened.[26] This progress, despite the neglect of important parts of the bargain, testifies to the fact that the NPT has an intrinsic security value to nonnuclear weapon states. Notably, the internationally certified nonnuclear status of countries reduces the likelihood of these states being attacked by nuclear arms, and it solves security dilemmas among regional powers that wish to make their nuclear restraint conditional on that of other states in the region.

Some important problems remain to be solved. In particular, there have been cases of treaty violations, and several critical states remain outside the NPT.[27] Despite safeguards by the IAEA, Iraq was able to engage in a large nuclear weapons program. Following defeat in war against a UN-approved coalition in 1990–1991, Iraq was forced to declare its activities to UNSCOM and the IAEA. Its nuclear program, which was still several years away from production of a functioning nuclear weapon, was eliminated. In 1993 the IAEA discovered that North Korea, an NPT member, was violating its treaty obligations by operating undeclared and unsafeguarded nuclear facilities and trying to divert plutonium from civilian to military projects. Since 1994, this compliance problem has been addressed outside the NPT. In May 1998, India, which had already conducted a nuclear test in 1974, exploded several nuclear devices, prompting its rival Pakistan into a series of tests as well. Both countries, which have remained outside the NPT and have thus not formally violated international law by their activities, are now engaged in developing and testing delivery systems for their nuclear weapons. International efforts to freeze that beginning arms race and bring the two countries into the NPT have so far failed. Another long-standing holdout is Israel. As long as the regional security problems in the Middle East are not resolved, the likelihood of Israel giving up its nuclear arsenal is rather small.

Biological and Chemical Weapons

Reaffirming earlier laws of war, the 1925 Geneva Protocol outlawed the use of CBW. Many reservations made by the parties turned the protocol into a no-first-use agreement—states restricted their right to use CBW to situations of retaliation in kind. Several countries acquired large arsenals of chemical weapons, and some used these weapons in war. By contrast, biological weapons have been less attractive to military planners. Very few countries, at some point in their history, possessed biological weapons, and no country is known to have used them on a significant scale in war. For these reasons, and because they were already nuclear powers, the United States and the United Kingdom decided in the early 1970s to eliminate unilaterally their biological weapons. This unilateral action facilitated a multilateral solution. In 1972, the CD concluded a ban on biological weapons and decided to deal with chemical weapons subsequently.

The BWC, which has been in force since 1975, establishes a comprehensive ban on microbial or other biological as well as toxin weapons. The parties committed themselves not to develop, produce, stockpile, acquire by other means, retain, or transfer to any recipient such means of warfare or delivery vehicles for biological warfare agents. Countries are also barred from assisting or inducing anyone else to acquire the prohibited weapons. Countries must destroy or divert to peaceful uses all banned warfare agents and means of delivery. The convention does not provide for any mechanisms that would allow effective monitoring of states' compliance with their obligations. Neither did the BWC make use of a preexisting international organization (as the NPT parties did with the IAEA) or establish a new international organization (as did the parties of the CWC) for that purpose. The decision not to establish a monitoring system was partly an acknowledgment that the former Soviet Union and many other countries were unwilling to accept any mandatory on-site inspections, and partly the result of the low military value biological weapons were, at that time, thought to have.

The BWC records the intention of the parties to conclude a ban on chemical weapons as soon as possible. "Soon" was to mean twenty years. In 1992 the CWC was signed. It entered into force in 1997 and bans the development, production, acquisition by other means, stockpiling or retention of chemical weapons, and their transfer to anyone. To prevent any ambiguities that reservations to the 1925 Geneva Protocol had left, the use and preparation for use of chemical weapons are also prohibited. Assistance to and inducement of others to acquire chemical weapons are banned. All parties must destroy their chemical weapons and the facilities that produce them. In contrast to the BWC, the CWC established a large monitoring machinery, including mandatory on-site inspections, to ascertain the destruction of proscribed items and make sure that the parties comply with the other obligations, such as not to develop and produce chemical weapons. This monitoring system is administered by the Organization for the Prohibition of Chemical Weapons (OPCW).

In contrast to the NPT, the BWC and CWC provide for the total elimination of entire classes of weaponry and for equal rights and obligations of the parties. Nevertheless, the BWC and CWC contain some provisions designed to fine-tune the respective incentive structures so as to maximize adherence and compliance. Developing countries in particular tend to have fewer means of protection against CBW. Under the BWC, the parties are expected to assist other parties, in accordance with the UN Charter, should these become victims of a treaty violation. The CWC goes somewhat further in encouraging cooperation among the parties in the development and uses of protective measures, and in specifying more clearly when and how assistance should be provided. The OPCW is to play an active role in this regard. None of these provisions has been formally invoked by the parties because no instances of CBW use have occurred since the treaty's entry into force.

Both regimes encourage the parties to cooperate more closely in the civilian uses of chemistry and biology. There is no evidence that the two regimes have significantly promoted such cooperation. They remain strongly focused on disarmament and have not been able to support or even expand on existing free trade regimes, development assistance efforts, or transnational or intergovernmental research cooperation. The CWC is more explicit than the BWC in urging the parties to lift restrictions on trade in dual-use items among each other. At the same time, the CWC imposes increasingly tough restrictions on trade in dual-use chemicals with nonparties. These provisions are designed to gradually tighten the screw on nonmembers and make treaty membership more attractive. Because a wide range of chemicals and technologies will be affected, and international trade in such items is important to developing and developed economies, these provisions are likely to have a significant impact on countries' incentives to join the regime.

The intrinsic security value of the two regimes as well as the equal rights and obligations enshrined in them has generated strong incentives for states to join. More than 140 states are party to the BWC, and more than 130 states to the CWC. The large majority of states have complied with their treaty obligations.[28] The most serious violations of the BWC have occurred in Russia, which, by its own admission, has developed and produced biological weapons even after joining the BWC. Despite intensive bilateral efforts between the United States and Russia to remedy the situation, doubts about Russia's compliance with the BWC continue.[29] Russia promised but did not allow international on-site inspections to investigate allegations. Since its entry into force, the CWC has not suffered from significant violations. Some major implementation problems remain to be solved, however. For more than two years beyond the deadline, the United States failed to bring its civilian chemical industry under the regime's monitoring system. Russia in particular has been unable to meet its obligations to destroy its chemical weapons and related production facilities within agreed time frames. Moreover, several parties (such as Iran and Pakistan) are suspected of having submitted incomplete declarations on their chemical weapons activities.[30]

Iraq, not a party to the BWC, accumulated a considerable arsenal of biological and toxin weapons. After its defeat in the 1991 Gulf War, the largest part of the biological weapons potential was eliminated under the supervision of the UNSCOM. The same holds for Iraq's large arsenal of chemical weapons. After a renewed escalation of the conflict in 1998, Iraq terminated its cooperation with UNSCOM and the latter broke down. Its successor, the UN Monitoring, Verification, and Inspection Commission (UNMOVIC), is not yet fully operational. In the meantime, there is strong evidence that Iraq is trying to rebuild its chemical and biological weapons program. Whereas Iraq's military nuclear program has been largely eliminated and would take many years to rebuild, the country's chemical and biological weapons ambitions pose a more important risk in the medium to long term.[31] The most important absentees from the CWC are some Arab countries. They have linked their adherence to the convention to the denuclearization of Israel. Another critical state remaining outside the BWC and CWC is North Korea.

Export Control Regimes

The globalization of production and trade in military goods and dual-use items, in combination with socioeconomic disarray in the former Soviet Union, poses a serious challenge to states' capacities for controlling illicit activities associated with WMD.[32] The challenge is particularly great in this case because a very high interdiction rate is essential. In preventing drug trade or money laundering, interdiction rates of 20 percent are usually considered a success. In controlling WMD activities, such an interdiction rate would have catastrophic consequences.

In response to these challenges, Western countries, sometimes in association with other states, have established international regimes designed to harmonize national export controls[33] and to prevent free riding—that is, situations in which some countries profit from other countries' restraint by exporting military or dual-use goods or services to would-be proliferators, thereby undercutting the export control efforts of all countries.[34] The regimes discussed below are meant to increase the effectiveness of the three global regimes for NBC weapons. In some instances, however, disputes about their compatibility with the global regimes have arisen.

Zangger Committee and Nuclear Supplier Club.   The Zangger Committee (also named Nuclear Exporters Committee) is an informal intergovernmental grouping of thirty-three states. It was established in 1971 to develop a common understanding of what constitutes nuclear material and equipment, and to develop procedures for regulating exports of such items so that NPT parties can fulfill their obligation not to assist anyone in developing, producing, or acquiring nuclear weapons. The NPT does not contain any specific regulations on how to handle exports of nuclear materials and related technology. The Zangger Committee maintains a trigger list, so called because it is supposed to trigger the need for IAEA safeguards when listed items are exported to nonnuclear weapon states. The work of the committee has remained technical and definitional. Its members have never been able to agree on which specific IAEA safeguards should be required before trigger-list items can be exported.

Based on a disputed interpretation of the NPT and nuclear safeguards rules, some NPT members used to export dual-use technology to non-NPT states without making their exports contingent on full-scope safeguards. The latter are IAEA safeguards applied to the entire nuclear fuel cycle of the importer country, not only facilities where the imported goods are used. This practice created perverse incentives: NPT members importing dual-use goods had to accept full-scope safeguards, whereas nonmembers were able to acquire these good with fewer strings attached. In 1978 the United States took the lead in solving this problem by making all nuclear exports to non-NPT countries conditional on full-scope safeguards. But only in April 1992 did the members of another export control regime, that operated by the Nuclear Suppliers Group (NSG), adopt this policy at the international level. The NSG, set up in

1977 after India's nuclear test, is an informal group of thirty-four countries that seeks to harmonize national export control policies. For that purpose, it has developed guidelines that are applied to lists of nuclear items. No consensus has yet been reached on a protocol to tie nuclear trade to new and more stringent safeguards under discussion at the IAEA (INFCIRC 540).

Australia Group. Set up in 1985, this informal group of thirty states coordinates national export controls on precursor substances for chemical weapons and equipment that could be used for the production of CBW, and it maintains a control list of critical items.[35] The Australia Group also serves as a forum for states to exchange information on CBW proliferation issues. In 1993 it adopted a "no undercut" policy: whenever a country denies an export license, it notifies the other members of the group and provides information on the good, destination, and end-user. Unless the denying state gives its consent, other states are not allowed to undercut this restraint by delivering the notified items to the country or any other actor of concern.

The original objective of the Australia Group was to prevent further proliferation of CBW while the CWC was being negotiated and efforts to improve monitoring of compliance with the BWC were under way. Despite entry into force of the CWC in 1997, which has established an export control scheme of its own, the Australia Group has continued to operate. One of the key questions to be resolved is the extent to which parties currently maintaining restrictions on trade in dual-use items with some other parties to the BWC and CWC will have to lift these restrictions in accordance with the treaty obligations to facilitate the peaceful uses of chemistry and biology. Most developing countries demand that the Australia Group eliminate its export restrictions among parties to the CWC and BWC. The members of the Australia Group, by contrast, prefer to maintain their freedom of choice regarding countries to which export restrictions apply. They suspect some members of the two treaties of engaging in illicit activities. In particular they point to the case of Iraq, suggesting that determined proliferator states could circumvent the CWC's controls. They also point to the fact that efforts to equip the BWC with an effective compliance system have not yet been successful. It is unlikely that the Australia Group will disband anytime soon. The BWC and the CWC bar countries from assisting other countries in the acquisition of CBW but do not specify how this obligation is to be implemented. Neither do the two treaties explicitly prohibit supply-side mechanisms, such as the Australia Group, that operate outside the global conventions.

Missile Technology Control Regime (MTCR). The member states of the MTCR, most of them Western countries, seek to prevent the further spread of missiles, unmanned air vehicles, and related technology capable of carrying a 500-kilogram payload at least 300 kilometers, as well as systems for the delivery of WMD. The regime's controls cover ballistic missiles, cruise missiles, space launch vehicles, sounding rockets, drones, and remotely piloted vehicles. MTCR members maintain a set of rules that guide their individual export licensing regulations in this field.

* * *

The supply-side regimes just discussed operate in conjunction with global regimes as well as unilateral, bilateral, and regional arms control arrangements. Hence it is difficult to determine the extent to which these regimes have, in and of themselves, been effective. Evidence about the supplier networks of Iraq, Iran, and Pakistan, for example, suggests that there are limits to preventing determined proliferators from acquiring critical materials and technologies on global markets. The first problem with regard to the effectiveness of export controls is that not all suppliers of relevant military or dual-use items are members of export control regimes. North Korea and China, for example, have been important exporters of missiles and related technology, particularly to Pakistan. Second, some members of export control regimes have not fulfilled their promises. Russia, for example, has seriously diminished the effectiveness of MTCR by selling missile technology to Iran, India, and other countries. Third, a tension exists between free trade and nonproliferation efforts: even among states with strict export control regulations, full control of all critical exports could halt international trade in some areas and impose great costs on exporters and importers; thus there are limits to the political acceptability of stringent export controls also for countries in the Organization for Economic Cooperation and Development (OECD). Much less is known about the performance of the Australia Group than about the MTCR's effectiveness, in part because in the case of the Australia Group illegally exported materials do not usually show up in weapon tests where acquired technologies can be picked up by intelligence services, in contrast to missile technology. Most analysts believe, however, that the policies of the Australia Group have performed somewhat better than those of the MTCR.[36]

Despite these weaknesses in export control regimes, experience with the Australia Group and MTCR suggests that an important regulatory turnaround was achieved in the 1990s.[37] No doubt, determined proliferators are still able to acquire critical items on global markets, but at a massively higher price than they could without these controls. The best solution to risks posed by WMD is global prohibition regimes, such as the CWC and BWC. But as long as the obligations set forth in these regimes have not been fully accepted and implemented by all states and gaps in their control systems for imports and exports of dual-use goods remain, international export control regimes can be an effective way of filling the gaps.

Challenges Ahead

Four challenges are likely to dominate future governance efforts in the policy area under investigation: first, attracting the remaining holdouts of the NPT, BWC, and

CWC; second, ascertaining implementation and compliance with the three global regimes for WMD, including the commitment by nuclear weapon states to eliminate these weapons; third, finding the right balance between arms control objectives and mutually beneficial expansion of trade in dual-use items for civilian purposes; and fourth, preventing WMD terrorism.

The first and second tasks are the more traditional ones. Their importance has not decreased with the end of the Cold War. On the one hand, the number of holdout countries has significantly diminished, and violations of treaty obligations have been extremely rare. On the other hand, the remaining holdouts are the really tough cases. In addition, glaring loopholes in the compliance system of the BWC have not yet been closed, and the NPT and CWC provisions have not yet been fully implemented. What has changed in this regard since the end of East-West conflict are constraints on the set of policies that supporters of the three WMD regimes can use in ascertaining adherence and compliance by problematic countries. The cases of Iraq, North Korea, and Ukraine examined further below demonstrate that the possibilities of applying positive and negative incentives on a wider scale may have increased. This may be reason for hope that there is room for more innovative policies in solving the remaining governance problems of an intergovernmental nature.

As to the third challenge, since private actors have increasingly become part of the proliferation problem they must logically also become part of the solution. The rapid expansion of international trade, foreign direct investment, and global industrial activity has increased the possibilities for illegal transactions. How can governments forge effective partnerships with firms in the global marketplace so as to maximize the benefits of international trade and investment while ascertaining the effectiveness of global regimes for WMD? Finally, and closely related to the third challenge, WMD or materials and technology for their production could fall into the hands of terrorist groups.

LESSONS LEARNED

Some policies for WMD have worked better than others. An examination of the four stages of the policy cycle—agenda setting, negotiation, implementation, and responses to noncompliance—sheds light on why.

Agenda Setting

International efforts to eliminate WMD or slow their spread have usually been spurred by armed conflicts in which these weapons were used or their use was threatened. Nuclear issues have been on the international agenda ever since the United States dropped two atomic bombs on Japan in 1945. But concrete negotiations on nuclear arms control were initiated only after the Cuban missile crisis, which in 1962 brought the world to the brink of a nuclear war between the United States and the Soviet Union.

Chemical and biological means of warfare found their way onto the international agenda in the 1920s, after chemical weapons had been used on a massive scale in World War I. The absence of larger-scale CBW use in World War II and the emergence of nuclear weapons pushed CBW issues into the background until the late 1960s, when the United States began to employ large amounts of tear gas and herbicides in the Vietnam War, activities that many opponents regarded as chemical warfare.[38]

The war between Iran and Iraq in the second half of the 1980s and the war between Iraq and a UN-endorsed alliance in 1990–1991 gave a considerable boost to global disarmament and nonproliferation efforts. First, pictures of chemical warfare victims went around the world, increasing public aversion against this means of warfare and forcing politicians to act. Second, these two wars demonstrated to the United States, France, and some other countries that were reluctant to give up chemical weapons that they could win a war against a possessor of such weapons without having to resort to deterrence or retaliation in kind. Thus they encouraged governments to opt for a comprehensive ban on chemical weapons. Third, the two wars demonstrated to developing countries that use of CBW was most likely among less developed countries because protection was largely a question of money and technology, thus rapid conclusion of the CWC and strengthening of the BWC were manifestly in their best interest. Fourth, these wars exposed significant gaps in export control systems of OECD countries and in the IAEA safeguards system. All these lessons promoted a variety of international efforts in the late 1980s and 1990s, including negotiations on the CWC; efforts to strengthen the BWC; the creation of supply-side controls through the Australia Group, the Nuclear Suppliers Group, and MTCR, and reforms in the IAEA safeguards system. From these observations and the analysis above, we can derive three conclusions regarding agenda-setting processes in regard to WMD.

First, agendas in WMD negotiations have to a great extent been shaped by events outside the main negotiating forums, particularly armed conflicts. Negotiations on international measures usually started when the problem had become virulent. The only measures that might be regarded as truly preventive are nuclear weapon–free zones (for example, in Latin America and the South Pacific) and demilitarized geographic areas, such as Antarctica, the seabed, and celestial bodies.

Second, the historical record of international efforts to remove the risks posed by WMD shows that governments have maintained a strong grip on the agenda. Compared with agenda-setting processes in international trade, human rights, or environmental policy, nongovernmental actors have been only very indirectly involved in identifying and framing problems and possible solutions. In Western countries, during most of the Cold War NGOs (such as the Pugwash Group or Greenpeace) usually adopted positions that were at odds with the positions of their governments. Only in a few Western countries, notably the United States, have NGOs been actively involved with governments in developing negotiating agendas and proposals. In the former communist states, governments controlled the few NGOs active in this area, a situation that still prevails in countries such as China, North Korea, and Vietnam. In developing countries, hardly any NGOs focus on arms control issues. In sum, NGOs have not had much visible imprint on negotiating agendas. Rather they have exerted their influence in indirect ways via public opinion and transfers of ideas to negotiators through debate and studies.

After the end of the Cold War, governments did begin to involve nongovernmental actors to a greater extent. Ironically, however, just at that time many NGOs thought that the arms problem was basically resolved and that more urgent matters, such as environmental problems, democracy, human rights, and questions of globalization, needed their attention. As a result, the possibilities of NGOs to influence states' bargaining agendas and positions with regard to WMD are greater today than they were during the Cold War, but the capacities of many NGOs in this area have shrunk significantly. The latter development has been compounded by the fact that in many cases negotiations have moved into complex technical areas that NGOs could, with the exception of some NGOs in large Western countries, only follow and influence if they allocated significant resources for that purpose.[39]

In contrast, since the late 1980s, organizations representing business interests have significantly influenced the negotiating agenda. Prior to the 1980s Western governments had insisted on verifiable agreements, requesting foolproof monitoring mechanisms that would generate full information on the other parties' behavior in the area of concern. Business interest groups, such as chemical manufacturers' associations and the pharmaceutical industry, succeeded in changing this position. They convinced Western governments of the downside of intrusive compliance mechanisms, such as threats to confidential business information and the excessive costs of originally envisaged monitoring procedures. Ironically, just as former communist countries fully heeded Cold War–era Western requests for very intrusive inspections, Western governments were withdrawing to proposals for more modest compliance mechanisms, not least under the influence of business interests.[40]

Third, the way in which bargaining issues are initially framed at the agenda-setting stage has an important bearing on outcomes, including the performance of international regimes. The big military and economic powers have so far shaped the agenda in ways that have promoted asymmetrical solutions (implying unequal rights and obligations) to WMD risks, notably in the case of the NPT and export control arrangements.

The framing of global agreements on WMD in terms similar to the NPT, which essentially ascertained a nuclear weapons oligopoly of some states, would be impossible today. The effectiveness of the NPT has depended on circumstances that do not exist in the case of other WMD. The NPT was the product of a world in which two superpowers had a strong influence on most other states with nuclear capabilities, and where ownership of nuclear weapons was a very remote possibility for most states. Controls on the supply and demand side of the nuclear problem have been easier to achieve than controls on other WMD also because of the relatively few suppliers of nuclear materials and know-how and a considerable shrinking of global markets for civilian nuclear power over the past twenty years. In addition, the intrinsic security value of remaining nonnuclear has become increasingly evident to most states. Thus, challenges to the NPT regime have been limited to very few states, notably India, Iraq, Israel, North Korea, and Pakistan.

In the agenda-setting and bargaining process for chemical weapons, the United States and France originally proposed a regime structure with possessor and nonpossessor states. They wished to maintain a "security stockpile" of chemical weapons, to be used for retaliation if they were threatened or attacked with chemical weapons by other countries. This proposal met with stern opposition by most other members of the Conference on Disarmament and was eventually buried. Existing asymmetric arrangements, such as those of the Australia Group and the MTCR, are encountering persistent opposition by many importing countries. These arrangements are aimed at confining international exchanges of certain materials and technologies to states that are defined by the supplier group as "countries in good standing." In essence, they constitute supplier cartels. In the medium to long term, the effectiveness of these asymmetric regimes is likely to erode if they cannot be reframed in a more balanced and cooperative fashion.[41]

Negotiation

Among the countless lessons that might be drawn from negotiating responses to risks posed by WMD, the following ones are particularly relevant. The first lesson concerns the institutional setting in which regulatory regimes have been devised. The second relates to the specific features of export control regimes. The third extends to the negotiation of monitoring arrangements, a key element of any arms control negotiation. The fourth lesson concerns incentive structures designed to maximize adherence to global regulatory regimes.

Institutional Setting. All three global regimes for WMD have been negotiated in the Conference on Disarmament or its predecessors. That said, the NPT and the BWC were firmly based on bilateral bargains between the two superpowers, which were "multilateralized" by means of a global accord, worked out in the CD. The CD has been kept institutionally separate from the UN system to limit membership of the conference, but pressure to expand participation has grown over time. And so has the number of members, which increased from around forty in the 1980s to more than sixty in the 1990s. Membership decisions have, at least implicitly, been shaped by a trade-off problem. On the one hand, the difficulties of reaching agreement grow with the size of the negotiating body, particularly if decisions are subject to the consensus rule, which is the case in the CD. On the other hand, the more countries are involved in negotiations, the higher is the likelihood that a particular bargain will be effectively implemented.[42]

The end of the Cold War has led to more heterogeneous interests of countries, not least because the Warsaw Pact fell apart, the nonaligned movement lost much of its cohesion, and the logic of economic competition has caused much variance in the positions also of Western countries. In addition, negotiations in the Conference moved into areas where a larger number of countries had weapons capabilities, making their participation essential to the effectiveness of policies. Expansion of CD membership may thus have been necessary. On the other hand, negotiations on the CTBT have exposed the limits of negotiating arms control and disarmament accords in large forums under a consensus rule.

The CWC was the first global prohibition regime for WMD that was fully designed in a multilateral forum. To some extent, this success was more accident than intention. During much of the Cold War, the positions of the two superpowers on monitoring of compliance remained far apart, blocking any rapprochement on this issue. Shortly after bilateral progress came within reach and a bilateral agreement on chemical weapons reductions was concluded between the two countries in 1990, the Soviet Union fell apart. A small coalition of Western states, building on a draft convention that had been in the making for some years, took advantage of the political paralysis in former Warsaw Pact countries and a very heterogeneous coalition of developing countries. It submitted a series of proposals and succeeded in quickly convincing other countries to sign on. This speedy negotiation left a number of issues, such as the destruction of chemical weapons in Russia and details of monitoring civilian chemical facilities, unresolved. These issues would surface again in the implementation phase.

Attempts to strike a bargain on nuclear testing at similar speed failed in the mid-to-late 1990s. In the case of the CTBT, a small group of countries (including India and Iran) blocked progress in the negotiations. A coalition of proponents of a comprehensive ban on nuclear testing carried the negotiating text out of the CD, finalized the draft, and put it up for signature in the UN system. This failure of the CD to ultimately strike a bargain once again exposed the difficulties of negotiating in a large multilateral forum under a consensus rule. The disadvantages of moving out of the CD are evident: the CTBT might attract fewer states than it could have, had the agreement been reached in the CD. The advantages of the approach taken are thought to be twofold: first, the agreement was not delayed any further and is more stringent; second, growing adherence to the CTBT will gradually increase the political pressure on holdout countries, such as India and Pakistan, to join the agreement. It is too early to say whether these potential advantages will materialize. In part, the negotiating parties may themselves have undermined their strategy by making entry into force contingent on ratification by all states participating in the CD and possessing nuclear reactors (forty-four in total). Those favoring such a clause thought that it would amplify the political pressure on holdouts the closer the number of parties moved toward forty-four. But it could make the entire regime hostage to a single holdout country. The parties, having recognized this problem, have made allowances for a provisional entry into force, should the signatories decide so. Because the U.S. Congress (in contrast to the Russian Duma) refused to ratify the CTBT, the entire process remains paralyzed.

Experience with the CWC negotiations and failure to conclude the CTBT in the CD suggest that the golden age of negotiating global regimes for WMD in the CD is over. Negotiations in that forum on comparatively much less significant measures such as a cutoff of fissile-material production are stalled.[43] It appears that further measures to reduce or eliminate WMD or prevent their further spread will be negotiated not in the CD but in smaller forums that are assembled in an ad hoc fashion, probably in combination with more unilateral policies and negotiations within the structures of the three existing global regimes for WMD.[44] This changing cooperative structure has the advantage of allowing for the case-specific composition of negotiating groups and the exclusion of permanent naysayers that tend to lower standards. But the disadvantages of this approach should not be ignored. Permanent negotiating bodies allow for quasi-permanent interaction of the countries involved. This may preserve negotiated substance over longer periods of time when progress is slow and negotiations are affected by extended bottoms in governments' attention cycles. In ad hoc forums, slow progress can lead to breakdowns more quickly, and the entire negotiating machinery needs to be assembled anew when governments decide to pick up the pieces and start again.

Export Control Regimes. In striking contrast to the NPT, BWC, and CWC, export control regimes—in particular those operated by the Nuclear Suppliers Group, the Australia Group, and the MTCR—are informal and based on restricted membership. There are several reasons for these features. First, these regimes are supply-side solutions. States producing and exporting certain materials or technologies coordinate their decisions on which countries are eligible to receive defined goods and services, and under what conditions. Apart from the fact that states are free to choose their trading partners, supplier countries wish to remain flexible in deciding on trade restrictions. Consequently, countries subject to export restrictions are not involved in decision making by the supplier group. Second, because it tends to rely on a "good" and "bad" country distinction and thus smacks of discrimination, international cooperation on export controls is politically sensitive. Supplier countries are often not interested in explaining publicly and in detail why they ban exports of critical goods to certain countries, hence another reason not to formalize export control regimes. The informal nature of these regimes also allows their members to coopt other supplier states on a flexible basis. Third, the export control regimes for WMD serve increasingly as platforms for exchanging intelligence information on proliferation issues. The no-undercut policies of some of these regimes even requires extensive exchanges of sensitive information on exporters, importers, and measures taken to safeguard against proliferation. Members of export control regimes have little interest in having those suspected of proliferation present in such exchanges.

Although the logic of informality and restricted membership appears compelling, there is a fundamental problem. Those actors—states, firms, and other actors—who are located on the demand side of the proliferation problem are not involved in efforts to solve it. Strategies of denial, such as those practiced by export control regimes, can raise the price of certain military or dual-use goods. But they will only rarely prevent determined proliferators from obtaining access to these goods on global markets.[45] The ability of Iraq, North Korea, Pakistan, and other countries to purchase key technologies for their WMD programs abroad testifies to this problem. In contrast to actors receiving positive incentives, actors targeted by export controls have an incentive to hide or distort information on their intentions and behavior and cheat. Moreover, rising prices due to export restrictions tend to create black markets. Higher prices attract new suppliers who attempt to free ride on the restraint of others. Black markets, by their very nature, also reduce the transparency of global transactions in the arms and dual-use sector. Difficulties encountered by Western countries in convincing China, North Korea, Russia, and other states to restrict their exports of dual-use technology to suspected proliferator countries underline this problem. Finally, cases such as North Korea and Iran show that demand-side problems can generate additional supply-side problems when suspected proliferator countries seek to reduce their costs of weapons development by exporting military or dual-use technology to yet other countries seeking to acquire WMD. Supplier networks between Israel and South Africa and between North Korea and Pakistan illustrate this problem. Such networks are virtually impossible to eliminate through the existing export control regimes.

In theory, all these problems could be resolved if states could agree on a formal global regime open to all countries that was based on cooperation and not denial.

Ideally, such a global regime would facilitate economic exchange among its members, install a sweeping denial regime with regard to those few countries remaining outside the regime, and establish an effective monitoring system among members whereby the peaceful end use of exported goods could be ascertained. Such a regime does not yet exist. It is therefore impossible to judge whether it would, in practice, perform better than existing arrangements.

There are three basic obstacles to successfully negotiating such regulations. First, for states determined to pursue WMD programs, such a proposal will be a nonstarter. They are a priori not interested in a regime that seeks to ascertain the peaceful end use of dual-use goods. Regime-based positive and negative incentives, even on a large scale, may not be sufficient to convince such states otherwise.[46] Second, as long as nuclear weapon states remain unwilling to implement their NPT commitment to eliminate these arms, some other states will not accept an obligation to become or remain nonnuclear. For example, India is unlikely to eliminate its nuclear program as long as China maintains nuclear weapons. Third, nonstate actors, such as terrorist groups, that may seek to acquire WMD will still not be involved and, by their very nature, cannot be involved in such an effort. In that case, the traditional denial strategies with all the problems involved will still have to apply.

To date, the CWC is the only global WMD regime that operates a formal export control mechanism. Exports and imports of chemicals defined in three lists are subject to such controls. Transfers of the most critical chemicals, called Schedule 1 chemicals, are heavily restricted and must be announced to the OPCW prior to exports. Exports of such substances to nonparties is prohibited. Since April 2000, exports of Schedule 2 chemicals—the second most critical to the purposes of the CWC—to nonparties are also prohibited. In April 2003, the CWC's parties will decide whether such a restriction will also apply to Schedule 3 chemicals, which are widely used for civilian purposes but could be precursors for chemical weapons. Pending prohibition of exports to nonparties, end-user certificates are required from such states. The OPCW records all transfers of listed chemicals by the CWC's parties. It can ask the parties to explain discrepancies and inspect the end use of such chemicals in member states if they are used in declared facilities. Serious cases of illegal diversion to nondeclared facilities are subject to challenge inspections, which can be initiated only by and in member-states. Specific procedures ensure that information on imports and exports is treated confidentially by the Technical Secretariat of the OPCW. Member states receive detailed information from that body only if there are discrepancies and doubts about compliance.

This control system is still a far cry from a comprehensive global export control system for WMD. For example, transfers of Schedule 2 and 3 chemicals have to be declared only once a year; some critical chemicals are not in the lists; only chemicals, but not technologies that could be used for the production of chemical weapons, are controlled; there is no mechanism for inspections of end users in states not parties to the CWC; bookkeeping practices of CWC members diverge, so that there have been in practice great discrepancies in import-export balances; finally, the system applies only to one category of WMD. Despite these weaknesses, the CWC's export control system provides a useful starting point for building more cooperative regimes that marry the objectives of free trade and nonproliferation.

Negotiating Monitoring Arrangements. To achieve substantive arms control and disarmament measures, security dilemma problems must be overcome. Solutions to such problems—for example, through step-by-step approaches—usually hinge on states' ability to negotiate effective monitoring systems. The negotiators of the NPT left the task to the IAEA, a preexisting international body. For reasons pointed out above, the BWC did not contain any monitoring provisions.

In at least three respects, negotiating monitoring provisions for the CWC posed a much greater challenge than designing monitoring mechanisms for the NPT. First, the number of installations worldwide producing or processing critical items is far greater in the chemical than in the nuclear field. In addition to monitoring of military installations, a large number of civilian sites where dual-use items are produced or used require surveillance. Second, chemical weapons programs, due to the nature of the activity, are smaller in scale than nuclear weapons programs. Thus they are harder to detect and require more intrusive inspections. Third, because all states are equally obliged to disarm, monitoring activities cover all parties to the CWC. In the case of the NPT, the nuclear powers have remained largely outside the IAEA safeguards regime because the key task has been to prevent the have-nots from pursuing nuclear weapons programs. For these reasons, the focus here is on the CWC experience.

For many years, negotiations on monitoring provisions for the CWC were stalled by the unwillingness of former communist countries to accept mandatory and intrusive on-site inspections. When these opponents reversed their position in the late 1980s, substantive negotiations on monitoring mechanisms began. In assessing what lessons might be learned from these negotiations, three issues seem particularly relevant: trial inspections; the scope and cost efficiency of monitoring activity; and challenge inspections.

Two sorts of concerns worried even those generally favorable to concluding a ban on chemical weapons with intrusive on-site monitoring. Military secrets unrelated to the CWC could be compromised as a result of inspections. Moreover, chemical industries, which annually invest billions of dollars into research and development and face heavy commercial competition, were afraid that their business secrets could fall into the wrong hands and that their production processes could be slowed or interrupted by inspections. To address these concerns, some members of the CD invited delegations from other countries to a series of experimental inspections in military facilities and civilian chemical plants. This step was unprecedented. It alleviated concerns about the protection of confidential military and business information and was at least partly responsible for remarkably reducing opposition of military and business circles to monitoring mechanisms proposed for the CWC. Moreover, it allowed testing of inspection procedures under quasi-real conditions—most important, procedures to protect confidential business information and procedures for conducting challenge inspections (see below). This testing was not enough to fine-tune all procedures, but it saved the OPCW from having to undertake even more preparatory work for implementing the CWC's monitoring system later on.

Economically efficient monitoring systems should target predominantly those countries where the probability and expected consequences of noncompliance are the greatest. This implies that a substantial part of monitoring should focus on ascertaining the elimination of prohibited weapons. Under the CWC, possessor states of chemical weapons incur a substantial part of the cost of such monitoring, in addition to the costs of weapons elimination per se—some sort of "proliferator pays" principle thus prevails. By contrast, in the case of monitoring compliance with the obligation not to develop or produce chemical weapons, this efficiency criterion has been impossible to meet. Because it is politically unacceptable to classify countries as good or bad and focus monitoring on those that are thought to be bad—the approach taken in export control regimes—the entire routine inspections effort under the CWC is geared to facilities whose riskiness is ranked according to the chemicals they produce or process, irrespective of the presumed intentions of the respective country or firm.[47] Routine inspections are inspections that are carried out regularly at facilities previously declared by the parties to the OPCW according to criteria of risk the chemicals produced or processed there pose. As a result, highly industrialized countries shoulder by far the greatest burden in terms of receiving inspections. As long as the challenge inspection mechanism of the CWC, which targets the most risky states, appears to be effective, those countries that receive more routine inspections than are, in terms of risk to the CWC, necessary are likely to accept the mentioned inefficiency (see below).

The cases of Iraq and North Korea, but also unresolved compliance issues with Russia under the BWC, suggest that routine monitoring of previously declared facilities cannot assure the parties of each other's compliance under all circumstances. The most important monitoring mechanism to fill the gap is challenge inspections. A challenge inspection is an inspection that is carried out upon a specific request by one party on the territory of another party. Such requests are meant to clarify suspicions about illegal activity on the territory of the requested party. The negotiators of the CWC were the first, and so far only, ones successful in designing such a mechanism for a global arms control treaty. After former Warsaw Pact countries had accepted the Western formula of "anytime, anywhere, with no right of refusal by the requested party"—a measure of unprecedented intrusiveness—second thoughts about such a radical scheme emerged. Worries centered on the possibility that challenge inspections could be used for espionage purposes or simply to embarrass a party to the CWC.

How can such problems be excluded without taking the teeth out of the mechanism? The CWC's negotiators found an innovative way of solving the problem. Instead of installing a political filter for deciding on challenge inspections, any request for a challenge inspection will result in inspectors of the OPCW going to the requested country. But access to the relevant site is "managed." Managed access means that inspectors and host country representatives approach the inspection target step-by-step on the basis of negotiations, guided by procedures laid out in OPCW rules for such cases. The main advantage of this approach is that it allows for practical bargaining among experts on site, instead of diplomatic rows in the OPCW far away from the inspection target. Moreover, even if full inspection of the requested site is not possible, at least some information will be gathered.[48] No request for a challenge inspection has so far been put forward under the CWC. It is therefore too early to judge how the managed access approach would perform under stress.

Incentive Structures. As noted above the designers of the NPT, BWC, and CWC regimes have included in these regimes incentives that go beyond the intrinsic security benefits the regimes create by reducing NBC arsenals and preventing the further spread of such weapons. These incentives are meant to attract as many states as possible by making regime membership more beneficial than nonmembership, and to increase the likelihood that regime members will comply with their obligations.

The most important additional incentives associated with all three global WMD regimes are trade measures. As noted above, all three regimes contain clauses that urge the parties to facilitate peaceful uses of nuclear, chemical, and biological materials and technologies, as well as international trade for that purpose. Trade provisions associated with the NPT and the CWC have been the most effective in terms of making membership attractive. In the case of the NPT, these incentives have been established and applied largely outside the treaty, particularly through the NSG. There is evidence that increasingly strong export restrictions have been critical in several countries' decisions to join the NPT as nonnuclear weapon states. For example, in the mid-1970s Switzerland joined the NPT because it had decided that nuclear weapons were, from a military standpoint, not in its best interest, but also because it faced a cutoff of nuclear supplies for its civilian nuclear power industry by the United States and other countries. There is also evidence that the NSG's policy, adopted in 1992, of allowing certain nuclear exports only on the condition of full-scope safeguards has been crucial in motivating Brazil and Argentina to join the NPT. In addition to developing their military nuclear programs, both countries were pursuing the construction of nuclear power plants and would have suffered from the new measures.

The trade provisions of the CWC have had a powerful effect on states' willingness to join the treaty. A large number of countries use or produce chemicals included in the CWC's three lists of substances that might be used for chemical weapons purposes. The convention bans trade in Schedule 1 chemicals—the most risky ones in terms of the convention's objectives—with nonparties and provides for increasingly tough constraints up to outright bans on trade in Schedule 2 and 3 chemicals with nonparties. In the ratification debates of many industrialized countries, these trade measures have figured prominently as strong arguments in favor of adherence. Also in some developing countries, the effect is hard to overlook. Algeria, Morocco, and Tunisia, which together with South Africa are the dominant importers and only exporters of Schedule 2 and 3 chemicals in Africa, abandoned the linkage between adherence to the CWC and Israel's joining of the NPT, which has been strongly advocated by the League of Arab States, and joined the CWC.

The principal problem that remains is defining the relationship between the CWC's trade provisions and the measures of the Australia Group. The trade incentives for those CWC parties currently facing Australia Group restrictions will materialize to the full extent only when the remaining restrictions are lifted. As long as the constraints imposed by the Australia Group on some CWC parties or would-be parties are not abolished, the incentive to comply with the CWC's rules or join the regime respectively will be less than optimal. The likely solution to this problem is that the Australia Group members will watch how critical countries behave under the CWC regime and lift restrictions on a case-by-case basis for CWC members in good standing. With increasing membership and compliance with the CWC, the CWC's own trade regulations will, if everything works well, eventually make the Australia Group obsolete.

Implementation

Five questions are key in considering the implementation process of WMD regimes. First, how has the failure of the five nuclear powers to eliminate their nuclear weapons affected the prospects of successfully implementing the three global WMD regimes? Second, has the performance of different monitoring mechanisms under the three global WMD regimes varied, and if so why? Third, how do states proceed from the collection of information through extant monitoring mechanisms to political and legal assessments of compliance? Fourth, has assistance or compensation been used to facilitate accession to WMD regimes by critical countries or to help parties facing implementation problems? If yes, how have such policies performed? Fifth, how great is the risk of terrorism with WMD, and how has that risk been dealt with in the past?

Failure of Nuclear Disarmament.   Perhaps the most difficult implementation problem emanates from the failure of the five nuclear powers under the NPT to eliminate their nuclear weapons. This failure cannot be defined as noncompliance in a legal sense because the NPT did not specify a time frame for denuclearization. But the unwillingness of nuclear powers to fulfill their commitment violates the spirit of the treaty. The military doctrines of these powers have not changed significantly even after their renewed pledges made at the 1995 and 2000 NPT conferences to negotiate nuclear disarmament in good faith, as stated in the NPT.[49] Four nuclear powers under the NPT (and probably also the three nuclear powers not in the NPT—India, Israel, and Pakistan) continue to regard the use of these weapons against states attacking them or their allies with any weapon as an acceptable military option. The unwillingness of the nuclear weapon states to denuclearize undermines the legitimacy of their pressure on the remaining holdouts of the NPT, on the parties violating their treaty obligations, and on nonstate actors pursuing WMD ambitions. If eight countries, including the largest one on Earth, evidently regard nuclear weapons as useful, why should other countries not do the same? This problem has, at least indirectly, also increased the incentive of some states not to join the global chemical weapons ban.[50] As long as the five nuclear powers under the NPT do not take decisive steps toward nuclear disarmament, they will have little leverage on India, Israel, and Pakistan in that regard.

The argument that the five nuclear powers under the NPT could safely forgo these weapons in return for increased performance of global prohibition regimes for WMD gained increasing support in the 1990s.[51] Many analysts consider that the conventional arsenals of the five states are sufficient to deter or defeat any attack by conventional, chemical, or biological weapons. It is evident that the elimination of the existing nuclear arsenals cannot be accomplished overnight. Most supporters of such a policy thus argue that it should proceed in steps, including an international agreement not to use nuclear weapons under any circumstance, the deactivation of all nuclear warheads, the elimination of tactical nuclear weapons, and finally the disarmament of strategic nuclear weapons.

Monitoring Mechanisms. In the late 1980s and 1990s, the views of most governments converged on the position that effective monitoring of compliance with regime rules for WMD requires mandatory and intrusive on-site inspections. In principle, one might argue that the more extensive and intrusive monitoring is the better. However, monitoring activity imposes direct costs (financing of inspections and analysis of their results) and indirect costs (false alarms, compromising of unrelated military and business secrets). As a result, each additional dollar invested in monitoring leads, from some abstract point on, to declining marginal benefits in terms of being useful for ascertaining implementation and compliance. In practice, this optimization problem is impossible to solve systematically. There is no ideal monitoring mechanism against which the performance of existing mechanisms can be judged.[52] Because of that, and because there is no clearly observable difference across the NPT,

BWC, and CWC in the extent of compliance—whereas the features of the respective monitoring systems differ substantially—it is impossible to make any sweeping claims about variation in monitoring systems causing different levels of implementation or compliance.

The only safe assertion is that monitoring systems including routine and challenge inspections are likely to be more effective. Experience with existing monitoring arrangements shows that a considerable extent of routine monitoring plus significant inputs from national intelligence agencies are indispensable to assemble a broader picture of implementation problems and to trigger challenge inspections at the right time and place. Violations of the NPT, such as those by Iraq and North Korea, would probably not have occurred or would have been detected much earlier had the NPT parties been able to make use of a challenge inspection mechanism similar to that provided for in the CWC.

The BWC has been plagued by a series of allegations of noncompliance, only some of which, those by the former Soviet Union and Russia, have been clarified to a limited extent. In the late 1980s, the UN Security Council installed a mechanism by which allegations of use of chemical and biological weapons could be investigated by the UN Secretary-General. Some investigations were carried out but, particularly in the case of biological warfare, did not lead to conclusive results. Attempts to negotiate a special protocol to the BWC that would add a monitoring mechanism to that regime have been under way for several years, but agreement is not yet in sight. Many countries, including the United States and many developing countries, are unwilling to accept intrusive on-site monitoring of compliance because of concerns about the protection of business secrets and other information unrelated to compliance with the BWC. Indeed routine inspections on the basis of national declarations may, in the case of the BWC, not be feasible because of the small-scale nature of biological activities. If politically acceptable, a new monitoring scheme for the BWC might, in contrast to the NPT and CWC, have to rely almost exclusively on declarations by the parties and on challenge inspection procedures.

Among the most serious implementation problems in regard to routine inspections under the CWC have been long delays by the United States and some other countries in submitting their declarations on civilian facilities producing or processing listed chemicals. By contrast, the United States and Russia, the two largest possessors of chemical weapons, have complied with their obligation to declare all military activities and facilities in the chemical weapons field.

Assessing Compliance. The technical units of the IAEA and the OPCW, through their monitoring activities, generate enormous amounts of information. The right to draw more sweeping conclusions from these data as to the compliance of individual parties has not been given to these units but to political bodies of the respective organizations. On one hand, this setup spares the technical units from excessive interference by the governments of state parties, for example, as regards the hiring of inspectors and the modalities of individual inspections. On the other hand, it turns the assessment of compliance into a sensitive political, and not so much a legal or technical, issue. In the NPT and CWC regime, this problem has not been fully resolved. In the BWC there are no specific procedures for assessing compliance. The IAEA understands itself as a technical body and has never passed a judgment on important compliance issues. In the most extreme case to date, the IAEA stated that it was unable to implement its safeguards in North Korea. The question was then referred to the UN Security Council. Similarly, the OPCW has never taken a formal decision on the compliance of a party, even though the Conference of the States Parties of the OPCW could do so with a two-thirds majority.

Assistance Mechanisms. Assistance mechanisms have been established within and outside the global regulatory regimes for nuclear and chemical weapons. Assistance can, in principle, constitute a means of attracting new members, facilitating implementation by existing members, or resolving compliance problems. The boundaries among these three types of assistance are often fluid.

In the nuclear field, assistance to Ukraine in the order of several hundred million dollars has been the most prominent example of an assistance effort designed to facilitate the adherence of a state to the NPT. When the former Soviet Union fell apart, the United States, Russia, and many other countries requested the denuclearization of Ukraine (and of Belarus and Kazakhstan as well) as quickly as possible.[53] Ukraine first signaled its willingness to comply with the request, but from March 1992 on it began to withdraw from this position. U.S. and Russian efforts to force Ukraine into handing over the nuclear arms on its territory were of limited effect. Negative incentives, such as threats to turn Ukraine into a pariah state, to cut off energy supplies, to disrupt other economic relationships, or even to question the territorial integrity of Ukraine appeared to make Ukraine cling even harder to its nuclear bargaining chip and hold out for more in negotiations with the United States and Russia. Only when, from 1993 on, the United States extended its cooperative agenda with Ukraine beyond the nuclear disarmament issue in the narrow sense and Russia softened its hitherto heavy-handed approach did the prospects of Ukraine's denuclearization improve. In late 1994, Ukraine joined the NPT as a nonnuclear weapon state, and by the end of May 1996, the last nuclear warhead had been removed from Ukraine's territory.

The agreements paving the way to Ukraine's successful denuclearization were accompanied by a substantial set of positive incentives. First, the United States pledged more than $900 million in dismantlement assistance and economic aid to Ukraine and promised to mobilize assistance from other sources. Dismantlement assistance has been delivered in the framework of the United States' Cooperative Threat Reduction (CTR) program. Second, some other Western countries also pledged more limited assistance. Third, Russia delivered 100 tons of fuel rods for Ukraine's nuclear power plants and promised further deliveries. Fourth, Russia promised to cancel some of Ukraine's debt for oil and gas deliveries. Fifth, three of the five declared nuclear powers—Russia, the United Kingdom, and the United States—issued specific security assurances to Ukraine similar to those issued to all nonnuclear weapon states in the context of the NPT. That Ukraine did not become the world's third largest nuclear power represents an outstanding success in international nonproliferation efforts. Positive incentives contributed to this outcome.[54]

Assistance to facilitate implementation has been less spectacular. The most important effort has come from the United States assisting Russia—the possessor of the world's largest stockpile of chemical weapons—in the destruction of its chemical arsenal according to the time frames outlined in the CWC. Russia faces enormous difficulties in overcoming political, legal, and financial hurdles in its chemical demilitarization program. In addition, the IAEA, with the support of its member states, provides much technical assistance to the NPT parties in developing and implementing nuclear safeguards.

Finally, experience with assistance to resolve compliance problems is limited. Assistance to Russia, provided primarily by the United States, has been instrumental in establishing more accurate inventories of nuclear material, securing critical installations to prevent illegal removal of nuclear material or even weapons, controlling exports of military and dual-use items, and dealing with excess fissile material from dismantled nuclear weapons.[55] Due to the broad range of assistance activity, assessing the overall effectiveness of this policy option is impossible. The evidence suggests, however, that assistance has contributed to solving a number of implementation problems that could not have been resolved through negative incentives alone.[56]

WMD Terrorism. Expert opinions diverge substantially over how likely it is that WMD could be produced or acquired and used by terrorist groups or other nongovernmental actors.[57] Most analysts regard the probability of acquisition or use of nuclear weapons by terrorists as extremely low, that of CBW acquisition or use as somewhat higher but still very low. Potential damage, should WMD be used by terrorist groups, is high. Whatever the risk, this issue raises an implementation and compliance problem under the three global WMD regimes. Under all three, the parties are obliged not to assist anyone in developing, producing, or acquiring WMD. They are also committed not to allow prohibited activities within their jurisdictions. Consequently, virtually all terrorist activity involving WMD is likely to constitute an unintended violation of global rules for WMD—unless it involves terrorism sponsored by a state not party to the regimes. The latter risk is very small because of the high risk of massive retaliation imposed by those affected on the sponsor state.

WMD terrorism not sponsored by a state is somewhat more likely, but only one such attack occurred in the 1990s. Had the CWC been in force at that time, the poison gas attacks by the Japanese sect Aum Shinrikyo in the Tokyo subway in 1995 would have constituted an unintended violation of the CWC by Japan. This incident would not have caused a great problem within the CWC, however, because the violation affected only the country that had been unable to exert effective controls on proliferation within its territory. More serious problems could be expected if a terrorist group used WMD outside its "host" country, or if such activity were sponsored by the "host" country. No such violations of the three global WMD regimes have occurred.

Because of their very low probability but great potential damage, risks of WMD terrorism have to be taken very seriously. Measures are already in effect to reduce these risks, including export controls on dual-use items; monitoring of critical nuclear and chemical facilities by the IAEA and the OPCW; bilateral assistance programs in the former Soviet Union to prevent illegal diversion of WMD and related materials; monitoring and enforcement activity by domestic police forces and national intelligence agencies; and international cooperation among enforcement agencies. The most effective response to the risks posed by WMD terrorism lies in the intensification of international collaboration in the framework of global WMD regimes and export control arrangements, domestic enforcement activity, and information exchanges among national intelligence services. Most essential are national and international surveillance systems that enable countries to identify motivations and acquisition activities of terrorist groups at a very early stage.

Responses to Noncompliance

Most states enter into global regimes for WMD because they perceive an intrinsic security benefit of being regime members, and because these regimes deliver some additional benefits, such as facilitated trade in dual-use items. From this perspective, global governance structures for WMD can, to a large extent, be considered self-enforcing: states not interested in complying do not join. A substantial portion of noncompliance in a legal sense is thus likely to be unintended.[58] In some rare cases, however, deliberate violations of the NPT, BWC, and international norms against chemical warfare have occurred. How effective have international policies to change the behavior of noncomplying actors been? In this section, I restrict the analysis to responses to deliberate violations of regime rules.

The textbook-like, top-down model of arms control—in which international organizations evaluate inspection data, decide on whether a state has complied with its obligations, and if not proceed to enforcement action—does not exist in the real world. To those who have studied international politics, the absence of supranational enforcement power is a well-known corollary of the anarchic self-help structure of the international system.[59] Moreover, unlike in the case of the World Trade

Organization, the European Union, or some international organizations set up to implement environmental or resource policies, international bodies in the WMD field have abstained from formally deciding on whether a party is guilty of a treaty violation and what punishment is to be imposed on the culprit. Only in minor cases of noncompliance, such as missed deadlines for declarations or nonpayment of contributions to international organizations, have international bodies associated with the global regimes for WMD formally responded to noncompliance. With reference to the fact that the UN Security Council has the prerogative in questions of international peace and security—and the most serious violations of global regimes for WMD belong to this category of issues—all WMD global regimes provide for referral of grave compliance issues to the Security Council.

The cases of North Korea and Iraq have been the most extreme cases of noncompliance with global WMD regimes. And because responses have varied greatly across the two cases, this section focuses on them in more detail.

North Korea. In March 1993, North Korea, formally a nonnuclear weapon state member of the NPT, announced its intention to withdraw from the treaty.[60] It took this step after having inhibited the monitoring of its nuclear facilities by the IAEA and the failure of several initiatives to ease tensions on the Korean peninsula. In addition it was experiencing mounting economic difficulties and diplomatic isolation. Obviously, North Korea was betting that the United States and the international community would agree to address some of its political and economic concerns in exchange for a commitment not to withdraw from the NPT. After some saber rattling by both sides, North Korea entered into high-level talks with the United States, which began in early June 1993.

The ensuing bargaining process resulted in an Agreed Framework, concluded on October 21, 1994. It includes three provisions. First, North Korea remains a party to the NPT, although with unique status: it does not (yet) accept full-scope safeguards, as every nonnuclear weapon state under the NPT normally would. It committed itself to seal its nuclear reprocessing facility, halt operation of its 5-megawatt heavy water reactor and forgo refueling it, and suspend construction of two larger reactors that could produce weapon-grade plutonium. Eight thousand fuel rods, which were initially intended to be reprocessed, were placed in special storage canisters and are to be shipped out of the country. The IAEA is allowed to continue its monitoring of declared North Korean nuclear facilities. Second, in return, an international consortium is to build two modern light water reactors (LWRs) that do not produce weapon-grade plutonium. These reactors are financed mainly by South Korea and Japan. North Korea's energy shortages would, in the meantime, be relieved by shipments of heavy fuel oil—50,000 tons in the first year, then ten times as much annually for approximately a five-year period. Third, the transaction proceeds in the form of reciprocal steps, and the accord gives both sides more or less equal leverage against reneging. Only after completion of the first LWR, but before the delivery of key nuclear components, will North Korea allow full inspections of its facilities by the IAEA. It will then become clear whether North Korea had in fact embarked upon a full-scale nuclear weapons program, or whether, at the other extreme, the North had simply bluffed the United States and its allies into a deal worth around $6 billion.

Assessments regarding the effectiveness and efficiency of the Agreed Framework in denuclearizing North Korea are difficult because information on decision-making processes in North Korea is extremely scarce, and because implementation of the Agreed Framework is at an early stage. North Korea has stopped the construction of two reactors, closed its reprocessing facility, and allowed all fuel rods to be placed in canisters. So the short-term—and possibly only—prospects of arresting Pyongyang's nuclear program with the help of positive incentives look good. The more difficult task of eliminating this program still lies ahead.

As a result of the Agreed Framework, North Korea's nuclear weapons capabilities are to be virtually eliminated. From this perspective, the United States, South Korea, Japan, and the international community as a whole could be major beneficiaries of the deal. The cost of the LWRs is rather low in comparison to the possible consequences that a failure to reach an agreement might have had—for example, the acquisition of nuclear weapons by South Korea (and in response perhaps also Japan) or even a war on the Korean peninsula. Without the agreement, North Korea may have refueled its 5-megawatt reactor and completed, operated, and refueled the 50- and 200-megawatt reactors. North Korea may have also begun to reprocess spent fuel from all three reactors and obtained enough weapon-grade plutonium for dozens of nuclear weapons annually. This outcome would have debilitated the NPT, not to mention the IAEA. Analyses of the case suggest that North Korea, using the only bargaining chip it had, might indeed have taken this course in the absence of substantial positive incentives.[61]

As to the efficiency of the transaction, many problems have plagued the process, which, not surprisingly, has been slow and bumpy. For example, there is evidence that North Korea has engaged in overly risky nuclear and missile activities in the expectation of scaring the other side into paying a higher price. Critics of the Agreed Framework have also claimed that the deal amounts to extortion and is bound to motivate other countries to request rewards for abandoning illegal behavior. Nonetheless, these problems have not derailed progress toward the denuclearization of North Korea. In addition, it remains questionable whether other strategies for soliciting the cooperation of North Korea (that is, no action, additional sanctions, or even threats of military action) would have led to a firmer and earlier commitment to denuclearization. Given the history of North-South relations on the Korean peninsula, it should come as no surprise if the Agreed Framework were put into practice imperfectly by all parties, and if the process were extended beyond the target date originally envisaged.

Iraq. After its defeat in the Persian Gulf War, Iraq unconditionally accepted a UN Security Council resolution that mandates the total elimination of all WMD and associated programs in Iraq. This resolution took effect in April 1991 and was implemented by the UN Special Commission for Iraq with the assistance of the IAEA. The enforcement of WMD obligations in Iraq, whose totalitarian leadership remained in place, was much more difficult than expected. When forced to, the Iraqi leadership cooperated with UNSCOM, but it has never genuinely abandoned its interest in the possession of WMD. Only under repeated threats of bombing, and with the help of Iraqi defectors and Western countries' intelligence services, was UNSCOM able to track down most of Iraq's WMD stockpiles and facilities and destroy what had not already been destroyed during Desert Storm. The Iraqi nuclear weapons program was eliminated and would take many years to rebuild. The largest part of the country's chemical weapons and missiles with a range greater than 150 kilometers has also been eliminated. By contrast, what remain unaccounted for are important elements of Iraq's biological weapons program.[62]

In 1998 UNSCOM's activities came to a halt. Frustrated with the slow implementation of Iraq's disarmament obligations and its gross violation of human rights, the U.S. administration had decided to expand the aim of its policies from eliminating WMD and improving human rights to removing the regime of Saddam Hussein altogether. With no lifting of sanctions in sight, bombing raids by the United States and the United Kingdom, and the discovery of abuse of UNSCOM by U.S. intelligence agencies, Iraq refused to cooperate further with UNSCOM. The successor to UNSCOM, the UN Monitoring, Verification and Inspection Commission (UNMOVIC), a much weaker organization by design, is not yet fully operational. Intelligence services report that Iraq is again seeking to acquire critical technologies for WMD on international markets. Whether economic sanctions, continuing selective bombing of Iraqi targets by the United States and the United Kingdom, and monitoring by UNMOVIC will, in the long run, prevent Iraq from rebuilding its chemical and biological weapons and missile capability remains questionable.

What are the general lessons to be learned from using positive incentives to attract holdout countries or solve compliance problems, in contrast to negative incentives (economic sanctions, military action at the extreme)?[63] The analysis of cases such as Ukraine and North Korea shows that employing positive incentives raises several problems: encouraging the cooperation of a laggard or obstructionist state in arms control by means of positive incentives can set an undesirable precedent. It might cause other holdouts or regime members to ask for special treatment as well, leading to a spiral of requests and counterrequests that may end in the demise of the entire regime. Positive incentives carry the risk of extortion by a critical state. Extortion implies inefficiency: the recipient state would have behaved in a desirable manner even in the absence of positive incentives or a smaller amount thereof. In other words, providers of positive incentives pay more than necessary. Positive incentives can motivate the recipient to engage in overly risky behavior because she expects to be rewarded or bailed out if she puts herself and others at risk. For positive incentives to function properly, the recipient must be rational in the sense of cost-benefit calculating, not norm- or habit-driven or plainly irrational. Information and monitoring problems can complicate the negotiation and implementation of exchanges of positive incentives for arms control measures. Burden-sharing problems are to be expected on the provider side. "Hard cases" could turn out to be simply too costly to be solved through the application of positive incentives alone. States such as India, Pakistan, Israel, and some Arab countries are likely to belong to this category. When a proliferator is strongly motivated by security concerns, its economic situation is not desperate, and its political and economic elites are inward-oriented, even large-scale positive incentives may not change the proliferator's mind.

Nonetheless, positive incentives do exhibit some features that render them potentially advantageous: they can affect the behavior of recipients relatively quickly, thus contributing to the solution of urgent and possibly irreversible problems. They are less antagonistic than sanctions. When recipients do not have the means to implement arms control measures, positive incentives will work better than threatening sanctions. Incentives can be applied even without clear-cut legal standards of arms control compliance. They can be conceived of as a means for driving recipients toward more desirable behavior. Penalties, by contrast, require decisions about when specific actors have "crossed the line." Last but not least, positive incentives can motivate recipient states to provide information on their problems in implementing international arms control obligations. If a recipient country has no problem, it will not receive assistance. In contrast to situations involving threats of negative incentives, secrecy does not pay.

CONCLUSIONS AND RECOMMENDATIONS

Regulatory responses to risks posed by WMD have often been sparked by armed conflicts where use or threats of use of WMD have occurred. The agenda for WMD has evolved very slowly. The only truly preventive measures have been those establishing nuclear weapon–free zones and demilitarized geographic areas. Efforts to strengthen existing constraints of that nature and establish new ones are to be commended. Such regulations may look unnecessary at the time of their establishment. Their main advantage, however, lies in locking in a beneficial status quo, and making it more difficult to reverse established nonproliferation norms at some point in the future, should anyone try.

NGOs have in most cases influenced agenda-setting processes, negotiations, and the implementation of arms control agreements only very indirectly, through their influence on public opinion and policy makers. Governments have only rarely involved NGOs in bargaining processes and implementation of WMD control measures. Since the end of the Cold War, most NGOs have reduced their capacity to influence policy agendas for WMD. Ironically, this withdrawal comes at a time when their influence could be somewhat greater than during the Cold War and when many of the risks posed by WMD persist.[64] The only nongovernmental actors that have clearly expanded their influence since the late 1980s are business interest groups.

The effectiveness of asymmetric global rules for nuclear weapons hinges on several unique circumstances that do not exist with regard to other WMD. Regimes such as the Australia Group and the MTCR, which are framed as supplier cartels, are under persistent pressure from importer countries. The availability of dual-use technology on global markets has increased for a variety of reasons, for example, because of unsuccessful attempts to integrate civilian and military production to compensate for declining military procurement after the Cold War, and by the increasing flows of technology from the civilian to the military sectors rather than vice versa, as was the case in the past. Dual-use technologies are increasingly relevant to civilian economic activities in both industrialized and developing countries. Under these circumstances, traditional denial regimes that divide the world into "good" and "bad" countries are unlikely to perform well in the long term if they run against the interests of large numbers of private and public participants in ever more integrated global markets.

Such asymmetric regulations need to be recast in a more balanced and cooperative form. Solutions require a new framing of the global agenda for WMD, moving from one of denial to one that cooperatively asserts that economic advantages of global free trade in dual-use goods and services can be combined with safeguards against their abuse for military purposes. Countries currently operating international export control arrangements should try to integrate these arrangements in the three global WMD regimes. Substantive trade regulations should be introduced into the NPT and BWC. Existing trade regulations, such as those in the CWC, should be strengthened.

The CWC's export control system provides a useful nucleus for a larger effort. States should try to expand on this system in several directions. First, all end users of the most critical dual-use materials and technologies, also those located in nonparties, should be subject to effective monitoring. Second, information flows should become more regular and faster, approaching real-time exchanges if possible. One option worthy of further discussion is comprehensive electronic systems that can track exports and imports of dual-use items and make much more use of information provided by market participants. Third, as long as there is no clear violation of international rules, proprietary information should be protected. Fourth, if the system works well, more goods and technologies could be added to the control lists, gradually making denial regimes, such as the Australia Group and MTCR, obsolete.[65]

The negotiation of the CWC may well have been the last large-scale and successful effort to create an important global regime for WMD in the Conference on Disarmament. Further negotiations are likely to be conducted in ad hoc forums with more flexible composition.

In contrast to the three global treaty-based regimes, export control arrangements are informal and membership is restricted. Existing export control regimes suffer from several problems. In the best case, they can contribute to increasing the effectiveness of global treaty-based regimes but cannot effectively replace them. They should be transformed from denial systems to more collaborative systems if they are to perform well in the long run.

Experimental inspections involving government and industry representatives have been highly effective in overcoming impasses in CWC negotiations on difficult monitoring issues. They have helped in removing some concerns about undesirable side effects of monitoring and allowed for quasi-real testing of procedures under negotiation. Thus they have helped in getting the CWC's monitoring system off to a quicker and more effective start.

Routine monitoring under the CWC and the NPT involves considerable inefficiencies due to the lack of focus of inspections on the more risky countries. Removing these inefficiencies is, for political reasons, unacceptable to many countries. As long as the challenge (or special) inspection procedure, which in the case of the CWC involves an innovative "managed access" approach, proves effective, these inefficiencies are likely to be tolerated by countries that bear inspection burdens they think do not correspond to risk. Challenge inspections on the basis of managed access should also be introduced into the NPT regime and the BWC. Ongoing negotiations on such procedures could make more systematic use of trial inspections to test the practicalities of various proposals.

Trade measures associated with the NPT and CWC have had a powerful impact on states' willingness to join these regimes. If trade restrictions maintained outside the three regimes, particularly those of the Australia Group, the MTCR, and the NSG, can be integrated in the CWC's and NPT regime's trade regulations, the attractiveness of these regimes will increase. Such integration should be combined with the establishment of more comprehensive trade regulations within WMD regimes that also regulate trade in dual-use technologies among regime members.

Failure of the five nuclear weapon powers under the NPT to take decisive steps toward nuclear disarmament has negative consequences for the viability of all three WMD regimes. As a first step to restore confidence in their commitment, the five states should conclude a treaty unconditionally banning the use of nuclear weapons, deactivate all nuclear weapons, eliminate all tactical nuclear arms, ratify the CTBT, fully implement START II and III, and begin negotiations on comprehensive nuclear disarmament that also involve other nuclear powers.

It is difficult to trace differences in the performance of WMD regimes back to differences in monitoring systems. The track record suggests, however, that monitoring arrangements of global WMD regimes are likely to be more effective if they comprise elements of routine monitoring of declared activities and facilities as well as challenge inspections to fill the remaining gaps. The analysis of negotiation processes has shown that it is possible to design procedures for preventing abusive requests for challenge inspections without taking the teeth out of such inspections. The NPT regime should be strengthened by a challenge inspection procedure that, in contrast to the existing possibility of special inspections, operates at the request of regime parties without right of refusal by the requested state. Negotiations on a new compliance system for the BWC, possibly including rather little routine monitoring but a strong mechanism for challenge inspections, should be brought to a close as soon as possible. Insufficient compliance by several countries, including the United States, with their obligation to declare critical civilian chemical facilities and subject them to inspections threatens to undermine the routine monitoring system of the CWC and therefore also confidence of the parties in the regime. This implementation failure should be redressed as quickly as possible.

Political bodies of the IAEA and the OPCW may engage in legal and political assessments of data collected by the technical bodies of these organizations. So far these bodies have shied away from formally deciding on whether a country has complied with its commitments. Most critical issues of that nature are referred to the UN Security Council, where they usually dissipate. This situation makes it more difficult to build up political pressure against countries violating their obligations and should be changed.

Assistance beyond the one provided for as an integral part of WMD regimes has been crucial in attracting some important holdout countries and in facilitating implementation of regime rules. The most important cases of this kind are incentives that facilitated Ukraine's denuclearization and assistance to Russia for its chemical demilitarization project and for controlling more effectively nuclear materials on its territory. The case of Ukraine testifies to the potential of positive incentives as a means of solving nuclear proliferation problems at relatively low cost. Assistance to Russia, Ukraine, and other critical parts of the former Soviet Union for the purpose of controlling fissile materials, nuclear technology, and know-how, missile technology and other precursors, as well as the elimination of existing chemical weapons, should be put on a more solid footing. Also, the amounts spent to date are far from sufficient, even though it would seem that a few billion dollars would be a small price for definitively solving a major proliferation problem.

The risk posed by terrorist activity in the realm of WMD is, at present, largely a matter of informed guessing. The probability of acquisition and use of WMD by terrorist groups is rather small; expected damage if use occurs can range from very small to enormous. Most experts believe that risk in regard to nuclear weapons is much smaller than in regard to chemical and biological weapons. Only one larger-scale instance of recent terrorist use of chemical weapons (the one in Japan) is known, and its effects were limited. Scientific innovation, particularly in biology, may increase WMD risks emanating from nonstate actors. Such risks must be addressed in terms of compliance problems under the three global WMD regimes and must be reduced through tighter controls on trade in dual-use technologies, better surveillance of terrorist groups, and internationally coordinated law enforcement activity.

Global regimes for WMD are, to a large extent, self-enforcing: states join these regimes because compliance is in their self-interest. The anarchic self-help nature of the international system makes collective enforcement in cases of noncompliance extremely rare. Problems of noncompliance are, in practice, often dealt with through negotiations within or outside WMD regimes whose rules have been violated. Solutions tend to involve a variety of rewards and punishments.

It has become increasingly evident that negative incentives alone, the traditional recipe for dealing with holdout countries and treaty violations, have frequently been of limited effect. The use of positive incentives involves difficulties of its own, such as problems of moral hazard and extortion. The analysis of cases where positive incentives have been used shows, however, that such incentives have several important advantages. For example, they motivate the target country to provide more information about the problem at hand. They are also more conducive to a cooperative climate than negative incentives because of their less confrontational nature.

Despite their advantages, positive incentives are no panacea. States such as India, Pakistan, Israel, Iraq, and some other Arab countries are unlikely to buy into global prohibitions of WMD or comply with their obligations as a result of positive incentives alone. Proliferators who are strongly motivated by security concerns, whose economic situation is not desperate, and whose political and economic elites are inward-oriented and antiliberal may not respond favorably even to large positive incentives. Perhaps to a greater extent than has been done in the past, positive incentives will have to be combined with negative incentives in these cases to change the minds of decision makers in these countries.

The most important violations of global WMD regimes have been those by Iraq, North Korea, and Russia. Implementation of the Agreed Framework with North Korea should be pursued because there is no viable alternative for solving the problem. Other countries that have been able to free ride on the prospective benefits of North Korea's denuclearization should been encouraged to participate. Even if the Agreed Framework is being implemented much slower than initially planned, and even if this deal may have incited North Korea to request more money for further inspections and restraint on exports of missile technology, the denuclearization of North Korea is worth the price. In the case of Iraq, the transition from UNSCOM to UNMOVIC is associated with a significant weakening of international efforts to control Iraq's WMD activity. Whether economic sanctions, destruction of Iraq's military capability through bombing, and UNMOVIC's monitoring will, in the long run, prevent Iraq from resuming its WMD programs is questionable.

By and large, international efforts to reduce the risks of nuclear, biological, and chemical warfare have been relatively effective. This does not imply that complacency is recommended. All three global regimes, as well as international measures associated with them, suffer from a variety of weaknesses. Perhaps the most important challenges are: establishing parity in the nuclear field by achieving the elimination of all nuclear weapons, and integrating denial regimes into global WMD regimes so as to transform these denial regimes into truly cooperative and thus more effective mechanisms on a global scale.

NOTES

1. In the year 2000, the United States had around 10,500 warheads, Russia around 20,000, the United Kingdom 185, France 450, and China 400. See Joseph Cirincione, ed., *Repairing the Regime: Preventing the Spread of Weapons of Mass Destruction* (Washington, D.C.: Carnegie Endowment for International Peace, 2000), app. 5.
2. This phenomenon is often referred to as the "nuclear winter." See Owen Greene, Ian Percival, and Irene Ridge, *Nuclear Winter: The Evidence and the Risks* (New York: Polity Press, 1985).
3. Russia possesses around 40,000 metric tons of chemical warfare agents, the United States around 30,000 tons.
4. See Susan Wright, ed., *Current Problems of Biological Warfare and Disarmament* (Geneva: UN Institute for Disarmament Research, 1999); and Brad Roberts, *Weapons Proliferation and World Order After the Cold War* (The Hague: Kluwer, 1996). See also the Nonproliferation Program web site of the Carnegie Endowment for International Peace, <http://www.ceip.org/files/projects/npp/npp_home.ASP >; and the web site of the Center for Nonproliferation Studies, Monterey Institute of International Studies, <http://www.cns.miis.edu>.
5. See Barry Buzan, ed., *The International Politics of Deterrence* (New York: St. Martin's Press, 1987); Daniel Frei and Christian Catrina, *Risks of Unintentional Nuclear War* (Geneva: UN Institute for Disarmament Research, 1982); and Stephen J. Cimbala, ed., *Deterrence and Nuclear Proliferation in the Twenty-first Century* (Westport, Conn.: Praeger, 2000).
6. During the confrontation between the United States and North Korea in the first half of the 1990s over North Korea's nuclear program, U.S. decision makers discussed the option of a preventive destruction of that country's nuclear facilities. That plan was rejected, among other reasons, because of the large-scale war on the Korean peninsula that would have followed such an attack.
7. See Thomas C. Schelling and Morton H. Halperin, *Strategy and Arms Control* (New York: Twentieth Century Fund, 1961).

8. See Joseph Rotblat, *Nuclear Weapons: The Road to Zero* (Boulder, Colo.: Westview Press, 1998); and Cirincione, *Repairing the Regime.*

9. See Scott D. Sagan and Kenneth N. Waltz, *The Spread of Nuclear Weapons: A Debate* (New York: W. W. Norton, 1995); and Colin S. Gray, *The Second Nuclear Age* (Boulder, Colo.: Lynne Rienner, 1999).

10. See Colin S. Gray, *House of Cards: Why Arms Control Must Fail* (Ithaca, N.Y.: Cornell University Press, 1992).

11. See Daniel Frei, *Perceived Images: U.S. and Soviet Assumptions and Perceptions in Disarmament* (Totowa, N.J.: Rowman and Allanheld, 1986).

12. See Robert Axelrod, *The Evolution of Cooperation* (New York: Basic Books, 1984).

13. See Thomas Bernauer, *The Chemistry of Regime Formation: Explaining International Cooperation for a Comprehensive Ban on Chemical Weapons* (Aldershot: Dartmouth, 1993).

14. See John J. Mearsheimer, "Back to the Future: Instability in Europe After the Cold War," *International Security*, vol. 15, no. 1 (Summer 1990), pp. 5–56.

15. See Kenichi Ohmae, *The End of the Nation State: The Rise of Regional Economies* (London: HarperCollins, 1995).

16. See Graham T. Allison et al., *Avoiding Nuclear Anarchy: Containing the Threat of Loose Russian Nuclear Weapons and Fissile Material* (Cambridge, Mass.: MIT Press, 1996); Amy Smithson, *Toxic Archipelago: Preventing Proliferation from the Former Soviet Chemical and Biological Weapons Complexes* (Washington, D.C.: Stimson Center, 1999); and Scott Jones and Keith Wolfe, eds., "In Word and in Deed: Nonproliferation Export Controls in the Former Soviet Union," paper presented at the annual convention of the International Studies Association, Toronto, Canada, 1997.

17. See Wolfgang H. Reinicke, *Global Public Policy: Governing Without Government* (Washington, D.C.: Brookings Institution Press, 1998); and Richard A. Falkenrath, Robert D. Newman, and Bradley A. Thayer, *America's Achilles' Heel: Nuclear, Biological, and Chemical Terrorism and Covert Attack* (Cambridge, Mass.: MIT Press, 1998).

18. See Thomas Bernauer, *Staaten im Weltmarkt* (Opladen: Leske and Budrich, 2000).

19. See Michael Barletta and Amy Sands, eds., *Nonproliferation Regimes at Risk* (Monterey, Calif.: Center for Nonproliferation Studies, 1999).

20. See Cirincione, *Repairing the Regime.*

21. See Gary T. Gardner, *Nuclear Nonproliferation: A Primer* (Boulder, Colo.: Lynne Rienner Publishers, 1994); Jozef Goldblat, *The Nuclear Nonproliferation Regime: Assessment and Prospects* (The Hague: Martinus Nijhoff Publishers and Stockholm International Peace Research Institute, 1995); and *SIPRI Yearbooks* (Oxford, U.K.: Oxford University Press, various years).

22. See Gardner, *Nuclear Nonproliferation; Jozef Goldblat, Arms Control: A Guide to Negotiations and Agreements* (London: Sage, 1994); and Goldblat, *The Nuclear Nonproliferation Regime.*

23. See Goldblat, *The Nuclear Nonproliferation Regime;* and Cirincione, *Repairing the Regime.*

24. See Rebecca Johnson, "The NPT Review: Disaster Averted," *Bulletin of the Atomic Scientists*, vol. 56, no. 4 (July 2000), pp. 52–7.

25. See George Bunn and Roland M. Timerbaev, "Security Assurances to Non-Nuclear Weapon States," *Nonproliferation Review*, vol. 1, no. 1 (Fall 1993), pp. 11–20. See also <http://www.ceip.org/files/projects/npp/npp_home.ASP>.

26. See Allison et al. *Avoiding Nuclear Anarchy*. See also <http://www.cns.miis.edu>.

27. See Cirincione, *Repairing the Regime*; Thomas Bernauer and Dieter Ruloff, eds., *The Politics of Positive Incentives in Arms Control* (Columbia, S.C.: University of South Carolina Press, 1999); and Leon V. Sigal, *Disarming Strangers: Nuclear Diplomacy with North Korea* (Princeton, N.J.: Princeton University Press, 1998).

28. See *SIPRI Yearbooks*.

29. See <http://www.cns.miis.edu>.

30. Ibid.; also Henry L. Stimson Center web site, <http://www.stimson.org>.

31. See Graham S. Pearson, *The UNSCOM Saga* (New York: St. Martin's Press, 1999); and Richard Butler, "Inspecting Iraq," in Cirincione, *Repairing the Regime*, pp. 175–84. See also <http://www.cns.miis.edu>.

32. See Reinicke, *Global Public Policy*.

33. See Cirincione, *Repairing the Regime*; Roberts, *Weapons Proliferation and World Order After the Cold War*; Gary K. Bertsch, Richard T. Cupitt, and Steven Elliott-Gower, eds., *International Cooperation on Nonproliferation Export Controls: Prospects for the 1990s and Beyond* (Ann Arbor, Mich.: University of Michigan Press, 1994); and Müller, "Nuklearschmuggel und Terrorismus mit Kernwaffen."

34. See Todd Sandler, *Collective Action: Theory and Applications* (Ann Arbor, Mich.: University of Michigan Press, 1992); and Todd Sandler, *Global Challenges: An Approach to Environmental, Political, and Economic Problems* (Cambridge, U.K.: Cambridge University Press, 1997).

35. This list has also been adopted by the members of the Wassenaar Arrangement and the European Union. The Wassenaar Arrangement is another international regime that controls the export of conventional weapons and dual-use technologies.

36. See Cirincione, *Repairing the Regime*. See also <http://www.cns.miis.edu>.

37. A trend, particularly manifest in the 1970s and 1980s, in which proliferators tried to play off individual exporters against each other and in which governments and firms relaxed their restraints in order not to lose clients, has in part been reversed.

38. The U.S. administration insisted that under a controversial interpretation of the 1925 Geneva Protocol, use of these substances in war was permitted, but this clearly put the United States on the defensive. Former communist countries were hoping to exploit the accusation against the United States for propaganda purposes. For countries that did not possess chemical weapons, this public outcry was a welcome opportunity to initiate talks on a worldwide ban on such means of warfare. This is how the CBW problem moved onto the agenda of the Geneva-based multilateral disarmament conference.

39. For examples of proposals made by different U.S. academic institutions with regard to denuclearization in the former Soviet Union that had a significant influence on U.S. policy in this area, see Allison et al., *Avoiding Nuclear Anarchy*. See also <http://www.cns.miis.edu>.

40. See Bernauer, *The Chemistry of Regime Formation*.

41. See Reinicke, *Global Public Policy*.

42. Cast in the terminology of political economy, the trade-off is one of transaction costs (that is, costs of negotiating an agreement) versus external effects (that is, costs imposed on actors not involved in the bargaining process), which can negatively affect the performance of a regulatory regime. See Bernauer, *The Chemistry of Regime Formation.*

43. It may be recalled that the global ban on antipersonnel land mines was concluded outside the CD, even though the latter forum has had the issue on its agenda.

44. See Jeffrey A. Larsen and Gregory J. Rattray, eds., *Arms Control Toward the Twenty-first Century* (Boulder, Colo.: Lynne Rienner Publishers, 1996).

45. See Bertsch, Cupitt, and Elliott-Gower, *International Cooperation on Nonproliferation Export Controls.*

46. See Bernauer and Ruloff, *The Politics of Positive Incentives in Arms Control;* and Sigal, *Disarming Strangers.*

47. A similar approach is used for IAEA safeguards under the NPT.

48. Without the "managed access" procedure, the requested country might—as North Korea did in the case of the NPT—simply bar the inspectors from entering the country. The NPT safeguards provide for special inspections on request by the IAEA and with the agreement of the party to be inspected, without specifying this procedure in detail. North Korea has so far been the only case in which a request for such an inspection has been made.

49. In 1996, the International Court of Justice expressed the opinion that there is an international obligation to eliminate nuclear weapons, to negotiate nuclear disarmament, and to bring such negotiations to a conclusion.

50. Some Arab states have argued that they will not give up the option of chemical weapons as long as Israel possesses nuclear weapons.

51. See Rotblat, *Nuclear Weapons;* and Ronald Walker, "What Is to Be Done About Nuclear Weapons?" *Security Dialogue,* vol. 31, no. 2 (2000), pp. 179–84.

52. See Bernauer and Ruloff, *The Politics of Positive Incentives in Arms Control.*

53. Ibid.

54. If the United States had opted for a broader cooperative agenda with Ukraine earlier in the process, and if Russia had displayed a more conciliatory attitude, it is possible that Ukraine would have agreed to the withdrawal of tactical and strategic nuclear weapons in exchange for even a smaller amount of positive incentives (but not without), and probably earlier. Overall, therefore, the transactions in this case have probably been relatively effective and efficient. Some problems with regard to long-term commitments by the United States and other Western countries persist, however. Western economic assistance to Ukraine has not materialized at the level that was promised in the run-up to the Rada's vote on START I (February 3, 1994) and NPT accession (November 16, 1994). How long the CTR program, which has played a vital role in the denuclearization of Ukraine, will continue is unclear. Denuclearization assistance by other countries has remained scarce, and it is unclear whether these countries will fill the gap should the U.S. assistance dry up. Continued support for Ukraine is desirable if not indispensable, not least because the risk of transfers of nuclear materials, know-how, and missiles to problematic countries or nongovernmental actors will persist even after the nuclear weapons stockpile in Ukraine has been removed.

55. See Allison et al., *Avoiding Nuclear Anarchy*; and John M. Shields and William C. Potter, eds., *Dismantling the Cold War: U.S. and NIS Perspectives on the Nunn-Lugar Cooperative Threat Reduction Program* (Cambridge, Mass.: MIT Press, 1997). See also <http://www.cns.miis.edu>.

56. See Bernauer and Ruloff, *The Politics of Positive Incentives in Arms Control*.

57. See Müller, "Nuklearschmuggel und Terrorismus mit Kernwaffen"; Falkenrath, Newman, and Thayer, *America's Achilles' Heel*; Bruce Hoffman, *Terrorism and Weapons of Mass Destruction* (Santa Monica, California: RAND, 1999); and Stuart E. Johnson, ed., *The Niche Threat: Deterring the Use of Chemical and Biological Weapons* (Washington, D.C.: National Defense University Press, 1997).

58. See Abram Chayes and Antonia Handler Chayes, *The New Sovereignty: Compliance with International Regulatory Agreements* (Cambridge, Mass.: Harvard University Press, 1995).

59. See Kenneth A. Oye, *Cooperation Under Anarchy* (Princeton, N.J.: Princeton University Press, 1986).

60. This section draws on work by Amy Smithson, "North Korea: A Case in Progress," in Bernauer and Ruloff, *The Politics of Positive Incentives in Arms Control*, pp. 73–110; and Sigal, *Disarming Strangers*.

61. See Smithson, "North Korea: A Case in Progress"; and Sigal, *Disarming Strangers*.

62. See Butler, "Inspecting Iraq"; and Pearson, *The UNSCOM Saga*. See also <http://www.cns.miis.edu>.

63. This section draws on Bernauer and Ruloff, *The Politics of Positive Incentives in Arms Control*.

64. Important exceptions are some think tanks and academic institutions in the United States.

65. For a detailed proposal of that nature, see Reinicke, *Global Public Policy*, p. 186.

SUGGESTED ADDITIONAL READING

Bernauer, Thomas, and Dieter Ruloff, eds. *The Politics of Positive Incentives in Arms Control.* Columbia, S.C.: University of South Carolina Press, 1999.

Cirincione, Joseph, ed. *Repairing the Regime: Preventing the Spread of Weapons of Mass Destruction.* Washington, D.C.: Carnegie Endowment for International Peace, 2000.

Gardner, Gary T. *Nuclear Nonproliferation: A Primer.* Boulder, Colo.: Lynne Rienner Publishers, 1994.

Goldblat, Jozef. *Arms Control: A Guide to Negotiations and Agreements.* London: Sage, 1994.

Goldblat, Jozef, ed. *Nuclear Disarmament: Obstacles to Banishing the Bomb.* New York: St. Martin's Press, 2000.

Hoffman, Bruce. *Terrorism and Weapons of Mass Destruction: An Analysis of Trends and Motivations.* Santa Monica, Calif.: RAND, 1999.

Jones, Rodney W., and Mark G. McDonough. *Tracking Nuclear Proliferation.* Washington D.C.: Carnegie Endowment for International Peace, 1998.

Larsen, Jeffrey A., and Gregory J. Rattray, eds. *Arms Control Toward the 21st Century.* Boulder, Colo.: Lynne Rienner Publishers, 1996.

Roberts, Brad. *Weapons Proliferation and World Order After the Cold War*. The Hague: Kluwer, 1996.

SIPRI (yearbook). *Armaments, Disarmament and International Security*. Oxford, U.K.: Oxford University Press.

Wright, Susan, ed. *Current Problems of Biological Warfare and Disarmament*. Geneva: UN Institute for Disarmament Research, 1999.

Internet sites

Center for Nonproliferation Studies, Monterey Institute of International Studies <http://cns.miis.edu> This institution also publishes the *Nonproliferation Review*.

Henry L. Stimson Center, Washington D.C. <http://www.stimson.org> This institution also publishes the *CBW Chronicle*.

The Carnegie Endowment for International Peace, Non-Proliferation Project <http://www.ceip.org/npp>

Program for Promoting Nuclear Non-Proliferation <http://www.soton.ac.uk/~ppnn>

Part III

Conclusions

17

From Agenda to Accord

P. J. Simmons and Chantal de Jonge Oudraat

IF THIS BOOK HAD BEEN WRITTEN in 1961 or 1971, aside from being a good deal thinner, it would have emphasized two sets of protagonists: sovereign states and the international organizations they controlled. With few exceptions, those states and institutions defined which international issues received serious notice and determined how they would be addressed. Increasingly over the last quarter century, the exceptions have become the rule. In every phase of managing global issues, free agents have gained significant influence.

Nonstate actors is the accepted—but not felicitous—term for these free agents; it only explains the authority they lack, not the burgeoning influence they exercise. By whatever name, these new notables—from the private sector, from the galaxies of nongovernmental organizations (NGOs), from communities of scholars, scientists, and similar experts—are helping to draft blueprints of the global architecture. States remain the master builders, but the new global management structure—sometimes effective, often not—is increasingly a device built by many hands pulling many levers. Among the common threads to be found in the preceding chapters, this remarkable development is one of the strongest.

Overall, our case studies show a wide range of works in progress. As global issues assume greater importance, long-established methods of carrying on relations among states are making room for updated, sometimes improvised, diplomatic arrangements. New issues demand attention. And new dynamics are propelling the action.

SETTING THE INTERNATIONAL AGENDA

The emergence of new players is relatively recent. The predominance of powerful, wealthy states in agenda setting is, as the case studies show, a pattern of long standing.[1] Throughout most of the last century and into this one, the world's most powerful states have been the primary gatekeepers and architects of the global issues agenda—with the United States as *primus inter pares*. Their long-term ascendancy largely reflects the economic, military, and diplomatic clout they can use to persuade, entice, or threaten others to follow their lead.[2] In contrast, small and medium-sized states, as well as developing countries, usually influence the agenda more incrementally and indirectly—mainly by trying to steer the major powers in a particular direction or by asserting their interests inside multilateral institutions where consensus requirements elevate their standing.

Powerful states, the record indicates, exercise their authority as much in reaction to events and pressures as in the pursuit of predetermined national or collective interests. Frequently these pacesetters engage with global issues only after challenges become too large or threatening to ignore. Indeed, many of the major advances in governance to which the authors point in this volume came in the wake of crises. The United States became an energetic advocate of an ambitious international trade regime only in the aftermath of the post-Depression tariff wars and on the threshold of the Cold War, a competition that required bringing the U.S. economy and those of its allies up to full strength. Economic crises were, writes Robert Litan (chapter 5), the "mother of invention" for "two of the major efforts to address cross-border economic volatility: the creation of the Bretton Woods system . . . and more recently the development of common international prudential financial standards for financial institutions—especially banks." The savagery of World War II and the Holocaust, to take another example, galvanized private organizations that, in turn, convinced the initially skeptical, victorious states that human rights issues were matters of global concern, deserving of their own place on the international agenda.

The decisive dominance of the great powers, however, has eroded in recent decades as lesser states, multinational corporations, NGOs, and ad hoc coalitions of special interests have gained access to and mastery of the levers of international politics and public opinion. The information revolution has greatly enhanced private actors' sway relative to previously paramount states, including the United States. For development assistance and global environmental issues, the interaction of many actors seems more important than the role of any single participant. In human rights, Dinah Shelton (chapter 11) sees NGOs as having been the "engine for virtually every advance" on the international agenda, with small and medium-sized states sometimes exerting more influence than the military and economic powerhouses. Canada's reputation for moral authority, for instance, certainly had a hand in its success in bringing together a coalition of small and medium-sized powers to pull the landmine issue out of the Geneva-based Conference on Disarmament where it had languished for years.

Much of this phenomenon is familiar. Civil society actors—individuals, NGOs, businesses—have been influencing agendas and more across borders for centuries. In colonial times, corporations like the East India Company acted by charter as the prime agents for the colonial expansion of the British Empire. Holding the power to make laws, tax, and wage war within its territory, by the eighteenth century the company was acting as the private government of the Indian subcontinent.[3] In the early 1800s, the British and Foreign Anti-Slavery Society, a transnational citizen group that would easily fit the United Nations' 1994 umbrella definition of an NGO, was a driving force behind government action against the slave trade.[4] Charismatic leaders of developing countries—Nasser, Sukarno, Nehru, and others—have commanded global attention and organized at least temporarily influential coalitions like the Non-Aligned Movement. A single book, Rachel Carson's *Silent Spring*, spurred environmental activism around the world. The 1975 Helsinki Accords offer a notable example of civil society turning a superpower agenda on its head. Long promoted by the Soviet Union as a diplomatic confirmation of the post-war status quo, the agreement turned out to be best known for its human-rights provisions and their unexpected use by Soviet and East European dissidents and Western human rights groups to defy the status quo.

What is new in recent decades is the rise in the number and diversity of actors with claims on the global policy agenda, the boom in their networking and communications potential, and the extension of their influence onto such previously privileged turf as trade, finance, and communications. Private actors, not states, have changed the parameters of the ongoing debate over what works in the way of assistance to developing countries and economies, demanding high priority for such objectives as microcredit, the empowerment of women, and sustainable development. In addition to familiar, visible street protests, NGOs—singly, in national and transnational coalitions, and jointly, in multisector advocacy networks—launch e-mail and fax campaigns to pressure decision makers, devise media strategies, and construct web sites to educate publics. The authors suggest that NGOs have been most influential in spotlighting corruption, environment, human rights, labor rights, refugee, and intrastate violence issues. And as the chapters on communications, corruption, finance, health, trade, pollution, labor rights, and weapons of mass destruction note, businesses and business groups are increasingly positioning themselves as independent players on the international scene.

In short, the near-monopoly once held by the most powerful states—singly or together—over the content and direction of the international agenda is less and less assured. The treatment of core issues—including nuclear arms and international trade—still largely follows the dictates of traditional powers. But in a number of other areas, different thinkers are pushing ideas until their time comes. The consequences for coherent global governance of multiplying agenda setters are impossible to assess confidently, but if full participation is rightly identified as a prerequisite for good governance, the trend toward inclusiveness may prove to be a healthy if initially confusing one.

Explaining the Exceptions

When authors discuss the "important" or "key" role of actors other than powerful states, they usually refer to behind-the-scenes or step-by-step maneuvers that inject new issues in the way that drip irrigation waters crops. International organizations, for example, generate support for action over time through their educational programs, annual reports, field activities, and technical assistance programs. Experts with specialized technical, regulatory, and scientific knowledge bring their weight to bear in important but subtle ways. Businesses and corporations usually exert power over global agendas by influencing the policies of dominant states. And most NGO successes result from slow-and-steady siege tactics rather than full-out assault.

Occasionally, though, outsiders rapidly overcome great-power inertia or opposition and win a place on the agenda for a previously orphaned issue. When that reversal happens, it reflects a remarkable—and not easily replicated—confluence of forces and circumstances. A dramatic case in point was the successful effort that brought a transnational NGO coalition and several small and medium-sized states together in a campaign to put negotiations for a ban on anti-personnel landmines on a diplomatic fast track. The result was a treaty negotiated in less than fourteen months and signed by 122 states in December 1997. The feat was all the more noteworthy because it was achieved without the backing—indeed over the initial opposition—of the usual suspects in Washington, Moscow, Paris, London, and Beijing.[5]

The pivotal influence of the Nobel Peace Prize–winning International Campaign to Ban Landmines (ICBL) infused new energy and hope into numerous advocacy groups around the world. It also raised a prickly question. If civil society groups and their allies in second-tier states could sidestep traditional multilateral settings and succeed in the face of initially strong opposition by all the great powers, why can environmentalists, human rights activists, and other smaller states not do the same?

The answer—still being debated by analysts and campaigners alike—is far from clear. What is certain is that the ICBL success flowed from the intermingling of many separate forces. Among them were support from such key political figures as U.S. Senator Patrick Leahy and UN Secretary-General Kofi Annan, the strenuous involvement of Canada, and minimal private sector opposition. Additionally, the inherent clarity and humanitarian nature of the issue; a celebrity advocate of the magnitude of the late Princess Diana; a compelling, clear, and circumscribed goal all combined with excellent teamwork, timing, and more to force an issue to prominence and resolution.

The anti-landmine campaign owes its success, in other words, to so many different factors that it would seem to be a singular exercise rather than a model. Examining the different ingredients at work, however, it is possible to separate out five elements that were not only crucial in this one instance but can also go far to determine the success of similar projects that other outsiders have launched or might:

- Effective choices in framing issues so as to grab public and elite attention;
- Partnerships including key players capable of effecting change at a particular moment because of their bureaucratic, symbolic, or moral authority;
- Cohesiveness of coalitions;
- Money; and
- Timing—either intentional or serendipitous.

Effective Framing. The power to frame issues can serve to inform or mislead, to promote constructive responses or to derail them, to break ideological deadlocks or to reinforce them, to pursue public interests or selfish ones. When advocates introduce issues in ways that capture the attention and sympathy of the general public and/or of government and corporate elites—particularly in influential countries—they can decisively affect when and how issues reach the international agenda. For the anti-landmine advocates, for instance, selling their vision to the public as a humanitarian priority was easy given the horrific effects of landmines on innocent civilians, including children. From that decision flowed an effective communications and media strategy that won wide attention and generated a powerful emotional response.

Powerful states' ample communications machinery and access to air time nationally and internationally have long given them the widest opportunities to frame issues, but corporations, business lobbies, and well-funded interest groups have also done well in this regard. They can purchase airtime and print space and hire specialized personnel to give their arguments an effective spin. The information revolution and globalization, moreover, are making it easier for more actors with fewer resources and less access to elites to publicize their own arguments and concerns.

Dramatic reductions in the cost of transportation and communications mean that massive outreach is no longer a monopoly of big companies or organizations with deep pockets. Today, smaller, poorer groups with creative flair can use cellular telephones, computers, and faxes or can put representatives on the road to network and organize campaigns rapidly and effectively. Granted, a serious digital and economic divide between developed and developing countries still excludes many potential participants. As Shelton points out, "the paucity of African NGOs with capacity to attract international media coverage accounts for less attention to African human rights problems." But overall, the number of actors with the ability to network and reach large audiences continues to rise. With that expansion comes more competition for attention.

Effective choices about how to define and present global issues to capture public and policy-making attention are central to effective agenda setting. The settings or frames that seem to work best are those that:

- Possess the emotional resonance to appeal to values of fairness, justice, and responsibility;

- Incite fear;
- Touch the immediate interests of citizens, government decision makers, and businesses; and
- Couple problems with solutions and show remedies to be possible, practical, and affordable.[6]

The message has to be a powerful one. Particularly in information-overloaded wealthy countries, single-issue, emotional, or sensational presentations that arouse feelings of empathy, anger about injustice or unfairness, or fear produce the strongest responses—a reality not lost on publicity- and money-hungry groups with self-interested, short-term motives. Not all global issues, however, can generate passion. Emotion-laden issues like dolphins and sweatshops do. Topics like money laundering and income inequality that are harder to personalize are among the many less "camera-ready" issues that get crowded out and side-tracked.

Kathleen Newland (chapter 13) notes that historical analogies have worked well in bringing home the plight of refugees: "A refugee outflow is more likely to get the attention of Western politicians and publics if the perpetrator can be portrayed as a latter day Hitler (Pol Pot) or Stalin (Saddam Hussein) and the threat to the targeted population is cast as genocidal." Brian Langille (chapter 12) argues that emotional presentations have at times worked well for labor rights advocacy groups, but only with clamorous concerns that involve high-profile, brand-name corporations such as Nike.

Emotion-laden charges do not have to be accurate to have effect. In 1995, Greenpeace grabbed the media spotlight by predicting an environmental disaster when the Royal Dutch/Shell Group planned to dispose of its Brent Spar oil rig by sinking it in the North Sea. Independent scientific analyses had concluded that the environmental effects would be inconsequential. Greenpeace got the issue onto the international agenda, and Shell backed down.

Casting global issues in terms of core national economic and security interests, especially in rich and influential countries, has also had some success. Advocates' and scholars' arguments over the last decade framing poverty, transboundary crime, infectious disease, and environmental issues in terms of security threats helped to put these concerns on the agenda of governments in Western countries and, through them, involve the OECD, G-8, and other multilateral institutions.[7]

Presentations that couple problems with solutions have been especially important in getting policy makers' attention. Phil Williams (chapter 3) argues that when the G-8 issued forty recommendations on transnational crime, the effect was to send a strong message that remedial measures would work. Peter Richardson (chapter 2) asserts that the success of the transnational anti-corruption movement was due in large measure to the way the issue was framed. Not only did the movement provide solid data and analysis to demonstrate that corruption is a significant impediment to economic growth, but it also defined workable, corrective steps.

Power of Partnerships. To win respect and, beyond that, action, unofficial actors do well to find a state's shoulders on which to stand. The coordinator and members of the anti-landmine campaign, for instance, readily attribute its success to the highly effective partnership they achieved with governments and government officials, noting Canada first and foremost. Founded in mutual respect and shared goals, that coalition came to include the International Committee of the Red Cross (ICRC) and UN agencies, valuable door-openers in parts of the world like East Asia, the Middle East, and parts of Africa where civil society is less vigorous.[8] Within the team effort, though, the link with Canada and other small and medium-sized states was decisive in moving from the agenda to the accord stage.

Many other NGO successes occurred when they engaged the support of catalytic decision makers or organizations possessing great bureaucratic or symbolic influence. Peter Richardson attributes much of the success of the anticorruption movement, for instance, to activists' ability to link up with powerful states (the United States), international organizations (World Bank, International Monetary Fund, Organization for Economic Cooperation and Development), and businesses with leverage in and outside the United States. On development assistance, Gwin (chapter 4) argues that the Jubilee 2000 campaign to relieve the debt of the poorest countries was aided by three major players—the Pope, the U.S. Treasury secretary, and the president of the World Bank. Similarly, as Williams notes, domestic NGOs and transnational networks succeed when they get major states to focus on crime issues and when they work with powerful institutions like Interpol. ECPAT (End Child Prostitution in Asian Tourism), for example, successfully pushed key states to act on human rights issues associated with crime.

In the international trade arena, when business and labor interests come together, they form redoubtable coalitions. Aggarwal writes:

> When faced with growing imports from Japan in the 1950s, the U.S. textile industry pressed for protection. . . . Although labor and business were at odds on many matters, they came together on the protection issue. Using access to Congress and pointing to job losses, the coalition was able to halt progress on trade acts that authorized the president to negotiate tariff reductions. In addition, they used the Tariff Commission mechanism to investigate imports to produce new information in support of their protectionist cause. (chapter 6)

Cohesiveness Within Coalitions. Crusades require disciplined crusaders, and the most productive NGOs have been the ones with motivated, responsive members. Richardson (chapter 2), for instance, describes how the approximately eighty far-flung national chapters of Transparency International develop priorities based on local settings but keep an eye on the global effort. The anti-landmine effort, a network that consisted of hundreds of highly skilled nongovernmental groups, managed to avoid internal clashes over priorities by maintaining a remarkably steady focus on a total ban with no exceptions and no loopholes. The uncelebrated leaders of these diverse groups were willing to set aside their separate goals because they recognized that if the game was to be won, not everyone could be team captain. Such lessons in unity are vitally important when the information revolution is increasing the communications power of private organizations relative to that of states. If nongovernmental groups use their newfound strength simply to trumpet individual interests more loudly, the resulting cacophony could drown out any unifying message.

Money. "Who pays the piper," the proverb declares, "calls the tune." Civil society groups, businesses, and even governments with substantial resources to invest in publicizing an issue have clear, though not definitive, advantages in the marketplace of ideas. Relatively few NGOs, however, are well funded. Corporate interests can and do outspend them, as happened in the run-up to the Kyoto negotiations. An extensive, negative ad campaign on prime-time television in the United States characterized the proposed treaty as unfair because it did not require developing countries to control greenhouse gas emissions. That criticism drowned out the pro-Kyoto arguments advanced by environmental groups without the funds to buy comparable access to the public.

The equation is not always so one-sided. Dinah Shelton found that one reason for Amnesty International's success in promoting three international treaties against the death penalty is the substantial funding that the advocacy group has for its global operations. Foundation contributions to NGOs, she adds, translate into influence on the human rights agenda. The Rockefeller Foundation's strong interest in weapons of mass destruction, for instance, "shaped the Arms Watch Program of Human Rights Watch" to the point that a program initially focused only on arms exports to human rights violators expanded into "a separate division on arms control. . . ." The supposedly hand-to-mouth, anti-landmine campaign also had a large enough budget to mount a successful media operation, one that dovetailed with the efforts of the prestigious ICRC.

In one imaginative maneuver, noted by Peter Sand (chapter 7), millions of dollars raised and deployed by Greenpeace and other NGOs opposed to commercial whaling worked a sea change in the membership and outlook of the International Whaling Commission (IWC). Persuading non-whaling states to join the organization—even paying their membership fees in some cases—the NGO action nearly tripled the size of the IWC, from fourteen members in 1972 to thirty-nine in 1982. What some observers saw as an institutional coup d'état put non-whaling interests in control of the commission and over time altered the focus of the IWC from managing whaling to saving whales.[9]

The influence of money is unremarkable. The exceptional cases of civil society activists having the funds to amplify their views are just that—exceptional. The reality is that official and corporate interests hold the upper hand in this area. On trade issues, for example, business interests have been instrumental in pushing for open markets following deregulation and internationalization, with bankers, investors, and other market-movers giving strong backing to agenda changes that labor groups, environmentalists, and others hotly oppose. When businesses unite in determined support of or opposition to a proposed shift in the agenda, advocates face an uphill battle and, to succeed, need to call on all the other strategic factors that can give them an edge.

Timing. The last of those factors is the genius to make the right choice at the right time—when to launch a campaign, when to float a policy proposal, when to expend political capital in support of an idea and so on. Striking while irons are hot can turn an otherwise limited move into an action that tips the scale decisively toward change. If, for example, big states are strongly united for or against an issue or agenda item, lesser states and/or NGOs may stand little chance of attracting attention, even with brilliant ideas and high-decibel megaphones. On the other hand, moments when individual governments are weaker, such as immediately after an election, or when groups of states are fractured—as they were at the 1999 World Trade Organization (WTO) Seattle Ministerial—present windows of opportunity for less powerful actors. They can turn what in other contexts might be an incremental action into one that makes a decisive opening for change.[10] In one remarkable stroke of luck, a small group of U.S. Senators hoping to educate lawmakers and the public about the potential dangers of climate change happened to organize hearings to present scientific evidence on a summer day in 1988 that turned out to be the hottest on record—in what was then the hottest decade on record.

To win a place on the global issues agenda for an unorthodox or neglected concern does not require that all the planets be in perfect alignment. Dedication in the ranks can compensate for some lack of sophistication in the propaganda. If all the ingredients are present, however, the chances of outsiders transforming their concerns into the subjects of an international negotiation rise impressively.

NEGOTIATING INTERGOVERNMENTAL AGREEMENTS

As the number and variety of performers have ballooned in recent decades, so has the complexity of international negotiations. By way of contrast, in the early days of the Congress of Vienna, only a handful of leaders from the four great European powers—and not any of the 215 minor German princelings also in attendance—shaped decisions. A little more than a century later the Versailles Peace Conference brought together just twenty-seven states, the victors of World War I. The founders of the United Nations in 1945 numbered fifty-one. Today 189 UN members can vote in the General Assembly.

Inflation in the number of sovereign states claiming a seat at international gatherings is, however, only one complicating factor in a process that is rarely smooth. Another is the emergence of the influential nonstate agents discussed in the preceding section who may not even have expert or observer status but who can, from off stage, significantly affect the climate of negotiations and the latitude of the negotiators. A third determinant of mounting complexity, arguably the strongest of the forces at work, is the almost encyclopedic range of subject matter under discussion. Contemporary trade talks no longer deal only with tariff reductions but also with the size of openings in commercial fishing nets, guarantees on the repatriation of investments, and restrictions on exporting hazardous waste. Arms control pacts may hinge on debates about the frequency of inspections and the certification of inspectors. Negotiations on the global commons can reach from the wastes of Antarctica to the chill of the stratosphere.

Where states meet states to try to find shared interests and transform them into formal mutual obligations, even the preliminary steps are elaborate. They involve decisions on institutional settings, participants, and decision-making procedures. Separately or collectively, the participants have to define their goals going in and some of their bargaining strategies, how broadly or narrowly they wish to set the substantive focus of the exercise, how or whether to propose confidence-building measures and to put compensation packages on the table. Either at this preparatory stage or soon thereafter, one or more participants must assume a leadership role just to keep the negotiation on track, steering the process toward concrete ends and shepherding the others through workable compromises to an outcome all parties can consider their own.

All Power to Whom?

In most institutional settings, the great powers hold decisive leverage and exert it quite overtly. Discriminatory or weighted voting controls negotiations on international peace and security issues, as well as decisions on some international economic issues. The permanent members of the UN Security Council—China, France, Russia, the United Kingdom, and the United States—have veto power over all Security Council decisions on peace and security issues. This practice has not always led to successful negotiations or quick decisions; indeed, it has often held up bargaining and UN action. The International Monetary Fund (IMF) and the World Bank also employ discriminatory voting procedures, with voting power in their top councils based on members' capital contributions. The arrangement ensures that those who furnish the most resources have proportionate influence over collective decisions. It also gives powerful states an added reason—beyond their interest in international financial stability and the export earnings that development credits generate for them—to support the system.[11]

Another great-power gambit is the threat to pull out of an international agency—possibly undermining its finances and effectiveness—if the institution's plans and conduct stray too far from the great power's interests. The U.S. decision to leave the UN Educational, Scientific, and Cultural Organization (UNESCO) in 1985 is one example of the threat being put into practice. A discontented principal player, though, has another option: pushing others to agree to shift consideration of an issue from one negotiating forum to another more receptive to its interests, a maneuver sometimes called forum switching.

Often, however, great powers exert their influence through the power of persuasion, prevailing when the international context favors them, when their credibility on a given issue is high, or when timing or other considerations work in their favor. As Aggarwal points out, other powers accepted U.S. hegemony more easily during the post–World War II recovery phase and within the overarching Cold War context. Even then, of course, the U.S. ability to set the agenda did not automatically lead to trade agreements. Similarly, as Gwin notes of a different policy universe, although the economically powerful states that provide the lion's share of development assistance—mainly Organization for Economic Cooperation and Development (OECD) countries—can often dictate agendas and priorities, they cannot always force their will on aid recipients.

Although powerful and rich states continue to dominate many international negotiations, other players, formerly mere spectators, can now maneuver their way into key slots. The blurring of older geopolitical divides enables weaker states to exert leverage through coalitions. More fluid than Cold War alliances, such coalitions are now common in multilateral negotiations. Small and medium-sized powers enjoy greater ability to stall or block negotiations until their interests are acknowledged, if not fully satisfied. Thomas Bernauer (chapter 16) observes that countries such as India and Iran—states critical of the nuclear status quo—have spearheaded blocking coalitions in negotiations in the mid-1990s of the Comprehensive Test Ban Treaty.

The interventions are not necessarily negative. Canada's role in the effort to ban landmines put it at the head of a partnership with other small and medium-sized powers and transnational civil society groups. Among the determinants of power in addressing many global challenges, knowledge, expertise, reputation, and persuasive ability can be as decisive as wealth or military muscle. In global commons negotiations, Christopher Joyner finds that:

> Given the close association between international economics, communications, maritime, and environmental matters, the dominant players in commons space regimes are likely to be developed states. But salient exceptions occur. . . . In

Antarctic Treaty meetings, Chile and Argentina, by virtue of being claimant states and closest to the continent, play exceptional roles. (chapter 9)

Aggarwal sees that in trade negotiations, as well, small and middle-sized powers have sometimes maneuvered successfully "by alternating between the roles of 'supporter' and 'spoiler' of hegemonic initiatives." Developing countries that opposed negotiations on trade in services also balked at Northern pressure to negotiate extensive market-opening reforms in the area of financial services. "Over a protracted negotiation period of ten years," he writes, "the United States withdrew its offer several times and pressured countries individually to wear down the anti–financial services coalition." The tactic failed, at least during the Uruguay Round, and talks did not produce a financial services agreement until 1999.

Advancing a solution rather than blocking one, a lesser state (Poland) was able to couple its goals with those of a more activist international organization secretariat to propel important negotiations forward. During talks on the UN Convention Against Transnational Organized Crime, when governments were focused on principle rather than practical measures, the frustrated Polish government tipped the debate toward specific negotiations. "Initially," says Phil Williams, "developing countries supported the idea of moving to a convention against transnational organized crime." Several Western countries that had conceptual and legal reservations also feared that any negotiated convention would be hollow and toothless, written to accommodate the least committed parties. "During 1995 and 1996," however, the tide began to turn when a "survey by the UN Secretariat revealed that a majority of states favored the idea," Williams records, and "a Group of Senior Experts [established by the G-8] developed forty recommendations to help combat transnational organized crime." Those inputs, overcoming much of the previous skepticism, paved the way for Poland to put forward a draft framework in September 1996, "transform[ing] the discussion from an abstract debate about desirability to a more specific focus on what the convention would look like." The outcome was a document that put the emphasis on fundamental problems, focusing on organized crime, rather than single offenses such as trade in endangered species or trade in sex.

NGOs have been highly influential behind the scenes at least since the 1945 negotiations on the UN Charter. The great powers' original draft contained no reference to human rights, as Shelton reads the record, but under pressure from NGOs—particularly American ones—the subject gained prominent mention in the charter. That victory then gave impetus to follow-on talks from which the detailed 1948 Universal Declaration on Human Rights emerged. Even earlier, European and U.S.-based peace groups lobbied at various international peace conferences, and NGOs such as the Institut de Droit International and the International Law Association, both formed in 1873, contributed substantially to the development of international law.[12]

More recently, some NGOs have won formal observer status at international organizations and negotiations, enabling them to make declarations and submit written documents to the official delegations. The United Nations, in particular, has generally facilitated NGO access to negotiations. World conferences such as the 1992 UN Conference on the Environment and Development in Rio de Janeiro and the 1994 Cairo Conference on Population and Development have been particularly instrumental in giving NGOs a voice.

In preparations for Rio, where the draft of Agenda 21 represented the thinking of many environmental advocacy groups, some NGOs helped to forge a coalition of almost forty small island states inside climate change negotiations. The U.K.-based Centre for International Environmental Law, moreover, became a de facto negotiator at the table and in the hallways—drafting policy statements and coordinating coalition positions and strategy.[13] In negotiating on real battlefields rather than assembly halls, NGOs have sometimes succeeded as intermediaries between warring parties because, Sisk notes, they are usually perceived as well-intentioned neutrals. During the civil war in Mozambique, for instance, an Italian NGO, the Comunità di Sant'Egidio, was instrumental—along with the United Nations, the Organization of African Unity, and the United States—in arranging the informal meetings between the warring parties that eventually led to a peace settlement in 1990.

Outside the decorous bargaining sessions, NGOs have flexed their muscles in street protests against global financial liberalization, issues toward which they had traditionally been indifferent. As party crashers in 1997, 600 or so boisterous organizations—labor unions, environmentalists, and consumer groups—from nearly seventy countries helped scuttle negotiations for a Multilateral Agreement on Investment.[14] Allied again with well-funded labor groups and others, NGOs assailed the WTO Seattle ministerial meeting in December 1999, bringing the trade talks to a halt. These interventions have had the effect of breaking the monopoly of buttoned-up financial technocrats on decisions that are not just about capital and credit but, in the eyes of NGOs, about exploiting labor and natural resources. In the arms control field, NGOs achieved near partner status with states in the Ottawa Process negotiations leading to the 1997 convention banning anti-personnel landmines. In that case, the NGO presence took the form of speeches inside the hall, participation in shaping decisions in hallways and meeting rooms, and formal comments on drafts.

Private sector interests, too, can exercise great sway over the course of many multilateral negotiations, traditionally by molding the policies of powerful states in advance of diplomatic encounters and through independent activity for or against the official position of the countries where they are headquartered. Transnational corporations take an active role in areas such as telecommunications, trade and labor negotiations, and even in arms control talks, where the chemical industry became a crucial participant in developing the Chemical Weapons Convention of 1993. The coincidence of private and governmental interests has allowed firms to enshrine their views of intellectual property rights, for instance, in WTO rules and to match European Union (EU) standards in some fields to industry wishes. On climate change issues, in contrast, many energy firms have vigorously opposed the government line and lobbied heavily at Kyoto against various proposals for mandatory reduction in emissions of greenhouse gases.

Where there is smoke, however, the fire is not necessarily a conflagration. Separately, neither the second-rank states nor the private sector lobbies nor the most effective advocacy groups have achieved more than intermittent successes in shaping global bargains that the great powers opposed or discounted. Nor should anyone expect the major players to cede their dominance or discretion easily or soon. What is significant instead is the nibbling on the margins, the movement away from monopoly negotiating clout to broader sharing of responsibility.

Choosing the Type of Agreement

Negotiated agreements run such a gamut of possible shapes and weights that it is not unusual for participants to enter into talks uncertain of how ambitious a bargain, if any, can be struck. The possibilities include framework accords—comprehensive in their scope—or partial ones that focus on either single issues or a narrow spectrum of related issues. The outcome, as well, can be a legally binding instrument or a nonbinding agreement also known as soft law.

Broader or Narrower? Broad framework agreements, such as the 1985 Vienna Convention for the Protection of the Ozone Layer, can provide structure, coherence, and momentum to subsequent negotiations and actions. As crowbars that open up bargaining space, they are particularly useful in issue areas where knowledge is sparse, where resource implications are uncertain, and where negotiating environments are quickly changing. A framework accord or a convention that anticipates follow-on protocols to be concluded separately can impart some thrust to the bargaining process, codify political intent and commitment, and also allow for regional diversity. Their main shortcomings—not unlike those of formal treaty making in general— include the protracted periods of time required to produce real behavioral change and the role they play in reinforcing tendencies to seek lowest common denominators. Importantly, they can also foster a false sense of accomplishment.

Partial or single-issue agreements are sometimes easier to negotiate. Most of the arms control negotiations in the 1960s and 1970s were designed to produce such circumscribed agreements—such as a ban on nuclear testing or the militarization of space. Thomas Bernauer believes that partial approaches in the arms control field— such as export controls—have helped to curb proliferation of weapons of mass destruction when global prohibition regimes are out of reach or existing agreements have not been fully implemented. Trade negotiations have also been dominated by single-issue and step-by-step efforts. In the late 1940s, states that could not agree on a broad trade liberalization declaration could assent to a piecemeal approach. Similarly, in the health field, international interventions often focus on specific diseases— for example, smallpox, polio, malaria, or AIDS. This expedient, argues Octavio Gómez Dantés (chapter 10), reflects a tendency to treat symptoms without addressing underlying causes. Attempts to adopt more encompassing approaches, as seen in campaigns to focus on primary health care, have generally failed.

The choice of a general Framework Convention on Climate Change to be followed by specific protocols was, among other things, a reaction against the seemingly endless UN Law of the Sea (UNLOS) Treaty negotiations. That comprehensive, closely detailed pact, ultimately rejected by the United States and opposed by other key powers, came out of negotiations that James K. Sebenius in 1991 characterized as "universally inclusive with respect to issues and participants." Because the talks "virtually required consensus on a comprehensive package deal," the ultimate results were in effect held "hostage to the most reluctant party on the most difficult issue." In contrast, climate change negotiations sought to build on the success of the framework-plus-protocol model for ozone-layer action. "This step-by-step framework-protocol alternative has attractive negotiating features," Sebenius noted, ". . . but it is worth recalling that the failure of precisely this approach—negotiation of separate 'miniconventions,' analogous to protocols—in earlier LOS conferences (in 1958 and 1960) indirectly led back to the comprehensive package approach of the 1973 LOS conference."[15]

Although the broad sweep of a framework agreement can build a foundation for action and foster new thinking, it does not automatically spur progress beyond the initial agreement. As a practical matter, therefore, states are likely to tackle single issues—even global ones—as a more manageable approach better designed to achieve concrete resolutions. The resulting challenge is to give purposeful direction and momentum to the negotiation of limited pacts so that, in increments, they further a strategic vision.

Binding or Nonbinding? The apparent dichotomy between legally binding agreements and those that impose no such obligations is sometimes more semantic than significant. In practice, negotiators often produce agreements that entail varying degrees of commitment. The binding nature of a bargain does not necessarily ensure its effectiveness, and voluntary rules or standards occasionally prove highly effective. As implements for managers of global issues, the two forms of accord can be compared to flat-head and Phillips screwdrivers—tools to be used according to circumstances and the job to be done.

Quicker and easier to negotiate because they usually need not go through lengthy legislative ratification processes, nonbinding agreements have a high degree of flexibility, making them more easily renegotiated or abandoned. Among their deficits is the risk that they will sap momentum in dealing with issues that require further, urgent, and tough action. When they are declaratory rather than operational, as Joyner points out, the process of negotiating them may be useful when consensus is lacking and when large numbers of parties are involved.[16] Such declarations have been utilized in all of the issue areas considered in this book. The 1948 Universal Declaration on Human Rights, the 1975 Final Act of the Conference on Security and Cooperation in Europe, and the environmental action program adopted by the Rio Conference in 1992 (Agenda 21) are all examples. Along with broad promises to settle disputes peacefully, the parties to the Final Act also accepted and implemented a few specific and useful operational obligations, ranging from military confidence-building measures to the rights of business representatives and accredited journalists to multiple entry-and-exit visas.

Operational—as opposed to hortatory—instruments can be used to test solutions to specific problems and may serve as interim steps toward binding agreements. Particularly effective in rapidly changing technical environments, they have been used frequently in the environmental field, often preceding hard-law treaty commitments, and in the telecommunications sector, where technical standards have to be updated frequently. Export controls during the Cold War were based on soft-law agreements; so is much of the international cooperative effort in law enforcement and international finance. The Basel Committee, for example, operates without a constitution or formal bylaws, and all of its policy decisions are voluntary and nonbinding.

Some of these nonbinding pacts have generated very real results.[17] Ten European countries, for example, agreed in 1984 that they would voluntarily exceed requirements of the 1979 Geneva Convention on Long-Range Transboundary Air Pollution. They undertook to reduce their sulphur dioxide emissions by as much as thirty percent—an action that created a "bandwagon effect" and soon led to all parties formally adopting stricter requirements.[18]

Matching Effectiveness with Inclusiveness

The Trojan War stemmed from the failure of a bridal couple to invite Eris, the deity of discord, to their nuptials. Her revenge was the gift of a golden apple, a trophy for which the three chief goddesses disastrously competed. The mythical episode suggests a moral for policy makers organizing global rites: exclude at your peril. Unfortunately, the reverse is also sensible practice: include at your peril. The truth is that questions on the length and breadth of international invitation lists admit of no immutable answers. A highly participatory negotiation can be difficult to keep orderly. Secret-handshake gatherings, on the other hand, run the risk of reaching accords that non-initiates will neither accept nor carry out.

And beyond choosing which states to put on the door list, organizers increasingly have to decide whether and where to place unofficial representatives with a claim to admission. Seating them only as observers to be seen but not heard can deny the negotiation the benefit of their knowledge. It may also prejudice effective action they might otherwise contribute in the implementation stage. But mingling NGOs, scholars, and representatives of private enterprise with officials on an equal footing can also confuse the proceedings and diminish the commitment of the state participants.

As the next pages illustrate, the complications of global diplomatic etiquette are multiplying, and with them so have the options for imaginative response. None of those discussed below appears to be uniformly applicable. In their variety, instead, is an indication that experimentation can be fruitful.

Global or Circumscribed? Logic would seem to dictate that global issues be handled in global assemblies, but experience does not teach such crisp lessons. Established after World War II to deal with problems affecting the entire international community, the United Nations would seem almost foreordained as the sponsor for global negotiations on a range of issues including international security. While UN-forged agreements led to effective collective action in some crucial areas—conflicts in Cyprus and El Salvador, for instance—the hope that the United Nations would be the primary site for negotiating international peace and security agreements has not been realized. Argentina and Chile, for instance, eventually chose the Pope over the UN as mediator of their dispute over the Beagle Strait.[19] Even on some unquestionably global concerns, the role of the United Nations and other large multilateral forums has been circumscribed. For instance, the 66-member Geneva-based Conference on Disarmament—set up in 1979 as the sole multilateral forum for disarmament negotiations—was preempted on landmine and CTBT negotiations in 1996.

The United Nations and large multilateral forums like the Conference on Disarmament, nonetheless, give negotiations conducted under their auspices great legitimacy and permit small and medium-sized countries to weigh in where their interests might be affected. Moreover, the permanent or quasi-permanent nature of many UN forums provides continuity and facilitates ongoing exchanges of ideas. Continuity does foster the accumulation of knowledge, and the United Nations offers a mechanism for learning and socialization. Finally, it allows for a flexible mix of formal and informal negotiations in a setting that helps to keep channels of communication open even when negotiating positions are far apart.

Set against those positive features are a number of drawbacks. Discussions under UN auspices rarely produce quick results. Negotiations involving a great number of participants are inherently arduous, requiring the reconciliation of many interests through complex tradeoffs that require a more informal setting than the United Nations generally offers. A common result is a scaling-down of aspirations to produce limited agreements based on lowest common denominators. Finally, under the consensus rule—de rigueur in most UN forums—coalitions of small powers can hold up negotiations and play spoiler roles.

Given the difficulties of bargaining in a crowded bazaar, negotiators often prefer regional or other limited encounters, even bilateral ones. With fewer participants and a higher likelihood that the members of the club will be like-minded, such sessions can be easier to move forward. When, for instance, a small group of countries (including India and Iran) blocked progress during CTBT negotiations, a coalition of like-minded states favoring a comprehensive ban on nuclear testing yanked negotiations out of the original venue, redrafted the treaty, then put it up for signature in the UN General Assembly.[20] The failure to conclude the CTBT in the Conference on Disarmament (CD), contends Thomas Bernauer, suggests "that the golden age of negotiating global regimes for WMD [weapons of mass destruction] in the CD is over." The type of cooperative structure represented by the CTBT experience "has the advantage of allowing for the case-specific composition of negotiating groups and the exclusion of permanent naysayers that tend to lower standards."

The disadvantage of ostracizing eligible participants can come when talk shifts to action. Leaving certain actors out of negotiations to stem proliferation of WMD, Bernauer reflects further, has sometimes hindered implementation: "[T]hose actors—states, firms, and other actors—that are located on the demand side of the proliferation problem are not involved in efforts to solve it." Development assistance strategies that only reflect donors' interests also prove hard to execute, distinctly harder than those that emerge in tune with local priorities, cultivate a sense of ownership among recipients, and delegate to local groups and institutions the responsibility for implementation and accountability for results.

An additional risk is that success in regional and limited negotiations may halt progress on the global front. Indeed, if global problems are dealt with regionally, those in the region may have little incentive to push for further, deeper progress. For example, Aggarwal argues that the conclusion of regional agreements in the trade arena may actually undercut global trade agreements.[21]

Making Room for Nonstate Participants.   Even though outsiders, as noted earlier, have inserted themselves into some multilateral negotiations, the practice was usually infrequent and informal until the late 1980s. Times have changed.

No longer simply tolerating participation by nonstate actors, governments sometimes invite them, hoping that the additional players, including businesses likely to both benefit from and play important parts in implementation, will help produce more effective agreements. Peter Haas, for instance, describes how business groups in "multilateral environmental negotiations and institutions helped generate better information about policy options, technical feasibility, and environmental benefits and thus shaped more effective treaties and compliance." Enforcement of the International Convention for the Prevention of Pollution from Ships (MARPOL) design standards to reduce operational oil pollution from tankers, he adds, "falls, in practice, to the insurance industry, because insurance providers do not want to be liable for oil spill cleanups or for paying for faulty tankers. Consequently shipyards and tanker owners have no choice but to comply with the state written regime." Implementation of the Montreal Protocol to halt depletion of the ozone layer has progressed well, partly because the process of consultation and scientific advice surrounding the negotiations included such major chemical manufacturers as Dupont from the start.

Haas also discusses the delicate balance needed in deciding whether the inclusion of businesses in drafting environmental agreements risks weakening the provisions and, if so, whether that tradeoff promotes better outcomes. "[N]ot all target groups," he observes, "contribute to compliance. In the 1970s and 1980s, most target groups opposed any international regimes and, when present in the negotiations, tried to dismiss the need for a regime or urged voluntary measures." Recording the intransigent opposition of timber companies to international efforts to promote sustainable tropical forestry, Haas emphasizes the need for a workable match "between the potential for market gains for the target groups and compliance."

As insiders at a negotiation, NGOs, too, can be either useful or distracting. On the positive side, they can break deadlocks in case of impasse. During the Law of the Sea negotiations, Quaker and Methodist NGOs organized a workshop to introduce developed and developing country delegates to a Massachusetts Institute of Technology computer model of deep-ocean mining. The model

> came to be widely accepted in the face of the great uncertainty felt by the delegates about the engineering and economic aspects of deep-seabed mining. . . . Indeed, the delegates over time came to make frequent use of the model for learning, mutual education, and invention of new options—and even as a political excuse to move from frozen positions.[22]

The risk of distraction, however, grows with the number of interest groups circling the hall. As one of the editors of this volume has written elsewhere:

> [O]pening up the floodgates to allow equal access to every group would frustrate decision making. More than 1,500 NGOs were accredited at the 1992 United Nations Conference on the Environment and Development in Rio de Janeiro, for example. Trying to include them all was impossible, so in the final days of the conference, government delegates increasingly retreated behind closed doors. On the other hand, narrowing the field is extraordinarily difficult because no one

algorithm or set of criteria can objectively rank the worth of [outside groups] to a participatory process.[23]

Common practice has involved accrediting qualified outside groups and giving them limited access as observers. Under the United Nations' formal but flexible system for NGO participation in the Economic and Social Council (ECOSOC), the Council

> ranks NGOs according to three tiers of status. . . . The small percentage of those with [top access] have more opportunities to attend meetings, submit written advice, and occasionally speak at conferences. . . . In 1998, more than 1,500 NGOs [had] top status, versus 978 in 1995, and 41 in 1948. NGOs want more, governments want less, but the system generally works.[24]

Another route into the negotiating process is through membership in government delegations, a status sometimes granted to civil society groups and to businesses. Typically, the crossover from private spokesman to temporary public servant occurs where the interests of the outsiders and those of the government coincide. Telecommunications is one such field. U.S. delegations to the International Telecommunications Union (ITU), for instance, not only routinely include corporate representatives and an occasional academic or industry analyst, but also businesspersons frequently serve as ambassadors and heads of delegations to treaty-making conferences. According to William Drake (chapter 1), the spread of liberalization and market entry has made hybrid delegations more common, "particularly among the industrialized and upper income developing countries that account for most of the global industry's revenues."

Although these hybrid delegations increase the supply of expertise during negotiations and can increase the level of stakeholder support for negotiated outcomes, such inclusiveness has its risks. In reviewing the practice, Drake observes that multisectoral delegations can be more difficult for governments to manage. Furthermore, he adds,

> some delegation members may not be fully aware of the relevant institutional history and the bargaining strategies in play. In addition, lacking a certain deftness in multilateral negotiations, they may fail to sing from the same hymnal in explaining their delegation's positions and hence get played off against one another by crafty counterparts. (chapter 1)

Additionally, a backlash that may prove temporary but is currently under way comes from many countries objecting to what they see as interlopers—companies that act on a global scale—sitting in on serious interstate discussions. Drake, in fact, notes that such objections arise particularly when, as is often the case, the guests are part of U.S. delegations. Ironically, some of the same states that supported intimate NGO participation during the negotiations of the 1997 treaty to ban landmines—for example, France—were later annoyed by the activism of NGOs during the 1998 negotiations in Rome on establishing a permanent International Criminal Court. They subsequently condoned initiatives to restrict NGO participation in multilateral negotiations.[25] For example, NGO participation at the 2000 conference on the advancement of women, commonly known as "Beijing Plus Five," in the UN Commission on Human Rights, and in the CD has been curtailed. States have also put the brakes on NGO participation in the 2001 negotiations on a small arms convention. By the end of the 1990s, while representatives of states and officials of international organizations were paying lip service to the importance of NGOs, they were also making it more difficult for NGOs to have formal access to global negotiations.[26]

A different sort of problem can arise when experts, scholars, and scientists with both public and private credentials serve as members of national delegations to international conferences where the technical nature of many agenda items requires their presence and knowledge. An unfortunate political downside to this practice is the disadvantage it can impose on developing countries at gatherings where expertise holds sway and they arrive almost empty-handed. Such a gap was a factor in the Law of the Sea talks and has been a problem in arms control negotiations. To bridge such divides, international organizations can help to share the intellectual wealth more fairly by assembling specialized information, serving as central reference points, and providing technical assistance to one and all. For example, the International Panel on Climate Change (IPCC)—set up under the auspices of the UN Environment Program (UNEP) and the World Meteorological Organization (WMO)—brought together experts and scientists from both North and South. It was instrumental in identifying the problem of global warming and in creating a common frame of reference with respect to the problem.[27]

Looking ahead, innovation—in terms of the inclusion of nonstate players—appears more and more likely to modify tradition. The current trend seems to be running toward inclusiveness. Increasingly in official negotiations on global issues, it is reasonable to expect that national delegations will have some distinctly nonofficial tinges.

Keys to Compromise

As the range of subject matter and the diversity of participants involved in efforts to manage global issues both increase, some long-standing techniques have been reworked as devices to facilitate agreement. A practice that once involved the exchange of hostages—often royal ones—between antagonistic kingdoms now, in the form of confidence-building measures (CBMs), involves the exchange of information and even inspectors. Compensation packages now appear as arrangements to lighten the burdens on economically weaker participants.

Confidence Building. The fear that some parties may cheat on an agreement can be lively enough to stymie diplomacy. In such circumstances, extra effort needs to go into building trust. CBMs such as exchanges of experts and information to increase transparency can increase mutual knowledge and may ease the course of negotiations.[28]

CBMs have been widely used in arms control. The term came into common usage through the 1975 Final Act of the Conference on Security and Cooperation in Europe. It referred to a set of military measures—for instance, inviting observers to military exercises of a specified size and giving advance notification of major troop movements—that sought to reduce the risk of unintended war and surprise attack. Having come over time to encompass the aim of enhancing knowledge about capabilities and intentions, CBMs also seek to reduce suspicions and misperceptions so that uncertainty shrinks and the resulting environment facilitates further talks. Among the measures in use are data exchanges and experiments with methods to verify agreements. Although they are not panaceas, some CBMs can make significant contributions to negotiations on many global issues, and unlike other instruments, they have few, if any, downsides.

Trial inspections, for instance, are often very effective in increasing confidence that proposed solutions are workable. As Thomas Bernauer notes, the trial inspections in military facilities and civilian chemical plants organized during the chemical weapons negotiations "alleviated concerns about the protection of confidential military and business information and [were] at least partly responsible for remarkably reducing opposition of military and business circles against monitoring mechanisms proposed for the CWC [Chemical Weapons Convention]."

Compensation. A successful negotiation requires that most participants perceive the results as equitable. When costs are unevenly distributed under an accord, measures to compensate the disadvantaged may sweeten the deal. Differential obligations and incentives (including financial incentives and technical assistance) enable negotiators to even things out. Such bonuses are not always irresistible. According to Thomas Bernauer, Kathleen Newland, and Joanna Spear, if the reasons for not participating are what the holdouts see as non-negotiable interests—for example, fundamental security concerns—differential obligations and incentives will not break the impasse.

Differential undertakings that assign asymmetric rights and obligations take into account disparities among the parties and look forward to ways to improve the odds of successful implementation, particularly in the increasingly common situation of signatory states too poor or bureaucratically ill-equipped to shoulder the duties they agree on paper to assume. Fostering equitable, rather than equal, burdens and entitlements, they have been widely used in the environmental field.[29] The 1987 Montreal Protocol on Substances that Deplete the Ozone Layer, for instance, extended up to ten years extra time for economies in transition and developing countries to come into compliance; moreover, the parties set up a fund in 1990 to assist poorer countries with implementation. The Montreal Protocol Fund was linked to the Global Environment Facility (GEF), created as an experiment in 1991 and restructured after the 1992 Earth Summit, which provides supplementary financing as a stimulus to states that would not invest in sustainable development projects without such help. Arms control negotiations have also used various forms of compensation. According to Bernauer, an important attraction to developing countries deciding whether or not to join the Nuclear Nonproliferation Treaty (NPT) and the CWC is the prospect that as members they could have access to commerce in nuclear and chemical materials and technologies for peaceful use.

One of the keys to devising successful compensation packages is having a clear understanding of the economic and political conditions of the would-be beneficiaries. As several authors in this book point out, differential obligations and incentives are most effective when they deal with specific capacity problems and are doled out on a case-by-case basis.

Three main concerns circumscribe the use of differential obligations and incentives. First, compensation packages may be too costly. Second, providing incentives to one party may provoke requests from others, leading, in turn, to burden-sharing problems—deciding who will pay to underwrite the incentives. Ever since 1994, for instance, the Montreal Protocol Fund has been able to approve only a small fraction of funding proposals.[30] Third, parties may engage in extortion, especially when compensation packages are offered from positions of weakness. In the early 1990s, many foreign policy observers, particularly in the United States, believed that North Korea engaged in such blackmail.[31]

ART OF THE POSSIBLE

Given the variety of issues on the global agenda and their tendency to resist neat, conceptual packaging, the rapidity of political and economic change, and the number and diversity of actors claiming roles, the most productive negotiating strategy will keep a range of options open. Twenty-first century diplomacy, like politics, will most of all be the art of the possible. Although no hard and fast rules apply, some general findings emerge from this book.

First, if interim solutions are better than none, a regional or limited deal is usually easier to reach and, with the right follow-up, can set the pattern for something broader. Second, to cement a bargain, CBMs are one of the few negotiating instruments with no inherent downsides. They can do much to promote trust and facilitate negotiations as long as they do not substitute for real engagement and action. Third, in other circumstances, compensation strategies become essential when negotiations involve uneven benefits and costs, as more and more of them do. Sweeteners then are needed to give the parties incentives to carry out their undertakings. Fourth, as between a legal contract and a declaratory one or a broad framework agreement and a single-issue compact, the choice should be a pragmatic one based primarily on what will work and what can be obtained. And finally, since conference tables are not favorable environments for Utopians, an insistence on optimum results can miss the opportunity for progress.

Constant and variegated change is the only predictable pattern for the coming age. Adapting to it will be a basic survival mechanism for the diplomats, business leaders, and citizen standard-bearers who will be working to reach consensus. The overarching lesson of this review of mechanisms for agenda setting and negotiation is that no single compass always points the right way; no one technique will always assure agreement or that agreements will be effective. The corollary to that judgment is the evident virtue of constant experimentation, of trial and error in building coalitions and designing accords. It is generally true, however, that it is at the early stages of global diplomacy that the odds are raised or lowered for success further along the road—when implementing agreements and ensuring compliance constitute the acid test of success.

Those are the challenges discussed in the next and final chapter.

NOTES

1. For this book, an issue is "on the global policy agenda" when it is widely recognized by decision makers, including business leaders and/or publics as being worthy of action. One way to measure success in agenda setting is the amount of time devoted to an issue at high-level political meetings (for example, G-8 meetings), the number of media references to it, and the cooperative actions taken to address it.

2. Nowhere is the influence of powerful states on agenda setting more evident than in the areas of arms control, the military, and humanitarian intervention. Thomas Bernauer claims that great-power dominance in agenda setting on weapons of mass destruction has led to inherently "asymmetrical" ways of framing issues that reflect underlying inequalities. As for conventional weapons, Joanna Spear notes that the unilateral actions of key states heavily influence the agenda and perceptions about what governance efforts are possible. Timothy Sisk argues that powerful states' interests matter most in determining which intrastate conflicts get attention. U.S. and Chinese geopolitical interests vis-à-vis India, for example, help to explain why thoroughgoing discussion of the Kashmir question remains largely off-limits to the UN Security Council, despite UN involvement in the dispute since 1947.

3. John Braithwaite and Peter Drahos, *Global Business Regulation* (Cambridge, U.K.: Cambridge University Press, 2000), p. 147.

4. As one of the editors notes, "A 1994 United Nations document, for example, describes an 'NGO as a non-profit entity whose members are citizens or associations of citizens of one or more countries and whose activities are determined by the collective will of its members in response to the needs of the members of one or more communities with which the NGO cooperates.' This formulation embraces just about every kind of group except for private businesses, revolutionary or terrorist groups, and political parties." See P. J. Simmons, "Learning to Live with NGOs," *Foreign Policy*, no. 112 (Fall 1998), pp. 83–4.

5. See Robert Lawson, "The Ottawa Process: Fast-Track Diplomacy and the International Movement to Ban Anti-Personnel Landmines," in Fen Olser Hampson and Maureen Appel Molot, eds., *Leadership and Dialogue* (Toronto: Oxford University Press Canada, 1998), pp. 81–98.

6. A multiyear study on what frames work best in the United States is being conducted by the Aspen Institute–Rockefeller Brothers Fund's Global Interdependence Initiative. See Susan Bales, "Communicating Global Interdependence," at <http://www. aspeninst.org>.

7. For a review of the literature contributing to this wave of discussion on "new" security threats, see Ann M. Florini and P. J. Simmons, "North America," in Paul B. Stares, ed., *The New Security Agenda: A Global Survey* (Tokyo: Japan Center for International Exchange, 1998), pp. 23–74.

8. See Don Hubert, "The Landmine Ban: A Case Study in Humanitarian Advocacy," Occasional Paper no. 42 (Providence, R.I.: Thomas J. Watson Institute for International Studies, Brown University, 2000).

9. See Steinar Andresen, "The Making and Implementation of Whaling Policies: Does Participation Make a Difference?" in David G. Victor, Kal Raustiala, and Eugene B. Skolnikoff, eds., *The Implementation and Effectiveness of International Environmental Commitments* (Cambridge, Mass.: MIT Press, 1998), pp. 439–40.

10. See Jessica Mathews, "What Did and Didn't Happen in Seattle," *Chemistry Business* (July/August 2000).

11. The unequal nature of these decision-making procedures is regularly questioned. Developing countries as well as many NGOs believe that decision-making power on global issues should not be based solely on military might or financial resources.

12. See Ann M. Florini and P. J. Simmons, "What the World Needs Now," in Ann M. Florini, ed., *The Third Force: The Rise of Transnational Civil Society* (Washington, D.C.: Carnegie Endowment for International Peace, 2000), p. 9.

13. Abram Chayes and Antonia Handler Chayes, *The New Sovereignty: Compliance with International Regulatory Agreements* (Cambridge, Mass.: Harvard University Press, 1995), pp. 260–61.

14. See Stephen J. Kobrin, "The MAI and the Clash of Globalizations," *Foreign Policy*, no. 112 (Fall 1998), pp. 97–109.

15. James K. Sebenius, "Crafting a Winning Coalition: Negotiating a Regime to Control Global Warming," in Jessica Mathews, ed., *Greenhouse Warming: Negotiating a Global Regime* (Washington, D.C.: World Resources Institute, 1991), p. 76.

16. Many other ways exist to characterize soft-law agreements. For a more general discussion on soft versus hard law, see Dinah Shelton, ed., *Commitment and Compliance: The Role of Non-Binding Norms in the International System* (Oxford, U.K.: Oxford University Press,

2000). See also Charles Lipson, "Why Are Some International Agreements Informal?" *International Organization*, vol. 45, no. 4 (Autumn 1991), pp. 489–538; and Anthony Clark Arend, *Legal Rules and International Society* (Oxford, U.K.: Oxford University Press, 1999).

17. Three recent multi-regime studies catalogue the benefits of soft law instruments: Edith Brown Weiss and Harold K. Jacobson, eds., *Engaging Countries: Strengthening Compliance with International Environmental Accords* (Cambridge, Mass.: MIT Press, 1998); Victor, Raustiala, and Skolnikoff, eds., *The Implementation and Effectiveness of International Environmental Agreements*; and Dinah Shelton, ed., *Commitment and Compliance: The Role of Non-binding Norms in the International Legal System* (Oxford, U.K.: Oxford University Press, 2000).

18. Peter H. Sand, "International Cooperation: The Environmental Experience," in Jessica Tuchman Mathews, ed., *Global Environment: The Challenge of Shared Leadership* (New York: W.W. Norton, 1991), p. 248.

19. See "Cascon Case CAR: Chile-Argentina [Beagle Channel] 1977–85" at <http://web.mit.edu/cascon/cases/case_car.html>.

20. Bernauer, chapter 16.

21. See also Robert Z. Lawrence, "Regionalism and the WTO: Should the Rules Be Changed?" in Jeffrey J. Schott, *The World Trading System: Challenges Ahead* (Washington, D.C.: Institute for International Economics, December 1996), pp. 41–61.

22. Sebenius, "Crafting a Winning Coalition," p. 88.

23. Simmons, "Learning to Live with NGOs," p. 90.

24. Ibid., pp. 90–3.

25. See Ann M. Florini, "Lessons Learned," in Florini, ed., *The Third Force*, pp. 214–16; and James A. Paul, *NGOs and the United Nations* (New York: Global Policy Forum, June 1999) at <http://www.globalpolicy.org/ngos>.

26. Scaling back on world conferences (under U.S. pressure) and UN financial troubles are also to blame for diminishing NGO access. However, the thrust of denying NGOs access to multilateral negotiations comes from states influential in the United Nations.

27. Scientists, however, sometimes act more as agents of their national governments than as impartial experts. See Lawrence E. Susskind, *Environmental Diplomacy: Negotiating More Effective Global Agreements* (Oxford, U.K.: Oxford University Press, 1994), pp. 62–81; and Albert Weale and Andrea Williams, "National Science and International Policy," in Arild Underdal, ed., *The Politics of International Environmental Management* (Dordrecht: Kluwer Academic Publishers, 1998), pp. 83–99.

28. On transparency, see Bernard I. Finel and Kristin M. Lord, eds., *Power and Conflict in the Age of Transparency* (New York: Palgrave, 2000). Finel and Lord warn, however, that too much transparency can also undermine sensitive international negotiations and lead to misunderstandings (see pp. 343–44). Indeed, transparency and CBMs may be dangerous when parties are aggressive and not intent on reaching agreements. See also Ann M. Florini, "The End of Secrecy," *Foreign Policy*, no. 111 (Summer 1998), pp. 13–28.

29. See Sand, "International Cooperation," pp. 247–48.

30. The dilemma arose partly because rich parties were slow to pay pledged contributions. See Edith Brown Weiss, "The Five International Treaties: A Living History," in Weiss and Jacobson, eds., *Engaging Countries*, p. 150.

31. For more on the problems of incentives, see Thomas Bernauer, "Positive Incentives in Nuclear Nonproliferation and Beyond," in Bernauer and Ruloff, eds., *The Politics of Positive Incentives in Arms Control*, pp. 160–61.

18

From Accord to Action

P. J. Simmons and Chantal de Jonge Oudraat

CONVERTING THE INTENT behind negotiated agreements and strategies into practical action is like running a marathon over a course pitted with obstacles after the cheering crowds have gone home. Implementation is hard, unglamorous work, but it is also the essence of global problem solving. Identifying the pressing challenges and furnishing a negotiated response to them is so much wasted effort if, after the signing ceremony, the parties return to business as usual. To ensure effective follow-through when consequences, commitment, and resources are unevenly distributed among signatories requires cajolery, collaboration, arm-twisting, encouragement, and the sophistication to know how much of each will work when. The one doomed approach is complacency.

Too often, however, the work of carrying out an accord gets insufficient or misdirected notice. Enforcement in the relatively few cases of willful noncompliance gets disproportionate attention, for example. Just as important is the need to identify and help parties who want to abide by agreements but—due to technical, economic, or human resource constraints—cannot. As agreements proliferate, covering wider terrain and more complex substance, shortfalls in compliance are becoming more common. The increasing frequency of such shortfalls reflects the reality that many weaker and younger states' governments lack the administrative, legal, judicial, and enforcement capacity to oversee and reverse the conduct of private actors whose behavior they are supposed to change.

In such situations, help should be close at hand. Unfortunately, it is not. Often, the international community drops the ball at the design stage, underestimating the impact of built-in weaknesses in an accord. To compound the difficulty, most international organizations charged with monitoring, analysis, assistance, and other implementation activities are abysmally underfunded and overburdened. Our contribu-

690

tors consistently highlight the need to devote significantly more attention and greater resources to managing implementation.

MAKING INTERGOVERNMENTAL AGREEMENTS WORK

The roll call of implementation agents begins with states. As signatories of agreements, they are responsible for putting the terms into effect, first of all, on their territory. The summons to action, however, reaches further. International organizations are also convoked to serve as information coordinators, monitors, and verifiers of intergovernmental agreements. Additionally, they organize technical and capacity-building assistance to countries that otherwise would not be able to implement agreements. Civil society groups and experts closely involved with the issues in play are auxiliary forces, sometimes indispensable ones, in moving along implementation.

Activist nongovernmental organizations (NGOs), pressuring governments from inside and out to comply with agreements, also promote societal changes necessary to make agreements work. Large, well-funded NGOs provide supplementary and respected information on global problems, help to assess the overall effectiveness of international agreements, provide early warning of trouble, and channel technical assistance to help developing countries implement and comply with agreements. Businesses occasionally carry out implementation tasks that states and international organizations cannot accomplish alone. Although often at the root of the problems to be addressed, they wield vast influence, resources, and the ability to shape markets—forces that can alleviate or even remedy threats to well-being. Finally, experts possessing specialized technical, regulatory, and scientific knowledge supply much of the practical expertise, education, and analysis that undergird effective implementation of agreements and goals.

With or without complementary action from other agents, signatory states with the strongest interest in realizing the aims of an agreement carry the chief responsibility for advancing it. Among the techniques that work best, leading by example stands out for its relative simplicity and occasional dramatic impact. Creating a bandwagon effect encourages more parties to take implementation and compliance seriously. A second means of developing momentum is evaluation of the parties' performance, but such appraisals require a nuanced approach. To be productive where compliance is faulty, judgments have to weigh causes, distinguishing between willful and inadvertent failures, between those due to weak resolve or inadequate means, or combinations of these deficiencies.

Without understanding the motivations at work, it is impossible to determine intelligently which response—assistance, coaxing, penalizing, or all three—is most likely to correct the situation. Properly carried out, evaluation is the fundamental means of determining how well or poorly an agreement is working and of isolating the most serious shortcomings to be resolved. Where the flaws in the agreement itself are fatal, evaluation can prevent the parties from wasting more effort on a lost cause and may send them back to the starting line for a new try. More often, though, implementation is feasible—if the parties pursue it with determination and imagination.

Leadership by Example

States can, for instance, generate a follow-the-leader effect if they change their behavior unilaterally. Similarly, state and nonstate actors often try to sway influential private sector actors to abide by or exceed norms in hopes that others will follow suit. The power of example of the major states and corporate actors is central in helping to raise awareness and support for a norm or, through practice, to elevate initially aspirational precepts into sets of binding rules.

A recent, vivid example of the momentum that action by the great powers can generate came in June 2000, when the United States allowed the Financial Action Task Force (FATF) to include Israel, a close U.S. ally, on the FATF's "naming and shaming" list of fifteen countries lacking adequate safeguards against money laundering. According to David Ignatius, U.S. support for that decision, considered long overdue by other countries, demonstrated that the United States was "serious about cracking down on money laundering." The decision set off an extraordinary ripple effect. U.S. allies, satisfied that the United States was no longer playing favorites, began pressuring their friends too—France on Monaco, Great Britain on the Caymans and Bahamas, and so on. Standard & Poor's lowered its bond rating for a top bank in Liechtenstein, and several U.S. and European financial institutions ended relationships with banks in some listed countries. Quite soon, even the listed countries, including Israel, began changing their policies.[1]

Nothing guarantees, however, that the example set by great powers will always be positive. When leading states do not follow governance norms, they set the pattern for others. As Kathleen Newland points out,

> increasingly restrictionist [immigration] policies on the part of European and North American states have been imitated and cited as justification for similar policies in places as distant as Thailand and Tanzania. If wealthy and stable countries cannot bear the burden of proportionally much smaller flows of refugees and asylum seekers, how should poor and struggling countries be expected to cope? (chapter 13)

In the case of the international telecommunications regime, William Drake (chapter 1) reports, private firms, many of them U.S.-based, had long chafed at a variety of restrictions. The information revolution had increased their power, and with their backing, Washington not only disregarded rules it opposed but called regularly for "thorough liberalization." Drake writes,

> the growing noncompliance of leading firms and the United States has eroded other players' commitment to the rules, a problem complicated by the difficulty of detecting some types of cheating. . . . And when the United States left the fold and authorized private competitors to Intelsat, other countries—after a period of decrying American unilateralism—began to do the same thing. (chapter 1)

In another instance of private sector interests steering government away from prompt, good-faith implementation, some chemical and pharmaceutical makers carped that the monitoring provisions of the Chemical Weapons Convention (CWC) were too costly on one hand and too likely to compromise trade secrets on the other. Accepting that view, says Thomas Bernauer, the U.S. government, while scrupulous in reporting its military activities, failed

> for more than two years beyond the deadline . . . to bring its civilian chemical industry under the regime's monitoring system. . . . Ironically, just as former communist countries fully heeded Cold War–time Western requests for very intrusive inspections, Western governments were withdrawing to proposals for more modest compliance mechanisms, not least under the influence of business interests. (chapter 16)

In important areas, however, exemplary conduct has advanced important goals and processes. Bernauer describes, for instance, the positive effect of the decision by the United States and United Kingdom in the early 1970s unilaterally to eliminate their biological weapons. Their move gained broader acceptance for what became the 1972 multilateral agreement to ban biological weapons. That agreement, in turn, freed international negotiators to move on to chemical weapons issues. Another similar initiative in the field of arms control was the decision that various states made to create agreed-upon zones free of nuclear weapons. Their move helped to reinforce the obligations of non-nuclear signatories of the Nuclear Nonproliferation Treaty (NPT).

Evaluating Performance

Since the international community can hardly count on individual members to lead on every front, it needs collective mechanisms to serve its will, not least in fostering compliance. Review processes that help to deter parties from flouting norms or agreements can serve that purpose well. First, they provide information that flags parties to potential noncompliance before it occurs, helping to preclude unintentional shortcomings or violations. Second, they help to nip in the bud misconduct by parties that might intentionally fall short of obligations but fear the negative political or economic repercussions of exposure. Third, by providing regular opportunities for parties, implementors, and stakeholders to interact, ongoing review activities help to instill the trust and build the personal relationships that can be key to effective cooperation.[2]

Periodic and even continual evaluation of the ways that parties to an agreement fulfill their obligations is a proven technique for improving performance. It is often perceived, however, as primarily a device to catch cheaters. The practice of monitoring, assessing, and verifying parties' behavior—collectively referred to here as "performance review"—can and should be positive activity above all. It can and should encourage progress not just by detecting noncompliance but also by uncovering the reasons that parties are succeeding or failing and by identifying both potential remedies in the second instance and openings for further movement in the first.[3] It can and it should, but too often it does not. The reviewing agencies may be short of cash or staff or time. The signatory parties, busy fighting fires elsewhere and facing no deadlines, let matters slide.

That neglect is a mistake. At its best, collective stock-taking brings nations and their representatives closer, builds mutual trust, and provides the reassurance essential for further joint action. Procedures for monitoring and verification can demonstrate, for instance, that the parties actually respect the same rules or norms, a minimal reassurance without which rivals would hardly undertake significant arms control or competitors accept trade pacts and anticorruption measures.

One outcome can even be a new consensus on broadening or tightening norms and rules. In 1989, for example, governments adopted a voluntary system to ensure that exports of the most hazardous chemicals and pesticides took place only with the prior informed consent of importing nations. The elaborate system for implementation review that developed involved experts, public interest NGOs, and industry groups. Over time, feedback from learning by doing led to refinements in the voluntary system and eventual support for a binding international convention. In September 1998, ninety-five governments signed the Convention on the Prior Informed Consent (PIC) Procedure for Hazardous Chemicals and Pesticides in International Trade.[4] The combined benefits of review for enhanced trust and cooperation may be especially important where norms or rules are highly contested, including human rights, labor rights, environment, trade, and weapons, or in dealing with issues such as international crime where continual information sharing is essential.[5]

The most effective review practices, however, are those that dig deep enough to reveal why parties are or are not living up to the provisions of a given agreement. Positive performance can sometimes be traced to the benefits a state expects for good conduct—added security, access to markets, technical or financial assistance, prestige, and other rewards. Governmental indifference or a sense of grievance, on the other hand, might be roadblocks to compliance, although a state's fear of damaging its reputation or suffering material harm can often overcome the conflict between an international accord and local priorities or values.[6] Most frequently in the developing world, however, nations with strong *intent* to comply find that they do not have the necessary *capacity*. In some cases, they cannot afford the extensive, costly measures embodied in certain agreements. Or they lack the expertise to draft effective implementing legislation, the administrative institutions and human resources to put new rules into practice, and the enforcement power to control troublesome private conduct. Evaluation procedures need to produce an in-depth analysis of compliance or noncompliance so that, in the latter event, workable remedies—positive or punitive—can be based on accurate information.

Concealment or reticence, however, impedes such inquiries. For most issues, parties have at least some incentive to restrict information either because they do not want to be caught in violation of agreements or the information sought is proprietary, linked to other secrets, or potentially embarrassing. Performance review systems vary greatly in levels of intrusiveness and sophistication. Highly intrusive information gathering and verification systems are relatively uncommon, and, of the issues in this book, apply only to some regimes in the fields of arms control, trade, environment, and the global commons.

Additionally, performance review faces several other serious obstacles. First, most systems must rely heavily on self-reporting. Second, information is sometimes technically difficult or costly to obtain. Third, data must be evaluated and assessed in a timely, credible, and impartial way, often by understaffed agencies. Yet member states expect much of these groups, charging them with heavy responsibilities usually without providing adequate resources.[7]

Even the World Trade Organization (WTO) secretariat, operating with an annual budget of $80 million and perceived by many as a bureaucratic Godzilla, is actually grievously overburdened. Vinod Aggarwal (chapter 6) describes its Trade Policy Review Mechanism (TPRM) as designed "to examine the impact of member policies on other countries" and to provide greater transparency of national laws and practices. Member states' calls on the TPRM, however, strain the WTO's limited resources, especially in the legal and economic analyses divisions.[8]

The Convention on International Trade in Endangered Species (CITES) has done as well as it has by tapping into networks of environmental NGOs, giving them substantive investigative duties and legal standing. Information flows that were previously informal and sporadic are becoming regularized, sometimes even formalized. The trusted NGO network TRAFFIC (Trade Records Analysis of Flora and Fauna in Commerce) once volunteered supplementary information to the CITES secretariat, but by 1980 had signed a long-term contract with the secretariat as official monitors of wildlife trade. (See Peter Sand, chapter 7.) The International Committee of the Red Cross (ICRC), a long-established NGO, has formal monitoring responsibilities for the 1949 Geneva Conventions and the 1997 landmine ban. In that latter area, a more recent network of 115 researchers in ninety-five countries in an NGO coalition called Landmine Monitor carries out a "quasi-formal role in monitoring the implementation" of the Ottawa Convention.[9] Largely funded by governments with whom it collaborates extensively, Landmine Monitor produces an annual report—even covering countries that are not parties to the ban—that runs to a thousand pages.

Although this study finds no single technique for performance review to be failproof, four complementary courses of action dependably turn in worthwhile results:

- Use of independent experts and data;
- Transparency and open review;
- Mechanisms to protect sensitive information; and
- Uniform evaluation standards and trusted analysis.[10]

Use of Independent Experts and Data. Given the high risk of compliance assessments becoming politicized, systems that set up independent experts or bodies for data collection and analysis can enhance the credibility of performance analysis.[11] For example, some environmental agreements charge independent panels of scientists with gathering data and gauging compliance, taking what Peter Haas (chapter 8) argues is the most reliable route to credible review. Similarly, the committee of twenty independent legal experts that meets annually to examine member states' reports to the ILO is authorized to request additional information and call for changes in domestic law.

Independent experts have been notably important in areas of great normative contention such as human rights. There, the absence of a generally accepted methodology for comparing states' human rights practices leads many nations to criticize reporting as subjective and biased. Shelton points to one of the most important innovations to deal with this problem: the use of "thematic" mechanisms and rapporteurs. The former establish a common standard for comparison of many states on a single issue, rather than courting an accusation of unfairness for singling out an individual state for uncomfortably close scrutiny. The effectiveness of these mechanisms is largely a function of the appointed thematic rapporteurs, however. In practice, they vary considerably in their expertise, commitment, and the level of resources available to them.

Transparency and Open Review. For the same reasons cited above, procedures that allow others to judge and comment on information that is collected are central to the effectiveness of many review systems, especially those that rely on self-reporting. These systems offer a dual benefit. First, the knowledge that others will examine the data closely provides an incentive for parties to report accurately. Second, open review provides opportunities to obtain supplementary information, an important consideration not only when dishonest reporting is all too likely, but also when good data are not technically easy to obtain. Joanna Spear (chapter 15) points out, for example, that changes in defense technologies make it harder for actors to monitor the international weapons trade. No longer "about supply of whole weapons," it is "more about the supply of modular systems, weapons kits (to be assembled in-country), production facilities, software programs, and dual-use goods."

One particularly effective technique of this kind, used predominantly in the labor and human rights fields, has been to establish procedures to call on state representatives to answer questions about the reports they submit—sometimes under the glare of the media, as with the UN Human Rights Committee. States feel intense pressure to appear for these discussions, for fear of negative publicity if they do not. The OECD Convention on Combating Bribery recently followed this lead, devising a "self- and mutual-evaluation" process that includes an independent Working Group on Bribery authorized to question individual countries and accept comments from businesses and civil society groups. (See Peter Richardson, chapter 2.)

Ultimately, it appears that a combination of political will and the international context in which human rights bodies operate determines the success of this type of reporting procedure. Shelton argues that it has been effective in human rights matters because of the quality of leadership on the UN Human Rights Committee, a high degree of transparency, extensive NGO involvement, and the quasi-judicial but nonconfrontational nature of the process. However, Shelton notes that public questioning procedures led by the African Commission on Human Rights have not met with the same kind of success due to the lack of political support from the Organization for African Unity (OAU) and the dearth of African NGOs.[12]

Open review procedures, moreover, can help to expose weaknesses in information gathering and even breakdowns in reporting, as occurred when the International Whaling Commission's reciprocal observer scheme lent itself to a mutual cover-up by Japanese and Russian whalers who concealed each other's practices. Another major indirect benefit is the springboard that the procedures can provide for creative responses by nonstate actors.

Mechanisms to Protect Sensitive Information. Parties are reluctant to agree to intrusive monitoring unless they have assurances that sensitive information will be protected. In the human rights field, on-site visits are sometimes possible only when visitors—the ICRC, for instance—promise confidentiality. Labor rights NGOs also conduct confidential interviews to uncover anti-union practices and other violations.

Although the practice is controversial, Shelton believes that many individuals have benefited as a result.

One of the innovations in arms control to protect confidentiality while still getting useful information has been to use so-called "managed access" to sites being inspected. The highly sophisticated monitoring and verification system of the CWC, administered by the Organization for the Prohibition of Chemical Weapons (OPCW), was designed in this way.[13] At parties' request, the OPCW may perform on-site challenge inspections in a country suspected of violating the treaty. To address the twin demands of those wanting an intrusive mechanism and those concerned about protecting sensitive security or business information, "inspectors and host country representatives approach the inspection target step-by-step on the basis of negotiations, guided by procedures laid out in OPCW rules for such cases." Thomas Bernauer (Chapter 16) argues that the "main advantage of this approach is that it allows for practical bargaining among experts on site, instead of diplomatic rows in the OPCW far away from the inspection target. Moreover, even if full inspection of the requested site is not possible, at least some information will be gathered." An interesting aside is that the CWC monitoring system also incorporates an innovative "proliferator pays" principle, whereby states possessing chemical weapons incur substantial costs associated with monitoring.

Uniform Evaluation Standards and Trusted Analysis.   As described earlier, determining a common set of evaluation standards is often challenging—especially where criteria are inherently subjective or where agreements' obligations are broad and ill-defined. Still, most authors in this study stress the importance and power of uniform evaluation standards, suggesting that the value of developing them is worth the effort. Peter Richardson (chapter 2), for example, argues that one of the keys to the shaming strategy of Transparency International (TI) is that it is based on comparing the performance of many states, not just singling out selected wrongdoers. Shelton attributes the success of thematic human rights rapporteurs partially to the common standard against which states are judged. Catherine Gwin (chapter 4) argues that effective implementation evaluation in development assistance should begin with a clear statement of objectives and a limited number of appropriate indicators.

Although international organizations are theoretically best placed to provide impartial evaluation, budgetary and political constraints can limit their effectiveness. In some areas, communications, in particular private monitoring, reporting, and analysis, are extensive. Such monitoring is not always perceived, however, as impartial. State-owned communications enterprises may see critiques by private firms as biased, and the dominant position of English-speaking countries can be a source of resentment. Thus, while private monitoring is essential to the communications field, it is also imperfect.

Managing Capacity Shortfalls

Effective governance requires recognizing that some states and other actors are, in practical terms, less equal than others. It is not uncommon in environmental and refugee affairs, with human and labor rights issues and with efforts to combat crime and corruption to find parties who lack the necessary capacity to undertake demanding domestic implementation measures.[14] The frequency of such shortfalls is an important international reality because in cases where capacity gaps defeat implementation, the influence of most other techniques for promoting compliance is nullified.

Turning a blind eye to inadequate implementation or actual noncompliance is one response to the reality. More demanding on the international community but more likely to produce positive change over time is a strategy built around strengthening the capacity of the weaker parties. Incentives and capacity assistance—in the form of access to resources, markets, funding, technical assistance, and other means—are appropriate correctives when strong intentions are undercut by inadequate means.

Many of the instruments for providing support, however, are independent actors that conduct their work without reference to multilateral agreements on specific issues—including international organizations such as the World Bank, regional development banks, the World Health Organization (WHO), the UN Development Program (UNDP), and the UN Environment Program (UNEP). What they contribute may help states build capacity to implement an accord. If so, however, the benefit is an incidental one. When the linkage between assistance and implementation is direct, available resources are often inadequate. In the area of global communications, for example, Drake refers to technical and development assistance provided by the developed states to alleviate painful short-term adjustment costs that developing countries face when implementing International Telecommunications Union (ITU) recommendations, opening markets under the General Agreement on Trade and Services (GATS), or even changing frequency spectrum assignments.

In the environmental field, at least, incentives have helped induce states to participate in treaties regarding trade in endangered species, ozone depletion, and the protection of World Heritage Sites. More broadly, the restructuring of the experimental Global Environment Facility (GEF) in 1994 created a funding entity specifically linked with the 1992 conventions on biodiversity and global climate change, as well as the Montreal Protocol. In practice, the GEF works closely with the World Bank and UNDP—relationships that, at one remove, connect those agencies to the goals enunciated at the Rio Earth Summit.

National and private development assistance organizations, similarly, may contribute significantly to building capacity without reference, however, to any treaties. Collaboration among WHO, Rotary International, and the Bill and Melinda Gates Foundation to eradicate polio is an ambitious example of such an undertaking. More narrowly, but actually linked to the World Heritage Convention, the privately financed United Nations Foundation has granted the UN Educational, Scientific, and Cultural Organization (UNESCO) $2.9 million over four years to strengthen capacity through staff training and regular salary payments of five endangered wildlife sanctuaries near Lake Kivu in the Upper Congo. In a less direct kind of intervention that also serves environmental protection goals but not specific accords, both bilateral and private debt-for-nature swaps have permitted creditors to reward countries for their conservation efforts by writing off a portion of their foreign debt. Total swaps to date amount to over $1 billion.[15]

Elastic schedules for compliance—longer and sometimes less demanding deadlines for weaker parties—have proved in some circumstances to be appropriate incentives. Such flexibility has been built into some global accords as practical responses to implementation and compliance capacity problems. Both the Montreal Protocol and the agreement on Trade-Related Aspects of Intellectual Property Rights (TRIPs), for example, give developing countries an extended period of time to implement commitments.

As for weak states, Peter Sand (chapter 7) notes that the findings of a series of effectiveness surveys conducted since 1992 point to shortfalls in "administrative capacity" more than to lax criminal enforcement in cases of environmental noncompliance. "Capacity building at the local level—including professional training and managerial infrastructure—has thus become a high priority for technical assistance under several conservation agreements," he writes. It is even specifically labeled "as compliance assistance, for example, in article 23 of the 1992 Convention for the Protection of the Marine Environment of the North-East Atlantic. . . ." Even if some critics see these payments as eroding respect for law, the threat or actuality of withdrawing the subsidies can be productive moves that get attention and promote compliance. The World Heritage Fund, Sand notes, is one agency "where reporting duties and compliance controls—in return for financial assistance—are gradually being tightened."

In efforts to prevent states from acquiring weapons of mass destruction, Thomas Bernauer (chapter 16) points out that assistance may motivate states to provide information about implementation problems. Although limited experience with incentives in arms control makes it difficult to assess overall effectiveness, Bernauer nonetheless believes that evidence suggests "assistance has contributed to solving a number of implementation problems that could not have been resolved through negative incentives alone." U.S. bilateral assistance to Russia, he believes, has been "instrumental in establishing more accurate inventories of nuclear material, securing critical installations to prevent illegal removal of nuclear material or even weapons, controlling exports of military and dual-use items, and dealing with excess fissile material from dismantled nuclear weapons."

Along somewhat similar lines, Phil Williams (chapter 3) calls for closer linkage of anti-crime efforts to development aid, arguing that sanctioning states that lack genuine law-enforcement capacity only weakens them and makes them more inviting targets for organized criminals. Many states that support the anti–money laundering regime, for example, have little or no capacity to oversee and regulate their banking sectors. Williams argues:

> the predominant effort of governance has been to encourage compliance through capacity building rather than the imposition of penalties. This makes sense. If a state is weak, external sanctions are likely simply to exacerbate the weakness, making the state an even easier target for criminal organizations (as has been demonstrated in Serbia, where sanctions actually facilitated the criminalization of the state). The problem, however, is that capacity building is a slow process and one in which the results are not easy to measure. (chapter 3)

Positive incentives and assistance—cynics might regard them as high-level bribes—carry drawbacks. Sometimes they feed an atmosphere of entitlement that weakens an entire regime. Bernauer warns that recipient states may try to exact more than they deserve in exchange for joining an international agreement. Newland notes a similar hazard with refugee problems. In response to resistance by Turkey, Malaysia, and Macedonia to receiving large numbers of refugees, the international community undertook "exceptional measures" to bow to their objections. "[R]ewarding noncompliance," Newland fears, "will encourage recalcitrance in the future."

Responding to Willful Noncompliance

What can the international community do in response to intentional transgression? The authors of this study found no convincing evidence that specific responses have proven regularly effective. Not only is it extremely difficult to predict what actions will induce states to change their ways, but some such actions can also impose significant costs on those who act (for instance, the interruption of familiar trade relations). Only in the relatively few cases of agreements that include highly specific, binding provisions—the Montreal Protocol and some trade pacts—is noncompliance easily established, much less corrected.

The trade sanctions written into the Montreal Protocol have, for instance, been successfully invoked against Russia, prompting not punishment but World Bank assistance in a program to phase out chlorofluorocarbon production. CITES, which established its widely admired sanctions procedures several years after the original pact was signed, has reversed noncompliance on several occasions by tagging countries from Bolivia to Greece for violations. The Convention on Long-Range Transboundary Air Pollution (LRTAP) was in force for eighteen years before its parties, too, adopted provisions to identify and react to noncompliance. Interestingly, Norway and Slovenia, the first two countries to be brought up on charges, actually turned themselves in both to get help with their problems and to stimulate the development of the enforcement regime.[16]

Most multilateral agreements, however, contain no defined punitive measures to be invoked in cases of noncompliance. The signatory states that would have to enforce them resist such strong provisions for two reasons. They fear having the tables turned and the penalties applied to them or that the political, military, and economic costs of trying to impose such measures would be too high. Also, it can be difficult to agree on air-tight definitions of what constitutes either required or improper conduct. In the field of arms control, as Thomas Bernauer shows, cheating can often be hard to document. Similarly, in refugee affairs, many states interpret their obligations so differently that noncompliance is hard to establish.

Additionally, Peter Sand writes of situations when limited or temporary noncompliance may be tolerable compared to the risk of losing the participation of the party concerned. Some agreements even build in such latitude, giving parties the right to make reservations—that is, to set aside certain agreed-upon requirements. The opt-out clauses in the International Whaling Commission procedures and the reservation procedures of CITES are examples. Such systems of tolerated noncompliance can be successful, in Sand's view, because they establish latitude at the negotiating stage for minority dissents and defections.[17]

Another reason for not establishing tougher, tighter discipline in international regimes is the refusal of most of the world's nations, even in the face of global challenges, to accept limits on state sovereignty. Few if any leaders would care to announce that, in the global interest, they had handed over the management of their forests to outsiders or forgone exploration for oil in the habitats of endangered species. Member states of the European Union (EU) are a notable exception, having agreed to accept rulings of the European Court of Justice (ECJ) as superseding domestic laws. One result is that the court in Luxembourg has a record of effective enforcement that no other regional tribunal can match.

Finally, states may lack the resolve to set up strong enforcement mechanisms because the pacts themselves may be only ephemeral expressions of harmony where discord remains wide and deep. Intense ideological and philosophical disagreements persist, for instance, between developed and developing countries over definitions of labor rights and the means to uphold them, with developing countries seeing protectionism in requirements that infringe on their ability to trade or attract investment.

In the absence of consensus over the meaning of noncompliance and the means of dealing with it, the international community nonetheless has workable options. Shaming a miscreant or bringing a dispute before a judicial body, penalizing misconduct with economic restrictions or, in rare cases, applying force in the name of security are all responses that can move states toward good faith implementation. The tools are likely to work better in combination than alone, and they are likely to be inapplicable in the multiplying cases where systemic or developmental weaknesses block theoretically willing parties from shouldering heavy burdens. Such noncompliance can only be managed, gradually reversed, not forcibly eradicated. To the extent that global undertakings increasingly ask weaker parties to assume obligations equal to those the stronger ones can carry, the future is likely to see an expansion of efforts to boost capacity rather than to sanction default.

Publicizing Noncompliance. Shaming has become an increasingly popular tool in the arsenal of reactions to noncompliance. As a strategy used in connection with almost every issue area addressed in this book, shaming is a soft version of coercion. It amounts to publicizing misconduct in one state, perhaps, to an international audience and even to international organizations. The practice has often been useful in identifying and correcting substandard and even abusive conduct. The porous nature of national defenses against the flow of even embarrassing information, moreover, could further ease the process of exposing violations and calling those responsible to account. Where NGOs operate as imaginative and energetic whistle-blowers, their pressure for transparency has at times advanced compliance.

Threatened and actual public exposure, however, is most effective with respect to relatively minor violations and with actors concerned about their international reputations. For example, Dinah Shelton reports that the threat of public exposure often makes governments release political prisoners, locate supposedly missing persons, or allow dissidents to leave. The risk of being included on any of a number of public "naming and shaming lists"—such as FATF's list of jurisdictions with systemic problems—can also sometimes be enough to steer parties' behavior in the direction of compliance. Phil Williams recalls how G-7's FATF succeeded in getting cooperation from Austria on money laundering after publicly identifying noncompliant actions. In that case the infraction was relatively minor, the principle in question was not in dispute, and the target country was interested in maintaining its good name.

The technique has less impact on states preoccupied with overriding security problems (South Africa during the apartheid era) or indifferent to their international standing (Burma, Iraq, and Liberia, for example) and less impact overall if other actions do not follow public exposure. It has the most impact when the effect of a tarnished reputation would be a market-based vote of no confidence by consumers, investors, lenders, and the like.

In the areas of environmental protection, human rights, and labor rights, NGOs have generated the loudest cries and gotten the most attention. The UN Working Group on Arbitrary Detentions, Dinah Shelton reports, found that international NGOs brought almost three out of four of the cases it considered in 1995. In the human rights field, the tactic dates back about a quarter of a century. Jewish organizations in the United States and elsewhere seized on the Soviet Union's 1975 Helsinki Accords commitment to facilitate family reunification specifically and "freer movement and contacts" generally as a lever to use in campaigns to win exit visas for Soviet Jews. Fed by a flow of information about human rights abuses from groups of dissenters within the Soviet Union, Western partisans mounted vigorous propaganda assaults on Moscow, raising the noise level of what was derogated as public diplomacy too high for advocates of détente. Despite that discomfort, the Helsinki partisans successfully lobbied the United States to echo their charges at various review meetings where Conference on Security and Cooperation in Europe (now the Organization for Security Cooperation in Europe, or OSCE) states reviewed implementation of the Final Act. Although Soviet authorities insisted that they were not bowing to outside pressure, as complaints mounted they released a number of high-profile political prisoners—one, two, or a few at a time—and between 1968 and 1989 allowed 365,628 Jews to emigrate to Israel and the West, as compared to under 12,000 between 1951 and 1967.[18]

The dirty-linen tactic turns up in a number of imaginative variants. By ranking states, TI's corruption index garners enormous publicity and enables citizens' groups to press low-ranking states and transnational actors—private and public, financial and political—for action where it appears most needed. When activism combines with shaming to generate financial consequences, the impact can be significant. For example, NGO boycotts (actions that could be termed as either shaming or sanctions or both) to protest South Africa's apartheid policies raised consciousness and depressed some sales. The Greenpeace 1988 campaign against buying seafood from whaling countries resulted in a total loss to Icelandic seafood exports estimated at US$30 million."[19]

Shaming appears to be the technique *par excellence* for unofficial actors to take speaking roles in the theater of global diplomacy. NGOs have been its most energetic practitioners, sometimes with the primary aim of spurring compliant but complacent states and institutions to act against wrongdoers. This NGO capacity for viewing situations loudly and with alarm in hopes of prompting wider public outcry, perhaps financial backlash, and eventually international action is not to be disparaged as Chicken-Little megalomania. It is actually closely comparable to the kind of reactions to noncompliance used by many regimes—the International Labor Organization (ILO), for instance, which can invoke only public shaming when countries violate International Labor Conventions.

Complaint Procedures.　　Most familiar as a judicial strategy in the face of noncompliance are mechanisms for legal dispute settlement—in the main, arbitration, referral to the World Court (ICJ), and referral to treaty-specific judicial arrangements. Aside from the generally slow pace of argument and action, the primary weakness in relying on judicial machinery in international controversies is that all the parties involved usually must consent to the referral and agree to honor whatever judgment is rendered.

The graver the quarrel the less likely is such reciprocal courtesy. When Nicaragua complained successfully to the ICJ that U.S. mining of its ports constituted a breach of international law, for example, the Reagan administration refused to recognize the ICJ's authority, to attend or give evidence, and to pay court-ordered reparations to the plaintiff.[20] Many arms control treaties provide for the possibility of referral to the ICJ, but it has never taken on a case involving disarmament. Although it established a Chamber for Environmental Matters in 1993 in response to the growing number of environmental treaties, the new body has yet to consider any cases.

Arbitration is a much more effective legal procedure for advancing compliance in a quasi-judicial setting. Long-established, and commonly used, arbitration enables disputing parties to set up panels or tribunals limited to a specific case and in place for a limited period of time with a mutual pledge to accept the judgment rendered. Some environment treaties give states the option (not yet used) to make such procedures compulsory upon signature or ratification.[21] Arbitration is also provided for in regional accords such as the North American Free Trade Agreement (NAFTA). Unlike many other international agreements, which only allow states to initiate legal proceedings, NAFTA allows companies (foreign investors) to take complaints about breaches of obligations by a NAFTA party to an international arbitration panel.

Some treaties come into force with built-in mechanisms for dispute resolution: sometimes actual courts, sometimes more loosely defined adjudication machinery that often overlaps with treaty-specific bodies to oversee implementation, and sometimes permitting individuals and corporations as well as states to bring cases before them (such arrangements include the especially noteworthy International Tribunal for the Law of the Sea).[22] Since it started operating in 1996, this body has dealt with a wide variety of cases and built a generally good record of compliance with its decisions.

Regional conventions have focused on the creation of individual complaint and redress procedures. The European Human Rights Court (EHCR) has been extremely effective in getting redress for individuals and in forcing states to change their laws and policies. Dinah Shelton finds that EHRC rulings, particularly on prisoners, mental patients, and detention, have led many countries to change their penal and criminal codes. The quality of EHRC decisions has given the court considerable credibility and legitimacy that has also generated a high degree of compliance. As she also notes, however, the writ of the EHRC runs among generally homogeneous nations in Western Europe, which have committed themselves over time to accept a wide range of common institutions. The same cannot yet be said for the status of other regional courts, except for the EHRC's cousin in the Americas, which Shelton argues has been effective, albeit more slowly.

International trade is the field where a rule-based approach to controversies over compliance has advanced the furthest. Though relatively new, WTO procedures for settling disputes have been working well—not only in adjudicating between powerful contending parties but also in equalizing the odds between weak countries and strong ones. The mechanism, for instance, permits small countries to join forces and compel powerful countries to comply with WTO rulings by imposing countervailing duties. However, the WTO gets drawn onto more unsettled ground when confronted by controversies over which no global consensus has been reached, including environmental and labor matters. As Aggarwal notes,

> The continuing controversy and escalating protectionism between the EU and the United States over hormone-fed beef, despite a ruling from the WTO in favor of the latter, demonstrate the limits of dispute settlement mechanisms in the absence of shared norms on proper justification of national regulation for health and safety reasons. (chapter 6)

As clashes over issues that had little or no perceived connection to trade a generation ago become more frequent, the strain on the WTO and its members is likely to rise.

Economic Sanctions. The WTO has a highly unusual place among international agreements, explicitly providing for punitive action after legal dispute settlement mechanisms have failed. For example, in 1999 the United States was allowed to adopt retaliatory measures against Europe when the latter refused to amend its banana-import rules. The United States slapped a 100 percent tariff worth $520 million on some European luxury goods. Restrictions by the Europeans on hormone-treated beef were met by a U.S. threat to impose tariffs worth $900 million on European goods.

As a general proposition, however, disciplinary remedies established within multilateral accords are both infrequent and usually weak. A notable exception is CITES, whose Standing Committee can urge member states to suspend wildlife trade with culprits.[23] "Over the past fifteen years, th[e] procedure was invoked at least twelve times, most recently against Greece, Guyana, and Senegal," writes Peter Sand. He adds,

> In the case of the United Arab Emirates, the country withdrew from the convention after being targeted by an embargo in 1987, then re-adhered when the embargo was lifted in 1990. CITES sanctions have even been used against nonmem-

ber countries, to penalize persistent refusal to provide "comparable documents" pursuant to article 10 of the treaty. (chapter 7)

Embargos against El Salvador and Equatorial Guinea were only removed when the two joined the convention, changing "from free riders into 'forced riders.'"[24]

Flowing from the UN Charter, economic sanctions imposed by the UN Security Council can carry great weight. The Security Council has the authority to use sanctions to try to force compliance with its resolutions and to restore and maintain international peace and security. When it exercises this discretionary power, however, it acts on the basis of broad concerns, rather than in the context of a particular multilateral agreement.

Until close to the turn of the century, the Security Council seemed to be following a rising curve in imposing economic sanctions and arms embargoes on both state and nonstate actors to prevent, manage, or resolve violent conflict and to stop gross abuses of human rights. It even authorized sanctions to force the extradition of individuals alleged to have been involved in terrorist attacks. Although these measures have often entailed tremendous costs to target countries, they have mostly failed to change the political behavior of their leaders. Moreover, they have had unintended negative social and humanitarian effects, leading many to question their choice as a policy instrument.[25] These problems notwithstanding, sanctions remain attractive to many policy makers as seemingly inexpensive and low-risk ways of showing concern and taking action short of military force.

Targeted financial sanctions that became the subject of much attention in the last half of the 1990s held the theoretical promise of avoiding excessive costs to neighboring states as well as to the population at large. Unfortunately for the theory, these so-called "smart" sanctions—often used to curb flight or travel by suspected miscreants—have encountered formidable implementation problems. The speed at which financial assets can be transferred, the many ways in which true ownership can be concealed, and the fact that many countries lack the technology and the domestic legislation to monitor financial transactions are just some of the problems that confound such targeted sanctions.

More generally, sanction regimes have suffered from four main problems.[26] First, those imposing the penalty have often imperfectly assessed the strengths and weaknesses of their targets, characteristics that will dictate whether the target is able to withstand economic pressure and devise countermeasures. Second, economic sanctions have often been imposed in isolation, independent of other instruments.

Third, sanction regimes have suffered from poor implementation. States have often interpreted sanction resolution language differently. Moreover, because few states have the expertise or resources needed to establish or maintain effective monitoring mechanisms, circumvention has been easy, and multinational corporations have flouted many UN economic sanction regimes. Also, states, such as those adjoining Rhodesia in the 1960s and Serbia in the 1990s, can hesitate to enforce sanctions against their neighbors, fearing countermeasures. Similarly, insufficient compensation to third parties for lost economic opportunities undercuts their enthusiasm for sanction regimes. Finally, noncompliance typically has had no adverse consequences: The Security Council would not adopt secondary sanctions against states that fail to enforce the first set.[27]

Fourth, as Joanna Spear and Phil Williams note, arms embargoes and economic sanctions have had important "balloon" effects—that is, they have led to the emergence of black markets (as in Yugoslavia, Iraq, and Haiti) and the stimulation of local industrial capacities (as in South Africa). Faced with an arms embargo from 1977 to 1994 and a hostile security environment for most of this period, South Africa created a booming indigenous arms industry.

Sanction regimes will continue to falter until these weaknesses—third-party noncompliance, most importantly—can be remedied by building and maintaining a broad international consensus on the legitimacy of coercive action and by compensating third parties that experience collateral damage from sanction regimes. Sanction regimes also need an interested supporting party to take the lead in defining their precise objectives and keeping the relevant international actors focused on them.

Eye on Effectiveness

The process of defining and responding to noncompliance might benefit if all those involved stepped far enough back to judge their work as a whole. If the governance arrangements established by a treaty, for instance, are not working and making a difference, if they are outdated or poorly targeted, it hardly matters who is following or ignoring them. The parties in such cases will need to consider adjustments in rules or implementation priorities or may have to rethink completely the overall framework and strategy. Such an exercise may shed light on why certain serious compliance problems arise, such as the still unresolved "paper satellite issue" described in the communications chapter involving parties that violate the spirit of an agreement but remain in formal compliance. The process of reviewing an agreement's overall effectiveness can also help actors anticipate obstacles, build awareness about serious flaws in approach, or even generate the requisite will for renegotiating specific terms or entire frameworks if necessary.

An interesting example of an ingenious response strategy was one adopted by the IMO that shifted "enforcement [of its requirements on oil dumping] onto gatekeepers on whom principals depend but who have no limited interest in rule-breaking. . . ."[28]

The move, as business regulation experts Braithwaite and Drahos described it, included designing "into the regime a requirement that regulated actors pay for gatekeepers to audit their compliance, and those gatekeepers [be] monitored in a way that ensures that competence, integrity, and diligence are the best way for them to flourish." Since states ignored their duties to prosecute ships that spilled oil, they continued,

> [W]hat worked was shifting the enforcement target from the ships which benefited from the pollution to builders, insurers and classification societies which did not. Insurers would not insure ships that were not classified, classification societies would not classify ships without segregated ballast tanks and crude oil washing to prevent oil spills, and builders would not be silly enough to build ships which could not be classified or insured. Globally, 98 percent compliance with IMO requirements to install technologies, which dramatically reduced oil discharges at sea, was obtained.[29]

Summing up the impact of incentives that hit polluters in the bottom line, they observed: "Where mighty states could not succeed in reducing oil spills at sea, Lloyd's of London could."[30]

Systems that review effectiveness are critically important for issues that are poorly understood, dynamic in nature, prone to surprises, or where untested strategies may produce unintended consequences. The nonlinear effects of environmental degradation—for instance, the overharvesting of one species that can produce the unexpected collapse of an entire ecosystem—make it hard to devise rules that cover all possible contingencies. Rule makers, therefore, need to be ready when new discoveries arise—when, perhaps, scientists find that a seemingly benign chemical designed to replace an ozone-depleting one turns out to accelerate global warming.

Such unintended consequences haunt many global governance initiatives. In conventional weapons, they have manifested themselves in a balloon effect whereby certain prohibitions actually prompted technological innovations that defeated the purpose of the prohibitions. Efforts against transnational organized crime have led to similar "restriction-opportunity" dilemmas, when limitations on activities or goods have paradoxically opened the way for the creation of new criminal markets or the enlargement of existing markets. The results include new opportunities for criminals to circumvent restrictions and the higher prices and increased profits—real or potential—that lure new scofflaw suppliers into the game.

Useful as systematic devices for focusing on governance effectiveness could be, they exist in only a few settings. In this regard, the environmental field boasts some of the most significant and sophisticated forms of institutionalized governance learning and adaptation—what David Victor terms "systems for implementation review" (SIRs).[31] Ideally, SIRs contribute to an ongoing process of "social learning" and allow for a "rolling process of intermediate or self-adjusting agreements that respond to growing scientific understanding."[32] The Montreal Protocol, for example, provides a means for modifying parties' obligations, without the need for re-ratification in light of major changes in scientific understanding of ozone depletion—an innovation that led parties to jump quickly from a 50 to 100 percent phaseout of ozone-depleting chemicals. The Intergovernmental Panel on Climate Change, a multinational group of scientists, meets regularly to assess the state of scientific knowledge and advise parties to the Framework Convention on Climate Change and issues a complete formal review every five years. Regular reviews of CITES allow for changes in the species listed in the convention's appendices and offer recommendations for improving regime performance.[33]

Similar innovations are appearing in other fields. In 2000 the UN High Commissioner for Refugees (UNHCR) initiated a process of "global consultations" to address problems of interpretation and gaps in the coverage of existing refugee law.[34] Gwin points to the Special Program of Assistance for Africa as an important move in development assistance where donors could share information and coordinate their activities. "Free of formality," she writes, "donors were able to test ideas, develop mutual understandings, and engage in frank and open exchanges on African economic and social policy issues." An added novelty was the "peer pressure" that developed in the course of the meetings and resulted in upgrading the procedures that donors followed and in speeding the disbursement of structural adjustment aid. At the same time, other authors lament the absence of good measures of effectiveness in their fields. Williams criticizes global anti-crime efforts as being long on conventions, laws, and regulations and short on implementation. He calls for better monitoring and effectiveness yardsticks "to ensure states bring criminal laws in line with international review processes within the anti-crime community."

BEYOND INTERGOVERNMENTAL AGREEMENTS

As this volume makes clear, a host of intergovernmental agreements—multilateral, minilateral, regional, and bilateral—already exist. They do not, however, hold a monopoly on the management of global issues, and many of them do not perform impressively or even well as problem-solving mechanisms. Some have too narrow a focus or too vague a mandate; others have become outdated, have been undercut by other agreements, or hobbled by inadequate incentives or enforcement authority. To compensate, business leaders, citizen activists and NGOs, governmental elites, international organizations, and others have launched supplementary rule-making and problem-solving actions—alone and in partnerships that span national boundaries and sectoral lines.[35]

Applying many of the techniques described earlier to enhance implementation and compliance with intergovernmental agreements, these policy entrepreneurs operate in the civic space left open by ineffective government-led action or designs. Self-selected coalitions of private actors monitor and enforce their own negotiated rules. Some global private authorities, such as private bond-rating agencies, in effect force governments to accept their rules. Government elites compare techniques and then imitate each other—the result sometimes being common (and higher) criteria on issues of global concern such as human rights and banking standards. Activist networks selectively target and change the behavior of influential public and private players in ways that others follow. NGOs, private foundations, and businesses—beyond serving merely as contract agents for states and international organizations—increasingly provide services and money and normative values where governments and international organizations do not.

These supplemental efforts are not a sideshow. Rather, they represent both a new style and a new substance in global issues management. Made possible to a large degree by the emergence of a globalizing world, they are also among the agents able to steer the course of globalization. Some have already made a serious dent in global problem solving and, thanks to imaginative experiments in governance, some are developing interesting, practical approaches to other problems. The overall potential of these alternative activities is still not widely understood, and it is too early to draw sweeping lessons from them. Detractors argue that many of these efforts engage only self-selected participants and stretch the limits of democratic accountability. Another potentially serious drawback is that some small-scale victories may obscure broader defeats—misleading publics and letting governments off the hook.

Still, these supplementary approaches offer genuine promise as new weapons in the arsenal of intergovernmental cooperation. They hold special appeal in areas where the only international agreements that exist are nonbinding ones and where traditional state-based approaches make little headway against private conduct that gives rise to or exacerbates particular problems. The more cutting-edge initiatives—some of them described below—are helping to force a reconceptualization about who does what in governance and how.

Implementation by Imitation

"Implementation by imitation"—when state and business actors follow each other's practices to the letter or with some variation—comes in two main forms.

Transgovernmentalism. Anne Marie Slaughter argues that "functionally distinct parts" of governments—courts, regulatory agencies, executives, and legislatures—are "networking with their counterparts abroad, creating a dense web of relations that constitutes a new, transgovernmental order." Some of these relations materialize as formal agreements and organizations among government actors—like the Basle Committee of Central Bankers. Slaughter also describes a fairly new kind of intergovernmental imitation that springs from informal networking of government elites—mainly but not exclusively taking place among liberal democracies. These activities, combined with other forms of intergovernmentalism, are, according to Slaughter, helping in a fast, flexible, and effective way to fill some of the regulatory loopholes that global forces bring into being.[36]

Some government officials, for instance, have collaborated "directly with their counterparts in other countries, not bothering to work by means of the usual diplomatic filters." This practice has long occurred in exchanges among law enforcement officials, who share knowledge and adapt each other's techniques in ways that enhance enforcement of national laws. Slaughter states: "Transgovernmental regulation . . . produces rules concerning issues that each nation already regulates within its borders: crime, securities fraud, pollution, tax evasion. . . . Regulators benefit from coordinating their enforcement efforts with those of their foreign counterparts and from ensuring that other nations adopt similar approaches."[37]

National courts are interacting with one another and with supranational tribunals in ways that "accommodate differences but acknowledge and reinforce common values." Slaughter points out that in the process, "Judges are building a global community of law. They share values and interests based on their belief in the law as distinct but not divorced from politics and their view of themselves as professionals who must be insulated from direct political influence. At its best, this global community reminds each participant that his or her professional performance is being monitored and supported by a larger audience." Supreme Court justices, for example, research and accept each other's decisions as precedents. Slaughter continues: "The Israeli Supreme Court and the German and Canadian constitutional courts have long researched U.S. Supreme Court precedents in reaching their own conclusions on questions like freedom of speech, privacy rights, and due process. Fledgling constitutional courts in Central and Eastern Europe and in Russia are eagerly following suit."[38]

Private Sector Imitation. As Braithwaite and Drahos argue in their decade-long study on global business regulation, global regulatory norms "follow globalizing self-regulatory practice." In all areas of their study—some covered in this book including environment, drugs, trade, labor, global finance, telecommunications business regulation—they found that "state regulation follows industry self-regulatory practice more than the reverse, although the reverse is very important." This, they argue, "has always been so, and as we have moved from the era of the indicative planning state to the new regulatory state, it has become even more true."[39] The ongoing process mirrors the development of modern commercial law from its roots in medieval guild rules and practices. Now, codes of conduct that a particular industry develops become standards for wider business governance, just as "best practices" adopted by insurance firms become the norm for their clients and others.[40]

In some cases, powerful enterprises dictate industry practice, leaving others no choice but to fall in line, following a pattern of top-down rule making by global-level private authorities, such as private bond-rating agencies. Such authorities, according to Craig Murphy, include oligopolies in reinsurance, accounting, and consulting, as well as "global and regional cartels in industries as diverse as mining and electrical products."[41] This exercise of authority is one of the reasons why Braithwaite and Drahos assert that besides the United States and the European Commission (EC), global lawmakers today "are the men who run the largest corporations."[42]

It is no wonder, then, that NGOs, international organizations, individual governments, and other forces lobby or make common cause with top corporations, aiming for the corporations that set industry norms. Oxfam International, for example, owns a considerable number of shares in GlaxoSmithKline (GSK), one of the world's biggest drug companies.[43] Individual NGOs, albeit predominantly U.S.-based, are forming strategic partnerships with business to help develop more environmentally friendly technologies and production processes—Conservation International with Starbucks, Environmental Defense with McDonald's, The Natural Step with Home Depot, and on and on. "Green" architects like Bill McDonough are working with major architectural firms to reengineer the way skyscrapers are designed. TI (itself an NGO-business partnership) and others worked with Shell to develop a voluntary but strict code of business ethics in line with the OECD convention on combating bribery. This flurry of NGO-business partnerships is happening because individuals and groups hope that if they convince what Braithwaite calls the "motors of transformation" to change, others may follow. To date, successes have been small scale but significant: When McDonald's stopped packaging food in Styrofoam containers, for instance, other multinational fast-food chains followed.

A remarkable and far-reaching recent demonstration of business sensitivity to pressure occurred in early March 2001, when the drug conglomerate Merck reversed its determined opposition and announced it would dramatically cut the price of AIDS drugs to developing countries to one-tenth the level charged in developed countries. A week later, Bristol-Myers Squibb, the third largest U.S. drug company, did the same, with strong indications that many others would follow. The decisions to use differential pricing—consistent with the TRIPs agreement and supported by WHO, the EC, and the WTO—came in the wake of enormous pressure from critics who charged that by protecting drug patents, the industry was reaping enormous profits at the expense of poor, desperately sick people.[44] Although many activists took full credit, Merck and Bristol-Myers Squibb's decisions were the result of many factors. Among them were threats from Indian drug companies to sell cheap, generic versions of various anti-AIDS medicines to African plague states and behind-the-scenes pressure from and negotiations with WHO and the UN AIDS Program (UNAIDS) secretariats. Added pressure came from respected scientists and Yale University, which held the patent on one of the drugs, competitiveness, and other forces.[45] Admittedly, the decision does not solve the AIDS crisis—treatment of infection is only one aspect of the problem, and even at reduced prices such treatment will still be out of reach for millions. Even so, industry's about-face on pricing makes a huge dent in the obstacles to treating the disease in poorer countries. The precedent is unlikely to be limited to AIDS medications or even to drugs.

Selective Self-Regulation Among the Willing

As global firms come under more pressure to tally social and environmental considerations on their bottom lines, they are increasingly agreeing to voluntary, industry-wide codes and standards. Interest groups generate much of the pressure behind business self-regulation, but some also comes from business associations that want to ensure a level playing field so the costs of reform do not put them at a disadvantage relative to competitors. The pattern is a time-tested one that, according to Virginia Haufler, has seen different kinds of business associations negotiating with each other technical standards, business best practices, and norms of doing business.[46] The process has, she argues, produced a large body of maritime law, guidelines on information privacy, and rules for rating securities. Government officials often provide the impetus and leadership for industry self-regulation; indeed, they are often central to success. Some governments have even agreed to subject themselves to voluntary codes alongside business.

Sometimes self-regulation comes in the form of multi-actor negotiated agreements that subject members to rules, monitoring, and enforcement on the lines of intergovernmental agreements. These rules may be set in hybrid organizations—with voting representatives from government, industry, and sometimes NGOs—and then adopted by the consenting.[47] The International Organization for Standardization (ISO), for instance, sets voluntary business standards that can quickly become industry norms. Formal certification and consumer labeling schemes, described by Brian Langille (chapter 12) and Peter Sand (chapter 7), also exist to set rules that reward complying businesses. The Forest Stewardship Council, for example, issues a consumer label to wood products if it finds that they came from forests managed in an environmentally sustainable way.

In the labor rights field, the U.S. Department of Labor in 1996—recognizing that ILO efforts had met minimal success in eliminating child labor and sweatshops—called upon U.S.-based multinational apparel and footwear manufacturers, labor unions, and NGOs to develop voluntary standards on working conditions. The resulting initiative, called the Apparel Industry Partnership (AIP), developed a complex monitoring program run by a new NGO, the Fair Labor Association (FLA). The FLA accredits independent monitors to monitor participating companies and certify compliance with AIP's code.[48] Progress, however, has been mixed, not least because of the difficulty of replicating labor standards developed in one country across the far-flung territory where multinational employers operate. Organized labor eventually pulled out of the process, and great splits divide the NGO community. Meanwhile, the number of participating companies has grown very slowly, "partly because of the lessening of public governmental pressure and partly because of increasing competition in labels and codes of conduct from other companies and networks."[49]

To influence the behavior of firms and governments confronting corruption in different localities in developing countries, the transnational anticorruption movement pioneered the innovative use of "islands of integrity"—mini-governance arrangements with built-in incentives and sanctions that cover large contracts, industry segments, or entire cities. (See Peter Richardson, chapter 2.) Industry participants promise to comply with rules that require disclosure of payments to third parties and allow monitoring; government participants must publicize criteria and evaluation data for bids. If bidders cheat, governments remove them from consideration for future contracts, and other parties may attempt to invoke arbitration proceedings.

Self-regulation can also be done "bottom-up"—with fewer players and on an informal basis. Although small in scale, this is the level where many exciting developments and experiments are taking place—some of them codified in formal agreements. In October 2000, BP (formerly British Petroleum, now advertising with the slogan "Beyond Petroleum" and calling itself an "Energy Company") announced that to meet its pledge to cut greenhouse gas emissions ahead of Kyoto Protocol mandates, it had joined six other leading U.S., Canadian, and French multinationals to develop an inter-firm emissions trading system.[50]

The one-man crusade of Reverend Leon H. Sullivan, an influential American clergyman, provides a remarkable example—if not in formal negotiations—of a tightly focused concern giving birth to a widespread undertaking. The 1977 principles or guidelines that bore his name were standards of treatment for workers in apartheid-era South Africa that he persuaded almost all American companies doing business there to accept. Based on them, New York City Comptroller, Harrison Goldin, launched the MacBride Principles, which requested American companies with subsidiaries in Northern Island to commit to a series of nondiscrimination and affirmative action principles. These earlier efforts helped inspire the UN Secretary-General to pen the 1999 Global Compact laying down ethical precepts of labor relations for multinational corporations, an unusual case of moving from the particular to the general.[51]

Regulation by Revelation

Transparency is not just a central component in the effort to nudge states into compliance with interstate agreements; it is a more broadly powerful tool in the hands of citizen activists.[52] Thanks to the information revolution, transparency is becoming an influential force in shaping business and government behavior when no interstate agreement exists.[53] Widely used in local and national settings to target behavior of particular governments or firms, it can also be applied transnationally. At its most powerful, it can deter bad behavior in ways that eliminate the need for formal regulation. More often, however, it steers actors toward desired behavior until formal regulatory agreements are in place.

TI's use of its Corruption Perception Index (CPI) has been held up as a model by transparency advocates. Many credit the threat that investors will pull out of corruption-ridden countries at the bottom of the list with helping to deter governments from demanding bribes as a matter of routine. Less known are TI's national survey instruments, described by Peter Richardson (chapter 2), that help expose domestic publics to the extent of corruption in their countries and uncover specific problem areas. Some TI chapters conduct "service delivery surveys" of consumers of public services and then publish "report cards" that rate individual government agencies based on "the incidence and magnitude of bribes typically demanded and paid." Among other techniques, TI also developed "Big Mac Indexes" that "reveal unexplainable cost discrepancies within a country for similar commodities (such as school lunches, aspirins in a hospital, and others)." A Big Mac survey conducted by TI/Argentina revealed that

> a school lunch in Buenos Aires cost the equivalent of $5. A comparable lunch in Mendoza, which had been implementing anticorruption measures, cost the equivalent of $0.80. Within days of publication of the survey's result, the cost of a school lunch in Buenos Aires was more than halved. (chapter 2)

Richardson claims that the use of comparative indexes has been central to TI's success. Similar efforts are under way in rating multinational corporations on their social and environmental performance. After years of environmental NGOs singling out individual corporations for negative action—Greenpeace raising a furor, described earlier, about Shell's plans to sink the Brent Spar oil rig, for example—or roundly criticizing all timber or oil companies, practices are changing. The U.S.-based NGO Council on Economic Priorities (CEP) developed a system to rate hundreds of brand-name multinational corporations according to a common and extensive set of social and environmental criteria. The rankings—graded A to D—are published in "Shopping for a Better World" to help consumers reward good behavior and punish its opposite. CEP's rating system is all the more important given the tendency for more companies to claim in advertisements more credit than they deserve for social and environmental performance—a practice now widespread enough to have earned its own name, "greenwashing."

The use of transparency generates its share of fears and criticisms—especially when employed by nonstate actors who are "unelected, unaccountable, and sometimes less transparent than the institutions they monitor."[54] The biggest fear, perhaps, is that information can be misused or misrepresented, for as Ann Florini put it, "transparency reveals behavior, not intent." Information taken out of context, or not grounded in good analysis, can lead to mistaken conclusions. Simply posting information about companies' toxic releases on the Internet, for example, without explaining how much of a toxic chemical causes harm to humans or ecosystems, might spark undeserved criticism or lead well-intentioned citizen groups to spend precious energy, time, and money fighting battles of marginal significance.

Direct Action Partnerships

In a decade (the 1990s) when lending by the World Bank averaged about $20 billion a year, the fact that by 1994 NGOs were funneling $8 billion annually in assistance to developing countries established them as significant and rarely silent partners in global issues management.[55] They are not alone. Multinational corporations, often following standard operating procedures for good community relations, have undertaken corporate philanthropy in the developing world for years. As long as it is not short-lived, such charitable engagement can have a positive effect in local communities in which the companies operate. BP, for instance, provides solar-powered refrigerators in Zambia to store antimalarial vaccines.[56]

Still somewhat scattershot, the activities of NGOs and corporations are nonetheless taking on a fairly new dimension as private actors team up with governments and international organizations to form what Wolfgang Reinicke calls "global public policy networks" or "cross-sectoral networks." These partnerships undertake direct palliative and preventative action on domestic problems that contribute seriously to global ones or that are major symptoms of global problems. Such networks can be seen as offspring of the information revolution that nurtures informal, international support groups by putting individuals and organizations with matching concerns in touch with one another and with the know-how they share or seek.[57] The Roll Back Malaria (RBM) initiative, for instance, was set up in 1998 to coordinate public and private efforts against a disease that kills roughly one million people, mostly in Sub-Sahara Africa, every year, "more people than any other communicable disease except tuberculosis."[58] Directed by about ten staff members at the WHO, the RBM involves the World Bank, UN Children's Fund (UNICEF), UNDP, NGOs, businesses, bilateral development agencies, and the media. It is not a source of financing;

rather, it gives developing countries "access to knowledge, technology, and financial resources through global partnerships."[59]

Like all other actors catalogued here, international organizations seek to help address, even correct, serious shortfalls in implementation. In the interest of alleviating global poverty and improving health care, for example, the United Nations has helped to build a network of partners, including major corporations and foundations, into a Health InterNetwork. Its goal is to establish 10,000 online sites connecting hospitals and clinics in developing countries with up-to-date medical information.[60] Likewise, the United Nations is working with Swedish communications firm Ericsson, the Red Cross, and others to provide mobile phones and microwave links for humanitarian relief workers in areas affected by natural disasters and emergencies.[61]

NGOs have been providing services on their own for quite some time. The venerable ICRC, for example, delivers health care to political prisoners. It is granted access in exchange for keeping silent about any human-rights violations that its members witness.[62] Oxfam International and dozens of other cross-national NGOs provide rapid relief during and after complex humanitarian disasters—with and without UN partners. More and more private actors are getting into the game, often to fill gaps or provide more rapid intervention than older institutions can and sometimes to push innovative actions that more conventional international bureaucracies might simply study to death.

The Medicines for Malaria Venture (MMV), for example, "was launched to solve the problem of private sector underinvestment in vaccine research and production and thus to respond to a steady decrease in private involvement in malaria prevention and control since the 1960s." Joining philanthropic entities, the pharmaceutical industry, and the public sector, it "seeks to create incentives for the development of new drugs and vaccines and thus to spur the development of new medicines that would otherwise never be brought to market. Its goal is "to secure the registration (every 5 years, on average) of one new antimalarial drug affordable to the worst-hit populations and capable of countering the growing resistance to existing vaccines." Inaugural partners included the WHO, the International Federation of Pharmaceutical Manufacturers Associations, the government of the Netherlands, the Rockefeller Foundation, and many others. "It is structured as an entrepreneurial, not-for-profit business venture that will funnel royalties from its products into a general fund to offset the need for future donations."[63]

Reinicke and Deng argue that

> [t]risectoral networks can also support the deepening of existing markets to include those who would otherwise not have access. Microlending networks are a case in point. Microlending—the extension of small loans to poor individuals and small businesses—is regarded as one of the most effective tools yet invented for combating poverty. Microlending networks bring together NGOs, the public sec-

tor (donor agencies and international organizations), and commercial banks to support such financing.

These networks do "more than deliver a financial service. . . . They also generate sociopolitical outcomes, strengthen self-governance capabilities at the local level (through the financing of educational programs and, in some cases, the delivery of health care), and empower the poor."[64]

HALF FULL, HALF EMPTY

Where, in all the words that have preceded these closing ones, is there hope that global responses can match the profound, perplexing challenges of the new millennium? Nowhere and everywhere. The authors of this book see the mixed record of international action and they acknowledge that no one strategy or set of forces has been, is, or will be definitive or enduring. They also see, however, that new avenues are constantly opening and ingenious experiments are replacing threadbare custom.

In the midst of charting a passage into globalization, still treading shaky ground, the world's nations and their citizens can no longer take ideological certainties as their guide. Nor is any well-indexed user's manual available for the inexact art of managing global issues. Yet, some prescriptions do apply to diplomacy as practiced by official envoys and by their unofficial adjuncts from the corporate world and civil society.

One broad observation relates to every stage of the process. Whether pushing an issue to prominence or pushing recalcitrants to comply, combining forces and techniques is by far a more promising and frequently a more productive course than trying to rely on a single lever or formulation. Silver bullet solutions are a recipe for losing ground. Building coalitions and mixing options are a slow and often frustrating way to make a difference, but for many global challenges, it is often the only effective way.

In this context, it is essential to recognize the spreading tendency of issues to overlap one another, requiring problem solvers to identify and analyze both positive and negative connections. Development is the cause of ecologically harmful use of natural resources. Or it is the cure. Or both. Making environment and development part of the same equation for many national and international policy makers is at least a crucial step toward a coherent approach. Balancing penalties and rewards makes them a more effective tool in promoting compliance. Looking at the record of responses to global challenges, the authors document examples of successes and failures with binding and nonbinding regimes, with universal and minilateral approaches, with comprehensive frameworks and incremental steps. Often the choice of tactic and instrument is based on what is possible at the negotiating table, not what is rational or optimal. In any case, success does not necessarily flow from the mechanical design of an agreement. Progress is more likely to reflect the kinds of goals that the parties set, how realistic their commitments are, and the attention and resources that are devoted to implementation. Finally, whatever approach is taken at the start, continuous, sharp-eyed scrutiny of performance makes much of the difference between lip service and genuine implementation.

Those positive lessons deserve, as corollaries, two significant findings about the role of global information flows and the involvement of business and NGOs in problem solving. These are the diplomatic wild cards now being played from the first sighting of a global-scale issue onwards. The availability of information and its rapid movement turn the theoretical virtue of transparency into very practical pressure wielded by both official and unofficial actors.

It is hard to overstate the difference these two factors can make in the recognition and disposition of a global challenge. It is easy, on the contrary, to imagine some of the possible consequences for the policies of Hitler's European neighbors of an Internet invented in 1933 linking a human rights network as vigorous as the one now in place.

Blessings, though, rarely come unmixed. The same historic currents that have brought private actors into scene-stealing prominence in the dramas of international diplomacy have also made private conduct that states have difficulty controlling a major concern of that diplomacy. In illicit weapons trade, crime, corruption, and environmental degradation, public servants are usually only peripheral to the action. Some of the movers and shakers are simply crooks. Others are officers of powerful corporations, the assets of which outstrip the economies of many countries.

The significance of this altered order is that private actors whose conduct largely defines a problem are indispensable to its solution. Ironically, however, many discussions that stress the need for public-private partnerships and for non-state-centric strategies to address such global issues reflect an old-fashioned commitment to governmental initiative. The very term *nonstate actor* reflects this bias. Applying such verbs as "to involve," "to enlist," or "to sub-contract" to nonstate actors suggests a hierarchical disposition and a measure of state control in coordinating the process that may not always match reality or advance effective policy. Often states will and should be the coordinators or main actors in partnerships. But in many cases, that pecking order will be neither possible nor desirable.

The wider challenge is to design incentives that encourage private operators who break or stretch the law to change their behavior and how they perceive their self-interest. Some states can use tax incentives to nudge corporations into more socially responsible roles. Others may need to concentrate on strengthening respect for the rule of law so as to nourish the growth of vigorous markets and civil society. In both instances and in others yet to be devised, the goal is to foster coalitions of public and private forces that strengthen all parties in dealing with global challenges.

In many of the most urgent problem areas, however, states are and will remain the arbiters of action and the only actors that matter. The world is changing, but it is not being stood on its head. As the pace picks up, though, governments remain slow to agree on firm actions equal to the scale of the problems at hand. Indeed, sometimes by the time multilateral groupings of states move out of first gear, their agreements only formalize or legitimate regulatory procedures that have been informally in place long enough to be standard practice.

Even trail-blazing international accords—particularly dealing with environmental threats—often do not go far enough in establishing goals and obligations. Negotiating the Kyoto Protocol—a feat in itself—was, for instance, only a tiny step in the right direction. Even in the unlikely event that it enters into force and gets 100 percent compliance anytime soon, it will only slow the pace of advancing climate change. The increasingly common fallback on soft law and nonbinding commitments will prove little more than camouflage for inaction unless the parties move beyond annual meetings and calls for patience to action on multiple fronts that formalizes demanding commitments and motivates real behavioral change over time.

So, is there hope that today's six-billion-plus inhabitants of the Earth will, as their numbers grow, see the global threats to their well-being shrink? The answer can be a qualified yes. Old habits are changing. New agents of change are gaining strength. In the positive gifts that globalization brings and in the experiments being developed and launched in global diplomacy, there is plenty of reason for optimism. Of the cautious sort.

One sound reason for caution is the unsolved question of leadership, not just who can or will exercise it but how nations and their peoples can be led when risks rise from many quarters but no single threat menaces individual or common security. The authors of this book who weighed the role of leadership assigned it preeminent importance. Nothing of significance, they found, happens without leaders causing it to happen. That truism, however, needs modifiers— disinterested leadership? collective leadership? sustained leadership? forceful leadership? patient leadership?—to define the quality of direction required to contain or redirect global challenges.

One near certainty is that the lone gunslinger image of leadership is as dated as the John Wayne films that made the conceit iconic. The burdens in terms of resources and resolve, imagination, and analytical capacity are heavier than even the wealthiest state can carry forward unaccompanied. It is like counting on an All-Star athlete to plan and execute every play, to be coach and cheerleader, umpire and team manager.

Recognizing the need for a cooperative model of leadership, however, does not make the concept practical. It will need to be practiced long and hard and with numerous parties before the international community determines how to share responsibility and exert it effectively at the same time. Inside the many multilateral organizations that are both meeting places and instrumentalities of collective governance, the experiment is under way. The admission of nonstate actors to what used to be closed-door consultations and their incorporation in a variety of implementation strategies assigns a portion of power to new players. The more that they earn and carry out such assignments, the more respect and even responsibilities they are likely to earn. Even efforts to put together post–Cold War military coalitions against the Iraqi and Serb leadership have shown not only how difficult such endeavors are to launch, but also that it can be possible to mount them.

The temptation to believe that the United States, as the colossus of the times, could step out in front on issue after issue and draw legions of willing followers in its wake is beguiling but mistaken. The first flaw lies in the "willing followers" part of the equation. Globalization intrudes on sovereignty. It does not eradicate it. Nations more jealous of their freedom of action than responsive to the specter of common dangers may want to be led—but only on their own terms and at the pace they think they can keep up.

The other reason to be wary of over-reliance on U.S. leadership is that it has shown itself repeatedly uncertain. For every feat of wise and resolute guidance in international affairs, there is an almost Newtonian instance of going it alone or not joining up at all. Unilateral actions such as the withdrawals from the ILO and UNESCO or the 1998 bombing sorties against Iraq, no matter how justified by policy and circumstances, introduce fears in the international community that more shoes remain to be dropped. Failing to support the Law of the Sea agreement, the framework convention on biodiversity, the accord on banning landmines, and the initiative to establish an international criminal tribunal, during the 1990s Washington displayed some of its historical ambivalence about the degree of its involvement with other states.

Many factors shape this inconsistent performance. Deep-rooted isolationist sentiments were not obliterated at Pearl Harbor. The widespread conviction that as Lincoln's "last best hope of earth," the United States is always in the right does not always dictate foreign policy, but it often punishes U.S. officials and supposed allies who are seen to lack that certainty. A measure of fatigue after the Cold War marathon is a political reality. And, like every other globally wired nation, the United States suffers from information overload, receiving more cries for help, more reports of danger, and consequently more appeals for leadership than its government and society can effectively handle.

In a world growing interdependent on almost every level, the likelihood is that U.S. leadership will win deference today and resentment tomorrow. That has been the pattern for decades. It seems unlikely to change. What has changed is the sort of challenge that is growing with globalization and for which urgent, effective responses are as necessary as they are still infrequent.

However it is to be accomplished, whoever will lead it, the move from geographic and political alliances to global and multilateral cooperation will shape that future. Collaboration is not a luxury for use only in the right technical or functional settings.

It is, instead, a necessary survival tool to manage new challenges and new opportunities in a steadily changing global setting.

NOTES

1. See David Ignatius, "Crackdown on Global Theft," *Washington Post*, December 3, 2000, p. B7. Ignatius notes that an important element of influence on Israel was that the listing decision had "crucial backing" of a credible figure in U.S.-Israeli relations, Stuart Eizenstat, who had credibility because of the Holocaust compensation issue. The ripple effect was strengthened by the simultaneous publication of the Organization for Economic Cooperation and Development's (OECD's) own "Hall of Shame list of 35 tax havens."

2. For a discussion of socialization in compliance, see Dinah Shelton, ed., *Commitment and Compliance: The Role of Non-binding Norm in the International Legal System* (Oxford, U.K.: Oxford University Press, 2000), p. 539.

3. For an outstanding discussion and chart illustrating the range of factors that affect a country's intent and capacity to comply with interstate agreements, see Harold K. Jacobson and Edith Brown Weiss, "Assessing the Record and Designing Strategies to Engage Countries," in Edith Brown Weiss and Harold K. Jacobson, eds., *Engaging Countries: Strengthening Compliance with International Environmental Accords* (Cambridge, Mass.: MIT Press, 1998), pp. 511–54.

4. See David G. Victor, "'Learning by Doing' in the Nonbinding International Regime to Manage Trade in Hazardous Chemicals and Pesticides," in David G. Victor, Kal Raustiala, and Eugene B. Skolnikoff, eds., *The Implementation and Effectiveness of International Environmental Commitments* (Cambridge, Mass.: MIT Press, 1998), pp. 221–81. See also <http://www.fao.org/AG/AGP/AGPP/Pesticid/PIC/pichome.htm>.

5. Formal, regularized meetings take place and are considered important for parties dealing with weapons of mass destruction (WMD) and conventional weapons; Bernauer (chapter 16) and Spear (chapter 15) cite the International Atomic Energy Agency (IAEA), the Organization for the Prohibition of Chemical Weapons (OPCW), and the Conference on Disarmament as key forums. Haas notes that these ongoing exchanges help facilitate the creation of a "culture of compliance" with environmental values. Environmental scientists and experts meet regularly both through formal mechanisms such as the Intergovernmental Panel on Climate Change and through participation in epistemic communities.

6. Jacobson and Weiss, "Assessing the Record," pp. 511–54.

7. As Chayes, Chayes, and Mitchell argue, "It is no coincidence that the regimes with the most impressive compliance experience," such as the International Monetary Fund (IMF) and the OECD, "depend on substantial, well-staffed, and well-functioning international organizations." See Abram Chayes, Antonia Handler Chayes, and Ronald B. Mitchell, "Managing Compliance: A Comparative Perspective," in Weiss and Jacobson, *Engaging Countries*, p. 58.

8. Aggarwal (chapter 6) adds: "Ironically, the United States has resisted budgetary increases despite indications that it stands to benefit disproportionately."

9. Oliver Meier and Clare Tenner, "Civil Society Monitoring: NGOs and the Verification of International Agreements," in VERTIC, *Verification 2002* (London: Verification Research, Training, and Information Centre, forthcoming).

10. A fifth, highly intuitive one is that reporting questionnaires and surveys should include clear guidelines for states on reporting, detailing what information should be submitted. We do not discuss this finding at length here because only Shelton discusses it in this book. Still, Shelton echoes other studies on compliance that stress clarity in reporting requirements as a key component of getting effective national reporting. See, for example, Jacobson and Weiss, "Assessing the Record," pp. 545, 553.

11. The chapters on development assistance, communications, environment, labor, and trade suggest that the use of independent means for data collection is important.

12. Shelton notes that this has not been all bad. Ironically, it has led to a situation whereby the African Commission has had more time to focus on individual communications and gross violations.

13. In contrast, the Biological Weapons Convention does not have any monitoring mechanism, a lacuna widely considered to be a major flaw and impediment to overall regime effectiveness.

14. "Capacity gaps" do not always make it impossible to implement necessary measures to comply with governance demands; but they do often create conditions in which decision makers believe it imprudent or unrealistic to give compliance with global governance the same attention as other urgent and domestic priorities.

15. See Peter Sand (chapter 7); and interview with Thomas E. Lovejoy.

16. Duncan Brack, "International Environmental Disputes" (London: Royal Institute of International Affairs, March 2001), p. 16. See <http://www.riia.org/Research/eep/eeparticle.html>.

17. See Peter Sand (chapter 7); and Albert O. Hirschman, *Exit, Voice, and Loyalty: Responses to Decline in Firms, Organizations, and States* (Cambridge, Mass.: Harvard University Press, 1970), pp. 77–101.

18. Thomas Naylor, "On Swiss Bankers: Reconciliation not Retribution," at <http://www.dukenews.duke.edu/swiss605/htm>.

19. See Steinar Andresen, "The Making and Implementation of Whaling Policies: Does Participation Make a Difference?" in David G. Victor, Kal Raustiala, and Eugene B. Skolnikoff, eds., *The Implementation and Effectiveness of International Environmental Commitments: Theory and Practice* (Cambridge, Mass.: MIT Press, 1998), pp. 458–59.

20. In 1986 the court found that the United States had violated customary international law as well as a 1956 bilateral Treaty of Friendship, Commerce, and Navigation, by laying mines and hence blocking access to Nicaraguan ports. Refusing throughout to take part in the case, the United States also vetoed two UN Security Council resolutions that required full compliance with the court's judgment of June 26, 1986.

21. See, for example, the 1985 Vienna Convention on Substances that Deplete the Ozone Layer, the 1992 UN Framework Convention on Climate Change, and the 1992 Convention on Biological Diversity. However, as noted by Peter Sand, no country has yet seized an arbitration panel to enforce an environmental treaty.

22. For example, individuals can petition the ECJ in cases that directly violate EU treaty law. Corporations are allowed to petition the tribunal for the Law of the Sea. The tribunal also allows for *amicus curiae* briefs—that is, communications from third parties, including nonstate actors. Many regional human rights courts allow individuals to seek redress.

23. The treaty does not contain formal trade sanction provisions; it only says that parties can take "stricter measures," individually or collectively.

24. This term was coined by Charles Pearson; see Steve Charnovitz, "Encouraging Environmental Cooperation Through the Pelly Amendment," *Journal of Environment and Development*, vol. 3 (1994), pp. 3–28, at p. 4.

25. See, for example, Joy Gordon, "A Peaceful, Silent, Deadly Remedy: The Ethics of Economic Sanctions," *Ethics and International Affairs*, vol. 13 (1999), pp. 123–50; John and Karl Mueller, "Sanctions of Mass Destruction," *Foreign Affairs*, vol. 78, no. 3 (May/June 1999), pp. 43–53.

26. See Chantal de Jonge Oudraat, "Making Economic Sanctions Work," *Survival*, vol. 42, no. 3 (Autumn 2000), pp. 105–27.

27. In the early 2000s, the Security Council took a harder stance and considered imposing secondary sanctions on noncompliant actors.

28. John Braithwaite and Peter Drahos, *Global Business Regulation* (Cambridge, U.K.: Cambridge University Press, 2000).

29. Ibid., p. 618.

30. Ibid., pp. 618–9. The authors base their summary on a study by Ronald B. Mitchell, *Intentional Oil Pollution at Sea: Environmental Policy and Treaty Compliance* (Cambridge, Mass.: MIT Press, 1994).

31. SIRs are the institutional arrangements through which parties to an agreement share information, review both the performance of member states and the regime itself, handle noncompliance issues, and adjust the commitments of member states.

32. Jessica T. Mathews, "Redefining Security," *Foreign Affairs*, vol. 68, no. 2 (Spring 1989), p. 176.

33. Peter Haas has argued that these types of review systems should be implemented at the global level and believes a Global Environmental Organization would further that end.

34. Newland, however, adds that "refugee advocates . . . have expressed concern that instances of retreat from core principles of international protection are often presented as legitimate issues of interpretation."

35. See Jessica Mathews, "Power Shift," *Foreign Affairs*, vol. 76, no. 1 (January/February 1997), pp. 50–66; Jessica Mathews, "What Did and Didn't Happen in Seattle," *Chemistry Business* (July/August 2000); Jessica Mathews, "In a New World, But Stiffly," *Newsday*, September 10, 2000; Anne Marie Slaughter, "The Real New World Order," *Foreign Affairs*, vol. 76, no. 5 (September/October 1997), pp. 183–97; Braithwaite and Drahos, *Global Business Regulation*; Virginia Haufler, *A Public Role for the Private Sector: Industry Self-Regulation in a Global Economy* (Washington, D.C.: Carnegie Endowment for International Peace, 2001); Ann M. Florini, ed., *The Third Force: The Rise of Transnational Civil Society* (Washington, D.C.: Carnegie Endowment for International Peace, 2000); Wolfgang Reinicke and Francis Deng, *Critical Choices: The United Nations, Networks,*

and the Future of Global Governance (Ottawa: International Development Research Centre, 2000); and Gordon Smith and Moise Naím, *Altered States: Globalization, Sovereignty, and Governance* (Ottawa: International Development Research Centre, 2000). Trisectoral networks are described by Wolfgang Reinicke as "Global Public Policy Networks" in his *Critical Choices*.

36. See Slaughter, "The Real New World Order," pp. 183–97.

37. Ibid.

38. Ibid.

39. Braithwaite and Drahos, *Global Business Regulation*, p. 481.

40. Haufler, *A Public Role for the Private Sector*.

41. Craig Murphy, "Global Governance: Poorly Done and Poorly Understood," *International Affairs*, vol. 76, no. 5 (September/October 1997), p. 794.

42. Braithwaite and Drahos, *Global Business Regulation*, p. 629.

43. Sebastian Mallaby, "Activists, Acting Governmental," *Washington Post*, February 26, 2001, p. A19.

44. See Paul Bluestein and Barton Gellman, "HIV Drug Prices Cut for Poorer Countries; Other Firms May Follow Merck's Lead," *Washington Post*, March 8, 2001, p. A1; and Karen DeYoung and Bill Brubaker, "Another Firm Cuts HIV Drug Prices: Sub-Saharan Africa Is the Focus of Bristol-Meyers Move," *Washington Post*, March 15, 2001, p. A1.

45. In the words of one scientist closest to the ground: "I am struck by all the steps that led us to today: the work of Dr. [J. P.] Horwitz on anticancer compounds, my own work and that of Dr. [Tai-Shun] Lin, the timely tests performed by Dr. [Raymond F.] Schinazi, the inquiries made by Doctors Without Borders to Bristol-Myers, which then led to Yale and some Yale law students and the campus paper and then back to Bristol-Myers, whose executive vice president John L. McGoldrick said on March 14 that his company hoped to 'energize a groundswell of action' to fight AIDS in Africa. I find it hard to see any pattern in all this, except perhaps that there is a moral urge among people that, however coincidentally, can sometimes bring results." See William Prusoff, "The Scientist's Story," *New York Times*, March 19, 2001, p. A19. See also Mike Moore, "Yes, Drugs for the Poor—and Patents as Well," *International Herald Tribune*, February 22, 2001, p. 6.

46. See Virginia Haufler, unpublished discussion papers for Carnegie Endowment study group on Role of the Private Sector, 1998; also Haufler, *A Public Role for the Private Sector*.

47. The ILO is technically a hybrid international organization, too, with labor, employer, and government delegates.

48. See Reinicke and Deng, *Critical Choices*, pp. 40–1; and Brian Langille (chapter 12). Langille argues that this monitoring process is not ideal: whereas the ILO is widely accepted for its "credibility, democratic legitimacy, expertise, competence, and budgetary ability to monitor compliance," the opposite may be true with industry-negotiated monitoring systems.

49. Reinicke and Deng, *Critical Choices*, pp. 42–3.

50. Peter Behr, "Big Firms Join to Share Greenhouse-Gas Cuts," *Washington Post*, October 18, 2000.

51. For analyses on the effectiveness of the Sullivan and MacBride principles, see Christopher McCrudden, "Human Rights Codes for Transnational Corporations: The Sullivan and

MacBride Principles," in Shelton, ed., *Commitment and Compliance*, pp. 418–49; and Chester A. Crocker, *High Noon in Southern Africa: Making Peace in a Rough Neighborhood* (New York: W.W. Norton, 1992).

52. Florini coined the term, "Regulation by Revelation." See Ann M. Florini, "The End of Secrecy," *Foreign Policy*, no. 111 (Summer 1998).

53. Today, anyone can buy commercial space satellite photography with one-meter resolution "for a price that will fall rapidly in the years ahead." Mathews, "In a New World, But Stiffly." See also Ann Florini and Yahya Dehqanzada, "Commercial Satellite Imagery Comes of Age," *Issues in Science and Technology*, vol. 16, no. 1 (Fall 1999).

54. Florini, "The End of Secrecy," pp. 60–1.

55. See World Bank, <http://www.worldbank.org/html/extdr/pb/10things.html>; and P. J. Simmons, "Learning to Live with NGOs," *Foreign Policy*, no. 112 (Fall 1998), p. 87.

56. Jeffrey E. Garten, "Globalism Doesn't Have to Be Cruel," *Business Week*, February 9, 2001, p. 26.

57. Reinicke and Deng, *Critical Choices*, p. 47. The Consultative Group on International Agricultural Research (CGIAR) is one of the oldest examples, set up in 1971. An alliance of fifty-eight donor states and organizations and co-sponsored by UN Food and Agriculture Organization (FAO), UNDP, UNEP, and the World Bank, CGIAR works in partnership with research institutions in developed and developing countries to share scientific knowledge on feeding the hungry in developing countries.

58. WHO Fact Sheet No. 94, Revised October 1998. See <http://www.who.int/inf-fs/en/fact094.html>.

59. Reinicke and Deng, *Critical Choices*, p. 49.

60. The initiative is supported by the WebMD Foundation, WHO, the UN Foundation, and others. See <http://www.un.org/millennium/media/health_kit.htm>.

61. See "Ericsson Pledges Support for Improved Disaster Response" at <http://www.ericsson.com/infocenter/news/Disaster_response.html>.

62. Simmons, "Learning to Live with NGOs," p. 87.

63. Reinicke and Deng, *Critical Choices*, pp. 54–5.

64. Ibid., p. 56.

Acronyms

ACA	Agency for the Control of Armaments
ADM	Antidumping Measures
AFTA	ASEAN Free Trade Agreement
AIP	Apparel Industry Partnership
AP	Antipersonnel
APEC	Asia-Pacific Economic Cooperation
ARF	ASEAN Regional Forum
ASEAN	Association of Southeast Asian Nations
ASEM	Asia Europe Meeting
ASOC	Antarctic and Southern Ocean Coalition
ATCP	Antarctic Treaty Consultative Party
ATS	Antarctic Treaty System
BPI	Bribe Payers Index
BTA	Basic Telecommunications Agreement
BWC	Biological Weapons Convention
CAT	Conventional Arms Transfer
CBD	Convention on Biological Diversity
CBW	Chemical and Biological Weapons
CCAMLR	Convention on the Conservation of Antarctic Marine Living Resources
CCC	Customs Cooperation Council
CCD	Convention to Combat Desertification
CCPR	Covenant on Civil and Political Rights
CCW	Convention on Conventional Weapons
CD	Conference on Disarmament
CDF	Comprehensive Development Framework

CEDAW	Convention on the Elimination of All Forms of Discrimination Against Women
CEP	Council on Economic Priorities
CERD	Convention on the Elimination of All Forms of Racial Discrimination
CESCR	International Covenant on Economic, Social, and Cultural Rights
CFA	Committee on Freedom of Association
CFE	Conventional Armed Forces in Europe
CFCs	Chlorofluorocarbons
CG	Consultation Group
CGIAR	Consultative Group on International Agricultural Research
CHM	Common Heritage of Mankind
CIE	Committee of Independent Experts
CIESIN	Center for International Earth Sciences Information Network
CITES	Convention on International Trade in Endangered Species
CMS	Convention on the Conservation of Migratory Species of Wild Animals
CNN	Cable Network News
CoCom	Coordinating Committee for Multilateral Export Controls
COFO	Committee on Forestry
COLREGS	Convention on the International Regulations for Preventing Collisions at Sea
COMSAT	Communications Satellite Organization
COPUOS	United Nations Committee on Peaceful Uses of Outer Space
CPI	Corruption Perceptions Index
CSBM	Confidence- and Security-Building Measure
CSCE	Conference on Security and Cooperation in Europe
CTBT	Comprehensive Test Ban Treaty
CTR	Cooperative Threat Reduction
CVI	Children's Vaccine Initiative
CWC	Chemical Weapons Convention
DAC	Development Assistance Committee
DBS	Direct Broadcast Satellites
DSM	Dispute Settlement Mechanism
DSU	Dispute Settlement Understanding
ESAAMLG	Eastern and Southern African Anti–Money Laundering Group
EC	European Community
ECHR	European Convention on Human Rights
ECJ	European Court of Justice
ECOMOG	Economic Community Cease-fire Monitoring Group [of ECOWAS]

ECOSOC	United Nations Economic and Social Council
ECOWAS	Economic Community of West African States
ECPAT	End Child Prostitution in Asian Tourism
EEC	European Economic Community
EEZ	Exclusive Economic Zone
EFTA	European Free Trade Area
ENTRI	Environmental Treaties and Resource Indicators
EPI	Expanded Program on Immunization
ESAF	Enhanced Structural Adjustment Facility
EU	European Union
EVSL	Early Voluntary Sectoral Liberalization
FAO	Food and Agriculture Organization
FARC	Revolutionary Armed Forces of Colombia
FATF	Financial Action Task Force
FCC	U.S. Federal Communications Commission
FCCC	Framework Convention on Climate Change
FCPA	Foreign Corrupt Practices Act
FDI	Foreign Direct Investment
FFA	South Pacific Forum Fisheries Agency
FINCEN	Financial Crimes Enforcement Network
FIS	Islamic Salvation Front
FIUS	Financial Intelligence Units
FLA	Fair Labor Association
FSA	Financial Services Agreement
FSC	Forest Stewardship Council[a]
FSC	Forum for Security Cooperation[b]
FTA	Free Trade Agreement
FTAA	Free Trade Area of the Americas
G-7	Group of Seven Industrialized Countries
G-8	Group of Eight Industrialized Countries
G-77	Group of Seventy-Seven
GATS	General Agreement of Trade in Services
GATT	General Agreement on Tariffs and Trade
GAVI	Global Alliance for Vaccines and Immunization
GBT	Group on Basic Telecommunications
GDP	Gross Domestic Product
GEF	Global Environment Facility

---

a. Chapter 7 (Sand).
b. Chapter 15 (Spear).

GEO	Global Environmental Organization
GESAMP	Group of Experts on Scientific Aspects of Marine Environment Protection
GNP	Gross National Product
GOBI	UNICEF's Growth Surveillance, Oral Rehydration, Breastfeeding, and Immunization Initiative
GPA	Global Program on AIDS
GPS	Global Positioning Systems
GRECO	Council of Europe's Group of States Against Corruption
GSN	Global Survival Network
GSO	Geostationary Orbit
GTZ	German Technical Assistance Program
HAI	Health Action International
HNP	Health, Nutrition, and Population [World Bank]
IADB	Inter-American Development Bank
IAEA	International Atomic Energy Agency
IANSA	International Action Network on Small Arms
IAP	Individual Action Program
IBI	Intergovernmental Bureau for Informatics
IBRD	International Bank for Reconstruction and Development
ICANN	Internet Corporation for Assigned Names and Numbers
ICBL	International Campaign to Ban Landmines
ICC	International Chamber of Commerce
ICJ	International Court of Justice
ICRC	International Committee of the Red Cross
IDA	International Development Association
IEEPA	International Emergency Economic Powers Act
IETF	Internet Engineering Task Force
IFI	International Financial Institution
IFRB	International Frequency Registration Board
IFTF	International Fur Trade Federation
IGO	Intergovernmental Organization
IGY	International Geophysical Year
IIASA	International Institute for Applied Systems Analysis
ILO	International Labor Organization
IMDG	International Maritime Dangerous Goods
IMEC	Industrialized Market Economy Countries
IMF	International Monetary Fund
IMPEL	Network on the Implementation and Enforcement of Environmental Law
IMO	International Maritime Organization

INECE	International Network for Environment Compliance and Enforcement
INF	Intermediate-Range Nuclear Forces
INFACT	Infant Formula Action Coalition
INL	International Narcotics and Law Enforcement Bureau
INMARSAT	International Maritime Satellite Organization
INTELSAT	International Telecommunications Satellite Organization
IOC	Intergovernmental Oceanographic Commission
IOPC	International Oil Pollution Compensation Funds
IP	Internet Protocol
IPCC	Intergovernmental Panel on Climate Change
ISO	International Standards Organization
IT	Information Technology
ITA	Information Technology Agreement
ITLOS	International Tribunal for the Law of the Sea
ITO	International Trade Organization
ITTO	International Tropical Timber Organization
ITU	International Telecommunications Union
IUCN	World Conservation Union
IWC	International Whaling Commission
KLA	Kosovo Liberation Army
LAFTA	Latin American Free Trade Area
LAWASIA	The Law Association for Asia and the Pacific
LRTAP	Long-Range Transboundary Air Pollution
LTA	Long Term Arrangement on Cotton Textiles
LTTE	Liberation Tigers of Tamil Elam
LWR	Light Water Reactor
MAI	Multilateral Agreement on Investment
MARPOL	International Convention for the Prevention of Pollution from Ships
MBFR	Mutual and Balanced Force Reductions
MDB	Multilateral Development Bank
MFA	Multi-Fiber Arrangement
MLAT	Mutual Legal Assistance Treaty
MMV	Medicines for Malaria Venture
MOU	Memorandum of Understanding
MSC	Marine Stewardship Council
MSY	Maximum Sustainable Yield
MTCR	Missile Technology Control Regime
MTEF	Medium Term Expenditure Framework
NAALC	North American Agreement on Labor Cooperation

NAFTA	North American Free Trade Agreement
NAMMCO	North Atlantic Marine Mammal Commission
NAO	National Administrative Office
NATO	North Atlantic Treaty Organization
NBC	Nuclear, Biological and Chemical [Weapons]
NCB	National Central Bureau
NCDDR	National Committee for Disarmament, Demobilization, and Reintegration
NGO	Nongovernmental Organization
NIEO	New International Economic Order
NPT	Nuclear Nonproliferation Treaty
NSG	Nuclear Suppliers Group
NTM	National Technical Means
OAS	Organization of American States
OAU	Organization for African Unity
ODA	Official Development Assistance
OECD	Organization for Economic Cooperation and Development
OIHP	Office International d'Hygiène Publique
OMA	Orderly Marketing Agreement
OPCW	Organization for the Prohibition of Chemical Weapons
OPEC	Organization of the Petroleum Exporting Countries
OSCE	Organization for Security and Cooperation in Europe
PEFC	Pan European Forest Certification
PFP	Policy Framework Paper
PIC	Convention on the Prior Informed Consent Procedure for Hazardous Chemicals and Pesticides
PKK	Kurdistan Workers Party
ProMED	Program to Monitor Emerging Diseases
PRSP	Poverty Reduction Strategy Papers
PTO	Public Telecommunications Operator
PTT	(Ministries of) Posts, Telegraphs, and Telephones
RBM	Rollback Malaria
RDB	Regional Development Bank
RRC	Regional Radiocommunication Conference
SA	Social Accountability
SADC	Southern African Development Community
SALT	Strategic Arms Limitation Treaty
SCAR	Scientific Committee on Antarctic Research
SFOR	NATO's Stabilization Force in Bosnia
SGM	Safeguard Measure
SIR	System for Implementation Review

SOLAS	International Convention for the Safety of Life at Sea
SPA	Special Program of Assistance for Africa
START	Strategic Arms Reduction Treaty
SWAps	Sectorwide Approaches
TB	Tuberculosis
TDF	Transborder Data Flows
TI	Transparency International
TMB	Textiles Monitoring Body
TNC	Transnational Corporation
TPRM	Trade Policy Review Mechanism
TRAFFIC	Trade Records Analysis of Flora and Fauna in Commerce
TRIPs	Trade-Related Aspects of Intellectual Property Rights
TSB	Textiles Surveillance Board
UDHR	Universal Declaration of Human Rights
UDRP	Uniform Domain Name Dispute
UN	United Nations
UNAIDS	United Nations AIDS Program
UNCC	United Nations Compensation Commission
UNCED	United Nations Conference on Environment and Development
UNCHE	United Nations Conference on the Human Environment
UNCITRAL	United Nations Commission on International Trade Law
UNCLOS	United Nations Conferences on the Law of the Sea
UNCSD	United Nations Commission on Sustainable Development
UNCTAD	United Nations Conference on Trade and Development
UNDP	United Nations Development Program
UNECE	United Nations Economic Commission for Europe
UNEP	United Nations Environment Program
UNESCO	United Nations Educational, Scientific, and Cultural Organization
UNFF	United Nations Forum on Forests
UNFPA	United Nations Population Activities Fund
UNHCR	United Nations High Commissioner for Refugees
UNICEF	United Nations Children's Fund
UNITE	Union of Needle Trades, Industrial, and Textile Employees
UNMOVIC	United Nations Monitoring, Verification, and Inspection Commission
UNSCOM	United Nations Special Commission for Iraq
USTR	United States Trade Representative
VER	Voluntary Export Restraint
VERTIC	Verification Research, Training, and Information Centre
WARC	World Administrative Radio Conference

WCMC	World Conservation Monitoring Centre
WCO	World Customs Organization
WEU	Western European Union
WGB	Working Group on Bribery
WHC	Convention for Protection of World Cultural and Natural Heritage
WHF	World Heritage Fund
WHO	World Health Organization
WIPO	World Intellectual Property Organization
WMD	Weapons of Mass Destruction
WMO	World Meteorological Organization
WTO	Warsaw Treaty Organization[c]
WTO	World Trade Organization
WWF	World Wildlife Fund

c. Chapter 15 (Spear).

Index

Contributors

Vinod K. Aggarwal is Professor in the Department of Political Science, Affiliated Professor of Business and Public Policy in the Haas School of Business, and Director of the Berkeley Asia Pacific Economic Cooperation Study Center at the University of California, Berkeley. Previously, he was Chairman of the Political Economy of Industrial Societies Program (1991–1994). He is also the founder and editor-in-chief of the journal *Business and Politics* and has authored or edited numerous books and articles.

Thomas Bernauer is an Associate Professor of International Relations at the Swiss Federal Institute of Technology (ETH). His research group forms part of the Center for International Studies, a joint venture of ETH and the University of Zurich. Previously, he served as a Research Associate at the UN Institute for Disarmament Research in Geneva (1988–1992). Before joining ETH, he was a Postdoctoral Research Fellow at Harvard University for two years and a Senior Lecturer at the University of Zurich. He received his Ph.D. from the University of Zurich.

Chantal de Jonge Oudraat is an Associate at the Carnegie Endowment for International Peace. Previously, she was a Research Affiliate at the Belfer Center for Science and International Affairs at Harvard University (1994–1998) and Senior Research Associate at the UN Institute for Disarmament Research in Geneva (1981–1994). She is an Executive Board Member and Vice-President of Women in International Security. She has written widely on arms control, economic sanctions, the use of force, and peacekeeping. She holds a Ph.D. in political science from the University of Paris II (Panthéon).

William J. Drake is a Senior Associate and the Director of the Project on the Information Revolution and World Politics at the Carnegie Endowment for International Peace. Previously, he was Associate Director of the Communication, Culture, and Technology Program at Georgetown University. Among his publications are *Toward Sustainable Competition in Global Telecommunications* (Aspen Institute, 1999); and the edited volumes *Telecommunications in the Information Age* (U.S. Information Agency, 1998) and *The New Information Infrastructure: Strategies for US Policy* (The Twentieth Century Fund, 1995). He received his Ph.D. in political science from Columbia University.

Octavio Gómez-Dantés is Director of Health Policy at the Center for Health Systems Research in the National Institute of Public Health of Mexico. He has served as Director of Evaluation at the Ministry of Health in Mexico, Advisor to the National Academy of Medicine in Mexico, and Coordinator of the Unit for International Studies in Public Health at the National Institute of Public Health. He received his Masters in Public Health and his Masters in Health Policy and Management from the Harvard School of Public Health.

Catherine Gwin is a consultant to the World Bank's Operations Evaluation Department. Previously, she was Senior Vice President of the Overseas Development Council, directing the international policy research program. She has been Special Program Adviser to the Rockefeller Foundation, Senior Associate at the Carnegie Endowment for International Peace, on the staff of the U.S. International Development Cooperation Agency, and Executive Director of the Council on Foreign Relations 1980s Project. She has written on the issue of international development assistance, the role of the multilateral development banks, and the history of U.S.–World Bank relations.

Peter M. Haas is Professor of Political Science at the University of Massachusetts at Amherst. He has consulted for the Commission on Global Governance, the UN Environment Program, U.S. Department of State, among others. He has published widely on international environmental subjects and international relations theory, including *Saving the Mediterranean* (Columbia University Press, 1990), *Knowledge, Power and International Policy Coordination* (editor, University of South Carolina Press, 1997), and *Institutions for the Earth: Sources of Effective International Environmental Protection* (coeditor, MIT Press, 1993).

Christopher C. Joyner is Professor of International Law in the Government Department at Georgetown University. He has also taught at the George Washington University, Dartmouth College, and the University of Virginia, and served as a Senior Research Fellow at the Marine Policy Center, Woods Hole Oceanographic Institution, and the Institute of Antarctic and Southern Ocean Studies at the University of Tasmania. He has published extensively on international legal issues, including *Governing the Commons: The Antarctic Regime and Environmental Protection* (University of South Carolina Press, 1998) and *The United Nations and International Law* (Cambridge University Press, 1997).

Brian Langille is a Professor of Law at the University of Toronto and Dean of Graduate Studies. He has also taught at Dalhousie Law School. He is an experienced arbitrator and mediator, having served as advisor to various Canadian governments, member of the Canadian delegation to the International Labor Organization, rapporteur for the OECD, and editor of the *International Labor Law Reports*. He was educated at Acadia University, Dalhousie Law School, and Oxford University.

Robert E. Litan is Vice President of the Brookings Institution, where he also serves as the Director of Economic Studies. He is the Cabot Family Chairholder in Economics and Co-Editor of the *Brookings-Wharton Papers on Financial Services*. He has served as the Deputy Assistant Attorney-General of the Antitrust Division of the U.S. Justice Department, Associate Director of the Office of Management and Budget, Partner at Powell, Goldstein, Frazer & Murphy, and Visiting Lecturer in banking law at Yale Law School. He received his Ph.D. and J.D. from Yale University.

Kathleen Newland is Co-Director of the Migration Policy Institute in Washington, D.C. Previously she was Co-Director of the International Migration Policy Program at the Carnegie Endowment for International Peace. She also chairs the Women's Commission for Refugee Women and Children and serves on the Board of the International Rescue Committee. She has been an independent consultant to the UN High Commissioner for Refugees, the UN Secretary-General, the International Labor Organization, and the World Bank. She also was a member of the international relations faculty of the London School of Economics (1988–1992).

Peter Richardson is a board member of the U.S. national chapter of Transparency International (TI) and an advisor to TI's international secretariat. He is also a board member of the international NGO Pact and Washington, D.C.'s Institute for Learning in Retirement. Previously, he worked in various positions at the World Bank (1971–1996), was an associate at McKinsey & Company (1968–1970), and served at the U.S. Agency for International Development (1959–1968). He received a J.D. from Harvard Law School.

Peter H. Sand is Lecturer in transnational environmental law at the University of Munich, Germany. He has served as Senior Legal Officer at the Food and Agriculture Organization, as Assistant Director-General of the World Conservation Union,

Chief of the Environmental Law Unit at the UN Environment Program, and Legal Adviser for Environmental Affairs at the World Bank. He was formerly an Associate Professor of law at McGill University in Montreal, Canada, and Visiting Professor at the Universities of Addis Ababa, Geneva, and Paris.

Dinah L. Shelton is Professor of International Law at the University of Notre Dame Law School, where she directs the doctoral program at the Center for Civil and Human Rights and is a Fellow of the Kroc Institute for International Peace Studies. She has lectured throughout the world and has served on the Executive Council of the American Society of International Law, the International Institute of Human Rights, and various other international law and human rights associations.

P. J. Simmons is an Associate at the Carnegie Endowment for International Peace. Previously, he was the founding Director of the Environmental Change and Security Project at the Woodrow Wilson International Center for Scholars. He also worked at the National Security Council's Global Environmental Affairs directorate and at the National Security Archive. He was educated at Tufts University and the Johns Hopkins School of Advanced International Studies. He was a Fulbright scholar in Yugoslavia (1989–1990) and is a term member of the Council on Foreign Relations.

Timothy D. Sisk is an Associate Professor at the University of Denver Graduate School of International Studies. He has served as a Program Officer and Research Scholar at the U.S. Institute of Peace (1989–1998), a Legislative Assistant with the U.S. Senate (1984–1989), and a Research Fellow at the Norwegian Nobel Institute (1995). He was a Fulbright Scholar in 1991 and a Distinguished Fulbright Lecturer in 1998. He received his Ph.D. in political science from the George Washington University in 1992.

Joanna Spear is Senior Lecturer in War Studies and Director of the Graduate Research Programme at the Department of War Studies, King's College London. Previously, she was Director of the Graduate Programme in International Studies at the University of Sheffield. She has also taught at the Universities of Birmingham and York and held postdoctoral fellowships at Harvard University. She is currently writing a book on the defense trade in the post–Cold War period. She received her Ph.D. from Southampton University.

Phil Williams is Professor of International Security at the Graduate School of Public and International Affairs at the University of Pittsburgh. From 1992 until April 2001 he was Director of the University's Ridgway Center for International Security Studies. In the academic year of 2001–2002, he is Visiting Scientist at CERT/CC at

Carnegie Mellon University. Previously, he has taught at the Universities of Aberdeen and Southampton and in the 1980s directed several projects on international security at the Royal Institute for International Affairs. He has written extensively on transnational organized crime and money laundering. He has his Ph.D. in political science from the University of Southampton, England.